Data Compression

Second Edition

Springer
New York
Berlin
Heidelberg
Barcelona
Hong Kong
London
Milan
Paris
Singapore
Tokyo

David Salomon

Data Compression

The Complete Reference

Second Edition

With 301 Figures, 5 in Full Color

 Springer

David Salomon
Department of Computer Science
California State University, Northridge
Northridge, CA 91330-8281
USA
david.salomon@csun.edu

Library of Congress Cataloging-in-Publication Data
Salomon, D. (David), 1938–
    Data compression: the complete reference/David Salomon.—2nd ed.
        p. cm.
    Includes bibliographical references and index.
    ISBN 0-387-95045-1 (alk. paper)
        1. Data compression (Computer science)   I. Title.
    QA76.9.D33 S25 2000
    005.74′6—dc21   00-040048

Printed on acid-free paper.

Production managed by Francine McNeill; manufacturing supervised by Jeffrey Taub.
Photocomposed copy prepared from the author's TeX files.
Printed and bound by Maple-Vail Book Manufacturing Group, York, PA.
Printed in the United States of America.

9 8 7 6 5 4 3 2 1

ISBN 0-387-95045-1   SPIN 10767882

Springer-Verlag   New York Berlin Heidelberg
A member of BertelsmannSpringer Science+Business Media GmbH

To my family, without whose help, patience, and support
this book would not have been written.

Preface to the Second Edition

This second edition has come about for three reasons. The first one is the many favorable readers' comments, of which the following is an example:

> I just finished reading your book on data compression. Such joy. And as it contains many algorithms in a volume only some 20 mm thick, the book itself serves as a fine example of data compression!
>
> —Fred Veldmeijer, 1998

The second reason is the errors found by the author and by readers in the first edition. They are listed in the book's web site (see below), and they have been corrected in the second edition.

The third reason is the title of the book (originally chosen by the publisher). This title had to be justified by making the book a complete reference. As a result, many compression methods and much background material have been added to the book in this edition. The most important additions and changes are the following:

■ Three new chapters have been added. The first is Chapter 5, on the relatively young (and relatively unknown) topic of wavelets and their applications to image and audio compression. The chapter opens with an intuitive explanation of wavelets, using the continuous wavelet transform (CWT). It continues with a detailed example that shows how the Haar transform is used to compress images. This is followed by a general discussion of filter banks and the discrete wavelet transform (DWT), and a listing of the wavelet coefficients of many common wavelet filters. The chapter concludes with a description of important compression methods that either use wavelets or are based on wavelets. Included among them are the Laplacian pyramid, set partitioning in hierarchical trees (SPIHT), embedded coding using zerotrees (EZW), the WSQ method for the compression of fingerprints, and JPEG 2000, a new, promising method for the compression of still images (Section 5.19).

■   The second new chapter, Chapter 6, discusses video compression. The chapter opens with a general description of CRT operation and basic analog and digital video concepts. It continues with a general discussion of video compression, and it concludes with a description of MPEG-1 and H.261.

■   Audio compression is the topic of the third new chapter, Chapter 7. The first topic in this chapter is the properties of the human audible system and how they can be exploited to achieve lossy audio compression. A discussion of a few simple audio compression methods follows, and the chapter concludes with a description of the three audio layers of MPEG-1, including the very popular mp3 format.

Other new material consists of the following:

■   Conditional image RLE (Section 1.4.2).

■   Scalar quantization (Section 1.6).

■   The QM coder used in JPEG, JPEG 2000, and JBIG is now included in Section 2.16.

■   Context-tree weighting is discussed in Section 2.19. Its extension to lossless image compression is the topic of Section 4.24.

■   Section 3.4 discusses a sliding buffer method called repetition times.

■   The troublesome issue of patents is now also included (Section 3.25).

■   The relatively unknown Gray codes are discussed in Section 4.2.1, in connection with image compression.

■   Section 4.3 discusses intuitive methods for image compression, such as subsampling and vector quantization.

■   The important concept of *image transforms* is discussed in Section 4.4. The discrete cosine transform (DCT) is described in detail. The Karhunen-Loève transform, the Walsh-Hadamard transform, and the Haar transform are introduced. Section 4.4.5 is a short digression, discussing the discrete sine transform, a poor, unknown cousin of the DCT.

■   JPEG-LS, a new international standard for lossless and near-lossless image compression, is the topic of the new Section 4.7.

■   JBIG2, another new international standard, this time for the compression of bi-level images, is now found in Section 4.10.

■   Section 4.11 discusses EIDAC, a method for compressing simple images. Its main innovation is the use of two-part contexts. The intra context of a pixel P consists of several of its near neighbors in its bitplane. The inter context of P is made up of pixels that tend to be correlated with P even though they are located in different bitplanes.

■   There is a new Section 4.12 on vector quantization followed by sections on adaptive vector quantization and on block truncation coding (BTC).

■ Block matching is an adaptation of LZ77 (sliding window) for image compression. It can be found in Section 4.14.

■ Differential pulse code modulation (DPCM) is now included in the new Section 4.23.

■ An interesting method for the compression of discrete-tone images is block decomposition (Section 4.25).

■ Section 4.26 discusses binary tree predictive coding (BTPC).

■ Prefix image compression is related to quadtrees. It is the topic of Section 4.27.

■ Another image compression method related to quadtrees is *quadrisection*. It is discussed, together with its relatives *bisection* and *octasection*, in Section 4.28.

■ The section on WFA (Section 4.31) was wrong in the first edition and has been completely rewritten with much help from Karel Culik and Raghavendra Udupa.

■ Cell encoding is included in Section 4.33.

■ DjVu is an unusual method, intended for the compression of scanned documents. It was developed at Bell Labs (Lucent Technologies) and is described in Section 5.17.

■ The new JPEG 2000 standard for still image compression is discussed in the new Section 5.19.

■ Section 8.4 is a description of the sort-based context similarity method. This method uses the context of a symbol in a way reminiscent of ACB. It also assigns ranks to symbols, and this feature relates it to the Burrows-Wheeler method and also to symbol ranking.

■ Prefix compression of sparse strings has been added to Section 8.5.

■ FHM is an unconventional method for the compression of curves. It uses Fibonacci numbers, Huffman coding, and Markov chains, and it is the topic of Section 8.9.

■ Sequitur, Section 8.10, is a method especially suited for the compression of semi-structured text. It is based on context-free grammars.

■ Section 8.11 is a detailed description of edgebreaker, a highly original method for compressing the connectivity information of a triangle mesh. This method and its various extensions may become the standard for compressing polygonal surfaces, one of the most common surface types used in computer graphics. Edgebreaker is an example of a *geometric compression* method.

■ All the appendices have been deleted because of space considerations. They are freely available, in PDF format, at the book's web site. The appendices are (1) the ASCII code (including control characters); (2) space-filling curves; (3) data structures (including hashing); (4) error-correcting codes; (5) finite-state automata (this topic is needed for several compression methods, such as WFA, IFS, and dynamic Markov coding); (6) elements of probability; and (7) interpolating polynomials.

■ The answers to the exercises have also been deleted and are available at the book's web site.

Currently, the book's web site is part of the author's web site, which is located at `http://www.ecs.csun.edu/~dxs/`. Domain name `BooksByDavidSalomon.com` has been reserved and will always point to any future location of the web site. The author's email address is `david.salomon@csun.edu`, but it is planned that any email sent to ⟨*anyname*⟩`@BooksByDavidSalomon.com` will be forwarded to the author.

Readers willing to put up with eight seconds of advertisement can be redirected to the book's web site from `http://welcome.to/data.compression`. Email sent to `data.compression@welcome.to` will also be redirected.

Those interested in data compression in general should consult the short section titled "Joining the Data Compression Community," at the end of the book, as well as the two URLs `http://www.internz.com/compression-pointers.html` and `http://www.hn.is.uec.ac.jp/~arimura/compression_links.html`.

Northridge, California   David Salomon

Preface to the
First Edition

Historically, data compression was not one of the first fields of computer science. It seems that workers in the field needed the first 20 to 25 years to develop enough data before they felt the need for compression. Today, when the computer field is about 50 years old, data compression is a large and active field, as well as big business. Perhaps the best proof of this is the popularity of the Data Compression Conference (DCC, see end of book).

Principles, techniques, and algorithms for compressing different types of data are being developed at a fast pace by many people and are based on concepts borrowed from disciplines as varied as statistics, finite-state automata, space-filling curves, and Fourier and other transforms. This trend has naturally led to the publication of many books on the topic, which poses the question, Why another book on data compression?

The obvious answer is, Because the field is big and getting bigger all the time, thereby "creating" more potential readers and rendering existing texts obsolete in just a few years.

The original reason for writing this book was to provide a clear presentation of both the principles of data compression and all the important methods currently in use, a presentation geared toward the nonspecialist. It is the author's intention to have descriptions and discussions that can be understood by anyone with some background in the use and operation of computers. As a result, the use of mathematics is kept to a minimum and the material is presented with many examples, diagrams, and exercises. Instead of trying to be rigorous and prove every claim, the text many times says "it can be shown that ..." or "it can be proved that ...."

The exercises are an especially important feature of the book. They complement the material and should be worked out by anyone who is interested in a full understanding of data compression and the methods described here. Almost all the answers are provided (at the book's web page), but the reader should obviously try to work out each exercise before peeking at the answer.

Acknowledgments

I would like especially to thank Nelson Beebe, who went meticulously over the entire text of the first edition and made numerous corrections and suggestions. Many thanks also go to Christopher M. Brislawn, who reviewed Section 5.18 and gave us permission to use Figure 5.64; to Karel Culik and Raghavendra Udupa, for their substantial help with weighted finite automata (WFA); to Jeffrey Gilbert, who went over Section 4.25 (block decomposition); to John A. Robinson, who reviewed Section 4.26 (binary tree predictive coding); to Øyvind Strømme, who reviewed Section 5.10; to Frans Willems and Tjalling J. Tjalkins, who reviewed Section 2.19 (context-tree weighting); and to Hidetoshi Yokoo, for his help with Sections 3.15 and 8.4.

The author would also like to thank Paul Amer, Guy Blelloch, Mark Doyle, Hans Hagen, Emilio Millan, Haruhiko Okumura, and Vijayakumaran Saravanan, for their help with errors.

We seem to have a natural fascination with shrinking and expanding objects. Since our practical ability in this respect is very limited, we like to read stories where people and objects dramatically change their natural size. Examples are *Gulliver's Travels* by Jonathan Swift (1726), *Alice in Wonderland* by Lewis Carroll (1865), and *Fantastic Voyage* by Isaac Asimov (1966).

Fantastic Voyage started as a screenplay written by the famous writer Isaac Asimov. While the movie was being produced (it was released in 1966), Asimov rewrote it as a novel, correcting in the process some of the most glaring flaws in the screenplay. The plot concerns a group of medical scientists placed in a submarine and shrunk to microscopic dimensions. They are then injected into the body of a patient in an attempt to remove a blood clot from his brain by means of a laser beam. The point is that the patient, Dr. Benes, is the scientist who improved the miniaturization process and made it practical in the first place.

Because of the success of both the movie and the book, Asimov later wrote *Fantastic Voyage II: Destination Brain*, but the latter novel proved a flop.

But before we continue here is a question that you might have already asked: "OK, but why should I be interested in data compression?" Very simple: "DATA COMPRESSION SAVES YOU MONEY!" More interested now? We think you should be. Let us give you an example of data compression application that you see every day. Exchanging faxes every day...

From `http://www.rasip.etf.hr/research/compress/index.html`

Northridge, California

David Salomon

Contents

Contents

Each memorable verse of a true poet has
two or three times the written content
—Alfred de Musset

Introduction

Giambattista della Porta, a Renaissance scientist, was the author in 1558 of *Magia Naturalis* (Natural Magic), a book in which he discusses many subjects, including demonology, magnetism, and the camera obscura. The book mentions an imaginary device that has since become known as the "sympathetic telegraph." This device was to have consisted of two circular boxes, similar to compasses, each with a magnetic needle. Each box was to be labeled with the 26 letters, instead of the usual directions, and the main point was that the two needles were supposed to be magnetized by the *same lodestone*. Porta assumed that this would somehow coordinate the needles such that when a letter was dialed in one box, the needle in the other box would swing to point to the same letter.

Needless to say, such a device does not work (this, after all, was about 300 years before Samuel Morse), but in 1711 a worried wife wrote to the *Spectator*, a London periodical, asking for advice on how to bear the long absences of her beloved husband. The adviser, Joseph Addison, offered some practical ideas, then mentioned Porta's device, adding that a pair of such boxes might enable her and her husband to communicate with each other even when they "were guarded by spies and watches, or separated by castles and adventures." Mr. Addison then added that, in addition to the 26 letters, the sympathetic telegraph dials should contain, when used by lovers, "several entire words which always have a place in passionate epistles." The message "I love you," for example, would, in such a case, require sending just three symbols instead of ten.

> A woman seldom asks advice before she has bought her wedding clothes.
> —Joseph Addison

This advice is an early example of *text compression* achieved by using short codes for common messages and longer codes for other messages. Even more importantly, this shows how the concept of data compression comes naturally to people who are interested in communications. We seem to be preprogrammed with the idea of sending as little data as possible in order to save time.

Data compression is the process of converting an input data stream (the source stream or the original raw data) into another data stream (the output, or the compressed, stream) that has a smaller size. A stream is either a file or a buffer in memory. Data compression is popular because of two reasons: (1) People like to accumulate data and hate to throw anything away. No matter how big a storage device one has, sooner or later it is going to overflow. Data compression seems useful because it delays this inevitability. (2) People hate to wait a long time for data transfers. When sitting at the computer, waiting for a Web page to come in, or for a file to download, we naturally feel that anything longer than a few seconds is a long time to wait.

Data compression has come of age in the last 20 years. Both the quantity and the quality of the body of literature in this field provides ample proof of this. However, the need for compressing data has been felt in the past, even before the advent of computers, as the following quotation suggests:

> I have made this letter longer than usual
> because I lack the time to make it shorter.
> —Blaise Pascal (1623–1662)

There are many known methods for data compression. They are based on different ideas, are suitable for different types of data, and produce different results, but they are all based on the same principle, namely, they compress data by removing *redundancy* from the original data in the source file. Any nonrandom collection data has some structure, and this structure can be exploited to achieve a smaller representation of the data, a representation where no structure is discernible. The terms *redundancy* and *structure* are used in the professional literature, as well as *smoothness*, *coherence*, and *correlation*; they all refer to the same thing. Thus, redundancy is an important concept in any discussion of data compression.

In typical English text, for example, the letter E appears very often, while Z is rare (Tables 1 and 2). This is called *alphabetic redundancy*, and suggests assigning variable-size codes to the letters, with E getting the shortest code and Z, the longest one. Another type of redundancy, *contextual redundancy*, is illustrated by the fact that the letter Q is almost always followed by the letter U (i.e., that certain digrams and trigrams are more common in plain English than others). Redundancy in images is illustrated by the fact that in a nonrandom image, adjacent pixels tend to have similar colors.

Section 2.1 discusses the theory of information and presents a definition of redundancy. However, even if we don't have a precise definition for this term, it is intuitively clear that a variable-size code has less redundancy than a fixed-size code (or no redundancy at all). Fixed-size codes make it easier to work with text, so they are useful, but they are redundant.

The idea of compression by reducing redundancy suggests the *general law* of data compression, which is to "assign short codes to common events (symbols or phrases) and long codes to rare events." There are many ways to implement this law, and an analysis of any compression method shows that, deep inside, it works by obeying the general law.

Compressing data is done by changing its representation from inefficient (i.e., long) to efficient (short). Compression is thus possible only because data is normally represented in the computer in a format that is longer than absolutely necessary. The reason that inefficient (long) data representations are used is that they make it easier to process the data, and data processing is more common and more important than data compression. The ASCII code for characters is a good example of a data representation that is longer than absolutely necessary. It uses 7-bit codes because fixed-size codes are easy to work with. A variable-size code, however, would be more efficient, since certain characters are used more than others and so could be assigned shorter codes.

In a world where data is always represented by its shortest possible format there would therefore be no way to compress data. Instead of writing books on data compression, authors in such a world would write books on how to determine the shortest format for different types of data.

A Word to the Wise ...

The main aim of the field of data compression is, of course, to develop methods for better and better compression. However, one of the main dilemmas of the *art* of data compression is when to stop looking for better compression. Experience shows that fine-tuning an algorithm to squeeze out the last remaining bits of redundancy from the data gives diminishing returns. Modifying an algorithm to improve compression by 1% may increase the run time by 10% and the complexity of the program by more than that. A good way out of this dilemma was taken by Fiala and Greene (Section 3.7). After developing their main algorithms A1 and A2, they modified them to produce less compression at a higher speed, resulting in algorithms B1 and B2. They then modified A1 and A2 again, but in the opposite direction, sacrificing speed to get slightly better compression.

The principle of compressing by removing redundancy also answers the following question: "Why is it that an already compressed file cannot be compressed further?" The answer, of course, is that such a file has little or no redundancy, so there is nothing to remove. An example of such a file is random text. In such text, each letter occurs with equal probability, so assigning them fixed-size codes does not add any redundancy. When such a file is compressed, there is no redundancy to remove. (Another answer is that, if it were possible to compress an already compressed file, then successive compressions would reduce the size of the file until it becomes a single byte, or even a single bit. This, of course, is ridiculous since a single byte cannot contain the information present in an arbitrarily large file.) The reader should also consult page 724 for an interesting twist on the topic of compressing random data.

Since random data has been mentioned, let's say a few more words about it. Normally, it is rare to have a file with random data, but there is one good example—an already compressed file. Someone owning a compressed file normally knows that it is already compressed and would not attempt to compress it further but there is one exception—data transmission by modems. Modern modems contain hardware to automatically compress the data they send, and if that data is already compressed, there will not be further compression. There may even be expansion. This is why a modem should monitor the compression ratio "on the fly" and, if it is low, should stop compressing and should send the rest of the data uncompressed. The V.42bis protocol (Section 3.18) is a good example of this technique. Section 2.7 discusses "techniques" for compressing random data.

◇ **Exercise 1:** (Fun.) Find English words that contain all five vowels "aeiou" in their original order.

   Data compression has become so important that some researchers (see, for example, [Wolff 99]) have proposed the SP theory (for "simplicity" and "power"), which suggests that all computing is compression! Specifically, it says, Data compression may be interpreted as a process of removing unnecessary complexity (redundancy) in information, and thus maximizing simplicity while preserving as much as possible of its nonredundant descriptive power. SP theory is based on the following conjectures:

■   All kinds of computing and formal reasoning may usefully be understood as information compression by pattern matching, unification, and search.

■   The process of finding redundancy and removing it may always be understood at a fundamental level as a process of searching for patterns that match each other, and merging or unifying repeated instances of any pattern to make one.

   This book discusses many compression methods, some suitable for text and others for graphical data (still images or movies). Most methods are classified into four categories: run length encoding (RLE), statistical methods, dictionary-based (sometimes called LZ) methods, and transforms. Chapters 1 and 8 describe methods based on other principles.

   Before delving into the details, we discuss important data compression terms.

■   The *compressor* or *encoder* is the program that compresses the raw data in the input stream and creates an output stream with compressed (low-redundancy) data. The *decompressor* or *decoder* converts in the opposite direction. Notice that the term *encoding* is very general and has wide meaning, but since we discuss only data compression, we use the name *encoder* to mean data compressor. The term *codec* is sometimes used to describe both the encoder and decoder. Similarly, the term *companding* is short for "compressing/expanding."

■   The term "stream" is used throughout this book instead of "file." "Stream" is a more general term because thc compressed data may be transmitted directly to the decoder, instead of being written to a file and saved. Also, the data to be compressed may be downloaded from a network instead of being input from a file.

■   For the original input stream we use the terms *unencoded*, *raw*, or *original* data. The contents of the final, compressed, stream is considered the *encoded* or *compressed* data. The term *bitstream* is also used in the literature to indicate the compressed stream.

Letter	Freq.	Prob.		Letter	Freq.	Prob.
A	51060	0.0721		E	86744	0.1224
B	17023	0.0240		T	64364	0.0908
C	27937	0.0394		I	55187	0.0779
D	26336	0.0372		S	51576	0.0728
E	86744	0.1224		A	51060	0.0721
F	19302	0.0272		O	48277	0.0681
G	12640	0.0178		N	45212	0.0638
H	31853	0.0449		R	45204	0.0638
I	55187	0.0779		H	31853	0.0449
J	923	0.0013		L	30201	0.0426
K	3812	0.0054		C	27937	0.0394
L	30201	0.0426		D	26336	0.0372
M	20002	0.0282		P	20572	0.0290
N	45212	0.0638		M	20002	0.0282
O	48277	0.0681		F	19302	0.0272
P	20572	0.0290		B	17023	0.0240
Q	1611	0.0023		U	16687	0.0235
R	45204	0.0638		G	12640	0.0178
S	51576	0.0728		W	9244	0.0130
T	64364	0.0908		Y	8953	0.0126
U	16687	0.0235		V	6640	0.0094
V	6640	0.0094		X	5465	0.0077
W	9244	0.0130		K	3812	0.0054
X	5465	0.0077		Z	1847	0.0026
Y	8953	0.0126		Q	1611	0.0023
Z	1847	0.0026		J	923	0.0013

Frequencies and probabilities of the 26 letters in a prepublication version of this book, containing 708,672 letters (upper- and lowercase) comprising approximately 145,000 words.

Most, but not all, experts agree that the most common letters in English, in order, are ETAOINSHRDLU (normally written as two separate words ETAOIN SHRDLU). However, see [Fang 66] for a different viewpoint. The most common digrams (2-letter combinations) are TH, TA, RE, IA, AK, EJ, EK, ER, GJ, AD, YU, RX, and KT. The most frequently appearing letters *beginning* words are S, P, C, and the most frequent final letters are E, Y, S.

Table 1: Probabilities of English Letters.

Char.	Freq.	Prob.	Char.	Freq.	Prob.	Char.	Freq.	Prob.
e	85537	0.099293	x	5238	0.006080	F	1192	0.001384
t	60636	0.070387	|	4328	0.005024	H	993	0.001153
i	53012	0.061537	-	4029	0.004677	B	974	0.001131
s	49705	0.057698	)	3936	0.004569	W	971	0.001127
a	49008	0.056889	(	3894	0.004520	+	923	0.001071
o	47874	0.055573	T	3728	0.004328	!	895	0.001039
n	44527	0.051688	k	3637	0.004222	#	856	0.000994
r	44387	0.051525	3	2907	0.003374	D	836	0.000970
h	30860	0.035823	4	2582	0.002997	R	817	0.000948
l	28710	0.033327	5	2501	0.002903	M	805	0.000934
c	26041	0.030229	6	2190	0.002542	;	761	0.000883
d	25500	0.029601	I	2175	0.002525	/	698	0.000810
m	19197	0.022284	^	2143	0.002488	N	685	0.000795
\	19140	0.022218	:	2132	0.002475	G	566	0.000657
p	19055	0.022119	A	2052	0.002382	j	508	0.000590
f	18110	0.021022	9	1953	0.002267	@	460	0.000534
u	16463	0.019111	[	1921	0.002230	Z	417	0.000484
b	16049	0.018630	C	1896	0.002201	J	415	0.000482
.	12864	0.014933	]	1881	0.002183	O	403	0.000468
1	12335	0.014319	'	1876	0.002178	V	261	0.000303
g	12074	0.014016	S	1871	0.002172	X	227	0.000264
0	10866	0.012613	_	1808	0.002099	U	224	0.000260
,	9919	0.011514	7	1780	0.002066	?	177	0.000205
&	8969	0.010411	8	1717	0.001993	K	175	0.000203
y	8796	0.010211	`	1577	0.001831	%	160	0.000186
w	8273	0.009603	=	1566	0.001818	Y	157	0.000182
$	7659	0.008891	P	1517	0.001761	Q	141	0.000164
}	6676	0.007750	L	1491	0.001731	>	137	0.000159
{	6676	0.007750	q	1470	0.001706	*	120	0.000139
v	6379	0.007405	z	1430	0.001660	<	99	0.000115
2	5671	0.006583	E	1207	0.001401	"	8	0.000009

Frequencies and probabilities of the 93 characters in a prepublication version of this book, containing 861,462 characters.

Table 2: Frequencies and Probabilities of Characters.

> ### The Gold Bug
>
> Here, then, we have, in the very beginning, the groundwork for something more than a mere guess. The general use which may be made of the table is obvious—but, in this particular cipher, we shall only very partially require its aid. As our predominant character is 8, we will commence by assuming it as the "e" of the natural alphabet. To verify the supposition, let us observe if the 8 be seen often in couples—for "e" is doubled with great frequency in English—in such words, for example, as "meet," "fleet," "speed," "seen," "been," "agree," etc. In the present instance we see it doubled no less than five times, although the cryptograph is brief.
>
> —Edgar Allan Poe

■ A *nonadaptive* compression method is rigid and does not modify its operations, its parameters, or its tables in response to the particular data being compressed. Such a method is best used to compress data that is all of a single type. Examples are the Group 3 and Group 4 methods for facsimile compression (Section 2.13). They are specifically designed for facsimile compression and would do a poor job compressing any other data. In contrast, an *adaptive* method examines the raw data and modifies its operations and/or its parameters accordingly. An example is the adaptive Huffman method of Section 2.9. Some compression methods use a 2-pass algorithm, where the first pass reads the input stream to collect statistics on the data to be compressed, and the second pass does the actual compressing using parameters set by the first pass. Such a method may be called *semiadaptive*. A data compression method can also be *locally adaptive*, meaning it adapts itself to local conditions in the input stream and varies this adaptation as it moves from area to area in the input. An example is the move-to-front method (Section 1.5).

■ *Lossy/lossless compression:* Certain compression methods are lossy. They achieve better compression by losing some information. When the compressed stream is decompressed, the result is not identical to the original data stream. Such a method makes sense especially in compressing images, movies, or sounds. If the loss of data is small, we may not be able to tell the difference. In contrast, text files, especially files containing computer programs, may become worthless if even one bit gets modified. Such files should be compressed only by a lossless compression method. [Two points should be mentioned regarding text files: (1) If a text file contains the source code of a program, many blank spaces can normally be eliminated, since they are disregarded by the compiler anyway. (2) When the output of a word processor is saved in a text file, the file may contain information about the different fonts used in the text. Such information may be discarded if the user wants to save just the text.]

■ *Symmetrical compression* is the case where the compressor and decompressor use basically the same algorithm but work in "opposite" directions. Such a method makes sense for general work, where the same number of files are compressed as are decompressed. In an asymmetric compression method either the compressor or the decompressor may have to work significantly harder. Such methods have their uses and are not necessarily bad. A compression method where the compressor executes a slow, complex algorithm and the decompressor is simple is a natural choice when files are compressed into an archive, where they will be decompressed and used very often. The opposite case is useful in environments where files are updated all the time and backups made. There is a small chance that a backup file will be used, so the decompressor isn't used very often.

> Like the ski resort full of girls hunting for husbands and husbands hunting for girls, the situation is not as symmetrical as it might seem.
> —Alan Lindsay Mackay, lecture, Birckbeck College, 1964

⋄ **Exercise 2:** Give an example of a compressed file where good compression is important but the speed of both compressor and decompressor isn't important.

■   A data compression method is called *universal* if the compressor and decompressor do not know the statistics of the input stream. A universal method is *optimal* if the compressor can produce compression factors that asymptotically approach the entropy of the input stream for long inputs.

■   Most compression methods operate in the *streaming mode*, where the codec inputs a byte or several bytes, processes them, and continues until an end-of-file is sensed. Some methods, such as Burrows-Wheeler (Section 8.1), work in the *block mode*, where the input stream is read block by block and each block is encoded separately. The block size in this case should be a user-controlled parameter, since its size may greatly affect the performance of the method.

■   Most compression methods are *physical*. They look only at the bits in the input stream and ignore the meaning of the data items in the input (e.g., the data items may be words, pixels, or sounds). Such a method translates one bit stream into another, shorter, one. The only way to make sense of the output stream (to decode it) is by knowing how it was encoded. Some compression methods are *logical*. They look at individual data items in the source stream and replace common items with short codes. Such a method is normally special-purpose and can be used successfully on certain types of data only. The pattern substitution method described on page 22 is an example of a logical compression method.

■   *Compression performance*: Several quantities are commonly used to express the performance of a compression method.

1. The *compression ratio* is defined as

$$\text{Compression ratio} = \frac{\text{size of the output stream}}{\text{size of the input stream}}.$$

A value of 0.6 means that the data occupies 60% of its original size after compression. Values greater than 1 mean an output stream bigger than the input stream (negative compression). The compression ratio can also be called bpb (bit per bit), since it equals the number of bits in the compressed stream needed, on average, to compress one bit in the input stream. In image compression, the same term, bpb stands for "bits per pixel." In modern, efficient text compression methods, it makes sense to talk about bpc (bits per character), the number of bits it takes, on average, to compress one character in the input stream.

Two more terms should be mentioned in connection with the compression ratio. The term *bitrate* (or "bit rate") is a general term for bpb and bpc. Thus, the main goal of data compression is to represent any given data at low bit rates. The term *bit budget* refers to the functions of the individual bits in the compressed stream. Imagine a compressed stream where 90% of the bits are variable-size codes of certain symbols, and the remaining 10% are used to encode certain tables. The bit budget for the tables is 10%.

2. The inverse of the compression ratio is called the *compression factor*:

$$\text{Compression factor} = \frac{\text{size of the input stream}}{\text{size of the output stream}}.$$

In this case values greater than 1 indicates compression, and values less than 1 imply expansion. This measure seems natural to many people, since the bigger the factor, the better the compression. This measure is distantly related to the sparseness ratio, a performance measure discussed in Section 5.6.2.

3. The expression $100 \times (1 - \text{compression ratio})$ is also a reasonable measure of compression performance. A value of 60 means that the output stream occupies 40% of its original size (or that the compression has resulted in savings of 60%).

4. In image compression, the quantity bpp (bits per pixel) is commonly used. It equals the number of bits needed, on average, to compress one pixel of the image. This quantity should always be compared with the bpp before compression.

5. The *compression gain* is defined as

$$100 \log_e \frac{\text{reference size}}{\text{compressed size}},$$

where the reference size is either the size of the input stream or the size of the compressed stream produced by some standard lossless compression method. For small numbers x it is true that $\log_e(1 + x) \approx x$, so a small change in a small compression gain is very similar to the same change in the compression ratio. Because of the use of the logarithm, two compression gains can be compared simply by subtracting them. The unit of the compression gain is called *percent log ratio* and is denoted by $\frac{o}{o}$.

6. The speed of compression can be measured in *cycles per byte* (CPB). This is the average number of machine cycles it takes to compress one byte. This measure is important when compression is done by special hardware.

7. Other quantities, such as mean square error (MSE) and peak signal to noise ratio (PSNR), are used to measure the distortion caused by lossy compression of images and movies. Section 4.2.2 provides information on those.

■   The *Calgary Corpus* is a set of 18 files traditionally used to test data compression programs. They include text, image, and object files, for a total of more than

Name	Size	Description	Type
bib	111,261	A bibliography in UNIX *refer* format	Text
book1	768,771	Text of T. Hardy's *Far From the Madding Crowd*	Text
book2	610,856	Ian Witten's *Principles of Computer Speech*	Text
geo	102,400	Geological seismic data	Data
news	377,109	A Usenet news file	Text
obj1	21,504	VAX object program	Obj
obj2	246,814	Macintosh object code	Obj
paper1	53,161	A technical paper in *troff* format	Text
paper2	82,199	Same	Text
pic	513,216	Fax image (a bitmap)	Image
progc	39,611	A source program in C	Source
progl	71,646	A source program in LISP	Source
progp	49,379	A source program in Pascal	Source
trans	93,695	Document teaching how to use a terminal	Text

Table 3: The Calgary Corpus.

3.2 million bytes (Table 3). The corpus can be downloaded by anonymous FTP from `ftp://ftp.cpsc.ucalgary.ca/pub/projects/text.compression.corpus`.

■ The *Canterbury Corpus* is another collection of files, introduced in 1997 to provide an alternative to the Calgary corpus for evaluating lossless compression methods. The concerns leading to the new corpus were as follows:

1. The Calgary corpus has been used by many researchers to develop, test and compare many compression methods, and there is a chance that new methods would unintentionally be fine-tuned to that corpus. They may do well on the Calgary corpus documents but poorly on other documents.

2. The Calgary corpus was collected in 1987 and is getting old. "Typical" documents change during a decade (e.g., html documents did not exist until recently), and any body of documents used for evaluation purposes should be examined from time to time.

3. The Calgary corpus is more or less an arbitrary collection of documents, whereas a good corpus for algorithm evaluation should be selected carefully.

The Canterbury corpus started with about 800 candidate documents, all in the public domain. They were divided into 11 classes, representing different types of documents. A representative "average" document was selected from each class by compressing every file in the class using different methods and selecting the file whose compression was closest to the average (as determined by regression). The corpus is summarized in Table 4 and can be freely obtained by anonymous ftp from `http://corpus.canterbury.ac.nz`.

The last three files constitute the beginning of a random collection of larger files. More files are likely to be added to it.

■ The *probability model*. This concept is important in statistical data compression methods. When such a method is used, a model for the data has to be constructed

Description	File name	Size (bytes)
English text (*Alice in Wonderland*)	alice29.txt	152,089
Fax images	ptt5	513,216
C source code	fields.c	11,150
Spreadsheet files	kennedy.xls	1,029,744
SPARC executables	sum	38,666
Technical document	lcet10.txt	426,754
English poetry ("Paradise Lost")	plrabn12.txt	481,861
HTML document	cp.html	24,603
LISP source code	grammar.lsp	3,721
GNU manual pages	xargs.1	4,227
English play (*As You Like It*)	asyoulik.txt	125,179
Complete genome of the *E. coli* bacterium	E.Coli	4,638,690
The King James version of the Bible	bible.txt	4,047,392
The CIA World Fact Book	world192.txt	2,473,400

Table 4: The Canterbury Corpus.

before compression can begin. A typical model is built by reading the entire input stream, counting the number of times each symbol appears (its frequency of occurrence), and computing the probability of occurrence of each symbol. The data stream is then input again, symbol by symbol, and is compressed using the information in the probability model. A typical model is shown in Table 2.44, page 103.

> In a symbol there is concealment and yet revelation: here therefore, by Silence and by Speech acting together, comes a double significance.
>
> —Thomas Carlyle (1795–1881)

Reading the entire input stream twice is slow, so practical compression methods use estimates, or adapt themselves to the data as it is being input and compressed. It is easy to input large quantities of, say, English text and calculate the frequencies and probabilities of every character. This information can serve as an approximate model for English text, and can be used by text compression methods to compress any English text. It is also possible to start by assigning equal probabilities to all the symbols in an alphabet, then reading symbols and compressing them, and, while doing that, also counting frequencies and changing the model as compression progresses. This is the principle behind *adaptive compression methods*.

The concept of *data reliability* (page 90) is in some sense the opposite of data compression. Nevertheless, the two concepts are very often related since any good data compression program should generate reliable code and so should be able to use error-detecting and error-correcting codes. (There is an appendix on error-correcting codes in the book's web site.)

The intended readership of this book is those who have a basic knowledge of computer science; who know something about programming and data structures;

who feel comfortable with terms such as *bit, mega, ASCII, file, I/O,* and *binary search*; and who want to understand how data is compressed. The necessary mathematical background is minimal, and is limited to logarithms, matrices, polynomials, differentiation/integration, and the concept of probability. This book is not intended to be a guide to software implementors and contains few programs.

In addition to the bibliography at the end of the book, there are short, specialized bibliographies following most sections. The following URLs contain useful lists of data compression pointers:

`http://www.hn.is.uec.ac.jp/~arimura/compression_links.html` and
`http://www.internz.com/compression-pointers.html`.

Reference [Okumura 98] discusses the history of data compression in Japan.

The symbol "␣" is used to indicate a blank space in places where spaces may lead to ambiguity.

The author would like to thank Peter D. Smith for his help. He has read the entire manuscript, corrected many errors, and provided many helpful suggestions and comments. In addition, J. Robert Henderson is to be thanked for his mathematical help, and John M. Motil for helpful ideas and comments.

Readers who would like to get an idea of the effort it took to write this book should consult the colophon.

The author welcomes any comments, suggestions, and corrections. They should be sent to `david.salomon@csun.edu`. In the future, when this address is no longer active, readers should try ⟨*anything*⟩`@BooksByDavidSalomon.com`.

Bibliography

Fang I. (1966) "It Isn't ETAOIN SHRDLU; It's ETAONI RSHDLC," *Journalism Quarterly* **43**:761–762.

Okumura, Haruhiko (1998) URL `http://www.matsusaka-u.ac.jp/~okumura/` directory `compression/history.html`.

Wolff, Gerry (1999) URL `http://www.sees.bangor.ac.uk/~gerry/sp_summary.html`.

> A blond in a red dress can do without introductions—but not without a bodyguard.
>
> —Rona Jaffe

1
Basic Techniques

1.1 Intuitive Compression

Data compression is achieved by reducing redundancy, but this also makes the data less reliable, more prone to errors. Making data more reliable, on the other hand, is done by adding check bits and parity bits, a process that increases the size of the codes, thereby increasing redundancy. Data compression and data reliability are thus opposites, and it is interesting to note that the latter is a relatively recent field, whereas the former existed even before the advent of computers. The sympathetic telegraph, discussed in the Preface, the Braille code of 1820 (Section 1.1.1), and the Morse code of 1838 (Table 2.1) use simple forms of compression. It therefore seems that reducing redundancy comes naturally to anyone who works on codes, but increasing it is something that "goes against the grain" in humans. This section discusses simple, intuitive compression methods that have been used in the past. Today these methods are mostly of historical interest, since they are generally inefficient and cannot compete with the modern compression methods developed during the last 15–20 years.

1.1.1 Braille

This well-known code, which enables the blind to read, was developed by Louis Braille in the 1820s and is still in common use today, after being modified several times. Many books in Braille are available from the National Braille Press. The Braille code consists of groups (or cells) of 3×2 dots each, embossed on thick paper. Each of the 6 dots in a group may be flat or raised, so the information content of a group is equivalent to 6 bits, resulting in 64 possible groups. Since the letters (Table 1.1), digits, and punctuation marks don't require all 64 codes, the remaining groups are used to code common words—such as **and**, **for**, and **of**—and common strings of letters—such as **ound**, **ation** and **th** (Table 1.2).

A B C D E F G H I J K L M

N O P Q R S T U V W X Y Z

Table 1.1: The 26 Braille Letters.

and for of the with ch gh sh th

Table 1.2: Some Words and Strings in Braille.

Redundancy in Everyday Situations

Even though we don't unnecessarily increase redundancy in our data, we use redundant data all the time, mostly without noticing it. Here are some examples:

All natural languages are redundant. A Portuguese who does not speak Italian may read an Italian newspaper and still understand most of the news because he recognizes the basic form of many Italian verbs and nouns and because most of the text he does not understand is superfluous (i.e., redundant).

PIN is an acronym for "Personal Identification Number," but banks always ask you for your "PIN number." SALT is an acronym for "Strategic Arms Limitations Talks," but TV announcers in the 1970s kept talking about the "SALT Talks." These are just two examples illustrating how natural it is to be redundant in everyday situations. More examples can be found at URL `http://www.corsinet.com/braincandy/twice.html`

⋄ **Exercise 1.1:** Find a few more everyday redundant phrases.

The amount of compression achieved by Braille is small but important, since books in Braille tend to be very large (a single group covers the area of about ten printed letters). Even this modest compression comes with a price. If a Braille book is mishandled or gets old and some dots become flat, serious reading errors may result since every possible group is used. (Brailler, a Macintosh shareware program by Mark Pilgrim, is a good choice for anyone wanting to experiment with Braille.)

1.1.2 Irreversible Text Compression

Sometimes it is acceptable to "compress" text by simply throwing away some information. This is called *irreversible text compression* or *compaction*. The decompressed text will not be identical to the original, so such methods are not general purpose; they can only be used in special cases.

A run of consecutive blank spaces may be replaced by a single space. This may be acceptable in literary texts and in most computer programs, but it should not be used when the data is in tabular form.

In extreme cases all text characters except letters and spaces may be thrown away, and the letters may be case flattened (converted to all lower- or all uppercase).

This will leave just 27 symbols, so a symbol can be encoded in 5 instead of the usual 8 bits. The compression ratio is $5/8 = .625$, not bad, but the loss may normally be too great. (An interesting example of similar text is the last chapter of *Ulysses* by James Joyce. In addition to letters, digits, and spaces, this long chapter contains only a few punctuation marks.)

⬦ **Exercise 1.2:** A character set including the 26 uppercase letters and the space can be coded with 5-bit codes, but that would leave five unused codes. Suggest a way to use them.

1.1.3 Ad Hoc Text Compression

Here are some simple, intuitive ideas for cases where the compression must be reversible (lossless).

■ If the text contains many spaces but they are not clustered, they may be removed and their positions indicated by a bit-string that contains a 0 for each text character that is not a space and a 1 for each space. Thus, the text

`Here are some ideas,`

is encoded as the bit-string "0000100010000100000" followed by the text

`Herearesomeideas.`

If the number of blank spaces is small, the bit-string will be sparse, and the methods of Section 8.5 can be used to compress it considerably.

■ Since ASCII codes are essentially 7 bits long, the text may be compressed by writing 7 bits per character instead of 8 on the output stream. This may be called *packing*. The compression ratio is, of course, $7/8 = 0.875$.

■ The numbers $40^3 = 64,000$ and $2^{16} = 65,536$ are not very different and satisfy the relation $40^3 < 2^{16}$. This can serve as the basis of an intuitive compression method for a small set of symbols. If the data to be compressed is text with at most 40 different characters (such as the 26 letters, 10 digits, a space, and three punctuation marks), then this method produces a compression factor of $24/16 = 1.5$. Here is how it works.

Given a set of 40 characters and a string of characters from the set, we group the characters into triplets. Since each character can take one of 40 values, a trio of characters can have one of $40^3 = 64,000$ values. Since $40^3 < 2^{16}$, such a value can be expressed in 16 bits, or two bytes. Without compression, each of the 40 characters requires one byte, so our intuitive method produces a compression factor of $3/2 = 1.5$. (This is one of those rare cases where the compression factor is constant and is known in advance.)

■ If the text includes just uppercase letters, digits, and some punctuation marks, the old 6-bit CDC display code (Table 1.3) may be used. This code was commonly used in second-generation computers (and even a few third-generation ones). These computers did not need more than 64 characters because they did not have any CRT screens and they sent their output to printers that could print only a limited set of characters.

Bits				Bit positions 210				
543	0	1	2	3	4	5	6	7
0		A	B	C	D	E	F	G
1	H	I	J	K	L	M	N	O
2	P	Q	R	S	T	U	V	W
3	X	Y	Z	0	1	2	3	4
4	5	6	7	8	9	+	-	*
5	/	(	)	$	=	sp	,	.
6	≡	[	]	:	≠	_	∨	∧
7	↑	↓	<	>	≤	≥	¬	;

Table 1.3: The CDC Display Code.

■   Another old code worth mentioning is the Baudot code (Table 1.4). This was a 5-bit code developed by J. M. E. Baudot in about 1880 for telegraph communication. It became popular and, by 1950 was designated as the International Telegraph Code No. 1. It was used in many first- and second-generation computers. The code uses 5 bits per character but encodes more than 32 characters. Each 5-bit code can be the code of two characters, a letter and a figure. The "letter shift" and "figure shift" codes are used to shift between letters and figures.

Using this technique, the Baudot code can represent $32 \times 2 - 2 = 62$ characters (each code can have two meanings except the LS and FS codes). The actual number of characters is, however, less than that, since 5 of the codes have one meaning each, and some codes are not assigned.

The Baudot code is not reliable because no parity bit is used. A bad bit can transform a character into another. In particular, a bad bit in a shift character causes a wrong interpretation of all the characters following, up to the next shift.

■   If the data include just integers, each decimal digit may be represented in 4 bits, with 2 digits packed in a byte. Data consisting of dates may be represented as the number of days since January 1, 1900 (or some other convenient start date). Each date may be stored as a 16- or 24-bit number (2 or 3 bytes). If the data consists of date/time pairs, a possible compressed representation is the number of seconds since a convenient start date. If stored as a 32-bit number (4 bytes) it can be sufficient for about 136 years.

■   Dictionary data (or any list sorted lexicographically) can be compressed using the concept of *front compression*. This is based on the observation that adjacent words in such a list tend to share some of their initial characters. A word can thus be compressed by dropping the n characters it shares with its predecessor in the list and replacing them with n.

Table 1.5 shows a short example taken from a word list used to create anagrams. It is clear that it is easy to get significant compression with this simple method (see also [Robinson 81] and [Nix 81]).

■   The MacWrite word processor [Young 85] uses a special 4-bit code to code the most common 15 characters "␣etnroaisdlhcfp" plus an escape code. Any of

Letters	Code	Figures	Letters	Code	Figures
A	10000	1	Q	10111	/
B	00110	8	R	00111	-
C	10110	9	S	00101	SP
D	11110	0	T	10101	na
E	01000	2	U	10100	4
F	01110	na	V	11101	'
G	01010	7	W	01101	?
H	11010	+	X	01001	,
I	01100	na	Y	00100	3
J	10010	6	Z	11001	:
K	10011	(	LS	00001	LS
L	11011	=	FS	00010	FS
M	01011	)	CR	11000	CR
N	01111	na	LF	10001	LF
O	11100	5	ER	00011	ER
P	11111	%	na	00000	na

LS, Letter Shift; FS, Figure Shift.
CR, Carriage Return; LF, Line Feed.
ER, Error; na, Not Assigned; SP, Space.

Table 1.4: The Baudot Code.

The 9/19/89 Syndrome

How can a date, such as 11/12/71, be represented inside a computer? One way to do this is to store the number of days since January 1, 1900 in an integer variable. If the variable is 16 bits long (including 15 magnitude bits and one sign bit), it will overflow after $2^{15} = 32K = 32,768$ days, which is September 19, 1989. This is precisely what happened on that day in several computers (see the January, 1991 issue of the *Communications of the ACM*). Notice that doubling the size of such a variable to 32 bits would have delayed the problem until after $2^{31} = 2$ giga days have passed, which would occur sometime in the fall of year 5,885,416.

---

these 15 characters is encoded by 4 bits. Any other character is encoded as the escape code followed by the 8 bits ASCII code of the character; a total of 12 bits. Each paragraph is coded separately, and if this results in expansion, the paragraph is stored as plain ASCII. One more bit is added to each paragraph to indicate whether or not it uses compression.

a	a
aardvark	1ardvark
aback	1back
abaft	3ft
abandon	3ndon
abandoning	7ing
abasement	3sement
abandonment	3ndonment
abash	3sh
abated	3ted
abate	5
abbot	2bot
abbey	3ey
abbreviating	3reviating
abbreviate	9e
abbreviation	9ion

Table 1.5: Front Compression.

The principle of parsimony values a theory's ability to compress a maximum of information into a minimum of formalism. Einstein's celebrated $E = mc^2$ derives part of its well-deserved fame from the astonishing wealth of meaning it packs into its tiny frame. Maxwell's equations, the rules of quantum mechanics, and even the basic equations of the general theory of relativity similarly satisfy the parsimony requirement of a fundamental theory: They are compact enough to fit on a T-shirt. By way of contrast, the human genome project, requiring the quantification of hundreds of thousands of genetic sequences, represents the very antithesis of parsimony.

—Hans Christian von Baeyer, *Maxwell's Demon*, 1998

1.2 Run Length Encoding

The idea behind this approach to data compression is this: If a data item d occurs n consecutive times in the input stream, replace the n occurrences with the single pair nd. The n consecutive occurrences of a data item are called a *run length* of n, and this approach to data compression is called *run length encoding* or RLE. We apply this idea first to text compression then to image compression.

1.3 RLE Text Compression

Just replacing "2.␣all␣is␣too␣well" with "2.␣a2␣is␣t2␣we2" will not work. Clearly, the decompressor should have a way to tell that the first "2" is part of the text while the others are repetition factors for the letters "o" and "l". Even the string "2.␣a2l␣is t2o␣we2l" does not solve this problem (and also does not provide any compression). One way to solve this problem is to precede each repetition with a special escape character. If we use the character "@" as the escape character, then the string "2.␣a@2l␣is␣t@2o we@2l" can be decompressed unambiguously. However, it is longer than the original string, since it replaces two consecutive letters with three characters. We have to adopt the convention that only three or more repetitions of the same character will be replaced with a repetition factor. Figure 1.6a is a flowchart for such a simple run-length text compressor.

After reading the first character, the count is 1 and the character is saved. Subsequent characters are compared with the one already saved and, if they are identical to it, the repeat-count is incremented. When a different character is read, the operation depends on the value of the repeat count. If it is small, the saved character is written on the compressed file and the newly read character is saved. Otherwise, an "@" is written, followed by the repeat-count and the saved character.

Decompression is also straightforward. It is shown in Figure 1.6b. When an "@" is read, the repetition count n and the actual character are immediately read, and the character is written n times on the output stream.

The main problems with this method are the following:

1. In plain English text there are not many repetitions. There are many "doubles" but a "triple" is rare. The most repetitive character is the space. Dashes or asterisks may also repeat sometimes. In mathematical texts, some digits may repeat. The following "paragraph" is a contrived example.

> The abbott from Abruzzi accedes to the demands of all abbesses from Narragansett and Abbevilles from Abyssinia. He will accommodate them, abbreviate his sabbatical, and be an accomplished accessory.

2. The character "@" may be part of the text in the input stream, in which case a different escape character must be chosen. Sometimes the input stream may contain every possible character in the alphabet. An example is an object file, the result of compiling a program. Such a file contains machine instructions and can be thought of as a string of bytes that can have any values. The MNP5 method described below and in Section 2.10 provides a solution.

3. Since the repetition count is written on the output stream as a byte, it is limited to counts of up to 255. This limitation can be softened somewhat when we realize that the existence of a repetition count means that there is a repetition (at least three identical consecutive characters). We may adopt the convention that a repeat count of 0 means three repeat characters. This implies that a repeat count of 255 means a run of 258 identical characters.

> There are three kinds of lies: lies, damned lies, and statistics.
> (Attributed by Mark Twain to Benjamin Disraeli)

The MNP class 5 method is commonly used for data compression by modems. It has been developed by Microcom, Inc., a maker of modems (MNP stands for Microcom Network Protocol) and it uses a combination of run length and adaptive frequency encoding. The latter technique is described in Section 2.10, but here is how MNP5 solves problem 2 above.

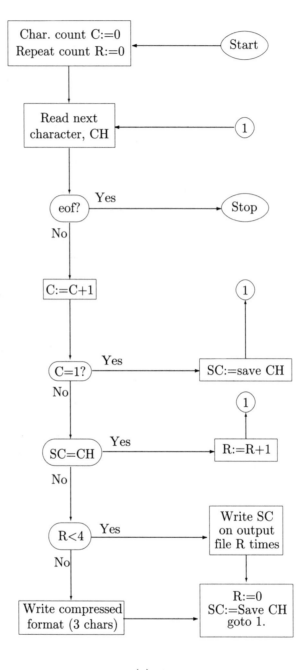

(a)

Figure 1.6: RLE. Part I: Compression.

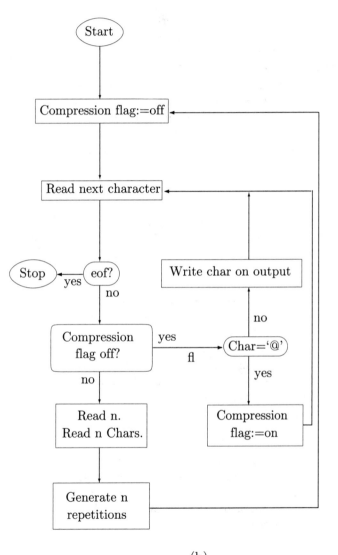

(b)

Figure 1.6: RLE. Part II: Decompression.

When three or more identical consecutive bytes are found in the input stream, the compressor writes three copies of the byte on the output stream, followed by a repetition count. When the decompressor reads three identical consecutive bytes, it knows that the next byte is a repetition count (which may be 0, indicating just three repetitions). A disadvantage of the method is that a run of three characters in the input stream results in four characters written to the output stream: expansion! A run of four characters results in no compression. Only runs longer than 4 characters get compressed. Another slight problem is that the maximum count is artificially limited in MNP5 to 250 instead of 255.

To get an idea of the compression ratios produced by RLE, we assume a string of N characters that needs to be compressed. We assume that the string contains M repetitions of average length L each. Each of the M repetitions is replaced by 3 characters (escape, count, and data), so the size of the compressed string is $N - M \times L + M \times 3 = N - M(L - 3)$ and the compression factor is

$$\frac{N}{N - M(L - 3)}.$$

(For MNP5 just substitute 4 for 3.) Examples: $N = 1000, M = 10, L = 3$ yield a compression factor of $1000/[1000 - 10(4 - 3)] = 1.01$. A better result is obtained in the case $N = 1000, M = 50, L = 10$, where the factor is $1000/[1000 - 50(10 - 3)] = 1.538$.

A variant of run length encoding for text is *digram encoding*. This method is suitable for cases where the data to be compressed consists only of certain characters, e.g., just letters, digits, and punctuation. The idea is to identify commonly occurring pairs of characters and to replace a pair (a digram) with one of the characters that cannot occur in the data (e.g., one of the ASCII control characters). Good results can be obtained if the data can be analyzed beforehand. We know that in plain English certain pairs of characters, such as "E␣", "␣T", "TH", and "␣A", occur often. Other types of data may have different common digrams. The sequitur method of Section 8.10 is an example of a method that compresses data by locating repeating digrams (as well as longer repeated phrases) and replacing them with special symbols.

A similar variant is *pattern substitution*. This is suitable for compressing computer programs, where certain words, such as `for`, `repeat`, and `print`, occur often. Each such word is replaced with a control character or, if there are many such words, with an escape character followed by a code character. Assuming that code "a" is assigned to the word `print`, the text "m:␣print,b,a;" will be compressed to "m:␣@a,b,a;".

1.3.1 Relative Encoding

This is another variant, sometimes called *differencing* (see [Gottlieb 75]). It is used in cases where the data to be compressed consists of a string of numbers that do not differ by much, or in cases where it consists of strings that are similar to each other. An example of the former is telemetry. The latter case is used in facsimile data compression described in Section 2.13 and also in LZW compression (Section 3.10.4).

In telemetry, a sensing device is used to collect data at certain intervals and transmit it to a central location for further processing. An example is temperature values collected every hour. Successive temperatures normally do not differ by much, so the sensor needs to send only the first temperature, followed by differences. Thus the sequence of temperatures $70, 71, 72.5, 73.1, \ldots$ can be compressed to $70, 1, 1.5, 0.6, \ldots$. This compresses the data, since the differences are small and can be expressed in fewer bits.

Notice that the differences can be negative and may sometimes be large. When a large difference is found, the compressor sends the actual value of the next measurement instead of the difference. Thus the sequence $110, 115, 121, 119, 200, 202, \ldots$ can be compressed to $110, 5, 6, -2, 200, 2, \ldots$. Unfortunately, we now need to distinguish between a difference and an actual value. This can be done by the compressor creating an extra bit (a flag) for each number sent, accumulating those bits, and sending them to the decompressor from time to time, as part of the transmission. Assuming that each difference is sent as a byte, the compressor should follow (or precede) a group of 8 bytes with a byte consisting of their 8 flags.

Another practical way to send differences mixed with actual values is to send pairs of bytes. Each pair is either an actual 16-bit measurement (positive or negative) or two 8-bit signed differences. Thus actual measurements can be between 0 and $\pm 32K$ and differences can be between 0 and ± 255. For each pair, the compressor creates a flag: 0 if the pair is an actual value, 1 if it is a pair of differences. After 16 pairs are sent, the compressor sends the 16 flags.

Example: The sequence of measurements $110, 115, 121, 119, 200, 202, \ldots$ is sent as $(110), (5, 6), (-2, -1), (200), (2, \ldots)$, where each pair of parentheses indicates a pair of bytes. The -1 has value 11111111_2, which is ignored by the decompressor (it indicates that there is only one difference in this pair). While sending this information, the compressor prepares the flags $01101\ldots$, which are sent after the first 16 pairs.

Relative encoding can be generalized to the lossy case, where it is called *differential encoding*. An example of a differential encoding method is differential pulse code modulation (or DPCM, Section 4.23).

1.4 RLE Image Compression

RLE is a natural candidate for compressing graphical data. A digital image consists of small dots called *pixels*. Each pixel can be either one bit, indicating a black or a white dot, or several bits, indicating one of several colors or shades of gray. We assume that the pixels are stored in an array called a *bitmap* in memory, so the bitmap is the input stream for the image. Pixels are normally arranged in the bitmap in scan lines, so the first bitmap pixel is the dot at the top left corner of the image, and the last pixel is the one at the bottom right corner.

Compressing an image using RLE is based on the observation that if we select a pixel in the image at random, there is a good chance that its neighbors will have the same color (see also Sections 4.27 and 4.29). The compressor thus scans the bitmap row by row, looking for runs of pixels of the same color. If the bitmap starts, e.g., with 17 white pixels, followed by 1 black one, followed by 55 white ones, etc., then only the numbers $17, 1, 55, \ldots$ need be written on the output stream.

The compressor assumes that the bitmap starts with white pixels. If this is not true, then the bitmap starts with zero white pixels, and the output stream should start with 0. The resolution of the bitmap should also be saved at the start of the output stream.

The size of the compressed stream depends on the complexity of the image. The more detail, the worse the compression. However, Figure 1.7 shows how scan lines go through a uniform area. A line enters through one point on the perimeter of the area and exits through another point, and these two points are not "used" by any other scan lines. It is now clear that the number of scan lines traversing a uniform area is roughly equal to half the length (measured in pixels) of its perimeter. Since the area is uniform, each scan line contributes one number to the output stream. The compression ratio of a uniform area thus roughly equals the ratio

$$\frac{\text{half the length of the perimeter}}{\text{total number of pixels in the area}}.$$

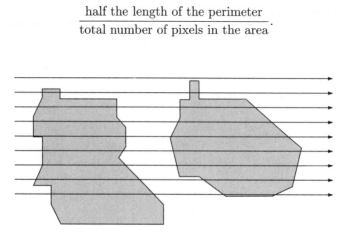

Figure 1.7: Uniform Areas and Scan Lines.

◇ **Exercise 1.3:** What would be the compressed file in the case of the following 6×8 bitmap?

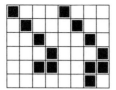

RLE can also be used to compress grayscale images. Each run of pixels of the same intensity (gray level) is encoded as a pair (run length, pixel value). The run length usually occupies one byte, allowing for runs of up to 255 pixels. The pixel value occupies several bits, depending on the number of gray levels (typically between 4 and 8 bits).

Example: An 8-bit deep grayscale bitmap that starts with

$$12, 12, 12, 12, 12, 12, 12, 12, 12, 35, 76, 112, 67, 87, 87, 87, 5, 5, 5, 5, 5, 5, 1, \ldots$$

is compressed into $\boxed{9}$,12,35,76,112,67,$\boxed{3}$,87, $\boxed{6}$,5,1,..., where the boxed numbers indicate counts. The problem is to distinguish between a byte containing a grayscale value (such as 12) and one containing a count (such as $\boxed{9}$). Here are some solutions (although not the only possible ones):

1. If the image is limited to just 128 grayscales, we can devote one bit in each byte to indicate whether the byte contains a grayscale value or a count.

2. If the number of grayscales is 256, it can be reduced to 255 with one value reserved as a flag to precede every byte with a count. If the flag is, say, 255, then the sequence above becomes

$$255, 9, 12, 35, 76, 112, 67, 255, 3, 87, 255, 6, 5, 1, \ldots.$$

3. Again, one bit is devoted to each byte to indicate whether the byte contains a grayscale value or a count. This time, however, these extra bits are accumulated in groups of 8, and each group is written on the output stream preceding (or following) the 8 bytes it "belongs to."

Example: the sequence $\boxed{9}$,12,35,76,112,67,$\boxed{3}$,87,$\boxed{6}$,5,1,... becomes

$\boxed{10000010}$,9,12,35,76,112,67,3,87,$\boxed{100.....}$,6,5,1,... .

The total size of the extra bytes is, of course, 1/8 the size of the output stream (they contain one bit for each byte of the output stream), so they increase the size of that stream by 12.5%.

4. A group of m pixels that are all different is preceded by a byte with the negative value $-m$. The sequence above is encoded by

$9, 12, -4, 35, 76, 112, 67, 3, 87, 6, 5, ?, 1, \ldots$ (the value of the byte with ? is positive or negative depending on what follows the pixel of 1). The worst case is a sequence of pixels (p_1, p_2, p_2) repeated n times throughout the bitmap. It is encoded as $(-1, p_1, 2, p_2)$, four numbers instead of the original three! If each pixel requires one byte, then the original three bytes are expanded into four bytes. If each pixel requires three bytes, then the original three pixels (comprising 9 bytes) are compressed into $1 + 3 + 1 + 3 = 8$ bytes.

Three more points should be mentioned:

1. Since the run length cannot be 0, it makes sense to write the [run length minus one] on the output stream. Thus the pair $(3, 87)$ means a run of *four* pixels with intensity 87. This way, a run can be up to 256 pixels long.

2. In color images it is common to have each pixel stored as three bytes, representing the intensities of the red, green, and blue components of the pixel. In such a case, runs of each color should be encoded separately. Thus the pixels $(171, 85, 34)$, $(172, 85, 35)$, $(172, 85, 30)$, and $(173, 85, 33)$ should be separated into the three sequences $(171, 172, 172, 173, \ldots)$, $(85, 85, 85, 85, \ldots)$, and $(34, 35, 30, 33, \ldots)$. Each sequence should be run-length encoded separately. This means that any method for compressing grayscale images can be applied to color images as well.

3. It is preferable to encode each row of the bitmap individually. Thus if a row ends with four pixels of intensity 87 and the following row starts with 9 such pixels, it is better to write $\ldots, 4, 87, 9, 87, \ldots$ on the output stream rather than $\ldots, 13, 87, \ldots$. It is even better to write the sequence $\ldots, 4, 87, \text{eol}, 9, 87, \ldots$, where "eol" is a special

end-of-line code. The reason is that sometimes the user may decide to accept or reject an image just by examining its general shape, without any details. If each line is encoded individually, the decoding algorithm can start by decoding and displaying lines $1, 6, 11, \ldots$, continue with lines $2, 7, 12, \ldots$, etc. The individual rows of the image are interlaced, and the image is built on the screen gradually, in several steps. This way, it is possible to get an idea of what is in the image at an early stage. Figure 1.8c shows an example of such a scan.

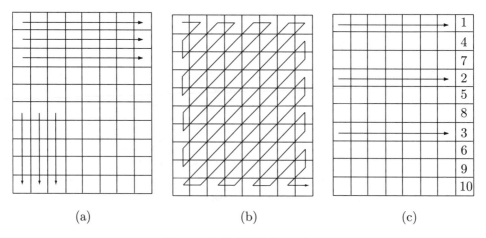

(a)   (b)   (c)

Figure 1.8: RLE Scanning.

Another advantage of individual encoding of rows is to make it possible to extract just part of an encoded image (such as rows k through l). Yet another application is to merge two compressed images without having to decompress them first.

If this idea (encoding each bitmap row individually) is adopted, then the compressed stream must contain information on where each bitmap row starts in the stream. This can be done by writing a header at the start of the stream that contains a group of 4 bytes (32 bits) for each bitmap row. The kth such group contains the offset (in bytes) from the start of the stream to the start of the information for row k. This increases the size of the compressed stream but may still offer a good trade-off between space (size of compressed stream) and time (time to decide whether to accept or reject the image).

⋄ **Exercise 1.4:** There is another, obvious, reason why each bitmap row should be coded individually. What is it?

Figure 1.9a lists Matlab code to compute run lengths for a bi-level image. The code is very simple. It starts by flattening the matrix into a one-dimensional vector, so the run lengths continue from row to row.

Disadvantage of image RLE: When the image is modified, the run lengths normally have to be completely redone. The RLE output can sometimes be bigger than pixel-by-pixel storage (i.e., an uncompressed image, a raw dump of the bitmap)

```
% Returns the run lengths of
% a matrix of 0s and 1s
function R=runlengths(M)
[c,r]=size(M);
for i=1:c;
 x(r*(i-1)+1:r*i)=M(i,:);
end
N=r*c;
y=x(2:N);
u=x(1:N-1);
z=y+u;
j=find(z==1);
i1=[j N];
i2=[0 j];
R=i1-i2;

the test
M=[0 0 0 1; 1 1 1 0; 1 1 1 0]
runlengths(M)

produces
3    4    1    3    1
```

(a)   (b)

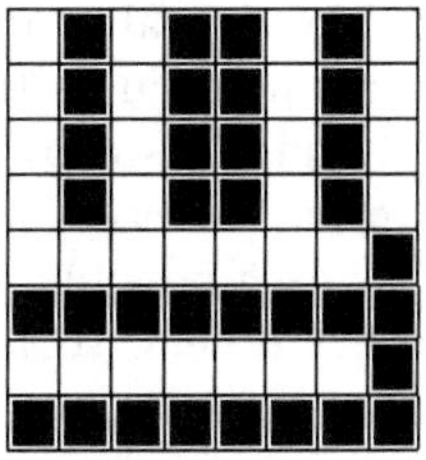

Figure 1.9: (a) Matlab Code To Compute Run Lengths; (b) A Bitmap.

for complex pictures. Imagine a picture with many vertical lines. When it is scanned horizontally, it produces very short runs, resulting in very bad compression, or even in expansion. A good, practical RLE image compressor should be able to scan the bitmap by rows, columns, or in zigzag (Figure 1.8a,b) and it may automatically try all three ways on every bitmap compressed to achieve the best compression.

◇ **Exercise 1.5:** Given the 8×8 bitmap of Figure 1.9b, use RLE to compress it, first row by row, then column by column. Describe the results in detail.

1.4.1 Lossy Image Compression

It is possible to get even better compression ratios if short runs are ignored. Such a method loses information when compressing an image, but sometimes this is acceptable to the user. (Notable examples where no loss is acceptable are X-ray images and astronomical images taken by large telescopes, where the price of an image is astronomical.)

A lossy run length encoding algorithm should start by asking the user for the longest run that should still be ignored. If the user specifies, for example, 3, then the program merges all runs of 1, 2, or 3 identical pixels with their neighbors. The compressed data "6,8,1,2,4,3,11,2" would be saved, in this case, as "6,8,7,16" where

7 is the sum $1 + 2 + 4$ (three runs merged) and 16 is the sum $3 + 11 + 2$. This makes sense for large high-resolution images where the loss of some detail may be invisible to the eye, but may significantly reduce the size of the output stream (see also Chapter 4).

1.4.2 Conditional Image RLE

Facsimile compression (Section 2.13) uses a modified Huffman code, but it can also be considered a modified RLE. This section discusses another modification of RLE, proposed in [Gharavi 87]. Assuming an image with n grayscales, the method starts by assigning an n-bit code to each pixel depending on its near neighbors. It then concatenates the n-bit codes into a long string, and calculates run lengths. The run lengths are assigned prefix codes (Huffman or otherwise, Section 2.3) that are written on the compressed stream.

The method considers each scan line in the image a second-order Markov model. In such a model the value of the current data item depends on just two of its past neighbors, not necessarily the two immediate ones. Figure 1.10 shows the two neighbors A and B used by our method to predict the current pixel X (compare this with the lossless mode of JPEG, Section 4.6.7). A set of training images is used to count—for each possible pair of values of the neighbors A, B—how many times each value of X occurs. If A and B have similar values, it is natural to expect that X will have a similar value. If A and B have very different values, we expect X to have many different values, each with a low probability. The counts thus produce the conditional probabilities $P(X|A, B)$ (the probability of the current pixel having value X if we already know that its neighbors have values A and B). Table 1.11 lists a small part of the results obtained by counting this way several training images with 4-bit pixels.

Each pixel in the image to be compressed is assigned a new four-bit code depending on its conditional probability as indicated by the table. Imagine a current pixel X with value 1 whose neighbors have values $A = 3$, $B = 1$. The table indicates that the conditional probability $P(1|3, 1)$ is high, so X should be assigned a new 4-bit code with few runs (i.e., codes that contain consecutive 1's or consecutive 0's). On the other hand, the same $X = 1$ with neighbors $A = 3$ and $B = 3$ can be assigned a new 4-bit code with many runs, since the table indicates that the conditional probability $P(1|3, 3)$ is low. The method therefore uses conditional probabilities to detect common pixels (hence the name *conditional RLE*), and assigns them codes with few runs.

Examining all 16 four-bit codes W_1 through W_{16}, we find that the two codes 0000 and 1111 have one run each, while 0101 and 1010 have four runs each. The codes should thus be arranged in order of increasing runs. For 4-bit codes we end up with the four groups

$$W_1 \text{ to } W_2 : 0000, 1111,$$
$$W_3 \text{ to } W_8 : 0001, 0011, 0111, 1110, 1100, 1000,$$
$$W_9 \text{ to } W_{14} : 0100, 0010, 0110, 1011, 1101, 1001,$$
$$W_{15} \text{ to } W_{16} : 0101, 1010.$$

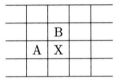

Figure 1.10: Neighbors Used To Predict X.

A	B		W1	W2	W3	W4	W5	W6	W7 ...
2	15	value:	4	3	10	0	6	8	1 ...
		count:	21	6	5	4	2	2	1 ...
3	0	value:	0	1	3	2	11	4	15 ...
		count:	443	114	75	64	56	19	12 ...
3	1	value:	1	2	3	4	0	5	6 ...
		count:	1139	817	522	75	55	20	8 ...
3	2	value:	2	3	1	4	5	6	0 ...
		count:	7902	4636	426	264	64	18	6 ...
3	3	value:	3	2	4	5	1	6	7 ...
		count:	33927	2869	2511	138	93	51	18 ...
3	4	value:	4	3	5	2	6	7	1 ...
		count:	2859	2442	240	231	53	31	13 ...

Table 1.11: Conditional Counting of 4-Bit Pixels.

The codes of group i have i runs each. The codes in each group are selected such that the codes in the second half of a group are the complements of those in the first half.

⋄ **Exercise 1.6:** Use this principle to construct the 32 five-bit codes.

The method can now be described in detail. The image is scanned in raster order. For each pixel X, its neighbors A and B are located, and the table is searched for this triplet. If the triplet is found in column i, then code W_i is selected. The first pixel has no neighbors, so if its value is i, code W_i is selected for it. If X is located at the top row of the image, it has an A neighbor but not a B neighbor, so this case is handled differently. Imagine a pixel $X = 2$ at the top row with a neighbor $A = 3$. All the rows in the table with $A = 3$ are examined, in this case, and the one with the largest count for $X = 2$ is selected. In our example this is the row with count 7902, so code W_1 is selected. Pixels X with no A neighbors (on the left column) are treated similarly.

Rule of complementing: After the code for X has been selected, it is compared with the preceding code. If the least-significant bit of the preceding code is 1, the current code is complemented. This is supposed to reduce the number of runs. As an example, consider the typical sequence of 4-bit codes $W_2, W_4, W_1, W_6, W_3, W_2, W_1$

$$1111, 0011, 0000, 1110, 0001, 1111, 0000.$$

When these codes are concatenated, the resulting 28-bit string has eight runs. After applying the rule above, the codes become

$$1111, 1100, 0000, 1110, 0001, 0000, 0000,$$

a string with just six runs.

◇ **Exercise 1.7:** Do the same for the code sequence W_1, W_2, W_3, W_6, W_1, W_4, W_2.

A	B		W1	W2	W3	W4	W5	W6	W7 ...
2	15	value:	4	3	10	0	6	8	1 ...
		code:	01	00	111	110	1011	1010	10010 ...
3	0	value:	0	1	3	2	11	4	15 ...
		code:	11	10	00	010	0110	011111	011101 ...
3	1	value:	1	2	3	4	0	5	6 ...
		code:	0	11	100	1011	10100	101010	10101111 ...
3	2	value:	2	3	1	4	5	6	0 ...
		code:	0	11	100	1011	10100	101010	10101111 ...
3	3	value:	3	2	4	5	1	6	7 ...
		code:	0	11	100	1011	101001	1010000	10101000 ...
3	4	value:	4	3	5	2	6	7	1 ...
		code:	11	10	00	0111	0110	0100	010110 ...

Table 1.12: Prefix Codes For 4-Bit Pixels.

A variation of this method uses the counts of Table 1.11 but not its codes and not run lengths. Instead, it assigns a prefix code to the current pixel X depending on its neighbors A and B. Table 1.12 is an example. Each row has a different set of prefix codes constructed according to the counts of the row.

Bibliography

Gharavi, H. (1987) "Conditional Run-Length and Variable-Length Coding of Digital Pictures," *IEEE Transactions on Communications*, COM-35(6):671–677, June.

1.4.3 The BinHex 4.0 Format

BinHex 4.0 is a file format for safe file transfers, designed by Yves Lempereur for use on the Macintosh computer. Before delving into the details of the format, the reader should understand why such a format is useful. ASCII is a 7-bit code. Each character is coded into a 7-bit number, which allows for 128 characters in the ASCII table (Appendix A). The ASCII standard recommends adding an eighth bit as parity to every character for increased reliability. However, the standard does not specify odd or even parity, and many computers simply ignore the extra bit or even set it to 0. As a result, when files are transferred in a computer network, some transfer programs may ignore the eighth bit and transfer just seven bits per character. This isn't so bad when a text file is being transferred but when the file is binary, no bits should be ignored. This is why it is safer to transfer text files, rather than binary files, over computer networks.

The idea of BinHex is to translate any file to a text file. The BinHex program reads an input file (text or binary) and produces an output file with the following format:

1. The comment:

(This␣file␣must␣be␣converted␣with␣BinHex␣4.0)

2. A header including the items listed in Table 1.13.

3. The input file is then read and RLE is used as the first step. Character 90_{16} is used as the RLE marker, and the following examples speak for themselves:

Source string	Packed string
00 11 22 33 44 55 66 77	00 11 22 33 44 55 66 77
11 22 22 22 22 22 22 33	11 22 90 06 33
11 22 90 33 44	11 22 90 00 33 44

(The character 00 indicates no run.) Runs of lengths 3–255 characters are encoded this way.

Field	Size
Length of FileName (1–63)	byte
FileName	("Length" bytes)
Version	byte
Type	long
Creator	long
Flags (And $F800)	word
Length of Data Fork	long
Length of Resource Fork	long
CRC	word
Data Fork	("Data Length" bytes)
CRC	word
Resource Fork	("Rsrc Length" bytes)
CRC	word

Table 1.13: The BinHex Header.

⋄ **Exercise 1.8:** How is the string "11 22 90 00 33 44" encoded?

4. Encoding into 7-bit ASCII characters. The input file is considered a stream of bits. As the file is being read, it is divided into blocks of 6 bits, and each block is used as a pointer to the BinHex table below. The character that's pointed at in this table is written on the output file. The table is

!"#$%&'()*+,-012345689@ABCDEFGHIJKLMNPQRSTUVXYZ['abcdefhijklmpqr

The output file is organized in "lines" of 64 characters each (except, perhaps, the last line). Each line is preceded and followed by a pair of colons ":". The following is a quotation from the designer:

"The characters in this table have been chosen for maximum noise protection."

◇ **Exercise 1.9:** Manually convert the string "123ABC" to BinHex. Ignore the comment and the file header.

1.5 Move-to-Front Coding

The basic idea of this method [Bentley 86] is to maintain the alphabet A of symbols as a list where frequently occurring symbols are located near the front. A symbol "s" is encoded as the number of symbols that precede it in this list. Thus if A=("t", "h", "e", "s",...) and the next symbol in the input stream to be encoded is "e", it will be encoded as 2, since it is preceded by two symbols. There are several possible variants to this method; the most basic of them adds one more step: After symbol "s" is encoded, it is moved to the front of list A. Thus, after encoding "e", the alphabet is modified to A=("e", "t", "h", "s",...). This move-to-front step reflects the hope that once "e" has been read from the input stream, it will be read many more times and will, at least for a while, be a common symbol. The move-to-front method is *locally adaptive*, since it adapts itself to the frequencies of symbols in local areas of the input stream.

The method thus produces good results if the input stream satisfies this hope, i.e., if it contains concentrations of identical symbols (if the local frequency of symbols changes significantly from area to area in the input stream). We call this "the concentration property." Here are two examples that illustrate the move-to-front idea. Both assume the alphabet A=("a", "b", "c", "d", "m", "n", "o", "p").

1. The input stream "abcddcbamnopponm" is encoded as $C = (0, 1, 2, 3, 0, 1, 2, 3, 4, 5, 6, 7, 0, 1, 2, 3)$ (Table 1.14a). Without the move-to-front step it is encoded as $C' = (0, 1, 2, 3, 3, 2, 1, 0, 4, 5, 6, 7, 7, 6, 5, 4)$ (Table 1.14b). Both C and C' contain codes in the same range $[0, 7]$, but the elements of C are smaller on the average, since the input starts with a concentration of "abcd" and continues with a concentration of "mnop". (The average value of C is 2.5, while that of C' is 3.5.)

2. The input stream "abcdmnopabcdmnop" is encoded as $C = (0, 1, 2, 3, 4, 5, 6, 7, 7, 7, 7, 7, 7, 7, 7, 7)$ (Table 1.14c). Without the move-to-front step it is encoded as $C' = (0, 1, 2, 3, 4, 5, 6, 7, 0, 1, 2, 3, 4, 5, 6, 7)$ (Table 1.14d). The average of C is now 5.25, greater than that of C', which is 3.5. The move-to-front rule creates a worse result in this case, since the input does not contain concentrations of identical symbols (it does not satisfy the concentration property).

Before getting into further details, it is important to understand the advantage of having small numbers in C. This feature makes it possible to efficiently encode C with either Huffman or arithmetic coding (Chapter 2). Here are four ways to do this:

1. Assign Huffman codes to the integers in the range $[0, n]$ such that the smaller integers get the shorter codes. Here is an example of such a code for the integers 0 through 7:

    0—0, 1—10, 2—110, 3—1110, 4—11110, 5—111110, 6—1111110, 7—1111111.

2. Assign codes to the integers such that the code of integer $i \geq 1$ is its binary code preceded by $\lfloor \log_2 i \rfloor$ zeros. Table 1.15 shows some examples.

a	abcdmnop	0	a	abcdmnop	0	a	abcdmnop	0	a	abcdmnop	0
b	abcdmnop	1	b	abcdmnop	1	b	abcdmnop	1	b	abcdmnop	1
c	bacdmnop	2	c	abcdmnop	2	c	bacdmnop	2	c	abcdmnop	2
d	cbadmnop	3	d	abcdmnop	3	d	cbadmnop	3	d	abcdmnop	3
d	dcbamnop	0	d	abcdmnop	3	m	dcbamnop	4	m	abcdmnop	4
c	dcbamnop	1	c	abcdmnop	2	n	mdcbanop	5	n	abcdmnop	5
b	cdbamnop	2	b	abcdmnop	1	o	nmdcbaop	6	o	abcdmnop	6
a	bcdamnop	3	a	abcdmnop	0	p	onmdcbap	7	p	abcdmnop	7
m	abcdmnop	4	m	abcdmnop	4	a	ponmdcba	7	a	abcdmnop	0
n	mabcdnop	5	n	abcdmnop	5	b	aponmdcb	7	b	abcdmnop	1
o	nmabcdop	6	o	abcdmnop	6	c	baponmdc	7	c	abcdmnop	2
p	onmabcdp	7	p	abcdmnop	7	d	cbaponmd	7	d	abcdmnop	3
p	ponmabcd	0	p	abcdmnop	7	m	dcbaponm	7	m	abcdmnop	4
o	ponmabcd	1	o	abcdmnop	6	n	mdcbapon	7	n	abcdmnop	5
n	opnmabcd	2	n	abcdmnop	5	o	nmdcbapo	7	o	abcdmnop	6
m	nopmabcd	3	m	abcdmnop	4	p	onmdcbap	7	p	abcdmnop	7
	mnopabcd						ponmdcba				
	(a)			(b)			(c)			(d)	

Table 1.14: Encoding With and Without Move-to-Front.

i	Code	Size
1	1	1
2	010	3
3	011	3
4	00100	5
5	00101	5
6	00110	5
7	00111	5
8	0001000	7
9	0001001	7
$\vdots$	$\vdots$	$\vdots$
15	0001111	7
16	000010000	9

Table 1.15: Examples of Variable-Size Codes.

⋄ **Exercise 1.10:** What is the total size of the code of i in this case?

3. Use adaptive Huffman coding (Section 2.9).

4. For maximum compression, perform two passes over C, the first pass counting frequencies of codes and the second one performing the actual encoding. The frequencies counted in pass 1 are used to compute probabilities and assign Huffman codes to be used later by pass 2.

It can be shown that the move-to-front method performs, in the worst case, slightly worse than Huffman coding. At best, it performs significantly better.

As has been mentioned earlier, it is easy to come up with variations of the basic idea of move-to-front. Here are some of them.

1. Move-ahead-k. The element of A matched by the current symbol is moved ahead k positions instead of all the way to the front of A. The parameter k can be specified by the user, with a default value of either n or 1. This tends to reduce performance (i.e., to increase the average size of the elements of C) for inputs that satisfy the concentration property, but it works better for other inputs. Notice that assigning $k = n$ is identical to move-to-front. The case $k = 1$ is especially simple, since it only requires swapping an element of A with the one preceding it.

◇ **Exercise 1.11:** Use move-ahead-k to encode each of the strings "abcddcbamnop-ponm" and "abcdmnopabcdmnop" twice, with $k = 1$ and $k = 2$.

2. Wait-c-and-move. An element of A is moved to the front only after it has been matched c times to symbols from the input stream (not necessarily c consecutive times). Each element of A should have a counter associated with it, to count the number of matches. This method makes sense in implementations where moving and rearranging elements of A is slow.

3. Normally, a symbol read from the input is a byte. If the input stream consists of text, however, it may make sense to treat each **word**, not each character, as a symbol. Consider the simple case where the input consists of just lower-case letters, spaces, and one end-of-text marker at the end. We can define a word as a string of letters followed by a space or by the end-of-text marker. The number of words in this case can be huge, so the alphabet list A should start empty, and words should be added as they are being input and encoded. We use the text

$$\text{the}_\sqcup\text{boy}_\sqcup\text{on}_\sqcup\text{my}_\sqcup\text{right}_\sqcup\text{is}_\sqcup\text{the}_\sqcup\text{right}_\sqcup\text{boy}$$

as an example.

The first word input is "the". It is not found in A, since A is empty, so it is added to A. The encoder emits 0 (the number of words preceding "the" in A) followed by "the". The decoder also starts with an empty A. The 0 tells it to select the first word in A but since A is empty, the decoder knows to expect the 0 to be followed by a word. It adds this word to A.

The next word is "boy". It is added to A, so A=("the", "boy") and the encoder emits "1boy". The word "boy" is moved to the front of A, so A=("boy", "the"). The decoder reads the 1, which refers to the second word of A, but the decoder's A has only one word in it so far. The decoder thus knows that a new word must follow the 1. It reads this word and adds it to the front of A. Table 1.16 summarizes the encoding steps for this example.

List A may grow very large in this variant, but any practical implementation has to limit its size. This is why the last item of A (the least recently used item) has to be deleted when A exceeds its size limit. This is another difference between this variant and the basic move-to-front method.

Word	A (before adding)	A (after adding)	Code emitted
the	()	(the)	0the
boy	(the)	(the, boy)	1boy
on	(boy, the)	(boy, the, on)	2on
my	(on, boy, the)	(on, boy, the, my)	3my
right	(my, on, boy, the)	(my, on, boy, the, right)	4right
is	(right, my, on, boy, the)	(right, my, on, boy, the, is)	5is
the	(is, right, my, on, boy, the)	(is, right, my, on, boy, the)	5
right	(the, is, right, my, on, boy)	(the, is, right, my, on, boy)	2
boy	(right, the, is, my, on, boy)	(right, the, is, my, on, boy)	5
	(boy, right, the, is, my, on)		

Table 1.16: Encoding Multiple-Letter Words.

⬦ **Exercise 1.12:** Decode "the␣boy␣on␣my␣right␣is␣the␣right␣boy" and summarize the steps in a table.

Bibliography

Bentley, J. L. et al. (1986) "A Locally Adaptive Data Compression Algorithm," *Communications of the ACM* **29**(4):320–330, April.

Gottlieb, D., et al. (1975) *A Classification of Compression Methods and their Usefulness for a Large Data Processing Center*, Proceedings of National Computer Conference **44**:453–458.

Nix, R. (1981) "Experience With a Space Efficient Way to Store a Dictionary," *Communications of the ACM* **24**(5):297–298.

Robinson, P., and D. Singer (1981) "Another Spelling Correction Program," *Communications of the ACM* **24**(5):296–297.

Young, D. M. (1985) "MacWrite File Format," *Wheels for the Mind* **1**:34, Fall.

1.6 Scalar Quantization

The dictionary definition of the term "quantization" is "to restrict a variable quantity to discrete values rather than to a continuous set of values." In the field of data compression, quantization is used in two ways:

1. If the data to be compressed are in the form of large numbers, quantization is used to convert them to small numbers. Small numbers take less space than large ones, so quantization generates compression. On the other hand, small numbers generally contain less information than large ones, so quantization results in lossy compression.

2. If the data to be compressed are analog (i.e., a voltage that changes with time) quantization is used to digitize it into small numbers. The smaller the numbers the better the compression, but also the greater the loss of information. This aspect of quantization is used by several speech compression methods.

In the discussion here we assume that the data to be compressed is in the form of numbers, and that it is input, number by number, from an input stream (or a source). Section 4.12 discusses a generalization of discrete quantization to cases where the data consists of sets (called vectors) of numbers rather than of individual numbers.

The first example is naive discrete quantization of an input stream of 8-bit numbers. We can simply delete the least-significant four bits of each data item. This is one of those rare cases where the compression factor (=2) is known in advance and does not depend on the data. The input data is made of 256 different symbols, while the output data consists of just 16 different symbols. This method is simple but not very practical because too much information is lost in order to get the unimpressive compression factor of 2.

In order to develop a better approach we assume again that the data consists of 8-bit numbers, and that they are unsigned. Thus, input symbols are in the range $[0, 255]$ (if the input data is signed, input symbols have values in the range $[-128, +127]$). We select a spacing parameter s and compute the sequence of uniform quantized values $0, s, 2s, \ldots, ks, 255$, such that $(k+1)s > 255$ and $ks \leq 255$. Each input symbol S is quantized by converting it to the nearest value in this sequence. Selecting $s = 3$, e.g., produces the uniform sequence $0,3,6,9,12,\ldots,252,255$. Selecting $s = 4$ produces $0,4,8,12,\ldots,252,255$ (since the next multiple of 4, after 252, is 256).

A similar approach is to select quantized values such that any number in the range $[0, 255]$ will be no more than d units distant from one of the data values that are being quantized. This is done by dividing the range into segments of size $2d+1$ and centering them on the range $[0, 255]$. If $d = 16$, e.g., then the range $[0, 255]$ is divided into seven segments of size 33 each, with 25 numbers remaining. We can thus start the first segment 12 numbers from the start of the range, which produces the 10-number sequence 12, 33, 45, 78, 111, 144, 177, 210, 243, and 255. Any number in the range $[0, 255]$ is at most 16 units distant from any of these numbers. If we want to limit the quantized sequence to just eight numbers (so each can be expressed in 3 bits) we can apply this method to compute the sequence 8, 41, 74, 107, 140, 173, 206, and 239.

The quantized sequences above make sense in cases where each symbol appears in the input data with equal probability (cases where the source is *memoryless*). If the input data is not uniformly distributed, the sequence of quantized values should be distributed in the same way as the data.

Imagine, e.g., an input stream of 8-bit unsigned data items where most are zero or close to zero and few are large. A good sequence of quantized values for such data should have the same distribution, i.e., many small values and few large ones. One way of computing such a sequence is to select a value for the length parameter l and to construct a "window" of the form

$$1 \underbrace{b \ldots bb}_{l},$$

where each b is a bit, and place it under each of the 8 bit positions of a data item. If the window sticks out on the right, some of the l bits are truncated. As the window is moved to the left, zero bits are appended to it. Table 1.17 illustrates this construction with $l = 2$. It is easy to see how the resulting quantized values start with initial spacing of one unit, continue with spacing of two units and four units, until the last four values are spaced by 32 units. The numbers 0 and 255 should be manually added to such a quasi-logarithmic sequence to make it more general.

bbbbbbbb		bbbbbbbb	
1	1	.	
10	2	.	
11	3	.	
100	4	100|000	32
101	5	101|000	40
110	6	110|000	48
111	7	111|000	56
100|0	8	100|0000	64
101|0	10	101|0000	80
110|0	12	110|0000	96
111|0	14	111|0000	112
100|00	16	100|00000	128
101|00	20	101|00000	160
110|00	24	110|00000	192
111|00	28	111|00000	224

Table 1.17: A Logarithmic Quantization Table.

Scalar quantization is an example of a lossy compression method, where it is easy to control the trade-off between compression ratio and the amount of loss. However, because it is so simple, its use is limited to cases where much loss can be tolerated. Many image compression methods are lossy, but scalar quantization is not suitable for image compression because it creates annoying artifacts in the decompressed image. Imagine an image with an almost uniform area where all pixels have values 127 or 128. If 127 is quantized to 111 and 128 is quantized to 144, then the result, after decompression, may resemble a checkerboard where adjacent pixels alternate between 111 and 144. This is why *vector quantization* is used in practice, instead of scalar quantization, for lossy (and sometimes lossless) compression of images and sound. See also Section 4.1.

Comparisons date. Adoption screams. Coordinates maps. Darn!
as composite. Is mono-spaced art. Composed as train.
Promised as on act. Oops and matrices. Promised to a scan.

—Anagrams of *data compression*

Compression algorithms are often described as squeezing,
squashing, crunching or imploding data, but these are not
very good descriptions of what is actually happening.

—James D. Murray and William Vanryper (1994)

2
Statistical Methods

The methods discussed so far have one common feature, they assign fixed-size codes to the symbols (characters or pixels) they operate on. In contrast, statistical methods use variable-size codes, with the shorter codes assigned to symbols or groups of symbols that appear more often in the data (have a higher probability of occurrence). Designers and implementors of variable-size codes have to deal with the two problems of (1) assigning codes that can be decoded unambiguously and (2) assigning codes with the minimum average size.

Samuel Morse used variable-size codes when he designed his well-known telegraph code (Table 2.1). It is interesting to note that the first version of his code, developed by Morse during a transatlantic voyage in 1832, was more complex than the version he settled on in 1843. The first version sent short and long dashes that were received and drawn on a strip of paper, where sequences of those dashes represented numbers. Each word (not each letter) was assigned a code number, and Morse produced a code book (or dictionary) of those codes in 1837. This first version was thus a primitive form of compression. Morse later abandoned this version in favor of his famous dots and dashes, developed together with Alfred Vail.

> Morse established the first long-distance line, between Washington and Baltimore, which opened on May 24, 1844 with a message selected by Miss Annie Ellsworth, daughter of the commissioner of patents—the last phrase of the twenty-third verse of the twenty–third chapter of the book of Numbers: "What hath God wrought!"
>
> —George B. Dyson, *Darwin Among the Machines* (1997)

Most of this chapter is devoted to the different statistical algorithms (Shannon-Fano, Huffman, arithmetic coding, and others). However, we start with a short presentation of important concepts from *information theory*. These lead to a definition of redundancy, so that later we can clearly see and calculate how redundancy is reduced, or eliminated, by the different methods.

A	.-	N	-.	1	.----	Period	.-.-.-
B	-...	O	---	2	..---	Comma	--..--
C	-.-.	P	.--.	3	...--	Colon	---...
Ch	----	Q	--.-	4	....-	Question mark	..--..
D	-..	R	.-.	5	.....	Apostrophe	.----.
E	.	S	...	6	-....	Hyphen	-....-
F	..-.	T	-	7	--...	Dash	-..-.
G	--.	U	..-	8	---..	Parentheses	-.--.-
H	....	V	...-	9	----.	Quotation marks	.-..-.
I	..	W	.--	0	-----		
J	.---	X	-..-				
K	-.-	Y	-.--				
L	.-..	Z	--..				
M	--						

If the duration of a dot is taken to be one unit, then that of a dash is three units. The space between the dots and dashes of one character is one unit, between characters it is three units, and between words six units (five for automatic transmission). To indicate that a mistake has been made and for the receiver to delete the last word, send "........" (eight dots).

Table 2.1: The Morse Code for English.

2.1 Information Theory Concepts

We intuitively know what information is. We constantly receive and send information in the form of text, speech, and images. We also feel that information is an elusive nonmathematical quantity that cannot be precisely defined, captured, and measured. The standard dictionary definitions of information are (1) knowledge derived from study, experience, or instruction; (2) knowledge of a specific event or situation; intelligence; (3) a collection of facts or data; (4) the act of informing or the condition of being informed; communication of knowledge.

Imagine a person who does not know what information is. Would those definitions make it clear to them? Probably not.

The importance of information theory is that it quantifies information. It shows how to measure information, so that we can answer the question "how much information is included in this piece of data?" with a precise number! Quantifying information is based on the observation that the information content of a message is equivalent to the amount of *surprise* in the message. If I tell you something that you already know (for example, "you and I work here"), I haven't given you any information. If I tell you something new (for example, "we both have got an increase"), I have given you some information. If I tell you something that really surprises you (for example, "only I have got an increase"), I have given you more information, regardless of the number of words I have used, and of how you feel about my information.

We start with a simple, familiar event that's easy to analyze, namely the toss of a coin. There are two results, so the result of any toss is initially uncertain. We have to actually throw the coin in order to resolve the uncertainty. The result is heads or tails, which can also be expressed as a yes or no, or as a 0 or 1; a bit.

A single bit resolves the uncertainty in the toss of a coin. What makes this example important is the fact that it can easily be generalized. Many real-life problems can be resolved, and their solutions expressed, by means of several bits. The principle of doing so is to find the minimum number of yes/no questions that must be answered in order to arrive at the result. Since the answer to a yes/no question can be expressed with 1 bit, the number of questions will equal the number of bits it takes to express the information contained in the result.

A slightly more complex example is a deck of 64 cards. For simplicity let's ignore their traditional names and simply number them 1 to 64. Consider the event of A drawing one card and B having to guess what it was. The guess is a number between 1 and 64. What is the minimum number of yes/no questions that are necessary? Those who are familiar with the technique of *binary search* know the answer. Using this technique, B should divide the range 1–64 in two, and should start by asking "is the result between 1 and 32?" If the answer is no, then the result is in the range 33 to 64. This range is then divided by two and B's next question should be "is the result between 33 and 48?" This process continues until the range used by B reduces to a single number.

It does not take much to see that exactly six questions are necessary to get at the result. This is because 6 is the number of times 64 can be divided in half. Mathematically, this is equivalent to writing $6 = \log_2 64$. This is why the **logarithm** is the mathematical function that quantifies information.

Another approach to the same problem is to ask the question; Given a nonnegative integer N, how many digits does it take to express it? The answer, of course, depends on N. The greater N, the more digits are needed. The first 100 nonnegative integers (0 to 99) can be expressed by two decimal digits. The first 1000 such integers can be expressed by three digits. Again it does not take long to see the connection. The number of digits required to represent N equals approximately $\log N$. The base of the logarithm is the same as the base of the digits. For decimal digits, use base 10; for binary ones (bits), use base 2. If we agree that the number of digits it takes to express N is proportional to the information content of N, then again the logarithm is the function that gives us a measure of the information.

⋄ **Exercise 2.1:** What is the precise size, in bits, of the binary integer i?

Here is another approach to quantifying information. We are all familiar with the ten decimal digits. We know that the value of a digit in a number depends on its position. Thus the value of the digit 4 in the number 14708 is 4×10^3, or 4000, since it is in position 3 (positions are numbered from right to left, starting from 0). We are also familiar with the two binary digits (bits) 0 and 1. The value of a bit in a binary number similarly depends on its position, except that powers of 2 are used. Mathematically, there is nothing special about 2 or 10. We can use the number 3 as the basis of our arithmetic. This would require the three digits, 0, 1, and 2 (we might call them *trits*). A trit t at position i would have a value of $t \times 3^i$.

⋄ **Exercise 2.2:** Actually, there is something special about 10. We use base-10 numbers because we have ten fingers. There is also something special about the use of 2 as the basis for a number system. What is it?

Given a decimal (base 10) or a ternary (base 3) number with k digits, a natural question is; how much information is included in this k-digit number? We answer this by calculating how many bits it takes to express the same number. Assuming that the answer is x, then $10^k - 1 = 2^x - 1$. This is because $10^k - 1$ is the largest k-digit decimal number and $2^x - 1$ is the largest x-bit binary number. Solving the equation above for x as the unknown is easily done using logarithms and yields

$$x = k\frac{\log 10}{\log 2}.$$

We can use any base for the logarithm, as long as we use the same base for $\log 10$ and $\log 2$. Selecting base 2 simplifies the result, which becomes $x = k\log_2 10 \approx 3.32k$. This shows that the information included in one decimal digit equals that contained in about 3.32 bits. In general, given numbers in base n, we can write $x = k\log_2 n$, which expresses the fact that the information included in one base-n digit equals that included in $\log_2 n$ bits.

⋄ **Exercise 2.3:** How many bits does it take to express the information included in one trit?

We now turn to a transmitter, a piece of hardware that can transmit data over a communications line (a channel). In practice, such a transmitter sends binary data (a modem is a good example). However, in order to obtain general results, we assume that the data is a string made up of occurrences of the n symbols a_1 through a_n. Such a set is an n-symbol alphabet. Since there are n symbols, we can think of each as a base-n digit, which means that it is equivalent to $\log_2 n$ bits. As far as the hardware is concerned, this means that it must be able to transmit at n discrete levels.

If the transmitter takes $1/s$ time units to transmit a single symbol, then the speed of the transmission is s symbols per time unit. A common example is $s = 28800$ baud (*baud* is the term for "bits per second"), which translates to $1/s \approx 34.7\mu\text{sec}$ (where the Greek letter μ stands for "micro" and $1\mu\text{sec} = 10^{-6}\text{sec}$). In one time unit the transmitter can send s symbols, which as far as information content is concerned, is equivalent to $s\log_2 n$ bits. We denote by $H = s\log_2 n$ the amount of information, measured in bits, transmitted in each time unit.

The next step is to express H in terms of the probabilities of occurrence of the n symbols. We assume that symbol a_i occurs in the data with probability P_i. The sum of the probabilities equals, of course, unity: $P_1 + P_2 + \cdots + P_n = 1$. In the special case where all n probabilities are equal, $P_i = P$, we get $1 = \sum P_i = nP$, implying that $P = 1/n$, and resulting in $H = s\log_2 n = s\log_2(1/P) = -s\log_2 P$. In general, the probabilities are different, and we want to express H in terms of all of them. Since symbol a_i occurs a fraction P_i of the time in the data, it occurs on the average sP_i times each time unit, so its contribution to H is $-sP_i\log_2 P_i$. The sum of the contributions of all n symbols to H is thus $H = -s\sum_1^n P_i\log_2 P_i$.

As a reminder, H is the amount of information, in bits, sent by the transmitter in one time unit. The amount of information contained in one base-n symbol is thus H/s (because it takes time $1/s$ to transmit one symbol), or $-\sum_1^n P_i \log_2 P_i$. This quantity is called the *entropy* of the data being transmitted. In analogy we can define the entropy of a single symbol a_i as $-P_i \log_2 P_i$. This is the smallest number of bits needed, on average, to represent the symbol.

(Information theory was developed, in the late 1940s, by Claude Shannon, of Bell Labs, and he chose the term *entropy* because this term is used in thermodynamics to indicate the amount of disorder in a physical system.)

> Since I think it is better to take the names of such quantities as these, which are important for science, from the ancient languages, so that they can be introduced without change into all the modern languages, I propose to name the magnitude S the *entropy* of the body, from the Greek word "trope" for "transformation." I have intentionally formed the word "entropy" so as to be as similar as possible to the word "energy" since both these quantities which are to be known by these names are so nearly related to each other in their physical significance that a certain similarity in their names seemed to me advantageous.
>
> —Rudolph Clausius, 1865 (translated by Hans C. von Baeyer)

The entropy of the data depends on the individual probabilities P_i, and is largest (see Exercise 2.4) when all n probabilities are equal. This fact is used to define the redundancy R in the data. It is defined as the difference between a symbol set's largest possible entropy and its actual entropy. Thus

$$R = -\log_2(1/P) - \left(-\sum_1^n P_i \log_2 P_i\right) = -\log_2 n + \sum_1^n P_i \log_2 P_i.$$

The test for fully compressed data (no redundancy) is thus $\sum_1^n P_i \log_2 P_i = \log_2 n$.

⋄ **Exercise 2.4:** Analyze the entropy of a two-symbol set.

Given a string of characters, the probability of a character can be calculated by counting the frequency of the character and dividing by the length of the string. Once the probabilities of all the characters are known, the entropy of the entire string can be calculated. With current availability of powerful mathematical software, it is easy to calculate the entropy of a given string. The *Mathematica* code

```
Frequencies[list_]:=Map[{Count[list,#],#}&, Union[list]];
Entropy[list_]:=-Plus @@ N[# Log[2,#]]& @
 (First[Transpose[Frequencies[list]]]/Length[list]);
Characters["swiss miss"]
Entropy[%]
```

does that and shows that, for example, the entropy of the string swiss␣miss is 1.96096.

You have two chances—
One of getting the germ
And one of not.
And if you get the germ
You have two chances—
One of getting the disease
And one of not.
And if you get the disease
You have two chances—
One of dying
And one of not.
And if you die—
Well, you still have two chances.

—Unknown

2.1.1 Algorithmic Information Content

Imagine the following three sequences:

$$S_1 = 100100100100100100100100100100100010 \ldots,$$
$$S_2 = 0101101101101011011010110110110101011 \ldots,$$
$$S_3 = 0111001001111001000010110000001101111 \ldots.$$

The first sequence, S_1, is just a repetition of the simple pattern 100. S_2 is less regular. It can be described as a 01, followed by r_1 repetitions of 011, followed by another 01, followed by r_2 repetitions of 011, etc., where $r_1 = 3$, $r_2 = 2$, $r_3 = 4$, and the other r_i's are not shown. S_3 is more difficult to describe, since it does not seem to have any apparent regularity; it seems random. Notice that the meaning of the ellipsis is clear in the case of S_1 (just repeat the pattern "100"), less clear in S_2 (what are the other r_i's?), and completely unknown in S_3 (is it random?).

We now assume that these sequences are very long (say, 999,999 bits each), and each continues "in the same way." How can we define the complexity of such a binary sequence, at least qualitatively? One way to do so, called the Kolmogorov-Chaitin complexity (KCC), is to define the complexity of a binary string S as the length, in bits, of the shortest computer program that, when executed, will generate S (display, print, or write it on file). This definition is also called the *algorithmic information content* of S.

A program P_1 to generate S_1 could just loop 333,333 times and print "100" in each iteration. Alternatively, it could loop 111,111 times and print "100100100" in each iteration. Such a program is very short (especially when compared with the length of the sequence it generates), concurring with our intuitive feeling that S_1 has low complexity.

A program P_2 to generate string S_2 should know the values of all the r_i's. They could either be built in or input by the user at run time. The program initializes a variable i to 1. It then prints "01", loops r_i times printing "011" in each iteration, increments i by 1, and repeats this behavior until 999,999 bits have been printed. Such a program is longer than P_1, reflecting our intuitive feel that S_2 is more complex than S_1.

A program P_3 to generate S_3 should (assuming that we cannot express this string in any regular way) simply print all 999,999 bits of the sequence. Such a program is as long as the sequence itself, implying that the KCC of S_3 is as large as S_3.

Using this definition of complexity, Gregory Chaitin showed (see [Chaitin 77] or [Chaitin 97]) that most binary strings of length n are random; their complexities are close to n. However, the "interesting" (or "practical") binary strings, those that are used in practice to represent text, images, and sound, and are compressed all the time, are similar to S_2. They are not random and exhibit some regularity, which makes it possible to compress them. Very regular strings, such as S_1, are rare in practice.

Algorithmic information content is a measure of the amount of information included in a message. It is related to the KCC and is different from the way information is measured in information theory. Shannon's information theory defines the amount of information in a string by considering the amount of *surprise* this information contains when revealed. Algorithmic information content, on the other hand, measures information that has already been revealed. An example may serve to illustrate this difference. Imagine two persons A (well-read, sophisticated and knowledgeable) and B (inexperienced and naive), reading the same story. There are few surprises in the story for A. He has already read many similar stories and can predict the development of the story line, the behavior of the characters, and even the end. The opposite is true for B. As he reads, he is surprised by the (to him) unexpected twists and turns that the story takes and by the (to him) unpredictable behavior of the characters. The question is; How much information does the story really contain?

Shannon's information theory tells us that the story contains less information for A than for B, since it contains fewer surprises for A than for B. Recall that A's mind already has memories of similar plots and characters. As they read more and more, however, both A and B get more and more familiar and thus less and less surprised (although at different rates). Thus, they get less and less (Shannon's type of) information. At the same time, as more of the story is revealed to them, their minds' complexities increase (again at different rates). Thus, they get more algorithmic information content. The sum of Shannon's information and KCC is thus constant (or close to constant).

This example suggests a way to measure the information content of the story in an absolute way, regardless of the particular reader. It is the *sum* of Shannon's information and the KCC. This measure has been proposed by the physicist Wojciech Zurek [Zurek 89], who termed it "physical entropy."

Got a bit of bad news today. Let go. Been made redundant.
—Donal O'Kelly as Bimbo in *The Van* (1996)

Bibliography

Chaitin, Gregory J. (1977) "Algorithmic Information Theory," *IBM Journal of Research and Development*, **21**:350–359, July.

Chaitin, Gregory J. (1997) *The Limits of Mathematics*, Singapore, Springer-Verlag.

Zurek, Wojciech (1989) "Thermodynamic Cost of Computation, Algorithmic Complexity, and the Information Metric," *Nature*, **341**(6238):119–124, Sept 14.

2.2 Variable-Size Codes

Consider the four symbols a_1, a_2, a_3, and a_4. If they appear in our data strings with equal probabilities ($= 0.25$), then the entropy of the data is $-4(0.25 \log_2 0.25) = 2$. Two is the smallest number of bits needed, on the average, to represent each symbol in this case. We can simply assign our symbols the four 2-bit codes 00, 01, 10, and 11. Since the probabilities are equal, the redundancy is zero and the data cannot be compressed below 2 bits/symbol.

Next, consider the case where the four symbols occur with different probabilities as shown in Table 2.2, where a_1 appears in the data (on average) about half the time, a_2 and a_3 have equal probabilities, and a_4 is rare. In this case, the data has entropy $-(0.49 \log_2 0.49 + 0.25 \log_2 0.25 + 0.25 \log_2 0.25 + 0.01 \log_2 0.01) \approx -(-0.050 - 0.5 - 0.5 - 0.066) = 1.57$. The smallest number of bits needed, on average, to represent each symbol has dropped to 1.57.

Symbol	Prob.	Code1	Code2
a_1	.49	1	1
a_2	.25	01	01
a_3	.25	010	000
a_4	.01	001	001

Table 2.2: Variable-Size Codes.

If we again assign our symbols the four 2-bit codes 00, 01, 10, and 11, the redundancy would be $R = -1.57 + \log_2 4 = 0.43$. This suggests assigning *variable-size codes* to the symbols. Code1 of Table 2.2 is designed such that the most common symbol, a_1, is assigned the shortest code. When long data strings are transmitted using Code1, the average size (the number of bits per symbol) is $1 \times 0.49 + 2 \times 0.25 + 3 \times 0.25 + 3 \times 0.01 = 1.77$, which is very close to the minimum. The redundancy in this case is $R = 1.77 - 1.57 = 0.2$ bits per symbol. An interesting example is the 20-symbol string $a_1 a_3 a_2 a_1 a_3 a_3 a_4 a_2 a_1 a_1 a_2 a_2 a_1 a_1 a_3 a_1 a_1 a_2 a_3 a_1$, where the four symbols occur with (approximately) the right frequencies. Encoding this string with Code1 yields the 37 bits:

$$1|010|01|1|010|010|001|01|1|1|01|01|1|1|010|1|1|01|010|1$$

(without the vertical bars). Using 37 bits to encode 20 symbols yields an average size of 1.85 bits/symbol, not far from the calculated average size. (The reader should bear in mind that our examples are short. To get results close to the best that's theoretically possible, an input stream with at least thousands of symbols is needed.)

However, when we try to *decode* the binary string above, it becomes obvious that Code1 is bad. The first bit is 1, and since only a_1 is assigned this code, it (a_1) must be the first symbol. The next bit is 0, but the codes of a_2, a_3, and a_4 all start with a 0, so the decoder has to read the next bit. It is 1, but the codes of both a_2 and a_3 start with 01. The decoder does not know whether to decode the string as $1|010|01\ldots$, which is $a_1a_3a_2\ldots$, or as $1|01|001\ldots$, which is $a_1a_2a_4\ldots$. Code1 is thus *ambiguous*. In contrast, Code2, which has the same average size as Code1, can be decoded unambiguously.

The property of Code2 that makes it so much better than Code1 is called the *prefix property*. This property requires that once a certain bit pattern has been assigned as the code of a symbol, no other codes should start with that pattern (the pattern cannot be the *prefix* of any other code). Once the string "1" was assigned as the code of a_1, no other codes could start with 1 (i.e., they all had to start with 0). Once "01" was assigned as the code of a_2, no other codes could start with 01. This is why the codes of a_3 and a_4 had to start with 00. Naturally, they became 000 and 001.

Designing variable-size codes is thus done by following two principles: (1) Assign short codes to the more frequent symbols and (2) obey the prefix property. Following these principles produces short, unambiguous codes, but not necessarily the best (i.e., shortest) ones. In addition to these principles, an algorithm is needed that always produces a set of shortest codes (ones with minimum average size). The only input to such an algorithm is the frequencies (or the probabilities) of the symbols of the alphabet. Two such algorithms, the Shannon-Fano method and the Huffman method, are discussed in Sections 2.6 and 2.8.

(It should be noted that not all statistical compression methods assign variable-size codes to the individual symbols of the alphabet. A notable exception is arithmetic coding, Section 2.14.)

2.3 Prefix Codes

A prefix code is a variable-size code that satisfies the prefix property. The binary representation of the integers does not satisfy the prefix property. Another disadvantage of this representation is that the size n of the set of integers has to be known in advance, since it determines the code size, which is $1 + \lfloor \log_2 n \rfloor$. In some applications, a prefix code is required to code a set of integers whose size is not known in advance. Several such codes, most of which are due to P. Elias [Elias 75], are presented here.

2.3.1 The Unary Code

The *unary code* of the nonnegative integer n is defined as $n-1$ ones followed by a single 0 (Table 2.3) or, alternatively, as $n-1$ zeros followed by a single one. The length of the unary code for the integer n is thus n bits.

⋄ **Exercise 2.5:** Discuss the use of the unary code as a variable-size code.

n	Code	Alt. Code
1	0	1
2	10	01
3	110	001
4	1110	0001
5	11110	00001

Table 2.3: Some Unary Codes.

It is also possible to define general unary codes, also known as start-step-stop codes. Such a code depends on a triplet (start, step, stop) of integer parameters and is defined as follows: Codewords are created to code symbols used in the data, such that the nth codeword consists of n ones, followed by one 0, followed by all the combinations of a bits where $a = \text{start} + n \times \text{step}$. If $a = \text{stop}$, then the single 0 preceding the a bits is dropped. The number of codes for a given triplet is finite and depends on the choice of parameters. Tables 2.4 and 2.5 show the 680 codes of (3,2,9) and the 2044 codes of (2,1,10) (see also Table 4.104). These codes are discussed in Section 3.7 in connection with the LZFG compression method, and in Section 4.14 for block matching lossless image compression.

n	$a = $ $3 + n \cdot 2$	nth codeword	Number of codewords	Range of integers
0	3	$0xxx$	$2^3 = 8$	0–7
1	5	$10xxxxx$	$2^5 = 32$	8–39
2	7	$110xxxxxxx$	$2^7 = 128$	40–167
3	9	$111xxxxxxxxx$	$2^9 = 512$	168–679
		Total	680	

Table 2.4: The General Unary Code (3,2,9).

n	$a = $ $2 + n \cdot 1$	nth codeword	Number of codewords	Range of integers
0	2	$0xx$	4	0–3
1	3	$10xxx$	8	4–11
2	4	$110xxxx$	16	12–27
3	5	$1110xxxxx$	32	28–59
	...	...		...
8	10	$\underbrace{11...1}_{8}\underbrace{xx...x}_{10}$	1024	1020–2043
		Total	2044	

Table 2.5: The General Unary Code (2,1,10).

The number of different general unary codes is

$$\frac{2^{\text{stop}+\text{step}} - 2^{\text{start}}}{2^{\text{step}} - 1}.$$

Notice that this expression increases exponentially with parameter "stop," so large sets of these codes can be generated with small values of the three parameters.

⬦ **Exercise 2.6:** What codes are defined by the parameters $(n, 1, n)$ and what by $(0, 0, \infty)$?

⬦ **Exercise 2.7:** How many codes are produced by the triplet $(1, 1, 30)$?

⬦ **Exercise 2.8:** Derive the general unary code for (10,2,14).

2.3.2 Other Prefix Codes

Four more prefix codes are described in this section. We use $B(n)$ to denote the binary representation of integer n. Thus $|B(n)|$ is the length, in bits, of this representation. We also use $\overline{B}(n)$ to denote $B(n)$ without its most significant bit (which is always 1).

Code C_1 is made of two parts. To code the positive integer n we first generate the unary code of $|B(n)|$ (the size of the binary representation of n), then append $\overline{B}(n)$ to it. An example is $n = 16 = 10000_2$. The size of B(16) is 5, so we start with the unary code 11110 (or 00001) and append $\overline{B}(16) = 0000$. The complete code is thus 11110|0000 (or 00001|0000). Another example is $n = 5 = 101_2$ whose code is 110|01. The length of $C_1(n)$ is $2\lfloor \log_2 n \rfloor + 1$ bits. Notice that this code is identical to the general unary code $(0, 1, \infty)$.

Code C_2 is a rearrangement of C_1 where each of the $1 + \lfloor \log_2 n \rfloor$ bits of the first part (the unary code) of C_1 is followed by one of the bits of the second part. Thus code $C_2(16) = 101010100$ and $C_2(5) = 10110$.

Code C_3 starts with $|B(n)|$ coded in C_2, followed by $\overline{B}(n)$. Thus 16 is coded as $C_2(5) = 11101$ followed by $\overline{B}(16) = 0000$, and 5 is coded as code $C_2(3) = 110$ followed by $\overline{B}(5) = 01$. The size of $C_3(n)$ is $1 + \lfloor \log_2 n \rfloor + 2\lfloor \log_2(1 + \lfloor \log_2 n \rfloor) \rfloor$.

Code C_4 consists of several parts. We start with $B(n)$. To the left of this we write the binary representation of $|B(n)| - 1$ (the length of n, minus 1). This continues recursively, until a 2-bit number is written. A zero is then added to the right of the entire number, to make it decodable. To encode 16, we start with 10000, add $|B(16)| - 1 = 4 = 100_2$ to the left, then $|B(4)| - 1 = 2 = 10_2$ to the left of that and finally, a zero on the right. The result is 10|100|10000|0. To encode 5, we start with 101, add $|B(5)| - 1 = 2 = 10_2$ to the left, and a zero on the right. The result is 10|101|0.

⬦ **Exercise 2.9:** How does the zero on the right make the code decodable?

Table 2.6 shows examples of the four codes above as well as $B(n)$ and $\overline{B}(n)$. The lengths of the four codes shown in the table increases as $\log_2 n$, in contrast to the length of the unary code, which increases as n. These codes are therefore good choices in cases where the data consists of integers n with probabilities that satisfy certain conditions. Specifically, the length L of the unary code of n is $L = n = \log_2 2^n$, so it is ideal for the case where $P(n) = 2^{-L} = 2^{-n}$. The length of code $C_1(n)$ is $L = 1 + 2\lfloor \log_2 n \rfloor = \log_2 2 + \log_2 n^2 = \log_2(2n^2)$, so it is ideal for the case where

$$P(n) = 2^{-L} = \frac{1}{2n^2}.$$

n	Unary	$B(n)$	$\overline{B}(n)$	C_1	C_2	C_3	C_4
1	0	1		1|	1	1|	0
2	10	10	0	10|0	100	100|0	10|0
3	110	11	1	10|1	110	100|1	11|0
4	1110	100	00	110|00	10100	110|00	10|100|0
5	11110	101	01	110|01	10110	110|01	10|101|0
6	111110	110	10	110|10	11100	110|10	10|110|0
7	...	111	11	110|11	11110	110|11	10|111|0
8		1000	000	1110|000	1010100	10100|000	11|1000|0
9		1001	001	1110|001	1010110	10100|001	11|1001|0
10		1010	010	1110|010	1011100	10100|010	11|1010|0
11		1011	011	1110|011	1011110	10100|011	11|1011|0
12		1100	100	1110|100	1110100	10100|100	11|1100|0
13		1101	101	1110|101	1110110	10100|101	11|1101|0
14		1110	110	1110|110	1111100	10100|110	11|1110|0
15		1111	111	1110|111	1111110	10100|111	11|1111|0
16		10000	0000	11110|0000	101010100	10110|0000	10|100|10000|0
31		11111	1111	11110|1111	111111110	10110|1111	10|100|11111|0
32		100000	00000	111110|00000	10101010100	11100|00000	10|101|100000|0
63		111111	11111	111110|11111	11111111110	11100|11111	10|101|111111|0
64		1000000	000000	1111110|000000	1010101010100	11110|000000	10|110|1000000|0
127		1111111	111111	1111110|111111	1111111111110	11110|111111	10|110|1111111|0
128		10000000	0000000	11111110|0000000	101010101010100	1010100|0000000	10|111|10000000|0
255		11111111	1111111	11111110|1111111	111111111111110	1010100|1111111	10|111|11111111|0

Table 2.6: Some Prefix Codes.

n	Unary	C_1	C_3
1	0.5	0.5000000	
2	0.25	0.1250000	0.2500000
3	0.125	0.0555556	0.0663454
4	0.0625	0.0312500	0.0312500
5	0.03125	0.0200000	0.0185482
6	0.015625	0.0138889	0.0124713
7	0.0078125	0.0102041	0.0090631
8	0.00390625	0.0078125	0.0069444

Table 2.7: Ideal Probabilities of Eight Integers for Three Codes.

The length of code $C_3(n)$ is

$$L = 1 + \lfloor \log_2 n \rfloor + 2\lfloor \log_2(1 + \lfloor \log_2 n \rfloor) \rfloor = \log_2 2 + 2\lfloor \log \log_2 2n \rfloor + \lfloor \log_2 n \rfloor,$$

so it is ideal for the case where

$$P(n) = 2^{-L} = \frac{1}{2n(\log_2 n)^2}.$$

Table 2.7 shows the ideal probabilities that the first eight positive integers should have for the three codes above to be used.

More prefix codes for the positive integers, appropriate for special applications, may be designed by the following general approach. Select positive integers v_i and combine them in a list V (which may be finite or infinite according to needs). The code of the positive integer n is prepared in the three following steps:

1. Find k such that

$$\sum_{i=1}^{k-1} v_i < n \leq \sum_{i=1}^{k} v_i.$$

2. Compute the difference

$$d = n - \sum_{i=1}^{k-1} v_i - 1.$$

The largest value of n is $\sum_1^k v_i$, so the largest value of d is $\sum_i^k v_i - \sum_1^{k-1} v_i - 1 = v_k - 1$, a number that can be written in $\lceil \log_2 v_k \rceil$ bits. The number d is encoded, using the standard binary code, either in this number of bits, or if $d < 2^{\lceil \log_2 v_k \rceil} - v_k$, it is encoded in $\lfloor \log_2 v_k \rfloor$ bits.

3. Encode n in two parts. Start with k encoded in some prefix code, and concatenate the binary code of d. Since k is coded in a prefix code, any decoder would know how many bits to read for k. After reading and decoding k, the decoder can compute the value $2^{\lceil \log_2 v_k \rceil} - v_k$ and thus knows how many bits to read for d.

A simple example is the infinite sequence $V = (1, 2, 4, 8, \ldots, 2^{i-1}, \ldots)$ with k coded in unary. The integer $n = 10$ satisfies

$$\sum_{i=1}^{3} v_i < 10 \leq \sum_{i=1}^{4} v_i,$$

so $k = 4$ (with unary code 1110) and $d = 10 - \sum_{i=1}^{3} v_i - 1 = 2$. The code of 10 is thus 1110|010.

See also the Golomb code, Section 2.4, the phased-in binary codes of Section 2.9.1, and the subexponential code of Section 4.18.1.

Bibliography

Elias, P. (1975) "Universal Codeword Sets and Representations of the Integers," *IEEE Transactions on Information Theory* IT-21(2):194–203, March.

Number Bases

Decimal numbers use base 10. The number 2037_{10}, e.g., has a value of $2 \times 10^3 + 0 \times 10^2 + 3 \times 10^1 + 7 \times 10^0$. We can say that 2037 is the sum of the digits 2, 0, 3, and 7, each weighted by a power of 10. Fractions are represented in the same way, using negative powers of 10. Thus $0.82 = 8 \times 10^{-1} + 2 \times 10^{-2}$ and $300.7 = 3 \times 10^2 + 7 \times 10^{-1}$.

Binary numbers use base 2. Such a number is represented as a sum of its digits, each weighted by a power of 2. Thus $101.11_2 = 1 \times 2^2 + 0 \times 2^1 + 1 \times 2^0 + 1 \times 2^{-1} + 1 \times 2^{-2}$.

Since there is nothing special about 10 or 2,* it should be easy to convince yourself that any positive integer $n > 1$ can serve as the basis for representing numbers. Such a representation requires n "digits" (if $n > 10$, we use the ten digits and the letters "A", "B", "C",...) and represents the number $d_3 d_2 d_1 d_0 . d_{-1}$ as the sum of the "digits" d_i, each multiplied by a power of n, thus $d_3 n^3 + d_2 n^2 + d_1 n^1 + d_0 n^0 + d_{-1} n^{-1}$. The base for a number system does not have to consist of powers of an integer but can be any *superadditive* sequence that starts with 1.

Definition: A superadditive sequence $a_0, a_1, a_2, \ldots$ is one where any element a_i is greater than the sum of all its predecessors. An example is 1, 2, 4, 8, 16, 32, 64,... where each element equals one plus the sum of all its predecessors. This sequence consists of the familiar powers of 2, so we know that any integer can be expressed by it using just the digits 0 and 1 (the two bits). Another example is 1, 3, 6, 12, 24, 50,..., where each element equals 2 plus the sum of all its predecessors. It is easy to see that any integer can be expressed by it using just the digits 0, 1, and 2 (the 3 trits).

Given a positive integer k, the sequence $1, 1 + k, 2 + 2k, 4 + 4k, \ldots, 2^i(1 + k)$ is superadditive, since each element equals the sum of all its predecessors plus k. Any nonnegative integer can be *uniquely* represented in such a system as a number $x \ldots xxy$, where x are bits and y is a single digit in the range $[0, k]$.

In contrast, a general superadditive sequence, such as 1, 8, 50, 3102 can be used to represent integers, but not uniquely. The number 50, e.g., equals $8 \times 6 + 1 + 1$, so it can be represented as $0062 = 0 \times 3102 + 0 \times 50 + 6 \times 8 + 2 \times 1$, but also as $0100 = 0 \times 3102 + 1 \times 50 + 0 \times 8 + 0 \times 1$.

It can be shown that $1 + r + r^2 + \cdots + r^k < r^{k+1}$ for any real number $r > 1$, which implies that the powers of any real number $r > 1$ can serve as the base of a number system using the digits $0, 1, 2, \ldots, d$ for some d.

The number $\phi = \frac{1}{2}(1 + \sqrt{5}) \approx 1.618$ is the well-known golden ratio. It can serve as the base of a number system using the two binary digits. Thus, e.g., $100.1_\phi = \phi^2 + \phi^{-1} \approx 3.23_{10}$.

Some real bases have special properties. For example, any positive integer R can be expressed as $R = b_1 F_1 + b_2 F_2 + b_3 F_3 + b_4 F_5 + \cdots$ (that's $b_4 F_5$, not $b_4 F_4$), where the b_i are either 0 or 1, and the F_i are the Fibonacci numbers $1, 2, 3, 5, 8, 13, \ldots$. This representation has the interesting property that the string $b_1 b_2 \ldots$ does not contain any adjacent 1's (this property is used by certain data compression methods; see Section 8.5.4). As an example, the integer 33 equals the sum $1 + 3 + 8 + 21$, so it is expressed in the Fibonacci base as the 7-bit number 1010101.

◇ **Exercise 2.10:** Show how the Fibonacci numbers can be used to construct a prefix code.

A nonnegative integer can be represented as a finite sum of binomial coefficients

$$n = \binom{a}{1} + \binom{b}{2} + \binom{c}{3} + \binom{d}{4} + \cdots, \quad \text{where } 0 \le a < b < c < d \cdots$$

are integers and $\binom{i}{n}$ is the binomial coefficient $\frac{i!}{n!(i-n)!}$. This is the *binomial number system*.

---

*Actually, there is. Two is the smallest integer that can be a base for a number system. Ten is the number of our fingers.

===

2.4 The Golomb Code

The *Golomb code* for nonnegative integers n [Golomb 66] can be an effective Huffman code. The code depends on the choice of a parameter b. The first step is to compute the two quantities

$$q = \left\lfloor \frac{n-1}{b} \right\rfloor, \quad r = n - qb - 1,$$

(where the notation $\lfloor x \rfloor$ implies truncation of x) following which the code is constructed of two parts; the first is the value of $q+1$, coded in unary (Exercise 2.5), and the second, the binary value of r coded in either $\lfloor \log_2 b \rfloor$ bits (for the small remainders) or in $\lceil \log_2 b \rceil$ bits (for the large ones). Choosing $b = 3$, e.g., produces three possible remainders, 0, 1, and 2. They are coded 0, 10, and 11, respectively. Choosing $b = 5$ produces the five remainders 0 through 4, which are coded 00, 01, 100, 101, and 110. Table 2.8 shows some examples of the Golomb code for $b = 3$ and $b = 5$.

n	1	2	3	4	5	6	7	8	9	10
$b = 3$	0|0	0|10	0|11	10|0	10|10	10|11	110|0	110|10	110|11	1110|0
$b = 5$	0|00	0|01	0|100	0|101	10|110	10|00	10|01	10|100	10|101	110|110

Table 2.8: Some Golomb Codes for $b = 3$ and $b = 5$.

Imagine an input data stream consisting of positive integers where the probability of integer n appearing in the data is $P(n) = (1-p)^{n-1}p$, for some $0 \le p \le 1$. It can be shown that the Golomb code is an optimal code for this data if b is chosen such that

$$(1-p)^b + (1-p)^{b+1} \le 1 < (1-p)^{b-1} + (1-p)^b.$$

Given the right data, it is easy to generate the best variable-size codes without going through the Huffman algorithm.

Section 4.7.1 illustrates the use of the Golomb code for lossless image compression.

Bibliography

Golomb, S. W. (1966) "Run-Length Encodings," *IEEE Transactions on Information Theory* IT-12(3):399–401.

In addition to the codes, Solomon W. Golomb has his "own" Golomb constant 0.6243299885435508709929363831008372441796426201805529286

2.5 The Kraft-MacMillan Inequality

This inequality is related to unambiguous variable-size codes. Its first part states that given an unambiguous variable-size code, with n codes of sizes L_i, then

$$\sum_{i=1}^{n} 2^{-L_i} \leq 1. \tag{2.1}$$

The second part states the opposite, namely, given a set of n positive integers $(L_1, L_2, \ldots, L_n)$ that satisfy equation (2.1), there exists an unambiguous variable-size code such that the L_i are the sizes of its individual codes. Together, both parts say that a code is unambiguous if and only if it satisfies relation (2.1).

This inequality can be related to the entropy by observing that the lengths L_i can always be written as $L_i = -\log_2 P_i + E_i$, where E_i is simply the amount by which L_i is greater than the entropy (the extra length of code i).

This implies that

$$2^{-L_i} = 2^{(\log_2 P_i - E_i)} = 2^{\log_2 P_i}/2^{E_i} = P_i/2^{E_i}.$$

In the special case where all the extra lengths are the same ($E_i = E$), the Kraft inequality says that

$$1 \geq \sum_{i=1}^{n} P_i/2^E = \left(\sum_{i=1}^{n} P_i\right) \bigg/ 2^E = 1/2^E \implies 2^E \geq 1 \implies E \geq 0.$$

An unambiguous code has non-negative extra length, meaning its length is greater than or equal to the length determined by its entropy.

Here is a simple example of the use of this inequality. Consider the simple case of n equal-length binary codes. The size of each code is $L_i = \log_2 n$ and the Kraft-MacMillan sum is

$$\sum_{1}^{n} 2^{-L_i} = \sum_{1}^{n} 2^{-\log_2 n} = \sum_{1}^{n} \frac{1}{n} = 1.$$

The inequality is satisfied, so such a code is unambiguous (uniquely decodable).

A more interesting example is the case of n codes where the first one is compressed and the second one expanded. We set $L_1 = \log_2 n - a$, $L_2 = \log_2 n + e$, and $L_3 = L_4 = \cdots = L_n = \log_2 n$, where a and e are positive. We show that $e > a$, which means that compressing a symbol by a factor a requires expanding another symbol by a larger factor. We can benefit from this only if the probability of the compressed symbol is greater than that of the expanded symbol.

$$\sum_{1}^{n} 2^{-L_i} = 2^{-L_1} + 2^{-L_2} + \sum_{3}^{n} 2^{-\log_2 n}$$

$$= 2^{-\log_2 n + a} + 2^{-\log_2 n - e} + \sum_{1}^{n} 2^{-\log_2 n} - 2 \times 2^{-\log_2 n}$$

$$= \frac{2^a}{n} + \frac{2^{-e}}{n} + 1 - \frac{2}{n}.$$

The Kraft-MacMillan inequality requires that

$$\frac{2^a}{n} + \frac{2^{-e}}{n} + 1 - \frac{2}{n} \leq 1, \quad \text{or} \quad \frac{2^a}{n} + \frac{2^{-e}}{n} - \frac{2}{n} \leq 0,$$

or $\quad 2^{-e} \leq 2 - 2^a, \quad$ implying $\quad -e \leq \log_2(2 - 2^a), \quad$ or $\quad e \geq -\log_2(2 - 2^a)$.

The inequality above implies $a \leq 1$ (otherwise, $2 - 2^a$ is negative) but a is also positive (since we assumed compression of symbol 1). The possible range of values of a is thus $(0, 1]$, and in this range $e > a$, proving the statement above. (It is easy to see that $a = 1 \rightarrow e \geq -\log_2 0 = \infty$, and $a = 0.1 \rightarrow e \geq -\log_2(2 - 2^{0.1}) \approx 0.10745$.)

It can be shown that this is just a special case of a general result that says; If you have an alphabet of n symbols, and you compress some of them by a certain factor, then the others must be expanded by a greater factor.

> Statistics show that there are more women in the world than anything else except insects.
> —Glenn Ford as Johnny Farrell in *Gilda* (1946)

2.6 Shannon-Fano Coding

Shannon-Fano coding was the first method developed for finding good variable-size codes. We start with a set of n symbols with known probabilities (or frequencies) of occurrence. The symbols are first arranged in descending order of their probabilities. The set of symbols is then divided into two subsets that have the same (or almost the same) probabilities. All symbols in one subset get assigned codes that start with a 0, while the codes of the symbols in the other subset start with a 1. Each subset is then recursively divided into two, and the second bit of all the codes is determined in a similar way. When a subset contains just two symbols, their codes are distinguished by adding one more bit to each. The process continues until no more subsets remain. Table 2.9 illustrates the Shannon-Fano code for a seven-symbol alphabet. Notice that the symbols themselves are not shown, only their probabilities.

The first step splits the set of seven symbols into two subsets, the first one with two symbols and a total probability of 0.45, the second one with the remaining five

symbols and a total probability of 0.55. The two symbols in the first subset are
assigned codes that start with 1, so their final codes are 11 and 10. The second
subset is divided, in the second step, into two symbols (with total probability 0.3
and codes that start with 01) and three symbols (with total probability 0.25 and
codes that start with 00). Step three divides the last three symbols into 1 (with
probability 0.1 and code 001) and 2 (with total probability 0.15 and codes that start
with 000).

	Prob.			Steps			Final
1.	0.25	1	1				:11
2.	0.20	1	0				:10
3.	0.15	0	1	1			:011
4.	0.15	0	1	0			:010
5.	0.10	0	0	1			:001
6.	0.10	0	0	0	1		:0001
7.	0.05	0	0	0	0		:0000

Table 2.9: Shannon-Fano Example.

The average size of this code is $0.25 \times 2 + 0.20 \times 2 + 0.15 \times 3 + 0.15 \times 3 + 0.10 \times 3 + 0.10 \times 4 + 0.05 \times 4 = 2.7$ bits/symbol. This is a good result because the entropy
(the smallest number of bits needed, on average, to represent each symbol) is

$$-\big(0.25 \log_2 0.25 + 0.20 \log_2 0.20 + 0.15 \log_2 0.15 + 0.15 \log_2 0.15$$
$$+ 0.10 \log_2 0.10 + 0.10 \log_2 0.10 + 0.05 \log_2 0.05\big) \approx 2.67.$$

⋄ **Exercise 2.11:** Repeat the above calculation but place the first split between the
third and fourth symbols. Calculate the average size of the code and show that it
is greater than 2.67 bits/symbol.

The code in the table in the answer to Exercise 2.11 has longer average size
because the splits, in this case, were not as good as those of Table 2.9. This
suggests that the Shannon-Fano method produces better code when the splits are
better, i.e., when the two subsets in every split have very close total probabilities.
Carrying this argument to its limit suggests that perfect splits yield the best code.
Table 2.10 illustrates such a case. The two subsets in every split have identical total
probabilities, yielding a code with the minimum average size (zero redundancy). Its
average size is $0.25 \times 2 + 0.25 \times 2 + 0.125 \times 3 + 0.125 \times 3 + 0.125 \times 3 + 0.125 \times 3 = 2.5$
bits/symbols, which is identical to its entropy. This means that it is the theoretical
minimum average size.

The conclusion is that this method produces best results when the symbols
have probabilities of occurrence that are (negative) powers of 2.

	Prob.		Steps		Final
1.	0.25	1	1		:11
2.	0.25	1	0		:10
3.	0.125	0	1	1	:011
4.	0.125	0	1	0	:010
5.	0.125	0	0	1	:001
6.	0.125	0	0	0	:000

Table 2.10: Shannon-Fano Balanced Example.

> Considine's Law. Whenever one word or letter can change the entire meaning of a sentence, the probability of an error being made will be in direct proportion to the embarrassment it will cause
>
> —Bob Considine

⋄ **Exercise 2.12:** Calculate the entropy of the codes of Table 2.10.

The Shannon-Fano method is easy to implement (see page 209 for its use in the Implode algorithm) but the code it produces is generally not as good as that produced by the Huffman method, described in Section 2.8.

2.7 The Counting Argument

Any compression method is limited. It cannot losslessly compress *all* files of size N, since some of these files are random.

Let's assume that an algorithm exists that can compress losslessly all files of size N bits (or larger, but we'll concentrate on N). There are 2^N files of size N bits, and compressing them with our algorithm must produce 2^N files of sizes $< N$. How many files are there of sizes $< N$? There are 2^{N-1} files of size $N-1$, 2^{N-2} files of size $N-2$, and so on, down to $2^{N-N} = 1$ file of size $N - N = 0$. The total number of all these files is

$$2^{N-1} + 2^{N-2} + \cdots + 1 = 2^N - 1,$$

instead of 2^N, so there must be at least two size-N different files compressed to the same smaller-size file, which means the algorithm is lossy.

This formula is easy to prove, and we provide three proofs.

1. By induction. We assume that $2^{N-1} + 2^{N-2} + \cdots + 1$ equals $2^N - 1$ and show that this implies that $2^N + 2^{N-1} + 2^{N-2} + \cdots + 1$ equals $2^{N+1} - 1$. The proof is straightforward

$$2^N + (2^{N-1} + 2^{N-2} + \cdots + 1) = 2^N + (2^N - 1) = 2 \cdot 2^N - 1 = 2^{N+1} - 1.$$

2. By the properties of binary numbers. Examining the binary representations of the numbers 2, 4, 8, and 16 shows that the binary representation of the integer 2^i consists of a single 1 followed by $i-1$ zeros. We therefore write our sum in the form

$$
\begin{array}{r}
\overbrace{10\ldots000}^{N-2} \\
\vdots \\
100 \\
10 \\
\underline{1} \\
1\ldots111 = X \\
\underline{1+} \\
\underbrace{10\ldots000}_{N-1} = 2^N.
\end{array}
$$

This shows that $X + 1 = 2^N$, or $X = 2^n - 1$.

3. We start with $2^{N-1}+2^{N-2}+\cdots+2+1 = X$, multiply both sides by 2, and add and subtract 1 to the left-hand side to obtain $2^n+2^{N-1}+2^{N-2}+\cdots+4+2+1-1 = 2X$, which can be written as $2^N + X - 1 = 2X$, proving once again that $X = 2^N - 1$.

Notice that this argument does not assume anything about the way the algorithm works.

⋄ **Exercise 2.13:** Imagine an input stream consisting of a string of n bits, being compressed by a compression method C. The resulting output stream should have fewer than n bits. Now apply the same method C to every n-bit string (there are 2^n of them). It is intuitively clear that some of the strings are random and will not compress. There is also a chance that method C will actually *expand* some of the strings. Show that any compression method C will have to expand at least some strings.

So how do people develop "algorithms" for compressing random files? Here are some ways:

1. It is possible to place all the data of any file P (even random) in the filename, creation date, author, version, and resources of another file Q. The actual data of file Q may be a single byte. It is possible to recreate file P from Q since Q contains (hidden) all the data of P, yet the size of Q (just the data, ignoring "technical" details such as the filename) is one byte.

2. Use variable-size codes that don't satisfy the prefix property (page 47). Such codes can be short and may be able to compress a random file. However, the decoder won't be able to tell how long each code is, making the compressed file undecodable and thus useless.

3. Find a pseudo-random number generator that uses a seed to generate a sequence of numbers whose concatenation will be the original, decompressed, file. The seed would thus be the compressed file. The counting argument (or other equivalent proofs) should discourage anyone from trying this, but some people persist.

4. Split the original file into blocks and treat each block as a large integer. Factorize each large integer, hoping that the total number of bits of all the factors will be less than that of the original large number. Again, this does not work.

The following case studies illustrate these points.

2.7.1 Case Study A: David James

Patent 5,533,051 "Method for Data Compression" was filed on March 12, 1993, and granted on July 2, 1996, to David C. James.

The patent abstract says: "Methods for compressing data including methods for compressing highly randomized data are disclosed."

The patent description says: "A second aspect of the present invention which further enhances its ability to achieve high compression percentages is its ability to be applied to data recursively. Specifically, the methods of the present invention are able to make multiple passes over a file, each time further compressing the file. Thus, a series of recursions are repeated until the desired compression level is achieved.

The direct bit encode method of the present invention is effective for reducing an input string by one bit regardless of the bit pattern of the input string."

Notice the evasive argument: "Of course, this does not take into account any overhead registers or other house-keeping type information which must be tracked. However such overhead tends to be negligible when processing the large quantities of data typically encountered in data compression applications."

And later: "Thus, one skilled in the art can see that by keeping the appropriate counters, the direct bit encode method of the present invention is effective for reducing an input string by one bit regardless of the bit pattern of the input string. Although a certain amount of "loss" is necessary in keeping and maintaining various counters and registers, for files which are sufficiently large, this overhead is insignificant compared to the savings obtained by the direct bit encode method."

It took the patent office three years to examine and grant this patent, which is similar in concept to a patent on a perpetual motion machine. Alas, the days when Einstein was a patent examiner are over.

2.7.2 Case Study B: Michael L. Cole

Patent 5,488,364 "Recursive data compression" was filed on February 28, 1994 and granted on January 30, 1996 to Michael L. Cole.

This is another recursive lossless compression algorithm that claims to compress random data. The patent summary states: "Averaged over a statistically significant sample of random input data, the first block will have a percentage of adjacent bits of the "1" state that is high relative to that of the original input data, and the second block will have a percentage of adjacent bits of the "0" state that is high relative to that of the original input data."

A careful examination of the method shows that the small compression achieved by these percentages is more than cancelled out by the extra bits needed for the patented "bit-reversal key" and "keyword."

⋄ **Exercise 2.14:** Explain why the following, simple, intuitive compression method does not work. The method is first illustrated by the 10-character redundant string "SWISS␣MISS" where the letter S appears five times and I appears twice. The first step is to isolate the different characters in the input and write them as a string, to be called the dictionary. In our example the dictionary is the five-character string "SWI␣M". In the second step the input is again scanned, compared to the dictionary, and bits are produced. If the current input character is identical to the current dictionary character, a 1-bit is generated. Otherwise a 0-bit is generated and we advance (circularly) to the next dictionary entry. Table 2.11 lists the 26-bit string obtained this way.

SWI␣M
11100
10000
10011
00100
10000
1

Table 2.11: Encoding SWISS␣MISS.

The compressed stream consists of the five-character dictionary, followed by the 26 bits, a total of 66 bits, or a little more than eight characters. Once this method is understood, it is not hard to see that it is not really necessary to output the dictionary. Given a large file, text, binary, or anything else, we can consider it a string of 8-bit bytes (if the file size is not a multiple of 8, it should be padded with some zeros before being compressed, and the number of zeros placed at the start of the compressed file). The dictionary can simply be the 256 8-bit bytes, so it is known to both encoder and decoder, and there is no need to include it in the compressed stream. What's wrong with this method?

⋄ **Exercise 2.15:** The following method can be used to compress strings of symbols. It works best when the string size is a power of two, but it can be extended to other sizes as well. Two exercises are embedded in the description that follows.

Let $\mathbf{v} = (v_1, v_2, v_3, v_4, v_5, v_6, v_7, v_8)$ be a vector whose components v_i can have values 1, 0, or -1. Since each component can take one of three values and since there are eight components, the total number of different vectors $\mathbf{v}$ is $3^8 = 6{,}561$. Thus, such a vector can be coded by 13-bit fixed-size codes (because 6,561 is between $2^{12} = 4{,}096$ and $2^{13} = 8{,}192$). We now describe *tree coding*, a seven-step method to code such vectors by using variable-size prefix codes as follows:

Step 1: Arrange the components of $\mathbf{v}$ as shown in Figure 2.12a, where v_1 is set apart from the other components, which form a complete binary tree with v_2 as its root. Denote the prefix code we are going to construct by C.

Step 2: If $v_1 = 0$, set the first bit of C to 0. If $v_1 = 1$, set the first two bits of C to 10. If $v_1 = -1$, set the first two bits of C to 11. (The last two codes consist of a 1-bit followed by the sign of v_1, 0 for positive, 1 for negative.) This takes care of v_1.

Step 3: Encode v_2 with the same code as v_1 and append this code to C.

Step 4: If the remaining nodes in the tree (i.e., the levels below v_2) are zero, append a 0-bit to C, and stop. Otherwise, append a 1-bit and go to step 5.

Step 5: Encode the next level of the tree (i.e., v_3 and v_4) and append the codes to C.

Step 6: (Similar to step 4.) If the remaining nodes in the tree (i.e., the levels below v_3 and v_4) are zero, append a 0-bit to C and stop. Otherwise, append a 1-bit and go to step 7.

Step 7: (Similar to step 5.) Encode the next level of the tree (i.e., v_5 through v_8) and append the codes to C.

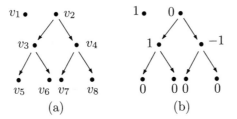

Figure 2.12: Illustrating Tree Coding.

This method can be applied to any vector with 2^n elements. Separating the first component ensures that the remaining ones will form a complete binary tree. We use the vector $\mathbf{v} = (1, 0, 1, -1, 0, 0, 0, 0)$ to illustrate the method.

Step 1: Figure 2.12b shows the tree.

Step 2: The first element v_1 is encoded to 10. We end up with $C = 10$.

Step 3: The second element v_2 is encoded to 0. We end up with $C = 100$.

Step 4: The remaining nodes are not all zero, so we append 1 to C, ending up with $C = 1001$.

Step 5: The codes for v_3 (10) and v_4 (11) are appended to C, resulting in $C = 10011011$.

Step 6: The four remaining elements, v_5 through v_8, are all zeros, so a zero is appended to C, resulting in the 9-bit code $C = 100110110$. The algorithm stops without executing step 7.

Decoding is the reverse of encoding. Thus, tree coding is symmetric.

Exercise 1: Show the first few steps in decoding the string 100110110.

It is easy to see that vectors with many trailing zeros are encoded by this method with fewer bits. In fact, the shortest zero-tree code is produced for vectors where every element is zero, and the longest code is produced when all the elements are nonzero. The longest code is longer than the 13-bit fixed-size code, as shown by the following exercise.

Exercise 2: Calculate the shortest and longest tree codes. (End of tree coding exercise.)

2.8 Huffman Coding

A commonly used method for data compression is Huffman coding. It serves as the basis for several popular programs used on personal computers. Some of them use just the Huffman method, while others use it as one step in a multistep compression process. The Huffman method [Huffman 52] is somewhat similar to the Shannon-Fano method. It generally produces better codes, and like the Shannon-Fano method, it produces best code when the probabilities of the symbols are negative powers of 2. The main difference between the two methods is that Shannon-Fano constructs its codes top to bottom (from the leftmost to the rightmost bits), while Huffman constructs a code tree from the bottom up (builds the codes from right to left). Since its development, in 1952, by D. Huffman, this method has been the subject of intensive research into data compression.

The method starts by building a list of all the alphabet symbols in descending order of their probabilities. It then constructs a tree, with a symbol at every leaf, from the bottom up. This is done in steps, where at each step the two symbols with smallest probabilities are selected, added to the top of the partial tree, deleted from the list, and replaced with an auxiliary symbol representing both of them. When the list is reduced to just one auxiliary symbol (representing the entire alphabet), the tree is complete. The tree is then traversed to determine the codes of the symbols.

This is best illustrated by an example. Given five symbols with probabilities as shown in Figure 2.13a, they are paired in the following order:

1. a_4 is combined with a_5 and both are replaced by the combined symbol a_{45}, whose probability is 0.2.
2. There are now four symbols left, a_1, with probability 0.4, and a_2, a_3, and a_{45}, with probabilities 0.2 each. We arbitrarily select a_3 and a_{45}, combine them and replace them with the auxiliary symbol a_{345}, whose probability is 0.4.
3. Three symbols are now left, a_1, a_2, and a_{345}, with probabilities 0.4, 0.2, and 0.4, respectively. We arbitrarily select a_2 and a_{345}, combine them and replace them with the auxiliary symbol a_{2345}, whose probability is 0.6.
4. Finally, we combine the two remaining symbols, a_1 and a_{2345}, and replace them with a_{12345} with probability 1.

The tree is now complete. It is shown in Figure 2.13a "lying on its side" with the root on the right and the five leaves on the left. To assign the codes, we arbitrarily assign a bit of 1 to the top edge, and a bit of 0 to the bottom edge, of every pair of edges. This results in the codes 0, 10, 111, 1101, and 1100. The assignments of bits to the edges is arbitrary.

The average size of this code is $0.4 \times 1 + 0.2 \times 2 + 0.2 \times 3 + 0.1 \times 4 + 0.1 \times 4 = 2.2$ bits/symbol, but even more importantly, the Huffman code is not unique. Some of the steps above were chosen arbitrarily, since there were more than two symbols with smallest probabilities. Figure 2.13b shows how the same five symbols can be combined differently to obtain a different Huffman code (11, 01, 00, 101, and 100). The average size of this code is $0.4 \times 2 + 0.2 \times 2 + 0.2 \times 2 + 0.1 \times 3 + 0.1 \times 3 = 2.2$ bits/symbol, the same as the previous code.

◇ **Exercise 2.16:** Given the eight symbols A, B, C, D, E, F, G, and H with probabilities 1/30, 1/30, 1/30, 2/30, 3/30, 5/30, 5/30, and 12/30, draw three different

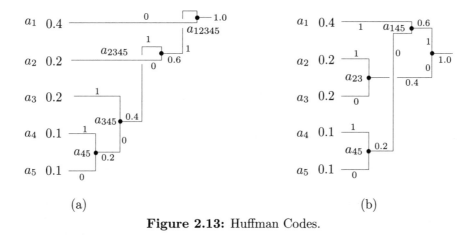

(a)   (b)

Figure 2.13: Huffman Codes.

Huffman trees with heights 5 and 6 for these symbols and calculate the average code size for each tree.

⋄ **Exercise 2.17:** Figure 2.14d shows another Huffman tree, with height 4, for the eight symbols introduced in Exercise 2.16. Explain why this tree is wrong.

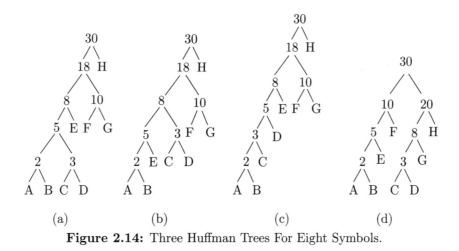

(a)   (b)   (c)   (d)

Figure 2.14: Three Huffman Trees For Eight Symbols.

It turns out that the arbitrary decisions made in constructing the Huffman tree affect the individual codes but not the average size of the code. Still, we have to answer the obvious question, "which of the different Huffman codes for a given set of symbols is best?" The answer, while not obvious, is simple: the code with the smallest variance. The variance of a code measures how much the sizes of the individual codes deviate from the average size (see page 370 for the definition of variance). The variance of code 2.13a is

$$0.4(1 - 2.2)^2 + 0.2(2 - 2.2)^2 + 0.2(3 - 2.2)^2 + 0.1(4 - 2.2)^2 + 0.1(4 - 2.2)^2 = 1.36,$$

while that of code 2.13b is

$$0.4(2 - 2.2)^2 + 0.2(2 - 2.2)^2 + 0.2(2 - 2.2)^2 + 0.1(3 - 2.2)^2 + 0.1(3 - 2.2)^2 = 0.16.$$

Code 2.13b is thus preferable (see below). A careful look at the two trees shows how to select the one we want. In the tree of Figure 2.13a, symbol a_{45} is combined with a_3, whereas in the tree of 2.13b it is combined with a_1. The rule is; when there are more than two smallest-probability nodes, select the ones that are lowest and highest in the tree and combine them. This will combine symbols of low probability with ones of high probability, thereby reducing the total variance of the code.

If the encoder simply writes the compressed stream on a file, the variance of the code makes no difference. A small-variance Huffman code is preferable only in cases where the encoder *transmits* the compressed stream, as it is being generated, over a communications line. In such a case, a code with large variance causes the encoder to generate bits at a rate that varies all the time. Since the bits have to be transmitted at a constant rate, the encoder has to use a buffer. Bits of the compressed stream are entered into the buffer as they are being generated and are moved out of it at a constant rate, to be transmitted. It is easy to see intuitively that a Huffman code with zero variance will enter bits into the buffer at a constant rate, so only a short buffer will be necessary. The larger the code variance, the less constant is the rate at which bits enter the buffer, requiring the encoder to use a larger buffer.

The following claim is sometimes found in the literature:

> It can be shown that the size of the Huffman code of a symbol a_i with probability P_i is always less than or equal to $\lceil -\log_2 P_i \rceil$.

Even though it is correct in many cases, this claim is not true in general. It seems to be a wrong corollary drawn by some authors from the Kraft-MacMillan inequality, Equation (2.1). The author is indebted to Guy Blelloch for pointing this out and also for the example of Table 2.15.

⋄ **Exercise 2.18:** Find an example where the size of the Huffman code of a symbol a_i is greater than $\lceil -\log_2 P_i \rceil$.

P_i	Code	$-\log_2 P_i$	$\lceil -\log_2 P_i \rceil$
.01	000	6.644	7
*.30	001	1.737	2
.34	01	1.556	2
.35	1	1.515	2

Table 2.15: A Huffman Code Example.

⋄ **Exercise 2.19:** It seems that the size of a code must also depend on the number n of symbols (the size of the alphabet). A small alphabet requires just a few codes, so they can all be short; a large alphabet requires many codes, so some must be long. This being so, how can we say that the size of the code of symbol a_i depends just on its probability P_i?

Figure 2.16 shows a Huffman code for the 26 letters.

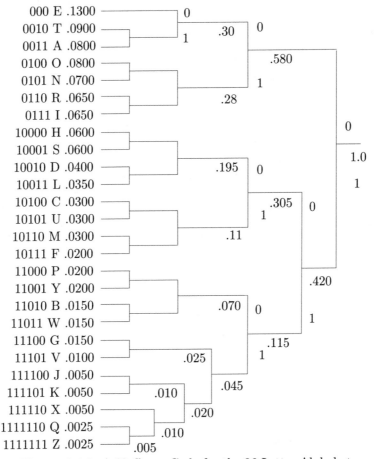

Figure 2.16: A Huffman Code for the 26-Letter Alphabet.

⋄ **Exercise 2.20:** Calculate the average size, entropy, and variance of this code.

⋄ **Exercise 2.21:** Discuss the Huffman codes for equal probabilities.

Exercise 2.21 shows that symbols with equal probabilities don't compress under the Huffman method. This is understandable, since strings of such symbols normally make random text, and random text does not compress. There may be special cases where strings of symbols with equal probabilities are not random and can be compressed. A good example is the string $a_1a_1 \ldots a_1a_2a_2 \ldots a_2a_3a_3 \ldots$ in which each symbol appears in a long run. This string can be compressed with RLE but not with Huffman codes.

Notice that the Huffman method cannot be applied to a two-symbol alphabet. In such an alphabet one symbol can be assigned the code 0 and the other code 1. The Huffman method cannot assign to any symbol a code shorter than one bit, so it cannot improve on this simple code. If the original data (the source) consists of individual bits, such as in the case of a bi-level (monochromatic) image, it is possible to combine several bits (perhaps four or eight) into a new symbol, and pretend that the alphabet consists of these (16 or 256) symbols. The problem with this approach is that the original binary data may have certain statistical correlations between the bits, and some of these correlations would be lost when the bits are combined into symbols. When a typical bi-level image (a painting or a diagram) is digitized by scan lines, a pixel is more likely to be followed by an identical pixel than by the opposite one. We thus have a file that can start with either a 0 or a 1 (each has 0.5 probability of being the first bit). A zero is more likely to be followed by another 0 and a 1 by another 1. Figure 2.17 is a finite-state machine illustrating this situation. If these bits are combined into, say, groups of eight, the bits inside a group will still be correlated, but the groups themselves will not be correlated by the original pixel probabilities. If the input stream contains, e.g., the two adjacent groups 00011100 and 00001110, they will be encoded independently, ignoring the correlation between the last 0 of the first group and the first 0 of the next group. Selecting larger groups improves this situation but increases the number of groups, which implies more storage for the code table and also longer time to calculate the table.

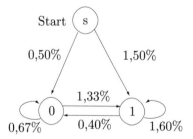

Figure 2.17: A Finite-State Machine.

◇ **Exercise 2.22:** How does the number of groups increase when the group size increases from s bits to $s + n$ bits?

A more complex approach to image compression by Huffman coding is to create several complete sets of Huffman codes. If the group size is, e.g., eight bits, then several sets of 256 codes are generated. When a symbol S is to be encoded, one of the sets is selected, and S is encoded using its code in that set. The choice of set depends on the symbol preceding S.

⋄ **Exercise 2.23:** Imagine an image with 8-bit pixels where half the pixels have values 127 and the other half, 128. Analyze the performance of RLE on the individual bitplanes of such an image, and compare it to what can be achieved with Huffman coding.

2.8.1 Huffman Decoding

Before starting the compression of a data stream, the compressor (encoder) has to determine the codes. It does that based on the probabilities (or frequencies of occurrence) of the symbols. The probabilities or frequencies have to appear on the compressed stream, so that any Huffman decompressor (decoder) will be able to decompress the stream. This is easy, since the frequencies are integers and the probabilities can be written as scaled integers. It normally adds just a few hundred bytes to the compressed stream. It is also possible to write the variable-size codes themselves on the stream, but this may be awkward, since the codes have different sizes. It is also possible to write the Huffman tree on the stream, but this may be longer than just the frequencies.

In any case, the decoder must know what's at the start of the stream, read it, and construct the Huffman tree for the alphabet. Only then can it read and decode the rest of the stream. The algorithm for decoding is simple. Start at the root and read the first bit off the compressed stream. If it is zero, follow the bottom edge of the tree; if it is one, follow the top edge. Read the next bit and move another edge toward the leaves of the tree. When the decoder gets to a leaf, it finds the original, uncompressed, code of the symbol (normally, its ASCII code), and that code is emitted by the decoder. The process starts again at the root with the next bit.

This process is illustrated for the five-symbol alphabet of Figure 2.18. The four-symbol input string "$a_4a_2a_5a_1$" is encoded into 1001100111. The decoder starts at the root, reads the first bit "1", and goes up. The second bit "0" sends it down, as does the third bit. This brings the decoder to leaf a_4, which it emits. It again returns to the root, reads 110, moves up, up, and down, to reach leaf a_2, and so on.

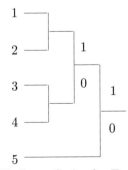

Figure 2.18: Huffman Codes for Equal Probabilities.

Bibliography

Huffman, David (1952) "A Method for the Construction of Minimum Redundancy Codes," *Proceedings of the IRE* **40**(9):1098–1101.

> Truth is stranger than fiction, but this is because fiction is obliged to stick to probability; truth is not.
>
> —Anonymous

2.8.2 Average Code Size

Figure 2.21a shows a set of five symbols with their probabilities and a typical Huffman tree. Symbol A appears 55% of the time and is assigned a 1-bit code, so it contributes $0.55 \cdot 1$ bits to the average code size. Symbol E appears only 2% of the time and is assigned a 4-bit Huffman code, so it contributes $0.02 \cdot 4 = 0.08$ bits to the code size. The average code size is therefore calculated to be

$$0.55 \cdot 1 + 0.25 \cdot 2 + 0.15 \cdot 3 + 0.03 \cdot 4 + 0.02 \cdot 4 = 1.7 \text{ bits per symbol.}$$

Surprisingly, the same result is obtained by adding the values of the four internal nodes of the Huffman code-tree $0.05 + 0.2 + 0.45 + 1 = 1.7$. This provides a way to calculate the average code size of a set of Huffman codes without any multiplications. Simply add the values of all the internal nodes of the tree. Table 2.19 illustrates why this works.

$$
\begin{aligned}
0.05 &= &&= 0.02 + 0.03 + \cdots \\
a_1 &= 0.05 + \ldots &&= 0.02 + 0.03 + \cdots \\
a_2 &= a_1 \quad + \ldots &&= 0.02 + 0.03 + \cdots \\
&\vdots \quad = \\
a_{d-2} &= a_{d-3} + \ldots &&= 0.02 + 0.03 + \cdots \\
1.0 &= a_{d-2} + \ldots &&= 0.02 + 0.03 + \cdots
\end{aligned}
$$

$$
\begin{aligned}
.05 &= &&.02 + .03 \\
.20 &= .05 + .15 &&= .02 + .03 + .15 \\
.45 &= .20 + .25 &&= .02 + .03 + .15 + .25 \\
1.0 &= .45 + .55 &&= .02 + .03 + .15 + .25 + .55
\end{aligned}
$$

Table 2.19: Composition of Nodes.   **Table 2.20:** Composition of Nodes.

(Internal nodes are shown in italics in this table.) The left column consists of the values of all the internal nodes. The right columns show how each internal node is the sum of some of the leaf nodes. Summing the values in the left column yields 1.7, and summing the other columns shows that this 1.7 is the sum of the four values 0.02, the four values 0.03, the three values 0.15, the two values 0.25, and the single value 0.55.

This argument can be extended for the general case. It is easy to show that, in a Huffman-like tree (a tree where each node is the sum of its children) the weighted sum of the leaves, where the weights are the distances of the leaves from the root, equals the sum of the internal nodes. (This property has been communicated to the author by John M. Motil.)

Figure 2.21b shows such a tree, where we assume that the two leaves 0.02 and 0.03 have d-bit Huffman codes. Inside the tree, these leaves become the children of internal node 0.05, which, in turn, is connected to the root by means of the $d - 2$ internal nodes a_1 through a_{d-2}. Table 2.20 has d rows and shows that the two values

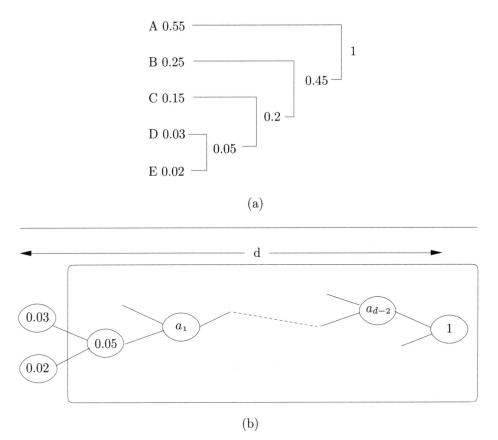

(a)

(b)

Figure 2.21: Huffman Code Trees.

0.02 and 0.03 are included in the various internal nodes exactly d times. Adding the values of all the internal nodes produces a sum that includes the contributions $0.02 \cdot d + 0.03 \cdot d$ from the 2 leaves. Since these leaves are arbitrary, it is clear that this sum includes similar contributions from all the other leaves, so this sum is the average code size. Since this sum also equals the sum of the left column, which is the sum of the internal nodes, it is clear that the sum of the internal nodes equals the average code size.

Notice that this proof does not assume that the tree is binary. The property illustrated here exists for any tree where a node contains the sum of its children.

2.8.3 Number of Codes

Since the Huffman code is not unique, the natural question is; How many different codes are there? Figure 2.22a shows a Huffman code-tree for six symbols, from which we can answer this question in two different ways.

Answer 1. The tree of 2.22a has five interior nodes, and in general, a Huffman code-tree for n symbols has $n - 1$ interior nodes. Each interior node has two edges coming out of it, labeled 0 and 1. Swapping the two labels produces a different

Huffman code-tree, so the total number of different Huffman code-trees is 2^{n-1} (in our example, 2^5 or 32). The tree of Figure 2.22b, for example, shows the result of swapping the labels of the two edges of the root. Table 2.23a,b show the codes generated by the two trees.

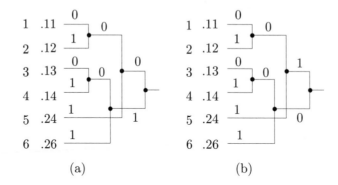

(a)   (b)

Figure 2.22: Two Huffman Code-Trees.

```
000 100 000
001 101 001
100 000 010
101 001 011
 01  11  10
 11  01  11
(a) (b) (c)
```

Table 2.23.

Answer 2. The six codes of Table 2.23a can be divided into the four classes $00x$, $10y$, 01, and 11, where x and y are 1-bit each. It is possible to create different Huffman codes by changing the first two bits of each class. Since there are four classes, this is the same as creating all the permutations of four objects, something that can be done in $4! = 24$ ways. In each of the 24 permutations it is also possible to change the values of x and y in four different ways (since they are bits) so the total number of different Huffman codes in our six-symbol example is $24 \times 4 = 96$.

The two answers are different because they count different things. Answer 1 counts the number of different Huffman code-trees, while answer 2 counts the number of different Huffman codes. It turns out that our example can generate 32 different code-trees but only 94 different codes instead of 96. This shows that there are Huffman codes that cannot be generated by the Huffman method! Table 2.23c shows such an example. A look at the trees of Figure 2.22 should convince the reader that the codes of symbols 5 and 6 must start with different bits, but in the code of Table 2.23c they both start with 1. This code is therefore impossible to generate by any relabeling of the nodes of the trees of Figure 2.22.

2.8.4 Ternary Huffman Codes

The Huffman code is not unique. Moreover, it does not have to be binary! The Huffman method can easily be applied to codes based on other numbers. Figure 2.24a shows a Huffman code tree for five symbols with probabilities 0.15, 0.15, 0.2, 0.25, and 0.25. The average code size is

$$2 \times .25 + 3 \times .15 + 3 \times .15 + 2 \times .20 + 2 \times .25 = 2.3 \,\text{bits/symbol}.$$

Figure 2.24b shows a ternary Huffman code tree for the same five symbols. The tree is constructed by selecting, at each step, three symbols with the smallest probabilities and merging them into one parent symbol, with the combined probability. The average code size of this tree is

$$2 \times .15 + 2 \times .15 + 2 \times .20 + 1 \times .25 + 1 \times .25 = 1.5 \,\text{trits/symbol}.$$

Notice that the ternary codes use the digits 0, 1, and 2.

◇ **Exercise 2.24:** Given seven symbols with probabilities .02, .03, .04, .04, .12, .26, and .49, construct binary and ternary Huffman code trees for them and calculate the average code size in each case.

2.8.5 Canonical Huffman Codes

Code 2.23c has a simple interpretation. It assigns the first four symbols the 3-bit codes 0, 1, 2, 3, and the last two symbols the 2-bit codes 2 and 3. This is an example of a *canonical Huffman code*. The word "canonical" means that this particular code has been selected from among the several (or even many) possible Huffman codes because its properties make it easy and fast to use.

Table 2.25 shows a slightly bigger example of a canonical Huffman code. Imagine a set of 16 symbols (whose probabilities are irrelevant and are not shown) such that four symbols are assigned 3-bit codes, five symbols are assigned 5-bit codes, and the remaining seven symbols, 6-bit codes. Table 2.25a shows a set of possible Huffman codes, while Table 2.25b shows a set of canonical Huffman codes. It is easy to see that the seven 6-bit canonical codes are simply the 6-bit integers 0 through 6. The five codes are the 5-bit integers 4 through 8, and the four codes are the 3-bit integers 3 through 6. We first show how these codes are generated and then how they are used.

The top row (length) of Table 2.26 lists the possible code lengths, from 1 to 6 bits. The second row (numl) lists the number of codes of each length, and the bottom row (first) lists the first code in each group. This is why the three groups of codes start with values 3, 4, and 0. To obtain the top two rows we need to compute the lengths of all the Huffman codes for the given alphabet (see below). The third row is computed by setting "first[6]:=0;" and iterating

<u>for</u> l:=5 <u>downto</u> 1 <u>do</u> first[l]:=$\lceil$(first[l+1]+numl[l+1])/2$\rceil$;

This guarantees that all the 3-bit prefixes of codes longer than 3 bits will be less than first[3] (which is 3), all the 5-bit prefixes of codes longer than 5 bits will be less than first[5] (which is 4), and so on.

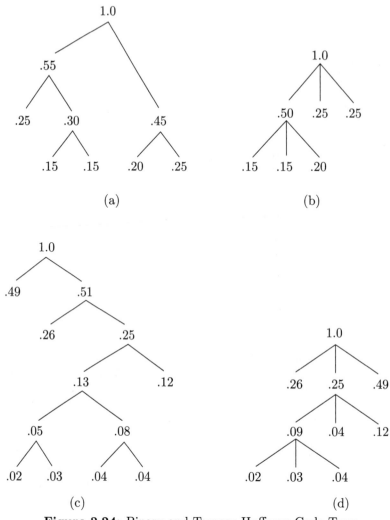

Figure 2.24: Binary and Ternary Huffman Code Trees.

Now for the use of these unusual codes. Canonical Huffman codes are useful in cases where the alphabet is large and where fast decoding is mandatory. Because of the way the codes are constructed, it is easy for the decoder to identify the length of a code by reading and examining input bits one by one. Once the length is known, the symbol can be found in one step. The pseudo-code below shows the rules for decoding:

```
l:=1; input v;
while v<first[l]
append next input bit to v; l:=l+1;
endwhile
```

	(a)	(b)		(a)	(b)
1:	000	011	9:	10100	01000
2:	001	100	10:	101010	000000
3:	010	101	11:	101011	000001
4:	011	110	12:	101100	000010
5:	10000	00100	13:	101101	000011
6:	10001	00101	14:	101110	000100
7:	10010	00110	15:	101111	000101
8:	10011	00111	16:	110000	000110

Table 2.25.

length:	1	2	3	4	5	6
numl:	0	0	4	0	5	7
first:	2	4	3	5	4	0

Table 2.26.

As an example, suppose the next code is 00110. As bits are input and appended to v, it goes through the values 0, 00=0, 001=1, 0011=3, 00110=6, while l is incremented from 1 to 5. All steps except the last satisfy v<first[l], so the last step determines the value of l (the code length) as 5. The symbol itself is found by subtracting v − first[5] = 6 − 4 = 2, so it is the third symbol (numbering starts at 0) in group l = 5 (symbol 7 of the 16 symbols).

It has been mentioned that canonical Huffman codes are useful in cases were the alphabet is large and fast decoding is important. A practical example is a collection of documents archived and compressed by a *word-based* adaptive Huffman coder (Section 8.6.1). In an archive a slow encoder is acceptable, but the decoder should be fast. When the individual symbols are words, the alphabet may be huge, making it impractical, or even impossible, to construct the Huffman code-tree. However, even with a huge alphabet, the number of different code lengths is small, rarely exceeding 20 bits (just the number of 20-bit codes is about a million). If canonical Huffman codes are used, and the maximum code length is L, then the code length l of a symbol is found by the decoder in at most L steps, and the symbol itself is identified in one more step.

> He uses statistics as a drunken man uses lamp-posts—for support rather than illumination.
>
> —Andrew Lang (1844–1912), *Treasury of Humorous Quotations*

The last point to be discussed is the encoder. In order to calculate the canonical Huffman code, the encoder needs to know the length of the Huffman code of every symbol. The main problem is the large size of the alphabet, which may make it impractical or even impossible to build the entire Huffman code-tree in memory.

The algorithm described here (see [Hirschberg 90] and [Sieminski 88]) solves this problem. It calculates the code sizes for an alphabet of n symbols using just one array of size $2n$. One-half of this array is used as a *heap*, so we start with a short description of this useful data structure.

A *binary tree* is a tree where every node has at most two children (i.e., it may have 0, 1, or 2 children). A *complete binary tree* is a binary tree where every node except the leaves has exactly two children. A *balanced binary tree* is a complete binary tree where some of the bottom-right nodes may be missing (see also page 113 for another application of those trees). A heap is a balanced binary tree where every leaf contains a data item and the items are ordered such that every path from a leaf to the root traverses nodes that are in sorted order, either nondecreasing (a max-heap) or nonincreasing (a min-heap). Figure 2.27 shows examples of min-heaps.

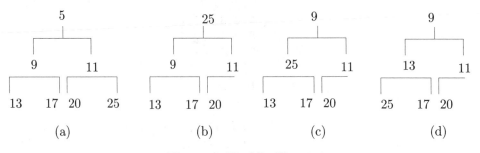

Figure 2.27: Min-Heaps.

A common operation on a heap is to remove the root and rearrange the remaining nodes to get back a heap. This is called *sifting* the heap. Figure 2.27a–d shows how a heap is sifted after the root (with data item 5) has been removed. Sifting starts by moving the bottom-right node to become the new root. This guarantees that the heap will remain a balanced binary tree. The root is then compared with its children and may have to be swapped with one of them in order to preserve the ordering of a heap. Several more swaps may be necessary to completely restore heap ordering. It is easy to see that the maximum number of swaps equals the height of the tree, which is $\lceil \log_2 n \rceil$.

The reason a heap must always remain balanced is that this makes it possible to store it in memory without using any pointers. The heap is said to be "housed" in an array. To house a heap in an array, the root is placed in the first array location (with index 1), the two children of the node at array location i are placed at locations $2i$ and $2i + 1$, and the parent of the node at array location j is placed at location $\lfloor j/2 \rfloor$. Thus the heap of Figure 2.27a is housed in an array by placing the nodes 5, 9, 11, 13, 17, 20, and 25 in the first seven locations of the array.

The algorithm uses a single array **A** of size $2n$. The frequencies of occurrence of the n symbols are placed in the top half of **A** (locations $n + 1$ through $2n$) and the bottom half of **A** (locations 1 through n) becomes a min-heap whose data items are pointers to the frequencies in the top half (Figure 2.28a). The algorithm then goes into a loop where in each iteration the heap is used to identify the 2 smallest frequencies and replace them with their sum. The sum is stored in the last heap position `A[h]`, and the heap shrinks by one position (Figure 2.28b). The loop repeats until the heap is reduced to just one pointer (Figure 2.28c).

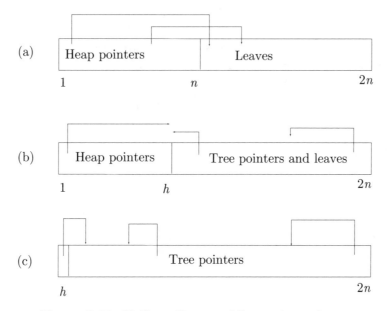

Figure 2.28: Huffman Heaps and Leaves in an Array.

We now illustrate this part of the algorithm using seven frequencies. The table below shows how the frequencies and the heap are initially housed in an array of size 14. Pointers are shown in italics, and the heap is delimited by square brackets.

1	2	3	4	5	6	7	8	9	10	11	12	13	14
[*14*	*12*	*13*	*10*	*11*	*9*	*8*]	25	20	13	17	9	11	5

The first iteration selects the smallest frequency (5), removes the root of the heap (pointer 14), and leaves `A[7]` empty.

1	2	3	4	5	6	7	8	9	10	11	12	13	14
[*12*	*10*	*13*	*8*	*11*	*9*]		25	20	13	17	9	11	5

The heap is sifted, and its new root (12) points to the second smallest frequency (9) in `A[12]`. The sum $5 + 9$ is stored in the empty location 7, and the three array locations `A[1]`, `A[12]`, and `A[14]` are set to point to that location.

1	2	3	4	5	6	7	8	9	10	11	12	13	14
[*7*	*10*	*13*	*8*	*11*	*9*]	5+9	25	20	13	17	*7*	11	*7*

The heap is now sifted.

1	2	3	4	5	6	7	8	9	10	11	12	13	14
[*13*	*10*	*7*	*8*	*11*	*9*]	14	25	20	13	17	*7*	11	*7*

The new root is 13, meaning that the smallest frequency (11) is stored at A[13]. The root is removed, and the heap shrinks to just five positions, leaving location 6 empty.

1	2	3	4	5	6	7	8	9	10	11	12	13	14
[10	11	7	8	9]		14	25	20	13	17	7	11	7

The heap is now sifted. The new root is 10, showing that the second smallest frequency, 13, is stored at A[10]. The sum $11 + 13$ is stored at the empty location 6, and the three locations A[1], A[13], and A[10] are set to point to 6.

1	2	3	4	5	6	7	8	9	10	11	12	13	14
[6	11	7	8	9]	11+13	14	25	20	6	17	7	6	7

◇ **Exercise 2.25:** Complete this loop.

The final result of the loop is

1	2	3	4	5	6	7	8	9	10	11	12	13	14
[2]	100	2	2	3	4	5	3	4	6	5	7	6	7

from which it is easy to figure out the code lengths of all seven symbols. To find the length of the code of symbol 14, e.g., we follow the pointers 7, 5, 3, 2 from A[14] to the root. Four steps are necessary, so the code length is 4.

◇ **Exercise 2.26:** Find the lengths of all the other codes.

Bibliography

Hirschberg, D., and D. Lelewer (1990) "Efficient Decoding of Prefix Codes," *Communications of the ACM* **33**(4):449–459.

Sieminski, A. (1988) "Fast Decoding of the Huffman Codes," *Information Processing Letters* **26**(5):237–241.

2.9 Adaptive Huffman Coding

The Huffman method assumes that the frequencies of occurrence of all the symbols of the alphabet are known to the compressor. In practice, the frequencies are seldom, if ever, known in advance. One solution is for the compressor to read the original data twice. The first time it just calculates the frequencies. The second time it compresses the data. Between the two passes, the compressor constructs the Huffman tree. Such a method is called semiadaptive (page 7), and is normally too slow to be practical. The method used in practice is called adaptive (or dynamic) Huffman coding. This method is the basis of the UNIX compact program. (See also Section 8.6.1 for a word-based version of adaptive Huffman coding.)

The main idea is for the compressor and the decompressor to start with an empty Huffman tree, and to modify it as symbols are being read and processed (in the case of the compressor the word "processed" means compressed; in the case of the decompressor, it means decompressed). The compressor and decompressor should modify the tree in the same way, so at any point in the process they should use the same codes, although those codes may change from step to step. We say that the compressor and decompressor are synchronized, or that they work in *lockstep* (although they don't necessarily work together; compression and decompression usually take place at different times). The term *mirroring* is perhaps a better choice. The decoder mirrors the operations of the encoder.

Initially, the compressor starts with an empty Huffman tree. No symbols have been assigned codes. The first symbol being input is simply written on the output stream in its uncompressed form. The symbol is then added to the tree, and a code assigned to it. The next time this symbol is encountered, its current code is written on the stream, and its frequency incremented by one. Since this modifies the tree, it (the tree) is examined to see whether it is still a Huffman tree (best codes). If not, it is rearranged, which entails changing the codes (Section 2.9.2).

The decompressor mirrors the same steps. When it reads the uncompressed form of a symbol, it adds it to the tree and assigns it a code. When it reads a compressed (variable-size) code, it uses the current tree to determine what symbol the code belongs to, and it updates the tree in the same way as the compressor.

The only subtle point is that the decompressor needs to know whether the item it has just input is an uncompressed symbol (normally, an 8-bit ASCII code, but see Section 2.9.1) or a variable-size code. To remove any ambiguity, each uncompressed symbol is preceded by a special, variable-size *escape code*. When the decompressor reads this code, it knows that the next 8 bits are the ASCII code of a symbol that appears in the compressed stream for the first time.

The trouble is that the escape code should not be any of the variable-size codes used for the symbols. Since these codes are being modified every time the tree is rearranged, the escape code should also be modified. A natural way to do this is to add an empty leaf to the tree, a leaf with a zero frequency of occurrence, that's always assigned to the 0-branch of the tree. Since the leaf is in the tree, it gets a variable-size code assigned. This code is the escape code preceding every uncompressed symbol. As the tree is being rearranged, the position of the empty leaf—and thus its code—change, but this escape code is always used to identify uncompressed symbols in the compressed stream. Figure 2.29 shows how the escape code moves as the tree grows.

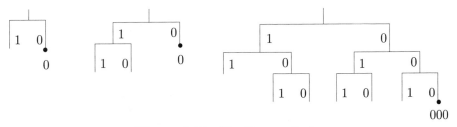

Figure 2.29: The Escape Code.

This method is used to compress/decompress data in the V.32 protocol for 14,400 baud modems.

> Escape is not his plan. I must face him. Alone.
> —David Prowse as Lord Darth Vader in *Star Wars* (1977)

2.9.1 Uncompressed Codes

If the symbols being compressed are ASCII characters, they may simply be assigned their ASCII codes as uncompressed codes. In the general case where there can be any symbols, uncompressed codes of two different sizes can be assigned by a simple method. Here is an example for the case $n = 24$. The first 16 symbols can be assigned the numbers 0 through 15 as their codes. These numbers require only 4 bits, but we encode them in 5 bits. Symbols 17 through 24 can be assigned the numbers $17 - 16 - 1 = 0$, $18 - 16 - 1 = 1$ through $24 - 16 - 1 = 7$ as 4-bit numbers. We end up with the sixteen 5-bit codes $00000, 00001, \ldots, 01111$, followed by the eight 4-bit codes $0000, 0001, \ldots, 0111$.

In general, we assume an alphabet that consists of the n symbols $a_1, a_2, \ldots, a_n$. We select integers m and r such that $2^m \leq n < 2^{m+1}$ and $r = n - 2^m$. The first 2^m symbols are encoded as the $(m + 1)$-bit numbers 0 through $2^m - 1$. The remaining symbols are encoded as m-bit numbers such that the code of a_k is $k - 2^m - 1$. This code is also called a *phased-in binary code* (see page 202 for an application of these codes).

2.9.2 Modifying the Tree

The main idea is to check the tree each time a symbol is input. If the tree is no longer a Huffman tree, it should be updated. A glance at Figure 2.30a shows what it means for a binary tree to be a Huffman tree. The tree in the figure contains five symbols: A, B, C, D, and E. It is shown with the symbols and their frequencies (in parentheses) after 16 symbols have been input and processed. The property that makes it a Huffman tree is that if we scan it level by level, scanning each level from left to right, and going from the bottom (the leaves) to the top (the root), the frequencies will be in sorted, nondescending order. Thus the bottom left node (A) has the lowest frequency, and the top right one (the root) has the highest frequency. This is called the *sibling property*.

$\diamond$ **Exercise 2.27:** Why is this the criterion for a tree to be a Huffman tree?

Here is a summary of the operations necessary to update the tree. The loop starts at the current node (the one corresponding to the symbol just input). This node is a leaf that we denote by X, with frequency of occurrence F. Each iteration of the loop involves three steps:

1. Compare X to its successors in the tree (from left to right and bottom to top). If the immediate successor has frequency $F + 1$ or greater, the nodes are still in sorted order and there is no need to change anything. Otherwise, some successors of X have identical frequencies of F or smaller. In this case, X should be swapped with the last node in this group (except that X should not be swapped with its parent).
2. Increment the frequency of X from F to $F + 1$. Increment the frequencies of all its parents.
3. If X is the root, the loop stops; otherwise, the loop repeats with the parent of node X.

Figure 2.30b shows the tree after the frequency of node A has been incremented from 1 to 2. It is easy to follow the three rules above to see how incrementing the frequency of A results in incrementing the frequencies of all its parents. No swaps are needed in this simple case because the frequency of A hasn't exceeded the frequency of its immediate successor B. Figure 2.30c shows what happens when A's frequency has been incremented again, from 2 to 3. The three nodes following A, namely, B, C, and D, have frequencies of 2, so A is swapped with the last of them, D. The frequencies of the new parents of A are then incremented, each is compared to its successor, but no more swaps are needed.

Figure 2.30d shows the tree after the frequency of A has been incremented to 4. Once we decide that A is the current node, its frequency (which is still 3) is compared to that of its successor (4), and the decision is not to swap. A's frequency is incremented, followed by incrementing the frequencies of its parents.

In Figure 2.30e, A is again the current node. Its frequency (4) equals that of its successor, so they should be swapped. This is shown in Figure 2.30f, where A's frequency is 5. The next loop iteration examines the parent of A, with frequency 10. It should be swapped with its successor E (with frequency 9), which leads to the final tree of Figure 2.30g.

2.9.3 Counter Overflow

The frequency counts are accumulated in the Huffman tree in fixed-size fields, and such fields may overflow. A 16-bit unsigned field can accommodate counts of up to $2^{16} - 1 = 65,535$. A simple solution is to watch the count field of the root each time it is incremented and, when it reaches its maximum value, to *rescale* all frequency counts by dividing them by 2 (integer division). In practice, this is done by dividing the count fields of the leaves, then updating the counts of the interior nodes. Each interior node gets the sum of the counts of its children. The problem is that the counts are integers, and integer division reduces precision. This may change a Huffman tree to one that does not satisfy the sibling property.

A simple example is shown in Figure 2.30h. After the counts of the leaves are halved, the three interior nodes are updated as shown in Figure 2.30i. The latter tree, however, is no longer a Huffman tree, since the counts are no longer in sorted order. The solution is to rebuild the tree each time the counts are rescaled, which does not happen very often. A Huffman data compression program intended for general use should thus have large count fields that would not overflow very often. A 4-byte count field overflows at $2^{32} - 1 \approx 4.3 \times 10^9$.

It should be noted that after rescaling the counts, the new symbols being read and compressed have more effect on the counts than the old symbols (those counted before the rescaling). This turns out to be fortuitous since it is known from experience that the probability of appearance of a symbol depends more on the symbols immediately preceding it than on symbols that appeared in the distant past.

2.9.4 Code Overflow

An even more serious problem is code overflow. This may happen when many symbols are added to the tree and it becomes high. The codes themselves are not stored in the tree, since they change all the time, and the compressor has to figure out the code of a symbol X each time X is input. Here are the details of this:

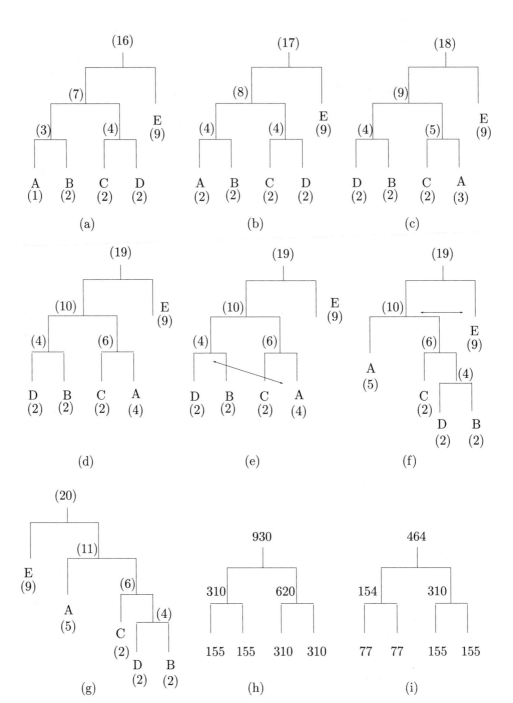

Figure 2.30: Updating the Huffman Tree.

1. The encoder has to locate symbol X in the tree. The tree has to be implemented as an array of structures, each a node, and the array is searched linearly.

2. If X is not found, the escape code is emitted, followed by the uncompressed code of X. X is then added to the tree.

3. If X is found, the compressor moves from node X back to the root, building the code bit by bit as it goes along. Each time it goes from a left child to a parent, a "1" is appended to the code. Going from a right child to a parent appends a "0" bit to the code (or vice versa, but this should be consistent because it is mirrored by the decoder). Those bits have to be accumulated someplace, since they have to be emitted in the *reverse order* in which they are created. When the tree gets taller, the codes get longer. If they are accumulated in a 16-bit integer, then codes longer than 16 bits would cause a malfunction.

One solution is to accumulate the bits of a code in a linked list, where new nodes can be created, limited in number only by the amount of available memory. This is general but slow. Another solution is to accumulate the codes in a large integer variable (perhaps 50 bits wide) and document a maximum code size of 50 bits as one of the limitations of the program.

Fortunately, this problem does not affect the decoding process. The decoder reads the compressed code bit by bit and uses each bit to go one step left or right down the tree until it reaches a leaf node. If the leaf is the escape code, the decoder reads the uncompressed code of the symbol off the compressed stream (and adds the symbol to the tree). Otherwise, the uncompressed code is found in the leaf node.

⋄ **Exercise 2.28:** Given the 11-symbol string "sir␣sid␣is␣" apply the adaptive Huffman method to it. For each symbol input, show the output, the tree after the symbol has been added to it, the tree after being rearranged (if necessary), and the list of nodes traversed left to right and bottom up.

2.9.5 A Variant

This variant of the adaptive Huffman method is simpler but less efficient. The idea is to calculate a set of n variable-size codes based on equal probabilities, to assign those codes to the n symbols at random, and to change the assignments "on the fly," as symbols are being read and compressed. The method is not efficient since the codes are not based on the actual probabilities of the symbols in the input stream. However, it is simpler to implement and also faster than the adaptive method described above, because it has to swap rows in a table, rather than update a tree, when updating the frequencies of the symbols.

The main data structure is an $n \times 3$ table where the three columns store the names of the n symbols, their frequencies of occurrence so far, and their codes. The table is always kept sorted by the second column. When the frequency counts in the second column change, rows are swapped, but only columns 1 and 2 are moved. The codes in column 3 never change. Figure 2.31 shows an example of four symbols and the behavior of the method when the string "a_2, a_4, a_4" is compressed.

Figure 2.31a shows the initial state. After the first symbol a_2 is read, its count is incremented, and since it is now the largest count, rows 1 and 2 are swapped

Name	Count	Code	Name	Count	Code	Name	Count	Code	Name	Count	Code
a_1	0	0	a_2	1	0	a_2	1	0	a_4	2	0
a_2	0	10	a_1	0	10	a_4	1	10	a_2	1	10
a_3	0	110	a_3	0	110	a_3	0	110	a_3	0	110
a_4	0	111	a_4	0	111	a_1	0	111	a_1	0	111
	(a)			(b)			(c)			(d)	

Figure 2.31: Four Steps in a Huffman Variant.

(Figure 2.31b). After the second symbol a_4 is read, its count is incremented and rows 2 and 4 are swapped (Figure 2.31c). Finally, after reading the last symbol a_4, its count is the largest, so rows 1 and 2 are swapped (Figure 2.31d).

The only point that can cause a problem with this method is overflow of the count fields. If such a field is k bits wide, its maximum value is $2^k - 1$, so it will overflow when incremented for the 2^kth time. This may happen if the size of the input stream is not known in advance, which is very common. Fortunately, we do not really need to know the counts, we just need them in sorted order, making it easy to solve this problem.

One solution is to count the input symbols and, after $2^k - 1$ symbols are input and compressed, to (integer) divide all the count fields by 2 (or shift them one position to the right, if this is easier).

Another, similar, solution is to check each count field every time it is incremented and, if it has reached its maximum value (if it consists of all ones), to integer divide all the count fields by 2 as above. This approach requires fewer divisions but more complex tests.

Whatever solution is adopted should be used by both the compressor and decompressor.

Bibliography

Knuth, D. E. (1985) "Dynamic Huffman Coding," *Journal of Algorithms* **6**:163–180.

Vitter, Jeffrey S. (1987) "Design and Analysis of Dynamic Huffman Codes," *Journal of the ACM* **34**(4):825–845, October.

I think you're begging the question," said Haydock, "and I can see looming ahead one of those terrible exercises in probability where six men have white hats and six men have black hats and you have to work it out by mathematics how likely it is that the hats will get mixed up and in what proportion. If you start thinking about things like that, you would go round the bend. Let me assure you of that!

—Agatha Christie, *The Mirror Crack'd*

2.10 MNP5

Microcom, Inc., a maker of modems, has developed a protocol (called MNP, for Microcom Networking Protocol) for use in its modems. Among other things, the MNP protocol specifies how to unpack bytes into individual bits before they are sent by the modem, how to transmit bits serially in the synchronous and asynchronous modes, and what modulation techniques to use. Each specification is called a *class*, and classes 5 and 7 specify methods for data compression. These methods (especially MNP5) have become very popular and are currently used by most modern modems.

The MNP5 method is a two-stage process that starts with run-length encoding, followed by adaptive frequency encoding.

The first stage has been described on page 19 and is repeated below. When three or more identical consecutive bytes are found in the source stream, the compressor emits three copies of the byte onto its output stream, followed by a repetition count. When the decompressor reads three identical consecutive bytes, it knows that the next byte is a repetition count (which may be zero, indicating just three repetitions). A disadvantage of the method is that a run of three characters in the input stream results in four characters written to the output stream (expansion). A run of four characters results in no compression. Only runs longer than four characters do actually get compressed. Another, slight, problem is that the maximum count is artificially limited to 250 instead of to 255.

The second stage operates on the bytes in the partially compressed stream generated by the first stage. Stage 2 is similar to the method of Section 2.9.5. It starts with a table of 256×2 entries, where each entry corresponds to one of the 256 possible 8-bit bytes 00000000 to 11111111. The first column, the frequency counts, is initialized to all zeros. Column 2 is initialized to variable-size codes, called *tokens*, that vary from a short "000|0" to a long "111|11111110". Column 2 with the tokens is shown in Table 2.32 (which shows column 1 with frequencies of zero). Each token starts with a 3-bit header, followed by some code bits.

The code bits (with three exceptions) are the two 1-bit codes 0 and 1, the four 2-bit codes 0 through 3, the eight 3-bit codes 0 through 7, the sixteen 4-bit codes, the thirty-two 5-bit codes, the sixty-four 6-bit codes, and the one hundred and twenty-eight 7-bit codes. This provides for a total of $2 + 4 + 8 + 16 + 32 + 64 + 128 = 254$ codes. The three exceptions are the first two codes "000|0" and "000|1", and the last code, which is "111|11111110" instead of the expected "111|11111111".

When stage 2 starts, all 256 entries of column 1 are assigned frequency counts of zero. When the next byte B is read from the input stream (actually, it is read from the output of the first stage), the corresponding token is written to the output stream, and the frequency of entry B is incremented by 1. Following this, tokens may be swapped to ensure that table entries with large frequencies always have the shortest tokens (see the next section for details). Notice that only the tokens are swapped, not the frequency counts. Thus the first entry always corresponds to byte "00000000" and contains its frequency count. The token of this byte, however, may change from the original "000|0" to something longer if other bytes achieve higher frequency counts.

Byte	Freq.	Token	Byte	Freq.	Token	Byte	Freq.	Token	Byte	Freq.	Token
0	0	000|0	9	0	011|001	26	0	111|1010	247	0	111|1110111
1	0	000|1	10	0	011|010	27	0	111|1011	248	0	111|1111000
2	0	001|0	11	0	011|011	28	0	111|1100	249	0	111|1111001
3	0	001|1	12	0	011|100	29	0	111|1101	250	0	111|1111010
4	0	010|00	13	0	011|101	30	0	111|1110	251	0	111|1111011
5	0	010|01	14	0	011|110	31	0	111|1111	252	0	111|1111100
6	0	010|10	15	0	011|111	32	0	101|00000	253	0	111|1111101
7	0	010|11	16	0	111|0000	33	0	101|00001	254	0	111|1111110
8	0	011|000	17	0	111|0001	34	0	101|00010	255	0	111|11111110

18 to 25 and 35 to 246 continue in the same pattern.

Table 2.32: The MNP5 Tokens.

The frequency counts are stored in 8-bit fields. Each time a count is incremented, the algorithm checks to see whether it has reached its maximum value. If yes, all the counts are scaled down by (integer) dividing them by 2.

Another, subtle, point has to do with interaction between the two compression stages. Recall that each repetition of three or more characters is replaced, in stage 1, by three repetitions, followed by a byte with the repetition count. When these four bytes arrive at stage 2, they are replaced by tokens, but the fourth one does not cause an increment of a frequency count.

Example: Suppose that the character with ASCII code 52 repeats six times. Stage 1 will generate the four bytes "52, 52, 52, 6," and stage 2 will replace each with a token, will increment the entry for "52" (entry 53 in the table) by 3, but will not increment the entry for "6" (which is entry 7 in the table). (The three tokens for the three bytes of "52" may all be different, since tokens may be swapped after each "52" is read and processed.)

The output of stage 2 consists of tokens of different sizes, from four to 11 bits. This output is packed in groups of eight bits, which get written into the output stream. At the end, a special code consisting of eleven bits of 1 (the flush token) is written, followed by as many 1-bits as necessary, to complete the last group of eight bits.

The efficiency of MNP5 is a result of both stages. The efficiency of stage 1 depends heavily on the original data. Stage 2 also depends on the original data, but to a smaller extent. Stage 2 tends to identify the most frequent characters in the data and assign them the short codes. A look at Table 2.32 shows that 32 of the 256 characters have tokens that are 7 bits or fewer in length, thus resulting in compression. The other 224 characters have tokens that are 8 bits or longer. When one of these characters is replaced by a long token, the result is no compression, or even expansion.

The efficiency of MNP5 thus depends on how many characters dominate the original data. If all characters occur at the same frequency, expansion will result. In the other extreme case, if only four characters appear in the data, each will be assigned a 4-bit token, and the compression factor will be 2.

⋄ **Exercise 2.29:** Assuming that all 256 characters appear in the original data with the same probability (1/256 each), what will the expansion factor in stage 2 be?

2.10.1 Updating the Table

The process of updating the table of MNP5 codes by swapping rows can be done in two ways:

1. Sorting the entire table every time a frequency is incremented. This is simple in concept but too slow in practice, since the table is 256 entries long.

2. Using pointers in the table, and swapping pointers such that items with large frequencies will point to short codes. This approach is illustrated in Figure 2.33. The figure shows the code table organized in four columns labeled F, P, Q, and C. Columns F and C contain the frequencies and codes; columns P and Q contain pointers that always point to each other, so if P[i] contains index j (i.e., points to Q[j]), then Q[j] points to P[i]. The following paragraphs correspond to the nine different parts of the figure.

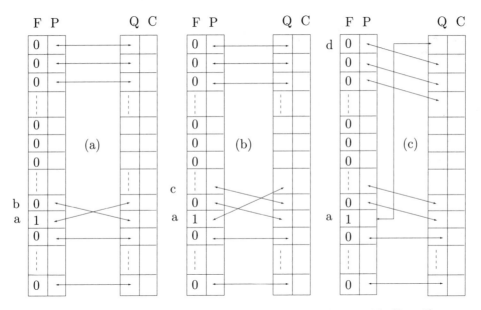

Figure 2.33: Swapping Pointers in the MNP5 Code Table (Part I).

(a) The first data item a is read and F[a] is incremented from 0 to 1. The algorithm starts with pointer P[a], which contains, say, j. The algorithm examines pointer Q[j-1], which initially points to entry F[b], the one right above F[a]. Since F[a]>F[b], entry a has to be assigned a short code, and this is done by swapping pointers P[a] and P[b] (and also the corresponding Q pointers).

(b) The same process is repeated. The algorithm again starts with pointer P[a], which now points higher, to entry b. Assuming that P[a] contains the index k, the algorithm examines pointer Q[k-1], which points to entry c. Since F[a]>F[c], entry a should be assigned a code shorter than that of c. This again is done by swapping pointers, this time P[a] and P[c].

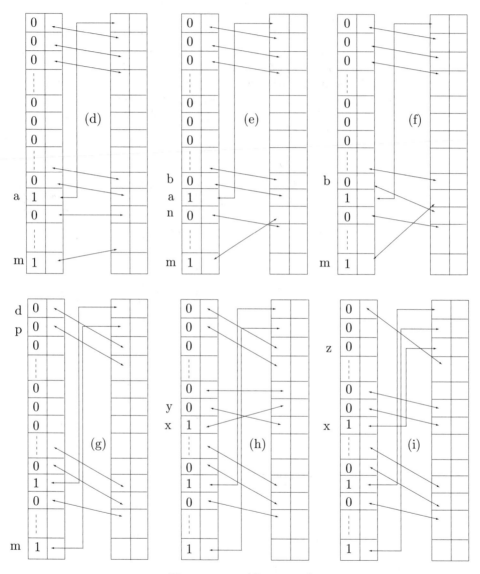

Figure 2.33 (Continued)

(c) This process is repeated and, since F[a] is greater than all the frequencies above it, pointers are swapped until P[a] points to the top entry, d. At this point entry a has been assigned the shortest code.

(d) We now assume that the next data item has been input, and F[m] incremented to 1. Pointers P[m] and the one above it are swapped as in (a) above.

(e) After a few more swaps, P[m] is now pointing to entry n (the one just below a). The next step performs j:=P[m]; b:=Q[j-1], and the algorithm compares F[m] to F[b]. Since F[m]>F[b], pointers are swapped as shown in Figure 2.33f.

(f) After the swap, P[m] is pointing to entry a and P[b] is pointing to entry n.

(g) After some more swaps, pointer P[m] points to the second entry p. This is how entry m is assigned the second-shortest code. Pointer P[m] is not swapped with P[a], since they have the same frequencies.

(h) We now assume that the third data item has been input and F[x] incremented. Pointers P[x] and P[y] are swapped.

(i) After some more swaps, pointer P[x] points to the third table entry z. This is how entry x is assigned the third shortest code.

Assuming that F[x] is incremented next, the reader is invited to try to figure out how P[x] is swapped, first with P[m] and then with P[a], so that entry x is assigned the shortest code.

The pseudo-code of Figure 2.34 summarizes the pointer swapping process.

```
F[i]:=F[i]+1;
repeat forever
 j:=P[i];
 if j=1 then exit;
 j:=Q[j-1];
 if F[i]<=F[j] then exit
   else
     tmp:=P[i]; P[i]:=P[j]; P[j]:=tmp;
     tmp:=Q[P[i]]; Q[P[i]]:=Q[P[j]]; Q[P[j]]:=tmp
 endif;
end repeat
```

Figure 2.34: Swapping Pointers in MNP5.

Are no probabilities to be accepted, merely because they are not certainties?

—Jane Austen, *Sense and Sensibility*

2.11 MNP7

More complex and sophisticated than MNP5, MNP7 combines run length encoding with a two-dimensional variant of adaptive Huffman coding. Stage 1 identifies runs and emits three copies of the run character, followed by a 4-bit count of the remaining characters in the run. A count of zero implies a run of length 3, and a count of 15 (the largest possible in a 4-bit nibble), a run of length 18. Stage 2 starts by assigning to each character a complete table with many variable-size codes. When a character C is read, one of the codes in its table is selected and output, depending on the *character preceding* C in the input stream. If this character is, say, P, then the frequency count of the pair (digram) PC is incremented by 1, and table rows may be swapped, using the same algorithm as for MNP5, to move the pair to a position in the table that has a shorter code.

MNP7 is thus based on a first-order Markov model, where each item is processed depending on the item and one of its predecessors. In a k-order Markov model, an item is processed depending on itself and k predecessors (not necessarily the k immediate ones).

Here are the details. Each of the 256 8-bit bytes gets a table of codes assigned, of size 256×2, where each row corresponds to one of the 256 possible bytes. Column 1 of the table is initialized to the integers 0 through 255, and column 2 (the frequency counts) is initialized to all zeros. The result is 256 tables, each a double column of 256 rows (Table 2.35a). Variable-size codes are assigned to the rows, such that the first code is 1-bit long, and the others get longer towards the bottom of the table. The codes are stored in an additional code table that never changes.

	Current character					
	0	1	2	...	254	255
	0 0	0 0	0 0	...	0 0	0 0
	1 0	1 0	1 0	...	1 0	1 0
	2 0	2 0	2 0	...	2 0	2 0
	3 0	3 0	3 0	...	3 0	3 0
Preced.	:	:	:		:	:
Char.	254 0	254 0	254 0	...	254 0	254 0
	255 0	255 0	255 0	...	255 0	255 0

```
...a  b  c  d  e...
   t  l  h  o  d
   h  e  o  a  r
   c  u  r  e  s
   :  :  :  :  :
```

(a)   (b)

Table 2.35: The MNP7 Code Tables.

When a character C is read (the current character to be compressed), its value is used as a pointer, to select one of the 256 tables. The first column of the table is searched, to find the row with the 8-bit value of the preceding character P. Once the row is found, the code from the same row in the code table is emitted and the count in the second column is incremented by 1. Rows in the table may be swapped if the new count of the digram PC is large enough.

After enough characters have been input and rows swapped, the tables start reflecting the true digram frequencies of the data. Table 2.35b shows a possible state assuming that the digrams `ta`, `ha`, `ca`, `lb`, `eb`, `ub`, `hc`, etc., are common. Since the top digram is encoded into 1 bit, MNP7 can be very efficient. If the original data consists of text in a natural language, where certain digrams are very common, MNP7 normally produces a high compression ratio.

> His only other visitor was a woman: the woman who had attended his reading. At the time she had seemed to him to be the only person present who had paid the slightest attention to his words. With kittenish timidity she approached his table. Richard bade her welcome, and meant it, and went on meaning it as she extracted from her shoulder pouch a copy of a novel written not by Richard Tull but by Fyodor Dostoevsky. *The Idiot.* Standing beside him, leaning over him, her face awfully warm and near, she began to leaf through its pages, explaining. The book too was stained, not by gouts of blood but by the vying colors of two highlighting pens, one blue, one pink. And not just two pages but the whole six hundred. Every time the letters *h* and *e* appeared together, as in *the, then, there,* as in *forehead, Pashlishtchev, sheepskin,* they were shaded in blue. Every time the letters *s, h,* and *e* appeared together, as in *she, sheer, ashen, sheepskin,* etc., they were shaded in pink. And since every *she* contained a *he,* the predominance was unarguably and unsurprisingly masculine. Which was exactly her point. "You see?" she said with her hot breath, breath redolent of metallic medications, of batteries and printing-plates. "You see?"... The organizers knew all about this woman—this unfortunate recurrence, this indefatigable drag—and kept coming over to try and coax her away.
>
> —Martin Amis, *The Information*

2.12 Reliability

The most obvious disadvantage of variable-size codes is their vulnerability to errors. The prefix property is used to decode those codes, so an error in a single bit can cause the decompressor to lose synchronization and be unable to decode the rest of the compressed stream. In the worst case, the decompressor may even read, decode, and interpret the rest of the compressed data incorrectly, without realizing that a problem has occurred.

Example: Using the code of Figure 2.16 the string "CARE" is coded into "10100 0011 0110 000" (without the spaces). Assuming the error "10$\boxed{0}$00 0011 0110 000", the decompressor will not notice any problem but will decode the string as "HARE".

◇ **Exercise 2.30:** What will happen in the case "11$\boxed{1}$11 0011 0110 000 ..." (the string "WARE ..." with one bad bit)?

People who use Huffman codes have noticed long ago that these codes recover quickly after an error. However, if they are used to code run lengths, then this property does not help, since all runs would be shifted after an error.

A simple way of adding reliability to variable-size codes is to break a long compressed stream, as it is being transmitted, into groups of 7 bits and add a parity bit to each group. This way the decompressor will at least be able to detect a problem and output an error message or ask for a retransmission. It is, of course, possible to add more than one parity bit to a group of data bits, thus making it more reliable. However, reliability is, in a sense, the opposite of compression. Compression is done by decreasing redundancy, while reliability is achieved by increasing it. The more reliable a piece of data is, the less compressed it is, so care should be taken when the two operations are going to be used together.

Some Important Standards Groups and Organizations

ANSI (American National Standards Institute) is the private sector voluntary standardization system for the United States. Its members are professional societies, consumer groups, trade associations, and some government regulatory agencies (it is thus a federation). It collects and distributes standards developed by its members. Its mission is the enhancement of global competitiveness of U.S. business and the American quality of life by promoting and facilitating voluntary consensus standards and conformity assessment systems and promoting their integrity.

It was founded in 1918 by five engineering societies and three government agencies, and it remains a private, nonprofit membership organization whose nearly 1,400 members are private and public sector organizations.

ANSI is located at 11 West 42nd Street, New York, NY 10036, USA. See also `http://web.ansi.org/`.

ISO (International Organization for Standardization, Organisation Internationale de Normalisation) is an agency of the United Nations whose members are standards organizations of some 100 member countries (one organization from each country). It develops a wide range of standards for industries in all fields.

Established in 1947, its mission is "to promote the development of standardization in the world with a view to facilitating the international exchange of goods and services, and to developing cooperation in the spheres of intellectual, scientific, technological and economic activity." This is the forum where it is agreed, for example, how thick your bank card should be, so every country in the world follows a compatible standard. The ISO is located at 1, rue de Varembé, CH-1211 Geneva 20, Switzerland, `http://www.iso.ch/`.

ITU (International Telecommunication Union) is another United Nations agency developing standards for telecommunications. Its members are mostly companies that make telecommunications equipment, groups interested in standards, and government agencies involved in telecommunications. It is located in Place des Nations, CH-1211 Geneva 20, Switzerland, `http://www.itu.ch/`.

IEC (International Electrotechnical Commission) is a nongovernmental international organization that prepares and publishes international standards for all electrical, electronic, and related technologies. The IEC was founded, in 1906, as a result of a resolution passed at the International Electrical Congress held in St. Louis (USA) in 1904. The membership consists of more than 50 participating countries, including all the world's major trading nations and a growing number of industrializing countries.

The IEC's mission is to promote, through its members, international cooperation on all questions of electrotechnical standardization and related matters, such as the assessment of conformity to standards, in the fields of electricity, electronics and related technologies.

The IEC is located at 3, rue de Varembé, P.O. Box 131, CH-1211, Geneva 20, Switzerland, `http://www.iec.ch/`.

QIC (Quarter-Inch Cartridge) is an international trade association, incorporated in 1987, to encourage and promote the widespread use of quarter-inch cartridge technology. Its mission includes the promotion of QIC technology among computer users, resellers, dealers, OEMs, system integrators, industry analysts, trade and technical press, and the formulation of development standards for compatibility among various manufacturers' drives, cartridges, and subsystems.

QIC's promotional activity emphasizes cost effectiveness, reliability and ease of use as it establishes product class standards that bolster continued user confidence and technology migration for the future.

The QIC is an outgrowth of the Working Group for Quarter-Inch Cartridge Drive Compatibility (also known as QIC), an informal organization begun in 1982 by several drive manufacturers.

Executive membership in QIC is open to all manufacturers of quarter-inch cartridge drives and media; makers of heads, critical components, and software can become Technology Members; and any interested party with a commitment to QIC technology is welcome to become an Associate of the organization.

It is located at 311 East Carrillo Street, Santa Barbara, CA 93101, USA (`http://www.qic.org/`).

> Mr. Elisha Wright, who labored under the impression that he was a local wit, used to say that nobody in Avonlea ever thought of looking in the Charlottetown dailies for weather probabilities. No; they just asked Uncle Abe what it was going to be tomorrow and expected the opposite.
>
> —Lucy Maud Montgomery, *Anne of Avonlea*

2.13 Facsimile Compression

Data compression is especially important when images are transmitted over a communications line because the user is typically waiting at the receiver, eager to see something quickly. Documents transferred between fax machines are sent as bitmaps, so a standard data compression method was needed when those machines became popular. Several methods were developed and proposed by the ITU-T.

The ITU-T is one of four permanent parts of the International Telecommunications Union (ITU), based in Geneva, Switzerland (`http://www.itu.ch/`). It issues recommendations for standards applying to modems, packet switched interfaces, V.24 connectors, etc. Although it has no power of enforcement, the standards it recommends are generally accepted and adopted by industry. Until March 1993, the ITU-T was known as the Consultative Committee for International Telephone and Telegraph (Comité Consultatif International Télégraphique et Téléphonique, or CCITT).

| CCITT: Can't Conceive Intelligent Thoughts Today |

The first data compression standards developed by the ITU-T were T2 (also known as Group 1) and T3 (Group 2). These are now obsolete and have been replaced by T4 (Group 3) and T6 (Group 4). Group 3 is currently used by all fax machines designed to operate with the Public Switched Telephone Network (PSTN). These are the machines we have at home, and at the time of writing, they operate at maximum speeds of 9,600 baud. Group 4 is used by fax machines designed to operate on a digital network, such as ISDN. They have typical speeds of 64K baud. Both methods can produce compression ratios of 10:1 or better, reducing the transmission time of a typical page to about a minute with the former, and a few seconds with the latter.

2.13.1 One-Dimensional Coding

A fax machine scans a document line by line, converting each line to small black and white dots called *pels* (from Picture ELement). The horizontal resolution is always 8.05 pels per millimeter (about 205 pels per inch). An 8.5-inch-wide scan line is thus converted to 1728 pels. The T4 standard, though, recommends to scan only about 8.2 inches, thus producing 1664 pels per scan line (these numbers, as well as those in the next paragraph, are all to within ±1% accuracy).

The vertical resolution is either 3.85 scan lines per millimeter (standard mode) or 7.7 lines/mm (fine mode). Many fax machines have also a very-fine mode, where they scan 15.4 lines/mm. Table 2.36 assumes a 10-inch-high page (254 mm), and shows the total number of pels per page, and typical transmission times for the three modes without compression. The times are long, which shows how important data compression is in fax transmissions.

Scan lines	Pels per line	Pels per page	Time (sec.)	Time (min.)
978	1664	1.670M	170	2.82
1956	1664	3.255M	339	5.65
3912	1664	6.510M	678	11.3

Ten inches equal 254 mm. The number of pels is in the millions, and the transmission times, at 9600 baud without compression, are between 3 and 11 minutes, depending on the mode. However, if the page is shorter than 10 inches, or if most of it is white, the compression factor can be 10:1 or better, resulting in transmission times of between 17 and 68 seconds.

Table 2.36: Fax Transmission Times.

To derive the Group 3 code, the ITU-T counted all the run lengths of white and black pels in a set of eight "training" documents that they felt represent typical text and images sent by fax and used the Huffman algorithm to assign a variable-size code to each run length. (The eight documents are described in Table 2.37. They are not shown, since they are copyrighted by the ITU-T.) The most common run lengths were found to be 2, 3, and 4 black pixels, so they were assigned the shortest codes (Table 2.38). Next come run lengths of 2–7 white pixels, which were assigned slightly longer codes. Most run lengths were rare and were assigned long, 12-bit codes. Group 3 thus uses a combination of RLE and Huffman coding.

Image	Description
1	Typed business letter (English)
2	Circuit diagram (hand drawn)
3	Printed and typed invoice (French)
4	Densely typed report (French)
5	Printed technical article including figures and equations (French)
6	Graph with printed captions (French)
7	Dense document (Kanji)
8	Handwritten memo with very large white-on-black letters (English)

Table 2.37: The Eight CCITT Training Documents.

⋄ **Exercise 2.31:** A run length of 1664 white pels was assigned the short code 011000. Why is this length so common?

Since run lengths can be long, the Huffman algorithm was modified. Codes were assigned to run lengths of 1 to 63 pels (they are the termination codes in Table 2.38a) and to run lengths that are multiples of 64 pels (the make-up codes in Table 2.38b). Group 3 is thus a *modified Huffman code* (also called MH). The code of a run length is either a single termination code (if the run length is short) or one or more make-up codes, followed by one termination code (if it is long). Here are some examples:

1. A run length of 12 white pels is coded as 001000.
2. A run length of 76 white pels ($= 64 + 12$) is coded as 11011|001000 (without the vertical bar).
3. A run length of 140 white pels ($= 128 + 12$) is coded as 10010|001000.
4. A run length of 64 black pels ($= 64 + 0$) is coded as 0000001111|0000110111.
5. A run length of 2561 black pels ($2560 + 1$) is coded as 000000011111|010.

⋄ **Exercise 2.32:** There are no runs of length zero. Why, then, were codes assigned to runs of zero black and white pels?

⋄ **Exercise 2.33:** An 8.5-inch-wide scan line results in 1728 pels, so how can there be a run of 2561 consecutive pels?

Each scan line is coded separately, and its code is terminated by the special 12-bit EOL code 000000000001. Each line also gets one white pel appended to it on the left when it is scanned. This is done to remove any ambiguity when the line is decoded on the receiving end. After reading the EOL for the previous line, the receiver assumes that the new line starts with a run of white pels, and it ignores the first of them. Examples:

1. The 14-pel line ⬛⬛⬛ ⬜ ⬛⬛ ⬜⬜⬜⬜⬜⬜⬜ is coded as the run lengths 1w 3b 2w 2b 7w EOL, which become 000111|10|0111|11|1111|000000000001. The decoder ignores the single white pel at the start.

2. The line ⬜⬜ ⬛⬛⬛⬛⬛ ⬜⬜⬜⬜ ⬛⬛ is coded as the run lengths 3w 5b 5w 2b EOL, which becomes the binary string 1000|0011|1100|11|000000000001.

◇ **Exercise 2.34:** The group 3 code for a run length of five black pels (0011) is also the prefix of the codes for run lengths of 61, 62, and 63 white pels. Explain this.

The Group 3 code has no error correction, but many errors can be detected. Because of the nature of the Huffman code, even one bad bit in the transmission can cause the receiver to get out of synchronization, and to produce a string of wrong pels. This is why each scan line is encoded separately. If the receiver detects an error, it skips bits, looking for an EOL. This way, one error can cause at most one scan line to be received incorrectly. If the receiver does not see an EOL after a certain number of lines, it assumes a high error rate, and it aborts the process, notifying the transmitter. Since the codes are between 2 and 12 bits long, the receiver detects an error if it cannot decode a valid code after reading 12 bits.

Each page of the coded document is preceded by one EOL and is followed by six EOL codes. Because each line is coded separately, this method is a *one-dimensional coding* scheme. The compression ratio depends on the image. Images with large contiguous black or white areas (text or black and white images) can be highly compressed. Images with many short runs can sometimes produce negative compression. This is especially true in the case of images with shades of gray (such as scanned photographs). Such shades are produced by halftoning, which covers areas with many alternating black and white pels (runs of length one).

◇ **Exercise 2.35:** What is the compression ratio for runs of length one (strictly alternating pels)?

The T4 standard also allows for fill bits to be inserted between the data bits and the EOL. This is done in cases where a pause is necessary, or where the total number of bits transmitted for a scan line must be a multiple of 8. The fill bits are zeros.

Example: The binary string 000111|10|0111|11|1111|000000000001 becomes

$$000111|10|0111|11|1111|00|0000000001$$

after two zeros are added as fill bits, bringing the total length of the string to 32 bits $(= 8 \times 4)$. The decoder sees the two zeros of the fill, followed by the eleven zeros of the EOL, followed by the single 1, so it knows that it has encountered a fill followed by an EOL.

See http://www.cis.ohio-state.edu/htbin/rfc/rfc804.html for a description of group 3.

(a)

Run length	White code-word	Black code-word	Run length	White code-word	Black code-word
0	00110101	0000110111	32	00011011	000001101010
1	000111	010	33	00010010	000001101011
2	0111	11	34	00010011	000011010010
3	1000	10	35	00010100	000011010011
4	1011	011	36	00010101	000011010100
5	1100	0011	37	00010110	000011010101
6	1110	0010	38	00010111	000011010110
7	1111	00011	39	00101000	000011010111
8	10011	000101	40	00101001	000001101100
9	10100	000100	41	00101010	000001101101
10	00111	0000100	42	00101011	000011011010
11	01000	0000101	43	00101100	000011011011
12	001000	0000111	44	00101101	000001010100
13	000011	00000100	45	00000100	000001010101
14	110100	00000111	46	00000101	000001010110
15	110101	000011000	47	00001010	000001010111
16	101010	0000010111	48	00001011	000001100100
17	101011	0000011000	49	01010010	000001100101
18	0100111	0000001000	50	01010011	000001010010
19	0001100	00001100111	51	01010100	000001010011
20	0001000	00001101000	52	01010101	000000100100
21	0010111	00001101100	53	00100100	000000110111
22	0000011	00000110111	54	00100101	000000111000
23	0000100	00000101000	55	01011000	000000100111
24	0101000	00000010111	56	01011001	000000101000
25	0101011	00000011000	57	01011010	000001011000
26	0010011	000011001010	58	01011011	000001011001
27	0100100	000011001011	59	01001010	000000101011
28	0011000	000011001100	60	01001011	000000101100
29	00000010	000011001101	61	00110010	000001011010
30	00000011	000001101000	62	00110011	000001100110
31	00011010	000001101001	63	00110100	000001100111

(b)

Run length	White code-word	Black code-word	Run length	White code-word	Black code-word
64	11011	0000001111	1344	011011010	0000001010011
128	10010	000011001000	1408	011011011	0000001010100
192	010111	000011001001	1472	010011000	0000001010101
256	0110111	000001011011	1536	010011001	0000001011010
320	00110110	000000110011	1600	010011010	0000001011011
384	00110111	000000110100	1664	011000	0000001100100
448	01100100	000000110101	1728	010011011	0000001100101
512	01100101	0000001101100	1792	00000001000	same as
576	01101000	0000001101101	1856	00000001100	white
640	01100111	0000001001010	1920	00000001101	from this
704	011001100	0000001001011	1984	000000010010	point
768	011001101	0000001001100	2048	000000010011	
832	011010010	0000001001101	2112	000000010100	
896	011010011	0000001110010	2176	000000010101	
960	011010100	0000001110011	2240	000000010110	
1024	011010101	0000001110100	2304	000000010111	
1088	011010110	0000001110101	2368	000000011100	
1152	011010111	0000001110110	2432	000000011101	
1216	011011000	0000001110111	2496	000000011110	
1280	011011001	0000001010010	2560	000000011111	

Table 2.38: Group 3 and 4 Fax Codes: (a) Termination Codes. (b) Make-Up Codes.

At the time of writing, the T.4 and T.6 recommendations can also be found at ftp site `src.doc.ic.ac.uk/computing/ccitt/ccitt-standards/1988/` as files `7_3_01.ps.gz` and `7_3_02.ps.gz`.

2.13.2 Two-Dimensional Coding

Two-dimensional coding was developed because one-dimensional coding does not produce good results for images with gray areas. Two-dimensional coding is optional on fax machines that use Group 3 but is the only method used by machines intended to work on a digital network. When a fax machine using Group 3 supports two-dimensional coding as an option, each EOL is followed by one extra bit, to indicate the compression method used for the next scan line. That bit is 1 if the next line is encoded with one-dimensional coding, and 0 if it is encoded with two-dimensional coding.

The two-dimensional coding method is also called MMR, for *modified modified READ*, where READ stands for *relative element address designate*. The term "modified modified" is used because this is a modification of one-dimensional coding, which itself is a modification of the original Huffman method. The two-dimensional coding method works by comparing the current scan line (called the *coding line*) to its predecessor (which is called the *reference line*) and recording the differences between them, the assumption being that two consecutive lines in a document will normally differ by just a few pels. The method assumes that there is an all-white line above the page, which is used as the reference line for the first scan line of the page. After coding the first line, it becomes the reference line, and the second scan line is coded. As in one-dimensional coding, each line is assumed to start with a white pel, which is ignored by the receiver.

The two-dimensional coding method is less reliable than one-dimensional coding, since an error in decoding a line will cause errors in decoding all its successors and will propagate through the entire document. This is why the T.4 (Group 3) standard includes a requirement that after a line is encoded with the one-dimensional method, at most $K - 1$ lines will be encoded with the two-dimensional coding method. For standard resolution $K = 2$, and for fine resolution $K = 4$. The T.6 standard (Group 4) does not have this requirement, and uses two-dimensional coding exclusively.

Scanning the coding line and comparing it to the reference line results in three cases, or modes. The mode is identified by comparing the next run length on the reference line [$(b_1 b_2)$ in Figure 2.40] with the current run length $(a_0 a_1)$ and the next one $(a_1 a_2)$ on the coding line. Each of these three runs can be black or white. The three modes are as follows (see also the flow chart of Figure 2.43):

1. **Pass mode**. This is the case where $(b_1 b_2)$ is to the left of $(a_1 a_2)$ and b_2 is to the left of a_1 (Figure 2.40a). This mode does not include the case where b_2 is above a_1. When this mode is identified, the length of run $(b_1 b_2)$ is coded using the codes of Table 2.39 and is transmitted. Pointer a_0 is moved below b_2, and the four values b_1, b_2, a_1, and a_2 are updated.

2. **Vertical mode**. $(b_1 b_2)$ overlaps $(a_1 a_2)$ by not more than three pels (Figure 2.40b1, b2). Assuming that consecutive lines do not differ by much, this is the most common case. When this mode is identified, one of seven codes is pro-

duced (Table 2.39) and is transmitted. Pointers are updated as in case 1 above. The performance of the two-dimensional coding method depends on this case being common.

3. **Horizontal mode.** (b_1b_2) overlaps (a_1a_2) by more than three pels (Figure 2.40c1, c2). When this mode is identified, the lengths of runs (a_0a_1) and (a_1a_2) are coded using the codes of Table 2.39 and are transmitted. Pointers are updated as in cases 1 and 2 above.

Mode	Run length to be encoded	Abbre-viation	Codeword
Pass	b_1b_2	P	0001+coded length of b_1b_2
Horizontal	a_0a_1, a_1a_2	H	001+coded length of a_0a_1 and a_1a_2
Vertical	$a_1b_1 = 0$	V(0)	1
	$a_1b_1 = -1$	VR(1)	011
	$a_1b_1 = -2$	VR(2)	000011
	$a_1b_1 = -3$	VR(3)	0000011
	$a_1b_1 = +1$	VL(1)	010
	$a_1b_1 = +2$	VL(2)	000010
	$a_1b_1 = +3$	VL(3)	0000010
Extension			0000001000

Table 2.39: 2D Codes for the Group 4 Method.

When scanning starts, pointer a_0 is set to an imaginary white pel on the left of the coding line, and a_1 is set to point to the first black pel on the coding line. (Since a_0 corresponds to an imaginary pel, the first run length is $|a_0a_1| - 1$.) Pointer a_2 is set to the first white pel following that. Pointers b_1, b_2 are set to point to the start of the first and second runs on the reference line, respectively.

After identifying the current mode and transmitting codes according to Table 2.39, a_0 is updated as shown in the flow chart, and the other four pointers are updated relative to the new a_0. The process continues until the end of the coding line is reached. The encoder assumes an extra pel on the right of the line, with a color opposite that of the last pel.

The extension code in Table 2.39 is used to abort the encoding process prematurely, before reaching the end of the page. This is necessary if the rest of the page is transmitted in a different code or even in uncompressed form.

⋄ **Exercise 2.36:** Manually figure out the code generated from the two lines below.

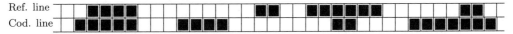

Table 2.42 summarizes the codes emitted by the group 4 encoder. Figure 2.41 is a tree with the same codes. Each horizontal branch corresponds to another zero and each vertical branch, to another 1.

> ...and you thought "impressive" statistics were 36–24–36.
>
> —Advertisement, *The American Statistician*, November 1979

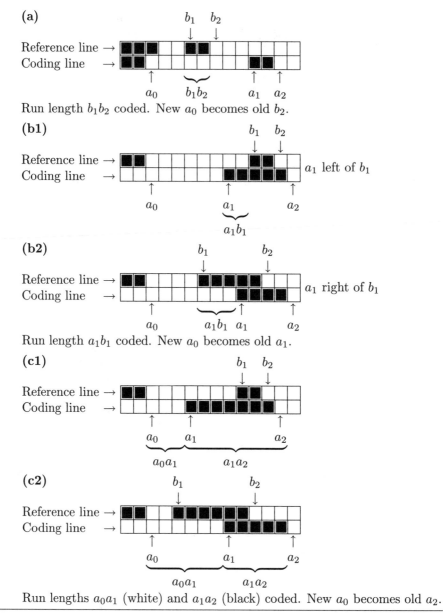

Figure 2.40: Five Run Length Configurations: (a) Pass Mode. (b) Vertical Mode. (c) Horizontal Mode.

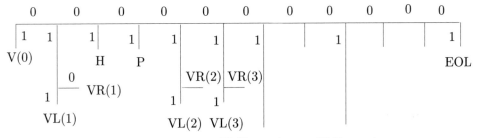

Figure 2.41: Tree of Group 3 Codes.

Mode	Elements to Be Coded		Notation	Codeword
Pass	b_1, b_2		P	0001
Horizontal	a_0a_1, a_1a_2		H	$001 + M(a_0a_1) + M(a_1a_2)$
Vertical	a_1 just under b_1	$a_1b_1 = 0$	V(0)	1
	a_1 to	$a_1b_1 = 1$	VR(1)	011
	the right	$a_1b_1 = 2$	VR(2)	000011
	of b_1	$a_1b_1 = 3$	VR(3)	0000011
	a_1 to	$a_1b_1 = 1$	VL(1)	010
	the left	$a_1b_1 = 2$	VL(2)	000010
	of b_1	$a_1b_1 = 3$	VL(3)	0000010
2D Extensions 1D Extensions				0000001xxx 000000001xxx
EOL				000000000001
1D Coding of Next Line 2D Coding of Next Line				EOL+'1' EOL+'0'

Table 2.42: Group 4 Codes.

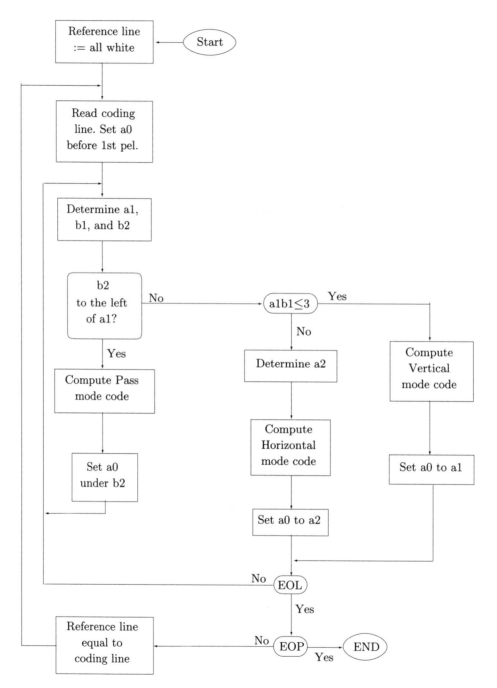

Figure 2.43: MMR Flow Chart.

Bibliography

Anderson, K. L., et al., (1987) "Binary-Image-Manipulation Algorithm in the Image View Facility," *IBM Journal of Research and Development* **31**(1):16–31, January.

Hunter, R., and A. H. Robinson (1980) "International Digital Facsimile Coding Standards," *Proceedings of the IEEE* **68**(7):854–867, July.

Marking, Michael P. (1990) "Decoding Group 3 Images," *The C Users Journal* pp. 45–54, June.

McConnell, Kenneth R. (1992) *FAX: Digital Facsimile Technology and Applications*, Norwood, MA, Artech House.

> ...and more than half of you (49 percent) have already checked out SmartBrowsing!
>
> —From the Netscape newsletter, October 1998

2.14 Arithmetic Coding

The Huffman method is more efficient than the Shannon-Fano method, but either method rarely produces the best variable-size code. Section 2.8 shows that these methods produce best results (codes whose average size equals the entropy) only when the symbols have probabilities of occurrence that are negative powers of 2. This is because these methods assign a code with an integral number of bits to each symbol in the alphabet. A symbol with probability 0.4 should ideally be assigned a 1.32-bit code, since $-\log_2 0.4 \approx 1.32$. The Huffman method, however, normally assigns such a symbol a code of 1 or 2 bits.

Arithmetic coding overcomes this problem by assigning one (normally long) code to the entire input stream, instead of assigning codes to the individual symbols. The method reads the input stream symbol by symbol and appends more bits to the code each time a symbol is input and processed. To understand the method, it is useful to imagine the resulting code as a number in the range $[0, 1)$. [The notation $[a, b)$ means the range of real numbers from a to b, not including b. The range is "closed" at a and "open" at b.] Thus the code "9746509" should be interpreted as "0.9746509", although the "0." part will not be included in the output stream.

The first step is to calculate, or at least to estimate, the frequencies of occurrence of each symbol. For best results, the exact frequencies are calculated by reading the entire input stream in the first pass of a two-pass compression job. If the program has good estimates of the frequencies from a different source, the first pass may be omitted.

The first example involves the three symbols a_1, a_2, and a_3, with probabilities $P_1 = 0.4$, $P_2 = 0.5$, and $P_3 = 0.1$, respectively. The interval $[0, 1)$ is divided among the three symbols by assigning each a subinterval proportional in size to its probability. The order of the subintervals is immaterial. In our example, the three symbols are assigned the subintervals $[0, 0.4)$, $[0.4, 0.9)$, and $[0.9, 1.0)$. To encode the string "$a_2a_2a_2a_3$", we start with the interval $[0, 1)$. The first symbol a_2 reduces this interval to the subinterval from its 40% point to its 90% point.

The result is $[0.4, 0.9)$. The second a_2 reduces $[0.4, 0.9)$ in the same way (see note below) to $[0.6, 0.85)$, the third a_2 reduces this to $[0.7, 0.825)$, and the a_3 reduces this to the stretch from the 90% point of $[0.7, 0.825)$ to its 100% point, producing $[0.8125, 0.8250)$. The final code our method produces can be any number in this final range.

(Note: The subinterval $[0.6, 0.85)$ is obtained from the interval $[0.4, 0.9)$ by $0.4 + (0.9 - 0.4) \times 0.4 = 0.6$ and $0.4 + (0.9 - 0.4) \times 0.9 = 0.85$.)

With this example in mind, it should be easy to understand the following rules, which summarize the main steps of arithmetic coding:

1. Start by defining the "current interval" as $[0, 1)$.
2. Repeat the following two steps for each symbol s in the input stream:
    2.1. Divide the current interval into subintervals whose sizes are proportional to the symbols' probabilities.
    2.2. Select the subinterval for s and define it as the new current interval.
3. When the entire input stream has been processed in this way, the output should be any number that uniquely identifies the current interval (i.e., any number inside the current interval).

For each symbol processed, the current interval gets smaller, so it takes more bits to express it, but the point is that the final output is a single number and does not consist of codes for the individual symbols. The average code size can be obtained by dividing the size of the output (in bits) by the size of the input (in symbols). Notice also that the probabilities used in step 2.1 may change all the time, since they may be supplied by an adaptive probability model (Section 2.15).

> A theory has only the alternative of being right or wrong. A model has a third possibility: it may be right, but irrelevant.
> —Eigen Manfred, *The Physicist's Conception of Nature*

The next example is a little more involved. We show the compression steps for the short string "SWISS⎵MISS". Table 2.44 shows the information prepared in the first step (the *statistical model* of the data). The five symbols appearing in the input may be arranged in any order. For each symbol, its frequency is first counted, followed by its probability of occurrence (the frequency divided by the string size, 10). The range $[0, 1)$ is then divided among the symbols, in any order, with each symbol getting a chunk, or a subrange, equal in size to its probability. Thus "S" gets the subrange $[0.5, 1.0)$ (of size 0.5), whereas the subrange of "I" is of size 0.2 $[0.2, 0.4)$. The cumulative frequencies column is used by the decoding algorithm on page 108.

The symbols and frequencies in Table 2.44 are written on the output stream before any of the bits of the compressed code. This table will be the first thing input by the decoder.

The encoding process starts by defining two variables, Low and High, and setting them to 0 and 1, respectively. They define an interval [Low, High). As symbols

Char	Freq	Prob.	Range	CumFreq
		Total CumFreq=		10
S	5	$5/10 = 0.5$	$[0.5, 1.0)$	5
W	1	$1/10 = 0.1$	$[0.4, 0.5)$	4
I	2	$2/10 = 0.2$	$[0.2, 0.4)$	2
M	1	$1/10 = 0.1$	$[0.1, 0.2)$	1
␣	1	$1/10 = 0.1$	$[0.0, 0.1)$	0

Table 2.44: Frequencies and Probabilities of Five Symbols.

are being input and processed, the values of Low and High are moved closer together, to narrow the interval.

After processing the first symbol "S", Low and High are updated to 0.5 and 1, respectively. The resulting code for the entire input stream will be a number in this range ($0.5 \leq$ Code < 1.0). The rest of the input stream will determine precisely where, in the interval $[0.5, 1)$, the final code will lie. A good way to understand the process is to imagine that the new interval $[0.5, 1)$ is divided among the five symbols of our alphabet using the same proportions as for the original interval $[0, 1)$. The result is the five subintervals $[0.5, 0.55)$, $[0.55, 0.60)$, $[0.60, 0.70)$, $[0.70, 0.75)$, and $[0.75, 1.0)$. When the next symbol W is input, the third of those subintervals is selected, and is again divided into five subsubintervals.

As more symbols are being input and processed, Low and High are being updated according to

```
NewHigh:=OldLow+Range*HighRange(X);
NewLow:=OldLow+Range*LowRange(X);
```

where Range=OldHigh−OldLow and LowRange(X), HighRange(X) indicate the low and high limits of the range of symbol X, respectively. In the example above, the second input symbol is W, so we update Low $:= 0.5 + (1.0 - 0.5) \times 0.4 = 0.70$, High $:= 0.5 + (1.0 - 0.5) \times 0.5 = 0.75$. The new interval $[0.70, 0.75)$ covers the stretch $[40\%, 50\%)$ of the subrange of S. Table 2.45 shows all the steps involved in coding the string "SWISS␣MISS" (the first three steps are illustrated graphically in Figure 2.58a). The final code is the final value of Low, 0.71753375, of which only the eight digits 71753375 need be written on the output stream (but see later for a modification of this statement).

The decoder works in the opposite way. It starts by inputting the symbols and their ranges, and reconstructing Table 2.44. It then inputs the rest of the code. The first digit is "7", so the decoder immediately knows that the entire code is a number of the form $0.7\ldots$. This number is inside the subrange $[0.5, 1)$ of S, so the first symbol is S. The decoder then eliminates the effect of symbol S from the code by subtracting the lower limit 0.5 of S and dividing by the width of the subrange of S (0.5). The result is 0.4350675, which tells the decoder that the next symbol is W (since the subrange of W is $[0.4, 0.5)$).

To eliminate the effect of symbol X from the code, the decoder performs the operation Code:=(Code-LowRange(X))/Range, where Range is the width of the

Char.		The calculation of low and high
S	L	$0.0 + (1.0 - 0.0) \times 0.5 = 0.5$
	H	$0.0 + (1.0 - 0.0) \times 1.0 = 1.0$
W	L	$0.5 + (1.0 - 0.5) \times 0.4 = 0.70$
	H	$0.5 + (1.0 - 0.5) \times 0.5 = 0.75$
I	L	$0.7 + (0.75 - 0.70) \times 0.2 = 0.71$
	H	$0.7 + (0.75 - 0.70) \times 0.4 = 0.72$
S	L	$0.71 + (0.72 - 0.71) \times 0.5 = 0.715$
	H	$0.71 + (0.72 - 0.71) \times 1.0 = 0.72$
S	L	$0.715 + (0.72 - 0.715) \times 0.5 = 0.7175$
	H	$0.715 + (0.72 - 0.715) \times 1.0 = 0.72$
␣	L	$0.7175 + (0.72 - 0.7175) \times 0.0 = 0.7175$
	H	$0.7175 + (0.72 - 0.7175) \times 0.1 = 0.71775$
M	L	$0.7175 + (0.71775 - 0.7175) \times 0.1 = 0.717525$
	H	$0.7175 + (0.71775 - 0.7175) \times 0.2 = 0.717550$
I	L	$0.717525 + (0.71755 - 0.717525) \times 0.2 = 0.717530$
	H	$0.717525 + (0.71755 - 0.717525) \times 0.4 = 0.717535$
S	L	$0.717530 + (0.717535 - 0.717530) \times 0.5 = 0.7175325$
	H	$0.717530 + (0.717535 - 0.717530) \times 1.0 = 0.717535$
S	L	$0.7175325 + (0.717535 - 0.7175325) \times 0.5 = 0.71753375$
	H	$0.7175325 + (0.717535 - 0.7175325) \times 1.0 = 0.717535$

Table 2.45: The Process of Arithmetic Encoding.

subrange of X. Table 2.46 summarizes the steps for decoding our example string (notice that it has two rows per symbol).

The next example is of three symbols with probabilities as shown in Table 2.47a. Notice that the probabilities are very different. One is large (97.5%) and the others much smaller. This is a case of *skewed probabilities*.

Encoding the string $a_2a_2a_1a_3a_3$ produces the strange numbers (accurate to 16 digits) in Table 2.48, where the two rows for each symbol correspond to the Low and High values, respectively. Figure 2.52 lists the *Mathematica* code that computed the table.

At first glance, it seems that the resulting code is longer than the original string, but Section 2.14.3 shows how to figure out the true compression achieved by arithmetic coding.

Decoding this string is shown in Table 2.49 and involves a special problem. After eliminating the effect of a_1, on line 3, the result is 0. Earlier, we implicitly assumed that this means the end of the decoding process, but now we know that there are two more occurrences of a_3 that should be decoded. These are shown on lines 4, 5 of the table. This problem always occurs when the last symbol in the input

Char.	Code−low		Range	
S	0.71753375 − 0.5	= 0.21753375	/0.5	= 0.4350675
W	0.4350675 − 0.4	= 0.0350675	/0.1	= 0.350675
I	0.350675 − 0.2	= 0.150675	/0.2	= 0.753375
S	0.753375 − 0.5	= 0.253375	/0.5	= 0.50675
S	0.50675 − 0.5	= 0.00675	/0.5	= 0.0135
␣	0.0135 − 0	= 0.0135	/0.1	= 0.135
M	0.135 − 0.1	= 0.035	/0.1	= 0.35
I	0.35 − 0.2	= 0.15	/0.2	= 0.75
S	0.75 − 0.5	= 0.25	/0.5	= 0.5
S	0.5 − 0.5	= 0	/0.5	= 0

Table 2.46: The Process of Arithmetic Decoding.

Char	Prob.	Range		Char	Prob.	Range	
a_1	0.001838	[0.998162,	1.0)	eof	0.000001	[0.999999,	1.0)
a_2	0.975	[0.023162, 0.998162)		a_1	0.001837	[0.998162, 0.999999)	
a_3	0.023162	[0.0,	0.023162)	a_2	0.975	[0.023162, 0.998162)	
				a_3	0.023162	[0.0,	0.023162)
		(a)				(b)	

Table 2.47: (Skewed) Probabilities of Three Symbols.

a_2	$0.0 + (1.0 - 0.0) \times 0.023162 = 0.023162$
	$0.0 + (1.0 - 0.0) \times 0.998162 = 0.998162$
a_2	$0.023162 + .975 \times 0.023162 = 0.04574495$
	$0.023162 + .975 \times 0.998162 = 0.99636995$
a_1	$0.04574495 + 0.950625 \times 0.998162 = 0.99462270125$
	$0.04574495 + 0.950625 \times 1.0 = 0.99636995$
a_3	$0.99462270125 + 0.00174724875 \times 0.0 = 0.99462270125$
	$0.99462270125 + 0.00174724875 \times 0.023162 = 0.994663171025547$
a_3	$0.99462270125 + 0.0000404697755474 9998 \times 0.0 = 0.99462270125$
	$0.99462270125 + 0.0000404697755474 9998 \times 0.023162 = 0.994623638610941$

Table 2.48: Encoding the String $a_2 a_2 a_1 a_3 a_3$.

Char.	Code−low		Range	
a_2	$0.99462270125 - 0.023162$	$= 0.97146170125$	$/0.975$	$= 0.99636995$
a_2	$0.99636995 - 0.023162$	$= 0.97320795$	$/0.975$	$= 0.998162$
a_1	$0.998162 - 0.998162$	$= 0.0$	$/0.00138$	$= 0.0$
a_3	$0.0 - 0.0$	$= 0.0$	$/0.023162$	$= 0.0$
a_3	$0.0 - 0.0$	$= 0.0$	$/0.023162$	$= 0.0$

Table 2.49: Decoding the String $a_2a_2a_1a_3a_3$.

a_3	$0.0 + (1.0 - 0.0) \times 0.0 = 0.0$
	$0.0 + (1.0 - 0.0) \times 0.023162 = 0.023162$
a_3	$0.0 + .023162 \times 0.0 = 0.0$
	$0.0 + .023162 \times 0.023162 = 0.000536478244$
a_3	$0.0 + 0.000536478244 \times 0.0 = 0.0$
	$0.0 + 0.000536478244 \times 0.023162 = 0.000012425909087528$
a_3	$0.0 + 0.000012425909087528 \times 0.0 = 0.0$
	$0.0 + 0.000012425909087528 \times 0.023162 = 0.00000028780890628532 35$
eof	$0.0 + 0.00000028780890628532 35 \times 0.999999 = 0.00000028780861847641 72$
	$0.0 + 0.00000028780890628532 35 \times 1.0 = 0.00000028780890628532 35$

Table 2.50: Encoding the String $a_3a_3a_3a_3$eof.

Char.	Code−low		Range	
a_3	$0.00000028780861847641 72 - 0$	$= 0.00000028780861847641 72$	$/0.023162$	$= 0.0000124258966616189 1247$
a_3	$0.0000124258966616189 1247 - 0$	$= 0.0000124258966616189 1247$	$/0.023162$	$= 0.000536477707521756$
a_3	$0.000536477707521756 - 0$	$= 0.000536477707521756$	$/0.023162$	$= 0.023161976838$
a_3	$0.023161976838 - 0.0$	$= 0.023161976838$	$/0.023162$	$= 0.999999$
eof	$0.999999 - 0.999999$	$= 0.0$	$/0.000001$	$= 0.0$

Table 2.51: Decoding the String $a_3a_3a_3a_3$eof.

stream is the one whose subrange starts at zero. In order to distinguish between such a symbol and the end of the input stream, we need to define an additional symbol, the end-of-input (or end-of-file, eof). This symbol should be added, with a small probability, to the frequency table (see Table 2.47b), and it should be encoded at the end of the input stream.

Tables 2.50 and 2.51 show how the string $a_3a_3a_3a_3$eof is encoded into the number 0.00000028780861847641 72, and then decoded properly. Without the eof symbol, a string of all a_3s would have been encoded into a 0.

```
lowRange={0.998162,0.023162,0.};
highRange={1.,0.998162,0.023162};
low=0.; high=1.;
enc[i_]:=Module[{nlow,nhigh,range},
range=high-low;
nhigh=low+range highRange[[i]];
nlow=low+range lowRange[[i]];
low=nlow; high=nhigh;
Print["r=",N[range,25]," l=",N[low,17]," h=",N[high,17]]]
enc[2]
enc[2]
enc[1]
enc[3]
enc[3]
```

Figure 2.52: *Mathematica* Code For Table 2.48.

Notice how the low value is 0 until the eof is input and processed, and how the high value quickly approaches 0. Now is the time to mention that the final code does not have to be the final low value but can be any number between the final low and high values. In the example of $a_3a_3a_3a_3$eof, the final code can be the much shorter number 0.0000002878086 (or 0.0000002878087 or even 0.0000002878088).

◇ **Exercise 2.37:** Encode the string $a_2a_2a_2a_2$ and summarize the results in a table similar to Table 2.50. How do the results differ from those of the string $a_3a_3a_3a_3$?

If the size of the input stream is known, it is possible to do without an eof symbol. The encoder can start by writing this size (unencoded) on the output stream. The decoder reads the size, starts decoding, and stops when the decoded stream reaches this size. If the decoder reads the compressed stream byte by byte, the encoder may have to add some zeros at the end, to make sure the compressed stream can be read in groups of 8 bits.

2.14.1 Implementation Details

The encoding process described earlier is not practical, since it assumes that numbers of unlimited precision can be stored in **Low** and **High**. The decoding process described on page 103 ("The decoder then eliminates the effect of the **S** from the code by subtracting... and dividing ...") is simple in principle but also impractical. The code, which is a single number, is normally long and may also be very long. A 1 Mbyte file may be encoded into, say, a 500 Kbyte one that consists of a single number. Dividing a 500 Kbyte number is complex and slow.

Any practical implementation of arithmetic coding should use just integers (because floating-point arithmetic is slow and precision is lost), and they should not be very long (preferably just single precision). We describe such an implementation here, using two integer variables **Low** and **High**. In our example they are four decimal digits long, but in practice they might be 16 or 32 bits long. These variables hold the low and high limits of the current subinterval, but we don't let them grow too much. A glance at Table 2.45 shows that once the leftmost digits of Low and High become identical, they never change. We therefore shift such digits out of the two variables and write one digit on the output stream. This way, the two variables don't have to hold the entire code, just the most recent part of it. As digits are shifted out of the two variables, a zero is shifted into the right end of Low and a 9 into the right end of High. A good way to understand this is to think of each of the two variables as the left end of an infinitely long number. Low contains $xxxx00\ldots$, and High= $yyyy99\ldots$.

One problem is that High should be initialized to 1, but the contents of Low and High should be interpreted as fractions less than 1. The solution is to initialize High to 9999..., since the infinite fraction 0.999... equals 1.

(This is easy to prove. If $0.999\ldots < 1$, then their average $a = (1+0.999\ldots)/2$ would be a number between 0.999... and 1, but there is no way to write a. It is impossible to give it more digits than to 0.999..., since the latter already has an infinite number of digits. It is impossible to make the digits any bigger, since they are already 9's. This is why the infinite fraction 0.999... must be equal to 1.)

◇ **Exercise 2.38:** Write the number 0.5 in binary.

Table 2.53 describes the encoding process of the string "SWISS␣MISS". Column 1 shows the next input symbol. Column 2 shows the new values of Low and High. Column 3 shows these values as scaled integers, after High has been decremented by 1. Column 4 shows the next digit sent to the output stream. Column 5 shows the new values of Low and High after being shifted to the left. Notice how the last step sends the four digits 3750 to the output stream. The final output is 717533750.

Decoding is the opposite of encoding. We start with Low=0000, High=9999, and Code=7175 (the first four digits of the compressed stream). These are updated at each step of the decoding loop. Low and High approach each other (and both approach Code) until their most significant digits are the same. They are then shifted to the left, which separates them again, and Code is also shifted at that time. An index is calculated at each step and is used to search the cumulative frequencies column of Table 2.44 to figure out the current symbol.

Each iteration of the loop consists of the following steps:

1. Calculate index:=((Code-Low+1)x10-1)/(High-Low+1) and truncate it to the nearest integer. (The number 10 is the total cumulative frequency in our example.)
2. Use index to find the next symbol by comparing it to the cumulative frequencies column in Table 2.44. In the example below, the first value of index is 7.1759, truncated to 7. Seven is between the 5 and the 10 in the table, so it selects the "S".
3. Update Low and High according to

```
Low:=Low+(High-Low+1)LowCumFreq[X]/10;
High:=Low+(High-Low+1)HighCumFreq[X]/10-1;
```

where LowCumFreq[X] and HighCumFreq[X] are the cumulative frequencies of symbol X and of the symbol above it in Table 2.44.
4. If the leftmost digits of Low and High are identical, shift Low, High, and Code one position to the left. Low gets a 0 entered on the right, High gets a 9, and Code

1	2	3	4	5
S $L =$	$0+(1 - 0)\times0.5 = 0.5$	5000		5000
$H =$	$0+(1 - 0)\times1.0 = 1.0$	9999		9999
W $L =$	$0.5+(1 - .5)\times0.4 = 0.7$	7000	7	0000
$H =$	$0.5+(1 - .5)\times0.5 = 0.75$	7499	7	4999
I $L =$	$0 +(0.5 - 0)\times0.2 = 0.1$	1000	1	0000
$H =$	$0 +(0.5 - 0)\times0.4 = 0.2$	1999	1	9999
S $L =$	$0+(1 - 0)\times0.5 = 0.5$	5000		5000
$H =$	$0+(1 - 0)\times1.0 = 1.0$	9999		9999
S $L =$	$0.5+(1 - 0.5)\times0.5 = 0.75$	7500		7500
$H =$	$0.5+(1 - 0.5)\times1.0 = 1.0$	9999		9999
␣ $L =$	$.75+(1 - .75)\times0.0 = 0.75$	7500	7	5000
$H =$	$.75+(1 - .75)\times0.1 = .775$	7749	7	7499
M $L =$	$0.5+(.75 - .5)\times0.1 = .525$	5250	5	2500
$H =$	$0.5+(.75 - .5)\times0.2 = 0.55$	5499	5	4999
I $L =$	$.25+(.5 - .25)\times0.2 = 0.3$	3000	3	0000
$H =$	$.25+(.5 - .25)\times0.4 = .35$	3499	3	4999
S $L =$	$0.0+(0.5 - 0)\times0.5 = .25$	2500		2500
$H =$	$0.0+(0.5 - 0)\times1.0 = 0.5$	4999		4999
S $L =$	$.25+(.5 - .25)\times0.5 = .375$	3750	3750	
$H =$	$.25+(.5 - .25)\times1.0 = 0.5$	4999		4999

Table 2.53: Encoding "SWISS␣MISS" by Shifting.

gets the next input digit from the compressed stream.

Here are all the decoding steps for our example:

0. Initialize Low=0000, High=9999, and Code=7175.

1. index= $[(7175 - 0 + 1) \times 10 - 1]/(9999 - 0 + 1) = 7.1759 \rightarrow 7$. Symbol "S" is selected.
Low $= 0+(9999-0+1)\times 5/10 = 5000$. High $= 0+(9999-0+1)\times 10/10-1 = 9999$.

2. index= $[(7175 - 5000 + 1) \times 10 - 1]/(9999 - 5000 + 1) = 4.3518 \rightarrow 4$. Symbol "W" is selected.
Low $= 5000 + (9999 - 5000 + 1) \times 4/10 = 7000$. High $= 5000 + (9999 - 5000 + 1) \times 5/10 - 1 = 7499$.
After the 7 is shifted out, we have Low=0000, High=4999, and Code=1753.

3. index= $[(1753 - 0 + 1) \times 10 - 1]/(4999 - 0 + 1) = 3.5078 \rightarrow 3$. Symbol "I" is selected.
Low $= 0+ (4999-0+1) \times 2/10 = 1000$. High $= 0+(4999-0+1) \times 4/10-1 = 1999$.
After the 1 is shifted out, we have Low=0000, High=9999, and Code=7533.

4. index= $[(7533 - 0 + 1) \times 10 - 1]/(9999 - 0 + 1) = 7.5339 \rightarrow 7$. Symbol "S" is selected.
Low $= 0+(9999-0+1)\times 5/10 = 5000$. High $= 0+(9999-0+1)\times 10/10-1 = 9999$.

5. $\texttt{index}= [(7533 - 5000 + 1) \times 10 - 1]/(9999 - 5000 + 1) = 5.0678 \to 5$. Symbol "S" is selected.
$\texttt{Low} = 5000 + (9999 - 5000 + 1) \times 5/10 = 7500$. $\texttt{High} = 5000 + (9999 - 5000 + 1) \times 10/10 - 1 = 9999$.

6. $\texttt{index}= [(7533 - 7500 + 1) \times 10 - 1]/(9999 - 7500 + 1) = 0.1356 \to 0$. Symbol "⌴" is selected.
$\texttt{Low} = 7500 + (9999 - 7500 + 1) \times 0/10 = 7500$. $\texttt{High} = 7500 + (9999 - 7500 + 1) \times 1/10 - 1 = 7749$.

After the 7 is shifted out, we have $\texttt{Low}=5000$, $\texttt{High}=7499$, and $\texttt{Code}=5337$.

7. $\texttt{index}= [(5337 - 5000 + 1) \times 10 - 1]/(7499 - 5000 + 1) = 1.3516 \to 1$. Symbol "M" is selected.
$\texttt{Low} = 5000 + (7499 - 5000 + 1) \times 1/10 = 5250$. $\texttt{High} = 5000 + (7499 - 5000 + 1) \times 2/10 - 1 = 5499$.

After the 5 is shifted out we have $\texttt{Low}=2500$, $\texttt{High}=4999$, and $\texttt{Code}=3375$.

8. $\texttt{index}= [(3375 - 2500 + 1) \times 10 - 1]/(4999 - 2500 + 1) = 3.5036 \to 3$. Symbol "I" is selected.
$\texttt{Low} = 2500 + (4999 - 2500 + 1) \times 2/10 = 3000$. $\texttt{High} = 2500 + (4999 - 2500 + 1) \times 4/10 - 1 = 3499$.

After the 3 is shifted out we have $\texttt{Low}=0000$, $\texttt{High}=4999$, and $\texttt{Code}=3750$.

9. $\texttt{index}= [(3750 - 0 + 1) \times 10 - 1]/(4999 - 0 + 1) = 7.5018 \to 7$. Symbol "S" is selected.
$\texttt{Low} = 0 + (4999 - 0 + 1) \times 5/10 = 2500$. $\texttt{High} = 0 + (4999 - 0 + 1) \times 10/10 - 1 = 4999$.

10. $\texttt{index}= [(3750 - 2500 + 1) \times 10 - 1]/(4999 - 2500 + 1) = 5.0036 \to 5$. Symbol "S" is selected.
$\texttt{Low} = 2500 + (4999 - 2500 + 1) \times 5/10 = 3750$. $\texttt{High} = 2500 + (4999 - 2500 + 1) \times 10/10 - 1 = 4999$.

⋄ **Exercise 2.39:** How does the decoder know to stop the loop at this point?

1	2			3	4	5
1	L=0+(1	−	0)×0.0	= 0.0	000000	0	000000
	H=0+(1	−	0)×0.023162	= 0.023162	023162	0	231629
2	L=0+(0.231629 − 0)×0.0			= 0.0	000000	0	000000
	H=0+(0.231629 − 0)×0.023162			= 0.00536478244	005364	0	053649
3	L=0+(0.053649 − 0)×0.0			= 0.0	000000	0	000000
	H=0+(0.053649 − 0)×0.023162			= 0.00124261813	001242	0	012429
4	L=0+(0.012429 − 0)×0.0			= 0.0	000000	0	000000
	H=0+(0.012429 − 0)×0.023162			= 0.00028788049	000287	0	002879
5	L=0+(0.002879 − 0)×0.0			= 0.0	000000	0	000000
	H=0+(0.002879 − 0)×0.023162			= 0.00006668339	000066	0	000669

Table 2.54: Encoding $a_3a_3a_3a_3a_3$ by Shifting.

2.14.2 Underflow

Table 2.54 shows the steps in encoding the string $a_3a_3a_3a_3a_3$ by shifting. This table is similar to Table 2.53, and it illustrates the problem of underflow. Low and High approach each other, and since Low is always 0 in this example, High loses its significant digits as it approaches Low.

Underflow may happen not just in this case but in any case where Low and High need to converge very closely. Because of the finite size of the Low and High variables, they may reach values of, say, 499996 and 500003 and from there, instead of reaching values where their most significant digits are identical, they reach the values 499999 and 500000. Since the most significant digits are different, the algorithm will not output anything, there will not be any shifts, and the next iteration will only add digits beyond the first six ones. Those digits will be lost, and the first six digits will not change. The algorithm will iterate without generating any output until it reaches the eof.

The solution is to detect such a case early and *rescale* both variables. In the example above, rescaling should be done when the two variables reach values of 49xxxx and 50yyyy. Rescaling should squeeze out the second most significant digits, end up with 4xxxx0 and 5yyyy9, and increment a counter cntr. The algorithm may have to rescale several times before the most significant digits become equal. At that point, the most significant digit (which can be either 4 or 5) should be output, followed by cntr zeros (if the two variables converged to 4) or nines (if they converged to 5).

2.14.3 Final Remarks

All the examples so far have been in decimal, since the computations involved are easier to understand in this number base. It turns out that all the algorithms and rules described above apply to the binary case as well and can be used with only one change: Every occurrence of 9 (the largest decimal digit) should be replaced by 1 (the largest binary digit).

The examples above don't seem to show any compression at all. It seems that the three example strings "SWISS␣MISS", "$a_2a_2a_1a_3a_3$", and "$a_3a_3a_3a_3$eof" are encoded into very long numbers. In fact, it seems that the length of the final code depends on the probabilities involved. The long probabilities of Table 2.47a generate long numbers in the encoding process, whereas the shorter probabilities of Table 2.44 result in the more reasonable Low and High values of Table 2.45. This behavior demands an explanation.

> I am ashamed to tell you to how many figures I carried these computations, having no other business at that time.
>
> —Isaac Newton

To figure out the kind of compression achieved by arithmetic coding, we have to consider two facts: (1) In practice, all the operations are performed on binary numbers, so we have to translate the final results to binary before we can estimate the efficiency of the compression; (2) since the last symbol encoded is the eof, the final code does not have to be the final value of Low; it can be any value between Low and High. This makes it possible to select a shorter number as the final code that's being output.

Table 2.45 encodes the string "SWISS␣MISS" into the final Low and High values 0.71753375 and 0.717535. The approximate binary values of these numbers are 0.10110111101100000100101010111 and 0.10110111101100000101111111011, so we can select the number "10110111101100000100" as our final, compressed output. The ten-symbol string has thus been encoded into a 20-bit number. Does this represent good compression?

The answer is yes. Using the probabilities of Table 2.44, it is easy to calculate the probability of the string "SWISS␣MISS". It is $P = 0.5^5 \times 0.1 \times 0.2^2 \times 0.1 \times 0.1 = 1.25 \times 10^{-6}$. The entropy of this string is therefore $-\log_2 P = 19.6096$. Twenty bits is thus the minimum needed in practice to encode the string.

The symbols in Table 2.47a have probabilities 0.975, 0.001838, and 0.023162. These numbers require quite a few decimal digits, and as a result, the final Low and High values in Table 2.48 are the numbers 0.99462270125 and 0.994623638610941. Again it seems that there is no compression, but an analysis similar to the above shows compression that's very close to the entropy.

The probability of the string "$a_2a_2a_1a_3a_3$" is $0.975^2 \times 0.001838 \times 0.023162^2 \approx 9.37361 \times 10^{-7}$, and $-\log_2 9.37361 \times 10^{-7} \approx 20.0249$.

The binary representations of the final values of Low and High in Table 2.48 are 0.1111111010011111110010111111001 and 0.1111111010011111110100111101. We can select any number between these two, so we select 1111111010011111100, a 19-bit number. (This should have been a 21-bit number, but the numbers in Table 2.48 have limited precision and are not exact.)

◇ **Exercise 2.40:** Given the three symbols a_1, a_2, and eof, with probabilities $P_1 = 0.4$, $P_2 = 0.5$, and $P_{eof} = 0.1$, encode the string "$a_2a_2a_2$eof" and show that the size of the final code equals the (practical) minimum.

The following argument shows why arithmetic coding can, in principle, be a very efficient compression method. We denote by s a sequence of symbols to be encoded, and by b the number of bits required to encode it. As s gets longer, its probability $P(s)$ gets smaller and b gets larger. Since the logarithm is the information function, it is easy to see that b should grow at the same rate that $\log_2 P(s)$ shrinks. Their product should, therefore, be constant, or close to a constant. Information theory shows that b and $P(s)$ satisfy the double inequality

$$2 \leq 2^b P(s) < 4,$$

which implies

$$1 - \log_2 P(s) \leq b < 2 - \log_2 P(s). \tag{2.2}$$

As s gets longer, its probability $P(s)$ shrinks, the quantity $-\log_2 P(s)$ becomes a large positive number, and the double inequality of Equation (2.2) shows that in the limit, b approaches $-\log_2 P(s)$. This is why arithmetic coding can, in principle, compress a string of symbols to its theoretical limit.

Bibliography

Moffat, Alistair, Radford Neal, and Ian H. Witten (1998) "Arithmetic Coding Revisited," *ACM Transactions on Information Systems*, **16**(3):256–294, July.

Witten, Ian H., Radford M. Neal, and John G. Cleary (1987) "Arithmetic Coding for Data Compression," *Communications of the ACM*, **30**(6):520–540.

2.15 Adaptive Arithmetic Coding

Two features of arithmetic coding make it easy to extend:

1. The main encoding step is

```
Low:=Low+(High-Low+1)LowCumFreq[X]/10;
High:=Low+(High-Low+1)HighCumFreq[X]/10-1;
```

This means that in order to encode symbol X, the encoder should be given the cumulative frequencies of the symbol and of the one above it (see Table 2.44 for an example of cumulative frequencies). This also implies that the frequency of X (or, equivalently, its probability) could be changed each time it is encoded, provided that the encoder and the decoder agree on how to do this.

2. The order of the symbols in Table 2.44 is unimportant. They can even be swapped in the table during the encoding process as long as the encoder and decoder do it in the same way.

With this in mind, it is easy to understand how adaptive arithmetic coding works. The encoding algorithm has two parts: the probability model and the arithmetic encoder. The model reads the next symbol from the input stream and invokes the encoder, sending it the symbol and the two required cumulative frequencies. The model then increments the count of the symbol and updates the cumulative frequencies. The point is that the symbol's probability is determined by the model from its *old* count, and the count is incremented only after the symbol has been encoded. This makes it possible for the decoder to mirror the encoder's operations. The encoder knows what the symbol is even before it is encoded, but the decoder has to decode the symbol in order to find out what it is. The decoder can therefore use only the old counts when decoding a symbol. Once the symbol has been decoded, the decoder increments its count and updates the cumulative frequencies in exactly the same way as the encoder.

The model should keep the symbols, their counts (frequencies of occurrence), and their cumulative frequencies in an array. This array should be kept in sorted order of the counts. Each time a symbol is read and its count is incremented, the model updates the cumulative frequencies, then checks to see whether it is necessary to swap the symbol with another one, to keep the counts in sorted order.

It turns out that there is a simple data structure that allows for both easy search and update. This structure is a balanced binary tree housed in an array. (A balanced binary tree is a complete binary tree where some of the bottom-right nodes may be missing.) The tree should have a node for every symbol in the alphabet and, since it is balanced, its height is $\lceil \log_2 n \rceil$, where n is the size of the alphabet. For $n = 256$ the height of the balanced binary tree is 8, so starting at the root and searching for a node takes at most eight steps. The tree is arranged such that the most probable symbols (the ones with high counts) are located near the root, which speeds up searches. Table 2.55a shows an example of a ten-symbol alphabet with counts. Table 2.55b shows the same symbols sorted by count.

a_1	a_2	a_3	a_4	a_5	a_6	a_7	a_8	a_9	a_{10}
11	12	12	2	5	1	2	19	12	8

(a)

a_8	a_2	a_3	a_9	a_1	a_{10}	a_5	a_4	a_7	a_6
19	12	12	12	11	8	5	2	2	1

(b)

Table 2.55: A Ten-Symbol Alphabet With Counts.

The sorted array "houses" the balanced binary tree of Figure 2.57a. This is a simple, elegant way to build a tree. A balanced binary tree can be housed in an array without the use of any pointers. The rule is that the first array location (with index 1) houses the root, the two children of the node at array location i are housed at locations $2i$ and $2i + 1$, and the parent of the node at array location j is housed at location $\lfloor j/2 \rfloor$. It is easy to see how sorting the array has placed the symbols with largest counts at and near the root.

In addition to a symbol and its count, another value is now added to each tree node, the total counts of its left subtree. This will be used to compute cumulative frequencies. The corresponding array is shown in Table 2.56a.

Assume that the next symbol read from the input stream is a_9. Its count is incremented from 12 to 13. The model keeps the array in sorted order by searching for the farthest array element left of a_9 that has a count smaller than that of a_9. This search can be a straight linear search if the array is short enough, or a binary search if the array is long. In our case, symbols a_9 and a_2 should be swapped (Table 2.56b). Figure 2.57b shows the tree after the swap. Notice how the left-subtree counts have been updated.

a_8	a_2	a_3	a_9	a_1	a_{10}	a_5	a_4	a_7	a_6
19	12	12	12	11	8	5	2	2	1
40	16	8	2	1	0	0	0	0	0

(a)

a_8	a_9	a_3	a_2	a_1	a_{10}	a_5	a_4	a_7	a_6
19	13	12	12	11	8	5	2	2	1
41	16	8	2	1	0	0	0	0	0

(b)

Tables 2.56: A Ten-Symbol Alphabet With Counts.

Finally, here is how the cumulative frequencies are computed from this tree. When the cumulative frequency for a symbol X is needed, the model follows the tree branches from the root to the node containing X while adding numbers into an integer `af`. Each time a right branch is taken from an interior node N, `af` is incremented by the two numbers (the count and the left-subtree count) found in that node. When a left branch is taken, `af` is not modified. When the node containing X is reached, the left-subtree count of X is added to `af`, and `af` then contains the quantity `LowCumFreq[X]`.

As an example, we trace the tree of Figure 2.57a from the root to symbol a_6, whose cumulative frequency is 28. A right branch is taken at node a_2, adding 12 and 16 to `af`. A left branch is taken at node a_1, adding nothing to `af`. When reaching a_6, its left-subtree count, 0, is added to `af`. The result in `af` is $12 + 16 = 28$, as can be verified from Figure 2.57c. The quantity `HighCumFreq[X]` is obtained by adding the count of a_6 (which is 1) to `LowCumFreq[X]`.

To trace the tree and find the path from the root to a_6, the algorithm performs the following steps:

1. Find a_6 in the array housing the tree by means of a binary search. In our example the node with a_6 is found at array location 10.

2. Integer-divide 10 by 2. The remainder is 0, which means that a_6 is the left child of its parent. The quotient is 5, which is the array location of the parent.

3. Location 5 of the array contains a_1. Integer-divide 5 by 2. The remainder is 1, which means that a_1 is the right child of its parent. The quotient is 2, which is the array location of a_1's parent.

4. Location 2 of the array contains a_2. Integer-divide 2 by 2. The remainder is 0, which means that a_2 is the left child of its parent. The quotient is 1, the array location of the root, so the process stops.

The PPM compression method, Section 2.18, is a good example of a statistical model that invokes an arithmetic encoder in the way described here.

> The driver held out a letter. Boldwood seized it and opened it, expecting another anonymous one—so greatly are people's ideas of probability a mere sense that precedent will repeat itself. "I don't think it is for you, sir," said the man, when he saw Boldwood's action. "Though there is no name I think it is for your shepherd."
>
> —Thomas Hardy, *Far From The Madding Crowd*

2.16 The QM Coder

JPEG (Section 4.6) is an important image compression method. It uses arithmetic coding, but not in the way described in Section 2.14. The arithmetic coders of JPEG, JPEG 2000, and JBIG (Section 4.9) are called the QM-coder. It is designed for simplicity and speed, so it is limited to input symbols that are single bits and it uses an approximation instead of a multiplication. It also uses fixed-precision integer arithmetic, so it has to resort to *renormalization* of the probability interval

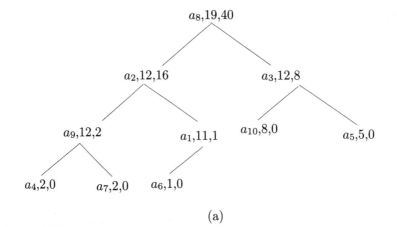

(a)

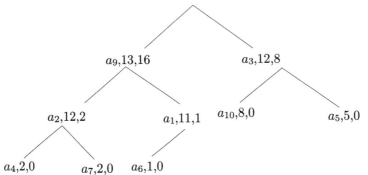

(b)

a_4	2	0—1
a_9	12	2—13
a_7	2	14—15
a_2	12	16—27
a_6	1	28—28
a_1	11	29—39
a_8	19	40—58
a_{10}	8	59—66
a_3	12	67—78
a_5	5	79—83

(c)

Figure 2.57: Adaptive Arithmetic Coding.

from time to time, in order for the approximation to remain close to the true multiplication.

⋄ **Exercise 2.41:** The QM-coder is limited to input symbols that are single bits. Suggest a way to convert an arbitrary set of symbols to a stream of bits.

The main idea behind the QM-coder is to classify each input symbol (which is a single bit) as either the more probable symbol (MPS) or the less probable symbol (LPS). Before the next bit is input, the QM-encoder uses a statistical model to determine whether a 0 or a 1 is more probable at that point. It then inputs the next bit and classifies it according to its actual value. If the model predicts, for example, that a 0 is more probable, and the next bit turns out to be a 1, the encoder classifies it as an LPS. It is important to understand that the only information encoded in the compressed stream is whether the next bit is MPS or LPS. When the stream is decoded, all that the decoder knows is whether the bit that has just been decoded is an MPS or an LPS. The decoder has to use the same statistical model to determine the current relation between MPS/LPS and 0/1. This relation changes, of course, from bit to bit, since the model is updated identically (in lockstep) by the encoder and decoder each time a bit is input by the former or decoded by the latter.

The statistical model also computes a probability Qe for the LPS, so the probability of the MPS is $(1 - Qe)$. Since Qe is the probability of the *less probable* symbol, it is in the range $[0, 0.5]$. The encoder divides the probability interval A into two subintervals according to Qe and places the LPS subinterval (whose size is $A \times Qe$) above the MPS subinterval [whose size is $A(1 - Qe)$], as shown in Figure 2.58b. Notice that the two subintervals in the figure are closed at the bottom and open at the top. This should be compared with the way a conventional arithmetic encoder divides the same interval (Figure 2.58a, where the numbers are taken from Table 2.45).

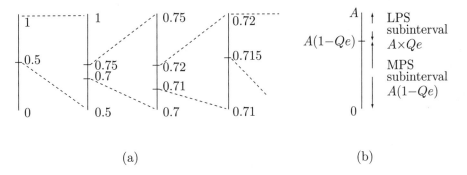

(a)   (b)

Figure 2.58: Division of the Probability Interval.

In conventional arithmetic coding, the interval is narrowed all the time, and the final output is any number inside the final subinterval. In the QM-coder, for simplicity, each step adds the bottom of the selected subinterval to the output-so-far. We denote the output string by C. If the current bit read from the input is the MPS, the bottom of the MPS subinterval (i.e., the number 0) is added to C.

If the current bit is the LPS, the bottom of the LPS subinterval [i.e., the number $A(1 - Qe)$] is added to C. After C is updated in this way, the current probability interval A is shrunk to the size of the selected subinterval. The probability interval is always in the range $[0, A)$, and A gets smaller at each step. This is the main principle of the QM-encoder, and it is expressed by the rules

$$
\begin{aligned}
\text{After MPS:} \quad & C \text{ is unchanged,} \quad A \leftarrow A(1 - Qe), \\
\text{After LPS:} \quad & C \leftarrow C + A(1 - Qe), \quad A \leftarrow A \times Qe.
\end{aligned} \tag{2.3}
$$

These rules set C to point to the bottom of the MPS or the LPS subinterval, depending on the classification of the current input bit. They also set A to the new size of the subinterval.

Table 2.59 lists the values of A and C when four symbols, each a single bit, are encoded. We assume that they alternate between an LPS and an MPS and that $Qe = 0.5$ for all four steps (normally, of course, the statistical model yields different values of Qe all the time). It is easy to see how the probability interval A shrinks from 1 to 0.0625, and how the output C grows from 0 to 0.625. Table 2.61 is similar, but uses $Qe = 0.1$ for all four steps. Again A shrinks, to 0.0081, and C grows, to 0.981. Figures 2.60 and 2.62 illustrate graphically the division of the probability interval A into an LPS and an MPS.

⋄ **Exercise 2.42:** Repeat these calculations for the case where all four symbols are LPS and $Qe = 0.5$, then for the case where they are MPS and $Qe = 0.1$.

The principle of the QM-encoder is simple and easy to understand, but it involves two problems. The first is the fact that the interval A, which starts at 1, shrinks all the time and requires high precision to distinguish it from zero. The solution to this problem is to maintain A as an integer and double it every time it gets too small. This is called *renormalization*. It is fast, since it is done by a logical left shift; no multiplication is needed. Each time A is doubled, C is also doubled. The second problem is the multiplication $A \times Qe$ used in subdividing the probability interval A. A fast compression method should avoid multiplications and divisions and should try to replace them with additions, subtractions, and shifts. It turns out that the second problem is also solved by renormalization. The idea is to keep the value of A close to 1, so that Qe will not be very different from the product $A \times Qe$. The multiplication is *approximated* by Qe.

How can we use renormalization to keep A close to 1? The first idea that comes to mind is to double A when it gets just a little below 1, say to 0.9. The problem is that doubling 0.9 yields 1.8, closer to 2 than to 1. If we let A get below 0.5 before doubling it, the result will be less than 1. It does not take long to realize that 0.75 is a good minimum value for renormalization. If A reaches this value at a certain step, it is doubled, to 1.5. If it reaches a smaller value, such as 0.6 or 0.55, it ends up even closer to 1 when doubled.

If A reaches a value less than 0.5 at a certain step, it has to be renormalized by doubling it several times, each time also doubling C. An example is the second row of Table 2.61, where A shrinks from 1 to 0.1 in one step, because of a very small probability Qe. In this case, A has to be doubled three times, from 0.1 to 0.2, to 0.4, to 0.8, in order to bring it into the desired range $[0.75, 1.5)$. We conclude that

Symbol	C	A
Initially	0	1
s1 (LPS)	$0 + 1(1 - 0.5) = 0.5$	$1 \times 0.5 = 0.5$
s2 (MPS)	unchanged	$0.5 \times (1 - 0.5) = 0.25$
s3 (LPS)	$0.5 + 0.25(1 - 0.5) = 0.625$	$0.25 \times 0.5 = 0.125$
s4 (MPS)	unchanged	$0.125 \times (1 - 0.5) = 0.0625$

Table 2.59: Encoding Four Symbols With $Qe = 0.5$.

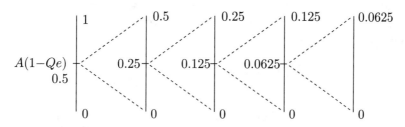

Figure 2.60: Division of the Probability Interval.

Symbol	C	A
Initially	0	1
s1 (LPS)	$0 + 1(1 - 0.1) = 0.9$	$1 \times 0.1 = 0.1$
s2 (MPS)	unchanged	$0.1 \times (1 - 0.1) = 0.09$
s3 (LPS)	$0.9 + 0.09(1 - 0.1) = 0.981$	$0.09 \times 0.1 = 0.009$
s4 (MPS)	unchanged	$0.009 \times (1 - 0.1) = 0.0081$

Table 2.61: Encoding Four Symbols With $Qe = 0.1$.

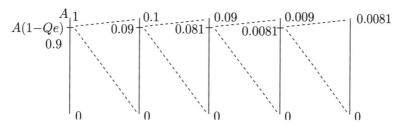

Figure 2.62: Division of the Probability Interval.

A can go down to 0 (or very close to 0) and can be at most 1.5 (actually, less than 1.5, since our intervals are always open at the high end).

⋄ **Exercise 2.43:** In what case does A always have to be renormalized?

Approximating the multiplication $A \times Qe$ by Qe changes the main rules of the QM-encoder to

After MPS: C is unchanged, $A \leftarrow A(1 - Qe) \approx A - Qe$,
After LPS: $C \leftarrow C + A(1 - Qe) \approx C + A - Qe$, $A \leftarrow A \times Qe \approx Qe$.

In order to include renormalization in these rules, we have to choose an integer representation for A where real values in the range $[0, 1.5)$ are represented as integers. Since many current computers have 16-bit words, it makes sense to choose a representation where 0 is represented by a word of 16 zero bits and 1.5 is represented by the smallest 17-bit number, which is

$$2^{16} = 65536_{10} = 10000_{16} = 1\underbrace{0\ldots0}_{16}{}_2.$$

This way we can represent 65536 real values in the range $[0, 1.5)$ as 16-bit integers, where the largest 16-bit integer, 65535, represents a real value slightly less than 1.5. Here are a few important examples of such values:

$$0.75 = 1.5/2 = 2^{15} = 32768_{10} = 8000_{16}, \quad 1 = 0.75(4/3) = 43690_{10} = AAAA_{16},$$
$$0.5 = 43690/2 = 21845_{10} = 5555_{16}, \quad 0.25 = 21845/2 = 10923_{10} = 2AAB_{16}.$$

(The optimal value of 1 in this representation is $AAAA_{16}$, but the way we associate the real values of A with the 16-bit integers is somewhat arbitrary. The important thing about this representation is to achieve accurate interval subdivision, and the subdivision is done by either $A \leftarrow A - Qe$ or $A \leftarrow Qe$. The accuracy of the subdivision depends, therefore, on the relative values of A and Qe, and it has been found experimentally that the average value of A is $B55A_{16}$, so this value, instead of $AAAA_{16}$, is associated in the JPEG QM-coder with $A = 1$. The difference between the two values $AAAA$ and $B55A$ is $AB0_{16} = 2736_{10}$. The JBIG QM-coder uses a slightly different value for 1.)

Renormalization can now be included in the main rules of the QM-encoder, which become

$$
\begin{aligned}
&\text{After MPS: } C \text{ is unchanged, } \quad A \leftarrow A - Qe, \\
&\qquad\qquad \text{if } A < 8000_{16} \text{ renormalize } A \text{ and } C. \\
&\text{After LPS: } C \leftarrow C + A - Qe, \quad A \leftarrow Qe, \\
&\qquad\qquad \text{renormalize } A \text{ and } C.
\end{aligned}
\tag{2.4}
$$

Tables 2.63 and 2.64 list the results of applying these rules to the examples shown in Tables 2.59 and 2.61, respectively.

Symbol	C	A	Renor. A	Renor. C
Initially	0	1		
s1 (LPS)	$0 + 1 - 0.5 = 0.5$	0.5	1	1
s2 (MPS)	unchanged	$1 - 0.5 = 0.5$	1	2
s3 (LPS)	$2 + 1 - 0.5 = 2.5$	0.5	1	5
s4 (MPS)	unchanged	$1 - 0.5 = 0.5$	1	10

Table 2.63: Renormalization Added to Table 2.59.

Symbol	C	A	Renor. A	Renor. C
Initially	0	1		
s1 (LPS)	$0 + 1 - 0.1 = 0.9$	0.1	0.8	0.8
s2 (MPS)	unchanged	$0.8 - 0.1 = 0.7$	1.4	1.6
s3 (LPS)	$1.6 + 1.4 - 0.1 = 2.9$	0.1	0.8	23.2
s4 (MPS)	unchanged	$0.8 - 0.1 = 0.7$	1.4	46.4

Table 2.64: Renormalization Added to Table 2.61.

⋄ **Exercise 2.44:** Repeat these calculations with renormalization for the case where all four symbols are LPS and $Qe = 0.5$. Following this, repeat the calculations for the case where they are all MPS and $Qe = 0.1$. (Compare this exercise with Exercise 2.42.)

The next point that has to be considered in the design of the QM-encoder is the problem of *interval inversion*. This is the case where the size of the subinterval allocated to the MPS becomes smaller than the LPS subinterval. This problem may occur when Qe is close to 0.5, and is a result of the approximation to the multiplication. It is illustrated in Table 2.65, where four MPS symbols are encoded with $Qe = 0.45$. In the third row of the table the interval A is doubled from 0.65 to 1.3. In the fourth row it is reduced to 0.85. This value is greater than 0.75, so no renormalization takes place, yet the subinterval allocated to the MPS becomes $A - Qe = 0.85 - 0.45 = 0.40$, which is smaller than the LPS subinterval, which is $Qe = 0.45$. Clearly, the problem occurs when $Qe > A/2$, a relation that can also be expressed as $Qe > A - Qe$.

Symbol	C	A	Renor. A	Renor. C
Initially	0	1		
s1 (MPS)	0	$1 - 0.45 = 0.55$	1.1	0
s2 (MPS)	0	$1.1 - 0.45 = 0.65$	1.3	0
s3 (MPS)	0	$1.3 - 0.45 = 0.85$		
s4 (MPS)	0	$0.85 - 0.45 = 0.40$	0.8	0

Table 2.65: Illustrating Interval Inversion.

The solution is to interchange the two subintervals whenever the LPS subinterval becomes greater than the MPS subinterval. This is called *conditional exchange*. The condition for interval inversion is $Qe > A - Qe$, but since $Qe \leq 0.5$, we get $A - Qe < Qe \leq 0.5$, and it becomes obvious that both Qe and $A - Qe$ (i.e., both the LPS and MPS subintervals) are less than 0.75, so renormalization must take place. This is why the test for conditional exchange is performed only *after* the encoder has decided that renormalization is needed. The new rules for the QM-encoder are shown in Figure 2.66.

```
After MPS:
    C is unchanged
    A ← A − Qe;           % The MPS subinterval
    if A < 8000₁₆ then  % if renormalization needed
      if A < Qe then      % if inversion needed
      C ← C + A;          % point to bottom of LPS
      A ← Qe              % Set A to LPS subinterval
      endif;
    renormalize A and C;
    endif;

After LPS:
    A ← A − Qe;           % The MPS subinterval
    if A ≥ Qe then  % if interval sizes not inverted
    C ← C + A;            % point to bottom of LPS
    A ← Qe               % Set A to LPS subinterval
    endif;
    renormalize A and C;
```

Figure 2.66: QM-Encoder Rules With Interval Inversion.

The QM-Decoder: The QM-decoder is the reverse of the QM-encoder. For simplicity we ignore renormalization and conditional exchange, and we assume that the QM-encoder operates by the rules of Equation (2.3). Reversing the way C is updated in those rules yields the rules for the QM-decoder (the interval A is updated in the same way):

$$
\begin{aligned}
&\text{After MPS:} \quad C \text{ is unchanged,} \quad A \leftarrow A(1 - Qe), \\
&\text{After LPS:} \quad C \leftarrow C - A(1 - Qe), \quad A \leftarrow A \times Qe.
\end{aligned}
\tag{2.5}
$$

These rules are demonstrated using the data of Table 2.59. The four decoding steps are as follows:

Step 1: $C = 0.625$, $A = 1$, the dividing line is $A(1 - Qe) = 1(1 - 0.5) = 0.5$, so the LPS and MPS subintervals are $[0, 0.5)$ and $[0.5, 1)$. Since C points to the upper subinterval, an LPS is decoded. The new C is $0.625 - 1(1 - 0.5) = 0.125$ and the new A is $1 \times 0.5 = 0.5$.

Step 2: $C = 0.125$, $A = 0.5$, the dividing line is $A(1 - Qe) = 0.5(1 - 0.5) = 0.25$, so the LPS and MPS subintervals are $[0, 0.25)$ and $[0.25, 0.5)$, and an MPS is decoded. C is unchanged and the new A is $0.5(1 - 0.5) = 0.25$.

Step 3: $C = 0.125$, $A = 0.25$, the dividing line is $A(1 - Qe) = 0.25(1 - 0.5) = 0.125$, so the LPS and MPS subintervals are $[0, 0.125)$ and $[0.125, 0.25)$, and an LPS is decoded. The new C is $0.125 - 0.25(1 - 0.5) = 0$ and the new A is $0.25 \times 0.5 = 0.125$.

Step 4: $C = 0$, $A = 0.125$, the dividing line is $A(1 - Qe) = 0.125(1 - 0.5) = 0.0625$, so the LPS and MPS subintervals are $[0, 0.0625)$ and $[0.0625, 0.125)$, and an MPS is decoded. C is unchanged and the new A is $0.125(1 - 0.5) = 0.0625$.

⋄ **Exercise 2.45:** Use the rules of Equation (2.5) to decode the four symbols encoded in Table 2.61.

Probability Estimation: The QM-encoder uses a novel, interesting, and little-understood method for estimating the probability Qe of the LPS. The first method that comes to mind in trying to estimate the probability of the next input bit is to initialize Qe to 0.5 and update it by counting the numbers of zeros and ones that have been input so far. If, for example, 1000 bits have been input so far, and 700 of them were zeros, then 0 is the current MPS, with probability 0.7, and the probability of the LPS is $Qe = 0.3$. Notice that Qe should be updated *before* the next input bit is read and encoded, since otherwise the decoder would not be able to mirror this operation (the decoder does not know what the next bit is). This method produces good results, but is slow, since Qe should be updated often (ideally, for each input bit), and the calculation involves a division (dividing $700/1000$ in our example).

The method used by the QM-encoder is based on a table of preset Qe values. Qe is initialized to 0.5 and is modified when renormalization takes place, not for every input bit. Table 2.67 illustrates the process. The Qe index is initialized to zero, so the first value of Qe is $0AC1_{16}$ or very close to 0.5. After the first MPS renormalization, the Qe index is incremented by 1, as indicated by column "Incr MPS." A Qe index of 1 implies a Qe value of $0A81_{16}$ or 0.49237, slightly smaller than the original, reflecting the fact that the renormalization occurred because of an MPS. If, for example, the current Qe index is 26, and the next renormalization is LPS, the index is decremented by 3, as indicated by column "Decr LPS," reducing Qe to 0.00421. The method is not applied very often, and it involves only table lookups and incrementing or decrementing the Qe index: fast, simple operations.

The column labeled "MPS exch" in Table 2.67 contains the information for the conditional exchange of the MPS and LPS definitions at $Qe = 0.5$. The zero value at the bottom of column "Incr MPS" should also be noted. If the Qe index is 29 and an MPS renormalization occurs, this zero causes the index to stay at 29 (corresponding to the smallest Qe value).

Table 2.67 is used here for illustrative purposes only. The JPEG QM-encoder uses Table 2.68, which has the same format but is harder to understand, since its Qe values are not listed in sorted order. This table was prepared using probability estimation concepts based on Bayesian statistics (see appendix in book's web site).

We now justify this probability estimation method with an approximate calculation that suggests that the Qe values obtained by this method will adapt to

Qe index	Hex Qe	Dec Qe	Decr LPS	Incr MPS	MPS exch	Qe index	Hex Qe	Dec Qe	Decr LPS	Incr MPS	MPS exch
0	0AC1	0.50409	0	1	1	15	0181	0.07050	2	1	0
1	0A81	0.49237	1	1	0	16	0121	0.05295	2	1	0
2	0A01	0.46893	1	1	0	17	00E1	0.04120	2	1	0
3	0901	0.42206	1	1	0	18	00A1	0.02948	2	1	0
4	0701	0.32831	1	1	0	19	0071	0.02069	2	1	0
5	0681	0.30487	1	1	0	20	0059	0.01630	2	1	0
6	0601	0.28143	1	1	0	21	0053	0.01520	2	1	0
7	0501	0.23456	2	1	0	22	0027	0.00714	2	1	0
8	0481	0.21112	2	1	0	23	0017	0.00421	2	1	0
9	0441	0.19940	2	1	0	24	0013	0.00348	3	1	0
10	0381	0.16425	2	1	0	25	000B	0.00201	2	1	0
11	0301	0.14081	2	1	0	26	0007	0.00128	3	1	0
12	02C1	0.12909	2	1	0	27	0005	0.00092	2	1	0
13	0281	0.11737	2	1	0	28	0003	0.00055	3	1	0
14	0241	0.10565	2	1	0	29	0001	0.00018	2	0	0

Table 2.67: Probability Estimation Table (Illustrative).

and closely approach the correct LPS probability of the binary input stream. The method updates Qe each time a renormalization occurs, and we know, from Equation (2.4), that this happens every time an LPS is input, but not for all MPS values. We therefore imagine an ideal balanced input stream where for each LPS bit there is a sequence of consecutive MPS bits. We denote the true (but unknown) LPS probability by q, and we try to show that the Qe values produced by the method for this ideal case are close to q.

Equation (2.4) lists the main rules of the QM-encoder, and shows how the probability interval A is decremented by Qe each time an MPS is input and encoded. Imagine a renormalization that brings A to a value A_1 (between 1 and 1.5), followed by a sequence of N consecutive MPS bits that reduce A in steps of Qe from A_1 to a value A_2 that requires another renormalization (i.e., A_2 is less than 0.75). It is clear that

$$N = \left\lfloor \frac{\Delta A}{Qe} \right\rfloor,$$

where $\Delta A = A_1 - A_2$. Since q is the true probability of an LPS, the probability of having N MPS bits in a row is $P = (1 - q)^N$. This implies $\ln P = N \ln(1 - q)$, which, for a small q, can be approximated by

$$\ln P \approx N(-q) = -\frac{\Delta A}{Qe}q, \text{ or } P \approx \exp\left(-\frac{\Delta A}{Qe}q\right). \tag{2.6}$$

Since we are dealing with an ideal balanced input stream, we are interested in the value $P = 0.5$, because it implies equal numbers of LPS and MPS renormalizations. From $P = 0.5$ we get $\ln P = -\ln 2$, which, when combined with Equation (2.6),

Qe index	Hex Qe	Next-Index LPS	MPS	MPS exch	Qe index	Hex Qe	Next-Index LPS	MPS	MPS exch
0	5A1D	1	1	1	57	01A4	55	58	0
1	2586	14	2	0	58	0160	56	59	0
2	1114	16	3	0	59	0125	57	60	0
3	080B	18	4	0	60	00F6	58	61	0
4	03D8	20	5	0	61	00CB	59	62	0
5	01DA	23	6	0	62	00AB	61	63	0
6	00E5	25	7	0	63	008F	61	32	0
7	006F	28	8	0	64	5B12	65	65	1
8	0036	30	9	0	65	4D04	80	66	0
9	001A	33	10	0	66	412C	81	67	0
10	000D	35	11	0	67	37D8	82	68	0
11	0006	9	12	0	68	2FE8	83	69	0
12	0003	10	13	0	69	293C	84	70	0
13	0001	12	13	0	70	2379	86	71	0
14	5A7F	15	15	1	71	1EDF	87	72	0
15	3F25	36	16	0	72	1AA9	87	73	0
16	2CF2	38	17	0	73	174E	72	74	0
17	207C	39	18	0	74	1424	72	75	0
18	17B9	40	19	0	75	119C	74	76	0
19	1182	42	20	0	76	0F6B	74	77	0
20	0CEF	43	21	0	77	0D51	75	78	0
21	09A1	45	22	0	78	0BB6	77	79	0
22	072F	46	23	0	79	0A40	77	48	0
23	055C	48	24	0	80	5832	80	81	1
24	0406	49	25	0	81	4D1C	88	82	0
25	0303	51	26	0	82	438E	89	83	0
26	0240	52	27	0	83	3BDD	90	84	0
27	01B1	54	28	0	84	34EE	91	85	0
28	0144	56	29	0	85	2EAE	92	86	0
29	00F5	57	30	0	86	299A	93	87	0
30	00B7	59	31	0	87	2516	86	71	0
31	008A	60	32	0	88	5570	88	89	1
32	0068	62	33	0	89	4CA9	95	90	0
33	004E	63	34	0	90	44D9	96	91	0
34	003B	32	35	0	91	3E22	97	92	0
35	002C	33	9	0	92	3824	99	93	0
36	5AE1	37	37	1	93	32B4	99	94	0
37	484C	64	38	0	94	2E17	93	86	0
38	3A0D	65	39	0	95	56A8	95	96	1
39	2EF1	67	40	0	96	4F46	101	97	0
40	261F	68	41	0	97	47E5	102	98	0
41	1F33	69	42	0	98	41CF	103	99	0
42	19A8	70	43	0	99	3C3D	104	100	0
43	1518	72	44	0	100	375E	99	93	0
44	1177	73	45	0	101	5231	105	102	0
45	0E74	74	46	0	102	4C0F	106	103	0
46	0BFB	75	47	0	103	4639	107	104	0
47	09F8	77	48	0	104	415E	103	99	0
48	0861	78	49	0	105	5627	105	106	1
49	0706	79	50	0	106	50E7	108	107	0
50	05CD	48	51	0	107	4B85	109	103	0
51	04DE	50	52	0	108	5597	110	109	0
52	040F	50	53	0	109	504F	111	107	0
53	0363	51	54	0	110	5A10	110	111	1
54	02D4	52	55	0	111	5522	112	109	0
55	025C	53	56	0	112	59EB	112	111	1
56	01F8	54	57	0					

Table 2.68: The QM-Encoder Probability Estimation Table.

yields

$$Qe = \frac{\Delta A}{\ln 2} q.$$

This is fortuitous because $\ln 2 \approx 0.693$ and ΔA is typically a little less than 0.75. We can say that for our ideal balanced input stream, $Qe \approx q$, providing one justification for our estimation method. Another justification is provided by the way P depends on Qe [shown in Equation (2.6)]. If Qe gets larger than q, P also gets large, and the table tends to move to smaller Qe values. In the opposite case, the table tends to select larger Qe values.

2.17 Text Compression

Before delving into the details of the next method, here is a general discussion of text compression. Most text compression methods are either statistical or dictionary based. The latter class breaks the text into fragments that are saved in a data structure called a dictionary. When a fragment of new text is found to be identical to one of the dictionary entries, a pointer to that entry is written on the compressed stream, to become the compression of the new fragment. The former class, on the other hand, consists of methods that develop statistical *models* of the text.

A common statistical method consists of a modeling stage followed by a coding stage. The model assigns probabilities to the input symbols, and the coding stage then actually codes the symbols based on those probabilities. The model can be static or dynamic (adaptive). Most models are based on one of the following two approaches.

Frequency: The model assigns probabilities to the text symbols based on their frequencies of occurrence, such that commonly occurring symbols are assigned short codes. A static model uses fixed probabilities, whereas a dynamic model modifies the probabilities "on the fly" while text is being input and compressed.

Context: The model considers the context of a symbol when assigning it a probability. Since the decoder does not have access to future text, both encoder and decoder must limit the context to past text, i.e., to symbols that have already been input and processed. In practice, the context of a symbol is the N symbols preceding it. We thus say that a context-based text compression method uses the context of a symbol to **predict** it (i.e., to assign it a probability). Technically, such a method is said to use an "order-N" Markov model. The PPM method, Section 2.18, is an excellent example of a context-based compression method, although the concept of context can also be used to compress images.

Some modern context-based text compression methods perform a transformation on the input data and then apply a statistical model to assign probabilities to the transformed symbols. Good examples of such methods are the Burrows-Wheeler method, Section 8.1, also known as the Burrows-Wheeler transform, or *block sorting*; the technique of symbol ranking, Section 8.2; and the ACB method, Section 8.3, which uses an associative dictionary.

2.18 PPM

The PPM method is a sophisticated, state of the art compression method originally developed by J. Cleary and I. Witten [Cleary 84], with extensions and an implementation by A. Moffat [Moffat 90]. The method is based on an encoder that maintains a statistical model of the text. The encoder inputs the next symbol S, assigns it a probability P, and sends S to an adaptive arithmetic encoder, to be encoded with probability P.

The simplest *statistical model* counts the number of times each symbol has occurred in the past and assigns the symbol a probability based on that. Assume that 1217 symbols have been input and encoded so far, and 34 of them were the letter q. If the next symbol is a q, it is assigned a probability of 34/1217 and its count is incremented by 1. Next time q is seen, it will be assigned a probability of $35/t$, where t is the total number of symbols input up to that point (not including the last q).

The next model up is a *context-based* statistical model. The idea is to assign a probability to symbol S depending not just on the frequency of the symbol but on the contexts in which it has occurred so far. The letter h, for example, occurs in "typical" English text (Table 1) with a probability of about 5%. On average, we expect to see an h about 5% of the time. However, if the current symbol is t, there is a high probability (about 30%) that the next symbol will be h, since the digram th is common in English. We say that the model of typical English **predicts** an h in such a case. If the next symbol is in fact h, it is assigned a large probability. In cases where an h is the second letter of an unlikely digram, say xh, the h is assigned a smaller probability. Notice that the word "predicts" is used here to mean "estimate the probability of." A similar example is the letter u, which has a probability of about 2%. When a q is encountered, however, there is a probability of more than 99% that the next letter will be a u.

⋄ **Exercise 2.46:** We know that in English, a q must be followed by a u. Why not just say that the probability of the digram qu is 100%?

A *static* context-based modeler always uses the same probabilities. It contains static tables with the probabilities of all the possible digrams (or trigrams) of the alphabet and uses the tables to assign a probability to the next symbol S depending on the symbol (or, in general, on the context) C preceding it. We can imagine S and C being used as indices for a row and a column of a static frequency table. The table itself can be constructed by accumulating digram or trigram frequencies from large quantities of text. Such a modeler is simple, produces good results on average, but has two problems. The first is that some input streams may be statistically very different from the data originally used to prepare the table. A static encoder may create considerable expansion in such a case. The second problem is zero probabilities.

What if after reading and analyzing huge amounts of English text, we still have never encountered the trigram qqz? The cell corresponding to qqz in the trigram frequency table will contain zero. The arithmetic encoder, Sections 2.14 and 2.15, requires all symbols to have nonzero probabilities. Even if a different encoder, such as Huffman, is used, all the probabilities involved must be nonzero.

(Recall that the Huffman method works by combining two low-probability symbols into one high-probability one. If two zero-probability symbols are combined, the resulting symbol will have the same zero probability.) Another reason why a symbol must have nonzero probability is that its entropy (the smallest number of bits into which it can be encoded) depends on $\log_2 P$, which is undefined for $P = 0$ (but gets very large when $P \rightarrow 0$). This *zero-probability problem* faces any model, static or adaptive, that uses probabilities of occurrence of symbols to achieve compression. Two simple solutions are traditionally adopted for this problem, but neither has any theoretical justification.

1. After analyzing a large quantity of data and counting frequencies, go over the frequency table, looking for empty cells. Each empty cell is assigned a frequency count of 1, and the total count is also incremented by 1. This method pretends that every digram and trigram has been seen at least once.

2. Add 1 to the total count and divide this single 1 among all the empty cells. Each will get a count that's less than 1 and, as a result, a very small probability. This assigns a very small probability to anything that hasn't been seen in the training data used for the analysis.

An *adaptive* context-based modeler also maintains tables with the probabilities of all the possible digrams (or trigrams or even longer contexts) of the alphabet, and uses the tables to assign a probability to the next symbol S depending on a few symbols immediately preceding it (its context C). The tables are updated all the time as more data is being input, which adapts the probabilities to the particular data being compressed.

Such a model is slower and more complex than the static one but produces better compression, since it uses the correct probabilities even when the input has data with probabilities much different from the average.

A text that skews letter probabilities is called a *lipogram*. (Would a computer program without any `goto` statements be considered a lipogram?) There are just a few examples of literary works that are lipograms:

1. Perhaps the best-known lipogram in English is *Gadsby*, a full-length novel [Wright 39], by Ernest Vincent Wright (1872–1939), that does not contain any occurrences of the letter E.

2. *Alphabetical Africa* by Walter Abish (W. W. Norton, 1974) is a readable lipogram where the reader is supposed to discover the unusual writing style while reading. This style has to do with the initial letters of words. The book consists of 52 chapters. In the first, all words begin with `a`; in the second, words start with either `a` or `b`, etc., until, in chapter 26, all letters are allowed at the start of a word. In the remaining 26 chapters, the letters are taken away one by one. Various readers have commented on how little or how much they have missed the word "the" and how they felt on finally seeing it (in chapter 20).

3. The novel *La Disparition* is a 1969 French lipogram by Georges Perec (1936–1982) that does not contain the letter E (this letter actually appears several times, outside the main text, in words that the publisher had to include, and these are all printed in red). *La Disparition* has been translated to English, where it is called *A Void*, by Gilbert Adair (Harper Collins, 1994).

A Quotation from the Preface to *Gadsby*

People as a rule will not stop to realize what a task such an attempt actually is. As I wrote along, in long-hand at first, a whole army of little E's gathered around my desk, all eagerly expecting to be called upon. But gradually as they saw me writing on and on, without even noticing them, they grew uneasy; and, with excited whisperings among themselves, began hopping up and riding on my pen, looking down constantly for a chance to drop off into some word; for all the world like sea birds perched, watching for a passing fish! But when they saw that I had covered 138 pages of typewriter size paper, they slid off unto the floor, walking sadly away, arm in arm; but shouting back: "You certainly must have a hodge-podge of a yarn there without Us! Why, man! We are in every story ever written, *hundreds and thousands of times!* This is the first time we ever were shut out!"

—Ernest Vincent Wright

---

4. Gottlob Burmann, a German poet (1737–1805), created our next example of a lipogram. He wrote 130 poems, consisting of about 20,000 words, without the use of the letter R. It is also believed that during the last 17 years of his life he even omitted this letter from his daily conversation.

5. A Portuguese lipogram is found in five stories written by Alonso Alcala y Herrera, a Portuguese writer, in 1641, each suppressing one vowel.

6. Other examples, in Spanish, are found in the writings of Francisco Navarrete y Ribera (1659), Fernando Jacinto de Zurita y Haro (1654), and Manuel Lorenzo de Lizarazu y Berbuizana (also 1654).

An order-N adaptive context-based modeler reads the next symbol S from the input stream and considers the N symbols preceding S the current order-N context C of S. The model then estimates the probability P that S appears in the input data following the particular context C. Theoretically, the larger N, the better the probability estimate (the *prediction*). To get an intuitive feeling, imagine the case $N = 20,000$. It is hard to imagine a situation where a group of 20,000 symbols in the input stream is followed by a symbol S, but another group of the same 20,000 symbols, found later in the same input stream, is followed by a different symbol. Thus, N=20,000 allows the model to predict the next symbol (to estimate its probability) with high accuracy. However, large values of N have three disadvantages:

1. If we encode a symbol based on the 20,000 symbols preceding it, how do we encode the first 20,000 symbols in the input stream? They may have to be written on the output stream as raw ASCII codes, thereby reducing the overall compression.

2. For large values of N there may be too many possible contexts. If our symbols are the 7-bit ASCII codes, the alphabet size is $2^7 = 128$ symbols. There are therefore $128^2 = 16,384$ order-2 contexts, $128^3 = 2,097,152$ order-3 contexts, and so on. The number of contexts grows exponentially, since it is 128^N or, in general, A^N, where A is the alphabet size.

> I pounded the keys so hard that night that the letter e flew off the part of
> the machine that hits the paper. Not wanting to waste the night, I went next
> door to a neighbor who, I knew, had an elaborate workshop in his cellar. He
> attempted to solder my e back, but when I started to work again, it flew off like
> a bumblebee. For the rest of the night I inserted each e by hand, and in the
> morning I took the last dollars from our savings account to buy a new typewriter.
> Nothing could be allowed to delay the arrival of my greatest triumph.
>
> —Sloan Wilson, *What Shall We Wear to This Party*, 1976

◇ **Exercise 2.47:** What is the number of order-2 and -3 contexts for an alphabet of
size $2^8 = 256$?

For a small alphabet, larger values of N can be used. For a 16-symbol alphabet
there are $16^4 = 65,536$ order-4 contexts and $16^6 = 16,777,216$ order-6 contexts.

◇ **Exercise 2.48:** What could be a practical example of such an alphabet?

3. A very long context retains information about the nature of old data. Experience
shows that large data files contain different distributions of symbols in different parts
(a good example is a history book, where one chapter may commonly use words such
as "Greek," "Athens," and "Troy," while the following chapter may use "Roman,"
"empire," and "legion"). Better compression can therefore be achieved if the model
assigns less importance to information collected from old data and more weight to
fresh, recent data. Such an effect is achieved by a short context.

◇ **Exercise 2.49:** Show an example of a common binary file where different parts
may have different bit distributions.

As a result, relatively short contexts, in the range of 2 to 10, are used in
practice. Any practical algorithm requires a carefully designed data structure that
provides fast search and easy update, while holding many thousands of symbols and
strings (Section 2.18.5).

We now turn to the next point in the discussion. Assume a context-based
encoder that uses order-3 contexts. Early in the compression process the word
here was seen several times, but the word **there** is now seen for the first time.
Assume that the next symbol is the **r** of **there**. The encoder will not find any
instances of the order-3 context **the** followed by **r** (the **r** has 0 probability in this
context). The encoder may simply write **r** on the compressed stream as a literal,
resulting in no compression, but we know that **r** was seen several times in the past
following the order-2 context **he** (**r** has nonzero probability in this context). The
PPM method takes advantage of this knowledge.

> "uvulapalatopharangoplasty" is the name of a surgical procedure to correct sleep
> apnea. It is rumored to be the longest (English?) word without any e's.

2.18.1 PPM Principles

The central idea of PPM is to use this knowledge. The PPM encoder switches to a shorter context when a longer one has resulted in 0 probability. PPM thus starts with an order-N context. It searches its data structure for a previous occurrence of the current context C followed by the next symbol S. If it finds no such occurrence (i.e., if the probability of this particular C followed by this S is 0), it switches to order $N-1$, and tries the same thing. Let C' be the string consisting of the rightmost $N-1$ symbols of C. The PPM encoder searches its data structure for a previous occurrence current context C' followed by symbol S. PPM thus tries to use smaller and smaller parts of the context C, which is the reason for its name. The name PPM stands for "prediction with partial string matching." Here is the process in some detail.

The encoder reads the next symbol S from the input stream, looks at the current order-N context C (the last N symbols read), and, based on input data that has been seen in the past, determines the probability P that S will appear following the particular context C. The encoder then invokes an adaptive arithmetic coding algorithm to encode symbol S with probability P. In practice the adaptive arithmetic encoder is a procedure that receives the quantities `HighCumFreq[X]` and `LowCumFreq[X]` (Section 2.15) as parameters from the PPM encoder.

As an example, suppose that the current order-3 context is the string `the`, which has already been seen 27 times in the past, and was followed by the letters `r` (11 times), `s` (9 times), `n` (6 times), and `m` (just once). The encoder assigns these cases the probabilities $11/27$, $9/27$, $6/27$, and $1/27$, respectively. If the next symbol read is `r`, it is sent to the arithmetic encoder with a probability of $11/27$, and the probabilities are updated to $12/28$, $9/28$, $6/28$, and $1/28$.

What if the next symbol read is `a`? The context `the` was never seen followed by an `a`, so the probability of this case is 0. This zero-probability problem is solved in PPM by switching to a shorter context. The PPM encoder asks itself; How many times was the order-2 context `he` seen in the past, and by what symbols was it followed? The answer may be; Seen 54 times, followed by `a` (26 times), by `r` (12 times), etc. The PPM encoder now sends the `a` to the arithmetic encoder with a probability of $26/54$.

If the next symbol S was never seen before following the order-2 context `he`, the PPM encoder switches to order-1 context. Was S seen before following the string `e`? If yes, a nonzero probability is assigned to S depending on how many times it (and other symbols) was seen following `e`. Otherwise, the PPM encoder switches to order-0 context. It asks itself how many times symbol S was seen in the past, regardless of any contexts. If it was seen 87 times out of 574 symbols read, it is assigned a probability of $87/574$. If symbol S has never been seen before (a common situation at the start of any compression process), the PPM encoder switches to a mode called order -1 context, where S is assigned the fixed probability $1/(\text{size of the alphabet})$.

Table 2.69 shows contexts and frequency counts for orders 4 through 0 after the 11-symbol string `xyzzxyxyzzx` has been input and encoded. To understand the operation of the PPM encoder, let's assume that the 12th symbol is `z`. The order-

> To predict is one thing. To predict correctly is another.
>
> —Unknown

4 context is now **yzzx**, which earlier was seen followed by **y** but never by **z**. The encoder therefore switches to the order-3 context, which is **zzx**, but even this hasn't been seen earlier followed by **z**. The next lower context, **zx**, is of order 2, and it also fails. The encoder then switches to order 1, where it checks context **x**. Symbol **x** was found three times in the past but was always followed by **y**. Order 0 is checked next, where **z** has a frequency count of 4 (out of a total count of 11). Symbol **z** is thus sent to the adaptive arithmetic encoder, to be encoded with probability 4/11 (the PPM encoder "predicts" that it will appear 4/11 of the time).

Order 4	Order 3	Order 2	Order 1	Order 0
xyzz→x 2	xyz→z 2	xy→z 2	x→y 3	x 4
yzzx→y 1	yzz→x 2	→x 1	y→z 2	y 3
zzxy→x 1	zzx→y 1	yz→z 2	→x 1	z 4
zxyx→y 1	zxy→x 1	zz→x 2	z→z 2	
xyxy→z 1	xyx→y 1	zx→y 1	→x 2	
yxyz→z 1	yxy→z 1	yx→y 1		

(a)

Order 4	Order 3	Order 2	Order 1	Order 0
xyzz→x 2	xyz→z 2	xy→z 2	x→y 3	x 4
yzzx→y 1	yzz→x 2	xy→x 1	→z 1	y 3
→z 1	zzx→y 1	yz→z 2	y→z 2	z 5
zzxy→x 1	→z 1	zz→x 2	→x 1	
zxyx→y 1	zxy→x 1	zx→y 1	z→z 2	
xyxy→z 1	xyx→y 1	→z 1	→x 2	
yxyz→z 1	yxy→z 1	yx→y 1		

(b)

Table 2.69: (a) Contexts and Counts for "xyzzxyxyzzx".
(b) Updated After Another **z** Is Input.

Next we consider the PPM decoder. There is a fundamental difference between the way the PPM encoder and decoder work. The encoder can always look at the next symbol and base its next step on what that symbol is. The job of the decoder is to find out what the next symbol is. The encoder decides to switch to a shorter context based on what the next symbol is. The decoder cannot mirror this, since it does not know what the next symbol is. The algorithm needs an additional feature that will make it possible for the decoder to stay in lockstep with the encoder. The feature used by PPM is to reserve one symbol of the alphabet as an *escape symbol*. When the encoder decides to switch to a shorter context, it first writes the escape symbol (arithmetically encoded) on the output stream. The decoder can decode the escape symbol, since it is encoded in the present context. After decoding an escape, the decoder also switches to a shorter context.

The worst that can happen with an order-N encoder is to encounter a symbol S for the first time (this happens mostly at the start of the compression process). The symbol hasn't been seen before in any context, not even in order-0 context (i.e., by itself). In such a case the encoder ends up sending $N + 1$ consecutive escapes to be arithmetically encoded and output, switching all the way down to order -1, followed by the symbol S encoded with the fixed probability 1/(size of the alphabet). Since the escape symbol may be output many times by the encoder, it is important to assign it a reasonable probability. Initially, the escape probability should be high, but it should drop as more symbols are input and decoded, and more information is collected by the modeler about contexts in the particular data being compressed.

⋄ **Exercise 2.50:** The escape is just a symbol of the alphabet, reserved to indicate a context switch. What if the data uses every symbol in the alphabet and none can be reserved? A common example is image compression where a pixel is represented by a byte (256 gray scales or colors). Since pixels can have any values between 0 and 255, what value can be reserved for the escape symbol in this case?

Table 2.70 shows one way of assigning probabilities to the escape symbol (this is variant PPMC of PPM). The table shows the contexts (up to order 2) collected while reading and encoding the 14-symbol string `assanissimassa`. (In the movie "8 1/2," Italian children use this string as a magic spell. They pronounce it **assa-neesee-massa**.) We assume that the alphabet consists of the 26 letters, the blank space, and the escape symbol, a total of 28 symbols. The probability of a symbol in order -1 is thus 1/28. Notice that it takes 5 bits to encode 1 of 28 symbols without compression.

Each context seen in the past is placed in the table in a separate group together with the escape symbol. The order-2 context `as`, e.g., was seen twice in the past and was followed by `s` both times. It is assigned a frequency of 2 and is placed in a group together with the escape symbol, which is assigned frequency 1. The probabilities of `as` and the escape in this group are thus 2/3 and 1/3, respectively. Context `ss` was seen three times, twice followed by `a` and once by `i`. These two occurrences are assigned frequencies 2 and 1, and are placed in a group together with the escape, which is now assigned frequency 2 (because it is in a group of 2 members). The probabilities of the three members of this group are thus 2/5, 1/5, and 2/5, respectively.

The justification for this method of assigning escape probabilities goes like this: suppose that context `abc` was seen ten times in the past and was always followed by `x`. This suggests that the same context will be followed by the same `x` in the future, so the encoder will only rarely have to switch down to a lower context. The escape symbol can thus be assigned the small probability 1/11. However, if every occurrence of context `abc` in the past was followed by a different symbol (suggesting that the data varies a lot), then there is a good chance that the next occurrence will also be followed by a different symbol, forcing the encoder to switch to a lower context (and thus to emit an escape) more often. The escape is thus assigned the higher probability 10/20.

◇ **Exercise 2.51:** Explain the numbers 1/11 and 10/20.

Order 2			Order 1				Order 0		
Context	f	p	Context		f	p	Symbol	f	p
as→s	2	2/3	a→	s	2	2/5	a	4	4/19
esc	1	1/3	a→	n	1	1/5	s	6	6/19
			esc→		2	2/5	n	1	1/19
ss→a	2	2/5					i	2	2/19
ss→i	1	1/5	s→	s	3	3/9	m	1	1/19
esc	2	2/5	s→	a	2	2/9	esc	5	5/19
			s→	i	1	1/9			
sa→n	1	1/2	esc		3	3/9			
esc	1	1/2							
			n→	i	1	1/2			
an→i	1	1/2	esc		1	1/2			
esc	1	1/2							
			i→	s	1	1/4			
ni→s	1	1/2	i→	m	1	1/4			
esc	1	1/2	esc		2	2/4			
is→s	1	1/2	m→	a	1	1/2			
esc	1	1/2	esc		1	1/2			
si→m	1	1/2							
esc	1	1/2							
im→a	1	1/2							
esc	1	1/2							
ma→s	1	1/2							
esc	1	1/2							

Table 2.70: Contexts, Counts (f), and Probabilities (p) for "assanissimassa".

Order 0 consists of the five different symbols asnim seen in the input string, followed by an escape, which is assigned frequency 5. Probabilities thus range from 4/19 (for a) to 5/19 (for the escape symbol).

> Wall Street indexes predicted nine out of the last five recessions.
> —Paul A. Samuelson, *Newsweek* (19 September 1966)

2.18.2 Examples

We are now ready to look at actual examples of new symbols being read and encoded. We assume that the 14-symbol string `assanissimassa` has been completely input and encoded, so the current order-2 context is "sa". Here are four typical cases:

1. The next symbol is n. The PPM encoder finds that sa followed by n has been seen before and has probability 1/2. The n is encoded by the arithmetic encoder with this probability, which takes, since arithmetic encoding normally compresses at or close to the entropy, $-\log_2(1/2) = 1$ bit.

2. The next symbol is s. The PPM encoder finds that sa was not seen before followed by an s. The encoder thus sends the escape symbol to the arithmetic encoder, together with the probability (1/2) predicted by the order-2 context of sa. It thus takes 1 bit to encode this escape. Switching down to order 1, the current context becomes a, and the PPM encoder finds that an a followed by an s was seen before and currently has probability 2/5 assigned. The s is then sent to the arithmetic encoder to be encoded with probability 2/5, which produces another 1.32 bits. In total $1 + 1.32 = 2.32$ bits are generated to encode the s.

3. The next symbol is m. The PPM encoder finds that sa was never seen before followed by an m. It therefore sends the escape symbol to the arithmetic encoder, as in 2 above, generating 1 bit so far. It then switches to order 1, finds that a has never been seen followed by an m, so it sends another escape symbol, this time using the escape probability for the order-1 a, which is 2/5. This is encoded in 1.32 bits. Switching to order 0, the PPM encoder finds m, which has probability 1/19 and sends it to be encoded in $-\log_2(1/19) = 4.25$ bits. The total number of bits produced is thus $1 + 1.32 + 4.25 = 6.57$.

4. The next symbol is d. The PPM encoder switches from order 2 to order 1 to order 0 sending two escapes as in 3 above. Since d hasn't been seen before, it is not found in order 0, and the PPM encoder switches to order -1 after sending a third escape with the escape probability of order 0, 5/19 (this produces $-\log_2(5/19) = 1.93$ bits). The d itself is sent to the arithmetic encoder with its order -1 probability, which is 1/28, so it gets encoded in 4.8 bits. The total number of bits necessary to encode this first d is $1 + 1.32 + 1.93 + 4.8 = 9.05$, more than the 5 bits that would have been necessary without any compression.

⋄ **Exercise 2.52:** Suppose that case 4 above has actually occurred (i.e., the 15th symbol to be input was a d). Show the new state of the order-0 contexts.

⋄ **Exercise 2.53:** Suppose that case 4 above has actually occurred and the 16th symbol is also a d. How many bits would it take to encode this second d?

⋄ **Exercise 2.54:** Show how the results of the four cases above are affected if we assume an alphabet size of 256 symbols.

2.18.3 Exclusion

When switching down from order 2 to order 1, the PPM encoder can use the information found in order 2 in order to exclude certain order-1 cases that are now known to be impossible. This increases the order-1 probabilities and thus improves compression. The same thing can be done when switching down from any order. Here are two detailed examples.

In case 2 above, the next symbol is s. The PPM encoder finds that sa was seen before followed by n but not by s. The encoder sends an escape and switches to order 1. The current context becomes a, and the encoder checks to see whether an a followed by an s was seen before. The answer is yes (with frequency 2), but the fact that sa was seen before followed by n implies that the current symbol cannot be n (if it were, it would be encoded in order 2).

The encoder can thus *exclude* the case of an a followed by n in order-1 contexts [we can say that there is no need to reserve "room" (or "space") for the probability of this case, since it is impossible]. This reduces the total frequency of the order-1 group "a→" from 5 to 4, which increases the probability assigned to s from 2/5 to 2/4. Based on our knowledge from order 2, the s can now be encoded in $-\log_2(2/4) = 1$ bit instead of 1.32 (a total of two bits is produced, since the escape also requires 1 bit).

Another example is case 4 above, modified for exclusions. When switching from order 2 to order 1, the probability of the escape is, as before, 1/2. When in order-1, the case of a followed by n is excluded, increasing the probability of the escape from 2/5 to 2/4. After switching to order 0, both s and n represent impossible cases and can be excluded. This leaves the order-0 with the 4 symbols a, i, m, and escape, with frequencies 4, 2, 1, and 5, respectively. The total frequency is 12, so the escape is assigned probability 5/12 (1.26 bits) instead of the original 5/19 (1.93 bits). This escape is sent to the arithmetic encoder, and the PPM encoder switches to order −1. Here it excludes all five symbols asnim that have already been seen in order 1 and are therefore impossible in order −1. The d can now be encoded with probability $1/(28-5) \approx 0.043$ (4.52 bits instead of 4.8) or $1/(256-5) \approx 0.004$ (7.97 bits instead of 8), depending on the alphabet size.

> Exact and careful model building should embody constraints that the final answer had in any case to satisfy.
>
> —Francis Harry Compton Crick, *What Mad Pursuit*

2.18.4 PPMA and PPMB

The particular method described above for assigning escape probabilities is called PPMC. Two more methods, named PPMA and PPMB, have traditionally been used to assign escape probabilities in PPM. All three methods have been selected based on the vast experience that the developers had with data compression. None of the three is supported by any theory.

Suppose that a group of contexts in Table 2.70 has total frequencies n (excluding the escape symbol). PPMA assigns the escape symbol a probability of $1/(n+1)$. This is equivalent to always assigning it a count of 1. The other members of the group are still assigned their original probabilities of x/n, and these probabilities add up to 1 (not including the escape probability).

PPMB is similar to PPMC with one difference. It assigns a probability to symbol S following context C only after S has been seen **twice** in context C.

This is done by subtracting 1 from the frequency counts. If context abc, e.g., was seen three times, twice followed by x and once by y, then x is assigned probability $(2-1)/3$, and y (which should be assigned probability $(1-1)/3 = 0$) is not assigned any probability (i.e., does not get included in Table 2.70 or its equivalent). Instead, the escape symbol "gets" the two counts subtracted from x and y, and ends up being assigned probability 2/3. This method is based on the belief that "seeing twice is believing."

It should again be noted that the way escape probabilities are assigned in the three methods is based on experience and intuition, not on any underlying theory. Experience with the three variants of PPM shows that none is preferable. They produce compression ratios that normally differ by just a few percent. This is an encouraging result, since it shows that the basic PPM algorithm is robust and is not affected much by the precise way of assigning escape probabilities.

2.18.5 Implementation Details

The main problem in any practical implementation of PPM is to maintain a data structure where all contexts (orders 0 through N) of every symbol read from the input stream are stored and can be located fast. The structure described here is a special type of tree, called a *trie*. This is a tree in which the branching structure at any level is determined by just part of a data item, not by the entire item. In the case of PPM, an order-N context is a string that includes all the shorter contexts of orders $N-1$ through 0, so each context effectively adds just one symbol to the trie.

Figure 2.71 shows how such a trie is constructed for the string "zxzyzxxyzx" assuming $N = 2$. A quick glance shows that the tree grows in width but not in depth. Its depth remains $N+1 = 3$ regardless of how much input data has been read. Its width grows as more and more symbols are input, but not at a constant rate. Sometimes, no new nodes are added, such as in case 10, when the last x is read. At other times, up to three nodes are added, such as in cases 3 and 4, when the second z and the first y are added.

Level 1 of the trie (just below the root) contains one node for each symbol read so far. These are the order-1 contexts. Level 2 contains all the order-2 contexts, and so on. Every context can be found by starting at the root and sliding down to one of the leaves. In case 3, e.g., the two contexts are xz (symbol z preceded by the order-1 context x) and zxz (symbol z preceded by the order-2 context zx). In case 10, there are seven contexts ranging from xxy and xyz on the left to zxz and zyz on the right.

The numbers in the nodes are context counts. The "z,4" on the right branch of case 10 implies that z has been seen 4 times. The "x,3" and "y,1" below it mean that these four occurrences were followed by x three times and by y once. The circled nodes show the different orders of the context of the last symbol added to the trie. In case 3, e.g., the second z has just been read and added to the trie. It was added twice, below the x of the left branch and the x of the right branch (the latter is indicated by the arrow). Also, the count of the original z has been incremented to 2. This shows that the new z follows the two contexts x (of order 1) and zx (order 2).

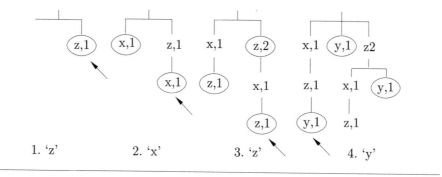

1. 'z'   2. 'x'   3. 'z'   4. 'y'

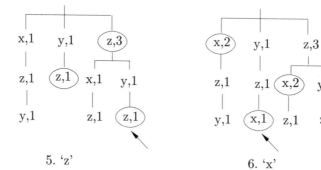

5. 'z'   6. 'x'

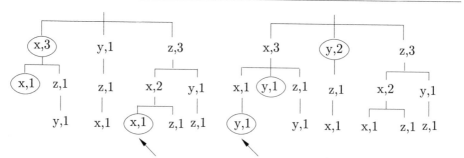

7. 'x'   8. 'y'

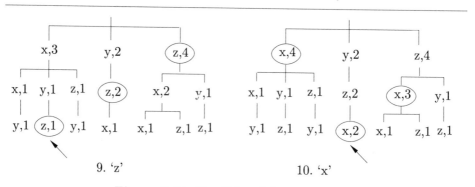

9. 'z'   10. 'x'

Figure 2.71: Ten Tries of "zxzyzxxyzx".

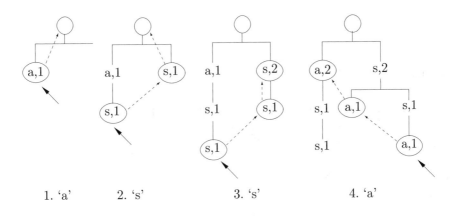

1. 'a'   2. 's'   3. 's'   4. 'a'

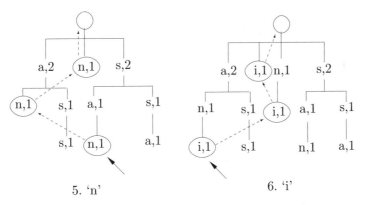

5. 'n'   6. 'i'

Figure 2.72: Part I. First Six Tries of "`assanissimassa`".

It should now be easy for the reader to follow the ten steps of constructing the tree and to understand intuitively how nodes are added and counts updated. Notice that three nodes (or, in general, $N + 1$ nodes, one at each level of the trie) are involved in each step (except the first few steps when the trie hasn't reached its final height yet). Some of the three are new nodes added to the trie; the others have their counts incremented.

The next point that should be discussed is how the algorithm decides which nodes to update and which to add. To simplify the algorithm, one more pointer is added to each node, pointing backward to the node representing the next shorter context. A pointer that points backwards in a tree is called a *vine pointer*.

Figure 2.72 shows the first ten steps in the of construction of the PPM trie for the 14-symbol string "`assanissimassa`". Each of the ten steps shows the new vine pointers (dashed lines in the figure) constructed by the trie updating algorithm while that step was handled. Notice that old vine pointers are not deleted; they are just not shown in later diagrams. In general, a vine pointer points from a node X on level n to a node with the same symbol X on level $n - 1$. All nodes on level 1 point to the root.

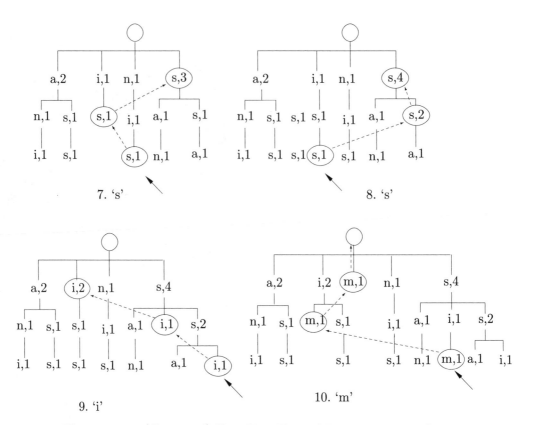

Figure 2.72: (Continued) Next Four Tries of "`assanissimassa`".

A node in the PPM trie thus contains the following fields:

1. The code (ASCII or other) of the symbol.
2. The count.
3. A down pointer, pointing to the leftmost child of the node. In Figure 2.72.10, e.g., the leftmost son of the root is "`a,2`". That of "`a,2`" is "`n,1`", and that of "`s,4`" is "`a,1`".
4. A right pointer, pointing to the next sibling of the node. The root has no right sibling. The next sibling of node "`a,2`" is "`i,2`" and that of "`i,2`" is "`m,1`".
5. A vine pointer. These are shown as arrows lines in Figure 2.72.

◇ **Exercise 2.55:** Complete the construction of this trie and show it after all 14 characters have been input.

At any step during the trie construction, one pointer, called the *base*, is maintained that points to the last node added or updated in the previous step. This is shown as a solid arrow in the figure. Suppose that symbol S has been input and the trie should now be updated. The algorithm for adding and/or updating nodes is as follows:

1. Follow the base pointer to node X. Follow the vine pointer from X to Y (notice that Y can be the root). Add S as a new child node of Y and set the base to point to it. However, if Y already has a child node with S, increment the count of that node by 1 (and also set the base to point to it). Call this node A.

2. Repeat the same step but without updating the base. Follow the vine pointer from Y to Z, add S as a new child node of Z, or update an existing child. Call this node B. If there is no vine pointer from A to B, install one. (If both A and B are old nodes, there will already be a vine pointer from A to B.)

3. Repeat until you have added (or incremented) a node at level 1.

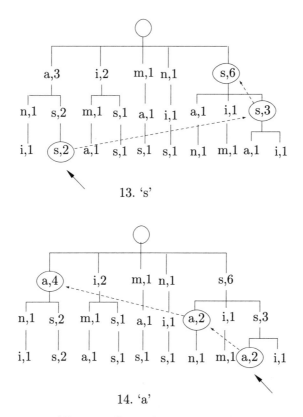

13. 's'

14. 'a'

Figure 2.72: (Continued) Final Two Tries of "assanissimassa".

During these steps the PPM encoder also collects the counts that are necessary to compute the probability of the new symbol S. Figure 2.72 shows the trie after the last two symbols s and a were added. In 2.72.13 a vine pointer was followed from node "s,2", to node "s,3", which already had the two children "a,1" and "i,1". The first child was incremented to "a,2". In 2.72.14, the subtree with the three nodes "s,3", "a,2" and "i,1" tells the encoder that a was seen following context ss twice, and i was seen following the same context once. Since the tree has two children, the escape symbol gets a count of 2, bringing the total count to 5. The probability of a is thus 2/5 (compare with Table 2.70). Notice that steps 11 and 12 are not shown. The serious reader should draw the tries for these steps as a voluntary exercise (i.e., without an answer).

It is now easy to see the reason why this particular trie is so useful. Each time a symbol is input, it takes the algorithm at most $N + 1$ steps to update the trie and collect the necessary counts by going from the base pointer toward the root. Adding a symbol to the trie and encoding it thus takes $O(N)$ steps regardless of the size of the trie. Since N is small (typically 4 or 5), an implementation can be made fast enough for practical use even if the trie is very large. If the user specifies that the algorithm should use exclusions, it becomes more complex, since it has to maintain, at each step, a list of symbols to be excluded.

As has been noted, between 0 and 3 nodes are added to the trie for each input symbol encoded (in general, between 0 and $N + 1$ nodes). The trie can thus grow very large and fill up any available memory space. One elegant solution, adopted in [Moffat 90], is to discard the trie when it gets full and start constructing a new one. In order to bring the new trie "up to speed" fast, the last 2048 input symbols are always saved in a circular buffer in memory and are used to construct the new trie. This reduces the amount of inefficient code generated when tries are replaced.

Bibliography

Cleary, J. G. and I. H. Witten (1984) "Data Compression Using Adaptive Coding and Partial String Matching," *IEEE Transactions on Communications* COM-32(4):396–402, April.

Moffat, A. (1990) "Implementing the PPM Data Compression Scheme," *IEEE Transactions on Communications* COM-38(11):1917–1921, November.

Wright, E. V. (1939) *Gadsby*, Los Angeles, Wetzel. Reprinted by University Microfilms, Ann Arbor, 1991.

Temporal reasoning involves both prediction and explanation. Prediction is projection forwards from causes to effects whilst explanation is projection backwards from effects to causes. That is, prediction is reasoning from events to the properties and events they cause, whilst explanation is reasoning from properties and events to events that may have caused them. Although it is clear that a complete framework for temporal reasoning should provide facilities for solving both prediction and explanation problems, prediction has received far more attention in the temporal reasoning literature than explanation.

—Murray Shanahan, *Proceedings IJCAI 1989*

2.19 Context-Tree Weighting

Whatever the input stream is, text, pixels, sound, or anything else, it can be considered a binary string. Ideal compression (i.e., compression at or very near the entropy of the string) would be achieved if we could use the bits that have been input so far in order to predict with certainty (i.e., with probability 1) the value of the next bit. In practice, the best we can hope for is to use past history to estimate the probability that the next bit will be 1. The context-tree weighting (CTW) method [Willems et al. 95] starts with a given bit-string $b_1^t = b_1 b_2 \ldots b_t$ and the d bits that precede it $c_d = b_{-d} \ldots b_{-2} b_{-1}$ (the context of b_1^t). The two strings c_d and b_1^t constitute the input stream. The method uses a simple algorithm to construct a tree of depth d based on the context, where each node corresponds to a substring of c_d. The first bit b_1 is then input and examined. If it is 1, the tree is updated to include the substrings of $c_d b_1$ and is then used to calculate (or estimate) the probability that b_1 will be 1 given context c_d. If b_1 is zero, the tree is updated differently and the algorithm again calculates (or estimates) the probability that b_1 will be zero given the same context. Bit b_1 and its probability are then sent to an arithmetic encoder, and the process continues with b_2. The context bits themselves are written on the compressed stream in raw format.

The depth d of the context tree is fixed during the entire compression process, and it should depend on the expected correlation among the input bits. If the bits are expected to be highly correlated, a small d may be enough to get good probability predictions and thus good compression.

In thinking of the input as a binary string, it is customary to use the term "source." We think of the bits of the inputs as coming from a certain information source. The source can be *memoryless* or it can have memory. In the former case, each bit is independent of its predecessors. In the latter case, each bit depends on some of its predecessors (and, perhaps, also on its successors, but these cannot be used because they are not available to the decoder), so they are correlated.

We start by looking at a memoryless source where each bit has probability $P_a(1)$ of being a 1 and probability $P_a(0)$ of being a 0. We set $\theta = P_a(1)$, so $P_a(0) = 1 - \theta$ (the subscript a stands for "actual" probability). The probability of a particular string b_1^t being generated by the source is denoted by $P_a(b_1^t)$, and it equals the product

$$P_a(b_1^t) = \prod_{i=1}^{t} P_a(b_i).$$

If string b_1^t contains a zeros and b ones, then $P_a(b_1^t) = (1 - \theta)^a \theta^b$.

Example: Let $t = 5$, $a = 2$, and $b = 3$. The probability of generating a 5-bit binary string with two zeros and three ones is $P_a(b_1^5) = (1 - \theta)^2 \theta^3$. Table 2.73 lists the values of $P_a(b_1^5)$ for seven values of θ from 0 to 1. It is easy to see that the maximum is obtained when $\theta = 3/5$. To understand these values intuitively we examine all 32 5-bit numbers. Ten of them consist of two zeros and three ones, so the probability of generating such a string is $10/32 = 0.3125$ and the probability of generating a particular string out of these 10 is 0.03125. This number is obtained for $\theta = 1/2$.

θ:	0	1/5	2/5	1/2	3/5	4/5	5/5
$P_a(2,3)$:	0	0.00512	0.02304	0.03125	0.03456	0.02048	0

Table 2.73: Seven Values of $P_a(2,3)$.

In real-life situations we don't know the value of θ, so we have to estimate it based on what has been input in the past. Assuming that the immediate past string b_1^t consists of a zeros and b ones, it makes sense to estimate the probability of the next bit being 1 by

$$P_e(b_{t+1} = 1|b_1^t) = \frac{b}{a+b},$$

where the subscript e stands for "estimate" (the expression above is read "the estimated probability that the next bit b_{t+1} will be a 1 given that we have seen string b_1^t is..."). The estimate above is intuitive and cannot handle the case $a = b = 0$. A better estimate, due to Krichevsky and Trofimov [Krichevsky 81], is called KT and is given by

$$P_e(b_{t+1} = 1|b_1^t) = \frac{b+1/2}{a+b+1}.$$

The KT estimate, like the intuitive estimate, predicts a probability of $1/2$ for any case where $a = b$. Unlike the intuitive estimate, however, it also works for the case $a = b = 0$.

The KT Boundary

All over the globe is a dark clay-like layer that was deposited around 65 million years ago. This layer is enriched with the rare element iridium. Older fossils found under this KT layer include many dinosaur species. Above this layer (younger fossils) there are no dinosaur species found. This suggests that something that happened around the same time as the KT boundary was formed killed the dinosaurs. Iridium is found in meteorites, so it is possible that a large iridium-enriched meteorite hit the earth, kicking up much iridium dust into the stratosphere. This dust then spread around the earth via air currents and was deposited on the ground very slowly, later forming the KT boundary.

This event has been called the "KT Impact" because it marks the end of the Cretaceous Period and the beginning of the Tertiary. The letter "K" is used because "C" represents the Carboniferous Period, which ended 215 million years earlier.

⋄ **Exercise 2.56:** Use the KT estimate to calculate the probability that the next bit will be a zero given string b_1^t as the context.

Example: We use the KT estimate to calculate the probability of the 5-bit string 01110. The probability of the first bit being zero is (since there is no context)

$$P_e(0|\text{null}) = P_e(0|_{a=b=0}) = \left(1 - \frac{0+1/2}{0+0+1}\right) = 1/2.$$

The probability of the entire string is the product

$$
\begin{aligned}
P_e(01110) &= P_e(2,3) \\
&= P_e(0|\text{null})P_e(1|0)P_e(1|01)P_e(1|011)P_e(0|0111) \\
&= P_e(0|_{a=b=0})P_e(1|_{a=1,b=0})P_e(1|_{a=b=1})P_e(1|_{a=1,b=2})P_e(0|_{a=1,b=3}) \\
&= \left(1 - \frac{0+1/2}{0+0+1}\right)\cdot\frac{0+1/2}{1+0+1}\cdot\frac{1+1/2}{1+1+1}\cdot\frac{2+1/2}{1+2+1}\cdot\left(1 - \frac{3+1/2}{1+3+1}\right) \\
&= \frac{1}{2}\cdot\frac{1}{4}\cdot\frac{3}{6}\cdot\frac{5}{8}\cdot\frac{3}{10} = \frac{3}{256} \approx 0.01172.
\end{aligned}
$$

In general, the KT estimated probability of a string with a zeros and b ones is

$$P_e(a,b) = \frac{1/2\cdot3/2\cdots(a-1/2)\cdot1/2\cdot3/2\cdots(b-1/2)}{1\cdot2\cdot3\cdots(a+b)}. \tag{2.7}$$

Table 2.74 lists some values of $P_e(a,b)$ calculated by Equation (2.7). Notice that $P_e(a,b) = P_e(b,a)$, so the table is symmetric.

	0	1	2	3	4	5
0	-	1/2	3/8	5/16	35/128	63/256
1	1/2	1/8	1/16	5/128	7/256	21/1024
2	3/8	1/16	3/128	3/256	7/1024	9/2048
3	5/8	5/128	3/256	5/1024	5/2048	45/32768
4	35/128	7/256	7/1024	5/2048	35/32768	35/65536
5	63/256	21/1024	9/2048	45/32768	35/65536	63/262144

Table 2.74: KT Estimates For Some $P_e(a,b)$.

Up until now we have assumed a memoryless source. In such a source the probability θ that the next bit will be a 1 is fixed. Any binary string, including random ones, is generated by such a source with equal probability. Binary strings that have to be compressed in real situations are generally not random and are generated by a non-memoryless source. In such a source θ is not fixed. It varies from bit to bit, and it depends on the past context of the bit. Since a context is a binary string, all the possible past contexts of a bit can be represented by a binary tree. Since a context can be very long, the tree can include just some of the last bits of the context, to be called the *suffix*. As an example consider the 42-bit string

$$S = 000101100111010110001101001011110010101100.$$

Let's assume that we are interested in suffixes of length 3. The first 3 bits of S don't have long enough suffixes, so they are written raw on the compressed stream. Next we examine the 3-bit suffix of each of the last 39 bits of S and count how many times each suffix is followed by a 1 and how many times by a 0. Suffix 001, for example, is followed twice by a 1 and three times by a 0. Figure 2.75a shows the entire suffix tree of depth 3 for this case (in general, this is not a complete binary tree). The suffixes are read from the leaves to the root, and each leaf is labeled with the probability of that suffix being followed by a 1-bit. Whenever the three most recently read bits are 001, the encoder starts at the root of the tree and follows the edges for 1, 0, and 0. It finds 2/5 at the leaf, so it should predict a probability of 2/5 that the next bit will be a 1, and a probability of $1 - 2/5$ that it will be a 0. The encoder then inputs the next bit, examines it, and sends it, with the proper probability, to be arithmetically encoded.

Figure 2.75b shows another simple tree of depth 2 that corresponds to the set of suffixes 00, 10, and 1. Each suffix (i.e., each leaf of the tree) is labeled with a probability θ. Thus, for example, the probability that a bit of 1 will follow the suffix $\ldots 10$ is 0.3. The tree is the *model* of the source, and the probabilities are the *parameters*. In practice, neither the model nor the parameters are known, so the CTW algorithm has to estimate them.

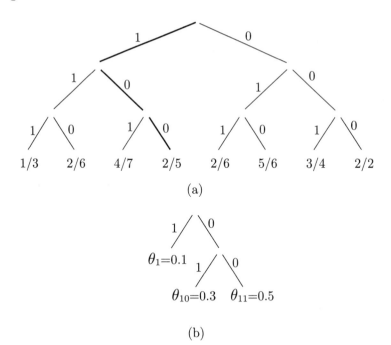

(a)

(b)

Figure 2.75: Two Suffix Trees.

Next we get one step closer to real-life situations. We assume that the model is known and the parameters are unknown, and we use the KT estimator to estimate the parameters. As an example we use the model of Figure 2.75b but without the probabilities. We use the string $10|0100110 = 10|b_1b_2b_3b_4b_5b_6b_7$, where the first two bits are the suffix, to illustrate how the probabilities are estimated with the KT estimator. Bits b_1 and b_4 have suffix 10, so the probability for leaf 10 of the tree is estimated as the KT probability of substring $b_1b_4 = 00$, which is $P_e(2,0) = 3/8$ (two zeros and no ones) from Table 2.74. Bits b_2 and b_5 have suffix 00, so the probability for leaf 00 of the tree is estimated as the KT probability of substring $b_2b_5 = 11$, which is $P_e(0,2) = 3/8$ (no zeros and two ones) from Table 2.74. Bits $b_3 = 0$, $b_6 = 1$, and $b_7 = 0$ have suffix 1, so the probability for leaf 1 of the tree is estimated as $P_e(2,1) = 1/16$ (two zeros and a single one) from Table 2.74. The probability of the entire string 0100110 given the suffix 10 is thus the product

$$\frac{3}{8} \cdot \frac{3}{8} \cdot \frac{1}{16} = \frac{9}{1024} \approx .0088.$$

◇ **Exercise 2.57:** Use this example to estimate the probabilities of the five strings 0, 00, 000, 0000, and 00000, assuming that each is preceded by the suffix 00.

In the last step we assume that the model, as well as the parameters, are unknown. We construct a binary tree of depth d. The root corresponds to the null context, and each node s corresponds to the substring of bits that were input following context s. Each node thus splits up the string. Figure 2.76a shows an example of a context tree for the string $10|0100110 = 10|b_1b_2b_3b_4b_5b_6b_7$.

Figure 2.76b shows how each node s contains the pair (a_s, b_s), the number of zeros and ones in the string associated with s. The root, for example, is associated with the entire string, so it contains the pair $(4,3)$. We still have to calculate or estimate a weighted probability P_w^s for each node s, the probability that should be sent to the arithmetic encoder to encode the string associated with s. This calculation is, in fact, the central part of the CTW algorithm. We start at the leaves because the only thing available in a leaf is the pair (a_s, b_s); there is no suffix. The best assumption that can therefore be made is that the substring consisting of a_s zeros and b_s ones that's associated with leaf s is memoryless, and the best weighted probability that can be defined for the node is the KT estimated probability $P_e(a_s, b_s)$. We therefore define

$$P_w^s \stackrel{\text{def}}{=} P_e(a_s, b_s) \quad \text{if depth}(s) = d. \tag{2.8}$$

Using the weighted probabilities for the leaves, we work our way recursively up the tree and calculate weighted probabilities for the internal nodes. For an internal node s we know a little more than for a leaf, since such a node has one or two children. The children, which are denoted by s_0 and s_1, have already been assigned weighted probabilities. We consider two cases. If the substring associated with suffix s is memoryless, then $P_e(a_s, b_s)$ is a good weighted probability for it. Otherwise the CTW method claims that the product $P_w^{s_0} P_w^{s_1}$ of the weighted probabilities of the child nodes is a good coding probability (a missing child node is considered, in such a case, to have weighted probability 1).

Since we don't know which of the above cases is true for a given internal node s, the best that we can do is to assign s a weighted probability that's the average

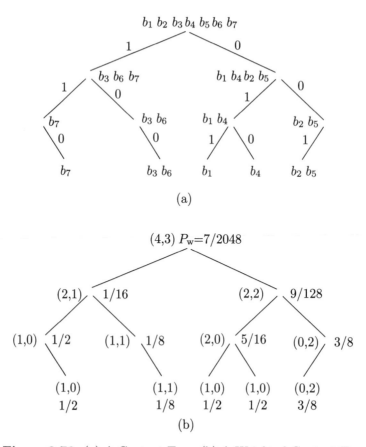

(a)

(b)

Figure 2.76: (a) A Context Tree. (b) A Weighted Context Tree.

of the two cases above, i.e.,

$$P_w^s \stackrel{\text{def}}{=} \frac{P_e(a_s, b_s) + P_w^{s_0} P_w^{s_1}}{2} \quad \text{if depth}(s) < d. \tag{2.9}$$

The last step that needs to be described is the way the context tree is updated when the next bit is input. Suppose that we have already input and encoded the string $b_1 b_2 \ldots b_{t-1}$. Thus, we have already constructed a context tree of depth d for this string, we have used Eqs. (2.8) and (2.9) to calculate weighted probabilities for the entire tree, and the root of the tree already contains a certain weighted probability. We now input the next bit b_t and examine it. Depending on what it is, we need to update the context tree for the string $b_1 b_2 \ldots b_{t-1} b_t$. The weighted probability at the root of the new tree will then be sent to the arithmetic encoder, together with bit b_t, and will be used to encode b_t.

If $b_t = 0$, then updating the tree is done by (1) incrementing the a_s counts for all nodes s, (2) updating the estimated probabilities $P_e(a_s, b_s)$ for all the nodes, and

(3) updating the weighted probabilities $P_w(a_s, b_s)$ for all the nodes. If $b_t = 1$, then all the b_s should be incremented, followed by updating the estimated and weighted probabilities as above. Figure 2.77a shows how the context tree of Figure 2.76b is updated when $b_t = 0$.

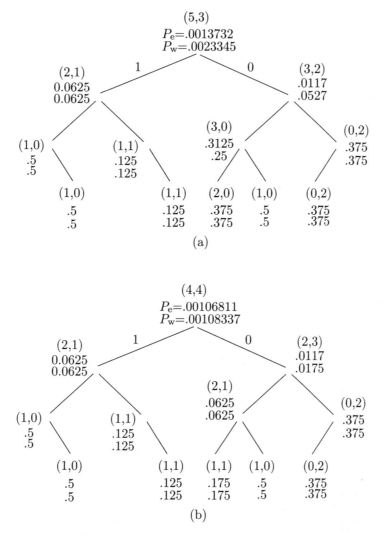

Figure 2.77: Context Trees For $b_t = 0, 1$.

⬦ **Exercise 2.58:** Show how the context tree of Figure 2.76b is updated when $b_t = 1$.

⬦ **Exercise 2.59:** Construct the context trees with depth 3 for the strings 000|0, 000|00, 000|1, and 000|11.

The depth d of the context tree is selected by the user (or is built into both encoder and decoder) and does not change during the compression job. The tree has to be updated for each input bit processed, but this requires updating at most $d+1$ nodes. The number of operations needed to process n input bits is thus linear in n.

2.19.1 CTW for Text Compression

The CTW method has so far been developed for compressing binary strings. In practice, we are normally interested in compressing text, image, and sound streams, and this section discusses one approach to applying CTW to text compression.

Each ASCII character consists of seven bits, and all 128 7-bit combinations are used. However, some combinations (such as E and T) are more common than others (such as Z, <, and certain control characters). Also, certain character pairs and triplets (such as TH and THE) appear more often than others. We therefore claim that if b_t is a bit in a certain ASCII character X, then the $t-1$ bits $b_1 b_2 \ldots b_{t-1}$ preceding it can act as context (even if some of them are not even parts of X but belong to characters preceding X). Experience shows that good results are obtained (1) with contexts of size 12, (2) when seven context trees are used, each to construct a model for one of the seven bits, and (3) if the original KT estimate is modified to the *zero-redundancy* estimate, defined by

$$P_e^z(a,b) \stackrel{\text{def}}{=} \frac{1}{2} P_e(a,b) + \frac{1}{4}\vartheta(a=0) + \frac{1}{4}\vartheta(b=0),$$

where $\vartheta(\text{true}) \stackrel{\text{def}}{=} 1$ and $\vartheta(\text{false}) \stackrel{\text{def}}{=} 0$.

Another experimental feature is a change in the definition of the weighted probabilities. The original definition, Equation (2.9), is used for the two trees on the ASCII borders (i.e., the ones for bits 1 and 7 of each ASCII code). The weighted probabilities for the five context trees for bits 2–6 are defined by $P_s^w = P_w^{s_0} P_w^{s_1}$.

This produces typical compression of 1.8 to 2.3 bits/character on the Calgary Corpus.

Paul Volf [Volf 97] has proposed other approaches to CTW text compression.

Bibliography

Krichevsky, R. E. and V. K. Trofimov (1981) "The Performance of Universal Coding," *IEEE Transactions on Information Theory*, IT-27:199–207, March.

Volf, Paul A. J. (1997) "A Context-Tree Weighting Algorithm for Text Generating Sources," in Storer, James A. (ed.), *DCC '97: Data Compression Conference*, Los Alamitos, CA, IEEE Computer Society Press, pp. 132–139, (Poster).

Willems, F. M. J., Y. M. Shtarkov and Tj. J. Tjalkens (1995) "The Context-Tree Weighting Method: Basic Properties," *IEEE Transactions on Information Theory*, IT-41:653–664, May.

> The excitement that a gambler feels when making a bet is equal to the amount he might win times the probability of winning it.
>
> —Blaise Pascal (1623–1662)

3
Dictionary Methods

Statistical compression methods use a statistical model of the data, and the quality of compression they achieve depends on how good that model is. Dictionary-based compression methods do not use a statistical model, nor do they use variable-size codes. Instead they select strings of symbols and encode each string as a *token* using a dictionary. The dictionary holds strings of symbols and it may be static or dynamic (adaptive). The former is permanent, sometimes allowing the addition of strings but no deletions, whereas the latter holds strings previously found in the input stream, allowing for additions and deletions of strings as new input is being read.

The simplest example of a static dictionary is a dictionary of the English language used to compress English text. Imagine a dictionary containing perhaps half a million words (without their definitions). A word (a string of symbols terminated by a space or a punctuation mark) is read from the input stream and the dictionary is searched. If a match is found, an index to the dictionary is written into the output stream. Otherwise, the uncompressed word itself is written. (This is an example of *logical compression*.)

As a result, the output stream contains indexes and raw words, and we need to distinguish between them. One way to do this is to use an extra bit in every item written. In principle, a 19-bit index is sufficient to specify an item in a $2^{19} = 524,288$-word dictionary. Thus, when a match is found, we can write a 20-bit token consisting of a flag bit (perhaps a zero) followed by a 19-bit index. When no match is found, a flag of 1 is written, followed by the size of the unmatched word, followed by the word itself.

Example: Assuming that the word **bet** is found in dictionary entry 1025, it is encoded as the 20-bit number 0|0000000010000000001. Assuming that the word **xet** is not found, it is encoded as 1|0000011|01111000|01100101|01110100. This is a 4-byte number where the 7-bit field 0000011 indicates that three more bytes follow.

Assuming that the size is written as a 7-bit number, and that an average word size is five characters, an uncompressed word occupies, on average, 6 bytes (= 48 bits) in the output stream. Compressing 48 bits into 20 is excellent, provided that it happens often enough. Thus, we have to answer the question; How many matches are needed in order to have overall compression? We denote the probability of a match (the case where the word is found in the dictionary) by P. After reading and compressing N words, the size of the output stream will be $N[20P + 48(1 - P)] = N[48 - 28P]$ bits. The size of the input stream is (assuming five characters per word) $40N$ bits. Compression is achieved when $N[48 - 28P] < 40N$, which implies $P > 0.29$. We need a matching rate of 29% or better to achieve compression.

◇ **Exercise 3.1:** What compression factor do we get with $P = 0.9$?

As long as the input stream consists of English text, most words will be found in a 500,000-word dictionary. Other types of data, however, may not do that well. A file containing the source code of a computer program may contain "words" such as cout, xor, and malloc that may not be found in an English dictionary. A binary file normally contains gibberish when viewed in ASCII, so very few matches may be found, resulting in considerable expansion instead of compression.

This shows that a static dictionary is not a good choice for a general-purpose compressor. It may, however, be a good choice for a special-purpose one. Consider a chain of hardware stores, for example. Their files may contain words such as nut, bolt, and paint many times, but words such as peanut, lightning, and painting will be rare. Special-purpose compression software for such a company may benefit from a small, specialized dictionary containing, perhaps, just a few hundred words. The computers in each branch would have a copy of the dictionary, making it easy to compress files and send them between stores and offices in the chain.

In general, an adaptive dictionary-based method is preferable. Such a method can start with an empty dictionary or with a small, default dictionary, add words to it as they are found in the input stream, and delete old words since a big dictionary means slow search. Such a method consists of a loop where each iteration starts by reading the input stream and breaking it up (parsing it) into words or phrases. It then should search the dictionary for each word and, if a match is found, write a token on the output stream. Otherwise, the uncompressed word should be written and also added to the dictionary. The last step in each iteration checks to see whether an old word should be deleted from the dictionary. This may sound complicated but it has two advantages:

1. It involves string search and match operations, rather than numerical computations. Many programmers prefer that.

2. The decoder is simple (this is an asymmetric compression method). In statistical compression methods, the decoder is normally the exact opposite of the encoder (symmetric compression). In an adaptive dictionary-based method, however, the decoder has to read its input stream, determine whether the current item is a token or uncompressed data, use tokens to obtain data from the dictionary, and output the final, uncompressed data. It does not have to parse the input stream in a complex way, and it does not have to search the dictionary to find matches. Many programmers like that, too.

Having one's name attached to a scientific discovery, technique, or phenomenon is considered a special honor in science. Having one's name associated with an entire field of science is even more so. This is what happened to Jacob Ziv and Abraham Lempel. In the 1970s these two researchers developed the first methods, LZ77 and LZ78, for dictionary-based compression. Their ideas have been a source of inspiration to many researchers, who generalized, improved, and combined them with RLE and statistical methods to form many commonly used lossless compression methods for text, images, and sound. This chapter describes the most common LZ compression methods used today and shows how they were developed from the basic ideas of Ziv and Lempel.

> I love the dictionary, Kenny, it's the only book with the words in the right place
> —Paul Reynolds as Colin Mathews in *Press Gang* (1989)

3.1 String Compression

In general, compression methods based on strings of symbols can be more efficient than methods that compress individual symbols. To understand this, the reader should first review Exercise 2.4. This exercise shows that in principle, better compression is possible if the symbols of the alphabet have very different probabilities of occurrence. We use a simple example to show that the probabilities of strings of symbols vary more than the probabilities of the individual symbols constituting the strings.

We start with a 2-symbol alphabet a_1 and a_2, with probabilities $P_1 = 0.8$ and $P_2 = 0.2$, respectively. The average probability is 0.5, and we can get an idea of the variance (how much the individual probabilities deviate from the average) by calculating the sum of absolute differences $|0.8 - 0.5| + |0.2 - 0.5| = 0.6$. Any variable-size code would assign 1-bit codes to the two symbols, so the average size of the code is 1 bit per symbol.

We now generate all the strings of two symbols. There are four of them, shown in Table 3.1a, together with their probabilities and a set of Huffman codes. The average probability is 0.25, so a sum of absolute differences similar to the one above yields

$$|0.64 - 0.25| + |0.16 - 0.25| + |0.16 - 0.25| + |0.04 - 0.25| = 0.78.$$

The average size of the Huffman code is $1 \times 0.64 + 2 \times 0.16 + 3 \times 0.16 + 3 \times 0.04 = 1.56$ bits per string, which is 0.78 bits per symbol.

In the next step we similarly create all eight strings of three symbols. They are shown in Table 3.1b, together with their probabilities and a set of Huffman codes. The average probability is 0.125, so a sum of absolute differences similar to the ones above yields

$$|0.512 - 0.125| + 3|0.128 - 0.125| + 3|0.032 - 0.125| + |0.008 - 0.125| = 0.792.$$

String	Probability	Code
a_1a_1	$0.8 \times 0.8 = 0.64$	0
a_1a_2	$0.8 \times 0.2 = 0.16$	11
a_2a_1	$0.2 \times 0.8 = 0.16$	100
a_2a_2	$0.2 \times 0.2 = 0.04$	101

(a)

Str. size	Variance of prob.	Avg. size of code
1	0.6	1
2	0.78	0.78
3	0.792	0.728

(c)

String	Probability	Code
$a_1a_1a_1$	$0.8 \times 0.8 \times 0.8 = 0.512$	0
$a_1a_1a_2$	$0.8 \times 0.8 \times 0.2 = 0.128$	100
$a_1a_2a_1$	$0.8 \times 0.2 \times 0.8 = 0.128$	101
$a_1a_2a_2$	$0.8 \times 0.2 \times 0.2 = 0.032$	11100
$a_2a_1a_1$	$0.2 \times 0.8 \times 0.8 = 0.128$	110
$a_2a_1a_2$	$0.2 \times 0.8 \times 0.2 = 0.032$	11101
$a_2a_2a_1$	$0.2 \times 0.2 \times 0.8 = 0.032$	11110
$a_2a_2a_2$	$0.2 \times 0.2 \times 0.2 = 0.008$	11111

(b)

Table 3.1: Probabilities and Huffman Codes for a Two-Symbol Alphabet.

The average size of the Huffman code in this case is $1 \times 0.512 + 3 \times 3 \times 0.128 + 3 \times 5 \times 0.032 + 5 \times 0.008 = 2.184$ bits per string, which equals 0.728 bits per symbol.

As we keep generating longer and longer strings, the probabilities of the strings differ more and more from their average, and the average code size gets better (Table 3.1c). This is why a compression method that compresses strings, rather than individual symbols, can, in principle, yield better results. This is also the reason why the various dictionary-based methods are in general better and more popular than the Huffman method and its variants (see also Section 4.12). The above conclusion is a fundamental result of rate-distortion theory, that part of information theory that deals with data compression.

3.2 LZ77 (Sliding Window)

The main idea of this method (which is sometimes referred to as LZ1) [Ziv 77] is to use part of the previously seen input stream as the dictionary. The encoder maintains a window to the input stream and shifts the input in that window from right to left as strings of symbols are being encoded. The method is thus based on a *sliding window*. The window below is divided into two parts. The part on the left is called the *search buffer*. This is the current dictionary, and it always includes symbols that have recently been input and encoded. The part on the right is the *look-ahead buffer*, containing text yet to be encoded. In practical implementations the search buffer is some thousands of bytes long, while the look-ahead buffer is only tens of bytes long. The vertical bar between the t and the e below represents the current dividing line between the two buffers. We thus assume that the text "sir␣sid␣eastman␣easily␣t" has already been compressed, while the text "eases␣sea␣sick␣seals" still needs to be compressed.

← coded text... $\boxed{\text{sir␣sid␣eastman␣easily␣t}\,|\,\text{eases␣sea␣sick␣seals}}$ ... ← text to be read

The encoder scans the search buffer backwards (from right to left) looking for a match to the first symbol e in the look-ahead buffer. It finds one at the e of the word `easily`. This `e` is at a distance (offset) of 8 from the end of the search buffer. The encoder then matches as many symbols following the two `e`'s as possible. Three symbols `eas` match in this case, so the length of the match is 3. The encoder then continues the backward scan, trying to find longer matches. In our case, there is one more match, at the word `eastman`, with offset 16, and it has the same length. The encoder selects the longest match or, if they are all the same length, the last one found and prepares the token (16, 3, "e").

Selecting the last match, rather than the first one, simplifies the encoder, since it only has to keep track of the last match found. It is interesting to note that selecting the first match, while making the program somewhat more complex, also has an advantage. It selects the smallest offset. It would seem that this is not an advantage, since a token should have room for the largest possible offset. However, it is possible to follow LZ77 with Huffman, or some other statistical coding of the tokens, where small offsets are assigned shorter codes. This method, proposed by Bernd Herd, is called LZH. Having many small offsets implies better compression in LZH.

⋄ **Exercise 3.2:** How does the decoder know whether the encoder selects the first match or the last match?

In general, an LZ77 token has three parts: offset, length, and next symbol in the look-ahead buffer (which, in our case, is the **second** `e` of the word `teases`). This token is written on the output stream, and the window is shifted to the right (or, alternatively, the input stream is moved to the left) four positions: three positions for the matched string and one position for the next symbol.

$$\ldots \mathtt{sir}_\sqcup \boxed{\mathtt{sid}_\sqcup\mathtt{eastman}_\sqcup\mathtt{easily}_\sqcup\mathtt{tease} \mid \mathtt{s}_\sqcup\mathtt{sea}_\sqcup\mathtt{sick}_\sqcup\mathtt{seals}\ldots} \ldots$$

If the backward search yields no match, an LZ77 token with zero offset and length and with the unmatched symbol is written. This is also the reason a token has to have a third component. Tokens with zero offset and length are common at the beginning of any compression job, when the search buffer is empty or almost empty. The first five steps in encoding our example are the following:

	`sir`$_\sqcup$`sid`$_\sqcup$`eastman`$_\sqcup$	⟹ (0,0,"s")
`s`	`ir`$_\sqcup$`sid`$_\sqcup$`eastman`$_\sqcup$`e`	⟹ (0,0,"i")
`si`	`r`$_\sqcup$`sid`$_\sqcup$`eastman`$_\sqcup$`ea`	⟹ (0,0,"r")
`sir`	$_\sqcup$`sid`$_\sqcup$`eastman`$_\sqcup$`eas`	⟹ (0,0,"$_\sqcup$")
`sir`$_\sqcup$	`sid`$_\sqcup$`eastman`$_\sqcup$`easi`	⟹ (4,2,"d")

⋄ **Exercise 3.3:** What are the next two steps?

Clearly, a token of the form $(0, 0, \ldots)$, which encodes a single symbol, does not provide good compression. It is easy to estimate its length. The size of the offset is $\lceil \log_2 S \rceil$, where S is the length of the search buffer. In practice, the search buffer may be a few thousand bytes long, so the offset size is typically 10–12 bits. The size of the "length" field is similarly $\lceil \log_2(L - 1) \rceil$, where L is the length of the look-ahead buffer (see below for the -1). In practice, the look-ahead buffer is only a few tens of bytes long, so the size of the "length" field is just a few bits. The size of the "symbol" field is typically 8 bits, but in general, it is $\lceil \log_2 A \rceil$, where A is the alphabet size. The total size of the 1-symbol token $(0, 0, \ldots)$ may typically be $11 + 5 + 8 = 24$ bits, much longer than the raw 8-bit size of the (single) symbol it encodes.

Here is an example showing why the "length" field may be longer than the size of the look-ahead buffer:

$$\ldots \text{Mr.}\underline{\ }\boxed{\text{alf}\underline{\ }\text{eastman}\underline{\ }\text{easily}\underline{\ }\text{grows}\underline{\ }\text{alf}}\,\boxed{\text{alfa}\underline{\ }\text{in}\underline{\ }\text{his}\underline{\ }}\text{garden}\ldots \;.$$

The first symbol a in the look-ahead buffer matches the 5 a's in the search buffer. It seems that the two extreme a's match with a length of 3 and the encoder should select the last (leftmost) of them and create the token (28,3,"a"). In fact, it creates the token (3,4,"␣"). The four-symbol string alfa in the look-ahead buffer is matched to the last three symbols alf in the search buffer **and** the first symbol a in the look-ahead buffer. The reason for this is that the decoder can handle such a token naturally, without any modifications. It starts at position 3 of its search buffer and copies the next four symbols, one by one, extending its buffer to the right. The first three symbols are copies of the old buffer contents, and the fourth one is a copy of the first of those three. The next example is even more convincing (and only somewhat contrived):

$$\cdots \boxed{\text{alf}\underline{\ }\text{eastman}\underline{\ }\text{easily}\underline{\ }\text{yells}\underline{\ }\text{A}}\,\boxed{\text{AAAAAAAAA}}\text{AAAAAH}\ldots \;.$$

The encoder creates the token (1,9,"A"), matching the first nine copies of A in the look-ahead buffer and including the tenth A. This is why, in principle, the length of a match can be up to the size of the look-ahead buffer minus 1.

The decoder is much simpler than the encoder (LZ77 is thus an asymmetric compression method). It has to maintain a buffer, equal in size to the encoder's window. The decoder inputs a token, finds the match in its buffer, writes the match and the third token field on the output stream, and shifts the matched string and the third field into the buffer. This implies that LZ77, or any of its variants, is useful in cases where a file is compressed once (or just a few times) and is decompressed often. A rarely used archive of compressed files is a good example.

At first it seems that this method does not make any assumptions about the input data. Specifically, it does not pay attention to any symbol frequencies. A little thinking, however, shows that because of the nature of the sliding window, the LZ77 method always compares the look-ahead buffer to the recently input text in the search buffer and never to text that was input long ago (and has thus been flushed out of the search buffer). The method thus implicitly assumes that patterns in the input data occur close together. Data that satisfies this assumption will compress well.

The basic LZ77 method was improved in several ways by researchers and programmers during the 1980s and 1990s. One way to improve it is to use variable-size "offset" and "length" fields in the tokens. Another way is to increase the sizes of both buffers. Increasing the size of the search buffer makes it possible to find better matches, but the tradeoff is an increased search time. A large search buffer thus requires a more sophisticated data structure that allows for fast search (Section 3.10.2). A third improvement has to do with sliding the window. The simplest approach is to move all the text in the window to the left after each match. A faster method is to replace the linear window with a *circular queue*, where sliding the window is done by resetting two pointers (Section 3.2.1). Yet another improvement is adding an extra bit (a flag) to each token, thereby eliminating the third field (Section 3.3).

3.2.1 A Circular Queue

The circular queue is a basic data structure. Physically, it is an array, but it is used differently. Figure 3.2 illustrates a simple example. It shows a 16-byte array with characters being appended at the "end" and others being deleted from the "start." Both the start and end positions move, and two pointers, s and e, point to them all the time. In (a) there are the 8 characters sid␣east, with the rest of the buffer empty. In (b) all 16 bytes are occupied, and e points to the end of the buffer. In (c), the first letter s has been deleted and the l of easily inserted. Notice how pointer e is now located *to the left* of s. In (d), the two letters id have been deleted just by moving the s pointer; the characters themselves are still present in the array but have been effectively deleted. In (e), the two characters y␣ have been appended and the e pointer moved. In (f), the pointers show that the buffer ends at teas and starts at tman. Inserting new symbols into the circular queue and moving the pointers is thus equivalent to shifting the contents of the queue. No actual shifting or moving is necessary, though.

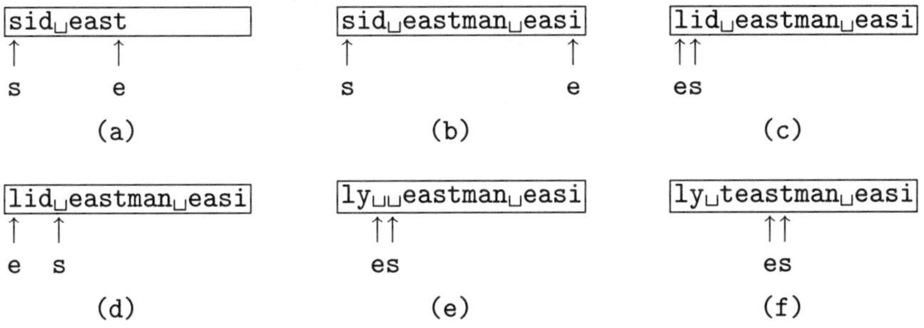

Figure 3.2: A Circular Queue.

More information on circular queues can be found in most texts on data structures.

> From the dictionary
> Sliding. To move over a surface while maintaining smooth, continuous contact.

Bibliography

Ziv, J. and A. Lempel (1977) "A Universal Algorithm for Sequential Data Compression," *IEEE Transactions on Information Theory*, IT-23(3):337–343.

3.3 LZSS

This version of LZ77 was developed by Storer and Szymanski in 1982 [Storer 82]. It improves LZ77 in three ways: (1) It holds the look-ahead buffer in a circular queue, (2) it holds the search buffer (the dictionary) in a binary search tree, and (3) it creates tokens with two fields instead of three.

A binary search tree is a binary tree where the left subtree of every node A contains nodes smaller than A, and the right subtree contains nodes greater than A. Since the nodes of our binary search trees contain strings, we first need to know how to compare two strings and decide which one is "bigger." This is easily understood by imagining that the strings appear in a dictionary or a lexicon, where they are sorted alphabetically. Clearly, the string `rote` precedes the string `said` since `r` precedes `s` (even though `o` follows `a`), so we consider `rote` smaller than `said`. This is called *lexicographic order* (ordering strings lexicographically).

What about the string "␣abc"? Most modern computers use ASCII codes to represent characters (although some use Unicode, discussed below, and some older IBM, Amdahl, Fujitsu, and Siemens mainframe computers use the old, 8-bit EBCDIC code developed by IBM), and in ASCII the code of a blank space precedes those of the letters, so a string that starts with a space will be smaller than any string that starts with a letter. In general, the *collating sequence* of the computer determines the sequence of characters arranged from small to big. Figure 3.3 shows two examples of binary search trees.

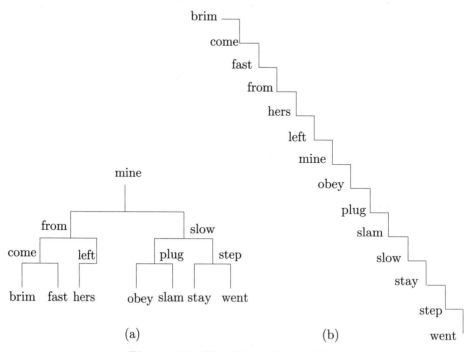

Figure 3.3: Two Binary Search Trees.

Unicode

A new international standard code, the Unicode, has been proposed, and is being developed by an international Unicode organization (`www.unicode.org`). Unicode uses 16-bit codes for its characters, so it provides for $2^{16} = 64K = 65,536$ codes. (Doubling the size of a code thus more than doubles the number of possible codes.) Unicode includes all the ASCII codes plus codes for characters in foreign languages (including complete sets of Korean, Japanese, and Chinese characters) and many mathematical and other symbols. Currently, about 39,000 out of the 65,536 possible codes have been assigned, so there is room for adding more symbols in the future.

The Microsoft Windows NT operating system has adopted Unicode, as have also AT&T Plan 9 and Lucent Inferno.

Notice the difference between the (almost) balanced tree in Figure 3.3a and the skewed one in Figure 3.3b. They contain the same 14 nodes, but they look and behave very differently. In the balanced tree any node can be found in at most four steps. In the skewed tree up to 14 steps may be needed. In either case, the maximum number of steps necessary to locate a node equals the height of the tree. For a skewed tree (which is really the same as a linked list), the height is the number of elements n; for a balanced tree, the height is $\lceil \log_2 n \rceil$, a much smaller number. More information on the properties of binary search trees may be found in any text on data structures.

Here is an example showing how a binary search tree can be used to speed up the search of the dictionary. We assume an input stream with the short sentence "sid␣eastman␣clumsily␣teases␣sea␣sick␣seals". To keep the example simple, we assume a window of a 16-byte search buffer followed by a 5-byte look-ahead buffer. After the first $16 + 5$ characters have been input, the sliding window is

$$\boxed{\texttt{sid␣eastman␣clum}}\texttt{sily␣teases␣sea␣sick␣seals}$$

with the string "teases␣sea␣sick␣seals" still waiting to be input.

The encoder scans the search buffer, creating the twelve five-character strings of Table 3.4 (twelve since $16 - 5 + 1 = 12$), which are inserted into the binary search tree, each with its offset.

The first symbol in the look-ahead buffer is s, so the encoder searches the tree for strings that start with an s. Two are found, at offsets 16 and 10, and the first of them, sid␣e (at offset 16) provides a longer match.

(We now have to sidetrack and discuss the case where a string in the tree completely matches that in the look-ahead buffer. In that case the encoder should go back to the search buffer, to attempt to match longer strings. In principle, the maximum length of a match can be $L - 1$.)

In our example, the match is of length 2, and the 2-field token $(16, 2)$ is emitted. The encoder now has to slide the window two positions to the right, and update the tree. The new window is

$$\texttt{si}\boxed{\texttt{d␣eastman␣clumsi}}\texttt{ly␣te}\texttt{ases␣sea␣sick␣seals}$$

sid␣e 16
id␣ea 15
d␣eas 14
␣east 13
eastm 12
astma 11
stman 10
tman␣ 09
man␣c 08
an␣cl 07
n␣clu 06
␣clum 05

Table 3.4: Five-Character Strings.

The tree should be updated by deleting strings sid␣e and id␣ea, and inserting the new strings clums and lumsi. If a longer, k-letter, string is matched, the window has to be shifted k positions, and the tree should be updated by deleting k strings and adding k new strings, but which ones?

A little thinking shows that the k strings to be deleted are the first ones in the search buffer before the shift, and the k strings to be added are the last ones in it after the shift. A simple procedure for updating the tree is to prepare a string consisting of the first five letters in the search buffer, find it in the tree, and delete it. Then slide the buffer one position to the right (or shift the data to the left), prepare a string consisting of the last five letters in the search buffer, and append it to the tree. This should be repeated k times.

Since each update deletes and adds the same number of strings, the tree size never changes. It always contains T nodes, where T is the length of the search buffer minus the length of the look-ahead buffer plus 1 ($T = S - L + 1$). The shape of the tree, however, may change significantly. As nodes are being added and deleted, the tree may change its shape between a completely skewed tree (the worst case for searching) and a balanced one, the ideal shape for searching.

The third improvement of LZSS over LZ77 is in the tokens created by the encoder. An LZSS token contains just an offset and a length. If no match was found, the encoder emits the uncompressed code of the next symbol instead of the wasteful three-field token $(0, 0, \ldots)$. To distinguish between tokens and uncompressed codes, each is preceded by a single bit (a flag).

In practice, the search buffer may be a few thousand bytes long, so the offset field would typically be 11–13 bits. The size of the look-ahead buffer should be selected such that the total size of a token would be 16 bits (2 bytes). For example, if the search buffer size is 2 Kbyte ($= 2^{11}$), then the look-ahead buffer should be 32 bytes long ($= 2^5$). The offset field would be 11 bits long and the length field, 5 bits (the size of the look-ahead buffer). With this choice of buffer sizes the encoder will emit either 2-byte tokens or 1-byte uncompressed ASCII codes. But what about the flag bits? A good practical idea is to collect eight output items (tokens and ASCII codes) in a small buffer, then output one byte consisting of the eight flags, followed by the eight items (which are 1 or 2 bytes long each).

3.3.1 Deficiencies

Before we discuss LZ78, let's summarize the deficiencies of LZ77 and its variants. It has already been mentioned that LZ77 uses the built-in implicit assumption that patterns in the input data occur close together. Data streams that don't satisfy this assumption compress poorly. A common example is text where a certain word, say "economy", occurs often but is uniformly distributed throughout the text. When this word is shifted into the look-ahead buffer, its previous occurrence may have already been shifted out of the search buffer. A better algorithm would save commonly occurring strings in the dictionary and not simply slide it all the time.

Another disadvantage of LZ77 is the limited size L of the look-ahead buffer. The size of matched strings is limited to $L - 1$, but L must be kept small, since the process of matching strings involves comparing individual symbols. If L were doubled in size, compression would improve, since longer matches would be possible, but the encoder would be much slower when searching for long matches. The size S of the search buffer is also limited. A large search buffer produces better compression but slows down the encoder, since searching takes longer (even with a binary search tree). Increasing the sizes of the two buffers also means creating longer tokens, thereby reducing the compression efficiency. With 2-byte tokens, compressing a 2-character string into one token results in 2 bytes plus 1 flag. Writing the two characters as two raw ASCII codes results in 2 bytes plus 2 flags, a very small difference in size. The encoder should, in such a case, use the latter choice and write the two characters in uncompressed form, saving time and wasting just one bit. We say that the encoder has a 2-byte *break even* point. With longer tokens, the break even point increases to 3 bytes.

Bibliography

Storer, J. A. and T. G. Szymanski (1982) "Data Compression via Textual Substitution," *Journal of the ACM* **29**:928–951.

3.4 Repetition Times

Frans Willems, one of the developers of context-tree weighting (Section 2.19), is also the developer of this original (although not very efficient) dictionary-based method. The input may consist of any symbols but the method is described here and also in [Willems 89] for binary input. The input symbols are grouped into words of length L each that are placed in a sliding buffer. The buffer is divided into a look-ahead buffer with words still to be compressed, and a search buffer containing the B most-recently processed words. The encoder tries to match the leftmost word in the look-ahead buffer to the contents of the search buffer. Only one word in the look-ahead buffer is matched in each step. If a match is found, the distance (offset) of the word from the start of the match is denoted by m and is encoded by a 2-part prefix code that's written on the compressed stream. Notice that there is no need to encode the number of symbols matched, since exactly one word is matched. If no match is found, a special code is written, followed by the L symbols of the unmatched word in raw format.

The method is illustrated by a simple example. We assume that the input symbols are bits. We select $L = 3$ for the length of words, and a search buffer of length $B = 2^L - 1 = 7$ containing the seven most-recently processed bits. The look-ahead buffer contains just the binary data, and the commas shown here are used only to indicate word boundaries.

$\leftarrow$ coded input... $\boxed{0100100}$ $\boxed{100,000,011,111,011,101,001}$...$\leftarrow$ input to be read

It is obvious that the leftmost word "100" in the look-ahead buffer matches the rightmost three bits in the search buffer. The repetition time (the offset) for this word is therefore $m = 3$. (The biggest repetition time is the length B of the search buffer, 7 in our example.) The buffer is now shifted one word (three bits) to the left to become

$\leftarrow$ ...010$\boxed{0100100}$ $\boxed{000,011,111,011,101,001,...}$...$\leftarrow$ input to be read

The repetition time for the current word "000" is $m = 1$ because each bit in this word is matched with the bit immediately to its left. Notice that it is possible to match the leftmost 0 of the next word "011" with the bit to its left, but this method matches exactly one word in each step. The buffer is again shifted L positions to become

$\leftarrow$ ...010010$\boxed{0100000}$ $\boxed{011,111,011,101,001,......}$...$\leftarrow$ input to be read

There is no match for the next word "011" in the search buffer, so m is set to a special value that we denote by 8* (meaning; greater than or equal 8). It is easy to verify that the repetition times of the remaining three words are 6, 4, and 8*.

Each repetition time is encoded by first determining two integers p and q. If $m = 8^*$, then p is set to L; otherwise p is selected as the integer that satisfies $2^p \le m < 2^{p+1}$. Notice that p is located in the interval $[0, L-1]$. The integer q is determined by $q = m - 2^p$, which places it in the interval $[0, 2^p - 1]$. Table 3.5 lists the values of m, p, q, and the prefix codes used for $L = 3$.

m	p	q	Prefix	Suffix	Length
1	0	0	00	none	2
2	1	0	01	0	3
3	1	1	01	1	3
4	2	0	10	00	4
5	2	1	10	01	4
6	2	2	10	10	4
7	2	3	10	11	4
8*	3	—	11	word	5

Table 3.5: Repetition Time Encoding Table for $L = 3$.

Once p and q are known, a prefix code for m is constructed and is written on the compressed stream. It consists of two parts, a prefix and a suffix, that are the binary values of p and q, respectively. Since p is in the interval $[0, L-1]$, the prefix requires $\log(L+1)$ bits. The length of the suffix is p bits. The case $p = L$ is different. Here, the suffix is the raw value (L bits) of the word being compressed.

The compressed stream for the seven words of our example consists of the seven codes

$$01|1, 00, 11|011, 00, 10|10, 10|00, 11|001, \ldots,$$

where the vertical bars separate the prefix and suffix of a code. Notice that the third and seventh words (011 and 001) are included in the codes in raw format.

It is easy to see why this method generates prefix codes. Once a code has been assigned (such as $01|0$, the code of $m = 2$), that code cannot be the prefix of any other code because (1) some of the other codes are for different values of p and thus do not start with 01, and (2) codes for the same p do start with 01 but must have different values of q, so they have different suffixes.

The compression performance of this method is inferior to that of LZ77, but it is interesting for two reasons.

1. It is universal and optimal. It does not use the statistics of the input stream, and its performance asymtotically approaches the entropy of the input as the input stream gets longer.

2. It is shown in [Cachin 98] that this method can be modified to include data hiding (steganography).

Bibliography

Cachin, Christian (1998) "An Information-Theoretic Model for Steganography," in *Proceedings of the Second International Workshop on Information Hiding*, D. Aucsmith, ed. vol. 1525 of *Lecture Notes in Computer Science*, Springer-Verlag, pp. 306–318.

Willems, F. M. J. (1989) "Universal Data Compression and Repetition Times," *IEEE Transactions on Information Theory*, IT-35(1):54–58, January.

3.5 QIC-122

QIC is an international trade association, incorporated in 1987, whose mission is to encourage and promote the widespread use of quarter-inch tape cartridge technology (hence the acronym QIC, see also `http://www.qic.org/html`).

The QIC-122 compression standard is an LZ77 variant that has been developed by QIC for text compression on 1/4-inch data cartridge tape drives. Data is read and shifted into a 2048-byte $(= 2^{11})$ input buffer from right to left, such that the first character is the leftmost one. When the buffer is full, or when all the data has been read into it, the algorithm searches from left to right for repeated strings. The output consists of raw characters and of tokens that represent strings already seen in the buffer. As an example, suppose that the following data have been read and shifted into the buffer:

ABAAAAAACABABABA..............

The first character A is obviously not a repetition of any previous string, so it is encoded as a raw (ASCII) character (see below). The next character B is also encoded as raw. The third character A is identical to the first character but is also encoded as raw since repeated strings should be at least two characters long. Only with the fourth character A we do have a repeated string. The string of five A's from position 4 to position 8 is identical to the one from position 3 to position 7. It is thus encoded as a string of length 5 at offset 1. The offset, in this method, is the distance between the start of the repeated string and the start of the original one.

The next character C at position 9 is encoded as raw. The string ABA at positions 10–12 is a repeat of the string at positions 1–3, so it is encoded as a string of length 3 at offset $10 - 1 = 9$. Finally, the string BABA at positions 13–16 is encoded with length 4 at offset 2, since it is a repetition of the string at positions 10–13.

⋄ **Exercise 3.4:** Suppose that the next four characters of data are CAAC

$$\boxed{\text{ABAAAAAACABABABACAAC}\ldots\ldots\ldots\ldots}$$

How will they be encoded?

A raw character is encoded as 0 followed by the 8 ASCII bits of the character. A string is encoded as a token that starts with 1 followed by the encoded offset, followed by the encoded length. Small offsets are encoded as 1, followed by 7 offset bits; large offsets are encoded as 0 followed by 11 offset bits (recall that the buffer size is 2^{11}). The length is encoded according to Table 3.7. The 9-bit string 110000000 is written, as an end marker, at the end of the output stream.

⋄ **Exercise 3.5:** How can the decoder identify the end marker?

When the search algorithm arrives at the right end of the buffer, it shifts the buffer to the left and inputs the next character into the rightmost position of the buffer. The decoder is the reverse of the encoder (symmetric compression).

Figure 3.6 is a precise description of the compression process, expressed in BNF, which is a metalanguage used to describe processes and formal languages unambiguously. BNF uses the following *metasymbols*:

::=   The symbol on the left is defined by the expression on the right.
<expr>   An expression still to be defined.
| A logical OR.
[]   Optional. The expression in the brackets may occur zero or more times.
()   A comment.
0,1   The bits 0 and 1.

Table 3.6 shows the results of encoding ABAAAAAACABABABA (a 16-symbol string). The reader can easily verify that the output stream consists of the 10 bytes

$$\text{20 90 88 38 1C 21 E2 5C 15 80.}$$

3.6 LZ78

The LZ78 method (which is sometimes referred to as LZ2) [Ziv 78] does not use any search buffer, look-ahead buffer, or sliding window. Instead, there is a dictionary of previously encountered strings. This dictionary starts empty (or almost empty), and its size is limited only by the amount of available memory. The encoder outputs two-field tokens. The first field is a pointer to the dictionary; the second is the code of a symbol. Tokens do not contain the length of a string, since this is implied in the dictionary. Each token corresponds to a string of input symbols, and that string is added to the dictionary after the token is written on the compressed stream. Nothing is ever deleted from the dictionary, which is both an advantage over LZ77

```
(QIC-122 BNF Description)
<Compressed-Stream>::=[<Compressed-String>] <End-Marker>
<Compressed-String>::= 0<Raw-Byte> | 1<Compressed-Bytes>
<Raw-Byte>          ::=<b><b><b><b><b><b><b><b> (8-bit byte)
<Compressed-Bytes> ::=<offset><length>
<offset>           ::= 1<b><b><b><b><b><b><b> (a 7-bit offset)
                         |
           0<b><b><b><b><b><b><b><b><b><b><b> (an 11-bit offset)
<length>           ::= (as per length table)
<End-Marker>       ::=110000000 (Compressed bytes with offset=0)
<b>                ::=0|1
```

Figure 3.6: BNF Definition of QIC-122.

Bytes	Length			Bytes	Length				
2	00			17	11	11	1001		
3	01			18	11	11	1010		
4	10			19	11	11	1011		
5	11	00		20	11	11	1100		
6	11	01		21	11	11	1101		
7	11	10		22	11	11	1110		
8	11	11	0000	23	11	11	1111	0000	
9	11	11	0001	24	11	11	1111	0001	
10	11	11	0010	25	11	11	1111	0010	
11	11	11	0011	:					
12	11	11	0100	37	11	11	1111	1110	
13	11	11	0101	38	11	11	1111	1111	0000
14	11	11	0110	39	11	11	1111	1111	0001
15	11	11	0111	etc.					
16	11	11	1000						

Table 3.7: Values of the <length> Field.

Raw byte "A"	0 01000001
Raw byte "B"	0 01000010
Raw byte "A"	0 01000001
String "AAAAA" offset=1	1 1 0000001 1100
Raw byte "C"	0 01000011
String "ABA" offset=9	1 1 0001001 01
String "BABA" offset=2	1 1 0000010 10
End-Marker	1 1 0000000

Table 3.8: Encoding the Example.

(since future strings can be compressed even by strings seen in the distant past) and a liability (since the dictionary tends to grow fast and to fill up the entire available memory).

The dictionary starts with the null string at position zero. As symbols are input and encoded, strings are added to the dictionary at positions 1, 2, and so on. When the next symbol x is read from the input stream, the dictionary is searched for an entry with the one-symbol string x. If none are found, x is added to the next available position in the dictionary, and the token (0, x) is output. This token indicates the string "null x" (a concatenation of the null string and x). If an entry with x is found (at position 37, say), the next symbol y is read, and the dictionary is searched for an entry containing the two-symbol string xy. If none are found, then string xy is added to the next available position in the dictionary, and the token (37, y) is output. This token indicates the string xy, since 37 is the dictionary position of string x. The process continues until the end of the input stream is reached.

In general, the current symbol is read and becomes a one-symbol string. The encoder then tries to find it in the dictionary. If the symbol is found in the dictionary, the next symbol is read and concatenated with the first to form a two-symbol string that the encoder then tries to locate in the dictionary. As long as those strings are found in the dictionary, more symbols are read and concatenated to the string. At a certain point the string is not found in the dictionary, so the encoder adds it to the dictionary and outputs a token with the last dictionary match as its first field, and the last symbol of the string (the one that caused the search to fail) as its second field. Table 3.9 shows the first 14 steps in encoding the string

$$\text{"sir}_\sqcup\text{sid}_\sqcup\text{eastman}_\sqcup\text{easily}_\sqcup\text{teases}_\sqcup\text{sea}_\sqcup\text{sick}_\sqcup\text{seals"}.$$

Dictionary		Token		Dictionary		Token
0	null					
1	"s"	(0, "s")		8	"a"	(0, "a")
2	"i"	(0, "i")		9	"st"	(1, "t")
3	"r"	(0, "r")		10	"m"	(0, "m")
4	"$\sqcup$"	(0, "$\sqcup$")		11	"an"	(8, "n")
5	"si"	(1, "i")		12	"$\sqcup$ea"	(7, "a")
6	"d"	(0, "d")		13	"sil"	(5, "l")
7	"$\sqcup$e"	(4, "e")		14	"y"	(0, "y")

Table 3.9: First 14 Encoding Steps in LZ78.

◇ **Exercise 3.6:** Complete Table 3.9.

In each step, the string added to the dictionary is the one being encoded, minus its last symbol. In a typical compression run, the dictionary starts with short strings, but as more text is being input and processed, longer and longer strings are added to it. The size of the dictionary can either be fixed or may be determined by the size of the available memory each time the LZ78 compression program is executed. A large dictionary may contain more strings and thus allow for longer matches, but the tradeoff is longer pointers (and thus bigger tokens) and slower dictionary search.

A good data structure for the dictionary is a tree, but not a binary one. The tree starts with the null string as the root. All the strings that start with the null string (strings for which the token pointer is zero) are added to the tree as children of the root. In the above example those are s, i, r, ⊔, d, a, m, y, e, c, and k. Each of them becomes the root of a subtree as shown in Figure 3.10. For example, all the strings that start with s (the four strings si, sil, st, and s(eof)) constitute the subtree of node s.

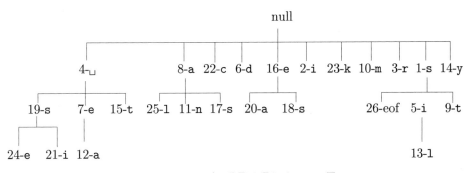

Figure 3.10: An LZ78 Dictionary Tree.

Assuming an alphabet with 8-bit symbols, there are 256 different symbols, so in principle, each node in the tree could have up to 256 children. The process of adding a child to a tree node should thus be dynamic. When the node is first created, it has no children and it should not reserve any memory space for them. As a child is added to the node, memory space should be claimed for it. Since no nodes are ever deleted, there is no need to reclaim memory space, which simplifies the memory management task somewhat.

Such a tree makes it easy to search for a string and to add strings. To search for sil, for example, the program looks for the child s of the root, then for the child i of s, and so on, going down the tree. Here are some examples:

1. When the s of sid is input in step 5, the encoder finds node "1-s" in the tree as a child of "null". It then inputs the next symbol i, but node s does not have a child i (in fact, it has no children at all at this point), so the encoder adds node "5-i" as a child of "1-s", which effectively adds the string si to the tree.

2. When the blank space between eastman and easily is input in step 12, a similar situation happens. The encoder finds node "4-⊔", inputs e, finds "7-e", inputs a, but "7-e" does not have "a" as a child, so the encoder adds node "12-a", which effectively adds the string "⊔ea" to the tree.

A tree of the type described here is called a *trie*. In general, a trie is a tree in which the branching structure at any level is determined by just part of a data item, not the entire item. In the case of LZ78, each string added to the tree effectively adds just one symbol, and does that by adding a branch.

Since the total size of the tree is limited, it may fill up during compression. This, in fact, happens all the time except when the input stream is unusually small. The original LZ78 method does not specify what to do in such a case, so here are some possible solutions.

1. The simplest solution is to freeze the dictionary at that point. No new nodes should be added, the tree becomes a static dictionary, but it can still be used to encode strings.

2. Delete the entire tree once it gets full and start with a new, empty tree. This solution effectively breaks the input into blocks, each with its own dictionary. If the content of the input varies from block to block, this solution will produce good compression, since it will eliminate a dictionary with strings that are unlikely to be used in the future. We can say that this solution implicitly assumes that future symbols will benefit more from new data than from old (the same implicit assumption used by LZ77).

3. The UNIX `compress` utility (Section 3.16) uses a more complex solution.

4. When the dictionary is full, delete some of the least recently used entries, to make room for new ones. Unfortunately there is no good algorithm to decide which entries to delete, and how many (but see the *reuse* procedure in Section 3.18).

The LZ78 decoder works by building and maintaining the dictionary in the same way as the encoder. It is thus more complex than the LZ77 decoder.

Bibliography

Ziv, J. and A. Lempel (1978) "Compression of Individual Sequences via Variable-Rate Coding," *IEEE Transactions on Information Theory* IT-24(5):530–536.

The Red Queen shook her head, "You may call it 'nonsense' if you like," she said, "but I've heard nonsense, compared with which that would be as sensible as a dictionary!"

—Lewis Carroll (1832–1898), *Through the Looking Glass*

3.7 LZFG

Edward Fiala and Daniel Greene have developed several related compression methods [Fiala 89] that are hybrids of LZ77 and LZ78. All their methods are based on the following scheme. The encoder generates a compressed file with tokens and literals (raw ASCII codes) intermixed. There are two types of tokens: a *literal* and a *copy*. A literal token indicates that a string of literals follow, a copy token points to a string previously seen in the data. For example, the string "the␣boy␣on␣my␣right␣is␣the␣right␣boy" produces, when encoded,

(literal 23)the␣boy␣on␣my␣right␣is␣(copy 4 23)(copy 6 13)(copy 3 29),

where the three copy tokens refer to the strings "the␣", "right␣", and "boy", respectively. The LZFG methods are best understood by considering how the decoder operates. The decoder starts with a large empty buffer in which it generates and shifts the decompressed stream. When the decoder inputs a (literal 23) token, it inputs the next 23 bytes as raw ASCII codes into the buffer, shifting the buffer such that the last byte input will be the rightmost one. When the decoder inputs (copy 4 23) it copies the string of length 4 that starts 23 positions from the right end of the buffer. The string is then appended to the buffer, while shifting it. Two LZFG methods, denoted by A1 and A2, are described here.

The A1 scheme employs 8-bit literal tokens and 16-bit copy tokens. A literal token has the format 0000nnnn, where nnnn indicates the number of ASCII bytes following the token. Since the 4-bit nnnn field can have values between 0 and 15, they are interpreted as meaning 1 to 16. The longest possible string of literals is thus 16 bytes. The format of a copy token is "sssspp...p", where the 4-bit nonzero ssss field indicates the length of the string to be copied, and the 12-bit "pp...p" field is a displacement showing where the string starts in the buffer. Since the ssss field cannot be zero, it can have values only between 1 and 15, and they are interpreted as string lengths between 2 and 16. Displacement values are in the range [0, 4095] and are interpreted as [1, 4096].

The encoder starts with an empty search buffer, 4,096 bytes long, and fills up the look-ahead buffer with input data. At each subsequent step it tries to create a copy token. If nothing matches in that step, the encoder creates a literal token. Suppose that at a certain point the buffer contains

←text already encoded..| ..   ..xyz|abcd..   ..|..← text yet to be input.

The encoder tries to match the string "abc..." in the look-ahead buffer to various strings in the search buffer. If a match is found (of at least two symbols); a copy token is written on the compressed stream and the data in the buffers is shifted to the left by the size of the match. If a match is not found, the encoder starts a literal with the a and left-shifts the data one position. It then tries to match "bcd..." to the search buffer. If it finds a match, a literal token is output, followed by a byte with the a, followed by a match token. Otherwise, the b is appended to the literal and the encoder tries to match from "cd..". Literals can be up to 16 bytes long, so the string "the␣boy␣on␣my..." above is encoded as

(literal 16)(literal 7)the␣boy␣on␣my␣right␣is␣(copy 4 23)(copy 6 13)(copy 3 29).

The A1 method borrows the idea of the sliding buffer from LZ77 but also behaves like LZ78, since it creates two-field tokens. This is why it can be considered a hybrid of the two original LZ methods. When A1 starts, it creates mostly literals, but when it gets up to speed (fills up its search buffer) it features strong adaptation, so more and more copy tokens appear in the compressed stream.

The A2 method uses a larger search buffer (up to 21K bytes long). This improves compression, since longer copies can be found, but raises the problem of token size. A large search buffer implies large displacements in copy tokens; long copies imply large "length" fields in those tokens. At the same time we expect both the displacement and "length" fields of a typical copy token to be small, since most matches are found close to the beginning of the search buffer. The solution is to use a variable-size code for those fields, and A2 uses the general unary codes of Section 2.3.1. The "length" field of a copy token is encoded with a (2,1,10) code (Table 2.5), making it possible to match strings up to 2,044 symbols long. Notice that the (2,1,10) code is between 3 and 18 bits long.

The first four codes of the $(2, 1, 10)$ code are 000, 001, 010, and 011. The last three of these codes indicate match lengths of two, three, and four, respectively (recall that the minimum match length is 2). The first one (code 000) is reserved to indicate a literal. The length of the literal then follows and is encoded with code $(0, 1, 5)$. A literal can thus be up to 63 bytes long, and the literal-length field in the token is encoded by between 1 and 10 bits. In case of a match, the "length" field is not 000 and is followed by the displacement field, which is encoded with the $(10,2,14)$ code (Table 3.11). This code has 21K values, and the maximum code size is 16 bits (but see points 2 and 3 below).

n	$a =$ $10 + n \cdot 2$	nth codeword	Number of codewords	Range of integers
0	10	$0 \underbrace{x...x}_{10}$	$2^{10} = 1K$	0–1023
1	12	$10 \underbrace{xx...x}_{12}$	$2^{12} = 4K$	1024–5119
2	14	$11 \underbrace{xx...xx}_{14}$	$2^{14} = 16K$	5120–21503
		Total	21504	

Table 3.11: The General Unary Code $(10, 2, 14)$.

Three more refinements are used by the A2 method, to achieve slightly better (1% or 2%) compression.

1. A literal of maximum length (63 bytes) can immediately be followed by another literal or by a copy token of any length, but a literal of fewer than 63 bytes must be followed by a copy token matching *at least three symbols* (or by the end-of-file). This fact is used to shift down the $(2,1,10)$ codes used to indicate the match length. Normally, codes 000, 001, 010, and 011 indicate no match, and matches of length 2, 3, and 4, respectively. However, a copy token following a literal token of fewer than 63 bytes uses codes 000, 001, 010, and 011 to indicate matches of length 3, 4, 5, and 6, respectively. This way the maximum match length can be 2,046 symbols instead of 2,044.

2. The displacement field is encoded with the $(10, 2, 14)$ code, which has 21K values and whose individual codes range in size from 11 to 16 bits. For smaller files, such large displacements may not be necessary, and other general unary codes may be used, with shorter individual codes. Method A2 thus uses codes of the form $(10 - d, 2, 14 - d)$ for $d = 10, 9, 8, \ldots, 0$. For $d = 1$, code $(9, 2, 13)$ has $2^9 + 2^{11} + 2^{13} = 10,752$ values, and individual codes range in size from 9 to 15 bits. For $d = 10$ code $(0, 2, 4)$ contains $2^0 + 2^2 + 2^4 = 21$ values, and codes are between 1 and 6 bits long. Method A2 starts with $d = 10$ [meaning it initially uses code $(0, 2, 4)$] and a search buffer of size 21 bytes. When the buffer fills up (indicating an input stream longer than 21 bytes), the A2 algorithm switches to $d = 9$ [code $(1, 2, 5)$] and increases the search buffer size to 42 bytes. This process continues until the entire input stream has been encoded or until $d = 0$ is reached [at which point code $(10,2,14)$ is used to the end]. A lot of work for a small gain in compression! (See the discussion of diminishing returns (*a word to the wise*) in the Preface.)

3. Each of the codes $(10 - d, 2, 14 - d)$ requires a search buffer of a certain size, from 21 up to 21K = 21,504 bytes, according to the number of codes it contains. If the user wants, for some reason, to assign the search buffer a different size, then some of the longer codes may never be used, which makes it possible to cut down a little the size of the individual codes. For example, if the user decides to use a search buffer of size 16K = 16,384 bytes, then code $(10, 2, 14)$ has to be used [because the next code $(9, 2, 13)$ contains just 10,752 values]. Code $(10, 2, 14)$ contains 21K = 21,504 individual codes, so the 5,120 longest codes will never be used. The last group of codes ("11" followed by 14 bits) in $(10, 2, 14)$ contains $2^{14} = 16,384$ different individual codes, of which only 11,264 will be used. Of the 11,264 codes the first 8,192 can be represented as "11" followed by $\lfloor \log_2 11,264 \rfloor = 13$ bits, and only the remaining 3,072 codes require $\lceil \log_2 11,264 \rceil = 14$ bits to follow the first "11". We thus end up with 8,192 15-bit codes and 3,072 16-bit codes, instead of 11,264 16-bit codes, a very small improvement.

These three improvements illustrate the great lengths that researchers are willing to go to in order to improve their algorithms ever so slightly.

> Experience shows that fine-tuning an algorithm to squeeze out the last remaining bits of redundancy from the data gives diminishing returns. Modifying an algorithm to improve compression by 1% may increase the run time by 10% (from the Preface).

The LZFG "corpus" of algorithms contains four more methods. B1 and B2 are similar to A1 and A2 but faster because of the way they compute displacements. However, some compression ratio is sacrificed. C1 and C2 go in the opposite direction. They achieve slightly better compression than A1 and A2 at the price of slower operation. (LZFG has been patented, an issue that's discussed in Section 3.25.)

Bibliography

Fiala, E. R., and D. H. Greene (1989), "Data Compression with Finite Windows," *Communications of the ACM* **32**(4):490–505.

3.8 LZRW1

Developed by Ross Williams [Williams 91] as a simple, fast LZ77 variant, LZRW1 is also related to method A1 of LZFG (Section 3.7). The main idea is to find a match in one step, using a hash table. This is fast but not very efficient, since the match found is not always the longest. We start with a description of the algorithm, follow with the format of the compressed stream, and conclude with an example.

The method uses the entire available memory as a buffer and encodes the input stream in blocks. A block is read into the buffer and is completely encoded, then the next block is read and encoded, and so on. The length of the search buffer is 4K and that of the look-ahead buffer is 16 bytes. These two buffers slide along the input block in memory from left to right. It is necessary to maintain only one pointer, p_src, pointing to the start of the look-ahead buffer. The pointer p_src is initialized to 1 and is incremented after each phrase is encoded, thereby moving both buffers to the right by the length of the phrase. Figure 3.12 shows how the search buffer starts empty, and then grows to 4K, then starts sliding to the right, following the look-ahead buffer.

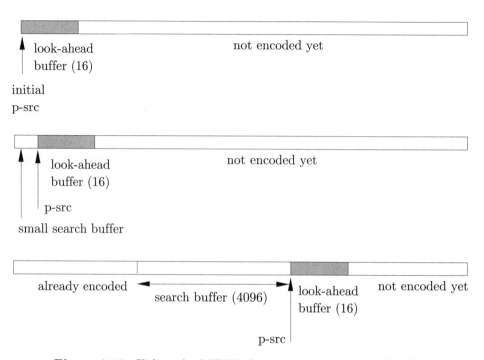

Figure 3.12: Sliding the LZRW1 Search- and Look-Ahead Buffers.

The leftmost three characters of the look-ahead buffer are hashed into a 12-bit number I, which is used to index an array of $2^{12} = 4,096$ pointers. A pointer P is retrieved and is immediately replaced in the array by I. If P points outside the search buffer, there is no match; the first character in the look-ahead buffer is output as a literal, and p_src is advanced by 1. The same thing is done if P points inside the search buffer but to a string that does not match the one in the look-ahead buffer. If P points to a match of at least three characters, the encoder finds the longest match (at most 16 characters), outputs a match item, and advances p_src by the length of the match. This process is depicted in Figure 3.14. An interesting point to note is that the array of pointers does not have to be initialized when the encoder starts, since the encoder checks every pointer. Initially, all pointers are random, but as they are replaced, more and more of them point to real matches.

The output of the LZRW1 encoder (Figure 3.15) consists of groups, each starting with a 16-bit *control word*, followed by 16 items. Each item is either an 8-bit literal or a 16-bit copy item (a match) consisting of a 4-bit length field b (where the length is $b + 1$) and a 12-bit offset (the a and c fields). The length field indicates lengths between 3 and 16. The 16 bits of the control word flag each of the 16 items that follow (a 0 flag indicates a literal and a flag of 1, a match item). The last group may contain fewer than 16 items.

The decoder is even simpler than the encoder, since it does not need the array of pointers. It maintains a large buffer using a `p_src` pointer in the same way as the encoder. The decoder reads a control word from the compressed stream and uses its 16 bits to read 16 items. A literal item is decoded by appending it to the buffer and incrementing `p_src` by 1. A copy item is decoded by subtracting the offset from `p_src`, fetching a string from the search buffer, of length indicated by the length field, and appending it to the buffer. Then `p_src` is incremented by the length.

Table 3.13 illustrates the first seven steps of encoding "that⊔thatch⊔thaws". The values produced by the hash function are arbitrary. Initially, all pointers are random (indicated by "any") but they are replaced by useful ones very quickly.

⋄ **Exercise 3.7:** Summarize the last steps in a table similar to Table 3.13 and write the final compressed stream in binary.

p_src	3 chars	Hash index	P	Output	Binary output
1	"tha"	4	any→4	t	01110100
2	"hat"	6	any→6	h	01101000
3	"at⊔"	2	any→2	a	01100001
4	"t⊔t"	1	any→1	t	01110100
5	"⊔th"	5	any→5	⊔	00100000
6	"tha"	4	4→4	4,5	0000|0011|00000101
10	"ch⊔"	3	any→3	c	01100011

Table 3.13: First Seven Steps of Encoding "that thatch thaws".

Tests done by the original developer indicate that LZRW1 performs about 10% worse than LZC (the UNIX `compress` utility) but is four times faster. Also, it performs about 4% worse than LZFG (the A1 method) but runs ten times faster. It is therefore suited for cases where speed is more important than compression performance. A 68000 assembly language implementation has required, on average, the execution of only 13 machine instructions to compress, and four instructions to decompress, 1 byte.

⋄ **Exercise 3.8:** Show a practical example where compression speed is more important than compression ratio.

Bibliography

Williams, Ross (1991),"An Extremely Fast Ziv-Lempel Data Compression Algorithm," in *Proceedings of the 1991 Data Compression Conference*, J. Storer, ed., Los Alamitos, CA, IEEE Computer Society Press, pp. 362–371.

Williams, Ross N., *Adaptive Data Compression*, Boston, Kluwer Academic Publishers, 1991.

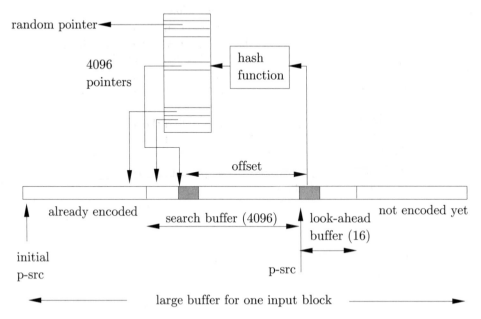

Figure 3.14: The LZRW1 Encoder.

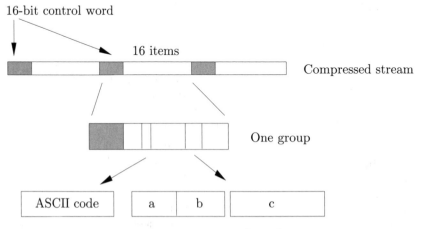

Figure 3.15: Format of the Output.

3.9 LZRW4

LZRW4 is a variant of LZ77, based on ideas of Ross Williams about possible ways to combine a dictionary method with prediction (Section 3.26). LZRW4 also borrows some ideas from LZRW1. It uses a 1 Mbyte buffer where both the search and look-ahead buffers slide from left to right. At any point in the encoding process, the order-2 context of the current symbol (the two most recent symbols in the search buffer) is used to predict the current symbol. The two symbols constituting the context are hashed to a 12-bit number I, which is used as an index to a $2^{12} = 4,096$-entry array A of partitions. Each partition contains 32 pointers to the input data in the 1 Mbyte buffer (each pointer is thus 20 bits long).

The 32 pointers in partition $A[I]$ are checked to find the longest match between the look-ahead buffer and the input data seen so far. The longest match is selected and is coded in 8 bits. The first 3 bits code the match length according to Table 3.16; the remaining 5 bits identify the pointer in the partition. Such an 8-bit number is called a *copy item*. If no match is found, a literal is encoded in 8 bits. For each item, an extra bit is prepared, a 0 for a literal and a 1 for a copy item. The extra bits are accumulated in groups of 16, and each group is output, as in LZRW1, preceding the 16 items it refers to.

3 bits:	000	001	010	011	100	101	110	111
length:	2	3	4	5	6	7	8	16

Table 3.16: Encoding the Length in LZRW4.

The partitions are updated all the time by moving "good" pointers toward the start of their partition. When a match is found, the encoder swaps the selected pointer with the pointer halfway toward the partition (Figure 3.17a,b). If no match is found, the entire 32-pointer partition is shifted to the left and the new pointer is entered on the right, pointing to the current symbol (Figure 3.17c).

3.10 LZW

This is a popular variant of LZ78, developed by Terry Welch in 1984 [Welch 84]. Its main feature is eliminating the second field of a token. An LZW token consists of just a pointer to the dictionary. To best understand LZW, we will temporarily forget that the dictionary is a tree, and will think of it as an array of variable-size strings. The LZW method starts by initializing the dictionary to all the symbols in the alphabet. In the common case of 8-bit symbols, the first 256 entries of the dictionary (entries 0 through 255) are occupied before any data is input. Because the dictionary is initialized, the next input character will always be found in the dictionary. This is why an LZW token can consist of just a pointer and does not have to contain a character code as in LZ77 and LZ78.

(LZW has been patented and its use requires a license. This issue is discussed in Section 3.25.)

The principle of LZW is that the encoder inputs symbols one by one and accumulates them in a string I. After each symbol is input and is concatenated to I, the dictionary is searched for string I. As long as I is found in the dictionary, the

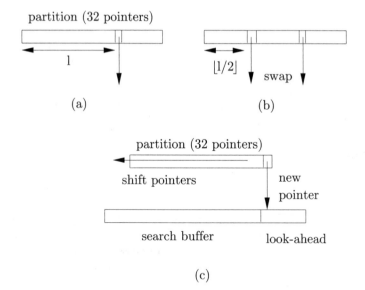

Figure 3.17: Updating An LZRW4 Partition.

process continues. At a certain point, adding the next symbol x causes the search to fail; string I is in the dictionary but string Ix (symbol x concatenated to I) is not. At this point the encoder (1) outputs the dictionary pointer that points to string I, (2) saves string Ix (which is now called a *phrase*) in the next available dictionary entry, and (3) initializes string I to symbol x. To illustrate this process, we again use the text string "sir␣sid␣eastman␣easily␣teases␣sea␣sick␣seals". The steps are as follows:

0. Initialize entries 0–255 of the dictionary to all 256 8-bit bytes.

1. The first symbol s is input and is found in the dictionary (in entry 115, since this is the ASCII code of s). The next symbol i is input, but si is not found in the dictionary. The encoder performs the following: (1) outputs 115, (2) saves string si in the next available dictionary entry (entry 256), and (3) initializes I to the symbol i.

2. The r of sir is input, but string ir is not in the dictionary. The encoder (1) outputs 105 (the ASCII code of i), (2) saves string ir in the next available dictionary entry (entry 257), and (3) initializes I to the symbol r.

Table 3.18 summarizes all the steps of this process. Table 3.19 shows some of the original 256 entries in the LZW dictionary plus the entries added during encoding of the string above. The complete output stream is (only the numbers are output, not the strings in parentheses) as follows:

115 (s), 105 (i), 114 (r), 32 (␣), 256 (si), 100 (d), 32 (␣), 101 (e), 97 (a), 115 (s), 116 (t), 109 (m), 97 (a), 110 (n), 262 (␣e), 264 (as), 105 (i), 108 (l), 121 (y), 32 (␣), 116 (t), 263 (ea), 115 (s), 101 (e), 115 (s), 259 (␣s), 263 (ea), 259 (␣s), 105 (i), 99 (c), 107 (k), 280 (␣se), 97 (a), 108 (l), 115 (s), eof.

I	in dict?	new entry	output	I	in dict?	new entry	output
s	Y			y	Y		
si	N	256-si	115 (s)	y␣	N	274-y␣	121 (y)
i	Y			␣	Y		
ir	N	257-ir	105 (i)	␣t	N	275-␣t	32 (␣)
r	Y			t	Y		
r␣	N	258-r␣	114 (r)	te	N	276-te	116 (t)
␣	Y			e	Y		
␣s	N	259-␣s	32 (␣)	ea	Y		
s	Y			eas	N	277-eas	263 (ea)
si	Y			s	Y		
sid	N	260-sid	256 (si)	se	N	278-se	115 (s)
d	Y			e	Y		
d␣	N	261-d␣	100 (d)	es	N	279-es	101 (e)
␣	Y			s	Y		
␣e	N	262-␣e	32 (␣)	s␣	N	280-s␣	115 (s)
e	Y			␣	Y		
ea	N	263-ea	101 (e)	␣s	Y		
a	Y			␣se	N	281-␣se	259 (␣s)
as	N	264-as	97 (a)	e	Y		
s	Y			ea	Y		
st	N	265-st	115 (s)	ea␣	N	282-ea␣	263 (ea)
t	Y			␣	Y		
tm	N	266-tm	116 (t)	␣s	Y		
m	Y			␣si	N	283-␣si	259 (␣s)
ma	N	267-ma	109 (m)	i	Y		
a	Y			ic	N	284-ic	105 (i)
an	N	268-an	97 (a)	c	Y		
n	Y			ck	N	285-ck	99 (c)
n␣	N	269-n␣	110 (n)	k	Y		
␣	Y			k␣	N	286-k␣	107 (k)
␣e	Y			␣	Y		
␣ea	N	270-␣ea	262 (␣e)	␣s	Y		
a	Y			␣se	Y		
as	Y			␣sea	N	287-␣sea	281 (␣se)
asi	N	271-asi	264 (as)	a	Y		
i	Y			al	N	288-al	97 (a)
il	N	272-il	105 (i)	l	Y		
l	Y			ls	N	289-ls	108 (l)
ly	N	273-ly	108 (l)	s	Y		
				s,eof	N		115 (s)

Table 3.18: Encoding "sir sid eastman easily teases sea sick seals".

0	NULL	110	n	262	⊔e	276	te
1	SOH	...		263	ea	277	eas
...		115	s	264	as	278	se
32	SP	116	t	265	st	279	es
...		...		266	tm	280	s⊔
97	a	121	y	267	ma	281	⊔se
98	b	...		268	an	282	ea⊔
99	c	255	255	269	n⊔	283	⊔si
100	d	256	si	270	⊔ea	284	ic
101	e	257	ir	271	asi	285	ck
...		258	r⊔	272	il	286	k⊔
107	k	259	⊔s	273	ly	287	⊔sea
108	l	260	sid	274	y⊔	288	al
109	m	261	d⊔	275	⊔t	289	ls

Table 3.19: An LZW Dictionary.

```
for i:=0 to 255 do
  append i as a 1-symbol string to the dictionary;
append λ to the dictionary;
di:=dictionary index of λ;
repeat
  read(ch);
  if <<di,ch>> is in the dictionary then
    di:=dictionary index of <<di,ch>>;
  else
    output(di);
    append <<di,ch>> to the dictionary;
    di:=dictionary index of ch;
  endif;
until end-of-input;
```

Figure 3.20: The LZW Algorithm.

Figure 3.20 is a pseudo-code listing of the algorithm. We denote by λ the empty string, and by <<a,b>> the concatenation of strings a and b.

The line "append <<di,ch>> to the dictionary" is of special interest. It is clear that in practice, the dictionary may fill up. This line should therefore include a test for a full dictionary, and certain actions for the case where it is full.

Since the first 256 entries of the dictionary are occupied right from the start, pointers to the dictionary have to be longer than 8 bits. A simple implementation would typically use 16-bit pointers, which allow for a 64K-entry dictionary (where $64K = 2^{16} = 65,536$). Such a dictionary will, of course, fill up very quickly in all but the smallest compression jobs. The same problem exists with LZ78, and any solutions used with LZ78 can also be used with LZW. Another interesting fact about LZW is that strings in the dictionary get only one character longer at a time. It therefore takes a long time to get long strings in the dictionary, and thus a chance to achieve really good compression. We can say that LZW adapts slowly to its input data.

◇ **Exercise 3.9:** Use LZW to encode the string "alf␣eats␣alfalfa". Show the encoder output and the new entries added by it to the dictionary.

◇ **Exercise 3.10:** Analyze the LZW compression of the string "aaaa...".

⎛ A `dirty icon` (anagram of "dictionary") ⎞

3.10.1 LZW Decoding

In order to undrestand how the LZW decoder works, we should first recall the three steps the encoder performs each time it writes something on the output stream. They are (1) it outputs the dictionary pointer that points to string I, (2) it saves string Ix in the next available entry of the dictionary, and (3) it initializes string I to symbol x.

The decoder starts with the first entries of its dictionary initialized to all the symbols of the alphabet (normally 256 symbols). It then reads its input stream (which consists of pointers to the dictionary) and uses each pointer to retrieve uncompressed symbols from its dictionary and write them on its output stream. It also builds its dictionary in the same way as the encoder (this fact is usually expressed by saying that the encoder and decoder are *synchronized*, or that they work in *lockstep*).

In the first decoding step, the decoder inputs the first pointer and uses it to retrieve a dictionary item I. This is a string of symbols, and it is written on the decoder's output stream. String Ix needs to be saved in the dictionary, but symbol x is still unknown; it will be the first symbol in the next string retrieved from the dictionary.

In each decoding step after the first, the decoder inputs the next pointer, retrieves the next string J from the dictionary, writes it on the output stream, isolates its first symbol x, and saves string Ix in the next available dictionary entry (after checking to make sure string Ix is not already in the dictionary). The decoder then moves J to I and is ready for the next step.

In our "sir␣sid..." example, the first pointer that's input by the decoder is 115. This corresponds to the string s, which is retrieved from the dictionary, gets stored in I and becomes the first thing written on the decoder's output stream. The next pointer is 105, so string i is retrieved into J and is also written on the output stream. J's first symbol is concatenated with I, to form string si, which does not exist in the dictionary, and is therefore added to it as entry 256. Variable J is moved to I, so I is now the string i. The next pointer is 114, so string r is retrieved from the dictionary into J and is also written on the output stream. J's first symbol is concatenated with I, to form string ir, which does not exist in the dictionary, and is added to it as entry 257. Variable J is moved to I, so I is now the string r. The next step reads pointer 32, writes "␣" on the output stream, and saves string "r␣".

⋄ **Exercise 3.11:** Decode the string "alf␣eats␣alfalfa" by using the encoding results from Exercise 3.9.

⋄ **Exercise 3.12:** Assume a two-symbol alphabet with the symbols a and b. Show the first few steps for encoding and decoding the string "ababab...".

3.10.2 LZW Dictionary Structure

Up until now, we have assumed that the LZW dictionary is an array of variable-size strings. To understand why a trie is a better data structure for the dictionary we need to recall how the encoder works. It inputs symbols and concatenates them into a variable I as long as the string in I is found in the dictionary. At a certain point the encoder inputs the first symbol x, which causes the search to fail (string Ix is not in the dictionary). It then adds Ix to the dictionary. This means that each string added to the dictionary effectively adds just one new symbol, x. (Phrased another way; for each dictionary string of more than one symbol, there exists a "parent" string in the dictionary that's one symbol shorter.)

A tree similar to the one used by LZ78 is thus a good data structure, since adding string Ix to such a tree is done by adding one node with x. The main problem is that each node in the LZW tree may have many children (the tree is multiway, not binary). Imagine the node for the letter a in entry 97. Initially it has no children, but if the string ab is added to the tree, node 97 gets one child. Later, when, say, the string ae is added, node 97 gets a second child, and so on. The data structure for the tree should therefore be designed such that a node could have any number of children, but without having to reserve any memory for them in advance.

One way of designing such a data structure is to house the tree in an array of nodes, each a structure with two fields: a symbol and a pointer to the parent node. A node has no pointers to any child nodes. Moving down the tree, from a node to one of its children, is done by a *hashing process* in which the pointer to the node and the symbol of the child are hashed to create a new pointer.

Suppose that string abc has already been input, symbol by symbol, and has been stored in the tree in the three nodes at locations 97, 266, and 284. Following that, the encoder has just input the next symbol d. The encoder now searches for string abcd, or, more specifically, for a node containing the symbol d whose parent is at location 284. The encoder hashes the 284 (the pointer to string abc) and the 100 (ASCII code of d) to create a pointer to some node, say, 299. The encoder then examines node 299. There are three possibilities:

1. The node is unused. This means that abcd is not yet in the dictionary and should be added to it. The encoder adds it to the tree by storing the parent pointer 284 and ASCII code 100 in the node. The result is the following:

Node				
Address :	97	266	284	299
Contents :	(-:"a")	(97:"b")	(266:"c")	(284:"d")
Represents:	"a"	"ab"	"abc"	"abcd"

2. The node contains a parent pointer of 284 and the ASCII code of d. This means that string abcd is already in the tree. The encoder inputs the next symbol, say e, and searches the dictionary tree for string abcde.

3. The node contains something else. This means that another hashing of a pointer and an ASCII code has resulted in 299, and node 299 already contains information from another string. This is called a *collision*, and it can be dealt with in several ways. The simplest way to deal with a collision is to increment pointer 299 and examine nodes 300, 301,... until an unused node is found, or until a node with (284:"d") is found.

In practice, we build nodes that are structures with three fields, a pointer to the parent node, the pointer (or index) created by the hashing process, and the code (normally ASCII) of the symbol contained in the node. The second field is necessary because of collisions. A node can thus be illustrated by

parent
index
symbol

We illustrate this data structure using string "ababab..." of Exercise 3.12. The dictionary is an array dict where each entry is a structure with the 3 fields parent, index, and symbol. We refer to a field by, e.g., dict[pointer].parent, where pointer is an index to the array. The dictionary is initialized to the two entries a and b. (To keep the example simple we use no ASCII codes. We assume that a has code 1 and b, code 2.) The first few steps of the encoder are as follows:

Step 0: Mark all dictionary locations from 3 on as unused.

Step 1: The first symbol a is input into variable I. What is actually input is the code of "a", which in our example is 1, so I = 1. Since this is the first symbol, the encoder assumes that it is in the dictionary and so does not perform any search.

Step 2: The second symbol b is input into J, so J = 2. The encoder has to search for string ab in the dictionary. It executes pointer:=hash(I,J). Let's assume that the result is 5. Field dict[pointer].index contains "unused", since location 5 is still empty, so string ab is not in the dictionary. It is added by executing

```
dict[pointer].parent:=I;
dict[pointer].index:=pointer;
dict[pointer].symbol:=J;
```

with `pointer`=5. J is moved into I, so I = 2.

/	/	/	/	1
1	2	-	-	5	...
a	b			b

Step 3: The third symbol a is input into J, so J = 1. The encoder has to search for string ba in the dictionary. It executes `pointer:=hash(I,J)`. Let's assume that the result is 8. Field `dict[pointer].index` contains "unused", so string ba is not in the dictionary. It is added as before by executing

```
dict[pointer].parent:=I;
dict[pointer].index:=pointer;
dict[pointer].symbol:=J;
```

with `pointer`=8. J is moved into I, so I = 1.

/	/	/	/	1	/	/	/	2	/
1	2	-	-	5	-	-	8	-	...
a	b			b			a	

Step 4: The fourth symbol b is input into J, so J=2. The encoder has to search for string ab in the dictionary. It executes `pointer:=hash(I,J)`. We know from step 2 that the result is 5. Field `dict[pointer].index` contains "5", so string ab is in the dictionary. The value of `pointer` is moved into I, so I = 5.

Step 5: The fifth symbol a is input into J, so J = 1. The encoder has to search for string aba in the dictionary. It executes as usual `pointer:=hash(I,J)`. Let's assume that the result is 8 (a collision). Field `dict[pointer].index` contains 8, which looks good, but field `dict[pointer].parent` contains 2 instead of the expected 5, so the hash function knows that this is a collision and string aba is not in dictionary entry 8. It increments `pointer` as many times as necessary until it finds a dictionary entry with `index`=8 and `parent`=5 or until it finds an unused entry. In the former case, string aba is in the dictionary, and `pointer` is moved to I. In the latter case aba is not in the dictionary, and the encoder saves it in the entry pointed at by `pointer`, and moves J to I.

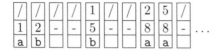

Example: The 15 hashing steps for encoding the string "alf␣eats␣alfalfa" are shown below. The encoding process itself is illustrated in detail in the answer to Exercise 3.9. The results of the hashing are arbitrary; they are not the results produced by a real hash function. The 12 trie nodes constructed for this string are shown in Figure 3.21.

1. Hash(1,97) → 278. Array location 278 is set to (97, 278, 1).
2. Hash(f,108) → 266. Array location 266 is set to (108, 266, f).

3. Hash($\sqcup$,102) $\rightarrow$ 269. Array location 269 is set to (102,269,$\sqcup$).

4. Hash(e,32) $\rightarrow$ 267. Array location 267 is set to $(32, 267, \text{e})$.

5. Hash(a,101) $\rightarrow$ 265. Array location 265 is set to $(101, 265, \text{a})$.

6. Hash(t,97) $\rightarrow$ 272. Array location 272 is set to $(97, 272, \text{t})$.

7. Hash(s,116) $\rightarrow$ 265. A collision! Skip to the next available location, 268, and set it to $(116, 265, \text{s})$. This is why the index needs to be stored.

8. Hash($\sqcup$,115) $\rightarrow$ 270. Array location 270 is set to $(115, 270, \sqcup)$.

9. Hash(a,32) $\rightarrow$ 268. A collision! Skip to the next available location, 271, and set it to $(32, 268, \text{a})$.

10. Hash(l,97) $\rightarrow$ 278. Array location 278 already contains index 278 and symbol l from step 1, so there is no need to store anything else or to add a new trie entry.

11. Hash(f,278) $\rightarrow$ 276. Array location 276 is set to $(278, 276, \text{f})$.

12. Hash(a,102) $\rightarrow$ 274. Array location 274 is set to $(102, 274, \text{a})$.

13. Hash(l,97) $\rightarrow$ 278. Array location 278 already contains index 278 and symbol l from step 1, so there is no need to do anything.

14. Hash(f,278) $\rightarrow$ 276. Array location 276 already contains index 276 and symbol f from step 11, so there is no need to do anything.

15. Hash(a,276) $\rightarrow$ 274. A collision! Skip to the next available location, 275, and set it to $(276, 274, \text{a})$.

Readers who have carefully followed the discussion up to this point will be happy to learn that the LZW decoder's use of the dictionary tree-array is simple and no hashing is needed. The decoder starts, like the encoder, by initializing the first 256 array locations. It then reads pointers from its input stream, and uses each to locate a symbol in the dictionary.

In the first decoding step, the decoder inputs the first pointer and uses it to retrieve a dictionary item I. This is a symbol that is now written by the decoder on its output stream. String Ix needs to be saved in the dictionary, but symbol x is still unknown; it will be the first symbol in the next string retrieved from the dictionary.

In each decoding step after the first, the decoder inputs the next pointer and uses it to retrieve the next string J from the dictionary and write it on the output stream. If the pointer is, say 8, the decoder examines field `dict[8].index`. If this field equals 8, then this is the right node. Otherwise, the decoder examines consecutive array locations until it finds the right one.

Once the right tree node is found, the **parent** field is used to go back up the tree and retrieve the individual symbols of the string *in reverse order*. The symbols are then placed in J in the right order (see below), the decoder isolates the first symbol x of J, and saves string Ix in the next available array location. (String I was found in the previous step, so only one node, with symbol x, needs be added.) The decoder then moves J to I, and is ready for the next step.

Retrieving a complete string from the LZW tree thus involves following the pointers in the **parent** fields. This is equivalent to moving *up* the tree, which is why the hash function is no longer needed.

Example: The previous example describes the 15 hashing steps in the encoding of string "alf$\sqcup$eats$\sqcup$alfalfa". The last step sets array location 275 to (276,274,a) and writes 275 (a pointer to location 275) on the compressed stream. When this

265	266	267	268	269	270	271	272	273	274	275	276	277	278
/	/	/	/	/	/	/	/	/	/	/	/	/	97
-	-	-	-	-	-	-	-	-	-	-	-	-	278
													1
/	108	/	/	/	/	/	/	/	/	/	/	/	97
-	266	-	-	-	-	-	-	-	-	-	-	-	278
	f												1
/	108	/	/	102	/	/	/	/	/	/	/	/	97
-	266	-	-	269	-	-	-	-	-	-	-	-	278
	f			⊔									1
/	108	32	/	102	/	/	/	/	/	/	/	/	97
-	266	267	-	269	-	-	-	-	-	-	-	-	278
	f	e		⊔									1
101	108	32	/	102	/	/	/	/	/	/	/	/	97
265	266	267	-	269	-	-	-	-	-	-	-	-	278
a	f	e		⊔									1
101	108	32	/	102	/	/	97	/	/	/	/	/	97
265	266	267	-	269	-	-	272	-	-	-	-	-	278
a	f	e		⊔			t						1
101	108	32	116	102	/	/	97	/	/	/	/	/	97
265	266	267	265	269	-	-	272	-	-	-	-	-	278
a	f	e	s	⊔			t						1
101	108	32	116	102	115	/	97	/	/	/	/	/	97
265	266	267	265	269	270	-	272	-	-	-	-	-	278
a	f	e	s	⊔	⊔		t						1
101	108	32	116	102	115	32	97	/	/	/	/	/	97
265	266	267	265	269	270	268	272	-	-	-	-	-	278
a	f	e	s	⊔	⊔	a	t						1
101	108	32	116	102	115	32	97	/	/	/	278	/	97
265	266	267	265	269	270	268	272	-	-	-	276	-	278
a	f	e	s	⊔	⊔	a	t				f		1
101	108	32	116	102	115	32	97	/	102	/	278	/	97
265	266	267	265	269	270	268	272	-	274	-	276	-	278
a	f	e	s	⊔	⊔	a	t		a		f		1
101	108	32	116	102	115	32	97	/	102	276	278	/	97
265	266	267	265	269	270	268	272	-	274	274	276	-	278
a	f	e	s	⊔	⊔	a	t		a	a	f		1

Figure 3.21: Growing An LZW Trie for "alf eats alfalfa".

stream is read by the decoder, pointer 275 is the last item input and processed by the decoder. The decoder finds symbol a in the symbol field of location 275 (indicating that the string stored at 275 ends with an a) and a pointer to location 276 in the parent field. The decoder then examines location 276 where it finds symbol f and parent pointer 278. In location 278 the decoder finds symbol l and a pointer to 97. Finally, in location 97 the decoder finds symbol a and a null pointer. The (reversed) string is thus afla. There is no need for the decoder to do any hashing or to use the index fields.

The last point to discuss is string reversal. Two commonly used approaches are outlined below:

1. Use a stack. A stack is a common data structure in modern computers. It is an array in memory that is accessed at one end only. At any time, the item that was last pushed into the stack will be the first one to be popped out (last-in-first-out, or LIFO). Symbols retrieved from the dictionary are pushed into the stack. When the last one has been retrieved and pushed, the stack is popped, symbol by symbol, into variable J. When the stack is empty, the entire string has been reversed. This is a common way to reverse a string.

2. Retrieve symbols from the dictionary and concatenate them into J *from right to left*. When done, the string will be stored in J in the right order. Variable J must be long enough to accommodate the longest possible string, but then it has to be long enough even when a stack is used.

◇ **Exercise 3.13:** What is the longest string that can be retrieved from the LZW dictionary during decoding?

3.10.3 LZW in Practice

The publication of the LZW algorithm, in 1984, has strongly affected the data compression community and has influenced many people to come up with implementations and variants of this method. Some of the most important LZW "spin-offs" are described below.

Bibliography

Phillips, Dwayne (1992) "LZW Data Compression," *The Computer Application Journal* Circuit Cellar Inc., **27**:36–48, June/July.

Welch, T. A. (1984) "A Technique for High-Performance Data Compression," *IEEE Computer* **17**(6):8–19, June.

3.10.4 Differencing

The idea of differencing, or relative encoding, has already been mentioned in Section 1.3.1. This idea turns out to be useful in LZW image compression, since most adjacent pixels don't differ by much. It is possible to implement an LZW encoder that computes the value of a pixel relative to its predecessor and then encodes this difference. The decoder should, of course, be compatible and should compute the absolute value of a pixel after decoding its relative value.

3.10.5 LZW Variants

A word-based LZW variant is described in Section 8.6.2.

LZW is an adaptive data compression method, but it is slow to adapt to its input, since strings in the dictionary get only one character longer at a time. Exercise 3.10 shows that a string of a million a's (which, of course, is highly redundant) produces dictionary phrases the longest of which contains only 1,414 a's.

The LZMW method, Section 3.11, is a variant of LZW that overcomes this problem. Its main principle is this: Instead of adding I plus one character of the next phrase to the dictionary, add I plus the entire next phrase to the dictionary.

The LZAP method, Section 3.12, is yet another variant based on this idea: Instead of just concatenating the last two phrases and placing the result in the dictionary, place all prefixes of the concatenation in the dictionary. More specifically, if S and T are the last two matches, add St to the dictionary for every nonempty prefix t of T, including T itself.

Table 3.22 summarizes the principles of LZW, LZMW, and LZAP and shows how they naturally suggest another variant, LZY.

Increment	Add a string to the dictionary	
string by	per phrase	per input char.
One character:	LZW	LZY
Several chars:	LZMW	LZAP

Table 3.22: Four Variants of LZW.

LZW adds one dictionary string per phrase and increments strings by one symbol at a time. LZMW adds one dictionary string per phrase and increments strings by several symbols at a time. LZAP adds one dictionary string per input symbol and increments strings by several symbols at a time. LZY, Section 3.13, fits the fourth cell of Table 3.22. It is a method that adds one dictionary string per input symbol and increments strings by one symbol at a time.

3.11 LZMW

This LZW variant, developed by V. Miller and M. Wegman [Miller and Wegman 85], is based on two principles:

1. When the dictionary gets full, the least recently used dictionary phrase is deleted. There are several ways to select this phrase, and the developers suggest that any reasonable way of doing so will work. One possibility is to identify all the dictionary phrases S for which there are no phrases Sa (nothing has been appended to S, meaning that S hasn't been used since it was placed in the dictionary) and delete the oldest of them. An auxiliary data structure has to be built and maintained in this case, pointing to dictionary phrases according to their age (the first pointer always points to the oldest phrase). The first 256 dictionary phrases should never be deleted.

2. Each phrase added to the dictionary is a concatenation of two strings, the previous match (S' below) and the current one (S). This is in contrast to LZW,

where each phrase added is the concatenation of the current match and the first symbol of the next match. The pseudo-code algorithm illustrates this:

```
Initialize Dict to all the symbols of alphabet A;
i:=1;
S':=null;
while i <= input size
 k:=longest match of Input[i] to Dict;
 Output(k);
 S:=Phrase k of Dict;
 i:=i+length(S);
 If phrase S'S is not in Dict, append it to Dict;
 S':=S;
endwhile;
```

By adding the concatenation S'S to the LZMW dictionary, dictionary phrases can grow by more than one symbol at a time. This means that LZMW dictionary phrases are more "natural" units of the input (e.g., if the input is text in a natural language, dictionary phrases will tend to be complete words or even several words in that language). This, in turn, implies that the LZMW dictionary generally adapts to the input faster than the LZW dictionary.

Table 3.23 illustrates the LZMW method by applying it to the string

"sir␣sid␣eastman␣easily␣teases␣sea␣sick␣seals".

LZMW adapts to its input faster than LZW but has the following three disadvantages:

1. The dictionary data structure cannot be the simple LZW trie, since not every prefix of a dictionary phrase is included in the dictionary. This means that the one-symbol-at-a-time search method used in LZW will not work. Instead, when a phrase S is added to the LZMW dictionary, every prefix of S must be added to the data structure, and every node in the data structure must have a tag indicating whether the node is in the dictionary or not.

2. Finding the longest string may require backtracking. If the dictionary contains "aaaa" and "aaaaaaaa", we have to reach the eighth symbol of phrase "aaaaaaab" to realize that we have to choose the shorter phrase. This implies that dictionary searches in LZMW are slower than in LZW. This problem does not apply to the LZMW decoder.

3. A phrase may be added to the dictionary twice. This again complicates the choice of data structure for the dictionary.

◇ **Exercise 3.14:** Use the LZMW method to compress the string "swiss␣miss".

◇ **Exercise 3.15:** Compress the string "yabbadabbadabbadoo" using LZMW.

Bibliography

Miller, V. S., and M. N. Wegman (1985) "Variations On a Theme by Ziv and Lempel," in A. Apostolico and Z. Galil, eds., NATO ASI series Vol. F12, *Combinatorial Algorithms on Words*, Springer, Berlin, pp. 131–140.

Step	Input	Output	S	Add to dict.	S'
	sir␣sid␣eastman␣easily␣teases␣sea␣sick␣seals				
1	s	115	s	—	—
2	i	105	i	256-si	s
3	r	114	r	257-ir	i
4	-	32	␣	258-r␣	r
5	si	256	si	259-␣si	␣
6	d	100	d	260-sid	si
7	-	32	␣	261-d␣	d
8	e	101	e	262-␣e	␣
9	a	97	a	263-ea	e
10	s	115	s	264-as	a
11	t	117	t	265-st	s
12	m	109	m	266-tm	t
13	a	97	a	267-ma	m
14	n	110	n	268-an	a
15	-e	262	␣e	269-n␣e	n
16	as	264	as	270-␣eas	␣e
17	i	105	i	271-asi	as
18	l	108	l	272-il	i
19	y	121	y	273-ly	l
20	-	32	␣	274-y␣	y
21	t	117	t	275-␣t	␣
22	ea	263	ea	276-tea	t
23	s	115	s	277-eas	ea
24	e	101	e	278-se	s
25	s	115	s	279-es	e
26	-	32	␣	280-s␣	s
27	se	278	se	281-␣se	␣
28	a	97	a	282-sea	se
29	-si	259	␣si	283-a␣si	a
30	c	99	c	284-␣sic	␣si
31	k	107	k	285-ck	c
32	-se	281	␣se	286-k␣se	k
33	a	97	a	287-␣sea	␣se
34	l	108	l	288-al	a
35	s	115	s	289-ls	l

Table 3.23: LZMW Example.

3.12 LZAP

LZAP is an extension of LZMW. The "AP" stands for "All Prefixes" [Storer 88]. LZAP adapts to its input fast, like LZMW, but eliminates the need for backtracking, a feature that makes it faster than LZMW. The principle is this: Instead of adding the concatenation S'S of the last two phrases to the dictionary, add all the strings S't where t is a prefix of S (including S itself). Thus if S' = a and S = bcd, add phrases ab,abc, and abcd to the LZAP dictionary. Table 3.24 shows the matches and the phrases added to the dictionary for yabbadabbadabbadoo.

Step	Input	Match	Add to dictionary
	yabbadabbadabbadoo		
1	y	y	—
2	a	a	256-ya
3	b	b	257-ab
4	b	b	258-bb
5	a	a	259-ba
6	d	d	260-ad
7	ab	ab	261-da, 262-dab
8	ba	ba	263-abb, 264-abba
9	dab	dab	265-bad, 266-bada, 267-badab
10	ba	ba	268-dabb, 269-dabba
11	d	d	270-bad
12	o	o	271-do
13	o	o	272-oo

Table 3.24: LZAP Example.

In step 7 the encoder concatenates d to the two prefixes of ab and adds the two phrases da and dab to the dictionary. In step 9 it concatenates ba to the three prefixes of dab and adds the resulting three phrases bad, bada, and badab to the dictionary.

LZAP adds more phrases to its dictionary than does LZMW, so it takes more bits to represent the position of a phrase. At the same time, LZAP provides a bigger selection of dictionary phrases as matches for the input string, so it ends up compressing slightly better than LZMW while being faster (because of the simpler dictionary data structure, which eliminates the need for backtracking). This kind of tradeoff is common in computer algorithms.

3.13 LZY

The LZW method is due to Dan Bernstein. The Y stands for "Yabba", which came from the input string originally used to test the algorithm. The LZY dictionary is initialized to all the single symbols of the alphabet. For every symbol C in the input stream, the decoder looks for the longest string P that precedes C and is already included in the dictionary. If the string PC is not in the dictionary, it is added to it as a new phrase.

As an example, the input `yabbadabbadabbadoo` causes the phrases `ya`, `ab`, `bb`, `ba`, `ad`, `da`, `abb`, `bba`, `ada`, `dab`, `abba`, `bbad`, `bado`, `ado`, and `oo` to be added to the dictionary.

While encoding the input, the encoder keeps track of the list of "matches-so-far" L. Initially, L is empty. If C is the current input symbol, the encoder (before adding anything to the dictionary) checks, for every string M in L, whether string MC is in the dictionary. If it is, then MC becomes a new match-so-far and is added to L. Otherwise, the encoder outputs the number of L (its position in the dictionary) and adds C, as a new match-so-far, to L.

Here is a pseudo-code algorithm for constructing the LZY dictionary. The author's personal experience suggests that implementing such an algorithm in a real programming language results in a deeper understanding of its operation.

```
Start with a dictionary containing all the symbols of the
  alphabet, each mapped to a unique integer.
M:=empty string.
Repeat
 Append the next symbol C of the input stream to M.
 If M is not in the dictionary, add it to the dictionary,
   delete the first character of M, and repeat this step.
Until end-of-input.
```

The output of LZY is not synchronized with the dictionary additions. Also, the encoder must be careful not to have the longest output match overlap itself. Because of this, the dictionary should consist of two parts, S and T, where only the former is used for the output. The algorithm is the following:

```
Start with S mapping each single character to a unique integer;
set T empty; M empty; and O empty.
Repeat
 Input the next symbol C. If OC is in S, set O:=OC;
 otherwise output S(O), set O:=C, add T to S,
   and remove everything from T.
 While MC is not in S or T, add MC to T (mapping to the next
    available integer), and chop off the first character of M.
 After M is short enough so that MC is in the dict., set M:=MC.
Until end-of-input.
Output S(O) and quit.
```

The decoder reads the compressed stream. It uses each code to find a phrase in the dictionary, it outputs the phrase as a string, then uses each symbol of the string to add a new phrase to the dictionary in the same way the encoder does. Here are the decoding steps:

```
Start with a dictionary containing all the symbols of the
  alphabet, each mapped to a unique integer.
M:=empty string.
Repeat
 Read D(O) from the input and take the inverse under D to find O.
```

As long as O is not the empty string, find the first character C
of O, and update (D,M) as above.

Also output C and chop it off from the front of O.
Until end-of-input.

Notice that encoding requires two fast operations on strings in the dictionary:
(1) testing whether string SC is in the dictionary if S's position is known and (2)
finding S's position given CS's position. Decoding requires the same operations
plus fast searching to find the first character of a string when its position in the
dictionary is given.

Table 3.25 illustrates LZY for the input string "abcabcabcabcabcabcabcx". It
shows the phrases added to the dictionary at each step, as well as the list of current
matches.

Step	Input	Add to dict.	Current matches
	abcabcabcabcabcabcabcx		
1	a	—	a
2	b	256-ab	b
3	c	257-bc	c
4	a	258-ca	a
5	b	—	ab, b
6	c	259-abc	bc, c
7	a	260-bca	ca, a
8	b	261-cab	ab, b
9	c	—	abc, bc, c
10	a	262-abca	bca, ca, a
11	b	263-bcab	cab, ab, b
12	c	264-cabc	abc, bc, c
13	a	—	abca, bca, ca, a
14	b	265-abcab	bcab, cab, ab, b
15	c	266-bcabc	cabc, abc, bc, c
16	a	267-cabca	abca, bca, ca, a
17	b	—	abcab, bcab, cab, ab, b
18	c	268-abcabc	bcabc, cabc, abc, bc, c
19	a	269-bcabca	cabca, abca, bca, ca, a
20	b	270-cabcab	abcab, bcab, cab, ab, b
21	c	—	abcabc, bcabc, cabc, abc, bc, c
22	x	271-abcabcx	x
23		272-bcabcx	
24		273-cabcx	
25		274-abcx	
26		275-bcx	
27		276-cx	

Table 3.25: LZY Example.

The encoder starts with no matches. When it inputs a symbol, it appends it to each match-so-far; any results that are already in the dictionary become the new matches-so-far (the symbol itself becomes another match). Any results that are not in the dictionary are deleted from the list and added to the dictionary.

Before reading the fifth c, for example, the matches-so-far are bcab, cab, ab, and b. The encoder appends c to each match. bcabc doesn't match, so the encoder adds it to the dictionary. The rest are still in the dictionary, so the new list of matches-so-far is cabc, abc, bc, and c.

When the x is input, the current list of matches-so-far is abcabc, bcabc, cabc, abc, bc, and c. None of abcabcx, bcabcx, cabcx, abcx, bcx, or cx are in the dictionary, so they are all added to it, and the list of matches-so-far is reduced to just a single x.

> Airman stops coed
> (anagram of "data compression")

3.14 LZP

This LZ77 variant is due to Charles Bloom [Bloom 96] (the P stands for "prediction"). It is based on the principle of context prediction, which says, "if a certain string 'abcde' has appeared in the input stream in the past and was followed by 'fg...', then when 'abcde' appears again in the input stream, there is a good chance that it will be followed by the same 'fg...'." Section 3.26 should be consulted for the relation between dictionary-based and prediction algorithms.

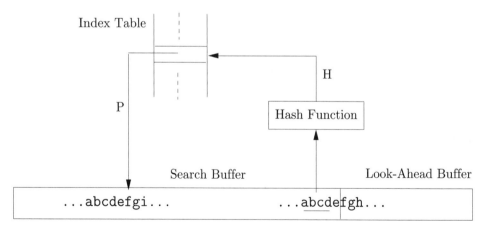

Figure 3.26: The Principle of LZP: Part I.

Figure 3.26 shows an LZ77 sliding buffer with "fgh..." as the current symbols (this string is denoted by S) in the look-ahead buffer, immediately preceded by abcde in the search buffer. The string abcde is called the *context* of "fgh..." and is denoted by C. In general, the context of a string S is the N-symbol string C immediately to the left of S. A context can be of any length N, and variants of LZP, discussed in Sections 3.14.3 and 3.14.4, use different values of N. The algorithm passes the context through a hash function and uses the result H as an index to a table of pointers called the *index table*. The index table contains pointers to various symbols in the search buffer. Index H is used to select a pointer P. In a typical case, P points to a previously seen string whose context is also abcde (see below for atypical cases). The algorithm then performs the following steps:

Step 1: It saves P and replaces it in the index table with a fresh pointer Q pointing to "fgh..." in the look-ahead buffer (Figure 3.26 Part II). An integer variable L is set to zero. It is used later to indicate the match length.

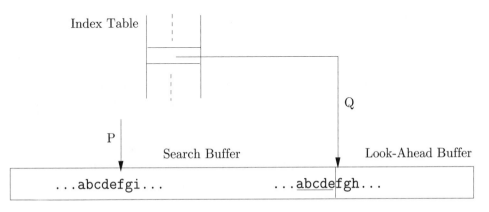

Figure 3.26: The Principle of LZP: Part II.

Step 2: If P is not a null pointer, the algorithm follows it and compares the string pointed at by P (string "fgi..." in the search buffer) to the string "fgh..." in the look-ahead buffer. Only two symbols match in our example, so the match length, L, is set to 2.

Step 3: If $L = 0$ (no symbols have been matched), the buffer is slid to the right (or, equivalently, the input is shifted to the left) **one position** and the first symbol of string S (the f) is written on the compressed stream as a raw ASCII code (a literal).

Step 4: If $L > 0$ (L symbols have been matched), the buffer is slid to the right L positions and the value of L is written on the compressed stream (after being suitably encoded).

In our example the single encoded value $L = 2$ is written on the compressed stream instead of the two symbols fg, and it is this step that produces compression. Clearly, the larger the value of L, the better the compression. Large values of L result when an N-symbol context C in the input stream is followed by the same long string S as a previous occurrence of C. This may happen when the input stream features high redundancy. In a random input stream each occurrence of the same context C is likely to be followed by another S, leading to $L = 0$ and thus to no compression. An "average" input stream results in more literals than L values being written on the output stream (see also Exercise 3.17).

The decoder inputs the compressed stream item by item and creates the decompressed output in a buffer B. The steps are:

Step 1: Input the next item I from the compressed stream.

Step 2: If I is a raw ASCII code (a literal), it is appended to buffer B, and the data in B is shifted to the left one position.

Step 3: If I is an encoded match length, it is decoded, to obtain L. The present context C (the rightmost N symbols in B) is hashed to an index H, which is used to select a pointer P from the index table. The decoder copies the string of L symbols starting at B[P] and appends it to the right end of B. It also shifts the data in B to the left L positions and replaces P in the index table with a fresh pointer, to keep in lockstep with the encoder.

Two points remain to be discussed before we are ready to look at a detailed example.

1. When the encoder starts, it places the first N symbols of the input stream in the search buffer, to become the first context. It then writes these symbols, as literals, on the compressed stream. This is the only special step needed to start the compression. The decoder starts by reading the first N items off the compressed stream (they should be literals), and placing them at the rightmost end of buffer B, to serve as the first context.

2. It has been mentioned before that in the typical case, P points to a previously seen string whose context is identical to the present context C. In an atypical case, P may be pointing to a string whose context is different. The algorithm, however, does not check the context and always behaves in the same way. It simply tries to match as many symbols as possible. At worst, zero symbols will match, leading to one literal written on the compressed stream.

3.14.1 Example

The input stream xyabcabcabxy is used to illustrate the operation of the LZP encoder. To simplify the example, we use $N = 2$.

1. To start the operation, the encoder shifts the first 2 symbols xy to the search buffer and outputs them as literals. It also initializes all locations of the index table to the null pointer.

2. The current symbol is a (the first a) and the context is xy. It is hashed to, say, 5, but location 5 of the index table contains a null pointer, so P is null (Figure 3.27a). Location 5 is set to point to the first a (Figure 3.27b), which is then output as a literal. The data in the encoder's buffer is shifted to the left.

3. The current symbol is the first b and the context is ya. It is hashed to, say, 7, but location 7 of the index table contains a null pointer, so P is null (Figure 3.27c). Location 7 is set to point to the first b (Figure 3.27d), which is then output as a literal. The data in the encoder's buffer is shifted to the left.

4. The current symbol is the first c and the context is ab. It is hashed to, say, 2, but location 2 of the index table contains a null pointer, so P is null (Figure 3.27e). Location 2 is set to point to the first c (Figure 3.27f), which is then output as a literal. The data in the encoder's buffer is shifted to the left.

5. The same happens two more times, writing the literals a and b on the compressed stream. The current symbol is now (the second) c, and the context is ab. This

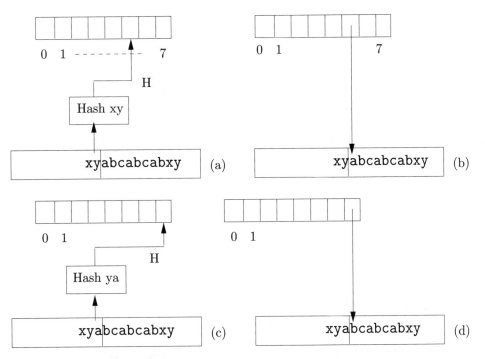

Figure 3.27: LZP Compression of "xyabcabcabxy": Part I.

context is hashed, as in step 4, to 2, so P points to "cabc...". Location 2 is set to point to the current symbol (Figure 3.27g), and the encoder tries to match strings cabcabxy and cabxy. The resulting match length is $L = 3$. The number 3 is written, encoded on the output, and the data is shifted three positions to the left.

6. The current symbol is the second x and the context is ab. It is hashed to 2, but location 2 of the index table points to the second c (Figure 3.27h). Location 2 is set to point to the current symbol, and the encoder tries to match strings cabxy and xy. The resulting match length is, of course, $L = 0$, so the encoder writes x on the compressed stream as a literal and shifts the data one position.

7. The current symbol is the second y and the context is bx. It is hashed to, say, 7. This is a hash collision, since context ya was hashed to 7 in step 3, but the algorithm does not check for collisions. It continues as usual. Location 7 of the index table points to the first b (or rather to the string bcabcabxy). It is set to point to the current symbol, and the encoder tries to match strings bcabcabxy and y, resulting in $L = 0$. The encoder writes y on the compressed stream as a literal and shifts the data one position.

8. The current symbol is the end-of-data, so the algorithm terminates.

⋄ **Exercise 3.16:** Write the LZP encoding steps for the input string "xyaaaa...".

Structures are the weapons of the mathematician.
—Nicholas Bourbaki

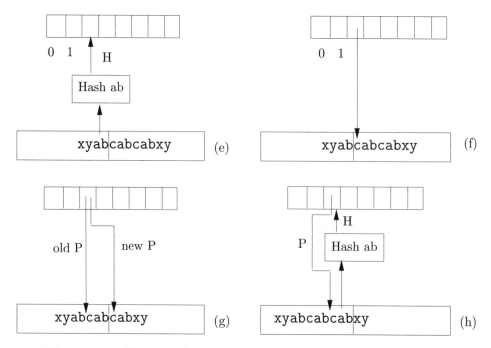

Figure 3.27 (Continued). LZP Compression of `xyabcabcabxy`: Part II.

3.14.2 Practical Considerations

Shifting the data in the buffer would require updating all the pointers in the index table. An efficient implementation should therefore adopt a better solution. Two approaches are described below, but other ones may also work.

1. Reserve a buffer as large as possible and compress the input stream in blocks. Each block is input into the buffer and is never shifted. Instead, a pointer is moved from left to right, to point at any time to the current symbol in the buffer. When the entire buffer has been encoded, the buffer is filled up again with fresh input. This approach simplifies the program but has the disadvantage that the data at the end of a block cannot be used to predict anything for the next block. Each block is encoded independently of the other ones, leading to poorer compression.

2. Reserve a large buffer and use it as a circular queue (Section 3.2.1). The data itself does not have to be shifted, but after encoding the current symbol the data is *effectively* shifted by updating the start and end pointers, and a new symbol is input and stored in the buffer. The algorithm is somewhat more complicated, but this approach has the advantage that the entire input is encoded as one stream. Every symbol benefits from the D symbols preceding it (where D is the total length of the buffer).

Imagine a pointer P in the index table pointing to some symbol X in the buffer. When the movement of the two pointers in the circular queue leaves X outside the queue, some new symbol Y will be input into the position occupied by X, and P will now be pointing to Y. When P is next selected by the hashing function and is used to match strings, the match will likely result in $L = 0$. However, the algorithm always replaces the pointer that it uses, so such a case should not degrade the algorithm's performance significantly.

3.14.3 LZP1 and LZP2

There are currently four versions of LZP, called LZP1 through LZP4. This section discusses the details of the first two. The context used by LZP1 is of order 3, i.e., it is the 3 bytes preceding the current one. The hash function produces a 12-bit index H and is best described by the following C code:

$$\texttt{H=((C>>11)\textasciicircum C)\&0xFFF}.$$

Since H is 12 bits, the index table should be $2^{12} = 4{,}096$ entries long. Each entry is 2 bytes (16 bits), but only 14 of the 16 bits are used. A pointer P selected in the index table thus points to a buffer of size $2^{14} = 16\text{K}$.

The LZP1 encoder creates a compressed stream with literals and L values mixed together. Each item must therefore be preceded by a flag indicating its nature. Since only two flags are needed, the simplest choice would be 1-bit flags. However, we have already mentioned that an "average" input stream results in more literals than L values, so it makes sense to assign a short flag (less than one bit) to indicate a literal, and a long flag (a wee bit longer than one bit) to indicate a length. The scheme used by LZP1 uses 1 to indicate two literals, 01 to indicate a literal followed by a match length, and 00 to indicate a match length.

⋄ **Exercise 3.17:** Let T indicate the probability of a literal in the compressed stream. For what value of T does the above scheme produce flags that are 1-bit long on average?

A literal is written on the compressed stream as an 8-bit ASCII code. Match lengths are encoded according to Table 3.28. Initially, the codes are 2 bits. When these are all used up, 3 bits are added, for a total of 5 bits, where the first 2 bits are 1's. When these are also all used, 5 bits are added, to produce 10-bit codes where the first 5 bits are 1's. From then on another group of 8 bits is added to the code whenever all the old codes have been used up. Notice how the pattern of all 1's is never used as a code and is reserved to indicate longer and longer codes. Notice also that a unary code or a general unary code (Section 2.3.1) might have been a better choice.

Length	Code	Length	Code
1	00	11	11|111|00000
2	01	12	11|111|00001
3	10	⋮	
4	11|000	41	11|111|11110
5	11|001	42	11|111|11111|00000000
6	11|010	⋮	
⋮		296	11|111|11111|11111110
10	11|110	297	11|111|11111|11111111|00000000

Table 3.28: Codes Used by LZP1 and LZP2 for Match Lengths.

The compressed stream consists of a mixture of literals (bytes with ASCII codes) and control bytes containing flags and encoded lengths. This is illustrated by the output of the example of Section 3.14.1. The input of this example is the string xyabcabcabxy, and the output items are x, y, a, b, c, a, b, 3, x, and y. The actual output stream consists of the single control byte "111 01|10 1" followed by 9 bytes with the ASCII codes of x, y, a, b, c, a, b, x, and y.

⋄ **Exercise 3.18:** Explain the contents of the control byte "111 01|10 1".

Another example of a compressed stream is the three literals x, y, and a followed by the four match lengths 12, 12, 12, and 10. We first prepare the flags

$$1 \ (\text{``x''}, \text{``y''}) \ 01 \ (\text{``a''}, 12) \ 00 \ (12) \ 00 \ (12) \ 00 \ (12) \ 00 \ (10),$$

then substitute the codes of 12 and 10,

$$1xy01a11|111|0000100|11|111|0000100|11|111|0000100|11|111|0000100|11|110,$$

and finally group together the bits that make up the control bytes. The result is

10111111 x, y, a, 00001001 11110000 10011111 00001001 11110000 10011110.

Notice that the first control byte is followed by the three literals.

The last point to be mentioned is the case: ...0 1yyyyyyy zzzzzzzz. The first control byte ends with the 0, and the second byte starts with the 1, of a pair 01. This indicates a literal followed by a match length. The match length is the yyy bits (at least some of them) in the second control byte. If the code of the match length is long, then the zzz bits or some of them may be part of the code. The literal is either the zzz byte or the byte following it.

LZP2 is identical to LZP1 except that literals are coded using nonadaptive Huffman codes. Ideally, two passes should be used; the first one counting the frequency of occurrence of the symbols in the input stream and the second doing the actual compression. In between the passes, the Huffman code table can be constructed.

3.14.4 LZP3 and LZP4

LZP3 is similar to both LZP1 and LZP2. It uses order-4 contexts and more sophisticated Huffman codes to encode both the match lengths and the literals. The LZP3 hash function is

$$\text{H=((C>>15)\^C)\&0xFFFF},$$

so H is a 16-bit index, to be used with an index table of size $2^{16} = 64$K. The index table contains, in addition to the pointers P, also the contexts C. Thus if a context C is hashed to an index H, the encoder expects to find the same context C in location H of the index table. This is called *context confirmation*. If the encoder finds something else, or if it finds a null pointer, it sets P to null and hashes an order-3 context. If the order-3 context confirmation also fails, the algorithm hashes the order-2 context, and if that also fails, the algorithm sets P to null and writes a literal on the compressed stream. This method thus attempts to find the highest-order context seen so far.

LZP4 uses order-5 contexts and a multistep lookup process. In step 1, the rightmost 4 bytes I of the context are hashed to create a 16-bit index H according to the following:

$$H=((I>>15)^I)\&0xFFFF.$$

Then H is used as an index to the index table that has 64K entries, each corresponding to one value of H. Each entry points to the start of a list linking nodes that have the same hash value. Suppose that the contexts abcde, xbcde, and mnopq hash to the same index H = 13 (i.e., the hash function computes the same index 13 when applied to bcde and nopq) and we are looking for context xbcde. Location 13 of the index table would point to a list with nodes for these contexts (and perhaps others that have also been hashed to 13). The list is traversed until a node is found with bcde. This node points to a second list linking a, x, and perhaps other symbols that precede bcde. The second list is traversed until a node with x is found. That node contains a pointer to the most recent occurrence of context xbcde in the search buffer. If a node with x is not found, a literal is written to the compressed stream.

This complex lookup procedure is used by LZP4 because a 5-byte context does not fit comfortably in a single word in most present computers.

Bibliography

Bloom, C. R. (1996), "LZP: A New Data Compression Algorithm," in *Proceedings of Data Compression Conference*, J. Storer, editor, Los Alamitos, CA, IEEE Computer Society Press, p. 425.

3.15 Repetition Finder

All the dictionary-based methods described so far have one thing in common: they use a large memory buffer as a dictionary that holds fragments of text found so far. The dictionary is used to locate strings of symbols that repeat. The method described here is different. Instead of a dictionary it uses a fixed-size array of integers to find previous occurrences of strings of text. The array size equals the square of the alphabet size, so it is not very large. The method is due to Hidetoshi Yokoo [Yokoo 91], who elected not to call it LZHY but left it nameless. The reason a name of the form LZxx was not used is that the method does not employ a traditional Ziv-Lempel dictionary. The reason it was left nameless is that it does not compress very well and should thus be considered the first step in a new field of research rather than a mature, practical method.

The method alternates between two modes, normal and repeat. It starts in the normal mode, where it inputs symbols and encodes them using adaptive Huffman. When it identifies a repeated string it switches to the "repeat" mode where it outputs an escape symbol, followed by the length of the repeated string.

Assume that the input stream consists of symbols $x_1 x_2 \ldots$ from an alphabet A. Both encoder and decoder maintain an array REP of dimensions $|A| \times |A|$ that is initialized to all zeros. For each input symbol x_i, the encoder (and decoder) compute a value y_i according to $y_i = i - \text{REP}[x_{i-1}, x_i]$, and then update $\text{REP}[x_{i-1}, x_i] := i$. The 13-symbol string

$$
\begin{array}{llllllllllllll}
x_i\colon & \text{X} & \text{A} & \text{B} & \text{C} & \text{D} & \text{E} & \text{Y} & \text{A} & \text{B} & \text{C} & \text{D} & \text{E} & \text{Z} \\
i\colon & 1 & & 3 & & 5 & & 7 & & 9 & & 11 & & 13
\end{array}
$$

results in the following y values:

$$
\begin{array}{llllllllllllll}
i = & 1 & 2 & 3 & 4 & 5 & 6 & 7 & 8 & 9 & 10 & 11 & 12 & 13 \\
y_i = & 1 & 2 & 3 & 4 & 5 & 6 & 7 & 8 & 6 & 6 & 6 & 6 & 13 \\
x_{i-1}x_i: & \text{XA} & \text{AB} & \text{BC} & \text{CD} & \text{DE} & \text{EY} & \text{YA} & \text{AB} & \text{BC} & \text{CD} & \text{DE} & \text{EZ}
\end{array}
$$

Table 3.29a shows the state of array REP after the eighth symbol has been input and encoded. Table 3.29b shows the state of REP after all 13 symbols have been input and encoded.

	A	B	C	D	E	...	X	Y	Z
A	3								
B		4							
C			5						
D				6					
E							7		
⋮									
X	2								
Y	8								
Z									

	A	B	C	D	E	...	X	Y	Z
A	9								
B		10							
C			11						
D				12					
E									13
⋮									
X	2								
Y	8								
Z									

Table 3.29: (a) REP at $i = 8$. (b) REP at $i = 13$.

Perhaps a better way to explain the way y is calculated is by means of

$$
y_i = \begin{cases}
1, & \text{for } i = 1, \\
i, & \text{for } i > 1 \text{ and first occurrence of } x_{i-1}x_i; \\
\min(k), & \text{for } i > 1 \text{ and } x_{i-1}x_i \text{ identical to } x_{i-k-1}x_{i-k}.
\end{cases}
$$

This shows that y is either i or is the distance k between the current string $x_{i-1}x_i$ and its most recent copy $x_{i-k-1}x_{i-k}$. However, recognizing a repetition of a string is done by means of array REP and without using any dictionary (which is the main point of this method).

When a string of length l repeats itself in the input, l consecutive identical values of y are generated, and this is the signal for the encoder to switch to the "repeat" mode. As long as consecutive different values of y are generated, the encoder stays in the "normal" mode, where it encodes x_i in adaptive Huffman and outputs it. When the encoder senses $y_{i+1} = y_i$, it outputs x_i in the normal mode, and then enters the "repeat" mode. In the example above this happens for $i = 9$, so the string "XABCDEYAB" is output in the normal mode.

Once in the "repeat" mode, the encoder inputs more symbols and calculates y values until it finds the first value that differs from y_i. In our example this happens at $i = 13$, when the Z is input. The encoder compresses the string "CDE" (corresponding to $i = 10, 11, 12$) in the "repeat" mode by outputting an (encoded) escape symbol, followed by the (encoded) length of the repeated string (3 in our example). The encoder then switches back to the normal mode, where it saves the y value for Z as y_i and inputs the next symbol.

The escape symbol must be an extra symbol, one that's not included in the alphabet A. Notice that only two y values, y_{i-1} and y_i, need be saved at any time. Notice also that the method is not very efficient, since it senses the repeating string "too late" and encodes the first two repeating symbols in the normal mode. In our example only three of the five repeating symbols are encoded in the "repeat" mode.

The decoder inputs and decodes the first nine symbols, decoding them into the string "XABCDEYAB" while updating array REP and calculating y values. When the escape symbol is input, i has the value 9 and y_i has the value 6. The decoder inputs and decodes the length, 3, and now it has to figure out the repeated string of length 3 using just the data in array REP, not any of the previously decoded input. Since $i = 9$ and y_i is the distance between this string and its copy, the decoder knows that the copy started at position $i - y_i = 9 - 6 = 3$ of the input. It scans REP, looking for a 3. It finds it at position REP[A,B], so it starts looking for a 4 in row B of REP. It finds it in REP[B,C], so the first symbol of the required string is "C". Looking for a 5 in row C, the decoder finds it in REP[C,D], so the second symbol is "D". Looking now for a 6 in row D, the decoder finds it in REP[D,E].

This is how a repeated string can be decoded without maintaining a dictionary.

Both encoder and decoder store values of i in REP, so an entry of REP should be at least 2 bytes long. This way i can have values of up to $64\text{K} - 1 \approx 65{,}500$, so the input has to be encoded in blocks of size 64K. For an alphabet of 256 symbols, the size of REP should thus be $256 \times 256 \times 2 = 128$ Kbytes, not very large. For larger alphabets REP may have to be uncomfortably large.

In the normal mode, symbols (including the escape) are encoded using adaptive Huffman (Section 2.9). In the repeat mode, lengths are encoded in a recursive prefix code denoted $Q_k(i)$, where k is a positive integer (see Section 2.3 for prefix codes). Assuming that i is an integer whose binary representation is 1α, the prefix code $Q_k(i)$ of i is defined by

$$Q_0(i) = 1^{|\alpha|}0\alpha, \qquad Q_k(i) = \begin{cases} 0, & i = 1, \\ 1Q_{k-1}(i - 1), & i > 1, \end{cases}$$

where $|\alpha|$ is the length of α and $1^{|\alpha|}$ is a string of $|\alpha|$ ones. Table 3.30 shows some of the proposed codes; however, any of the prefix codes of Section 2.3 can be used instead of the $Q_k(i)$ codes proposed here.

The developer of this method, Hidetoshi Yokoo, indicates that compression performance is not very sensitive to the precise value of k, and he proposes $k = 2$ for best overall performance.

As mentioned earlier, the method is not very efficient, which is why it should be considered the beginning of a new field of research where repeated strings are identified without the need for a large dictionary.

Bibliography

Yokoo, Hidetoshi (1991) "An Improvement of Dynamic Huffman Coding with a Simple Repetition Finder," *IEEE Transactions on Communications* **39**(1):8–10, January.

i	α	$Q_0(i)$	$Q_1(i)$	$Q_2(i)$
1	null	0	0	0
2	0	100	10	10
3	1	101	1100	110
4	00	11000	1101	11100
5	01	11001	111000	11101
6	10	11010	111001	1111000
7	11	11011	111010	1111001
8	000	1110000	111011	1111010
9	001	1110001	11110000	1111011

Table 3.30: Proposed Prefix Code.

3.16 UNIX Compression

In the large UNIX world, `compress` used to be the most common compression utility (although GNU `gzip` is now more popular; since it is free from patent claims, is faster, and provides superior compression). This utility (also called LZC) uses LZW with a growing dictionary. It starts with a small dictionary of just $2^9 = 512$ entries (with the first 256 of them already filled up). While this dictionary is being used, 9-bit pointers are written onto the output stream. When the original dictionary fills up, its size is doubled, to 1024 entries, and 10-bit pointers are used from this point. This process continues until the pointer size reaches a maximum set by the user (it can be set to between 9 and 16 bits, with 16 as the default value). When the largest allowed dictionary fills up, the program continues without changing the dictionary (which then becomes static), but with monitoring the compression ratio. If the ratio falls below a predefined threshold, the dictionary is deleted, and a new 512-entry dictionary is started. This way, the dictionary never gets "too out of date."

Decoding is done by the `uncompress` command, which implements the LZC decoder. Its main task is to maintain the dictionary in the same way as the encoder.

Two improvements to LZC, proposed by [Horspool 91], are listed below:

1. Encode the dictionary pointers with the phased-in binary codes of Section 2.9.1. Thus if the dictionary size is $2^9 = 512$ entries, pointers can be encoded in either 8 or 9 bits.

2. Determine all the impossible strings at any point. Suppose that the current string in the look-ahead buffer is "abcd..." and the dictionary contains strings abc and abca but not abcd. The encoder will output, in this case, the pointer to abc and will start encoding a new string starting with d. The point is that after decoding abc, the decoder knows that the next string cannot start with an a (if it did, an abca would have been encoded, instead of abc). In general, if S is the current string, then the next string cannot start with any symbol x that satisfies "Sx is in the dictionary."

This knowledge can be used by both the encoder and decoder to reduce redundancy even further. When a pointer to a string should be output, it should be coded, and the method of assigning the code should eliminate all the strings that are known to be impossible at that point. This may result in a somewhat shorter code but is probably too complex to justify its use in practice.

Bibliography

Horspool, N. R. (1991) "Improving LZW," in *Proceedings of the 1991 Data Compression Conference*, J. Storer Ed., Los Alamitos, CA, IEEE Computer Society Press, pp. 332–341.

3.17 GIF Images

GIF—the graphics interchange format—was developed by Compuserve Information Services in 1987 as an efficient, compressed graphics file format, which allows for images to be sent between different computers. The original version of GIF is known as GIF 87a. The current standard is GIF 89a and, at the time of writing, can be freely obtained as the file `http://delcano.mit.edu/info/gif.txt`. GIF is not a data compression method; it is a graphics file format that uses a variant of LZW to compress the graphics data. This section reviews only the data compression aspects of GIF.

In compressing data, GIF is very similar to `compress` and uses a dynamic, growing dictionary. It starts with the number of bits per pixel b as a parameter. For a monochromatic image, $b = 2$; for an image with 256 colors or shades of gray, $b = 8$. The dictionary starts with 2^{b+1} entries and is doubled in size each time it fills up, until it reaches a size of $2^{12} = 4,096$ entries, where it remains static. At such a point, the encoder monitors the compression ratio and may decide to discard the dictionary at any point and start with a new, empty one. When making this decision, the encoder emits the value 2^b as the *clear code*, which is the sign for the decoder to discard its dictionary.

The pointers, which get longer by 1 bit from one dictionary to the next, are accumulated and are output in blocks of 8-bit bytes. Each block is preceded by a header that contains the block size (255 bytes maximum) and is terminated by a byte of eight zeros. The last block contains, just before the terminator, the eof value, which is $2^b + 1$. An interesting feature is that the pointers are stored with their least significant bit on the left. Consider, for example, the following 3-bit pointers 3, 7, 4, 1, 6, 2, and 5. Their binary values are 011, 111, 100, 001, 110, 010, and 101, so they are packed in 3 bytes |10101001|11000011|11110...|.

The GIF format is commonly used today by web browsers, but it is not an efficient image compressor. GIF scans the image row by row, so it discovers pixel correlations within a row, but not between rows. We can say that GIF compression is inefficient because GIF is one-dimensional while an image is two-dimensional. An illustrative example is the two simple images of Figure 4.3a,b (Section 4.1). Saving both in GIF89 has resulted in file sizes of 1053 and 1527 bytes, respectively.

Most graphics file formats use some kind of compression. For more information on those files, see [Murray 94].

Bibliography

Blackstock, Steve (1987) "LZW and GIF Explained," public domain, available from URL "`http://www.ece.uiuc.edu/~ece291/class-resources/gpe/gif.txt.html`".

Murray, James D. and William vanRyper, (1994) *Encyclopedia of Graphics File Formats*, Sebastopol, CA, O'Reilly and Assoc.

3.18 The V.42bis Protocol

The V.42bis protocol is a set of rules, or a standard, published by the ITU-T (page 91) for use in fast modems. It is based on the existing V.32bis protocol and is supposed to be used for fast transmission rates, up to 57.6K baud. Thomborson [Thomborson 92] in a detailed reference for this standard. The ITU-T standards are recommendations, but they are normally followed by all major modem manufacturers. The standard contains specifications for data compression and error correction, but only the former is discussed here.

V.42bis specifies two modes: a *transparent* mode, where no compression is used, and a *compressed* mode using an LZW variant. The former is used for data streams that don't compress well and may even cause expansion. A good example is an already compressed file. Such a file looks like random data; it does not have any repetitive patterns, and trying to compress it with LZW will fill up the dictionary with short, two-symbol, phrases.

The compressed mode uses a growing dictionary, whose initial size is negotiated between the modems when they initially connect. V.42bis recommends a dictionary size of 2,048 entries. The minimum size is 512 entries. The first three entries, corresponding to pointers 0, 1, and 2, do not contain any phrases and serve as special codes. Code 0 (enter transparent mode—ETM) is sent when the encoder notices a low compression ratio, and it decides to start sending uncompressed data. (Unfortunately, V.42bis does not say how the encoder should test for low compression.) Code 1 is FLUSH, to flush data. Code 2 (STEPUP) is sent when the dictionary is almost full and the encoder decides to double its size. A dictionary is considered almost full when its size exceeds that of a special threshold (which is also negotiated by the modems).

When the dictionary is already at its maximum size and it becomes full, V.42bis recommends a *reuse* procedure. The least recently used phrase is located and deleted, to make room for a new phrase. This is done by searching the dictionary from entry 256 for the first phrase that is not a prefix to any other phrase. Suppose that the phrase abcd is found, and there are no phrases of the form abcdx for any x. This means that abcd has not been used since it was created, and that it is the oldest such phrase. It therefore makes sense to delete it, since it reflects an old pattern in the input stream. This way, the dictionary always reflects recent patterns in the input.

Bibliography

Thomborson, Clark (1992) "The V.42bis Standard for Data-Compressing Modems," *IEEE Micro* pp. 41–53, October.

> Time is the image of eternity
> —Diogenes Laertius

3.19 Zip and Gzip

The popular programs Zip and Gzip implement the so-called "deflation" algorithm, which uses a variation of LZ77 combined with static Huffman. It uses a 32 Kbyte-long sliding dictionary, and a look-ahead buffer of 258 bytes. When a string is not found in the dictionary it is emitted as a sequence of literal bytes.

The input stream is divided by the encoder into blocks. Block sizes are arbitrary, except that incompressible blocks are limited to 64 Kbytes. A block is terminated when the "deflate" encoder determines that it would be useful to start another block with fresh Huffman trees. (This is somewhat similar to UNIX compress.) Literals or match lengths are compressed with one Huffman tree, and match distances are compressed with another tree. The trees are stored in a compact form at the start of each block. The Huffman trees for each block are independent of those for previous or subsequent blocks.

Duplicated strings are found using a hash table. All input strings of length 3 are inserted in the hash table. A hash index is computed for the next 3 bytes. If the hash chain for this index is not empty, all strings in the chain are compared with the current input string, and the longest match is selected.

The hash chains are searched starting with the most recent strings, to favor small distances and thus take advantage of the Huffman encoding. The hash chains are singly linked. There are no deletions from the hash chains; the algorithm simply discards matches that are too old.

To avoid a worst-case situation, very long hash chains are arbitrarily truncated at a certain length, determined by a runtime option. As a result, Deflate does not always find the longest possible match, but it generally finds a match that's long enough.

Deflate also defers the selection of matches with a greedy evaluation mechanism. After a match of length N has been found, Deflate searches for a longer match at the next input byte. If a longer match is found, the previous match is truncated to a length of one (thus producing a single literal byte) and the longer match is emitted afterwards. Otherwise, the original match is kept, and the next match search is attempted only N steps later.

The greedy match evaluation is also controlled by a runtime parameter. If the current match is long enough, Deflate reduces the search for a longer match, thus speeding up the entire process. If compression ratio is more important than speed, Deflate attempts a complete second search even if the first match is already long enough.

The greedy match evaluation is not executed for the fastest compression modes. For these fast modes, new strings are inserted in the hash table only when no match was found, or when the match is not too long. This degrades the compression ratio but cuts down the run time of the algorithm, since there are both fewer insertions and fewer searches.

3.20 ARC and PKZip

ARC is a compression/archival/cataloging program developed by Robert A. Freed of System Enhancement Associates in the mid 1980s. It immediately became very popular among PC users, since it offered good compression and the ability to combine several files into one file, called an *archive*. Here are two situations where archiving is useful:

1. A group of files has to be up- or downloaded by modem. Archiving them into one large file can save transmission time since the modems on both sides have to go through a protocol for each file.

2. Storing hundreds of small files on a large hard disk can be space-consuming, since the bigger the disk, the larger the minimum block size. A typical 500 Mbyte disk may have a minimum block size of 5 Kbytes, so 100 small files of, say, 500 bytes each will occupy 500 Kbyte. When combined into an archive, the same information may occupy just 50 Kbyte.

Most modern archivers are self extracting. Such an archiver includes a small decompressor in the compressed file, so the file becomes a bit longer, but can decompress itself. In the PC world such archives have a suffix of ".SFX". On the Macintosh computer they are known as ".sea" files (for "self extracting archive").

ARC offers several compression methods, and the user can select any method for compressing a file. The general format of an ARC file is:

[[archive-mark + header-version + file header + file data]...] + archive-mark + end-of-arc-mark.

The archive-mark is the byte "1A". The file header is 27 bytes long and is defined by the following C structure:

```
typedef struct archive_file_header
  { char name[13]; /* file name */
    unsigned long size; /* size of compressed file */
    unsigned short date; /* file date */
    unsigned short time; /* file time */
    unsigned short crc; /* cyclic redundancy check */
    unsigned long length; /* true file length */
  };
```

The "name" field is the null-terminated file name.

The "size" is the number of bytes in the file data area following the header.

The "date" and "time" are stored in the same packed format as a DOS directory entry.

The "CRC" is a 16-bit code computed from the file data (Section 3.23).

The "length" is the actual uncompressed size of the file.

ARC uses the following compression methods:

1. No compression (obsolete).
2. Stored—The file is simply copied on the output stream with no compression.
3. Packed—(nonrepeat packing of text characters).
4. Squeezed (Huffman squeezing, after packing).
5. Crunched (Obsolete—12-bit static LZW without nonrepeat pack).

6. Crunched (Obsolete—12-bit static LZW with nonrepeat packing).

7. Crunched (Obsolete—after packing, using faster hash algorithm).

8. Crunched (Using dynamic LZW variations, after packing. The initial LZW code size is 9 bits with a maximum code size of 12 bits. Adaptive resets of the dictionary are implemented in this mode.)

9. Squashed (The file was compressed with Dynamic LZW compression without nonrepeat packing. The initial LZW code size is 9 bits with a maximum code size of 13 bits. Adaptive resets of the dictionary are implemented in this mode.)

PKArc is an improved version of ARC. It was developed by Phil Katz, who has founded the PKWare company ("`http://www.pkware.com`"), which markets the PKzip, PKunzip, PKlite, and PKArc software. The PK programs are faster and more general than ARC and also provide for more user control. As a result, ARC is no longer very popular. Several more PC compression programs are mentioned in Sections 3.21 and 3.22.

PKArc uses the same compression methods and file format as ARC. The other PK programs have several compression methods implemented, and the user can select any method to compress a file. Here is a short description of some of these methods:

1. *Shrinking.* This uses a version of dynamic LZW with partial clearing of the dictionary. The initial code size is 9 bits, with a maximum of 13 bits. Shrinking differs from other dynamic LZW implementations in two respects:

a. The code size is determined by the compressor and is increased by it from time to time. When the compressor decides to increment the code size, it emits the sequence 256, 1. This is a signal to the decompressor to do the same.

b. When the dictionary fills up it is not erased. Instead, the compressor clears all the leaves of the dictionary tree and emits the sequence 256, 2 as a signal for the decompressor. The code size is not increased. The cleared dictionary nodes are then reused

2. *Reducing.* This is a two-step method. It uses RLE followed by a statistical method. The statistical method prepares an array of "follower sets" $S(j)$, for $j = 0$ to 255, corresponding to the 256 possible bytes. Each set contains between 0 and 32 characters, to be denoted by $S(j)[0],\dots,S(j)[m]$, where $m < 32$. The sets are stored at the beginning of the output stream in reverse order, with $S(255)$ first and $S(0)$ last.

The sets are written on the output stream as $\{N(j),S(j)[0],\dots,S(j)[N(j)-1]\}$, where $N(j)$ is the size of set $S(j)$. $N(j)=0$ indicates an empty follower set $S(j)$. Each $N(j)$ is stored in 6 bits, followed by $N(j)$ 8-bit characters corresponding to $S(j)[0]$ through $S(j)[N(j)-1]$. If $N(j)=0$, then nothing is stored for $S(j)$, and the value of $N(j-1)$ immediately follows. Right after the follower sets, the output stream contains the compressed data stream, which is created by the compressor according to the pseudo-code below:

```
Last-Character:=0;
repeat
  if the follower set S(Last-Character) is empty then
  read 8 bits from the input stream, and
```

```
              write it on the output stream;
    else (the follower set S(Last-Character) is nonempty) then
      read 1 bit from the input stream;
      if this bit is not zero then
        read 8 bits from the input stream, and
                write it on the output stream;
      else (this bit is zero) then
        read B(N(Last-Character)) bits from the input stream,
                                    and assign it to i;
        Write value of S(Last-Character)[i] on output stream;
      endif;
    endif;
Last-Character:=last value written on the output stream;
until end-of-input
```

where $B(N(j))$ is defined as the minimal number of bits required to encode the value $N(j)-1$.

    The decompressor works as follows:

```
State:=0;
repeat
  read 8 bits from the input stream to C.
  case State of
0: if C is not equal DLE (ASCII 144) then write C on output stream;
   else if C is equal to DLE then let State <- 1; endif;
    endif;

1: if C is nonzero then
    V:=C;
    Len:=L(V);
    State:=F(Len);
    else if C is zero then
      copy the value 144 (decimal) to the output stream;
    State:=0;
     endif;

2: Len:=Len+C;
   State:=3;

3:   Move backwards D(V,C) bytes in the output stream
       (if this position is before the start of the output
       stream, then assume that all the data before the
       start of the output stream is filled with zeros).
       Write Len+3 bytes from this position to the output stream;
       State:=0;
   end case;
until end-of-input
```

The functions F, L, and D depend on the "compression factor" 1 through 4, and are defined as follows:

- For compression factor 1:
    L(X) equals the lower 7 bits of X.
    F(X)=2 if X equals 127; otherwise F(X) equals 3.
    D(X,Y) equals the (upper 1 bit of X)$\times 256 + Y + 1$.

- For compression factor 2:
    L(X) equals the lower 6 bits of X.
    F(X)=2 if X equals 63; otherwise F(X)=3.
    D(X,Y) equals the (upper 2 bits of X)$\times 256 + Y + 1$.

- For compression factor 3:
    L(X) equals the lower 5 bits of X.
    F(X)=2 if X equals 31; otherwise F(X)=3.
    D(X,Y) equals the (upper 3 bits of X)$\times 256 + Y + 1$.

- For compression factor 4:
    L(X) equals the lower 4 bits of X.
    F(X)=2 if X equals 15; otherwise F(X)=3.
    D(X,Y) equals the (upper 4 bits of X)$\times 256 + Y + 1$.

3. *Imploding.* This again is a combination of two methods. The first step compresses repeated byte sequences using a sliding dictionary (which is either 4 or 8 Kbytes long). The second step uses multiple Shannon-Fano trees to compress the output of the first step.

The Shannon-Fano trees are stored at the start of the output stream. Either two or three trees are stored. If three trees are stored, the first of them represents the encoding of the Literal characters, the second tree represents the encoding of the Length information, and the third represents the encoding of the Distance information. When two Shannon-Fano trees are stored, the Length tree is stored first, followed by the Distance tree.

If the "Literal" Shannon-Fano tree is present, it is used to represent every possible 8-bit byte, and it contains 256 values. This tree is used to compress any data not compressed by the sliding dictionary algorithm. When this tree is present, the Minimum Match Length for the sliding dictionary is 3. If this tree is absent, the Minimum Match Length is 2.

The "Length" Shannon-Fano tree is used to compress the "Length" part of the (length, distance) pairs from the sliding dictionary output. The "Length" tree contains 64 values, ranging from the Minimum Match Length, to 63 + Minimum Match Length.

The "Distance" Shannon-Fano tree is used to compress the "Distance" part of the (length, distance) pairs from the sliding dictionary output. This tree contains 64 values, ranging from 0 to 63, representing the upper 6 bits of the distance value. The distance values themselves will be between 0 and the sliding dictionary size, which is either 4K or 8K.

The Shannon-Fano trees themselves are stored in a compressed format. The first byte of the tree data contains the number of bytes of data representing the (compressed) Shannon-Fano tree minus 1. The remaining bytes contain the Shannon-Fano tree data encoded as follows:

High 4 bits: Number of values at this bit length +1. (1–16)
Low 4 bits: Bit Length needed to represent value +1. (1–16)

The Shannon-Fano codes can be constructed from the bit lengths using the following algorithm:

a. Sort the bit lengths in ascending order, while retaining the order of the original lengths stored in the file.
b. Generate the Shannon-Fano trees:

```
Code:=0;
CodeIncrement:=0;
LastBitLength:=0;
i:=number of Shannon-Fano codes -1 (either 255 or 63);

loop while i>=0
Code:=Code + CodeIncrement;
if BitLength(i) <> LastBitLength then
  LastBitLength=BitLength(i);
  CodeIncrement = 1 shifted left (16-LastBitLength);
 endif;
ShannonCode(i):=Code;
i:=i-1;
end loop;
```

c. Reverse the order of the bits in the above ShannonCode() array, so that the most significant bit becomes the least significant one.
d. Restore the order of Shannon-Fano codes as originally stored within the file.

The compressed data stream begins immediately after the compressed Shannon Fano data. It is created as follows:

```
repeat
  read 1 bit from input stream;
    if this bit is non-zero then (encoded data is literal data)
      if Literal Shannon-Fano tree is present
        read and decode symbol using Literal Shannon-Fano tree;
      else
        read 8 bits from input stream and write them on
        the output stream;
       endif;
    else                (encoded data is sliding dictionary match)
      if 8K dictionary size
       read 7 bits for offset Distance (lower 7 bits of offset);
      else
       read 6 bits for offset Distance (lower 6 bits of offset);
```

```
      endif;
    endif;
Using the Distance Shannon-Fano tree, read and decode the
upper 6 bits of the Distance value;

Using the Length Shannon-Fano tree, read and decode the Length;

Length:=Length + Minimum Match Length;

if Length = 63 + Minimum Match Length
   then read 8 bits from the input stream, and
     add this value to Length;
endif;

Move backwards Distance+1 bytes in the output stream, and copy
Length characters from this position to the output stream.
(if this position is before the start of the output stream,
then assume that all the data before the start of  the output
stream is filled with zeros).

until end-of-input;
```

> I do not know it—it is without name—it is a word unsaid, It is not in any dictionary, utterance, symbol.
>
> —Walt Whitman, *Leaves of Grass*

3.21 ARJ and LHArc

ARJ is a compression/archiving utility written by Robert K. Jung to compete with ARC and the various PK utilities. Here are some of its more powerful features:

1. It can search archives for any text without the user having to extract the archives.
2. It can save drive letter and pathname information.
3. It can sort the individual files within an archive.
4. It can merge two or more archives without decompressing and recompressing their files.
5. It can extract files directly to DOS devices.
6. It can synchronize an archive and a directory of files with just a few commands.
7. It can compare the contents of an archive and a directory of files byte for byte without extracting and decompressing the archive.
8. It allows duplicates of a file to be archived, producing several versions of a file within an archive.
9. It can display an archive's creation and modification dates and times.

LHArc, from Haruyasu Yoshizaki, and LHA, by Haruhiko Okumura and Haruyasu Yoshizaki use adaptive Huffman coding with features drawn from LZSS. A similar program, called ICE, for MS-DOS seems to be a faked version of either

LHarc or LHA. Reference [Okumura 98] has some information about LHArc and LHA as well as a history of data compression in Japan.

3.22 EXE Compressors

The LZEXE program is freeware originally written in the late 1980s by Fabrice Bellard as a special-purpose utility to compress EXE files (PC executable files). The idea is that an EXE file compressed by LZEXE can be decompressed **and** executed with one command. The decompressor does not write the decompressed file on the disk but loads it in memory, relocates addresses, and executes it! The decompressor uses memory that's eventually used by the program being decompressed, so it does not require any extra RAM. In addition, the decompressor is very small compared to decompressors in self extracting archives.

The algorithm is based on LZ. It uses a circular queue and a dictionary tree for finding string matches. The position and size of the match are encoded by an auxiliary algorithm based on the Huffman method. Uncompressed bytes are kept unchanged, since trying to compress them any further would have entailed a much more complex and larger decompressor. The decompressor is located at the end of the compressed EXE file and is 330 bytes long (in version 0.91). The main steps of the decoder are:

1. Check the CRC (Section 3.23) to ensure data reliability.
2. Locate itself in high RAM; then move the compressed code in order to leave sufficient room for the EXE file.
3. Decompress the code, check that it is correct, and adjust the segments if bigger than 64K.
4. Decompress the relocation table and update the relocatable addresses of the EXE file.
5. Run the program, updating the CS, IP, SS, and SP registers.

The idea of EXE compressors, introduced by LZEXE, was attractive to both users and software developers, so a few more have been developed:

1. PKlite, from PKWare, is a similar EXE compressor that can also compress .COM files.
2. DIET, by Teddy Matsumoto, is a more general EXE compressor that can compress data files. DIET can act as a monitor, permanently residing in RAM, watching for applications trying to read files from the disk. When an application tries to read a DIET-compressed data file, DIET senses it, and does the reading and decompressing in a process that's transparent to the application.

3.23 CRC

The idea of a parity bit is simple, old, and familiar to most computer practitioners. A parity bit is the simplest type of error detecting code. It adds reliability to a group of bits by making it possible for hardware to detect certain errors that occur when the group is stored in memory, is written on a disk, or is sent over communication lines between modems. A single parity bit does not make the group completely reliable. There are certain errors that cannot be detected with a parity bit, but experience shows that even a single parity bit can make data transmission reliable in most practical cases.

The 10^{12} Bit of π.

On September 22, 1997, Fabrice Bellard announced the calculation of the 1000 billionth (i.e., 10^{12}th) binary digit of π. This bit is "1." Bellard has modified the "miraculous" Bailey-Borwein-Plouffe algorithm that makes it possible to calculate a digit of π without having to calculate the preceding digits.

The computation employed more than twenty high-end workstations and PCs. A generic parallel computation program was developed to handle the communications between the server and the clients. It has been designed to handle huge computations with little communication between the server and the clients.

The first computation took 220 days of CPU time, and 12 days of real time. A second computation was performed to verify the first. Bellard and his team computed the digits starting at bit position $10^{12} - 9$ using the same formula. Since the intermediate results are not correlated, this is a good verification method. The second computation took 180 days of CPU time because of the use of a better (optimized) code. The computers used were mainly UltraSparc workstations, with some Pentium PCs, DEC Alpha 200 and 3000, and SGI10000 computers.

Any comments should be directed to Bellard at `bellard@email.enst.fr`

The parity bit is computed from a group of $n-1$ bits, then added to the group, making it n bits long. A common example is a 7-bit ASCII code that becomes 8 bits long after a parity bit is added. The parity bit "p" is computed by counting the number of "1" bits in the original group, and setting "p" to complete that number to either odd or even. The former is called odd parity and the latter, even parity.

Examples: Given the group of 7 bits 1010111, the number of "1" bits is 5, which is odd. Assuming odd parity, the value of "p" should be 0, leaving the total number of 1's odd. Similarly, the group 1010101 has 4 bits of "1", so its odd parity bit should also be a "1", bringing the total number of 1's to 5.

Imagine a block of data where the most significant bit (MSB) of each byte is an odd parity bit, and the bytes are written vertically (Table 3.31a).

When this block is read from a disk or is received by a modem, it may contain transmission errors, errors that have been caused by imperfect hardware or by electrical interference along the way. We can think of the parity bits as *horizontal reliability*. When the block is read, the hardware can check every byte, verifying the parity. This is done by simply counting the number of "1" bits in the byte. If this number is odd, the hardware assumes that the byte is good. This assumption is not always correct, since two bits may get corrupted during transmission (Table 3.31c). A single parity bit is thus useful (Table 3.31b) but does not provide full error detection capability.

A simple way to increase the reliability of a block of data is to compute vertical parities. The block is considered to be eight vertical columns, and an odd parity bit is computed for each column (Table 3.31d). If 2 bits in 1 byte go bad, the

1 01101001	1 01101001	1 01101001	1 01101001
0 00001011	0 00001011	0 00001011	0 00001011
0 11110010	0 11010010	0 11**010**110	0 11**010110**
0 01101110	0 01101110	0 01101110	0 01101110
1 11101101	1 11101101	1 11101101	1 11101101
1 01001110	1 01001110	1 01001110	1 01001110
0 11101001	0 11101001	0 11101001	0 11101001
1 11010111	1 11010111	1 11010111	1 11010111
			0 00011100
(a)	(b)	(c)	(d)

Table 3.31: Horizontal and Vertical Parities.

horizontal parity will not catch it, but 2 of the vertical ones will. Even the vertical bits do not provide complete error detection capability, but they are a simple way to significantly improve data reliability.

A CRC is a glorified vertical parity. CRC stands for Cyclical Redundancy Check (or Cyclical Redundancy Code) and is a rule that shows how to compute the vertical check bits (they are now called check bits, not just simple parity bits) from all the bits of the data. Here is how CRC-32 is computed (this is one of the many standards developed by the CCITT). The block of data is written as one long binary number. In our example this will be the 64-bit number

101101001|000001011|011110010|001101110|111101101|101001110|011101001|111010111.

The individual bits are considered the coefficients of a *polynomial* (see below for definition). In our example, this will be the degree-63 polynomial

$$P(x) = 1 \times x^{63} + 0 \times x^{62} + 1 \times x^{61} + 1 \times x^{60} + \cdots + 1 \times x^2 + 1 \times x^1 + 1 \times x^0$$
$$= x^{63} + x^{61} + x^{60} + \cdots + x^2 + x + 1.$$

This polynomial is then divided by the standard CRC-32 *generating polynomial*

$$\mathrm{CRC}_{32}(x) = x^{32} + x^{26} + x^{23} + x^{22} + x^{16} + x^{12} + x^{11} + x^{10} + x^8 + x^7 + x^5 + x^4 + x^2 + x^1 + 1.$$

When an integer M is divided by an integer N, the result is a quotient Q (which we will ignore) and a remainder R, which is in the range $[0, N-1]$. Similarly, when a polynomial $P(x)$ is divided by a degree-32 polynomial, the result is two polynomials, a quotient and a remainder. The remainder is a degree-31 polynomial, which means it has 32 coefficients, each a single bit. Those 32 bits are the CRC-32 code, which is appended to the block of data as 4 bytes. As an example, the CRC-32 of a recent version of the file with the text of this chapter is $586DE4FE_{16}$.

The CRC is sometimes called the "fingerprint" of the file. Of course, since it is a 32-bit number, there are only 2^{32} different CRCs. This number equals approximately 4.3 billion, so, in theory, there may be different files with the same

CRC, but in practice this is rare. The CRC is useful as an error detecting code because it has the following properties:

1. Every bit in the data block is used to compute the CRC. This means that changing even one bit may produce a different CRC.

2. Even small changes in the data normally produce very different CRCs. Experience with CRC-32 shows that it is very rare that introducing errors in the data does not change the CRC.

3. Any histogram of CRC-32 values for different data blocks is flat (or very close to flat). For a given data block, the probability of any of the 2^{32} possible CRCs being produced is practically the same.

Other common generating polynomials are $CRC_{12}(x) = x^{12} + x^3 + x + 1$ and $CRC_{16}(x) = x^{16} + x^{15} + x^2 + 1$. They generate the common CRC-12 and CRC-16 codes, which are 12 and 16 bits long, respectively.

Definition: A polynomial of degree n in x is the function

$$P_n(x) = \sum_{i=0}^{n} a_i x^i = a_0 + a_1 x + a_2 x^2 + \cdots + a_n x^n,$$

where a_i are the $n + 1$ coefficients (in our case, real numbers).

Bibliography

Ramabadran, Tenkasi V., and Sunil S. Gaitonde (1988) "A Tutorial on CRC Computations," *IEEE Micro* pp. 62–75, August.

3.24 Summary

The dictionary-based methods presented here are different but are based on the same principle. They read the input stream symbol by symbol and add phrases to the dictionary. The phrases are symbols or strings of symbols from the input. The main difference between the methods is in deciding what phrases to add to the dictionary. When a string in the input stream matches a dictionary phrase, the encoder outputs the position of the match in the dictionary. If that position requires fewer bits than the matched string, compression results.

In general, dictionary-based methods, when carefully implemented, give better compression than statistical methods. This is why many popular compression programs are dictionary based or involve a dictionary as one of several compression steps.

3.25 Data Compression Patents

It is generally agreed that an invention or a process is patentable but a mathematical concept, calculation, or proof is not. An algorithm seems to be an abstract mathematical concept that should not be patentable. However, once the algorithm is implemented in software (or in firmware) it may not be possible to separate the algorithm from its implementation. Once the implementation is used in a new product (i.e., an invention), that product—including the implementation (software or firmware) and the algorithm behind it—may be patentable. [Zalta 88] is a general discussion of algorithm patentability. Several common data compression algorithms, most notably LZW, have been patented; and the LZW patent is discussed here in some detail.

The Sperry Corporation was granted a patent on LZW in 1985 (even though the inventor, Terry Welch, left Sperry prior to that date). When Unisys acquired Sperry in 1986 it became the owner of this patent and is still requiring users to obtain (and pay for) a license to use it.

When CompuServe designed the GIF format in 1987 it decided to use LZW as the compression method for GIF files. It seems that CompuServe was not aware at that point that LZW was patented, nor was Unisys aware that the GIF format uses LZW. After 1987 many software developers became attracted to GIF and published programs to create and display images in this format. It became widely accepted and is now commonly used on the World-Wide Web, where it is one of the prime image formats for Web pages and browsers.

It was not until GIF had become a world-wide de facto standard that Unisys contacted CompuServe for a license. Naturally, CompuServe and other LZW users tried to challenge the patent. They applied to the United states Patent Office for a reexamination of the LZW patent, with the (perhaps surprising) result that on January 4, 1994, the patent was reconfirmed and CompuServe had to obtain a license (for an undisclosed sum) from Unisys later that year. Other important licensees of LZW (see [Rodriguez 95]) are Aldus (in 1991, for the TIFF graphics file format), Adobe (in 1990, for PostScript level II), and America Online and Prodigy (in 1995).

The Unisys LZW patent has significant implications for the World-Wide Web, where use of GIF format images is currently widespread. Similarly, the Unix **compress** utility uses LZW and therefore requires a license. The patent will run out either on December 10, 2002, or on June 20, 2003, depending on whether the GATT agreements grandfather in existing patents or not. The first date is 17 years from issuance of the patent (old U.S. law), and the second is 20 years from the date of first filing (a GATT requirement).

Unisys currently exempts old software products (those written or modified before January 1, 1995) from a patent license. Also exempt is any noncommercial and nonprofit software, old and new. Commercial software (even shareware) or firmware created after December 31, 1994, needs to be licensed if it supports the GIF format or implements LZW. A similar policy is enforced with regard to TIFF, where the cutoff date is July 1, 1995. Notice that computer users may legally keep and transfer GIF and any other files compressed with LZW; only the compression/decompression software requires a license.

More information on the Unisys LZW patent and license can be found at http://www.unisys.com.

An alternative to GIF is the Portable Network Graphics, PNG (pronounced "ping") graphics file format [Crocker 95], which was developed expressly to replace GIF, and avoid patent claims. PNG is simple, portable, with source code freely available, and is unencumbered by patent licenses. It has potential and promise in replacing GIF. However, any GIF-to-PNG conversion software still requires a Unisys license. The PNG home page is currently at http://www.cdrom.com/pub/png/. Unfortunately, PNG has never caught on.

The GNU `gzip` compression software (Section 3.16) should also be mentioned here as a popular substitute for `compress`, since it is free from patent claims, is faster, and provides superior compression.

The LZW U.S. patent number is 4,558,302, issued on Dec. 10, 1985. Here is the abstract filed as part of it (the entire filing constitutes 50 pages).

A data compressor compresses an input stream of data character signals by storing in a string table strings of data character signals encountered in the input stream. The compressor searches the input stream to determine the longest match to a stored string. Each stored string comprises a prefix string and an extension character where the extension character is the last character in the string and the prefix string comprises all but the extension character. Each string has a code signal associated therewith and a string is stored in the string table by, at least implicitly, storing the code signal for the string, the code signal for the string prefix and the extension character. When the longest match between the input data character stream and the stored strings is determined, the code signal for the longest match is transmitted as the compressed code signal for the encountered string of characters and an extension string is stored in the string table. The prefix of the extended string is the longest match and the extension character of the extended string is the next input data character signal following the longest match. Searching through the string table and entering extended strings therein is effected by a limited search hashing procedure. Decompression is effected by a decompressor that receives the compressed code signals and generates a string table similar to that constructed by the compressor to effect lookup of received code signals so as to recover the data character signals comprising a stored string. The decompressor string table is updated by storing a string having a prefix in accordance with a prior received code signal and an extension character in accordance with the first character of the currently recovered string.

Here are a few other patented compression methods, some of them mentioned elsewhere in this book:

1. "Textual Substitution Data Compression with Finite Length Search Windows," U.S. Patent 4,906,991, issued March 6, 1990 (the LZFG method).

2. "Search Tree Data Structure Encoding for Textual Substitution Data Compression Systems," U.S. Patent 5,058,144, issued Oct. 15, 1991.

The two patents above were issued to Edward Fiala and Daniel Greene.

3. "Apparatus and Method for Compressing Data Signals and Restoring the Compressed Data Signals." This is the LZ78 patent, assigned to Sperry Corporation by the inventors Willard L. Eastman, Abraham Lempel, Jacob Ziv, and Martin Cohn. U.S. Patent 4,464,650, issued August, 1984.

The following, from Ross Williams `http://www.ross.net/compression/` illustrates how thorny this issue of patents is.

Then, just when I thought all hope was gone, along came some software patents that drove a stake through the heart of the LZRW algorithms by rendering them unusable. At last I was cured! I gave up compression and embarked on a new life, leaving behind the world of data compression forever.

Bibliography

Crocker, Lee Daniel (1995) "PNG: The Portable Network Graphic Format," *Dr. Dobb's Journal of Software Tools* **20**(7):36–44.

Rodriguez, Karen (1995) "Graphics File Format Patent Unisys Seeks Royalties from GIF Developers," *InfoWorld*, January 9, **17**(2):3.

Zalta, Edward N. (1988) "Are Algorithms Patentable?" *Notices of the American Mathematical Society*, **35**(6):796–799.

3.26 A Unification

Dictionary-based methods and methods based on prediction approach the problem of data compression from two different directions. Any method based on prediction predicts (i.e., assigns probability to) the current symbol based on its order-N context (the N symbols preceding it). Such a method normally stores many contexts of different sizes in a data structure and has to deal with frequency counts, probabilities, and probability ranges. It then uses arithmetic coding to encode the entire input stream as one large number. A dictionary-based method, on the other hand, works differently. It identifies the next phrase in the input stream, stores it in its dictionary, assigns it a code, and continues with the next phrase. Both approaches can be used to compress data because each obeys the general law of data compression, namely, to assign short codes to common events (symbols or phrases) and long codes to rare events.

On the surface, the two approaches are completely different. A predictor deals with probabilities, so it can be highly efficient. At the same time, it can be expected to be slow, since it deals with individual symbols. A dictionary-based method deals with strings of symbols (phrases), so it gobbles up the input stream faster, but it ignores correlations between phrases, typically resulting in poorer compression.

The two approaches are similar because a dictionary-based method *does use* contexts and probabilities (although implicitly) just by storing phrases in its dictionary and searching it. The following discussion uses the LZW trie to illustrate this concept, but the argument is valid for every dictionary-based method, no matter what the details of its algorithm and its dictionary data structure.

Imagine the phrase "abcdef..." stored in an LZW trie (Figure 3.32a). We can think of the substring "abcd" as the order-4 context of "e". When the encoder finds another occurrence of "abcde..." in the input stream, it will locate our phrase in the dictionary, parse it symbol by symbol starting at the root, get to node "e", and continue from there, trying to match more symbols. Eventually, the encoder will get to a leaf, where it will add another symbol and allocate another code. We can think of this process as adding a new leaf to the subtree whose root is the "e" of "abcde...". Every time the string "abcde" becomes the prefix of a parse, both its subtree and its code space (the number of codes associated with it) get bigger by 1. It therefore makes sense to assign node "e" a probability depending on the size of its code space, and the above discussion shows that the size of the code space of node "e" (or, equivalently, string "abcde") can be measured by counting the number of nodes of the subtree whose root is "e". This is how probabilities can be assigned to nodes in any dictionary tree.

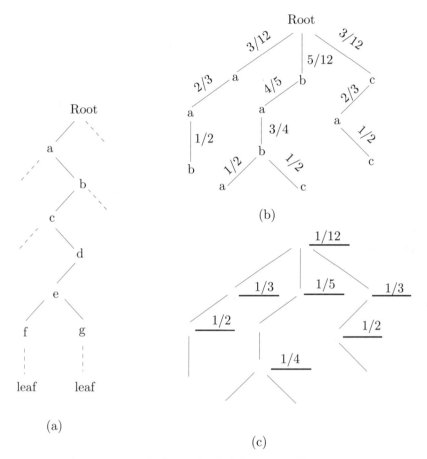

Figure 3.32: Defining Probabilities in a Dictionary Tree.

The ideas of Glen Langdon in the early 1980s (see [Langdon 83] but notice that his equation (8) is wrong; it should read $P(y|s) = c(s)/c(s \cdot y)$; [Langdon 84] is perhaps more useful) led to a simple way of associating probabilities not just to nodes but also to arcs in a dictionary tree. This is more useful, since the arc from node "e" to node "f", for example, signifies an "f" whose context is "abcde". The probability of this arc is thus the probability that an "f" will follow "abcde" in the input stream. The fact that these probabilities can be calculated in a dictionary tree shows that every dictionary-based data compression algorithm can be "simulated" by a prediction algorithm (but notice that the converse is not true). Algorithms based on prediction are, in this sense, more general, but the important fact is that these two seemingly different classes of compression methods can be unified by the observations listed here.

The process whereby a dictionary encoder slides down from the root of its dictionary tree, parsing a string of symbols, can now be given a different interpretation. We can visualize it as a sequence of making predictions for individual symbols, computing codes for them, and combining the codes into one longer code, which is eventually written on the compressed stream. It is as if the code generated by a dictionary encoder for a phrase is actually made up of small chunks, each a code for one symbol.

The rule for calculating the probability of the arc $e \to f$ is to count the number of nodes in the subtree whose root is "f" (including node "f" itself) and divide by the number of nodes in the subtree of "e". Figure 3.32b shows a typical dictionary tree with the strings "aab", "baba", "babc", and "cac". The probabilities associated with every arc are also shown and should be easy for the reader to verify. Note that the probabilities of sibling subtrees don't add up to 1. The probabilities of the three subtrees of the root, for example, add up to $11/12$. The remaining $1/12$ is assigned to the root itself and represents the probability that a fourth string will eventually start at the root. These "missing probabilities" are shown as horizontal lines in Figure 3.32c.

The two approaches, dictionary and prediction, can be combined in a single compression method. The LZP method of Section 3.14 is one example; the LZRW4 method (Section 3.9) is another. These methods work by considering the context of a symbol before searching the dictionary.

Bibliography

Langdon, Glen G. (1983) "A Note on the Ziv-Lempel Model for Compressing Individual Sequences," *IEEE Transactions on Information Theory* IT-29(2):284–287, March.

Langdon, Glen G. (1984) *On Parsing vs. Mixed-Order Model Structures for Data Compression*, IBM research report RJ-4163 (46091), Jan 18, 1984, San Jose.

> Comparisons date. Adoption screams. Co-ordinates maps.
> Darn! as composite. Is mono-spaced art. Composed as train.
> Promised as on act. Oops and matrices. Promised to a scan.
>
> —Anagrams of *data compression*

4
Image Compression

The first part of this chapter discusses digital images and general approaches to image compression. This is followed by a description of about 30 different compression methods. The author would like to start with the following observations:

1. Why were these particular methods included in the book, while others were ignored? The simple answer is this: Because of the documentation available to the author. Image compression methods that are well documented were included. Methods that are kept secret, or whose documentation was not clear to the author, were left out.

2. The treatment of the various methods is uneven. This, again, reflects the documentation available to the author. Some methods have been documented by their developers in great detail, and this is reflected in this chapter. Where no detailed documentation was available for a compression algorithm, only its basic principles are outlined here.

3. There is no attempt to compare the various methods described here. This is because most image compression methods have been designed for a particular type of image, and also because of the practical difficulties of getting all the software and adapting it to run on the same platform.

4. The compression methods described in this chapter are not arranged in any particular order. After a lot of thought and many trials, the author gave up any hope of sorting the compression methods in any reasonable way. Readers looking for any particular method can use the table of contents and the detailed index to find it easily.

A digital image is a rectangular array of dots, or picture elements, arranged in m rows and n columns. The expression $m \times n$ is called the *resolution* of the image, and the dots are called *pixels* (except in the cases of fax images and video compression, where they are referred to as *pels*). For the purpose of image compression it is useful to distinguish the following types of images:

1. A *bi-level* (or monochromatic) image. This is an image where the pixels can have one of two values, normally referred to as black and white. Each pixel in such an image is represented by one bit, so this is the simplest type of image.

2. A *grayscale* image. A pixel in such an image can have one of the n values 0 through $n - 1$, indicating one of 2^n shades of gray (or shades of some other color). The value of n is normally compatible with a byte size, i.e., it is 4, 8, 12, 16, 24, or some other convenient multiple of 4 or of 8. The set of the most-significant bits of all the pixels is the most-significant bitplane. Thus, a grayscale image has n bitplanes.

3. A *continuous-tone* image. This type of image can have many similar colors (or grayscales). When adjacent pixels differ by just one unit, it is hard or even impossible for the eye to distinguish their colors. As a result, such an image may contain areas with colors that seem to vary continuously as the eye moves along the area. A pixel in such an image is represented by either a single large number (in the case of many grayscales) or by three components (in the case of a color image). A continuous-tone image is normally a natural image (natural as opposed to artificial), and is obtained by taking a photograph with a digital camera, or by scanning a photograph or a painting. Figures 4.38 through 4.40 are typical examples of continuous-tone images.

4. A *discrete-tone* image (also called a graphical image or a synthetic image). This is normally an artificial image. It may have few colors or many colors, but it does not have the noise and blurring of a natural image. Examples of this type of image are a photograph of an artificial object or machine, a page of text, a chart, a cartoon, and the contents of a computer screen. (Not every artificial image is discrete-tone. A computer-generated image that's meant to look natural is a continuous-tone image in spite of being artificially generated.) Artificial objects, text, and line drawings have sharp, well-defined edges, and are therefore highly contrasted from the rest of the image (the background). Adjacent pixels in a discrete-tone image often are either identical or vary significantly in value. Such an image does not compress well with lossy methods, since the loss of just a few pixels may render a letter illegible, or change a familiar pattern to an unrecognizable one. Compression methods for continuous-tone images often do not handle the sharp edges of a discrete-tone image very well, so special methods are needed for efficient compression of these images. Notice that a discrete-tone image may be highly redundant, since the same character or pattern may appear many times in the image. Figure 4.41 is a typical example of a discrete-tone image.

5. A *cartoon-like* image. This is a color image that consists of uniform areas. Each area has a uniform color but adjacent areas may have very different colors. This feature may be exploited to obtain better compression.

It is intuitively clear that each type of image may feature redundancy, but they are redundant in different ways. This is why any given compression method may not perform well for all images, and why different methods are needed to compress the different image types. There are compression methods for bi-level images, for continuous-tone images, and for discrete-tone images. There are also methods that try to break an image up into continuous-tone and discrete-tone parts, and compress each separately.

> **From the Dictionary**
>
> Continuous (adjective).
> Etymology: Latin *continuus*, from *continere*, to hold together.
> Date: 1673.
> 1: marked by uninterrupted extension in space, time, or sequence
> 2: (in a function) having the property that the absolute value of the numerical difference between the value at a given point and the value at any point in a neighborhood of the given point can be made as close to zero as desired by choosing the neighborhood small enough
>
> Discrete (adjective).
> Etymology: Middle English, from Latin *discretus*.
> Date: 14th century.
> 1: constituting a separate entity: individually distinct
> 2a: consisting of distinct or unconnected elements: noncontinuous
> 2b: taking on or having a finite or countably infinite number of values.

4.1 Introduction

Modern computers employ graphics extensively. Window-based operating systems display the disk's file directory graphically. The progress of many system operations, such as downloading a file, may also be displayed graphically. Many applications provide a graphical user interface (GUI), which makes it easier to use the program and to interpret displayed results. Computer graphics is used in many areas in everyday life to convert many types of complex information to images. Images are thus important, but they tend to be big! Since modern hardware can display many colors, it is common to have a pixel represented internally as a 24-bit number, where the percentages of red, green, and blue occupy 8 bits each. Such a 24-bit pixel can specify one of $2^{24} \approx 16.78$ million colors. An image at a resolution of 512×512 that consists of such pixels thus occupies 786,432 bytes. At a resolution of 1024×1024 it becomes four times as big, requiring 3,145,728 bytes. Movies are also commonly used in computers, making for even bigger images. This is why image compression is so important. An important feature of image compression is that it can be lossy. An image, after all, exists for people to look at, so, when it is compressed, it is acceptable to lose image features to which the human eye is not sensitive. This is one of the main ideas behind the many lossy image compression methods described in this chapter.

In general, information can be compressed if it is redundant. It has been mentioned several times that data compression amounts to reducing or removing redundancy in the data. With lossy compression, however, we have a new concept, namely compressing by removing *irrelevancy*. An image can be lossy-compressed by removing irrelevant information even if the original image does not have any redundancy.

⋄ **Exercise 4.1:** It would seem that an image with no redundancy is always random (and therefore not interesting). Is that true?

The idea of losing image information becomes more palatable when we consider how digital images are created. Here are three examples: (1) A real-life image may be scanned from a photograph or a painting and digitized (converted to pixels). (2) An image may be recorded by a video camera that creates pixels and stores them directly in memory. (3) An image may be painted on the screen by means of a paint program. In all these cases, some information is lost when the image is digitized. The fact that the viewer is willing to accept this loss suggests that further loss of information might be tolerable if done properly.

(Digitizing an image involves two steps: *sampling* and *quantization*. Sampling an image is the process of dividing the two-dimensional original image into small regions: pixels. Quantization is the process of assigning an integer value to each pixel. Notice that digitizing sound involves the same two steps, with the difference that sound is one-dimensional.)

Here is a simple process to determine qualitatively the amount of data loss in a compressed image. Given an image A, (1) compress it to B, (2) decompress B to C, and (3) subtract $D = C - A$. If A was compressed without any loss and decompressed properly, then C should be identical to A and image D should be uniformly white. The more data was lost in the compression, the farther will D be from uniformly white.

How should an image be compressed? The main principles discussed so far were RLE, scalar quantization, statistical methods, and dictionary-based methods. By itself, none is very satisfactory for color or grayscale images (although they may be used in combination with other methods). Here is why:

Section 1.4.1 shows how RLE can be used for (lossless or lossy) compression of an image. This is simple, and it is used by certain parts of JPEG, especially by its lossless mode. In general, however, the other principles used by JPEG produce much better compression than does RLE alone. Facsimile compression (Section 2.13) uses RLE combined with Huffman coding and gets good results, but only for bi-level images.

Scalar quantization has been mentioned in Section 1.6. It can be used to compress images, but its performance is mediocre. Imagine an image with 8-bit pixels. It can be compressed with scalar quantization by cutting off the four least-significant bits of each pixel. This yields a compression ratio of 0.5, not very impressive, and at the same time reduces the number of colors (or grayscales) from 256 to just 16. Such a reduction not only degrades the overall quality of the reconstructed image, but may also create bands of different colors, a noticeable and annoying effect that's illustrated here.

Imagine a row of 12 pixels with similar colors, ranging from 202 to 215. In binary notation these values are

$$11010111 \; 11010110 \; 11010101 \; 11010011 \; 11010010 \; 11010001$$
$$11001111 \; 11001110 \; 11001101 \; 11001100 \; 11001011 \; 11001010.$$

Quantization will result in the 12 4-bit values

$$1101 \; 1101 \; 1101 \; 1101 \; 1101 \; 1101 \; 1100 \; 1100 \; 1100 \; 1100 \; 1100 \; 1100,$$

which will reconstruct the 12 pixels

$$11010000\ 11010000\ 11010000\ 11010000\ 11010000\ 11010000$$
$$11000000\ 11000000\ 11000000\ 11000000\ 11000000\ 11000000.$$

The first six pixels of the row now have the value $11010000_2 = 208$, while the next six pixels are $11000000_2 = 192$. If adjacent rows have similar pixels, the first six columns will form a band, distinctly different from the band formed by the next six columns. This banding, or contouring, effect is very noticeable to the eye, since our eyes are sensitive to edges and breaks in an image.

One way to eliminate this effect is called *improved gray-scale* (IGS) *quantization*. It works by adding to each pixel a random number generated from the four rightmost bits of previous pixels. Section 4.2.1 shows that the least-significant bits of a pixel are fairly random, so IGS works by adding to each pixel randomness that depends on the neighborhood of the pixel.

The method maintains an 8-bit variable, denoted by $\mathtt{rsm}$, that's initially set to zero. For each 8-bit pixel P to be quantized (except the first one), the IGS method does the following:

1. Set $\mathtt{rsm}$ to the sum of the eight bits of P and the four rightmost bits of $\mathtt{rsm}$. However, if P has the form $1111xxxx$, set $\mathtt{rsm}$ to P.
2. Write the four leftmost bits of $\mathtt{rsm}$ on the compressed stream. This is the compressed value of P. IGS is thus not exactly a quantization method, but a variation of scalar quantization.

The first pixel is quantized in the usual way, by dropping its four rightmost bits. Table 4.1 illustrates the operation of IGS.

Pixel	Value	$\mathtt{rsm}$	Compressed value
1	1010 0110	0000 0000	1010
2	1101 0010	1101 0010	1101
3	1011 0101	1011 0111	1011
4	1001 1100	1010 0011	1010
5	1111 0100	1111 0100	1111
6	1011 0011	1011 0111	1011

Table 4.1: Illustrating the IGS Method.

Vector quantization can be used more successfully to compress images. It is discussed in Section 4.12.

Statistical methods work best when the symbols being compressed have different probabilities. An input stream where all symbols have the same probability will not compress, even though it may not necessarily be random. It turns out that in a continuous-tone color or grayscale image, the different colors or shades of gray may often have roughly the same probabilities. This is why statistical methods are not a good choice for compressing such images, and why new approaches are needed.

Images with color discontinuities, where adjacent pixels have widely different colors, compress better with statistical methods, but it is not easy to predict, just by looking at an image, whether it has enough color discontinuities.

Dictionary-based compression methods also tend to be unsuccessful in dealing with continuous-tone images. Such an image typically contains adjacent pixels with similar colors, but does not contain repeating patterns. Even an image that contains repeated patterns such as vertical lines may lose them when digitized. A vertical line in the original image may become slightly slanted when the image is digitized (Figure 4.2), so the pixels in a scan row may end up having slightly different colors from those in adjacent rows, resulting in a dictionary with short strings.

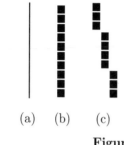

An ideal vertical rule is shown in (a). In (b), the rule is assumed to be perfectly digitized into ten pixels, laid vertically. However, if the image is placed in the digitizer slightly slanted, the digitizing process may be imperfect, and the resulting pixels might look as in (c).

(a)   (b)   (c)

Figure 4.2: Perfect and Imperfect Digitizing.

Another problem with dictionary compression of images is that such methods scan the image row by row, and may thus miss vertical correlations between pixels. An example is the two simple images of Figure 4.3a,b. Saving both in GIF89, a dictionary-based graphics file format (Section 3.17), has resulted in file sizes of 1053 and 1527 bytes, respectively, on the author's computer.

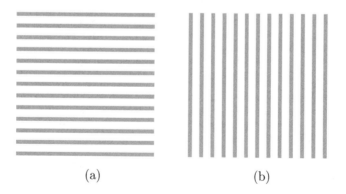

(a)   (b)

Figure 4.3: Dictionary Compression of Parallel Lines.

Traditional methods are therefore unsatisfactory for image compression, so this chapter discusses novel approaches. They are all different, but they remove redundancy from an image by using the following principle (see also Section 1.4):

The Principle of Image Compression. If we select a pixel in the image at random, there is a good chance that its neighbors will have the same color or very similar colors.

Image compression is therefore based on the fact that neighboring pixels are *highly correlated*. This correlation is also called *spatial redundancy*.

Here is a simple example that illustrates what can be done with correlated pixels. The following sequence of values gives the intensities of 24 adjacent pixels in a row of a continuous-tone image:

12, 17, 14, 19, 21, 26, 23, 29, 41, 38, 31, 44, 46, 57, 53, 50, 60, 58, 55, 54, 52, 51, 56, 60.

Only two of the 24 pixels are identical. Their average value is 40.3. Subtracting pairs of adjacent pixels results in the sequence

12, 5, −3, 5, 2, 4, −3, 6, 11, −3, −7, 13, 4, 11, −4, −3, 10, −2, −3, 1, −2, −1, 5, 4.

The two sequences are illustrated in Figure 4.4.

Figure 4.4: Values and Differences of 24 Adjacent Pixels.

The sequence of difference values has three properties that illustrate its compression potential: (1) The difference values are smaller than the original pixel values. Their average is 2.58. (2) They repeat. There are just 15 distinct difference values, so in principle they can be coded by four bits each. (3) They are *decorrelated*: adjacent difference values tend to be different. This can be seen by subtracting them, which results in the sequence of 24 second differences

12, −7, −8, 8, −3, 2, −7, 9, 5, −14, −4, 20, −11, 7, −15, 1, 13, −12, −1, 4, −3, 1, 6, 1.

They are larger than the differences themselves.

Figure 4.5 provides another illustration of the meaning of the words "correlated quantities." A 32×32 matrix A is constructed of random numbers, and its elements are displayed in part (a) as shaded squares. The random nature of the elements is obvious. The matrix is then inverted and stored in B, which is shown in part (b). This time, there seems to be more structure to the 32×32 squares. A direct calculation using Equation (4.1) shows that the cross-correlation between the top two rows of A is 0.0412, whereas the cross-correlation between the top two rows

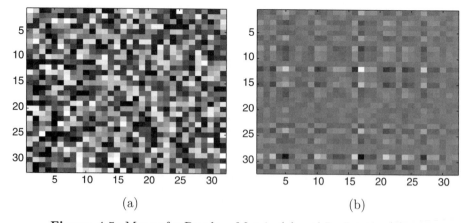

(a)   (b)

Figure 4.5: Maps of a Random Matrix (a) and Its Inverse (b).

```
n=32; a=rand(n); imagesc(a); colormap(gray)
b=inv(a); imagesc(b)
```

Matlab Code for Figure 4.5.

of B is -0.9831. The elements of B are correlated since each depends on *all* the elements of A

$$R = \frac{n \sum x_i y_i - \sum x_i \sum y_i}{\sqrt{[n \sum x_i^2 - (\sum x_i)^2][n \sum y_i^2 - (\sum y_i)^2]}}. \tag{4.1}$$

⋄ **Exercise 4.2:** Use mathematical software to illustrate the covariance matrices of (1) a matrix with correlated values and (2) a matrix with decorrelated values.

Once the concept of correlated quantities is clear, it is easy to answer the question; How can we test the values of pixels after they have been transformed to find out whether they are really decorrelated? The answer is, if a matrix M contains decorrelated values, the covariance of any of its rows with any of its columns is zero. As a result, the covariance matrix of M is diagonal. The statistical concepts of variance, covariance, and correlation are discussed in an appendix in the book's web site.

The principle of image compression has another aspect. We know from experience that the *brightness* of neighboring pixels is also correlated. Two adjacent pixels may have different colors. One may be mostly red and the other, mostly green. Yet if the red component of the first is bright, the green component of its neighbor will, in most cases, also be bright. This property can be exploited by converting pixel representations from RGB to three other components, one of which is the brightness, and the other two represent color. One such format (or *color space*) is YCbCr, where Y (the "luminance" component) represents the brightness of a pixel, and Cb and Cr define its color. This format is discussed in Section 4.6.1, but its advantage is easy to understand. The eye is sensitive to small changes in brightness but not to small changes in color. Thus, losing information in the Cb and Cr components compresseses the image while introducing distortions to which the eye is not sensitive. Losing information in the Y component, on the other hand, is very noticeable to the eye.

4.2 Approaches to Image Compression

An image compression method is normally designed for a specific type of image, and this section lists various approaches to compressing images of different types. Only the general principles are discussed here; specific methods are described in the rest of this chapter.

Approach 1: This is used for bi-level images. A pixel in such an image is represented by one bit. Applying the principle of image compression to a bi-level image therefore means that the immediate neighbors of a pixel P tend to be *identical* to P. Thus, it makes sense to use run length encoding (RLE) to compress such an image. A compression method for such an image may scan it in raster order (row by row) and compute the lengths of runs of black and white pixels. The lengths are encoded by variable-size (prefix) codes and are written on the compressed stream. An example of such a method is facsimile compression, Section 2.13.

It should be stressed that this is just an approach to bi-level image compression. The details of specific methods vary. For instance, a method may scan the image column by column or in zigzag (Figure 1.8b), it may convert the image to a quadtree (Section 4.27), or it may scan it region by region using a space-filling curve (Section 4.29).

Approach 2: Also for bi-level images. The principle of image compression tells us that the neighbors of a pixel tend to be similar to the pixel. We can extend this principle and conclude that if the current pixel has color c (where c is either black or white), then pixels of the same color seen in the past (and also those that will be found in the future) tend to have the same immediate neighbors.

This approach looks at n of the near neighbors of the current pixel and considers them an n-bit number. This number is the *context* of the pixel. In principle there can be 2^n contexts, but because of image redundancy we expect them to be distributed in a nonuniform way. Some contexts should be common and the rest will be rare.

The encoder counts how many times each context has already been found for a pixel of color c, and assigns probabilities to the contexts accordingly. If the current pixel has color c and its context has probability p, the encoder can use adaptive arithmetic coding to encode the pixel with that probability. This approach is used by JBIG (Section 4.9).

Next, we turn to grayscale images. A pixel in such an image is represented by n bits and can have one of 2^n values. Applying the principle of image compression to a grayscale image implies that the immediate neighbors of a pixel P tend to be similar to P, but are not necessarily identical. Thus, RLE should not be used to compress such an image. Instead, two approaches are discussed.

Approach 3: Separate the grayscale image into n bi-level images and compress each with RLE and prefix codes. The principle of image compression seems to imply intuitively that two adjacent pixels that are similar in the grayscale image will be identical in most of the n bi-level images. This, however, is not true, as the following example makes clear. Imagine a grayscale image with $n = 4$ (i.e.,

4-bit pixels, or 16 shades of gray). The image can be separated into four bi-level images. If two adjacent pixels in the original grayscale image have values 0000 and 0001, then they are similar. They are also identical in three of the four bi-level images. However, two adjacent pixels with values 0111 and 1000 are also similar in the grayscale image (their values are 7 and 8, respectively) but differ in all four bi-level images.

This problem occurs because the binary codes of adjacent integers may differ by several bits. The binary codes of 0 and 1 differ by one bit, those of 1 and 2 differ by two bits, and those of 7 and 8 differ by four bits. The solution is to design special binary codes such that the codes of any consecutive integers i and $i+1$ will differ by one bit only. An example of such a code is the *reflected Gray codes* of Section 4.2.1.

Approach 4: Use the *context* of a pixel to *predict* its value. The context of a pixel is the values of some of its neighbors. We can examine some neighbors of a pixel P, compute an average A of their values, and predict that P will have the value A. The principle of image compression tells us that our prediction will be correct in most cases, almost correct in many cases, and completely wrong in a few cases. We can say that the predicted value of pixel P represents the redundant information in P. We now calculate the difference

$$\Delta \stackrel{\mathrm{def}}{=} P - A,$$

and assign variable-size (prefix) codes to the different values of Δ such that small values (which we expect to be common) are assigned short codes and large values (which are expected to be rare) are assigned long codes. If P can have the values 0 through $m-1$, then values of Δ are in the range $[-(m-1), +(m-1)]$, and the number of codes needed is $2(m-1)+1$ or $2m-1$.

Experiments with a large number of images suggest that the values of Δ tend to be distributed according to the Laplace distribution (Figure 4.120b). A compression method can, therefore, use this distribution to assign a probability to each value of Δ, and thus use arithmetic coding to encode the Δ values very efficiently. This is the principle of the MLP method (Section 4.19).

The context of a pixel may consist of just one or two of its immediate neighbors. However, better results may be obtained when several neighbor pixels are included in the context. The average A in such a case should be weighted, with near neighbors assigned higher weights (see, for example, Table 4.118). Another important consideration is the decoder. In order for it to decode the image, it should be able to calculate the context of every pixel. This means that the context should contain only pixels that have already been encoded. If the image is scanned in raster order, the context should include only pixels located above the current pixel or on the same row and to its left.

Approach 5: Transform the values of the pixels, and encode the transformed values. The concept of a transform, as well as the most important transforms used in image compression, are discussed in Section 4.4. Chapter 5 is devoted to the wavelet transform. Recall that compression is achieved by reducing or removing redundancy. The redundancy of an image is caused by the correlation between pixels, so transforming the pixels to a representation where they are *decorrelated* eliminates the redundancy. It is also possible to think of a transform in terms of the entropy of the image. In a highly correlated image, the pixels tend to have equiprobable values, which results in maximum entropy. If the transformed pixels are decorrelated, certain pixel values become common, thereby having large probabilities, while others are rare. This results in small entropy. Quantizing the transformed values can produce efficient lossy image compression. We want the transformed values to be independent because coding independent values makes it simpler to construct a statistical model.

We now turn to color images. A pixel in such an image consists of three color components, such as red, green, and blue. Most color images are either continuous-tone or discrete-tone.

Approach 6: The principle of this approach is to separate a continuous-tone color image into three grayscale images and compress each of the three separately, using approaches 2, 3, or 4.

For a continuous-tone image, the principle of image compression implies that adjacent pixels have similar, although perhaps not identical, colors. However, similar colors do not mean similar pixel values. Consider, for example, 12-bit pixel values where each color component is expressed in four bits. Thus, the 12 bits 1000|0100|0000 represent a pixel whose color is a mixture of eight units of red (about 50%, since the maximum is 15 units), four units of green (about 25%), and no blue. Now imagine two adjacent pixels with values 0011|0101|0011 and 0010|0101|0011. They have similar colors, since only their red components differ, and only by one unit. However, when considered as 12-bit numbers, the two numbers 001101010011 and 001001010011 are very different, since they differ in one of their most significant bits.

An important feature of this approach is to use a luminance chrominance color representation instead of the more common RGB. The concepts of luminance and chrominance are discussed in Section 4.6.1 and in [Salomon 99]. The advantage of the luminance chrominance color representation is that the eye is sensitive to small changes in luminance but not in chrominance. This allows the loss of considerable data in the chrominance components, while making it possible to decode the image without a significant visible loss of quality.

Approach 7: A different approach is needed for discrete-tone images. Recall that such an image contains uniform regions, and a region may appear several times in the image. A good example is a screen dump. Such an image consists of text and icons. Each character of text and each icon is a region, and any region may appear several times in the image. A possible way to compress such an image is to scan it, identify regions, and find repeating regions. If a region B is identical to an already found region A, then B can be compressed by writing a pointer to A on the compressed stream. The block decomposition method (FABD, Section 4.25) is an example of how this approach can be implemented.

Approach 8: Partition the image into parts (overlapping or not) and compress it by processing the parts one by one. Suppose that the next unprocessed image part is part number 15. Try to match it with parts 1–14 that have already been processed. If part 15 can be expressed, e.g., as a combination of parts 5 (scaled) and

11 (rotated), then only the few numbers that specify the combination need be saved, and part 15 can be discarded. If part 15 cannot be expressed as a combination of already-processed parts, it is declared processed and is saved in raw format.

This approach is the basis of the various *fractal* methods for image compression. It applies the principle of image compression to image parts instead of to individual pixels. Applied this way, the principle tells us that "interesting" images (i.e., those that are being compressed in practice) have a certain amount of *self similarity*. Parts of the image are identical or similar to the entire image or to other parts.

Image compression methods are not limited to these basic approaches. This book discusses methods that use the concepts of context trees, Markov models (Section 8.8), and wavelets, among others. In addition, the concept of *progressive image compression* (Section 4.8) should be mentioned, since it adds another dimension to the compression of images.

Bibliography

Salomon, David (1999) *Computer Graphics and Geometric Modeling*, New York, Springer.

4.2.1 Gray Codes

An image compression method that has been developed specifically for a certain type of image can sometimes be used for other types. Any method for compressing bi-level images, for example, can be used to compress grayscale images by separating the bitplanes and compressing each individually, as if it were a bi-level image. Imagine, for example, an image with 16 grayscale values. Each pixel is defined by four bits, so the image can be separated into four bi-level images. The trouble with this approach is that it violates the general principle of image compression. Imagine two adjacent 4-bit pixels with values $7 = 0111_2$ and $8 = 1000_2$. These pixels have close values, but when separated into four bitplanes, the resulting 1-bit pixels are different in every bitplane! This is because the binary representations of the consecutive integers 7 and 8 differ in all four bit positions. In order to apply any bi-level compression method to grayscale images, a binary representation of the integers is needed where consecutive integers have codes differing by one bit only. Such a representation exists and is called *reflected Gray code* (RGC). This code is easy to generate with the following recursive construction:

Start with the two 1-bit codes $(0, 1)$. Construct two sets of 2-bit codes by duplicating $(0, 1)$ and appending, either on the left or on the right, first a zero, then a one, to the original set. The result is $(00, 01)$ and $(10, 11)$. We now reverse (reflect) the second set, and concatenate the two. The result is the 2-bit RGC $(00, 01, 11, 10)$; a binary code of the integers 0 through 3 where consecutive codes differ by exactly one bit. Applying the rule again produces the two sets $(000, 001, 011, 010)$ and $(110, 111, 101, 100)$, which are concatenated to form the 3-bit RGC. Note that the first and last codes of any RGC also differ by one bit. Here are the first three steps for computing the 4-bit RGC:

$$\text{Add a zero } (0000, 0001, 0011, 0010, 0110, 0111, 0101, 0100),$$
$$\text{Add a one } (1000, 1001, 1011, 1010, 1110, 1111, 1101, 1100),$$
$$\text{reflect } (1100, 1101, 1111, 1110, 1010, 1011, 1001, 1000).$$

43210	Gray	43210	Gray	43210	Gray	43210	Gray
00000	00000	01000	10010	10000	00011	11000	10001
00001	00100	01001	10110	10001	00111	11001	10101
00010	01100	01010	11110	10010	01111	11010	11101
00011	01000	01011	11010	10011	01011	11011	11001
00100	11000	01100	01010	10100	11011	11100	01001
00101	11100	01101	01110	10101	11111	11101	01101
00110	10100	01110	00110	10110	10111	11110	00101
00111	10000	01111	00010	10111	10011	11111	00001

Table 4.6: First 32 Binary and Reflected Gray Codes.

```
function b=rgc(a,i)
[r,c]=size(a);
b=[zeros(r,1),a; ones(r,1),flipud(a)];
if i>1, b=rgc(b,i-1); end;
```

Code For Table 4.6.

Table 4.6 shows how individual bits change when moving through the binary codes of the first 32 integers. The 5-bit binary codes of these integers are listed in the odd-numbered columns of the table, with the bits of integer i that differ from those of $i - 1$ shown in boldface. It is easy to see that the least-significant bit (bit b_0) changes all the time, bit b_1 changes for every other number, and, in general, bit b_k changes every k integers. The even-numbered columns list one of the several possible reflected Gray codes for these integers. The table also lists a recursive Matlab function to compute RGC.

⋄ **Exercise 4.3:** It is also possible to generate the reflected Gray code of an integer n with the following nonrecursive rule: Exclusive-OR n with a copy of itself that's logically shifted one position to the right. In the C programming language this is denoted by n^(n>>1). Use this expression to calculate a table similar to Table 4.6.

```
clear;
filename='parrots128'; dim=128;
fid=fopen(filename,'r');
img=fread(fid,[dim,dim])';
mask=1; % between 1 and 8



nimg=bitget(img,mask);
imagesc(nimg), colormap(gray)
```

Binary code

```
clear;
filename='parrots128'; dim=128;
fid=fopen(filename,'r');
img=fread(fid,[dim,dim])';
mask=1 % between 1 and 8
a=bitshift(img,-1);
b=bitxor(img,a);
nimg=bitget(b,mask);
imagesc(nimg), colormap(gray)
```

Gray Code

Figure 4.7: Matlab Code to Separate Image Bitplanes.

The conclusion is that the most-significant bitplanes of an image obey the principle of image compression more than the least-significant ones. When adjacent pixels have values that differ by one unit (such as p and $p+1$), chances are that the least-significant bits are different and the most-significant ones are identical. Any image compression method that compresses bitplanes individually should therefore treat the least-significant bitplanes differently from the most-significant ones, or should use RGC instead of the binary code to represent pixels. Figures 4.8, 4.9, and 4.10 (prepared by the Matlab code of Figure 4.7) show the eight bitplanes of the well-known "parrots" image in both the binary code (the left column) and in RGC (the right column). The bitplanes are numbered 8 (the leftmost or most-significant bits) through 1 (the rightmost or least-significant bits). It is obvious that the least significant bitplane doesn't show any correlations between the pixels; it is random or very close to random in both binary and RGC. Bitplanes 2 through 5, however, exhibit better pixel correlation in the Gray code. Bitplanes 6 through 8 look different in Gray code and binary, but seem to be highly correlated in either representation.

Figure 4.11 is a graphic representation of two versions of the first 32 reflected Gray codes. Part (b) shows the codes of Table 4.6, and part (c) shows the codes of Table 4.12. Even though both are Gray codes, they differ in the way the bits in each bitplane alternate between 0 and 1. In part (b), the bits of the most significant bitplane alternate four times between 0 and 1. Those of the second most significant bitplane alternate eight times between 0 and 1, and the bits of the remaining three bitplanes alternate 16, 2, and 1 times between 0 and 1. When the bitplanes are separated, the middle bitplane features the smallest correlation between the pixels, since the Gray codes of adjacent integers tend to have different bits in this bitplane. The Gray codes shown in Figure 4.11c, on the other hand, alternate more and more between 0 and 1 as we move from the most significant bitplanes to the least significant ones. The least significant bitplanes of this version feature less and less correlation between the pixels and therefore tend to be random. For comparison, Figure 4.11a shows the binary code. It is obvious that bits in this code alternate more often between 0 and 1.

⋄ **Exercise 4.4:** Even a cursory look at the Gray codes of Figure 4.11c shows that they exhibit some regularity. Examine these codes carefully, and find two features that may be used to calculate the codes.

⋄ **Exercise 4.5:** Figure 4.11 is a graphic representation of the binary codes and reflected Gray codes. Find a similar graphic representation of the same codes that illustrates the fact that the first and last codes also differ by just one bit.

Color images provide another example of using the same compression method across image types. Any compression method for grayscale images can be used to compress color images. In a color image, each pixel is represented by three color components (such as RGB). Imagine a color image where each color component is represented by one byte. A pixel is represented by three bytes, or 24 bits, but these bits should not be considered a single number. The two pixels 118|206|12 and 117|206|12 differ by just one unit in the first component, so they have very similar colors. Considered as 24-bit numbers, however, these pixels are very different, since

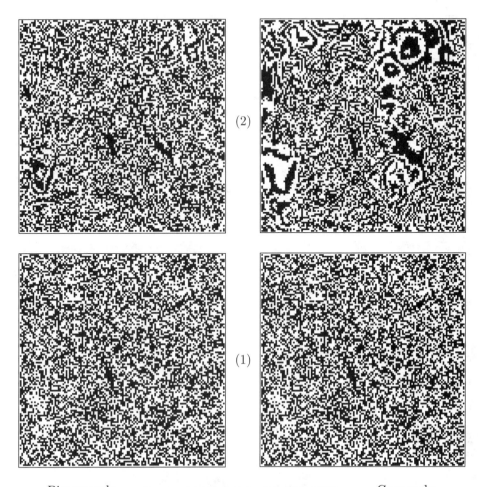

Binary code   Gray code

Figure 4.8: Bitplanes 1,2 of the Parrots Image.

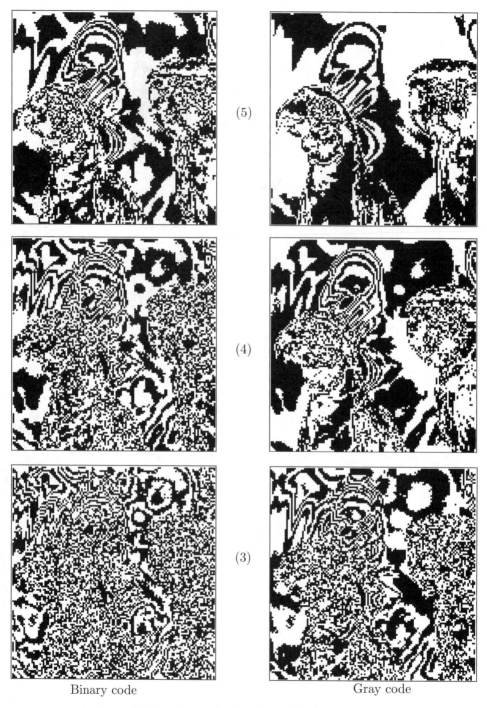

(5)

(4)

(3)

Binary code   Gray code

Figure 4.9: Bitplanes 3, 4, and 5 of the Parrots Image.

Figure 4.10: Bitplanes 6, 7, and 8 of the Parrots Image.

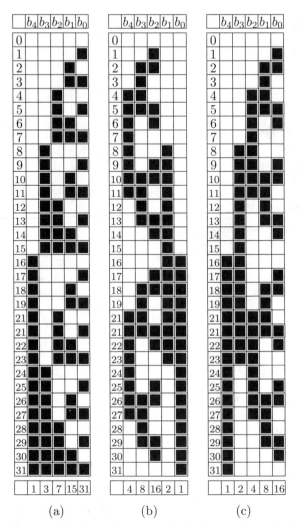

Table 4.11: First 32 Binary and Reflected Gray Codes.

> The binary Gray code is fun,
> For in it strange things can be done.
> Fifteen, as you know,
> Is one, oh, oh, oh,
> And ten is one, one, one, one.
>   —Anonymous

43210	Gray	43210	Gray	43210	Gray	43210	Gray
00000	00000	01000	01100	10000	11000	11000	10100
00001	00001	01001	01101	10001	11001	11001	10101
00010	00011	01010	01111	10010	11011	11010	10111
00011	00010	01011	01110	10011	11010	11011	10110
00100	00110	01100	01010	10100	11110	11100	10010
00101	00111	01101	01011	10101	11111	11101	10011
00110	00101	01110	01001	10110	11101	11110	10001
00111	00100	01111	01000	10111	11100	11111	10000

Table 4.12: First 32 Binary and Gray Codes.

```
a=linspace(0,31,32); b=bitshift(a,-1);
b=bitxor(a,b); dec2bin(b)
```

Code for Table 4.12.

they differ in one of their most-significant bits. Any compression method that treats these pixels as 24-bit numbers would consider these pixels very different, and its performance would suffer as a result. A compression method for grayscale images can be applied to compressing color images, but the color image should first be separated into three color components, and each component compressed individually as a grayscale image.

For an example of the use of RGC for image compression see Section 4.24.

History of Gray Codes

Gray codes are named after Frank Gray, who patented their use for shaft encoders in 1953 [Gray 53]. However, the work was performed much earlier, the patent being applied for in 1947. Gray was a researcher at Bell Telephone Laboratories. During the 1930s and 1940s he was awarded numerous patents for work related to television. According to [Heath 72] the code was first, in fact, used by J. M. E. Baudot for telegraphy in the 1870s (Section 1.1.3), though it is only since the advent of computers that the code has become widely known.

The Baudot code uses five bits per symbol. It can represent $32 \times 2 - 2 = 62$ characters (each code can have two meanings, the meaning being indicated by the **LS** and **FS** codes). It became popular and, by 1950, was designated the International Telegraph Code No. 1. It was used by many first- and second generation computers.

The August 1972 issue of *Scientific American* contains two articles of interest, one on the origin of binary codes [Heath 72], and another [Gardner 72] on some entertaining aspects of the Gray codes.

Bibliography

Gardner, Martin (1972) "Mathematical Games," *Scientific American*, **227**(2):106, August.

Gray, Frank (1953) "Pulse Code Communication," United States Patent 2,632,058, March 17.

Heath, F. G. (1972) "Origins of the Binary Code," *Scientific American*, **227**(2):76, August.

4.2.2 Error Metrics

Developers and implementers of lossy image compression methods need a standard metric to measure the quality of reconstructed images compared with the original ones. The better a reconstructed image resembles the original one, the bigger should be the value produced by this metric. Such a metric should also produce a dimensionless number, and that number should not be very sensitive to small variations in the reconstructed image. A common measure used for this purpose is the *peak signal to noise ratio* (PSNR). It is familiar to workers in the field, it is also simple to calculate, but it has only a limited, approximate relationship with the perceived errors noticed by the human visual system. This is why higher PSNR values imply closer resemblance between the reconstructed and the original images, but they do not provide a guarantee that viewers will like the reconstructed image.

Denoting the pixels of the original image by P_i and the pixels of the reconstructed image by Q_i (where $1 \le i \le n$), we first define the *mean square error* (MSE) between the two images as

$$\text{MSE} = \frac{1}{n} \sum_{i=1}^{n} (P_i - Q_i)^2. \tag{4.2}$$

It is the average of the square of the errors (pixel differences) of the two images. The *root mean square error* (RMSE) is defined as the square root of the MSE, and the PSNR is defined as

$$\text{PSNR} = 20 \log_{10} \frac{\max_i |P_i|}{\text{RMSE}}.$$

The absolute value is normally not needed, since pixel values are rarely negative. For a bi-level image, the numerator is 1. For a grayscale image with eight bits per pixel, the numerator is 255. For color images, only the luminance component is used.

Greater resemblance between the images implies smaller RMSE and, as a result, larger PSNR. The PNSR is dimensionless, since the units of both numerator and denominator are pixel values. However, because of the use of the logarithm, we say that the PSNR is expressed in *decibels* (dB, Section 7.1). The use of the logarithm also implies less sensitivity to changes in the RMSE. For example, dividing the RMSE by 10 multiplies the PSNR by 2. Notice that the PSNR has no absolute meaning. It is meaningless to say that a PSNR of, say, 25 is good. PSNR values are used only to compare the performance of different lossy compression methods or the effects of different parametric values on the performance of an algorithm. The MPEG committee, for example, uses an informal threshold of PSNR = 0.5 dB to decide whether to incorporate a coding optimization, since they believe that an improvement of that magnitude would be visible to the eye.

Typical PSNR values range between 20 and 40. Assuming pixel values in the range $[0, 255]$, an RMSE of 25.5 results in a PSNR of 20, and an RMSE of 2.55 results in a PSNR of 40. An RMSE of zero (i.e., identical images) results in an infinite (or, more precisely, undefined) PSNR. An RMSE of 255 results in a PSNR of zero, and RMSE values greater than 255 yield negative PSNRs.

⋄ **Exercise 4.6:** If the maximum pixel value is 255, can RMSE values be greater than 255?

Some authors define the PSNR as

$$ \text{PSNR} = 10 \log_{10} \frac{\max_i |P_i|^2}{\text{MSE}}. $$

In order for the two formulations to produce the same result, the logarithm is multiplied in this case by 10 instead of by 20, since $\log_{10} A^2 = 2 \log_{10} A$. Either definition is useful, because only relative PSNR values are used in practice. However, the use of two different factors is confusing.

A related measure is *signal to noise ratio* (SNR). This is defined as

$$ \text{SNR} = 20 \log_{10} \frac{\sqrt{\frac{1}{n} \sum_{i=1}^{n} P_i^2}}{\text{RMSE}}. $$

The numerator is the root mean square of the original image.

Figure 4.13 is a Matlab function to compute the PSNR of two images. A typical call is PSNR(A,B), where A and B are image files. They must have the same resolution and have pixel values in the range $[0, 1]$.

```
function PSNR(A,B)
if A==B
 error('Images are identical; PSNR is undefined')
end
max2_A=max(max(A)); max2_B=max(max(B));
min2_A=min(min(A)); min2_B=min(min(B));
if max2_A>1 | max2_B>1 | min2_A<0 | min2_B<0
   error('pixels must be in [0,1]')
end
differ=A-B;
decib=20*log10(1/(sqrt(mean(mean(differ.^2)))));
disp(sprintf('PSNR = +%5.2f dB',decib))
```

Figure 4.13: A Matlab Function to Compute PSNR.

Another relative of the PSNR is the *signal to quantization noise ratio (SQNR)*. This is a measure of the effect of quantization on signal quality. It is defined as

$$\text{SQNR} = 10 \log_{10} \frac{\text{signal power}}{\text{quantization error}},$$

where the quantization error is the difference between the quantized signal and the original signal.

Another approach to the comparison of an original and a reconstructed image is to generate the difference image and judge it visually. Intuitively, the difference image is $D_i = P_i - Q_i$, but such an image is hard to judge visually because its pixel values D_i tend to be small numbers. If a pixel value of zero represents white, such a difference image would be almost invisible. In the opposite case, where pixel values of zero represent black, such a difference would be too dark to judge. Better results are obtained by calculating

$$D_i = a(P_i - Q_i) + b,$$

where a is a magnification parameter (typically a small number such as 2) and b is half the maximum value of a pixel (typically 128). Parameter a serves to magnify small differences, while b shifts the difference image from extreme white (or extreme black) to a more comfortable gray.

4.3 Intuitive Methods

It is easy to come up with simple, intuitive methods for compressing images. They are inefficient and are described here for the sake of completeness.

4.3.1 Subsampling

Subsampling is perhaps the simplest way to compress an image. One approach to subsampling is simply to ignore some of the pixels. The encoder may, for example, ignore every other row and every other column of the image, and write the remaining pixels (which constitute 25% of the image) on the compressed stream. The decoder inputs the compressed data and uses each pixel to generate four identical pixels of the reconstructed image. This, of course, involves the loss of much image detail and is rarely acceptable. Notice that the compression ratio is known in advance.

A slight improvement is obtained when the encoder calculates the average of each block of four pixels and writes this average on the compressed stream. No pixel is totally ignored, but the method is still primitive, since a good lossy image compression method should lose data to which the eye is not sensitive.

Better results (but worse compression) are obtained when the color representation of the image is changed from the original (normally RGB) to luminance and chrominance. The encoder subsamples the two chrominance components of a pixel but not its luminance component. Assuming that each component uses the same number of bits, the two chrominance components use 2/3 of the image size. Subsampling them reduces this to 25% of 2/3, or 1/6. The size of the compressed image is thus 1/2 (for the uncompressed luminance component), plus 1/6 (for the two chrominance components) or 2/3 of the original size.

4.3.2 Quantization

Scalar quantization has been mentioned in Section 4.1. This is an intuitive, lossy method where the information lost is not necessarily the least important. Vector quantization can obtain better results, and an intuitive version of it is described here.

The image is partitioned into equal-size blocks (called *vectors*) of pixels, and the encoder has a list (called a *codebook*) of blocks of the same size. Each image block B is compared to all the blocks of the codebook and is matched with the "closest" one. If B is matched with codebook block C, then the encoder writes a pointer to C on the compressed stream. If the pointer is smaller than the block size, compression is achieved. Figure 4.14 shows an example.

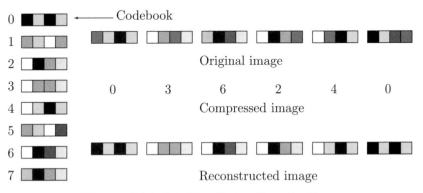

Figure 4.14: Intuitive Vector Quantization.

The details of selecting and maintaining the codebook and of matching blocks are discussed in Section 4.12. Notice that vector quantization is a method where the compression ratio is known in advance.

4.4 Image Transforms

The mathematical concept of a transform is a powerful tool in many areas and can also serve as an approach to image compression. Section 5.1 discusses this concept in general, as well as the Fourier transform. An image can be compressed by transforming its pixels (which are correlated) to a representation where they are *decorrelated*. Compression is achieved if the new values are smaller, on average, than the original ones. Lossy compression can be achieved by quantizing the transformed values. The decoder inputs the transformed values from the compressed stream and reconstructs the (precise or approximate) original data by applying the opposite transform. The transforms discussed in this section are *orthogonal*. Section 5.6.1 discusses *subband transforms*.

The term *decorrelated* means that the transformed values are independent of one another. As a result, they can be encoded independently, which makes it simpler to construct a statistical model. An image can be compressed if its representation has redundancy. The redundancy in images stems from pixel correlation. If we transform the image to a representation where the pixels are decorrelated, we have eliminated the redundancy and the image has been fully compressed.

We start with a simple example, where we scan an image in raster order and group pairs of adjacent pixels. Because the pixels are correlated, the two pixels (x, y) of a pair normally have similar values. We now consider the pairs of pixels as points in two-dimensional space, and plot them. We know that all the points of the form (x, x) are located on the 45° line $y = x$, so we expect our points to be concentrated around this line. Figure 4.15a shows the results of plotting the pixels of a typical image—where a pixel has values in the interval $[0, 255]$—in such a way. Most points form a cloud around this line, and only a few points are located away from it. We now transform the image by rotating all the points 45° clockwise about the origin, such that the 45° line now coincides with the x-axis (Figure 4.15b). This is done by the simple transformation [see Equation (4.48)]

$$(x^*, y^*) = (x, y) \begin{pmatrix} \cos 45° & -\sin 45° \\ \sin 45° & \cos 45° \end{pmatrix} = (x, y) \frac{1}{\sqrt{2}} \begin{pmatrix} 1 & -1 \\ 1 & 1 \end{pmatrix} = (x, y)\mathbf{R}, \quad (4.3)$$

where the rotation matrix $\mathbf{R}$ is orthonormal (i.e., the dot product of a row with itself is 1, the dot product of different rows is 0, and the same is true for columns). The inverse transfomation is

$$(x, y) = (x^*, y^*)\mathbf{R}^{-1} = (x^*, y^*)\mathbf{R}^T = (x^*, y^*)\frac{1}{\sqrt{2}} \begin{pmatrix} 1 & 1 \\ -1 & 1 \end{pmatrix}. \quad (4.4)$$

(The inverse of an orthonormal matrix is its transpose.)

It is obvious that most points end up having y-coordinates that are zero or close to zero, while the x-coordinates don't change much. Figure 4.16a,b shows that the distributions of the x and y coordinates (i.e., the odd-numbered and even-numbered pixels of an image) before the rotation don't differ by much. Figure 4.16c,d shows that the distribution of the x coordinates stays almost the same but the y coordinates are concentrated around zero.

Once the coordinates of points are known before and after the rotation, it is easy to measure the reduction in correlation. A simple measure is the sum $\sum_i x_i y_i$, also called the *cross-correlation* of points (x_i, y_i).

◇ **Exercise 4.7:** Given the five points $(5, 5)$, $(6, 7)$, $(12.1, 13.2)$, $(23, 25)$, and $(32, 29)$ rotate them 45° clockwise and calculate their cross-correlations before and after the rotation.

We can now compress the image by simply writing the transformed pixels on the compressed stream. If lossy compression is acceptable, then all the pixels can be quantized (Sections 1.6 and 4.12), resulting in even smaller numbers. We can also write all the odd-numbered pixels (those that make up the x coordinates of the pairs) on the compressed stream, followed by all the even-numbered pixels. These two sequences are called the *coefficient vectors* of the transform. The latter sequence consists of small numbers and may, after quantization, have runs of zeros, resulting in even better compression.

It can be shown that the total variance of the pixels does not change by the rotation, since a rotation matrix is orthonormal. However, since the variance of the new y coordinates is small, most of the variance is now concentrated in the

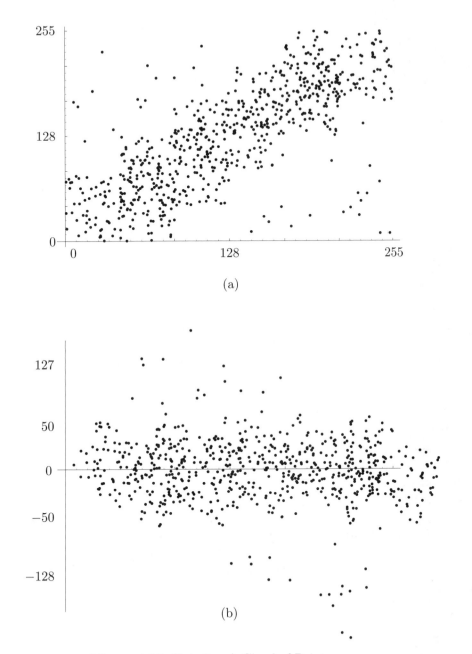

(a)

(b)

Figure 4.15: Rotating A Cloud of Points.

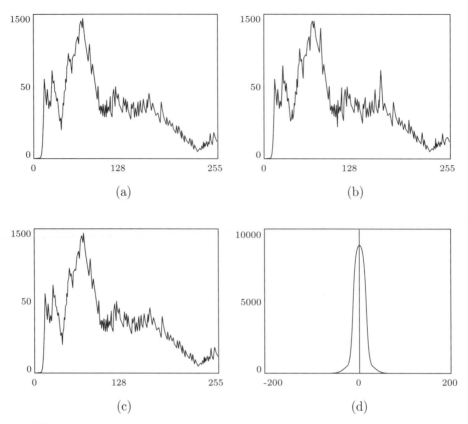

Figure 4.16: Distribution of Image Pixels Before and After Rotation.

x coordinates. The variance is sometimes called the *energy* of the distribution of pixels, so we can say that the rotation has concentrated (or compacted) the energy in the x coordinate and has created compression this way.

Concentrating the energy in one coordinate has another advantage. It makes it possible to quantize that coordinate more finely than the other coordinates. This type of quantization results in better (lossy) compression.

The following simple example illustrates the power of this basic transform. We start with the point $(4, 5)$, whose two coordinates are similar. Using Equation (4.3) the point is transformed to $(4, 5)\mathbf{R} = (9, 1)/\sqrt{2} \approx (6.36396, 0.7071)$. The energies of the point and its transform are $4^2 + 5^2 = 41 = (9^2 + 1^2)/2$. If we delete the smaller coordinate (4) of the point, we end up with an error of $4^2/41 = 0.39$. If, on the other hand, we delete the smaller of the two transform coefficients (0.7071), the resulting error is just $0.7071^2/41 = 0.012$. Another way to obtain the same error is to consider the reconstructed point. Passing $\frac{1}{\sqrt{2}}(9, 1)$ through the inverse transform [Equation (4.4)] results in the original point $(4, 5)$. Doing the same with $\frac{1}{\sqrt{2}}(9, 0)$ results in the approximate reconstructed point $(4.5, 4.5)$. The energy difference between the original and reconstructed points is the same small quantity

$$\frac{\left[(4^2 + 5^2) - (4.5^2 + 4.5^2)\right]}{4^2 + 5^2} = \frac{41 - 40.5}{41} = 0.0012.$$

This simple transform can easily be extended to any number of dimensions. Instead of selecting pairs of adjacent pixels we can select triplets. Each triplet becomes a point in three-dimensional space, and these points form a cloud concentrated around the line that forms $45°$ angles with the three coordinate axes. When this line is rotated such that it coincides with the x axis, the y and z coordinates of the transformed points become small numbers. The transformation is done by multiplying each point by a 3×3 rotation matrix, and such a matrix is, of course, orthonormal. The transformed points are then separated into three coefficient vectors, of which the last two consist of small numbers. For maximum compression each coefficient vector should be quantized separately.

This can be extended to more than three dimensions, with the only difference being that we cannot visualize spaces of dimensions higher than three. However, the mathematics can easily be extended. Some compression methods, such as JPEG, divide an image into blocks of 8×8 pixels each, and rotate each block twice, by means of Equation (4.9), as shown in Section 4.4.3. This double rotation produces a set of 64 transformed values, of which the first—termed the "DC coefficient"—is large, and the other 63 (called the "AC coefficients") are normally small. Thus, this transform concentrates the energy in the first of 64 dimensions. The set of DC coefficients and each of the sets of 63 AC coefficients should, in principle, be quantized separately (JPEG does this a little differently, though; see Section 4.6.5).

4.4.1 Orthogonal Transforms

Image transforms used in practice should be fast and preferably also simple to implement. This suggests the use of *linear transforms*. In such a transform, each transformed value c_i is a weighted sum of the data items (the pixels) d_j, where each item is multiplied by a weight (or a transform coefficient) w_{ij}. Thus, $c_i = \sum_j d_j w_{ij}$, for $i, j = 1, 2, \ldots, n$. For the case $n = 4$, this is expressed in matrix notation

$$\begin{pmatrix} c_1 \\ c_2 \\ c_3 \\ c_4 \end{pmatrix} = \begin{pmatrix} w_{11} & w_{12} & w_{13} & w_{14} \\ w_{21} & w_{22} & w_{23} & w_{24} \\ w_{31} & w_{32} & w_{33} & w_{34} \\ w_{41} & w_{42} & w_{43} & w_{44} \end{pmatrix} \begin{pmatrix} d_1 \\ d_2 \\ d_3 \\ d_4 \end{pmatrix}.$$

For the general case, we can write $\mathbf{C} = \mathbf{W} \cdot \mathbf{D}$. Each row of $\mathbf{W}$ is called a "basis vector."

The important issue is the determination of the values of the weights w_{ij}. The guiding principle is that we want the first transformed value c_1 to be large, and the remaining values $c_2, c_3, \ldots$ to be small. The basic relation $c_i = \sum_j d_j w_{ij}$ suggests that c_i will be large when each weight w_{ij} reinforces the corresponding data item d_j. This happens, for example, when the vectors w_{ij} and d_j have similar values and signs. Conversely, c_i will be small if all the weights w_{ij} are small and half of them have the opposite sign of d_j. Thus, when we get a large c_i we know that the basis vector w_{ij} resembles the data vector d_j. A small c_i, on the other hand, means that w_{ij} and d_j have different shapes. Thus, we can interpret the basis vectors w_{ij} as tools to extract features from the data vector.

In practice, the weights should be independent of the data items. Otherwise, the weights would have to be included in the compressed stream, for the use of the decoder. This, combined with the fact that our data items are pixel values, which are normally nonnegative, suggests a way to choose the basis vectors. The first vector, the one that produces c_1, should consist of positive, perhaps even identical, values. This will reinforce the nonnegative values of the pixels. Each of the other vectors should have half its elements positive and the other half, negative. When multiplied by nonnegative data items, such a vector tends to produce a small value. Recall that we can interpret the basis vectors as tools for extracting features from the data vector. A good choice would therefore be to have basis vectors that are very different from each other, and so can extract different features. This leads to the idea of basis vectors that are mutually orthogonal. If the transform matrix $\mathbf{W}$ is orthogonal, the transform itself is called orthogonal. Another observation that helps to select the basis vectors is that they should feature higher and higher frequencies, thus extracting higher-frequency features from the data as we go along, computing more transformed values.

These considerations are satisfied by the orthogonal matrix

$$\mathbf{W} = \begin{pmatrix} 1 & 1 & 1 & 1 \\ 1 & 1 & -1 & -1 \\ 1 & -1 & -1 & 1 \\ 1 & -1 & 1 & -1 \end{pmatrix}. \tag{4.5}$$

The first basis vector (the top row of $\mathbf{W}$) consists of all 1's, so its frequency is zero. Each of the subsequent vectors has two $+1$ and two -1, so they produce small transformed values, and their frequencies (measured as the number of sign changes along the basis vector) get higher. This matrix is similar to the Walsh-Hadamard transform [Equation (4.11)]. As an example, we transform the data vector $(4, 6, 5, 2)$

$$\begin{pmatrix} 1 & 1 & 1 & 1 \\ 1 & 1 & -1 & -1 \\ 1 & -1 & -1 & 1 \\ 1 & -1 & 1 & -1 \end{pmatrix} \begin{pmatrix} 4 \\ 6 \\ 5 \\ 2 \end{pmatrix} = \begin{pmatrix} 17 \\ 3 \\ -5 \\ 1 \end{pmatrix}.$$

The results are encouraging, since c_1 is large (compared to the original data items), and two of the remaining c_i's are small. However, the energy of the original data items is $4^2 + 6^2 + 5^2 + 2^2 = 81$, whereas the energy of the transformed values is $17^2 + 3^2 + (-5)^2 + 1^2 = 324$, four times as much. It is possible to conserve the energy by multiplying the transformation matrix $\mathbf{W}$ by the scale factor $1/2$. The new product $\mathbf{W} \cdot (4, 6, 5, 2)^T$ now produces $(17/2, 3/2, -5/2, 1/2)$. The energy is conserved, but it is concentrated in the first component, which contains $8.5^2/81 = 89\%$ of the total energy, compared to the original data, where the first component contained $4^2/81 \approx 20\%$ of the energy.

Another advantage of $\mathbf{W}$ is that it also performs the inverse transform. The product $\mathbf{W} \cdot (17/2, 3/2, -5/2, 1/2)^T$ reconstructs the original data $(4, 6, 5, 2)$.

We are now in a position to appreciate the power of a transform. We quantize the transformed vector $(8.5, 1.5, -2.5, 0.5)$ to the integers $(9, 1, -3, 0)$ and perform the inverse transform to get back $(3.5, 6.5, 5.5, 2.5)$. Another experiment is to completely delete the two smallest elements and to inverse-transform $(8.5, 0, -2.5, 0)$. This produces the reconstructed data $(3, 5.5, 5.5, 3)$, still very close to the original values. The conclusion is that even our simple transform is very useful. More sophisticated transforms produce results that can be quantized coarsely and still be used to reconstruct the original data to a high degree.

4.4.2 Two-Dimensional Transforms

Given two-dimensional data such as the 4×4 matrix

$$\mathbf{D} = \begin{pmatrix} 4 & 7 & 6 & 9 \\ 6 & 8 & 3 & 6 \\ 5 & 4 & 7 & 6 \\ 2 & 4 & 5 & 9 \end{pmatrix}$$

(where the first column is identical to the previous example), we can apply our simple one-dimensional transform. The result is

$$\mathbf{C}' = \mathbf{W} \cdot \mathbf{D} = \frac{1}{2} \begin{pmatrix} 1 & 1 & 1 & 1 \\ 1 & 1 & -1 & -1 \\ 1 & -1 & -1 & 1 \\ 1 & -1 & 1 & -1 \end{pmatrix}, \quad \mathbf{D} = \begin{pmatrix} 8.5 & 11.5 & 10.5 & 15 \\ 1.5 & 3.5 & -1.5 & 0 \\ -2.5 & -0.5 & 0.5 & 3 \\ 0.5 & -0.5 & 2.5 & 0 \end{pmatrix}.$$

Each column of $\mathbf{C}'$ is the transform of a column of $\mathbf{D}$. Notice how the top element of each column of $\mathbf{C}'$ is dominant. Also, all the columns have the same energy. We can consider $\mathbf{C}'$ the first stage in a two-stage process that produces the two-dimensional transform of matrix $\mathbf{D}$. The second stage should transform each *row* of $\mathbf{C}'$, and this is done by multiplying $\mathbf{C}'$ by the transpose $\mathbf{W}^T$. Our particular $\mathbf{W}$, however, is symmetric, so we end up with $\mathbf{C} = \mathbf{C}' \cdot \mathbf{W}^T = \mathbf{W} \cdot \mathbf{C} \cdot \mathbf{W}^T$ or

$$\mathbf{C} = \begin{pmatrix} 8.5 & 11.5 & 10.5 & 15 \\ 1.5 & 3.5 & -1.5 & 0 \\ -2.5 & -0.5 & 0.5 & 3 \\ 0.5 & -0.5 & 2.5 & 0 \end{pmatrix} \frac{1}{2} \begin{pmatrix} 1 & 1 & 1 & 1 \\ 1 & 1 & -1 & -1 \\ 1 & -1 & -1 & 1 \\ 1 & -1 & 1 & -1 \end{pmatrix}$$

$$= \begin{pmatrix} 22.75 & -2.75 & 0.75 & -3.75 \\ 1.75 & 3.25 & -0.25 & -1.75 \\ 0.25 & -3.25 & 0.25 & -2.25 \\ 1.25 & -1.25 & -0.75 & 1.75 \end{pmatrix}.$$

The top-left element is dominant. It contains 89% of the total energy of 579 in the original $\mathbf{D}$. The double-stage, two-dimensional transformation has reduced the correlation in both the horizontal and vertical dimensions.

The rest of this section discusses the following popular transforms:

1. The discrete cosine transform (DCT, Sections 4.4.3 and 4.6.2) is almost as efficient as the KLT in terms of energy compaction, and uses a fixed basis, regardless of the data. There are also fast methods for calculating the DCT. This method is used by JPEG and MPEG audio.

2. The Karhunen-Loève transform (KLT, Section 4.4.8) is the best one theoretically, in the sense of energy compaction (or, equivalently, pixel decorrelation). However, its coefficients are not fixed; they depend on the data to be compressed. Calculating these coefficients (the basis of the transform) is slow, as is the calculation of the transformed values themselves. Since the coefficients are data dependent, they have to be included in the compressed stream. For of these reasons, and because the DCT performs almost as well, the KLT is not generally used in practice.

3. The Walsh-Hadamard transform (WHT, Section 4.4.6) is fast to calculate (it requires only additions and subtractions), but its performance, in terms of energy compaction, is lower than that of the DCT.

4. The Haar transform [Stollnitz 96] is a simple, fast transform. It is the simplest wavelet transform and is discussed in Section 4.4.7 and in Chapter 5.

4.4.3 Discrete Cosine Transform

The *two-dimensional* DCT is the method used in practice, but the entire concept of DCT is easier to understand by looking at the one-dimensional DCT first. Figure 4.17 shows eight cosine waves, $w(f) = \cos(f\theta)$, for $0 \leq \theta \leq \pi$, with frequencies $f = 0, 1, \ldots, 7$. Each wave $w(f)$ is sampled at the eight points

$$\theta = \frac{\pi}{16}, \quad \frac{3\pi}{16}, \quad \frac{5\pi}{16}, \quad \frac{7\pi}{16}, \quad \frac{9\pi}{16}, \quad \frac{11\pi}{16}, \quad \frac{13\pi}{16}, \quad \frac{15\pi}{16}, \tag{4.6}$$

to form one basis vector $\mathbf{v}_f$, and the resulting eight vectors $\mathbf{v}_f$, $f = 0, 1, \ldots, 7$ (a total of 64 numbers), are shown in Table 4.18. They serve as the basis of the one-dimensional DCT. Notice the similarly between this table and matrix $\mathbf{W}$ of Equation (4.5).

It can be shown that these $\mathbf{v}_i$ vectors are orthonormal (because of the particular choice of the eight sample points), and it is also easy, with appropriate mathematical software, to check this by direct calculations. This set of eight orthonormal vectors can therefore be considered an 8×8 transformation matrix. Since this matrix is orthonormal, it is a rotation matrix. Thus, we can interpret the one-dimensional DCT as a rotation in eight dimensions (see the discussion of image transforms by means of rotations earlier in this section).

The one-dimensional DCT has another interpretation. We can consider the eight orthonormal vectors $\mathbf{v}_i$ the basis of a vector space, and express any other vector $\mathbf{p}$ in this space as a linear combination of the $\mathbf{v}_i$'s. As an example, we select the eight (correlated) numbers $\mathbf{p} = (.6, .5, .4, .5, .6, .5, .4, .55)$ as our test data. We express vector $\mathbf{p}$ as a linear combination $\mathbf{p} = \sum w_i \mathbf{v}_i$ of the eight basis vectors $\mathbf{v}_i$. Solving this system of eight equations yields the eight weights

$$w_0 = 0.506, \quad w_1 = 0.0143, \quad w_2 = 0.0115, \quad w_3 = 0.0439,$$
$$w_4 = 0.0795, \quad w_5 = -0.0432, \quad w_6 = 0.00478, \quad w_7 = -0.0077.$$

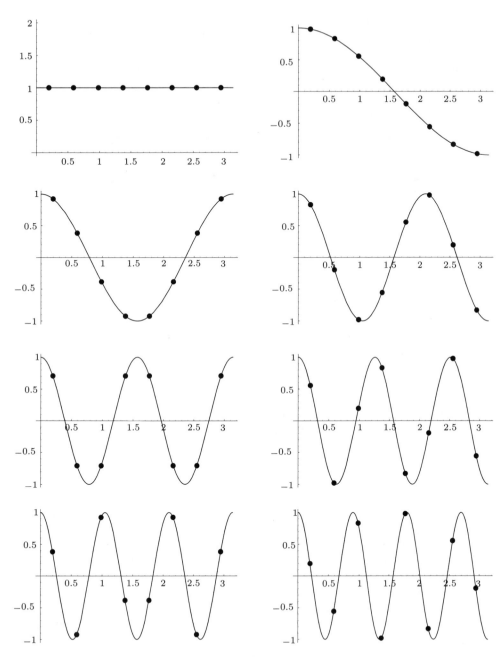

Figure 4.17: Calculating A One-Dimensional DCT.

θ	0.196	0.589	0.982	1.374	1.767	2.160	2.553	2.945
$\cos 0\theta$	1.	1.	1.	1.	1.	1.	1.	1.
$\cos 1\theta$	0.981	0.831	0.556	0.195	-0.195	-0.556	-0.831	-0.981
$\cos 2\theta$	0.924	0.383	-0.383	-0.924	-0.924	-0.383	0.383	0.924
$\cos 3\theta$	0.831	-0.195	-0.981	-0.556	0.556	0.981	0.195	-0.831
$\cos 4\theta$	0.707	-0.707	-0.707	0.707	0.707	-0.707	-0.707	0.707
$\cos 5\theta$	0.556	-0.981	0.195	0.831	-0.831	-0.195	0.981	-0.556
$\cos 6\theta$	0.383	-0.924	0.924	-0.383	-0.383	0.924	-0.924	0.383
$\cos 7\theta$	0.195	-0.556	0.831	-0.981	0.981	-0.831	0.556	-0.195

Table 4.18: Calculating A One-Dimensional DCT.

```
Table[N[t],{t,Pi/16,15Pi/16,Pi/8}]
dctp[pw_]:=Table[N[Cos[pw t]],{t,Pi/16,15Pi/16,Pi/8}]
dctp[0]
dctp[1]
...
dctp[7]
```

Code For Table 4.18.

```
dct[pw_]:=Plot[Cos[pw t], {t,0,Pi}, DisplayFunction->Identity,
  AspectRatio->Automatic];
dcdot[pw_]:=ListPlot[Table[{t,Cos[pw t]},{t,Pi/16,15Pi/16,Pi/8}],
  DisplayFunction->Identity]
Show[dct[0],dcdot[0], Prolog->AbsolutePointSize[4],
  DisplayFunction->$DisplayFunction]
...
Show[dct[7],dcdot[7], Prolog->AbsolutePointSize[4],
  DisplayFunction->$DisplayFunction]
```

Code For Figure 4.17.

Weight w_0 is not much different from the elements of **p**, but the other seven weights are much smaller. This is how the DCT (or any other orthogonal transform) produces compression. We can simply write the eight weights on the compressed stream, where they will occupy less space than the eight components of **p**. Quantizing the eight weights may increase compression considerably while resulting in just a small loss of data.

Figure 4.19 illustrates this linear combination graphically. Each of the eight $\mathbf{v}_i$'s is shown as a row of eight small, gray rectangles where a value of $+1$ is painted white and -1 is black. Each of the eight elements of vector **p** is expressed as the weighted sum of eight grayscales.

The simplest way to calculate the one-dimensional DCT in practice is by

$$G_f = \frac{1}{2} C_f \sum_{t=0}^{7} p_t \cos\left(\frac{(2t+1)f\pi}{16}\right), \tag{4.7}$$

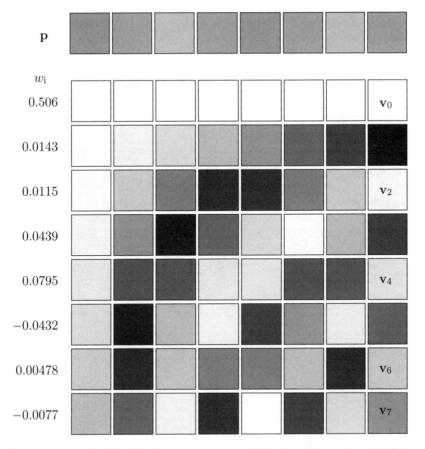

Figure 4.19: A Graphic Representation of the One-Dimensional DCT.

$$\text{where } C_f = \begin{cases} \frac{1}{\sqrt{2}}, & f = 0, \\ 1, & f > 0, \end{cases} \quad \text{for } f = 0, 1, \ldots, 7.$$

This starts with a set of eight data values p_t (pixels, sound samples, or other data) and produces a set of eight DCT coefficients G_f. It is straightforward but slow (Section 4.6.3 discusses faster versions). The decoder inputs the DCT coefficients in sets of eight, and uses the *inverse* DCT (IDCT) to reconstruct the original data values (also in groups of eight). The simplest way to calculate the IDCT is by

$$p_t = \frac{1}{2} \sum_{j=0}^{7} C_j G_j \cos\left(\frac{(2t+1)j\pi}{16}\right), \quad \text{for } t = 0, 1, \ldots, 7. \tag{4.8}$$

The following experiment illustrates the power of the DCT. We start with the set of eight data items $\mathbf{p} = (12, 10, 8, 10, 12, 10, 8, 11)$, apply the one-dimensional

DCT to them, and end up with the eight coefficients

28.6375, 0.571202, 0.46194, 1.757, 3.18198, −1.72956, 0.191342, −0.308709.

These can be used to precisely reconstruct the original data (except for small errors caused by limited machine precision). Our goal, however, is to compress the data even more by quantizing the coefficients. We first quantize them to $28.6, 0.6, 0.5, 1.8, 3.2, −1.8, 0.2, −0.3$, and apply the IDCT to get back

12.0254, 10.0233, 7.96054, 9.93097, 12.0164, 9.99321, 7.94354, 10.9989.

We then quantize the coefficients even more, to $28, 1, 1, 2, 3, −2, 0, 0$, and apply the IDCT to get back

12.1883, 10.2315, 7.74931, 9.20863, 11.7876, 9.54549, 7.82865, 10.6557.

Finally, we quantize the coefficients to $28, 0, 0, 2, 3, −2, 0, 0$, and still get back from the IDCT the sequence

11.236, 9.62443, 7.66286, 9.57302, 12.3471, 10.0146, 8.05304, 10.6842,

where the largest difference between an original value (12) and a reconstructed one (11.236) is 0.764 (or 6.4% of 12). The code that does all that is listed in Figure 4.20.

```
p={12.,10.,8.,10.,12.,10.,8.,11.};
c={.7071,1,1,1,1,1,1,1};
dct[i_]:=(c[[i+1]]/2)Sum[p[[t+1]]Cos[(2t+1)i Pi/16],{t,0,7}];
q=Table[dct[i],{i,0,7}] (* use precise DCT coefficients *)
q={28,0,0,2,3,-2,0,0}; (* or use quantized DCT coefficients *)
idct[t_]:=(1/2)Sum[c[[j+1]]q[[j+1]]Cos[(2t+1)j Pi/16],{j,0,7}];
ip=Table[idct[t],{t,0,7}]
```

Figure 4.20: Experiments With The One-Dimensional DCT.

Two-Dimensional DCT: We know from experience that the pixels of an image are correlated in two dimensions, not just in one dimension (a pixel is correlated with its neighbors on the left and right, and above and below). This is why image compression methods use the two-dimensional DCT, given by

$$G_{ij} = \frac{1}{\sqrt{2n}} C_i C_j \sum_{x=0}^{n-1} \sum_{y=0}^{n-1} p_{xy} \cos\left(\frac{(2y+1)j\pi}{2n}\right) \cos\left(\frac{(2x+1)i\pi}{2n}\right), \qquad (4.9)$$

for $0 \le i, j \le n - 1$. The image is broken up into blocks of $n \times n$ pixels p_{xy} (we use $n = 8$ as an example), and Equation (4.9) is used to produce a block of 8×8 DCT coefficients G_{ij} for each block of pixels. If lossy compression is required, the coefficients are quantized. The decoder reconstructs a block of (approximate or precise) data values by computing the inverse DCT (IDCT):

$$p_{xy} = \frac{1}{4} \sum_{i=0}^{7} \sum_{j=0}^{7} C_i C_j G_{ij} \cos\left(\frac{(2x+1)i\pi}{16}\right) \cos\left(\frac{(2y+1)j\pi}{16}\right),$$

$$\text{where } C_f = \begin{cases} \frac{1}{\sqrt{2}}, & f = 0, \\ 1, & f > 0. \end{cases} \tag{4.10}$$

The two-dimensional DCT can be interpreted in two different ways, as a rotation (actually, two separate rotations), and as a basis of an n-dimensional vector space. The first interpretation starts with a block of $n \times n$ pixels. It first considers each row of this block a point $(p_{x,0}, p_{x,1}, \ldots, p_{x,n-1})$ in n-dimensional space, and it rotates the point by means of the innermost sum

$$G1_{x,j} = C_j \sum_{y=0}^{n-1} p_{xy} \cos\left(\frac{(2y+1)j\pi}{2n}\right)$$

of Equation (4.9). This results in a block $G1_{x,j}$ of $n \times n$ coefficients where the first element of each row is dominant and the remaining elements are small. The outermost sum of Equation (4.9) is

$$G_{ij} = \frac{1}{\sqrt{2n}} C_i \sum_{x=0}^{n-1} G1_{x,j} \cos\left(\frac{(2x+1)i\pi}{2n}\right).$$

Here, the *columns* of $G1_{x,j}$ are considered points in n-dimensional space, and are rotated. The result is one large coefficient in the top-left corner of the block and $n^2 - 1$ small coefficients elsewhere. This interpretation looks at the two-dimensional DCT as two separate rotations in n dimensions. It is interesting to note that two rotations in n dimensions are faster than one rotation in n^2 dimensions, since the latter requires an $n^2 \times n^2$ rotation matrix.

The second interpretation (assuming $n = 8$) uses Equation (4.9) to create 64 blocks of 8×8 values each. The 64 blocks are then used as a basis of a 64-dimensional vector space (they are basis images). Any block B of 8×8 pixels can be expressed as a linear combination of the basis images, and the 64 weights of this linear combination are the DCT coefficients of B.

Figure 4.21 shows the graphic representation of the 64 basis images of the two-dimensional DCT for $n = 8$. A general element (i, j) in this figure is the 8×8 block obtained by calculating the product $\cos(i \cdot s) \cos(j \cdot t)$ where s and t are varied independently over the values listed in Equation (4.6). This figure can easily be generated by the *Mathematica* code shown with it. The alternative code shown is a modification of code in [Watson 94], and it requires the `GraphicsImage.m` package, which is not widely available.

Using appropriate software, it is easy to perform DCT calculations and display the results graphically. Figure 4.24a shows a random 8x8 data unit made up of zeros

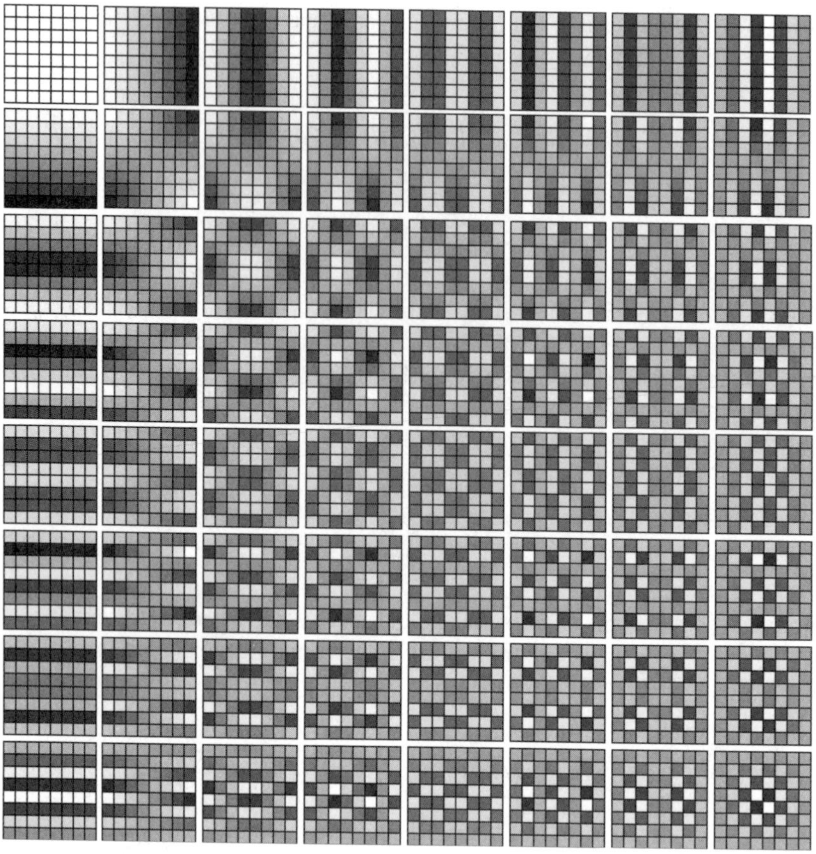

Figure 4.21: The 64 Basis Images of the Two-Dimensional DCT.

```
dctp[fs_,ft_]:=Table[SetAccuracy[N[(1.-Cos[fs s]Cos[ft t])/2],3],
  {s,Pi/16,15Pi/16,Pi/8},{t,Pi/16,15Pi/16,Pi/8}]//TableForm
dctp[0,0]
dctp[0,1]
...
dctp[7,7]
```

Code For Figure 4.21

```
Needs["GraphicsImage'"] (* Draws 2D DCT Coefficients *)
DCTMatrix=Table[If[k==0,Sqrt[1/8],Sqrt[1/4]Cos[Pi(2j+1)k/16]],
  {k,0,7}, {j,0,7}] //N;
DCTTensor=Array[Outer[Times, DCTMatrix[[#1]],DCTMatrix[[#2]]]&,
  {8,8}];
Show[GraphicsArray[Map[GraphicsImage[#, {-.25,.25}]&,
  DCTTensor,{2}]]]
```

Alternative Code For Figure 4.21

and ones. The same unit is shown in Figure 4.24b graphically, with 1 as white and 0 as black. Figure 4.24c shows the weights by which each of the 64 DCT coefficients has to be multiplied in order to reproduce the original data unit. In this figure, zero is shown in neutral gray, positive numbers are bright (notice how bright the DC coefficient is), and negative numbers are shown as dark. Figure 4.24d shows the weights numerically. The *Mathematica* code that does all that is also listed. Figure 4.25 is similar, but for a very regular data unit.

Next, we illustrate the performance of the two-dimensional DCT by applying it to two blocks of 8×8 values. The first block (Table 4.22) has highly correlated integer values in the range $[8, 12]$ and the second one, random values in the same range. The first block results in a large DC coefficient, followed by small (including 20 zeros) AC coefficients. In contrast, the coefficients for the second block (Table 4.23) include just one zero.

12	10	8	10	12	10	8	11	81	0	0	0	0	0	0	0
11	12	10	8	10	12	10	8	0	1.57	0.61	1.90	0.38	-1.81	0.20	-0.32
8	11	12	10	8	10	12	10	0	-0.61	0.71	0.35	0	0.07	0	0.02
10	8	11	12	10	8	10	12	0	1.90	-0.35	4.76	0.77	-3.39	0.25	-0.54
12	10	8	11	12	10	8	10	0	-0.38	0	-0.77	8.00	0.51	0	0.07
10	12	10	8	11	12	10	8	0	-1.81	-0.07	-3.39	-0.51	1.57	0.56	0.25
8	10	12	10	8	11	12	10	0	-0.20	0	-0.25	0	-0.56	-0.71	0.29
10	8	10	12	10	8	11	12	0	-0.32	-0.02	-0.54	-0.07	0.25	-0.29	-0.90

Table 4.22: Two-Dimensional DCT of a Block of Correlated Values.

8	10	9	11	11	9	9	12	79.12	0.98	0.64	-1.51	-0.62	-0.86	1.22	0.32
11	8	12	8	11	10	11	10	0.15	-1.64	-0.09	1.23	0.10	3.29	1.08	-2.97
9	11	9	10	12	9	9	8	-1.26	-0.29	-3.27	1.69	-0.51	1.13	1.52	1.33
9	12	10	8	8	9	8	9	-1.27	-0.25	-0.67	-0.15	1.63	-1.94	0.47	-1.30
12	8	9	9	12	10	8	11	-2.12	-0.67	-0.07	-0.79	0.13	-1.40	0.16	-0.15
8	11	10	12	9	12	12	10	-2.68	1.08	-1.99	-1.93	-1.77	-0.35	0	-0.80
10	10	12	10	12	10	10	12	1.20	2.10	-0.98	0.87	-1.55	-0.59	-0.98	2.76
12	9	11	11	9	8	8	12	-2.24	0.55	0.29	0.75	-2.40	-0.05	0.06	1.14

Table 4.23: Two-Dimensional DCT of a Block of Random Values.

Compressing an image with DCT can now be done as follows:

1. Dividing it into k blocks of $n \times n$ (typically 8×8) pixels each.

2. Applying the two-dimensional DCT to each block B_i. This expresses the block as a linear combination of the 64 basis images of Figure 4.21. The result is a block (we'll call it a vector) $W^{(i)}$ of 64 weights $w_j^{(i)}$ (where $j = 0, 1, \ldots, 63$).

3. The k vectors $W^{(i)}$ $(i = 1, 2, \ldots, k)$ are separated into 64 coefficient vectors $C^{(j)}$, where the k elements of $C^{(j)}$ are $\left(w_j^{(1)}, w_j^{(2)}, \ldots, w_j^{(k)} \right)$. The first coefficient vector $C^{(0)}$ consists of the k DC coefficients.

4. Each coefficient vector $C^{(j)}$ is quantized separately to produce a quantized vector $Q^{(j)}$, which is written on the compressed stream.

The decoder reads the 64 quantized coefficient vectors $Q^{(j)}$, uses them to construct k weight vectors $W^{(i)}$, and applies the IDCT to each weight vector, to reconstruct (approximately) the 64 pixels of block B_i. Notice that JPEG works differently.

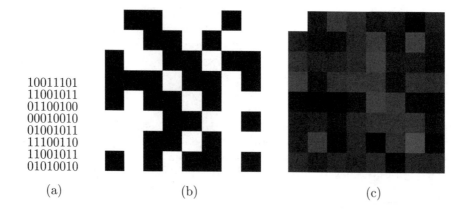

```
10011101
11001011
01100100
00010010
01001011
11100110
11001011
01010010
```

(a)   (b)   (c)

4.000	−0.133	0.637	0.272	−0.250	−0.181	−1.076	0.026
0.081	−0.178	−0.300	0.230	0.694	−0.309	0.875	−0.127
0.462	0.125	0.095	0.291	0.868	−0.070	0.021	−0.280
0.837	−0.194	0.455	0.583	0.588	−0.281	0.448	0.383
−0.500	−0.635	−0.749	−0.346	0.750	0.557	−0.502	−0.540
−0.167	0	−0.366	0.146	0.393	0.448	0.577	−0.268
−0.191	0.648	−0.729	−0.008	−1.171	0.306	1.155	−0.744
0.122	−0.200	0.038	−0.118	0.138	−1.154	0.134	0.148

(d)

Figure 4.24: A Two-Dimensional DCT Example.

```
DCTMatrix=Table[If[k==0,Sqrt[1/8],Sqrt[1/4]Cos[Pi(2j+1)k/16]],
  {k,0,7}, {j,0,7}] //N;
DCTTensor=Array[Outer[Times, DCTMatrix[[#1]],DCTMatrix[[#2]]]&,
  {8,8}];
img={{1,0,0,1,1,1,0,1},{1,1,0,0,1,0,1,1},
{0,1,1,0,0,1,0,0},{0,0,0,1,0,0,1,0},
{0,1,0,0,1,0,1,1},{1,1,1,0,0,1,1,0},
{1,1,0,0,1,0,1,1},{0,1,0,1,0,0,1,0}};
ShowImage[Reverse[img]]
dctcoeff=Array[(Plus @@ Flatten[DCTTensor[[#1,#2]] img])&,{8,8}];
dctcoeff=SetAccuracy[dctcoeff,4];
dctcoeff=Chop[dctcoeff,.001];
MatrixForm[dctcoeff]
ShowImage[Reverse[dctcoeff]]
```

Code For Figure 4.24.

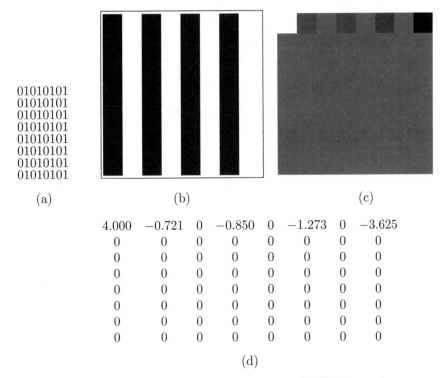

01010101
01010101
01010101
01010101
01010101
01010101
01010101
01010101

(a)   (b)   (c)

4.000	−0.721	0	−0.850	0	−1.273	0	−3.625
0	0	0	0	0	0	0	0
0	0	0	0	0	0	0	0
0	0	0	0	0	0	0	0
0	0	0	0	0	0	0	0
0	0	0	0	0	0	0	0
0	0	0	0	0	0	0	0
0	0	0	0	0	0	0	0

(d)

Figure 4.25: A Two-Dimensional DCT Example.

```
DCTMatrix=Table[If[k==0,Sqrt[1/8],Sqrt[1/4]Cos[Pi(2j+1)k/16]],
 {k,0,7}, {j,0,7}] //N;
DCTTensor=Array[Outer[Times, DCTMatrix[[#1]],DCTMatrix[[#2]]]&,
 {8,8}];
img={{0,1,0,1,0,1,0,1},{0,1,0,1,0,1,0,1},
 {0,1,0,1,0,1,0,1},{0,1,0,1,0,1,0,1},{0,1,0,1,0,1,0,1},
 {0,1,0,1,0,1,0,1},{0,1,0,1,0,1,0,1},{0,1,0,1,0,1,0,1}};
ShowImage[Reverse[img]]
dctcoeff=Array[(Plus @@ Flatten[DCTTensor[[#1,#2]] img])&,{8,8}];
dctcoeff=SetAccuracy[dctcoeff,4];
dctcoeff=Chop[dctcoeff,.001];
MatrixForm[dctcoeff]
ShowImage[Reverse[dctcoeff]]
```

Code For Figure 4.25.

⋄ **Exercise 4.8:** Show how the 64 values of Table 4.22 are correlated.

⋄ **Exercise 4.9:** Imagine an 8×8 block of values where all the odd-numbered rows consist of 1's and all the even-numbered rows contain zeros. What can we say about the DCT weights of this block?

⋄ **Exercise 4.10:** Calculate the one-dimensional DCT [Equation (4.7)] of the eight correlated values 11, 22, 33, 44, 55, 66, 77, and 88. Show how to quantize them, and calculate their IDCT from Equation (4.8).

4.4.4 Example

This example illustrates the difference in performance of the DCT on a continuous-tone image and a discrete-tone image. We start with the very correlated pattern of Table 4.26. This is an idealized example of a continuous-tone image, since adjacent pixels differ by a constant amount. The 64 DCT coefficients of this pattern are listed in Table 4.27. It is clear that there are just a few dominant coefficients. Table 4.28 lists the coefficients after they have been coarsely quantized. In fact, just four coefficients are nonzero. The results of performing the IDCT on these quantized coefficients are shown in Table 4.29. It is obvious that the four nonzero coefficients have reconstructed the original pattern to a high degree.

Tables 4.30 through 4.33 show the same process applied to a Y-shaped pattern, typical of a discrete-tone image. The quantization, shown in Table 4.32, is light. The coefficients have simply been truncated to the nearest integer. It is easy to see that the reconstruction, shown in Table 4.33, isn't as good as before. Quantities that should have been 10 are between 8.96 and 10.11. Quantities that should have been zero are as big as 0.86.

4.4.5 Discrete Sine Transform

Readers who have made it to this point may raise the question of why the cosine function, and not the sine, is used in the transform? Is it possible to use the sine function in a similar way to the DCT to create a discrete sine transform? Is there a DST, and if not, why? This short section discusses the differences between the sine and cosine functions and shows why these differences lead to a very ineffective sine transform.

A function $f(x)$ that satisfies $f(x) = -f(-x)$ is called *odd*. Similarly, a function for which $f(x) = f(-x)$ is called *even*. For an odd function, it is always true that $f(0) = -f(-0) = -f(0)$, so $f(0)$ must be 0. Most functions are neither odd nor even, but the trigonometric functions sine and cosine are important examples of odd and even functions, respectively. Figure 4.34 shows that even though the only difference between them is phase (i.e., the cosine is a shifted version of the sine), this difference is enough to reverse their parity. When the (odd) sine curve is shifted, it becomes the (even) cosine curve, which has the same shape.

To understand the difference between the DCT and the DST we examine the one-dimensional case. The one-dimensional DCT, Equation (4.7), employs the function $\cos((2t + 1)f\pi/16)$ for $f = 0, 1, \ldots, 7$. For the first term, where $f = 0$, this function becomes $\cos(0)$, which is 1. This term is the familiar and important DC coefficient, which produces the average of the eight data values being transformed.

00	10	20	30	30	20	10	00
10	20	30	40	40	30	20	10
20	30	40	50	50	40	30	20
30	40	50	60	60	50	40	30
30	40	50	60	60	50	40	30
20	30	40	50	50	40	30	20
10	20	30	40	40	30	12	10
00	10	20	30	30	20	10	00

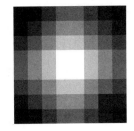

Table 4.26: A Highly-Correlated Pattern.

239	1.19	−89.76	−0.28	1.00	−1.39	−5.03	−0.79
1.18	−1.39	0.64	0.32	−1.18	1.63	−1.54	0.92
−89.76	0.64	−0.29	−0.15	0.54	−0.75	0.71	−0.43
−0.28	0.32	−0.15	−0.08	0.28	−0.38	0.36	−0.22
1.00	−1.18	0.54	0.28	−1.00	1.39	−1.31	0.79
−1.39	1.63	−0.75	−0.38	1.39	−1.92	1.81	−1.09
−5.03	−1.54	0.71	0.36	−1.31	1.81	−1.71	1.03
−0.79	0.92	−0.43	−0.22	0.79	−1.09	1.03	−0.62

Table 4.27: Its DCT Coefficients.

239	1	-90	0	0	0	0	0
0	0	0	0	0	0	0	0
-90	0	0	0	0	0	0	0
0	0	0	0	0	0	0	0
0	0	0	0	0	0	0	0
0	0	0	0	0	0	0	0
0	0	0	0	0	0	0	0
0	0	0	0	0	0	0	0

Table 4.28: Quantized Heavily to Just Four Nonzero Coefficients.

0.65	9.23	21.36	29.91	29.84	21.17	8.94	0.30
9.26	17.85	29.97	38.52	38.45	29.78	17.55	8.91
21.44	30.02	42.15	50.70	50.63	41.95	29.73	21.09
30.05	38.63	50.76	59.31	59.24	50.56	38.34	29.70
30.05	38.63	50.76	59.31	59.24	50.56	38.34	29.70
21.44	30.02	42.15	50.70	50.63	41.95	29.73	21.09
9.26	17.85	29.97	38.52	38.45	29.78	17.55	8.91
0.65	9.23	21.36	29.91	29.84	21.17	8.94	0.30

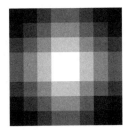

Table 4.29: Results of IDCT.

00	10	00	00	00	00	00	10
00	00	10	00	00	00	10	00
00	00	00	10	00	10	00	00
00	00	00	00	10	00	00	00
00	00	00	00	10	00	00	00
00	00	00	00	10	00	00	00
00	00	00	00	10	00	00	00
00	00	00	00	10	00	00	00

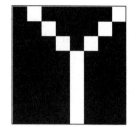

Table 4.30: A Pattern of Y.

13.75	−3.11	−8.17	2.46	3.75	−6.86	−3.38	6.59
4.19	−0.29	6.86	−6.85	−7.13	4.48	1.69	−7.28
1.63	0.19	6.40	−4.81	−2.99	−1.11	−0.88	−0.94
−0.61	0.54	5.12	−2.31	1.30	−6.04	−2.78	3.05
−1.25	0.52	2.99	−0.20	3.75	−7.39	−2.59	1.16
−0.41	0.18	0.65	1.03	3.87	−5.19	−0.71	−4.76
0.68	−0.15	−0.88	1.28	2.59	−1.92	1.10	−9.05
0.83	−0.21	−0.99	0.82	1.13	−0.08	1.31	−7.21

Table 4.31: Its DCT Coefficients.

13.75	−3	−8	2	3	−6	−3	6
4	−0	6	−6	−7	4	1	−7
1	0	6	−4	−2	−1	−0	−0
−0	0	5	−2	1	−6	−2	3
−1	0	2	−0	3	−7	−2	1
−0	0	0	1	3	−5	−0	−4
0	−0	−0	1	2	−1	1	−9
0	−0	−0	0	1	−0	1	−7

Table 4.32: Quantized Lightly by Truncating to Integer.

-0.13	8.96	0.55	-0.27	0.27	0.86	0.15	9.22
0.32	0.22	9.10	0.40	0.84	-0.11	9.36	-0.14
0.00	0.62	-0.20	9.71	-1.30	8.57	0.28	-0.33
-0.58	0.44	0.78	0.71	10.11	1.14	0.44	-0.49
-0.39	0.67	0.07	0.38	8.82	0.09	0.28	0.41
0.34	0.11	0.26	0.18	8.93	0.41	0.47	0.37
0.09	-0.32	0.78	-0.20	9.78	0.05	-0.09	0.49
0.16	-0.83	0.09	0.12	9.15	-0.11	-0.08	0.01

Table 4.33: The IDCT. Bad Results.

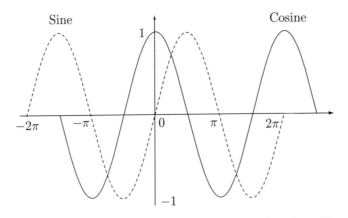

Figure 4.34: The Sine and Cosine as Odd and Even Functions, Respectively.

The DST is similarly based on the function $\sin((2t + 1)f\pi/16)$, resulting in a zero first term [since $\sin(0) = 0$]. The first term contributes nothing to the transform, so the DST does not have a DC coefficient.

The disadvantage of this can be seen when we consider the example of eight identical data values to be transformed. Such values are, of course, perfectly correlated. When plotted, they become a horizontal line. Applying the DCT to these values produces just a DC coefficient: All the AC coefficients are zero. The DCT compacts all the energy of the data into the single DC coefficient whose value is identical to the values of the data items. The IDCT can reconstruct the eight values perfectly (except for minor changes due to limited machine precision). Applying the DST to the same eight values, on the other hand, results in seven AC coefficients whose sum is a wave function that passes through the eight data points but oscillates between the points. This behavior, which is illustrated by Figure 4.35, has three disadvantages, namely (1) the energy of the original data values is not compacted, (2) the seven coefficients are not decorrelated (since the data points are perfectly correlated), and (3) quantizing the seven coefficients may greatly reduce the quality of the reconstruction done by the inverse DST.

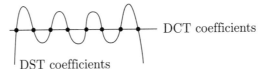

Figure 4.35: The DCT and DST of Eight Identical Data Values.

Example: Applying the DST to the eight identical values 100 results in the eight coefficients $(0, 256.3, 0, 90, 0, 60.1, 0, 51)$. Using these coefficients, the IDST can reconstruct the original values, but it is easy to see that the AC coefficients do not behave like those of the DCT. They are not getting smaller and smaller, and there are no runs of zeros between them. Applying the DST to the eight highly correlated values $11, 22, 33, 44, 55, 66, 77, 88$ results in the even worse set of coefficients $(0, 126.9, -57.5, 44.5, -31.1, 29.8, -23.8, 25.2)$. There is no energy compaction at all.

These arguments and examples, together with the fact (discussed in [Ahmed et al. 74]) that the DCT produces highly decorrelated coefficients, argue strongly for the use of the DCT as opposed to the DST in data compression.

⋄ **Exercise 4.11:** Use mathematical software to compute and display the 64 basis images of the DST for $n = 8$. The result should resemble Figure 4.21.

4.4.6 Walsh-Hadamard Transform

As mentioned earlier (page 250), this transform has low compression efficiency, so it is not used much in practice. It is, however, fast, since it can be computed with just additions, subtractions, and an occasional right shift (to efficiently divide by a power of 2).

Given an $N \times N$ block of pixels P_{xy} (where N must be a power of 2, $N = 2^n$), its two-dimensional WHT and inverse WHT are defined by Eqs. (4.11) and (4.12):

$$H(u,v) = \sum_{x=0}^{N-1} \sum_{y=0}^{N-1} P_{xy} g(x,y,u,v)$$

$$= \frac{1}{N} \sum_{x=0}^{N-1} \sum_{y=0}^{N-1} P_{xy} (-1)^{\sum_{i=0}^{n-1} [b_i(x)p_i(u) + b_i(y)p_i(v)]}, \tag{4.11}$$

$$P_{xy} = \sum_{u=0}^{N-1} \sum_{v=0}^{N-1} H(u,v) h(x,y,u,v)$$

$$= \frac{1}{N} \sum_{u=0}^{N-1} \sum_{v=0}^{N-1} H(u,v) (-1)^{\sum_{i=0}^{n-1} [b_i(x)p_i(u) + b_i(y)p_i(v)]}, \tag{4.12}$$

where $H(u,v)$ are the results of the transform (i.e., the WHT coefficients), the quantity $b_i(u)$ is bit i of the binary representation of the integer u, and $p_i(u)$ is defined in terms of the $b_j(u)$ by Equation (4.13):

$$p_0(u) = b_{n-1}(u),$$
$$p_1(u) = b_{n-1}(u) + b_{n-2}(u),$$
$$p_2(u) = b_{n-2}(u) + b_{n-3}(u), \tag{4.13}$$
$$\cdots$$
$$p_{n-1}(u) = b_1(u) + b_0(u).$$

(Recall that n is defined above by $N = 2^n$.) As an example consider $u = 6 = 110_2$. Bits zero, one, and two of 6 are 0, 1, and 1, respectively, so $b_0(6) = 0$, $b_1(6) = 1$, and $b_2(6) = 1$.

The quantities $g(x, y, u, v)$ and $h(x, y, u, v)$ are called the *kernels* (or *basis images*) of the WHT. These matrices are identical. Their elements are just $+1$ and -1, and they are multiplied by the factor $\frac{1}{N}$. As a result, the WHT transform consists in multiplying each image pixel by $+1$ or -1, summing, and dividing the sum by N. Since $N = 2^n$ is a power of 2, dividing by it can be done by shifting n positions to the right.

The WHT kernels are shown, in graphical form, for $N = 4$, in Figure 4.36, where white denotes $+1$ and black denotes -1 (the factor $\frac{1}{N}$ is ignored). The rows and columns of blocks in this figure correspond to values of u and v from 0 to 3, respectively. The rows and columns inside each block correspond to values of x and y from 0 to 3, respectively. The number of sign changes across a row or a column of a matrix is called the *sequency* of the row or column. The rows and columns in the figure are ordered in increased sequency. Some authors show similar but unordered figures, because this transform was defined by Walsh and by Hadamard in slightly different ways (see [Gonzalez 92] for more information).

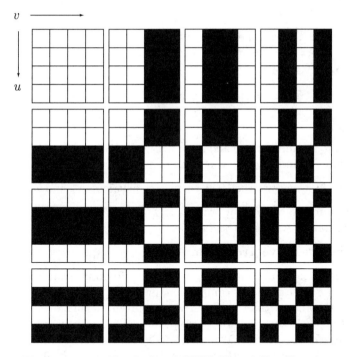

Figure 4.36: The Ordered WHT Kernel For $N = 4$.

Compressing an image with the WHT is done similarly to the DCT, except that Eqs. (4.11) and (4.12) are used, instead of Eqs. (4.9) and (4.10).

⋄ **Exercise 4.12:** Use mathematical software to compute and display the basis images of the WHT for $N = 8$.

4.4.7 Haar Transform

The Haar transform [Stollnitz 92] is based on the Haar functions $h_k(x)$, which are defined for $x \in [0, 1]$ and for $k = 0, 1, \ldots, N - 1$, where $N = 2^n$. Its application is also discussed in Chapter 5.

Before we discuss the actual transform, we have to mention that any integer k can be expressed as the sum $k = 2^p + q - 1$, where $0 \le p \le n - 1$, $q = 0$ or 1 for $p = 0$, and $1 \le q \le 2^p$ for $p \ne 0$. For $N = 4 = 2^2$, for example, we get $0 = 2^0 + 0 - 1$, $1 = 2^0 + 1 - 1$, $2 = 2^1 + 1 - 1$, and $3 = 2^1 + 2 - 1$.

The Haar basis functions are now defined as

$$h_0(x) \stackrel{\text{def}}{=} h_{00}(x) = \frac{1}{\sqrt{N}}, \quad \text{for } 0 \le x \le 1, \tag{4.14}$$

and

$$h_k(x) \stackrel{\text{def}}{=} h_{pq}(x) = \frac{1}{\sqrt{N}} \begin{cases} 2^{p/2}, & \frac{q-1}{2^p} \le x < \frac{q-1/2}{2^p}, \\ -2^{p/2}, & \frac{q-1/2}{2^p} \le x < \frac{q}{2^p}, \\ 0, & \text{otherwise for } x \in [0, 1]. \end{cases} \tag{4.15}$$

The Haar transform matrix $\mathbf{A}_N$ of order $N \times N$ can now be constructed. A general element i, j of this matrix is the basis function $h_i(j)$, where $i = 0, 1, \ldots, N-1$ and $j = 0/N, 1/N, \ldots, (N-1)/N$. For example,

$$\mathbf{A}_2 = \begin{pmatrix} h_0(0/2) & h_0(1/2) \\ h_1(0/2) & h_1(1/2) \end{pmatrix} = \frac{1}{\sqrt{2}} \begin{pmatrix} 1 & 1 \\ 1 & -1 \end{pmatrix} \tag{4.16}$$

(recall that $i = 1$ implies $p = 0$ and $q = 1$). Figure 4.37 shows code to calculate this matrix for any N, and also the Haar basis images for $N = 8$.

⋄ **Exercise 4.13:** Compute the Haar coefficient matrices $\mathbf{A}_4$ and $\mathbf{A}_8$.

Given an image block $\mathbf{P}$ of order $N \times N$ where $N = 2^n$, its Haar transform is the matrix product $\mathbf{A}_N \mathbf{P} \mathbf{A}_N$ (Section 5.6).

4.4.8 Karhunen-Loève Transform

The Karhunen-Loève transform (also called the Hotelling transform) has the best efficiency in the sense of energy compaction, but for of the reasons mentioned earlier, it has more theoretical than practical value. Given an image we break it up into k blocks of n pixels each, where n is typically 64 but can have other values, and k depends on the image size. We consider the blocks vectors and denote them by $\mathbf{b}^{(i)}$, for $i = 1, 2, \ldots, k$. The average vector is $\overline{\mathbf{b}} = (\sum_i \mathbf{b}^{(i)})/k$. A new set of vectors $\mathbf{v}^{(i)} = \mathbf{b}^{(i)} - \overline{\mathbf{b}}$ is defined, causing the average $(\sum \mathbf{v}^{(i)})/k$ to be zero. We denote the $n \times n$ KLT transform matrix that we are seeking by $\mathbf{A}$. The result of transforming a vector $\mathbf{v}^{(i)}$ is the weight vector $\mathbf{w}^{(i)} = \mathbf{A}\mathbf{v}^{(i)}$. The average of the $\mathbf{w}^{(i)}$ is also zero. We now construct a matrix $\mathbf{V}$ whose columns are the $\mathbf{v}^{(i)}$ vectors and another matrix $\mathbf{W}$ whose columns are the weight vectors $\mathbf{w}^{(i)}$:

$$\mathbf{V} = \left(\mathbf{v}^{(1)}, \mathbf{v}^{(2)}, \ldots, \mathbf{v}^{(k)} \right), \quad \mathbf{W} = \left(\mathbf{w}^{(1)}, \mathbf{w}^{(2)}, \ldots, \mathbf{w}^{(k)} \right).$$

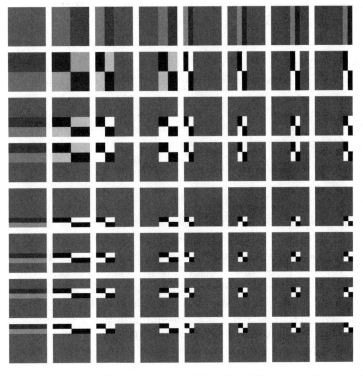

Figure 4.37: The Basis Images of the Haar Transform for $n = 8$.

```
Needs["GraphicsImage'"] (* Draws 2D Haar Coefficients *)
n=8;
h[k_,x_]:=Module[{p,q}, If[k==0, 1/Sqrt[n],            (* h_0(x) *)
 p=0; While[2^p<=k ,p++]; p--; q=k-2^p+1; (* if k>0, calc. p, q *)
 If[(q-1)/(2^p)<=x && x<(q-.5)/(2^p),2^(p/2),
  If[(q-.5)/(2^p)<=x && x<q/(2^p),-2^(p/2),0]]]];
HaarMatrix=Table[h[k,x], {k,0,7}, {x,0,7/n,1/n}] //N;
HaarTensor=Array[Outer[Times, HaarMatrix[[#1]],HaarMatrix[[#2]]]&,
 {n,n}];
Show[GraphicsArray[Map[GraphicsImage[#, {-2,2}]&, HaarTensor,{2}]]]
```

Code For Figure 4.37

Matrices $\mathbf{V}$ and $\mathbf{W}$ have n rows and k columns each. From the definition of $\mathbf{w}^{(i)}$ we get $\mathbf{W} = \mathbf{A} \cdot \mathbf{V}$.

The n coefficient vectors $\mathbf{c}^{(j)}$ of the Karhunen-Loève transform are given by

$$\mathbf{c}^{(j)} = \left(w_j^{(1)}, w_j^{(2)}, \ldots, w_j^{(k)} \right), \quad j = 1, 2, \ldots, n.$$

Thus, vector $\mathbf{c}^{(j)}$ consists of the jth elements of all the weight vectors $\mathbf{w}^{(i)}$, for $i = 1, 2, \ldots, k$ ($\mathbf{c}^{(j)}$ is the jth coordinate of the $\mathbf{w}^{(i)}$ vectors).

We now examine the elements of the matrix product $\mathbf{W} \cdot \mathbf{W}^T$ (this is an $n \times n$ matrix). A general element in row a and column b of this matrix is the sum of products

$$\left(\mathbf{W} \cdot \mathbf{W}^T\right)_{ab} = \sum_{i=1}^{k} w_a^{(i)} w_b^{(i)} = \sum_{i=1}^{k} c_i^{(a)} c_i^{(b)} = \mathbf{c}^{(a)} \bullet \mathbf{c}^{(b)}, \quad \text{for } a, b \in [1, n]. \quad (4.17)$$

The fact that the average of each $\mathbf{w}^{(i)}$ is zero implies that a general diagonal element $(\mathbf{W}\mathbf{W}^T)_{jj}$ of the product matrix is the variance (up to a factor k) of the jth element (or jth coordinate) of the $\mathbf{w}^{(i)}$ vectors. This, of course, is the variance of coefficient vector $\mathbf{c}^{(j)}$.

⋄ **Exercise 4.14:** Show why this is true!

The off-diagonal elements of $(\mathbf{W} \cdot \mathbf{W}^T)$ are the covariances of the $\mathbf{w}^{(i)}$ vectors (appendix in book's web site) such that element $\left(\mathbf{W} \cdot \mathbf{W}^T\right)_{ab}$ is the covariance of the ath and bth coordinates of the $\mathbf{w}^{(i)}$s. Equation (4.17) shows that this is also the dot product $\mathbf{c}^{(a)} \cdot \mathbf{c}^{(b)}$. One of the main aims of image transform is to decorrelate the coordinates of the vectors, and probability theory tells us that two coordinates are decorrelated if their covariance is zero (the other aim is energy compaction, but the two goals go hand in hand). Thus, our aim is to find a transformation matrix $\mathbf{A}$ such that the product $\mathbf{W} \cdot \mathbf{W}^T$ will be diagonal.

From the definition of matrix $\mathbf{W}$ we get

$$\mathbf{W} \cdot \mathbf{W}^T = (\mathbf{AV}) \cdot (\mathbf{AV})^T = \mathbf{A}(\mathbf{V} \cdot \mathbf{V}^T)\mathbf{A}^T.$$

Matrix $\mathbf{V} \cdot \mathbf{V}^T$ is symmetric, and its elements are the covariances of the coordinates of vectors $\mathbf{v}^{(i)}$, i.e.,

$$\left(\mathbf{V} \cdot \mathbf{V}^T\right)_{ab} = \sum_{i=1}^{k} v_a^{(i)} v_b^{(i)}, \quad \text{for } a, b \in [1, n].$$

Since $\mathbf{V} \cdot \mathbf{V}^T$ is symmetric, its eigenvectors are orthogonal. We therefore normalize these vectors (i.e., make them orthonormal) and choose them as the rows of matrix $\mathbf{A}$. This produces the result

$$\mathbf{W} \cdot \mathbf{W}^T = \mathbf{A}(\mathbf{V} \cdot \mathbf{V}^T)\mathbf{A}^T = \begin{pmatrix} \lambda_1 & 0 & 0 & \cdots & 0 \\ 0 & \lambda_2 & 0 & \cdots & 0 \\ 0 & 0 & \lambda_3 & \cdots & 0 \\ \vdots & \vdots & & \vdots & \vdots \\ 0 & 0 & \cdots & 0 & \lambda_n \end{pmatrix}.$$

This choice of $\mathbf{A}$ results in a diagonal matrix $\mathbf{W} \cdot \mathbf{W}^T$ whose diagonal elements are the eigenvalues of $\mathbf{V} \cdot \mathbf{V}^T$. Matrix $\mathbf{A}$ is the Karhunen-Loève transformation matrix; its rows are the basis vectors of the KLT, and the energies (variances) of the transformed vectors are the eigenvalues $\lambda_1, \lambda_2, \ldots, \lambda_n$ of $\mathbf{V} \cdot \mathbf{V}^T$.

The basis vectors of the KLT are calculated from the original image pixels, and are therefore data dependent. In a practical compression method, these vectors have to be included in the compressed stream, for the decoder's use, and this, combined with the fact that no fast method has been discovered for the calculation of the KLT, makes this transform less than ideal for practical applications.

Bibliography

Ahmed, N., T. Natarajan, and R. K. Rao (1974) "Discrete Cosine Transform," *IEEE Transactions on Computers* C-23:90–93.

Gonzalez, Rafael C., and Richard E. Woods (1992) *Digital Image Processing*, Reading, MA, Addison-Wesley.

Pennebaker, William B., and Joan L. Mitchell (1992) *JPEG Still Image Data Compression Standard*, New York, Van Nostrand Reinhold.

Rao, K.R. and P. Yip, *Discrete Cosine Transform—Algorithms, Advantages, Applications*, London, Academic Press, 1990.

Stollnitz, E. J., T. D. DeRose, and D. H. Salesin (1996) *Wavelets for Computer Graphics*, San Francisco, CA, Morgan Kaufmann.

Watson, Andrew (1994) "Image Compression Using the Discrete Cosine Transform," *Mathematica Journal*, **4**(1):81–88.

4.5 Test Images

New data compression methods that are developed and implemented have to be tested. Testing different methods on the same data makes it possible to compare their performance both in compression efficiency and in speed. This is why there are standard collections of test data such as the Calgary Corpus and the Canterbury Corpus (mentioned in the Preface), and the ITU-T set of eight training documents for fax compression (Section 2.13.1).

The need for standard test data has also been felt in the field of image compression, and there currently exist collections of still images commonly used by researchers and implementors in this field. Three of the four images shown here, namely "Lena," "mandril," and "peppers," are arguably the most well known of them. They are continuous-tone images, although "Lena" has some features of a discrete-tone image.

Each image is accompanied by a detail, showing individual pixels. It is easy to see why the "peppers" image is continuous-tone. Adjacent pixels that differ much in color are fairly rare in this image. Most neighboring pixels are very similar. In contrast, the "mandril" image, even though natural, is a bad example of a continuous-tone image. The detail (showing part of the right eye and the area around it) shows that many pixels differ considerably from their immediate neighbors because of the animal's facial hair in this area. This image compresses badly under any compression method. However, the nose area, with mostly blue and red, is continuous-tone. The "Lena" image is mostly pure continuous-tone, especially the wall and the bare skin areas. The hat is good continuous-tone, whereas the hair and the plume on the hat are bad continuous-tone. The straight lines on the wall and the curved parts of the mirror are features of a discrete-tone image.

Figure 4.38: Lena and Detail.

The "Lena" image is widely used by the image processing community, in addition to being popular in image compression. Because of the interest in it, its origin and history have been researched and are well documented. This image is part of the *Playboy* centerfold for November, 1972. It features the Swedish playmate Lena Soderberg (née Sjooblom), and it was discovered, clipped, and scanned in the early 1970s by an unknown researcher at the University of Southern California for use as a test image for his image compression research. It has since become the most important, well known, and commonly used image in the history of imaging and electronic communications. As a result, Lena is currently considered by many the First Lady of the Internet. *Playboy*, which normally prosecutes unauthorized users of its images, has found out about the unusual use of one of its copyrighted images, but decided to give its blessing to this particular "application."

Lena herself currently lives in Sweden. She was told of her "fame" in 1988, was surprised and amused by it, and was invited to attend the 50th Anniversary IS&T (the society for Imaging Science and Technology) conference in Boston in May 1997. At the conference she autographed her picture, posed for new pictures (available on the www) and gave a presentation (about herself, not compression).

The three images are widely available for downloading on the internet.

Figure 4.41 shows a typical discrete-tone image, with a detail shown in Figure 4.42. Notice the straight lines and the text, where certain characters appear several times (a source of redundancy). This particular image has few colors, but in general, a discrete-tone image may have many colors.

The village of Lena, Illinois is located approximately 9 miles west of Freeport, Illinois and 50 miles east of Dubuque, Iowa. We are on the edge of the rolling hills of Northwestern Illinois and only 25 miles south of Monroe, Wisconsin. The current population of Lena is approximately 2800 souls engaged in the farming business. (From http://www.lena.il.us/History.htm)

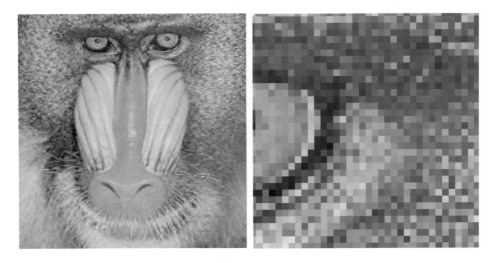

Figure 4.39: Mandril and Detail.

Figure 4.40: Peppers and Detail.

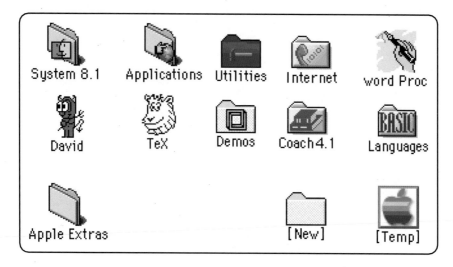

Figure 4.41: A Discrete-Tone Image.

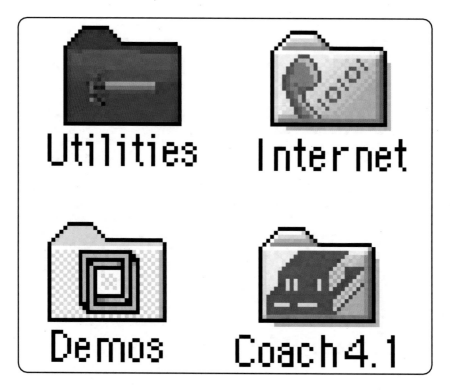

Figure 4.42: A Discrete-Tone Image (Detail).

4.6 JPEG

JPEG is a sophisticated lossy/lossless compression method for color or grayscale still images (not movies). It does not handle bi-level (black and white) images very well. It also works best on continuous-tone images, where adjacent pixels have similar colors. One advantage of JPEG is the use of many parameters, allowing the user to adjust the amount of the data lost (and thus also the compression ratio) over a very wide range. Often, the eye cannot see any image degradation even at compression ratios of 10:1 or 20:1. There are two main modes: lossy (also called baseline) and lossless (which typically produces compression ratios of around 0.5). Most implementations support just the lossy mode. This mode includes progressive and hierarchical coding.

JPEG is a compression method, not a complete standard for image representation. This is why it does not specify image features such as pixel aspect ratio, color space, or interleaving of bitmap rows.

JPEG has been designed as a compression method for continuous-tone images. The main goals of JPEG compression are the following:

1. High compression ratios, especially in cases where image quality is judged as very good to excellent.

2. The use of many parameters, allowing sophisticated users to experiment and achieve the desired compression/quality tradeoff.

3. Obtaining good results with any kind of continuous-tone image, regardless of image dimensions, color spaces, pixel aspect ratios, or other image features.

4. A sophisticated, but not too complex compression method, allowing software and hardware implementations on many platforms.

5. Several modes of operation: (a) Sequential mode: each image component (color) is compressed in a single left-to-right, top-to-bottom scan; (b) Progressive mode: the image is compressed in multiple blocks (known as "scans") to be viewed from coarse to fine detail; (c) Lossless mode: important for cases where the user decides that no pixels should be lost (the tradeoff is low compression ratio compared to the lossy modes); and (d) Hierarchical mode: the image is compressed at multiple resolutions allowing lower-resolution blocks to be viewed without first having to decompress the following higher-resolution blocks.

The word JPEG is an acronym that stands for Joint Photographic Experts Group. This was a joint effort by the CCITT and the ISO (the International Standards Organization) that started in June 1987 and produced the first JPEG draft proposal in 1991. The JPEG standard has proved successful and has become widely used for image compression, especially in web pages.

The main JPEG compression steps are outlined below, and each step is then described in detail later.

1. Color images are transformed from RGB into a luminance/chrominance color space (Section 4.6.1; this step is skipped for grayscale images). The eye is sensitive to small changes in luminance but not in chrominance, so the chrominance part can later lose much data, and thus be highly compressed, without visually impairing the overall image quality much. This step is optional but important since the remainder of the algorithm works on each color component separately. Without transforming

the color space, none of the three color components will tolerate much loss, leading to worse compression.

2. Color images are downsampled by creating low-resolution pixels from the original ones (this step is used only when hierarchical compression is needed; it is always skipped for grayscale images). The downsampling is not done for the luminance component. Downsampling is done either at a ratio of 2:1 both horizontally and vertically (the so-called 2h2v or "4:1:1" sampling) or at ratios of 2:1 horizontally and 1:1 vertically (2h1v or "4:2:2" sampling). Since this is done on two of the three color components, 2h2v reduces the image to $1/3 + (2/3) \times (1/4) = 1/2$ its original size, while 2h1v reduces it to $1/3 + (2/3) \times (1/2) = 2/3$ its original size. Since the luminance component is not touched, there is no noticeable loss of image quality. Grayscale images don't go through this step.

3. The pixels of each color component are organized in groups of 8×8 pixels called *data units*. If the number of image rows or columns is not a multiple of 8, the bottom row and the rightmost column are duplicated as many times as necessary. In the noninterleaved mode, the encoder handles all the data units of the first image component, then the data units of the second component, and finally those of the third component. In the interleaved mode the encoder processes the three top-left (#1) data units of the three image components, then the three data units #2, and so on.

4. The *discrete cosine transform* (DCT, Section 4.4.3) is then applied to each data unit to create an 8×8 map of frequency components (Section 4.6.2). They represent the average pixel value and successive higher-frequency changes within the group. This prepares the image data for the crucial step of losing information. Since DCT involves the transcendental function cosine, it must involve some loss of information due to the limited precision of computer arithmetic. This means that even without the main lossy step (step 5 below), there will be some loss of image quality, but it is normally small.

5. Each of the 64 frequency components in a data unit is divided by a separate number called its *quantization coefficient* (QC), and then rounded to an integer (Section 4.6.5). This is where information is irretrievably lost. Large QCs cause more loss, so the high-frequency components typically have larger QCs. Each of the 64 QCs is a JPEG parameter and can, in principle, be specified by the user. In practice, most JPEG implementations use the QC tables recommended by the JPEG standard for the luminance and chrominance image components (Table 4.52).

6. The 64 quantized frequency coefficients (which are now integers) of each data unit are encoded using a combination of RLE and Huffman coding (Section 4.6.6). An arithmetic coding variant known as the QM coder (Section 2.16) can optionally be used instead of Huffman coding.

7. The last step adds headers and all the JPEG parameters used, and outputs the result. The compressed file may be in one of three formats (1) the *interchange* format, in which the file contains the compressed image and all the tables needed by the decoder (mostly quantization tables and tables of Huffman codes), (2) the *abbreviated* format for compressed image data, where the file contains the compressed image and may contain no tables (or just a few tables), and (3) the *abbreviated* format for table-specification data, where the file contains just tables, and no compressed im-

age. The second format makes sense in cases where the same encoder/decoder pair is used, and they have the same tables built in. The third format is used in cases where many images have been compressed by the same encoder, using the same tables. When those images need to be decompressed, they are sent to a decoder preceded by one file with table-specification data.

The JPEG decoder performs the reverse steps. (Thus, JPEG is a symmetric compression method).

The progressive mode is a JPEG option. In this mode, higher-frequency DCT coefficients are written on the compressed stream in blocks called "scans." Each scan read and processed by the decoder results in a sharper image. The idea is to use the first few scans to quickly create a low-quality, blurred preview of the image, then either input the remaining scans or stop the process and reject the image. The tradeoff is that the encoder has to save all the coefficients of all the data units in a memory buffer before they are sent in scans, and also go through all the steps for each scan, slowing down the progressive mode.

Figure 4.43a shows an example of an image with resolution 1024×512. The image is divided into $128 \times 64 = 8192$ data units, and each is DCT transformed, becoming a set of 64 8-bit numbers. Figure 4.43b is a block whose depth corresponds to the 8,192 data units, whose height corresponds to the 64 DCT coefficients (the DC coefficient is the top one, numbered 0), and whose width corresponds to the eight bits of each coefficient.

After preparing all the data units in a memory buffer, the encoder writes them on the compressed stream in one of two methods, *spectral selection* or *successive approximation* (Figure 4.43c,d). The first scan in either method is the set of DC coefficients. If spectral selection is used, each successive scan consists of several consecutive (a *band* of) AC coefficients. If successive approximation is used, the second scan consists of the four most-significant bits of all AC coefficients, and each of the following four scans, numbers 3 through 6, adds one more significant bit (bits 3 through 0, respectively).

In the hierarchical mode, the encoder stores the image several times in the output stream, at several resolutions. However, each high-resolution part uses information from the low-resolution parts of the output stream, so the total amount of information is less than that required to store the different resolutions separately. Each hierarchical part may use the progressive mode.

The hierarchical mode is useful in cases where a high-resolution image needs to be output in low resolution. Older dot-matrix printers may be a good example of a low-resolution output device still in use.

The lossless mode of JPEG (Section 4.6.7) calculates a "predicted" value for each pixel, generates the difference between the pixel and its predicted value (see Section 1.3.1 for relative encoding), and encodes the difference using the same method (i.e., Huffman or arithmetic coding) used by step 5 above. The predicted value is calculated using values of pixels above and to the left of the current pixel (pixels that have already been input and encoded). The following sections discuss the steps in more detail:

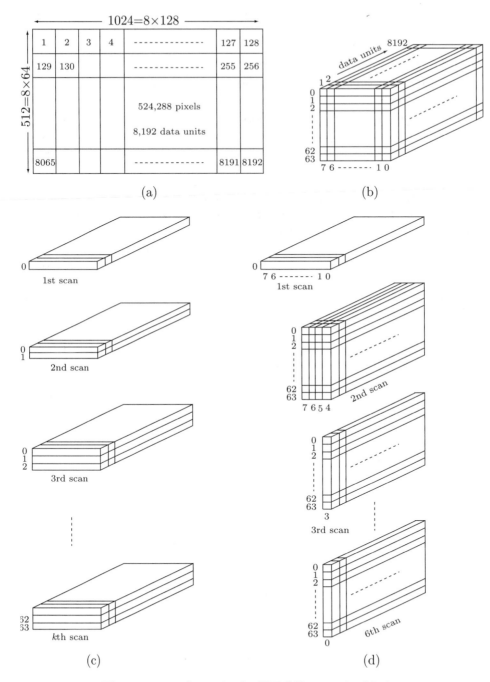

Figure 4.43: Scans in the JPEG Progressive Mode.

4.6.1 Luminance

The main international organization devoted to light and color is the International Committee on Illumination (Commission Internationale de l'Éclairage), abbreviated CIE. It is responsible for developing standards and definitions in this area. One of the early achievements of the CIE was its *chromaticity diagram* [Salomon 99], developed in 1931. It shows that no fewer than three parameters are required to define color. Expressing a certain color by the triplet (x, y, z) is similar to denoting a point in three-dimensional space, hence the term *color space*. The most common color space is RGB, where the three parameters are the intensities of red, green, and blue in a color. When used in computers, these parameters are normally in the range 0–255 (8 bits).

The CIE defines color as the perceptual result of light in the visible region of the spectrum, having wavelengths in the region of 400 nm to 700 nm, incident upon the retina (a nanometer, nm, equals 10^{-9} meter). Physical power (or radiance) is expressed in a spectral power distribution (SPD), often in 31 components each representing a 10 nm band.

The CIE defines brightness as the attribute of a visual sensation according to which an area appears to emit more or less light. The brain's perception of brightness is impossible to define, so the CIE defines a more practical quantity called *luminance*. It is defined as radiant power weighted by a spectral sensitivity function that is characteristic of vision. The luminous efficiency of the Standard Observer is defined by the CIE as a positive function of the wavelength, which has a maximum at about 555 nm. When a spectral power distribution is integrated using this function as a weighting function, the result is CIE luminance, which is denoted by Y. Luminance is an important quantity in the fields of digital image processing and compression.

Luminance is proportional to the power of the light source. It is similar to intensity, but the spectral composition of luminance is related to the brightness sensitivity of human vision.

The eye is very sensitive to small changes in luminance, which is why it is useful to have color spaces that use Y as one of their three parameters. A simple way to do this is to subtract Y from the Blue and Red components of RGB, and use the three components Y, B–Y, and R–Y as a new color space. The last two components are called chroma. They represent color in terms of the presence or absence of blue (Cb) and red (Cr) for a given luminance intensity.

Various number ranges are used in $B - Y$ and $R - Y$ for different applications. The YPbPr ranges are optimized for component analog video. The YCbCr ranges are appropriate for component digital video such as studio video, JPEG, JPEG 2000 and MPEG.

The YCbCr color space was developed as part of Recommendation ITU-R BT.601 (formerly CCIR 601) during the development of a worldwide digital component video standard. Y is defined to have a range of 16 to 235; Cb and Cr are defined to have a range of 16 to 240, with 128 equal to zero. There are several YCbCr sampling formats, such as 4:4:4, 4:2:2, 4:1:1, and 4:2:0, which are also described in the recommendation.

Conversions between RGB with a 16–235 range and YCbCr are linear and therefore simple. Transforming RGB to YCbCr is done by (notice the small weight assigned to blue):

$$Y = (77/256)R + (150/256)G + (29/256)B,$$
$$Cb = -(44/256)R - (87/256)G + (131/256)B + 128,$$
$$Cr = (131/256)R - (110/256)G - (21/256)B + 128;$$

while the opposite transformation is

$$R = Y + 1.371(Cr - 128),$$
$$G = Y - 0.698(Cr - 128) - 0.336(Cb - 128),$$
$$B = Y + 1.732(Cb - 128).$$

When performing YCbCr to RGB conversion, the resulting RGB values have a nominal range of 16–235, with possible occasional values in 0–15 and 236–255.

4.6.2 DCT

The general concept of a transform is discussed in Section 4.4. The discrete cosine transform is discussed in Section 4.4.3. Other examples of important transforms are the Fourier transform (Section 5.1), and the *wavelet transform* (Chapter 5). Both have applications in many areas and also have discrete versions (DFT and DWT).

The JPEG committee elected to use DCT because of its good performance, because it does not assume anything about the structure of the data (the DFT, for example, assumes that the data to be transformed is periodic), and because there are ways to speed it up (Section 4.6.3).

The following one-dimensional example shows the difference in performance between the DCT and the DFT. We start with the simple highly correlated sequence of eight numbers $(8, 16, 24, 32, 40, 48, 56, 64)$. It is shown graphically in Figure 4.44a. Applying the DCT to it yields $(100, -52, 0, -5, 0, -2, 0, 0.4)$. When this is quantized to $(100, -52, 0, -5, 0, 0, 0, 0)$ and transformed back, it produces $(8, 15, 24, 32, 40, 48, 57, 63)$: a sequence almost identical to the original input. Applying the DFT to the same input, on the other hand, yields $(36, 10, 10, 6, 6, 4, 4, 4)$. When this is quantized to $(36, 10, 10, 6, 0, 0, 0, 0)$ and is transformed back, it produces $(24, 12, 20, 32, 40, 51, 59, 48)$. This output is shown in Figure 4.44b and it illustrates the tendency of the Fourier transform to produce a periodic result.

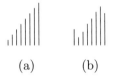

(a)   (b)

Figure 4.44: (a) One-Dimensional Input. (b) Its Inverse DFT.

The JPEG standard calls for applying the DCT not to the entire image but to data units (blocks) of 8×8 pixels. The reasons for this are (1) Applying DCT to all $n \times n$ pixels of an image produces better compression but also involves many arithmetic operations and is therefore slow. Applying DCT to data units reduces the overall compression ratio but is faster (Section 4.6.3). (2) Experience shows that, in a continuous-tone image, correlations between pixels are short range. A pixel in such an image has a value (color component or shade of gray) that's close to those of its near neighbors, but has nothing to do with the values of far neighbors. The JPEG DCT is thus done by Equation (4.9), duplicated here

$$
G_{ij} = \frac{1}{4} C_i C_j \sum_{x=0}^{7} \sum_{y=0}^{7} p_{xy} \cos\left(\frac{(2x+1)i\pi}{16}\right) \cos\left(\frac{(2y+1)j\pi}{16}\right),
$$

$$
\text{where } C_f = \begin{cases} \frac{1}{\sqrt{2}}, & f = 0, \\ 1, & f > 0, \end{cases} \quad \text{and } 0 \leq i, j \leq 7.
$$
(4.9)

The DCT is JPEG's key to lossy compression. The way to lose the unimportant image information is to reduce the size of the 64 DCT coefficients, especially the ones at the right bottom, by quantization. There is a very high chance that this won't degrade the image quality much. This does not always work, so in general, each of the 64 coefficients is divided by a different quantization coefficient (QC) in order to reduce its size, and all 64 QCs are parameters that can be controlled, in principle, by the user (Section 4.6.5).

The JPEG decoder works by computing the inverse DCT (IDCT), Equation (4.10), duplicated here:

$$
p_{xy} = \frac{1}{4} \sum_{i=0}^{7} \sum_{j=0}^{7} C_i C_j G_{ij} \cos\left(\frac{(2x+1)i\pi}{16}\right) \cos\left(\frac{(2y+1)j\pi}{16}\right),
$$

$$
\text{where } C_f = \begin{cases} \frac{1}{\sqrt{2}}, & f = 0; \\ 1, & f > 0. \end{cases}
$$
(4.10)

It takes the 64 quantized DCT results and calculates 64 pixels p_{xy}. If the QCs are the right ones, the new 64 pixels will be very similar to the original ones. Mathematically, the DCT is a one-to-one mapping of 64-point vectors from the image domain to the frequency domain. The IDCT is the reverse mapping. If the DCT and IDCT could be calculated with infinite precision and if the DCT coefficients were not quantized, the original 64 pixels could be exactly reconstructed.

4.6.3 Practical DCT

Equation (4.9) can be coded directly in any higher-level language. However, several improvements are possible, which speed it up considerably. Since this equation is the "heart" of JPEG, its fast calculation is essential. Here are some ideas.

1. Regardless of the image size, only 32 cosine functions are involved (see exercise below). They can be precomputed once and used repeatedly to calculate all the

8×8 data units. Calculating the expression

$$p_{xy} \cos\left(\frac{(2x+1)i\pi}{16}\right) \cos\left(\frac{(2y+1)j\pi}{16}\right)$$

now amounts to performing two multiplications. The double sum of (4.9) thus requires $64 \times 2 = 128$ multiplications and 63 additions.

⋄ **Exercise 4.15:** (Proposed by V. Saravanan.) Why are only 32 different cosine functions needed for the DCT?

2. A little algebraic tinkering shows that the double sum of (4.9) can be written as the matrix product $\mathbf{CPC}^T$, where $\mathbf{P}$ is the 8×8 matrix of the pixels, $\mathbf{C}$ is the matrix defined by

$$C_{ij} = \begin{cases} \frac{1}{\sqrt{8}}, & i = 0, \\ \frac{1}{2}\cos\left(\frac{(2j+1)i\pi}{16}\right), & i > 0, \end{cases}$$

and $\mathbf{C}^T$ is the transpose of $\mathbf{C}$.

Calculating one matrix element of the product $\mathbf{CP}$ thus requires eight multiplications and seven (but for simplicity let's say eight) additions. Multiplying the two 8×8 matrices $\mathbf{C}$ and $\mathbf{P}$ requires $64 \times 8 = 8^3$ multiplications and the same number of additions. Multiplying the product $\mathbf{CP}$ by $\mathbf{C}^T$ requires the same number of operations, so the DCT of one 8×8 data unit requires 2×8^3 multiplications (and the same number of additions). Assuming that the entire image consists of $n \times n$ pixels, and that $n = 8q$, there are $q \times q$ data units, so the DCT of all the data units requires $2q^2 8^3$ multiplications (and the same number of additions). In comparison, performing one DCT for the entire image would require $2n^3 = 2q^3 8^3 = (2q^2 8^3)q$ operations. By dividing the image into data units we reduce the number of multiplications (and also of additions) by a factor of q. Unfortunately, q cannot be too large, since that would mean very small data units.

We should remember that a color image consists of three components (normally RGB, but usually converted to YCbCr or YPbPr). Each is DCT-transformed separately, bringing the total number of arithmetic operations to $3 \times 2q^2 8^3 = 3,072q^2$. For a 512×512-pixel image, this means $3,072 \times 64^2 = 12,582,912$ multiplications (and the same number of additions).

3. Another way to speed up the DCT is to perform all the arithmetic operations on fixed-point (scaled integer), rather than floating-point, numbers. On many computers, operations on fixed-point numbers require (somewhat) sophisticated programming techniques but are considerably faster than floating-point operations (some high-performance computers—such as the CDC 6400, the CDC 7600, and the various Cray systems—are notable exceptions).

Arguably, the best DCT algorithm is described in [Feig and Linzer 90]. It uses 54 multiplications and 468 additions and shifts. Today, there are also various VLSI chips that perform this calculation efficiently. The interested reader should also check [Loeffler et al. 89] for a fast one-dimensional DCT algorithm that uses 11 multiplications and 29 additions.

4.6.4 Examples

Here are some examples of the results of applying the DCT to several data units. All the computations were done by the *Mathematica* code below (with different pixel values and different accuracies):

```
Clear[Pixl, G];
Cr[i_]:=If[i==0, 1/Sqrt[2], 1];
DCT[i_,j_]:={(1/4)Cr[i]Cr[j]Sum[Pixl[[x+1,y+1]]
            Cos[(2x+1)i Pi/16]Cos[(2y+1)j Pi/16],
  {x,0,7,1}, {y,0,7,1}]};
Pixl={{128,10,10,10,10,10,10,10},{10,128,10,10,10,10,10,10},
{10,10,128,10,10,10,10,10},{10,10,10,128,10,10,10,10},
 {10,10,10,10,128,10,10,10},{10,10,10,10,10,128,10,10},
 {10,10,10,10,10,10,128,10},{10,10,10,10,10,10,10,128}};
G=Table[N[DCT[m,n]], {m,0,7} ,{n,0,7}];
TableForm[SetAccuracy[G,2]]
```

1. A data unit with all 64 pixels set to 128 (corresponding to a flat surface) produces a DCT matrix with a DC coefficient of 1,024 and 63 AC coefficients of zero.

2. A data unit with vertical stripes (corresponding to a periodic surface) is transformed into a matrix with an upper nonzero row (Table 4.45).

3. A data unit with horizontal stripes is transformed into a matrix with a left nonzero column (Table 4.46).

4. Pixels with values 128 along the main diagonal produce a diagonal DCT matrix (Table 4.47).

5. Random pixels in the range 0–128, generated by

$$\text{Pixl=Table[128Random[],\{8\},\{8\}]}$$

(pixels shown in Table 4.48) produce a DCT matrix with all nonzero elements (Table 4.49), showing that it is harder to reconstruct such an irregular surface, but even here it is easy to see how they generally get smaller toward the bottom right corner.

6. Random pixels in the range 130–150 (corresponding to a flat, crinkled surface) generated by

$$\text{Pixl=Table[SetAccuracy[130+20Random[],0],\{8\},\{8\}]}$$

again produce a DCT matrix with all nonzero elements (Table 4.50), but here it is easy to see how just a few coefficients dominate.

The examples above show how DCT coefficients with low frequencies correspond to those parts of the image that are (more or less) uniform, while the high-frequency coefficients corresponds to image parts that feature sudden changes, such as the contours of objects.

4.6.5 Quantization

After each 8×8 matrix of DCT coefficients G_{ij} is calculated, it is quantized. This is the step where the information loss (except for some unavoidable loss because of finite precision calculations in other steps) occurs. Each number in the DCT coefficients matrix is divided by the corresponding number from the particular

10	128	10	10	128	10	10	128
10	128	10	10	128	10	10	128
10	128	10	10	128	10	10	128
10	128	10	10	128	10	10	128
10	128	10	10	128	10	10	128
10	128	10	10	128	10	10	128
10	128	10	10	128	10	10	128
10	128	10	10	128	10	10	128

434.	−57.47	63.86	−78.6	118.	−395.14	−154.17	38.4
0.	0.	0.	0.	0.	0.	0.	0.
0.	0.	0.	0.	0.	0.	0.	0.
0.	0.	0.	0.	0.	0.	0.	0.
0.	0.	0.	0.	0.	0.	0.	0.
0.	0.	0.	0.	0.	0.	0.	0.
0.	0.	0.	0.	0.	0.	0.	0.
0.	0.	0.	0.	0.	0.	0.	0.

Table 4.45: Vertical Stripes of Pixels.

10	10	10	10	10	10	10	10		434.	0.	0.	0.	0.	0.	0.	0.
128	128	128	128	128	128	128	128		−57.47	0.	0.	0.	0.	0.	0.	0.
10	10	10	10	10	10	10	10		63.86	0.	0.	0.	0.	0.	0.	0.
10	10	10	10	10	10	10	10		−78.6	0.	0.	0.	0.	0.	0.	0.
128	128	128	128	128	128	128	128		118.	0.	0.	0.	0.	0.	0.	0.
10	10	10	10	10	10	10	10		−395.14	0.	0.	0.	0.	0.	0.	0.
10	10	10	10	10	10	10	10		−154.17	0.	0.	0.	0.	0.	0.	0.
128	128	128	128	128	128	128	128		38.4	0.	0.	0.	0.	0.	0.	0.

Table 4.46: Horizontal Stripes of Pixels.

128	10	10	10	10	10	10	10		198.	0.	0.	0.	0.	0.	0.	0.
10	128	10	10	10	10	10	10		0.	118.	0.	0.	0.	0.	0.	0.
10	10	128	10	10	10	10	10		0.	0.	118.	0.	0.	0.	0.	0.
10	10	10	128	10	10	10	10		0.	0.	0.	118.	0.	0.	0.	0.
10	10	10	10	128	10	10	10		0.	0.	0.	0.	118.	0.	0.	0.
10	10	10	10	10	128	10	10		0.	0.	0.	0.	0.	118.	0.	0.
10	10	10	10	10	10	128	10		0.	0.	0.	0.	0.	0.	118.	0.
10	10	10	10	10	10	10	128		0.	0.	0.	0.	0.	0.	0.	118.

Table 4.47: A Diagonal Data Unit.

87.0786	64.4845	116.92	32.5291	51.4957	69.0415	116.617	71.904
84.4433	22.6334	71.2894	120.229	22.9243	53.2736	2.883	3.93644
72.4648	50.0736	103.744	0.103997	92.8995	124.246	59.1829	65.916
37.1069	125.542	113.893	73.1882	112.976	125.698	72.9573	97.6729
103.228	61.6884	84.5332	102.735	66.4958	109.423	32.2806	124.653
28.5424	118.875	25.5255	6.89471	78.9631	118.793	34.8613	4.75396
9.35065	22.1543	65.8646	103.447	1.18117	8.22679	31.2366	1.22152
121.952	37.2349	7.53621	99.5506	26.9121	26.4397	18.6029	45.1664

Table 4.48: A Highly Random Data Unit.

505.96	40.49	−29.3	13.94	−17.98	0.31	55.43	−30.16
77.14	−18.92	8.47	−0.92	−43.69	−1.03	44.39	57.22
−98.05	45.46	24.19	−14.92	38.26	104.08	−28.42	7.68
−4.99	−6.39	4.98	−0.71	−41.85	−10.51	−21.22	−3.35
103.43	−20.83	52.65	−21.53	35.92	−0.96	1.72	1.68
14.27	−39.92	−12.99	−35.13	−79.2	−21.92	−28.64	51.13
28.56	−29.91	46.51	82.37	−51.87	−74.69	0.29	44.55
3.6	−20.38	28.19	−25.66	29.47	40.77	45.77	23.52

Table 4.49: The DCT of Table 4.48.

136	131	135	139	135	138	139	145	1118	6	5	−6	7	4	−1	−5
139	146	132	146	135	133	138	134	−2	0	4	5	7	−5	−7	2
148	145	140	144	148	132	134	149	−10	−7	−5	−12	−2	6	2	−7
149	145	142	132	137	137	139	143	−4	−8	−3	3	−4	6	2	−3
149	140	132	139	150	146	145	130	−3	−4	4	11	0	0	4	6
141	137	144	145	131	133	134	149	3	−4	3	−6	−7	−2	7	2
132	143	146	146	133	146	144	135	0	−2	6	−11	15	−3	8	4
139	135	143	144	132	134	135	143	7	−3	−10	12	0	−1	−4	3

Table 4.50: A Slightly Random Data Unit and Its DCT Coefficient Matrix.

"quantization table" used, and the result is rounded to the nearest integer. As has already been mentioned, three such tables are needed, for the three color components. The JPEG standard allows for up to four tables, and the user can select any of the four for quantizing each color component. The 64 numbers constituting each quantization table are all JPEG parameters. In principle, they can all be specified and fine-tuned by the user for maximum compression. In practice, few users have the time or expertise to experiment with so many parameters, so JPEG software normally uses the two approaches below:

1. Default quantization tables. Two such tables, for the luminance (grayscale) and the chrominance components, are the result of many experiments performed by the JPEG committee. They are included in the JPEG standard and are reproduced here as Table 4.52. It is easy to see how the QCs in the table generally grow as we move from the upper left corner to the bottom right one. This is how JPEG reduces the DCT coefficients with high spatial frequencies.

2. A simple quantization table Q is computed, based on one parameter R supplied by the user. A simple expression such as $Q_{ij} = 1 + (i + j) \times R$ guarantees that QCs start small at the upper left corner and get bigger toward the bottom right corner.

Example: After dividing the 64 DCT coefficients of Table 4.49 by the quantization factors of Table 4.52 (luminance) and rounding to the nearest integer, most AC coefficients are zeros (this is Table 4.53a, but remember that this is a contrived example of random pixels). An even more drastic behavior is shown in Table 4.53b, which displays the results of quantizing the 64 DCT coefficients of Table 4.50 by the QCs of Table 4.52 (luminance). Of the 64 coefficients, only the first one is nonzero. It's hard to believe that anything resembling the original data unit could be reconstructed from a single DCT coefficient!

◇ **Exercise 4.16:** What is the result of applying the inverse DCT to the quantized coefficients of Table 4.53b?

The answer to Exercise 4.16 shows that the quantization Tables 4.52 are not always the best ones. To get a better reconstruction of the original data unit, Table 4.50, we tried a quantization table based on the expression $\text{Quant}(i, j) = 1 + (i + j) \times R$. Selecting $R = 2$ has produced the quantization coefficients of Table 4.54a and the quantized data unit of Table 4.54b. This table has only four nonzero coefficients, but these are enough to reconstruct the original data unit to a high precision (Table 4.51).

137	139	141	140	136	135	137	139
139	140	141	140	138	137	138	139
142	141	140	140	141	141	140	139
145	142	139	140	143	143	141	138
145	142	139	140	143	143	141	138
142	141	140	140	141	141	140	139
139	140	141	140	138	137	138	139
137	139	141	140	136	135	137	139

Table 4.51: Restored Data Unit of Table 4.50.

16	11	10	16	24	40	51	61
12	12	14	19	26	58	60	55
14	13	16	24	40	57	69	56
14	17	22	29	51	87	80	62
18	22	37	56	68	109	103	77
24	35	55	64	81	104	113	92
49	64	78	87	103	121	120	101
72	92	95	98	112	100	103	99

17	18	24	47	99	99	99	99
18	21	26	66	99	99	99	99
24	26	56	99	99	99	99	99
47	66	99	99	99	99	99	99
99	99	99	99	99	99	99	99
99	99	99	99	99	99	99	99
99	99	99	99	99	99	99	99
99	99	99	99	99	99	99	99

Luminance   Chrominance

Table 4.52: Recommended Quantization Tables.

32	4	−3	0	0	0	1	0
6	−2	0	0	−2	0	0	1
−7	3	2	0	0	2	0	0
0	0	0	0	0	0	0	0
6	0	1	0	0	0	0	0
0	−1	0	0	0	0	0	0
0	0	0	0	0	0	0	0
0	0	0	0	0	0	0	0

70	0	0	0	0	0	0	0
0	0	0	0	0	0	0	0
0	0	0	0	0	0	0	0
0	0	0	0	0	0	0	0
0	0	0	0	0	0	0	0
0	0	0	0	0	0	0	0
0	0	0	0	0	0	0	0
0	0	0	0	0	0	0	0

(a)   (b)

Table 4.53: (a) The Quantized Coefficients of Table 4.49. (b) Those of Table 4.50.

1	3	5	7	9	11	13	15
3	5	7	9	11	13	15	17
5	7	9	11	13	15	17	19
7	9	11	13	15	17	19	21
9	11	13	15	17	19	21	23
11	13	15	17	19	21	23	25
13	15	17	19	21	23	25	27
15	17	19	21	23	25	27	29

1118	2	0	0	0	0	0	0
0	0	0	0	0	0	0	0
-2	0	0	-1	0	0	0	0
0	0	0	0	0	0	0	0
0	0	0	0	0	0	0	0
0	0	0	0	0	0	0	0
0	0	0	0	0	0	0	0
0	0	0	0	0	0	0	0

(a)   (b)

Table 4.54: (a) The Quantization Table $1 + (i + j) \times 2$. (b) Quantized Coefficients Produced by (a).

Comparing the restored data unit in Table 4.51 to the original pixels of Table 4.50 shows that the maximum difference between an original pixel and a restored one is 10. Selecting $R < 2$ can improve the reconstruction significantly while adding just a few nonzero AC coefficients to the quantized data unit.

⋄ **Exercise 4.17:** Repeat this example for the case $R = 1$.

If the quantization is done right, very few nonzero numbers will be left in the DCT coefficients matrix, and they will typically be concentrated at the upper left corner. These numbers are the output of JPEG, but they are further compressed before being written on the output stream. In the JPEG literature this compression is called "entropy coding," and Section 4.6.6 shows in detail how it is done. Three techniques are used by entropy coding to compress the 8×8 matrix of integers:

1. The 64 numbers are collected by scanning the matrix in zigzags (Figure 1.8b). This produces a string of 64 numbers that starts with some nonzeros and typically ends with many consecutive zeros. Only the nonzero numbers are output (after further compressing them) and are followed by a special end-of block (EOB) code. This way there is no need to output the trailing zeros (we can say that the EOB is the run length encoding of all the trailing zeros). The interested reader should also consult Section 8.5 for other methods to compress binary strings with many consecutive zeros.

⋄ **Exercise 4.18:** What is the zigzag sequence of the 64 coefficients of Table 4.54b?

⋄ **Exercise 4.19:** Suggest a practical way of writing a loop that traverses an 8×8 matrix in zigzag.

2. The nonzero numbers are compressed using Huffman coding (Section 4.6.6).
3. The first of those numbers (the DC coefficient, page 247) is treated differently from the others (the AC coefficients).

> She had just succeeded in curving it down into a graceful zigzag, and was going to dive in among the leaves, which she found to be nothing but the tops of the trees under which she had been wandering, when a sharp hiss made her draw back in a hurry.
> —Lewis Carroll, *Alice in Wonderland*

4.6.6 Coding

We first discuss point 3 above. Each 8×8 matrix of quantized DCT coefficients contains one DC coefficient [at position $(0, 0)$, the top left corner] and 63 AC coefficients. The DC coefficient is a measure of the average value of the 64 original pixels, constituting the data unit. Experience shows that in a continuous-tone image, adjacent data units of pixels are normally correlated in the sense that the average values of the pixels in adjacent data units are close. We already know that the DC coefficient of a data unit is a multiple of the average of the 64 pixels constituting the unit. This implies that the DC coefficients of adjacent data units don't differ much. JPEG outputs the first one (encoded), followed by *differences* (also encoded) of the DC coefficients of consecutive data units. The concept of differencing is discussed in Section 1.3.1.

Example: If the first three 8×8 data units of an image have quantized DC coefficients of 1118, 1114, and 1119, then the JPEG output for the first data unit is 1118 (Huffman encoded, see below) followed by the 63 (encoded) AC coefficients of that data unit. The output for the second data unit will be $1114 - 1118 = -4$ (also Huffman encoded), followed by the 63 (encoded) AC coefficients of that data unit, and the output for the third data unit will be $1119 - 1114 = 5$ (also Huffman encoded), again followed by the 63 (encoded) AC coefficients of that data unit. This way of handling the DC coefficients is worth the extra trouble, since the differences are small.

Coding the DC differences is done using Table 4.55, so first here are a few words about this table. Each row has a row number (on the left), the unary code for the row (on the right), and several columns in between. Each row contains greater numbers (and also more numbers) than its predecessor but not the numbers contained in previous rows. Row i contains the range of integers $[-(2^i-1), +(2^i-1)]$ but is missing the middle range $[-(2^{i-1} - 1), +(2^{i-1} - 1)]$. The rows thus get very long, which means that a simple two-dimensional array is not a good data structure for this table. In fact, there is no need to store these integers in a data structure, since the program can figure out where in the table any given integer x is supposed to reside by analyzing the bits of x.

The first DC coefficient to be encoded in our example is 1118. It resides in row 11 column 930 of the table (column numbering starts at zero), so it is encoded as 111111111110|01110100010 (the unary code for row 11, followed by the 11-bit binary value of 930). The second DC difference is -4. It resides in row 3 column 3 of Table 4.55, so it is encoded as 1110|011 (the unary code for row 3, followed by the 3-bit binary value of 3).

$\diamond$ **Exercise 4.20:** How is the third DC difference, 5, encoded?

Point 2 above has to do with the precise way the 63 AC coefficients of a data unit are compressed. It uses a combination of RLE and either Huffman or arithmetic coding. The idea is that the sequence of AC coefficients normally contains just a few nonzero numbers, with runs of zeros between them, and with a long run of trailing zeros. For each nonzero number x, the encoder (1) finds the number Z of consecutive zeros preceding x; (2) finds x in Table 4.55 and prepares its row and column numbers (R and C); (3) the pair (R, Z) [that's (R, Z), not (R, C)] is used as row and column numbers for Table 4.58; and (4) the Huffman code found in that position in the table is concatenated to C (where C is written as an R-bit number) and the result is (finally) the code emitted by the JPEG encoder for the AC coefficient x and all the consecutive zeros preceding it.

The Huffman codes in Table 4.58 are not the ones recommended by the JPEG standard. The standard recommends the use of Tables 4.56 and 4.57 and says that up to four Huffman code tables can be used by a JPEG codec, except that the baseline mode can use only two such tables. The actual codes in Table 4.58 are

0:	0									0
1:	-1	1								10
2:	-3	-2	2	3						110
3:	-7	-6	-5	-4	4	5	6	7		1110
4:	-15	-14	...	-9	-8	8	9	10 ...	15	11110
5:	-31	-30	-29	...	-17	-16	16	17 ...	31	111110
6:	-63	-62	-61	...	-33	-32	32	33 ...	63	1111110
7:	-127	-126	-125	...	-65	-64	64	65 ...	127	11111110
⋮			⋮						
14:	-16383	-16382	-16381	...	-8193	-8192	8192	8193 ...	16383	111111111111110
15:	-32767	-32766	-32765	...	-16385	-16384	16384	16385 ...	32767	1111111111111110
16:	32768									1111111111111111

Table 4.55: Coding the Differences of DC Coefficients.

thus arbitrary. The reader should notice the EOB code at position $(0,0)$, and the ZRL code at position $(0,15)$. The former indicates end-of-block, and the latter is the code emitted for 15 consecutive zeros when the number of consecutive zeros exceeds 15. These codes are the ones recommended for the luminance AC coefficients of Table 4.56. The EOB and ZRL codes recommended for the chrominance AC coefficients of Table 4.57 are 00 and 1111111010, respectively.

As an example consider the sequence

$$1118, 2, 0, -2, \underbrace{0, \ldots, 0}_{13}, -1, 0, \ldots$$

of exercise 4.18. The first AC coefficient 2 has no zeros preceding it, so $Z = 0$. It is found in Table 4.55 in row 2, column 2, so $R = 2$ and $C = 2$. The Huffman code in position $(R, Z) = (2, 0)$ of Table 4.58 is 01, so the final code emitted for 2 is 01|10. The next nonzero coefficient, -2, has one zero preceding it, so $Z = 1$. It is found in Table 4.55 in row 2, column 1, so $R = 2$ and $C = 1$. The Huffman code in position $(R, Z) = (2, 1)$ of Table 4.58 is 11011, so the final code emitted for 2 is 11011|01.

⋄ **Exercise 4.21:** What code is emitted for the last nonzero AC coefficient, -1?

Finally, the sequence of trailing zeros is encoded as 1010 (EOB), so the output for the above sequence of AC coefficients is 0110110111011101010101010. We saw earlier that the DC coefficient is encoded as 111111111110|1110100010, so the final output for the entire 64-pixel data unit is the 46-bit number

111111111110011101000100110110111101110101010100.

These 46 bits encode one color component of the 64 pixels of a data unit. Let's assume that the other two color components are also encoded into 46-bit numbers. If each pixel originally consists of 24 bits, then this corresponds to a compression factor of $64 \times 24/(46 \times 3) \approx 11.13$; very impressive!

(Notice that the DC coefficient of 1118 has contributed 23 of the 46 bits. Subsequent data units code differences of their DC coefficient, which may take fewer than 10 bits instead of 23. They may feature much higher compression factors as a result.)

	R				
Z	**1** **6**	**2** **7**	**3** **8**	**4** **9**	**5** **A**
0	00 1111000	01 11111000	100 1111110110	1011 1111111110000010	11010 1111111110000011
1	1100 1111111110000100	11011 1111111110000101	11110001 1111111110000110	111110110 1111111110000111	1111110110 1111111110001000
2	11100 111111110001010	11111001 111111110001011	1111110111 111111110001100	111111110100 111111110001101	111111110001001 111111110001110
3	111010 1111111110010001	111110111 1111111110010010	111111110101 1111111110010011	1111111110001111 1111111110010100	1111111110010000 1111111110010101
4	111011 1111111110011001	1111111000 1111111110011010	1111111110010110 1111111110011011	1111111110010111 1111111110011100	1111111110011000 1111111110011101
5	1111010 1111111110100001	11111110111 1111111110100010	1111111110011110 1111111110100011	1111111110011111 1111111110100100	1111111110100000 1111111110100101
6	1111011 1111111110101001	111111110110 1111111110101010	1111111110100110 1111111110101011	1111111110100111 1111111110101100	1111111110101000 1111111110101101
7	11111010 1111111110110001	111111110111 1111111110110010	1111111110101110 1111111110110011	1111111110101111 1111111110110100	1111111110110000 1111111110110101
8	111111000 1111111110111001	111111111000000 1111111110111010	1111111110110110 1111111110111011	1111111110110111 1111111110111100	1111111110111000 1111111110111101
9	111111001 1111111111000010	1111111110111110 1111111111000011	1111111110111111 1111111111000100	1111111111000000 1111111111000101	1111111111000001 1111111111000110
A	111111010 1111111111001011	1111111111000111 1111111111001100	1111111111001000 1111111111001101	1111111111001001 1111111111001110	1111111111001010 1111111111001111
B	1111111001 1111111111010100	1111111111010000 1111111111010101	1111111111010001 1111111111010110	1111111111010010 1111111111010111	1111111111010011 1111111111011000
C	1111111010 1111111111011101	1111111111011001 1111111111011110	1111111111011010 1111111111011111	1111111111011011 1111111111100000	1111111111011100 1111111111100001
D	11111111000 1111111111100110	1111111111100010 1111111111100111	1111111111100011 1111111111101000	1111111111100100 1111111111101001	1111111111100101 1111111111101010
E	1111111111101011 1111111111110000	1111111111101100 1111111111110001	1111111111101101 1111111111110010	1111111111101110 1111111111110011	1111111111101111 1111111111110100
F	11111111001 1111111111111001	1111111111110101 1111111111111010	1111111111110110 1111111111111011	1111111111110111 1111111111111101	1111111111111000 1111111111111110

Table 4.56: Recommended Huffman Codes For Luminance AC Coefficients.

	R				
Z	1 / 6	2 / 7	3 / 8	4 / 9	5 / A
0	01 111000	100 1111000	1010 111110100	11000 1111110110	11001 111111110100
1	1011 111111110101	111001 111111110001000	11110110 111111110001001	111110101 111111110001010	11111110110 111111110001011
2	11010 1111111110001100	11110111 1111111110001101	1111110111 1111111110001110	111111110110 1111111110001111	111111111000010 1111111110010000
3	11011 1111111110010010	11111000 1111111110010011	1111111000 1111111110010100	111111110111 1111111110010101	1111111110010001 1111111110010110
4	111010 1111111110011010	111110110 1111111110011011	1111111110010111 1111111110011100	1111111110011000 1111111110011101	1111111110011001 1111111110011110
5	111011 1111111110100010	1111111001 1111111110100011	1111111110011111 1111111110100100	1111111110100000 1111111110100101	1111111110100001 1111111110100110
6	1111001 1111111110101010	11111110111 1111111110101011	1111111110100111 1111111110101100	1111111110101000 1111111110101101	1111111110101001 1111111110101110
7	1111010 1111111110110010	11111111000 1111111110110011	1111111110101111 1111111110110100	1111111110110000 1111111110110101	1111111110110001 1111111110110110
8	11111001 1111111110111011	1111111110110111 1111111110111100	1111111110111000 1111111110111101	1111111110111001 1111111110111110	1111111110111010 1111111110111111
9	111110111 1111111111000100	1111111111000000 1111111111000101	1111111111000001 1111111111000110	1111111111000010 1111111111000111	1111111111000011 1111111111001000
A	111111000 1111111111001101	1111111111001001 1111111111001110	1111111111001010 1111111111001111	1111111111001011 1111111111010000	1111111111001100 1111111111010001
B	111111001 1111111111010110	1111111111010010 1111111111010111	1111111111010011 1111111111011000	1111111111010100 1111111111011001	1111111111010101 1111111111011010
C	111111010 1111111111011111	1111111111011011 1111111111100000	1111111111011100 1111111111100001	1111111111011101 1111111111100010	1111111111011110 1111111111100011
D	11111111001 1111111111101000	1111111111100100 1111111111101001	1111111111100101 1111111111101010	1111111111100110 1111111111101011	1111111111100111 1111111111101100
E	11111111100000 1111111111110001	1111111111101101 1111111111110010	1111111111101110 1111111111110011	1111111111101111 1111111111110100	1111111111110000 1111111111110101
F	111111111000011 1111111111111010	11111111010110 1111111111111011	1111111111110111 1111111111111100	1111111111111000 1111111111111101	1111111111111001 1111111111111110

Table 4.57: Recommended Huffman Codes For Chrominance AC Coefficients.

The same tables (Tables 4.55 and 4.58) used by the encoder should, of course, be used by the decoder. The tables may be predefined and used by a JPEG codec as defaults, or they may be specifically calculated for a given image in a special pass preceding the actual compression. The JPEG standard does not specify any code tables, so any JPEG codec must use its own.

R Z:	0	1	. . .	15
0:	1010			11111111001(ZRL)
1:	00	1100	...	1111111111110101
2:	01	11011	...	1111111111110110
3:	100	1111001	...	1111111111110111
4:	1011	111110110	...	1111111111111000
5:	11010	11111110110	...	1111111111111001
⋮	⋮			

Table 4.58: Coding AC Coefficients.

Some JPEG variants use a particular version of arithmetic coding, called the QM coder (Section 2.16), that is specified in the JPEG standard. This version of arithmetic coding is adaptive, so it does not need Tables 4.55 and 4.58. It adapts its behavior to the image statistics as it goes along. Using arithmetic coding may produce 5–10% better compression than Huffman for a typical continuous-tone image. However, it is more complex to implement than Huffman coding, so in practice it is rare to find a JPEG codec that uses it.

4.6.7 Lossless Mode

The lossless mode of JPEG uses differencing (Section 1.3.1) to reduce the values of pixels before they are compressed. This particular form of differencing is called *predicting*. The values of some near neighbors of a pixel are subtracted from the pixel to get a small number, which is then compressed further using Huffman or arithmetic coding. Figure 4.59a shows a pixel X and three neighbor pixels A, B, and C. Figure 4.59b shows eight possible ways (predictions) to combine the values of the three neighbors. In the lossless mode, the user can select one of these predictions, and the encoder then uses it to combine the three neighbor pixels and subtract the combination from the value of X. The result is normally a small number, which is then entropy-coded in a way very similar to that described for the DC coefficient in Section 4.6.6.

Predictor 0 is used only in the hierarchical mode of JPEG. Predictors 1, 2, and 3 are called "one-dimensional." Predictors 4, 5, 6, and 7 are "two-dimensional."

It should be noted that the lossless mode of JPEG has never been very successful. It produces typical compression factors of 2, and is thus inferior to other lossless image compression methods. Because of this, popular JPEG implementations do not even implement this mode. Even the lossy (baseline) mode of JPEG does not perform well when asked to limit the amount of loss to a minimum. As

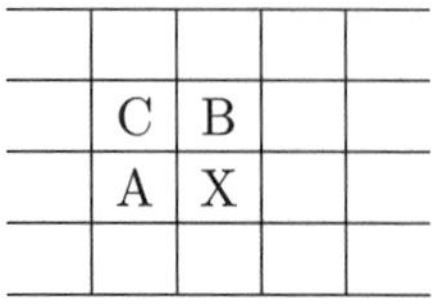

Selection value	Prediction
0	no prediction
1	A
2	B
3	C
4	$A + B - C$
5	$A + ((B - C)/2)$
6	$B + ((A - C)/2)$
7	$(A + B)/2$

C	B		
A	X		

(a)   (b)

Figure 4.59: Pixel Prediction in the Lossless Mode.

a result, some JPEG implementations do not allow parameter settings that result in minimum loss. The strength of JPEG is in its ability to generate highly compressed images that when decompressed are indistinguishable from the original. Recognizing this, the ISO has decided to come up with another standard for lossless compression of continuous-tone images. This standard is now commonly known as JPEG-LS and is described in Section 4.7.

4.6.8 The Compressed File

A JPEG encoder outputs a compressed file that includes parameters, markers, and the compressed data units. The parameters are either 4 bits (these always come in pairs), one byte, or two bytes long. The markers serve to identify the various parts of the file. Each is two bytes long, where the first byte is X'FF' and the second one is not 0 or X'FF'. A marker may be preceded by a number of bytes with X'FF'. Table 4.61 lists all the JPEG markers (the first four groups are start-of-frame markers). The compressed data units are combined into MCUs (minimal coded unit), where an MCU is either a single data unit (in the noninterleaved mode) or three data units from the three image components (in the interleaved mode).

Figure 4.60 shows the main parts of the JPEG compressed file (parts in square brackets are optional). The file starts with the SOI marker and ends with the EOI marker. In-between these markers, the compressed image is organized in frames. In the hierarchical mode there are several frames, and in all other modes there is only one frame. In each frame the image information is contained in one or more scans, but the frame also contains a header and optional tables (which, in turn, may include markers). The first scan may be followed by an optional DNL segment (define number of lines), which starts with the DNL marker and contains the number of lines in the image that's represented by the frame. A scan starts with optional tables, followed by the scan header, followed by several entropy-coded segments (ECS), which are separated by (optional) restart markers (RST). Each ECS contains one or more MCUs, where an MCU is, as explained earlier, either a single data unit or three such units.

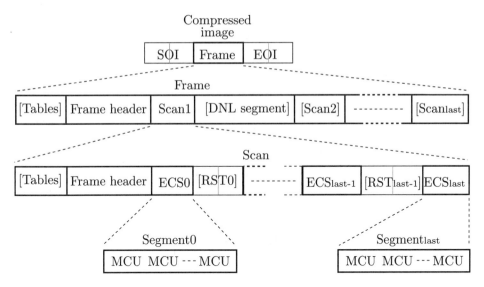

Figure 4.60: JPEG File Format.

4.6.9 JFIF

It has been mentioned earlier that JPEG is a compression method, not a graphics file format, which is why it does not specify image features such as pixel aspect ratio, color space, or interleaving of bitmap rows. This is where JFIF comes in.

JFIF (JPEG File Interchange Format) is a graphics file format that makes it possible to exchange JPEG-compressed images between computers. The main features of JFIF are the use of the YCbCr triple-component color space for color images (only one component for grayscale images) and the use of a *marker* to specify features missing from JPEG, such as image resolution, aspect ratio, and features that are application-specific.

The JFIF marker (called the APP0 marker) starts with the zero-terminated string `JFIF`. Following this, there is pixel information and other specifications (see below). Following this, there may be additional segments specifying JFIF extensions. A JFIF extension contains more platform-specific information about the image.

Each extension starts with the zero-terminated string `JFXX`, followed by a 1-byte code identifying the extension. An extension may contain application-specific information, in which case it starts with a different string, not `JFIF` or `JFXX` but something that identifies the specific application or its maker.

The format of the first segment of an APP0 marker is as follows:

1. APP0 marker (4 bytes): `FFD8FFE0`.
2. Length (2 bytes): Total length of marker, including the 2 bytes of the "length" field but excluding the APP0 marker itself (field 1).
3. Identifier (5 bytes): $4A46494600_{16}$. This is the `JFIF` string that identifies the APP0 marker.

Value	Name	Description
\multicolumn{3}{Nondifferential, Huffman coding}		
FFC0	SOF_0	Baseline DCT
FFC1	SOF_1	Extended sequential DCT
FFC2	SOF_2	Progressive DCT
FFC3	SOF_3	Lossless (sequential)
Differential, Huffman coding		
FFC5	SOF_5	Differential sequential DCT
FFC6	SOF_6	Differential progressive DCT
FFC7	SOF_7	Differential lossless (sequential)
Nondifferential, arithmetic coding		
FFC8	JPG	Reserved for extensions
FFC9	SOF_9	Extended sequential DCT
FFCA	SOF_{10}	Progressive DCT
FFCB	SOF_{11}	Lossless (sequential)
Differential, arithmetic coding		
FFCD	SOF_{13}	Differential sequential DCT
FFCE	SOF_{14}	Differential progressive DCT
FFCF	SOF_{15}	Differential lossless (sequential)
Huffman table specification		
FFC4	DHT	Define Huffman table
Arithmetic coding conditioning specification		
FFCC	DAC	Define arith coding conditioning(s)
Restart interval termination		
FFD0–FFD7	RST_m	Restart with modulo 8 count m
Other markers		
FFD8	SOI	Start of image
FFD9	EOI	End of image
FFDA	SOS	Start of scan
FFDB	DQT	Define quantization table(s)
FFDC	DNL	Define number of lines
FFDD	DRI	Define restart interval
FFDE	DHP	Define hierarchical progression
FFDF	EXP	Expand reference component(s)
FFE0–FFEF	APP_n	Reserved for application segments
FFF0–FFFD	JPG_n	Reserved for JPEG extensions
FFFE	COM	Comment
Reserved markers		
FF01	TEM	For temporary private use
FF02–FFBF	RES	Reserved

Table 4.61: JPEG Markers.

4. Version (2 bytes): Example: 0102_{16} specifies version 1.02.

5. Units (1 byte): Units for the X and Y densities. 0 means no units; the Xdensity and Ydensity fields specify the pixel aspect ratio. 1 means that Xdensity and Ydensity are dots per inch, 2, that they are dots per cm.

6. Xdensity (2 bytes), Ydensity (2 bytes): Horizontal and vertical pixel densities (both should be nonzero).

7. Xthumbnail (1 byte), Ythumbnail (1 byte): Thumbnail horizontal and vertical pixel counts.

8. (RGB)n (3n bytes): Packed (24-bit) RGB values for the thumbnail pixels. $n =$ Xthumbnail $\times$ Ythumbnail.

The syntax of the JFIF extension APP0 marker segment is as follows:

1. APP0 marker.

2. Length (2 bytes): Total length of marker, including the 2 bytes of the "length" field but excluding the APP0 marker itself (field 1).

3. Identifier (5 bytes): $4A46585800_{16}$ This is the **JFXX** string identifying an extension.

4. Extension code (1 byte): 10_{16} = Thumbnail coded using JPEG. 11_{16} = Thumbnail coded using 1 byte/pixel (monochromatic). 13_{16} = Thumbnail coded using 3 bytes/pixel (eight colors).

5. Extension data (variable): This field depends on the particular extension.

Bibliography

Blinn, J. F. (1993) "What's the Deal with the DCT," *IEEE Computer Graphics and Applications* pp. 78–83, July.

Feig, Ephraim N., and Elliot Linzer (1990) "Discrete Cosine Transform Algorithms for Image Data Compression," in *Proceedings Electronic Imaging '90 East*, pages 84–87, Boston, MA.

Loeffler, C., A. Ligtenberg, and G. Moschytz (1989) "Practical Fast 1-D DCT Algorithms with 11 Multiplications," *Proceedings of the International Conference on Acoustics, Speech, and Signal Processing (ICASSP '89)*, pp. 988–991.

Pennebaker, William B., and Joan L. Mitchell (1992) *JPEG Still Image Data Compression Standard*, Van Nostrand Reinhold.

Rao, K. R., and P. Yip (1990) *Discrete Cosine Transform—Algorithms, Advantages, Applications*, London, Academic Press.

Wallace, Gregory K. (1991) "The JPEG Still Image Compression Standard," *Communications of the ACM* **34**(4):30–44, April.

Zhang, Manyun (1990) *The JPEG and Image Data Compression Algorithms* (Ph.D. dissertation).

4.7 JPEG-LS

As has been mentioned in Section 4.6.7, the lossless mode of JPEG is inefficient and often is not even implemented. As a result, the ISO, in cooperation with the IEC, has decided to develop a new standard for the lossless (or near-lossless) compression of continuous-tone images. The result is recommendation ISO/IEC CD 14495, popularly known as JPEG-LS. The principles of this method are described here, but it should be noted that it is not simply an extension or a modification of JPEG. This is a new method, designed to be simple and fast. It does not use the DCT, does not use arithmetic coding, and uses quantization in a limited way, and only in its near-lossless option. JPEG-LS is based on ideas developed in [Weinberger et al. 96] for their LOCO-I compression method. JPEG-LS examines several of the previously seen neighbors of the current pixel, uses them as the *context* of the pixel, uses the context to predict the pixel and to select a probability distribution out of several such distributions, and uses that distribution to encode the prediction error with a special Golomb code. There is also a run mode, where the length of a run of identical pixels is encoded.

The context used to predict the current pixel x is shown in Figure 4.62. The encoder examines the context pixels and decides whether to encode the current pixel x in the *run mode* or in the *regular mode*. If the context suggests that the pixels y, z,...following the current pixel are likely to be identical, the encoder selects the run mode. Otherwise, it selects the regular mode. In the near-lossless mode the decision is slightly different. If the context suggests that the pixels following the current pixel are likely to be almost identical (within the tolerance parameter NEAR), the encoder selects the run mode. Otherwise, it selects the regular mode. The rest of the encoding process depends on the mode selected.

	c	b	d	
	a	x	y	z

Figure 4.62: Context for Predicting x.

In the regular mode, the encoder uses the values of context pixels a, b, and c to predict pixel x, and subtracts the prediction from x to obtain the *prediction error*, denoted by *Errval*. This error is then *corrected* by a term that depends on the context (this correction is done to compensate for systematic biases in the prediction), and encoded with a Golomb code. The Golomb coding depends on all four pixels of the context and also on prediction errors that were previously encoded for the same context (this information is stored in arrays A and N, mentioned in Section 4.7.1). If near-lossless compression is used, the error is quantized before it is encoded.

In the run mode, the encoder starts at the current pixel x and finds the longest run of pixels that are identical to context pixel a. The encoder does not extend this run beyond the end of the current image row. Since all the pixels in the run are identical to a (and a is already known to the decoder) only the length of the run needs be encoded, and this is done with a 32-entry array denoted by J (Section 4.7.1). If near-lossless compression is used, the encoder selects a run of pixels that are close to a within the tolerance parameter NEAR.

The decoder is not substantially different from the encoder, so JPEG-LS is a nearly symmetric compression method. The compressed stream contains data segments (with the Golomb codes and the encoded run lengths), marker segments (with information needed by the decoder), and markers (some of the reserved markers of JPEG are used). A marker is a byte of all ones followed by a special code, signaling the start of a new segment. If a marker is followed by a byte whose most significant bit is 0, that byte is the start of a marker segment. Otherwise, that byte starts a data segment.

4.7.1 The Encoder

JPEG-LS is normally used as a lossless compression method. In this case, the reconstructed value of a pixel is identical to its original value. In the near lossless mode, the original and the reconstructed values may differ. In every case we denote the reconstructed value of a pixel p by Rp.

When the top row of an image is encoded, context pixels b, c, and d are not available and should therefore be considered zero. If the current pixel is located at the start or the end of an image row, either a and c, or d are not available. In such a case, the encoder uses for a or d the reconstructed value Rb of b (or zero if this is the top row), and for c the reconstructed value that was assigned to a when the first pixel of the previous line was encoded. This means that the encoder has to do part of the decoder's job and has to figure out the reconstructed values of certain pixels.

The first step in determining the context is to calculate the three *gradient* values

$$D1 = Rd - Rb, \quad D2 = Rb - Rc, \quad D3 = Rc - Ra.$$

If the three values are zero (or, for near-lossless, if their absolute values are less than or equal to the tolerance parameter NEAR), the encoder selects the run mode, where it looks for the longest run of pixels identical to Ra. Step 2 compares the three gradients Di to certain parameters and calculates three region numbers Qi according to certain rules (not shown here). Each region number Qi can take one of the nine integer values in the interval $[-4, +4]$, so there are $9 \times 9 \times 9 = 729$ different region numbers. The third step uses the absolute values of the three region numbers Qi (there are 365 of them, since one of the 729 values is zero) to calculate an integer Q in the range $[0, 364]$. The details of this calculation are not specified by the JPEG-LS standard, and the encoder can do it in any way it chooses. The integer Q becomes the context for the current pixel x. It is used to index arrays A and N in Figure 4.66.

After determining the context Q, the encoder predicts pixel x in two steps. The first step calculates the prediction Px based on *edge rules*, as shown in Figure 4.63. The second step corrects the prediction, as shown in Figure 4.64, based on the quantity SIGN (determined from the signs of the three regions Qi), the correction values $C[Q]$ (derived from the bias and not discussed here), and parameter MAXVAL.

```
if(Rc>=max(Ra,Rb)) Px=min(Ra,Rb);
  else
   if(Rc<=min(Ra,Rb)) Px=max(Ra,Rb)
     else Px=Ra+Rb-Rc;
   endif;
endif;
```

```
if(SIGN=+1) Px=Px+C[Q]
        else Px=Px-C[Q]
  endif;
  if(Px>MAXVAL) Px=MAXVAL
     else if(Px<0) Px=0 endif;
  endif;
```

Figure 4.63: Edge Detecting.   **Figure 4.64:** Prediction Correcting.

To understand the edge rules, let's consider the case where $b \le a$. In this case the edge rules select b as the prediction of x in many cases where a vertical edge exists in the image just left of the current pixel x. Similarly, a is selected as the prediction in many cases where a horizontal edge exists in the image just above x. If no edge is detected, the edge rules compute a prediction of $a + b - c$, and this has a simple geometric interpretation. If we interpret each pixel as a point in three-dimensional space, with the pixel's intensity as its height, then the value $a + b - c$ places the prediction Px on the same plane as pixels a, b, and c.

Once the prediction Px is known, the encoder computes the prediction error $Errval$ as the difference $x - Px$ but reverses its sign if the quantity SIGN is negative.

In the near-lossless mode the error is quantized, and the encoder uses it to compute the reconstructed value Rx of pixel x the way the decoder will do it in the future. The encoder needs this reconstructed value to encode future pixels. The basic quantization step is

$$Errval \leftarrow \frac{Errval + \text{NEAR}}{2 \times \text{NEAR} + 1}.$$

It uses parameter NEAR, but it involves more details that are not shown here. The basic reconstruction step is

$$Rx \leftarrow Px + \text{SIGN} \times Errval \times (2 \times \text{NEAR} + 1).$$

The prediction error (after possibly being quantized) now goes through a range reduction (whose details are omitted here) and is finally ready for the important step of encoding.

The Golomb code was introduced in Section 2.4, where its main parameter was denoted by b. JPEG-LS denotes this parameter by m. Once m has been selected, the Golomb code of the nonnegative integer n consists of two parts, the unary code of the integer part of n/m and the binary representation of n mod m. These codes are ideal for integers n that are distributed geometrically (i.e., when the probability of n is $(1 - r)r^n$, where $0 < r < 1$). For any such geometric distribution there exists a value m such that the Golomb code based on it yields the shortest possible average code length. The special case where m is a power of 2 ($m = 2^k$) leads to simple encoding/decoding operations. The code for n consists, in such a case, of the k least-significant bits of n, preceded by the unary code of the remaining most-significant bits of n. This particular Golomb code is denoted by $G(k)$.

As an example we compute the $G(2)$ code of $n = 19 = 10011_2$. Since $k = 2$, m is 4. We start with the two least-significant bits, 11, of n. They equal the integer 3, which is also $n \bmod m$ ($3 = 19 \bmod 4$). The remaining most-significant bits, 100, are also the integer 4, which is the integer part of the quotient n/m ($19/4 = 4.75$). The unary code of 4 is 00001, so the $G(2)$ code of $n = 19$ is 00001|11.

In practice, we always have a finite set of nonnegative integers, where the largest integer in the set is denoted by I. The maximum length of $G(0)$ is $I + 1$, and since I can be large, it is desirable to limit the size of the Golomb code. This is done by the special Golomb code $LG(k, glimit)$ which depends on the two parameters k and $glimit$. We first form a number q from the most significant bits of n. If $q < glimit - \lceil \log I \rceil - 1$, the $LG(k, glimit)$ code is simply $G(k)$. Otherwise, the unary code of $glimit - \lceil \log I \rceil - 1$ is prepared (i.e., $glimit - \lceil \log I \rceil - 1$ zeros followed by a single 1). This acts as an escape code and is followed by the binary representation of $n - 1$ in $\lceil I \rceil$ bits.

Our prediction errors are not necessarily positive. They are differences, so they can also be zero or negative, but the various Golomb codes were designed for nonnegative integers. This is why the prediction errors must be mapped to nonnegative values before they can be coded. This is done by

$$MErrval = \begin{cases} 2Errval, & Errval \geq 0, \\ 2|Errval| - 1, & Errval < 0. \end{cases} \qquad (4.18)$$

This mapping interleaves negative and positive values in the sequence

$$0, -1, +1, -2, +2, -3, \ldots.$$

Table 4.65 lists some prediction errors, their mapped values, and their $LG(2, 32)$ codes assuming an alphabet of size 256 (i.e., $I = 255$ and $\lceil \log I \rceil = 8$).

The next point to be discussed is how to determine the value of the Golomb code parameter k. This is done adaptively. Parameter k depends on the context, and the value of k for a context is updated each time a pixel with that context is found. The calculation of k can be expressed by the single C-language statement

```
for (k=0; (N[Q]<<k)<A[Q]); k++);
```

where A and N are arrays indexed from 0 to 364. This statement uses the context Q as an index to the two arrays. It initializes k to 0 and goes into a loop. In each iteration it shifts array element $N[Q]$ by k positions to the left and compares it to element $A[Q]$. If the shifted value of $N[Q]$ is greater than or equal to $A[Q]$, the current value of k is chosen. Otherwise, k is incremented by 1 and the test repeated.

After k has been determined, the prediction error $Errval$ is mapped, by means of Equation (4.18), to $MErrval$, which is encoded using code $LG(k, LIMIT)$. The quantity LIMIT is a parameter. Arrays A and N (together with an auxiliary array

Prediction error	Mapped value	Code
0	0	1 00
−1	1	1 01
1	2	1 10
−2	3	1 11
2	4	01 00
−3	5	01 01
3	6	01 10
−4	7	01 11
4	8	001 00
−5	9	001 01
5	10	001 10
−6	11	001 11
6	12	0001 00
−7	13	0001 01
7	14	0001 10
−8	15	0001 11
8	16	00001 00
−9	17	00001 01
9	18	00001 10
−10	19	00001 11
10	20	000001 00
−11	21	000001 01
11	22	000001 10
−12	23	000001 11
12	24	0000001 00
...		
50	100	000000000000
		000000000001
		01100011

Table 4.65: Prediction Errors, Their Mappings, and $LG(2, 32)$ Codes.

```
B[Q]=B[Q]+Errval*(2*NEAR+1);
A[Q]=A[Q]+abs(Errval);
if(N[Q]=RESET) then
 A[Q]=A[Q]>>1; B[Q]=B[Q]>>1; N[Q]=N[Q]>>1
endif;
N[Q]=N[Q]+1;
```

Figure 4.66: Updating Arrays A, B, and N.

B) are then updated as shown in Figure 4.66 (RESET is a user-controlled parameter).

Encoding in the run mode is done differently. The encoder selects this mode when it finds consecutive pixels x whose values Ix are identical and equal to the reconstructed value Ra of context pixel a. For near-lossless compression, pixels in the run must have values Ix that satisfy

$$|Ix - Ra| \leq \text{NEAR}.$$

A run is not allowed to continue beyond the end of the current image row. The length of the run is encoded (there is no need to encode the value of the run's pixels, since it equals Ra), and if the run ends before the end of the current row, its encoded length is followed by the encoding of the pixel immediately following it (the pixel *interrupting* the run). The two main tasks of the encoder in this mode are (1) run scanning and run length encoding and (2) run interruption coding. Run scanning is shown in Figure 4.67. Run length encoding is shown in Figures 4.68 (for run segments of length rm) and 4.69 (for segments of length less than rm). Here are some of the details.

```
RUNval=Ra;
RUNcnt=0;
while(abs(Ix-RUNval)<=NEAR)
 RUNcnt=RUNcnt+1;
 Rx=RUNval;
 if(EOLine=1) break
   else GetNextSample()
 endif;
endwhile;
```

Figure 4.67: Run Scanning.

```
while(RUNcnt>=(1<<J[RUNindex]))
 AppendToBitStream(1,1);
 RUNcnt=RUNcnt-(1<<J[RUNindex]);
 if(RUNindex<31)
  RUNindex=RUNindex+1;
endwhile;
```

Figure 4.68: Run Encoding: I.

```
if(EOLine=0) then
 AppendToBitStream(0,1);
 AppendToBitStream
  (RUNcnt,J[RUNindex]);
 if(RUNindex>0)
  RUNindex=RUNindex-1;
 endif;
else if(RUNcnt>0)
 AppendToBitStream(1,1);
```

Figure 4.69: Run Encoding: II.

The encoder uses a 32-entry table J containing values that are denoted by rk. J is initialized to the 32 values

$$0, 0, 0, 0, 1, 1, 1, 1, 2, 2, 2, 2, 3, 3, 3, 3, 4, 4, 5, 5, 6, 6, 7, 7, 8, 9, 10, 11, 12, 13, 14, 15.$$

For each value rk, we use the notation $rm = 2^{rk}$. The 32 quantities rm are called *code-order*. The first 4 rms have values $2^0 = 1$. The next four have values $2^1 = 2$. The next four, $2^2 = 4$, up to the last rm, whose value is $2^{15} = 32768$. The encoder executes the procedure of Figure 4.67 to determine the run length, which it stores in variable `RUNlen`. This variable is then encoded by breaking it up into chunks whose sizes are the values of consecutive rms. For example, if `RUNlen` is 6, it can be expressed in terms of the rms as $1 + 1 + 1 + 1 + 2$, so it is equivalent to the first five rms. It is encoded by writing five bits of 1 on the compressed stream. Each of those bits is written by the statement `AppendToBitStream(1,1)` of Figure 4.68. Each time a 1 is written, the value of the corresponding rm is subtracted from `RUNlen`. If `RUNlen` is originally 6, it goes down to 5, 4, 3, 2, and 0.

It may happen, of course, that the length `RUNlen` of a run is not equal to an integer number of rms. An example is a `RUNlen` of 7. This is encoded by writing five bits of 1, followed by a *prefix* bit, followed by the remainder of `RUNlen` (in our example, a 1), written on the compressed stream as an rk-bit number (the current rk in our example is 2). This last operation is performed by the procedure call `AppendToBitStream(RUNcnt,J[RUNindex])` of Figure 4.69. The prefix bit is 0 if the run is interrupted by a different pixel. It is 1 if the run is terminated by the end of an image row.

The second main task of the encoder, encoding the interruption pixel, is similar to encoding the current pixel and is not discussed here.

Bibliography

Weinberger, M. J., G. Seroussi, and G. Sapiro (1996) "LOCO-I: A Low Complexity, Context-Based, Lossless Image Compression Algorithm," in *Proceedings of Data Compression Conference*, J. Storer, editor, Los Alamitos, CA, IEEE Computer Society Press, pp. 140–149.

4.8 Progressive Image Compression

Most modern image compression methods are either progressive or optionally so. Progressive compression is an attractive choice when compressed images are transmitted over a communications line and are decompressed and viewed in real time. When such an image is received and decompressed, the decoder can very quickly display the entire image in a low-quality format, and improve the display quality as more and more of the image is being received and decompressed. A user watching the image develop on the screen can normally recognize most of the image features after only 5–10% of it has been decompressed.

This should be compared to raster-scan image compression. When an image is raster scanned and compressed, a user normally cannot tell much about the image when only 5–10% of it has been decompressed and displayed. Since images are supposed to be viewed by humans, progressive compression makes sense even in cases where it is slower or less efficient than nonprogressive.

Perhaps a good way to think of progressive image compression is to imagine that the encoder compresses the most important image information first, then compresses less important information and appends it to the compressed stream, and so on. This explains why all progressive image compression methods have a natural lossy option; simply stop compressing at a certain point. The user can control the amount of loss by means of a parameter that tells the encoder how soon to stop the progressive encoding process. The sooner encoding is stopped, the better the compression ratio and the higher the data loss.

Another advantage of progressive compression becomes apparent when the compressed file has to be decompressed several times and displayed with different resolutions. The decoder can, in each case, stop the decompression when the image has reached the resolution of the particular output device used.

Progressive image compression has already been mentioned, in connection with JPEG (page 275). JPEG uses DCT to break the image up into its spatial frequency components, and it compresses the low-frequency components first. The decoder can therefore display these parts quickly, and it is these low-frequency parts that contain the general image information. The high-frequency parts contain image details. JPEG thus encodes spatial frequency data progressively.

It is useful to think of progressive decoding as the process of improving image features over time, and this can be done in three ways:

1. Encode spatial frequency data progressively. An observer watching such an image being decoded sees the image changing from blurred to sharp. Methods that work this way typically feature medium speed encoding and slow decoding. This type of progressive compression is sometimes called *SNR progressive* or *quality progressive*.
2. Start with a gray image and add colors or shades of gray to it. An observer watching such an image being decoded will see all the image details from the start, and will see them improve as more color is continuously added to them. Vector quantization methods (Section 4.12) use this kind of progressive compression. Such a method normally features slow encoding and fast decoding.
3. Encode the image in layers, where early layers consist of a few large low-resolution pixels, followed by later layers with smaller higher-resolution pixels. A person watching such an image being decoded will see more detail added to the image over time. Such a method thus adds detail (or resolution) to the image as it is being decompressed. This way of progressively encoding an image is called *pyramid coding* or *hierarchical coding*. Most progressive methods use this principle, so this section discusses general ideas for implementing pyramid coding. Figure 4.71 illustrates the three progressive methods mentioned here. It should be contrasted with Figure 4.70, which illustrates sequential decoding.

Assuming that the image size is $2^n \times 2^n = 4^n$ pixels, the simplest method that comes to mind, in trying to do progressive compression, is to calculate each pixel of layer $i-1$ as the average of a group of 2×2 pixels of layer i. Thus layer n is the entire image, layer $n-1$ contains $2^{n-1} \times 2^{n-1} = 4^{n-1}$ large pixels of size 2×2, and so on, down to layer 1, with $4^{n-n} = 1$ large pixel, representing the entire image. If the image isn't too large, all the layers can be saved in memory. The pixels are then written on the compressed stream in reverse order, starting with layer 1. The single pixel of layer 1 is the "parent" of the four pixels of layer 2, each of which is the parent of four pixels in layer 3, and so on. The total number of pixels in the pyramid is 33% more than the original number!

$$4^0 + 4^1 + \cdots + 4^{n-1} + 4^n = (4^{n+1} - 1)/3 \approx 4^n(4/3) \approx 1.33 \times 4^n = 1.33(2^n \times 2^n),$$

Figure 4.70: Sequential Decoding.

A simple way to bring the total number of pixels in the pyramid down to 4^n is to include only three of the four pixels of a group in layer i, and to compute the value of the 4th pixel using the parent of the group (from the preceding layer, $i-1$) and its three siblings.

Example: Figure 4.72c shows a 4×4 image that becomes the third layer in its progressive compression. Layer two is shown in Figure 4.72b, where, for example, pixel 81.25 is the average of the four pixels 90, 72, 140, and 23 of layer three. The single pixel of layer one is shown in Figure 4.72a.

The compressed file should contain just the numbers

$$54.125,\ 32.5, 41.5, 61.25,\ 72, 23, 140,\ 33, 18, 21,\ 18, 32, 44,\ 70, 59, 16,$$

(properly encoded, of course), from which all the missing pixel values can easily be calculated. The missing pixel 81.25, e.g., can be calculated from $(x + 32.5 + 41.5 + 61.25)/4 = 54.125$.

A small complication with this method is that averages of integers may be nonintegers. If we want our pixel values to remain integers we either have to lose precision or to keep using longer and longer integers. Assuming that pixels are represented by eight bits, adding four 8-bit integers produces a 10-bit integer. Dividing it by four, to create the average, reduces the sum back to an 8-bit integer, but some precision may be lost. If we don't want to lose precision, we should represent our second-layer pixels as 10-bit numbers and our first-layer (single) pixel as a 12-bit number. Figure 4.72d,e,f shows the results of rounding off our pixel values and thus losing some image information. The contents of the compressed file in this case should be

$$54,\ 33, 42, 61,\ 72, 23, 140,\ 33, 18, 21,\ 18, 32, 44,\ 70, 59, 16.$$

Figure 4.71: Progressive Decoding.

(a)

$$54.125$$

(b)

81.25	32.5
61.25	41.5

(c)

90	72	58	33
140	23	21	18
100	70	72	18
16	59	44	32

(d)

$$54$$

(e)

81	33
61	42

(f)

90	72	58	33
140	23	21	18
100	70	72	18
16	59	44	32

(g)

max
$$140$$

(h)

max 140	min 21
min 16	max 72

(i)

90	72	58	33
140	23	21	18
100	70	72	18
16	59	44	32

Figure 4.72: Progressive Image Compression.

The first missing pixel, 81, of layer three can be calculated from the equation $(x + 33 + 42 + 61)/4 = 54$, which yields the (slightly wrong) value 80.

⋄ **Exercise 4.22:** Show that the sum of four n-bit numbers is an $(n+2)$-bit number.

A better method is to let the parent of a group help in calculating the values of its four children. This can be done by calculating the differences between the parent and its children, and writing the differences (suitably coded) in layer i of the compressed stream. The decoder decodes the differences, then uses the parent from layer $i - 1$ to compute the values of the four pixels. Either Huffman or arithmetic coding can be used to encode the differences. If all the layers are calculated and saved in memory, then the distribution of difference values can be found and used to achieve the best statistical compression.

If there is no room in memory for all the layers, a simple adaptive model can be implemented. It starts by assigning a count of 1 to every difference value (to avoid the zero-probability problem). When a particular difference is calculated, it is assigned a probability and is encoded according to its count, and its count is then updated. It is a good idea to update the counts by incrementing them by a value greater than 1, since this way the original counts of 1 become insignificant very quickly.

Some improvement can be achieved if the parent is used to help calculate the values of three child pixels, and then these three plus the parent are used to calculate the value of the fourth pixel of the group. If the four pixels of a group are a, b, c, and d, then their average is $v = (a+b+c+d)/4$. The average becomes part of layer $i - 1$, and layer i need contain only the three differences $k = a - b$, $l = b - c$, and $m = c - d$. Once the decoder has read and decoded the three differences, it can use their values, together with the value of v from the previous layer, to compute the values of the four pixels of the group. Calculating v by a division by 4 still causes the loss of two bits, but this 2-bit quantity can be isolated before the division, and retained by encoding it separately, following the three differences.

The improvements mentioned above are based on the well-known fact that small numbers are easy to compress (page 32).

The parent pixel of a group does not have to be its average. One alternative is to select the maximum (or the minimum) pixel of a group as the parent. This has the advantage that the parent is identical to one of the pixels in the group. The encoder has to encode just three pixels in each group, and the decoder decodes three pixels (or differences) and uses the parent as the fourth pixel, to complete the group. When encoding consecutive groups in a layer, the encoder should alternate between selecting the maximum and the minimum as parents, since always selecting the same creates progressive layers that are either too dark or too bright. Figure 4.72g,h,i shows the three layers in this case.

The compressed file should contain the numbers

$$140, \ (0), 21, 72, 16, \ (3), 90, 72, 23, \ (3), 58, 33, 18, \ (0), 18, 32, 44, \ (3), 100, 70, 59,$$

where the numbers in parentheses are two bits each. They tell where (in what quadrant) the parent from the previous layer should go. Notice that quadrant numbering is $\left(\begin{smallmatrix} 0 & 1 \\ 3 & 2 \end{smallmatrix}\right)$.

Selecting the median of a group is a little slower than selecting the maximum or the minimum, but it improves the appearance of the layers during progressive decompression. In general, the median of a sequence $(a_1, a_2, \ldots, a_n)$ is an element a_i such that half the elements (or very close to half) are smaller than a_i and the other half are bigger. If the four pixels of a group satisfy $a < b < c < d$, then either b or c can be considered the median pixel of the group. The main advantage of selecting the median as the group's parent is that it tends to smooth large differences in pixel values that may occur because of one extreme pixel. In the group 1, 2, 3, 100, for example, selecting 2 or 3 as the parent is much more representative than selecting the average. Finding the median of four pixels requires a few comparisons, but calculating the average requires a division by 4 (or, alternatively, a right shift).

Once the median has been selected and encoded as part of layer $i - 1$, the remaining three pixels can be encoded in layer i by encoding their (three) differences, preceded by a 2-bit code telling which of the four is the parent. Another small advantage of using the median is that once the decoder reads this 2-bit code, it knows how many of the three pixels are smaller and how many are bigger than the median. If the code says, for example, that one pixel is smaller, and the other two are bigger than the median, and the decoder reads a pixel that's smaller than the median, it knows that the next two pixels decoded will be bigger than the median. This knowledge changes the distribution of the differences, and it can be taken advantage of by using three count tables to estimate probabilities when the differences are encoded. One table is used when a pixel is encoded that the decoder will know is bigger than the median. Another table is used to encode pixels that the decoder will know are smaller than the median, and the third table is used for pixels where the decoder will not know in advance their relations to the median.

This improves compression by a few percent and is another example of how adding more features to a compression method brings diminishing returns.

Some of the important progressive image compression methods used in practice are described in the rest of this chapter.

4.8.1 Growth Geometry Coding

The idea of growth geometry coding deserves its own section, since it combines image compression and progressive image transmission in an original and unusual way. This idea is due to Amalie J. Frank [Frank et al. 80], the originator of other image compression methods. The method is designed for progressive lossless compression of bi-level images. The idea is to start with some *seed* pixels and apply geometric rules to grow each seed pixel into a pattern of pixels. The encoder has the harder part of the job. It has to select the seed pixels, the growth rule for each seed, and the number of times the rule should be applied (the number of generations). Only this data is written on the compressed stream. Often, a group of seeds shares the same rule and the same number of generations. In such a case, the rule and number of generations are written once, following the coordinates of the seed pixels of the group. The decoder's job is simple. It reads the first group of seeds, applies the rule once, reads the next group and adds it to the pattern so far, applies the rule again, and so on. Compression is achieved if the number of seeds is small compared to the total image size, i.e., if each seed pixel is used to generate, on average, many image pixels.

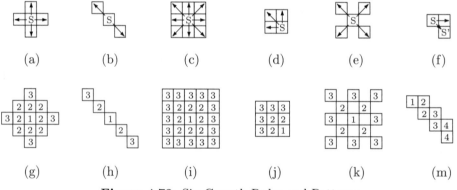

Figure 4.73: Six Growth Rules and Patterns.

Figure 4.73a–f shows six simple growth rules. Each adds some immediate neighbor pixels to the seed S, and the same rule is applied to these neighbors in the next generation (they become *secondary* seed pixels). Since a pixel can have up to eight immediate neighbors, there can be 256 such rules. Figure 4.73g–m shows the results of applying these rules twice (i.e., for two generations) to a single seed pixel. The pixels are numbered one plus the generation number. The growth rules can be as complex as necessary. For example, Figure 4.73m assumes that only pixel S' becomes a secondary seed. The resulting pattern of pixels may be solid or may have "holes" in it, as in Figure 4.73k.

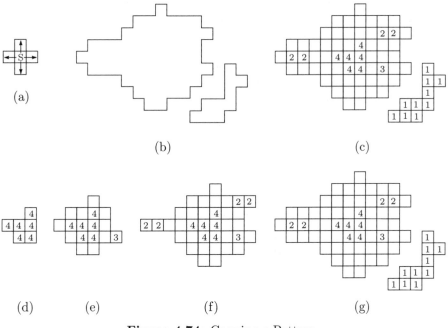

Figure 4.74: Growing a Pattern.

Figure 4.74 shows an example of how a simple growth rule (itself shown in Figure 4.74a) is used to grow the disconnected pattern of Figure 4.74b. The seed pixels are shown in Figure 4.74c. They are numbered 1–4 (one more than the number of generations). The decoder first inputs the six pixels marked 4 (Figure 4.74d). The growth rule is applied to them, producing the pattern of Figure 4.74e. The single pixel marked 3 is then input, and the rule applied again, to pixels 3 and 4, to form the pattern of Figure 4.74f. The four pixels marked 2 are input, and the rule applied again, to form the pattern of Figure 4.74g. Finally, the ten pixels marked 1 are read, to complete the image. The number of generations for these pixels is zero; they are not used to grow any other pixels, and so they do not contribute to the image compression. Notice that the pixels marked 4 go through three generations.

In this example, the encoder wrote the seed pixels on the compressed stream in order of decreasing number of generations. In principle, it is possible to complicate matters as much as desired. It is possible to use different growth rules for different groups of pixels (in such a case, the growth rules must tell unambiguously who the parent of a pixel P is, so that the decoder will know what growth rule to use for P), to stop growth if a pixel comes to within a specified distance of other pixels, to change the growth rule when a new pixel bumps into another pixel, to reverse direction in such a case and start erasing pixels, or to use any other algorithm. In practice, however, complex rules need more bits to encode them, so perhaps simple rules can lead to better compression.

⋄ **Exercise 4.23:** Simple growth rules have another advantage. What is it?

Figure 4.75 illustrates a simple approach to the design of a recursive encoder that identifies the seed pixels in layers. We assume that the only growth rule used is the one shown in Figure 4.75a. All the black (foreground) pixels are initially marked 1, and the white (background) pixels (not shown in the figure) are marked 0. The encoder scans the image and marks by 2 each 1-pixel that can grow. In order for a 1-pixel to grow it must be surrounded by 1-pixels on all four sides. The next layer consists of the resulting 2-pixels, shown in Figure 4.75c. The encoder next looks for 1-pixels that do not have at least one flanking 2-pixel. These are seed pixels. There are 10 of them, marked with a gray background in Figure 4.75c.

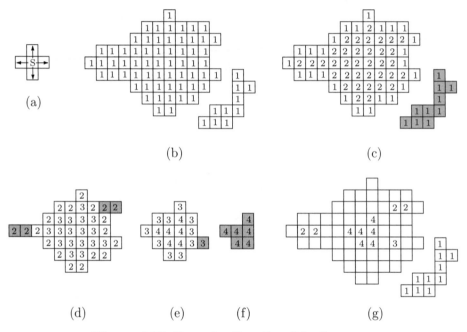

Figure 4.75: Recursive Encoding Of a Pattern.

The same process is applied to the layer of 2-pixels. The encoder scans the image and marks by 3 each 2-pixel that can grow. The next (third) layer consists of the resulting 3-pixels, shown in Figure 4.75d. The encoder next looks for 2-pixels that do not have at least one flanking 3-pixel. These are seed pixels. There are four of them, marked with a gray background in Figure 4.75d.

Figure 4.75e shows the fourth layer. It consists of six 4-pixels and one seed 3-pixel (marked in gray). Figure 4.75f shows the six seed 4-pixels, and the final seed pixels are shown in Figure 4.75g.

This basic algorithm can be extended in a number of ways, most notably by using several growth rules for each layer, instead of just one.

Bibliography

Frank, Amalie J., J. D. Daniels, and Diane R. Unangst (1980) "Progressive Image Transmission Using a Growth-Geometry Coding," *Proceedings of the IEEE*, **68**(7):897–909.

4.9 JBIG

No single compression method can efficiently compress every type of data. This is why new special-purpose methods are being developed all the time. JBIG is one of them. It has been developed specifically for progressive compression of bi-level images. Such images, also called monochromatic or black and white, are common in applications where drawings (technical or artistic), with or without text, need to be saved in a database and retrieved. It is customary to use the terms "foreground" and "background" instead of black and white, respectively.

The term "progressive compression" means that the image is saved in several "layers" in the compressed stream, at higher and higher resolutions. When such an image is decompressed and viewed, the viewer first sees an imprecise, rough, image (the first layer) followed by improved versions of it (later layers). This way, if the image is the wrong one, it can be rejected at an early stage, without having to retrieve and decompress all of it. Section 4.8 shows how each high-resolution layer uses information from the preceding lower-resolution layer, so there is no duplication of data. This feature is supported by JBIG, where it is an option called *deterministic prediction*.

Even though JBIG was designed for bi-level images, where each pixel is one bit, it is possible to apply it to grayscale images by separating the bitplanes and compressing each individually, as if it were a bi-level image. RGC (*reflected Gray code*) should be used, instead of the standard binary code, as discussed in Section 4.2.1.

The name JBIG stands for Joint Bi-Level Image Processing Group. This is a group of experts from several international organizations, formed in 1988 to recommend such a standard. The official name of the JBIG method is "ITU-T recommendation T.82." ITU is the International Telecommunications Union (part of the United Nations). The ITU-T is the telecommunication standardization sector of the ITU. JBIG uses multiple arithmetic coding to compress the image, and this part of JBIG, which is discussed below, is separate from the progressive compression part discussed in Section 4.9.1.

An important feature of the definition of JBIG is that the operation of the encoder is not defined in detail. The JBIG standard discusses the details of the decoder and the format of the compressed file. It is implied that any encoder that generates a JBIG file is a valid JBIG encoder. The JBIG2 method of Section 4.10 adopts the same approach, since this allows implementers to come up with sophisticated encoders that analyze the original image in ways that could not have been envisioned at the time the standard was defined.

One feature of arithmetic coding is that it is easy to separate the statistical model (the table with frequencies and probabilities) from the encoding and decoding operations. It is easy to encode, for example, the first half of a data stream using one model, and the second half using another model. This is called *multiple arithmetic coding*, and it is especially useful in encoding images, since it takes advantage of any local structures and interrelationships that might exist in the image. JBIG uses multiple arithmetic coding with many models, each a two-entry table that gives the probabilities of a white and a black pixel. There are between 1,024 and 4,096 such models, depending on the image resolution used.

A bi-level image is made up of foreground (black) and background (white) dots called *pixels*. The simplest way to compress such an image using arithmetic coding is to count the frequency of black and white pixels, and compute their probabilities. In practice, however, the probabilities change from region to region in the image, and this fact can be used to produce better compression. Certain regions, such as the margins of a page, may be completely white, while other regions, such as the center of a complex diagram, or a large, thick rule, may be predominantly or completely black.

Consider an image with 25% black pixels. Its entropy is $-0.25 \log_2 0.25 - 0.75 \log_2 0.75 \approx 0.8113$. The best that we can hope for is to represent each pixel with 0.81 bits instead of the original 1 bit: an 81% compression ratio (or 0.81 bpp). Now assume that we discover that 80% of the image is predominantly white, with just 10% black pixels, and the remaining 20% have 85% black pixels. The entropies of these parts are $-0.1 \log_2 0.1 - 0.9 \log_2 0.9 \approx 0.47$ and $-0.85 \log_2 0.85 - 0.15 \log_2 0.15 \approx 0.61$, so if we encode each part separately, we can have 0.47 bpp 80% of the time and 0.61 bpp the remaining 20%. On the average this results in 0.498 bpp, or a compression ratio of about 50%; much better than 81%!

We assume that a white pixel is represented by a 0 and a black one by a 1. In practice, we don't know in advance how many black and white pixels exist in each part of the image, so the JBIG encoder stops at every pixel and examines a *template* made of the 10 neighboring pixels marked "X" and "A" above it and to its left (those that have already been input; the ones below and to the right are still unknown). It interprets the values of these 10 pixels as a 10-bit integer which is then used as a pointer to a statistical model, which, in turn, is used to encode the current pixel (marked by a "?"). There are $2^{10} = 1{,}024$ 10-bit integers, so there should be 1,024 models. Each model is a small table consisting of the probabilities of black and white pixels (just one probability needs be saved in the table, since the probabilities add up to 1).

Figure 4.76a,b shows the two templates used for the lowest-resolution layer. The encoder decides whether to use the three-line or the two-line template and sets parameter `LRLTWO` in the compressed file to 0 or 1, respectively, to indicate this choice to the decoder. (The two-line template results in somewhat faster execution, while the three-line template produces slightly better compression.) Figure 4.76c shows the 10-bit template 0001001101, which becomes the pointer 77. The pointer shown in Figure 4.76d for pixel Y is 0000100101 or 37. Whenever any of the pixels used by the templates lies outside the image, the JBIG edge convention mentioned earlier should be used.

Figure 4.77 shows the four templates used for all the other layers. These templates reflect the fact that when any layer, except the first one, is decoded the low-resolution pixels from the preceding layer are known to the decoder. Each of the four templates is used to encode (and later decode) one of the four high-resolution pixels of a group. The context (pointer) generated in these cases consists of 12 bits, 10 taken from the template's pixels and two generated to indicate which of the four pixels in the group is being processed. The number of statistical models should thus be $2^{12} = 4096$. The two bits indicating the position of a high-resolution pixel in its group are 00 for the top-left pixel (Figure 4.77a), 01 for the top-right

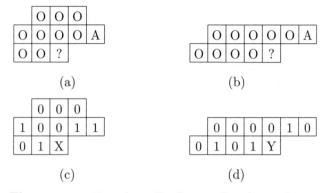

Figure 4.76: Templates For Lowest-Resolution Layer.

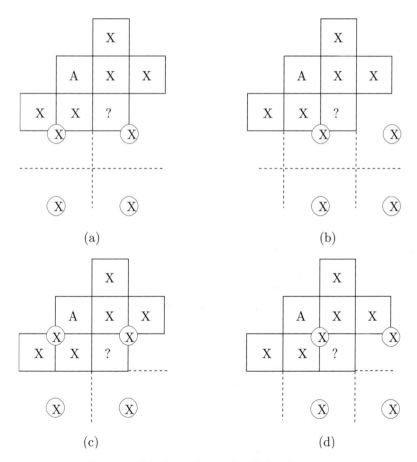

Figure 4.77: Templates For Other Layers.

(Figure 4.77b), 10 for the bottom-left (Figure 4.77c), and 11 for the bottom-right pixel (Figure 4.77d).

The use of these templates implies that the JBIG probability model is a 10th-order or a 12th-order Markov model.

The template pixels labeled "A" are called *adaptive pixels* (AP). The encoder is allowed to use as AP a pixel other than the one specified in the template, and it uses two parameters T_x and T_y (one byte each) in each layer to indicate to the decoder the actual location of the AP in that layer. (The AP is not allowed to overlap one of the "X" pixels in the template.) A sophisticated JBIG encoder may notice, for example, that the image uses halftone patterns where a black pixel normally has another black pixel three rows above it. In such a case the encoder may decide to use the pixel three rows above "?" as the AT. Figure 4.78 shows the image area where the AP may reside. Parameter M_x can vary in the range $[0, 127]$, while M_y can take the values 0 through 255.

M_x, M_y	$\cdots$	$2, M_y$	$1, M_y$	$0, M_y$	$-1, M_y$	$-2, M_y$	$\cdots$	$-M_x, M_y$
$\vdots$		$\vdots$		$\vdots$				
$M_x, 1$	$\cdots$	$2, 1$	$1, 1$	$0, 1$	$-1, 1$	$-2, 1$	$\cdots$	$-M_x, 1$
$M_x, 0$	$\cdots$	$2, 0$	$1, 0$	?				

Figure 4.78: Coordinates And Allowed Positions of AT Pixels.

4.9.1 Progressive Compression

One advantage of the JBIG method is its ability to generate low-resolution versions (layers) of the image in the compressed stream. The decoder decompresses these layers progressively, from the lowest to the highest resolution.

We first look at the order of the layers. The encoder is given the entire image (the highest-resolution layer), so it is natural for it to construct the layers from high to low resolution and write them on the compressed file in this order. The decoder, on the other hand, has to start by decompressing and displaying the lowest-resolution layer, so it is easiest for it to read this layer first. As a result, either the encoder or the decoder should use buffering to reverse the order of the layers. If fast decoding is important, the encoder should use buffers to accumulate all the layers, then write them on the compressed file from low to high resolutions. The decoder then reads the layers in the right order. In cases where fast encoding is important (such as an archive that's being updated often but is rarely decompressed and used), the encoder should write the layers in the order in which they are generated (from high to low) and the decoder should use buffers. The JBIG standard allows either method, and the encoder has to set a bit denoted by HITOLO in the compressed file to either zero (layers are in low to high order) or one (the opposite case). It is implied that the encoder decides what the resolution of the lowest layer should be (it doesn't have to be a single pixel). This decision may be based on user input or on information built in the encoder about the specific needs of a particular environment.

Progressive compression in JBIG also involves the concept of *stripes*. A stripe is a narrow horizontal band consisting of L scan lines of the image, where L is a user-controlled JBIG parameter. As an example, if L is chosen such that the height of a stripe is 8 mm (about 0.3 inches), then there will be about 36 stripes in an 11.5-inch-high image. The encoder writes the stripes on the compressed file in one of two ways, setting parameter SET to indicate this to the decoder. Either all the stripes of a layer are written on the compressed file consecutively, followed by the stripes of the next layer, and so on (SET=0), or the top stripes of all the layers are first written, followed by the second stripes of all the layers, and so on (SET=1). If the encoder sets SET=0, then the decoder will decompress the image progressively, layer by layer, and in each layer stripe by stripe. Figure 4.79 illustrates the case of an image divided into four stripes and encoded in three layers (from low-resolution 150 dpi to high-resolution 600 dpi). Table 4.80 lists the order in which the stripes are output for the four possible values of parameters HITOLO and SET.

0	4	8
1	5	9
2	6	10
3	7	11

| layer 1 | layer 2 | layer 3 |
| 150 dpi | 300 dpi | 600 dpi |

Figure 4.79: Four Stripes and Three Layers In a JBIG Image.

HITOLO	SEQ	Order
0	0	0,1,2,3,4,5,6,7,8,9,10,11
0	1	0,4,8,1,5,9,2,6,10,3,7,11
1	0	8,9,10,11,4,5,6,7,0,1,2,3
1	1	8,4,0,9,5,1,10,6,2,11,7,3

Table 4.80: The Four Possible Orders of Layers.

The basic idea of progressive compression is to group four high-resolution pixels into one low-resolution pixel, a process called *downsampling*. The only problem is to determine the value (black or white) of that pixel. If all four original pixels have the same value, or even if three are identical, the solution is obvious (follow the majority). When two pixels are black and the other two are white, we can try one of the following solutions:

1. Create a low-resolution pixel that's always black (or always white). This is a bad solution, since it may eliminate important details of the image, making it impractical or even impossible for an observer to evaluate the image by viewing the low-resolution layer.

2. Assign a random value to the new low-resolution pixel. This solution is also bad, since it may add too much noise to the image.

3. Give the low-resolution pixel the color of the top-left of the four high-resolution pixels. This prefers the top row and the left column, and has the drawback that thin lines can sometimes be completely missing from the low-resolution layer. Also, if the high-resolution layer uses halftoning to simulate grayscales, the halftone patterns may be corrupted.

4. Assign a value to the low-resolution pixel that depends on the four high-resolution pixels **and** on some of their nearest neighbors. This solution is used by JBIG. If most of the near neighbors are white, a white low-resolution pixel is created; otherwise, a black low-resolution pixel is created. Figure 4.81a shows the 12 high-resolution neighboring pixels and the three low-resolution ones that are used in making this decision. A, B, and C are three low-resolution pixels whose values have already been determined. Pixels d, e, f, g, and, j are on top or to the left of the current group of four pixels. Pixel "?" is the low-resolution pixel whose value needs to be determined.

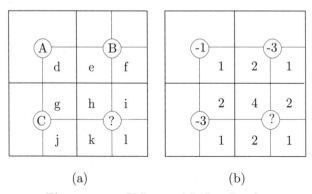

(a)   (b)

Figure 4.81: HiRes and LoRes Pixels.

Figure 4.81b shows the weights assigned to the various pixels involved in the determination of pixel "?". The weighted sum of the pixels can also be written as

$$4h + 2(e + g + i + k) + (d + f + j + l) - 3(B + C) - A$$
$$= 4h + 2(i + k) + l + (d - A) + 2(g - C) + (j - C) + 2(e - B) + (f - B). \tag{4.19}$$

The second line of Equation (4.19) shows how the value of pixel "?" depends on differences such as $d - A$ (a difference of a high-resolution pixel and the adjacent low-resolution one). Assuming equal probabilities for black and white pixels, the first line of Equation (4.19) can have values between zero (when all 12 pixels are white) and 9 (when all are black), so the rule is to assign pixel "?" the value 1 (black) if expression (4.19) is greater than 4.5 (if it is 5 or more), and the value 0 (white) otherwise (if it is 4 or less). This expression thus acts as a filter that preserves the density of the high-resolution pixels in the low-resolution image.

◇ **Exercise 4.24:** We normally represent a black (or "foreground") pixel with a binary 1, and a white (or "background") pixel with a binary 0. How will the resolution reduction method above change if we use 0 to represent black and 1 to represent white?

Since the image is divided into groups of 4×4 pixels, it should have an even number of rows and columns. The JBIG *edge convention* says that an image can be extended if and when necessary by adding columns of 0 pixels at the left and right, rows of 0 pixels at the top, and by replicating the bottom row as many times as necessary.

The JBIG method of resolution reduction has been carefully designed and extensively tested. It is known to produce excellent results for text, drawings, halftoned grayscales, as well as for other types of images.

JBIG also includes exceptions to the above rule in order to preserve edges (132 exceptions), preserve vertical and horizontal lines (420 exceptions), periodic patterns in the image (10 exceptions, for better performance in regions of transition to and from periodic patterns), and dither patterns in the image (12 exceptions that help preserve very low density or very high density dithering, i.e., isolated background or foreground pixels). The last two groups are used to preserve certain shading patterns and also patterns generated by halftoning. Each exception is a 12-bit number. Table 4.82 lists some of the exception patterns.

Figure 4.83 shows three typical exception patterns. A pattern of six zeros and three ones, as in Figure 4.83a, is an example exception, introduced to preserve horizontal lines. It means that the low-resolution pixel marked "C" should be complemented (assigned the opposite of its normal value). The normal value of this pixel depends, of course, on the three low-resolution pixels above it and to the left. Since these three pixels can have 8 different values, this pattern covers eight exceptions. Reflecting 4.83a about its main diagonal produces a pattern (actually, eight patterns) that's natural to use as an exception to preserve vertical lines in the original image. Figure 4.83a thus corresponds to 16 of the 420 line-preservation exceptions.

The pattern of Figure 4.83b was developed in order to preserve thick horizontal, or near-horizontal, lines. A two-pixel-wide high-resolution horizontal line, e.g., will result in a low-resolution line whose width alternates between one and two low-resolution pixels. When the upper row of the high-resolution line is scanned, it will result in a row of low-resolution pixels because of Figure 4.83a. When the next high-resolution row is scanned, the two rows of the thick line will generate alternating low-resolution pixels because pattern 4.83b requires a zero in the bottom-left low-resolution pixel in order to complement the bottom-right low-resolution pixel.

Pattern 4.83b leaves two pixels unspecified, so it counts for four patterns. Its

The 10 periodic pattern preservation exceptions are (in hex)

5c7 36d d55 b55 caa aaa c92 692 a38 638.

The 12 dither pattern preservation exceptions are

fef fd7 f7d f7a 145 142 ebd eba 085 082 028 010.

The 132 edge-preservation exception patterns are

a0f 60f 40f 20f e07 c07 a07 807 607 407 207 007 a27 627 427 227 e1f 61f e17 c17 a17 617 e0f c0f 847 647 447 247 e37 637 e2f c2f a2f 62f e27 c27 24b e49 c49 a49 849 649 449 249 049 e47 c47 a47 e4d c4d a4d 84d 64d 44d 24d e4b c4b a4b 64b 44b e69 c69 a69 669 469 269 e5b 65b e59 c59 a59 659 ac9 6c9 4c9 2c9 ab6 8b6 e87 c87 a87 687 487 287 507 307 cf8 8f8 ed9 6d9 ecb ccb acb 6cb ec9 cc9 949 749 549 349 b36 336 334 f07 d07 b07 907 707 3b6 bb4 3b4 bb2 3a6 b96 396 d78 578 f49 d49 b49 ff8 df8 5f8 df0 5f0 5e8 dd8 5d8 5d0 db8 fb6 bb6

where the 12 bits of each pattern are numbered as in the diagram.

Table 4.82: Some JBIG Exception Patterns.

reflection is also used, to preserve thick vertical lines, so it counts for 8 of the 420 line-preservation exceptions.

Figure 4.83c complements a low-resolution pixel in cases where there is 1 black high-resolution pixel among 11 white ones. This is common when a grayscale image is converted to black and white by halftoning. This pattern is 1 of the 12 dither preservation exceptions.

The JBIG method for reducing resolution seems complicated—especially since it includes so many exceptions—but is actually simple to implement, and also executes very fast. The decision whether to paint the current low-resolution pixel black or white depends on 12 of its neighboring pixels, 9 high-resolution pixels, and

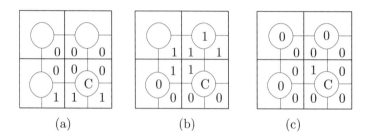

Figure 4.83: Some JBIG Exception Patterns.

3 low-resolution ones. Their values are combined into a 12-bit number, which is used as a pointer to a 4,096-entry table. Each entry in the table is one bit, which becomes the value of the current low-resolution pixel. This way, all the exceptions are already included in the table and don't require any special treatment by the program.

It has been mentioned in Section 4.8 that compression is improved if the encoder writes on the compressed stream only three of the four pixels of a group in layer i. This is enough because the decoder can compute the value of the 4th pixel from its three siblings and the parent of the group (the parent is from the preceding layer, $i-1$). Equation (4.19) shows that in JBIG, a low-resolution pixel is not calculated as a simple average of its four high-resolution "children," so it may not be possible for the JBIG decoder to calculate the value of, say, high-resolution pixel k from the values of its three siblings h, i, and l and their parent. The many exceptions used by JBIG also complicate this calculation. As a result, JBIG uses special tables to tell both encoder and decoder which high-resolution pixels can be inferred from their siblings and parents. Such pixels are not compressed by the encoder, but all the other high-resolution pixels of the layer are. This method is referred to as *deterministic prediction* (DP), and is a JBIG option. If the encoder decides to use it, it sets parameter DPON to one.

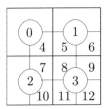

Figure 4.84: Pixel Numbering For Deterministic Prediction.

Figure 4.84 shows the pixel numbering used for deterministic prediction. Before it compresses high-resolution pixel 8, the encoder combines the values of pixels 0–7 to form an 8-bit pointer to the first DP table. If the table entry is 2, then pixel 8 should be compressed, since the decoder cannot infer it from its neighbors. If the table entry is 0 or 1, the encoder ignores pixel 8. The decoder prepares the same pointer (since pixels 0–7 are known when pixel 8 should be decoded). If the table entry is 0 or 1, the decoder assigns this value to pixel 8; otherwise (if the table entry is 2), the next pixel value is decoded from the compressed file and is assigned to pixel 8. Notice that of the 256 entries of Table 4.85 only 20 are not 2. Pixel 9 is handled similarly, except that the pointer used consists of pixels 0–8, and it points to an entry in the second DP table. This table, shown in 4.86, consists of 512 entries, of which 108 are not 2. The JBIG standard also specifies the third DP table, for pixel 10 (1024 entries, of which 526 are not 2), and the fourth table, for pixel 11 (2048 entries, of which 1044 are not 2). The total size of the four tables is 3840 entries, of which 1698 (or about 44%) actually predict pixel values.

Pointer	Value
0–63	02222222 22222222 22222222 22222222 02222222 22222222 22222222 22222222
64–127	02222222 22222222 22222222 22222222 00222222 22222222 22222222 22222222
128–191	02222222 22222222 00222222 22222222 02020222 22222222 02022222 22222222
192–255	00222222 22222222 22222222 22222221 02020022 22222222 22222222 22222222

Table 4.85: Predicting Pixel 8.

Pointer	Value
0–63	22222222 22222222 22222222 22000000 02222222 22222222 00222222 22111111
64–127	22222222 22222222 22222222 21111111 02222222 22111111 22222222 22112221
128–191	02222222 22222222 02222222 22222222 00222222 22222200 20222222 22222222
192–255	02222222 22111111 22222222 22222102 11222222 22222212 22220022 22222212
256–319	20222222 22222222 00220222 22222222 20000222 22222222 00000022 22222221
320–383	20222222 22222222 11222222 22222221 22222222 22222221 22221122 22222221
384–447	20020022 22222222 22000022 22222222 20202002 22222222 20220002 22222222
448–511	22000022 22222222 00220022 22222221 21212202 22222222 22220002 22222222

Table 4.86: Predicting Pixel 9.

Bibliography

Pennebaker, W. B., and J. L. Mitchell (1988) "Probability Estimation for the Q-coder," *IBM Journal of Research and Development* **32**(6):717–726.

Pennebaker, W. B., et al. (1988) "An Overview of the Basic Principles of the Q-coder Adaptive Binary Arithmetic Coder," *IBM J. of Research and Development* **32**(6):737–752.

4.10 JBIG2

They have done it again! The Joint Bi-Level Image Processing Group has produced another standard for the compression of bi-level images. The new standard is called JBIG2, implying that the old standard should be called JBIG1. At the time of writing (late 1998) JBIG2 is just a draft (which is why there is no bibliography at the end of this section), but it is expected to be approved by the ISO and the ITU-T in 1999. Current information about JBIG2 can be found at http://www.jpeg.org/public/jbigpt2.htm. Comments and questions to the JBIG committee can be sent to jbig2@parc.xerox.com. The JBIG2 standard is expected to offer:

1. Large increases in compression performance (typically 3–5 times better than Group 4/MMR, and 2–4 times better than JBIG1).

2. Special compression methods for text, halftones, and other bi-level image parts.

3. Lossy and lossless compression.

4. Two modes of progressive compression. Mode 1 is quality-progressive compression, where the decoded image progresses from low to high quality. Mode 2 is content-progressive coding, where important image parts (such as text) are decoded first, followed by less-important parts (such as halftone patterns).

5. Multipage document compression.

6. Flexible format, designed for easy embedding in other image file formats, such as TIFF.

7. Fast decompression: Using some coding modes, images can be decompressed at over 250 million pixels/second in software.

The JBIG2 standard describes the principles of the compression and the format of the compressed file. It does not get into the operation of the encoder. Any encoder that produces a JBIG2 compressed file is a valid JBIG2 encoder. It is hoped that this will encourage software developers to implement sophisticated JBIG2 encoders. The JBIG2 decoder reads the compressed file, which contains dictionaries and image information, and decompresses it into the *page buffer*. The image is then displayed or printed from the page buffer. Several auxiliary buffers may also be used by the decoder.

A document to be compressed by JBIG2 may consist of more than one page. The main feature of JBIG2 is that is distinguishes among text, halftone images, and everything else on the page. The JBIG2 encoder should somehow scan the page before doing any encoding, and identify *regions* of three types:

1. Text regions. These contain text, normally arranged in rows. The text does not have to be in any specific language, and may consist of unknown symbols, dingbats, musical notation, or hieroglyphs. The encoder treats each symbol as a rectangular bitmap, which it places in a dictionary. The dictionary is compressed by either arithmetic coding or MMR (Section 2.13.2) and written, as a segment, on the compressed file. Similarly, the text region itself is encoded and written on the compressed file as another segment. To encode a text region the encoder prepares the relative coordinates of each symbol (the coordinates relative to the preceding symbol), and a pointer to the symbol's bitmap in the dictionary. (It is also possible to have pointers to several bitmaps and specify the symbol as an aggregation of those bitmaps, such as logical AND, OR, or XOR.) This data also is encoded before being written on the compressed file. Compression is achieved if the same symbol occurs several times. Notice that the symbol may occur in different text regions and even on different pages. The encoder should make sure that the dictionary containing this symbol's bitmap will be retained by the decoder for as long as necessary. Lossy compression is achieved if the same bitmap is used for symbols that are slightly different.

2. Halftone regions. A bi-level image may contain a grayscale image done in halftone [Salomon 99]. The encoder scans such a region cell by cell (halftone cells, also called patterns, are typically 3×3 or 4×4 pixels). A halftone dictionary is created by collecting all the different cells and converting each to an integer (typically 9 bits or 16 bits). The dictionary is compressed and is written on the compressed file. Each cell in the halftone region is then replaced by a pointer to the dictionary. The same dictionary can be used to decode several halftone dictionaries, perhaps located on different pages of the document. The encoder should label each dictionary so the decoder would know how long to retain it.

3. Generic regions. Any region not identified by the encoder as text or halftone becomes a generic region. Such a region may contain a large character, line art, math expressions, or even noise (specks and dirt). A generic region is compressed with either arithmetic coding or MMR. When the former is used, the probability

of each pixel is determined by its context (i.e., some pixels above it and to its left that have already been encoded).

A page may contain any number of regions, and they may overlap. The regions are determined by the encoder, whose operation is not specified by the JBIG2 standard. As a result, a simple JBIG2 encoder may encode any page as one large generic region, while a sophisticated encoder may spend time analyzing the contents of a page and identifying several regions, thereby leading to better compression. Figure 4.87 is an example of a page with four text regions, one halftone region, and two generic region (a sheared face and fingerprints).

1. Text regions. These contain text, normally arranged in rows. The text does not have to be in any specificlanguage, and may consist of unknown symbols, dingbats, music notes, or hieroglyphs. The encoder treats each symbol as a rectangular bitmap which it places in a dictionary. The dictionary is compressed by either arithmetic coding or MMR and written, as a segment, on the compressed file. Similarly, the text region itself is encoded and written on the compressed file as another segment. To encode a text region the encoder prepares the relative coordinates of each symbol (the coordinates relative to the preceding symbol), and a pointer to the symbol's bitmap in the dictionary. (It is also possible to have pointers to several bitmaps and specify the symbol as an aggregation of those bitmaps, suchas logical AND, OR, or XOR.) This data also is encoded before being written on the compressed file. Compression is achieved if the same symbol occurs several times. Notice that thesymbol may occur in different text regions

2. Halftone regions. A bi-level image may contain a grayscale image done in halftone. The encoder scans such a region cell by cell (halftone cells, also called patterns, are typically. A halftone dictionary is created by collecting all the different cells, and converting each to an integer (typically 9 bits or 16 bits).

Example of shearing

Lena in halftone (2 by 2 inches)

Figure 4.87: Typical JBIG2 Regions.

The fact that the JBIG2 standard does not specify the encoder is also used to generate lossy compression. A sophisticated encoder may decide that dropping certain pixels would not deteriorate the appearance of the image significantly. The encoder therefore drops those bits and creates a small compressed file. The decoder operates as usual and does not know whether the image that's being decoded is lossy or not. Another approach to lossy compression is for the encoder to identify symbols that are very similar and replace them by pointers to the same bitmap in the symbol dictionary (this approach is risky, since symbols that differ by just a few pixels may be completely different to a human reader, think of "e" and "c" or "i" and "l"). An encoder may also be able to identify specks and dirt in the document and optionally ignore them.

JBIG2 introduces the concept of region *refinement*. The compressed file may include instructions directing the decoder to decode a region A from the compressed file into an auxiliary buffer. That buffer may later be used to refine the decoding of another region B. When B is found in the compressed file and is decoded into the page buffer, each pixel written in the page buffer is determined by pixels decoded from the compressed file *and* by pixels in the auxiliary buffer. One example of region refinement is a document where certain text regions contains the words "Top Secret" in large, gray type, centered as a background. A simple JBIG2 encoder may consider each of the pixels constituting "Top Secret" part of some symbol. A sophisticated encoder may identify the common background, treat it as a generic region, and compress it as a region refinement, to be applied to certain text regions by the decoder. Another example of region refinement is a document where certain halftone regions have dark background. A sophisticated encoder may identify the dark background in those regions, treat it as a generic region, and place instructions in the compressed file telling the decoder to use this region to refine certain halftone regions. Thus, a simple JBIG2 encoder may never use region refinement, but a sophisticated one may use this concept to add special effects to some regions.

The decoder starts by initializing the page buffer to a certain value, 0 or 1, according to a code read from the compressed file. It then inputs the rest of the file segment by segment and executes each segment by a different procedure. There are seven main procedures.

1. The procedure to decode segment headers. Each segment starts with a header that includes, among other things, the segment's type, the destination of the decoded output from the segment, and what other segments must be used in decoding this segment.

2. A procedure to decode a generic region. This is invoked when the decoder finds a segment describing such a region. The segment is compressed with either arithmetic coding or MMR, and the procedure decompresses it (pixel by pixel in the former case and runs of pixels in the latter). In the case of arithmetic coding, previously decoded pixels are used to form a prediction context. Once a pixel is decoded, the procedure does not simply store it in the page buffer, but combines it with the pixel already in the page buffer according to a logical operation (AND, OR, XOR, or XNOR) specified in the segment.

3. A procedure to decode a generic refinement region. This is similar to the above except that it modifies an auxiliary buffer instead of the page buffer.

4. A procedure to decode a symbol dictionary. This is invoked when the decoder finds a segment containing such a dictionary. The dictionary is decompressed and

is stored as a list of symbols. Each symbol is a bitmap that is either explicitly specified in the dictionary or is specified as a refinement (i.e., a modification) of a known symbol (a preceding symbol from this dictionary or a symbol from another existing dictionary) or is specified as an aggregate (a logical combination) of several known symbols).

5. A procedure to decode a symbol region. This is invoked when the decoder finds a segment describing such a region. The segment is decompressed and it yields triplets. The triplet for a symbol contains the coordinates of the symbol relative to the preceding symbol and a pointer (index) to the symbol in the symbol dictionary. Since the decoder may keep several symbol dictionaries at any time, the segment should indicate which dictionary is to be used. The symbol's bitmap is brought from the dictionary, and the pixels are combined with the pixels in the page buffer according to the logical operation specified by the segment.

6. A procedure to decode a halftone dictionary. This is invoked when the decoder finds a segment containing such a dictionary. The dictionary is decompressed and is stored as a list of halftone patterns (fixed-size bitmaps).

7. A procedure to decode a halftone region. This is invoked when the decoder finds a segment describing such a region. The segment is decompressed into a set of pointers (indexes) to the patterns in the halftone dictionary.

Some of these procedures are described below in more detail

4.10.1 Generic Region Decoding

This procedure reads several parameters from the compressed file (Table 4.88, where "I" stands for integer and "B" stands for bitmap), the first of which, **MMR**, specifies the compression method used in the segment about to be decoded. Either arithmetic coding or MMR can be used. The former is similar to arithmetic coding in JBIG1 and is described below. The latter is used as in fax compression (Section 2.13).

If arithmetic coding is used, pixels are decoded one by one and are placed row by row in the generic region being decoded (part of the page buffer), whose width and height are given by parameters **GBW** and **GBH**, respectively. They are not simply stored there but are logically combined with the existing background pixels. Recall that the decompression process in arithmetic coding requires knowledge of the probabilities of the items being decompressed (decoded). These probabilities are obtained in our case by generating a template for each pixel being decoded, using the template to generate an integer (the context of the pixel), and using that integer as a pointer to a table of probabilities. Parameter **GBTEMPLATE** specifies which of four types of templates should be used. Figure 4.89a–d shows the four templates that correspond to **GBTEMPLATE** values of 0–3, respectively (notice that the two 10-bit templates are identical to templates used by JBIG1, Figure 4.76b,d). The pixel labeled "O" is the one being decoded, and the "X" and the "A_i" are known pixels. If "O" is near an edge of the region, its missing neighbors are assumed to be zero.

The values of the "X" and "A_i" pixels (one bit per pixel) are combined to form a context (an integer) of between 10 and 16 bits. It is expected that the bits will be collected top to bottom and left to right, but the standard does not spec-

Name	Type	Size	Signed?	Description
MMR	I	1	N	MMR or arithcoding used
GBW	I	32	N	Width of region
GBH	I	32	N	Height of region
GBTEMPLATE	I	2	N	Template number
TPON	I	1	N	Typical prediction used?
USESKIP	I	1	N	Skip some pixels?
SKIP	B			Bitmap for skipping
GBATX$_1$	I	8	Y	Relative X coordinate of A_1
GBATY$_1$	I	8	Y	Relative Y coordinate of A_1
GBATX$_2$	I	8	Y	Relative X coordinate of A_2
GBATY$_2$	I	8	Y	Relative Y coordinate of A_2
GBATX$_3$	I	8	Y	Relative X coordinate of A_3
GBATY$_3$	I	8	Y	Relative Y coordinate of A_3
GBATX$_4$	I	8	Y	Relative X coordinate of A_4
GBATY$_4$	I	8	Y	Relative Y coordinate of A_4

Table 4.88: Parameters For Decoding a Generic Region.

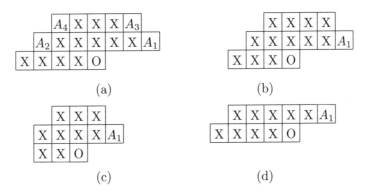

(a) (b)

(c) (d)

Figure 4.89: Four Templates For Generic Region Decoding.

ify that. The two templates of Figure 4.90a,b, e.g., should produce the contexts 1100011100010111 and 1000011011001, respectively. Once a context has been computed, it is used as a pointer to a probability table, and the probability found is sent to the arithmetic decoder to decode pixel "O."

The encoder specifies which of the four template types should be used. A simple rule of thumb is to use large templates for large regions.

An interesting feature of the templates is the use of the A_i pixels. They are called *adaptive* or AT pixels and can be located in positions other than the ones shown. Figure 4.89 shows their normal positions, but a sophisticated encoder may discover, for example, that the pixel three rows above the current pixel "O" is always identical to "O." The encoder may thus tell the decoder (by means of pa-

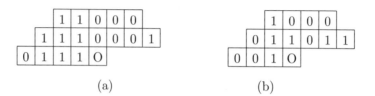

(a)   (b)

Figure 4.90: Two Templates.

rameters **GBATX**$_i$ and **GBATY**$_i$) to look for A_1 at address $(0, -3)$ relative to "O." Figure 4.91 shows the permissible positions of the AT pixels relative to the current pixel, and their coordinates. Notice that an AT pixel may also be located at one of the "X" positions of the template.

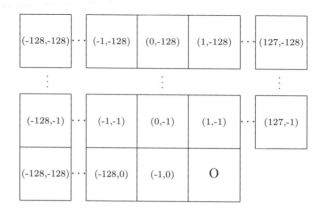

Figure 4.91: Coordinates and Allowed Positions of AT Pixels.

⋄ **Exercise 4.25:** What are the relative coordinates of the AT pixels in the four types of templates shown in Figure 4.89?

The **TPON** parameter controls the so-called *typical prediction* feature. A typical row is defined as a row identical to its predecessor. If the encoder notices that certain rows of the generic region being encoded are typical, it sets **TPON** to 1, then writes a code in the compressed file before each row, indicating whether it is typical. If the decoder finds **TPON** set to 1, it has to decode and check a special code preceding each row of pixels. When the code of a typical row is found, the decoder simply generates it as a copy of its predecessor.

The two parameters **USESKIP** and **SKIP** control the *skip* feature. If the encoder discovers that the generic region being encoded is sparse (i.e., most of its pixels are zero), it sets **USESKIP** to 1 and sets **SKIP** to a bitmap of size **GBW** × **GBH**, where each 1 bit indicates a zero-bit in the generic region. The encoder then compresses only the 1 bits of the generic region.

4.10.2 Symbol Region Decoding

This procedure is invoked when the decoder starts reading a new segment from the compressed file and identifies it as a symbol-region segment. The procedure starts by reading many parameters from the segment. It then inputs the coded information for each symbol and decodes it (using either arithmetic coding or MMR). This information contains the coordinates of the symbol relative to its row and the symbol preceding it, a pointer to the symbol in the symbol dictionary, and possibly also refinement information. The coordinates of a symbol are denoted by S and T. Normally, S is the x-coordinate and T is the y-coordinate of a symbol. However, if parameter **TRANSPOSED** has the value 1, the meaning of S and T is reversed. In general, T is considered the height of a row of text and S is the coordinate of a text symbol in its row.

⋄ **Exercise 4.26:** What is the advantage of transposing S and T?

Symbols are encoded and written on the compressed file by strips. A strip is normally a row of symbols but can also be a column. The encoder makes that decision and sets parameter **TRANSPOSED** to 0 or 1 accordingly. The decoder therefore starts by decoding the number of strips, then the strips themselves. For each strip the compressed file contains the strip's T coordinate relative to the preceding strip, followed by coded information for the symbols constituting the strip. For each symbol this information consists of the symbol's S coordinate (the gap between it and the preceding symbol), its T coordinate (relative to the T coordinate of the strip), its ID (a pointer to the symbol dictionary), and refinement information (optionally). In the special case where all the symbols are vertically aligned on the strip, their T coordinates will be zero.

Once the absolute coordinates (x, y) of the symbol in the symbol region have been computed from the relative coordinates, the symbol's bitmap is retrieved from the symbol dictionary and is combined with the page buffer. However, parameter **REFCORNER** indicates which of the four corners of the bitmap should be placed at position (x, y). Figure 4.92 shows examples of symbol bitmaps aligned in different ways.

If the encoder decides to use MMR to encode a region, it selects one of 15 Huffman code tables defined by the JBIG2 standard and sets a parameter to indicate to the decoder which table is used. The tables themselves are built into both encoder and decoder. Table 4.93 shows two of the 15 tables. The OOB value (out of bound) is used to terminate a list in cases where the length of the list is not known in advance.

4.10.3 Halftone Region Decoding

This procedure is invoked when the decoder starts reading a new segment from the compressed file and identifies it as a halftone-region segment. The procedure starts by reading several parameters from the segment and setting all the pixels in the halftone region to the value of background parameter **HDEFPIXEL**. It then inputs the coded information for each halftone pattern and decodes it using either arithmetic coding or MMR. This information consists of a pointer to a halftone pattern in the halftone dictionary. The pattern is retrieved and is logically combined with the background pixels that are already in the halftone region. Parameter **HCOMBOP** specifies the logical combination. It can have one of the values REPLACE, OR, AND, XOR, and XNOR.

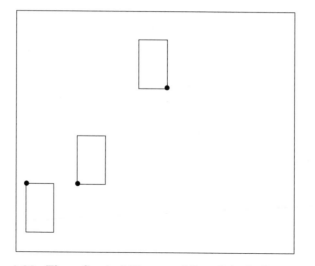

Figure 4.92: Three Symbol Bitmaps Aligned At Different Corners.

Value	Code
0–15	0+Value encoded as 4 bits
16–271	10+(Value − 16) encoded as 8 bits
272–65807	110+(Value − 272) encoded as 16 bits
65808–∞	111+(Value − 65808) encoded as 32 bits

Value	Code
0	0
1	10
2	110
3–10	1110+(Value − 3) encoded as 3 bits
11–74	11110+(Value − 11) encoded as 6 bits
75–∞	111110+(Value − 75) encoded as 32 bits
OOB	11111

Table 4.93: Two Huffman Code Tables For JBIG2 Decoding.

Notice that the region information read by the decoder from the compressed file does not include the positions of the halftone patterns. The decoder adds the patterns to the region at consecutive grid points of the *halftone grid*, which is itself defined by four parameters. Parameters **HGX** and **HGY** specify the origin of the grid relative to the origin of the halftone region. Parameters **HRX** and **HRY** specify the orientation of the grid by means of an angle θ. The last two parameters can be interpreted as the horizontal and vertical components of a vector **v**. In this interpretation θ is the angle between **v** and the x-axis. The parameters can also be interpreted as the cosine and sine of θ, respectively. (Strictly speaking, they are multiples of the sine and cosine, since $\sin^2 \theta + \cos^2 \theta$ equals unity, but the sum

$\mathbf{HRX^2 + HRY^2}$ can have any value.) Notice that these parameters can also be negative and are not limited to integer values. They are written on the compressed file as integers whose values are 256 times the real values. Thus, for example, if **HRX** should be -0.15, it is written as the integer -38 because $-0.15 \times 256 = -38.4$. Figure 4.94a shows typical relations between a page, a halftone region, and a halftone grid. Also shown are the coordinates of three points on the grid.

The decoder performs a double loop in which it varies m_g from zero to $\mathbf{HGH}-1$ and for each value of m_g it varies n_g from zero to $\mathbf{HGW} - 1$ (parameters **HGH** and **HGW** are the number of horizontal and vertical grid points, respectively). At each iteration the pair (n_g, m_g) constitutes the coordinates of a grid point. This point is mapped to a point (x, y) in the halftone region by the relation

$$
\begin{aligned}
x &= \mathbf{HGX} + m_g \times \mathbf{HRY} + n_g \times \mathbf{HRX}, \\
y &= \mathbf{HGY} + m_g \times \mathbf{HRX} - n_g \times \mathbf{HRY}.
\end{aligned}
\tag{4.20}
$$

To understand this relation the reader should compare it to a rotation of a point (n_g, m_g) through an angle θ about the origin. Such a rotation is expressed by

$$
(x, y) = (n_g, m_g) \begin{pmatrix} \cos\theta & -\sin\theta \\ \sin\theta & \cos\theta \end{pmatrix} = (n_g \cos\theta + m_g \sin\theta, m_g \cos\theta - n_g \sin\theta).
\tag{4.21}
$$

A comparison of Eqs. (4.20) and (4.21) shows that they are identical if we associate **HRX** with $\cos\theta$ and **HRY** with $\sin\theta$ (Equation (4.20) also adds the origin of the grid relative to the region, so it results in a point (x, y) whose coordinates are relative to the origin of the region).

It is expected that the grid would normally be identical to the region, i.e., its origin would be $(0, 0)$ and its rotation angle would be zero. This is achieved by setting **HGX**, **HGY**, and **HRY** to zero and setting **HRX** to the width of a halftone pattern. However, all four parameters may be used, and a sophisticated JBIG2 encoder may improve the overall compression quality by trying different combinations.

Once point (x, y) has been calculated, the halftone pattern is combined with the halftone region such that its top-left corner is at location (x, y) of the region. Since parts of the grid may lie outside the region, any parts of the pattern that lie outside the region are ignored (see gray areas in Figure 4.94b). Notice that the patterns themselves are oriented with the region, not with the grid. Each pattern is a rectangle with horizontal and vertical sides. The orientation of the grid affects only the position of the top-left corner of each pattern. As a result, the patterns added to the halftone region generally overlap by an amount that's greatly affected by the orientation and position of the grid. This is also illustrated by the three examples of Figure 4.94b.

4.10.4 The Overall Decoding Process

The decoder starts by reading general information for page 1 of the document from the compressed file. This information tells the decoder to what background value (0 or 1) to set the page buffer initially, and which of the four combination operators

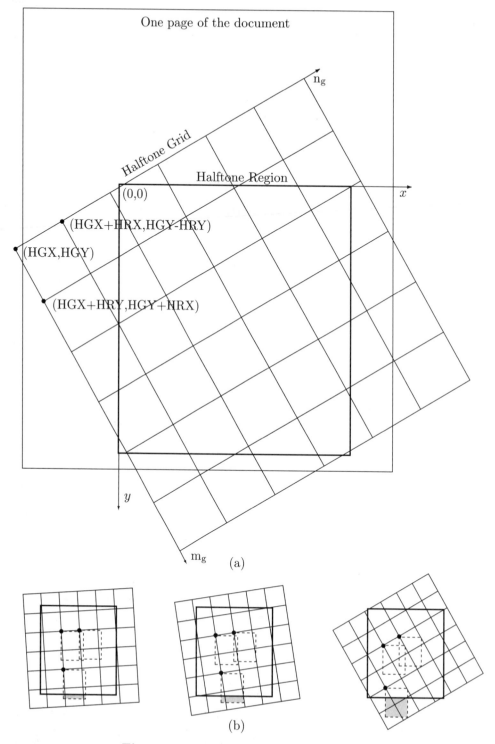

Figure 4.94: Halftone Grids and Regions.

OR, AND, XOR, and XNOR to use when combining pixels with the page buffer. The decoder then reads segments from the compressed file until it encounters the page information for page 2 or the end of the file. A segment may specify its own combination operator, which overrides the one for the entire page. A segment can be a dictionary segment or an image segment. The latter has one of four types:

1. An immediate direct image segment. The decoder uses this type to decode a region directly into the page buffer.
2. An intermediate direct image segment. The decoder uses this type to decode a region into an auxiliary buffer.
3. An immediate refinement image segment. The decoder uses this type to decode an image and combine it with an existing region in order to refine that region. The region being refined is located in the page buffer, and the refinement process may use an auxiliary buffer (which is then deleted).
4. An intermediate refinement image segment. The decoder uses this type to decode an image and combine it with an existing region in order to refine that region. The region being refined is located in an auxiliary buffer.

We therefore conclude that an immediate segment is decoded into the page buffer and an intermediate segment involves an auxiliary buffer.

4.11 Simple Images: EIDAC

Image compression methods based on transforms perform best on continuous-tone images. There is, however, an important class of images where transform-based methods, such as JPEG (Section 4.6) and the various wavelet methods (Chapter 5), produce mediocre compression. This is the class of *simple images*. A simple image is one that uses a small fraction of all the possible grayscales or colors available to it. A common example is a bi-level image where each pixel is represented by eight bits. Such an image uses just two colors out of a palette of 256 possible colors. Another example is a grayscale image scanned from a bi-level image. Most pixels will be black or white, but some pixels may have other shades of gray. A cartoon is also an example of a simple image (especially a cheap cartoon, where just a few colors are used). A typical cartoon consists of uniform areas, so it may use a small number of colors out of a potentially large palette.

EIDAC is an acronym that stands for *embedded image-domain adaptive compression*. This method is especially designed for the compression of simple images and combines high compression factors with lossless performance (although lossy compression is an option). The method is also progressive. It compresses each bitplane separately, going from the most significant bitplane (MSBP) to the least-significant one (LSBP). The decoder reads the data for the MSBP first, and immediately generates a rough "black-and-white" version of the image. This version is improved each time a bitplane is read and decoded. Lossy compression is achieved if some of the LSBPs are ignored by the encoder.

The encoder scans each bitplane in raster order and uses several near neighbors of the current pixel X as the context of X, to determine a probability for X. Pixel X and its probability are then sent to an adaptive arithmetic encoder that does the actual encoding. Thus, EIDAC resembles JBIG and CALIC, but there is an important difference. EIDAC uses a *two-part context* for each pixel. The first part is an *intra* context, consisting of several neighbors of the pixel in the same bitplane. The second part is an *inter* context, whose pixels are selected from the already encoded bitplanes (recall that encoding is done from the MSBP to the LSBP).

To see why an inter context makes sense, consider a grayscale image scanned from a bi-level image. Most pixel values will be 255 ($1111\ 1111_2$) or 0 ($0000\ 0000_2$), but some pixels may have values close to these, such as 254 ($1111\ 1110_2$) or 1 ($0000\ 0001_2$). Figure 4.95a shows (in binary) the eight bitplanes of the six pixels 255 255 254 0 1 0. It is clear that there are spatial correlations between the bitplanes. A bit position that has a zero in one bitplane tends to have zeros in the other bitplanes. Another example is a pixel P with value "0101xxxx" in a grayscale image. In principle, the remaining four bits can have any of 16 different values. In a simple image, however, the remaining four bits will have just a few values. There is therefore a good chance that pixels adjacent to P will have values similar to P and will thus be good predictors of P in all the bitplanes.

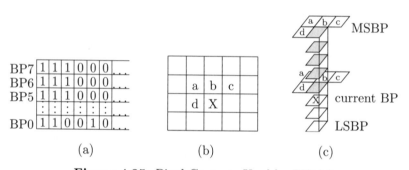

Figure 4.95: Pixel Contexts Used by EIDAC.

The intra context actually used by EIDAC is shown in Figure 4.95b. It consists of four of the already-seen nearest neighbors of the current pixel X. The inter context is shown in Figure 4.95c. It consists of (1) the same four neighbors in the bitplane immediately above the current bitplane, (2) the same four neighbors in the MSBP, and (3) the pixels in the same position as X in all the bitplanes above it (five shaded pixels in the figure). Thus, a pixel in the MSBP has no inter context, while the inter context of a pixel in the LSBP consists of $4 + 4 + 7 = 15$ pixels. Other contexts can be selected, which means that a general implementation of EIDAC should include three items of side information in the compressed stream. The first item is the dimensions of the image, the second one is the way the contexts are selected, and the third item is a flag indicating whether *histogram compaction* is used (if it is used, the flag should be followed by the new codes). This useful feature is described here.

A simple image is one that has a small number of colors or grayscales out of a large available palette of colors. Imagine a simple image with eight bits per pixel. If the image has just 27 colors, each can be assigned a 5-bit code instead of the original 8-bit value. This feature is referred to as histogram compaction. When histogram compaction is used, the new codes for the colors have to be included in the compressed stream, where they constitute overhead. Generally, histogram compaction improves compression, but in rare cases the overhead may be bigger than the savings due to histogram compaction.

Bibliography

Yoo, Youngjun, Younggap Kwon, and Antonio Ortega (1998) "Embedded Image-Domain Adaptive Compression of Simple Images," *Proceedings of the 32nd Asilomar Conference on Signals, Systems, and Computers*, Pacific Grove, CA, Nov. 1998.

4.12 Vector Quantization

This is a generalization of the scalar quantization method (Section 1.6). It is used for both image and sound compression. In practice, vector quantization is commonly used to compress data that have been digitized from an analog source, such as sampled sound and scanned images (drawings or photographs). Such data is called *digitally sampled analog data* (DSAD). Vector quantization is based on two facts:

1. We know (from Section 3.1) that compression methods that compress strings, rather than individual symbols, can, in principle, produce better results.
2. Adjacent data items in an image (i.e., pixels) and in digitized sound (i.e., samples; see Section 7.1) are correlated. There is a good chance that the near neighbors of a pixel P will have the same values as P or very similar values. Also, consecutive sound samples rarely differ by much.

We start with a simple, intuitive vector quantization method for image compression. Given an image, we divide it into small blocks of pixels, typically 2×2 or 4×4. Each block is considered a vector. The encoder maintains a list (called a *codebook*) of vectors and compresses each block by writing on the compressed stream a pointer to the block in the codebook. The decoder has the easy task of reading pointers, following each pointer to a block in the codebook, and joining the block to the image-so-far. Vector quantization is thus an asymmetric compression method.

In the case of 2×2 blocks, each block (vector) consists of four pixels. If each pixel is one bit, then a block is four bits long and there are only $2^4 = 16$ different blocks. It is easy to store such a small, permanent codebook in both encoder and decoder. However, a pointer to a block in such a codebook is, of course, four bits long, so there is no compression gain by replacing blocks with pointers. If each pixel is k bits, then each block is $4k$ bits long and there are 2^{4k} different blocks. The codebook grows very fast with k (for $k = 8$, for example, it is $256^4 = 2^{32} = 4$ Tera entries) but the point is that we again replace a block of $4k$ bits with a $4k$-bit pointer, resulting in no compression gain. This is true for blocks of any size.

Once it becomes clear that this simple method won't work, the next thing that comes to mind is that any given image may not contain every possible block. Given 8-bit pixels, the number of 2×2 blocks is $2^{2 \cdot 2 \cdot 8} = 2^{32} \approx 4.3$ billion, but any particular image may contain a few thousand different blocks. Thus, our next version of vector quantization starts with an empty codebook and scans the image block by block. The codebook is searched for each block. If the block is already in the codebook, the encoder outputs a pointer to the block in the (growing) codebook. If the block is not in the codebook, it is added to the codebook and a pointer is output.

The problem with this simple method is that each block added to the codebook has to be written on the compressed stream. This greatly reduces the effectiveness of the method and may lead to low compression and even to expansion. There is also the small added complication that the codebook grows during compression, so the pointers get longer, but this is not hard for the decoder to handle.

The problems outlined above are the reason why image vector quantization is lossy. If we accept lossy compression, then the size of the codebook can be greatly reduced. Here is an intuitive lossy method for image compression by vector quantization. Analyze a large number of different "training" images and find the B most-common blocks. Build a codebook with these B blocks into both encoder and decoder. Each entry of the codebook is a block. To compress an image, scan it block by block, and for each block find the codebook entry that best matches it, and output a pointer to that entry. The size of the pointer is, of course, $\lceil \log_2 B \rceil$, so the compression ratio (which is known in advance) is

$$\frac{\lceil \log_2 B \rceil}{\text{block size}}.$$

One problem with this approach is how to match image blocks to codebook entries. Here are a few common measures. Let $B = (b_1, b_2, \ldots, b_n)$ and $C = (c_1, c_2, \ldots, c_n)$ be a block of image pixels and a codebook entry, respectively (each is a vector of n bits). We denote the "distance" between them by $d(B, C)$ and measure it in three different ways as follows:

$$d_1(B, C) = \sum_{i=0}^{n} |b_i - c_i|,$$

$$d_2(B, C) = \sum_{i=0}^{n} (b_i - c_i)^2, \qquad (4.22)$$

$$d_3(B, C) = \text{MAX}_{i=0}^{n} |b_i - c_i|.$$

The third measure $d_3(B, C)$ is easy to interpret. It finds the component where B and C differ most, and it returns this difference. The first two measures are easy to visualize in the case $n = 3$. Measure $d_1(B, C)$ becomes the distance between the two three-dimensional vectors B and C when we move along the coordinate axes. Measure $d_2(B, C)$ becomes the Euclidean (straight line) distance between the two vectors. The quantities $d_i(B, C)$ can also be considered measures of distortion.

Another problem with this approach is the quality of the codebook. In the case of 2×2 blocks with 8-bit pixels the total number of blocks is $2^{32} \approx 4.3$ billion. If we decide to limit the size of our codebook to, say, a million entries, it will contain only 0.023% of the total number of blocks (and still be 32 million bits, or about 4 Mb long). Using this codebook to compress an "atypical" image may result in a large distortion regardless of the distortion measure used. When the compressed image is decompressed, it may look so different from the original as to render our method useless. A natural way to solve this problem is to modify the original codebook entries in order to *adapt* them to the particular image being compressed. The final codebook will have to be included in the compressed stream, but since it has been adapted to the image, it may be small enough to yield a good compression ratio, yet close enough to the image blocks to produce an acceptable decompressed image.

Such an algorithm has been developed by Linde, Buzo, and Gray [Linde, Buzo, and Gray 80]. It is known as the LBG algorithm and it is the basis of many vector quantization methods for the compression of images and sound (see, for example, Section 4.30). Its main steps are the following:

Step 0: Select a threshold value ϵ and set $k = 0$ and $D^{(-1)} = \infty$. Start with an initial codebook with entries $C_i^{(k)}$ (where k is currently zero, but will be incremented in each iteration). Denote the image blocks by B_i (these blocks are also called *training vectors*, since the algorithm uses them to find the best codebook entries).

Step 1: Pick up a codebook entry $C_i^{(k)}$. Find all the image blocks B_m that are closer to C_i than to any other C_j. Phrased more precisely; find the set of all B_m that satisfy

$$d(B_m, C_i) < d(B_m, C_j) \quad \text{for all } j \neq i.$$

This set (or *partition*) is denoted by $P_i^{(k)}$. Repeat for all values of i. It may happen that some partitions will be empty, and we deal with this problem below.

Step 2: Select an i and calculate the distortion $D_i^{(k)}$ between codebook entry $C_i^{(k)}$ and the set of training vectors (partition) $P_i^{(k)}$ found for it in Step 1. Repeat for all i, then calculate the average $D^{(k)}$ of all the $D_i^{(k)}$. A distortion $D_i^{(k)}$ for a certain i is calculated by computing the distances $d(C_i^{(k)}, B_m)$ for all the blocks B_m in partition $P_i^{(k)}$, then calculating the average distance. Alternatively, $D_i^{(k)}$ can be set to the minimum of the distances $d(C_i^{(k)}, B_m)$.

Step 3: If $(D^{(k-1)} - D^{(k)})/D^{(k)} \leq \epsilon$, halt. The output of the algorithm is the last set of codebook entries $C_i^{(k)}$. This set can now be used to (lossy) compress the image with vector quantization. In the first iteration k is zero, so $D^{(k-1)} = D^{(-1)} = \infty > \epsilon$. This guarantees that the algorithm will not stop at the first iteration.

Step 4: Increment k by 1 and calculate new codebook entries $C_i^{(k)}$; each equals the average of the image blocks (training vectors) in partition $P_i^{(k-1)}$ that was computed in Step 1. (This is how the codebook entries are adapted to the particular image.) Go to Step 1.

A full understanding of such an algorithm calls for a detailed example, parts of which should be worked out by the reader in the form of exercises. In order to easily visualize the example, we assume that the image to be compressed consists of 8-bit pixels, and we divide it into small, two-pixel blocks. Normally, a block should be square, but the advantage of our two-pixel blocks is that they can be plotted on paper as two-dimensional points, thereby rendering the data (as well as the entire example) more visual. Examples of blocks are $(35, 168)$ and $(250, 37)$; we interpret the two pixels of a block as the (x, y) coordinates of a point.

Our example assumes an image consisting of 24 pixels, organized in the 12 blocks $B_1 = (32, 32)$, $B_2 = (60, 32)$, $B_3 = (32, 50)$, $B_4 = (60, 50)$, $B_5 = (60, 150)$, $B_6 = (70, 140)$, $B_7 = (200, 210)$, $B_8 = (200, 32)$, $B_9 = (200, 40)$, $B_{10} = (200, 50)$, $B_{11} = (215, 50)$, and $B_{12} = (215, 35)$ (Figure 4.96). It is clear that the 12 points are concentrated in four regions. We select an initial codebook with the four entries $C_1^{(0)} = (70, 40)$, $C_2^{(0)} = (60, 120)$, $C_3^{(0)} = (210, 200)$, and $C_4^{(0)} = (225, 50)$ (shown as x in the diagram). These entries were selected more or less at random but we show later how the LBG algorithm selects them methodically, one by one. Because of the graphical nature of the data, it is easy to determine the four initial partitions. They are $P_1^{(0)} = (B_1, B_2, B_3, B_4)$, $P_2^{(0)} = (B_5, B_6)$, $P_3^{(0)} = (B_7)$, and $P_4^{(0)} = (B_8, B_9, B_{10}, B_{11}, B_{12})$. Table 4.97 shows how the average distortion $D^{(0)}$ is calculated for the first iteration (we use the Euclidean distance function). The result is

$$\begin{aligned} D^{(0)} =&(1508 + 164 + 1544 + 200 + 900 + 500 \\ &+ 200 + 449 + 725 + 625 + 100 + 325)/12 \\ =&603.33. \end{aligned}$$

Step 3 indicates no convergence, since $D^{(-1)} = \infty$, so we increment k to 1 and calculate four new codebook entries $C_i^{(1)}$ (rounded to the nearest integer for simplicity)

$$\begin{aligned} C_1^{(1)} &= (B_1 + B_2 + B_3 + B_4)/4 = (46, 41), \\ C_2^{(1)} &= (B_5 + B_6)/2 = (65, 145), \\ C_3^{(1)} &= B_7 = (200, 210), \\ C_4^{(1)} &= (B_8 + B_9 + B_{10} + B_{11} + B_{12})/5 = (206, 41). \end{aligned} \tag{4.23}$$

They are shown in Figure 4.98.

⬦ **Exercise 4.27:** Perform the next iteration.

⬦ **Exercise 4.28:** Use the four codebook entries of Equation (4.23) to perform the next iteration of the LBG algorithm.

Even though the algorithm reduces the average distortion from one iteration to the next, it does not guarantee that the codebook entries will converge to the optimum set. They may converge to a less-than-optimum set, and this aspect of the algorithm depends heavily on the initial choice of codebook entries (i.e., on the values of $C_i^{(0)}$). We therefore discuss this aspect of the LBG algorithm next. The original LBG algorithm proposes a computationally intensive *splitting technique* where the initial codebook entries $C_i^{(0)}$ are selected in several steps as follows:

Step 0: Set $k = 1$ and select a codebook with k entries (i.e., one entry) $C_1^{(0)}$ that's an average of all the image blocks B_m.

Step 1: In a general iteration there will be k codebook entries $C_i^{(0)}$, $i = 1, 2, \ldots, k$. Split each entry (which is a vector) into the two similar entries $C_i^{(0)} \pm e$ where e is a fixed *perturbation vector*. Set $k \leftarrow 2k$. (Alternatively, we can use the two vectors $C_i^{(0)}$ and $C_i^{(0)} + e$, a choice that leads to smaller overall distortion.)

Step 2: If there are enough codebook entries, stop the splitting process. The current set of k codebook entries can now serve as the initial set $C_i^{(0)}$ for the LBG algorithm above. If more entries are needed, execute the LBG algorithm on the current set of k entries, to converge them to a better set; then go to step 1.

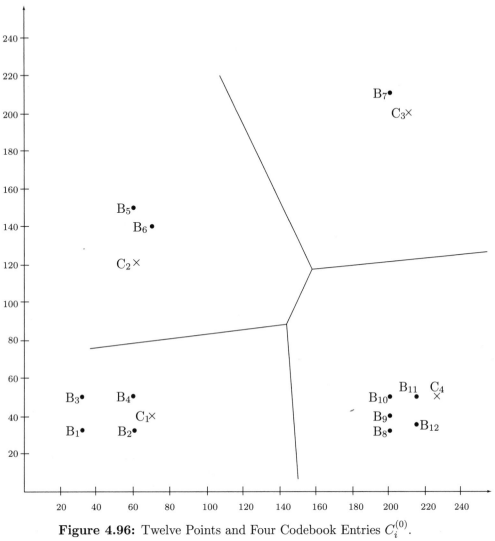

Figure 4.96: Twelve Points and Four Codebook Entries $C_i^{(0)}$.

$$
\begin{array}{lll}
\text{I:} & (70-32)^2 + (40-32)^2 = 1508, & (70-60)^2 + (40-32)^2 = 164, \\
 & (70-32)^2 + (40-50)^2 = 1544, & (70-60)^2 + (40-50)^2 = 200, \\
\text{II:} & (60-60)^2 + (120-150)^2 = 900, & (60-70)^2 + (120-140)^2 = 500, \\
\text{III:} & (210-200)^2 + (200-210)^2 = 200, & \\
\text{IV:} & (225-200)^2 + (50-32)^2 = 449, & (225-200)^2 + (50-40)^2 = 725, \\
 & (225-200)^2 + (50-50)^2 = 625, & (225-215)^2 + (50-50)^2 = 100, \\
 & (225-215)^2 + (50-35)^2 = 325. &
\end{array}
$$

Table 4.97: Twelve Distortions For $k = 0$.

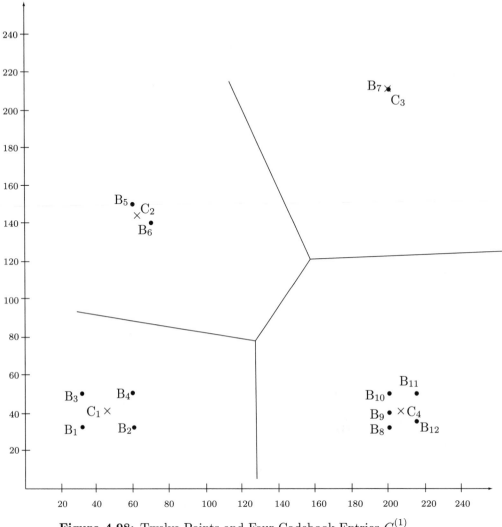

Figure 4.98: Twelve Points and Four Codebook Entries $C_i^{(1)}$.

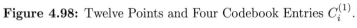

$$
\begin{aligned}
\text{I:}\quad & (46-32)^2+(41-32)^2=277, & (46-60)^2+(41-32)^2=277, \\
& (46-32)^2+(41-50)^2=277, & (46-60)^2+(41-50)^2=277, \\
\text{II:}\quad & (65-60)^2+(145-150)^2=\ 50, & (65-70)^2+(145-140)^2=\ 50, \\
\text{III:}\quad & (210-200)^2+(200-210)^2=200, \\
\text{IV:}\quad & (206-200)^2+(41-32)^2=117, & (206-200)^2+(41-40)^2=\ 37, \\
& (206-200)^2+(41-50)^2=117, & (206-215)^2+(41-50)^2=162, \\
& (206-215)^2+(41-35)^2=117.
\end{aligned}
$$

Table 4.99: Twelve Distortions For $k=1$.

This process starts with one codebook entry $C_1^{(0)}$ and uses it to create two entries, then four, eight, and so on. The number of entries is always a power of 2. If a different number is needed, then the last time Step 1 is executed, it can split just some of the entries. For example, if 11 codebook entries are needed, then the splitting process is repeated until eight entries have been computed. Step 1 is then invoked to split just three of the eight entries, ending up with 11 entries.

One more feature of the LBG algorithm needs to be clarified. Step 1 of the algorithm says; "Find all the image blocks B_m that are closer to C_i than to any other C_j. They become partition $P_i^{(k)}$." It may happen that no image blocks are close to a certain codebook entry C_i, which creates an empty partition $P_i^{(k)}$. This is a problem, since the average of the image blocks included in partition $P_i^{(k)}$ is used to compute a better codebook entry in the next iteration. A good solution is to delete codebook entry C_i and replace it with a new entry chosen at random from one of the image blocks included in the biggest partition $P_j^{(k)}$.

If an image block is an n-dimensional vector, then the process of constructing the partitions in Step 1 of the LBG algorithm divides the n-dimensional space into Voronoi regions [Salomon 99] with a codebook entry C_i at the center of each region. Figs. 4.97 and 4.98 show the Voronoi regions in the first two iterations of our example. In each iteration the codebook entries are moved, thereby changing the Voronoi regions.

Tree-Structured VQ: The LBG algorithm is computationally intensive, since computing the partitions in Step 1 requires many comparisons. Each image block B_m has to be compared to all the codebook entries C_j in order to find the closest entry C_i. Thus, a straightforward algorithm requires n steps per image block, where n is the number of codebook entries. The tree structure described here reduces this to $\log_2 n$ steps per image block. This variant is called *tree-structured vector quantization* (TSVQ). The idea is to use the individual bits of the pixels constituting an image block to locate the block in space. In our example, each block consists of two 8-bit pixels that are naturally considered the (x, y) coordinates of the block in the plane (the two-dimensional space). In general, a block consists of k pixels, and may therefore be considered a point in k-dimensional space.

We divide the plane into four quadrants numbered 00, 01, 10, and 11 as shown in Figure 4.100a. The most-significant bits of the x and y coordinates of a point determine its quadrant. Thus, all the image blocks with values $(0\ldots, 0, \ldots)$ are located in quadrant 00, all the image blocks of the form $(1\ldots, 0, \ldots)$ are located in quadrant 10, and so on. We now divide each quadrant into four subquadrants and it is not hard to see how the second-most-significant bits of the coordinates of a point determine its subquadrant. Figure 4.100b shows the four subquadrants of quadrant 00 and the first two most-significant bits of the points located in them. Similarly, Figure 4.100c shows the four subsubquadrants of subquadrant 10 and how the three most-significant bits of a point determine its subsubquadrant.

Since our points (image blocks) have 8-bit coordinates, we can pinpoint the location of each point down to a subquadrant of order 8. We now construct a quadtree (Section 4.27) of depth eight where each leaf is associated with a codebook entry. Given an image block $B_m = (x, y)$ we use consecutive pairs of bits from x

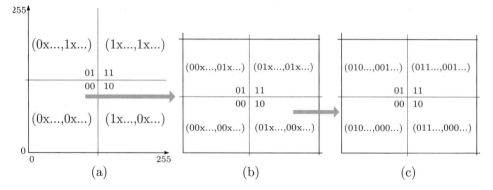

Figure 4.100: Quadrant Numbering.

and y to go down the tree. When we get to a leaf, we place B_m in the partition of the codebook entry found in that leaf. As an example, consider image block B_4 above. Its coordinates are $(60, 50) = (00111100, 00110010)$. The eight pairs of bits taken, from left to right, from the two coordinates are $(0, 0)$, $(0, 0)$, $(1, 1)$, $(1, 1)$, $(1, 0)$, $(1, 0)$, $(0, 1)$, and $(0, 0)$. They determine which of the four branches of the quadtree should be taken in each of the eight steps going down the tree. When we get to the bottom we find codebook entry C_1, so we include image block B_4 in partition P_1.

⋄ **Exercise 4.29:** What is the area of a subquadrant of order 8?

Bibliography

Linde, Y., A. Buzo, and R. M. Gray (1980) "An Algorithm For Vector Quantization Design," *IEEE Transactions on Communications*, COM-28:84–95, January.

4.13 Adaptive Vector Quantization

The basic vector quantization method described in Section 4.12 uses either a fixed codebook, or the LBG (or similar) algorithm to construct the codebook as it goes along. In all these cases the codebook consists of fixed-size entries, identical in size to the image block. The adaptive method described here, due to Constantinescu and Storer [Constantinescu and Storer 94a,b], uses variable-size image blocks and codebook entries. The codebook is called *dictionary*, as in the various LZ methods, because this method bears a slight resemblance to them. The method combines the single-pass, adaptive dictionary used by the various dictionary-based algorithms with the distance measures used by the different vector quantization methods to obtain good approximations of data blocks.

At each step of the encoding process, the encoder selects an image block (a rectangle of any size), matches it to one of the dictionary entries, outputs a pointer to that entry, and updates the dictionary by adding one or more entries to it. The new entries are based on the current image block. The case of a full dictionary has to be taken care of, and is discussed below.

Some authors refer to such a method as *textual substitution*, since it substitutes pointers for the original data.

Extensive experimentation by the developers yielded compression ratios that equal or even surpass those of JPEG. At the same time, the method is fast (since it performs just one pass), simple (it starts with an empty dictionary, so no training is required), and reliable (the amount of loss is controlled easily and precisely by a single tolerance parameter). The decoder's operation is similar to that of a vector quantization decoder, so it is fast and simple.

The encoder has to select the image blocks carefully, making sure that they cover the entire image, that they cover it in a way that the decoder can mimic, and that there is not too much overlap between the different blocks. In order to select the blocks the encoder selects one or more *growing points* at each iteration, and uses one of them in the next iteration as the corner of a new image block. The block starts small and is increased in size (is "grown" from the corner) by the encoder as long as it can be matched with a dictionary entry. A growing point is denoted by G and is a triplet (x, y, q), where x and y are the coordinates of the point and q indicates the corner of the image block where the point is located. We assume that q values of 0, 1, 2, and 3 indicate the top-left, top-right, bottom-left, and bottom-right corners, respectively (thus, q is a 2-bit number). An image block B anchored at a growing point G is denoted by $B = (G, w, h)$, where w and h are the width and height of the block, respectively.

We list the main steps of the encoder and decoder, then discuss each in detail. The encoder's main steps are as follows:

Step 1: Initialize the dictionary D to all the possible values of the image pixels. Initialize the pool of growing points (GPP) to one or more growing points using one of the algorithms discussed below.

Step 2: Repeat Steps 3–7 until the GPP is empty.

Step 3: Use a growing algorithm to select a growing point G from GPP.

Step 4: Grow an image block B with G as its corner. Use a matching algorithm to match B, as it is being grown, to a dictionary entry with user-controlled fidelity.

Step 5: Once B has reached the maximum size where it still can be matched with a dictionary entry d, output a pointer to d. The size of the pointer depends on the size (number of entries) of D.

Step 6: Delete G from the GPP and use an algorithm to decide which new growing points (if any) to add to the GPP.

Step 7: If D is full, use an algorithm to delete one or more entries. Use an algorithm to update the dictionary based on B.

The operation of the encoder depends, therefore, on several algorithms. Each algorithm should be developed, implemented, and its performance tested with many test images. The decoder is much simpler and faster. Its main steps are as follows:

Step 1: Initialize the dictionary D and the GPP as in Step 1 of the encoder.

Step 2: Repeat Steps 3–5 until GPP is empty.

Step 3: Use the encoder's growing algorithm to select a growing point G from the GPP.

Step 4: Input a pointer from the compressed stream, use it to retrieve a dictionary entry d, and place d at the location and position specified by G.

Step 5: Update D and the GPP as in Steps 6–7 of the encoder.

The remainder of this section discusses the various algorithms needed, and shows an example.

Algorithm: Select a growing point G from the GPP. The simplest methods are LIFO (which probably does not yield good results) and FIFO (which is used in the example below), but the coverage methods described here may be better, since they determine how the image will be covered with blocks.

Wave Coverage: This algorithm selects from among all the growing points in the GPP the point $G = (x_s, y_s, 0)$ that satisfies

$$x_s + y_s \le x + y, \quad \text{for any } G(x, y, 0) \text{ in } GPP$$

(notice that the growing point selected has $q = 0$, so it is located at the upper-left corner of an image block). When this algorithm is used, it makes sense to initialize the GPP with just one point, the top-left corner of the image. If this is done, then the wave coverage algorithm will select image blocks that cover the image in a wave that moves from the upper-left to the lower-right corners of the image (Figure 4.101a).

Circular Coverage: Select the growing point G whose distance from the center of the image is minimal among all the growing points G in the GPP. This covers the image with blocks located in a growing circular region around the center (Figure 4.101b).

Diagonal Coverage: This algorithm selects from among all the growing points in the GPP the point $G = (x_s, y_s, q)$ that satisfies

$$|x_s - y_s| \le |x - y|, \quad \text{for any } G(x, y, p) \text{ in } GPP$$

(notice that the growing point selected may have any q). The result will be blocks that start around the main diagonal and move away from it in two waves that run parallel to it.

Algorithm: Matching an image block B (with a growing point G as its corner) to a dictionary entry. It seems that the best approach is to start with the smallest block B (just a single pixel) and try to match bigger and bigger blocks to the dictionary entries, until the next increase of B does not find any dictionary entry to match B to the tolerance specified by the user. The following parameters control the matching:

1. The distance measure. Any of the measures proposed in Equation (4.22) can be used.

2. The tolerance. A user-defined real parameter t that's the maximum allowed distance between an image block B and a dictionary entry.

3. The type of coverage. Since image blocks have different sizes and grow from the growing point in different directions, they can overlap (Figure 4.101a). Imagine that an image block B has been matched, but it partly covers some other blocks. We can compute the distance using just those parts of B that don't overlap any other blocks. This means that the first block that covers a certain image area will determine the quality of the decompressed image in that area. This can be called *first coverage*. The opposite is *last coverage*, where the distance between an image

block B and a dictionary entry is computed using all of B (except those parts that lie outside the image), regardless of any overlaps. It is also possible to have *average coverage*, where the distance is computed for all of B, but in a region of overlap, any pixel value used to calculate the distance will be the average of pixel values from all the image blocks in the region.

4. The elementary subblock size l. This is a "normalization" parameter that compensates for the different block sizes. We know that image blocks can have different sizes. It may happen that a large block will match a certain dictionary entry to within the tolerance, while some regions within the block will match poorly (and other regions will yield a very good match). An image block should therefore be divided into subblocks of size $l \times l$ (where the value of l depends on the image size, but is typically 4 or 5) and each dictionary entry should similarly be divided. The matching algorithm should calculate the distance between each image subblock and the corresponding dictionary entry subblock. The maximum of these distances should be selected as the distance between the image block and the dictionary entry.

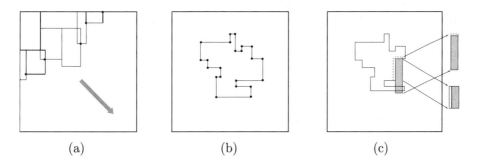

(a)   (b)   (c)

Figure 4.101: (a) Wave Coverage. (b) Growing Points. (c) Dictionary Update.

Algorithm: GPP update. A good policy is to choose as new growing points those points located at or near the borders of the partially encoded image (Figure 4.101b). This causes new image blocks to be adjacent to old ones. This policy makes sense because an old block has contributed to new dictionary entries and those entries are perfect candidates to match a new, adjacent block, since adjacent blocks generally don't differ much. Initially, when the partially encoded image is small, consisting mainly of single-pixel blocks, this policy adds two growing points to the GPP for each small block added to the encoded image. Those are the points below and to the right of the image block (see example below). Another good location for new growing points is any new concave corners that have been generated by adding the recent image block to the partially encoded image (Figure 4.101a,b). We show below that when a new image block is grown from such a corner point, it contributes two or three new entries to the dictionary.

Algorithm: Dictionary update. This is based on two principles: (1) Each matched block added to the image-so-far should be used to add one or more dictionary entries; (2) the new entries added should contain pixels in the image-encoded-so-far (so the decoder can update its dictionary in the same way). Denoting the currently matched block by B, a simple policy is to add to the dictionary the two blocks obtained by adding one column of pixels to the left of B and one row of pixels above it. Sometimes, as Figure 4.101c shows, the row or column can be added to just part of B. Later experiments with the method added a third block to the dictionary, the block obtained by adding the column to the left of B *and* the row above it. Since image blocks B start small and square, this third dictionary entry is also square. Adding this third block improves compression performance significantly.

Algorithm: Dictionary deletion. The dictionary keeps growing but it can grow only so much. When it reaches its maximum size, we can select from among the following ideas: (1) Delete the least recently used (LRU) entry (except that the original entries, all the possible pixel values, should not be deleted); (2) freeze the dictionary (i.e., don't add any new entries); and (3) delete the entire dictionary (except the original entries) and start afresh.

⋄ **Exercise 4.30:** Suggest another approach to dictionary deletion. (Hint: See Section 3.16.)

Experiments performed by the method's developers suggest that the basic algorithm is robust and does not depend much on the particular choice of the algorithms above, except for two choices that seem to improve compression performance significantly:

1. Wave coverage seems to offer better performance than circular or diagonal coverage.

2. Visual inspection of many decompressed images shows that the loss of data is more visible to the eye in image regions that are smooth (i.e., uniform or close to uniform). The method can thus be improved by using a smaller tolerance parameter for such regions. A simple measure A of smoothness is the ratio V/M, where V is the variance of the pixels in the region (see page 370 for the definition of variance) and M is their mean. The larger A, the more active (i.e., the less smooth) is the region. The tolerance t is determined by the user, and the developers of the method suggest the use of smaller tolerance values for smooth regions as follows:

$$\text{if} \begin{cases} A \le 0.05, & \text{use } 0.4t, \\ 0.05 < A \le 0.1, & \text{use } 0.6t, \\ A > 0.1, & \text{use } t. \end{cases}$$

Example: We select an image that consists of 4-bit pixels. The nine pixels at the top-left corner of this image are shown in Figure 4.102a. They have image coordinates ranging from $(0,0)$ to $(2,2)$. The first 16 entries of the dictionary D (locations 0 through 15) are initialized to the 16 possible values of the pixels. The GPP is initialized to the top-left corner of the image, position $(0,0)$. We assume that the GPP is used as a (FIFO) queue. Here are the details of the first few steps.

Step 1: Point $(0,0)$ is popped out of the GPP. The pixel value at this position is 8. Since the dictionary contains just individual pixels, not blocks, this point can be matched only with the dictionary entry containing 8. This entry happens to be located in dictionary location 8, so the encoder outputs the pointer 8. This match does not have any concave corners, so we push the point on the right of the matched block, $(0,1)$, and the point below it, $(1,0)$, into the GPP.

Step 2: Point $(1,0)$ is popped out of the GPP. The pixel value at this position is 4. The dictionary still contains just individual pixels, not any bigger blocks, so this point can be matched only with the dictionary entry containing 4. This entry is located in dictionary location 4, so the encoder outputs the pointer 4. The match does not have any concave corners, so we push the point on the right of the matched block, $(1,1)$, and the point below it, $(2,0)$, into the GPP. The GPP now contains (from most recent to least recent) points $(1,1)$, $(2,0)$, and $(0,1)$. The dictionary is updated by appending to it (at location 16) the block $\boxed{\begin{smallmatrix}8\\4\end{smallmatrix}}$ as shown in Figure 4.102b.

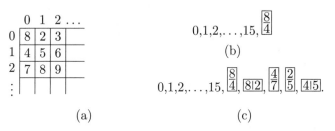

(a) (b) (c)

Figure 4.102: An Image and A Dictionary.

Step 3: Point $(0,1)$ is popped out of the GPP. The pixel value at this position is 2. The dictionary contains the 16 individual pixel values and one bigger block. The best match for this point is with the dictionary entry containing 2, which is at dictionary location 2, so the encoder outputs the pointer 2. The match does not have any concave corners, so we push the point on the right of the matched block, $(0,2)$, and the point below it, $(1,1)$, into the GPP. The GPP is now (from most recent to least recent) points $(0,2)$, $(1,1)$, and $(2,0)$. The dictionary is updated by appending to it (at location 17) the block $\boxed{8|2}$ (Figure 4.102c).

⋄ **Exercise 4.31:** Do the next two steps.

Bibliography

Constantinescu, C., and J. A. Storer (1994a) "Online Adaptive Vector Quantization with Variable Size Codebook Entries," *Information Processing and Management*, **30**(6)745–758.

Constantinescu, C., and J. A. Storer (1994b) "Improved Techniques for Single-Pass Adaptive Vector Quantization," *Proceedings of the IEEE*, **82**(6)933–939, June.

4.14 Block Matching

The LZ77 sliding window method for compressing text (Section 3.2) can be applied to images as well. This section describes such an application for the lossless compression of images. It follows the ideas outlined in [Storer and Helfgott 97]. Figure 4.103a shows how a search buffer and a look-ahead buffer can be made to slide in raster order along an image. The principle of image compression (Section 4.1) says that the neighbors of a pixel P tend to have the same value as P or very similar values. Thus, if P is the leftmost pixel in the look-ahead buffer, there is a good chance that some of its neighbors on the left (i.e., in the search buffer) will have the same value as P. There is also a chance that a string of neighbor pixels in the search buffer will match P and the string of pixels that follow it in the look-ahead buffer. Experience also suggests that in any nonrandom image there is a good chance of having identical strings of pixels in several different locations in the image.

Since near-neighbors of a pixel are located also above and below it and not just on the left and right, it makes sense to use "wide" search and look-ahead buffers and to compare blocks of, say, $4{\times}4$ pixels instead of individual pixels (Figure 4.103b). This is the reason for the name *block matching*. When this method is used, the number of rows and columns of the image should be divisible by 4. If the image doesn't satisfy this, up to three artificial rows and/or columns should be added. Two reasonable *edge conventions* are (1) add columns of zero pixels on the left and rows of zero pixels on the top of the image, (2) duplicate the rightmost column and the bottom row as many times as needed.

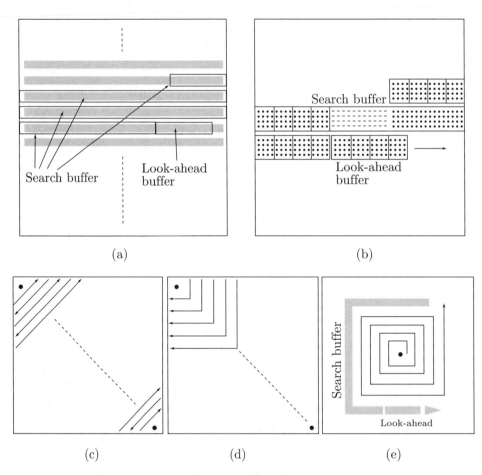

Figure 4.103: Block Matching (LZ77 For Images).

Figure 4.103c,d,e shows three other ways of sliding the window in the image. The $-45°$-diagonal traversal visits pixels in the order (1,1), (1,2), (2,1), (1,3), (2,2),

(3,1),.... In the rectilinear traversal pixels are visited in the order (1,1), (1,2), (2,2), (2,1), (1,3), (2,3), (3,3), (3,2), (3,1),.... The circular traversal visits pixels in order of increasing distance from the center.

The encoder proceeds as in LZ77. It finds all blocks in the search buffer that match the current 4×4 block in the look-ahead buffer and selects the longest match. A token is emitted (i.e., written on the compressed stream), and both buffers are advanced. In the original LZ77 the token consists of an offset (distance), match length, and next symbol in the look-ahead buffer (and the buffers are advanced by one plus the length of the match). The third item guarantees that progress will be made even in cases where no match was found. When LZ77 is extended to images, the third item of a token is the next pixel block in the look-ahead buffer. Thus, the method should be modified to output tokens without this third item, and three ways of doing this are outlined here.

⋄ **Exercise 4.32:** What's wrong with including the next block of pixels in the token?

1. The output stream consists of 2-field tokens (offset, length). When no match is found, a token of the form (0,0) is output, followed by the raw unmatched block of pixels (this is common at the start of the compression process, when the search buffer is empty or almost so). The decoder can easily mimic this.

2. The output stream consists of variable-size tags, some of which are followed by either a 2-field token or by a raw block of 16 pixels. This method is especially appropriate for bi-level images, where a pixel is represented by a single bit. We know from experience that in a "typical" bi-level image there are more uniform white areas than uniform black ones (the doubting reader should see the eighth of the ITU-T fax training documents, listed in Table 2.37, for an example of an atypical image). The tag can therefore be assigned one of the following four values: 0 if the current block in the look-ahead buffer is all white, 10 if the current block is all black, 110 if a match was found (in which case the tag is followed by an offset and a length, encoded in either fixed size or variable size), and 111 if no match was found (in this case the tag is followed by the 16-bit raw pixel block).

3. This is similar to 2 above, but on discovering a current all-white or all-black pixel block, the encoder looks for a run of such blocks. If it finds n consecutive all-white blocks, it generates a tag of 0 followed by the encoded value of n. Similarly, a tag of 10 precedes an encoded count of a run of all-black pixel blocks. Since large values of n are rare, it makes sense to use a variable-size code such as the general unary codes of Section 2.3.1. A simple encoder can always use the same unary code, for example, the (2,1,10) code, which has 2044 values. A sophisticated encoder may use the image resolution to estimate the maximum size of a run of identical blocks, select a proper value for k based on this, and use code $(2, 1, k)$. The value of k being used would have to be included in the header of the compressed file, for the decoder's use. Table 4.104 lists the number of codes of each of the general unary codes $(2, 1, k)$ for $k = 2, 3, \ldots, 11$. This table was calculated by the single *Mathematica* statement `Table[2^(k+1)-4,{k,2,11}]`.

The offset can be a single number, the distance of the matched string of pixel blocks from the edge of the search buffer. This has the advantage that the maximum value of the distance depends on the size of the search buffer. However, since the

k	:	2	3	4	5	6	7	8	9	10	11
$(2,10,k)$:		4	12	28	60	124	252	508	1020	2044	4092

Table 4.104: Number Of General Unary Codes $(2, 1, k)$ For $k = 2, 3, \ldots, 11$.

search buffer may meander through the image in a complicated way, the decoder may have to work hard to determine the image coordinates from the distance. An alternative is to use as offset the image coordinates (row and column) of the matched string instead of its distance. This makes it easy for the decoder to find the matched string of pixel blocks, but it decreases compression performance, since the row and column may be large numbers and since the offset does not depend on the actual distance (offsets for a short distance and for a long distance would require the same number of bits). An example may shed light on this point. Imagine an image with a resolution of 1K × 1K. The numbers of rows and columns are 10 bits each, so coding an offset as the pair (row, column) requires 20 bits. A sophisticated encoder, however, may decide, based on the image size, to select a search buffer of $256K = 2^{18}$ locations (25% of the image size). Coding the offsets as distances in this search buffer would require 18 bits, a small gain.

4.14.1 Implementation Details

The method described below for finding a match is just one of many possible methods. It is simple and fast, but is not guaranteed to find the best match. It is similar to the method used by LZP (Section 3.14) to find matches. Notice that finding matches is a task performed by the encoder. The decoder's task is to use the token to locate a string of pixel blocks, and this is straightforward.

The encoder starts with the current pixel block B in the look-ahead buffer. It hashes the values of the pixels of B to create a pointer p to an index table T. In $T[p]$ the encoder normally finds a pointer q pointing to the search buffer S. Block B is compared with $S[q]$. If they are identical, the encoder finds the longest match. If B and $S[q]$ are different, or if $T[p]$ is invalid (does not contain a pointer to the search buffer), there is no match. In any of these cases, a pointer to B is stored in $T[p]$, replacing its former contents. Once the encoder finds a match or decides that there is no match, it encodes its findings using one of the methods outlined above.

The index table T is initialized to all invalid entries, so initially there are no matches. As more and more pointers to pixel blocks B are stored in T, the index table becomes more useful, since more of its entries contain meaningful pointers.

Another implementation detail has to do with the header of the compressed file. It should include information that depends on the image or on the particular method used by the encoder. Such information is obviously needed by the decoder. The main items included in the header are the image resolution, number of bitplanes, the block size (4 in the examples above), and the method used for sliding the buffers. Other items that may be included are the sizes of the search and look-ahead buffers (they determine the sizes of the offset and the length fields of a token), the edge convention used, the format of the compressed file (one of the three methods outlined above), and whether the offset is a distance or a pair of image coordinates,

Step 2: Point $(1, 0)$ is popped out of the GPP. The pixel value at this position is 4. The dictionary still contains just individual pixels, not any bigger blocks, so this point can be matched only with the dictionary entry containing 4. This entry is located in dictionary location 4, so the encoder outputs the pointer 4. The match does not have any concave corners, so we push the point on the right of the matched block, $(1, 1)$, and the point below it, $(2, 0)$, into the GPP. The GPP now contains (from most recent to least recent) points $(1, 1)$, $(2, 0)$, and $(0, 1)$. The dictionary is updated by appending to it (at location 16) the block $\frac{8}{4}$ as shown in Figure 4.102b.

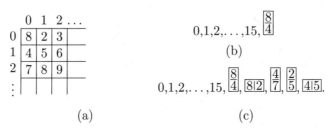

(a)   (b)   (c)

Figure 4.102: An Image and A Dictionary.

Step 3: Point $(0, 1)$ is popped out of the GPP. The pixel value at this position is 2. The dictionary contains the 16 individual pixel values and one bigger block. The best match for this point is with the dictionary entry containing 2, which is at dictionary location 2, so the encoder outputs the pointer 2. The match does not have any concave corners, so we push the point on the right of the matched block, $(0, 2)$, and the point below it, $(1, 1)$, into the GPP. The GPP is now (from most recent to least recent) points $(0, 2)$, $(1, 1)$, and $(2, 0)$. The dictionary is updated by appending to it (at location 17) the block $\boxed{8|2}$ (Figure 4.102c).

⋄ **Exercise 4.31:** Do the next two steps.

Bibliography

Constantinescu, C., and J. A. Storer (1994a) "Online Adaptive Vector Quantization with Variable Size Codebook Entries," *Information Processing and Management*, **30**(6)745–758.

Constantinescu, C., and J. A. Storer (1994b) "Improved Techniques for Single-Pass Adaptive Vector Quantization," *Proceedings of the IEEE*, **82**(6)933–939, June.

4.14 Block Matching

The LZ77 sliding window method for compressing text (Section 3.2) can be applied to images as well. This section describes such an application for the lossless compression of images. It follows the ideas outlined in [Storer and Helfgott 97]. Figure 4.103a shows how a search buffer and a look-ahead buffer can be made to slide in raster order along an image. The principle of image compression (Section 4.1) says that the neighbors of a pixel P tend to have the same value as P or very similar values. Thus, if P is the leftmost pixel in the look-ahead buffer, there is a good chance that some of its neighbors on the left (i.e., in the search buffer) will have the same value as P. There is also a chance that a string of neighbor pixels in the search buffer will match P and the string of pixels that follow it in the look-ahead buffer. Experience also suggests that in any nonrandom image there is a good chance of having identical strings of pixels in several different locations in the image.

Since near-neighbors of a pixel are located also above and below it and not just on the left and right, it makes sense to use "wide" search and look-ahead buffers and to compare blocks of, say, 4×4 pixels instead of individual pixels (Figure 4.103b). This is the reason for the name *block matching*. When this method is used, the number of rows and columns of the image should be divisible by 4. If the image doesn't satisfy this, up to three artificial rows and/or columns should be added. Two reasonable *edge conventions* are (1) add columns of zero pixels on the left and rows of zero pixels on the top of the image, (2) duplicate the rightmost column and the bottom row as many times as needed.

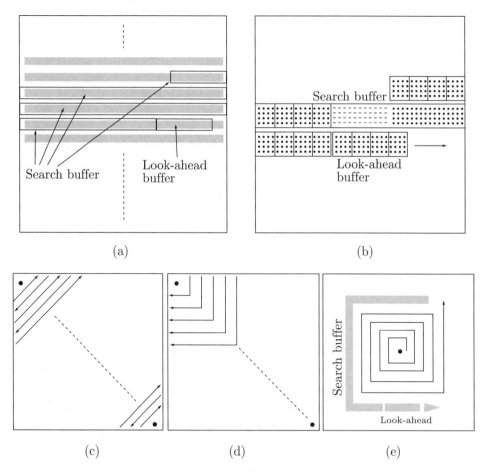

(a)   (b)

(c)   (d)   (e)

Figure 4.103: Block Matching (LZ77 For Images).

Figure 4.103c,d,e shows three other ways of sliding the window in the image. The $-45°$-diagonal traversal visits pixels in the order (1,1), (1,2), (2,1), (1,3), (2,2),

⋄ **Exercise 4.33:** Indicate one more item that a sophisticated encoder may have to include in the header.

Bibliography

Storer, James A. and Harald Helfgott (1997) "Lossless Image Compression by Block Matching," *The Computer Journal* **40**(2/3):137–145.

4.15 Block Truncation Coding

Quantization is an important technique for data compression in general and for image compression in particular. Any quantization method should be based on a principle that determines what data items to quantize and by how much. The principle used by the *block truncation coding* (BTC) method and its variants is to quantize pixels in an image while preserving the first two or three *statistical moments*. The main reference is [Dasarathy 95], which includes an introduction and copies of the main papers in this area. In the basic BTC method, the image is divided into blocks (normally 4×4 or 8×8 pixels each). Assuming that a block contains n pixels with intensities p_1 through p_n, the first two moments are the mean and variance, defined as

$$\bar{p} = \frac{1}{n} \sum_{i=1}^{n} p_i, \tag{4.24}$$

and

$$\overline{p^2} = \frac{1}{n} \sum_{i=1}^{n} p_i^2, \tag{4.25}$$

respectively. The standard deviation of the block is

$$\sigma = \sqrt{\overline{p^2} - \bar{p}}. \tag{4.26}$$

The principle of the quantization is to select three values, a threshold p_{thr}, a high value p^+, and a low value p^-. Each pixel is replaced by either p^+ or p^-, such that the first two moments of the new pixels (i.e., their mean and variance) will be identical to the original moments of the pixel block. The rule of quantization is that a pixel p_i is quantized to p^+ if it is greater than the threshold, and is quantized to p^- if it is less than the threshold (if p_i equals the threshold, it can be quantized to either value). Thus,

$$p_i \leftarrow \begin{cases} p^+, & \text{if } p_i \geq p_{\text{thr}}, \\ p^-, & \text{if } p_i < p_{\text{thr}}. \end{cases}$$

Intuitively, it is clear that the mean $\bar{p}$ is a good choice for the threshold. The high and low values can be calculated by writing equations that preserve the first two moments, and solving them. We denote by n^+ the number of pixels in the current block that are greater than or equal to the threshold. Similarly, n^- stands for the number of pixels less than the threshold. The sum $n^+ + n^-$ equals, of course, the number of pixels n in the block. Once the mean $\bar{p}$ has been computed, both n^+ and n^- are easy to calculate. Preserving the first two moments is expressed by the two equations

$$n\bar{p} = n^- p^- - n^+ p^+, \quad n\overline{p^2} = n^- (p^-)^2 - n^+ (p^+)^2. \tag{4.27}$$

These are easy to solve even though they are nonlinear, and the solutions are

$$p^- = \bar{p} - \sigma \sqrt{\frac{n^+}{n^-}}, \quad p^+ = \bar{p} + \sigma \sqrt{\frac{n^-}{n^+}}. \tag{4.28}$$

These solutions are generally real numbers, but they have to be rounded to the nearest integer, which implies that the mean and variance of the quantized block may be somewhat different from the original ones. Notice that the solutions are located on the two sides of the mean $\bar{p}$ at distances that are proportional to the standard deviation σ of the pixel block.

Example: We select the $4{\times}4$ block of 8-bit pixels

$$\begin{pmatrix} 121 & 114 & 56 & 47 \\ 37 & 200 & 247 & 255 \\ 16 & 0 & 12 & 169 \\ 43 & 5 & 7 & 251 \end{pmatrix}.$$

The mean is $\bar{p} = 98.75$, so we count $n^+ = 7$ pixels greater than the mean and $n^- = 16 - 7 = 9$ pixels less than the mean. The standard deviation is $\sigma = 92.95$, so the high and low values are

$$p^+ = 98.75 + 92.95\sqrt{\frac{9}{7}} = 204.14, \quad p^- = 98.75 - 92.95\sqrt{\frac{7}{9}} = 16.78.$$

They are rounded to 204 and 17, respectively. The resulting block is

$$\begin{pmatrix} 204 & 204 & 17 & 17 \\ 17 & 204 & 204 & 204 \\ 17 & 17 & 17 & 204 \\ 17 & 17 & 17 & 204 \end{pmatrix},$$

and it is clear that the original $4{\times}4$ block can be compressed to the 16 bits

$$\begin{pmatrix} 1 & 1 & 0 & 0 \\ 0 & 1 & 1 & 1 \\ 0 & 0 & 0 & 1 \\ 0 & 0 & 0 & 1 \end{pmatrix},$$

plus the two 8-bit values 204 and 17; a total of $16 + 2{\times}8$ bits, compared to the $16{\times}8$ bits of the original block. The compression factor is

$$\frac{16{\times}8}{16 + 2{\times}8} = 4.$$

⋄ **Exercise 4.34:** Do the same for the 4×4 block of 8-bit pixels

$$\begin{pmatrix} 136 & 27 & 144 & 216 \\ 172 & 83 & 43 & 219 \\ 200 & 254 & 1 & 128 \\ 64 & 32 & 96 & 25 \end{pmatrix}.$$

It is clear that the compression factor of this method is known in advance, since it depends on the block size n and on the number of bits b per pixel. In general, the compression factor is

$$\frac{bn}{n + 2b}.$$

Figure 4.105 shows the compression factors for b values of 2, 4, 8, 12, and 16 bits per pixel, and for block sizes n between 2 and 16.

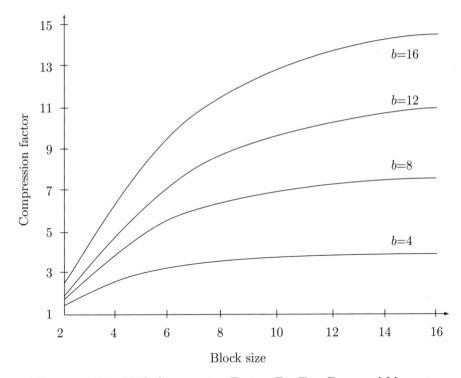

Figure 4.105: BTC Compression Factors For Two Preserved Moments.

The basic BTC method is simple and fast. Its main drawback is the way it loses image information, which is based on pixel intensities in each block, and not on any properties of the human visual system. Because of this, images compressed under BTC tend to have a blocky character when decompressed and reconstructed. This led many researchers to develop enhanced and extended versions of the basic BTC, some of which are briefly mentioned here.

1. Encode the results before writing them on the compressed stream. In basic BTC, each original block of n pixels becomes a block of n bits plus two numbers. It is possible to accumulate B blocks of n bits each, and encode the Bn bits using run length encoding (RLE). This should be followed by $2B$ values, and those can be encoded with prefix codes.

2. Sort the n pixels p_i of a block by increasing intensity values, and denote the sorted pixels by s_i. The first n^- pixels s_i have values that are less than the threshold, and the remaining n^+ pixels s_i have larger values. The high and low values, p^+ and p^-, are now the values that minimize the square-error expression

$$\sum_{i=1}^{n^--1} \left(s_i - p^-\right)^2 + \sum_{i=n^-}^{n^+} \left(s_i - p^+\right)^2. \tag{4.29}$$

These values are

$$p^- = \frac{1}{n^-} \sum_{i=1}^{n^--1} s_i \text{ and } p^+ = \frac{1}{n^+} \sum_{i=n^-}^{n^+} s_i.$$

The threshold in this case is determined by searching all $n-1$ possible threshold values and choosing the one that produces the lowest value for the square-error expression of Equation (4.29).

3. Sort the pixels as in 2 above, and change Equation (4.29) to a similar one using absolute values instead of squares:

$$\sum_{i=1}^{n^--1} |s_i - p^-| + \sum_{i=n^-}^{n^+} |s_i - p^+|. \tag{4.30}$$

The high and low values p^+ and p^- should be, in this case, the medians of the low and high intensity sets of pixels, respectively. Thus, p^- should be the median of the set $\{s_i | i = 1, 2, \ldots, n^- - 1\}$, and p^+ should be the median of the set $\{s_i | i = n^-, \ldots, n^+\}$. The threshold value is determined as in 2 above.

4. This is an extension of the basic BTC method, where *three* moments are preserved, instead of two. The three equations that result make it possible to calculate the value of the threshold, in addition to those of the high (p^+) and low (p^-) parameters. The third moment is

$$\overline{p^3} = \frac{1}{n} \sum_{i=1}^{n} p_i^3, \tag{4.31}$$

and its preservation gives rise to the equation

$$n\overline{p^3} = n^- \left(p^-\right)^3 - n^+ \left(p^+\right)^3. \tag{4.32}$$

Solving the three equations (4.27) and (4.32) with p^-, p^+, and n^+ as the unknowns yields

$$n^+ = \frac{n}{2} \left(1 + \frac{\alpha}{\sqrt{\alpha^2 + 4}}\right),$$

where

$$\alpha = \frac{3\bar{p}(\overline{p^2}) - \overline{p^3} - 2(\bar{p})^3}{\sigma^3}.$$

And the threshold p_{thr} is selected as pixel p_{n+}.

5. BTC is a lossy compression method where the data being lost is based on the mean and variance of the pixels in each block. This loss has nothing to do with the human visual system [Salomon 99], or with any general features of the image being compressed, so it may cause artifacts and unrecognizable regions in the decompressed image. One especially annoying feature of the basic BTC is that straight edges in the original image become jagged in the reconstructed image.

The *edge following* algorithm [Ronson and Dewitte 82] is an extension of basic BTC, where this tendency is minimized by identifying pixels that are on an edge, and using an additional quantization level for blocks containing such pixels. Each pixel in such a block is quantized into one of *three* different values instead of the usual two. This reduces the compression factor but improves the visual appearance of the reconstructed image.

Another extension of the basic BTC is a three-stage process, proposed in [Dewitte and Ronson 83] where the first stage is basic BTC, resulting in a binary matrix and two numbers. The second stage classifies the binary matrix into one of three categories as follows:

a. The block has no edges (indicating a uniform or near-uniform region).

b. There is a single edge across the block.

c. There is a pair of edges across the block.

The classification is done by counting the number of transitions from 0 to 1 and from 1 to 0 along the four edges of the binary matrix. Blocks with zero transitions or with more than four transitions are considered category *a* (no edges). Blocks with two transitions are considered category *b* (a single edge), and blocks with four transitions, category *c* (two edges).

Stage three matches the classified block of pixels to a particular model depending on its classification. Experiments with this method suggest that about 80% of the blocks belong in category *a*, 12% are category *b*, and 8% belong in category *c*. The fact that category *a* blocks are so common means that the basic BTC can be used in most cases, and the particular models used for categories *b* and *c* improve the appearance of the reconstructed image without significantly degrading the compression time and compression factor.

6. The original BTC is based on the principle of preserving the first two statistical moments of a pixel block. The variant described here changes this principle to preserving the first two *absolute moments*. The first absolute moment is given by

$$\overline{p_a} = \frac{1}{n} \sum_{i=1}^{n} |p_i - \bar{p}|,$$

and it can be shown that this implies

$$p^+ = \bar{p} + \frac{n\overline{p_a}}{2n^+} \quad \text{and} \quad p^- = \bar{p} - \frac{n\overline{p_a}}{2n^-},$$

which shows that the high and low values are simpler than those used by the basic BTC. They are obtained from the mean by adding and subtracting quantities that are proportional to the absolute first moment $\overline{p_a}$ and inversely proportional to the numbers n^+ and n^- of pixels on both sides of this mean. Moreover, these high and low values can also be written as

$$p^+ = \frac{1}{n^+} \sum_{p_i \geq \bar{p}} p_i \quad \text{and} \quad p^- = \frac{1}{n^-} \sum_{p_i < \bar{p}} p_i,$$

simplifying their computation even more.

In addition to these improvements and extensions there are BTC variants that deviate significantly from the basic idea. The *three-level BTC* is a good example of the latter. It quantizes each pixel p_i into one of three values, instead of the original two. This, of course, requires two bits per pixel, thereby reducing the compression factor. The method starts by scanning all the pixels in the block and finding the range Δ of intensities

$$\Delta = \max(p_i) - \min(p_i), \text{ for } i = 1, 2, \ldots, n.$$

Two mean values, high and low, are defined as

$$\overline{p_h} = \max(p_i) - \Delta/3 \quad \text{and} \quad \overline{p_l} = \min(p_i) + \Delta/3.$$

The three quantization levels, high, low, and mid, are now given by

$$p^+ = \tfrac{1}{2}\left[\overline{p_h} + \max(p_i)\right], \quad p^- = \tfrac{1}{2}\left[\overline{p_l} + \min(p_i)\right], \quad p^{\mathrm{m}} = \tfrac{1}{2}\left[\overline{p_l} + \overline{p_h}\right].$$

A pixel p_i is compared to p^+, p^-, and p^{m} and is quantized to the nearest of these values. It takes two bits to express the result of quantizing p_i, so the original block of n b-bit pixels becomes a block of $2n$ bits. In addition, the values of $\max(p_i)$ and $\min(p_i)$ have to be written on the compressed stream as two b-bit numbers. The resulting compression factor is

$$\frac{bn}{2n + 2b},$$

lower than in basic BTC. Figure 4.106 shows the compression factors for $b = 4, 8, 12,$ and 16 and for n values in the range $[2, 16]$.

In spite of worse compression, the three-level BTC has an overall better performance than the basic BTC because it requires simpler calculations (in particular, the second moment is not needed) and because its reconstructed images are of higher quality and don't have the blocky appearance typical of images compressed and decompressed under basic BTC.

Bibliography

Dasarathy, Belur V. (ed.) (1995) *Image Data Compression: Block Truncation Coding (BTC) Techniques*, Los Alamitos, CA, IEEE Computer Society Press.

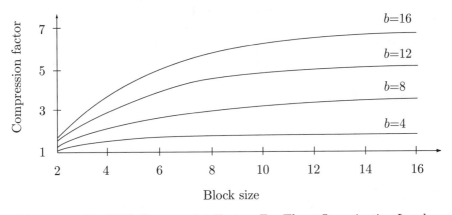

Figure 4.106: BTC Compression Factors For Three Quantization Levels.

Dewitte, J. and J. Ronson (1983) "Original Block Coding Scheme for Low Bit Rate Image Transmission," in *Signal Processing II: Theories and Applications—Proceedings of EU-SIPCO 83*, H. W. Schussler, ed., Amsterdam, Elsevier Science Publishers B. V. (North-Holland), pp. 143–146.

Ronson, J. and J. Dewitte (1982) "Adaptive Block Truncation Coding Scheme Using an Edge Following Algorithm," *Proceedings of the IEEE International Conference on Acoustics, Speech, and Signal Processing*, Piscataway, NJ, IEEE Press, pp. 1235–1238.

4.16 Context-Based Methods

Most image-compression methods are based on the observation that for any randomly selected pixel in the image, its near neighbors tend to have the same value as the pixel (or similar values). A context-based image compression method generalizes this observation. It is based on the idea that the context of a pixel can be used to predict (estimate the probability of) the pixel.

Such a method compresses an image by scanning it pixel by pixel, examining the context of every pixel, and assigning it a probability depending on how many times the same context was seen in the past. The pixel and its assigned probability are then sent to an arithmetic encoder that does the actual encoding. The methods described here are due to Langdon [Langdon 81] and Moffat [Moffat 91], and apply to monochromatic (bi-level) images. The context of a pixel consists of some of its neighbor pixels that have already been seen. The diagram below shows a possible seven-pixel context (the pixels marked P) made up of five pixels above and two on the left of the current pixel X. The pixels marked "?" haven't been input yet, so they cannot be included in the context.

·	·	P	P	P	P	P	·	·
·	·	P	P	X	?	?	?	?

The main idea is to use the values of the seven context pixels as a 7-bit index to a frequency table, and find the number of times a 0 pixel and a 1 pixel were seen in the past with the same context. Here is an example:

·	·	1	0	0	1	1	·	·
·	·	0	1	X	?	?	?	?

Since $1001101_2 = 77$, location 77 of the frequency table is examined. We assume that it contains a count of 15 for a 0 pixel and a count of 11 for a 1 pixel. The current pixel is thus assigned probability $15/(15 + 11) \approx 0.58$ if it is 0 and $11/26 \approx 0.42$ if it is 1.

77
· · ·	15	· · ·
· · ·	11	· · ·

One of the counts at location 77 is then incremented, depending on what the current pixel is. Figure 4.107 shows ten possible ways to select contexts. They range from a 1-bit, to a 22-bit context. In the latter case, there may be $2^{22} \approx 4.2$ million contexts, most of which will rarely, if ever, occur in the image. Instead of maintaining a huge, mostly empty array, the frequency table can be implemented as a binary search tree or a hash table. For short, 7-bit, contexts, the frequency table can be an array, resulting in fast search.

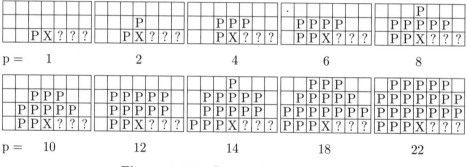

Figure 4.107: Context Pixel Patterns.

Experience shows that longer contexts result in better compression, up to about 12–14 bits. Contexts longer than that result in worse compression, indicating that a pixel in a typical image does not "relate" to distant pixels (correlations between pixels are typically limited to a distance of 1–2).

As usual for a context-based compression method, care should be taken to avoid zero probabilities. The frequency table should thus be initialized to nonzero values, and experience shows that the precise way of doing this does not affect the compression performance significantly. It seems best to initialize every table entry to 1.

When the process starts, the first pixels to be scanned don't have any neighbors above them or to the left. A simple way to handle this is to assume that any nonexistent neighbors are zeros. It is as if the image was extended by adding as many rows of zero pixels as necessary on top and as many zero columns on the left.

The 2-bit context of Figure 4.107 is now used, as an example, to encode the first row of the 4×4 image

$$
\begin{array}{c|cccc}
 & 0\ 0\ 0\ 0 \\
\hline
0 & 1\ 0\ 1\ 1 \\
0 & 0\ 1\ 0\ 1 \\
0 & 1\ 0\ 0\ 1 \\
0 & 0\ 0\ 1\ 0 \\
\end{array}
$$

The results are summarized in Table 4.108.

Number	Pixel	Context	*Counts*	Probability	*Newcounts*
1	1	00=0	1, 1	$1/(1+1) = 1/2$	1, 2
2	0	01=1	1, 1	1/2	2, 1
3	1	00=0	1, 2	2/3	1, 3
4	1	01=1	2, 1	1/3	2, 2

Table 4.108: Counts and Probabilities for First Four Pixels.

⋄ **Exercise 4.35:** Continue Table 4.108 for the next row of four pixels 0101.

The contexts of Figure 4.107 are not symmetric about the current pixel, since they must use pixels that have already been input ("past" pixels). If the algorithm scans the image by rows, those will be the pixels above and to the left of the current pixel. In practical work it is impossible to include "future" pixels in the context (since the decoder wouldn't have their values when decoding the current pixel), but for experiments, where there is no need to actually decode the compressed image, it is possible to store the entire image in memory so that the encoder can examine any pixel at any time. Experiments performed with symmetric contexts have shown that compression performance can improve by as much as 30%. (The MLP method, Section 4.19, provides an interesting twist to the question of a symmetric context.)

⋄ **Exercise 4.36:** (Easy.) Why is it possible to use "future" pixels in an experiment but not in practice? It would seem that the image, or part of it, could be stored in memory and the encoder could use any pixel as part of a context?

One disadvantage of a large context is that it takes the algorithm longer to "learn" it. A 20-bit context, for example, allows for about a million different contexts. It takes many millions of pixels to collect enough counts for all those contexts, which is one reason large contexts do not result in better compression. One way to improve our method is to implement a *two-level* algorithm that uses a long context only if that context has already been seen Q times or more (where Q is a parameter, typically set to a small value such as 2 or 3). If a context has been seen fewer than Q times, it is deemed unreliable, and only a small subset of it is used to predict the current pixel. Figure 4.109 shows four such contexts, where the pixels of the subset are labeled S. The notation p, q means a two-level context of p bits with a subset of q bits.

	P	P	P	P	P	
	S	S	S	S	P	
	S	S	X	?	?	?

$p, q =$ 12,6

			P			
	P	P	S	P	P	
	S	S	S	S	S	
P	S	S	X	?	?	?

14,8

		P	P	P		
	P	S	S	S	P	
P	S	S	S	S	S	P
P	S	S	X	?	?	?

18,10

	P	P	P	P	P	
P	P	S	S	S	P	P
P	S	S	S	S	S	P
P	S	S	X	?	?	?

22,10

Figure 4.109: Two-Level Context Pixel Patterns.

Experience shows that the 18, 10 and 22, 10 contexts result in better, although not revolutionary, compression.

Bibliography

Langdon, G., and J. Rissanen (1981) "Compression of Black White Images with Arithmetic Coding," *IEEE Transactions on Communications* COM-29(6):858–867, June.

Moffat, A. (1991) "Two-Level Context Based Compression of Binary Images," in *Proceedings of the 1991 Data Compression Conference*, J. Storer ed., Los Alamitos, CA, IEEE Computer Society Press, pp. 382–391.

4.17 FELICS

FELICS is an acronym for Fast, Efficient, Lossless Image Compression System [Howard 93]. It is a special-purpose compression method designed for grayscale images and it competes with the lossless mode of JPEG (Section 4.6.7). It is fast and it generally produces good compression. However, it cannot compress an image to below one bit per pixel, so it is not a good choice for bi-level or for highly redundant images.

The principle of FELICS is to code each pixel with a variable-size code based on the values of two of its previously seen neighbor pixels. Figure 4.110a shows the two known neighbors A and B of some pixels P. For a general pixel, these are the neighbors above it and to its left. For a pixel in the top row, these are its two left neighbors (except for the first two pixels of the image). For a pixel in the leftmost column, these are the first two pixels of the line above it. Notice that the first two pixels of the image don't have any previously seen neighbors, but since there are only two of them, they can be output without any encoding, causing just a slight degradation in the overall compression.

◇ **Exercise 4.37:** What model is used by FELICS to predict the current pixel?

Consider the two neighbors A and B of a pixel P. We use A, B, and P to denote both the three pixels and their intensities (grayscale values). We denote by L and H the neighbors with the smaller and the larger intensities, respectively. Pixel P should be assigned a variable-size code depending on where the intensity P is located relative to L and H. There are three cases:

1. The intensity of pixel P is between L and H (it is located in the central region of Figure 4.110b). This case is known experimentally to occur in about half the pixels, and P is assigned, in this case, a code that starts with 0. (A special case occurs when L = H. In such a case, the range [L, H] consists of one value only, and the chance that P will have that value is small.) The probability that P will be in this central region is almost, but not completely, flat, so P should be assigned a binary

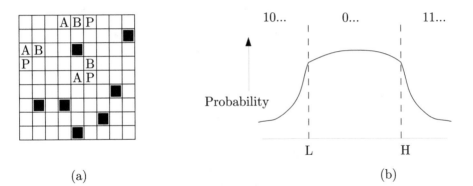

Figure 4.110: (a) The Two Neighbors. (b) The Three Regions.

code that has about the same size in the entire region but is slightly shorter at the center of the region.

2. The intensity of P is lower than L (P is in the left region). The code assigned to P in this case starts with 10.

3. P's intensity is greater than H. P is assigned a code that starts with 11.

When pixel P is in one of the outer regions, the probability that its intensity will differ from L or H by much is small, so P can be assigned a long code in these cases.

The code assigned to P should thus depend heavily on whether P is in the central region or in one of the outer regions. Here is how the code is assigned when P is in the central region. We need $H - L + 1$ variable-size codes that will not differ much in size and will, of course, satisfy the prefix property. We set $k = \lfloor \log_2(H - L + 1) \rfloor$ and compute integers a and b by

$$a = 2^{k+1} - (H - L + 1), \quad b = 2(H - L + 1 - 2^k).$$

Example: If $H - L = 9$, then $k = 3$, $a = 2^{3+1} - (9+1) = 6$, and $b = 2(9+1-2^3) = 4$. We now select the a codes $2^k - 1$, $2^k - 2, \ldots$ expressed as k-bit numbers, and the b codes 0, 1, 2, ... expressed as $(k + 1)$-bit numbers. In the example above, the a codes are $8 - 1 = 111$, $8 - 2 = 110$, through $8 - 6 = 010$, and the b codes, 0000, 0001, 0010, and 0011. The a short codes are assigned to values of P in the middle of the central region, and the b long codes are assigned to values of P closer to L or H. Notice that b is even, so the b codes can always be divided evenly. Table 4.111 shows how ten such codes can be assigned in the case $L = 15$, $H = 24$.

When P is in one of the outer regions, say the upper one, the value $P - H$ should be assigned a variable-size code whose size can grow quickly as $P - H$ gets bigger. One way to do this is to select a small nonnegative integer m (typically 0, 1, 2, or 3) and to assign the integer n a 2-part code. The second part is the lower m bits of n, and the first part is the unary code of [n without its lower m bits] (see Exercise 2.5 for the unary code). Example: If $m = 2$, then $n = 1101_2$ is assigned the code 110|01, since 110 is the unary code of 11. This code is a special case of the Golomb code (Section 2.4), where the parameter b is a power of 2 (2^m). Table 4.112

Pixel P	Region code	Pixel code
L=15	0	0000
16	0	0010
17	0	010
18	0	011
19	0	100
20	0	101
21	0	110
22	0	111
23	0	0001
H=24	0	0011

Table 4.111: The Codes for the Central Region.

shows some examples of this code for $m = 0, 1, 2, 3$ and $n = 1, 2, \ldots, 9$. The value of m used in any particular compression job can be selected, as a parameter, by the user.

Pixel P	P–H	Region code	$m =$ 0	1	2	3
H+1=25	1	11	0	00	000	0000
26	2	11	10	01	001	0001
27	3	11	110	100	010	0010
28	4	11	1110	101	011	0011
29	5	11	11110	1100	1000	0100
30	6	11	111110	1101	1001	0101
31	7	11	1111110	11100	1010	0110
32	8	11	11111110	11101	1011	0111
33	9	11	111111110	111100	11000	10000
...	...	...	...	...		
...	...	...	...	...	...	

Table 4.112: The Codes for an Outer Region.

⋄ **Exercise 4.38:** Given the 4×4 bitmap of Figure 4.113, calculate the FELICS codes for the three pixels with values 8, 7, and 0.

```
2   5   7  12
3   0  11  10
2   1   8  15
4  13  11   9
```

Figure 4.113: A 4×4 Bitmap.

Bibliography

Howard, P. G. and J. S. Vitter, (1993) "Fast and Efficient Lossless Image Compression," in *Proceedings of the 1993 Data Compression Conference*, J. Storer ed., Los Alamitos, CA, IEEE Computer Society Press, pp. 351–360.

4.18 Progressive FELICS

The original FELICS method can easily be extended to progressive compression of images because of its main principle. FELICS scans the image in raster order (row by row) and encodes a pixel based on the values of two of its (previously seen and encoded) neighbors. Progressive FELICS works similarly, but it scans the pixels in levels. Each level uses the k pixels encoded in all previous levels to encode k more pixels, so the number of encoded pixels doubles after each level. Assuming that the image consists of $n \times n$ pixels, and the first level starts with just four pixels, consecutive levels result in

$$4, 8, \ldots, \frac{n^2}{8}, \frac{n^2}{4}, \frac{n^2}{2}, n^2$$

pixels. Thus, the number of levels is the number of terms, $2 \log_2 n - 1$, in this sequence. (This property is easy to prove. The first term can be written

$$4 = \frac{n^2}{2^{-2} n^2} = \frac{n^2}{2^{2 \log n - 2}}.$$

Terms in the sequence thus contain powers of 2 that go from 0 to $2 \log_2 n - 2$, showing that there are $2 \log_2 n - 1$ terms.)

Figure 4.114 shows the pixels encoded in most of the levels of a 16×16-pixel image. Figure 4.115 shows how the pixels of each level are selected. In Figure 4.115a there are $8 \times 8 = 64$ pixels, one quarter of the final number, arranged in a square grid. Each group of four pixels is used to encode a new pixel, so Figure 4.115b has 128 pixels, half the final number. The image of Figure 4.115b is then rotated 45° and scaled by factors of $\sqrt{2} \approx 1.414$ in both directions, to produce Figure 4.115c, which is a square grid that looks exactly like Figure 4.115a. The next step (not shown in the figure) is to use every group of 4×4 pixels in Figure 4.115c to encode a pixel, thereby encoding the remaining 128 pixels. In practice, there is no need to actually rotate and scale the image; the program simply alternates between xy and diagonal coordinates.

Each group of four pixels is used to encode the pixel at its center. Notice that in early levels the four pixels of a group are far from each other and are thus not correlated, resulting in poor compression. However, the last two levels encode 3/4 of the total number of pixels, and these levels contain compact groups. Two of the four pixels of a group are selected to encode the center pixel, and are designated L and H. Experience shows that the best choice for L and H is the two median pixels (page 307), the ones with the middle values (i.e., not the maximum or the minimum pixels of the group). Ties can be resolved in any way, but it should be consistent. If the two medians in a group are the same, then the median and the minimum (or the median and the maximum) pixels can be selected. The two selected pixels, L and

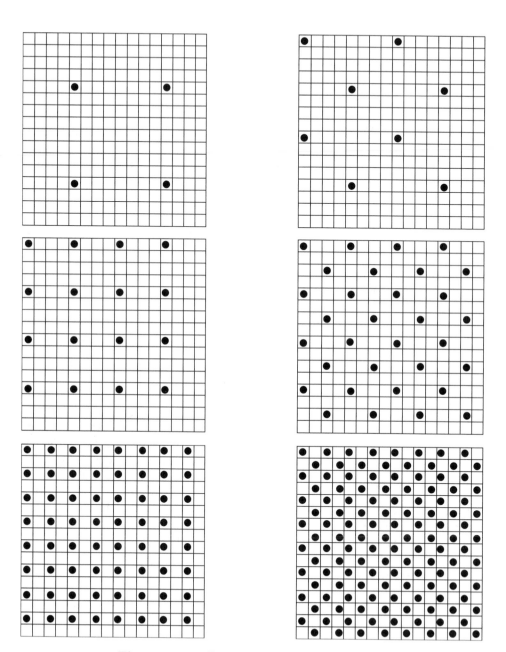

Figure 4.114: Some Levels of a 16×16 Image.

H, are used to encode the center pixel in the same way FELICS uses two neighbors to encode a pixel. The only difference is that a new prefix code (Section 4.18.1) is used, instead of the Golomb code.

⋄ **Exercise 4.39:** Why is it important to resolve ties in a consistent way?

4.18.1 Subexponential Code

In early levels, the four pixels used to encode a pixel are far from each other. As more levels are progressively encoded the groups get more compact, so their pixels get closer. The encoder uses the absolute difference between the L and H pixels in a group (the *context* of the group) to encode the pixel at the center of the group, but a given absolute difference means more for late levels than for early ones, because the groups of late levels are smaller, so their pixels are more correlated. The encoder should thus scale the difference by a weight parameter s that gets heavier from level to level. The specific value of s is not critical, and experiments recommend the value 12.

The prefix code used by progressive FELICS is called *subexponential*. Like the Golomb code (Section 2.4), this new code depends on a parameter $k \geq 0$. The main feature of the subexponential code is its length. For integers $n < 2^{k+1}$ the code length increases linearly with n, but for larger n, it increases logarithmically. The subexponential code of the nonnegative integer n is computed in two steps. In the first step, values b and u are calculated by

$$b = \begin{cases} k & \text{if } n < 2^k; \\ \lfloor \log_2 n \rfloor & \text{if } n \geq 2^k; \end{cases} \quad \text{and} \quad u = \begin{cases} 0 & \text{if } n < 2^k; \\ b - k + 1 & \text{if } n \geq 2^k. \end{cases}$$

In the second step, the unary code of u (in $u + 1$ bits), followed by the b least significant bits of n, becomes the subexponential code of n. The total size of the code is thus

$$u + 1 + b = \begin{cases} k + 1 & \text{if } n < 2^k, \\ 2\lfloor \log_2 n \rfloor - k + 2 & \text{if } n \geq 2^k. \end{cases}$$

Table 4.116 shows examples of the subexponential code for various values of n and k. It can be shown that for a given n, the code lengths for consecutive values of k differ by at most 1.

If the value of the pixel to be encoded lies between those of L and H, the pixel is encoded as in FELICS. If it lies outside the range $[L, H]$, the pixel is encoded by using the subexponential code where the value of k is selected by the following rule: Suppose that the current pixel P to be encoded has context C. The encoder maintains a cumulative total, for some reasonable values of k, of the code length the encoder would have if it had used that value of k to encode all pixels encountered so far in context C. The encoder then uses the k value with the smallest cumulative code length to encode P.

Bibliography

Howard, P. G., and J. S. Vitter (1994) "Fast Progressive Lossless Image Compression," Proceedings of the Image and Video Compression Conference, *IS&T/SPIE 1994 Symposium on Electronic Imaging: Science & Technology*, 2186, San Jose, CA, pp. 98–109. February.

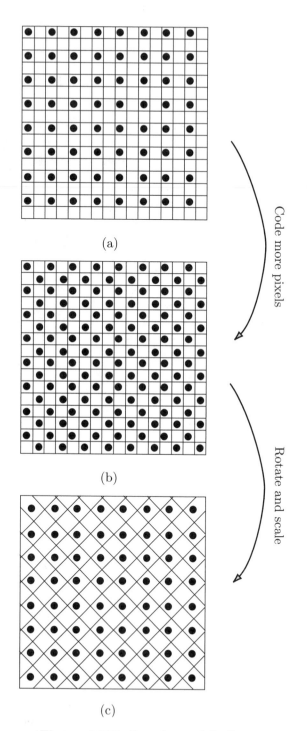

(a)

Code more pixels

(b)

Rotate and scale

(c)

Figure 4.115: Rotation and Scaling.

n	$k = 0$	$k = 1$	$k = 2$	$k = 3$	$k = 4$	$k = 5$
0	0|	0|0	0|00	0|000	0|0000	0|00000
1	10|	0|1	0|01	0|001	0|0001	0|00001
2	110|0	10|0	0|10	0|010	0|0010	0|00010
3	110|1	10|1	0|11	0|011	0|0011	0|00011
4	1110|00	110|00	10|00	0|100	0|0100	0|00100
5	1110|01	110|01	10|01	0|101	0|0101	0|00101
6	1110|10	110|10	10|10	0|110	0|0110	0|00110
7	1110|11	110|11	10|11	0|111	0|0111	0|00111
8	11110|000	1110|000	110|000	10|000	0|1000	0|01000
9	11110|001	1110|001	110|001	10|001	0|1001	0|01001
10	11110|010	1110|010	110|010	10|010	0|1010	0|01010
11	11110|011	1110|011	110|011	10|011	0|1011	0|01011
12	11110|100	1110|100	110|100	10|100	0|1100	0|01100
13	11110|101	1110|101	110|101	10|101	0|1101	0|01101
14	11110|110	1110|110	110|110	10|110	0|1110	0|01110
15	11110|111	1110|111	110|111	10|111	0|1111	0|01111
16	111110|0000	11110|0000	1110|0000	110|0000	10|0000	0|10000

Table 4.116: Some Subexponential Codes.

4.19 MLP

Text compression methods can use context to predict (i.e., to estimate the probability of) the next character of text. Using context to predict the intensity of the next pixel in image compression is more complex for two reasons: (1) An image is two-dimensional, allowing for many possible contexts, and (2) a digital image is normally the result of digitizing an analog image. The intensity of any individual pixel is thus determined by the details of digitization and may differ from the "ideal" intensity.

The multilevel progressive method (MLP) described here [Howard and Vitter 92a], is a computationally intensive, lossless method for compressing grayscale images. It uses context to predict the intensities of pixels, then uses arithmetic coding to encode the difference between the prediction and the actual value of a pixel (the error). The Laplace distribution is used to estimate the probability of the error. The method combines four separate steps: (1) pixel sequencing, (2) prediction (image modeling), (3) error modeling (by means of the Laplace distribution), and (4) arithmetically encoding the errors.

MLP is also progressive, encoding the image in levels, where the pixels of each level are selected as in progressive FELICS. When the image is decoded, each level adds details to the entire image, not just to certain parts, so a user can view the image as it is being decoded and decide in real time whether to accept or reject it. This feature is useful when an image has to be selected from a large archive of compressed images. The user can browse through images very fast, without having to wait for any image to be completely decoded. Another advantage of progressive compression is that it provides a natural lossy option. The encoder may be told to stop encoding before it reaches the last level (thereby encoding only half the total number of pixels) or before it reaches the next to last level (encoding only a quarter of the total number of pixels). Such an option results in excellent compression ratio but a loss of image data. The decoder may be told to use interpolation to determine the intensities of any missing pixels.

Like any compression method for grayscale images, MLP can be used to compress color images. The original color image should be separated into three color components, and each component compressed individually as a grayscale image. Following is a detailed description of the individual MLP encoding steps.

> What we know is not much. What we do not know is immense.
> —(Allegedly Laplace's last words.)

4.19.1 Pixel Sequencing

Pixels are selected in levels, as in progressive FELICS, where each level encodes the same number of pixels as all the preceding levels combined, thereby doubling the number of encoded pixels. This means that the last level encodes half the number of pixels, the level preceding it encodes a quarter of the total number, and so on. The first level should start with at least four pixels, but may also start with 8, 16, or any desired power of 2.

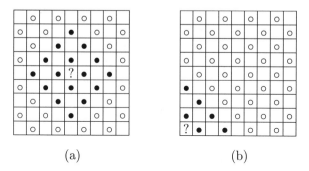

(a)   (b)

Figure 4.117: (a) 16 Neighbors. (b) 6 Neighbors.

> Man follows only phantoms.
> —(Allegedly Laplace's last words.)

4.19.2 Prediction

A pixel is predicted by calculating a weighted average of 16 of its known neighbors. Keep in mind that pixels are not raster scanned but are encoded (and thus also decoded) in levels. When decoding the pixels of level L, the MLP decoder has already decoded all the pixels of all the preceding levels, and it can use their values (gray levels) to predict values of pixels of L. Figure 4.117a shows the situation when the MLP encoder processes the last level. Half the pixels have already been encoded in previous levels, so they will be known to the decoder when the last level is decoded. The encoder can thus use a diamond-shaped group of 4×4 pixels (shown in black) from previous levels to predict the pixel at the center of the group. This group becomes the *context* of the pixel. Compression methods that scan the image in raster order can use only pixels above and to the left of pixel P to predict P. Because of the progressive nature of MLP, it can use a symmetric context, which produces more accurate predictions. On the other hand, the pixels of the context are not near neighbors and may even be (in early levels) far from the predicted pixel.

> It's hard to predict, especially the future.
> —Niels Bohr.

Table 4.118 shows the 16 weights used for a group. They are calculated by bicubic polynomial interpolation (appendix in the book's web site) and are normalized such that they add up to 1. (Notice that in Table 4.118a the weights are not normalized; they add up to 256. When these integer weights are used, the weighted sum should be divided by 256.) To predict a pixel near an edge, where some of the 16 neighbors are missing (as in Figure 4.117b), only those neighbors that exist are used, and their weights are renormalized, to bring their sum to 1.

$$
\begin{array}{cccc}
 & 1 & & \\
-9 & & -9 & \\
-9 & 81 & & -9 \\
1 & 81 & 81 & 1 \\
-9 & 81 & & -9 \\
 & -9 & -9 & \\
 & 1 & &
\end{array}
\qquad
\begin{array}{cccc}
 & 0.0039 & & \\
-0.0351 & & -0.0351 & \\
-0.0351 & 0.3164 & & -0.0351 \\
0.0039 & 0.3164 & 0.3164 & 0.0039 \\
-0.0351 & 0.3164 & & -0.0351 \\
 & -0.0351 & -0.0351 & \\
 & 0.0039 & &
\end{array}
$$

Table 4.118: 16 Weights. (a) Integers. (b) Normalized.

⋄ **Exercise 4.40:** Why do the weights have to add up to 1?

⋄ **Exercise 4.41:** Show how to renormalize the six weights needed to predict the pixel at the bottom left corner of Figure 4.117b.

The encoder predicts all the pixels of a level by using the diamond-shaped group of 4×4 (or fewer) "older" pixels around each pixel of the level. This is the *image model* used by MLP.

4.19.3 Error Modeling

Assume that the weighted sum of the 16 near-neighbors of pixel P equals R. R is thus the value predicted for P. The prediction error, E, is simply the difference

R − P. Assuming an image with 16 gray levels (4 bits per pixel) the largest value
of E is 15 (when R = 15 and P = 0) and the smallest is −15. Depending on the
image, we can expect most of the errors to be small integers, either zero or close
to it. Few errors will be ±15 or close to that. Experiments with a large number
of images (see, e.g., [Netravali 80]) have produced the error distribution shown in
Figure 4.120a. This is a symmetric, narrow curve, with a sharp peak, indicating
that most errors are small and are thus concentrated at the top. Such a curve has
the shape of the well-known Laplace distribution (appendix in the book's web site)
with mean 0.

				x		
V	0	2	4	6	8	10
3:	0.408248	0.0797489	0.015578	0.00304316	0.00059446	0.000116125
4:	0.353553	0.0859547	0.020897	0.00508042	0.00123513	0.000300282
5:	0.316228	0.0892598	0.025194	0.00711162	0.00200736	0.000566605
1,000:	0.022360	0.0204475	0.018698	0.0170982	0.0156353	0.0142976

Table 4.119: Some Values of the Laplace Distribution with $V = 3, 4, 5$, and 1,000.

Table 4.119 shows some values for the Laplace distributions with $m = 0$ and
$V = 3, 4, 5$, and 1,000. Figure 4.120b shows the graphs of the first three of those. It
is clear that as V grows, the graph becomes lower and wider, with a less-pronounced
peak.

The factor $1/\sqrt{2V}$ is included in the definition of the Laplace distribution in
order to scale the area under the curve of the distribution to 1. Because of this,
it is easy to use the curve of the distribution to calculate the probability of any
error value. Figure 4.120c shows a gray strip, 1 unit wide, under the curve of the
distribution, centered at an error value of k. The area of this strip equals the
probability of any error E having the value k. Mathematically, the area is the
integral

$$P_V(k) = \int_{k-.5}^{k+.5} \frac{1}{\sqrt{2V}} \exp\left(-\sqrt{\frac{2}{V}}|x|\right) dx, \qquad (4.33)$$

and this is the key to encoding the errors. With 4-bit pixels, error values are in
the range $[-15, +15]$. When an error k is obtained, the MLP encoder encodes
it arithmetically with a probability computed by Equation (4.33). In practice,
both encoder and decoder should have a table with all the possible probabilities
precomputed.

The only remaining point to discuss is what value of the variance V should
be used in Equation (4.33). Both encoder and decoder need to know this value.
It is clear, from Figure 4.120b, that using a large variance (which corresponds to
a low, flat distribution) results in too low a probability estimate for small error
values k. The arithmetic encoder would produce an unnecessarily long code in such
a case. On the other hand, using a small variance (which corresponds to a high,
narrow distribution) would allocate too low probabilities to large error values k.
The choice of variance is thus important. An ideal method to estimate the variance

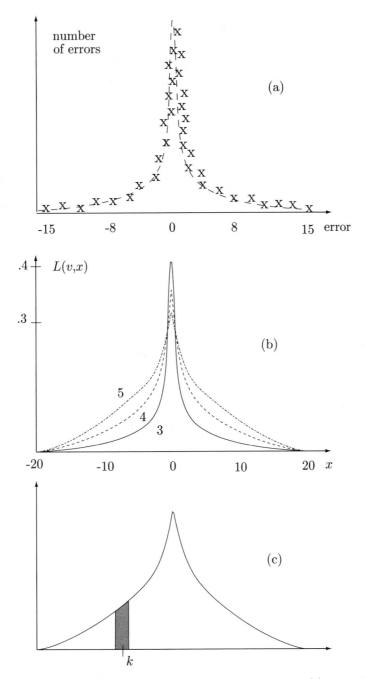

Figure 4.120: (a) Error Distribution. (b) Laplace Distributions. (c) Probability of k.

should assign the best variance value to each error and should involve no overhead (i.e., no extra data should be written on the compressed stream to help the decoder estimate the variances). Here are some approaches to variance selection:

1. The Laplace distribution was adopted as the MLP error distribution after many experiments with real images. The distribution obtained by all those images has a certain value of V, and this value should be used by MLP. This is a simple approach, which can be used in fast versions of MLP. However, it is not adaptive (since it always uses the same variance), and thus does not result in best compression performance for all images.

2. (A two-pass compression job.) Each compression should start with a pass where all the error values are computed and their variance calculated (see below). This variance should be used, after the first pass, to calculate a table of probabilities from Equation (4.33). The table should be used in the second pass where the error values are encoded and written on the compressed stream. Compression performance would be excellent, but any two-pass job is slow. Notice that the entire table can be written at the start of the compressed stream, thereby greatly simplifying the task of the decoder.

$\diamond$ **Exercise 4.42:** Show an example where this approach is practical (i.e., when slow encoding is unimportant but a fast decoder and excellent compression are important).

3. Every time an error is obtained and is about to be arithmetically coded, use some method to estimate the variance associated with that error. Quantize the estimate and use a number of precomputed probability tables, one for each quantized variance value, to compute the probability of the error. This is computationally intensive but may be a good compromise between approaches 1 and 2 above.

We now need to discuss how the variance of an error can be estimated, and we start with an explanation of the concept of variance. Variance is a statistical concept defined for a sequence of values $a_1, a_2, \ldots, a_n$. It measures how elements a_i vary by calculating the differences between them and the average A of the sequence, which is given, of course, by $A = (1/n) \sum a_i$. This is why the curves of Figure 4.120b that correspond to smaller variances are narrower; their values are concentrated near the average, which in this case is zero. The sequence $(5, 5, 5)$, e.g., has average 5 and variance 0, since every element of the sequence equals the average. The sequence $(0, 5, 10)$ also has average 5 but should have a nonzero variance, since two of its elements differ from the average. In general, the variance of the sequence a_i is defined as the nonnegative quantity

$$ V = \sigma^2 = E(a_i - A)^2 = \frac{1}{n} \sum_{1}^{n} (a_i - A)^2, $$

so the variance of $(0, 5, 10)$ is $(0 - 5)^2 + (5 - 5)^2 + (10 - 5)^2 = 50$. Statisticians also use a quantity called *standard deviation* (denoted by σ) that is defined as the square root of the variance.

We now discuss several ways to estimate the variance of a prediction error E.

3.1. Equation (4.33) gives the probability of an error E with value k, but this probability depends on V. We can consider $P_V(k)$ a function of the two variables V and k, and find the optimal value of V by solving the equation $\partial P_V(k)/\partial V = 0$. The solution is $V = 2k^2$, but this method is not practical, since the decoder does not know k (it is trying to decode k so it can find the value of pixel P), and thus cannot mirror the operations of the encoder. It is possible to write the values of all the variances on the compressed stream, but this would significantly reduce the compression ratio. This method can be used to encode a particular image in order to find the best compression ratio of the image and compare it to what is achieved in practice.

3.2. While the pixels of a level are being encoded, consider their errors E to be a sequence of numbers, and find its variance V. Use V to encode the pixels of the next level. The number of levels is never very large, so all the variance values can be written (arithmetically encoded) on the compressed stream, resulting in fast decoding. The variance used to encode the first level should be a user-controlled parameter whose value is not critical, since that level contains just a few pixels. Since MLP quantizes a variance to one of 37 values (see below), each variance written on the compressed stream is encoded in just $\log_2 37 \approx 5.21$ bits, a negligible overhead. The obvious disadvantage of this method is that it disregards local concentrations of identical or very similar pixels in the same level.

3.3. (Similar to 3.2.) While the pixels of a level are being encoded, collect the prediction errors of each block of $b \times b$ pixels and use them to calculate a variance that will be used to encode the pixels inside this block in the next level. The variance values for a level can also be written on the compressed stream following all the encoded errors for that level, so the decoder could use them without having to compute them. Parameter b should be adjusted by experiments, and the authors recommend the value $b = 16$. This method entails significant overhead and thus may degrade compression performance.

3.4. (This is a later addition to MLP; see [Howard and Vitter 92b].) A *variability index* is computed, by both the encoder and decoder, for each pixel. This index should depend on the amount by which the pixel differs from its near neighbors. The variability indexes of all the pixels in a level are then used to adaptively estimate the variances for the pixels, based on the assumption that pixels with similar variability index should use Laplace distributions with similar variances. The method proceeds in the following steps:

1. Variability indexes are calculated for all the pixels of the current level, based on values of pixels in the preceding levels. This is done by the encoder and is later mirrored by the decoder. After several tries, the developers of MLP have settled on a simple way to calculate the variability index. It is calculated as the variance of the four nearest neighbors of the current pixel (the neighbors are from preceding levels, so the decoder can mirror this operation).

2. The variance estimate V is set to some initial value. The choice of this value is not critical, as V is going to be updated later often. The decoder chooses this value in the same way.

3. The pixels of the current level are sorted in variability index order. The decoder can mirror this even though it still does not have the values of these pixels (the

decoder has already calculated the values of the variability index in step 1, since they depend on pixels of previous levels).

4. The encoder loops over the sorted pixels in decreasing order (from large variability indexes to small ones). For each pixel:

4.1. The encoder calculates the error E of the pixel and sends E and V to the arithmetic encoder. The decoder mirrors this step. It knows V, so it can decode E.

4.2. The encoder updates V by

$$V \leftarrow f \times V + (1 - f)E^2,$$

where f is a smoothing parameter (experience suggests a large value, such as 0.99, for f). This is how V is adapted from pixel to pixel, using the errors E. Because of the large value of f, V is decreased in small steps. This means that latter pixels (those with small variability indexes) will get small variances assigned. The idea is that compressing pixels with large variability indexes is less sensitive to accurate values of V.

As the loop progresses, V gets assigned more accurate values, and these are used to compress pixels with small variability indexes, which are more sensitive to variance values. Notice that the decoder can mirror this step, since it has already decoded E in step 4.1. Notice also that the arithmetic encoder writes the encoded error values on the compressed stream in decreasing variability index order, not row by row. The decoder can mirror this too, since it has already sorted the pixels in this order in step 3.

This method gives excellent results but is even more computationally intensive than the original MLP (end of method 3.4).

Using one of the four methods above, variance V is estimated. Before using V to encode error E, V is quantized to one of 37 values as shown in Table 4.122. For example, if the estimated variance value is 0.31, it is quantized to 7. The quantized value is then used to select one of 37 precomputed probability tables (in our example Table 7, precomputed for variance value 0.290, is selected) prepared using Equation (4.33), and the value of error E is used to index that table. (The probability tables are not shown here.) The value retrieved from the table is the probability that's sent to the arithmetic encoder, together with the error value, to arithmetically encode error E.

MLP is thus one of the many compression methods that implement a model to estimate probabilities and use arithmetic coding to do the actual compression.

Table 4.121 is a pseudo-code summary of MLP encoding.

Bibliography

Howard, Paul G., and J. S. Vitter (1992a), "New Methods for Lossless Image Compression Using Arithmetic Coding," *Information Processing and Management*, **28**(6):765–779.

Howard, Paul G., and J. S. Vitter (1992b), "Error Modeling for Hierarchical Lossless Image Compression," in *Proceedings of the 1992 Data Compression Conference*, J. Storer, ed., Los Alamitos, CA, IEEE Computer Society Press, pp. 269–278.

Netravali, A. and J. O. Limb (1980) "Picture Coding: A Preview," *Proceedings of the IEEE*, **68**:366–406.

```
for each level L do
 for every pixel P in level L do
  Compute a prediction R for P using a group from level L-1;
  Compute E=R-P;
  Estimate the variance V to be used in encoding E;
  Quantize V and use it as an index to select a Laplace table LV;
  Use E as an index to table LV and retrieve LV[E];
  Use LV[E] as the probability to arithmetically encode E;
 endfor;
 Determine the pixels of the next level (rotate & scale);
endfor;
```

Table 4.121: MLP Encoding.

Variance range	Var. used	Variance range	Var. used	Variance range	Var. used
0.005–0.023	0.016	2.882–4.053	3.422	165.814–232.441	195.569
0.023–0.043	0.033	4.053–5.693	4.809	232.441–326.578	273.929
0.043–0.070	0.056	5.693–7.973	6.747	326.578–459.143	384.722
0.070–0.108	0.088	7.973–11.170	9.443	459.143–645.989	540.225
0.108–0.162	0.133	11.170–15.627	13.219	645.989–910.442	759.147
0.162–0.239	0.198	15.627–21.874	18.488	910.442–1285.348	1068.752
0.239–0.348	0.290	21.874–30.635	25.875	1285.348–1816.634	1506.524
0.348–0.502	0.419	30.635–42.911	36.235	1816.634–2574.021	2125.419
0.502–0.718	0.602	42.911–60.123	50.715	2574.021–3663.589	3007.133
0.718–1.023	0.859	60.123–84.237	71.021	3663.589–5224.801	4267.734
1.023–1.450	1.221	84.237–118.157	99.506	5224.801–7247.452	6070.918
1.450–2.046	1.726	118.157–165.814	139.489	7247.452–10195.990	8550.934
2.046–2.882	2.433				

Table 4.122: Thirty-Seven Quantized Variance Values.

4.20 PPPM

The reader should review the PPM method, Section 2.18, before reading this section. The PPPM method uses the ideas of MLP (Section 4.19). It is also (remotely) related to the context-based image compression method of Section 4.16.

PPM encodes a symbol by comparing its present context to other similar contexts and selecting the longest match. The context selected is then used to estimate the symbol's probability in the present context. This way of context matching works well for text, where we can expect strings of symbols to repeat exactly, but it does not work well for images, since a digital image is normally the result of digitizing an analog image. Assume that the current pixel has intensity 118 and its context is the two neighboring pixels with values 118 and 120. It is possible that 118 was never seen in the past with the context 118, 120 but was seen with contexts 119, 120 and 118, 121. Clearly, these contexts are close enough to the current one to justify using one of them. Once a closely matching context has been found, it is used to estimate the variance (not the probability) of the current prediction error. This idea serves as one principle of the Prediction by Partial Precision Matching (PPPM) method [Howard and Vitter 92a]. The other principle is to use the Laplace distribution to estimate the probability of the prediction error, as done in MLP.

Figure 4.123: Prediction and Variance-Estimation Contexts for PPPM.

Figure 4.123 shows how prediction is done in PPPM. Pixels are raster-scanned, row by row. The two pixels labeled C are used to predict the one labeled P. The prediction R is simply the rounded average of the two C pixels. Pixels in the top or left edges are predicted by one neighbor only. The top-left pixel of the image is encoded without prediction. After predicting the value of P, the encoder calculates the error $E = R - P$ and uses the Laplace distribution to estimate the probability of the error, as in MLP.

The only remaining point to discuss is how PPPM estimates the variance of the particular Laplace distribution that should be used to obtain the probability of E. PPPM uses the four neighbors labeled C and S in Figure 4.123. These pixels have already been encoded, so their values are known. They are used as the variance-estimation context of P. Assume that the 4 values are 3, 0, 7, and 5, expressed as 4-bit numbers. They are combined to form the 16-bit key 0011|0000|0111|0101, and the encoder uses a hash table to find all the previous occurrences of this context. If this context occurred enough times in the past (more than the value of a threshold parameter), the statistics of these occurrences are used to obtain a mean m and a variance V. if the context did not occur enough times in the past, the least-significant bit of each of the four values is dropped to obtain the 12-bit key 001|000|011|010, and the encoder hashes this value. The encoder thus iterates in a loop until it finds m and V. (It turns out that using the errors of the C and S pixels as a key, instead of their values, produces slightly better compression, so this is what PPPM actually does.)

Once m and V are obtained, the encoder quantizes V and uses it to select one of 37 Laplace probability tables, as in MLP. The encoder then adds $E + m$ and sends this value to be arithmetically encoded with the probability obtained from the Laplace table. To update the statistics, the PPPM encoder uses a lazy approach. It updates the statistics of the context actually used plus, if applicable, the context with one additional bit of precision.

One critical point is the number of times a context had to be seen in the past to be considered meaningful and not random. The PPMB method, Section 2.18.4, "trusts" a context if it has been seen twice. For an image, a threshold of 10–15 is more reasonable.

4.21 CALIC

Sections 4.16 through 4.20 describe context-based image compression methods that have one feature in common: They determine the context of a pixel using some of its neighbor pixels that have already been seen. Normally, these are some of the pixels above and to the left of the current pixel, leading to asymmetric context. It seems intuitive that a symmetric context, one that predicts the current pixel using pixels all around it, would produce better compression, so attempts have been made to develop image compression methods that use such contexts.

The MLP method, Section 4.19, provides an interesting twist to the problem of symmetric context. The CALIC method described here uses a different approach. The name CALIC ([Wu 95] and [Wu 96]) stands for Context-based, Adaptive, Lossless Image Compression. It uses three passes to create a symmetric context around the current pixel, and it uses quantization to reduce the number of possible contexts to something manageable. The method has been developed for compressing grayscale images (where each pixel is a c-bit number representing a shade of gray), but like any other method for grayscale images, it can handle a color image by separating it into three color components and treating each component as a grayscale image.

4.21.1 Three Passes

Assume an image $I[i, j]$ consisting of H rows and W columns of pixels. Both encoder and decoder perform three passes over the image. The first pass calculates averages of pairs of pixels. It looks only at pixels $I[i, j]$ where i and j have the same parity (i.e., both are even or both are odd). The second pass uses these averages to actually encode the same pixels. The third pass uses the same averages plus the pixels of the second pass to encode all pixels $I[i, j]$ where i and j have different parities (one is odd and the other is even).

The first pass calculates the $W/2 \times H/2$ values $\mu[i, j]$ defined by

$$\mu[i, j] = (I[2i, 2j] + I[2i + 1, 2j + 1])/2, \text{ for } 0 \le i < H/2, \, 0 \le j < W/2. \quad (4.34)$$

(In the original CALIC papers i and j denote the columns and rows, respectively. We use the standard notation where the first index denotes the rows.) Each $\mu[i, j]$ is thus the average of two diagonally adjacent pixels. Table 4.124 shows the pixels (in boldface) involved in this calculation for an 8×8-pixel image. Each pair that's used to calculate a value $\mu[i, j]$ is connected with an arrow. Notice that the two original pixels cannot be fully reconstructed from the average because 1 bit may be lost by the division by 2 in Equation (4.34).

The newly calculated values $\mu[i, j]$ are now considered the pixels of a new, small, $W/2 \times H/2$-pixel image (a quarter of the size of the original image). This image is raster-scanned and each of its pixels is predicted by four of its neighbors, three centered above it and one on its left. If $x = \mu[i, j]$ is the current pixel, it is

0,0	0,1	**0,2**	0,3	**0,4**	0,5	**0,6**	0,7
1,0	**1,1**	1,2	**1,3**	1,4	**1,5**	1,6	**1,7**
2,0	2,1	**2,2**	2,3	**2,4**	2,5	**2,6**	2,7
3,0	**3,1**	3,2	**3,3**	3,4	**3,5**	3,6	**3,7**
4,0	4,1	**4,2**	4,3	**4,4**	4,5	**4,6**	4,7
5,0	**5,1**	5,2	**5,3**	5,4	**5,5**	5,6	**5,7**
6,0	6,1	**6,2**	6,3	**6,4**	6,5	**6,6**	6,7
7,0	**7,1**	7,2	**7,3**	7,4	**7,5**	7,6	**7,7**

Table 4.124: The 4×4 Values $\mu[i, j]$ for an 8×8-Pixel Image.

predicted by the quantity

$$\hat{x} = \frac{1}{2}\mu[i - 1, j] + \frac{1}{2}\mu[i, j - 1] + \frac{1}{4}\mu[i - 1, j + 1] - \frac{1}{4}\mu[i - 1, j - 1]. \quad (4.35)$$

(The coefficients 1/2, 1/4, and −1/4, as well as the coefficients used in the other passes, were determined by linear regression, using a set of "training" images. The idea is to find the set of coefficients a_k that gives the best compression for those images, then round them to integer powers of 2, and build them into the algorithm.) The error value $x - \hat{x}$ is then encoded.

The second pass involves the same pixels as the first pass (half the pixels of the original image), but this time each of them is individually predicted. They are raster scanned, and assuming that $x = I[2i, 2j]$ denotes the current pixel, it is predicted using five known neighbor pixels above it and to its left, and three averages μ, known from the first pass, below it and to its right:

$$\hat{x} = 0.9\mu[i, j] + \frac{1}{6}(I[2i + 1, 2j - 1] + I[2i - 1, 2j - 1] + I[2i - 1, 2j + 1])$$
$$- 0.05(I[2i, 2j - 2] + I[2i - 2, 2j]) - 0.15(\mu[i, j + 1] + \mu[i + 1, j]). \quad (4.36)$$

Figure 4.125a shows the five pixels (gray dots) and three averages (slanted lines) involved. The task of the encoder is again to encode the error value $x - \hat{x}$ for each pixel x.

◇ **Exercise 4.43:** Pixel $I[2i - 1, 2j + 1]$ is located below $x = I[2i, 2j]$, so how does the decoder know its value when x is decoded?

The third pass involves the remaining pixels:

$$I[2i, 2j + 1] \text{ and } I[2i + 1, 2j], \quad \text{for } 0 \le i < H/2, \quad 0 \le j < W/2. \quad (4.37)$$

Each is predicted by an almost symmetric context of six pixels (Figure 4.125b) consisting of all of its four-connected neighbors and two of its eight-connected neighbors. If $x = I[i, j]$ is the current pixel, it is predicted by

$$\hat{x} = \frac{3}{8}\left(I[i, j - 1] + I[i - 1, j] + I[i, j + 1] + I[i + 1, j]\right)$$
$$- \frac{1}{4}\left(I[i - 1, j - 1] + I[i - 1, j + 1]\right). \quad (4.38)$$

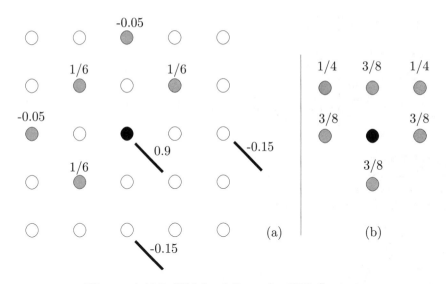

Figure 4.125: Weighted Sums for 360° Contexts.

The decoder can mimic this operation, since the pixels below and to the right of x are known to it from the second pass.

Notice that each of the last two passes of the decoder creates half of the image pixels. CALIC can thus be considered a progressive method where the two progressive steps increase the resolution of the image.

4.21.2 Context Quantization

In each of the three passes, the error values $x - \hat{x}$ are arithmetically encoded, which means that they have to be assigned probabilities. Assume that pixel x is predicted by the n pixel neighbors $x_1, x_2, \ldots, x_n$. The values of n for the three passes are 4, 8, and 6, respectively. In order to assign a probability to x the encoder has to count the number of times x was found in the past with every possible n-pixel context. If a pixel is stored as a c-bit number (representing a shade of gray), then the number of possible contexts for a pixel is $2^{n \cdot c}$. Even for $c = 4$ (just 16 shades of gray) this number is $2^{8 \cdot 4} \approx 4.3$ billion, too large for a practical implementation. CALIC reduces the number of contexts in several steps. It first creates the single n-bit number $t = t_n \ldots t_1$ by

$$t_k = \begin{cases} 0, & \text{if } x_k \geq \hat{x}, \\ 1, & \text{if } x_k < \hat{x}. \end{cases}$$

Next it calculates the quantity

$$\Delta = \sum_{k=1}^{n} w_k |x_k - \hat{x}|,$$

where the coefficients w_k were calculated in advance, by using the same set of training images, and are built into the algorithm. The quantity Δ is called the *error strength discriminant* and is quantized to one of L integer values d, where L is typically set to 8. Once $\hat{x}$ and the n neighbors $x_1, x_2, \ldots, x_n$ are known, both t and the quantized value d of Δ can be calculated, and they become the indices of the context. This reduces the number of contexts to $L \cdot 2^n$, which is at most $8 \cdot 2^8 = 2{,}048$. The encoder maintains an array S of d rows and t columns where context counts are kept. The following is a summary of the steps performed by the CALIC encoder.

```
For all passes
INITIALIZATION: N(d,t):=1; S(d,t):=0; d=0,1,...,L, t=0,1,...,2ⁿ;
PARAMETERS: aₖ and wₖ are assigned their values;
for all pixels x in the current pass do
```
$\quad$ 0: $\hat{x} = \sum_{k=1}^{n} a_k \cdot x_k$;
$\quad$ 1: $\Delta = \sum_{k=1}^{n} w_k(x_k - \hat{x})$;
$\quad$ 2: $d = \texttt{Quantize}(\Delta)$;
$\quad$ 3: Compute $t = t_n \ldots t_2 t_1$;
$\quad$ 4: $\bar{\epsilon} = S(d,t)/N(d,t)$;
$\quad$ 5: $\dot{x} = \hat{x} + \bar{\epsilon}$;
$\quad$ 6: $\epsilon = x - \dot{x}$;
$\quad$ 7: $S(d,t) := S(d,t) + \epsilon$; $N(d,t) := N(d,t) + 1$;
$\quad$ 8: <u>if</u> $N(d,t) \geq 128$ <u>then</u>
$\qquad\quad$ $S(d,t) := S(d,t)/2$; $N(d,t) := N(d,t)/2$;
$\quad$ 9: <u>if</u> $S(d,t) < 0$ encode$(-\epsilon, d)$ <u>else</u> encode(ϵ, d);
```
endfor;
end.
```

Bibliography

Wu, Xiaolin (1995), "Context Selection and Quantization for Lossless Image Coding," in Storer, James A., and Martin Cohn (eds.), *DCC '95, Data Compression Conference*, Los Alamitos, CA, IEEE Computer Society Press, p. 453.

Wu, Xiaolin (1996), "An Algorithmic Study on Lossless Image Compression," in Storer, James A. (ed.), *DCC '96, Data Compression Conference*, Los Alamitos, CA, IEEE Computer Society Press.

4.22 Differential Lossless Compression

There is always a tradeoff between speed and performance, so there is always a demand for fast compression methods as well as for methods that are slow but very efficient. The differential method of this section, due to Sayood and Anderson [Sayood 92], belongs to the former class. It is fast and simple to implement, while offering good, albeit not spectacular, performance.

$\quad$ The principle is to compare each pixel p to a *reference pixel*, which is one of its previously encoded immediate neighbors, and encode p in two parts: a prefix, which is the number of most significant bits of p that are identical to those of the reference pixel, and a suffix, which is the remaining least significant bits of p. For example, if the reference pixel is 10110010 and p is 10110100, then the prefix is 5, since the 5 most significant bits of p are identical to those of the reference pixel, and the suffix is 00. Notice that the remaining three least significant bits are 100 but the suffix does not have to include the 1, since the decoder can easily deduce its value.

⋄ **Exercise 4.44:** How can the decoder do this?

The prefix in our example is 5, and in general it is an integer in the range $[0, 8]$, and compression can be improved by encoding the prefix further. Huffman coding is a good choice for this purpose, with either a fixed set of nine Huffman codes or with adaptive codes. The suffix can be any number of between 0 and 8 bits, so there are 256 possible suffixes. Since this number is relatively large, and since we expect most suffixes to be small, it is reasonable to write the suffix on the output stream unencoded.

This method encodes each pixel using a different number of bits. The encoder generates bits until it has 8 or more of them, then outputs a byte. The decoder can easily mimic this. All that it has to know is the location of the reference pixel and the Huffman codes. In the example above, if the Huffman code of 6 is, say, 010, the code of p will be the 5 bits 010|00.

The only remaining point to discuss is the selection of the reference pixel. It should be close to the current pixel p, and it should be known to the decoder when p is decoded. The rules adopted by the developers of this method for selecting the reference pixel are therefore simple. The very first pixel of an image is written on the output stream unencoded. For every other pixel in the first (top) scan line, the reference pixel is selected as its immediate left neighbor. For the first (leftmost) pixel on subsequent scan lines, the reference pixel is the one above it. For every other pixel, it is possible to select the reference pixel in one of three ways: (1) the pixel immediately to its left; (2) the pixel above it; and (3) the pixel on the left, except that if the resulting prefix is less than a predetermined threshold, the pixel above it.

An example of case 3 is a threshold value of 3. Initially, the reference pixel for p is chosen to be its left neighbor, but if this results in a prefix value of 0, 1, or 2, the reference pixel is changed to the one above p, regardless of the prefix value that is then produced.

This method assumes 1 byte per pixel (256 colors or grayscale values). If a pixel is expressed by 3 bytes, the image should be separated into three parts, and the method applied individually to each part.

⋄ **Exercise 4.45:** Can this method be used for images with 16 grayscale values (where each pixel is 4 bits, and a byte contains two pixels)?

Bibliography

Sayood, K., and K. Robinson (1992) "A Differential Lossless Image Compression Scheme," *IEEE Transactions on Signal Processing* **40**(1):236–241, January.

4.23 DPCM

The DPCM compression method is a member of the family of differential encoding compression methods, which itself is a generalization of the simple concept of relative encoding (Section 1.3.1). It is based on the well-known fact that neighboring pixels in an image (and also adjacent samples in digitized sound, Section 7.2) are correlated. Correlated values are generally similar, so their differences are small, resulting in compression. Table 4.126 lists 25 consecutive values of $\sin \theta_i$, calculated for θ_i values from 0 to 360° in steps of 15°. The values therefore range from -1 to $+1$, but the 24 differences $\sin \theta_{i+1} - \sin \theta_i$ (also listed in the table) are all in the range $[-0.259, 0.259]$. The average of the 25 values is zero, as is the average of the 24 differences. However, the variance of the differences is smaller, since they are all closer to their average.

Figure 4.127a shows a histogram of a hypothetical image that consists of 8-bit pixels. For each pixel value between 0 and 255 there is a different number of pixels. Figure 4.127b shows a histogram of the differences of consecutive pixels. It is easy to see that most of the differences (which, in principle, can be in the range $[0, 255]$) are small; only a few are outside the range $[-50, +50]$.

Differential encoding methods calculate the differences $d_i = a_i - a_{i-1}$ between consecutive data items a_i, and encode the d_i's. The first data item, a_0, is either encoded separately or is written on the compressed stream in raw format. In either case the decoder can decode and generate a_0 in exact form. In principle, any suitable method, lossy or lossless, can be used to encode the differences. In practice, quantization is often used, resulting in lossy compression. The quantity encoded is not the difference d_i but a similar, quantized number that we denote by $\hat{d}_i$. The difference between d_i and $\hat{d}_i$ is the *quantization error* q_i. Thus, $\hat{d}_i = d_i + q_i$.

It turns out that the lossy compression of differences introduces a new problem, namely, the accumulation of errors. This is easy to see when we consider the operation of the decoder. The decoder inputs encoded values of $\hat{d}_i$, decodes them, and uses them to generate "reconstructed" values $\hat{a}_i$ (where $\hat{a}_i = \hat{a}_{i-1} + \hat{d}_i$) instead of the original data values a_i. The decoder starts by reading and decoding a_0. It then inputs $\hat{d}_1 = d_1 + q_1$ and calculates $\hat{a}_1 = a_0 + \hat{d}_1 = a_0 + d_1 + q_1 = a_1 + q_1$. The next step is to input $\hat{d}_2 = d_2 + q_2$ and to calculate $\hat{a}_2 = \hat{a}_1 + \hat{d}_2 = a_1 + q_1 + d_2 + q_2 = a_2 + q_1 + q_2$. The decoded value $\hat{a}_2$ contains the sum of two quantization errors. In general, the decoded value $\hat{a}_n$ equals

$$\hat{a}_n = a_n + \sum_{i=1}^{n} q_i,$$

and includes the sum of n quantization errors. Sometimes, the errors q_i are signed and tend to cancel each other out in the long run. However, in general this is a problem.

The solution is easy to understand once we realize that the encoder and the decoder operate on different pieces of data. The encoder generates the exact differences d_i from the original data items a_i, while the decoder generates the reconstructed $\hat{a}_i$ using only the quantized differences $\hat{d}_i$. The solution is therefore to modify the encoder to calculate differences of the form $d_i = a_i - \hat{a}_{i-1}$. A general difference

sin(t) :	0	0.259	0.500	0.707	0.866	0.966	1.000	0.966
diff :	−	0.259	0.241	0.207	0.159	0.100	0.034	−0.034

sin(t) :	0.866	0.707	0.500	0.259	0	−0.259	−0.500	−0.707
diff :	−0.100	−0.159	−0.207	−0.241	−0.259	−0.259	−0.241	−0.207

sin(t) :	−0.866	−0.966	−1.000	−0.966	−0.866	−0.707	−0.500	−0.259	0
diff :	−0.159	−0.100	−0.034	0.034	0.100	0.159	0.207	0.241	0.259

Table 4.126: 25 Sine Values and 24 Differences.

```
S=Table[N[Sin[t Degree]], {t,0,360,15}]
Table[S[[i+1]]-S[[i]], {i,1,24}]
```

Code For Table 4.126

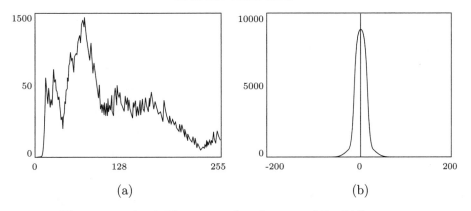

(a) (b)

Figure 4.127: A Histogram of an Image and Its Differences.

d_i is therefore calculated by subtracting the most recent reconstructed value $\hat{a}_{i-1}$ (which both encoder and decoder have) from the current original item a_i.

The decoder now starts by reading and decoding a_0. It then inputs $\hat{d}_1 = d_1 + q_1$ and calculates $\hat{a}_1 = a_0 + \hat{d}_1 = a_0 + d_1 + q_1 = a_1 + q_1$. The next step is to input $\hat{d}_2 = d_2 + q_2$ and calculate $\hat{a}_2 = \hat{a}_1 + \hat{d}_2 = \hat{a}_1 + d_2 + q_2 = a_2 + q_2$. The decoded value $\hat{a}_2$ contains just the single quantization error q_2, and in general, the decoded value $\hat{a}_i$ equals $a_i + q_i$, so it contains just quantization error q_i. We say that the *quantization noise* in decoding $\hat{a}_i$ equals the noise generated when a_i was quantized.

Figure 4.128a summarizes the operations of both encoder and decoder. It shows how the current data item a_i is saved in a storage unit (a delay), to be used for encoding the next item a_{i+1}.

The next step in developing a general differential encoding method is to take advantage of the fact that the data items being compressed are correlated. This means that in general, an item a_i depends on *several* of its near neighbors, not just on the preceding item a_{i-1}. Better prediction (and, as a result, smaller differences) can therefore be obtained by using N of the previously seen neighbors to encode the

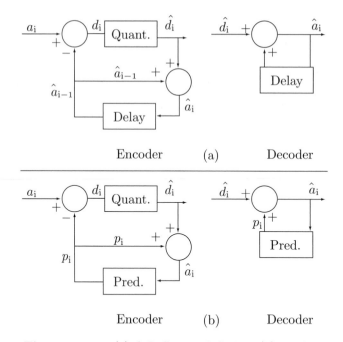

Figure 4.128: (a) A Differential Codec. (b) DPCM.

current item a_i (where N is a parameter). We therefore would like to have a function $p_i = f(\hat{a}_{i-1}, \hat{a}_{i-2}, \ldots, \hat{a}_{i-N})$ to predict a_i (Figure 4.128b). Notice that f has to be a function of the $\hat{a}_{i-j}$, not the a_{i-j}, since the decoder has to calculate the same f. Any method using such a predictor is called *differential pulse code modulation*, or DPCM. In practice, DPCM methods are used mostly for sound compression, but are illustrated here in connection with image compression.

The simplest predictor is linear. In such a predictor the value of the current pixel a_i is predicted by a weighted sum of N of its previously seen neighbors (in the case of an image these are the pixels above it or to its left):

$$p_i = \sum_{j=1}^{N} w_j a_{i-j},$$

where w_j are the weights, which still need to be determined.

Figure 4.129a shows a simple example for the case $N = 3$. Let's assume that a pixel X is predicted by its three neighbors A, B, and C according to the simple weighted sum

$$X = 0.35A + 0.3B + 0.35C. \tag{4.39}$$

Figure 4.129b shows 16 8-bit pixels, part of a bigger image. We use Equation (4.39) to predict the nine pixels at the bottom right. The predictions are shown in Figure 4.129c. Figure 4.129d shows the differences between the pixel values a_i and their predictions p_i.

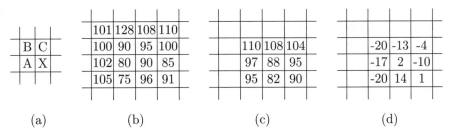

Figure 4.129: Predicting Pixels and Calculating Differences.

The weights used in Equation (4.39) have been selected more or less arbitrarily and are for illustration purposes only. However, they make sense, since they add up to unity.

⋄ **Exercise 4.46:** Why should the weights add up to 1? (This is an easy exercise, but it is important, since weights that add up to unity are very common. Such weights are called *barycentric*.)

In order to determine the best weights we denote by e_i the prediction error for pixel a_i,

$$e_i = a_i - p_i = a_i - \sum_{j=1}^{N} w_j a_{i-j}, \quad i = 1, 2, \ldots, n,$$

where n is the number of pixels to be compressed (in our example nine of the 16 pixels), and we find the set of weights w_j that minimizes the sum

$$E = \sum_{i=1}^{n} e^2 = \sum_{i=1}^{n} \left(a_i - \sum_{j=1}^{N} w_j a_{i-j} \right)^2.$$

We denote by $\mathbf{a} = (90, 95, 100, 80, 90, 85, 75, 96, 91)$ the vector of the nine pixels to be compressed. We denote by $\mathbf{b}^{(k)}$ the vector consisting of the kth neighbors of the six pixels. Thus

$$\mathbf{b}^{(1)} = (100, 90, 95, 102, 80, 90, 105, 75, 96),$$

$$\mathbf{b}^{(2)} = (101, 128, 108, 100, 90, 95, 102, 80, 90),$$

$$\mathbf{b}^{(3)} = (128, 108, 110, 90, 95, 100, 80, 90, 85).$$

The total square prediction error is

$$E = \left| \mathbf{a} - \sum_{j=1}^{3} w_j \mathbf{b}^{(j)} \right|^2,$$

where the vertical bars denote the absolute value of the vector between them. To minimize this error, we need to find the linear combination of vectors $\mathbf{b}^{(j)}$ that's closest to **a**. Readers familiar with the algebraic concept of vector spaces know that this is done by finding the orthogonal projection of **a** on the vector space spanned by the $\mathbf{b}^{(j)}$'s, or, equivalently, by finding the difference vector

$$\mathbf{a} - \sum_{j=1}^{3} w_j \mathbf{b}^{(j)}$$

that's orthogonal to all the $\mathbf{b}^{(j)}$. Two vectors are orthogonal if their dot product is zero, which produces the M (in our case, 3) equations

$$\mathbf{b}^{(k)} \cdot \left(\mathbf{a} - \sum_{j=1}^{M} w_j \mathbf{b}^{(j)} \right) = 0, \quad \text{for } 1 \le k \le M,$$

or, equivalently,

$$\sum_{j=1}^{M} w_j \left(\mathbf{b}^{(k)} \cdot \mathbf{b}^{(j)} \right) = \left(\mathbf{b}^{(k)} \cdot \mathbf{a} \right), \quad \text{for } 1 \le k \le M.$$

The *Mathematica* code of Figure 4.130 produces, for our example, the solutions $w_1 = 0.1691$, $w_2 = 0.1988$, and $w_3 = 0.5382$. Note that they add up to 0.9061, not to 1, and this is discussed in the following exercise.

```
a={90.,95,100,80,90,85,75,96,91};
b1={100,90,95,102,80,90,105,75,96};
b2={101,128,108,100,90,95,102,80,90};
b3={128,108,110,90,95,100,80,90,85};
Solve[{b1.(a-w1 b1-w2 b2-w3 b3)==0,
b2.(a-w1 b1-w2 b2-w3 b3)==0,
b3.(a-w1 b1-w2 b2-w3 b3)==0},{w1,w2,w3}]
```

Figure 4.130: Solving For Three Weights.

⋄ **Exercise 4.47:** Repeat this calculation for the six pixels 90, 95, 100, 80, 90, and 85. Discuss your results.

Adaptive DPCM: This is commonly used for sound compression. In ADPCM the quantization step size adapts to the changing frequency of the sound being compressed. The predictor also has to adapt itself and recalculate the weights according to changes in the input. Several versions of ADPCM exist. A popular version is the IMA ADPCM standard (Section 7.5), which specifies the compression of PCM from 16 down to four bits per sample. ADPCM is fast, but it introduces noticeable quantization noise and achieves unimpressive compression factors of about four.

4.24 Context-Tree Weighting

The context-tree weighting method of Section 2.19 can be applied to images. The method described here [Ekstrand 96] proceeds in five steps as follows:

Step 1, prediction. This step uses differencing to predict pixels and is similar to the lossless mode of JPEG (Section 4.6.7). The four immediate neighbors A, B, C, and D of the current pixel X (Figure 4.131) are used to calculate a linear prediction P of X according to

$$L = aA + bB + cC + dD, \quad P = X - \lfloor L + 1/2 \rfloor, \quad \text{for } a + b + c + d = 1.$$

The four weights should add up to 1 and are selected such that a and c are assigned slightly greater values than b and d. A possible choice is $a = c = 0.3$ and $b = d = 0.2$, but experience seems to suggest that the precise values are not critical.

Figure 4.131: Pixel Prediction.

The values of P are mostly close to zero and are normally Laplace distributed (Figure 4.120).

Step 2, Gray encoding. Our intention is to apply the CTW method to the compression of grayscale or color images. In the case of a grayscale image we have to separate the bitplanes and compress each individually, as if it were a bi-level image. A color image has to be separated into its three components and each component compressed separately as a grayscale image. Section 4.2.1 discusses *reflected Gray codes* (RGC) and shows how their use preserves pixel correlations after the different bitplanes are separated.

Step 3, serialization. The image is converted to a bit stream that will be arithmetically encoded in step 5. Perhaps the best way of doing this is to scan the image line by line for each bitplane. The bit stream therefore starts with all the bits of the first (least-significant) bitplane, continues with the bits of the second least-significant bitplane, and so on. Each bit in the resulting bit stream has as context (its neighbors on the left) bits that originally were above it or to its left in the two-dimensional bitplane. An alternative is to start with the first lines of all the bitplanes, continue with the second lines, and so on.

Step 4, estimation. The bitstream is read bit by bit and a context tree constructed and updated. The weighted probability at the root of the tree is used to predict the current bit, and both the probability and the bit are sent to the arithmetic encoder (Step 5). The tree should be deep, since the prediction done in Step 1 reduces the correlation between pixels. On the other hand, a deep CTW tree slows down the encoder, since more nodes should be updated for each new input bit.

Step 5, encoding. This is done by a standard adaptive arithmetic encoder.

Bibliography

Ekstrand, Nicklas (1996) "Lossless Compression of Gray Images via Context Tree Weighting," in Storer, James A. (ed.), *DCC '96: Data Compression Conference*, Los Alamitos, CA, IEEE Computer Society Press, pp. 132–139, April.

4.25 Block Decomposition

Readers of this chapter may have noticed that most image compression methods have been designed for, and perform best on, continuous-tone images, where adjacent pixels normally have similar intensities or colors. The method described here is intended for the lossless compression of discrete-tone images, be they bilevel, grayscale, or color. Such images are (with few exceptions) artificial, having been obtained by scanning a document, or grabbing a computer screen. The pixel colors of such an image do not vary continuously or smoothly, but have a small set of values, such that adjacent pixels may differ much in intensity or color.

The method works by searching for, and locating, identical blocks of pixels. A copy B of a block A is compressed by preparing the height, width, and location (image coordinates) of A, and compressing those four numbers by means of Huffman codes. The method is called *Flexible Automatic Block Decomposition* (FABD) [Gilbert 98]. Finding identical blocks of pixels is a natural method for image compression, since an image is a two-dimensional structure. The GIF graphics file format (Section 3.17), for example, scans an image row by row to compress it. It is therefore a one-dimensional method, so its efficiency as an image compressor is not very high. The JBIG method of Section 4.9 considers pixels individually, and examines just the local neighborhood of a pixel. It does not attempt to discover correlations in distant parts of the image (at least, not explicitly).

FABD, on the other hand, assumes that identical parts (blocks) of pixels may appear several times in the image. In other words, it assumes that images have a *global two-dimensional redundancy*. It also assumes that large, uniform blocks of pixels will exist in the image. Thus, FABD performs well on images that satisfy these assumptions, such as discrete-tone images. The method scans the image in raster order, row by row, and divides it into (possibly overlapping) sets of blocks. There are three types of blocks namely, copied blocks, solid fill blocks, and punts.

> Basically "punting" is often used as slang (at least in Massachusetts, where I am from) to mean "give up" or do something suboptimal—in my case the punting is a sort of catch-all to make sure that pixels that cannot efficiently take part in a fill or copy block are still coded.
>
> —Jeffrey M. Gilbert

A copied block B is a rectangular part of the image that has been seen before (which is located above, or on the same line but to the left of, the current pixel). It can have any size. A solid fill block is a rectangular uniform region of the image. A punt is any image area that's neither a copied block nor a solid fill one. Each of these three types is compressed by preparing a set of parameters that fully describe the block, and writing their Huffman codes on the compressed stream. Here is a general description of the operations of the encoder.

The encoder proceeds from pixel to pixel. It looks at the vicinity of the current pixel P to see if its future neighbors (those to the right and below P) have the same color. If yes, the method locates the largest uniform block of which P is the top-left corner. Once such a block has been identified, the encoder knows the width and height of the block. It writes the Huffman codes of these two quantities on the compressed stream, followed by the color of the block, and preceded by a code specifying a solid fill block. The four values

$$\text{fill-block code, width, height, pixel value,}$$

are thus written, encoded, on the output. Figure 4.132a shows a fill block with dimensions 4×3 at pixel B.

If the near neighbors of P have different values, the encoder starts looking for an identical block among past pixels. It considers P the top-left corner of a block with unspecified dimensions, and it searches pixels seen in the past (those above or to the left of P) to find the largest block A that will match P. If it finds such a block, then P is designated a copy block of A. Since A has already been compressed, its copy block P can be fully identified by preparing its dimensions (width and height) and source location (the coordinates of A). The five quantities

$$\text{copy-block code, width, height, } A_x, A_y,$$

are thus written, suitably encoded, on the output. Notice that there is no need to write the coordinates of P on the output, since both encoder and decoder proceed pixel by pixel in raster order. Figure 4.132a shows a copy block with dimensions 3×4 at pixel P. This is a copy of block A whose image coordinates are $(2, 2)$, so the quantities

$$\text{copy-block code, 3, 4, 2, 2,}$$

should be written, encoded, on the output.

If no identical block A can be found (we propose below that blocks should have a certain minimum size, such as 4×4), the encoder marks pixel P and continues with the next pixel. P thus becomes a punt pixel. Suppose that P and the four pixels following it are punts, but the next one starts a copy or a fill block. The encoder prepares the quantities

$$\text{punt-block code, 5, } P_1, P_2, P_3, P_4, P_5,$$

where the P_i are the punt pixels, and writes them, encoded, on the output. Figure 4.132a shows how the first six pixels of the image are all different and thus form a punt block. The seventh pixel, marked x, is identical to the first pixel, and thus has a chance of starting a fill or a copy block.

In each of these cases, the encoder marks the pixels of the current block "encoded," and skips them in its raster scan of the image. Figure 4.132a shows how the scan order is affected when a block is identified.

The decoder scans the image in raster order. For each pixel P it inputs the next block code from the compressed stream. This can be the code of a copy block, a fill block, or a punt block. If this is the code of a copied block, the decoder knows that it will be followed by a pair of dimensions and a pair of image coordinates. Once the decoder inputs those, it knows the dimensions of the block and where to copy it from. The block is copied and is anchored with P as its top-left corner. The decoder

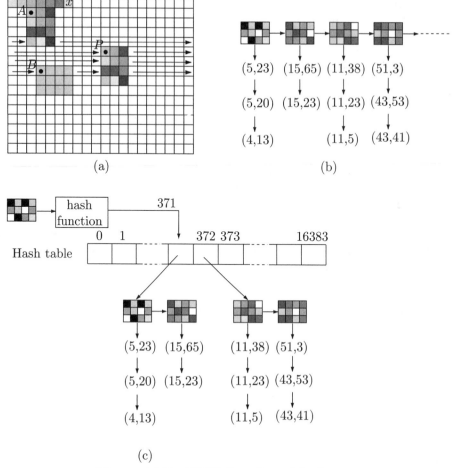

Figure 4.132: FABD Encoding of An Image.

continues its raster scan, but it skips all pixels of the newly constructed block (and any other blocks constructed previously). If the next block code is that of a fill block or a punt block, the decoder generates the block of pixels, and continues with the raster scan, skipping already generated pixels. The task of the decoder is thus very simple, making this method ideal for use by web browsers, where fast decoding is a must.

It is now clear that FABD is a highly asymmetric method. The job of the decoder is mostly to follow pointers and to copy pixels, but the encoder has to identify fill and copy blocks. In principle, the encoder has to scan the entire image for each pixel P, looking for bigger and bigger blocks identical to those that start at P. If the image consists of n pixels, this implies n^2 searches, where each search has to examine several, possibly even many, pixels. For $n = 10^6$, the number of searches is 10^{12} and the number of pixels examined may be 2–3 orders of magnitude bigger. This kind of exhaustive search may take hours on current computers and has to be drastically improved before the method can be considered practical. The discussion below explores ways of speeding up the encoder's search. The following two features are obvious:

1. The search examines only past pixels, not future ones. Searching the entire image has to be done for the last pixels only. There are no searches at all for the first pixel. This reduces the total number of searches from n^2 to $n^2/2$ on average. In fact, the actual implementation of FABD tries to start blocks only at uncoded pixel locations—which reduces the number of searches from n^2 to $n^2/\text{average block size}^2$.

2. There is no search for the pixels of a solid fill block. The process of identifying such a block is simple and fast.

There still remains a large number of searches, and they are speeded up by the following technique. The minimum block size can be limited to 4×4 pixels without reducing the amount of compression, since blocks smaller than 4×4 aren't much bigger than a single pixel. This suggests constructing a list with all the 4×4 pixel patterns found so far in the image (in reverse order, so that recently found patterns are placed at the start of the list). If the current pixel is P, the encoder constructs the 4×4 block B starting at P, and searches this list for occurrences of B. The list may be extremely long. For a bilevel image, where each pixel is one bit, the total number of 16-bit patterns is $2^{16} = 65,536$. For an image with 8-bit pixels, the total number of such patterns is $2^{8\cdot16} = 2^{128} \approx 3.4 \cdot 10^{38}$. Not every pattern must occur in a given image, but the number of patterns that do occur may still be large, and more improvements are needed. Here are three:

3. The list of patterns should include each pattern found so far *only once*. Our list is now called the main list, and it becomes a list of lists. Each element of the main list starts with a unique 4×4 pattern, followed by a match-list of image locations where this pattern was found so far. Figure 4.132b shows an example. Notice how each pattern points to a match-list of coordinates that starts with recently found pixels. A new item is always added to the start of a match-list, so those lists are naturally maintained in sorted order. The elements of a match list are sorted by (descending) rows and, within a row, by column.

4. Hashing can be used to locate a 4×4 pattern in the main list. The bits of a pattern are hashed into a 14-bit number that's used as a pointer (for 1-bit pixels, there are 16 bits in a pattern. The actual implementation of FABD assumes 8-bit pixels, resulting in 128-bit patterns). It points to an element in an array of pointers (the hash table). Following a pointer from the hash table brings the encoder to the start of a match-list. Because of hash collisions, more than one 16-bit pattern may hash into the same 14-bit number, so each pointer in the hash table actually points to a (normally short) list whose elements are match-lists. Figure 4.132c shows an example.

5. If the image has many pixels and large redundancy, some match lists may be long. The total compression time depends heavily on a fast search of the match lists, so it makes sense to limit those searches. A practical implementation may have a parameter k that limits the depth of the search of a match list. Thus, setting $k = 1000$ limits the search of a match list to its 1000 top elements. This reduces the search time while having only a minimal detrimental effect on the final compression

ratio. Experience shows that even values as low as $k = 50$ can be useful. Such a value may increase the compression ratio by a few percent, while cutting down the compression time of a typical $1K \times 1K$ image to just a few seconds. Another beneficial effect of limiting the search depth has to do with hard-to-compress regions in the image. Such regions may be rare, but tend nevertheless to increase the total compression time significantly.

Denoting the current pixel by P, the task of the encoder is to (1) construct the 4×4 block B of which P is the upper-left corner, (2) hash the 16 pixel values of B into a 14-bit pointer, (3) follow the pointer to the hash table and, from there, to a short main list, (4) search this main list linearly, to find a match list that starts with B, and (5) search the first k items in this match list. Each item is the start location of a block that matches P by at least 4×4 pixels. The largest match is selected.

The last interesting feature of FABD has to do with transforming the quantities that should be encoded, before the actual encoding. This is based on the *spatial locality* of discrete-tone images. This property implies that a block will normally be copied from a nearby source block. Also, a given region will tend to have just a few colors, even though the image in general may have many colors.

Thus, spatial locality suggests the use of *relative image coordinates*. If the current pixel is located at, say, $(81, 112)$ and it is a copy of a block located at $(41, 10)$, then the location of the source block is expressed by the pair $(81 - 41, 112 - 10)$ of relative coordinates. Relative coordinates are thus small numbers and are also distributed nonuniformly. Thus, they compress well with Huffman coding.

Spatial locality also suggests the use of *color age*. This is a simple way to assign relative codes to colors. The age of a color C is the number of unique colors located between the current instance of C and its previous instance. As an example, given the sequence of colors

green, yellow, red, red, red, green, red,

their color ages are

?, ?, ?, 0, 0, 2, 1.

It is clear that color ages in an image with spatial locality are small numbers. The first time a color is seen it does not have an age, so it is encoded raw.

Experiments with FABD on discrete-tone images yield compression of between 0.04 bpp (for bilevel images) and 0.65 bpp (for 8-bit images).

The author is indebted to Jeff Gilbert for reviewing this section.

Bibliography

Gilbert, Jeffrey M., and Robert W. Brodersen (1998) "A Lossless 2-D Image Compression Technique for Synthetic Discrete-Tone Images," in *Proceedings of the 1998 Data Compression Conference*, J. Storer ed., Los Alamitos, CA, IEEE Computer Society Press, pp. 359–368, March. This is also available from `http://infopad.eecs.berkeley.edu/~gilbertj` in PDF format.

4.26 Binary Tree Predictive Coding

The concept of *image pyramid* is central to this method. BTPC also uses quantization for its lossy option. The method is intended for lossless and lossy compression of all types of images and was designed to meet the following criteria:

1. It should be able to compress continuous-tone (photographic), discrete-tone (graphical), and mixed images as well as the standard methods for each.

2. The lossy option should not require a fundamental change in the basic algorithm.

3. When the same image is compressed several times, losing more and more data each time, the result should visually appear as a gradual blurring of the decompressed images, not as sudden changes in image quality.

4. A software implementation should be efficient in its time and memory requirements. The decoder's memory requirements should be just a little more than the image size. The decoding time (number of steps) should be a small multiple of the image size.

5. A hardware implementation of both encoder and decoder should allow for fine-grain parallelism. In the ideal case, each processor should be able to process one bit of the image.

There are two versions, BTPC1 and BTPC2. The details of both are described here, and the name BTPC is used for features that are common to both.

The main innovation of BTPC is the use of a *binary image pyramid*. The technique repeatedly decomposes the image into two components, a low band L, which is recursively decomposed, and a high band H. The low band is a low-resolution part of the image. The high band contains differences between L and the original image. These differences are later used by the decoder to reconstruct the image from L. If the original image is highly correlated, L will contain correlated (i.e., highly redundant) values, but will still contribute to the overall compression, since it is small. On the other hand, the differences that are the contents of H will be decorrelated (i.e., with little or no redundancy left), will be small numbers, and will have a histogram that peaks around zero. Thus, their entropy will be small, making it possible to compress them efficiently with an entropy coder. Since the difference values in H are small, it is natural to obtain lossy compression by quantizing them, a process that generates many zeros.

The final compression ratio depends on how small L is and how decorrelated the values of H are. The main idea of the binary pyramid used by BTPC is to decompose the original image into two bands L_1 and H_1, decompose L_1 into bands L_2 and H_2, and continue decomposing the low bands until bands L_8 and H_8 are obtained. The eight high bands and the last low band L_8 are written on the compressed stream after being entropy encoded. They constitute the binary image pyramid, and they are used by the BTPC decoder to reconstruct the original image.

It is natural for the encoder to write them in the order $L_1, H_1, H_2, \ldots, H_8$. The decoder, however, needs them in the opposite order, so it makes sense for the encoder to collect these matrices in memory and write them in reverse order. The decoder needs just one memory buffer, the size of the original image, plus some more memory to input a row of H_i from the compressed stream. The elements of the row are used to process pixels in the buffer, and the next row is then input.

If the original image has $2^n \times 2^n = N$ pixels, then band H_1 contains $N/2$ elements, band H_2 has $N/4$ elements, and bands L_8 and H_8 have $N/2^8$ elements each. The total number of values to be encoded is therefore

$$(N/2 + N/2^2 + N/2^3 + \cdots + N/2^8) + N/2^8 = N(1 - 2^{-8}) + N/2^8 = N.$$

If the original image size has $2^{10} \times 2^{10} = 2^{20}$ pixels, then bands L_8 and H_8 have $2^{12} = 4096$ elements each. When dealing with bigger images, it may be better to continue beyond L_8 and H_8 down to matrices of size 2^{10} to 2^{12}.

Figure 4.133 illustrates the details of the BTPC decomposition. Figure 4.133a shows an 8×8 highly correlated grayscale image (note how pixel values grow from 1 to 64). The first low band L_1 is obtained by removing every even pixel on every odd-numbered row and every odd pixel on every even-numbered row. The result (shown in Figure 4.133b) is a rectangular lattice with eight rows and four pixels per column. It contains half the number of pixels in the original image. Since its elements are pixels, we call it a *subsampled band*. The positions of the removed pixels are labeled H_1 and their values are shown in small type in Figure 4.133c. Each H_1 is calculated by subtracting the original pixel value at that location from the average of the L_1 pixels directly above and below it. For example, the H_1 value 3 in the top row, column 2, is obtained by subtracting the original pixel 2 from the average $(10 + 0)/2 = 5$ (we use a simple *edge rule* where any missing pixels along edges of the image are considered zero for the purpose of predicting pixels). The H_1 value -33 at the bottom-left corner is obtained by subtracting 57 from the average $(0 + 49)/2 = 24$. For simplicity, we use just integers in these examples. A real implementation, however, should deal with real values. Also, the prediction methods actually used by BTPC1 and BTPC2 are more sophisticated than the simple method shown here. They are discussed below. The various H_i bands are called *difference bands*.

Among the difference bands, H_1 is the finest (because it contains the most values), and H_8 is the coarsest. Similarly, L_8 (which is the only subsampled band written on the compressed stream) is the coarsest subsampled band.

Figure 4.133d shows how the second low band L_2 is obtained from L_1 by removing the pixels on even-numbered rows. The result is a square pattern containing half the number of pixels in L_1. The positions of the H_2 values are also shown. Notice that they don't have neighbors above or below, so we use two diagonal neighbors for prediction (again, the actual prediction used by BTPC1 and BTPC2 is different). For example, the H_2 value -5 in Figure 4.134a was obtained by subtracting the original pixel 16 from the prediction $(23 + 0)/2 = 11$. The next low band, L_3 (Figure 4.133e), is obtained from L_2 in the same way that L_1 is obtained from the original image. Band L_4 (Figure 4.133f) is obtained from L_3 in the same way that L_2 is obtained from L_1. Each band contains half the number of pixels of its predecessor. It is also obvious that the four near neighbors of a value H_i are located on its four corners for even values of i and on its four sides for odd values of i.

⋄ **Exercise 4.48:** Calculate the values of L_i and H_i, for $i = 2, 3, 4$. For even values of i use the average of the bottom-left and top-right neighbors for prediction. For odd values of i use the average of the neighbors above and below.

```
1  2  3  4  5  6  7  8      1  H1 3  H1 5  H1 7  H1      1   3   3   2   5   1   7   0
9  10 11 12 13 14 15 16     H1 10 H1 12 H1 14 H1 16     0   10  0   12  0   14  0   16
17 18 19 20 21 22 23 24     17 H1 19 H1 21 H1 23 H1     17  0   19  0   21  0   23  0
25 26 27 28 29 30 31 32     H1 26 H1 28 H1 30 H1 32     0   26  0   28  0   30  0   32
33 34 35 36 37 38 39 40     33 H1 35 H1 37 H1 39 H1     33  0   35  0   37  0   39  0
41 42 43 44 45 46 47 48     H1 42 H1 44 H1 46 H1 48     0   42  0   44  0   46  0   48
49 50 51 52 53 54 55 56     49 H1 51 H1 53 H1 55 H1     49  0   51  0   53  0   55  0
57 58 59 60 61 62 63 64     H1 58 H1 60 H1 62 H1 64     -33 58 -34 60 -35 62 -36 64

            (a)                           (b)                           (c)


1  .  3  .  5  .  7  .      1  .  H3 .  5  .  H3 .      1  .  .  .  5  .  .  .
.  H2 .  H2 .  H2 .  H2     .  .  .  .  .  .  .  .      .  .  .  .  .  .  .  .
17 .  19 .  21 .  23 .      H3 .  19 .  H3 .  23 .      .  .  H4 .  .  .  H4 .
.  H2 .  H2 .  H2 .  H2     .  .  .  .  .  .  .  .      .  .  .  .  .  .  .  .
33 .  35 .  37 .  39 .      33 .  H3 .  37 .  H3 .      33 .  .  .  37 .  .  .
.  H2 .  H2 .  H2 .  H2     .  .  .  .  .  .  .  .      .  .  .  .  .  .  .  .
49 .  51 .  53 .  55 .      H3 .  51 .  H3 .  55 .      .  .  H4 .  .  .  H4 .
.  H2 .  H2 .  H2 .  H2     .  .  .  .  .  .  .  .      .  .  .  .  .  .  .  .

            (d)                           (e)                           (f)
```

Figure 4.133: An 8×8 Image and Its First Three L Bands.

```
1  .  3  .  5  .  7  .      1  .  7  .  5  .  5  .      1  .  .  .  5  .  .  .
.  0  .  0  .  0  .  -5     .  .  .  .  .  .  .  .      .  .  .  .  .  .  .  .
17 .  19 .  21 .  23 .      15 .  19 .  11 .  23 .      .  .  0  .  .  .  -5 .
.  0  .  0  .  0  .  -13    .  .  .  .  .  .  .  .      .  .  .  .  .  .  .  .
33 .  35 .  37 .  39 .      33 .  0  .  37 .  0  .      33 .  .  .  37 .  .  .
.  0  .  0  .  0  .  -21    .  .  .  .  .  .  .  .      .  .  .  .  .  .  .  .
49 .  51 .  53 .  55 .      -33 . 51 .  -35 . 55 .      .  .  -33 . .  .  -55 .
.  -33 . -34 . -35 . -64    .  .  .  .  .  .  .  .      .  .  .  .  .  .  .  .

            (a)                           (b)                           (c)
```

Figure 4.134: (a) Bands L_2 and H_2. (b) Bands L_3 and H_3. (c) Bands L_4 and H_4.

$\diamond$ **Exercise 4.49:** Use Figure 4.134a to calculate the entropy of band H_2.

The next step in BTPC encoding is to turn the binary pyramid into a binary tree, similar to the bintree of Section 4.27.1. This is useful, since many H_i values tend to be zeros, especially when lossy compression is used. If a node v in this tree is zero and all its children are zeros, the children will not be written on the compressed stream and v will contain a special termination code telling the decoder to substitute zeros for the children. The rule used by BTPC to construct the tree tells how to associate a difference value in H_i with its two children in H_{i-1}:

1. If i is even, a value in H_i has one child $i/2$ rows above it and another child $i/2$ columns to its left in H_{i-1}. Thus, the 0 in H_4 of Figure 4.134c has the two children

7 and 15 in H_3 of Figure 4.134b. Also, the -33 in H_4 has the two children 0 and -33 in H_3

2. For odd i, if the parent (in H_{i-1}) of a value v in H_i is located below v, then the two children of v are located in H_{i-1}, $(i-1)/2$ rows below it and $(i-1)/2$ columns to its left and right. For example, the 5 in H_3 of Figure 4.134b has its parent (the -5 of H_4) below it, so its two children 0 and -5 are located one row below and one column to its left and right in the H_2 band of Figure 4.134a.

3. For odd i, if the parent (in H_{i-1}) of a value v in H_i is to the right of v, then the two children of v are located in H_{i-1}, $(i-1)/2$ rows below it. One is $(i-1)/2$ columns to its right and the other is $3(i-1)/2$ columns to its right. For example, the -33 of H_3 has its parent (the -33 of H_4) to its right, so its children are the -33 and -34 of H_2. They are located one row below it, and one and three columns to its right.

These rules seem arbitrary, but they have the advantage that the descendants of a difference value form either a square or a rectangle around it. For example, the descendants of the 0 value of H_4 (shown in Figure 4.135 in boldface) are (1) its two children, the 7 and 15 of H_3, (2) their four children, the four top-left zeros of H_2 (shown in italics), and (3) the eight grandchildren in H_1 (shown in small type). These 14 descendants are shown in Figure 4.135.

$$
\begin{array}{ccccccccc}
. & 3 & 7 & 2 & . & . & . & . \\
0 & \mathit{0} & 0 & \mathit{0} & . & . & . & . \\
15 & 0 & \mathbf{0} & 0 & . & . & . & . \\
0 & \mathit{0} & 0 & \mathit{0} & . & . & . & . \\
. & . & . & . & . & . & . & . \\
. & . & . & . & . & . & . & . \\
. & . & . & . & . & . & . & . \\
. & . & . & . & . & . & . & . \\
\end{array}
$$

Figure 4.135: The Fourteen Descendants of the Zero of H_4.

Not all these descendants are zeros, but if they were, the zero value of H_4 would have a special zero-termination code associated with it. This code tells the decoder that this value and all its descendants are zeros and are not written on the compressed stream. BTPC2 adds another twist to the tree. It uses the leaf codeword for left siblings in H_1 to indicate that both siblings are zero. This slightly improves the encoding of H_1.

Experiments show that turning the binary pyramid into a binary tree increases the compression factor significantly.

It should now be clear why BTPC is a natural candidate for implementation on a parallel computer. Each difference value input by the decoder from a difference band H_i is used to calculate a pixel in subsampled band L_i, and these calculations can be done in parallel, since they are independent (except for competition for memory accesses).

We now turn to the pixel prediction used by BTPC. The goal is to have simple prediction, using just two or four neighbors of a pixel, while minimizing the prediction error. Figure 4.133 shows how each H_i difference value is located at the center of a group of four pixels that are known to the decoder from the decoding of bands H_{i-1}, H_{i-2}, etc. It is therefore a good idea for the encoder to use this group to predict the H_i value. Figure 4.136a,b shows that there are three ways to estimate an H_i value at the center X of a group where A and C are two opposite pixels, and B and D are the other two. Two estimations are the linear predictions $(A + C)/2$ and $(B + D)/2$, and the third is the bilinear $(A + B + C + D)/4$. Based on the results of experiments, the developers of BTPC1 decided to use the following rule for prediction (notice that the decoder can mimic this rule):

Rule: If the two extreme (i.e., the largest and smallest) pixels of A, B, C, and D are opposite each other in the prediction square, use the average of the other two opposite pixels (i.e., the middle two of the four values). Otherwise, use the average of the two opposite pixels closest in value to each other.

A D	A	1 6	1
X	D X B	X	9 X 5
B C	C	4 9	3
(a)	(b)	(c)	(d)

Figure 4.136: The Four Neighbors Used to Predict an H_i Value X.

The two extreme values in Figure 4.136c are 1 and 9. They are opposite each other, so the prediction is the average 5 of the other two opposite pixels 4 and 6. In Figure 4.136d, on the other hand, the two extreme values, which are the same 1 and 9, are not opposite each other, so the prediction is the average, 2, of the 1 and 3, since they are the opposite pixels closest in value.

⋄ **Exercise 4.50:** It seems that the best prediction is obtained when the encoder tries all three ways to estimate X and selects the best one. Why not use this prediction?

When BTPC2 was developed, extensive experiments were performed, resulting in more sophisticated prediction. BTPC2 selects one of 13 different predictions, depending on the values and positions of the four pixels forming the prediction square. These pixels are assigned names a, b, c, and d in such a way that they satisfy $a < b < c < d$. The 13 cases are summarized in Table 4.138.

As has been mentioned, BTPC has a natural lossy option that quantizes the prediction differences (the H_i values). The main aim of the quantization is to increase the number of zero differences, so it uses a double-size zero zone, illustrated in Figure 4.137. The quantizer step size in this figure is 3, so the values 3, 4, and 5 are quantized to 4 (quantization bin 1). The values -6, -7, and -8 are quantized to -7 (bin -2), but the values 0, 1, and 2 are quantized to 0 (bin 0), as are the values 0, -1, and -2.

The amount of quantization varies from level to level in the pyramid. The first difference band H_1 (the finest one) is the most coarsely quantized, since it is half the

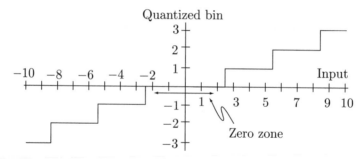

Figure 4.137: Quantization in BTPC.

Num	Name	Pixels	Closest-Opposite-Pair (BTPC1) Prediction	Adaptive (BTPC2) Prediction
0	Flat	a a a a	a	a
1	High point	a a a b	a	a
2	Line	a b b a	a or b	a or b (note1)
3	Aligned edge	a a b b	$(a+b)/2$	a or b (note2)
4	Low	a b b b	b	b
5	Twisted edge	a a b c	$(a+b)/2$	$(a+b)/2$
6	Valley	a b c a	a	a or $(a+b)/2$ (note1)
7	Edge	a b b c	b	b
8	Doubly twisted edge	a b c b	$(a+b)/2$ or $(b+c)/2$	b
9	Twisted edge	a b c c	$(b+c)/2$	$(b+c)/2$
10	Ridge	a c c b	c	c or $(a+b)/2$ (note1)
11	Edge	a b c d	$(b+c)/2$	$(b+c)/2$
12	Doubly twisted edge	a b d c	$(a+c)/2$ or $(b+d)/2$	$(b+c)/2$
13	Line	a c d b	$(a+b)/2$ or $(c+d)/2$	$(a+b)/2$ or $(c+d)/2$ (note1)

Note 1: Flag is needed to indicate choice
Note 2: Depending on other surrounding values

Table 4.138: Thirteen Predictions Used by BTPC2.

image size and since its difference values affect single pixels. Any quantization errors in this level do not propagate to the following difference bands. The main decision in the quantization process is how to vary the quantization step size s from level to level. The principle is to set the step size s_i of the current level H_i such that any value that would be quantized to 0 with the step s_{i-1} of the preceding level using exact prediction (no quantization), is quantized to 0 with the inexact prediction actually obtained by step size s_i. If we can calculate the range of prediction error caused by earlier quantization errors, then the right value for s_i is the preceding step size s_{i-1} plus the maximum error in the prediction.

Since this type of calculation is time-consuming, BTPC determines the step size s_i for level i by scaling down the preceding step size s_{i-1} by a constant factor a. Thus, $s_i = a\, s_{i-1}$, where the constant a satisfies $a < 1$. Its value was determined by experiment to be in the range 0.75 to 0.8.

The last step in BTPC compression is the entropy coding of L_8 and the eight difference bands H_i. BTPC1 does not include an entropy coder. Its output can be sent to any available adaptive lossless coder, such as Huffman, arithmetic or dictionary-based. BTPC2 includes an integrated adaptive Huffman coder. This coder is reset for each difference band, since each band is quantized differently, so their statistics are different. If the coder is not reset at the start of a band H_i, it may produce bad compression while getting adapted to the statistical model of H_i.

The binary tree structure introduces another feature that should be taken into account. When a leaf is found with a zero-termination code, it means that the current difference value and all its descendants are zero. However, if an interior node with a zero value is found in the binary tree, and if its left child is a leaf, then its right child cannot be a leaf (since otherwise, the parent would have two zero children and would itself be a leaf). As a result, a right child whose parent is zero and whose left sibling is a leaf is special in some sense. Because of this property, BTPC2 uses three adaptive Huffman coders for each difference band, one for left children, another for "normal" right children, and the third for "special" right children.

Bibliography

Robinson, John A. (1997) "Efficient General-Purpose Image Compression with Binary Tree Predictive Coding," *IEEE Transactions on Image Processing*, **6**,4:601–607 April.

4.27 Quadtrees

A quadtree compression of an image is based on the principle of image compression (Section 1.4) that states; If we select a pixel in the image at random, there is a good chance that its immediate neighbors will have the same or similar color. The quadtree method scans the bitmap, area by area, looking for areas composed of identical pixels (uniform areas). This should be compared to RLE image compression (Section 1.4), where only neighbors on the same scan row are checked, even though neighbors on the same column may also be identical or very similar.

The input consists of bitmap pixels, and the output is a tree (a quadtree, where each node is either a leaf or has exactly four children). The size of the quadtree depends on the complexity of the image. For complex images the tree may be bigger than the original bitmap (expansion). The method starts by constructing a single node, the root of the final quadtree. It divides the bitmap into four quadrants, each to become a child of the root. A uniform quadrant (one where all the pixels have the same color) is saved as a leaf child of the root. A nonuniform quadrant is saved as an (interior node) child of the root. Any nonuniform quadrants are then recursively divided into four smaller subquadrants that are saved as four sibling nodes of the quadtree. Figure 4.139 shows a simple example:

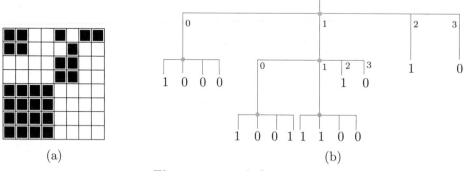

(a)   (b)

Figure 4.139: A Quadtree.

The 8×8 bitmap in 4.139a produces the 21-node quadtree of 4.139b. Sixteen nodes are leaves (each containing the color of one quadrant, 0 for white, 1 for black), and the other five (the gray circles) are interior nodes containing four pointers each. The quadrant numbering used is $\binom{0\,1}{2\,3}$ (but see Exercise 4.60 for a more natural numbering scheme).

The size of a quadtree depends on the complexity of the image. Assuming a bitmap size of $2^N \times 2^N$, one extreme case is where all the pixels are identical. The quadtree in this case consists of just one node, the root. The other extreme case is where each quadrant, even the smallest one, is nonuniform. The lowest level of the quadtree has, in such a case, $2^N \times 2^N = 4^N$ nodes. The level directly above it has a quarter of that number (4^{N-1}), and the level above that one has 4^{N-2} nodes. The total number of nodes in this case is $4^0 + 4^1 + \cdots + 4^{N-1} + 4^N = (4^{N+1} - 1)/3 \approx 4^N(4/3) \approx 1.33 \times 4^N = 1.33(2^N \times 2^N)$. In this worst case the quadtree contains about 33% more nodes than the number of pixels (the bitmap size). Such an image therefore generates considerable expansion when converted to a quadtree.

A nonrecursive approach to generating a quadtree starts by building the complete quadtree assuming that all quadrants are nonuniform and then checking the assumption. Every time a quadrant is tested and found to be uniform, the four nodes corresponding to its four quarters are deleted from the quadtree. This process proceeds from the bottom (the leaves) up towards the root. The main steps are the following:

1. A complete quadtree of height N is constructed. It contains levels $0, 1, \ldots, N$ where level k has 4^k nodes.

2. All $2^N \times 2^N$ pixels are copied from the bitmap into the leaves (the lowest level) of the quadtree.

3. The tree is scanned level by level, from the bottom (level N) to the root (level 0). When level k is scanned, its 4^k nodes are examined in groups of four, the four nodes in each group having a common parent. If the four nodes in a group are leaves and have the same color (i.e., if they represent a uniform quadrant), they are deleted and their parent is changed from an interior node to a leaf having the same color.

Here is a simple analysis of the time complexity of this approach. A complete quadtree has about 1.33×4^N nodes, and since each is tested once, the number of operations (in step 3) is 1.33×4^N. Step 1 also requires 1.33×4^N operations, and step 2 requires 4^N operations. The total number of operations is thus $(1.33 + 1.33 + 1) \times 4^N = 3.66 \times 4^N$. We are faced with comparing the first method, which requires $1/3 \times 4^N$ steps, with the second method, which needs 3.66×4^N operations. Since N usually varies in the narrow range 8–12, the difference is not very significant. Similarly, an analysis of storage requirements shows that the first method uses just the amount of memory required by the final quadtree, whereas the second one uses all the storage needed for a complete quadtree.

The following discussion shows the relation between the positions of pixels in a quadtree and in the image. Imagine a complete quadtree. Its bottom row consists of all the $2^n \times 2^n$ pixels of the image. Suppose we scan these pixels from left to right and number them. We show how the number of a pixel can be used to determine its (x, y) image coordinates.

Each quadrant, subquadrant, or pixel (or, in short, each subsquare) obtained by a quadtree partitioning of an image can be represented by a string of the quaternary (base 4) digits 0, 1, 2, and 3. The longer the string, the smaller the subsquare it represents. We denote such a string by $d_i d_{i-1} \ldots d_0$, where $0 \leq i \leq n$. We assume that the quadrant numbering of Figure 4.152a (Section 4.31) is extended recursively to subsquares of all sizes. Figure 4.152b shows how each of the 16 subquadrants produced from the four original ones is identified by a 2-digit quaternary number. After another subdivision, each of the resulting subsubquadrants is identified by a 3-digit number, and so on. The black area in Figure 4.152c, for example, is identified by the quaternary integer 1032, and the gray area is identified by the integer 2011_4.

Consecutive quaternary numbers are easy to generate. We simply have to increment the digit 3_4 to the 2-digit number 10_4. The first n-digit quaternary numbers are (notice that there are $4 \times 2^{2n-2} = 2^n \times 2^n$ of them)

$$0, 1, 2, 3, 10, 11, 12, 13, 20, 21, 22, 23, 30, 31, 32, 33, 100, 101, 102, 103, \ldots,$$
$$\ldots, 130, 131, 132, 133, 200, \ldots, \underbrace{33 \ldots 3}_{n}.$$

Figure 4.140a shows a complete quadtree for a $2^2 \times 2^2$ image. The 16 pixels constitute the bottom row, and their quaternary numbers are listed. Once we know how to locate a pixel in the image by its quaternary number, we can construct the quadtree with a bottom-up, left-to-right approach. Here are the details. We start with the four pixels with quaternary numbers 00, 01, 02, and 03. They become the

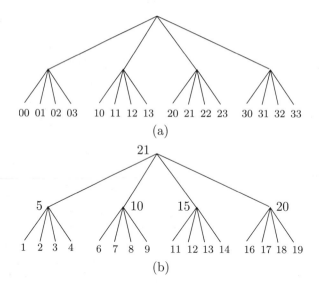

Figure 4.140: A Quadtree For a $2^2 \times 2^2$ Image.

bottom-left part of the tree and are numbered 1–4 in Figure 4.140b. We construct their parent node (numbered 5 in Figure 4.140b). If the four pixels are uniform, they are deleted from the quadtree. We do the same with the next group of pixels, whose quaternary numbers are 10, 11, 12, and 13. They become pixels 6–9, with a parent numbered 10 in Figure 4.140b. If they are uniform, they are deleted. This is repeated until four parents, numbered 5, 10, 15, and 20, are constructed. Their parent (numbered 21) is then created, and the four nodes are checked. If they are uniform, they are deleted. The process continues until the root is created and its four children nodes checked, and, if necessary, deleted. This a recursive approach whose advantage is that no extra memory is needed. Any unnecessary nodes of the quadtree are deleted as soon as they and their parent are created.

```
x:=0; y:=0;
for k:= n − 1 step −1 to 0 do
  if digit(k)=1 or 3 then y := y + 2^k;
  if digit(k)=2 or 3 then x := x + 2^k
endfor;
```

Figure 4.141: Pseudo-Code to Locate a Pixel in an Image.

Given a square image with $2^n \times 2^n$ pixels, each pixel is identified by an n-digit quaternary number. Given such a number $d_{n-1}d_{n-2}\ldots d_0$, we show how to locate "its" pixel in the image. We assume that a pixel has image coordinates (x, y), with the origin of the coordinate system at the bottom-left corner of the image. We start at the origin and scan the quaternary digits from left to right. A digit of 1 tells us to move up to reach our target pixel. A digit of 2 signals a move to the right, and a digit of 3 directs us to move up and to the right. A digit of 0 corresponds to no movement. The amount of the move halves from digit to digit. The leftmost digit corresponds to a move of 2^{n-1} rows and/or columns, the second digit from the left corresponds to a move of 2^{n-2} rows and/or columns, and so on, until the rightmost digit corresponds to moving just $1 (= 2^0)$ pixels (or none, if this digit is a 0). The pseudo-code of Figure 4.141 summarizes this process

It should also be noted that quadtrees are a special case of the Hilbert curve, discussed in Section 4.29.

4.27.1 Bintrees

Instead of partitioning the image into quadrants, it can be recursively split in halves. This is the principle of the bintree method. Figure 4.142a–e shows the 8×8 image of Figure 4.139a and the first four steps in its bintree partitioning. Figure 4.142f shows part of the resulting bintree. It is easy to see how the bintree method alternates between vertical and horizontal splits, and how the subimages being generated include all those produced by a quadtree plus other ones. As a compression method, bintree partitioning is less efficient than quadtree, but it may be useful in cases where many subimages are needed. A case in point is the WFA method of Section 4.31. The original method uses a quadtree to partition an image into nonoverlapping subsquares, and compresses the image by matching a subsquare with a linear combination of other (possibly bigger) subsquares. An extension of WFA (page 433) uses bintrees to obtain more subimages and thus better compression.

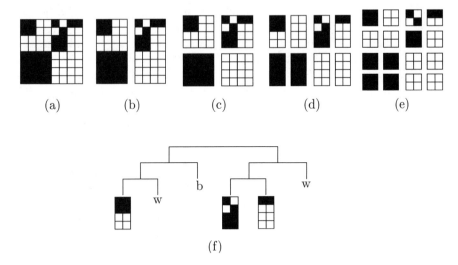

Figure 4.142: A Bintree For an 8×8 Image.

4.27.2 Composite and Difference Values

The average of a set of integers is a good representative of the integers in the set, but is not always an integer. The median of such a set is an integer but is not always a good representative. The progressive image method described in this section, due to K. Knowlton [Knowlton 80], uses the concepts of *composite* and *differentiator* to encode an image progressively. The image is encoded in layers, where early layers consist of a few large, low-resolution blocks, followed by later layers with smaller, higher-resolution blocks. The image is divided into layers using the method of bintrees (Section 4.27.1). The entire image is divided into two vertical halves, each is divided into two horizontal quadrants, and so on.

The first layer consists of a single uniform area, the size of the entire image. We call it the *zeroth* progressive approximation. The next layer is the *first* approximation. It consists of two uniform rectangles (or cells), one above the other, each half the size of the image. We can consider them the two children of the single cell of the zeroth approximation. In the *second* approximation, each of these cells is divided into two children, which are two smaller cells, laid side by side. If the original image has 2^n pixels, then they are the cells of the nth approximation, which constitutes the last layer.

If the image has 16 grayscales, then each pixel consists of four bits, describing its intensity. The pixels are located at the bottom of the bintree (they are the leaves of the tree), so each cell in the layer immediately above the leaves is the parent of two pixels. We want to represent such a cell by means of two 4-bit numbers. The first number, called the *composite*, should be similar to an average. It should be a representative of both pixels taken as a unit. The second number, called the *differentiator*, should reflect the difference between the pixels. Using the composite and differentiator (which are 4-bit integers) it should be possible to reconstruct the two pixels.

Figure 4.143a,b,c shows how two numbers $v_1 = 30$ and $v_2 = 03$ can be considered the vectors $(3, 0)$ and $(0, 3)$, and how their sum $v_1 + v_2 = (3, 3)$ and difference $v_1 - v_2 = (3, -3)$ correspond to a 45° rotation of the vectors. The sum can be considered, in a certain sense, the average of the vectors, and the difference can be used to reconstruct them. However, the sum and difference of binary vectors are, in general, not binary. The sum and difference of the vectors $(0, 0, 1, 1)$ and $(1, 0, 1, 0)$, for example, are $(1, 0, 2, 1)$ and $(-1, 0, 0, 1)$.

The method proposed here for determining the composite and differentiator is illustrated by Figure 4.143d. Its 16 rows and 16 columns correspond to the 16 grayscales of our hypothetical image. The diagram is divided into 16 narrow strips of 16 locations each. The strips are numbered 0 through 15, and these numbers (shown in boldface) are the composite values. The 16 locations within each strip are also numbered 0 through 15 (this numbering is shown for strips 3 and 8), and they are the differentiators. Given two adjacent cells, $v_1 = 0011$ and $v_2 = 0100$ in one of the approximations, we use their values as (x, y) table coordinates to determine the composite $3 = 0011$ and differentiator $7 = 0111$ of their parent.

Once a pair of composite and differentiator values are given, Figure 4.143d can be used to reconstruct the two original values. It is obvious that such a diagram can be designed in many different ways, but the important feature of this particular diagram is the way it determines the composite values. They are always close to the true average of v_1 and v_2. The elements along the main diagonal, for example, satisfy $v_1 = v_2$, and the diagram is designed such that the composite values c for these elements are $c = v_1 = v_2$. The diagram is constructed by laying a narrow,

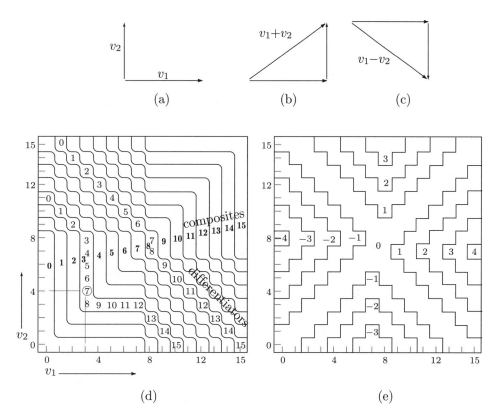

Figure 4.143: Determining Composite and Differentiator Values.

1-unit, strip of length 16 around the bottom-left corner, and adding similar strips that are symmetric about the main diagonal.

Most of the time, the composite value determined by this diagram for a pair v_1 and v_2 of 4-bit numbers is their true average, or it differs from the true average by 1. Only in 82 out of the 256 possible pairs (v_1, v_2) does the composite value differ from the true average $(v_1 + v_2)/2$ by more than 1. This is about 32%. The deviations of the composite values from the true averages are shown in Figure 4.143e. The maximum deviation is 4, and it occurs in just two cases.

Since the composite values are so close to the average, they are used to color the cells of the various approximations, which makes for realistic-looking progressive images. This is the main feature of the method.

Figure 4.144 shows the binary tree resulting from the various approximations. The root represents the entire image, and the leaves are the individual pixels. Every pair of pixels becomes a pair (c, d) of composite and differentiator values in the level above the leaves. Every pair of composite values in that level becomes a pair (c, d) in the level above it, and so on, until the root becomes one such pair. If the image contains 2^n pixels, then the bottom level (the leaves) contains 2^n nodes. The level above it contains 2^{n-1} nodes, and so on. Displaying the image progressively is done by the progressive decoder in steps as follows:

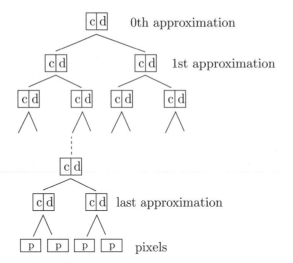

Figure 4.144: Successive Approximation in a Binary Tree.

1. The pair (c_0, d_0) for the root is input and the image is displayed as one large uniform block (0th approximation) of intensity c_0.

2. Values c_0 and d_0 are used to determine, from Figure 4.143d, the two composite values c_{10} and c_{11}. The first approximation, consisting of two large uniform cells with intensities c_{10} and c_{11}, is displayed, replacing the 0th approximation. Two differentiator values d_{10} and d_{11} for the next level (2nd approximation) are input.

3. Values c_{10} and d_{10} are used to determine, from Figure 4.143d, the two composite values c_{20} and c_{21}. Values c_{11} and d_{11} are similarly used to determine the two composite values c_{22} and c_{23}. The second approximation, consisting of four large cells with intensities c_{20}, c_{21}, c_{22}, and c_{23}, is displayed, replacing the 1st approximation. Four differentiator values d_{2i} for the next level (3rd approximation) are input.

4. This process is repeated until, in the last step, the 2^{n-1} composite values for the next to last approximation are determined and displayed. The 2^{n-1} differentiator values for these composites are now input, and each of the 2^{n-1} pairs (c, d) is used to compute a pair of pixels. The 2^n pixels are displayed, completing the progressive generation of the image.

These steps show that the image file should contain the value c_0, the value d_0, the two values d_{10} and d_{11}, the four values d_{20}, d_{21}, d_{22}, and d_{23}, and so on, up to the 2^{n-1} differentiator values for the next to last approximation. The total is one composite value and $2^n - 1$ differentiator values. The image file thus contains 2^n 4-bit values, so its size equals that of the original image. The method discussed so far is for progressive image transmission and does not yet include any compression.

⋄ **Exercise 4.51:** Given the eight pixel values 3, 4, 5, 6, 6, 4, 5, and 8, build a tree similar to the one of Figure 4.144 and list the contents of the progressive image file.

The encoder starts with the original image pixels (the leaves of the binary tree) and prepares the tree from bottom to top. The image file, however, should start with the root of the tree, so the encoder must keep all the levels of the tree in memory while the tree is being generated. Fortunately, this does not require any extra memory. The original pixel values are not needed after the first step, and can be discarded, leaving room for the composite and differentiator values. The composite values are used in the second step and can later also be discarded. Only the differentiator values have to saved for all the steps, but they can be stored in the memory space originally taken by the image.

It is clear that the first few approximations are too coarse to show any recognizable image. However, they involve very few cells and are computed and displayed quickly. Each approximation has twice the number of cells of its predecessor, so the time it takes to display an approximation increases geometrically. Since the computations involved are simple, we can estimate the time needed to generate and display an approximation by considering the time it takes to input the values needed for the following approximation; the time for computations can be ignored. Assuming a transmission speed of 28,800 baud, the zeroth approximation (input two 4-bit values) takes $8/28800 \approx 0.00028$ sec., the first approximation (input another two 4-bit values) takes the same time. The second approximation (four 4-bit values) takes 0.000556 sec., and the tenth approximation (input 2^{10} 4-bit numbers) takes 0.14 sec. Following approximations take 0.28, 0.56, 1.04, and 2.08 seconds.

It is also possible to develop the image progressively in a nonuniform way. The simplest way to encode an image progressively is to compute the differentiator values of each approximation in raster order and write them on the image file in this order. However, if we are interested in the center of the image, we may change this order, as long as we do it in the same way for the encoder and decoder. The encoder may write the differentiator values for the center of the image first, followed by the remaining differentiator values. The decoder should mimic this. It should start each approximation by displaying the center of the image, followed by the rest of the approximation.

The image file generated by this method can be compressed by entropy coding the individual values in it. All the values (except one) in this file are differentiators, and experiments indicate that these values are normally distributed. For 4-bit pixels, differentiator values are in the range 0 through 15, and Table 4.145 lists typical counts and Huffman codes for each of the 16 values. This reduces the data from four bits per differentiator to about 2.7 bits/value.

Another way to compress the image file is to quantize the original pixels from 16 to 15 intensity levels and use the extra pixel value as a termination code, indicating a uniform cell. When the decoder inputs this value from the image file, it does not split the cell further.

4.27.3 Progressive Bintree Compression

Various techniques for progressive image representation are discussed in Section 4.8. Section 4.27.2 describes an application of bintrees for the progressive transmission of grayscale images. This section (based on [Knowlton 80]) outlines a similar method for bi-level images. We illustrate the method on an image with resolution 384×512. The image is divided into blocks of size 3×2 each. There are $128 = 2^7$ rows and $256 = 2^8$ columns of these 6-tuples, so their total number is $2^{15} = 32,768$.

diff. value	count	Huffman code
0	27	00000000
1	67	00000001
2	110	0000001
3	204	000001
4	485	00001
5	1564	0001
6	4382	001
7	8704	01
8	10206	11
9	4569	101
10	1348	1001
11	515	10001
12	267	100001
13	165	1000001
14	96	10000001
15	58	10000000

Table 4.145: Possible Huffman Codes for 4-bit Differentiator Values.

The encoder constructs a binary tree by dividing the entire image into two horizontal halves, splitting each into two vertical quadrants, and continuing in this way, down to the level of 6-tuples. In practice, this is done from the bottom up, following which the tree is written on the output file top to bottom. Figure 4.146 shows the final tree. Each node is marked as either uniform black (b, with prefix code 10), uniform white ($w = 11$), or mixed ($m = 0$). A mixed node also contains another prefix code, following the 0, specifying one of five shades of gray. A good set of these codes is

110 for 16.7%,   00 for 33.3%,   01 for 50%,   10 for 66.7%, and 111 for 83.3%.

Five codes are needed, since a group of six pixels can have between zero and six white pixels, corresponding to seven shades of gray. Two shades, namely black and white, do not occur in a mixed 6-tuple, so only the five shades above need be specified. The average size of these codes is 2.4 bits, so a mixed (m) tree node has on average 3.4 bits, the code 0 followed by 2 or 3 bits.

When the decoder inputs one of these levels, it splits each block of the preceding level into two smaller blocks and uses the codes to paint them black, white, or one of five shades of gray.

The bottom two levels of the tree are different. The next to last level contains 2^{15} nodes, one for each 6-tuple. A node in this level contains one of seven codes, specifying the number of white pixels in the 6-tuple. When the decoder gets to this level, each block is already a 6-tuple, and it is painted the right shade of gray, according to the number of the white pixels in the 6-tuple. When the decoder gets to the last level, it already knows how many white pixels each 6-tuple contains. It only needs to be told *where* these white pixels are located in the 6-tuple. This is

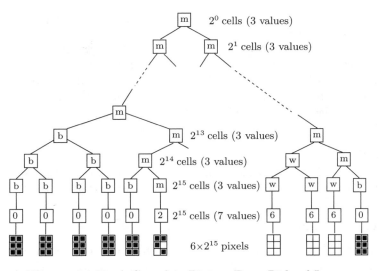

Figure 4.146: A Complete Bintree For a Bi-level Image.

also done by means of codes. If a 6-tuple contains just one white pixel, that pixel may be located in one of six positions, so six 3-bit codes are needed. A 6-tuple with five white pixels also requires a 3-bit code. If a 6-tuple contains two white pixels, they may be located in the 6-tuple in 15 different ways, so 15 4-bit codes are needed. A 6-tuple with four white pixels also requires a 4-bit code. When a 6-tuple contains three white pixels, they may form 20 configurations, so 20 prefix (variable-size) codes are used, ranging in size from 3 to 5 bits.

⋄ **Exercise 4.52:** Show the 15 6-tuples with two white pixels.

The size of the binary tree of Figure 4.146 can now be estimated. The top levels (excluding the bottom three levels) contain between 1 and 2^{14} nodes, for a total of $2^{15} - 1 \approx 2^{15}$. The third level from the bottom contains 2^{15} nodes, so the total number of nodes so far is 2×2^{15}. Each of these nodes contains either a 2-bit code (for uniform b and w nodes) or a 3.4-bit code (for m nodes). Assuming that half the nodes are mixed, the average is 2.7 bits per node. The total number of bits so far is $2 \times 2^{15} \times 2.7 = 5.4 \times 2^{15}$. This almost equals the original size of the image (which is 6×2^{15}), and we still have two more levels to go!

The next to last level contains 2^{15} nodes with a 3-bit code each (one of seven shades of gray). The bottom level also contains 2^{15} nodes with 3, 4, or 5-bit codes each. Assuming a 4-bit average code size for this level, the total size of the tree is

$$(5.4 + 3 + 4) \times 2^{15} = 12.4 \times 2^{15},$$

more than twice the image size! Compression is achieved by pruning the tree, similar to a quadtree, such that any b or w node located high in the tree becomes a leaf. Experiments indicate a typical compression factor of 6, implying that the tree is reduced in size from twice the image size to 1/6 the image size: a factor of

12. [Knowlton 80] describes a more complex coding scheme that produces typical compression factors of 8.

One advantage of the method proposed here is the fact that it produces gray blocks for tree nodes of type m (mixed). This means that the method can be used even with a bi-level display. A block consisting of black and white pixels looks gray when we watch it from a distance, and the amount of gray is determined by the mixture of black and white pixels in the block. Methods that attempt to get nice-looking gray blocks on a bi-level display are known as *dithering* [Salomon 99].

Bibliography

Knowlton, Ken (1980) "Progressive Transmission of Grey-Scale and Binary Pictures by Simple, Efficient, and Lossless Encoding Schemes," *Proceedings of the IEEE*, **68**(7):885–896, July.

4.27.4 Prefix Compression

Prefix compression is a variant of quadtrees proposed in [Anedda 88] (see also Section 8.5.5). We start with a $2^n \times 2^n$ image. Each quadrant in the quadtree of this image is numbered 0, 1, 2, or 3, a two-bit number. Each subquadrant has a two-digit (i.e., a four-bit) number and each subsubquadrant, a 3-digit number. As the quadrants get smaller, their numbers get longer. When this numbering scheme is carried down to individual pixels, the number of a pixel turns out to be n digits, or $2n$ bits, long. Prefix compression is designed for bi-level images with text or diagrams where the number of black pixels is relatively small. It is not suitable for grayscale, color, or any image that contains many black pixels, such as a painting. The method is best explained by an example. Figure 4.147 shows the pixel numbering in an 8×8 image (i.e., $n = 3$) and also a simple 8×8 image containing of 18 black pixels. Each pixel number is three digits long, and they range from 000 to 333.

000 001 010 011	100 101 110 111
002 003 012 013	102 103 112 113
020 021 030 031	120 121 130 131
022 023 032 033	122 123 132 133
200 201 210 211	300 301 310 311
202 203 212 213	302 303 312 313
220 221 230 231	320 321 330 331
222 223 232 233	322 323 332 333

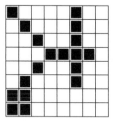

Figure 4.147: Example of Prefix Compression.

The first step is to use quadtree methods to figure the three-digit id numbers of the 18 black pixels. They are 000 101 003 103 030 121 033 122 123 132 210 301 203 303 220 221 222 223.

The next step is to select a *prefix* value P. We select $P = 2$, a choice that's justified below. The code of a pixel is now divided into P prefix digits followed by $3 - P$ suffix digits. The last step goes over the sequence of black pixels and selects all the pixels with the same prefix. The first prefix is 00, so all the pixels that start with 00 are selected. They are 000 and 003. They are removed from the original sequence and are compressed by writing the token $00|1|0|3$ on the output stream. The first part of this token is a prefix (00), the second part is a count (1), and the rest are the suffixes of the two pixels having prefix 00. Notice that a count of one implies two pixels. The count is always one less than the number of pixels being counted. Sixteen pixels now remain in the original sequence, and the first of them has prefix 10. The two pixels with this prefix are removed and compressed by writing the token $10|1|1|3$ on the output stream. This continues until the original sequence is empty. The final result is the 9-token string

$$00|1|0|3, 10|1|1|3, 03|1|0|3, 12|2|1|2|3, 13|0|2, 21|0|0, 30|1|1|3, 20|0|3, 22|3|0|1|2|3$$

(without the commas). Such a string can be decoded uniquely, since each segment starts with a two-digit prefix, followed by a one-digit count c, followed by $c + 1$ one-digit suffixes.

In general, the prefix is P digits long, and the count and each suffix are $n - P$ digits each. The maximum number of suffixes in a segment is therefore 4^{n-P}. The maximum size of a segment is thus $P + (n - P) + 4^{n-P}(n - P)$ digits. Each segment corresponds to a different prefix. A prefix has P digits, each between 0 and 3, so the maximum number of segments is 4^P. The entire compressed string thus occupies at most

$$4^P \left[P + (n - P) + 4^{n-P}(n - P) \right] = n \cdot 4^P + 4^n(n - P)$$

digits. To find the optimum value of P we differentiate the expression above with respect to P,

$$\frac{d}{dP} \left[n \cdot 4^P + 4^n(n - P) \right] = n \cdot 4^P \ln 4 - 4^n,$$

and set the derivative to zero. The solution is

$$4^P = \frac{4^n}{n \cdot \ln 4}, \quad \text{or } P = \log_4 \left[\frac{4^n}{n \cdot \ln 4} \right] = \frac{1}{2} \log_2 \left[\frac{4^n}{n \cdot \ln 4} \right].$$

For $n = 3$ this yields

$$P \approx \frac{1}{2} \log_2 \left[\frac{4^3}{3 \times 1.386} \right] = \frac{\log_2 15.388}{2} = 3.944/2 = 1.97.$$

This is why $P = 2$ was selected earlier.

A downside of this method is that some pixels may be assigned numbers with different prefixes even though they are near neighbors. This happens when they are located in different quadrants. An example is pixels 123 and 301 of Figure 4.147.

Improvement: The count field was arbitrarily set to one digit (two bits). The maximum count is thus $3 (= 11_2)$, i.e., four pixels. It is possible to have a variable-size count field containing a variable-size code, such as the unary code of Section 2.3.1. This way a single token could compress any number of pixels.

Bibliography

Anedda, C. and L. Felician (1988) "P-Compressed Quadtrees for Image Storing," *The Computer Journal*, **31**(4):353–357.

4.28 Quadrisection

A quadtree exploits the redundancy in an image by examining smaller and smaller quadrants, looking for uniform areas. The method of *quadrisection* is related to quadtrees, since it uses the quadtree principle for dividing an image into subimages. However, quadrisection does not divide an image into four parts, but rather reshapes the image in steps by increasing the number of its rows and decreasing the number of its columns. The method is lossless. It performs well for bi-level images and is illustrated here for such an image, but can also be applied to grayscale (and thus to color) images.

The method assumes that the original image is a $2^k \times 2^k$ square matrix M_0, and it reshapes M_0 into a sequence of matrices $M_1, M_2, \ldots, M_{k+1}$ with fewer and fewer columns. These matrices naturally have more and more rows, and the quadrisection method achieves compression by searching for and removing duplicate rows. The more rows and the fewer columns a matrix has, the better the chance of having duplicate rows. The end result is a matrix M_{k+1} with one column and not more than 64 rows. This matrix is treated as a short string and is written at the end of the compressed stream, to help in decoding and recovering the original image M_0. The compressed stream must also contain information on how to reconstruct each matrix M_{j-1} from its successor M_j. This information is in the form of an *indicator vector* denoted by I_{j-1}. Thus, the output consists of all the I_j vectors (each arithmetically encoded into a string w_j), followed by the bits of M_{k+1}^T (the transpose of the last, single-column, matrix, in raw format). This string is preceded by a prefix that indicates the value of k, the sizes of all the w_j's, and the size of M_{k+1}^T.

Here is the encoding process in a little more detail. We assume that the original image is a $2^k \times 2^k$ square matrix M_0 of 4^k pixels, each a single bit. The encoder uses an operation called *projection* (discussed below) to construct a sequence of matrices M_1, M_2, up to M_{k+1}, such that M_j has 4^{k-j+1} columns. This implies that M_1 has $4^{k-1+1} = 4^k$ columns and therefore just one row. Matrix M_2 has 4^{k-1} columns and therefore four rows. Matrix M_3 has 4^{k-2} columns, but may have fewer than eight rows, since any duplicate rows are removed from M_2 before M_3 is constructed. The number of rows of M_3 is four times the number of *distinct* rows of M_2. Indicator vector I_2 is constructed at the same time as M_3 to indicate those rows of M_2 that are duplicates. The size of I_2 equals the number of rows of M_2, and the elements of I_2 are nonnegative integers. The decoder uses I_2 to reconstruct M_2 from M_3.

All the I_j indicator vectors are needed by the decoder. Since the size of I_j equals the number of rows of matrix M_j, and since these matrices have more and more rows, the combined sizes of all the indicator vectors I_j may be large. However, most elements of a typical indicator vector I_j are zeros, so these vectors can be highly compressed with arithmetic coding. Also, the first few indicator vectors are normally all zeros, so they may all be replaced by one number indicating how many of them there are.

⋄ **Exercise 4.53:** Even though we haven't yet described the details of the method (specifically, the projection operation), it is possible to logically deduce (or guess) the answer to this exercise. The question is; We know that images with little or no correlation will not compress. Yet the size of the last matrix, M_{k+1}, is small (64 bits or fewer) regardless of the image being compressed. Can quadrisection somehow compress images that other methods cannot?

The decoder starts by decoding the prefix, to obtain the sizes of all the compressed strings w_j. It then decompresses each w_j to obtain an indicator vector I_j. The decoder knows how many indicator vectors there are, since j goes from 1 to k. After decoding all the indicator vectors, the decoder reads the rest of the compressed stream and considers it the bits of M_{k+1}. The decoder then uses the indicator vectors to reconstruct matrices M_k, $M_{k-1}, \ldots$ all the way down to M_0.

The projection operation is the heart of quadrisection. It is described here in three steps.

Step 1: An indicator vector I for a matrix M with r rows contains r components, one for each row of M. Each distinct row of M has a zero component in I, and each duplicate row has a positive component. If, for example, row 8 is a duplicate of the fifth distinct row, then the 8th component of I will be 5. Notice that the fifth distinct row is not necessarily row five. As an example, the indicator vector for matrix M of Equation (4.40) is $I = (0, 0, 0, 3, 0, 4, 3, 1)$:

$$M_3 = \begin{bmatrix} 1001 \\ 1101 \\ 1011 \\ 1011 \\ 0000 \\ 0000 \\ 1011 \\ 1001 \end{bmatrix}. \tag{4.40}$$

Step 2: Given a row vector v of length m, where m is a power of 2, we perform the following: (1) Divide it into $\sqrt{m}$ segments of length $\sqrt{m}$ each. (2) Arrange the segments as a matrix of size $\sqrt{m} \times \sqrt{m}$. (3) Divide it into four quadrants, each a matrix of size $\sqrt{m}/2 \times \sqrt{m}/2$. (4) Label the quadrants 1, 2, 3, and 4 according to $\left(\begin{smallmatrix} 1 & 2 \\ 3 & 4 \end{smallmatrix}\right)$, and (5) unfold each into a vector v_i of length $\sqrt{m}$. As an example consider the vector

$$v = (0, 1, 2, 3, 4, 5, 6, 7, 8, 9, 10, 11, 12, 13, 14, 15),$$

of length $16 = 2^4$. It first becomes the 4×4 matrix

$$M = \begin{pmatrix} 0 & 1 & 2 & 3 \\ 4 & 5 & 6 & 7 \\ 8 & 9 & 10 & 11 \\ 12 & 13 & 14 & 15 \end{pmatrix}.$$

Partitioning M yields the four 2×2 matrices

$$M_1 = \begin{pmatrix} 0 & 1 \\ 4 & 5 \end{pmatrix}, \quad M_2 = \begin{pmatrix} 2 & 3 \\ 6 & 7 \end{pmatrix}, \quad M_3 = \begin{pmatrix} 8 & 9 \\ 12 & 13 \end{pmatrix}, \quad \text{and } M_4 = \begin{pmatrix} 10 & 11 \\ 14 & 15 \end{pmatrix}.$$

Each is unfolded, to produce the four vectors

$$v_1 = (0, 1, 4, 5), \quad v_2 = (2, 3, 6, 7), \quad v_3 = (8, 9, 12, 13), \text{ and } v_4 = (10, 11, 14, 15).$$

This step illustrates the relation between quadrisection and quadtrees.

Step 3: This finally describes the projection operation. Given an $n \times m$ matrix M where m (the number of columns) is a power of 2, we first construct an indicator vector I for it. Vector I will have n components, for the n rows of M. If M has r distinct rows, vector I will have r zeros corresponding to these rows. We construct the projected matrix M' with $4r$ rows and $m/4$ columns in the following steps: (3.1) Ignore all duplicate rows of M (i.e., all rows corresponding to nonzero elements of I). (3.2) For each of the remaining r distinct rows of M construct four vectors v_i as shown in Step 2 above, and make them into the next four rows of M'. We use the notation

$$M \xrightarrow{I} M',$$

to indicate this projection.

Example: Given the 16×16 matrix M_0 of Figure 4.148 we concatenate its rows to construct matrix M_1 with one row and 256 columns. This is always our starting point, regardless of whether the rows of M_0 are distinct or not. Since M_1 has just one row, its indicator vector is $I_1 = (0)$.

```
0 0 0 0 0 0 0 0 1 0 0 0 0 0 0 0
0 0 0 0 0 0 0 1 1 0 0 0 0 0 0 0
0 0 0 0 0 0 1 1 1 1 0 0 0 0 0 0
0 0 0 0 0 0 1 1 0 1 1 1 0 0 0 0
0 0 0 0 0 0 1 1 1 1 1 0 0 0 0 0
0 0 0 0 1 1 1 1 1 1 0 0 0 0 0 0
0 0 1 1 1 1 1 1 1 1 0 0 0 0 0 0
0 1 1 1 1 1 1 1 1 1 0 0 0 0 0 0
0 1 1 1 1 1 1 1 1 0 0 0 0 0 0 0
1 1 1 1 1 1 1 1 1 0 0 0 0 0 0 0
1 1 1 1 1 1 1 1 0 0 0 0 0 0 0 0
1 1 1 1 1 0 1 1 1 0 0 0 0 0 0 0
1 1 1 1 1 0 0 1 1 0 0 0 0 0 0 0
1 1 1 1 1 1 0 1 1 0 0 0 0 0 0 0
0 1 1 1 1 1 0 1 1 0 0 0 0 0 0 0
0 1 1 1 1 1 0 1 1 1 0 0 1 1 1 1
```

Figure 4.148: A 16×16 Matrix M_0.

Matrix M_2 is easily projected from M_1. It has four rows and 64 columns

$$M_2 = \begin{bmatrix} 0000000000000001000000110000001100000011000011110011111011111111 \\ 1000000010000000110000001110000111000001100000011000000011000000 \\ 0111111111111111111111111111011111111001111111010111110101111101 \\ 1000000010000000000000001000000010000000100000011001111 \end{bmatrix}.$$

All four rows of M_2 are distinct, so its indicator vector is $I_2 = (0, 0, 0, 0)$. Notice how each row of M_2 is an 8×8 submatrix of M_0. The top row, for example, is the upper-left 8×8 corner of M_0.

To project M_3 from M_2 we perform Step 2 above on each row of M_2, converting it from a 1×64 to a 4×16 matrix. Matrix M_3 thus consists of four parts, each 4×16, so its size is 16×16:

$$M_3 = \begin{bmatrix} 0000000000000000 \\ 0000000100110011 \\ 0000000000110111 \\ 0011111111111111 \\ \hline 1000100011000111 \\ 0000000000000000 \\ 1110110011001100 \\ 0000000000000000 \\ \hline 0111111111111111 \\ 1111111111111011 \\ 1111111101110111 \\ 1001110111011101 \\ \hline 1000100000001000 \\ 0000000000000000 \\ 1000100010001100 \\ 0000000000001111 \end{bmatrix}.$$

Notice how each row of M_3 is a 4×4 submatrix of M_0. The top row, for example, is the upper-left 4×4 corner of M_0, and the second row is the upper-second-from-left 4×4 corner. Examining the 16 rows of M_3 results in the indicator vector $I_3 = (0, 0, 0, 0, 0, 1, 0, 1, 0, 0, 0, 0, 0, 1, 0, 0)$ (i.e., rows 6, 8, and 14 are duplicates of row 1). This is how the next projection creates some compression. Projecting M_3 to M_4 is done by ignoring rows 6, 8, and 14. M_4 (Equation (4.41)) thus has $4 \times 13 = 52$ rows and four columns (a quarter of the number of M_3). It therefore has $52 \times 4 = 208$ elements instead of 256.

It is clear that with so many short rows, M_4 must have many duplicate rows. An examination indicates only 12 distinct rows, and produces vector I_4:

$$I_4 = (0, 1, 1, 1, 1, 0, 1, 0, 1, 1, 2, 3, 0, 3, 3, 3 | 0, 1, 0, 4, 3, 0, 3, 1 |$$
$$0, 3, 3, 3, 3, 3, 0, 3, 3, 3, 0, 3, 0, 10, 3, 10 | 5, 1, 0, 1, 5, 1, 11, 1, 1, 1, 4, 4).$$

Projecting M_4 to obtain M_5 is done as before. Matrix M_5 has $4 \times 12 = 48$ rows and only one column (a quarter of the number of columns of M_4). This is therefore the final matrix M_{k+1}, whose transpose will be the last part of the compressed stream.

⋄ **Exercise 4.54:** Calculate matrix M_5.

The compressed stream consists therefore of a prefix, followed by the value of $k (= 4)$, followed by I_1, I_2, I_3, and I_4, arithmetically encoded, followed by the 48 bits of M_5^T. There is no need to encode those last bits, since there may be at most 64 of them (see exercise below). Moreover, since I_1 and I_2 are zeros, there is no need to write them on the output. All that the encoder has to write instead is the number 3 (encoded) to point out that the first indicator vector included in the output is I_3.

The prefix consists of 4 (k), 3 (index of first nonzero indicator vector), and the encoded lengths of indicator vectors I_3 and I_4. After decoding this, the decoder can decode the two indicator vectors, read the remaining compressed stream as M_5^T, then use all this data to reconstruct M_4, M_3, M_2, M_1, and M_0.

⋄ **Exercise 4.55:** Show why M_5 cannot have more than 64 elements.

Extensions: Quadrisection is used to compress two-dimensional data, and can therefore be considered the second method in a succession of three compression methods the first and third of which are *bisection* and *octasection*. Following is a short description of these two methods.

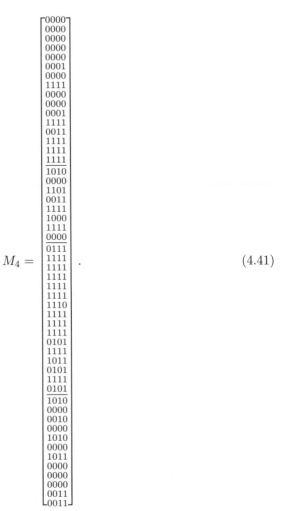

$$M_4 = \begin{bmatrix} \vdots \end{bmatrix}. \tag{4.41}$$

Bisection is an extension (or rather a reduction) of quadrisection for the case where the data is one-dimensional (typical examples are sampled speech, a binary string, or text). We assume that the data consists of a string L_0 of 2^k data items, where an item can be a single bit, an ASCII code, a speech sample, or anything else, but all items have the same size.

The encoder iterates k times, varying j from 1 to k. In iteration j, a list L_j is created by bisecting the elements of the preceding list L_{j-1}. An indicator vector I_j is constructed for L_j. The duplicate elements of L_j are then deleted (this is where we get compression).

Each of the two elements of the first constructed list L_1 is therefore a block of 2^{k-1} data items (half the number of the data items in L_0). Indicator vector I_1 also has two elements. Each element of L_2 is a block of 2^{k-2} data items, but the number of elements of L_2 is not necessarily four. It can be smaller depending on how many distinct elements L_1 has. In the last step, where $j = k$, list L_k is created, where each element is a block of size $2^{k-k} = 1$. Thus, each element of L_k is one of the original data items of L_0. It is not necessary to construct indicator vector I_k (the last indicator vector generated is I_{k-1}).

The compressed stream consists of k, followed by indicator vectors I_1, I_2, through I_{k-1} (compressed), followed by L_k (raw). Since the first few indicator vectors tend to be all zeros, they can be replaced by a single number indicating the index of the first nonzero indicator vector.

Example: The 32-element string L_0 where each data element is a single bit:

$$L_0 = (0,1,1,1,0,0,1,0,1,1,0,0,0,0,1,0,0,1,1,0,1,1,1,1,0,1,0,1,1,0,1,0).$$

The two halves of L_0 are distinct, so L_1 consists of two elements

$$L_1 = (0111001011000010, 0110111101011010),$$

and the first indicator vector is $I_1 = (0,0)$. The two elements of L_1 are distinct, so L_2 has four elements,

$$L_2 = (01110010, 11000010, 01101111, 01011010),$$

and the second indicator vector is $I_2 = (0,0,0,0)$. The four elements of L_2 are distinct, so L_3 has eight elements,

$$L_3 = (0111, 0010, 1100, 0010, 0110, 1111, 0101, 1010),$$

and the third indicator vector is $I_3 = (0,0,0,2,0,0,0,0)$. Seven elements of L_3 are distinct, so L_4 has 14 elements,

$$L_4 = (01, 11, 00, 10, 11, 00, 01, 10, 11, 11, 01, 01, 10, 10),$$

and the fourth indicator vector is $I_4 = (0,0,0,0,2,3,1,4,2,2,1,1,4,4)$. Only four elements of L_4 are distinct, so L_5 has eight elements, $L_5 = (0,1,1,1,0,0,1,0)$.

The output therefore consists of $k = 5$, indicator vectors $I_1 = (0,0)$, $I_2 = (0,0,0,0)$, $I_3 = (0,0,0,2,0,0,0,0)$, and $I_4 = (0,0,0,0,2,3,1,4,2,2,1,1,4,4)$ (encoded), followed by $L_5 = (0,1,1,1,0,0,1,0)$. Since the first nonzero indicator vector is I_3, we can omit both I_1 and I_2 and replace them with the integer 3.

⋄ **Exercise 4.56:** Describe the operations of the decoder for this example.

⋄ **Exercise 4.57:** Use bisection to encode the 32-bit string

$$L_0 = (0101010101010101\ 1010101010101010).$$

The discussion above shows that if the original data to be compressed is a bit string of length 2^k, then L_{k-1} is a list of pairs of bits. L_{k-1} can therefore have at most four distinct elements, so L_k, whose elements are single bits, can have at most eight elements. This, of course, does not mean that any binary string L_0 can be compressed into eight bits. The reader should bear in mind that the compressed stream must also include the nonzero indicator vectors. If the elements of L_0 are not bits, then L_k could, in principle, be as long as L_0.

Example: A source string $L_0 = (a_1, a_2, \ldots, a_{32})$ where the a_i's are distinct data items, such as ASCII characters. L_1 consists of two elements,

$$L_1 = (a_1 a_2 \ldots a_{16}, \, a_{17} a_{18} \ldots a_{32}),$$

and the first indicator vector is $I_1 = (0, 0)$. The two elements of L_1 are distinct, so L_2 has four elements,

$$L_2 = (a_1 a_2 \ldots a_8, \, a_9 a_{10} \ldots a_{16}, \, a_{17} a_{18} \ldots a_{24}, \, a_{25} a_{26} \ldots a_{32}),$$

and the second indicator vector is $I_2 = (0, 0, 0, 0)$. All four elements of L_2 are distinct, so

$$L_3 = (a_1 a_2 a_3 a_4, \, a_5 a_6 a_7 a_8, \, a_9 a_{10} a_{11} a_{12}, \ldots, \, a_{29} a_{30} a_{31} a_{32}).$$

Continuing this way, it is easy to see that all indicator vectors will be zero, and L_5 will have the same 32 elements as L_0. The result will be no compression at all.

If the length L of the original data is not a power of two, we can still use bisection by considering the following: There is some integer k such that $2^{k-1} < L < 2^k$. If L is close to 2^k, we can add $d = 2^k - L$ zeros to the original string L_0, compress it by bisection, and write d on the compressed stream, so the decoder can delete the d zeros. If L is close to 2^{k-1} we divide L_0 into a string L_0^1 with the first 2^{k-1} items, and string L_0^2 with the remaining items. The former string can be compressed with bisection and the latter can be compressed by either appending zeros to it or splitting it recursively.

Octasection is an extension of both bisection and quadrisection for three-dimensional data. Examples of such data are a movie (a sequence of images), a grayscale image, and a color image. Such an image can be viewed as a three-dimensional matrix where the third dimension is the bits constituting each pixel (the bitplanes). We assume that the data is a rectangular box P of dimensions $2^{k_1} \times 2^{k_2} \times 2^{k_3}$, where each entry is a data item (a single bit or several bits) and all entries have the same size. The encoder performs k iterations, where $k = \min(k_1, k_2, k_3)$, varying j from 1 to k. In iteration j, a list L_j is created, by subdividing each element of the preceding list L_{j-1} into eight smaller rectangular boxes. An indicator vector I_j is constructed for L_j. The duplicate elements of L_j are then deleted (this is where we get compression).

The compressed stream consists, as before, of all the (arithmetically encoded) indicator vectors, followed by the last list L_k.

Bibliography

Kieffer, J., G. Nelson, and E-H. Yang (1996a) "Tutorial on the quadrisection method and related methods for lossless data compression." Available for downloading at URL http://www.ece.umn.edu/users/kieffer/index.html.

Kieffer, J., E-H. Yang, G. Nelson, and P. Cosman (1996b) "Lossless compression via bisection trees." Available from URL http://www.ece.umn.edu/users/kieffer/index.html.

4.29 Space-Filling Curves

A space-filling curve is a parametric function $\mathbf{P}(t)$ that passes through every point in a given two-dimensional area, normally the unit square, when its parameter t varies in the range $[0,1]$. For any value t_0, the value of $\mathbf{P}(t_0)$ is a point $[x_0, y_0]$ in the unit square. Mathematically, such a curve is a mapping from the interval $[0,1]$ to the two-dimensional interval $[0,1] \times [0,1]$. To understand how such a curve is constructed it is best to think of it as the limit of an infinite sequence of curves $\mathbf{P}_1(t)$, $\mathbf{P}_2(t), \ldots$, which are drawn inside the unit square, where each curve is derived from its predecessor by a process of *refinement*. The details of the refinement depend on the specific curve. An appendix in the book's web site discusses two well-known space-filling curves: the Hilbert curve and the Sierpiński curve. Since the sequence of curves is infinite, it is impossible to compute all its components. Fortunately, we are interested in a curve that passes through every pixel in a bitmap, not through every mathematical point in the unit square. Since the number of pixels is finite, it is possible to construct such a curve in practice.

To understand why such curves are useful for image compression, the reader should recall the principle that has been mentioned several times in the past, namely, if we select a pixel in an image at random, there is a good chance that its neighbors will have the same color. Both RLE image compression and the quadtree method are based on this principle, but they are not always efficient, as Figure 4.149 shows. This 8×8 bitmap has two concentrations of pixels, but neither RLE nor the quadtree method compress it very well, since there are no long runs and since the pixel concentrations happen to cross quadrant boundaries.

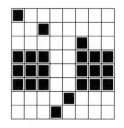

Figure 4.149: An 8×8 Bitmap.

Better compression may be produced by a method that scans the bitmap area by area instead of line by line or quadrant by quadrant. This is why space-filling curves provide a new approach to image compression. Such a curve visits every point in a given area, and does that by visiting all the points in a subarea, then moves to the next subarea and traverses it, and so on. We use the Hilbert curve (six figures in an appendix in the book's web site) as an example. Each curve H_i is constructed by making four copies of the previous curve H_{i-1}, shrinking them, rotating them, and connecting them. The new curve ends up covering the same area as its predecessor. This is the refinement process for the Hilbert curve.

Scanning an 8×8 bitmap in a Hilbert curve results in the sequence of pixels

$$(0,0), (0,1), (1,1), (1,0), (2,0), (3,0), (3,1), (2,1),$$
$$(2,2), (3,2), (3,3), (2,3), (1,3), (1,2), (0,2), (0,3),$$
$$(0,4), (1,4), (1,5), (0,5), (0,6), (0,7), (1,7), (1,6),$$
$$(2,6), (2,7), (3,7), (3,6), (3,5), (2,5), (2,4), (3,4),$$
$$(4,4), (5,4), (5,5), (4,5), (4,6), (4,7), (5,7), (5,6),$$
$$(6,6), (6,7), (7,7), (7,6), (7,5), (6,5), (6,4), (7,4),$$
$$(7,3), (7,2), (6,2), (6,3), (5,3), (4,3), (4,2), (5,2),$$
$$(5,1), (4,1), (4,0), (5,0), (6,0), (6,1), (7,1), (7,0).$$

An appendix in the book's web site discusses space-filling curves in general and shows methods for fast traversal of some curves. Here we would like to point out that quadtrees (Section 4.27) are a special case of the Hilbert curve, a fact illustrated by six figures in that appendix.

⋄ **Exercise 4.58:** Scan the 8×8 bitmap of Figure 4.149 using a Hilbert curve. Calculate the runs of identical pixels and compare them to the runs produced by RLE.

Bibliography

Prusinkiewicz, P., and A. Lindenmayer (1990) *The Algorithmic Beauty of Plants*, New York, Springer Verlag.

Prusinkiewicz, P., A. Lindenmayer, and F. D. Fracchia (1991) "Synthesis of Space-Filling Curves on the Square Grid," in *Fractals in the Fundamental and Applied Sciences*, edited by Peitgen, H.-O. et al., Amsterdam, Elsevier Science Publishers, pp. 341–366.

Sagan, Hans (1994) *Space-Filling Curves*, New York, Springer-Verlag.

4.30 Hilbert Scan and VQ

The space-filling Hilbert curve (appendix in book's web site) is used in this method [Sampath and Ansari 93] as a preprocessing step for the lossy compression of images (notice that the authors use the term "Peano scan," but they actually use the Hilbert curve). The Hilbert curve is used to transform the original image into another, highly correlated, image. The compression itself is done by a vector quantization algorithm that exploits the correlation produced by the preprocessing step.

In the preprocessing step, an original image of size $M \times N$ is partitioned into small blocks of $m \times m$ pixels each (with $m = 8$ typically) that are scanned in Hilbert curve order. The result is a linear (one-dimensional) sequence of blocks, which is then rearranged into a new two-dimensional array of size $\frac{M}{m} \times Nm$. This process results in bringing together (or clustering) blocks that are highly correlated. The "distance" between adjacent blocks is now smaller than the distance between blocks that are raster-scan neighbors in the original image.

The distance between two blocks B_{ij} and C_{ij} of pixels is measured by the *mean absolute difference*, a quantity defined by

$$\frac{1}{m^2} \sum_{i=1}^{m} \sum_{j=1}^{m} |B_{ij} - C_{ij}|.$$

It turns out that the mean absolute difference of adjacent blocks in the new, rearranged, image is about half that of adjacent blocks in a raster scan of the original image. The reason for this is that the Hilbert curve is space filling. Points that are close on the curve are close in the image. Conversely, points that are close in the image are normally close on the curve. Thus, the Hilbert curve acts as an image transform. This fact is the main innovation of the method described here.

As an example of a Hilbert scan, imagine an image of size $M \times N = 128 \times 128$. If we select $m = 8$, we get $16 \times 16 = 256$ blocks that are scanned and made into a one-dimensional array. After rearranging, we end up with a new image of size 2×128 blocks or $\frac{128}{8} \times 128 \cdot 8 = 16 \times 1024$ pixels. Figure 4.150 shows how the blocks are Hilbert scanned to produce the sequence shown in Figure 4.151. This sequence is then rearranged. The top row of the rearranged image contains blocks 1, 17, 18, 2, 3, 4, ..., and the bottom row contains blocks 138, 154, 153, 169, 185, 186, ...

The new, rearranged image is now partitioned into new blocks of $4 \times 4 = 16$ pixels each. The 16 pixels of a block constitute a vector. (Notice that the vector has 16 components, each of which can be one or more bits, depending on the size of a pixel.) The LBG algorithm (Section 4.12) is used for the vector quantization of those vectors. This algorithm calls for an initial codebook, so the implementors chose five images, scanned them at a resolution of 256×256, and used them as training images, to generate three codebooks, consisting of 128, 512, and 1024 codevectors, respectively.

The main feature of the particular vector quantization algorithm used here is that the Hilbert scan results in adjacent blocks that are highly correlated. As a result, the LBG algorithm frequently assigns the same codevector to a *run* of blocks, and this fact can be used to highly compress the image. Experiments indicate that as many as 2–10 consecutive blocks (for images with details) and 30–70 consecutive blocks (for images with high spatial redundancy) may participate in such a run. Therefore, the method precedes each codevector with a code indicating the length of the run (one block or several). There are two versions of the method, one with a fixed-size code and the other with a variable-size prefix code.

When a fixed-size code is used preceding each codevector, the main question is the size of the code. A long code, such as 6 bits, allows for runs of up to 64 consecutive blocks with the same codevector. On the other hand, if the image has small details, the runs would be shorter and some of the 6 bits would be wasted. A short code, such as 2 bits, allows for runs of up to four blocks only, but fewer bits are wasted in the case of a highly detailed image. A good solution is to write the size of the code (which is typically 2–6 bits) at the start of the compressed stream, so the decoder knows what it is. The encoder can then be very sophisticated, trying various code sizes before settling on one and using it to compress the image.

Using prefix codes can result in slightly better compression, especially if the encoder can perform a two-pass job to determine the frequency of each run before anything is compressed. In such a case, the best Huffman codes can be assigned to the runs, resulting in best compression.

Further improvement can be achieved by a variant of the method that uses *dynamic codebook partitioning*. This is again based on adjacent blocks being very similar. Even if such blocks end up with different codevectors, those codevectors

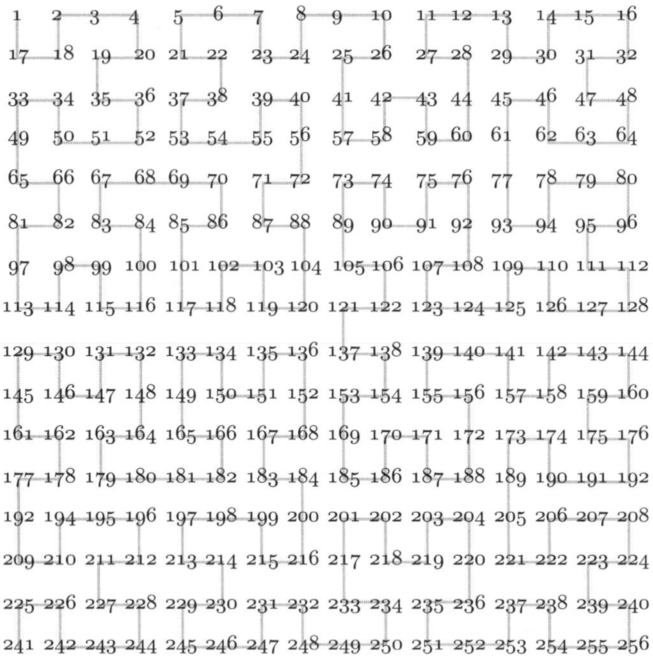

Figure 4.150: Hilbert Scan of 16×16 Blocks.

1, 17, 18, 2, 3, 4, 20, 19, 35, 36, 52, 51, 50, 34, 33, 49,
65, 66, 82, 81, 97, 113, 114, 98, 99, 115, 116, 100, 84, 83, 67, 68,
69, 70, 86, 85, 101, 117, 118, 102, 103, 119, 120, 104, 88, 87, 71, 72,
56, 40, 39, 55, 54, 53, 37, 38, 22, 21, 5, 6, 7, 23, 24, 8,
9, 10, 26, 25, 41, 57, 58, 42, 43, 59, 60, 44, 28, 27, 11, 12,
13, 29, 30, 14, 15, 16, 32, 31, 47, 48, 64, 63, 62, 46, 45, 61,
77, 93, 94, 78, 79, 80, 96, 95, 111, 112, 128, 127, 126, 110, 109, 125,
124, 123, 107, 108, 92, 76, 75, 91, 90, 74, 73, 89, 105, 106, 122, 121,
137, 138, 154, 153, 169, 185, 186, 170, 171, 187, 188, 172, 156, 155, 139, 140,
141, 157, 158, 142, 143, 144, 160, 159, 175, 176, 192, 191, 190, 174, 173, 189,
205, 221, 222, 206, 207, 208, 224, 223, 239, 240, 256, 255, 254, 238, 237, 253,
252, 251, 235, 236, 220, 204, 203, 219, 218, 202, 201, 217, 233, 234, 250, 249,
248, 232, 231, 247, 246, 245, 229, 230, 214, 213, 197, 198, 199, 215, 216, 200,
184, 183, 167, 168, 152, 136, 135, 151, 150, 134, 133, 149, 165, 166, 182, 181,
180, 179, 163, 164, 148, 132, 131, 147, 146, 130, 129, 145, 161, 162, 178, 177,
192, 209, 210, 194, 195, 196, 212, 211, 227, 228, 244, 243, 242, 226, 225, 241

Figure 4.151: The Resulting 256 Blocks.

may be very similar. This variant selects the codevectors for the first block in the usual way, using the entire codebook. It then selects a set of the next best codevectors that could have been used to code this block. This set becomes the *active part* of the codebook. (Notice that the decoder can mimic this selection.) The second block is then compared to the first block and the distance between them measured. If this distance is less than a given threshold, the codevector for the second block is selected from the active set. Since the active set is much smaller than the entire codebook, this leads to much better compression. However, each codevector must be preceded by a bit telling the decoder whether the codevector was selected from the entire codebook or just from the active set.

If the distance is greater than the threshold, a codevector for the second block is selected from the entire codebook, and a new active set is chosen, to be used (hopefully) for the third block.

If the Hilbert scan really ends up with adjacent blocks that are highly correlated, a large fraction of the blocks are coded from the active sets, thereby considerably improving the compression. A typical codebook size is 128–1024 entries, whereas the size of an active set may be just four codevectors. This reduces the size of a codebook pointer from 7–10 bits to 2 bits.

The choice of the threshold for this variant is important. It seems that an adaptive threshold adjustment may work best, but the developers don't indicate how this may be implemented.

Bibliography

Sampath, A., and A. C. Ansari (1993) "Combined Peano Scan and VQ Approach to Image Compression," *Image and Video Processing*, Bellingham, WA, SPIE vol. 1903, pp. 175–186.

4.31 Finite Automata Methods

Finite automata methods are somewhat similar to the IFS method of Section 4.32. They are based on the fact that images used in practice have a certain amount of self-similarity, i.e., it is often possible to find a part of the image that looks the same (or almost the same) as another part, except perhaps for size, brightness, or contrast. It is shown in Section 4.32 that IFS uses affine transformations to match image parts. The methods described here, on the other hand, try to describe a subimage as a weighted sum of other subimages.

Two methods are described in this section, *weighted finite automata* (or WFA) and *generalized finite automata* (or GFA). Both are due to Karel Culik, the former in collaboration with Jarkko Kari, and the latter with Vladimir Valenta. The term "automata" is used because these methods represent the image to be compressed in terms of a graph that is very similar to graphs used to represent finite-state automata (also called finite-state machines, see Section 8.8).

4.31.1 Weighted Finite Automata

WFA starts with an image to be compressed. It locates image parts that are identical or very similar to the entire image or to other parts, and constructs a graph that reflects the relationships between these parts and the entire image. The various components of the graph are then compressed and become the compressed image.

The image parts used by WFA are obtained by a quadtree partitioning of the image. Any quadrant, subquadrant, or pixel in the image can be represented by a string of the digits 0, 1, 2, and 3. The longer the string, the smaller the image area (subsquare) it represents. We denote such a string by $a_1 a_2 \ldots a_k$.

Quadtrees were introduced in Section 4.27. We assume that the quadrant numbering of Figure 4.152a is extended recursively to subquadrants. Figure 4.152b shows how each of the 16 subquadrants produced from the 4 original ones are identified by a 2-digit string of the digits 0, 1, 2, and 3. After another subdivision, each of the resulting subsubquadrants is identified by a 3-digit string, and so on. The black area in Figure 4.152c, for example, is identified by the string 1032.

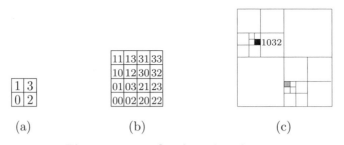

(a)   (b)   (c)

Figure 4.152: Quadrant Numbering.

◇ **Exercise 4.59:** What string identifies the gray area of Figure 4.152c?

Instead of constantly saying "quadrant, subquadrant, or subsubquadrant," we use the term "subsquare" throughout this section.

◇ **Exercise 4.60:** (Proposed by Karel Culik.) What is special about the particular quadrant numbering of Figure 4.152a?

If the image size is $2^n \times 2^n$, then a single pixel is represented by a string of n digits, and a string $a_1 a_2 \ldots a_k$ of k digits represents a subsquare of size $2^{n-k} \times 2^{n-k}$ pixels. Once this is grasped, it is not hard to see how any type of image, bi-level, grayscale, or color, can be represented by a graph. Mathematically, a graph is a set of nodes (or vertices) connected by edges. A node may contain data, and an edge may have a label. The graphs used in WFA represent finite automata, so the term *state* is used instead of node or vertex.

The WFA encoder starts by generating a graph that represents the image to be compressed. One state in this graph represents the entire image, and each of the other states represents a subimage. The edges show how certain subimages can be expressed as linear combinations of the entire (scaled) image or of other subimages. Since the subimages are generated by a quadtree, they do not overlap. The basic rule for connecting states with edges is; If quadrant a (where a can be 0, 1, 2, or 3) of subimage i is identical to subimage j, construct an edge from state i to state j, and label it a. In an arbitrary image it is not very common to find two identical subimages, so the rule above is extended to; If subsquare a of subimage i can be obtained by multiplying all the pixels of subimage j by a constant w, construct an edge from state i to state j, label it a, and assign it a weight w. We use the notation $a(w)$ or, if $w = 1$, just a.

A sophisticated encoding algorithm may discover that subsquare a of subimage i can be expressed as the weighted sum of subimages j and k with weights u and w, respectively. In such a case, two edges should be constructed. One from i to j, labeled $a(u)$, and another, from i to k, labeled $a(w)$. In general, such an algorithm may discover that a subsquare of subimage i can be expressed as a weighted sum (or a linear combination) of several subimages, with different weights. In such a case, an edge should be constructed for each term in the sum.

We denote the set of states of the graph by Q and the number of states by m.

Notice that the weights do not have to add up to 1. They can be any real numbers, and can be greater than 1 or negative. Figure 4.153b is the graph of a simple 2×2 chessboard. It is clear that we can ignore subsquares 1 and 2, since they are all white. The final graph includes states for subsquares that are not all white, and it has two states. State 1 is the entire image, and state 2 is an all black subimage. Since subsquares 0 and 3 are identical to state 2, there are two edges (shown as one edge) from state 1 to state 2, where the notation $0, 3(1)$ stands for $0(1)$ and $3(1)$. Since state 2 represents subsquares 0 and 3, it can be named q_0 or q_3.

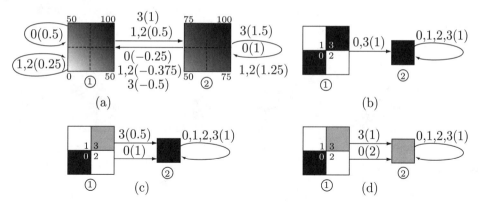

Figure 4.153: Graphs For Simple Images.

Figure 4.153c shows the graph of a 2×2 chessboard where quadrant 3 is 50% gray. This is also a two-state graph. State 2 of this graph is an all-black image and is identical to quadrant 0 of the image (we can also name it q_0). This is why there is an edge labeled $0(1)$. State 2 can also generate quadrant 3, if multiplied by 0.5, and this is expressed by the edge $3(0.5)$. Figure 4.153d shows another two-state graph representing the same image. This time, state 2 (which may be named q_3) is a 50%-gray image, and the weights are different.

Figure 4.153a shows an example of a weighted sum. The image (state 1) varies smoothly from black in the top-right corner to white in the bottom-left corner. The graph contains one more state, state 2, which is identical to quadrant 3 (we can also name it q_3). It varies from black in the top-right corner to 50% gray in the bottom-left corner, with 75% gray in the other two corners. Quadrant 0 of the image is obtained when the entire image is multiplied by 0.5, so there is an edge from state 1 to itself labeled 0(0.5). Quadrants 1 and 2 are identical and are obtained as a weighted sum of the entire image (state 1) multiplied by 0.25 and of state 2 (quadrant 3) multiplied by 0.5. The four quadrants of state 2 are similarly obtained as weighted sums of states 1 and 2.

The average grayness of each state is easy to figure out in this simple case. For example, the average grayness of state 1 of Figure 4.153a is 0.5 and that of quadrant 3 of state 2 is $(1 + 0.75)/2 = 0.875$. The average grayness is used later and is called the *final distribution*.

Notice that the two states of Figure 4.153a have the same size. In fact, nothing has been said so far about the sizes and resolutions of the image and the various subimages. The process of constructing the graph does not depend on the resolution, which is why WFA can be applied to *multiresolution images*, i.e., images that may exist in several different resolutions.

Figure 4.154 is another example. The original image is state 1 of the graph, and the graph has four states. State 2 is quadrant 0 of the image (so it may be called q_0). State 3 represents (the identical) quadrants 1 and 2 of the image (it may be called q_1 or q_2). It should be noted that, in principle, a state of a WFA graph does not have to correspond to any subsquare of the image. However, the recursive inference algorithm used by WFA generates a graph where each state corresponds to a subsquare of the image.

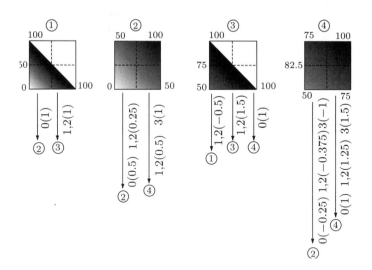

Figure 4.154: A Four-State Graph.

⋄ **Exercise 4.61:** In Figure 4.154, state 2 of the graph is represented in terms of itself and of state 4. Show how to represent it in terms of itself and an all-black state.

A multiresolution image M may, in principle, be represented by an intensity function $f_M(x, y)$ that gives the intensity of the image at point (x, y). For simplicity, we assume that x and y vary independently in the range $[0, 1]$, that the intensity varies between 0 (white) and 1 (black), and that the bottom-left corner of the image is located at the origin [i.e., it is point $(0, 0)$]. Thus, the subimage of state 2 of Figure 4.154 is defined by the function

$$f(x, y) = \frac{x + y}{2}.$$

⋄ **Exercise 4.62:** What function describes the image of state 1 of Figure 4.154?

Since we are dealing with multiresolution images, the intensity function f must be able to generate the image at any resolution. If we want, for example, to lower the resolution to one-fourth the original one, each new pixel should be computed from a set of four original ones. The obvious value for such a "fat" pixel is the average of the four original pixels. This implies that at low resolutions, the intensity function f should compute the average intensity of a region in the original image. In general, the value of f for a subsquare w should satisfy

$$f(w) = \frac{1}{4} \left[f(w0) + f(w1) + f(w2) + f(w3) \right].$$

Such a function is called *average preserving* (ap). It is also possible to increase the resolution, but the details created in such a case would be artificial.

Given an arbitrary image, however, we generally do not know its intensity function. Also, any given image has limited, finite resolution. Thus, WFA proceeds as follows: It starts with a given image with resolution $2^n \times 2^n$. It uses an inference algorithm to construct its graph, then extracts enough information from the graph to be able to reconstruct the image at its original or any lower resolution. The information obtained from the graph is compressed and becomes the compressed image.

The first step in extracting information from the graph is to construct four *transition matrices* W_0, W_1, W_2, and W_3 according to the following rule: If there is an edge labeled q from state i to state j, then element (i, j) of transition matrix W_q is set to the weight w of the edge. Otherwise, $(W_q)_{i,j}$ is set to zero. An example is the four transition matrices resulting from the graph of Figure 4.155. They are

$$W_0 = \begin{pmatrix} 0.5 & 0 \\ 0 & 1 \end{pmatrix}, \ W_1 = \begin{pmatrix} 0.5 & 0.25 \\ 0 & 1 \end{pmatrix}, \ W_2 = \begin{pmatrix} 0.5 & 0.25 \\ 0 & 1 \end{pmatrix}, \ W_3 = \begin{pmatrix} 0.5 & 0.5 \\ 0 & 1 \end{pmatrix}.$$

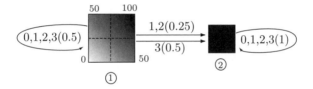

Figure 4.155: A Two-State Graph.

The second step is to construct a column vector F of size m called the *final distribution* (this is not the same as the intensity function f). Each component of F is the average intensity of the subimage associated with one state of the graph. Thus, for the two-state graph of Figure 4.155 we get

$$F = (0.5, 1)^T.$$

⋄ **Exercise 4.63:** Write the four transition matrices and the final distribution for the graph of Figure 4.154.

In the third step we define quantities $\psi_i(a_1 a_2 \ldots a_k)$. As a reminder, if the size of the original image is $2^n \times 2^n$, then the string $a_1 a_2 \ldots a_k$ (where $a_i = 0, 1, 2$, or 3) defines a subsquare of size $2^{n-k} \times 2^{n-k}$ pixels. The definition is

$$\psi_i(a_1 a_2 \ldots a_k) = (W_{a1} \cdot W_{a2} \cdots W_{ak} \cdot F)_i. \tag{4.42}$$

Thus, $\psi_i(a_1 a_2 \ldots a_k)$ is the ith element of the column $(W_{a1} \cdot W_{a2} \cdots W_{ak} \cdot F)^T$; it is a number.

Each transition matrix W_a has dimensions $m \times m$ (where m the number of states of the graph) and F is a column of size m. For any given string $a_1 a_2 \ldots a_k$ there are therefore m numbers $\psi_i(a_1 a_2 \ldots a_k)$, for $i = 1, 2, \ldots, m$. We use the two-state graph of Figure 4.155 to calculate some ψ_i's:

$$\psi_i(0) = (W_0 \cdot F)_i = \begin{pmatrix} 0.5 & 0 \\ 0 & 1 \end{pmatrix} \begin{pmatrix} 0.5 \\ 1 \end{pmatrix}_i = \begin{pmatrix} 0.25 \\ 1 \end{pmatrix}_i,$$

$$\psi_i(01) = (W_0 \cdot W_1 \cdot F)_i = \begin{pmatrix} 0.5 & 0 \\ 0 & 1 \end{pmatrix} \begin{pmatrix} 0.5 & 0.25 \\ 0 & 1 \end{pmatrix} \begin{pmatrix} 0.5 \\ 1 \end{pmatrix}_i = \begin{pmatrix} 0.25 \\ 1 \end{pmatrix}_i,$$

$$\psi_i(1) = (W_1 \cdot F)_i = \begin{pmatrix} 0.5 & 0.25 \\ 0 & 1 \end{pmatrix} \begin{pmatrix} 0.5 \\ 1 \end{pmatrix}_i = \begin{pmatrix} 0.5 \\ 1 \end{pmatrix}_i, \tag{4.43}$$

$$\psi_i(00) = (W_0 \cdot W_0 \cdot F)_i = \begin{pmatrix} 0.5 & 0 \\ 0 & 1 \end{pmatrix} \begin{pmatrix} 0.5 & 0 \\ 0 & 1 \end{pmatrix} \begin{pmatrix} 0.5 \\ 1 \end{pmatrix}_i = \begin{pmatrix} 0.125 \\ 1 \end{pmatrix}_i,$$

$$\psi_i(03) = (W_0 \cdot W_3 \cdot F)_i = \begin{pmatrix} 0.5 & 0 \\ 0 & 1 \end{pmatrix} \begin{pmatrix} 0.5 & 0.5 \\ 0 & 1 \end{pmatrix} \begin{pmatrix} 0.5 \\ 1 \end{pmatrix}_i = \begin{pmatrix} 0.375 \\ 1 \end{pmatrix}_i,$$

$$\psi_i(33\ldots3) = (W_3 \cdot W_3 \cdots W_3 \cdot F)_i$$
$$= \begin{pmatrix} 0.5 & 0.5 \\ 0 & 1 \end{pmatrix} \begin{pmatrix} 0.5 & 0.5 \\ 0 & 1 \end{pmatrix} \cdots \begin{pmatrix} 0.5 & 0.5 \\ 0 & 1 \end{pmatrix} \begin{pmatrix} 0.5 \\ 1 \end{pmatrix}_i$$
$$= \begin{pmatrix} 0 & 1 \\ 0 & 1 \end{pmatrix} \begin{pmatrix} 0.5 \\ 1 \end{pmatrix}_i = \begin{pmatrix} 1 \\ 1 \end{pmatrix}_i.$$

⋄ **Exercise 4.64:** Calculate ψ_i at the center of the image.

Notice that each $\psi_i(w)$ is identified by two quantities, its subscript i (which corresponds to a state of the graph) and a string $w = a_1 a_2 \ldots a_k$ that specifies a subsquare of the image. The subsquare can be as big as the entire image or as small as a single pixel. The quantity ψ_i (where no subsquare is specified) is called the *image* of state i of the graph. The name *image* makes sense, since for each subsquare

w, $\psi_i(w)$ is a number, so ψ_i consists of several numbers from which the pixels of the image of state i can be computed and displayed. The WFA encoding algorithms described in this section generate a graph where each state is a subsquare of the image. In principle, however, some states of the graph may not correspond to any subsquare of the image. An example is state 2 of the graph of Figure 4.155. It is all black, even though the image does not have an all-black subsquare.

Figure 4.156 shows the image of Figure 4.155 at resolutions 2×2, 4×4, and 256×256.

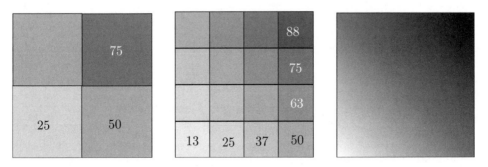

Figure 4.156: Image $f = (i + j)/2$ at Three Resolutions.

⬦ **Exercise 4.65:** Use mathematical software to compute a matrix such as those of Figure 4.156.

We now introduce the *initial distribution* $I = (I_1, I_2, \ldots, I_m)$, a row vector with m elements. If we set it to $I = (1, 0, 0, \ldots, 0)$, then the dot product $I \cdot \psi(a_1 a_2 \ldots a_k)$ [where the notation $\psi(q)$ stands for a vector with the m values $\psi_1(q)$ through $\psi_m(q)$] gives the average intensity $f(a_1 a_2 \ldots a_k)$ of the subsquare specified by $a_1 a_2 \ldots a_k$. This intensity function can also be expressed as the matrix product

$$f(a_1 a_2 \ldots a_k) = I \cdot W_{a1} \cdot W_{a2} \cdots W_{ak} \cdot F. \tag{4.44}$$

In general, the initial distribution specifies the image defined by a WFA as a linear combination $I_1 \psi_1 + \cdots + I_n \psi_n$ of "state images." If $I = (1, 0, 0, \ldots, 0)$, then the image defined is ψ_1, the image corresponding to the first state. This is always the case for the image resulting from the inference algorithm described later in this section.

Given a WFA, we can easily find another WFA for the image obtained by zooming to the subsquare with address $a_1 a_2 \ldots a_k$. We just replace the initial distribution I by $I \cdot W_{a1} \cdot W_{a2} \cdots W_{ak}$.

To prove this, consider the subsquare (pixel) with address $b_1 b_2 \ldots b_m$ in the zoomed square. It corresponds to the subsquare in the entire image with address $a_1 a_2 \ldots a_k b_1 b_2 \ldots b_m$. Hence, its grayness value computed by the original WFA is $I W_{a1} W_{a2} \ldots W_{ak} W_{b1} W_{b2} \ldots W_{bm} F$.

Using the new WFA for the corresponding subsquare, we get the same value, namely $I' W_{b1} W_{b2} \ldots W_{bm} F$, where $I' = I W_{a1} W_{a2} \ldots W_{ak}$ (proof provided by Karel Culik).

For the ψ_i's computed in Equation (4.43) the dot products of the form $I \cdot \psi(a_1 a_2 \dots a_k)$ yield

$$f(0) = I \cdot \psi(0) = (1, 0) \begin{pmatrix} 0.25 \\ 1 \end{pmatrix} = I_1 \psi_1(0) + I_2 \psi_2(0) = 0.25,$$

$$f(01) = I \cdot \psi(01) = 1 \times 0.25 + 0 \times 1 = 0.25,$$

$$f(1) = I \cdot \psi(1) = 0.5,$$

$$f(00) = I \cdot \psi(00) = 0.125,$$

$$f(03) = I \cdot \psi(03) = 0.375,$$

$$f(33 \dots 3) = I \cdot \psi(33 \dots 3) = 1.$$

$\diamond$ **Exercise 4.66:** Calculate the ψ_i's and the corresponding f values for subsquares 0, 01, 1, 00, 03, and 3 of the five-state graph of Figure 4.154.

Equation (4.42) is the definition of $\psi_i(a_1 a_2 \dots a_k)$. It shows that this quantity is the ith element of the column vector $(W_{a1} \cdot W_{a2} \cdots W_{ak} \cdot F)^T$. We now examine the reduced column vector $(W_{a2} \cdots W_{ak} \cdot F)^T$. Its ith element is, according to the definition of ψ_i, the quantity $\psi_i(a_2 \dots a_k)$. Thus, we conclude that

$$\psi_i(a_1 a_2 \dots a_k)$$
$$= (W_{a1})_{i,1} \psi_1(a_2 \dots a_k) + (W_{a1})_{i,2} \psi_2(a_2 \dots a_k) + \cdots + (W_{a1})_{i,m} \psi_m(a_2 \dots a_k),$$

or, if we denote the string $a_2 \dots a_k$ by w,

$$\psi_i(a_1 w) = (W_{a1})_{i,1} \psi_1(w) + (W_{a1})_{i,2} \psi_2(w) + \cdots + (W_{a1})_{i,m} \psi_m(w)$$
$$= \sum_{j=1}^{m} (W_{a1})_{i,j} \psi_j(w). \tag{4.45}$$

The quantity $\psi_i(a_1 w)$ (which corresponds to quadrant a_1 of subsquare w) can be expressed as a linear combination of the quantities $\psi_j(w)$, where $j = 1, 2, \dots, m$. This justifies calling ψ_i the *image* of state i of the graph. We say that subsquare a_1 of image $\psi_i(w)$ can be expressed as a linear combination of images $\psi_j(w)$, for $j = 1, 2, \dots, m$. This is how the self similarity of the original image enters the picture.

Equation (4.45) is recursive, since it defines a smaller image in terms of larger ones. The largest image is, of course, the original image, for which w is null (we denote the null string by ϵ). This is where the recursion starts

$$\psi_i(a) = (W_a)_{i,1} \psi_1(\epsilon) + (W_a)_{i,2} \psi_2(\epsilon) + \cdots + (W_a)_{i,m} \psi_m(\epsilon)$$
$$= \sum_{j=1}^{m} (W_a)_{i,j} \psi_j(\epsilon), \quad \text{for } a = 0, 1, 2, 3. \tag{4.46}$$

On the other hand, Equation (4.42) shows that $\psi_i(\epsilon) = F_i$, so Equation (4.46) becomes

$$\psi_i(a) = \sum_{j=1}^{m}(W_a)_{i,j}F_j, \quad \text{for } a = 0, 1, 2, 3. \tag{4.47}$$

It should now be clear that if we know the four transition matrices and the final distribution, we can compute the images $\psi_i(w)$ for strings w of any length (i.e., for subsquares of any size). Once an image $\psi_i(w)$ is known, the average intensity $f(w)$ of subsquare w can be computed by Equation (4.44) (which requires knowledge of the initial distribution).

The problem of representing an image f in WFA is thus reduced to finding vectors I and F and matrices W_0, W_1, W_2, and W_3 that will produce f (or an image close to it). Alternatively, we can find I and images $\psi_i(\epsilon)$ for $i = 1, 2, \ldots, m$.

Here is an informal approach to this problem. We can start with a graph consisting of one state and select this state as the entire image, $\psi_1(\epsilon)$. We now concentrate on quadrant 0 of the image and try to determine $\psi_1(0)$. If quadrant 0 is identical, or similar enough, to (a scaled version of) the entire image, we can write

$$\psi_1(0) = \psi_1(\epsilon) = \sum_{j=1}^{m}(W_0)_{1,j}\psi_j(\epsilon),$$

which is true if the first row of W_0 is $(1, 0, 0, \ldots, 0)$. We have determined the first row of W_0, even though we don't yet know its size (it is m but m hasn't been determined yet). If quadrant 0 is substantially different from the entire image, we add $\psi_1(0)$ to the graph as a new state, state 2 (i.e., we increment m by 1) and call it $\psi_2(0)$. The result is

$$\psi_1(0) = \psi_2(0) = \sum_{j=1}^{m}(W_0)_{1,j}\psi_j(0),$$

which is true if the first row of W_0 is $(0, 1, 0, \ldots, 0)$. We have again determined the first row of W_0, even though we still don't know its size.

Next, we process the remaining three quadrants of $\psi_1(\epsilon)$ and the four quadrants of $\psi_2(0)$. Let's examine, for example, the processing of quadrant three $[\psi_2(03)]$ of $\psi_2(0)$. If we can express it (precisely or close enough) as the linear combination

$$\psi_2(03) = \alpha\psi_1(3) + \beta\psi_2(3) = \sum_{j}(W_0)_{2,j}\psi_j(3),$$

then we know that the second row of W_0 must be $(\alpha, \beta, 0, \ldots, 0)$. If we cannot express $\psi_2(03)$ as a linear combination of already known ψ's, then we declare it a new state $\psi_3(03)$, and this implies $(W_3)_{2,3} = 1$, and also determines the second row of W_0 to be $(0, 0, 1, 0, \ldots, 0)$.

This process continues until all quadrants of all the ψ_j's have been processed. This normally generates many more ψ_i's, all of which are subsquares of the image.

This intuitive algorithm is now described more precisely, using pseudo-code. It constructs a graph from a given multiresolution image f one state at a time.

The graph has the minimal number of states (to be denoted by m) but a relatively large number of edges. Since m is minimal, the four transition matrices (whose dimensions are $m \times m$) are small. However, since the number of edges is large, most of the elements of these matrices are nonzero. The image is compressed by writing the transition matrices (in compressed format) on the compressed stream, so the sparser the matrices, the better the compression. Thus, this algorithm does not produce good compression and is described here because of its simplicity. We denote by i the index of the first unprocessed state, and by γ, a mapping from states to subsquares. The steps of this algorithm are as follows:

Step 1: Set $m = 1$, $i = 1$, $F(q_1) = f(\epsilon)$, $\gamma(q_1) = \epsilon$.

Step 2: Process q_i, i.e., for $w = \gamma(q_i)$ and $a = 0, 1, 2, 3$, do:

    Step 2a: Start with $\psi_j = f_{\gamma(q_j)}$ for $j = 1, \ldots, m$ and try to find real numbers $c_1, \ldots, c_m$ such that $f_{wa} = c_1\psi_1 + \cdots + c_m\psi_m$. If such numbers are found, they become the m elements of row q_i of transition matrix W_a, i.e., $W_a(q_i, q_j) = c_j$ for $j = 1, \ldots, m$.

    Step 2b: If such numbers cannot be found, increment the number of states $m = m + 1$, and set $\gamma(q_m) = wa$, $F(q_m) = f(wa)$ (where F is the final distribution), and $W_a(q_i, q_m) = 1$.

Step 3: Increment the index of the next unprocessed state $i = i + 1$. If $i \leq m$, go to Step 2.

Step 4: The final step. Construct the initial distribution I by setting $I(q_1) = 1$ and $I(q_j) = 0$ for $j = 2, 3, \ldots, m$.

[Litow and Olivier 95] presents another inference algorithm that also yields a minimum-state WFA and uses only additions and inner products.

The real breakthrough in WFA compression came when a better inference algorithm was developed. This algorithm is the most important part of the WFA method. It generates a graph that may have more than the minimal number of states, but that has a small number of edges. The four transition matrices may be large, but they are sparse, resulting in better compression of the matrices and hence better compression of the image. The algorithm starts with a given finite-resolution image A, and generates its graph by matching subsquares of the image to the entire image or to other subsquares. An important point is that this algorithm can be lossy, with the amount of the loss controlled by a user-defined parameter G. Larger values of G "permit" the algorithm to match two parts of the image even if they poorly resemble each other. This naturally leads to better compression. The metric used by the algorithm to match two images (or image parts) f and g is the square of the L2 metric, a common measure where the distance $d_k(f, g)$ is defined as

$$d_k(f, g) = \sum_w [f(w) - g(w)]^2,$$

where the sum is over all subsquares w.

The algorithm tries to produce a small graph. If we denote the size of the graph by (size A), the algorithm tries to keep as small as possible the value of

$$d_k(f, f_A) + G \cdot (\text{size } A)$$

The quantity m indicates the number of states, and there is a multiresolution image ψ_i for each state $i = 1, 2, \ldots, m$. The pseudo-code of Figure 4.157 describes a recursive function $make\_wfa(i, k, max)$ that tries to approximate ψ_i at level k as well as possible by adding new edges and (possibly) new states to the graph. The function minimizes the value of the cost quantity

$$cost = d_k(\psi_i, \psi_i') + G \cdot s,$$

where ψ_i' is the current approximation to ψ_i and s is the increase in the size of the graph caused by adding new edges and states. If $cost > max$, the function returns ∞ otherwise, it returns $cost$.

When the algorithm starts, m is set to 1 and ψ is set to f, where f is the function that needs to be approximated at level k. The algorithm then calls $make\_wfa(1, k, \infty)$, which calls itself. For each of the four quadrants, the recursive call $make\_wfa(i, k, max)$ tries to approximate $(\psi_i)_a$ for $a = 0, 1, 2, 3$ in two different ways, as a linear combination of the functions of existing states (step 1), and by adding a new state and recursively calling itself (steps 2 and 3). The better of the two results is then selected (in steps 4 and 5).

---

function $make\_wfa(i, k, max)$;
If $max < 0$, return ∞;
$cost \leftarrow 0$;
if $k = 0$, $cost \leftarrow d_0(f, 0)$
else do steps 1–5 with $\psi = (\psi_i)_a$ for $a = 0, 1, 2, 3$;

    1. Find $r_1, r_2, \ldots r_m$ such that the value of

$$cost1 \leftarrow d_{k-1}(\psi, r_1\psi_1 + \cdots + r_n\psi_n) + G \cdot s$$

is small, where s denotes the increase in the size of the graph caused by adding edges from state i to states j with nonzero weights r_j and label a, and d_{k-1} denotes the distance between two multiresolution images at level $k - 1$ (quite a mouthful).
    2. Set $m_0 \leftarrow m$, $m \leftarrow m + 1$, $\psi_m \leftarrow \psi$ and add an edge with label a and weight 1 from state i to the new state m. Let s denote the increase in the size of the graph caused by the new state and new edge.
    3. Set $cost2 \leftarrow G \cdot s + make\_wfa(m, k - 1, min(max - cost, cost1) - G \cdot s)$;
    4. If $cost2 \leq cost1$, set $cost \leftarrow cost + cost2$;
    5. If $cost1 < cost2$, set $cost \leftarrow cost + cost1$, remove all outgoing edges from states $m_0 + 1, \ldots, m$ (added during the recursive call), as well as the edge from state i added in step 2. Set $m \leftarrow m_0$ and add the edges from state i with label a to states $j = 1, 2, \ldots, m$ with weights r_j whenever $r_j \neq 0$.

If $cost \leq max$, return($cost$), else return(∞).

Figure 4.157: The WFA Recursive Inference Algorithm.

The algorithm constructs an initial distribution $I = (1, 0, \dots, 0)$ and a final distribution $F_i = \psi_i(\epsilon)$ for all states i.

Next, we discuss how the elements of the graph can be compressed. Step 2 creates an edge whenever a new state is added to the graph. They form a tree, and their weights are always 1, so each edge can be coded in four bits. Each of the four bits indicates which of two alternatives was selected for the label in steps 4–5.

Step 1 creates edges that represent linear combinations (i.e., cases where subimages are expressed as linear combinations of other subimages). Both the weight and the endpoints need be stored. Experiments indicate that the weights are normally distributed, so they can be efficiently encoded with prefix codes. Storing the endpoints of the edges is equivalent to storing four sparse binary matrices, so run length encoding can be used.

The WFA decoder reads vectors I and F and the four transition matrices W_a from the compressed stream and decompresses them. Its main task is to use them to reconstruct the original $2^n \times 2^n$ image A (precisely or approximately), i.e., to compute $f_A(w)$ for all strings $w = a_1 a_2 \dots a_n$ of size n. The original WFA decoding algorithm is fast but has storage requirements of order $m4^n$, where m is the number of states of the graph. The algorithm consists of four steps as follows:

Step 1: Set $\psi_p(\epsilon) = F(p)$ for all $p \in Q$.

Step 2: Repeat Step 3 for $i = 1, 2, \dots, n$.

Step 3: For all $p \in Q$, $w = a_1 a_2 \dots a_{i-1}$, and $a = 0, 1, 2, 3$, compute

$$\psi_p(aw) = \sum_{q \in Q} W_a(p, q) \cdot \psi_q(w).$$

Step 4: For each $w = a_1 a_2 \dots a_n$ compute

$$f_A(w) = \sum_{q \in Q} I(q) \cdot \psi_q(w).$$

This decoding algorithm was improved by Raghavendra Udupa, Vinayaka Pandit, and Ashok Rao [Udupa, Pandit, and Ashok 99]. They define a new multiresolution function Φ_p for every state p of the WFA graph by

$$\Phi_p(\epsilon) = I(p),$$
$$\Phi_p(wa) = \sum_{q \in Q} (W_a)_{q,p} \Phi_q(w), \text{ for } a = 0, 1, 2, 3,$$

or, equivalently,

$$\Phi_p(a_1 a_2 \dots a_k) = (I\, W_{a1} \dots W_{ak})_p,$$

where $\Phi_p(wa)$ is the sum of the weights of all the paths with label wa ending in p. The weight of a path starting at state i is the product of the initial distribution of i and the weights of the edges along the path wa.

One result of this definition is that the intensity function f can be expressed as a linear combination of the new multiresolution functions Φ_p,

$$f(w) = \sum_{q \in Q} \Phi_q(w) F(q),$$

but there is a more important observation! Suppose that both $\Phi_p(u)$ and $\psi_p(w)$ are known for all states $p \in Q$ of the graph and for all strings u and w. Then the intensity function of subsquare uw can be expressed as

$$f(uw) = \sum_{p \in Q} \Phi_p(u) \psi_p(w).$$

This observation is used in the improved 6-step algorithm that follows to reduce both the space and time requirements. The input to the algorithm is a WFA A with resolution $2^n \times 2^n$, and the output is an intensity function $f_A(w)$ for every string w up to length n.

Step 1: Select nonnegative integers $n1$ and $n2$ satisfying $n1+n2 = n$. Set $\Phi_p = I(p)$ and $\psi_p = F(p)$ for all $p \in Q$.
Step 2: For $i = 1, 2, \ldots, n1$ do Step 3.
Step 3: For all $p \in Q$ and $w = a_1 a_2 \ldots a_{i-1}$ and $a = 0, 1, 2, 3$, compute

$$\Phi_p(aw) = \sum_{q \in Q} (W_a)_{q,p} \Phi_q(w).$$

Step 4: For $i = 1, 2, \ldots, n2$ do Step 5.
Step 5: For all $p \in Q$ and $w = a_1 a_2 \ldots a_{i-1}$ and $a = 0, 1, 2, 3$, compute

$$\psi_p(aw) = \sum_{q \in Q} (W_a)_{p,q} \psi_q(w).$$

Step 6: For each $u = a_1 a_2 \ldots a_{n1}$ and $w = b_1 b_2 \ldots b_{n2}$, compute

$$f_A(uw) = \sum_{q \in Q} \Phi_q(u) \psi_q(w).$$

The original WFA decoding algorithm is a special case of the above algorithm for $n1 = 0$ and $n2 = n$. For the case where $n = 2l$ is an even number, it can be shown that the space requirement of this algorithm is of order $m4^{n1} + m4^{n2}$. This expression has a minimum when $n1 = n2 = n/2 = l$, implying a space requirement of order $m4^l$.

Another improvement on the original WFA is the use of *bintrees* (Section 4.27.1). This idea is due to Ullrich Hafner [Hafner 95]. Recall that WFA uses quadtree methods to partition the image into a set of nonoverlapping subsquares. These can be called (in common with the notation used by IFS) the *range images*. Each range image is then matched, precisely or approximately, to a linear combination of other images that become the *domain images*. Using bintree methods to partition the image results in finer partitioning and an increase in the number of domain images available for matching. In addition, the compression of the transition matrices and of the initial and final distributions is improved. Each node in a bintree has two children compared to four children in a quadtree. A subimage can therefore be identified by a string of bits instead of a string of the digits 0–3. This also means that there are just two transition matrices W_0 and W_1.

WFA compression works particularly well for color images, since it constructs a single WFA graph for the three color components of each pixel. Each component has its own initial state, but other states are shared. This normally saves many states because the color components of pixels in real images are not independent. Experience indicates that the WFA compression of a typical image may create, say, 300 states for the Y color component, 40 states for I, and only about 5 states for the Q component (see appendix in book's web site for color components). Another property of WFA compression is that it is relatively slow for high-quality compression, since it builds a large automaton, but is faster for low-quality compression, since the automaton constructed in such a case is small.

Bibliography

Culik, Karel II and Jarkko Kari (1993) "Image Compression Using Weighted Finite Automata," *Computer and Graphics*, **17**,3:305–313.

Culik, Karel II and J. Kari (1994) "Image-Data Compression Using Edge-Optimizing Algorithm for WFA Inference," *Journal of Information Processing and Management*, **30**,6:829–838.

Culik, Karel II and Jarkko Kari (1994) "Inference Algorithm for Weighted Finite Automata and Image Compression," in *Fractal Image Encoding and Compression*, Y. Fisher, editor, New York, NY, Springer-Verlag.

Culik, Karel II and Jarkko Kari (1995) "Finite State Methods for Compression and Manipulation of Images," in *DCC '96, Data Compression Conference*, J. Storer, editor, Los Alamitos, CA, IEEE Computer Society Press, pp. 142–151.

Hafner, Ullrich (1995) "Asymmetric Coding in (m)-WFA Image Compression," Report 132, Department of Computer Science, University of Würzburg, December. (Available at `http://www-info2.informatik.uni-wuerzburg.de/staff/ulli/home/publications/` file `tr132.ps.gz`.)

Litow, Bruce, and Olivier de Val (1995) "The Weighted Finite Automaton Inference Problem," Technical report 95-1, James Cook University, Queensland.

Udupa, Raghavendra U., Vinayaka D. Pandit, and Ashok Rao (1999), Private Communication (available from the authors or from the author of this book).

4.31.2 Generalized Finite Automata

The graphs constructed and used by WFA represent finite-state automata with "weighted inputs." Without weights, finite automata specify multiresolution bi-level images. At resolution $2^k \times 2^k$, a finite automaton specifies an image that is black in those subsquares whose addresses are accepted by the automaton. It is well known that every nondeterministic automaton can be converted to an equivalent deterministic one. This is not the case for WFA, where nondeterminism gives much more power. This is why an image with a smoothly varying gray scale, such as the one depicted in Figure 4.155, can be represented by a simple, two-state automaton. This is also why WFA can efficiently compress a large variety of grayscale and color images.

For bi-level images the situation is different. Here nondeterminism might provide more concise description. However, experiments show that a nondeterministic automaton does not improve the compression of such images by much, and is slower to construct than a deterministic one. This is why the *generalized finite automata* (GFA) method was originally developed. We also show how it is extended for color images. The algorithm to generate the GFA graph is completely different from the one used by WFA. In particular, it is not recursive (in contrast to the edge-optimizing WFA algorithm of Figure 4.157, which is recursive). GFA also uses three types of transformations, rotations, flips, and complementation, to match image parts.

A GFA graph consists of states and of edges connecting them. Each state represents a subsquare of the image, with the first state representing the entire image. If quadrant q of the image represented by state i is identical (up to a scale factor) to the image represented by state j, then an edge is constructed from i to j and is labeled q. More generally, if quadrant q of state i can be made identical to state j by applying transformation t to the image of j, then an edge is constructed from i to j and is labeled q, t or (q, t). There are 16 transformations, shown in Figure 4.159. Transformation 0 is the identity, so it may be omitted when an edge is labeled. Transformations 1–3 are 90° rotations, and transformations 4–7 are rotations of a reflection of transformation 0. Transformations 8–15 are the reverse videos of 0–7, respectively. Each transformation t is thus specified by a 4-bit number.

Figure 4.158: Image for Exercise 4.67.

Figure 4.160 shows a simple bi-level image and its GFA graph. Quadrant 3 of state 0, for example, has to go through transformation 1 in order to make it identical to state 1, so there is an edge labeled $(3, 1)$ from state 0 to state 1.

⋄ **Exercise 4.67:** Construct the GFA of the image of Figure 4.158 using transformations, and list all the resulting edges in a table.

Images used in practice are more complex and less self-similar than the examples shown here, so the particular GFA algorithm discussed here (although not GFA in general) allows for a certain amount of data loss in matching subsquares of the image. The distance $d_k(f, g)$ between two images or subimages f and g of resolution $2^k \times 2^k$ is defined as

$$d_k(f, g) = \frac{\sum_{w=a1a2...ak} |f(w) - g(w)|}{2^k \times 2^k}.$$

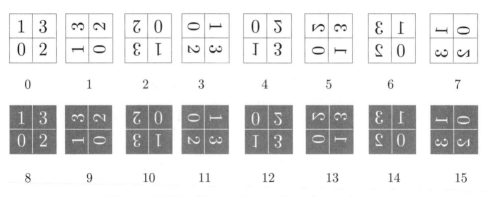

Figure 4.159: Sixteen Image Transformations.

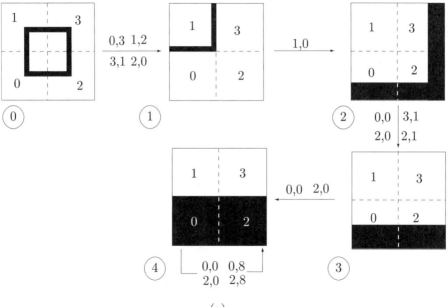

(a)

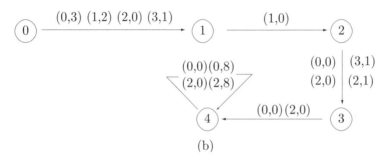

(b)

Figure 4.160: A Five-State GFA.

The numerator of this expression counts the number of pixels that differ in the two images, while the denominator is the total number of pixels in each image. The distance is thus the percentage of pixels that differ in the two images (we assume that 0 and 1 represent white and black pixels, respectively). The four-step algorithm described here for constructing the graph also uses an error parameter input by the user to control the amount of loss.

Step 1: Generate state 0 as the entire image (i.e., subsquare ϵ). We select the initial distribution as $I = (1, 0, 0, \ldots, 0)$, so state 0 will be the only one displayed. The final distribution is a vector of all ones.

Step 2: Process each state as follows: Let the next unprocessed state be q, representing subsquare w. Partition w into its four quadrants $w0$, $w1$, $w2$, and $w3$, and perform Step 3 for each of the four wa's.

Step 3: Denote the image of subsquare wa by ψ'. If $\psi' = 0$, there is no edge from state q with label a. Otherwise, examine all the states generated so far and try to find a state p and a transformation t such that $t(\psi_p)$ (the image of state p transformed by t) will be similar enough to image ψ'. This is expressed by $d_k(\psi', t(\psi_p)) \leq$ error. If such p and t are found, construct an edge $q(a, t)p$. Otherwise, add a new, unprocessed, state r to ψ' and construct a new edge $q(a, 0)r$.

Step 4: If there are any unprocessed states left, go to Step 2. Otherwise stop.

Step 3 may involve many searches, since many states may have to be examined up to 16 times until a match is found. Therefore, the algorithm uses two versions for this search, a *first fit* and a *best fit*. Both approaches proceed from state to state, apply each of the 16 transformations to the state, and calculate the distance between each transformed state and ψ'. The first fit approach stops when it finds the first transformed state that fits, while the best fit conducts the full search and selects the state and transformation that yield the best fit. The former is thus faster, while the latter produces better compression.

The GFA graph for a real, complex image may have a huge number of states, so the GFA algorithm discussed here has an option where vector quantization is used. This option reduces the number of states (and thus speeds up the process of constructing the graph) by treating subsquares of size 8×8 differently. When this option is selected, the algorithm does not try to find a state similar to such a small subsquare, but rather encodes the subsquare with vector quantization (Section 4.12). An 8×8 subsquare has 64 pixels, and the algorithm uses a 256-entry codebook to code them. It should be noted that in general, GFA does not use quantization or any specific codebook. The vector quantization option is specific to the implementation discussed here.

After constructing the GFA graph, its components are compressed and written on the compressed stream in three parts. The first part is the edge information created in step 3 of the algorithm. The second part is the state information (the indices of the states), and the third part is the 256 codewords used in the vector quantization of small subsquares. All three parts are arithmetically encoded.

GFA decoding is done as in WFA, except that the decoder has to consider possible transformations when generating new image parts from existing ones.

GFA has been extended to color images. The image is separated into individual bitplanes and a graph is constructed for each. However, common states in these graphs are stored only once, thereby improving compression. A little thinking shows that this works best for color images consisting of several areas with well-defined boundaries (i.e., discrete-tone or cartoon-like images). When such an image is separated into its bitplanes, they tend to be similar. A subsquare q in bitplane 1, for example, may be identical to the same subsquare in, say, bitplane 3. The graphs for these bitplanes can thus share the state for subsquare q.

The GFA algorithm is then applied to the bitplanes, one by one. When working on bitplane b, Step 3 of the algorithm searches through all the states of all the graphs constructed so far for the preceding $b - 1$ bitplanes. This process can be viewed in two different ways. The algorithm may construct n graphs, one for each bitplane, and share states between them. Alternatively, it may construct just one graph with n initial states.

Experiments show that GFA works best for images with a small number of colors. Given an image with many colors, quantization is used to reduce the number of colors.

Bibliography

Culik, Karel II, and V. Valenta (1996), "Finite Automata Based Compression of Bi-Level Images," in Storer, James A. (ed.), *DCC '96, Data Compression Conference*, Los Alamitos, CA, IEEE Computer Society Press, pp. 280–289.

Culik, Karel II, and V. Valenta (1997), "Finite Automata Based Compression of Bi-Level and Simple Color Images," *Computer and Graphics*, **21**:61–68.

Culik, Karel II, and V. Valenta (1997), "Compression of Silhouette-like Images Based on WFA," *Journal of Universal Computer Science*, **3**:1100–1113.

4.32 Iterated Function Systems

Fractals have been popular since the 1970s and have many applications. One such application, relatively underused, is data compression. Applying fractals to data compression is done by means of *iterated function systems*, or IFS. Two references to IFS are [Barnsley 88] and [Fisher 95]. IFS compression can be very efficient, achieving excellent compression factors (32 is not uncommon), but it is lossy and also computationally intensive. The IFS encoder partitions the image into parts called ranges; it then matches each range to some other part called a domain, and produces an *affine transformation* from the domain to the range. The transformations are written on the compressed stream, and they constitute the compressed image. We start with an introduction to two-dimensional affine transformations.

4.32.1 Affine Transformations

In computer graphics, a complete two-dimensional image is built part by part and is normally edited before it is considered satisfactory. Editing is done by selecting a figure (part of the drawing) and applying a transformation to it. Typical transformations (Figure 4.161) are moving or sliding (translation), reflecting or flipping (mirror image), zooming (scaling), rotating, and shearing.

The transformation can be applied to every pixel of the figure. Alternatively, it can be applied to a few key points that completely define the figure (such as the

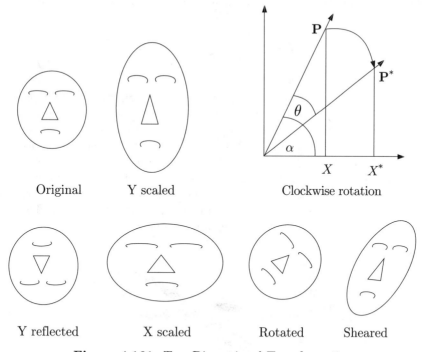

Figure 4.161: Two-Dimensional Transformations.

four corners of a rectangle), following which the figure is reconstructed from the transformed key points.

We use the notation $\mathbf{P} = (x, y)$ for a two-dimensional point, and $\mathbf{P}^* = (x^*, y^*)$ for the transformed point. The simplest linear transformation is $x^* = ax + cy$, $y^* = bx + dy$, in which each of the new coordinates is a *linear combination* of the two old ones. This transformation can be written $\mathbf{P}^* = \mathbf{PT}$, where $\mathbf{T}$ is the 2×2 matrix $\left(\begin{smallmatrix} a & b \\ c & d \end{smallmatrix}\right)$.

To understand the functions of the four matrix elements, we start by setting $b = c = 0$. The transformation becomes $x^* = ax$, $y^* = dy$. Such a transformation is called *scaling*. If applied to all the points of an object, all the x dimensions are scaled by a factor a, and all the y dimensions by a factor d. Note that a and d can also be less than 1, causing shrinking of the object. If any of a or d equals -1, the transformation is a *reflection*. Any other negative values cause both scaling and reflection.

Note that scaling an object by factors of a and d changes its area by a factor of $a \times d$, and that this factor is also the value of the determinant of the scaling matrix $\left(\begin{smallmatrix} a & 0 \\ 0 & d \end{smallmatrix}\right)$.

(Scaling, reflection, and other geometrical transformations can be extended to three dimensions, where they become much more complex.)

Below are examples of matrices for scaling and reflection. In a, the y-coordinates are scaled by a factor of 2. In b, the x-coordinates are reflected. In c, the x dimensions are shrunk to 0.001 their original values. In d, the figure is shrunk to a vertical line:

$$a = \begin{pmatrix} 1 & 0 \\ 0 & 2 \end{pmatrix}, \quad b = \begin{pmatrix} -1 & 0 \\ 0 & 1 \end{pmatrix}, \quad c = \begin{pmatrix} .001 & 0 \\ 0 & 1 \end{pmatrix}, \quad d = \begin{pmatrix} 0 & 0 \\ 0 & 1 \end{pmatrix}.$$

The next step is to set $a = 1$, $d = 1$ (no scaling or reflection), and explore the effect of b and c on the transformations. The transformation becomes $x^* = x + cy$, $y^* = bx + y$. We first select matrix $\begin{pmatrix} 1 & 1 \\ 0 & 1 \end{pmatrix}$ and use it to transform the rectangle whose four corners are $(1, 0)$, $(3, 0)$, $(1, 1)$, and $(3, 1)$. The corners are transformed to $(1, 1)$, $(3, 3)$, $(1, 2)$, $(3, 4)$. The original rectangle has been *sheared* vertically, and got transformed into a parallelogram. A similar effect occurs when we try the matrix $\begin{pmatrix} 1 & 0 \\ 1 & 1 \end{pmatrix}$. The quantities b and c are thus responsible for *shearing*. Figure 4.162 shows the connection between shearing and the operation of scissors. The word shearing comes from the concept of shear in mechanics.

Figure 4.162: Scissors and Shearing.

⋄ **Exercise 4.68:** Apply the shearing transformation $\begin{pmatrix} 1 & -1 \\ 0 & 1 \end{pmatrix}$ to the four points $(1, 0)$, $(3, 0)$, $(1, 1)$, and $(3, 1)$. What are the transformed points? What geometrical figure do they represent?

The next important transformation is *rotation*. Figure 4.161 illustrates rotation. It shows a point $\mathbf{P}$ rotated clockwise through an angle θ to become $\mathbf{P}^*$. Simple trigonometry yields $x = R \cos \alpha$ and $y = R \sin \alpha$. From this we get the expressions for x^* and y^*:

$$x^* = R \cos(\alpha - \theta) = R \cos \alpha \cos \theta + R \sin \alpha \sin \theta = x \cos \theta + y \sin \theta,$$
$$y^* = R \sin(\alpha - \theta) = -R \cos \alpha \sin \theta + R \sin \alpha \cos \theta = -x \sin \theta + y \cos \theta.$$

Thus the rotation matrix in two dimensions is

$$\begin{pmatrix} \cos \theta & -\sin \theta \\ \sin \theta & \cos \theta \end{pmatrix}, \tag{4.48}$$

which also equals

$$\begin{pmatrix} \cos \theta & 0 \\ 0 & \cos \theta \end{pmatrix} \begin{pmatrix} 1 & -\tan \theta \\ \tan \theta & 1 \end{pmatrix}.$$

This proves that any rotation in two dimensions is a combination of scaling (and, perhaps, reflection) and shearing, an unexpected result that's true for all angles satisfying $\tan\theta \neq \infty$.

Matrix $\mathbf{T}_1$ below rotates anticlockwise. Matrix $\mathbf{T}_2$ reflects about the line $y = x$, and matrix $\mathbf{T}_3$ reflects about the line $y = -x$. Note the determinants of these matrices. In general, a determinant of $+1$ indicates pure rotation, whereas a determinant of -1 indicates pure reflection. (As a reminder, $\det \left(\begin{smallmatrix} a & b \\ c & d \end{smallmatrix}\right) = ad - bc$.)

$$\mathbf{T}_1 = \begin{pmatrix} \cos\theta & \sin\theta \\ -\sin\theta & \cos\theta \end{pmatrix}, \qquad \mathbf{T}_2 = \begin{pmatrix} 0 & 1 \\ 1 & 0 \end{pmatrix}, \qquad \mathbf{T}_3 = \begin{pmatrix} 0 & -1 \\ -1 & 0 \end{pmatrix}.$$

4.32.2 A $90°$ Rotation

In the case of a $90°$ clockwise rotation, the rotation matrix is

$$\begin{pmatrix} \cos(90) & -\sin(90) \\ \sin(90) & \cos(90) \end{pmatrix} = \begin{pmatrix} 0 & -1 \\ 1 & 0 \end{pmatrix}. \tag{4.49}$$

A point $\mathbf{P} = (x, y)$ is thus transformed to the point $(y, -x)$. For a counterclockwise $90°$ rotation, (x, y) is transformed to $(-y, x)$. This is called the *negate and exchange* rule.

4.32.3 Translations

Unfortunately, our simple 2×2 matrix cannot generate all the necessary transformations! Specifically, it cannot generate *translation*. This is proved by realizing that any object containing the origin will, after any of the transformations above, still contain the origin (the result of $(0,0) \times \mathbf{T}$ is $(0,0)$ for any matrix $\mathbf{T}$).

One way to implement translation (which can be expressed by $x^* = x + m$, $y^* = y + n$), is to generalize our transformations to $\mathbf{P}^* = \mathbf{PT} + (m, n)$, where $\mathbf{T}$ is the familiar 2×2 transformation matrix $\left(\begin{smallmatrix} a & b \\ c & d \end{smallmatrix}\right)$. A more elegant approach, however, is to stay with $\mathbf{P}^* = \mathbf{PT}$ and to generalize $\mathbf{T}$ to the 3×3 matrix

$$\mathbf{T} = \begin{pmatrix} a & b & 0 \\ c & d & 0 \\ m & n & 1 \end{pmatrix}.$$

This approach is called *homogeneous coordinates* and is commonly used in projective geometry. It makes it possible to unify all the two-dimensional transformations within one matrix. Notice that only six of the nine elements of matrix $\mathbf{T}$ above are variables. Our points should now be the triplets $\mathbf{P} = (x, y, 1)$.

It is easy to see that the transformations discussed above can change lengths and angles. Scaling changes the lengths of objects. Rotation and shearing change angles. One thing that's preserved, though, is parallel lines. A pair of parallel lines will remain parallel after any scaling, reflection, rotation, shearing, and translation. A transformation that preserves parallelism is called *affine*.

The final conclusion of this section is that any affine two-dimensional transformation can be fully specified by only six numbers!

The Golden Ratio

Imagine a straight segment of length l. We divide it into two parts a and b such that $a + b = l$ and $l/a = a/b$.

The ratio a/b is a constant called the *golden ratio* and denoted by ϕ. It is one of the important mathematical constants, such as π and e, and was already known to the ancient Greeks. It is believed that geometric figures can be made more pleasing to the human eye if they involve this ratio. One example is the golden rectangle, with sides of dimensions x and $x\phi$. Many classical buildings and paintings involve this ratio. [Huntley 70] is a lively introduction to the golden ratio. It illustrates properties such as

$$\phi = \sqrt{1 + \sqrt{1 + \sqrt{1 + \sqrt{1 + \cdots}}}} \quad \text{and} \quad \phi = 1 + \cfrac{1}{1 + \cfrac{1}{1 + \frac{1}{\cdots}}}.$$

The value of ϕ is easy to calculate: $l/a = a/b = \phi \Rightarrow (a + b)/a = a/b = \phi \Rightarrow 1 + b/a = \phi \Rightarrow 1 + 1/\phi = \phi \Rightarrow \phi^2 - \phi - 1 = 0$. The last equation is easy to solve, yielding $\phi = (1 + \sqrt{5})/2 \approx 1.618\ldots$

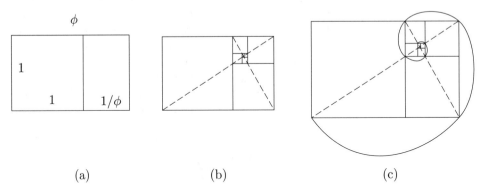

(a)   (b)   (c)

Figure 4.163: The Golden Ratio.

The equation $\phi = 1 + 1/\phi$ illustrates another unusual property of ϕ. Imagine the golden rectangle with sides 1 and ϕ (Figure 4.163a). Such a rectangle can be divided into a 1×1 square and a smaller golden rectangle of dimensions $1 \times 1/\phi$. The smaller rectangle can now be divided into a $1/\phi \times 1/\phi$ square and an even smaller golden rectangle (Figure 4.163b). When this process continues, the rectangles converge to a point. Figure 4.163c shows how a logarithmic spiral can be drawn through corresponding corners of the rectangles.

Affine transformations can be defined in different ways. One important definition is that a transformation of points in space is affine if it preserves *barycentric sums* of the points. A barycentric sum of points $\mathbf{P}_i$ has the form $\sum w_i \mathbf{P}_i$, where w_i are numbers and $\sum w_i = 1$, so if $\mathbf{P} = \sum w_i \mathbf{P}_i$ and if $\sum w_i = 1$, then any affine transformation $\mathbf{T}$ satisfies

$$\mathbf{TP} = \sum_1^n w_i \mathbf{TP}_i.$$

4.32.4 IFS Definition

A simple example of IFS is the set of three transformations

$$\mathbf{T}_1 = \begin{pmatrix} .5 & 0 & 0 \\ 0 & .5 & 0 \\ 8 & 8 & 1 \end{pmatrix}, \quad \mathbf{T}_2 = \begin{pmatrix} .5 & 0 & 0 \\ 0 & .5 & 0 \\ 96 & 16 & 1 \end{pmatrix}, \quad \mathbf{T}_3 = \begin{pmatrix} .5 & 0 & 0 \\ 0 & .5 & 0 \\ 120 & 60 & 1 \end{pmatrix}. \quad (4.50)$$

We first discuss the concept of the *fixed point*. Imagine the sequence $\mathbf{P}_1 = \mathbf{P}_0 \mathbf{T}_1$, $\mathbf{P}_2 = \mathbf{P}_1 \mathbf{T}_1, \ldots$, where transformation $\mathbf{T}_1$ is applied repeatedly to create a sequence of points $\mathbf{P}_1, \mathbf{P}_2, \ldots$. It is easy to prove that $\lim_{i \to \infty} \mathbf{P}_i = (2m, 2n) = (16, 16)$. This point is called the *fixed point* of $\mathbf{T}_1$, and *it does not depend* on the particular starting point $\mathbf{P}_0$ selected.

Proof: $\mathbf{P}_1 = \mathbf{P}_0 \mathbf{T}_1 = (.5x_0 + 8, .5y_0 + 8)$, $\mathbf{P}_2 = \mathbf{P}_1 \mathbf{T}_1 = (0.5(0.5x_0 + 8) + 8, .5(0.5y_0 + 8) + 8)$. It is easy to see (and to prove by induction) that $x_n = 0.5^n x_0 + 0.5^{n-1}8 + 0.5^{n-2}8 + \cdots + 0.5^1 8 + 8$. In the limit $x_n = 0.5^n x_0 + 8 \sum_{i=0}^{\infty} 0.5^i = 0.5^n x_0 + 8 \times 2$, which approaches the limit $8 \times 2 = 16$ for large n regardless of x_0.

Now it is easy to show that for the transformations above, with scale factors of 0.5 and no shearing, each new point in the sequence moves half the remaining distance toward the fixed point. Given a point $\mathbf{P}_i = (x_i, y_i)$, the point midway between $\mathbf{P}_i$ and the fixed point $(16, 16)$ is

$$\left(\frac{x_i + 16}{2}, \frac{y_i + 16}{2} \right) = (0.5x_i + 8, 0.5y_i + 8) = (x_{i+1}, y_{i+1}) = \mathbf{P}_{i+1}.$$

Consequently, for the particular transformations above there is no need to use the transformation matrix. At each step of the iteration, point $\mathbf{P}_{i+1}$ is obtained by $(\mathbf{P}_i + (2m, 2n))/2$. For other transformations, matrix multiplication is necessary to compute point $\mathbf{P}_{i+1}$.

In general, every affine transformation where the scale and shear factors are less than 1 has a fixed point, but it may not be easy to find it.

The principle of IFS is now easy to describe. A set of transformations (an IFS code) is selected. A sequence of points is calculated and plotted by starting with an arbitrary point $\mathbf{P}_0$, selecting a transformation from the set at random, and applying it to $\mathbf{P}_0$, transforming it into a point $\mathbf{P}_1$, and then randomly selecting another transformation and applying it to $\mathbf{P}_1$, thereby generating point $\mathbf{P}_2$, and so on.

Every point is plotted on the screen as it is calculated, and gradually, the object begins to take shape before the viewer's eyes. The shape of the object is called the

IFS *attractor*, and it depends on the IFS code (the transformations) selected. The shape also depends slightly on the particular selection of $\mathbf{P}_0$. It is best to choose $\mathbf{P}_0$ as one of the fixed points of the IFS code (if they are known in advance). In such a case, all the points in the sequence will lie inside the attractor. For any other choice of $\mathbf{P}_0$, a finite number of points will lie outside the attractor, but eventually they will move into the attractor and stay there.

It is surprising that the attractor does not depend on the precise order of the transformations used. This result has been proved by the mathematician John Elton.

Another surprising property of IFS is that the random numbers used don't have to be uniformly distributed; they can be weighted. Transformation $\mathbf{T}_1$, for example, may be selected at random 50% of the time, transformation $\mathbf{T}_2$, 30%, and $\mathbf{T}_3$, 20%. The shape being generated does not depend on the probabilities, but the computation time does. The weights should add up to 1 (a normal requirement for a set of mathematical weights), and none can be zero.

The three transformations of Equation (4.50) above create an attractor in the form of a Sierpiński triangle (Figure 4.164a). The translation factors determine the coordinates of the three triangle corners. The six transformations of Table 4.165 create an attractor in the form of a fern (Figure 4.164b). The notation used in Table 4.165 is $\begin{pmatrix} a & b \\ c & d \end{pmatrix} + \begin{pmatrix} m \\ n \end{pmatrix}$.

The Sierpiński triangle, also known as the Sierpiński gasket (Figure 4.164a), is defined recursively. Start with any triangle, find the midpoint of each edge, connect the three midpoints to obtain a new triangle fully contained in the original one, and cut the new triangle out. The newly created hole now divides the original triangle into three smaller ones. Repeat the process on each of the smaller triangles. At the limit, there is no area left in the triangle. It resembles Swiss cheese without any cheese, just holes.

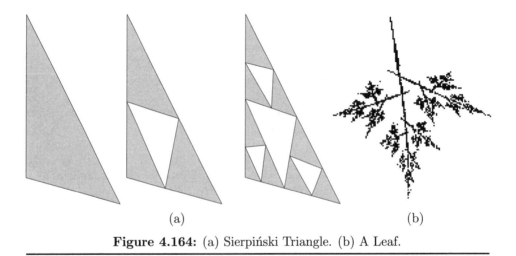

(a)   (b)

Figure 4.164: (a) Sierpiński Triangle. (b) A Leaf.

The program of Figure 4.166 calculates and displays IFS attractors for any given set of transformations. It runs on the Macintosh computer.

4.32.5 IFS Principles

Before we describe how IFS is used to compress real-life images, let's look at IFS from a different point of view. Figure 4.167 shows three images: a person, the letter "T", and the Sierpiński gasket (or triangle). The first two images are transformed in a special way. Each image is shrunk to half its size, then copied three times, and the three copies are arranged in the shape of a triangle. When this transformation is applied a few times to an image, it is still possible to discern the individual copies of the original image. However, when it is applied many times, the result is the Sierpiński gasket (or something very close to it, depending on the number of iterations and on the resolution of the output device). The point is that each transformation shrinks the image (the transformations are *contractive*), so the final result does not depend on the shape of the original image. The shape can be that of a person, a letter, or anything else; the final result depends only on the particular transformation applied to the image. A different transformation will create a different result, which again will not depend on the particular image being transformed. Figure 4.167d, for example, shows the results of transforming the letter "T" by reducing it, making three copies, arranging them in a triangle, and flipping the top copy. The final image obtained at the limit, after applying a certain transformation infinitely many times, is called the *attractor* of the transformation.

The following sets of numbers create especially interesting patterns.

1. A frond.

```
5
    0  -28    0   29  151   92
   64    0    0   64   82    6
   -2   37  -31   29   85  103
   17  -51  -22    3  183  148
   -1   18  -18   -1   88  147
```

2. A coastline

```
4
  -17  -26   34  -12   84   53
   25  -20   29   17  192   57
   35    0    0   35   49    3
   25   -6    6   25  128   28
```

3. A leaf (Figure 4.164b)

```
4
    2   -7   -2   48  141   83
   40    0   -4   65   88   10
   -2   45  -37   10   82  132
  -11  -60  -34   22  237  125
```

4. A Sierpiński Triangle

```
3
   50    0    0   50    0    0
   50    0    0   50  127   79
   50    0    0   50  127    0
```

⋄ **Exercise 4.69:** The three affine transformations of example 4 above (the Sierpiński triangle) are different from those of Equation (4.50). What's the explanation?

The result of each transformation is an image containing all the images of all the previous transformations. If we apply the same transformation many times, it is possible to zoom on the result, to magnify it many times, and still see details of the original images. In principle, if we apply the transformation an infinite number of times, the final result will show details at *any* magnification. It will be a fractal.

The case of Figure 4.167c is especially interesting. It seems that the original image is simply shown four times, without any transformations. A little thinking,

	a	b	c	d	m	n		a	b	c	d	m	n
1:	0	−28	0	29	151	92	4:	64	0	0	64	82	6
2:	−2	37	−31	29	85	103	5:	0	−80	−22	1	243	151
3:	−1	18	−18	−1	88	147	6:	2	−48	0	50	160	80

Table 4.165: All numbers are shown as integers, but $a, b, c,$ and d should be divided by 100, to make them less than 1. The values m and n are the translation factors.

```
PROGRAM IFS;
USES ScreenIO, Graphics, MathLib;
CONST LB = 5; Width = 490; Height = 285;
(* LB=left bottom corner of window *)
VAR i,k,x0,y0,x1,y1,NumTransf: INTEGER;
Transf: ARRAY[1..6,1..10] OF INTEGER;
Params:TEXT;
filename:STRING;
BEGIN (* main *)
Write('params file='); Readln(filename);
Assign(Params,filename); Reset(Params);
Readln(Params,NumTransf);
FOR i:=1 TO NumTransf DO
Readln(Params,Transf[1,i],Transf[2,i],Transf[3,i],
 Transf[4,i],Transf[5,i],Transf[6,i]);
 OpenGraphicWindow(LB,LB,Width,Height,'IFS shape');
 SetMode(paint);
 x0:=100; y0:=100;
 REPEAT
 k:=RandomInt(1,NumTransf+1);
 x1:=Round((x0*Transf[1,k]+y0*Transf[2,k])/100)+Transf[5,k];
 y1:=Round((x0*Transf[3,k]+y0*Transf[4,k])/100)+Transf[6,k];
 Dot(x1,y1); x0:=x1; y0:=y1;
 UNTIL Button()=TRUE;
  ScBOL; ScWriteStr('Hit a key & close this window to quit');
  ScFreeze;
END.
```

Figure 4.166: Calculate and Display IFS Attractors.

however, shows that our particular transformation transforms this image to itself. The original image is already the Sierpiński gasket, and it gets transformed to itself because it is self-similar.

◇ **Exercise 4.70:** Explain the geometrical meaning of the combined three affine transformations below and show the attractor they converge to

$$
w_1 \begin{pmatrix} x \\ y \end{pmatrix} = \begin{pmatrix} 1/2 & 0 \\ 0 & 1/2 \end{pmatrix} \begin{pmatrix} x \\ y \end{pmatrix},
$$

$$
w_2 \begin{pmatrix} x \\ y \end{pmatrix} = \begin{pmatrix} 1/2 & 0 \\ 0 & 1/2 \end{pmatrix} \begin{pmatrix} x \\ y \end{pmatrix} + \begin{pmatrix} 0 \\ 1/2 \end{pmatrix},
$$

$$
w_3 \begin{pmatrix} x \\ y \end{pmatrix} = \begin{pmatrix} 1/2 & 0 \\ 0 & 1/2 \end{pmatrix} \begin{pmatrix} x \\ y \end{pmatrix} + \begin{pmatrix} 1/2 \\ 0 \end{pmatrix}.
$$

The Sierpiński gasket is thus easy to compress because it is self-similar; it is easy to find parts of it that are identical to the entire image. In fact, every part of it is identical to the entire image. Figure 4.168 shows the bottom-right part of the gasket surrounded by dashed lines. It is easy to see the relation between this part and the entire image. Their shapes are identical, up to a scale factor. The size of this part is half the size of the image, and we know where it is positioned relative to the entire image (we can measure the displacement of its bottom-left corner from the bottom-left corner of the entire image).

This points to a possible way to compress real images. If we can divide an image into parts such that each part is identical (or at least very close) to the entire image up to a scale factor, then we can highly compress the image by IFS. All that we need is the scale factor (actually two scale factors, in the x and y directions) and the displacement of each part relative to the entire image [the (x, y) distances between one corner of the part and the same corner of the image]. Sometimes we may find a part of the image that has to be reflected in order to become identical to the entire image. In such a case we also need the reflection coefficients. We can thus compress an image by figuring out the transformations that transform each part (called "range") into the entire image. The transformation for each part is expressed by a few numbers, and these numbers become the compressed stream.

It is easy to see that this simple approach will not work on real-life images. Such images are complex, and it is generally impossible to divide such an image into parts that will all be identical (or even very close) to the entire image. A different approach is needed to make IFS practical. The approach used by any practical IFS algorithm is to partition the image into nonoverlapping parts called *ranges*. They can be of any size and shape, but in practice it is easiest to work with squares, rectangles, or triangles. For each range R_i, the encoder has to find a *domain* D_i that's very similar, or even identical in shape, to the range but is bigger. Once such a domain is found, it is easy to figure out the transformation w_i that will transform the domain into the range $R_i = w_i(D_i)$. Two scale factors have to be determined (the scaling is shrinking, since the domain is bigger than the range) as well as the displacement of the domain relative to the range [the (x, y) distances between one corner of the domain and the same corner of the range]. Sometimes,

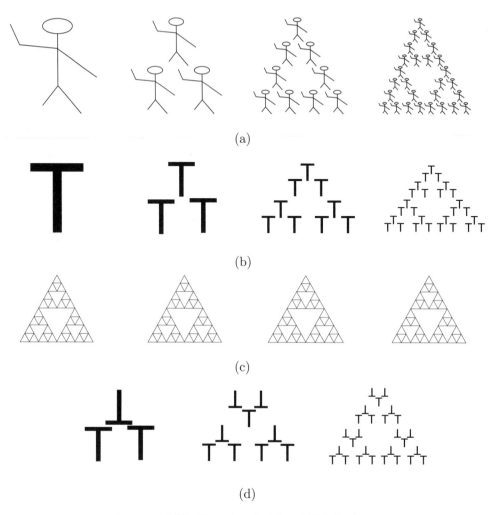

Figure 4.167: Creating the Sierpiński Gasket.

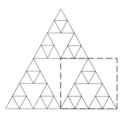

Figure 4.168: A Self-Similar Image.

the domain has to be rotated and/or reflected to make it identical to the range, and the transformation should, of course, include these factors as well. This approach to IFS image compression is called PIFS (for partitioned IFS).

4.32.6 IFS Decoding

Before looking into the details of PIFS encoding, let's try to understand how the PIFS decoder works. All that the decoder has is the set of transformations, one per range. It does not know the shapes of any ranges or domains. In spite of this, decoding is very simple. It is based on the fact, mentioned earlier, that a contractive transformation creates a result that does not depend on the shape of the initial image used. We can thus create any range R_i by applying contractive transformation w_i many times to *any* bigger shape D_i (except an all-white shape).

The decoder thus starts by setting all the domains to arbitrary shapes (e.g., it can initially set the entire image to black). It then goes into a loop where in each iteration it applies every transformation w_i once. The first iteration applies the transformations to domains D_i that are all black. This creates ranges R_i that may already, after this single iteration, slightly resemble the original ranges. This iteration changes the image from the initial all black to something resembling the original image. In the second iteration the decoder applies again all the w_i transformations, but this time they are applied to domains that are no longer all black. The domains already somewhat resemble the original ones, so the second iteration results in better-looking ranges, and thus in a better image. Experience shows that only 8–10 iterations are normally needed to get a result closely resembling the original image.

It is important to realize that this decoding process is resolution independent! Normally, the decoder starts with an initial image whose size is identical to that of the original image. It can, however, start with an all-black image of any size. The affine transformations used to encode the original image do not depend on the resolution of the image or on the resolutions of the ranges. Decoding an image at, say, twice its original size will create a large, smooth image, with details not seen in the original and without pixelization (without jagged edges or "fat" pixels). The extra details will, of course, be artificial. They may not be what one would see when looking at the original image through a magnifying glass, but the point is that PIFS decoding is resolution independent; it creates a natural-looking image at any size, and it does not involve pixelization.

The resolution-independent nature of PIFS decoding also means that we have to be careful when measuring the compression performance. After compressing a 64 Kb image into, say, 2 Kb, the compression factor is 32. Decoding the 2 Kb compressed file into a large, 2 Mb, image (with a lot of artificial detail) does not mean that we have changed the compression factor to 2M/2K=1024. The compression factor is still the same 32.

4.32.7 IFS Encoding

PIFS decoding is thus easy, if somewhat magical, but we still need to see the details of PIFS encoding. The first point to consider is how to select the ranges and find the domains. Here are some possibilities:

1. Suppose that the original image has resolution 512×512. We can select as ranges the nonoverlapping groups of 16×16 pixels. There are $32 \times 32 = 1024$ such groups. The domains should be bigger than the ranges, so we may select as domains all the 32×32 groups of pixels in the image (they may, of course, overlap). There are $(512-31) \times (512-31) = 231{,}361$ such groups. The encoder should compare each range to all 231,361 domains. Each comparison involves eight steps, since a range may be identical to a rotation or a reflection of a domain (Figure 4.159). The total number of steps in comparing ranges and domains is thus $1{,}024 \times 231{,}361 \times 8 = 1{,}895{,}309{,}312$. If each step takes a microsecond, the total time required is 1,895 seconds, or about 31 minutes.

◇ **Exercise 4.71:** Repeat the computation above for a 256×256 image with ranges of size 8×8 and domains of size 16×16.

If the encoder is looking for a domain to match range R_i and it is lucky to find one that's identical to R_i, it can proceed to the next range. In practice, however, domains identical to a given range are very rare, so the encoder has to compare all $231{,}361 \times 8$ domains to each range R_i and select the one that's closest to R_i (PIFS is, in general, a lossy compression method). We thus have to answer two questions: When is a domain identical to a range (remember: they have different sizes) and how do we measure the "distance" between a domain and a range?

To compare a 32×32-pixel domain to a 16×16-pixel range, we can either choose one pixel from each 2×2 square of pixels in the domain (this is called subsampling) or average each 2×2 square of pixels in the domain and compare it to one pixel of the range (averaging).

To decide how close a range R_i is to a domain D_j, we have to use one of several *metrics*. A metric is a function that measures "distance" between, or "closeness" of, two mathematical quantities. Experience recommends the use of the *rms* (root mean square) metric

$$M_{\mathrm{rms}}(R_i, D_j) = \sqrt{\sum_{x,y} \left[R_i(x,y) - D_j(x,y) \right]^2}. \tag{4.51}$$

This involves a square root calculation, so a simpler metric may be

$$M_{\max}(R_i, D_j) = \max |R_i(x,y) - D_j(x,y)|$$

(the largest difference between a pixel of R_i and a pixel of D_j). Whatever metric is used, a comparison of a range and a domain involves subsampling (or averaging) followed by a metric calculation.

After comparing range R_i to all the (rotated and reflected) domains, the encoder selects the domain with the smallest metric and calculates the transformation that will bring the domain to the range. This process is repeated for all ranges.

Even this simple way of matching parts of the image produces excellent results. Compression factors are typically in the 15–32 range and data loss is minimal.

⋄ **Exercise 4.72:** What's a reasonable way to estimate the amount of image information lost in PIFS compression?

The main disadvantage of this method of determining ranges and domains is the fixed size of the ranges. A method where ranges can have different sizes may lead to better compression ratios and less loss. Imagine an image of a hand with a ring on one finger. If the ring happens to be inside a large range R_i, it may be impossible to find any domain that will even come close to R_i. Too much data may be lost in such a case. On the other hand, if part of an image is fairly uniform, it may become a large range, since there is a better chance that it will match some domain. Clearly, large ranges are preferable, since the compressed stream contains one transformation per range. Quadtrees, discussed below, therefore offer a good solution.

Quadtrees: We start with a few large ranges, each a subquadrant. If a range does not match well any domain (the metric between it and any domain is greater than a user-controlled tolerance parameter), it is divided into four subranges, and each is matched separately. As an example, consider a 256×256-pixel image. We can choose for domains all the image squares of size 8, 12, 16, 24, 32, 48, and 64. We start with ranges that are subquadrants of size 32×32. Each range is compared with domains that are larger than itself (48 or 64). If a range does not match well, it is divided into four quadrants of size 16×16 each, and each is compared, as a new range, with all domains of sizes 24, 32, 48, and 64. This process continues until all ranges have been matched to domains. Large ranges result in better compression, but small ranges are easier to match, since they contain a few adjacent pixels, and we know from experience that adjacent pixels tend to be highly correlated in real-life images.

4.32.8 IFS for Grayscale Images

Up until now we have assumed that our transformations have to be affine. The truth is that any contractive transformations, even nonlinear ones, can be used for IFS. Affine transformations are used simply because they are linear and thus computationally simple. Also, up to now we have assumed a monochromatic image, where the only problem is to determine which pixels should be black. IFS can easily be extended to compress grayscale images (and therefore also color images; see below). The problem here is to determine which pixels to paint, and what gray level to paint each.

Matching a domain to a range now involves the intensities of the pixels in both. Whatever metric is used, it should use only those intensitie to determine the "closeness" of the domain and the range. Assume that a certain domain D contains n pixels with gray levels $a_1 \ldots a_n$, and the IFS encoder tries to match D to a range R containing n pixels with gray levels $b_1, \ldots, b_n$. The rms metric, mentioned earlier, works by finding two numbers, r and g (called the contrast and brightness controls), that will minimize the expression

$$Q = \sum_1^n \big((r \cdot a_i + g) - b_i\big)^2. \tag{4.52}$$

This is done by solving the two equations $\partial Q/\partial r = 0$ and $\partial Q/\partial g = 0$ for the unknowns r and g (see details below). Minimizing Q minimizes the difference in contrast and brightness between the domain and the range. The value of the rms metric is $\sqrt{Q}$ [compare with Equation (4.51)].

When the IFS encoder finally decides what domain to associate with the current range, it has to figure out the transformation w between them. The point is that r and g should be included in the transformation, so that the decoder will know what gray level to paint the pixels when the domain is recreated in successive decoding iterations. It is common to use transformations of the form

$$w \begin{pmatrix} x \\ y \\ z \end{pmatrix} = \begin{pmatrix} a & b & 0 \\ c & d & 0 \\ 0 & 0 & r \end{pmatrix} \begin{pmatrix} x \\ y \\ z \end{pmatrix} + \begin{pmatrix} l \\ m \\ g \end{pmatrix}. \tag{4.53}$$

A pixel (x, y) in the domain D is now given a third coordinate z (its gray level) and is transformed into a pixel (x^*, y^*, z^*) in the range R, where $z^* = z \cdot r + g$. Transformation (4.53) has another property. It is contractive if $r < 1$, regardless of the scale factors.

Any compression method for grayscale images can be extended to color images. It is only necessary to separate the image into three color components (preferably YIQ) and compress each individually as a grayscale image. This is how IFS can be applied to compression of color images.

The next point to consider is how to write the coefficients of a transformation w on the compressed stream. There are three groups of coefficients, the scale factors a, d, the reflection/rotation factors a, b, c, d, the displacement l, m, and the contrast/brightness controls r, g. If a domain is twice as large as a range, then the scale factors are always 0.5 and thus do not have to be written on the compressed stream. If the domains and ranges can have several sizes, then only certain scale factors are possible, and they can be encoded either arithmetically or by some prefix code. The particular rotation or reflection of the domain relative to the range can be coded in 3 bits, since there are only eight rotations/reflections possible. The displacement can be encoded by encoding the positions and sizes of the domain and range.

The quantities r and g are not distributed in any uniform way, and they are also real (floating-point) numbers that can have many different values. They should thus be quantized, i.e., converted to an integer in a certain range. Experience shows that the contrast r can be quantized into a 4- or 5-bit integer (i.e., 16 or 32 contrast values are enough in practice), whereas the brightness g should become a 6- or 7-bit integer (resulting in 64 or 128 brightness values).

Here are the details of calculating r and g that minimize Q and then calculating the (minimized) Q and the rms metric.

From Equation (4.52), we get

$$\frac{\partial Q}{\partial g} = 0 \rightarrow \sum 2(r \cdot a_i + g - b_i) = 0 \rightarrow ng + \sum (r \cdot a_i - b_i) = 0,$$

$$g = \frac{1}{n} \left[\sum b_i - r \sum a_i \right], \tag{4.54}$$

and

$$\frac{\partial Q}{\partial r} = 0 \rightarrow \sum 2(r \cdot a_i + g - b_i)a_i = 0 \rightarrow \sum (r \cdot a_i^2 + g \cdot a_i - a_i b_i) = 0,$$

$$r \sum a_i^2 + \frac{1}{n}\left[\sum b_i - r \sum a_i\right] \sum a_i - \sum a_i b_i = 0,$$

$$r \left[\sum a_i^2 - \frac{1}{n}\left(\sum a_i\right)^2\right] = \sum a_i b_i - \frac{1}{n} \sum a_i \sum b_i,$$

$$r = \frac{\sum a_i b_i - \frac{1}{n} \sum a_i \sum b_i}{\sum a_i^2 - \frac{1}{n}\left(\sum a_i\right)^2} = \frac{n \sum a_i b_i - \sum a_i \sum b_i}{n \sum a_i^2 - \left(\sum a_i\right)^2}. \qquad (4.55)$$

From the same Equation (4.52), we also get the minimized Q

$$Q = \sum_1^n (r \cdot a_i + g - b_i)^2 = \sum (r^2 a_i^2 + g^2 + b_i^2 + 2rga_i - 2ra_i b_i - 2gb_i)$$

$$= r^2 \sum a_i^2 + ng^2 + \sum b_i^2 + 2rg \sum a_i - 2r \sum a_i b_i - 2g \sum b_i. \qquad (4.56)$$

The following steps are needed to calculate the rms metric:
1. Compute the sums $\sum a_i$ and $\sum a_i^2$ for all domains.
2. Compute the sums $\sum b_i$ and $\sum b_i^2$ for all ranges.
3. Every time a range R and a domain D are compared, compute:
    3.1. The sum $\sum a_i b_i$.
    3.2. The quantities r and g from Equations (4.54) and (4.55) using the five sums above. Quantize r and g.
    3.3. Compute Q from Equation (4.56) using the quantized r, g and the five sums. The value of the rms metric for these particular R and D is $\sqrt{Q}$.

Finally, Figures 4.169 and 4.170 are pseudo-code algorithms outlining two approaches to IFS encoding. The former is more intuitive. For each range R it selects the domain that's closest to R. The latter tries to reduce data loss by sacrificing compression ratio. This is done by letting the user specify the minimum number T of transformations to be generated. (Each transformation w is written on the compressed stream using roughly the same number of bits, so the size of that stream is proportional to the number of transformations.) If every range has been matched, and the number of transformations is still less than T, the algorithm continues by taking ranges that have already been matched and partitioning them into smaller ones. This increases the number of transformations but reduces the data loss, since smaller ranges are easier to match with domains.

> He gathered himself together and then banged his fist on the table. "To hell with art, I say."
> "You not only say it, but you say it with tiresome iteration," said Clutton severely.
>
> —W. Somerset Maugham, *Of Human Bondage*

```
t:=some default value; [t is the tolerance]
push(entire image); [stack contains ranges to be matched]
repeat
 R:=pop();
 match all domains to R, find the one (D) that's closest to R,
  pop(R);
 if metric(R,D)<t then
   compute transformation w from D to R and output it;
 else partition R into smaller ranges and push them
       into the stack;
  endif;
until stack is empty;
```

Figure 4.169: IFS Encoding: Version I.

```
input T from user;
push(entire image); [stack contains ranges to be matched]
repeat
 for every unmatched R in the stack find the best matching domain D,
  compute the transformation w, and push D and w into the stack;
 if the number of ranges in the stack is <T then
    find range R with largest metric (worst match)
    pop R, D and w from the stack
    partition R into smaller ranges and push them, as unmatched,
     into the stack;
  endif
until all ranges in the stack are matched;
output all transformations w from the stack;
```

Figure 4.170: IFS Encoding: Version II.

Bibliography

Barnsley, M., and Sloan, A. D. (1988) "A Better Way to Compress Images," *Byte magazine* pp. 215–222, January.

Barnsley, M., (1988) *Fractals Everywhere*, New York, Academic Press.

Demko, S., L. Hodges, and B. Naylor (1985) "Construction of Fractal Objects with Iterated Function Systems," *Computer Graphics* **19**(3):271–278, July.

Feder, Jens (1988) *Fractals*, New York, Plenum Press.

Fisher, Yuval (ed.), (1995) *Fractal Image Compression: Theory and Application*, New York, Springer-Verlag.

Mandelbrot, B., (1982) *The Fractal Geometry of Nature*, San Francisco, CA, W. H. Freeman.

Peitgen, H. -O., et al. (eds.) (1982) *The Beauty of Fractals*, Berlin, Springer-Verlag.

Peitgen, H. -O., and Dietmar Saupe (1985) *The Science of Fractal Images*, Berlin, Springer-Verlag.

Reghbati, H. K. (1981) "An Overview of Data Compression Techniques," *IEEE Computer* **14**(4):71–76.

4.33 Cell Encoding

Imagine an image stored in a bitmap and displayed on a screen. Let's start with the case where the image consists of just text, with each character occupying the same area, say 8×8 pixels (large enough for a 5×7 or a 6×7 character and some spacing). Assuming a set of 256 characters, each cell can be encoded as an 8-bit pointer pointing to a 256-entry table where each entry contains the description of an 8×8 character as a 64-bit string. The compression factor is thus 64/8, or eight to one. Figure 4.171 shows the letter "H" both as a bitmap and as a 64-bit string.

									0	1	0	0	0	0	1	0

$$
\begin{array}{cccccccc}
0 & 1 & 0 & 0 & 0 & 0 & 1 & 0 \\
0 & 1 & 0 & 0 & 0 & 0 & 1 & 0 \\
0 & 1 & 0 & 0 & 0 & 0 & 1 & 0 \\
0 & 1 & 1 & 1 & 1 & 1 & 1 & 0 \\
0 & 1 & 0 & 0 & 0 & 0 & 1 & 0 \\
0 & 1 & 0 & 0 & 0 & 0 & 1 & 0 \\
0 & 1 & 0 & 0 & 0 & 0 & 1 & 0 \\
0 & 0 & 0 & 0 & 0 & 0 & 0 & 0
\end{array}
$$

Figure 4.171: An 8×8 Letter H.

Cell encoding is not very useful for text (which can always be represented with eight bits per character), but this method can also be extended to an image that consists of straight lines only. The entire bitmap is divided into cells of, say, 8×8 pixels and is scanned cell by cell. The first cell is stored in entry 0 of a table and is encoded (i.e., written on the compressed file) as the pointer 0. Each subsequent cell is searched in the table. If found, its index in the table becomes its code and is written on the compressed file. Otherwise, it is added to the table. With 8×8

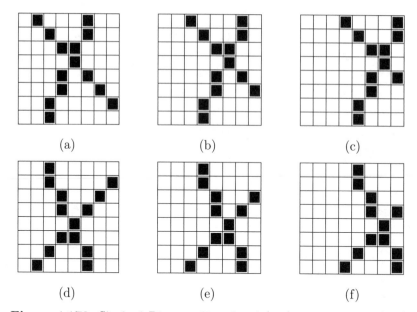

(a)   (b)   (c)

(d)   (e)   (f)

Figure 4.172: Six 8×8 Bitmaps Translated (a–c) and Reflected (d–f).

cells, each of the 64 pixels can be black or white, so the total number of different cells is $2^{64} \approx 1.8 \times 10^{19}$, a huge number. However, some patterns never appear, as they don't represent any possible combination of line segments. Also, many cells are translated or reflected versions of other cells (Figure 4.172). All this brings the total number of distinct cells to just 108 [Jordan and Barrett 74]. These 108 cells can be stored in ROM and used frequently to compress images.

Bibliography

Jordan, B. W., and R. C. Barrett (1974) "A Cell Organized Raster Display for Line Drawings," *Communications of the ACM,* **17**(2):70–77.

An ounce of image is worth a pound of performance.

—Anonymous

5
Wavelet Methods

5.1 Fourier Transform

The concept of a transform is familiar to mathematicians. It is a standard mathematical tool used to solve problems in many areas. The idea is to change a mathematical quantity (a number, a vector, a function, or anything else) to another form, where it may look unfamiliar but may exhibit useful features. The transformed quantity is used to solve a problem or to perform a calculation, and the result is then transformed back to the original form.

A simple, illustrative example is Roman numerals. The ancient Romans presumably knew how to operate on such numbers, but when we have to, say, multiply two Roman numerals, we may find it more convenient to transform them into modern (Arabic) notation, multiply, then transform the result back into a Roman numeral. Here is a simple example:

$$XCVI \times XII \rightarrow 96 \times 12 = 1152 \rightarrow MCLII.$$

Functions used in science and engineering often use *time* as their parameter. We therefore say that a function $g(t)$ is represented in the *time domain*. Since a typical function oscillates, we can think of it as being similar to a wave, and we may try to represent it as a wave (or as a combination of waves). When this is done, we denote the resulting function by $G(f)$, where f stands for the frequency of the wave, and we say that the function is represented in the *frequency domain*. This turns out to be a useful concept, since many operations on functions are easy to carry out in the frequency domain. Transforming a function between the time and frequency domains is easy when the function is *periodic*, but it can also be done for certain nonperiodic functions.

Definition: A function $g(t)$ is periodic if there exists a nonzero constant P such that $g(t + P) = g(t)$ for all values of t. The least such P is called the *period* of the function.

Figure 5.1 shows three periodic functions. The function of Figure 5.1a is a square pulse, that of Figure 5.1b is a sine wave, and the function of Figure 5.1c is more complex.

A periodic function has four important attributes: its amplitude, period, frequency, and phase. The amplitude of the function is the maximum value it has in any period. The frequency f is the inverse of the period ($f = 1/P$). It is expressed in cycles per second, or hertz (Hz). The phase is the least understood of the four attributes. It measures the position of the function within a period, and it is easy to visualize when a function is compared to its own copy. Consider the two sinusoids of Figure 5.1b. They are identical but out of phase. One follows the other at a fixed interval called the *phase difference*. We can write them as $g_1(t) = A\sin(2\pi ft)$ and $g_2(t) = A\sin(2\pi ft + \theta)$. The phase difference between them is θ, but we can also say that the first one has no phase, while the second one has a phase of θ. (This example also shows that the cosine is a sine function with a phase $\theta = \pi/2$.)

5.2 The Frequency Domain

To understand the concept of frequency domain, let's look at two simple examples. The function $g(t) = \sin(2\pi ft) + (1/3)\sin(2\pi(3f)t)$ is a combination of two sine waves with amplitudes 1 and 1/3, and frequencies f and $3f$, respectively. They are shown in Figure 5.2a,b. Their sum (Figure 5.2c) is also periodic, with frequency f (the smaller of the two frequencies f and $3f$). The frequency domain of $g(t)$ is a function consisting of just the two points $(f, 1)$ and $(3f, 1/3)$ (Figure 5.2h). It indicates that the original (time domain) function is made up of frequency f with amplitude 1, and frequency $3f$ with amplitude 1/3.

This example is extremely simple, since it involves just two frequencies. When a function involves several frequencies that are integer multiples of some lowest frequency, the latter is called the *fundamental frequency* of the function.

Not every function has a simple frequency domain representation. Consider the single square pulse of Figure 5.2d. Its time domain is

$$g(t) = \begin{cases} 1, & -a/2 \le t \le a/2, \\ 0, & \text{elsewhere,} \end{cases}$$

but its frequency domain is Figure 5.2e. It consists of all the frequencies from 0 to ∞, with amplitudes that drop continuously. This means that the time domain representation, even though simple, consists of all possible frequencies, with lower frequencies contributing more, and higher ones, less and less.

In general, a periodic function can be represented in the frequency domain as the sum of (phase shifted) sine waves with frequencies that are integer multiples (harmonics) of some fundamental frequency. However, the square pulse of Figure 5.2d is not periodic. It turns out that frequency domain concepts can be applied to a nonperiodic function, but only if it is nonzero over a finite range (like our square pulse). Such a function is represented as the sum of (phase shifted) sine waves with all kinds of frequencies, not just harmonics.

The *spectrum* of the frequency domain (sometimes also called the *frequency content* of the function) is the range of frequencies it contains. For the function

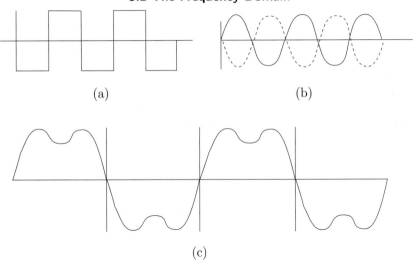

(a)　　　　　　　　　　　　(b)

(c)

Figure 5.1: Periodic Functions.

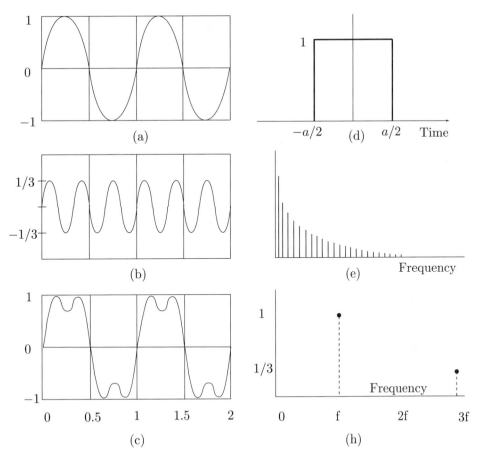

Figure 5.2: Time and Frequency Domains.

of Figure 5.2h, the spectrum is the two frequencies f and $3f$. For the one of Figure 5.2e, it is the entire range $[0, \infty]$. The *bandwidth* of the frequency domain is the width of the spectrum. It is $2f$ in our first example, and ∞ in the second one.

Another important concept to define is the *dc component* of the function. The time domain of a function may include a component of zero frequency. Engineers call this component the *direct current*, so the rest of us have adopted the term "dc component." Figure 5.3a is identical to Figure 5.2c except that it goes from 0 to 2, instead of from -1 to $+1$. The frequency domain (Figure 5.3b) now has an added point at $(0, 1)$, representing the dc component.

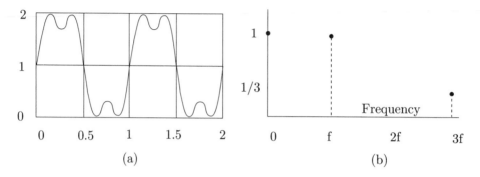

Figure 5.3: Time and Frequency Domains With a dc Component.

The entire concept of the two domains is due to the French mathematician Joseph Fourier. He proved a fundamental theorem that says that every periodic function, real or complex, can be represented as the sum of sine and cosine functions. He also showed how to transform a function between the time and frequency domains. If the shape of the function is far from a regular wave, its Fourier expansion will include an infinite number of frequencies. For a continuous function $g(t)$, the Fourier transform and its inverse are given by

$$G(f) = \int_{-\infty}^{\infty} g(t)[\cos(2\pi ft) - i \sin(2\pi ft)]\, dt,$$

$$g(t) = \int_{-\infty}^{\infty} G(f)[\cos(2\pi ft) + i \sin(2\pi ft)]\, df.$$

In computer applications, we normally have discrete functions that take just n (equally spaced) values. In such a case the discrete Fourier transform is

$$\begin{aligned}
G(f) &= \sum_{t=0}^{n-1} g(t)\left[\cos\left(\frac{2\pi ft}{n}\right) - i \sin\left(\frac{2\pi ft}{n}\right)\right] \\
&= \sum_{t=0}^{n-1} g(t)e^{-ift}, \quad 0 \le f \le n-1,
\end{aligned} \tag{5.1}$$

and its inverse

$$
g(t) = \frac{1}{n} \sum_{f=0}^{n-1} G(f) \left[\cos\left(\frac{2\pi f t}{n}\right) + i \sin\left(\frac{2\pi f t}{n}\right) \right]
$$

$$
= \sum_{t=0}^{n-1} G(f) e^{ift}, \quad 0 \le t \le n - 1.
$$

(5.2)

Note that $G(f)$ is complex, so it can be written $G(f) = \mathcal{R}(f) + i\mathcal{I}(f)$. For any value of f, the amplitude (or magnitude) of G is given by $|G(f)| = \sqrt{\mathcal{R}^2(f) + \mathcal{I}^2(f)}$.

A word on terminology. Generally, $G(f)$ is called the Fourier transform of $g(t)$. However, if $g(t)$ is periodic, then $G(f)$ is its Fourier series.

A function $f(t)$ is a *bandpass function* if its Fourier transform $F(\omega)$ is confined to a frequency interval $\omega_1 < |\omega| < \omega_2$, where $\omega_1 > 0$ and ω_2 is finite.

Note how the function in Figure 5.2c, obtained by adding the simple functions in Figure 5.2a,b, starts resembling a square pulse. It turns out that we can bring it closer to a square pulse (like the one in Figure 5.1a) by adding $(1/5)\sin(2\pi(5f)t)$, $(1/7)\sin(2\pi(7f)t)$, and so on. We say that the Fourier series of a square wave with amplitude A and frequency f is the infinite sum

$$
A \sum_{k=1,3,5,\dots}^{\infty} \frac{1}{k} \sin(2\pi k f t),
$$

where successive terms have smaller and smaller amplitudes.

Here are two examples that show the relation between a function $g(t)$ and its Fourier expansion $G(f)$. The first example is the step function of Figure 5.4a, defined by

$$
g(t) = \begin{cases} \pi/2, & \text{for } 2k\pi \le t < (2k+1)\pi, \\ -\pi/2, & \text{for } (2k+1)\pi \le t < (2k+2)\pi, \end{cases}
$$

where k is any integer (positive or negative). The Fourier expansion of $g(t)$ is

$$
G(f) = 2 \sum_{k=0}^{\infty} \frac{\sin[f(2k+1)]}{2k+1} = 2 \sin f + \frac{2 \sin 3f}{3} + \frac{2 \sin 5f}{5} + \cdots.
$$

Figure 5.5a shows the first three terms of this series, and Figure 5.5b shows three partial sums, of the first four, eight, and 13 terms. It is obvious that these partial sums quickly approach the original function.

The second example is the sawtooth function of Figure 5.4b, defined by $g(t) = t/2$ for every interval $[2k\pi, (2k+1)\pi)$. Its Fourier expansion is

$$
G(f) = \frac{\pi}{2} - \sum_{k=1}^{\infty} \frac{\sin(k f)}{k}.
$$

Figure 5.6 shows four partial sums, of the first three, five, nine, and 17 terms, of this expansion.

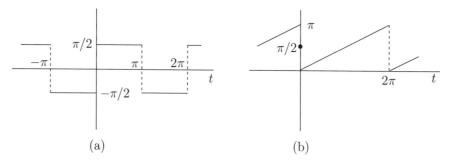

Figure 5.4: Two Functions $g(t)$ to be Transformed.

5.3 The Uncertainty Principle

The examples shown here illustrate an important relation between the time and frequency domains; namely, they are *complementary*. Each of them complements the other in the sense that when one of them is localized the other one must be global. Consider, for example, a pure sine wave. It has one frequency, so it is well localized in the frequency domain. However, it is infinitely long, so in the time domain it is global. On the other hand, a function may be localized in the time domain, such as the single spike of Figure 5.38a, but it will invariably be global in the frequency domain; its Fourier expansion will contain many (perhaps even infinitely many) frequencies. This relation between the time and frequency domains makes them complementary, and it is popularly described by the term *uncertainty relation* or *uncertainty principle*.

The Heisenberg uncertainty principle, first recognized in 1927 by Werner Heisenberg, is a very important physical principle. It says that position and momentum are complementary. The better we know the position of a particle of matter, the less certain we are of its momentum. The reason for this relation is the way we measure positions. In order to locate a particle in space, we have to see it (with our eyes or with an instrument). This requires shining light on the particle (either visible light or some other wavelength), and it is this light that disturbs the particle, moves it from its position and thus changes its momentum. We think of light as consisting of small units, photons, that don't have any mass but have momentum. When a photon hits a particle, it gives the particle a "kick," which moves it away. The larger the particle, the smaller the effects of the kick, but in principle, the complementary relation between position and momentum exists even for macroscopic objects.

It is important to realize that the uncertainty principle is part of nature; it is not just a result of our imperfect knowledge or primitive instruments. It is expressed by the relation

$$\Delta x \, \Delta p \geq \frac{\hbar}{2} = \frac{h}{4\pi},$$

where Δx and Δp are the uncertainties in the position and momentum of the particle, and h is the Planck constant (6.626176×10^{-27} erg·sec.). The point is that

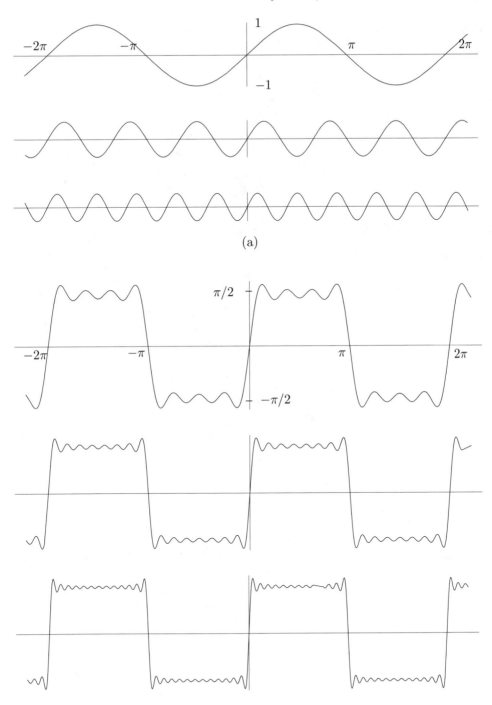

Figure 5.5: The First Three Terms and Three Partial Sums.

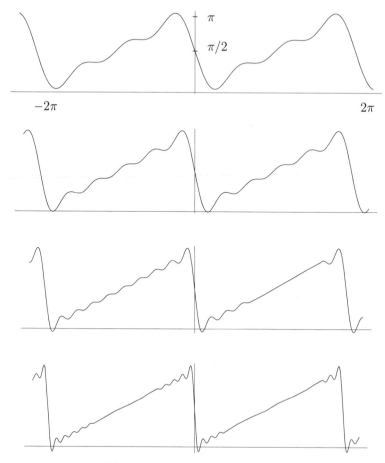

Figure 5.6: Four Partial Sums.

h is very small, so

$$\hbar \stackrel{\text{def}}{=} \frac{h}{2\pi} = 1.05 \times 10^{-34} = 0.00000000000000000000000000000000105 \,\text{joule·sec.}$$

(An erg and a joule are units of energy whose precise values are irrelevant for this discussion.) This is why we don't notice the position/momentum uncertainty in everyday life. A simple example should make this clear. Suppose that the mass of a moving ball is 0.15 Kg and we measure its velocity to a precision of 0.05 m/s (that is about 1 mph). Momentum is the product of mass and velocity, so if the uncertainty in the velocity of the ball is 0.05 m/s, the uncertainty in its momentum is $\Delta p = 0.15 \times 0.05 = 0.0075$ Kg·m/s The uncertainty principle says that $\Delta x \times 0.0075 \geq 1.05 \times 10^{-34}/2$, which implies that the uncertainty in the position of the ball is on the order of 70×10^{-34} m or 7×10^{-30} mm, too small to measure!

While we are discussing physics, here is another similarity between the time frequency domains and physical reality. Real objects (i.e., objects with mass) have a property called the "wave particle duality." This is true for all objects but is noticeable and can be measured only for microscopic particles. This property means that every object has a wave associated with it. The amplitude of this wave (actually, the square of the absolute value of the amplitude) in a given region describes the probability of finding the object in that region. When we observe the object, it will normally will be found in that region where its wave function has the highest amplitude.

The wave associated with an object is generally not spread throughout the entire universe, but is confined to a small region in space. This "localized" wave is called a *wave packet*. Such a packet does not have one particular wavelength, but consists of waves of many wavelengths. The momentum of an object depends on its wavelength, so an object that is localized in space doesn't have a specific, well-defined momentum; it has many momenta. In other words, there's an uncertainty in the momentum of the particle.

Nuggets of Uncertainty

A full discussion of Heisenberg's uncertainty principle may be found in the Appendix. Then again, it may not.

Uncertainty is the very essence of romance. It's what you don't know that intrigues you.

5.4 Fourier Image Compression

We now apply these concepts to digital images. Imagine a black and white photograph scanned line by line. For all practical purposes we can assume that the photograph has infinite resolution (its shades of gray can vary continuously). An ideal scan would therefore result in an infinite sequence of numbers that can be considered the values of a (continuous) intensity function $I(t)$. In practice, we can store only a finite amount of data in memory, so we have to select a finite number of values $I(1)$ through $I(n)$. This process is known as *sampling*.

Intuitively, sampling seems a tradeoff between quality and price. The bigger the sample, the better the quality of the final image, but more hardware (more memory and higher screen resolution) is required, resulting in higher costs. This intuitive conclusion, however, is not entirely true. Sampling theory tells us that we can sample an image and reconstruct it later in memory without loss of quality if we can do the following:

1. Transform the intensity function from the time domain $I(t)$ to the frequency domain $G(f)$.

2. Find the maximum frequency f_m.

3. Sample $I(t)$ at a rate slightly higher than $2f_m$ (e.g., if $f_m = 22,000$ Hz, generate samples at the rate of $44,100$ Hz).

4. Store the sampled values in the bitmap. The resulting image would be equal in quality to the original one on the photograph.

There are two points to consider. The first is that f_m could be infinite. In such a case, a value f_m should be selected such that frequencies that are greater than f_m do not contribute much (have low amplitudes). There is some loss of image quality in such a case. The second point is that the bitmap (and consequently, the resolution) may be too small for the sample generated in step 3. In such a case, a smaller sample has to be taken, again resulting in a loss of image quality.

The result above was proved by Harry Nyquist, and the quantity $2f_m$ is called the *Nyquist rate*. It is used in many practical situations. The range of human hearing, for instance, is between 16 Hz and 22,000 Hz. When sound is digitized at high quality (such as music recorded on a CD), it is sampled at the rate of 44,100 Hz. Anything lower than that results in distortions.

> Fourier is a mathematical poem.
> —William Thomson (Lord Kelvin)

The Fourier transform is useful and popular, having applications in many areas. It has, however, one drawback: It shows the frequency content of a function $f(t)$, but it does not specify where (i.e., for what values of t) the function has low and high frequencies. The reason for this is that the basis functions (sine and cosine) used by this transform are infinitely long. They pick up the different frequencies of $f(t)$ regardless of where they are located.

A better transform should specify the frequency content of $f(t)$ as a function of t. Instead of producing a one-dimensional function (in the continuous case) or a one-dimensional array of numbers (in the discrete case), it should produce a two-dimensional function or array of numbers $W(a, b)$ that describes the frequency content of $f(t)$ for different values of t. A column $W(a_i, b)$ of this array (where $i = 1, 2, \ldots, n$) lists the frequency spectrum of $f(t)$ for a certain value (or range of values) of t. A row $W(a, b_i)$ contains numbers that describe how much of a certain frequency (or range of frequencies) $f(t)$ has for any given t.

The *wavelet transform* is such a method. It has been developed, researched, and applied to many areas of science and engineering since the early 1980s, although its roots go much earlier. The main idea is to select a mother wavelet, a function that is nonzero in some small interval, and use it to explore the properties of $f(t)$ in that interval. The mother wavelet is then translated to another interval of t and used in the same way. Parameter b specifies the translation. Different frequency resolutions of $f(t)$ are explored by scaling the mother wavelet with a scale factor a.

Before getting into any details, we illustrate the relation between the "normal" (time domain) representation of a function and its two-dimensional transform by looking at standard musical notation. This notation, used in the West for hundreds of years, is two-dimensional. Notes are written on a stave in two dimensions, where the horizontal axis denotes the time (from left to right) and the vertical axis denotes the pitch. The higher the note on the stave, the higher the pitch of the tone played. In addition, the shape of a note indicates its duration. Figure 5.7a shows, from left to right, one whole note (called "C" in the U.S. and "do" in Europe), two half notes, three quarter notes, and two eighth notes. In addition to the stave and the notes, musical notation includes many other symbols and directions from the composer. However, the point is that the same music can also be represented by a one-dimensional function that simply describes the amplitude of the sound as a function of the time (Figure 5.7b). The two representations are mathematically equivalent, but are used differently in practice. The two-dimensional representation is used by musicians to actually perform the music. The one-dimensional representation is used to replay music that has already been performed and recorded.

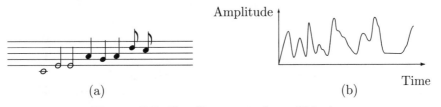

Figure 5.7: Two Representations of Music.

⋄ **Exercise 5.1:** Give another example of a common notation that has a familiar two-dimensional representation used by humans and an unfamiliar one-dimensional representation used by machines.

The principle of analyzing a function by time and by frequency can be applied to image compression because images contain areas that exhibit "trends" and areas with "anomalies." A trend is an image feature that involves just a few frequencies (it is localized in frequency) but is spread spatially. A typical example is an image area where the brightness varies gradually. An anomaly is an image feature that involves several frequencies but is localized spatially (it is concentrated in a small image area). An example is an edge.

We start by looking at functions that can serve as a wavelet, by defining the continuous wavelet transform (CWT) and its inverse, and illustrating the way the CWT works. We then show in detail how the Haar wavelet can be applied to the compression of images. This naturally leads to the concepts of filter banks and the *discrete wavelet transform* (Section 5.8). The *lifting scheme* for the calculation of the wavelet transform and its inverse are described in Section 5.11. This is followed by descriptions of several compression methods that either employ the wavelet transform or compress the coefficients that result from such a transform.

5.5 The CWT and Its Inverse

The continuous wavelet transform (CWT) of a function $f(t)$ involves a mother wavelet $\psi(t)$. The mother wavelet can be any real or complex continuous function that satisfies the following properties:

1. The total area under the curve of the function is zero, i.e.,

$$\int_{-\infty}^{\infty} \psi(t)\,dt = 0.$$

2. The total area of $|\psi(t)|^2$ is finite, i.e.

$$\int_{-\infty}^{\infty} |\psi(t)|^2 \, dt < \infty.$$

This condition implies that the integral of the square of the wavelet has to exist. We can also say that a wavelet has to be *square integrable*, or that it belongs to the set $\mathcal{L}^2(R)$ of all the square integrable functions.

3. The admissibility condition, discussed below.

   Property 1 suggests a function that oscillates above and below the t axis. Such a function tends to have a wavy appearance. Property 2 implies that the *energy* of the function is finite, suggesting that the function is localized in some finite interval and is zero, or almost zero, outside this interval. These properties justify the name "wavelet." An infinite number of functions satisfy these conditions, and some of them have been researched and are commonly used for wavelet transforms. Figure 5.8a shows the Morlet wavelet, defined as

$$\psi(t) = e^{-t^2} \cos\left(\pi t \sqrt{\frac{2}{\ln 2}}\right) \approx e^{-t^2} \cos(2.885\pi t).$$

This is a cosine curve whose oscillations are dampened by the exponential (or Gaussian) factor. More than 99% of its energy is concentrated in the interval $-2.5 \le t \le 2.5$. Figure 5.8b shows the so-called Mexican hat wavelet, defined as

$$\psi(t) = (1 - 2t^2)e^{-t^2}.$$

This is the second derivative of the (negative) Gaussian function $-0.5e^{-t^2}$.

The energy of a function

   A function $y = f(x)$ relates each value of the independent variable x with a value of y. Plotting these pairs of values results in a representation of the function as a curve in two dimensions. The *energy* of a function is defined in terms of the area enclosed by this curve and the x axis. It makes sense to say that a curve that stays close to the axis has little energy, while a curve that spends "time" away from the x axis has more energy. Negative values of y push the curve under the x axis, where its area is considered negative, so the energy of $f(t)$ is defined as the area under the curve of the nonnegative function $f(x)^2$. If the function is complex, its absolute value is used in area calculations, so the energy of $f(x)$ is defined as

$$\int_{-\infty}^{\infty} |f(x)|^2 dx.$$

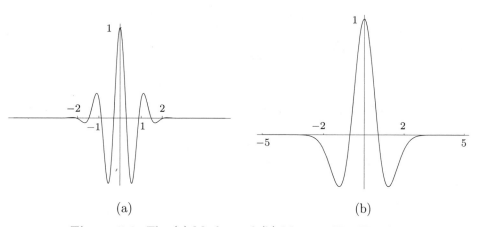

Figure 5.8: The (a) Morlet and (b) Mexican Hat Wavelets.

Once a wavelet $\psi(t)$ has been chosen, the CWT of a square integrable function $f(t)$ is defined as

$$W(a,b) = \int_{-\infty}^{\infty} f(t) \frac{1}{\sqrt{|a|}} \psi^* \left(\frac{t-b}{a} \right) dt. \qquad (5.3)$$

The transform is a function of the two real parameters a and b. The $*$ denotes the complex conjugate. If we define a function $\psi_{a,b}(t)$ as

$$\psi_{a,b}(t) = \frac{1}{\sqrt{|a|}} \psi \left(\frac{t-b}{a} \right),$$

we can write Equation (5.3) in the form

$$W(a,b) = \int_{-\infty}^{\infty} f(t) \psi_{a,b}(t) \, dt. \qquad (5.4)$$

Mathematically, the transform is the *inner product* of the two functions $f(t)$ and $\psi_{a,b}(t)$. The quantity $1/\sqrt{|a|}$ is a normalizing factor that ensures that the energy of $\psi(t)$ remains independent of a and b, i.e.,

$$\int_{-\infty}^{\infty} |\psi_{a,b}(t)|^2 \, dt = \int_{-\infty}^{\infty} |\psi(t)|^2 \, dt.$$

For any a, $\psi_{a,b}(t)$ is a copy of $\psi_{a,0}$ shifted b units along the time axis. Thus, b is a *translation parameter*. Setting $b = 0$ shows that

$$\psi_{a,0}(t) = \frac{1}{\sqrt{|a|}} \psi \left(\frac{t}{a} \right),$$

implying that a is a scaling (or a dilation) parameter. Values $a > 1$ stretch the wavelet, while values $0 < a < 1$ shrink it.

Since wavelets are used to transform a function, the inverse transform is needed. We denote by $\Psi(\omega)$ the Fourier transform of $\psi(t)$:

$$\Psi(\omega) = \int_{-\infty}^{\infty} \psi(t)e^{-i\omega t}\,dt.$$

If $W(a, b)$ is the CWT of a function $f(t)$ with a wavelet $\psi(t)$, then the inverse CWT is defined by

$$f(t) = \frac{1}{C} \int_{-\infty}^{\infty} \int_{-\infty}^{\infty} \frac{1}{|a|^2} W(a, b)\psi_{a,b}(t)\,da\,db,$$

where the quantity C is defined as

$$C = \int_{-\infty}^{\infty} \frac{|\Psi(\omega)|^2}{|\omega|}\,d\omega.$$

The inverse CWT exists if C is positive and finite. Since C is defined by means of Ψ, which itself is defined by means of the wavelet $\psi(t)$, the requirement that C be positive and finite imposes another restriction, called the *admissibility condition*, on the choice of wavelet.

The CWT is best thought of as an array of numbers that are inner products of $f(t)$ and $\psi_{a,b}(t)$. The rows of the array correspond to values of a, and the columns are indexed by b. The *inner product* of two functions $f(t)$ and $g(t)$ is defined as

$$\langle f(t), g(t) \rangle = \int_{-\infty}^{\infty} f(t)g^*(t)\,dt,$$

so the CWT is the inner product

$$\langle f(t), \psi_{a,b}(t) \rangle = \int_{-\infty}^{\infty} f(t)\psi_{a,b}(t)\,dt.$$

After this introduction, we are now in a position to explain the intuitive meaning of the CWT. We start with a simple example: the CWT of a sine wave, where the Mexican hat is chosen as the wavelet. Figure 5.9a shows a sine wave with two copies of the wavelet. Copy 1 is positioned at a point where the sine wave has a maximum. At this point there is a good match between the function being analyzed (the sine) and the wavelet. The wavelet *replicates* the features of the sine wave. As a result, the inner product of the sine and the wavelet is a large positive number. In contrast, copy 2 is positioned where the sine wave has a minimum. At that point the wave and the wavelet are almost mirror images of each other. Where the sine wave is positive, the wavelet is negative and vice versa. The product of the wave and the wavelet at this point is negative, and the CWT (the integral or the inner product) becomes a large negative number. In between points 1 and 2, the CWT drops from positive, to zero, to negative.

As the wavelet is translated along the sine wave, from left to right, the CWT alternates between positive and negative and produces the small wave shown in

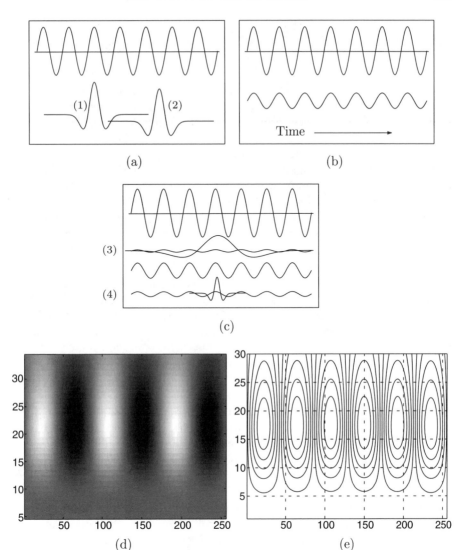

Figure 5.9: The Continuous Wavelet Transform of a Pure Sine Wave.

```
t=linspace(0,6*pi,256);        t=linspace(-10,10,256);
sinwav=sin(t);                 sombr=(1-2*t.^2).*exp(-t.^2);
plot(t,sinwav)                 plot(t,sombr)
cwt=CWT(sinwav,10,'Sombrero');
axis('ij'); colormap(gray);
imagesc(cwt')
x=1:256; y=1:30;
[X,Y]=meshgrid(x,y);
contour(X,Y,cwt',10)
```

Code for Figure 5.9.

Figure 5.9b. This shape is the result of the close match between the function being analyzed (the sine wave) and the analyzing wavelet. They have similar shapes and also similar frequencies.

We now extend the analysis to cover different frequencies. This is done by scaling the wavelet. Figure 5.9c shows (in part 3) what happens when the wavelet is stretched such that it covers several periods of the sine wave. Translating the wavelet from left to right does not affect the match between it and the sine wave by much, with the result that the CWT varies just a little. The wider the wavelet, the closer the CWT is to a constant. Notice how the amplitude of the wavelet has been reduced, thereby reducing its area and producing a small constant. A similar thing happens in part 4 of the figure, where the wavelet has shrunk and is much narrower than one cycle of the sine wave. Since the wavelet is so "thin," the inner product of it and the sine wave is always a small number (positive or negative) regardless of the precise position of the wavelet relative to the sine wave. We see that translating the wavelet does not much affect its match to the sine wave, resulting in a CWT that is close to a constant.

The results of translating the wavelet, scaling it, and translating again and again are summarized in Figure 5.9d. This is a density plot of the transform function $W(a, b)$ where the horizontal axis corresponds to values of b (translation) and the vertical axis corresponds to values of a (scaling). Figure 5.9e is a contour plot of the same $W(a, b)$. These diagrams show that there is a good match between the function and the wavelet at a certain frequency (the frequency of the sine wave). At other frequencies the match deteriorates, resulting in a transform that gets closer and closer to a constant.

This is how the CWT provides a time-frequency analysis of a function $f(t)$. The result is a function $W(a, b)$ of two variables that shows the match between $f(t)$ and the wavelet at different frequencies of the wavelet and at different times. It is obvious that the quality of the match depends on the choice of wavelet. If the wavelet is very different from $f(t)$ at any frequencies and any times, the values of the resulting $W(a, b)$ will all be small and will not exhibit much variation. As a result, when wavelets are used to compress images, different wavelets should be selected for different image types (bi-level, continuous-tone, and discrete-tone), but the precise choice of wavelet is still the subject of much research.

Since both our function and our wavelet are simple functions, it may be possible in this case to calculate the integral of the CWT as an indefinite integral, and come up with a closed formula for $W(a, b)$. In the general case, however, this is impossible, either in practice or in principle, and the calculations have to be done numerically.

The next example is slightly more complex and leads to a better understanding of the CWT. The function being analyzed this time is a sine wave with an accelerated frequency: the so-called *chirp*. It is given by $f(t) = \sin(t^2)$, and it is shown in Figure 5.10a. The wavelet is the same Mexican hat. Readers who have gone over the previous example carefully will have no trouble in interpreting the CWT of this example. It is given by Figure 5.10b,c and shows how the frequency of $f(t)$ increases with time.

The two examples above illustrate how the CWT is used to analyze the time frequency of a function $f(t)$. It is clear that the user needs experience both in order

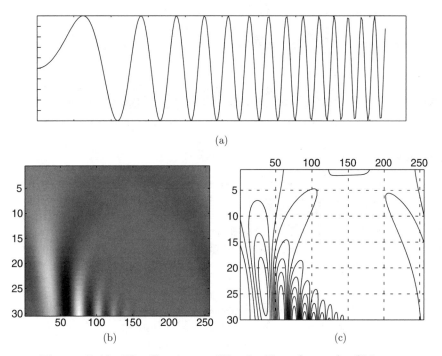

(a)

(b)   (c)

Figure 5.10: The Continuous Wavelet Transform of a Chirp.

to select the right wavelet for the job and in order to interpret the results. However, with the right experience, the CWT can be a powerful analytic tool in the hands of scientists and engineers.

⋄ **Exercise 5.2:** Experiment with the CWT by trying to work out the following analysis. Select the function $f(t) = 1 + \sin(\pi t + t^2)/8$ as your candidate for analysis. This is a sine wave that oscillates between $y = 1 - 1/8$ and $y = 1 + 1/8$ with a frequency $2\pi + t$ that increases with t. As the wavelet, select the Mexican hat. Plot several translated copies of the wavelet against $f(t)$, then use appropriate software, such as *Mathematica* or Matlab, to calculate and display the CWT.

Wavelets are also subject to the uncertainty principle (Section 5.3). The Haar wavelet is very well localized in the time domain but is spread in the frequency domain due to the appearance of sidebands in the Fourier spectrum. In contrast, the Mexican hat wavelet and especially the Morlet wavelet have more concentrated frequencies but are spread over time. An important result of the uncertainty principle is that it is impossible to achieve a complete simultaneous mapping of both time and frequency. Wavelets provide a compromise, or a near optimal solution, to this problem, and this is one feature that makes them superior to Fourier analysis.

We can compare wavelet analysis to looking at a complex object first from a distance, then closer, then through a magnifying glass, and finally through a microscope. When looking from a distance, we see the overall shape of the object, but not any small details. When looking through a microscope, we see small details, but not the overall shape. This is why it is important to analyze in different scales. When we change the scale of the wavelet, we get new information about the function being analyzed.

Bibliography

Lewalle, Jacques (1995) "Tutorial on Continuous Wavelet Analysis of Experimental Data," available anonymously from `ftp.mame.syr.edu/pub/jlewalle/tutor.ps.Z`.

Rao, Raghuveer M., and Ajit S. Bopardikar (1998) *Wavelet Transforms: Introduction To Theory and Applications*, Reading, MA, Addison-Wesley.

5.6 The Haar Transform

Information that is being wavelet transformed in practical situations, such as digitized sound and images, is discrete, consisting of individual numbers. This is why the discrete, and not the continuous, wavelet transform is used in practice. The discrete wavelet transform is described in general in Section 5.8, but we precede this discussion by presenting a simple example of this type of transform, namely, the Haar wavelet transform.

The use of the Haar transform for image compression is described here from a practical point of view. We first show how this transform is applied to the compression of grayscale images, then show how this method can be extended to color images. The Haar transform was introduced in Section 4.4.7.

The Haar transform uses a scale function $\phi(t)$ and a wavelet $\psi(t)$, both shown in Figure 5.11a, to represent a large number of functions $f(t)$. The representation is the infinite sum

$$f(t) = \sum_{k=-\infty}^{\infty} c_k \phi(t-k) + \sum_{k=-\infty}^{\infty} \sum_{j=0}^{\infty} d_{j,k} \psi(2^j t - k),$$

where c_k and $d_{j,k}$ are coefficients to be calculated.

The basic scale function $\phi(t)$ is the unit pulse

$$\phi(t) = \begin{cases} 1, & 0 \le t < 1, \\ 0, & \text{otherwise.} \end{cases}$$

The function $\phi(t-k)$ is a copy of $\phi(t)$, shifted k units to the right. Similarly, $\phi(2t-k)$ is a copy of $\phi(t-k)$ scaled to half the width of $\phi(t-k)$. The shifted copies are used to approximate $f(t)$ at different times t. The scaled copies are used to approximate $f(t)$ at higher resolutions. Figure 5.11b shows the functions $\phi(2^j t - k)$ for $j = 0, 1, 2$, and 3 and for $k = 0, 1, \ldots, 7$.

The basic Haar wavelet is the step function

$$\psi(t) = \begin{cases} 1, & 0 \le t < 0.5, \\ -1, & 0.5 \le t < 1. \end{cases}$$

From this we can see that the general Haar wavelet $\psi(2^j t - k)$ is a copy of $\psi(t)$ shifted k units to the right and scaled such that its total width is $1/2^j$.

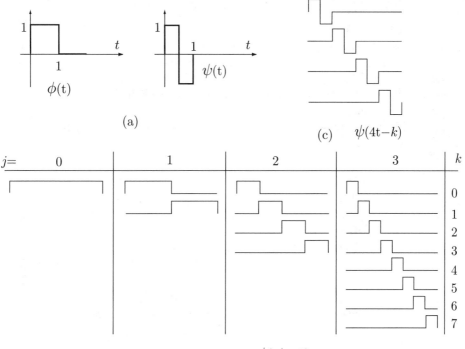

(a)

(c) $\psi(4\mathrm{t}-k)$

(b) $\phi(2^j\mathrm{t}-k)$

Figure 5.11: The Haar Basis Scale and Wavelet Functions.

◇ **Exercise 5.3:** Draw the four Haar wavelets $\psi(2^2 t - k)$ for $k = 0, 1, 2$, and 3.

Both $\phi(2^j t - k)$ and $\psi(2^j t - k)$ are nonzero in an interval of width $1/2^j$. This interval is their *support*. Since this interval tends to be short, we say that these functions have *compact support*.

We illustrate the basic transform on the simple step function

$$f(t) = \begin{cases} 5, & 0 \le t < 0.5, \\ 3, & 0.5 \le t < 1. \end{cases}$$

It is easy to see that $f(t) = 4\phi(t) + \psi(t)$. We say that the original steps $(5, 3)$ have been transformed to the (low resolution) average 4 and the (high resolution) detail -1. Using matrix notation, this can be expressed as $(5, 3)\mathbf{A}_2 = (4, -1)$, where $\mathbf{A}_2$ is the order-2 Haar transform matrix of Equation (4.16).

An image is a two-dimensional array of pixel values. To illustrate how the Haar transform is used to compress an image, we start with a single row of pixel values, i.e., a one-dimensional array of n values. For simplicity we assume that n is a power of 2. (We use this assumption throughout this chapter, but there is no loss of generality. If n has a different value, the data can be extended by appending zeros. After decompression, the extra data are removed.) Consider the array of eight values $(1, 2, 3, 4, 5, 6, 7, 8)$. We first compute the four averages $(1+2)/2 = 3/2$,

$(3 + 4)/2 = 7/2$, $(5 + 6)/2 = 11/2$, and $(7 + 8)/2 = 15/2$. It is impossible to reconstruct the original eight values from these four averages, so we also compute the four differences $(1 - 2)/2 = -1/2$, $(3 - 4)/2 = -1/2$, $(5 - 6)/2 = -1/2$, and $(7 - 8)/2 = -1/2$. These differences are called *detail coefficients*, and in this section the terms "difference" and "detail" are used interchangeably. We can think of the averages as a coarse resolution representation of the original image, and of the details as the data needed to reconstruct the original image from this coarse resolution. If the pixels of the image are correlated, the coarse representation will resemble the original pixels, while the details will be small. This explains why the Haar wavelet compression of images uses averages and details.

> Prolonged, lugubrious stretches of Sunday afternoon in a university town could be mitigated by attending Sillery's tea parties, to which anyone might drop in after half-past three. Action of some law of averages always regulated numbers at these gatherings to something between four and eight persons, mostly undergraduates, though an occasional don was not unknown.
>
> —Anthony Powell, *A Buyer's Market*

It is easy to see that the array $(3/2, 7/2, 11/2, 15/2, -1/2, -1/2, -1/2, -1/2)$ made of the four averages and four differences can be used to reconstruct the original eight values. This array has eight values, but its last four components, the differences, tend to be small numbers, which helps in compression. Encouraged by this, we repeat the process on the four averages, the large components of our array. They are transformed into two averages and two differences, yielding the array $(10/4, 26/4, -4/4, -4/4, -1/2, -1/2, -1/2, -1/2)$. The next, and last, iteration of this process transforms the first two components of the new array into one average (the average of all eight components of the original array) and one difference $(36/8, -16/8, -4/4, -4/4, -1/2, -1/2, -1/2, -1/2)$. The last array is the *Haar wavelet transform* of the original data items.

Because of the differences, the wavelet transform tends to have numbers smaller than the original pixel values, so it is easier to compress using RLE, perhaps combined with move-to-front and Huffman coding. Lossy compression can be obtained if some of the smaller differences are quantized or even completely deleted (changed to zero).

Before we continue, it is interesting (and also useful) to calculate the *complexity* of this transform, i.e., the number of necessary arithmetic operations as a function of the size of the data. In our example we needed $8+4+2 = 14$ operations (additions and subtractions), a number that can also be expressed as $16 = 2(8 - 1)$. In the general case, assume that we start with $N = 2^n$ data items. In the first iteration we need 2^n operations, in the second one we need 2^{n-1} operations, and so on, until the last iteration, where $2^{n-(n-1)} = 2^1$ operations are needed. Thus, the total number of operations is

$$\sum_{i=1}^{n} 2^i = \sum_{i=0}^{n} 2^i - 1 = \frac{1 - 2^{n+1}}{1 - 2} - 1 = 2^{n+1} - 2 = 2(2^n - 1) = 2(N - 1).$$

The Haar wavelet transform of N data items can therefore be performed with $2(N - 1)$ operations, so its complexity is $\mathcal{O}(N)$, an excellent result.

It is useful to associate with each iteration a quantity called *resolution*, which is defined as the number of remaining averages at the end of the iteration. The resolutions after each of the three iterations above are $4(= 2^2)$, $2(= 2^1)$, and $1(= 2^0)$. Section 5.6.3 shows that each component of the wavelet transform should be normalized by dividing it by the square root of the resolution. (This is the *orthonormal Haar transform*, also discussed in Section 4.4.7.) Thus, our example wavelet transform becomes

$$\left(\frac{36/8}{\sqrt{2^0}}, \frac{-16/8}{\sqrt{2^0}}, \frac{-4/4}{\sqrt{2^1}}, \frac{-4/4}{\sqrt{2^1}}, \frac{-1/2}{\sqrt{2^2}}, \frac{-1/2}{\sqrt{2^2}}, \frac{-1/2}{\sqrt{2^2}}, \frac{-1/2}{\sqrt{2^2}} \right).$$

If the normalized wavelet transform is used, it can be formally proved that ignoring the smallest differences is the best choice for lossy wavelet compression, since it causes the smallest loss of image information.

The two procedures of Figure 5.12 illustrate how the normalized wavelet transform of an array of n components (where n is a power of 2) can be computed. Reconstructing the original array from the normalized wavelet transform is illustrated by the pair of procedures of Figure 5.13.

These procedures seem at first to be different from the averages and differences discussed earlier. They don't compute averages, since they divide by $\sqrt{2}$ instead of by 2; the first one starts by dividing the entire array by $\sqrt{n}$, and the second one ends by doing the reverse. The final result, however, is the same as that shown above. Starting with array $(1, 2, 3, 4, 5, 6, 7, 8)$, the three iterations of procedure NWTcalc result in

$$\left(\frac{3}{\sqrt{2^4}}, \frac{7}{\sqrt{2^4}}, \frac{11}{\sqrt{2^4}}, \frac{15}{\sqrt{2^4}}, \frac{-1}{\sqrt{2^4}}, \frac{-1}{\sqrt{2^4}}, \frac{-1}{\sqrt{2^4}}, \frac{-1}{\sqrt{2^4}} \right),$$

$$\left(\frac{10}{\sqrt{2^5}}, \frac{26}{\sqrt{2^5}}, \frac{-4}{\sqrt{2^5}}, \frac{-4}{\sqrt{2^5}}, \frac{-1}{\sqrt{2^4}}, \frac{-1}{\sqrt{2^4}}, \frac{-1}{\sqrt{2^4}}, \frac{-1}{\sqrt{2^4}} \right),$$

$$\left(\frac{36}{\sqrt{2^6}}, \frac{-16}{\sqrt{2^6}}, \frac{-4}{\sqrt{2^5}}, \frac{-4}{\sqrt{2^5}}, \frac{-1}{\sqrt{2^4}}, \frac{-1}{\sqrt{2^4}}, \frac{-1}{\sqrt{2^4}}, \frac{-1}{\sqrt{2^4}} \right),$$

$$\left(\frac{36/8}{\sqrt{2^0}}, \frac{-16/8}{\sqrt{2^0}}, \frac{-4/4}{\sqrt{2^1}}, \frac{-4/4}{\sqrt{2^1}}, \frac{-1/2}{\sqrt{2^2}}, \frac{-1/2}{\sqrt{2^2}}, \frac{-1/2}{\sqrt{2^2}}, \frac{-1/2}{\sqrt{2^2}} \right).$$

5.6.1 Applying the Haar Transform

Once the concept of a wavelet transform is grasped, it's easy to generalize it to a complete two-dimensional image. This can be done in several ways that are

```
procedure NWTcalc(a:array of real, n:int);
 comment n is the array size (a power of 2)
 a:=a/√n comment divide entire array
 j:=n;
 while j≥ 2 do
  NWTstep(a, j);
  j:=j/2;
 endwhile;
end;

procedure NWTstep(a:array of real, j:int);
 for i=1 to j/2 do
  b[i]:=(a[2i-1]+a[2i])/√2;
  b[j/2+i]:=(a[2i-1]-a[2i])/√2;
 endfor;
 a:=b; comment move entire array
end;
```

Figure 5.12: Computing the Normalized Wavelet Transform.

```
procedure NWTreconst(a:array of real, n:int);
 j:=2;
 while j≤n do
  NWTRstep(a, j);
  j:=2j;
 endwhile
 a:=a√n; comment multiply entire array
end;

procedure NWTRstep(a:array of real, j:int);
 for i=1 to j/2 do
  b[2i-1]:=(a[i]+a[j/2+i])/√2;
  b[2i]:=(a[i]-a[j/2+i])/√2;
 endfor;
 a:=b; comment move entire array
end;
```

Figure 5.13: Restoring From a Normalized Wavelet Transform.

> We spake no word, Tho' each I ween did hear the other's soul.
> Not a wavelet stirred,
> And yet we heard
> The loneliest music of the weariest waves
> That ever roll.
>
> —Abram J. Ryan, *Poems*

discussed in Section 5.10. Here we show two such approaches, called the *standard decomposition* and the *pyramid decomposition*.

The former (Figure 5.14) starts by computing the wavelet transform of every row of the image. This results in a transformed image where the first column contains averages and all the other columns contain differences. The standard algorithm then computes the wavelet transform of every column. This results in one average value at the top-left corner, with the rest of the top row containing averages of differences, and with all other pixel values transformed into differences.

The latter method computes the wavelet transform of the image by alternating between rows and columns. The first step is to calculate averages and differences for all the rows (just one iteration, not the entire wavelet transform). This creates averages in the left half of the image and differences in the right half. The second step is to calculate averages and differences for all the columns, which results in averages in the top-left quadrant of the image and differences elsewhere. Steps 3 and 4 operate on the rows and columns of that quadrant, resulting in averages concentrated in the top-left subquadrant. Pairs of steps are repeatedly executed on smaller and smaller subsquares, until only one average is left, at the top-left corner of the image, and all other pixel values have been reduced to differences. This process is summarized in Figure 5.15.

The transforms described in Section 4.4 are orthogonal. They transform the original pixels into a few large numbers and many small numbers. In contrast, wavelet transforms, such as the Haar transform, are *subband transforms*. They partition the image into regions such that one region contains large numbers (averages in the case of the Haar transform) and the other regions contain small numbers (differences). However, these regions, which are called subbands, are more than just sets of large and small numbers. They reflect different geometrical artifacts of the image. To illustrate what this means, we examine a small, mostly-uniform image with one vertical line and one horizontal line. Figure 5.16a shows an 8×8 image with pixel values of 12, except for a vertical line with pixel values of 14 and a horizontal line with pixel values of 16.

Figure 5.16b shows the results of applying the Haar transform once to the columns of the image. The right half of this figure (the differences) is mostly zeros, reflecting the uniform nature of the image. However, traces of the vertical line can easily be seen (the notation $\underline{2}$ indicates a negative difference). Figure 5.16c shows the results of applying the Haar transform once to the rows of Figure 5.16b. The upper-right subband now contains traces of the vertical line, whereas the lower-left subband shows traces of the horizontal line. These subbands are denoted by HL

```
procedure StdCalc(a:array of real, n:int);
 comment array size is nxn (n = power of 2)
 for r=1 to n do NWTcalc(row r of a, n);
 endfor;
 for c=n to 1 do comment loop backwards
  NWTcalc(col c of a, n);
 endfor;
end;
procedure StdReconst(a:array of real, n:int);
 for c=n to 1 do comment loop backwards
  NWTreconst(col c of a, n);
 endfor;
 for r=1 to n do
  NWTreconst(row r of a, n);
 endfor;
end;
```

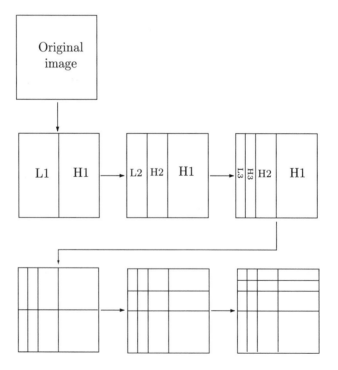

Figure 5.14: The Standard Image Wavelet Transform and Decomposition.

```
procedure NStdCalc(a:array of real, n:int);
 a:=a/√n̄ comment divide entire array
 j:=n;
 while j≥ 2 do
  for r=1 to j do NWTstep(row r of a, j);
  endfor;
  for c=j to 1 do comment loop backwards
   NWTstep(col c of a, j);
  endfor;
  j:=j/2;
 endwhile;
end;
procedure NStdReconst(a:array of real, n:int);
 j:=2;
 while j≤n do
  for c=j to 1 do comment loop backwards
   NWTRstep(col c of a, j);
  endfor;
  for r=1 to j do
   NWTRstep(row r of a, j);
  endfor;
  j:=2j;
 endwhile
 a:=a√n̄; comment multiply entire array
end;
```

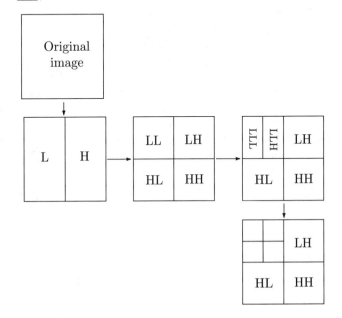

Figure 5.15: The Pyramid Image Wavelet Transform.

```
12 12 12 12 14 12 12 12     12 12 13 12 | 0 0 2 0     12 12 13 12 | 0 0 2 0
12 12 12 12 14 12 12 12     12 12 13 12 | 0 0 2 0     12 12 13 12 | 0 0 2 0
12 12 12 12 14 12 12 12     12 12 13 12 | 0 0 2 0     14 14 14 14 | 0 0 0 0
12 12 12 12 14 12 12 12     12 12 13 12 | 0 0 2 0     12 12 13 12 | 0 0 2 0
12 12 12 12 14 12 12 12     12 12 13 12 | 0 0 2 0      0  0  0  0 | 0 0 0 0
16 16 16 16 14 16 16 16     16 16 15 16 | 0 0 2 0      0  0  0  0 | 0 0 0 0
12 12 12 12 14 12 12 12     12 12 13 12 | 0 0 2 0      4  4  2  4 | 0 0 4 0
12 12 12 12 14 12 12 12     12 12 13 12 | 0 0 2 0      0  0  0  0 | 0 0 0 0
         (a)                      (b)                      (c)
```

Figure 5.16: An 8×8 Image and its Subband Decomposition.

and LH, respectively (Figures 5.15 and 5.55, although there is inconsistency in the use of this notation by various authors). The lower-right subband, denoted by HH, reflects diagonal image artifacts (which our example image lacks). Most interesting is the upper-left subband, denoted by LL, that consists entirely of averages. This subband is a one-quarter version of the entire image, containing traces of both the vertical and the horizontal lines.

⋄ **Exercise 5.4:** Construct a diagram similar to Figure 5.16 to show how subband HH reflects diagonal artifacts of the image.

Figure 5.55 shows four levels of subbands, where level 1 contains the detailed features of the image (also referred to as the high-frequency or fine-resolution wavelet coefficients) and the top level, level 4, contains the coarse image features (low-frequency or coarse-resolution coefficients). It is clear that the lower levels can be quantized coarsely without much loss of important image information, while the higher levels should be quantized finely. The subband structure is the basis of all the image compression methods that use the wavelet transform.

Figure 5.17 shows typical results of the pyramid wavelet transform. The original image is shown in Figure 5.17a, and Figure 5.17c is a general pyramid decomposition. In order to illustrate how the pyramid transform works, this image consists only of horizontal, vertical, and slanted lines. The four quadrants of Figure 5.17b show smaller versions of the image. The top-left subband, containing the averages, is similar to the entire image, while each of the other three subbands shows image details. Because of the way the pyramid transform is constructed, the top-right subband contains vertical details, the bottom-left subband contains horizontal details, and the bottom-right one contains the details of slanted lines. Figure 5.17c shows the results of repeatedly applying this transform. The image is transformed into subbands of horizontal, vertical, and diagonal details, while the top-left subsquare, containing the averages, is shrunk to a single pixel.

Section 4.4 discusses image transforms. It should be mentioned that there are two main types of transforms, *orthogonal* and *subband*. An orthogonal linear transform is done by computing the *inner product* of the data (pixel values or sound samples) with a set of *basis functions*. The result is a set of transform coefficients that can later be quantized or compressed with RLE, Huffman coding, or other methods. Several examples of important orthogonal transforms, such as

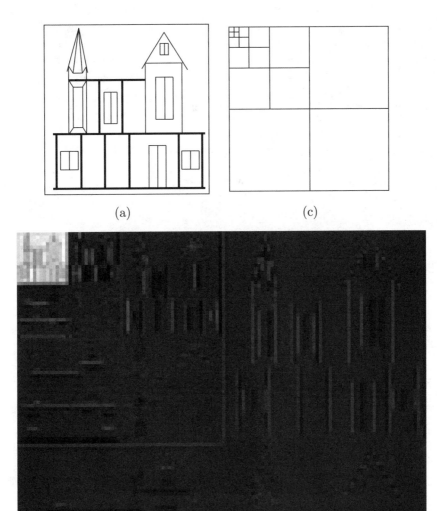

Figure 5.17: An Example of the Pyramid Image Wavelet Transform.

the DCT, the WHT, and the KLT, are described in detail in Section 4.4. The Fourier transform also belongs in this category. It is discussed in Section 5.1.

The other main type is the *subband transform*. It is done by computing a convolution of the data (Section 5.7 and appendix in the book's web site) with a set of *bandpass filters*. Each resulting subband encodes a particular portion of the frequency content of the data.

As a reminder, the discrete inner product of the two vectors f_i and g_i is defined by

$$\langle f, g \rangle = \sum_i f_i \, g_i.$$

The discrete convolution h is defined by Equation (5.5):

$$h_i = f \star g = \sum_j f_j \, g_{i-j}. \tag{5.5}$$

(Each element h_i of the discrete convolution h is the sum of products. It depends on i in the special way shown.)

Either method, standard or uniform, results in a transformed—although not yet compressed—image that has one average at the top-left corner and smaller numbers, differences, or averages of differences everywhere else. This can now be compressed using a combination of methods, such as RLE, move-to-front, and Huffman coding. If lossy compression is acceptable, some of the smallest differences can be quantized or even set to zeros, which creates run lengths of zeros, making the use of RLE even more attractive.

> Whiter foam than thine, O wave,
> Wavelet never wore,
> Stainless wave; and now you lave
> The far and stormless shore —
> Ever — ever — evermore!
> —Abram J. Ryan, *Poems*

Color Images: So far we have assumed that each pixel is a single number (i.e., we have a single-component image, in which all pixels are shades of the same color, normally gray). Any compression method for single-component images can be extended to color (three-component) images by separating the three components, then transforming and compressing each individually. If the compression method is lossy, it makes sense to convert the three image components from their original color representation, which is normally RGB, to the YIQ color representation. The Y component of this representation is called *luminance*, and the I and Q (the chrominance) components are responsible for the color information [Salomon 99]. The advantage of this color representation is that the human eye is most sensitive to Y and least sensitive to Q. A lossy method should therefore leave the Y component alone and delete some data from the I, and more data from the Q components, resulting in good compression and in a loss for which the eye is not that sensitive.

It is interesting to note that U.S. color television transmission also takes advantage of the YIQ representation. Signals are broadcast with bandwidths of 4 MHz for Y, 1.5 MHz for I, and only 0.6 MHz for Q.

5.6.2 Properties of the Haar Transform

The examples in this section illustrate some properties of the Haar transform, and of the discrete wavelet transform in general. Figure 5.18 shows a highly correlated 8×8 image and its Haar wavelet transform. Both the grayscale and numeric values of the pixels and the *transform coefficients* are shown. Because the original image is so correlated, the wavelet coefficients are small and there are many zeros.

⋄ **Exercise 5.5:** A glance at Figure 5.18 suggests that the last sentence is wrong. The wavelet transform coefficients listed in the figure are very large compared to the pixel values of the original image. In fact, we know that the top-left Haar transform coefficient should be the average of all the image pixels. Since the pixels of our image have values that are (more or less) uniformly distributed in the interval $[0, 255]$, this average should be around 128, yet the top-left transform coefficient is 1051. Explain this!

In a discrete wavelet transform, most of the wavelet coefficients are details (or differences). The details in the lower levels represent the fine details of the image. As we move higher in the subband level, we find details that correspond to coarser image features. Figure 5.19a illustrates this concept. It shows an image that is smooth on the left and has "activity" (i.e., adjacent pixels that tend to be different) on the right. Part (b) shows the wavelet transform of the image. Low levels (corresponding to fine details) have transform coefficients on the right, since this is where the image activity is located. High levels (coarse details) look similar but also have coefficients on the left side, since the image is not completely blank on the left.

The Haar transform is the simplest wavelet transform, but even this simple method illustrates the power of the wavelet transform. It turns out that the low levels of the discrete wavelet transform contain the unimportant image features, so quantizing or discarding these coefficients can lead to lossy compression that is both efficient and of high quality. Many times, the image can be reconstructed from very few transform coefficients without any noticeable loss of quality. Figure 5.20a–c shows three reconstructions of the simple 8×8 image of Figure 5.18. They were obtained from only 32, 13, and 5 wavelet coefficients, respectively.

Figure 5.21 is a similar example. It shows a bi-level image fully reconstructed from just 4% of its transform coefficients (653 coefficients out of 128×128).

Experimenting is the key to understanding these concepts. Proper mathematical software makes it easy to input images and experiment with various features of the discrete wavelet transform. In order to help the interested reader, Figure 5.22 lists a Matlab program that inputs an image, computes its Haar wavelet transform, discards a given percentage of the smallest transform coefficients, then computes the inverse transform to reconstruct the image.

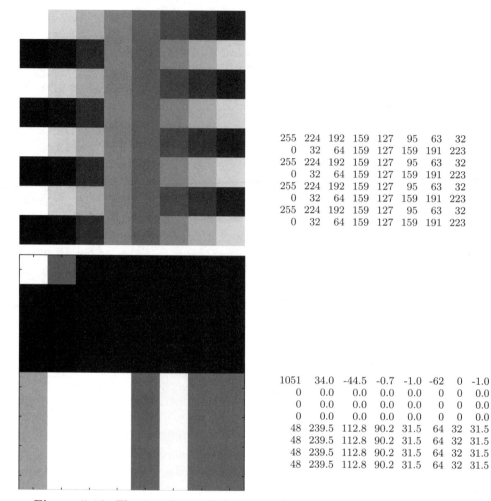

255	224	192	159	127	95	63	32
0	32	64	159	127	159	191	223
255	224	192	159	127	95	63	32
0	32	64	159	127	159	191	223
255	224	192	159	127	95	63	32
0	32	64	159	127	159	191	223
255	224	192	159	127	95	63	32
0	32	64	159	127	159	191	223

1051	34.0	-44.5	-0.7	-1.0	-62	0	-1.0
0	0.0	0.0	0.0	0.0	0	0	0.0
0	0.0	0.0	0.0	0.0	0	0	0.0
0	0.0	0.0	0.0	0.0	0	0	0.0
48	239.5	112.8	90.2	31.5	64	32	31.5
48	239.5	112.8	90.2	31.5	64	32	31.5
48	239.5	112.8	90.2	31.5	64	32	31.5
48	239.5	112.8	90.2	31.5	64	32	31.5

Figure 5.18: The 8×8 Image Reconstructed in Figure 5.20 and its Haar Transform.

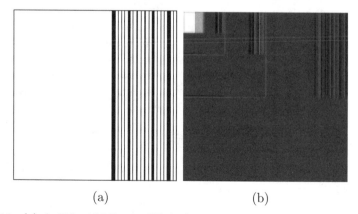

(a)   (b)

Figure 5.19: (a) A 128×128 Image With Activity On the Right. (b) Its Transform.

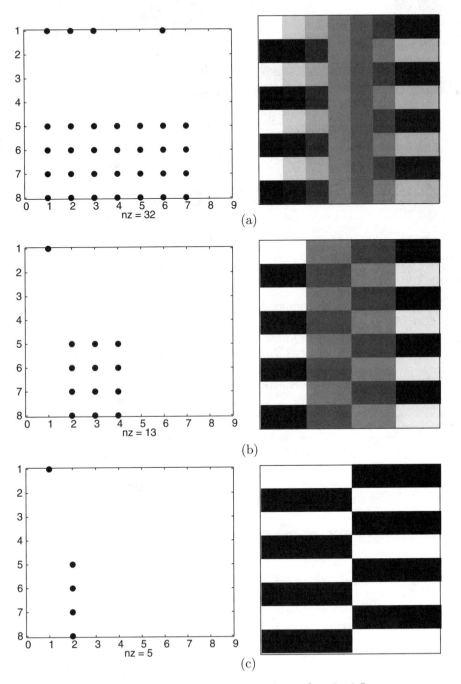

Figure 5.20: Three Lossy Reconstructions of an 8×8 Image.

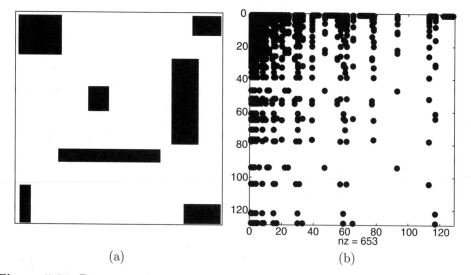

$$\text{(a)} \hspace{6cm} \text{(b)}$$

Figure 5.21: Reconstructing a 128×128 Simple Image From 4% of Its Coefficients.

Lossy wavelet image compression involves the discarding of coefficients, so the concept of *sparseness ratio* is defined to measure the amount of coefficients discarded. It is defined as the number of nonzero wavelet coefficients divided by the number of coefficients left after some are discarded. The higher the sparseness ratio, the fewer coefficients are left. Higher sparseness ratios lead to better compression but may result in poorly reconstructed images. The sparseness ratio is distantly related to *compression factor*, a compression measure defined in the Preface.

> And just like the wavelet that moans on the beach,
> And, sighing, sinks back to the sea,
> So my song—it just touches the rude shores of speech,
> And its music melts back into me.
> —Abram J. Ryan, *Poems*

The line "filename='lena128'; dim=128;" contains the image file name and the dimension of the image. The image files used by the author were in raw form and contained just the grayscale values, each as a single byte. There is no header, and not even the image resolution (number of rows and columns) is contained in the file. However, Matlab can read other types of files. The image is assumed to be square, and parameter "dim" should be a power of 2. The assignment "thresh=" specifies the percentage of transform coefficients to be deleted. This provides an easy was to experiment with lossy wavelet image compression.

File "harmatt.m" contains two functions that compute the Haar wavelet coefficients in a matrix form (Section 5.6.3).

```
clear; % main program
filename='lena128'; dim=128;
fid=fopen(filename,'r');
if fid==-1 disp('file not found')
else img=fread(fid,[dim,dim])'; fclose(fid);
end
thresh=0.0;        % percent of transform coefficients deleted
figure(1), imagesc(img), colormap(gray), axis off, axis square
w=harmatt(dim); % compute the Haar dim x dim transform matrix
timg=w*img*w';    % forward Haar transform
tsort=sort(abs(timg(:)));
tthresh=tsort(floor(max(thresh*dim*dim,1)));
cim=timg.*(abs(timg) > tthresh);
[i,j,s]=find(cim);
dimg=sparse(i,j,s,dim,dim);
% figure(2) displays the remaining transform coefficients
%figure(2), spy(dimg), colormap(gray), axis square
figure(2), image(dimg), colormap(gray), axis square
cimg=full(w'*sparse(dimg)*w);       % inverse Haar transform
density = nnz(dimg);
disp([num2str(100*thresh) '% of smallest coefficients deleted.'])
disp([num2str(density) ' coefficients remain out of ' ...
 num2str(dim) 'x' num2str(dim) '.'])
figure(3), imagesc(cimg), colormap(gray), axis off, axis square

File harmatt.m with two functions

function x = harmatt(dim)
num=log2(dim);
p = sparse(eye(dim)); q = p;
i=1;
while i<=dim/2;
 q(1:2*i,1:2*i) = sparse(individ(2*i));
 p=p*q; i=2*i;
end
x=sparse(p);

function f=individ(n)
x=[1, 1]/sqrt(2);
y=[1,-1]/sqrt(2);
while min(size(x)) < n/2
 x=[x, zeros(min(size(x)),max(size(x)));...
   zeros(min(size(x)),max(size(x))), x];
end
while min(size(y)) < n/2
 y=[y, zeros(min(size(y)),max(size(y)));...
   zeros(min(size(y)),max(size(y))), y];
end
f=[x;y];
```

Figure 5.22: Matlab Code for the Haar Transform of An Image.

(A technical note: A Matlab m file can contain commands or a function but not both. It may, however, contain more than one function, provided that only the top function is invoked from outside the file. All the other functions must be called from within the file. In our case, function harmatt(dim) calls function individ(n).)

◊ **Exercise 5.6:** Use the code of Figure 5.22 (or similar code) to compute the Haar transform of the "Lena" image (Figure 4.38) and reconstruct it three times by discarding more and more detail coefficients.

5.6.3 A Matrix Approach

The principle of the Haar transform is to calculate averages and differences. It turns out that this can be done by means of matrix multiplication. As an example, we look at the top row of the simple 8×8 image of Figure 5.18. Anyone with a little experience using matrices can construct a matrix that when multiplied by this vector creates a vector with four averages and four differences. Matrix A_1 of Equation (5.6) does that and, when multiplied by the top row of pixels of Figure 5.18, generates $(239.5, 15.5, 192, 159, 127, 95, 63, 32)$. Similarly, matrices A_2 and A_3 perform the second and third steps of the transform, respectively. The results are shown in Equation (5.7):

$$A_1 = \begin{pmatrix} \frac{1}{2} & \frac{1}{2} & 0 & 0 & 0 & 0 & 0 & 0 \\ 0 & 0 & \frac{1}{2} & \frac{1}{2} & 0 & 0 & 0 & 0 \\ 0 & 0 & 0 & 0 & \frac{1}{2} & \frac{1}{2} & 0 & 0 \\ 0 & 0 & 0 & 0 & 0 & 0 & \frac{1}{2} & \frac{1}{2} \\ \frac{1}{2} & -\frac{1}{2} & 0 & 0 & 0 & 0 & 0 & 0 \\ 0 & 0 & \frac{1}{2} & -\frac{1}{2} & 0 & 0 & 0 & 0 \\ 0 & 0 & 0 & 0 & \frac{1}{2} & -\frac{1}{2} & 0 & 0 \\ 0 & 0 & 0 & 0 & 0 & 0 & \frac{1}{2} & -\frac{1}{2} \end{pmatrix}, \quad A_1 \begin{pmatrix} 255 \\ 224 \\ 192 \\ 159 \\ 127 \\ 95 \\ 63 \\ 32 \end{pmatrix} = \begin{pmatrix} 239.5 \\ 175.5 \\ 111.0 \\ 47.5 \\ 15.5 \\ 16.5 \\ 16.0 \\ 15.5 \end{pmatrix}, \quad (5.6)$$

$$A_2 = \begin{pmatrix} \frac{1}{2} & \frac{1}{2} & 0 & 0 & 0 & 0 & 0 & 0 \\ 0 & 0 & \frac{1}{2} & \frac{1}{2} & 0 & 0 & 0 & 0 \\ \frac{1}{2} & -\frac{1}{2} & 0 & 0 & 0 & 0 & 0 & 0 \\ 0 & 0 & \frac{1}{2} & -\frac{1}{2} & 0 & 0 & 0 & 0 \\ 0 & 0 & 0 & 0 & 1 & 0 & 0 & 0 \\ 0 & 0 & 0 & 0 & 0 & 1 & 0 & 0 \\ 0 & 0 & 0 & 0 & 0 & 0 & 1 & 0 \\ 0 & 0 & 0 & 0 & 0 & 0 & 0 & 1 \end{pmatrix}, \quad A_3 = \begin{pmatrix} \frac{1}{2} & \frac{1}{2} & 0 & 0 & 0 & 0 & 0 & 0 \\ \frac{1}{2} & -\frac{1}{2} & 0 & 0 & 0 & 0 & 0 & 0 \\ 0 & 0 & 1 & 0 & 0 & 0 & 0 & 0 \\ 0 & 0 & 0 & 1 & 0 & 0 & 0 & 0 \\ 0 & 0 & 0 & 0 & 1 & 0 & 0 & 0 \\ 0 & 0 & 0 & 0 & 0 & 1 & 0 & 0 \\ 0 & 0 & 0 & 0 & 0 & 0 & 1 & 0 \\ 0 & 0 & 0 & 0 & 0 & 0 & 0 & 1 \end{pmatrix},$$

$$A_2 \begin{pmatrix} 239.5 \\ 15.5 \\ 192.0 \\ 159.0 \\ 127.0 \\ 95.0 \\ 63.0 \\ 32.0 \end{pmatrix} = \begin{pmatrix} 207.5 \\ 79.25 \\ 32.0 \\ 31.75 \\ 15.5 \\ 16.5 \\ 16.0 \\ 15.5 \end{pmatrix}, \quad A_3 \begin{pmatrix} 207.5 \\ 79.25 \\ 32.0 \\ 31.75 \\ 15.5 \\ 16.5 \\ 16.0 \\ 15.5 \end{pmatrix} = \begin{pmatrix} 143.375 \\ 64.125 \\ 32. \\ 31.75 \\ 15.5 \\ 16.5 \\ 16. \\ 15.5 \end{pmatrix}. \quad (5.7)$$

Instead of calculating averages and differences, all we have to do is construct matrices A_1, A_2, and A_3, multiply them to get $W = A_1 A_2 A_3$, and apply W to all the columns of the image I by multiplying $W \cdot I$:

$$W \begin{pmatrix} 255 \\ 224 \\ 192 \\ 159 \\ 127 \\ 95 \\ 63 \\ 32 \end{pmatrix} = \begin{pmatrix} \frac{1}{8} & \frac{1}{8} & \frac{1}{8} & \frac{1}{8} & \frac{1}{8} & \frac{1}{8} & \frac{1}{8} & \frac{1}{8} \\ \frac{1}{8} & \frac{1}{8} & \frac{1}{8} & \frac{1}{8} & \frac{-1}{8} & \frac{-1}{8} & \frac{-1}{8} & \frac{-1}{8} \\ \frac{1}{4} & \frac{1}{4} & \frac{-1}{4} & \frac{-1}{4} & 0 & 0 & 0 & 0 \\ 0 & 0 & 0 & 0 & \frac{1}{4} & \frac{1}{4} & \frac{-1}{4} & \frac{-1}{4} \\ \frac{1}{2} & \frac{-1}{2} & 0 & 0 & 0 & 0 & 0 & 0 \\ 0 & 0 & \frac{1}{2} & \frac{-1}{2} & 0 & 0 & 0 & 0 \\ 0 & 0 & 0 & 0 & \frac{1}{2} & \frac{-1}{2} & 0 & 0 \\ 0 & 0 & 0 & 0 & 0 & 0 & \frac{1}{2} & \frac{-1}{2} \end{pmatrix} \begin{pmatrix} 255 \\ 224 \\ 192 \\ 159 \\ 127 \\ 95 \\ 63 \\ 32 \end{pmatrix} = \begin{pmatrix} 143.375 \\ 64.125 \\ 32 \\ 31.75 \\ 15.5 \\ 16.5 \\ 16 \\ 15.5 \end{pmatrix}.$$

This, of course, is only half the job. In order to compute the complete transform, we still have to apply W to the rows of the product $W \cdot I$, and we do this by applying it to the columns of the transpose $(W \cdot I)^T$, then transposing the result. Thus, the complete transform is (see line `timg=w*img*w'` in Figure 5.22)

$$I_{\text{tr}} = \left(W(W \cdot I)^T \right)^T = W \cdot I \cdot W^T.$$

The inverse transform is done by

$$W^{-1}(W^{-1} \cdot I_{\text{tr}}^T)^T = W^{-1}\left(I_{\text{tr}} \cdot (W^{-1})^T \right),$$

and this is where the normalized Haar transform (mentioned on page 477) becomes important. Instead of calculating averages [quantities of the form $(d_i + d_{i+1})/2$] and differences [quantities of the form $(d_i - d_{i+1})/2$], it is better to use the quantities $(d_i + d_{i+1})/\sqrt{2}$ and $(d_i - d_{i+1})/\sqrt{2}$. This results is an *orthonormal* matrix W, and it is well known that the inverse of such a matrix is simply its transpose. Thus, we can write the inverse transform in the simple form $W^T \cdot I_{\text{tr}} \cdot W$ [see line `cimg=full(w'*sparse(dimg)*w)` in Figure 5.22].

In between the forward and inverse transforms, some transform coefficients may be quantized or deleted. Alternatively, matrix I_{tr} may be compressed by means of run length encoding and/or Huffman codes.

Function `individ(n)` of Figure 5.22 starts with a 2×2 Haar transform matrix (notice that it uses $\sqrt{2}$ instead of 2), then uses it to construct as many individual matrices A_i as necessary. Function `harmatt(dim)` combines those individual matrices to form the final Haar matrix for an image of `dim` rows and `dim` columns.

$\diamond$ **Exercise 5.7:** Perform the calculation $W \cdot I \cdot W^T$ for the 8×8 image of Figure 5.18.

Bibliography

Mulcahy, Colm (1996) "Plotting and Scheming with Wavelets," *Mathematics Magazine*, **69**(5):323–343, December. Also available as http://www.spelman.edu/~colm/csam.ps.

Mulcahy, Colm (1997) "Image Compression Using the Haar Wavelet Transform," *Spelman College Science and Mathematics Journal*, **1**(1):22–31, April. Also available as `http://www.spelman.edu/~colm/wav.ps`. (It has been claimed that any smart 15 year old could follow this introduction to wavelets.)

Stollnitz, E. J., T. D. DeRose, and D. H. Salesin (1996) *Wavelets for Computer Graphics*, San Francisco, CA, Morgan Kaufmann.

5.7 Filter Banks

The matrix approach to the Haar transform is used here to introduce the reader to the idea of *filter banks*. This section shows how the Haar transform can be interpreted as a bank of two filters, a lowpass and a highpass. We explain the terms "filter," "lowpass," and "highpass" and show how the idea of filter banks leads naturally to the concept of *subband transform*. The Haar transform, of course, is the simplest wavelet transform, so it is used here to illustrate the new concepts. However, using it as a filter bank may not be very efficient. Most practical applications of wavelet filters use more sophisticated sets of filter coefficients, but they are all based on the concept of filters and filter banks.

A *filter* is a linear operator defined in terms of its *filter coefficients* $h(0)$, $h(1)$, $h(2), \ldots$. It can be applied to an input vector x to produce an output vector y according to

$$y(n) = \sum_k h(k)x(n-k) = h \star x,$$

where the symbol $\star$ indicates a convolution (see appendix in the book's web site). Notice that the limits of the sum above have not been stated explicitly. They depend on the sizes of vectors x and h. Since our independent variable is the time t, it is convenient to assume that the inputs (and, as a result, also the outputs) come at all times $t = \ldots, -2, -1, 0, 1, 2, \ldots$. Thus, we use the notation

$$x = (\ldots, a, b, c, d, e, \ldots),$$

where the central value c is the input at time zero [$c = x(0)$], values d and e are the inputs at times 1 and 2, respectively, and $b = x(-1)$ and $a = x(-2)$. In practice, the inputs are always finite, so the infinite vector x will have only a finite number of nonzero elements.

Deeper insight into the behavior of a linear filter can be gained by considering the simple input $x = (\ldots, 0, 0, 1, 0, 0, \ldots)$. This input is zero at all times except at $t = 0$. It is called a *unit pulse* or a *unit impulse*. Even though the limits of the sum in the convolution have not been specified, it is easy to see that for any n there is only one nonzero term in the sum, so $y(n) = h(n)x(0) = h(n)$. We say that the output $y(n) = h(n)$ at time n is the *response* at time n to the unit impulse $x(0) = 1$. Since the number of filter coefficients $h(i)$ is finite, the filter is a *finite impulse response* or FIR.

Figure 5.23 shows the basic idea of a filter bank. It shows an *analysis bank* consisting of two filters, a lowpass filter H_0 and a highpass filter H_1. The lowpass filter employs convolution to remove the high frequencies from the input signal x and let the low frequencies go through. The highpass filter does the opposite. Together, they separate the input into *frequency bands*.

The input x can be a one-dimensional signal (a vector of real numbers, which is what we assume in this section) or a two-dimensional signal, an image. The elements $x(n)$ of x are fed into the filters one by one, and each filter computes and outputs one number $y(n)$ in response to $x(n)$. The number of responses is therefore double the number of inputs (since we have two filters); a bad result, since we are interested in data compression. To correct this situation, each filter is followed by a *downsampling* process where the odd-numbered outputs are thrown away. This operation is also called *decimation* and is represented by the boxes marked "$\downarrow 2$". After decimation, the number of outputs from the two filters together equals the number of inputs.

Notice that the filter bank described here, followed by decimation, performs exactly the same calculations as matrix $W = A_1 A_2 A_3$ of Section 5.6.3. Filter banks are just a more general way of looking at the Haar transform (or, in general, at the discrete wavelet transform). We look at this transform as a filtering operation, followed by decimation, and we can then try to find better filters.

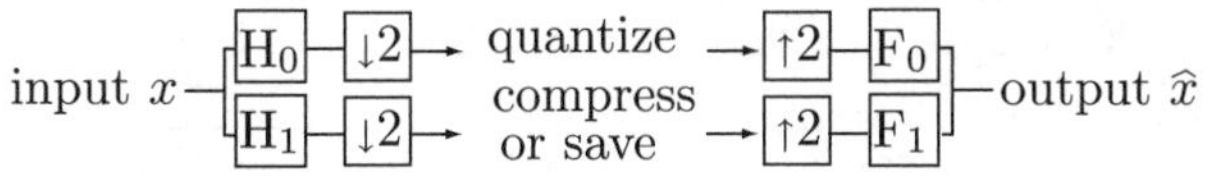

Figure 5.23: A Two-Channel Filter Bank.

The reason for having a bank of filters as opposed to just one filter is that several filters working together, with downsampling, can exhibit behavior that is impossible to get with just a single filter. The most important feature of a filter bank is its ability to reconstruct the input from the outputs $H_0 x$ and $H_1 x$, even though each has been decimated.

Downsampling is not time invariant. After downsampling, the output is the even-numbered values $y(0)$, $y(2)$, $y(4)$,..., but if we delay the inputs by one time unit, the new outputs will be $y(-1)$, $y(1)$, $y(3)$,..., and these are different from and independent of the original outputs. These two sequences of signals are two phases of vector y.

The outputs of the analysis bank are called *subband coefficients*. They can be quantized (if lossy compression is acceptable), and they can be compressed by means of RLE, Huffman, arithmetic coding, or any other method. Eventually, they are fed into the *synthesis bank*, where they are first upsampled (by inserting zeros for each odd-numbered coefficient that was thrown away), then passed through the inverse filters F_0 and F_1, and finally combined to form a single output vector $\hat{x}$. The output of each analysis filter (after decimation) is

$$(\downarrow y) = (\ldots, y(-4), y(-2), y(0), y(2), y(4), \ldots).$$

Upsampling inserts zeros for the decimated values, so it converts the output vector above to

$$(\uparrow y) = (\ldots, y(-4), 0, y(-2), 0, y(0), 0, y(2), 0, y(4), 0, \ldots).$$

Downsampling causes loss of data. Upsampling alone cannot compensate for it, because it simply inserts zeros for the missing data. In order to achieve lossless reconstruction of the original signal x, the filters have to be designed such that they compensate for this loss of data. One feature that is commonly used in the design of good filters is *orthogonality*. Figure 5.24 shows a set of orthogonal filters of size 4. The filters of the set are orthogonal because their dot product is zero

$$(a, b, c, d) \cdot (d, -c, b, -a) = 0.$$

Notice how similar H_0 and F_0 are (and also H_1 and F_1). It still remains, of course, to choose actual values for the four *filter coefficients* a, b, c, and d. A full discussion of this is outside the scope of this book, but Section 5.7.1 illustrates some of the methods and rules used in practice to determine the values of various filter coefficients. An example is the Daubechies D4 filter, whose values are listed in Equation (5.11).

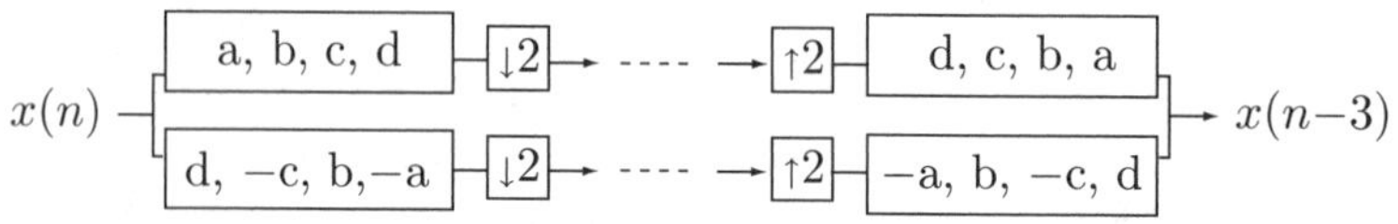

Figure 5.24: An Orthogonal Filter Bank with Four Filter Coefficients.

Simulating the operation of this filter manually shows that the reconstructed input is identical to the original input but lags three time units behind it.

A filter bank can also be *biorthogonal*, a less restricted type of filter. Figure 5.25 shows an example of such a set of filters that can reconstruct a signal exactly. Notice the similarity of H_0 and F_1 and also of H_1 and F_0.

Figure 5.25: A Biorthogonal Filter Bank With Perfect Reconstruction.

We already know, from the discussion in Section 5.6, that the outputs of the lowpass filter H_0 are normally passed through the analysis filter several times, creating shorter and shorter outputs. This recursive process can be illustrated as a tree (Figure 5.26). Since each node of this tree produces half the number of outputs as its predecessor, the tree is called a *logarithmic tree*. Figure 5.26 shows how the scaling function $\phi(t)$ and the wavelet $\psi(t)$ are obtained at the limit of the logarithmic tree. This is the connection between the discrete wavelet transform (using filter banks) and the CWT.

As we "climb" up the logarithmic tree from level i to the next finer level $i+1$, we compute the new averages from the new, higher-resolution scaling functions

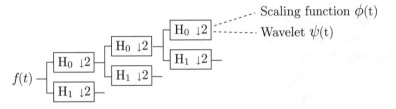

Figure 5.26: Scaling Function and Wavelet As Limits of a Logarithmic Tree.

$\phi(2^i t - k)$ and the new details from the new wavelets $\psi(2^i t - k)$

signal at level i (averages) $\searrow$

$+$ signal at level $i + 1$

details at level i (differences) $\nearrow$

Each level of the tree corresponds to twice the frequency (or twice the resolution) of the preceding level, which is why the logarithmic tree is also called a *multiresolution tree*. Successive filtering through the tree separates lower and lower frequencies.

People who do quantitative work with sound and music know that two tones at frequencies ω and 2ω sound like the same note and differ only by pitch. The frequency interval between ω and 2ω is divided into 12 subintervals (the so called *chromatic scale*), but Western music has a tradition of favoring just eight of the twelve tones that result from this division (a *diatonic scale*, made up of seven notes, with the eighth note as the "octave"). This is why the basic frequency interval used in music is traditionally called an *octave*. We therefore say that adjacent levels of the multiresolution tree differ in an octave of frequencies.

In order to understand the meaning of *lowpass* and *highpass* we need to work in the frequency domain, where the convolution of two vectors is replaced by a multiplication of their Fourier transforms. The vector $x(n)$ is in the time domain, so its frequency domain equivalent is its discrete Fourier transform (Equation (5.1))

$$X(\omega) \stackrel{\text{def}}{=} X(e^{i\omega}) = \sum_{-\infty}^{\infty} x(n)e^{-in\omega},$$

which is sometimes written in the z-domain,

$$X(z) = \sum_{-\infty}^{\infty} x(n)z^{-n},$$

where $z \stackrel{\text{def}}{=} e^{i\omega}$. The convolution by h in the time domain now becomes a multiplication by the function $H(\omega) = \sum h(n)e^{-in\omega}$ in the frequency domain, so we can express the output in the frequency domain by

$$Y(e^{i\omega}) = H(e^{i\omega})X(e^{i\omega}),$$

or, in reduced notation, $Y(\omega) = H(\omega)X(\omega)$, or, in the z-domain, $Y(z) = H(z)X(z)$. When all the inputs are $X(\omega) = 1$, the output at frequency ω is $Y(\omega) = H(\omega)$.

We can now understand the operation of the lowpass Haar filter. It works by averaging two consecutive inputs, so it produces the output

$$y(n) = \frac{1}{2}x(n) + \frac{1}{2}x(n-1). \tag{5.8}$$

This is a convolution with only the two terms $k = 0$ and $k = 1$ in the sum. The filter coefficients are $h(0) = h(1) = 1/2$, and we can call the output a *moving average*, since each $y(n)$ depends on the current input and its predecessor. If the input is the unit impulse $x = (\ldots, 0, 0, 1, 0, 0, \ldots)$, then the output is $y(0) = y(1) = 1/2$, or $y = (\ldots, 0, 0, 1/2, 1/2, 0, \ldots)$. The output values are simply the filter coefficients as we saw earlier.

We can look at this averaging filter as the combination of an identity operator and a delay operator. The output produced by the identity operator equals the current input, while the output produced by the delay is the input one time unit earlier. Thus, we write

$$\text{averaging filter} = \frac{1}{2}(\text{identity}) + \frac{1}{2}(\text{delay}).$$

In matrix notation this can be expressed by

$$
\begin{pmatrix} \cdots \\ y(-1) \\ y(0) \\ y(1) \\ \cdots \end{pmatrix}
=
\begin{pmatrix}
\cdots & & & \\
\frac{1}{2} & \frac{1}{2} & & \\
& \frac{1}{2} & \frac{1}{2} & \\
& & \frac{1}{2} & \frac{1}{2} \\
& & & \cdots
\end{pmatrix}
\begin{pmatrix} \cdots \\ x(-1) \\ x(0) \\ x(1) \\ \cdots \end{pmatrix}.
$$

The $1/2$ values on the main diagonal are copies of the weight of the identity operator. They all equal the $h(0)$ Haar filter coefficient. The $1/2$ values on the diagonal below are copies of the weights of the delay operator. They all equal the $h(1)$ Haar filter coefficient. Thus, the matrix is a *constant diagonal* matrix (or a *banded* matrix). A wavelet filter that has a coefficient $h(3)$ would correspond to a matrix where this filter coefficient appears on the second diagonal below the main diagonal. The rule of matrix multiplication produces the familiar convolution

$$y(n) = h(0)x(n) + h(1)x(n-1) + h(2)x(n-2) + \cdots = \sum_k h(k)x(n-k).$$

Notice that the matrix is lower triangular. The upper diagonal, which would naturally correspond to the filter coefficients $h(-1)$, $h(-2), \ldots$, is zero. All filter coefficients with negative indices must be zero, since such coefficients lead to outputs that precede the inputs in time. In the real world, we are used to a cause preceding its effect, so our finite impulse response filters should also be *causal*.

Summary: A causal FIR filter with $N+1$ filter coefficients $h(0), h(1), \ldots, h(N)$ (a filter with $N + 1$ "taps") has $h(i) = 0$ for all negative i and for $i > N$. When expressed in terms of a matrix, the matrix is lower triangular and banded. Such filters are commonly used and are important.

From the Dictionary

Tap (noun).
1. A cylindrical plug or stopper for closing an opening through which liquid is drawn, as in a cask; spigot.
2. A faucet or cock.
3. A connection made at an intermediate point on an electrical circuit or device.
4. An act or instance of wiretapping.

To illustrate the frequency response of a filter we select an input vector of the form

$$x(n) = e^{in\omega} = \cos(n\omega) + i\sin(n\omega), \text{ for } -\infty < n < \infty.$$

This is a complex function whose real and imaginary parts are a cosine and a sine, respectively, both with frequency ω. Recall that the Fourier transform of a pulse contains all the frequencies (Figure 5.2d,e), but the Fourier transform of a sine wave has just one frequency. The smallest frequency is $\omega = 0$, for which the vector becomes $x = (\ldots, 1, 1, 1, 1, 1, \ldots)$. The highest frequency is $\omega = \pi$, where the same vector becomes $x = (\ldots, 1, -1, 1, -1, 1, \ldots)$. The special feature of this input is that the output vector $y(n)$ is a multiple of the input.

For the moving average, the output (filter response) is

$$y(n) = \frac{1}{2}x(n) + \frac{1}{2}x(n-1) = \frac{1}{2}e^{in\omega} + \frac{1}{2}e^{i(n-1)\omega} = \left(\frac{1}{2} + \frac{1}{2}e^{-i\omega}\right)e^{in\omega} = H(\omega)x(n),$$

where $H(\omega) = (\frac{1}{2} + \frac{1}{2}e^{-i\omega})$ is the *frequency response function* of the filter. Since $H(0) = 1/2 + 1/2 = 1$, we see that the input $x = (\ldots, 1, 1, 1, 1, 1, \ldots)$ is transformed to itself. Also, $H(\omega)$ for small values of ω generates output that is very similar to the input. This filter "lets" the low frequencies go through, hence the name "lowpass filter." For $\omega = \pi$, the input is $x = (\ldots, 1, -1, 1, -1, 1, \ldots)$ and the output is all zeros (since the average of 1 and -1 is zero). This lowpass filter smooths out the high-frequency regions (the bumps) of the input signal.

Notice that we can write

$$H(\omega) = \left(\cos\frac{\omega}{2}\right)e^{i\omega/2}.$$

When we plot the magnitude $|H(\omega)| = \cos(\omega/2)$ of $H(\omega)$ (Figure 5.27a), it is easy to see that it has a maximum at $\omega = 0$ (the lowest frequency) and two minima at $\omega = \pm\pi$ (the highest frequencies).

The highpass filter uses differences to pick up the high frequencies in the input signal, and reduces or removes the smooth (low frequency) parts. In the case of the

Haar transform, the highpass filter computes

$$y(n) = \frac{1}{2}x(n) - \frac{1}{2}x(n-1) = h \star x,$$

where the filter coefficients are $h(0) = 1/2$ and $h(1) = -1/2$, or

$$h = (\ldots, 0, 0, 1/2, -1/2, 0, \ldots).$$

In matrix notation this can be expressed by

$$\begin{pmatrix} \cdots \\ y(-1) \\ y(0) \\ y(1) \\ \cdots \end{pmatrix} = \begin{pmatrix} \cdots & & & & \\ -\frac{1}{2} & \frac{1}{2} & & & \\ & -\frac{1}{2} & \frac{1}{2} & & \\ & & -\frac{1}{2} & \frac{1}{2} & \\ & & & \cdots & \end{pmatrix} \begin{pmatrix} \cdots \\ x(-1) \\ x(0) \\ x(1) \\ \cdots \end{pmatrix}.$$

The main diagonal contains copies of $h(0)$, and the diagonal below contains $h(1)$. Using the identity and delay operator, this can also be written

$$\text{highpass filter} = \frac{1}{2}(\text{identity}) - \frac{1}{2}(\text{delay}).$$

Again selecting input $x(n) = e^{in\omega}$, it is easy to see that the output is

$$y(n) = \frac{1}{2}e^{in\omega} - \frac{1}{2}e^{i(n-1)\omega} = \left(\frac{1}{2} - \frac{1}{2}e^{-i\omega}\right)e^{-i\omega/2} = \sin(\omega/2)\,ie^{-i\omega/2}.$$

This time the highpass response function is

$$H_1(\omega) = \frac{1}{2} - \frac{1}{2}e^{-i\omega} = \frac{1}{2}\left(e^{i\omega/2} - e^{-i\omega/2}\right)e^{-i\omega/2} = \sin(\omega/2)\,e^{-i\omega/2}.$$

The magnitude is $|H_1(\omega)| = |\sin\left(\frac{\omega}{2}\right)|$. It is shown in Figure 5.27b, and it is obvious that it has a minimum for frequency zero and two maxima for large frequencies.

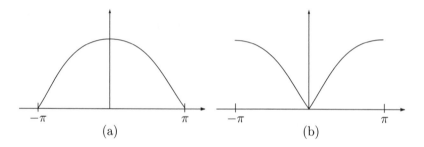

Figure 5.27: Magnitudes of (a) Lowpass and (b) Highpass Filters.

An important property of filter banks is that none of the individual filters are invertible, but the bank as a whole has to be designed such that the input signal could be perfectly reconstructed from the output in spite of the data loss caused by downsampling. It is easy to see, for example, that the constant signal $x = (\ldots, 1, 1, 1, 1, 1, \ldots)$ is transformed by the highpass filter H_1 to an output vector of all zeros. Obviously, there cannot exist an inverse filter H_1^{-1} that will be able to reconstruct the original input from a zero vector. The best that such an inverse transform can do is to use the zero vector to reconstruct another zero vector.

⋄ **Exercise 5.8:** Show an example of an input vector x that is transformed by the lowpass filter H_0 to a vector of all zeros.

Summary: The discussion of filter banks in this section should be compared to the discussion of image transforms in Section 4.4. Even though both sections describe transforms, they differ in their approach, since they describe different classes of transforms. Each of the transforms described in Section 4.4 is based on a set of *orthogonal* basis functions (or orthogonal basis images), and is computed as an inner product of the input signal with the basis functions. The result is a set of transform coefficients that are subsequently compressed either losslessly (by RLE or some entropy encoder) or lossily (by quantization followed by entropy coding).

This section deals with *subband transforms*, a different type of transform that is computed by taking the *convolution* of the input signal with a set of bandpass filters and decimating the results. Each decimated set of transform coefficients is a subband signal that encodes a specific range of the frequencies of the input. Reconstruction is done by upsampling, followed by computing the inverse transforms, and adding the resulting sets of outputs from the inverse filters.

The main advantage of subband transforms is that they isolate the different frequencies of the input signal, thereby making it possible for the user to precisely control the loss of data in each frequency range. In practice, such a transform decomposes an image into several subbands, corresponding to different image frequencies, and each subband can be quantized differently.

The main disadvantage of this type of transform is the introduction of artifacts, such as aliasing and ringing, into the reconstructed image, because of the downsampling. This is why the Haar transform is not satisfactory, and most of the research in this field has been aimed at finding better sets of filters.

Figure 5.28 shows a general subband filter bank with N bandpass filters and three stages. Notice how the output of the highpass filter H_0 of each stage is sent to the next stage for further decomposition, and how the combined output of the synthesis bank of a stage is sent to the top inverse filter of the synthesis bank of the preceding stage.

Bibliography

Simoncelli, Eero P. and Edward. H. Adelson (1990) "Subband Transforms," in John Woods, editor, *Subband Coding*, Boston, Kluwer Academic Press, 143–192.

Strang, Gilbert and Truong Nguyen (1996) *Wavelets and Filter Banks*, Wellesley, MA, Wellesley-Cambridge Press.

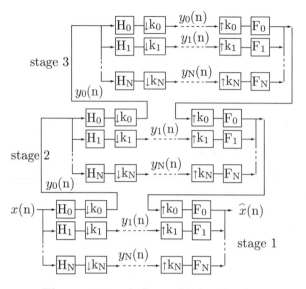

Figure 5.28: A General Filter Bank.

5.7.1 Deriving the Filter Coefficients

After presenting the basic operation of filter banks, the natural question is, How are the filter coefficients derived? A full answer is outside the scope of this book (see, for example, [Akansu and Haddad 92]), but this section provides a glimpse at the rules and methods used to figure out the values of various filter banks.

Given a set of two forward and two inverse N-tap filters H_0 and H_1, and F_0 and F_1 (where N is even), we denote their coefficients by

$$h_0 = \big(h_0(0), h_0(1), \ldots, h_0(N-1)\big), \quad h_1 = \big(h_1(0), h_1(1), \ldots, h_1(N-1)\big),$$
$$f_0 = \big(f_0(0), f_0(1), \ldots, f_0(N-1)\big), \quad f_1 = \big(f_1(0), f_1(1), \ldots, f_1(N-1)\big).$$

The four vectors h_0, h_1, f_0, and f_1 are the *impulse responses* of the four filters. The simplest set of conditions that these quantities have to satisfy is:

1. Normalization: Vector h_0 is normalized (i.e., its length is one unit).
2. Orthogonality: For any integer i that satisfies $1 \leq i < N/2$, the vector formed by the first $2i$ elements of h_0 should be orthogonal to the vector formed by the last $2i$ elements of the same h_0.
3. Vector f_0 is the reverse of h_0.
4. Vector h_1 is a copy of f_0 where the signs of the odd-numbered elements (the first, third, etc.) are reversed. We can express this by saying that h_1 is computed by coordinate multiplication of h_1 and $(-1, 1, -1, 1, \ldots, -1, 1)$.
5. Vector f_1 is a copy of h_0 where the signs of the even-numbered elements (the second, fourth, etc.) are reversed. We can express this by saying that f_1 is computed by coordinate multiplication of h_0 and $(1, -1, 1, -1, \ldots, 1, -1)$.

For two-tap filters, rule 1 implies

$$h_0^2(0) + h_0^2(1) = 1. \tag{5.9}$$

Rule 2 is not applicable because $N = 2$, so $i < N/2$ implies $i < 1$. Rules 3–5 yield

$$f_0 = \big(h_0(1), h_0(0)\big), \quad h_1 = \big(-h_0(1), h_0(0)\big), \quad f_1 = \big(h_0(0), -h_0(1)\big).$$

It all depends on the values of $h_0(0)$ and $h_0(1)$, but the single Equation (5.9) is not enough to determine them. However, it is not hard to see that the choice $h_0(0) = h_0(1) = 1/\sqrt{2}$ satisfies Equation (5.9).

For four-tap filters, rules 1 and 2 imply

$$h_0^2(0) + h_0^2(1) + h_0^2(2) + h_0^2(3) = 1, \quad h_0(0)h_0(2) + h_0(1)h_0(3) = 0, \tag{5.10}$$

and rules 3–5 yield

$$f_0 = \big(h_0(3), h_0(2), h_0(1), h_0(0)\big),$$
$$h_1 = \big(-h_0(3), h_0(2), -h_0(1), h_0(0)\big),$$
$$f_1 = \big(h_0(0), -h_0(1), h_0(2), -h_0(3)\big).$$

Again, Equation (5.10) is not enough to determine four unknowns, and other considerations (plus mathematical intuition) are needed to derive the four values. They are listed in Equation (5.11) (this is the Daubechies D4 filter).

⋄ **Exercise 5.9:** Write the five conditions above for an eight-tap filter.

Determining the N filter coefficients for each of the four filters H_0, H_1, F_0, and F_1 depends on $h_0(0)$ through $h_0(N-1)$, so it requires N equations. However, in each of the cases above, rules 1 and 2 supply only $N/2$ equations. Other conditions have to be imposed and satisfied before the N quantities $h_0(0)$ through $h_0(N-1)$ can be determined. Here are some examples:

Lowpass H_0 filter: We want H_0 to be a lowpass filter, so it makes sense to require that the frequency response $H_0(\omega)$ be zero for the highest frequency $\omega = \pi$.

Minimum phase filter: This condition requires the zeros of the complex function $H_0(z)$ to lie on or inside the unit circle in the complex plane.

Controlled collinearity: The linearity of the phase response can be controlled by requiring that the sum

$$\sum_i \big(h_0(i) - h_0(N-1-i)\big)^2$$

be a minimum.

Other conditions are discussed in [Akansu and Haddad 92].

Bibliography

Akansu, Ali, and R. Haddad (1992) *Multiresolution Signal Decomposition*, San Diego, CA, Academic Press.

5.8 The DWT

Information that is produced and analyzed in real-life situations is discrete. It comes in the form of numbers, rather than a continuous function. This is why the discrete rather than the continuous wavelet transform is the one used in practice. Recall that the CWT [Equation (5.3)] is the integral of the product $f(t)\psi^*(\frac{t-b}{a})$, where a, the scale factor, and b, the time shift, can be any real numbers. The corresponding calculation for the discrete case (the DWT) involves a *convolution* (see appendix in the book's web site), but experience shows that the quality of this type of transform depends heavily on two things, the choice of scale factors and time shifts, and the choice of wavelet.

In practice, the DWT is computed with scale factors that are negative powers of 2 and time shifts that are nonnegative powers of 2. Figure 5.29 shows the so-called *dyadic lattice* that illustrates this particular choice. The wavelets used are those that generate orthonormal (or biorthogonal) wavelet bases.

The main thrust in wavelet research has therefore been the search for wavelet families that form orthogonal bases. Of those wavelets, the preferred ones are those that have compact support, because they allow for DWT computations with *finite impulse response* (FIR) filters.

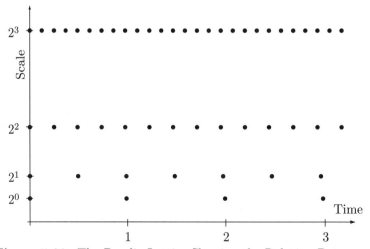

Figure 5.29: The Dyadic Lattice Showing the Relation Between Scale Factors and Time.

The simplest way to describe the discrete wavelet transform is by means of matrix multiplication, along the lines developed in Section 5.6.3. The Haar transform depends on two *filter coefficients* c_0 and c_1, both with a value of $1/\sqrt{2} \approx 0.7071$. The smallest transform matrix that can be constructed in this case is $\left(\begin{smallmatrix} 1 & 1 \\ 1 & -1 \end{smallmatrix}\right)/\sqrt{2}$. It is a 2×2 matrix, and it generates two transform coefficients, an average and a difference. (Notice that these are not exactly an average and a difference, because $\sqrt{2}$ is used instead of 2. Better names for them are *coarse detail* and *fine detail*, respectively.) In general, the DWT can use any set of wavelet filters, but it is computed in the same way regardless of the particular filter used.

We start with one of the most popular wavelets, the Daubechies D4. As its name implies, it is based on four filter coefficients c_0, c_1, c_2, and c_3, whose values are listed in Equation (5.11). The transform matrix W is [compare with matrix A_1, Equation (5.6)]

$$
W = \begin{pmatrix}
c_0 & c_1 & c_2 & c_3 & 0 & 0 & \cdots & 0 \\
c_3 & -c_2 & c_1 & -c_0 & 0 & 0 & \cdots & 0 \\
0 & 0 & c_0 & c_1 & c_2 & c_3 & \cdots & 0 \\
0 & 0 & c_3 & -c_2 & c_1 & -c_0 & \cdots & 0 \\
\vdots & \vdots & & & & \ddots & & \\
0 & 0 & \cdots & 0 & c_0 & c_1 & c_2 & c_3 \\
0 & 0 & \cdots & 0 & c_3 & -c_2 & c_1 & -c_0 \\
c_2 & c_3 & 0 & \cdots & 0 & 0 & c_0 & c_1 \\
c_1 & -c_0 & 0 & \cdots & 0 & 0 & c_3 & -c_2
\end{pmatrix}.
$$

When this matrix is applied to a column vector of data items $(x_1, x_2, \ldots, x_n)$, its top row generates the weighted sum $s_1 = c_0 x_1 + c_1 x_2 + c_2 x_3 + c_3 x_4$, its third row generates the weighted sum $s_2 = c_0 x_3 + c_1 x_4 + c_2 x_5 + c_3 x_6$, and the other odd-numbered rows generate similar weighted sums s_i. Such sums are *convolutions* of the data vector x_i with the four filter coefficients. In the language of wavelets, each of them is called a *smooth coefficient*, and together they are called an H smoothing filter.

In a similar way, the second row of the matrix generates the quantity $d_1 = c_3 x_1 - c_2 x_2 + c_1 x_3 - c_0 x_4$, and the other even-numbered rows generate similar convolutions. Each d_i is called a *detail coefficient*, and together they are called a G filter. G is not a smoothing filter. In fact, the filter coefficients are chosen such that the G filter generates small values when the data items x_i are correlated. Together, H and G are called *quadrature mirror filters* (QMF).

The discrete wavelet transform of an image can therefore be viewed as passing the original image through a QMF that consists of a pair of lowpass (H) and highpass (G) filters.

If W is an $n \times n$ matrix, it generates $n/2$ smooth coefficients s_i and $n/2$ detail coefficients d_i. The transposed matrix is

$$
W^T = \begin{pmatrix}
c_0 & c_3 & 0 & 0 & \cdots & & & & c_2 & c_1 \\
c_1 & -c_2 & 0 & 0 & \cdots & & & & c_3 & -c_0 \\
c_2 & c_1 & c_0 & c_3 & \cdots & & & & 0 & 0 \\
c_3 & -c_0 & c_1 & -c_2 & \cdots & & & & 0 & 0 \\
& & & & \ddots & & & & & \\
& & & & & c_2 & c_1 & c_0 & c_3 & 0 & 0 \\
& & & & & c_3 & -c_0 & c_1 & -c_2 & 0 & 0 \\
& & & & & & & c_2 & c_1 & c_0 & c_3 \\
& & & & & & & c_3 & -c_0 & c_1 & -c_2
\end{pmatrix}.
$$

It can be shown that in order for W to be orthonormal, the four coefficients have to satisfy the two relations $c_0^2 + c_1^2 + c_2^2 + c_3^2 = 1$ and $c_2 c_0 + c_3 c_1 = 0$. The other two equations used to calculate the four filter coefficients are $c_3 - c_2 + c_1 - c_0 = 0$ and $0 c_3 - 1 c_2 + 2 c_1 - 3 c_0 = 0$. They represent the vanishing of the first two moments of the sequence $(c_3, -c_2, c_1, -c_0)$. The solutions are

$$
\begin{aligned}
c_0 = (1 + \sqrt{3})/(4\sqrt{2}) \approx 0.48296, \quad & c_1 = (3 + \sqrt{3})/(4\sqrt{2}) \approx 0.8365, \\
c_2 = (3 - \sqrt{3})/(4\sqrt{2}) \approx 0.2241, \quad & c_3 = (1 - \sqrt{3})/(4\sqrt{2}) \approx -0.1294.
\end{aligned}
\tag{5.11}
$$

Using a transform matrix W is conceptually simple, but not very practical, since W should be of the same size as the image, which can be large. However, a look at W shows that it is very regular, so there is really no need to construct the full matrix. It is enough to have just the top row of W. In fact, it is enough to have just an array with the filter coefficients. Figure 5.30 is Matlab code that performs this calculation. Function `fwt1(dat,coarse,filter)` takes a row vector `dat` of 2^n data items, and another array, `filter`, with filter coefficients. It then calculates the first `coarse` levels of the discrete wavelet transform.

⋄ **Exercise 5.10:** Write similar code for the inverse one-dimensional discrete wavelet transform.

Plotting Functions: Wavelets are being used in many fields and have many applications, but the simple test of Figure 5.30 suggests another application, namely, plotting functions. Any graphics program or graphics software package has to include a routine to plot functions. This is done by calculating the function at certain points and connecting the points with straight segments. In regions where the function has small curvature (it resembles a straight line) only few points are needed, whereas in areas where the function has large curvature (it changes direction rapidly) more points are required. An ideal plotting routine should therefore be adaptive. It should select the points depending on the curvature of the function.

The curvature, however, may not be easy to calculate (it is essentially given by the second derivative of the function) which is why many plotting routines use instead the angle between consecutive segments. Figure 5.31 shows how a typical plotting routine works. It starts with a fixed number (say, 50) of points. This implies 49 straight segments connecting them. Before any of the segments is actually plotted, the routine measures the angles between consecutive segments. If an angle at point $\mathbf{P}_i$ is extreme (close to zero or close to $360°$, as it is around points 4 and 10 in the figure), then more points are calculated between points $\mathbf{P}_{i-1}$ and $\mathbf{P}_{i+1}$; otherwise (if the angle is closer to $180°$, as, for example, around points 5 and 9 in the figure), $\mathbf{P}_i$ is considered the only point necessary in that region.

Better and faster results may be obtained using a discrete wavelet transform. The function is evaluated at n points (where n, a parameter, is large), and the values are collected in a vector v. A discrete wavelet transform of v is then calculated, to produce n transform coefficients. The next step is to discard m of the smallest coefficients (where m is another parameter). We know, from the previous discussion, that the smallest coefficients represent small details of the function, so discarding them leaves the important details practically untouched. The inverse transform is

```
function wc1=fwt1(dat,coarse,filter)
%  The 1D Forward Wavelet Transform
%  dat must be a 1D row vector of size 2^n,
%  coarse is the coarsest level of the transform
%  (note that coarse should be <<n)
%  filter is an orthonormal quadrature mirror filter
%  whose length should be <2^(coarse+1)
n=length(dat); j=log2(n); wc1=zeros(1,n);
beta=dat;
for i=j-1:-1:coarse
  alfa=HiPass(beta,filter);
  wc1((2^(i)+1):(2^(i+1)))=alfa;
  beta=LoPass(beta,filter) ;
end
wc1(1:(2^coarse))=beta;

function d=HiPass(dt,filter) % highpass downsampling
d=iconv(mirror(filter),lshift(dt));
% iconv is matlab convolution tool
n=length(d);
d=d(1:2:(n-1));

function d=LoPass(dt,filter) % lowpass downsampling
d=aconv(filter,dt);
% aconv is matlab convolution tool with time-
% reversal of filter
n=length(d);
d=d(1:2:(n-1));

function sgn=mirror(filt)
% return filter coefficients with alternating signs
sgn=-((-1).^(1:length(filt))).*filt;
```

A simple test of fwt1 is

```
n=16; t=(1:n)./n;
dat=sin(2*pi*t)
filt=[0.4830 0.8365 0.2241 -0.1294];
wc=fwt1(dat,1,filt)
```

which outputs

```
dat=
0.3827   0.7071   0.9239 1.0000 0.9239 0.7071 0.3827 0
-0.3827 -0.7071 -0.9239 -1.0000 -0.9239 -0.7071 -0.3827 0
wc=
1.1365 -1.1365 -1.5685 1.5685 -0.2271 -0.4239 0.2271 0.4239
-0.0281 -0.0818 -0.0876 -0.0421 0.0281 0.0818 0.0876 0.0421
```

Figure 5.30: Code for the One-Dimensional Forward Discrete Wavelet Transform.

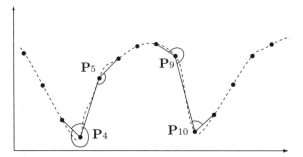

Figure 5.31: Using Angles Between Segments To Add More Points.

then performed on the remaining $n - m$ transform coefficients, resulting in $n - m$ new points that are then connected with straight segments. The larger m, the fewer segments necessary, but the worse the fit.

Readers who take the trouble to read and understand functions `fwt1` and `iwt1` (Figures 5.30 and 5.32) may be interested in their two-dimensional equivalents, functions `fwt2` and `iwt2`, which are listed in Figures 5.33 and 5.34, respectively, with a simple test routine.

Table 5.35 lists the filter coefficients for some of the most common wavelets currently in use. Notice that each of those sets should still be normalized. Following are the main features of each set:

■   The Daubechies family of filters maximize the smoothness of the father wavelet (the scaling function) by maximizing the rate of decay of its Fourier transform.

■   The Haar wavelet can be considered the Daubechies filter of order 2. It is the oldest filter. It is simple to work with, but it does not produce best results, since it is not continuous.

■   The Beylkin filter places the roots of the frequency response function close to the Nyquist frequency (page 466) on the real axis.

■   The Coifman filter (or "Coiflet") of order p (where p is a positive integer) gives both the mother and father wavelets $2p$ zero moments.

■   Symmetric filters (symmlets) are the most symmetric compactly supported wavelets with a maximum number of zero moments.

■   The Vaidyanathan filter does not satisfy any conditions on the moments but produces exact reconstruction. This filter is especially useful in speech compression.

Figures 5.36 and 5.37 are diagrams of some of those wavelets.

The Daubechies family of wavelets is a set of orthonormal, compactly supported functions where consecutive members are increasingly smoother. Some of them are shown in Figure 5.37. The term *compact support* means that these functions are zero (exactly zero, not just very small) outside a finite interval.

The Daubechies D4 wavelet is based on four coefficients, shown in Equation (5.11). The D6 wavelet is, similarly, based on six coefficients. They are calculated by solving six equations, three of which represent orthogonality requirements

```
function dat=iwt1(wc,coarse,filter)
% Inverse Discrete Wavelet Transform
dat=wc(1:2^coarse);
n=length(wc); j=log2(n);
for i=coarse:j-1
 dat=ILoPass(dat,filter)+ ...
  IHiPass(wc((2^(i)+1):(2^(i+1))),filter);
end

function f=ILoPass(dt,filter)
f=iconv(filter,AltrntZro(dt));

function f=IHiPass(dt,filter)
f=aconv(mirror(filter),rshift(AltrntZro(dt)));

function sgn=mirror(filt)
% return filter coefficients with alternating signs
sgn=-((-1).^(1:length(filt))).*filt;

function f=AltrntZro(dt)
% returns a vector of length 2*n with zeros
% placed between consecutive values
n =length(dt)*2; f =zeros(1,n);
f(1:2:(n-1))=dt;
```

A simple test of iwt1 is

```
n=16; t=(1:n)./n;
dat=sin(2*pi*t)
filt=[0.4830 0.8365 0.2241 -0.1294];
wc=fwt1(dat,1,filt)
rec=iwt1(wc,1,filt)
```

Figure 5.32: Code for the One-Dimensional Inverse Discrete Wavelet Transform.

```
function wc=fwt2(dat,coarse,filter)
%  The 2D Forward Wavelet Transform
%  dat must be a 2D matrix of size (2^n:2^n),
%  "coarse" is the coarsest level of the transform
%  (note that coarse should be <<n)
%  filter is an orthonormal qmf of length<2^(coarse+1)
q=size(dat); n = q(1); j=log2(n);
if q(1)~=q(2), disp('Nonsquare image!'), end;
wc = dat; nc = n;
for i=j-1:-1:coarse,
 top = (nc/2+1):nc; bot = 1:(nc/2);
 for ic=1:nc,
  row = wc(ic,1:nc);
  wc(ic,bot)=LoPass(row,filter);
  wc(ic,top)=HiPass(row,filter);
 end
 for ir=1:nc,
  row = wc(1:nc,ir)';
  wc(top,ir)=HiPass(row,filter)';
  wc(bot,ir)=LoPass(row,filter)';
 end
nc = nc/2;
end

function d=HiPass(dt,filter) % highpass downsampling
d=iconv(mirror(filter),lshift(dt));
% iconv is matlab convolution tool
n=length(d);
d=d(1:2:(n-1));

function d=LoPass(dt,filter) % lowpass downsampling
d=aconv(filter,dt);
% aconv is matlab convolution tool with time-
% reversal of filter
n=length(d);
d=d(1:2:(n-1));

function sgn=mirror(filt)
% return filter coefficients with alternating signs
sgn=-((-1).^(1:length(filt))).*filt;
```

A simple test of fwt2 and iwt2 is

```
filename='house128'; dim=128;
fid=fopen(filename,'r');
if fid==-1 disp('file not found')
 else img=fread(fid,[dim,dim])'; fclose(fid);
end
filt=[0.4830 0.8365 0.2241 -0.1294];
fwim=fwt2(img,4,filt);
figure(1), imagesc(fwim), axis off, axis square
rec=iwt2(fwim,4,filt);
figure(2), imagesc(rec), axis off, axis square
```

Figure 5.33: Code for the Two-Dimensional Forward Discrete Wavelet Transform.

```
function dat=iwt2(wc,coarse,filter)
% Inverse Discrete 2D Wavelet Transform
n=length(wc); j=log2(n);
dat=wc;
nc=2^(coarse+1);
for i=coarse:j-1,
 top=(nc/2+1):nc; bot=1:(nc/2); all=1:nc;
 for ic=1:nc,
  dat(all,ic)=ILoPass(dat(bot,ic)',filter)'  ...
   +IHiPass(dat(top,ic)',filter)';
 end % ic
 for ir=1:nc,
  dat(ir,all)=ILoPass(dat(ir,bot),filter)  ...
   +IHiPass(dat(ir,top),filter);
 end % ir
nc=2*nc;
end % i

function f=ILoPass(dt,filter)
f=iconv(filter,AltrntZro(dt));

function f=IHiPass(dt,filter)
f=aconv(mirror(filter),rshift(AltrntZro(dt)));

function sgn=mirror(filt)
% return filter coefficients with alternating signs
sgn=-((-1).^(1:length(filt))).*filt;

function f=AltrntZro(dt)
% returns a vector of length 2*n with zeros
% placed between consecutive values
n =length(dt)*2; f =zeros(1,n);
f(1:2:(n-1))=dt;
```

A simple test of fwt2 and iwt2 is

```
    filename='house128'; dim=128;
    fid=fopen(filename,'r');
    if fid==-1 disp('file not found')
     else img=fread(fid,[dim,dim])'; fclose(fid);
    end
    filt=[0.4830 0.8365 0.2241 -0.1294];
    fwim=fwt2(img,4,filt);
    figure(1), imagesc(fwim), axis off, axis square
    rec=iwt2(fwim,4,filt);
    figure(2), imagesc(rec), axis off, axis square
```

Figure 5.34: Code for the Two-Dimensional Inverse Discrete Wavelet Transform.

.099305765374	.424215360813	.699825214057	.449718251149	-.110927598348	-.264497231446
.026900308804	.155538731877	-.017520746267	-.088543630623	.019679866044	.042916387274
-.017460408696	-.014365807969	.010040411845	.001484234782	-.002736031626	.000640485329

Beylkin

.038580777748	-.126969125396	-.077161555496	.607491641386	.745687558934	.226584265197

Coifman 1-tap

.016387336463	-.041464936782	-.067372554722	.386110066823	.812723635450	.417005184424
-.076488599078	-.059434418646	.023680171947	.005611434819	-.001823208871	-.000720549445

Coifman 2-tap

-.003793512864	.007782596426	.023452696142	-.065771911281	-.061123390003	.405176902410
.793777222626	.428483476378	-.071799821619	-.082301927106	.034555027573	.015880544864
-.009007976137	-.002574517688	.001117518771	.000466216960	-.000070983303	-.000034599773

Coifman 3-tap

.000892313668	-.001629492013	-.007346166328	.016068943964	.026682300156	-.081266699680
-.056077313316	.415308407030	.782238930920	.434386056491	-.066627474263	-.096220442034
.039334427123	.025082261845	-.015211731527	-.005658286686	.003751436157	.001266561929
-.000589020757	-.000259974552	.000062339034	.000031229876	-.000003259680	-.000001784985

Coifman 4-tap

-.000212080863	.000358589677	.002178236305	-.004159358782	-.010131117538	.023408156762
.028168029062	-.091920010549	-.052043163216	.421566206729	.774289603740	.437991626228
-.062035963906	-.105574208706	.041289208741	.032683574283	-.019761779012	-.009164231153
.006764185419	.002433373209	-.001662863769	-.000638131296	.000302259520	.000140541149
-.000041340484	-.000021315014	.000003734597	.000002063806	-.000000167408	-.000000095158

Coifman 5-tap

.482962913145	.836516303738	.224143868042	-.129409522551

Daubechies 4-tap

.332670552950	.806891509311	.459877502118	-.135011020010	-.085441273882	.035226291882

Daubechies 6-tap

.230377813309	.714846570553	.630880767930	-.027983769417	-.187034811719	.030841381836
.032883011667	-.010597401785				

Daubechies 8-tap

.160102397974	.603829269797	.724308528438	.138428145901	-.242294887066	-.032244869585
.077571493840	-.006241490213	-.012580751999	.003335725285		

Daubechies 10-tap

.111540743350	.494623890398	.751133908021	.315250351709	-.226264693965	-.129766867567
.097501605587	.027522865530	-.031582039317	.000553842201	.004777257511	-.001077301085

Daubechies 12-tap

.077852054085	.396539319482	.729132090846	.469782287405	-.143906003929	-.224036184994
.071309219267	.080612609151	-.038029936935	-.016574541631	.012550998556	.000429577973
-.001801640704	.000353713800				

Daubechies 14-tap

.054415842243	.312871590914	.675630736297	.585354683654	-.015829105256	-.284015542962
.000472484574	.128747426620	-.017369301002	-.044088253931	.013981027917	.008746094047
-.004870352993	-.000391740373	.000675449406	-.000117476784		

Daubechies 16-tap

.038077947364	.243834674613	.604823123690	.657288078051	.133197385825	-.293273783279
-.096840783223	.148540749338	.030725681479	-.067632829061	.000250947115	.022361662124
-.004723204758	-.004281503682	.001847646883	.000230385764	-.000251963189	.000039347320

Daubechies 18-tap

.026670057901	.188176800078	.527201188932	.688459039454	.281172343661	-.249846424327
-.195946274377	.127369340336	.093057364604	-.071394147166	-.029457536822	.033212674059
.003606553567	-.010733175483	.001395351747	.001992405295	-.000685856695	-.000116466855
.000093588670	-.000013264203				

Daubechies 20-tap

Table 5.35: Filter Coefficients For Some Common Wavelets (Continues).

-.107148901418	-.041910965125	.703739068656	1.136658243408	.421234534204	-.140317624179
-.017824701442	.045570345896				

Symmlet 4-tap

.038654795955	.041746864422	-.055344186117	.281990696854	1.023052966894	.896581648380
.023478923136	-.247951362613	-.029842499869	.027632152958		

Symmlet 5-tap

.021784700327	.004936612372	-.166863215412	-.068323121587	.694457972958	1.113892783926
.477904371333	-.102724969862	-.029783751299	.063250562660	.002499922093	-.011031867509

Symmlet 6-tap

.003792658534	-.001481225915	-.017870431651	.043155452582	.096014767936	-.070078291222
.024665659489	.758162601964	1.085782709814	.408183939725	-.198056706807	-.152463871896
.005671342686	.014521394762				

Symmlet 7-tap

.002672793393	-.000428394300	-.021145686528	.005386388754	.069490465911	-.038493521263
-.073462508761	.515398670374	1.099106630537	.680745347190	-.086653615406	-.202648655286
.010758611751	.044823623042	-.000766690896	-.004783458512		

Symmlet 8-tap

.001512487309	-.000669141509	-.014515578553	.012528896242	.087791251554	-.025786445930
-.270893783503	.049882830959	.873048407349	1.015259790832	.337658923602	-.077172161097
.000825140929	.042744433602	-.016303351226	-.018769396836	.000876502539	.001981193736

Symmlet 9-tap

.001089170447	.000135245020	-.012220642630	-.002072363923	.064950924579	.016418869426
-.225558972234	-.100240215031	.667071338154	1.088251530500	.542813011213	-.050256540092
-.045240772218	.070703567550	.008152816799	-.028786231926	-.001137535314	.006495728375
.000080661204	-.000649589896				

Symmlet 10-tap

-.000062906118	.000343631905	-.000453956620	-.000944897136	.002843834547	.000708137504
-.008839103409	.003153847056	.019687215010	-.014853448005	-.035470398607	.038742619293
.055892523691	-.077709750902	-.083928884366	.131971661417	.135084227129	-.194450471766
-.263494802488	.201612161775	.635601059872	.572797793211	.250184129505	.045799334111

Vaidyanathan

Table 5.35: Continued.

and the other three, the vanishing of the first three moments. The result is shown in Equation (5.12):

$$
\begin{aligned}
c_0 &= (1 + \sqrt{10} + \sqrt{5 + 2\sqrt{10}})/(16\sqrt{2}) \approx .3326, \\
c_1 &= (5 + \sqrt{10} + 3\sqrt{5 + 2\sqrt{10}})/(16\sqrt{2}) \approx .8068, \\
c_2 &= (10 - 2\sqrt{10} + 2\sqrt{5 + 2\sqrt{10}})/(16\sqrt{2}) \approx .4598, \\
c_3 &= (10 - 2\sqrt{10} - 2\sqrt{5 + 2\sqrt{10}})/(16\sqrt{2}) \approx -.1350, \\
c_4 &= (5 + \sqrt{10} - 3\sqrt{5 + 2\sqrt{10}})/(16\sqrt{2}) \approx -.0854, \\
c_5 &= (1 + \sqrt{10} - \sqrt{5 + 2\sqrt{10}})/(16\sqrt{2}) \approx .0352.
\end{aligned}
\tag{5.12}
$$

Each member of this family has two more coefficients than its predecessor and is smoother. The derivation of these functions is outside the scope of this book and can be found in [Daubechies 88]. They are derived recursively, do not have a closed form, and are nondifferentiable at infinitely many points. Truly unusual functions!

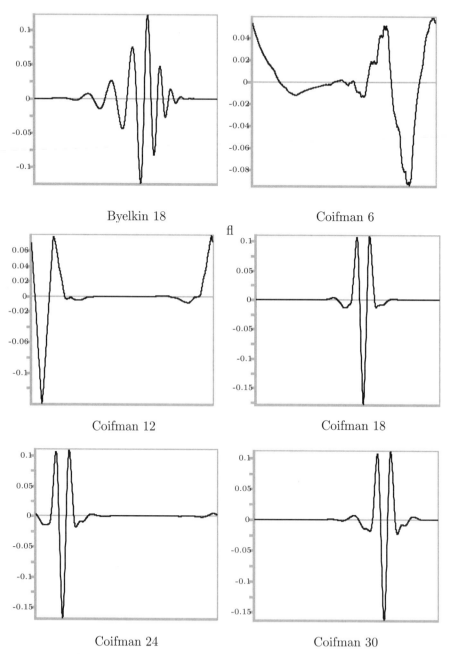

fl

Figure 5.36: Examples of Common Wavelets.

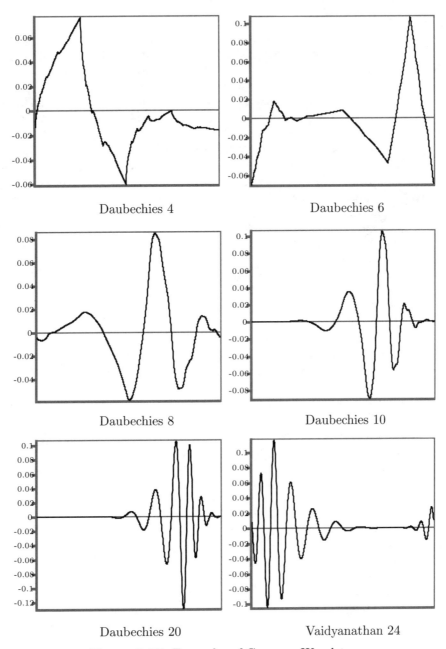

Figure 5.37: Examples of Common Wavelets.

Nondifferentiable Functions

Most functions used in science and engineering are smooth. They have a well-defined direction (or tangent) at every point. Mathematically, we say that they are *differentiable*. Some functions may have a few points where they suddenly change direction, and so do not have a tangent. The Haar wavelet is an example of such a function. A function may have many such "sharp" corners, even infinitely many. A simple example is an infinite square wave. It has infinitely many sharp points, but it does not look strange or unusual, since those points are separated by smooth areas of the function.

What is hard for us to imagine (and even harder to accept the existence of) is a function that is everywhere continuous but is nowhere differentiable! Such a function has no "holes" or "gaps." It continues without interruptions, but it changes its direction sharply at *every* point. It is as if it has a certain direction at point x and a different direction at the point that immediately follows x; except, of course, that a real number x does not have an immediate successor.

Such functions exist. The first was discovered in 1875 by Karl Weierstrass. It is the sum of the infinite series

$$W_{b,w}(t) = \frac{\sum_{n=0}^{\infty} w^n e^{2\pi i b^n t}}{\sqrt{1 - w^2}},$$

where $b > 1$ is a real number, w is written either as $w = b^h$, with $0 < h < 1$, or as $w = b^{d-2}$, with $1 < d < 2$, and $i = \sqrt{-1}$. Notice that $W_{b,w}(t)$ is complex; its real and imaginary parts are called the Weierstrass cosine and sine functions, respectively.

Weierstrass proved the unusual behavior of this function, and also showed that for $d < 1$ it is differentiable. In his time, such a function was so contrary to common sense and mathematical intuition that he did not publish his findings. Today, we simply call this function and others like it *fractals*.

⋄ **Exercise 5.11:** Use functions `fwt2` and `iwt2` of Figures 5.33 and 5.34 to blur an image. The idea is to compute the four-step subband transform of an image (thus ending up with 13 subbands), then set most of the transform coefficients to zero and heavily quantize some of the others. This, of course, results in a loss of image information, and in a nonperfectly reconstructed image. The aim of this exercise, however, is to have the inverse transform produce a *blurred image*. This illustrates an important property of the discrete wavelet transform, namely its ability to reconstruct images that degrade gracefully when more and more transform coefficients are zeroed or coarsely quantized. Other transforms, most notably the DCT, may introduce artifacts in the reconstructed image, but this property of the DWT makes it ideal for applications such as fingerprint compression (Section 5.18).

Bibliography

Daubechies, Ingrid (1988) "Orthonormal Bases of Compactly Supported Wavelets," *Communications on Pure and Applied Mathematics*, **41**:909–996.

DeVore R. et al. (1992) "Image Compression Through Wavelet Transform Coding," *IEEE Transactions on Information Theory* **38**(2):719–746, March.

Vetterli, M., and J. Kovacevic (1995) *Wavelets and Subband Coding*, Englewood Cliffs, NJ, Prentice-Hall.

5.9 Multiresolution Decomposition

The main idea of wavelet analysis, illustrated in detail in Section 5.5, is to analyze a function at different scales. A mother wavelet is used to construct wavelets at different scales (dilations) and translate each relative to the function being analyzed. The results of translating a wavelet depend on how much it matches the function being analyzed. Wavelets at different scales (resolutions) produce different results. The principle of multiresolution decomposition, due to Stephane Mallat and Yves Meyer, is to group all the wavelet transform coefficients for a given scale, display their superposition, and repeat for all scales.

Figure 5.39 lists a Matlab function `multres` for this operation, together with a test. Figure 5.38 shows two examples, a single spike and multiple spikes. It is easy to see how the fine-resolution coefficients are concentrated at the values of t that correspond to the spikes (i.e., the high activity areas of the data).

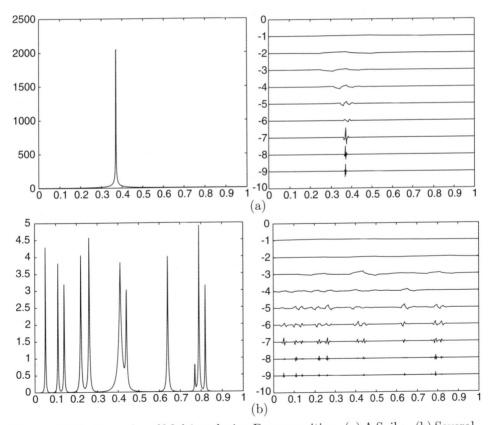

Figure 5.38: Examples of Multiresolution Decomposition. (a) A Spike. (b) Several Spikes.

```
function multres(wc,coarse,filter)
% A multi resolution plot of a 1D wavelet transform
scale=1./max(abs(wc));
n=length(wc); j=log2(n);
LockAxes([0 1 -(j) (-coarse+2)]);
t=(.5:(n-.5))/n;
for i=(j-1):-1:coarse
 z=zeros(1,n);
 z((2^(i)+1):(2^(i+1)))=wc((2^(i)+1):(2^(i+1)));
 dat=iwt1(z,i,filter);
 plot(t,-(i)+scale.*dat);
end
z=zeros(1,n);
z(1:2^(coarse))=wc(1:2^(coarse));
dat=iwt1(z,coarse,filter);
plot(t,(-(coarse-1))+scale.*dat);
UnlockAxes;
```

And a test routine

```
n=1024; t=(1:n)./n;
dat=spikes(t);                    % several spikes
%p=floor(n*.37); dat=1./abs(t-(p+.5)/n); % one spike
figure(1), plot(t,dat)
filt=[0.4830 0.8365 0.2241 -0.1294];
wc=fwt1(dat,2,filt);
figure(2), plot(t,wc)
figure(3)
multres(wc,2,filt);

function dat=spikes(t)
pos=[.05 .11 .14 .22 .26 .41 .44 .64  .77 .79 .82];
hgt=[5  5 4 4.5 5 3.9 3.3 4.6 1.1 5 4];
wth=[.005 .005 .006 .01 .01 .03 .01 .01  .005 .008 .005];
dat=zeros(size(t));
for i=1:length(pos)
dat=dat+hgt(i)./(1+abs((t-pos(i))./wth(i))).^4;
end;
```

Figure 5.39: Matlab Code for the Multiresolution Decomposition of a One-Dimensional Row Vector.

5.10 Various Image Decompositions

Section 5.6.1 shows two ways of applying a discrete wavelet transform to an image in order to partition it into several subbands. This section (based on [Strømme 99], which also contains comparisons of experimental results) discusses seven ways of doing the same thing, each involving a different algorithm and resulting in subbands with different energy compactions. Other decompositions are also possible (Section 5.18 describes a special, symmetric decomposition).

It is important to realize that the wavelet filters and the decomposition method are independent. The discrete wavelet transform of an image can use any set of wavelet filters and can decompose the image in any way. The only limitation is that there must be enough data points in the subband to cover all the filter taps. For example, if a 12-tap Daubechies filter is used, and the image and subband sizes are powers of two, then the smallest subband that can be produced has size 8×8. This is because a subband of size 16×16 is the smallest that can be multiplied by the 12 coefficients of this particular filter. Once such a subband is decomposed, the resulting 8×8 subbands are too small to be multiplied by 12 coefficients and be decomposed further.

1. Laplacian Pyramid: This technique for image decomposition is described in detail in Section 5.13. Its main feature is progressive image transmission. During decompression and image reconstruction, the user sees small, blurred images that grow and become sharper. The main reference is [Burt and Adelson 83].

The Laplacian pyramid is generated by subtracting an upsampled lowpass version of the image from the original image. The image is partitioned into a Gaussian pyramid (the lowpass subbands), and a Laplacian pyramid that consists of the detail coefficients (the highpass subbands). Only the Laplacian pyramid is needed to reconstruct the image. The transformed image is bigger than the original image, which is the main difference between the Laplacian pyramid decomposition and the pyramid decomposition (method 4).

2. Line: This technique is a simpler version of the standard wavelet decomposition (method 5). The wavelet transform is applied to each row of the image, resulting in smooth coefficients on the left (subband L1) and detail coefficients on the right (subband H1). Subband L1 is then partitioned into L2 and H2, and the process is repeated until the entire coefficient matrix is turned into detail coefficients, except the leftmost column, which contains smooth coefficients. The wavelet transform is then applied recursively to the leftmost column, resulting in one smooth coefficient at the top-left corner of the coefficient matrix. This last step may be omitted if the compression method being used requires that image rows be individually compressed (notice the distinction between the wavelet transform and the actual compression algorithm).

This technique exploits correlations only within an image row to calculate the transform coefficients. Also, discarding a coefficient that is located on the leftmost column may affect just a particular group of rows and may thus introduce artifacts into the reconstructed image.

Implementation of this method is simple, and execution is fast, about twice that of the standard decomposition. This type of decomposition is illustrated in Figure 5.40.

It is possible to apply this decomposition to the columns of the image, instead of to the rows. Ideally, the transform should be applied in the direction of highest image redundancy, and experience suggests that for natural images this is the horizontal direction. Thus, in practice, line decomposition is applied to the image rows.

3. Quincunx: Somewhat similar to the Laplacian pyramid, quincunx decomposition proceeds level by level and decomposes subband L_i of level i into subbands H_{i+1} and L_{i+1} of level $i + 1$. Figure 5.41 illustrates this type of decomposition. The method is due to Strømme and McGregor [Strømme and McGregor 97], who

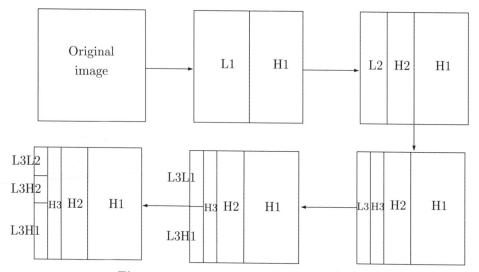

Figure 5.40: Line Wavelet Decomposition.

originally called it nonstandard decomposition. (See also [Starck et al. 83] for a different presentation of this method.) It is efficient and computationally simple. On average, it achieves more than four times the energy compaction of the line method.

Quincunx decomposition results in fewer subbands than most other wavelet decompositions, a feature that may lead to reconstructed images with slightly lower visual quality. The method is not used much in practice, but [Strømme 99] presents results that suggest that quincunx decomposition performs extremely well and may be the best performer in many practical situations.

4. Pyramid: The pyramid decomposition is by far the most common method used to decompose images that are wavelet transformed. It results in subbands with horizontal, vertical, and diagonal image details, as illustrated by Figure 5.17. The three subbands at each level contain horizontal, vertical, and diagonal image features at a particular scale, and each scale is divided by an octave in spatial frequency (division of the frequency by two).

Pyramid decomposition turns out to be a very efficient way of transferring significant visual data to the detail coefficients. Its computational complexity is about 30% higher than that of the quincunx method, but its image reconstruction abilities are higher. The reasons for the popularity of the pyramid method may be that (1) it is symmetrical, (2) its mathematical description is simple, and (3) it was used by the influential paper [Mallat 89].

Figure 5.42 illustrates pyramid decomposition. It is obvious that the first step is identical to that of quincunx decomposition. However, while the quincunx method leaves the high-frequency subband untouched, the pyramid method resolves it into two bands. On the other hand, pyramid decomposition involves more computations in order to spatially resolve the asymmetric high-frequency band into two symmetric high- and low-frequency bands.

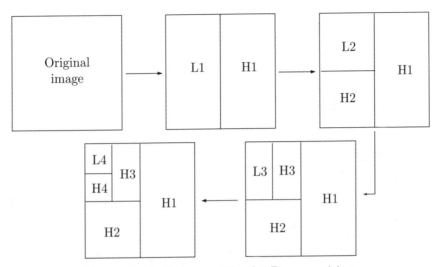

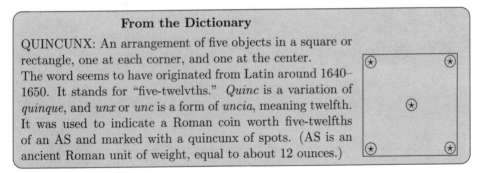

Figure 5.41: Quincunx Wavelet Decomposition.

From the Dictionary

QUINCUNX: An arrangement of five objects in a square or rectangle, one at each corner, and one at the center.
The word seems to have originated from Latin around 1640–1650. It stands for "five-twelvths." *Quinc* is a variation of *quinque*, and *unx* or *unc* is a form of *uncia*, meaning twelfth. It was used to indicate a Roman coin worth five-twelfths of an AS and marked with a quincunx of spots. (AS is an ancient Roman unit of weight, equal to about 12 ounces.)

---

5. Standard: The first step in the standard decomposition is to apply whatever discrete wavelet filter is being used to all the rows of the image, obtaining subbands L_1 and H_1. This is repeated on L_1 to obtain L_2 and H_2, and so on k times. This is followed by a second step where a similar calculation is applied k times to the columns. If $k = 1$, the decomposition alternates between rows and columns, but k may be greater than 1. The end result is to have one smooth coefficient at the top-left corner of the coefficient matrix. This method is somewhat similar to line decomposition. An important feature of standard decomposition is that when a coefficient is quantized, it may affect a long, thin rectangular area in the reconstructed image. Thus, very coarse quantization may result in artifacts in the reconstructed image in the form of horizontal rectangles.

Standard decomposition has the second-highest reconstruction quality of the seven methods described here. The reason for the improvement compared to the pyramid decomposition may be that the higher directional resolution gives thresholding a better chance to cover larger uniform areas. On the other hand, Standard decomposition is more expensive computationally than pyramid decomposition.

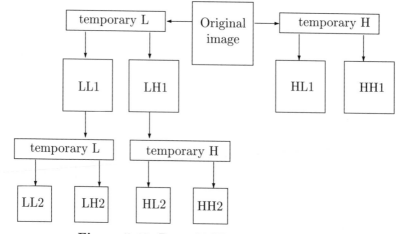

Figure 5.42: Pyramid Wavelet Decomposition.

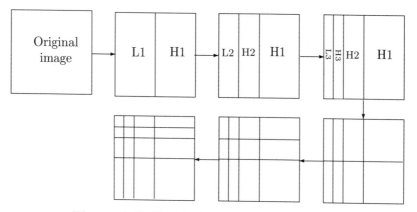

Figure 5.43: Standard Wavelet Decomposition.

6. Uniform Decomposition: This method is also called the *wavelet packet transform*. It is illustrated in Figure 5.44. In the case where the user elects to compute all the levels of the transform, the uniform decomposition becomes similar to the discrete Fourier transform (DFT) in that each coefficient represents a spatial frequency for the entire image. In such a case (where all the levels are computed), the removal of one coefficient in the transformed image affects the entire reconstructed image.

The computational cost of uniform decomposition is very high, since it effectively computes n^2 coefficients for every level of decomposition, where n is the side length of the (square) image. Despite having comparably high average reconstruction qualities, the perceptual quality of the image starts degrading at lower ratios than for the other decomposition methods. The reason for this is the same as for Fourier methods: Since the support for a single coefficient is global, its removal has the effect of blurring the reconstructed image. The conclusion is that the increased computational complexity of uniform decomposition does not result in increased quality of the reconstructed image.

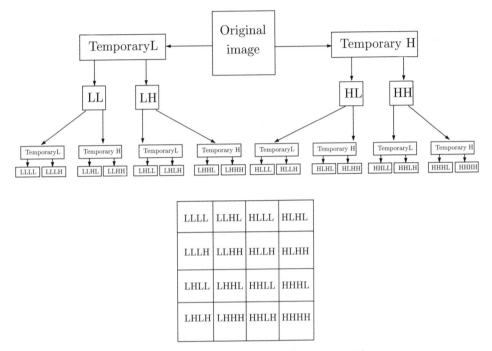

Figure 5.44: Uniform Wavelet Decomposition.

6.1. Full Wavelet Decomposition: (This is a special case of uniform decomposition.) Denote the original image by I_0. We assume that its size is $2^l \times 2^l$. After applying the discrete wavelet transform to it, we end up with a matrix I_1 partitioned into four subbands. The same discrete wavelet transform (i.e., using the same wavelet filters) is then applied recursively to each of the four subbands individually. The result is a coefficient matrix I_2 consisting of 16 subbands. When this process is carried out r times, the result is a coefficient matrix consisting of $2^r \times 2^r$ subbands, each of size $2^{l-r} \times 2^{l-r}$. The top-left subband contains the smooth coefficients (depending on the particular wavelet filter used, it may look like a small version of the original image) and the other subbands contain detail coefficients. Each subband corresponds to a frequency band, while each individual transform coefficient corresponds to a local spatial region. By increasing the recursion depth r, we can increase frequency resolution at the expense of spatial resolution.

This type of wavelet image decomposition has been proposed by Wong and Kuo [Wong and Kuo 93], who highly recommend its use. However, it seems that it has been ignored by researchers and implementers in the field of image compression.

7. Adaptive Wavelet Packet Decomposition: The uniform decomposition method is costly in terms of computations, and the adaptive wavelet packet method is potentially even more so. The idea is to skip those subband splits that do not contribute significantly to energy compaction. The result is a coefficient matrix with subbands of different (possibly even many) sizes. The bottom-right part of Figure 5.45 shows such a case (after [Meyer et al. 98], which shows the adaptive wavelet packet transform matrix for the bi-level "mandril" image, Figure 4.39).

The justification for this complex decomposition method is the prevalence of continuous-tone (natural) images. These images, which are discussed at the start of Chapter 4, are mostly smooth but normally also have some regions with high frequency data. Such regions should end up as many small subbands (to better enable an accurate spatial frequency representation of the image), with the rest of the image giving rise to a few large subbands. The bottom-left coefficient matrix in Figure 5.45 is an example of a very uniform image, resulting in just 10 subbands. (The test for a split depends on the absolute magnitude of the transform coefficients. Thus, the test can be adjusted so high that very few splits are done.)

The main problem in this type of decomposition is finding an algorithm that will determine which subband splits can be skipped. Such an algorithm uses entropy calculations and should be efficient. It should identify all the splits that do not have to be performed, and it should identify as many of them as possible. An inefficient algorithm may lead to the split of every subband, thereby performing many unnecessary computations and ending up with a coefficient matrix where every coefficient is a subband, in which case this decomposition reduces to the uniform decomposition.

This type of decomposition has the highest reproduction quality of all the methods discussed here, a feature that may justify the high computational costs in certain special applications. This quality, however, is not much higher than what is achieved with simpler decomposition methods, such as standard, pyramid, or quincunx.

Bibliography

Burt, Peter J., and Edward H. Adelson (1983) "The Laplacian Pyramid as a Compact Image Code," *IEEE Transactions on Communications*, COM-31(4):532–540, April.

Mallat, Stephane (1989) "A Theory for Multiresolution Signal Decomposition: The Wavelet Representation," *IEEE Trans. on Pattern Analysis and Machine Intelligence*, **11**(7):674–693, July.

Meyer, F. G., A. Averbuch, and J.O. Strömberg (1998) "Fast Adaptive Wavelet Packet Image Compression," submitted to the *IEEE Transactions on Image Processing*, revised June 1999.

Starck, J. L., F. Murtagh, and A. Bijaoui (1998) *Image Processing and Data Analysis: The Multiscale Approach*, Cambridge University Press.

Strømme, Øyvind and Douglas R. McGregor (1997) "Comparison of Fidelity of Reproduction of Images After Lossy Compression Using Standard and NonStandard Wavelet Decompositions," in *Proceedings of The First European Conference on Signal Analysis and Prediction (ECSAP 97)*, Prague, June. Also downloadable from
`http://homepages.strath.ac.uk/~cadu02/research/publications.html`.

Strømme, Øyvind (1999) *On The Applicability of Wavelet Transforms to Image and Video Compression*, Ph.D. thesis, University of Strathclyde, February.

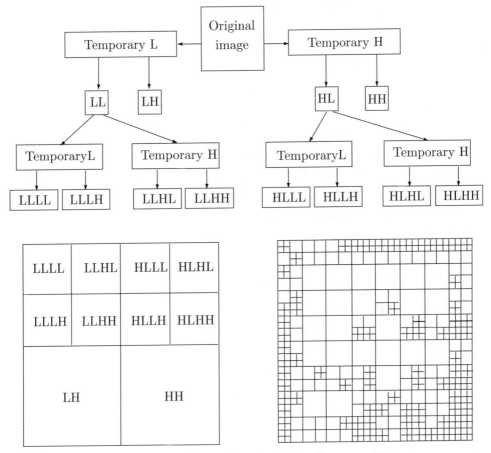

Figure 5.45: Adaptive Wavelet Packet Decomposition.

Wong, Kwo-Jyr, and C. C. Jay Kuo (1993) "A Full Wavelet Transform (FWT) Approach to Image Compression," *Image and Video Processing*, Bellingham, WA, SPIE volume 1903:153–164.

5.11 The Lifting Scheme

The lifting scheme is a useful way of looking at the discrete wavelet transform. It is easy to understand, since it performs all the operations in the time domain, rather than in the frequency domain, and has other advantages as well. This section illustrates the lifting approach using the Haar transform, which is already familiar to the reader, as an example. The following section extends the same approach to other transforms.

The Haar transform, described Section 5.6, is based on the calculations of averages and differences (details). Given two adjacent pixels a and b, the principle is to calculate the average $s = (a + b)/2$ and difference $d = b - a$. If a and b are similar, s will be similar to both and d will be small, i.e., require fewer bits to represent. This transform is reversible, since $a = s - d/2$ and $b = s + d/2$, and it can be written using matrix notation as

$$(s,d) = (a,b) \begin{pmatrix} 1/2 & -1 \\ 1/2 & 1 \end{pmatrix} = (a,b)\mathbf{A}, \quad (a,b) = (s,d) \begin{pmatrix} 1 & 1 \\ -1/2 & 1/2 \end{pmatrix} = (s,d)\mathbf{A}^{-1}.$$

Consider a row of 2^n pixel values $s_{n,l}$ for $0 \le l < 2^n$. There are 2^{n-1} pairs of pixels $s_{n,2l}$, $s_{n,2l+1}$ for $l = 0, 2, 4, \ldots, 2^{n-2}$. Each pair is transformed into an average $s_{n-1,l} = (s_{n,2l} + s_{n,2l+1})/2$ and a difference $d_{n-1,l} = s_{n,2l+1} - s_{n,2l}$. The result is a set s_{n-1} of 2^{n-1} averages and a set d_{n-1} of 2^{n-1} differences.

The same operations can be applied to the 2^{n-1} averages $s_{n-1,l}$ of set s_{n-1}, resulting in 2^{n-2} averages $s_{n-2,l}$ and 2^{n-2} differences $d_{n-2,l}$. After applying these operations n times we end up with a set s_0 consisting of one average $s_{0,0}$, and with n sets of differences $d_{j,l}$ where $j = 0, 1, \ldots, n-1$ and $l = 0, 1, \ldots, 2^j - 1$. Set j consists of j differences, so the total number of differences is

$$\sum_{j=0}^{n-1} 2^j = 2^n - 1.$$

Adding the single average $s_{0,0}$ brings the total number of results to 2^n, the same as the number of original pixel values. Notice that the final average $s_{0,0}$ is the average S of the original 2^n pixel values, so it can be called the DC component of the original values. In fact, if we look at any set s_j of averages $s_{j,l}$, $l = 0, 1, \ldots, 2^j - 1$, we find that its average

$$S = \frac{1}{2^j} \sum_{l=0}^{2^j-1} s_{j,l}$$

is the average of all the original 2^n pixel values. Thus, the average S of set s_j is independent of j. Figure 5.46a,b illustrates the transform and its inverse.

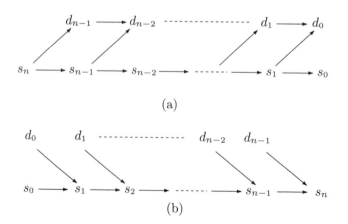

(a)

(b)

Figure 5.46: (a) The Haar Wavelet Transform and (b) Its Inverse.

The main idea in the lifting scheme is to perform all the necessary operations without using extra space. The entire transform is performed *in place*, replacing the original image. We start with a pair of consecutive pixels a and b. They are replaced with their average s and difference d by first replacing b with $d = b - a$, then replacing a with $s = a + d/2$ [since $d = b - a$, $a + d/2 = a + (b - a)/2$ equals $(a + b)/2$]. In the C language, this is written

$$\texttt{b-=a;} \quad \texttt{a+=b/2;}$$

⋄ **Exercise 5.12:** Write the reverse operations in C.

This is easy to apply to an entire row of pixels. Suppose that we have a row s_j with 2^j values and we want to transform it to a row s_{j-1} with 2^{j-1} averages and 2^{j-1} differences. The lifting scheme performs this transform in three steps, *split*, *predict*, and *update*.

The split operation splits row s_j into two separate sets denoted by even_{j-1} and odd_{j-1}. The former contains all the even values $s_{j,2l}$, and the latter contains all the odd values $s_{j,2l+1}$. The range of l is from zero to $2^j - 1$. This kind of splitting into odd and even values is called the *lazy wavelet transform*. We denote it by

$$(\text{even}_{j-1}, \text{odd}_{j-1}) := \text{Split}(s_j).$$

The predict operation uses the even set even_{j-1} to predict the odd set odd_{j-1}. This is based on the fact that each value $s_{j,2l+1}$ in the odd set is adjacent to the corresponding value $s_{j,2l}$ in the even set. Thus, the two values are correlated and either can be used to predict the other. Recall that a general difference $d_{j-1,l}$ is computed as the difference $d_{j-1,l} = s_{j,2l+1} - s_{j,2l}$ between an odd value and an adjacent even value (or between an odd value and its prediction), which is why we can define the prediction operator P as

$$d_{j-1} = \text{odd}_{j-1} - P(\text{even}_{j-1}).$$

The update operation U follows the prediction step. It calculates the 2^{j-1} averages $s_{j-1,l}$ as the sum

$$s_{j-1,l} = s_{j,2l} + d_{j-1,l}/2. \tag{5.13}$$

This operation is formally defined by

$$s_{j-1} = \text{even}_{j-1} + U(d_{j-1}).$$

⋄ **Exercise 5.13:** Use Equation (5.13) to prove that sets s_j and s_{j-1} have the same average.

The important point to notice is that all three operations can be performed in place. The even locations of set s_j are overwritten with the averages (i.e., with set even_{j-1}), and the odd locations are overwritten with the differences (set odd_{j-1}). The sequence of three operations can be summarized by

$$(\text{odd}_{j-1}, \text{even}_{j-1}) := \text{Split}(s_j); \quad \text{odd}_{j-1} - = P(\text{even}_{j-1}); \quad \text{even}_{j-1} + = U(\text{odd}_{j-1});$$

Figure 5.47a is a wiring diagram of this process.

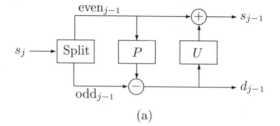

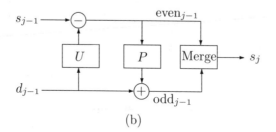

Figure 5.47: The Lifting Scheme. (a) Forward Transform. (b) Reverse Transform.

The reverse transform is similar. It is based on the three operations *undo update*, *undo prediction*, and *merge*.

Given two sets s_{j-1} and d_{j-1}, the "undo update" operation reconstructs the averages $s_{j,2l}$ (the even values of set s_j) by subtracting the update operation. It generates the set even_{j-1} by subtracting the sets $s_{j-1} - U(d_{j-1})$. Written explicitly, this operation becomes

$$s_{j,2l} = s_{j-1,l} - d_{j-1,l}/2, \text{ for } 0 \leq l < 2^j.$$

Given the two sets even_{j-1} and d_{j-1}, the "undo predict" operation reconstructs the differences $s_{j,2l+1}$ (the odd values of set s_j) by adding the prediction operator P. It generates the set odd_{j-1} by adding the sets $d_{j-1} + P(\text{even}_{j-1})$. Written explicitly, this operation becomes

$$s_{j,2l+1} = d_{j-1,l} + s_{j,2l}, \text{ for } 0 \leq l < 2^j.$$

Now that the two sets even_{j-1} and odd_{j-1} have been reconstructed, they are merged by the "merge" operation into the set s_j. This is the inverse lazy wavelet transform, formally denoted by

$$s_j = \text{Merge}(\text{even}_{j-1}, \text{odd}_{j-1}).$$

It moves the averages and the differences into the even and odd locations of s_j, respectively, without using any extra space. The three operations are summarized by

$$\text{even}_{j-1}- = U(\text{odd}_{j-1}); \quad \text{odd}_{j-1}+ = P(\text{even}_{j-1}); \quad s_j := \text{Merge}(\text{odd}_{j-1}, \text{even}_{j-1});$$

Figure 5.47b is a wiring diagram of this process.

The wiring diagrams show one of the important features of the lifting scheme, namely its inherent parallelism. Given an SIMD (single instruction, multiple data) computer with 2^n processing units, each unit can be "responsible" for one pixel value. Such a computer executes a single program where each instruction is executed in parallel by all the processing units. Another advantage of lifting is the simplicity of its inverse transform. It is simply the code for the forward transform, run backward. The main advantage of lifting is the fact that it is easy to extend. It has been presented here for the Haar transform, where averages and differences are calculated in a simple way. It can be extended to more complex cases, where the prediction and update operations are more complex.

5.11.1 The Linear Wavelet Transform

The reason for extending the lifting scheme beyond the Haar transform is that this transform does not produce high-quality results, since it uses such simple prediction. Recall that the "predict" operation uses the even set even_{j-1} to predict the odd set odd_{j-1}. This gives accurate prediction only in the (very rare) cases where the two sets are identical. We can say that the Haar transform eliminates order-zero correlation between pixels by using an order-one predictor. The Haar transform also preserves the average of all the pixels of the image, and this average can be called the *order-zero moment* of the image.

Better compression can be achieved by transforms that use better predictors, predictors that exploit correlations between several neighbor pixels and also preserve higher-order moments of the image. The predictor and update operations described here are of order two. This implies that the predictor will provide exact prediction if the image pixels vary linearly, and the update operation will preserve the first two (order-zero and order-one) moments. The principle is easy to describe. We again concentrate on a row s_j of pixel values. An odd-numbered value $s_{j,2l+1}$ is predicted as the average of its two immediate neighbors $s_{j,2l}$ and $s_{j,2l+2}$. To be able to reconstruct $s_{j,2l+1}$, we have to calculate a detail value $d_{j,l}$ that is no longer a simple difference but is given by

$$d_{j,l} = s_{j,2l+1} - \frac{1}{2}(s_{j,2l} + s_{j,2l+2}).$$

(This notation assumes that every pixel has two immediate neighbors. This is not true for pixels located on the boundaries of the image, so edge rules will have to be developed and justified.)

Figure 5.48 illustrates the meaning of the detail values in this case. Figure 5.48a shows the values of nine hypothetical pixels numbered 0 through 8. Figure 5.48b shows straight segments connecting the even-numbered pixels. This is the reason for the name "linear transform." In Figure 5.48c the odd-numbered pixels are predicted by these straight segments, and Figure 5.48d shows (in dashed bold) the difference between each odd-numbered pixel and its prediction. The equation of a straight line is $y = ax + b$, a polynomial of degree 1, which is why we can think of the detail values as the amount by which the pixel values deviate locally from a degree-1 polynomial. If pixel x had value $ax + b$, all the detail values would be

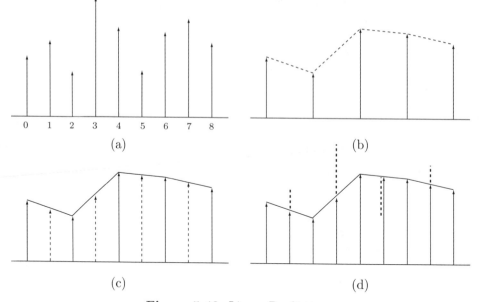

Figure 5.48: Linear Prediction.

zero. This is why we can say that the detail values capture the high frequencies of the image.

The "update" operation reconstructs the averages $s_{j-1,l}$ from the averages $s_{j,l}$ and the differences $d_{j-1,l}$. In the case of the Haar transform, this operation is defined by Equation (5.13): $s_{j-1,l} = s_{j,2l} + d_{j-1,l}/2$. In the case of the linear transform it is somewhat more complicated. We derive the update operation for the linear transform using the requirement that it preserves the zeroth-order moment of the image, i.e., the average of the averages $s_{j,l}$ should not depend on j. We try an update of the form

$$s_{j-1,l} = s_{j,2l} + A(d_{j-1,l-1} + d_{j-1,l}), \tag{5.14}$$

where A is an unknown coefficient. The sum of $s_{j-1,l}$ now becomes

$$\sum_l s_{j-1,l} = \sum_l s_{j,2l} + 2A \sum_l d_{j-1,l} = (1 - 2A) \sum_l s_{j,2l} + 2A \sum_l s_{j,2l+1},$$

so the choice $A = 1/4$ results in

$$\sum_{l=0}^{2^{j-1}-1} s_{j-1,l} = \left(1 - \frac{1}{2}\right) \sum_{l=0}^{2^j - 1} s_{j,2l} + \frac{2}{4} \sum_{l=0}^{2^j - 1} s_{j,2l+1} = \frac{1}{2} \sum_{l=0}^{2^j - 1} s_{j,l}.$$

Comparing this with Equation (5.15) shows that the zeroth-order moment of the image is preserved by the update operation of Equation (5.14). A direct check also verifies that

$$\sum_l l\, s_{j-1,l} = \frac{1}{2}\sum_l l\, s_{j,l},$$

which shows that this update operation also preserves the first-order moment of the image and is therefore of order 2.

Equation (5.15), duplicated below, is derived in the answer to Exercise 5.13:

$$\sum_{l=0}^{2^{j-1}-1} s_{j-1,l} = \sum_{l=0}^{2^{j-1}-1} (s_{j,2l} + d_{j-1,l}/2) = \frac{1}{2}\sum_{l=0}^{2^{j-1}-1} (s_{j,2l} + s_{j,2l+1}) = \frac{1}{2}\sum_{l=0}^{2^{j}-1} s_{j,l}.$$
$$(5.15)$$

The inverse linear transform reconstructs the even and odd average values by

$$s_{j,2l} = s_{j-1,l} - \frac{1}{4}(d_{j-1,l-1} + d_{j-1,l}), \text{ and } s_{j,2l+1} = d_{j,l} + \frac{1}{2}(s_{j,2l} + s_{j,2l+2}),$$

respectively.

Figure 5.49 summarizes the linear transform. The top row shows the even and odd averages $s_{j,l}$. The middle row shows how a detail value $d_{j-1,l}$ is calculated as the difference between an odd average $s_{j,2l+1}$ and half the sum of its two even neighbors $s_{j,2l}$ and $s_{j,2l+2}$. The bottom row shows how the next set s_{j-1} of averages is calculated. Each average $s_{j-1,l}$ in this set is the sum of an even average $s_{j,2l}$ and one-quarter of the two detail values $d_{j-1,l-1}$ and $d_{j-1,l}$. The figure also illustrates the main feature of the lifting scheme, namely how the even averages $s_{j,2l}$ are replaced by the next set of averages $s_{j-1,l}$ and how the odd averages $s_{j,2l+1}$ are replaced by the detail values $d_{j-1,l}$ (the dashed arrows indicate items that are not moved). All these operations are done in place.

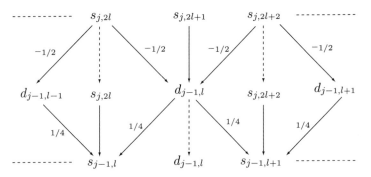

Figure 5.49: Summary of the Linear Wavelet Transform.

5.11.2 Interpolating Subdivision

The method of interpolating subdivision starts with a set s_0 of pixels where pixel $s_{0,k}$ (for $k = 0, 1, \ldots$) is stored in location k of an array a. It creates a set s_1 (twice the size of s_0) of pixels $s_{1,k}$ such that the even-numbered pixels $s_{1,2k}$ are simply the even-numbered pixels $s_{0,k}$ and each of the odd-numbered pixels $s_{1,2k+1}$ is obtained by interpolating some of the pixels (odd and/or even) of set s_0. The new content of array a is

$$s_{1,0} = s_{0,0},\ s_{1,1},\ s_{1,2} = s_{0,1},\ s_{1,3},\ s_{1,4} = s_{0,2},\ s_{1,5}, \ldots, s_{1,2k} = s_{0,k},\ s_{1,2k+1}, \ldots.$$

The original elements $s_{0,k}$ of s_0 are now stored in a in locations $2k = k{\cdot}2^1$. We say that set s_1 was created from s_0 by a process of subdivision (or refinement).

Next, set s_2 (twice the size of s_1) is created in the same way from s_1. The even-numbered pixels $s_{2,2k}$ are simply the even-numbered pixels $s_{1,k}$, and each of the odd-numbered pixels $s_{2,2k+1}$ is obtained by interpolating some of the pixels (odd and/or even) of set s_1. The new content of array a becomes

$$s_{2,0} = s_{1,0} = s_{0,0},\ s_{2,1},\ s_{2,2} = s_{1,1},\ s_{2,3},\ s_{2,4} = s_{1,2} = s_{0,1},\ s_{2,5}, \ldots$$
$$s_{2,2k} = s_{1,k},\ s_{2,2k+1}, \ldots, s_{2,4k} = s_{1,2k} = s_{0,k}, s_{2,4k+1}, \ldots.$$

The original elements $s_{0,k}$ of s_0 are now stored in a in locations $4k = k{\cdot}2^2$.

In a general subdivision step, a set s_j of pixel values $s_{j,k}$ is used to construct a new set s_{j+1}, twice as large. The even-numbered pixels $s_{j+1,2k}$ are simply the even-numbered pixels $s_{j,k}$, and each of the odd-numbered pixels $s_{j+1,2k+1}$ is obtained by interpolating some of the pixels (odd and/or even) of set s_j. The original elements $s_{0,k}$ of s_0 are now stored in a in locations $k{\cdot}2^j$.

We illustrate this refinement process by using linear interpolation. Each of the odd-numbered pixels $s_{1,2k+1}$ is calculated as the average of the two pixels $s_{0,k}$ and $s_{0,k+1}$ of set s_0. In general, we get

$$s_{j+1,2k} = s_{j,k}, \quad s_{j+1,2k+1} = \frac{1}{2}\left(s_{j,k} + s_{j,k+1}\right). \tag{5.16}$$

Figure 5.50a–d shows several steps in this process, starting with a set s_0 of four pixels (it is useful to visualize each pixel as a two-dimensional point). It is obvious that the pixel values converge to the *polyline* that passes through the original four points.

Given an image where the pixel values go up and down linearly (in a polyline), we can compress it by selecting the pixels at the corners of the polyline (i.e., those pixels where the value changes direction) and writing them on the compressed file. The image could then be perfectly reconstructed to any resolution by using linear subdivision to compute as many pixels as needed between corner pixels. Most images, however, feature more complex behavior of pixel values, so more complex subdivision is needed.

We now show how to extend linear subdivision to *polynomial subdivision*. Instead of computing an odd-numbered pixel $s_{j+1,2k+1}$ as the average of its two immediate level-j neighbors $s_{j,k}$ and $s_{j,k+1}$, we calculate it as a weighted sum of its **four** immediate level-j neighbors $s_{j,k-1}$, $s_{j,k}$, $s_{j,k+1}$, and $s_{j,k+2}$. It is obvious that the two closer neighbors $s_{j,k}$ and $s_{j,k+1}$ should be assigned more weight than the two extreme neighbors $s_{j,k-1}$ and $s_{j,k+2}$, but what should the weights be? The answer is provided in an appendix in the book's web site, where it is shown that

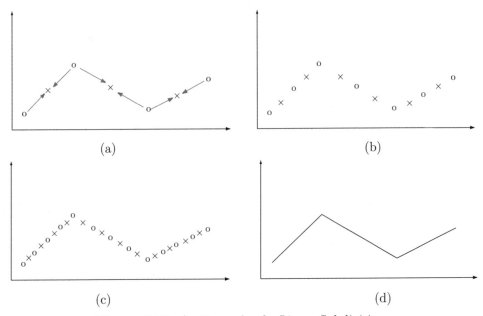

Figure 5.50: An Example of a Linear Subdivision.

the degree-3 (cubic) polynomial $\mathbf{P}(t)$ that interpolates four arbitrary points $\mathbf{P}_1$, $\mathbf{P}_2$, $\mathbf{P}_3$, and $\mathbf{P}_4$ is given by

$$\mathbf{P}(t) = (t^3, t^2, t, 1) \begin{pmatrix} -4.5 & 13.5 & -13.5 & 4.5 \\ 9.0 & -22.5 & 18 & -4.5 \\ -5.5 & 9.0 & -4.5 & 1.0 \\ 1.0 & 0 & 0 & 0 \end{pmatrix} \begin{pmatrix} \mathbf{P}_1 \\ \mathbf{P}_2 \\ \mathbf{P}_3 \\ \mathbf{P}_4 \end{pmatrix}. \tag{5.17}$$

We are going to place the new odd-numbered pixel $s_{j+1,2k+1}$ in the middle of the group of its four level-j neighbors, so it makes sense to assign it the value of the interpolating polynomial in the middle of its interval, i.e., $\mathbf{P}(0.5)$. Calculated from Equation (5.17), this value is

$$\mathbf{P}(0.5) = -0.0625\mathbf{P}_1 + 0.5625\mathbf{P}_2 + 0.5625\mathbf{P}_3 - 0.0625\mathbf{P}_4.$$

(Notice that the four weights add up to one. This is an example of barycentric functions, introduced in an appendix in the book's web site. Also, see an exercise in that appendix for an explanation of the negative weights.)

The subdivision rule in this case is [by analogy with Equation (5.16)]

$$s_{j+1,2k} = s_{j,k}, \quad s_{j+1,2k+1} = \mathbf{P}_{3,j,k-1}(0.5), \tag{5.18}$$

where the notation $\mathbf{P}_{3,j,k-1}(t)$ indicates the degree-3 interpolating polynomial for the group of four level-j pixels that starts at $s_{j,k-1}$. We define the *order* of this subdivision to be four (the number of interpolated pixels). Since linear subdivision

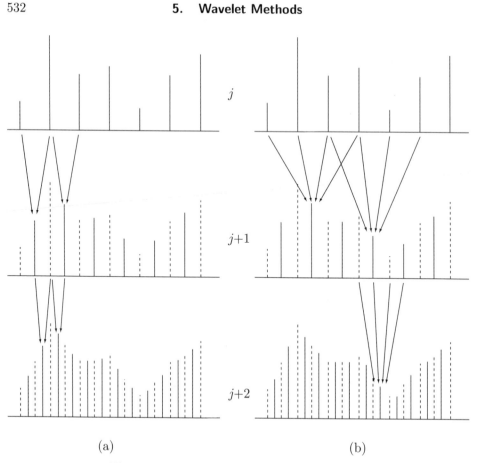

(a)   (b)

Figure 5.51: Linear and Cubic Subdivisions.

interpolates two pixels, its order is two. Figure 5.51 shows three levels of pixels generated by linear (5.51a) and by cubic (5.51b) subdivisions.

It is now obvious how interpolating subdivision can be extended to higher orders. Select an even integer n, derive the degree-$n-1$ polynomial $\mathbf{P}_{n-1,j,k-(n/2-1)}(t)$ that will interpolate the n level-j pixels

$$s_{j,k-(n/2-1)},\ s_{j,k-n/2},\ s_{j,k-n/2+1},\ldots,s_{j,k},\ s_{j,k+1},\ldots,s_{j,k+n/2},$$

calculate the midpoint $\mathbf{P}_{n-1,j,k-(n/2-1)}(0.5)$, and generate the level-$(j+1)$ pixels according to

$$s_{j+1,2k} = s_{j,k},\quad s_{j+1,2k+1} = \mathbf{P}_{n-1,j,k-(n/2-1)}(0.5), \qquad (5.19)$$

⋄ **Exercise 5.14:** Calculate the midpoint $\mathbf{P}(0.5)$ of the degree-5 interpolating polynomial for six points $\mathbf{P}_1$ through $\mathbf{P}_6$ as a function of the points.

5.11.3 Scaling Functions

The scaling functions $\phi_{j,k}(x)$ have been mentioned in Section 5.6, in connection with the Haar transform. Here we show how they are constructed for interpolating subdivision. Each coefficient $s_{j,k}$ computed in level j has a scaling function $\phi_{j,k}(x)$ associated with it, which is defined as follows: Select values n, j, and k. Set pixel $s_{j,k}$ to 1 and all other $s_{j,i}$ to 0 (this can be expressed as $s_{j,k} = \delta_{0,k}$). Use a subdivision scheme (based on n points) to compute levels $(j+1)$, $(j+2)$, etc. Each level has twice the number of pixels as its predecessor. In the limit, we end up with an infinite number of pixels. We can view these pixels as real numbers and define the range of the scaling function $\phi_{j,k}(x)$ as these numbers. Each pair of values j and k defines a different scaling function $\phi_{j,k}(x)$, but we can intuitively see that the scaling functions depend on j and k in simple ways. The shape of $\phi_{j,k}(x)$ does not depend on k, since we calculate ϕ by setting $s_{j,k} = 1$ and all other $s_{j,i} = 0$. Thus, the function $\phi_{j,8}(x)$ is a shifted copy of $\phi_{j,7}(x)$, a twice shifted copy of $\phi_{j,6}(x)$, etc. In general, we get $\phi_{j,k}(x) = \phi_{j,0}(x - k)$. To understand the dependence of $\phi_{j,k}(x)$ on j, the reader should recall the following sentence (from page 530)

The original elements $s_{0,k}$ of s_0 are now stored in a in locations $k \cdot 2^j$.

This implies that if we select a small value for j, we end up with a wide scaling function $\phi_{j,k}(x)$. In general, we have

$$\phi_{j,k}(x) = \phi_{0,0}(2^j x - k) \stackrel{\text{def}}{=} \phi(2^j x - k),$$

implying that all the scaling functions for different values of j and k are translations and dilations (scaling) of $\phi(x)$, the fundamental solution of the subdivision process. $\phi(x)$ is shown in Figure 5.52 for $n = 2, 4, 6$, and 8.

The main properties of $\phi(x)$ are compact support and smoothness (it can be nonzero only inside the interval $[-(n-1), n-1]$), but it also satisfies a *refinement relation* of the form

$$\phi(x) = \sum_{l=-n}^{n} h_l \phi(2x - l),$$

where h_l are called the *filter coefficients*. A change of variables allows us to write the same refinement relation in the form

$$\phi_{j,k}(x) = \sum_l h_{l-2k} \phi_{j+1,l}(x).$$

The odd-numbered filter coefficients are the coefficients of the interpolating polynomial at its midpoint $\mathbf{P}_{n-1,j,k-(n/2-1)}(0.5)$. The even-numbered coefficients are zero except for $l = 0$ (this property can be expressed as $h_{2l} = \delta_{0,l}$). The general expression for h_k is

$$h_k = \begin{cases} k \text{ even}, & \delta_{k,0}, \\ k \text{ odd}, & (-1)^{d+k} \frac{\Pi_{i=0}^{2d-1}(i-d+1/2)}{(k+1/2)(d+k)!(d-k-1)!}, \end{cases}$$

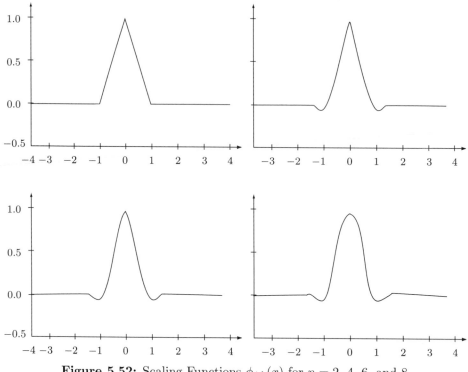

Figure 5.52: Scaling Functions $\phi_{j,k}(x)$ for $n = 2, 4, 6,$ and 8.

where $d = n/2$. For linear subdivision, the filter coefficients are $(1/2, 1, 1/2)$. For cubic interpolation the eight filter coefficients are $(-1/16, 0, 9/16, 1, 9/16, 0, -1/16)$. The filter coefficients are useful, since they allow us to write the interpolating subdivision in the form

$$s_{j+1,l} = \sum_k h_{l-2k} s_{j,k}.$$

Bibliography

Stollnitz, E. J., T. D. DeRose, and D. H. Salesin (1996) *Wavelets for Computer Graphics*, San Francisco, CA, Morgan Kaufmann.

Sweldens, Wim and Peter Schröder (1996), *Building Your Own Wavelets At Home*, SIG-GRAPH 96 Course Notes, available on the WWW.

5.12 The IWT

The DWT is simple but has an important drawback, namely, it uses noninteger filter coefficients, which results in noninteger transform coefficients. There are several ways to modify the basic DWT such that it produces integer transform coefficients. This section describes a simple *integer wavelet transform* (IWT) that can be used to decompose an image in any of the ways described in Section 5.10. The transform is reversible, i.e., the image can be fully reconstructed from the (integer) transform coefficients. This IWT can be used to compress the image either lossily (by quantizing the transform coefficients) or losslessly (by entropy coding the transform coefficients).

The principle of this transform is simple and is illustrated here for the one-dimensional case. Given a data vector of N integers x_i, where $i = 0, 1, \ldots, N - 1$, we define $k = N/2$ and we compute the transform vector y_i by calculating the odd and even components of y separately. We first discuss the case where N is even. The $N/2$ odd components y_{2i+1} (where $i = 0, 1, \ldots, k - 1$) are calculated as differences of the x_i's. They become the detail (high frequency) transform coefficients. Each of the even components y_{2i} (where i varies in the same range $[0, k-1]$) is calculated as a weighted average of five data items x_i. These $N/2$ numbers become the low-frequency transform coefficients, and are normally transformed again, into $N/4$ low-frequency and $N/4$ high-frequency coefficients.

The basic rule for the odd transform coefficients is

$$y_{2i+1} = -\frac{1}{2}x_{2i} + x_{2i+1} - \frac{1}{2}x_{2i+2},$$

except the last coefficient, where $i = k - 1$, which is calculated as the simple difference $y_{2k-1} = x_{2k-1} - x_{2k-2}$. This can be summarized as

$$y_{2i+1} = \begin{cases} x_{2i+1} - (x_{2i} + x_{2i+2})/2, & \text{for } i = 0, 1, \ldots, k - 2, \\ x_{2i+1} - x_{2i}, & \text{for } i = k - 1. \end{cases} \tag{5.20}$$

The even transform coefficients are calculated as the weighted average

$$y_{2i} = -\frac{1}{8}x_{2i-2} + \frac{1}{4}x_{2i-1} + \frac{3}{4}x_{2i} + \frac{1}{4}x_{2i+1} - \frac{1}{8}x_{2i+2},$$

except the first coefficient, where $i = 0$, which is calculated as

$$y_0 = \frac{3}{4}x_0 + \frac{1}{2}x_1 - \frac{1}{4}x_2.$$

In practice, this calculation is done by computing each even coefficient y_{2i} in terms of x_{2i} and the two odd coefficients y_{2i-1} and y_{2i+1}. This can be summarized by

$$y_{2i} = \begin{cases} x_{2i} + y_{2i+1}/2, & \text{for } i = 0, \\ x_{2i} + (y_{2i-1} + y_{2i+1})/4, & \text{for } i = 1, 2, \ldots, k - 1. \end{cases} \tag{5.21}$$

The inverse transform is easy to figure out. It uses the transform coefficients y_i to calculate data items z_i that are identical to the original x_i. It first computes the even elements

$$z_{2i} = \begin{cases} y_{2i} - y_{2i+1}/2, & \text{for } i = 0, \\ y_{2i} - (y_{2i-1} + y_{2i+1})/4, & \text{for } i = 1, 2, \ldots, k - 1, \end{cases} \tag{5.22}$$

then the odd elements

$$z_{2i+1} = \begin{cases} y_{2i+1} + (z_{2i} + z_{2i+2})/2, & \text{for } i = 0, 1, \ldots, k - 2, \\ y_{2i+1} + z_{2i}, & \text{for } i = k - 1. \end{cases} \tag{5.23}$$

Now comes the interesting part. The transform coefficients calculated by Equations (5.20) and (5.21) are not generally integers, because of the divisions by 2 and 4. The same is true for the reconstructed data items of Equations (5.22) and (5.23). The main feature of the particular IWT described here is the use of *truncation*. Truncation, denoted by the "floor" symbols $\lfloor$ and $\rfloor$, is used to produce integer transform coefficients y_i **and** also integer reconstructed data items z_i. Equations (5.20) through (5.23) are modified to

$$
y_{2i+1} = \begin{cases} x_{2i+1} - \lfloor (x_{2i} + x_{2i+2})/2 \rfloor, & \text{for } i = 0, 1, \ldots, k-2, \\ x_{2i+1} - x_{2i}, & \text{for } i = k-1. \end{cases}
$$

$$
y_{2i} = \begin{cases} x_{2i} + \lfloor y_{2i+1}/2 \rfloor, & \text{for } i = 0, \\ x_{2i} + \lfloor (y_{2i-1} + y_{2i+1})/4 \rfloor, & \text{for } i = 1, 2, \ldots, k-1. \end{cases}
$$

$$
z_{2i} = \begin{cases} y_{2i} - \lfloor y_{2i+1}/2 \rfloor, & \text{for } i = 0, \\ y_{2i} - \lfloor (y_{2i-1} + y_{2i+1})/4 \rfloor, & \text{for } i = 1, 2, \ldots, k-1, \end{cases} \tag{5.24}
$$

$$
z_{2i+1} = \begin{cases} y_{2i+1} + \lfloor (z_{2i} + z_{2i+2})/2 \rfloor, & \text{for } i = 0, 1, \ldots, k-2, \\ y_{2i+1} + z_{2i}, & \text{for } i = k-1. \end{cases}
$$

Because of truncation, some information is lost when the y_i are calculated. However, truncation is also used in the calculation of the z_i, which restores the lost information. Thus, Equation (5.24) is a true forward and inverse IWT that reconstructs the original data items exactly.

$\diamond$ **Exercise 5.15:** Given the data vector $x = (112, 97, 85, 99, 114, 120, 77, 80)$, use Equation (5.24) to calculate its forward and inverse integer wavelet transforms.

The same concepts can be applied to the case where the number N of data items is odd. We first define k by $N = 2k + 1$, then define the forward and inverse integer transforms by

$$
y_{2i+1} = x_{2i+1} - \lfloor (x_{2i} + x_{2i+2})/2 \rfloor, \text{ for } i = 0, 1, \ldots, k-1,
$$

$$
y_{2i} = \begin{cases} x_{2i} + \lfloor y_{2i+1}/2 \rfloor, & \text{for } i = 0, \\ x_{2i} + \lfloor (y_{2i-1} + y_{2i+1})4 \rfloor, & \text{for } i = 1, 2, \ldots, k-1, \\ x_{2i} + \lfloor y_{2i-1}/2 \rfloor, & \text{for } i = k. \end{cases}
$$

$$
z_{2i} = \begin{cases} y_{2i} - \lfloor y_{2i+1}/2 \rfloor, & \text{for } i = 0, \\ y_{2i} - \lfloor (y_{2i-1} + y_{2i+1})/4 \rfloor, & \text{for } i = 1, 2, \ldots, k-1, \\ y_{2i} - \lfloor y_{2i-1}/2 \rfloor, & \text{for } i = k, \end{cases}
$$

$$
z_{2i+1} = y_{2i+1} + \lfloor (z_{2i} + z_{2i+2})/2 \rfloor, \text{ for } i = 0, 1, \ldots, k-1.
$$

Notice that the IWT produces a vector y_i where the detail coefficients and the weighted averages are interleaved. The algorithm should be modified to place the averages in the first half of y and the details in the second half.

The extension of this transform to the two-dimensional case is obvious. The IWT is applied to the rows and the columns of the image using any of the image decomposition methods discussed in Section 5.10.

5.13 The Laplacian Pyramid

The main feature of the Laplacian pyramid method is progressive compression. The decoder inputs the compressed stream section by section, and each section improves the appearance on the screen of the image-so-far. The method uses both prediction and transform techniques, but its computations are simple and local (i.e., there is no need to examine or use values that are far away from the current pixel). The name "Laplacian" comes from the field of image enhancement, where it is used to indicate operations similar to the ones used here. We start with a general description of the method.

We denote by $g_0(i, j)$ the original image. A new, reduced image g_1 is computed from g_0 such that each pixel of g_1 is a weighted sum of a group of 5×5 pixels of g_0. Image g_1 is computed [see Equation (5.25)] such that it has half the number of rows and half the number of columns of g_0, so it is one-quarter the size of g_0. It is a blurred (or lowpass filtered) version of g_0. The next step is to expand g_1 to an image $g_{1,1}$ the size of g_0 by interpolating pixel values [Equation (5.26)]. A difference image (also called an error image) L_0 is calculated as the difference $g_0 - g_{1,1}$, and it becomes the bottom level of the Laplacian pyramid. The original image g_0 can be reconstructed from L_0 and $g_{1,1}$, and also from L_0 and g_1. Since g_1 is smaller than $g_{1,1}$, it makes sense to write L_0 and g_1 on the compressed stream. The size of L_0 equals that of g_0, and the size of g_1 is $1/4$ of that, so it seems that we get expansion, but in fact, compression is achieved, since the error values in L_0 are decorrelated to a high degree, and so are small (and therefore have small variance and low entropy) and can be represented with fewer bits than the original pixels in g_0.

In order to achieve progressive representation of the image, only L_0 is written on the output, and the process is repeated on g_1. A new, reduced image g_2 is computed from g_1 (the size of g_2 is $1/16$ that of g_0). It is expanded to an image $g_{2,1}$, and a new difference image L_1 is computed as the difference $g_1 - g_{2,1}$ and becomes the next level, above L_0, of the Laplacian pyramid. The final result is a sequence $L_0, L_1, \ldots, L_{k-1}, L_k$ where the first k items are difference images and the last one, L_k, is simply the (very small) reduced image g_k. These items constitute the Laplacian pyramid. They are written on the compressed stream in reverse order, so the decoder inputs L_k first, uses it to display a small, blurred image, inputs L_{k-1}, reconstructs and displays g_{k-1} (which is four times bigger), and repeats until g_0 is reconstructed and displayed. This process can be summarized by

$$g_k = L_k,$$
$$g_i = L_i + \text{Expand}(g_{i+1}) = L_i + g_{i+1,1}, \text{ for } i = k-1, k-2, \ldots, 2, 1, 0.$$

The user sees small, blurred images that grow and become sharper. The decoder can be modified to expand each intermediate image g_i (before it is displayed) several times, by interpolating pixel values, until it gets to the size of the original image g_0. This way, the user sees an image that progresses from very blurred to sharp, while remaining the same size. For example, image g_3, which is $1/64$th the size of g_0, can be brought to that size by expanding it three times, yielding the chain

$$g_{3,3} = \text{Expand}(g_{3,2}) = \text{Expand}(g_{3,1}) = \text{Expand}(g_3).$$

In order for all the intermediate g_i and L_i images to have well-defined dimensions, the original image g_0 should have $R = M_R 2^M + 1$ rows and $C = M_C 2^M + 1$ columns, where M_R, M_C, and M are integers. Selecting, for example, $M_R = M_C$ results in a square image. Image g_1 has dimensions $(M_R 2^{M-1}+1) \times (M_C 2^{M-1}+1)$, and image g_p has dimensions $(M_R 2^{M-p} + 1) \times (M_C 2^{M-p} + 1)$. An example is $M_R = M_C = 1$ and $M = 8$. The original image has, in this case, dimensions $(2^8 + 1) \times (2^8 + 1) = 257 \times 257$, and the reduced images g_1 through g_5 have dimensions $(2^7 + 1) \times (2^7 + 1) = 129 \times 129$, 65×65, 33×33, 17×17, and 9×9, respectively.

⋄ **Exercise 5.16:** Calculate the dimensions of the first six images g_0 through g_5 for the case $M_C = 3$, $M_R = 4$, and $M = 5$.

We now turn to the details of reducing and expanding images. Reducing an image g_{p-1} to an image g_p of dimensions $R_p \times C_p$ (where $R_p = M_R 2^{M-p} + 1$, and $C_p = M_C 2^{M-p} + 1$) is done by

$$g_p(i,j) = \sum_{m=-2}^{2} \sum_{n=-2}^{2} w(m,n) g_{p-1}(2i + m, 2j + n), \qquad (5.25)$$

where $i = 0, 1, \ldots, C_p - 1$, $j = 0, 1, \ldots, R_p - 1$, and p (the level) varies from 1 to $k - 1$. Each pixel of g_p is a weighted sum of 5×5 pixels of g_{p-1} with weights $w(m,n)$ that are the same for all levels p. Figure 5.53a illustrates this process in one dimension. It shows how each pixel in a higher level of the pyramid is generated as a weighted sum of five pixels from the level below it, and how each level has (about) half the number of pixels of its predecessor. Figure 5.53b is in two dimensions. It shows how a pixel in a high level is obtained from 25 pixels located one level below. Some of the weights are also shown. Notice that in this case each level has about $1/4$ the number of pixels of its predecessor.

The weights $w(m,n)$ (also called the generating kernel) are determined by first separating each in the form $w(m,n) = \hat{w}(m)\hat{w}(n)$, where the functions $\hat{w}(m)$ should be normalized,

$$\sum_{m=-2}^{2} \hat{w}(m) = 1,$$

and symmetric, $\hat{w}(m) = \hat{w}(-m)$. These two constraints are not enough to determine $\hat{w}(m)$, so we add a third one, called *equal contribution*, that demands that all the pixels at a given level contribute the same total weight $(= 1/4)$ to pixels at the next higher level. If we set $\hat{w}(0) = a$, $\hat{w}(-1) = \hat{w}(1) = b$, and $\hat{w}(-2) = \hat{w}(2) = c$, then the three constraints are satisfied if

$$w(0) = a, \quad \hat{w}(-1) = \hat{w}(1) = 0.25, \quad \hat{w}(-2) = \hat{w}(2) = 0.25 - a/2.$$

(The reader should compare this to the discussion of interpolating polynomials in an appendix in the book's web site.)

Experience recommends setting $a = 0.6$, which yields (see values of $w(m,n)$ in Table 5.54)

$$\hat{w}(0) = 0.6, \quad \hat{w}(-2) = \hat{w}(2) = 0.25, \quad \hat{w}(-1) = \hat{w}(1) = 0.25 - 0.3 = -0.05.$$

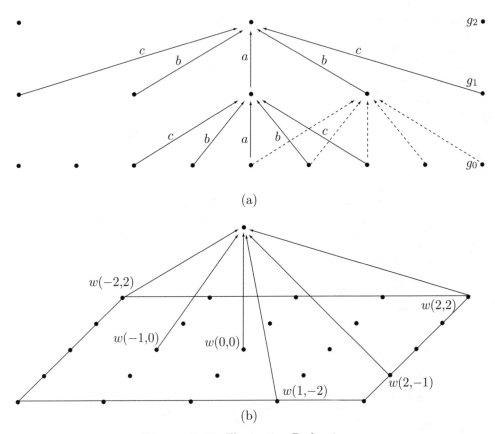

(a)

(b)

Figure 5.53: Illustrating Reduction.

The same weights used in reducing images are also used in expanding them. Expanding an image g_p of dimensions $R_p \times C_p$ (where $R_p = M_R 2^{M-p} + 1$, and $C_p = M_C 2^{M-p} + 1$) to an image $g_{p,1}$ that has the same dimensions as g_{p-1} (i.e., is four times bigger than g_p) is done by

$$g_{p,1}(i,j) = 4 \sum_{m=-2}^{2} \sum_{n=-2}^{2} w(m,n) g_p\big([i-m]/2, [j-n]/2\big), \qquad (5.26)$$

where $i = 0, 1, \ldots, C_p - 1$, $j = 0, 1, \ldots, R_p - 1$, and the sums include only terms for which both $(i-m)/2$ and $(j-n)/2$ are integers. As an example we compute the single pixel

$$g_{1,1}(4,5) = 4 \sum_{m=-2}^{2} \sum_{n=-2}^{2} w(m,n) g_1\big([4-m]/2, [5-n]/2\big).$$

Of the 25 terms of this sum, only six, namely those with $m = -2, 0, 2$ and $n = -1, 1$, satisfy the condition above and are included. The six terms correspond to

$$(m, n) = (-2, -1), (-2, 1), (0, -1), (0, 1), (2, -1), (2, 1),$$

and the sum is

$$4\big[w(-2, -1)g_1(3, 3) + w(-2, 1)g_1(3, 2) + w(0, -1)g_1(2, 3)$$
$$+ w(0, 1)g_1(2, 2) + w(2, -1)g_1(1, 3) + w(2, 1)g_1(1, 2)\big].$$

	−0.05	0.25	0.6	0.25	−0.05
−0.05	0.0025	−0.0125	−0.03	−0.01	0.0025
0.25		0.0625	0.15	0.0625	−0.0125
0.6			0.36	0.15	−0.03
0.25				0.0625	−0.0125
−0.05					0.0025

Table 5.54: Values of $w(m, n)$ For $a = 0.6$.

A lossy version of the Laplacian pyramid can be obtained by quantizing the values of each L_i image before it is encoded and written on the compressed stream.

Bibliography

Burt, Peter J., and Edward H. Adelson (1983) "The Laplacian Pyramid as a Compact Image Code," *IEEE Transactions on Communications*, COM-31(4):532–540, April.

5.14 SPIHT

Section 5.6 shows how the Haar transform can be applied several times to an image, creating regions (or subbands) of averages and details. The Haar transform is simple, and better compression can be achieved by other wavelet filters. It seems that different wavelet filters produce different results depending on the image type, but it is currently not clear what filter is the best for any given image type. Regardless of the particular filter used, the image is decomposed into subbands, such that lower subbands correspond to higher image frequencies (they are the highpass levels) and higher subbands correspond to lower image frequencies (lowpass levels), where most of the image energy is concentrated (Figure 5.55). This is why we can expect the detail coefficients to get smaller as we move from high to low levels. Also, there are spatial similarities among the subbands (Figure 5.17b). An image part, such as an edge, occupies the same spatial position in each subband. These features of the wavelet decomposition are exploited by the SPIHT (set partitioning in hierarchical trees) method [Said and Pearlman 96].

SPIHT was designed for optimal progressive transmission, as well as for compression. One of the important features of SPIHT (perhaps a unique feature) is that at any point during the decoding of an image, the quality of the displayed image is the best that can be achieved for the number of bits input by the decoder up to that moment.

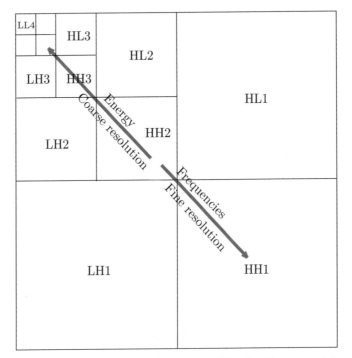

Figure 5.55: Subbands and Levels in Wavelet Decomposition.

Another important SPIHT feature is its use of embedded coding. This feature is defined as follows: If an (embedded coding) encoder produces two files, a large one of size M and a small one of size m, then the smaller file is identical to the first m bits of the larger file.

The following example aptly illustrates the meaning of this definition. Suppose that three users wait for you to send them a certain compressed image, but they need different image qualities. The first one needs the quality contained in a 10 Kb file. The image qualities required by the second and third users are contained in files of sizes 20 Kb and 50 Kb, respectively. Most lossy image compression methods would have to compress the same image three times, at different qualities, to generate three files with the right sizes. SPIHT, on the other hand, produces one file, and then three chunks—of lengths 10 Kb, 20 Kb, and 50 Kb, all starting at the beginning of the file—can be sent to the three users, thereby satisfying their needs.

We start with a general description of SPIHT. We denote the pixels of the original image $\mathbf{p}$ by $p_{i,j}$. Any set $\mathbf{T}$ of wavelet filters can be used to transform the pixels to wavelet coefficients (or transform coefficients) $c_{i,j}$. These coefficients constitute the transformed image $\mathbf{c}$. The transformation is denoted by $\mathbf{c} = \mathbf{T}(\mathbf{p})$. In a progressive transmission method, the decoder starts by setting the reconstruction image $\hat{\mathbf{c}}$ to zero. It then inputs (encoded) transform coefficients, decodes them, and uses them to generate an improved reconstruction image $\hat{\mathbf{c}}$, which, in turn, is used to produce a better image $\hat{\mathbf{p}}$. We can summarize this operation by $\hat{\mathbf{p}} = \mathbf{T}^{-1}(\hat{\mathbf{c}})$.

The main aim in progressive transmission is to transmit the most important image information first. This is the information that results in the largest reduction of the distortion (the difference between the original and the reconstructed images). SPIHT uses the mean squared error (MSE) distortion measure [Equation (4.2)]

$$D_{\mathrm{mse}}(\mathbf{p} - \hat{\mathbf{p}}) = \frac{|\mathbf{p} - \hat{\mathbf{p}}|^2}{N} = \frac{1}{N} \sum_i \sum_j (p_{i,j} - \hat{p}_{i,j})^2,$$

where N is the total number of pixels. An important consideration in the design of SPIHT is the fact that this measure is invariant to the wavelet transform, a feature that allows us to write

$$D_{\mathrm{mse}}(\mathbf{p} - \hat{\mathbf{p}}) = D_{\mathrm{mse}}(\mathbf{c} - \hat{\mathbf{c}}) = \frac{|\mathbf{p} - \hat{\mathbf{p}}|^2}{N} = \frac{1}{N} \sum_i \sum_j (c_{i,j} - \hat{c}_{i,j})^2. \qquad (5.27)$$

Equation (5.27) shows that the MSE decreases by $|c_{i,j}|^2/N$ when the decoder receives the transform coefficient $c_{i,j}$ (we assume that the exact value of the coefficient is received by the decoder, i.e., there is no loss of precision due to limitations imposed by computer arithmetic). It is now clear that the largest coefficients $c_{i,j}$ (largest in absolute value, regardless of their signs) contain the information that reduces the MSE distortion most, so a progressive encoder should send those coefficients first. This is one important principle of SPIHT.

Another principle is based on the observation that the most significant bits of a binary integer whose value is close to maximum tend to be ones. This suggests that the most significant bits contain the most important image information, and that they should be sent to the decoder first (or written first on the compressed stream).

The progressive transmission method used by SPIHT incorporates these two principles. SPIHT sorts the coefficients and transmits their most significant bits first. To simplify the description, we first assume that the sorting information is explicitly transmitted to the decoder; the next section discusses an efficient method to code this information.

We now show how the SPIHT encoder uses these principles to progressively transmit the wavelet coefficients to the decoder (or write them on the compressed stream), starting with the most important information. We assume that a wavelet transform has already been applied to the image (SPIHT is a coding method, so it can work with any wavelet transform) and that the transformed coefficients $c_{i,j}$ are already stored in memory. The coefficients are sorted (ignoring their signs) and the sorting information is contained in an array m such that array element $m(k)$ contains the (i, j) coordinates of a coefficient $c_{i,j}$, and such that $|c_{m(k)}| \geq |c_{m(k+1)}|$ for all values of k. Table 5.56 lists hypothetical values of 16 coefficients. Each is shown as a 16-bit number where the most significant bit (bit 15) is the sign and the remaining 15 bits (numbered 14 through 0, top to bottom) are the magnitude. The first coefficient $c_{m(1)} = c_{2,3}$ is $s1aci \ldots r$ (where s, a, etc., are bits). The second one $c_{m(2)} = c_{3,4}$ is $s1bdj \ldots s$, and so on.

k		1	2	3	4	5	6	7	8	9	10	11	12	13	14	15	16
	sign	s	s	s	s	s	s	s	s	s	s	s	s	s	s	s	s
msb	14	1	1	0	0	0	0	0	0	0	0	0	0	0	0	0	0
	13	a	b	1	1	1	1	0	0	0	0	0	0	0	0	0	0
	12	c	d	e	f	g	h	1	1	1	0	0	0	0	0	0	0
	11	i	j	k	l	m	n	o	p	q	1	0	0	0	0	0	0
	$\vdots$	$\vdots$	$\vdots$	$\vdots$													$\vdots$
lsb	0	r	s	t	u	v	w	x	y	$\cdots$		$\cdots$		$\cdots$			z
$m(k) =$	i,j	2,3	3,4	3,2	4,4	1,2	3,1	3,3	4,2	4,1	$\cdots$		$\cdots$		$\cdots$		4,3

Table 5.56: Transform Coefficients Ordered by Absolute Magnitudes.

The sorting information that the encoder has to transmit is the sequence $m(k)$, or

$$(2,3), (3,4), (3,2), (4,4), (1,2), (3,1), (3,3), (4,2), \ldots, (4,3).$$

In addition, it has to transmit the 16 signs, and the 16 coefficients in order of significant bits. A direct transmission would send the 16 numbers

$$ssssssssssssssss, \quad 1100000000000000, \quad ab11110000000000,$$
$$cdefgh1110000000, \quad ijklmnopq1000000, \ldots, rstuvwxy\ldots z,$$

but this is clearly wasteful. Instead, the encoder goes into a loop, where in each iteration it performs a *sorting step* and a *refinement step*. In the first iteration it transmits the number $l = 2$ (the number of coefficients $c_{i,j}$ in our example that satisfy $2^{14} \leq |c_{i,j}| < 2^{15}$) followed by the two pairs of coordinates $(2,3)$ and $(3,4)$ and by the signs of the first two coefficients. This is done in the first sorting pass. This information enables the decoder to construct approximate versions of the 16 coefficients as follows: Coefficients $c_{2,3}$ and $c_{3,4}$ are constructed as the 16-bit numbers $s100\ldots0$. The remaining 14 coefficients are constructed as all zeros. This is how the most significant bits of the largest coefficients are transmitted to the decoder first.

The next step of the encoder is the refinement pass, but this is not performed in the first iteration.

In the second iteration the encoder performs both passes. In the sorting pass it transmits the number $l = 4$ (the number of coefficients $c_{i,j}$ in our example that satisfy $2^{13} \leq |c_{i,j}| < 2^{14}$), followed by the four pairs of coordinates $(3,2)$, $(4,4)$, $(1,2)$, and $(3,1)$ and by the signs of the four coefficients. In the refinement step it transmits the two bits a and b. These are the 14th most significant bits of the two coefficients transmitted in the previous iteration.

The information received so far enables the decoder to improve the 16 approximate coefficients constructed in the previous iteration. The first six become

$$c_{2,3} = s1a0\ldots0, \ c_{3,4} = s1b0\ldots0, \ c_{3,2} = s0100\ldots0,$$

$$c_{4,4} = s0100\ldots0, \; c_{1,2} = s0100\ldots0, \; c_{3,1} = s0100\ldots0,$$

and the remaining 10 coefficients are not changed.

⋄ **Exercise 5.17:** Perform the sorting and refinement passes of the next (third) iteration.

The main steps of the SPIHT encoder should now be easy to understand. They are as follows:

Step 1: Given an image to be compressed, perform its wavelet transform using any suitable wavelet filter, decompose it into transform coefficients $c_{i,j}$, and represent the resulting coefficients with a fixed number of bits. (In the discussion that follows we use the terms *pixel* and *coefficient* interchangeably.) We assume that the coefficients are represented as 16-bit signed-magnitude numbers. The leftmost bit is the sign, and the remaining 15 bits are the magnitude. (Notice that the sign-magnitude representation is different from the 2's complement method, which is used by computer hardware to represent signed numbers.) Such numbers can have values from $-(2^{15} - 1)$ to $2^{15} - 1$. Set n to $\lfloor \log_2 \max_{i,j}(c_{i,j}) \rfloor$. In our case n will be set to $\lfloor \log_2(2^{15} - 1) \rfloor = 14$.

Step 2: Sorting pass: Transmit the number l of coefficients $c_{i,j}$ that satisfy $2^n \leq |c_{i,j}| < 2^{n+1}$. Follow with the l pairs of coordinates and the l sign bits of those coefficients.

Step 3: Refinement pass: Transmit the nth most significant bit of all the coefficients satisfying $|c_{i,j}| \geq 2^{n+1}$. These are the coefficients that were selected in previous sorting passes (not including the immediately preceding sorting pass).

Step 4: Iterate: Decrement n by 1. If more iterations are needed (or desired), go to Step 2.

The last iteration is normally performed for $n = 0$, but the encoder can stop earlier, in which case the least important image information (some of the least significant bits of all the wavelet coefficients) will not be transmitted. This is the natural lossy option of SPIHT. It is equivalent to scalar quantization, but it produces better results than what is usually achieved with scalar quantization, since the coefficients are transmitted in sorted order. An alternative is for the encoder to transmit the entire image (i.e., all the bits of all the wavelet coefficients) and the decoder can stop decoding when the reconstructed image reaches a certain quality. This quality can either be predetermined by the user or automatically determined by the decoder at run time.

5.14.1 Set Partitioning Sorting Algorithm

The method as described so far is simple, since we have assumed that the coefficients had been sorted before the loop started. In practice, the image may have $1\text{K} \times 1\text{K}$ pixels or more; there may be more than a million coefficients, so sorting all of them is too slow. Instead of sorting the coefficients, SPIHT uses the fact that sorting is done by comparing two elements at a time, and each comparison results in a simple yes/no result. Therefore, if both encoder and decoder use the same sorting algorithm, the encoder can simply send the decoder the sequence of yes/no results, and the decoder can use those to duplicate the operations of the encoder. This is true not just for sorting but for any algorithm based on comparisons or on any type of branching.

The actual algorithm used by SPIHT is based on the realization that there is really no need to sort *all* the coefficients. The main task of the sorting pass in each iteration is to select those coefficients that satisfy $2^n \le |c_{i,j}| < 2^{n+1}$. This task is divided into two parts. For a given value of n, if a coefficient $c_{i,j}$ satisfies $|c_{i,j}| \ge 2^n$, then we say that it is *significant*; otherwise, it is called *insignificant*. In the first iteration, relatively few coefficients will be significant, but their number increases from iteration to iteration, since n keeps getting decremented. The sorting pass has to determine which of the significant coefficients satisfies $|c_{i,j}| < 2^{n+1}$ and transmit their coordinates to the decoder. This is an important part of the algorithm used by SPIHT.

The encoder partitions all the coefficients into a number of sets T_k and performs the significance test

$$\max_{(i,j) \in T_k} |c_{i,j}| \ge 2^n \ ?$$

on each set T_k. The result may be either "no" (all the coefficients in T_k are insignificant, so T_k itself is considered insignificant) or "yes" (some coefficients in T_k are significant, so T_k itself is significant). This result is transmitted to the decoder. If the result is "yes," then T_k is partitioned by both encoder and decoder, using the same rule, into subsets and the same significance test is performed on all the subsets. This partitioning is repeated until all the significant sets are reduced to size 1 (i.e., they contain one coefficient each, and that coefficient is significant). This is how the significant coefficients are identified by the sorting pass in each iteration.

The significant test performed on a set T can be summarized by

$$S_n(T) = \begin{cases} 1, & \max_{(i,j) \in T} |c_{i,j}| \ge 2^n, \\ 0, & \text{otherwise.} \end{cases} \qquad (5.28)$$

The result, $S_n(T)$, is a single bit that is transmitted to the decoder. Since the result of each significance test becomes a single bit written on the compressed stream, the number of tests should be minimized. To achieve this goal, the sets should be created and partitioned such that sets expected to be significant will be large and sets expected to be insignificant will contain just one element.

5.14.2 Spatial Orientation Trees

The sets T_k are created and partitioned using a special data structure called a *spatial orientation tree*. This structure is defined in a way that exploits the spatial relationships between the wavelet coefficients in the different levels of the subband pyramid. Experience has shown that the subbands in each level of the pyramid exhibit spatial similarity (Figure 5.17b). Any special features, such as a straight edge or a uniform region, are visible in all the levels at the same location.

The spatial orientation trees are illustrated in Figure 5.57a,b for a 16×16 image. The figure shows two levels, level 1 (the highpass) and level 2 (the lowpass). Each level is divided into four subbands. Subband LL2 (the lowpass subband) is divided into four groups of 2×2 coefficients each. Figure 5.57a shows the top-left group, while Figure 5.57b shows the bottom-right one. In each group, each of the four coefficients (except the top-left one, marked in gray) becomes the root of a spatial orientation tree. The arrows show examples of how the various levels of these trees are related. The thick arrows indicate how each group of 4×4 coefficients in level 2 is the parent of four such groups in level 1. In general, a coefficient at location (i, j) in the image is the parent of the four coefficients at locations $(2i, 2j)$, $(2i + 1, 2j)$, $(2i, 2j + 1)$, and $(2i + 1, 2j + 1)$.

The roots of the spatial orientation trees of our example are located in subband LL2 (in general, they are located in the top-left LL subband, which can be of any size), but any wavelet coefficient, except the gray ones on level 1 (also except the leaves), can be considered the root of some spatial orientation subtree. The leaves of all those trees are located on level 1 of the subband pyramid.

In our example, subband LL2 is of size 4×4, so it is divided into four 2×2 groups, and three of the four coefficients of a group become roots of trees. Thus, the number of trees in our example is 12. In general, the number of trees is 3/4 the size of the highest LL subband.

Each of the 12 roots in subband LL2 in our example is the parent of four children located on the same level. However, the children of these children are located on level 1. This is true in general. The roots of the trees are located on the highest level and their children are on the same level, but from then on, the four children of a coefficient on level k are themselves located on level $k - 1$.

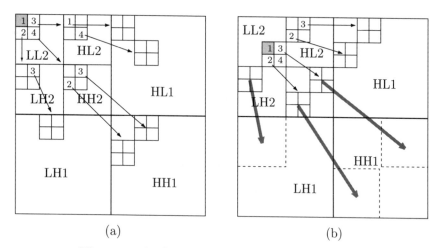

$$(a) \qquad\qquad\qquad\qquad (b)$$

Figure 5.57: Spatial Orientation Trees in SPIHT.

We use the terms *offspring* for the four children of a node, and *descendants* for the children, grandchildren, and all their descendants. The set partitioning sorting algorithm uses the following four sets of coordinates:

1. $\mathcal{O}(i, j)$: the set of coordinates of the four offspring of node (i, j). If node (i, j) is a leaf of a spatial orientation tree, then $\mathcal{O}(i, j)$ is empty.
2. $\mathcal{D}(i, j)$: the set of coordinates of the descendants of node (i, j).

3. $\mathcal{H}(i,j)$: the set of coordinates of the roots of all the spatial orientation trees (3/4 of the wavelet coefficients in the highest LL subband).

4. $\mathcal{L}(i,j)$: The difference set $\mathcal{D}(i,j) - \mathcal{O}(i,j)$. This set contains all the descendants of tree node (i,j), except its four offspring.

The spatial orientation trees are used to create and partition the sets T_k. The set partitioning rules are as follows:

1. The initial sets are $\{(i,j)\}$ and $\mathcal{D}(i,j)$, for all $(i,j) \in \mathcal{H}$ (i.e., for all roots of the spatial orientation trees). In our example there are 12 roots, so there will initially be 24 sets: 12 sets, each containing the coordinates of one root, and 12 more sets, each with the coordinates of all the descendants of one root.

2. If set $\mathcal{D}(i,j)$ is significant, then it is partitioned into $\mathcal{L}(i,j)$ plus the four single-element sets with the four offspring of (i,j). In other words, if any of the descendants of node (i,j) is significant, then its four offspring become four new sets and all its other descendants become another set (to be significance tested in rule 3).

3. If $\mathcal{L}(i,j)$ is significant, then it is partitioned into the four sets $\mathcal{D}(k,l)$, where (k,l) are the offspring of (i,j).

Once the spatial orientation trees and the set partitioning rules are understood, the coding algorithm can be described.

5.14.3 SPIHT Coding

It is important to have the encoder and decoder test sets for significance in the same way, so the coding algorithm uses three lists called *list of significant pixels* (LSP), *list of insignificant pixels* (LIP), and *list of insignificant sets* (LIS). These are lists of coordinates (i,j) that in the LIP and LSP represent individual coefficients, and in the LIS represent either the set $\mathcal{D}(i,j)$ (a type A entry) or the set $\mathcal{L}(i,j)$ (a type B entry).

The LIP contains coordinates of coefficients that were insignificant in the previous sorting pass. In the current pass they are tested, and those that test significant are moved to the LSP. In a similar way, sets in the LIS are tested in sequential order, and when a set is found to be significant, it is removed from the LIS and is partitioned. The new subsets with more than one coefficient are placed back in the LIS, to be tested later, and the subsets with one element are tested and appended to the LIP or the LSP, depending on the results of the test. The refinement pass transmits the nth most significant bit of the entries in the LSP.

Figure 5.58 shows this algorithm in detail. Figure 5.59 is a simplified version, for readers who are intimidated by too many details.

The decoder executes the detailed algorithm of Figure 5.58. It always works in *lockstep* with the encoder, but the following notes shed more light on its operation:

1. Step 2.2 of the algorithm evaluates all the entries in the LIS. However, step 2.2.1 appends certain entries to the LIS (as type-B) and step 2.2.2 appends other entries to the LIS (as type-A). It is important to realize that all these entries are also evaluated by step 2.2 in the same iteration.

2. The value of n is decremented in each iteration, but there is no need to bring it all the way to zero. The loop can stop after any iteration, resulting in lossy compression. Normally, the user specifies the number of iterations, but it is also

1. Initialization: Set n to $\lfloor \log_2 \max_{i,j}(c_{i,j}) \rfloor$ and transmit n. Set the LSP to empty. Set the LIP to the coordinates of all the roots $(i, j) \in \mathcal{H}$. Set the LIS to the coordinates of all the roots $(i, j) \in \mathcal{H}$ that have descendants.

2. Sorting pass:

   2.1 for each entry (i, j) in the LIP do:
      2.1.1 output $S_n(i, j)$;
      2.1.2 if $S_n(i, j) = 1$, move (i, j) to the LSP and output the sign of $c_{i,j}$;
   2.2 for each entry (i, j) in the LIS do:
      2.2.1 if the entry is of type A, then
   - output $S_n(\mathcal{D}(i, j))$;
   - if $S_n(\mathcal{D}(i, j)) = 1$, then
     * for each $(k, l) \in \mathcal{O}(i, j)$ do:
       · output $S_n(k, l)$;
       · if $S_n(k, l) = 1$, add (k, l) to the LSP, output the sign of $c_{k,l}$;
       · if $S_n(k, l) = 0$, append (k, l) to the LIP;
     * if $\mathcal{L}(i, j) \neq 0$, move (i, j) to the end of the LIS, as a type-B entry, and go to step 2.2.2; else, remove entry (i, j) from the LIS;

      2.2.2 if the entry is of type B, then
   - output $S_n(\mathcal{L}(i, j))$;
   - if $S_n(\mathcal{L}(i, j)) = 1$, then
     * append each $(k, l) \in \mathcal{O}(i, j)$ to the LIS as a type-A entry:
     * remove (i, j) from the LIS:

3. Refinement pass: for each entry (i, j) in the LSP, except those included in the last sorting pass (the one with the same n), output the nth most significant bit of $|c_{i,j}|$;

4. Loop: decrement n by 1 and go to step 2 if needed.

Figure 5.58: The SPIHT Coding Algorithm.

---

1. Set the threshold. Set LIP to all root nodes coefficients. Set LIS to all trees (assign type D to them). Set LSP to an empty set.

2. Sorting pass: Check the significance of all coefficients in LIP:
   2.1 If significant, output 1, output a sign bit, and move the coefficient to the LSP.
   2.2 If not significant, output 0.

3. Check the significance of all trees in the LIS according to the type of tree:
   3.1 For a tree of type D:
      3.1.1 If it is significant, output 1, and code its children:
         3.1.1.1 If a child is significant, output 1, then a sign bit, add it to the LSP
         3.1.1.2 If a child is insignificant, output 0 and add the child to the end of LIP.
         3.1.1.3 If the children have descendants, move the tree to the end of LIS as type L, otherwise remove it from LIS.
      3.1.2 If it is insignificant, output 0.
   3.2 For a tree of type L:
      3.2.1 If it is significant, output 1, add each of the children to the end of LIS as an entry of type D and remove the parent tree from the LIS.
      3.2.2 If it is insignificant, output 0.

4. Loop: Decrement the threshold and go to step 2 if needed.

Figure 5.59: A Simplified SPIHT Coding Algorithm.

possible to have the user specify the acceptable amount of distortion (in units of MSE), and the encoder can use Equation (5.27) to decide when to stop the loop.

3. The encoder knows the values of the wavelet coefficients $c_{i,j}$ and uses them to calculate the bits S_n (Equation (5.28)), which it transmits (i.e., writes on the compressed stream). These bits are input by the decoder, which uses them to calculate the values of $c_{i,j}$. The algorithm executed by the decoder is that of Figure 5.58 but with the word "output" changed to "input."

4. The sorting information, previously denoted by $m(k)$, is recovered when the coordinates of the significant coefficients are appended to the LSP in steps 2.1.2 and 2.2.1. This implies that the coefficients indicated by the coordinates in the LSP are sorted according to

$$\lfloor \log_2 |c_{m(k)}| \rfloor \geq \lfloor \log_2 |c_{m(k+1)}| \rfloor,$$

for all values of k. The decoder recovers the ordering because its three lists (LIS, LIP, and LSP) are updated in the same way as those of the encoder (remember that the decoder works in lockstep with the encoder). When the decoder inputs data, its three lists are identical to those of the encoder at the moment it (the encoder) output that data.

5. The encoder starts with the wavelet coefficients $c_{i,j}$; it never gets to "see" the actual image. The decoder, however, has to display the image and update the display in each iteration. In each iteration, when the coordinates (i, j) of a coefficient $c_{i,j}$ are moved to the LSP as an entry, it is known (to both encoder and decoder) that $2^n \leq |c_{i,j}| < 2^{n+1}$. As a result, the best value that the decoder can give the coefficient $\hat{c}_{i,j}$ that is being reconstructed is midway between 2^n and $2^{n+1} = 2 \times 2^n$. Thus, the decoder sets $\hat{c}_{i,j} = \pm 1.5 \times 2^n$ (the sign of $\hat{c}_{i,j}$ is input by the decoder just after the insertion). During the refinement pass, when the decoder inputs the actual value of the nth bit of $c_{i,j}$, it improves the value 1.5×2^n by adding 2^{n-1} to it (if the input bit was a 1) or subtracting 2^{n-1} from it (if the input bit was a 0). This way, the decoder can improve the appearance of the image (or, equivalently, reduce the distortion) during *both* the sorting and refinement passes.

It is possible to improve the performance of SPIHT by entropy coding the encoder's output, but experience shows that the added compression gained this way is minimal and does not justify the additional expense of both encoding and decoding time. It turns out that the signs and the individual bits of coefficients output in each iteration are uniformly distributed, so entropy coding them does not produce any compression. The bits $S_n(i, j)$ and $S_n(\mathcal{D}(i, j))$, on the other hand, are distributed nonuniformly and may gain from such coding.

5.14.4 Example

We assume that a 4×4 image has already been transformed, and the 16 coefficients are stored in memory as 6-bit signed-magnitude numbers (one sign bit followed by five magnitude bits). They are shown in Figure 5.60, together with the single spatial orientation tree. The coding algorithm initializes LIP to the one-element set $\{(1, 1)\}$, the LIS to the set $\{\mathcal{D}(1, 1)\}$, and the LSP to the empty set. The largest coefficient is 18, so n is set to $\lfloor \log_2 18 \rfloor = 4$. The first two iterations are shown.

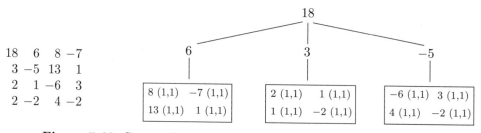

```
18   6   8 −7
 3  −5  13   1
 2   1  −6   3
 2  −2   4  −2
```

Figure 5.60: Sixteen Coefficients and One Spatial Orientation Tree.

Sorting Pass 1:

$2^n = 16$.

Is $(1,1)$ significant? yes: output a 1.

LSP $= \{(1,1)\}$, output the sign bit: 0.

Is $\mathcal{D}(1,1)$ significant? no: output a 0.

LSP $= \{(1,1)\}$, LIP $= \{\}$, LIS $= \{\mathcal{D}(1,1)\}$.

Three bits output.

Refinement pass 1: no bits are output (this pass deals with coefficients from sorting pass $n - 1$).

Decrement n to 3.

Sorting Pass 2:

$2^n = 8$.

Is $\mathcal{D}(1,1)$ significant? yes: output a 1.

Is $(1,2)$ significant? no: output a 0.

Is $(2,1)$ significant? no: output a 0.

Is $(2,2)$ significant? no: output a 0.

LIP $= \{(1,2),(2,1),(2,2)\}$, LIS $= \{\mathcal{L}(1,1)\}$.

Is $\mathcal{L}(1,1)$ significant? yes: output a 1.

LIS $= \{\mathcal{D}(1,2),\mathcal{D}(2,1),\mathcal{D}(2,2)\}$.

Is $\mathcal{D}(1,2)$ significant? yes: output a 1.

Is $(1,3)$ significant? yes: output a 1.

LSP $= \{(1,1),(1,3)\}$, output sign bit: 1.

Is $(2,3)$ significant? yes: output a 1.

LSP $= \{(1,1),(1,3),(2,3)\}$, output sign bit: 1.

Is $(1,4)$ significant? no: output a 0.

Is $(2,4)$ significant? no: output a 0.

LIP $= \{(1,2),(2,1),(2,2),(1,4),(2,4)\}$,

LIS $= \{\mathcal{D}(2,1),\mathcal{D}(2,2)\}$.

Is $\mathcal{D}(2,1)$ significant? no: output a 0.

Is $\mathcal{D}(2,2)$ significant? no: output a 0.

LIP $= \{(1,2),(2,1),(2,2),(1,4),(2,4)\}$,

LIS $= \{\mathcal{D}(2,1),\mathcal{D}(2,2)\}$,

LSP $= \{(1,1),(1,3),(2,3)\}$.

Fourteen bits output.

Refinement pass 2: After iteration 1, the LSP included entry $(1, 1)$, whose value is $18 = 10010_2$.

One bit is output.

Sorting Pass 3:

$2^n = 4$.

Is $(1, 2)$ significant? yes: output a 1.

LSP $= \{(1, 1), (1, 3), (2, 3), (1, 2)\}$, output a sign bit: 1.

Is $(2, 1)$ significant? no: output a 0.

Is $(2, 2)$ significant? yes: output a 1.

LSP $= \{(1, 1), (1, 3), (2, 3), (1, 2), (2, 2)\}$, output a sign bit: 0.

Is $(1, 4)$ significant? yes: output a 1.

LSP $= \{(1, 1), (1, 3), (2, 3), (1, 2), (2, 2), (1, 4)\}$, output a sign bit: 1.

Is $(2, 4)$ significant? no: output a 0.

LIP $= \{(2, 1), (2, 4)\}$.

Is $D(2, 1)$ significant? no: output a 0.

Is $D(2, 2)$ significant? yes: output a 1.

Is $(3, 3)$ significant? yes: output a 1.

LSP $= \{(1, 1), (1, 3), (2, 3), (1, 2), (2, 2), (1, 4), (3, 3)\}$, output a sign bit: 0.

Is $(4, 3)$ significant? yes: output a 1.

LSP $= \{(1, 1), (1, 3), (2, 3), (1, 2), (2, 2), (1, 4), (3, 3), (4, 3)\}$, output a sign bit: 1.

Is $(3, 4)$ significant? no: output a 0.

LIP $= \{(2, 1), (2, 4), (3, 4)\}$.

Is $(4, 4)$ significant? no: output a 0.

LIP $= \{(2, 1), (2, 4), (3, 4), (4, 4)\}$.

LIP $= \{(2, 1), (3, 4), (3, 4), (4, 4)\}$, LIS $= \{\mathcal{D}(2, 1)\}$,

LSP $= \{(1, 1), (1, 3), (2, 3), (1, 2), (2, 2), (1, 4), (3, 3), (4, 3)\}$.

Sixteen bits output.

Refinement Pass 3:

After iteration 2, the LSP included entries $(1, 1)$, $(1, 3)$, and $(2, 3)$, whose values are $18 = 10010_2$, $8 = 1000_2$, and $13 = 1101_2$. Three bits are output

After two iterations, a total of 37 bits has been output.

Bibliography

Said, A., and W. A. Pearlman (1996), "A New Fast and Efficient Image Codec Based on Set Partitioning in Hierarchical Trees," *IEEE Transactions on Circuits and Systems for Video Technology*, **6**(6):243–250, June.

5.14.5 QTCQ

Closely related to SPIHT, the QTCQ (quadtree classification and trellis coding quantization) method [Banister and Fischer 99] uses fewer lists than SPIHT and explicitly forms classes of the wavelet coefficients for later quantization by means of the ACTCQ and TCQ (arithmetic and trellis coded quantization) algorithms of [Joshi, Crump, and Fischer 93].

The method uses the spatial orientation trees originally developed by SPIHT. This type of tree is a special case of a quadtree. The encoding algorithm is iterative. In the nth iteration, if any element of this quadtree is found to be significant, then the four highest elements in the tree are defined to be in class n. They also become roots for four new quadtrees. Each of the four new trees is tested for significance, moving down each tree until all the significant elements are found. All the wavelet coefficients declared to be in class n are stored in a *list of pixels* (LP). The LP is initialized with all the wavelet coefficients in the lowest frequency subband (LFS). The test for significance is performed by the function $S_T(k)$, which is defined by

$$S_T(k) = \begin{cases} 1, & \max_{(i,j)\in k} |C_{i,j}| \geq T, \\ 0, & \text{otherwise,} \end{cases}$$

where T is the current threshold for significance and k is a tree of wavelet coefficients. The QTCQ encoding algorithm uses this test, and is listed in Figure 5.61.

The QTCQ decoder is similar. All the outputs in Figure 5.61 should be replaced by inputs, and ACTCQ encoding should be replaced by ACTCQ decoding.

1. <u>Initialization:</u>
   Initialize LP with all $C_{i,j}$ in LFS,
   Initialize LIS with all parent nodes,
   Output $n = \lfloor \log_2(\max |C_{i,j}|/q) \rfloor$.
   Set the threshold $T = q2^n$, where q is a quality factor.
2. <u>Sorting:</u>
   <u>for</u> each node k in LIS <u>do</u>
      output $S_T(k)$
      <u>if</u> $S_T(k) = 1$ <u>then</u>
        <u>for</u> each child of k <u>do</u>
         move coefficients to LP
         add to LIS as a new node
        <u>endfor</u>
        remove k from LIS
      <u>endif</u>
   <u>endfor</u>
3. <u>Quantization:</u> For each element in LP,
      quantize and encode using ACTCQ.
      (use TCQ step size $\Delta = \alpha \cdot q$).
4. <u>Update:</u> Remove all elements in LP. Set $T = T/2$. Go to step 2.

Figure 5.61: QTCQ Encoding.

The QTCQ implementation, as described in [Banister and Fischer 99], does not transmit the image progressively, but the authors claim that this property can be added to it.

Bibliography

Banister, Brian and Thomas R. Fischer (1999) "Quadtree Classification and TCQ Image Coding," in Storer, James A., and Martin Cohn (eds.) (1999) *DCC '99: Data Compression Conference*, Los Alamitos, CA, IEEE Computer Society Press, pp. 149–157.

Joshi, R. L., V. J. Crump, and T. R. Fischer (1993) "Image Subband Coding Using Arithmetic and Trellis Coded Quantization," *IEEE Transactions on Circuits and Systems Video Technology*, **5**(6):515–523, December.

5.15 CREW

The CREW method (compression with reversible embedded wavelets) was developed in 1994 by A. Zandi at Ricoh Silicon Valley for the high-quality lossy and lossless compression of medical images. It was later realized that he independently developed a method very similar to SPIHT (Section 5.14), which is why the details of CREW are not described here. The interested reader is referred to [Zandi 95], but more recent and detailed descriptions can be found at [CREW 00].

Bibliography

CREW 2000 is URL http://www.crc.ricoh.com/CREW/

Zandi A., J. Allen, E. Schwartz, and M. Boliek, 1995, "CREW: Compression with Reversible Embedded Wavelets," in Storer, James A., and Martin Cohn (eds.) *DCC '95: Data Compression Conference*, Los Alamitos, CA, IEEE Computer Society Press, pp. 212–221, March.

5.16 EZW

The SPIHT method is in some ways an extension of EZW, so this method, whose full name is "embedded coding using zerotrees of wavelet coefficients," is described here by outlining its principles and showing an example. Some of the details, such as the relation between parents and descendants in a spatial orientation tree, and the meaning of the term "embedded," are described in Section 5.14.

The EZW method, as implemented in practice, starts by performing the 9-tap symmetric quadrature mirror filter (QMF) wavelet transform [Adelson et al. 87]. The main loop is then repeated for values of the threshold that are halved at the end of each iteration. The threshold is used to calculate a *significance map* of significant and insignificant wavelet coefficients. Zerotrees are used to represent the significance map in an efficient way. The main steps are as follows:

1. Initialization: Set the threshold T to the smallest power of 2 that is greater than $\max_{(i,j)} |c_{i,j}|/2$, where $c_{i,j}$ are the wavelet coefficients.
2. Significance map coding: Scan all the coefficients in a predefined way and output a symbol when $|c_{i,j}| > T$. When the decoder inputs this symbol, it sets $c_{i,j} = \pm 1.5T$.
3. Refinement: Refine each significant coefficient by sending one more bit of its binary representation. When the decoder receives this, it increments the current coefficient value by $\pm 0.25T$.
4. Set $T = T/2$, and go to step 2 if more iterations are needed.

A wavelet coefficient $c_{i,j}$ is considered insignificant with respect to the current threshold T if $|c_{i,j}| < T$. The zerotree data structure is based on the following well-known experimental result: If a wavelet coefficient at a coarse scale (i.e., high in the image pyramid) is insignificant with respect to a given threshold T, then all of the coefficients of the same orientation in the same spatial location at finer scales (i.e., located lower in the pyramid) are very likely to be insignificant with respect to T.

In each iteration, all the coefficients are scanned in the order shown in Figure 5.62a. This guarantees that when a node is visited, all its parents will already have been scanned. The scan starts at the lowest frequency subband LL_n, continues with subbands HL_n, LH_n, and HH_n, and drops to level $n-1$, where it scans HL_{n-1}, LH_{n-1}, and HH_{n-1}. Each subband is fully scanned before the algorithm proceeds to the next subband.

Each coefficient visited in the scan is classified as a zerotree root (ZTR), an isolated zero (IZ), positive significant (POS), or negative significant (NEG). A zerotree root is a coefficient that is insignificant and all its descendants (in the same spatial orientation tree) are also insignificant. Such a coefficient becomes the root of a zerotree. It is encoded with a special symbol (denoted by ZTR), and the important point is that its descendants don't have to be encoded in the current iteration. When the decoder inputs a ZTR symbol, it assigns a zero value to the coefficients and to all its descendants in the spatial orientation tree. Their values get improved (refined) in subsequent iterations. An isolated zero is a coefficient that is insignificant but has some significant descendants. Such a coefficient is encoded with the special IZ symbol. The other two classes are coefficients that are significant and are positive or negative. The flowchart of Figure 5.62b illustrates this classification. Notice that a coefficient is classified into one of five classes, but the fifth class (a zerotree node) is not encoded.

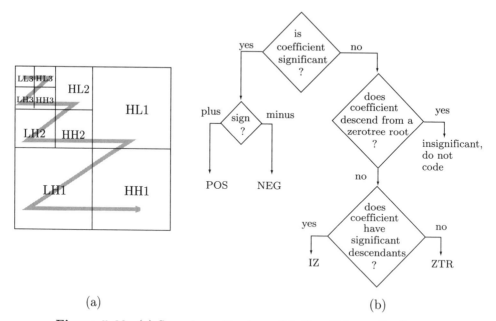

(a)   (b)

Figure 5.62: (a) Scanning a Zerotree. (b) Classifying a Coefficient

Coefficients in the lowest pyramid level don't have any children, so they cannot be the roots of zerotrees. Thus, they are classified into isolated zero, positive significant, or negative significant.

The zerotree can be viewed as a structure that helps find insignificance. Most methods that try to find structure in an image try to find significance. The IFS method of Section 4.32, for example, tries to locate image parts that are similar up to size and/or transformation, and this is much harder than to locate parts that are insignificant relative to other parts.

Two lists are used by the encoder (and also by the decoder, which works in lockstep) in the scanning process. The *dominant list* contains the coordinates of the coefficients that have not been found to be significant. They are stored in the order scan, by pyramid levels, and within each level by subbands. The *subordinate list* contains the *magnitudes* (not coordinates) of the coefficients that have been found to be significant. Each list is scanned once per iteration.

An iteration consists of a *dominant pass* followed by a *subordinate pass*. In the dominant pass, coefficients from the dominant list are tested for significance. If a coefficient is found significant, then (1) its sign is determined, (2) it is classified as either POS or NEG, (3) its magnitude is appended to the subordinate list, and (4) it is set to zero in memory (in the array containing all the wavelet coefficients). The last step is done so that the coefficient does not prevent the occurrence of a zerotree in subsequent dominant passes at smaller thresholds.

Imagine that the initial threshold is $T = 32$. When a coefficient $c_{i,j} = 63$ is encountered in the first iteration, it is found to be significant. Since it is positive, it is encoded as POS. When the decoder inputs this symbol, it does not know its value, but it knows that the coefficient is positive significant, i.e., it satisfies $c_{i,j} > 32$. The decoder also knows that $c_{i,j} \leq 64 = 2\times32$, so the best value that the decoder can assign the coefficient is $(32 + 64)/2 = 48$. The coefficient is then set to 0, so subsequent iterations will not identify it as significant.

We can think of the threshold T as an indicator that specifies a bit position. In each iteration, the threshold indicates the next less significant bit position. We can also view T as the current quantization width. In each iteration that width is divided by 2, so another less significant bit of the coefficients becomes known.

During a subordinate pass, the subordinate list is scanned and the encoder outputs a 0 or a 1 for each coefficient to indicate to the decoder how the magnitude of the coefficient should be improved. In the example of $c_{i,j} = 63$, the encoder transmits a 1, indicating to the decoder that the actual value of the coefficient is greater than 48. The decoder uses that information to improve the magnitude of the coefficient from 48 to $(48+64)/2 = 56$. If a 0 had been transmitted, the decoder would have refined the value of the coefficient to $(32 + 48)/2 = 40$.

The string of bits generated by the encoder during the subordinate pass is entropy encoded using a custom version of adaptive arithmetic coding (Section 2.15).

At the end of the subordinate pass, the encoder (and, in lockstep, also the decoder) sorts the magnitudes in the subordinate list in decreasing order.

The encoder stops the loop when a certain condition is met. The user may, for example, specify the desired bitrate (number of bits per pixel). The encoder knows the image size (number of pixels), so it knows when the desired bitrate has been reached or exceeded. The advantage is that the compression ratio is known (in fact, it is determined by the user) in advance. The downside is that too much information may be lost if the compression ratio is too high, thereby leading to a poorly reconstructed image. It is also possible for the encoder to stop in the midst of an iteration, when the exact bitrate specified by the user has been reached. However, in such a case the last codeword may be incomplete, leading to wrong decoding of one coefficient.

The user may also specify the bit budget (the size of the compressed stream) as a stopping condition. This is similar to specifying the bitrate. An alternative is for the user to specify the maximum acceptable distortion (the difference between the original and the compressed image). In such a case, the encoder iterates until the threshold becomes 1, and the decoder stops decoding when the maximum acceptable distortion is reached.

5.16.1 Example

This example follows the one in [Shapiro 93]. Figure 5.63a shows three levels of the wavelet transform of an 8×8 image. The largest value is 63, so the initial threshold can be anywhere in the range $(31, 64]$. We set it to 32. Table 5.63b lists the results of the first dominant pass.

| | Coeff. | | Reconstr. | |
Subband	value	Symbol	value	Note
LL3	63	POS	48	1
HL3	−34	NEG	−48	
LH3	−31	IZ	0	2
HH3	23	ZTR	0	3
HL2	49	POS	48	
HL2	10	ZTR	0	4
HL2	14	ZTR	0	
HL2	−13	ZTR	0	
LH2	15	ZTR	0	
LH2	14	IZ	0	5
LH2	−9	ZTR	0	
LH2	−7	ZTR	0	
HL1	7	Z	0	
HL1	13	Z	0	
HL1	3	Z	0	
LH1	−1	Z	0	
LH1	47	POS	48	6
LH1	−3	Z	0	
LH1	−2	Z	0	

63	−34	49	10	7	13	−12	7
−31	23	14	−13	3	4	6	−1
15	14	3	−12	5	−7	3	9
−9	−7	−14	8	4	−2	3	2
−5	9	−1	47	4	6	−2	2
3	0	−3	2	3	−2	0	4
2	−3	6	−4	3	6	3	6
5	11	5	6	0	3	−4	4

(a)   (b)

Figure 5.63: An EZW Example: Three Levels of an 8×8 Image.

Notes:

1. The top-left coefficient is 63. It is greater than the threshold, and it is positive, so a POS symbol is generated and is transmitted by the encoder (and the 63 is

changed to 0). The decoder assigns this POS symbol the value 48, the midpoint of the interval $[32, 64)$.

2. The coefficient 31 is insignificant with respect to 32, but it is not a zerotree root, since one of its descendants (the 47 in LH1) is significant. The 31 is therefore an isolated zero (IZ).

3. The 23 is less than 32. Also, all its descendants (the 3, -12, -14, and 8 in HH2, and all of HH1) are insignificant. The 23 is therefore a zerotree root (ZTR). As a result, no symbols will be generated by the encoder in the dominant pass for its descendants (this is why none of the HH2 and HH1 coefficients appear in the table).

4. The 10 is less than 32, and all its descendants (the -12, 7, 6, and -1 in HL1) are also less than 32. Thus, the 10 becomes a zerotree root (ZTR). Notice that the -12 is greater, in absolute value, than the 10, but is still less than the threshold.

5. The 14 is insignificant with respect to the threshold, but one of its children (they are -1, 47, -3, and 2) is significant. Thus, the 14 becomes an IZ.

6. The 47 in subband LH1 is significant with respect to the threshold, so it is coded as POS. It is then changed to zero, so that a future pass (with a threshold of 16) will code its parent, 14, as a zerotree root.

Four significant coefficients were transmitted during the first dominant pass. All that the decoder knows about them is that they are in the interval $[32, 64)$. They will be refined during the first subordinate pass, so the decoder will be able to place them either in $[32, 48)$ (if it receives a 0) or in $[48, 64)$ (if it receives a 1). The encoder generates and transmits the bits "1010" for the four significant coefficients 63, 34, 49, and 47. Thus, the decoder refines them to 56, 40, 56, and 40, respectively.

In the second dominant pass, only those coefficients not yet found to be significant are scanned and tested. The ones found significant are treated as zero when the encoder checks for zerotree roots. This second pass ends up identifying the -31 in LH3 as NEG, the 23 in HH3 as POS, the 10, 14, and -3 in LH2 as zerotree roots, and also all four coefficients in LH2 and all four in HH2 as zerotree roots. The second dominant pass stops at this point, since all other coefficients are known to be insignificant from the first dominant pass.

The subordinate list contains, at this point, the six magnitudes 63, 49, 34, 47, 31, and 23. They represent the 16-bit-wide intervals $[48, 64)$, $[32, 48)$, and $[16, 31)$. The encoder outputs bits that define a new subinterval for each of the three. At the end of the second subordinate pass, the decoder could have identified the 34 and 47 as being in different intervals, so the six magnitudes are ordered as 63, 49, 47, 34, 31, and 23. The decoder assigns them the refined values 60, 52, 44, 36, 28, and 20. (End of example.)

Bibliography

Adelson, E. H., E. Simoncelli, and R. Hingorani (1987) "Orthogonal Pyramid Transforms for Image Coding," *Proceedings SPIE*, vol. 845, Cambridge, MA, pp. 50–58, October.

Shapiro, Jerome M. (1993) "Embedded Image Coding Using Zerotrees of Wavelet Coefficients," *IEEE Transactions on Signal Processing*, **41**(12):3445–3462, October.

5.17 DjVu

Image compression methods are normally designed for one type of image. JBIG (Section 4.9), for example, has been designed for bi-level images, the FABD block decomposition method (Section 4.25) is intended for the compression of discrete-tone images, and JPEG (Section 4.6) works best on continuous-tone images. Certain images, however, combine the properties of all three image types. An important example of such an image is a scanned document containing text, line drawings, and regions with continuous-tone pictures, such as paintings or photographs. Libraries all over the world are currently digitizing their holdings by scanning and storing them in compressed format on disks and CD-ROMs. Organizations interested in making their documents available to the public (such as a mail-order firm with a colorful catalog, or a research institute with scientific papers) also have such documents. They can all benefit from an efficient lossy compression method that can highly compress such documents. Viewing such a document is normally done in a web browser, so such a method should feature fast decoding. Such a method is DjVu (pronounced "déjà vu"), from AT&T laboratories [ATT 96]. We start with a short summary of its performance.

> déjà vu—French for "already seen."

DjVu routinely achieves compression factors as high as 1000—which is 5 to 10 times better than competing image compression methods. Scanned pages at 300 dpi in full color are typically compressed from 25 Mb down to 30–60 Kb with excellent quality. Black-and-white pages are even smaller, typically compressed to 10–30 Kb. This creates high-quality scanned pages whose size is comparable to that of an average HTML page.

For color documents with both text and pictures, DjVu files are typically 5–10 times smaller than JPEG at similar quality. For black-and-white pages, DjVu files are typically 10–20 times smaller than JPEG and five times smaller than GIF. DjVu files are also about five times smaller than PDF files produced from scanned documents.

To help users read DjVu-compressed documents in a web browser, the developers have implemented a decoder in the form of a plug-in for standard web browsers. With this decoder (freely available for all popular platforms) it is easy to pan the image and zoom on it. The decoder also uses little memory, typically 2 Mbyte of RAM for images that normally require 25 Mbyte of RAM to fully display. The decoder keeps the image in RAM in a compact form, and decompresses, in real time, only the part that is actually displayed on the screen.

The DjVu method is progressive. The viewer sees an initial version of the document very quickly, and the visual quality of the display improves progressively as more bits arrive. For example, the text of a typical magazine page appears in just three seconds over a 56 Kbps modem connection. In another second or two, the first versions of the pictures and backgrounds appear. The final, full-quality, version of the page is completed after a few more seconds.

We next outline the main features of DjVu. The main idea is that the different elements of a scanned document, namely text, drawings, and pictures, have different perceptual characteristics. Digitized text and line drawings require high spatial resolution but little color resolution. Pictures and backgrounds, on the other hand, can be coded at lower spatial resolution, but with more bits per pixel (for high color resolution). We know from experience that text and line diagrams should be scanned and displayed at 300 dpi or higher resolution, since at any lower resolution text is barely legible and lines lose their sharp edges. Also, text normally uses one color, and drawings use few colors. Pictures, on the other hand, can be scanned and viewed at 100 dpi without much loss of picture detail if adjacent pixels can have similar colors (i.e., if the number of available colors is large).

DjVu therefore starts by decomposing the document into three components: mask, foreground, and background. The background component contains the pixels that constitute the pictures and the paper background. The mask contains the text and the lines in bi-level form (i.e., one bit per pixel). The foreground contains the color of the mask pixels. The background is a continuous-tone image and can be compressed at the low resolution of 100 dpi. The foreground normally contains large uniform areas and is also compressed as a continuous-tone image at the same low resolution. The mask is left at 300 dpi but can be efficiently compressed, since it is bi-level. The background and foreground are compressed with a wavelet-based method called IW44 ("IW" stands for "integer wavelet"), while the mask is compressed with JB2, a version of JBIG2 (Section 4.10) developed at AT&T.

The decoder decodes the three components, increases the resolution of the background and foreground components back to 300 dpi, and generates each pixel in the final decompressed image according to the mask. If a mask pixel is zero, the corresponding image pixel is taken from the background. If the mask pixel is one, the corresponding image pixel is generated in the color of the foreground pixel.

The rest of this section describes the image separation method used by DjVu. This is a multiscale bicolor clustering algorithm based on the concept of *dominant colors*. Imagine a document containing just black text on a white background. In order to obtain best results, such a document should be scanned as a grayscale, antialiased image. This results in an image that has mostly black and white pixels, but also gray pixels of various shades located at and near the boundaries of the text characters. It is obvious that the dominant colors of such an image are black and white. In general, given an image with several colors or shades of gray, its two dominant colors can be identified by the following algorithm:

Step 1: Initialize the background color b to white and the foreground f to black.

Step 2: Loop over all the pixels of the image. For each pixel calculate the distances f and b between the pixel's color and the current foreground and background colors. Select the shorter of the two distances and flag the pixel as either f or b accordingly.

Step 3: Calculate the average color of all the pixels that are flagged f. This becomes the new foreground color. Do the same for the background color.

Step 4: Repeat steps 2 and 3 until the two dominant colors converge (i.e., until they vary by less than the value of a preset threshold).

This algorithm is simple, and it converges rapidly. However, a real document seldom has two dominant colors, so DjVu uses two extensions of the above algorithm. The first extension is called *block bicolor clustering*. It divides the document into small rectangular blocks, and executes the clustering algorithm above in each block to get two dominant colors. Each block is then separated into a foreground and a background using these two dominant colors. This extension is not completely satisfactory because of the following problems involving the block size:

1. A block should be small enough to have a dominant foreground color. Imagine, for instance, a red word in a region of black text. Ideally, we want such a word to be in a block of its own, with red as one of the dominant colors of the block. If the blocks are large, this word may end up being a small part of a block whose dominant colors will be black and white; the red will effectively disappear.

2. On the other hand, a small block may be located completely outside any text area. Such a block contains just background pixels and should not be separated into background and foreground. A block may also be located completely inside a large character. Such a block is all foreground and should not be separated. In either case, this extension of the clustering algorithm will not find meaningfully dominant colors.

3. Experience shows that in a small block this algorithm does not always select the right colors for foreground and background.

The second extension is called *multiscale bicolor clustering*. This is an iterative algorithm that starts with a grid of large blocks and applies the block bicolor clustering algorithm to each. The result of this first iteration is a pair of dominant colors for each large block. In the second and subsequent iterations the grid is divided into smaller and smaller blocks, and each is processed with the original clustering algorithm. However, this algorithm is slightly modified, since it now attracts the new foreground and background colors of an iteration not toward black and white but toward the two dominant colors found in the previous iteration. Here is how it works:

1. For each small block b, identify the larger block B (from the preceding iteration) inside which b is located. Initialize the background and foreground colors of b to those of B.

2. Loop over the entire image. Compare the color of a pixel to the background and foreground colors of its block and tag the pixel according to the smaller of the two distances.

3. For each small block b, calculate a new background color by averaging (1) the colors of all pixels in b that are tagged as background, and (2) the background color that was used for b in this iteration. This is a weighted average where the pixels of (1) are given a weight of 80%, and the background color of (2) is assigned a weight of 20%. The new foreground color is calculated similarly.

4. Steps 2 and 3 are repeated until both background and foreground converge.

The multiscale bicolor clustering algorithm then divides each small block b into smaller blocks and repeats.

This process is usually successful in separating the image into the right foreground and background components. To improve it even more, it is followed by a variety of filters that are applied to the various foreground areas. They are designed to find and eliminate the most obvious mistakes in the identification of foreground parts.

> Vuja De—The feeling you've never been here.

Bibliography

ATT (1996) is URL `http://www.djvu.att.com/`.

Haffner, Patrick et al. (1998) "High-Quality Document Image Compression with DjVu," Journal of Electronic Imaging, **7**(3):410–425, SPIE. This is also available from URL `http://www.research.att.com/~leonb/biblio.html`.

5.18 WSQ, Fingerprint Compression

Most of us don't realize it, but fingerprints are "big business." The FBI started collecting fingerprints in the form of inked impressions on paper cards back in 1924, and today they have about 200 million cards, occupying an acre of filing cabinets in the J. Edgar Hoover building in Washington, D.C. (The FBI, like many of us, never throws anything away. They also have many "repeat customers," which is why "only" about 29 million out of the 200 million cards are distinct; these are the ones used for running background checks.) What's more, these cards keep accumulating at a rate of 30,000–50,000 new cards per day (this is per day, not per year)! There's clearly a need to digitize this collection, so it will occupy less space and will lend itself to automatic search and classification. The main problem is size (in bits). When a typical fingerprint card is scanned at 500 dpi, with eight bits/pixel, it results in about 10 Mb of data. Thus, the total size of the digitized collection would be more than 2000 terabytes (a terabyte is 2^{40} bytes).

⋄ **Exercise 5.18:** Use these numbers to estimate the size of a fingerprint card.

Compression is, therefore, a must. At first, it seems that fingerprint compression must be lossless because of the small but important details involved. However, lossless image compression methods produce typical compression ratios of 0.5, whereas in order to make a serious dent in the huge amount of data in this collection, compressions of about 1 bpp or better are needed. What is needed is a lossy compression method that results in graceful degradation of image details, and does not introduce any artifacts into the reconstructed image. Most lossy image compression methods involve the loss of small details and are therefore unacceptable, since small fingerprint details, such as sweat pores, are admissible points of identification in court. This is where wavelets come into the picture. Lossy wavelet compression, if carefully designed, can satisfy the criteria above and result in efficient compression where important small details are preserved or are at least identifiable. Figure 5.64a,b (obtained, with permission, from Christopher M. Brislawn), shows two examples of fingerprints and one detail, where ridges and sweat pores can clearly be seen.

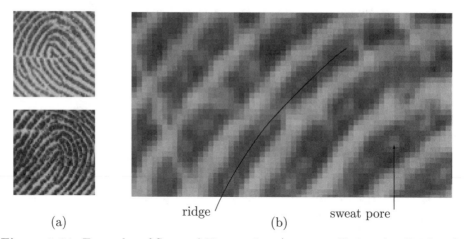

ridge   sweat pore

(a)   (b)

Figure 5.64: Examples of Scanned Fingerprints (courtesy Christopher Brislawn).

Compression is also necessary, since fingerprint images are routinely sent between law enforcement agencies. Overnight delivery of the actual card is too slow and risky (there are no backup cards), and sending 10 Mb of data through a 9600 baud modem takes about three hours.

The method described here [Bradley, Brislawn, and Hopper 1993] has been adopted by the FBI as its standard for fingerprint compression. It involves three steps: (1) a discrete wavelet transform, (2) adaptive scalar quantization of the wavelet transform coefficients, and (3) a two-pass Huffman coding of the quantization indices. This is the reason for the name *wavelet/scalar quantization*, or WSQ. The method typically produces compression factors of about 20. Decoding is the opposite of encoding, so WSQ is a symmetric compression method.

The first step is a symmetric discrete wavelet transform (SWT) using the symmetric filter coefficients listed in Table 5.65 (where $\mathcal{R}$ indicates the real part of a complex number). They are symmetric filters with 7 and 9 impulse response taps, and they depend on the two numbers x_1 (real) and x_2 (complex). The final standard adopted by the FBI uses the values

$$x_1 = A + B - \frac{1}{6}, \quad x_2 = \frac{-(A+B)}{2} - \frac{1}{6} + \frac{i\sqrt{3}(A-B)}{2},$$

where

$$A = \left(\frac{-14\sqrt{15}+63}{1080\sqrt{15}}\right)^{1/3}, \quad \text{and } B = \left(\frac{-14\sqrt{15}-63}{1080\sqrt{15}}\right)^{1/3}.$$

The wavelet image decomposition is different from those discussed in Section 5.10. It can be called symmetric and is shown in Figure 5.66. The SWT is first applied to the image rows and columns, resulting in $4 \times 4 = 16$ subbands. The SWT is then applied in the same manner to three of the 16 subbands, decomposing each into 16 smaller subbands. The last step is to decompose the top-left subband into four smaller ones.

Tap	Exact value	Approximate value
$h_0(0)$	$-5\sqrt{2}x_1(48|x_2|^2 - 16\mathcal{R}x_2 + 3)/32$	0.852698790094000
$h_0(\pm 1)$	$-5\sqrt{2}x_1(8|x_2|^2 - \mathcal{R}x_2)/8$	0.377402855612650
$h_0(\pm 2)$	$-5\sqrt{2}x_1(4|x_2|^2 + 4\mathcal{R}x_2 - 1)/16$	-0.110624404418420
$h_0(\pm 3)$	$-5\sqrt{2}x_1(\mathcal{R}x_2)/8$	-0.023849465019380
$h_0(\pm 4)$	$-5\sqrt{2}x_1/64$	0.037828455506995
$h_1(-1)$	$\sqrt{2}(6x_1 - 1)/16x_1$	0.788485616405660
$h_1(-2,0)$	$-\sqrt{2}(16x_1 - 1)/64x_1$	-0.418092273222210
$h_1(-3,1)$	$\sqrt{2}(2x_1 + 1)/32x_1$	-0.040689417609558
$h_1(-4,2)$	$-\sqrt{2}/64x_1$	0.064538882628938

Table 5.65: Symmetric Wavelet Filter Coefficients for WSQ.

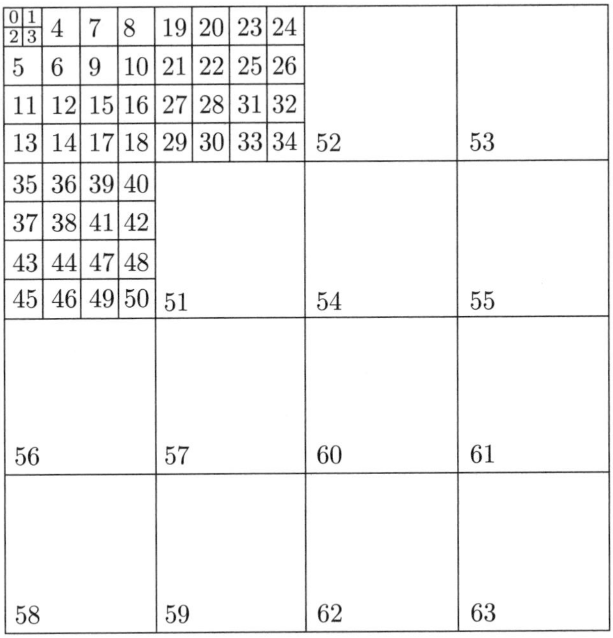

Figure 5.66: Symmetric Image Wavelet Decomposition.

The larger subbands (51–63) contain the fine-detail, high-frequency information of the image. They can later be heavily quantized without loss of any important information (i.e., information needed to classify and identify fingerprints). In fact, subbands 60–63 are completely discarded. Subbands 7–18 are important. They contain that portion of the image frequencies that corresponds to the ridges in a fingerprint. This information is important and should be quantized lightly.

The transform coefficients in the 64 subbands are floating-point numbers to be denoted by a. They are quantized to a finite number of floating-point numbers that are denoted by $\hat{a}$. The WSQ encoder maps a transform coefficient a to a quantization index p (an integer that is later mapped to a code that is itself Huffman encoded). The index p can be considered a pointer to the quantization bin where a lies. The WSQ decoder receives an index p and maps it to a value $\hat{a}$ that is close, but not identical, to a. This is how WSQ loses image information. The set of $\hat{a}$ values is a discrete set of floating-point numbers called the *quantized wavelet coefficients*. The quantization depends on parameters that may vary from subband to subband, since different subbands have different quantization requirements.

Figure 5.67 shows the setup of quantization bins for subband k. Parameter Z_k is the width of the zero bin, and parameter Q_k is the width of the other bins. Parameter C is in the range $[0, 1]$. It determines the reconstructed value $\hat{a}$. For $C = 0.5$, for example, the reconstructed value for each quantization bin is the center of the bin. Equation (5.29) shows how parameters Z_k and Q_k are used by the WSQ encoder to quantize a transform coefficient $a_k(m, n)$ (i.e., a coefficient in position (m, n) in subband k) to an index $p_k(m, n)$ (an integer), and how the WSQ decoder computes a quantized coefficient $\hat{a}_k(m, n)$ from that index:

$$
p_k(m, n) = \begin{cases} \left\lfloor \frac{a_k(m,n) - Z_k/2}{Q_k} \right\rfloor + 1, & a_k(m, n) > Z_k/2, \\ 0, & -Z_k/2 \le a_k(m, n) \le Z_k/2, \\ \left\lceil \frac{a_k(m,n) + Z_k/2}{Q_k} \right\rceil + 1, & a_k(m, n) < -Z_k/2, \end{cases}
$$

$$
\tag{5.29}
$$

$$
\hat{a}_k(m, n) = \begin{cases} \big(p_k(m, n) - C\big)Q_k + Z_k/2, & p_k(m, n) > 0, \\ 0, & p_k(m, n) = 0, \\ \big(p_k(m, n) + C\big)Q_k - Z_k/2, & p_k(m, n) < 0. \end{cases}
$$

The actual standard adopted by the FBI uses the value $C = 0.44$ and determines the bin widths Q_k and Z_k from the variances of the transform coefficients in the different subbands as follows:

Step 1: Let the width and height of subband k be denoted by X_k and Y_k, respectively. We compute the six quantities

$$
W_k = \left\lfloor \frac{3X_k}{4} \right\rfloor, \quad H_k = \left\lfloor \frac{7Y_k}{16} \right\rfloor,
$$

$$
x_{0k} = \left\lfloor \frac{X_k}{8} \right\rfloor, \quad x_{1k} = x_{0k} + W_k - 1,
$$

$$
y_{0k} = \left\lfloor \frac{9Y_k}{32} \right\rfloor, \quad y_{1k} = y_{0k} + H_k - 1.
$$

Step 2: Assuming that position $(0, 0)$ is the top-left corner of the subband, we use the subband region from position (x_{0k}, y_{0k}) to position (x_{1k}, y_{1k}) to estimate the variance σ_k^2 of the subband by

$$\sigma_k^2 = \frac{1}{W \cdot H - 1} \sum_{n=x_{0k}}^{x_{1k}} \sum_{m=y_{0k}}^{y_{1k}} \left(a_k(m, n) - \mu_k\right)^2,$$

where μ_k denotes the mean of $a_k(m, n)$ in the region.

Step 3: Parameter Q_k is computed by

$$q Q_k = \begin{cases} 1, & 0 \le k \le 3, \\ \frac{10}{A_k \log_e(\sigma_k^2)}, & 4 \le k \le 59, \text{ and } \sigma_k^2 \ge 1.01, \\ 0, & 60 \le k \le 63, \text{ or } \sigma_k^2 < 1.01, \end{cases}$$

where q is a proportionality constant that controls the bin widths Q_k and thus the overall level of compression. The procedure for computing q is complicated and will not be described here. The values of the constants A_k are

$$A_k = \begin{cases} 1.32, & k = 52, 56, \\ 1.08, & k = 53, 58, \\ 1.42, & k = 54, 57, \\ 1.08, & k = 55, 59, \\ 1, & \text{otherwise.} \end{cases}$$

Notice that the bin widths for subbands 60–63 are zero. As a result, these subbands, containing the finest detail coefficients, are simply discarded.

Step 4: The width of the zero bin is set to $Z_k = 1.2 Q_k$.

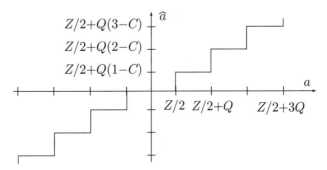

Figure 5.67: WSQ Scalar Quantization.

The WSQ encoder calculates the quantization indices $p_k(m, n)$ as shown, then maps them to the 254 codes shown in Table 5.68. These values are encoded with Huffman codes (using a two-pass process), and the Huffman codes are then written on the compressed stream. A quantization index $p_k(m, n)$ can be any integer, but most are small and there are many zeros. Thus, the codes of Table 5.68 are divided into three groups. The first group consists of 100 codes (codes 1 through 100) for run lengths of 1 to 100 zero indices. The second group is codes 107 through 254.

They specify small indices, in the range $[-73, +74]$. The third group consists of the six *escape* codes 101 through 106. They indicate large indices or run lengths of more than 100 zero indices. Code 180 (which corresponds to an index $p_k(m, n) = 0$) is not used, since this case is really a run length of a single zero. An escape code is followed by the (8-bit or 16-bit) raw value of the index (or size of the run length). Here are some examples:

An index $p_k(m, n) = -71$ is coded as 109. An index $p_k(m, n) = -1$ is coded as 179. An index $p_k(m, n) = 75$ is coded as 101 (escape for positive 8-bit indices) followed by 75 (in eight bits). An index $p_k(m, n) = -259$ is coded as 104 (escape for negative large indices) followed by 259 (the absolute value of the index, in 16 bits). An isolated index of zero is coded as 1, and a run length of 260 zeros is coded as 106 (escape for large run lengths) followed by 260 (in 16 bits). Indices or run lengths that require more than 16 bits cannot be encoded, but the particular choice of the quantization parameters and the wavelet transform practically guarantee that large indices will never be generated.

Code	Index or run length
1	run length of 1 zeros
2	run length of 2 zeros
3	run length of 3 zeros
⋮	
100	run length of 100 zeros
101	escape code for positive 8-bit index
102	escape code for negative 8-bit index
103	escape code for positive 16-bit index
104	escape code for negative 16-bit index
105	escape code for zero run, 8-bit
106	escape code for zero run, 16-bit
107	index value -73
108	index value -72
109	index value -71
⋮	
179	index value -1
180	unused
181	index value 1
⋮	
253	index value 73
254	index value 74

Table 5.68: WSQ Codes For Quantization Indices and Run Lengths.

The last step is to prepare the Huffman code tables. They depend on the image, so they have to be written on the compressed stream. The standard adopted by the FBI specifies that subbands be grouped into three blocks and all the subbands in a group use the same Huffman code table. This facilitates progressive transmission of the image. The first block consists of the low- and mid-frequency subbands 0–18. The second and third blocks contain the highpass detail subbands 19–51 and 52–59, respectively (recall that subbands 60–63 are completely discarded). Two Huffman code tables are prepared: one for the first block and the other for the second and third blocks.

A Huffman code table for a block of subbands is prepared by counting the number of times each of the 254 codes of Table 5.68 appears in the block. The counts are used to determine the length of each code and to construct the Huffman code tree. This is a two-pass job (one pass to determine the code tables and another pass to encode), and it is done in a way similar to the use of the Huffman code by JPEG (Section 4.6.6).

Bibliography

Bradley, Jonathan N., Christopher M. Brislawn, and Tom Hopper (1993) "The FBI Wavelet/Scalar Quantization Standard for Grayscale Fingerprint Image Compression," *Proc. of Visual Information Processing II*, Orlando, FL, SPIE v. 1961, pp. 293–304, April.

Brislawn, Christopher, Jonathan Bradley, R. Onyshczak, and Tom Hopper (1996) "The FBI Compression Standard for Digitized Fingerprint Images," in *Proceedings SPIE*, v. 2847, Denver, CO, pp. 344–355, August.

Federal Bureau of Investigations (1993) *WSQ Grayscale Fingerprint Image Compression Specification, ver. 2.0*, Document #IAFIS-IC-0110v2, Criminal Justice Information Services, February.

5.19 JPEG 2000

The data compression field is very active, with new approaches, ideas, and techniques being developed and implemented all the time. JPEG (Section 4.6) is widely used for image compression but is not perfect. The use of the DCT on 8×8 blocks of pixels results sometimes in a reconstructed image that has a blocky appearance (especially when the JPEG parameters are set for much loss of information). This is why the JPEG committee has decided, as early as 1995, to develop a new, wavelet-based standard for the compression of still images, to be known as JPEG 2000 (or JPEG Y2K). At the time of writing (mid 2000), this new standard is almost complete, so more and more information about it is becoming available. Its design, specification, and testing are supposed to be finalized sometime in 2001. Following is a list of areas where this new standard is expected to improve on existing methods:

■ High compression efficiency. Bitrates of less than 0.25 bpp are expected for highly-detailed grayscale images.

■ The ability to handle large images, up to $2^{32} \times 2^{32}$ pixels (the original JPEG can handle images of up to $2^{16} \times 2^{16}$).

■ Progressive image transmission (Section 4.8). The proposed standard can decompress an image progressively by SNR, resolution, color component, or region of interest.

■ Easy, fast access to various points in the compressed stream.

■   The decoder can pan/zoom the image while decompressing only parts of it.

■   The decoder can rotate and crop the image while decompressing it.

■   Error resilience. Error-correcting codes can be included in the compressed stream, to improve transmission reliability in noisy environments.

The main source of information on JPEG 2000 is [JPEG 00]. This section, however, is based on [ISO/IEC 00], the final committee draft (FCD), released in March, 2000. This document defines the compressed stream (referred to as the *bitstream*) and the operations of the decoder. It contains informative sections about the encoder, but any encoder that produces a valid bitstream is considered a valid JPEG 2000 encoder.

How does JPEG 2000 work? The following paragraph is a short summary of the algorithm. Certain steps are described in more detail in the rest of this section.

If the image being compressed is in color, it is divided into three components. Each component is partitioned into rectangular, nonoverlapping regions called *tiles*, that are compressed individually. A tile is compressed in four main steps. The first step is to compute a wavelet transform that results in subbands of wavelet coefficients. Two such transforms, an integer and a floating-point, are specified by the standard. There are $L + 1$ resolution levels of subbands, where L is a parameter determined by the encoder. In step two, the wavelet coefficients are quantized. This is done if the user specifies a target bitrate. The lower the bitrate, the coarser the wavelet coefficients have to be quantized. Step three uses the MQ coder (an encoder similar to the QM coder, Section 2.16) to arithmetically encode the wavelet coefficients. The EBCOT algorithm [Taubman 99] has been adopted for the encoding step. The principle of EBCOT is to divide each subband into blocks (termed *code-blocks*) that are coded individually. The bits resulting from coding several code-blocks become a *packet* and the packets are the components of the bitstream. The last step is to construct the bitstream. This step places the packets, as well as many *markers*, in the bitstream. The markers can be used by the decoder to skip certain areas of the bitstream and to reach certain points quickly. Using markers, the decoder can, e.g., decode certain code-blocks before others, thereby displaying certain regions of the image before other regions. Another use of the markers is for the decoder to progressively decode the image in one of several ways. The bitstream is organized in *layers*, where each layer contains higher-resolution image information. Thus, decoding the image layer by layer is a natural way to achieve progressive image transmission and decompression.

Before getting to the details, here is a short history of the development effort of JPEG 2000.

The history of JPEG 2000 starts in 1995, when Ricoh Inc. submitted the CREW algorithm (compression with reversible embedded wavelets, Section 5.15) to the ISO/IEC as a candidate for JPEG-LS (Section 4.7). CREW was not selected as the algorithm for JPEG-LS, but was sufficiently advanced to be considered a candidate for the new method then being considered by the ISO/IEC. This method, to become later known as JPEG 2000, was approved as a new, official work item, and a working group (WG1) set for it in 1996. In March, 1997 WG1 called for proposals, and started evaluating them. Of the many algorithms submitted, the

WTCQ method (wavelet trellis coded quantization) performed the best and was selected in November, 1997 as the reference JPEG 2000 algorithm. The WTCQ algorithm includes a wavelet transform and a quantization method.

In November, 1998 the EBCOT algorithm was presented to the working group by its developer, David Taubman, and was adopted as the method for encoding the wavelet coefficients. In March, 1999 the MQ coder was presented to the working group and was adopted by it as the arithmetic coder to be used in JPEG 2000. During 1999, the format of the bitstream was being developed and tested, with the result that by the end of 1999 all the main components of JPEG 2000 were in place. In December, 1999 the working group issued its committee draft (CD), and in March, 2000 it has issued its final committee draft (FCD), the document on which this section is based. Changes to the method are still possible but are getting less likely as time passes. JPEG 2000 is expected to be approved by the ISO and the IEC and to become an international standard in late 2000.

This section continues with details of certain conventions and operations of JPEG 2000. The aim is to illuminate the key concepts in order to give the reader a general understanding of this new international standard.

Color Components: A color image consists of three color components. The first step of the JPEG 2000 encoder is to transform the components by means of either a reversible component transform (RCT) or an irreversible component transform (ICT). Each transformed component is then compressed separately.

If the image pixels have unsigned values (which is the normal case), then the component transform (either RCT or ICT) is preceded by a DC level shifting. This process translates all pixel values from their original, unsigned interval $[0, 2^s - 1]$ (where s is the pixels' depth) to the signed interval $[-2^{s-1}, 2^{s-1} - 1]$ by subtracting 2^{s-1} from each value. For $s = 4$, e.g., the $2^4 = 16$ possible pixel values are transformed from the interval $[0, 15]$ to the interval $[-8, +7]$ by subtracting $2^{4-1} = 8$ from each value.

The RCT is a decorrelating transform. It can only be used with the integer wavelet transform (which is reversible). Denoting the pixel values of image component i (after a possible DC level shifting) by $I_i(x, y)$ for $i = 0, 1$, and 2, the RCT produces new values $Y_i(x, y)$ according to

$$Y_0(x, y) = \left\lfloor \frac{I_0(x, y) + 2I_1(x, y) + I_2(x, y)}{4} \right\rfloor,$$
$$Y_1(x, y) = I_2(x, y) - I_1(x, y),$$
$$Y_2(x, y) = I_0(x, y) - I_1(x, y).$$

Notice that the values of components Y_1 and Y_2 (but not Y_0) require one more bit than the original I_i values.

The ICT is also a decorrelating transform. It can only be used with the floating-point wavelet transform (which is irreversible). The ICT is defined by

$$Y_0(x, y) = 0.299I_0(x, y) + 0.587I_1(x, y) + 0.144I_2(x, y),$$
$$Y_1(x, y) = -0.16875I_0(x, y) - 0.33126I_1(x, y) + 0.5I_2(x, y),$$
$$Y_2(x, y) = 0.5I_0(x, y) - 0.41869I_1(x, y) - 0.08131I_2(x, y).$$

If the original image components are red, green, and blue, then the ICT is very similar to the YCbCr color representation (Section 6.2).

Tiles: Each (RCT or ICT transformed) color component of the image is partitioned into rectangular, nonoverlapping tiles. Since the color components may have different resolutions, they may use different tile sizes. Tiles may have any size, up to the size of the entire image (i.e., one tile). All the tiles of a given color component have the same size, except those at the edges. Each tile is compressed individually.

Figure 5.69a shows an example of image tiling. JPEG 2000 allows the image to have a vertical offset at the top and a horizontal offset on the left (the offsets can be zero). The origin of the tile grid (the top-left corner) can be located anywhere inside the intersection area of the two offsets. All the tiles in the grid are the same size, but those located on the edges, such as T0, T4, and T19 in the figure, have to be truncated. Tiles are numbered in raster order.

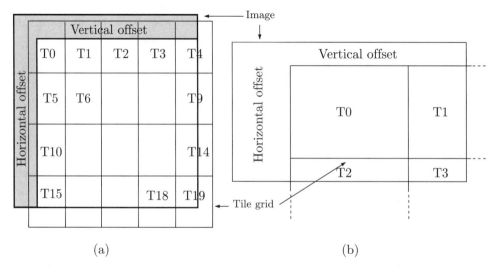

(a)   (b)

Figure 5.69: JPEG 2000 Image Tiling.

The main reason for having tiles is to enable the user to decode parts of the image (regions of interest). The decoder can identify each tile in the bitstream and decompress just those pixels included in the tile. Figure 5.69b shows an image with an aspect ratio (height/width) of 16:9 (the aspect ratio of high-definition television, HDTV, Section 6.3.1). The image is tiled with four tiles whose aspect ratio is 4:3 (the aspect ratio of current, analog television), such that tile T0 covers the central area of the image. This makes it easy to crop the image from the original aspect ratio to the 4:3 ratio.

Wavelet Transform: Two wavelet transforms are specified by the standard. They are the (9,7) floating-point wavelet (irreversible) and the (5,3) integer wavelet (reversible). Either transform allows for progressive transmission but only the integer transform can produce lossless compression.

We denote a row of pixels in a tile by P_k, P_{k+1}, through P_m. Because of the nature of the wavelet transforms used by JPEG 2000, a few pixels with indices less than k or greater than m may have to be used. Therefore, before any wavelet transform is computed for a tile, the pixels of the tile may have to be extended. The JPEG 2000 standard specifies a simple extension method termed *periodic symmetric extension*, which is illustrated by Figure 5.70. The figure shows a row of seven symbols "ABCDEFG" and how they are reflected to the left and to the right to extend the row by l and r symbols, respectively. Table 5.71 lists the minimum values of l and r as functions of the parity of k and m and of the particular transform used.

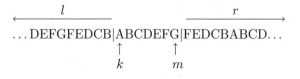

Figure 5.70: Extending a Row of Pixels.

k	l (5,3)	l (9,7)	m	r (5,3)	r (9,7)
even	2	4	odd	2	4
odd	1	3	even	1	3

Table 5.71: Minimum Left and Right Extensions.

We now denote a row of extended pixels in a tile by P_k, P_{k+1}, through P_m. Since the pixels have been extended, index values below k and above m can be used. The (5,3) integer wavelet transform computes wavelet coefficients $C(i)$ by computing the odd values $C(2i + 1)$ first, then using them to compute the even values $C(2i)$. The calculations are

$$C(2i + 1) = P(2i + 1) - \left\lfloor \frac{P(2i) + P(2i + 2)}{2} \right\rfloor, \quad \text{for } k - 1 \le 2i + 1 < m + 1,$$

$$C(2i) = P(2i) + \left\lfloor \frac{C(2i - 1) + C(2i + 1) + 2}{4} \right\rfloor, \quad \text{for } k \le 2i < m + 1.$$

The (9,7) floating-point wavelet transform is computed by executing four "lifting" steps followed by two "scaling" steps on the extended pixel values P_k through P_m. Each step is performed on all the pixels in the tile before the next step starts. Step 1 is performed for all i values satisfying $k - 3 \le 2i + 1 < m + 3$. Step 2 is performed for all i such that $k - 2 \le 2i < m + 2$. Step 3 is performed for $k - 1 \le 2i + 1 < m + 1$. Step 4 is performed for $k \le 2i < m$. Step 5 is done for $k \le 2i + 1 < m$. Finally, step 6 is executed for $k \le 2i < m$. The calculations are

$$C(2i + 1) = P(2i + 1) + \alpha[P(2i) + P(2i + 2)], \qquad \text{step 1}$$
$$C(2i) = P(2i) + \beta[C(2i - 1) + C(2i + 1)], \qquad \text{step 2}$$
$$C(2i + 1) = C(2i + 1) + \gamma[C(2i) + C(2i + 2)], \qquad \text{step 3}$$
$$C(2i) = C(2i) + \delta[C(2i - 1) + C(2i + 1)], \qquad \text{step 4}$$

$$C(2i + 1) = -K \times C(2i + 1), \qquad \text{step 5}$$
$$C(2i) = (1/K) \times C(2i), \qquad \text{step 6}$$

where the five constants (wavelet filter coefficients) used by JPEG 2000 are given by $\alpha = -1.586134342$, $\beta = -0.052980118$, $\gamma = 0.882911075$, $\delta = 0.443506852$, and $K = 1.230174105$.

These one-dimensional wavelet transforms are applied L times, where L is a parameter (either user-controlled or set by the encoder), and are interleaved on rows and columns to form L levels (or resolutions) of subbands. Resolution $L - 1$ is the original image (resolution 3 in Figure 5.72a) and resolution 0 is the lowest-frequency subband. The subbands can be organized in one of three ways, as illustrated in Figure 5.72a–c.

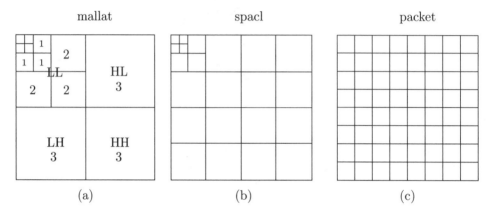

Figure 5.72: JPEG 2000 Subband Organization.

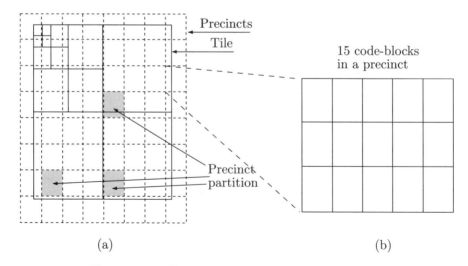

Figure 5.73: Subbands, Precincts, and Code-blocks.

Quantization: Each subband can have a different quantization step size. Each wavelet coefficient in the subband is divided by the quantization step size and the result truncated. The quantization step size may be determined iteratively in order to achieve a target bitrate (i.e., the compression factor may be specified in advance by the user) or in order to achieve a predetermined level of image quality. If lossless compression is desired, the quantization step is set to 1.

Precincts and Code-Blocks: Consider a tile in a color component. The original pixels are wavelet transformed, resulting in subbands of L resolution levels. Figure 5.73a shows one tile and four resolution levels. There are three subbands in each resolution level (except the lowest level). The total size of all the subbands equals the size of the tile. A grid of rectangles known as *precincts* is now imposed on the entire image as shown in Figure 5.73b. The origin of the precinct grid is anchored at the top-left corner of the image and the dimensions of a precinct (its width and height) are powers of 2. Notice that subband boundaries are generally not identical to precinct boundaries. We now examine the three subbands of a certain resolution and pick three precincts located in the same regions in the three subbands (the three gray rectangles in Figure 5.73a). These three precincts constitute a *precinct partition.* The grid of precincts is now divided into a finer grid of *code-blocks*, which are the basic units to be arithmetically coded. Figure 5.73b shows how a precinct is divided into 15 code-blocks. Thus, a precinct partition in this example consists of 45 code-blocks. A code-block is a rectangle of size 2^{xcb} (width) by 2^{ycb} (height) where $2 \leq xcb$, $ycb \leq 10$ and $xcb + ycb \leq 12$.

We can think of the tiles, precincts, and code-blocks as coarse, medium, and fine partitions of the image, respectively. Partitioning the image into smaller and smaller units helps in (1) creating memory-efficient implementations, (2) streaming, and (3) allowing easy access to many points in the bitstream. It is expected that simple JPEG 2000 encoders would ignore this partitioning and have just one tile, one precinct, and one code-block. Sophisticated encoders, on the other hand, may end up with a large number of code-blocks, thereby allowing the decoder to perform progressive decompression, fast streaming, zooming, panning, and other special operations while decoding only parts of the image.

Entropy Coding: The wavelet coefficients of a code-block are arithmetically coded by bitplane. The coding is done from the most-significant bitplane (containing the most important bits of the coefficients) to the least-significant bitplane. Each bitplane is scanned as shown in Figure 5.74. A context is determined for each bit, a probability is estimated from the context, and the bit and its probability are sent to the arithmetic coder.

Many image compression methods work differently. A typical image compression algorithm may use several neighbors of a pixel as its context, and encode the pixel (not just an individual bit) based on the context. Such a context can include only pixels that will be known to the decoder (normally pixels located above the current pixel, or to its left). JPEG 2000 is different in this respect. It encodes individual bits (this is why it uses the MQ coder, which encodes bits, not numbers) and it uses symmetric contexts. The context of a bit is computed from its eight near neighbors. However, since at decoding time the decoder will not know all the neighbors, the context cannot use the values of the neighbors. Instead, it uses the *significance* of the neighbors. Each wavelet coefficient has a 1-bit variable (a flag) associated with it, that indicates its significance. This the *significance state* of the coefficient. When the encoding of a code-block starts, all its wavelet coefficients are considered insignificant and all significance states are cleared.

Some of the most-significant bitplanes may be all zeros. The number of such bitplanes is stored in the bitstream, for the decoder's use. Encoding starts from the first bitplane that is not identically zero. That bitplane is encoded in one pass (a *cleanup pass*). Each of the less-significant bitplanes following it is encoded in three passes, referred to as the *significance propagation pass*, the *magnitude refinement pass*, and the *cleanup pass*. Each pass divides the bitplane into stripes that are four rows high each (Figure 5.74). Each stripe is scanned column by column from left to right. Each bit in the bitplane is encoded in one of the three passes. As mentioned above, encoding a bit involves (1) determining its context, (2) estimating a probability for it, and (3) sending the bit and its probability to the arithmetic coder.

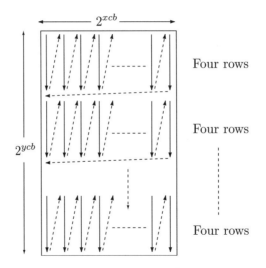

Figure 5.74: Stripes in a Code-Block.

The first encoding pass (significance propagation) of a bitplane encodes all the bits that belong to wavelet coefficients satisfying (1) the coefficient is insignificant and (2) at least one of its eight nearest neighbors is significant. If a bit is encoded in this pass, and if the bit is 1, its wavelet coefficient is marked as significant by setting its significance state to 1. Subsequent bits encoded in this pass (and the following two passes) will consider this coefficient significant.

It is clear that for this pass to encode *any* bits, some wavelet coefficients must be declared significant before the pass starts. This is why the first bitplane that is being encoded is encoded in just one pass, the cleanup pass. In that pass, all the bits of the bitplane are encoded. If a bit happens to be a 1, its coefficient is declared significant.

The second encoding pass (magnitude refinement) of a bitplane encodes all bits of wavelet coefficients that became significant in a *previous* bitplane. Thus, once a coefficient becomes significant, all its less-significant bits will be encoded one by one, each one in the second pass of a different bitplane.

The third and final encoding pass (cleanup) of a bitplane encodes all the bits not encoded in the first two passes. Let's consider a coefficient C in a bitplane B. If C is insignificant, its bit in B will not be encoded in the second pass. If all eight near neighbors of C are insignificant, the bit of C in bitplane B will not be encoded in the first pass either. That bit will therefore be encoded in the third pass. If the bit happens to be 1, C will become significant (the encoder will set its significance state to 1).

Wavelet coefficients are signed integers and have a sign bit. In JPEG 2000, they are represented in the *sign-magnitude* method. The sign bit is 0 for a positive (or a zero) coefficient and is 1 for a negative coefficient. The magnitude bits are the same, regardless of the sign. If a coefficient has one sign bit and eight bits of magnitude, then the value $+7$ is represented as $0|00000111$ and -7 is represented as $1|00000111$. The sign bit of a coefficient is encoded following the first 1 bit of the coefficient.

The behavior of the three passes is illustrated by a simple example. We assume four coefficients with values $10 = 0|00001010$, $1 = 0|00000001$, $3 = 0|00000011$, and $-7 = 1|00000111$. There are eight bitplanes numbered 7 through 0 from left (most significant) to right (least significant). The bitplane with the sign bits is initially ignored. The first four bitplanes 7–4 are all zeros, so encoding starts with bitplane 3 (Figure 5.75). There is just one pass for this bitplane, the cleanup pass. One bit from each of the four coefficients is encoded in this pass. The bit for coefficient 10 is 1, so this coefficient is declared significant (its remaining bits, in bitplanes 2, 1, and 0, will be encoded in pass 2). Also the sign bit of 10 is encoded following this 1. Next, bitplane 2 is encoded. Coefficient 10 is significant, so its bit in this bitplane (a zero) is encoded in pass 2. Coefficient 1 is insignificant, but one of its near neighbors (the 10) is significant, so the bit of 1 in bitplane 2 (a zero) is encoded in pass 1. The bits of coefficients 3 and -7 in this bitplane (a zero and a one, respectively) are encoded in pass 3. The sign bit of coefficient -7 is encoded following the 1 bit of that coefficient. Also, coefficient -7 is declared significant.

Bitplane 1 is encoded next. The bit of coefficient 10 is encoded in pass 2. The bit of coefficient 1 is encoded in pass 1, same as in bitplane 2. The bit of coefficient 3, however, is encoded in pass 1 since its near neighbor, the -7 is now significant. This bit is 1, so coefficient 3 becomes significant. This bit is the first 1 of coefficient 3, so the sign of 3 is encoded following this bit.

⋄ **Exercise 5.19:** Describe the encoding order of the last bitplane.

The context of a bit is determined in a different way for each pass. Here we show how it is determined for the significance propagation pass. The eight near neighbors of the current wavelet coefficient X are used to determine the context used in encoding each bit of X. One of nine contexts is selected and is used to estimate the probability of the bit being encoded. However, as mentioned earlier, it is the current *significance states* of the eight neighbors, not their values, that are

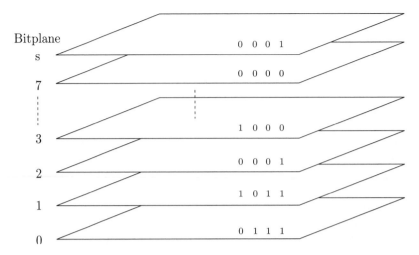

Bitplane s

7

3

2

1

0

Figure 5.75: Bitplanes of Four Coefficients in a Code-Block.

	Coefficients			
Bitplane	10	1	3	−7
sign	0	0	0	1
7	0	0	0	0
6	0	0	0	0
5	0	0	0	0
4	0	0	0	0
3	1	0	0	0
2	0	0	0	1
1	1	0	1	1
0	0	1	1	1

(a)

		Coefficients			
Bitplane	Pass	10	1	3	−7
3	cleanup	1+	0	0	0
2	significance		0		
2	refinement	0			
2	cleanup			0	1−
1	significance		0	1+	
1	refinement	1			1
1	cleanup				
0	significance		1+		
0	refinement	0		1	1
0	cleanup				

(b)

Table 5.76: Encoding Four Bitplanes of Four Coefficients.

used in the determination. Figure 5.77 shows the names assigned to the significance states of the eight neighbors. Table 5.78 lists the criteria used to select one of the nine contexts. Notice that those criteria depend on which of the four subbands (HH, HL, LH, or LL) are being encoded. Context 0 is selected when coefficient X has no significant near neighbors. Context 8 is selected when all eight neighbors of X are significant.

The JPEG 2000 standard specifies similar rules for determining the context of a bit in the refinement and cleanup passes, as well as for the context of a sign bit. Context determination in the cleanup pass is identical to that of the significance pass, with the difference that run-length coding is used if all four bits in a column of

D_0	V_0	D_1
H_0	X	H_1
D_2	V_1	D_3

Figure 5.77: Eight Neighbors.

LL and LH Subbands (vertical high pass)			HL Subband (horizontal high pass)			HH Subband (diagonal high pass)		Context
$\sum H_i$	$\sum V_i$	$\sum D_i$	$\sum H_i$	$\sum V_i$	$\sum D_i$	$\sum (H_i+V_i)$	$\sum D_i$	
2				2			≥ 3	8
1	≥ 1		≥ 1	1		≥ 1	2	7
1	0	≥ 1	0	1	≥ 1	0	2	6
1	0	0	0	1	0	≥ 2	1	5
0	2		2	0		1	1	4
0	1		1	0		0	1	3
0	0	≥ 2	0	0	≥ 2	≥ 2	0	2
0	0	1	0	0	1	1	0	1
0	0	0	0	0	0	0	0	0

Table 5.78: Nine Contexts For the Significance Propagation Pass.

a stripe are insignificant and each has only insignificant neighbors. In such a case, a single bit is encoded, to indicate whether the column is all zero or not. If not, then the column has a run of (between zero and three) zeros. In such a case, the length of this run is encoded. This run must, of course, be followed by a 1. This 1 does not have to encoded since its presence is easily deduced by the decoder. Normal (bit by bit) encoding resumes for the bit following this 1.

Once a context has been determined for a bit, it is used to estimate a probability for encoding the bit. This is done using a probability estimation table, similar to Table 2.67. Notice that JBIG and JBIG2 (Sections 4.9 and 4.10, respectively) use similar tables, but they use thousands of contexts, in contrast to the few contexts (nine or fewer) used by JPEG 2000.

Packets: After all the bits of all the coefficients of all the code-blocks of a precinct partition have been encoded into a short bitstream, a header is added to that bitstream, thereby turning it into a packet. Figure 5.73a,b shows a precinct partition consisting of three precincts, each divided into 15 code-blocks. Encoding this partition therefore results in a packet with 45 encoded code-blocks. The header contains all the information needed to decode the packet. If all the code-blocks in a precinct partition are identically zero, the body of the packet is empty. Recall that a precinct partition corresponds to the same spatial location in three subbands. As a result, a packet can be considered a quality increment for one level of resolution at a certain spatial location.

Layers: A layer is a set of packets. It contains one packet from each precinct partition of each resolution level. Thus, a layer is a quality increment for the entire image at full resolution.

Progressive Transmission: This is an important feature of JPEG 2000. The standard provides four ways of progressively transmitting and decoding an image: by resolution, quality, spatial location, and component. Progression is achieved simply by storing the packets in a specific order in the bitstream. For example, quality (also known as SNR) progression can be achieved by arranging the packets in layer, within each layer by component, within each component by resolution level, and within each resolution level by precinct partition. Resolution progression is achieved when the packets are arranged by precinct partition (innermost nesting), layer, image component, and resolution level (outermost nesting).

When an image is encoded, the packets are placed in the bitstream in a certain order, corresponding to a certain progression. If a user or an application require a different progression (and thus a different order of the packets), it should be easy to read the bitstream, identify the packets, and rearrange them. This process is known as *parsing*, and it is an easy task because of the many *markers* embedded in the bitstream. There are different types of markers and they are used for different purposes. Certain markers identify the type of progression used in the bitstream and others contain the lengths of all the packets. Thus, the bitstream can be parsed without having to decode any of it.

A typical example of parsing is printing a color image on a grayscale printer. In such a case, there is no point in sending the color information to the printer. A parser can use the markers to identify all the packets containing color information and discard them. Another example is decreasing the size of the bitstream (by increasing the amount of image loss). The parser has to identify and discard the layers that contribute the least to the image quality. This is done repeatedly, until the desired bitstream size is achieved.

The parser can be part of an *image server*. A client sends a request to such a server with the name of an image and a desired attribute. The server executes the parser to obtain the image with that attribute, and transmits the bitstream to the client.

Regions of Interest: A client may want to decode just part of an image, a region of interest (ROI). The parser should be able to identify the parts of the bitstream that correspond to the ROI and transmit just those parts. An ROI may be specified at compression time. In such a case, the encoder identifies the code-blocks located in the ROI and writes them early in the bitstream. In many cases, however, an ROI is specified to a parser after the image has been compressed. In such a case, the parser may use the tiles to identify the ROI. Any ROI will be contained in several tiles (perhaps just one), and the parser can identify those tiles and transmit to the client a bitstream consisting of just those tiles. This is one important application of tiles. Small tiles make it possible to specify small ROIs, but result in poor compression. Experience suggests that tiles of size $256{\times}256$ have a negligible negative impact on the compression ratio and are usually small enough to specify ROIs.

Since each tile is compressed individually, it is easy to find the tile's information in the bitstream. Each tile has a header and markers that make this easy. Any parsing that can be done on the entire image can also be performed on individual tiles. Other tiles can either be ignored or can be transmitted at a lower quality.

Alternatively, the parser can handle small ROIs by extracting from the bit-stream the information for individual code-blocks. The parser has to (1) determine what code-blocks contain a given pixel, (2) find the packets containing those code-blocks, (3) decode the packet headers, (4) use the header data to find the code-blocks information within each packet, and (5) transmit just this information to the decoder.

Summary: Current experimentation indicates that JPEG 2000 performs better than the original JPEG, especially for images where very low bitrates (large compression factors) or very high image quality are required. For lossless or near-lossless compression, JPEG 2000 offers only modest improvements over JPEG.

Bibliography

ISO/IEC (2000), International Standard IS 15444-1 "Information Technology—JPEG 2000 Image Coding System." This is the FDC (final committee draft) version 1.0, 16 March 2000.

JPEG 2000 Organization (2000) is at URL `http://www.jpeg.org/JPEG2000.htm`.

Taubman, David (1999) "High Performance Scalable Image Compression with EBCOT," to appear in *IEEE Transactions on Image Processing*. This is currently available from `http://maestro.ee.unsw.edu.au/~taubman/activities/preprints/ebcot.pdf`.

> reflections wobble in the
> mingling circles always spreading out
> the crazy web of wavelets makes sense
> seen from high above.
> the realm of fallen rock.

—Gary Snyder, *Mountains and Rivers Without End*

6
Video Compression

Sound recording and the movie camera were among the greatest inventions of Thomas Edison. They were later united when "talkies" were developed, and they are still used together in video recordings. This unification is one reason for the popularity of movies and video. With the rapid advances in computers in the 1980s and 1990s came multimedia applications, where pictures and sound are combined in the same file. Since such files tend to be large, compressing them became a natural application.

This chapter starts with basic discussions of analog and digital video, continues with the principles of video compression, and concludes with a description of two compression methods designed specifically for video, namely MPEG and H.261.

6.1 Analog Video

An analog video camera converts the image it "sees" through its lens to an electric voltage (a signal) that varies with time according to the intensity and color of the light emitted from the different image parts. Such a signal is called *analog*, since it is analogous (proportional) to the light intensity. The best way to understand this signal is to see how a television receiver responds to it.

> **From the Dictionary**
>
> Analog (adjective).
> being a mechanism that represents data by measurement of a continuously variable quantity (as electrical voltage)

6.1.1 The CRT

A television receiver (a CRT, or cathode ray tube, Figure 6.1a), is a glass tube with a familiar shape. In the back it has an electron gun (the cathode) that emits a stream of electrons. Its front surface is positively charged, so it attracts the electrons (which have a negative electric charge). The front is coated with a phosphor compound that converts the kinetic energy of the electrons hitting it to light. The flash of light only lasts a fraction of a second, so in order to get a constant display, the picture has to be refreshed several times a second. The actual refresh rate depends on the *persistence* of the compound (Figure 6.1b). For certain types of work, such as architectural drawing, long persistence is acceptable. For animation, short persistence is a must.

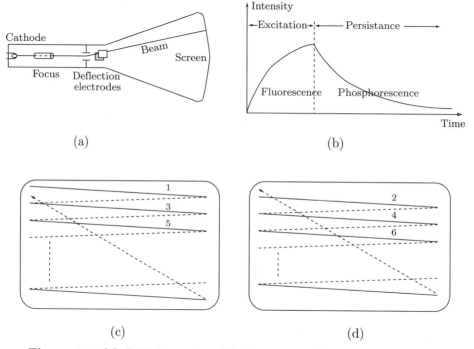

Figure 6.1: (a) CRT Operation. (b) Persistence. (c) Odd Scan Lines. (d) Even Scan Lines.

The early pioneers of motion pictures found, after much experimentation, that the minimum refresh rate required for smooth animation is 15 pictures (or frames) per second (fps), so they adopted 16 fps as the refresh rate for their cameras and projectors. However, when movies began to show fast action (such as in westerns), the motion pictures industry decided to increased the refresh rate to 24 fps, a rate that is used to this day. At a certain point it was discovered that this rate can artificially be doubled, to 48 fps (which produces smoother animation), by projecting each frame twice. This is done by employing a double-blade rotating shutter in the movie projector. The shutter exposes a picture, covers it, and exposes it again, all in 1/24 of a second, thereby achieving an effective refresh rate of 48 fps. Modern movie projectors have very bright lamps and can even use a triple-blade shutter, for an effective refresh rate of 72 fps.

The frequency of electric current in Europe is 50 Hz, so television standards used there, such as PAL and SECAM, employ a refresh rate of 25 fps. This is convenient for transmitting a movie on television. The movie, which was filmed at 24 fps, is shown at 25 fps, an undetectable difference.

The frequency of electric current in the United States is 60 Hz, so when television came, in the 1930s, it used a refresh rate of 30 fps. When color was added, in 1953, that rate was decreased by 1%, to 29.97 fps, because of the need for precise separation of the video and audio signal carriers. Because of interlacing, a complete television picture is made of two frames, so a refresh rate of 29.97 pictures per second requires a rate of 59.94 frames per second.

It turns out that the refresh rate for television should be higher than the rate for movies. A movie is normally watched in darkness, whereas television is watched in a lighted room, and human vision is more sensitive to flicker under conditions of bright illumination. This is why 30 (or 29.97) fps is better than 25.

The electron beam can be turned off and on very rapidly. It can also be deflected horizontally and vertically by two pairs (X and Y) of electrodes. Displaying a single point on the screen is done by turning the beam off, moving it to the part of the screen where the point should appear, and turning it on. This is done by special hardware in response to the analog signal received by the television set.

The signal instructs the hardware to turn the beam off, move it to the top-left corner of the screen, turn it on, and sweep a horizontal line on the screen. While the beam is swept horizontally along the top scan line, the analog signal is used to adjust the beam's intensity according to the image parts being displayed. At the end of the first scan line, the signal instructs the television hardware to turn the beam off, move it back and slightly down, to the start of the third (not the second) scan line, turn it on, and sweep that line. Moving the beam to the start of the next scan line is known as a *retrace*. The time it takes to retrace is the *horizontal blanking time*.

This way, one field of the picture is created on the screen line by line, using just the odd-numbered scan lines (Figure 6.1c). At the end of the last line, the signal contains instructions for a frame retrace. This turns the beam off and moves it to the start of the next field (the second scan line) to scan the field of even-numbered scan lines (Figure 6.1d). The time it takes to do the vertical retrace is the *vertical blanking time*. The picture is therefore created in two fields that together make a *frame*. The picture is said to be *interlaced*.

This process is repeated several times each second, to refresh the picture. This order of scanning (left to right, top to bottom, with or without interlacing) is called *raster scan*. The word raster is derived from the Latin *rastrum*, meaning rake, since this scan is done in a pattern similar to that left by a rake on a field.

A consumer television set uses one of three international standards. The standard used in the United States is called NTSC (National Television Standards Committee), although the new digital standard (Section 6.3.1) is fast becoming popular. NTSC specifies a television transmission of 525 lines (today, this would be $2^9 = 512$

lines, but since television was developed before the advent of computers with their preference for binary numbers, the NTSC standard has nothing to do with powers of two). Because of vertical blanking, however, only 483 lines are visible on the screen. Since the aspect ratio (width/height) of a television screen is 4:3, each line has a size of $\frac{4}{3}483 = 644$ pixels. The resolution of a standard television set is thus 483×644. This may be considered at best medium resolution. (This is the reason why text is so hard to read on a standard television.)

◇ **Exercise 6.1:** (Easy.) What would be the resolution if all 525 lines were visible on the screen?

The aspect ratio of 4:3 was selected by Thomas Edison when he built the first movie cameras and projectors, and was adopted by early television in the 1930s. In the 1950s, after many tests on viewers, the movie industry decided that people prefer larger aspect ratios and started making wide-screen movies, with aspect ratios of 1.85 or higher. Influenced by that, the developers of digital video opted (Section 6.3.1) for the large aspect ratio of 16:9. Exercise 6.4 compares the two aspect ratios, and Table 6.2 lists some common aspect ratios of television and film.

Image formats	Aspect ratio
NTSC, PAL, and SECAM TV	1.33
16 mm and 35 mm film	1.33
HDTV	1.78
Widescreen film	1.85
70 mm film	2.10
Cinemascope film	2.35

Table 6.2: Aspect Ratios of Television and Film.

The concept of *pel aspect ratio* is also useful and should be mentioned. We usually think of a pel (or a pixel) as a mathematical dot, with no dimensions and no shape. In practice, however, pels are printed or displayed, so they have shape and dimensions. The use of a shadow mask (see below) creates circular pels, but computer monitors normally display square or rectangular pixels, thereby creating a crisp, sharp image (because square or rectangular pixels completely fill up space). MPEG-1 (Section 6.5) even has a parameter `pel_aspect_ratio`, whose 16 values are listed in Table 6.26.

It should be emphasized that analog television does not display pixels. When a line is scanned, the beam's intensity is varied continuously. The picture is displayed line by line, but each line is continuous. The image displayed by analog television is, consequently, sampled only in the vertical dimension.

NTSC also specifies a refresh rate of 59.94 (or 60/1.001) frames per second and can be summarized by the notation 525/59.94/2:1, where the 2:1 indicates interlacing. The notation 1:1 indicates *progressive scanning* (not the same as progressive image compression). The PAL television standard (phase alternate line), used in Europe and Asia, is summarized by 625/50/2:1. The quantity $262.5 \times 59.94 =$

15734.25 KHz is called the *line rate* of the 525/59.94/2:1 standard. This is the product of the frame size (number of lines per frame) and the refresh rate.

It should be mentioned that NTSC and PAL are standards for color encoding. They specify how to encode the color into the analog black-and-white video signal. However, for historical reasons, television systems using 525/59.94 scanning normally employ NTSC color coding, whereas television systems using 625/50 scanning normally employ PAL color coding. This is why 525/59.94 and 625/50 are loosely called NTSC and PAL, respectively.

A word on color: Most color CRTs today use the *shadow mask* technique (Figure 6.3). They have three guns emitting three separate electron beams. Each beam is associated with one color, but the beams themselves, of course, consist of electrons and do not have any color. The beams are adjusted such that they always converge a short distance behind the screen. By the time they reach the screen they have diverged a bit, and they strike a group of three different (but very close) points called a *triad*.

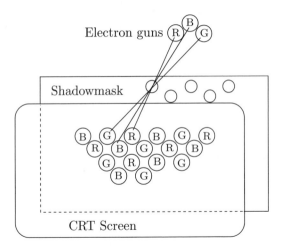

Figure 6.3: A Shadow Mask.

The screen is coated with dots made of three types of phosphor compounds that emit red, green, and blue light, respectively, when excited. At the plane of convergence there is a thin, perforated metal screen: the shadow mask. When the three beams converge at a hole in the mask, they pass through, diverge, and hit a triad of points coated with different phosphor compounds. The points glow at the three colors, and the observer sees a mixture of red, green, and blue whose precise color depends on the intensities of the three beams. When the beams are deflected a little, they hit the mask and are absorbed. After some more deflection, they converge at another hole and hit the screen at another triad.

At a screen resolution of 72 dpi (dots per inch) we expect 72 ideal, square pixels per inch of screen. Each pixel should be a square of side $25.4/72 \approx 0.353$ mm. However, as Figure 6.4a shows, each triad produces a wide circular spot, with a

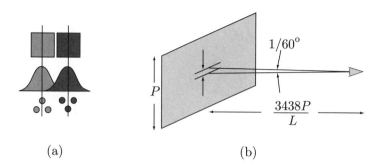

(a)   (b)

Figure 6.4: (a) Square and Circular Pixels. (b) Comfortable Viewing Distance.

diameter of 0.63 mm, on the screen. These spots highly overlap, and each affects the perceived colors of its neighbors.

When watching television, we tend to position ourselves at a distance from which it is comfortable to watch. When watching from a greater distance we miss some details, and when watching closer, the individual scan lines are visible. Experiments show that the comfortable viewing distance is determined by the rule: The smallest detail that we want to see should subtend an angle of about one minute of arc $(1/60)°$. We denote by P the height of the image and by L the number of scan lines. The relation between degrees and radians is $360° = 2\pi$ radians. Combining this with Figure 6.4b produces the expression

$$\frac{P/L}{\text{Distance}} = \left(\frac{1}{60}\right)° = \frac{2\pi}{360 \cdot 60} = \frac{1}{3438},$$

or

$$\text{Distance} = \frac{3438P}{L}. \tag{6.1}$$

If $L = 483$, the comfortable distance is $7.12P$. For $L = 1080$, Equation (6.1) suggests a distance of $3.18P$.

⬦ **Exercise 6.2:** Measure the height of the image on your television set and calculate the comfortable viewing distance from Equation (6.1). Compare it to the distance you actually use.

> All of the books in the world contain no more information than is broadcast as video in a single large American city in a single year. Not all bits have equal value.
>
> —Carl Sagan

6.2 Composite and Components Video

The common television receiver found in many homes receives from the transmitter a composite signal, where the luminance and chrominance components [Salomon 99] are multiplexed. This type of signal was designed in the early 1950s, when color was added to television transmissions. The basic black-and-white signal becomes the luminance (Y) component, and two chrominance components $C1$ and $C2$ are added. Those can be U and V, Cb and Cr, I and Q, or any other chrominance components. Figure 6.5a shows the main components of a transmitter and a receiver using a composite signal. The main point is that only one signal is needed. If the signal is sent on the air, only one frequency is needed. If it is sent on a cable, only one cable is used.

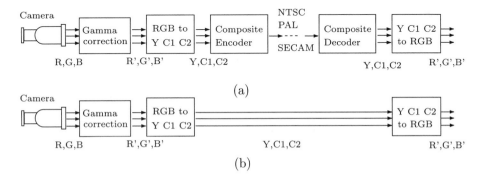

Figure 6.5: (a) Composite and (b) Component Television Transmission.

NTSC uses the YIQ components, which are defined by

$$Y = 0.299R' + 0.587B' + 0.114B',$$
$$I = 0.596R' - 0.274G' - 0.322B'$$
$$= -(\sin 33°)U + (\cos 33°)V,$$
$$Q = 0.211R' - 0.523G' + 0.311B'$$
$$= (\cos 33°)U + (\sin 33°)V.$$

At the receiver, the gamma-corrected $R'G'B'$ components are extracted using the inverse transformation

$$R' = Y + 0.956I + 0.621Q,$$
$$G' = Y - 0.272I - 0.649Q,$$
$$B' = Y - 1.106I + 1.703Q.$$

PAL uses the basic YUV color space, defined by

$$Y = 0.299R' + 0.587G' + 0.114B',$$
$$U = -0.147R' - 0.289G' + 0.436B' = 0.492(B' - Y),$$
$$V = 0.615R' - 0.515G' - 0.100B' = 0.877(R' - Y),$$

whose inverse transform is

$$R' = Y + 1.140V,$$
$$G' = Y - 0.394U - 0.580V,$$
$$B' = Y - 2.030U.$$

SECAM uses the composite color space $YDrDb$, defined by

$$Y = 0.299R' + 0.587G' + 0.114B',$$
$$Db = -0.450R' - 0.833G' + 1.333B' = 3.059U,$$
$$Dr = -1.333R' + 1.116G' - 0.217B' = -2.169V.$$

The inverse transformation is

$$R' = Y - 0.526Dr,$$
$$G' = Y - 0.129Db + 0.268Dr,$$
$$B' = Y + 0.665Db.$$

Composite video is cheap but has problems such as cross-luminance and cross-chrominance artifacts in the displayed image. High-quality video systems normally use *component video*, where three cables or three frequencies carry the individual color components (Figure 6.5b). A common component video standard is the ITU-R recommendation 601, which uses the YCbCr color space (page 570). In this standard, the luminance Y has values in the range $[16, 235]$, whereas each of the two chrominance components has values in the range $[16, 240]$ centered at 128, which indicates zero chrominance.

> Television, a medium. So called because it is neither rare nor well done.
>
> —Unknown

6.3 Digital Video

Digital video is the case where the original image is generated, in the camera, in the form of pixels. When reading this, we may intuitively feel that an image produced this way is inferior to an analog image. An analog image seems to have infinite resolution, whereas a digital image has a fixed, finite resolution that cannot be increased without loss of image quality. In practice, however, the high resolution of analog images is not an advantage, since we view them on a television screen or a computer monitor in a certain, fixed resolution. Digital video, on the other hand, has the following important advantages:

1. It can be easily edited. This makes it possible to produce special effects. Computer-generated images, such as spaceships or cartoon characters, can be combined with real-life action to produce complex, realistic-looking effects. The images

of an actor in a movie can be edited to make him look young at the beginning and old later. Editing software for digital video is already available for most computer platforms. Users can edit a video file and attach it to an email message, thus creating *vmail*. Multimedia applications, where text, sound, still images, and video are integrated, are common today and involve editing video.

2. It can be stored on any digital medium, such as hard disks, removable cartridges, CD-ROMs, or DVDs. An error-correcting code can be added, if needed, for increased reliability. This makes it possible to duplicate a long movie or transmit it between computers without loss of quality (in fact, without a single bit getting corrupted). In contrast, analog video is typically stored on tape, each copy is slightly inferior to the original, and the medium is subject to wear.

3. It can be compressed. This allows for more storage (when video is stored on a digital medium) and also for fast transmission. Sending compressed video between computers makes video telephony possible, which, in turn, makes video conferencing possible. Transmitting compressed video also makes it possible to increase the capacity of television cables and thus add channels.

Digital video is, in principle, a sequence of images, called frames, displayed at a certain *frame rate* (so many frames per second, or fps) to create the illusion of animation. This rate, as well as the image size and pixel depth, depend heavily on the application. Surveillance cameras, for example, use the very low frame rate of five fps, while HDTV displays 25 fps. Table 6.6 shows some typical video applications and their video parameters.

Application	Frame rate	Resolution	Pixel depth
Surveillance	5	640×480	12
Video telephony	10	320×240	12
Multimedia	15	320×240	16
Analog TV	25	640×480	16
HDTV	60	1920×1080	24

Table 6.6: Video Parameters For Typical Applications.

The table illustrates the need for compression. Even the most economic application, a surveillance camera, generates $5 \times 640 \times 480 \times 12 = 18{,}432{,}000$ bits per second! This is equivalent to more than 2.3 million bytes per second, and this information has to be saved for at least a few days before it can be deleted. Most video applications also involve sound. It is part of the overall video data and has to be compressed with the video image.

◇ **Exercise 6.3:** What video applications do not include sound?

A complete piece of video is sometimes called a *presentation*. It consists of a number of *acts*, where each act is broken down into several *scenes*. A scene is made of several *shots* or *sequences* of action, each a succession of *frames*, where there is a small change in scene and camera position between consecutive frames. The hierarchy is thus

$$\text{piece} \rightarrow \text{act} \rightarrow \text{scene} \rightarrow \text{sequence} \rightarrow \text{frame}.$$

6.3.1 High-Definition Television

The NTSC standard was created in the 1930s, for black-and-white television transmissions. Color was added to it in 1953, after four years of testing. NTSC stands
for National Television Standards Committee. This is a standard that specifies the
shape of the signal sent by a television transmitter. The signal is analog, with amplitude that goes up and down during each scan line in response to the black and
white parts of the line. Color was later added to this standard, but it had to be
added such that black-and-white television sets would be able to display the color
signal in black and white. The result was phase modulation of the black-and-white
carrier, a kludge (television engineers call it NSCT "never the same color twice").

With the explosion of computers and digital equipment in the last two decades
came the realization that a digital signal is a better, more reliable way of sending
images over the air. In such a signal the image is sent pixel by pixel, where each
pixel is represented by a number specifying its color. The digital signal is still a
wave, but the amplitude of the wave no longer represents the image. Rather, the
wave is *modulated* to carry binary information. The term modulation means that
something in the wave is modified to distinguish between the zeros and ones being
sent. An FM digital signal, for example, modifies (modulates) the frequency of the
wave. This type of wave uses one frequency to represent a binary zero and another
to represent a one. The DTV (Digital TV) standard uses a modulation technique
called 8-VSB (for *vestigial sideband*), which provides robust and reliable terrestrial
transmission. The 8-VSB modulation technique allows for a broad coverage area,
reduces interference with existing analog broadcasts, and is itself immune from
interference.

History of DTV: The Advanced Television Systems Committee (ATSC), established in 1982, is an international organization developing technical standards
for advanced video systems. Even though these standards are voluntary, they are
generally adopted by the ATSC members and other manufacturers. There are currently about eighty ATSC member companies and organizations, which represent
the many facets of the television, computer, telephone, and motion picture industries.

The ATSC Digital Television Standard adopted by the United States Federal
Communications Commission (FCC) is based on a design by the Grand Alliance
(a coalition of electronics manufacturers and research institutes) that was a finalist
in the first round of DTV proposals under the FCC's Advisory Committee on Advanced Television Systems (ACATS). The ACATS is composed of representatives of
the computer, broadcasting, telecommunications, manufacturing, cable television,
and motion picture industries. Its mission is to assist in the adoption of an HDTV
transmission standard and to promote the rapid implementation of HDTV in the
U.S.

The ACATS announced an open competition: Anyone could submit a proposed
HDTV standard, and the best system would be selected as the new television standard for the United States. To ensure fast transition to HDTV, the FCC promised
that every television station in the nation would be temporarily lent an additional
channel of broadcast spectrum.

The ACATS worked with the ATSC to review the proposed DTV standard, and gave its approval to final specifications for the various parts—audio, transport, format, compression, and transmission. The ATSC documented the system as a standard, and ACATS adopted the Grand Alliance system in its recommendation to the FCC in late 1995.

In late 1996, corporate members of the ATSC had reached an agreement on the DTV standard (Document A/53) and asked the FCC to approve it. On December 31, 1996, the FCC formally adopted every aspect of the ATSC standard except for the video formats. These video formats nevertheless remain a part of the ATSC standard, and are expected to be used by broadcasters and by television manufacturers in the foreseeable future.

HDTV Specifications: The NTSC standard in use since the 1930s specifies an interlaced image composed of 525 lines where the odd numbered lines $(1, 3, 5, \ldots)$ are drawn on the screen first, followed by the even numbered lines $(2, 4, 6, \ldots)$. The two fields are woven together and drawn in 1/30 of a second, allowing for 30 screen refreshes each second. In contrast, a noninterlaced picture displays the entire image at once. This *progressive scan* type of image is what's used by today's computer monitors.

The digital television sets that have been available since mid 1998 use an aspect ratio of 16/9 and can display both the interlaced and progressive-scan images in several different resolutions—one of the best features of digital video. These formats include 525-line progressive-scan (525P), 720-line progressive-scan (720P), 1050-line progressive-scan (1050P), and 1080-interlaced (1080I), all with square pixels.

Our present, analog, television sets cannot deal with the new, digital signal broadcast by television stations, but inexpensive converters will be available (in the form of a small box that can comfortably sit on top of a television set) to translate the digital signals to analog ones (and lose image information in the process).

The NTSC standard calls for 525 scan lines and an aspect ratio of 4/3. This implies $\frac{4}{3} \times 525 = 700$ pixels per line, yielding a total of $525 \times 700 = 367{,}500$ pixels on the screen. (This is the theoretical total, since only 483 lines are actually visible.) In comparison, a DTV format calling for 1080 scan lines and an aspect ratio of 16/9 is equivalent to 1920 pixels per line, bringing the total number of pixels to $1080 \times 1920 = 2{,}073{,}600$, about 5.64 times more than the NTSC interlaced standard.

⋄ **Exercise 6.4:** The NTSC aspect ratio is $4/3 = 1.33$ and that of DTV is $16/9 = 1.77$. Which one looks better?

In addition to the 1080×1920 DTV format, the ATSC DTV standard calls for a lower-resolution format with just 720 scan lines, implying $\frac{16}{9} \times 720 = 1280$ pixels per line. Each of these resolutions can be refreshed at one of three different rates: 60 frames/second (for live video) and 24 or 30 frames/second (for material originally produced on film). The refresh rates can be considered *temporal resolution*. The result is a total of six different formats. Table 6.7 summarizes the screen capacities and the necessary transmission rates of the six formats. With high-resolution and 60 frames per second the transmitter must be able to send 124,416,000 bits/sec (about 14.83 Mbyte/sec), which is why this format uses compression. (It uses MPEG-2.

Other video formats can also use this compression method.) The fact that DTV can have different spatial and temporal resolutions allows for tradeoffs. Certain types of video material (such as fast-moving horse- or car races) may look better at high refresh rates even with low spatial resolution, while other material (such as museum-quality paintings) should ideally be watched in high resolution even with low refresh rates.

lines × pixels	total # of pixels	refresh rate		
		24	30	60
1080 × 1920	2,073,600	49,766,400	62,208,000	124,416,000
720 × 1280	921,600	22,118,400	27,648,000	55,296,000

Table 6.7: Resolutions and Capacities of Six DTV Formats.

Digital Television (DTV) is a broad term encompassing all types of digital transmission. HDTV is a subset of DTV indicating 1080 scan lines. Another type of DTV is standard definition television (SDTV), which has picture quality slightly better than a good analog picture. (SDTV has resolution of 640×480 at 30 frames/sec and an aspect ratio of 4:3.) Since generating an SDTV picture requires fewer pixels, a broadcasting station will be able to transmit multiple channels of SDTV within its 6 MHz allowed frequency range. HDTV also incorporates Dolby Digital sound technology to bring together a complete presentation.

Figure 6.8 shows the most important resolutions used in various video systems. Their capacities range from 19,000 pixels to more than two million pixels.

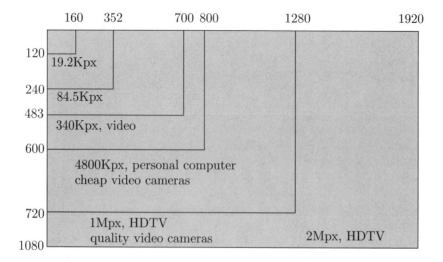

Figure 6.8: Various Video Resolutions.

> Sometimes cameras and television are good to people and sometimes they aren't. I don't know if its the way you say it, or how you look.
>
> —Vice President Dan Quayle

6.4 Video Compression

Video compression is based on two principles. The first is the spatial redundancy that exists in each frame. The second is the fact that most of the time, a video frame is very similar to its immediate neighbors. This is called *temporal redundancy*. A typical technique for video compression should therefore start by encoding the first frame using a still image compression method. It should then encode each successive frame by identifying the differences between the frame and its predecessor, and encoding these differences. If the frame is very different from its predecessor (as happens with the first frame of a shot), it should be coded independently of any other frame. In the video compression literature, a frame that is coded using its predecessor is called *inter frame* (or just *inter*), while a frame that is coded independently is called *intra frame* (or just *intra*).

Video compression is normally lossy. Encoding a frame F_i in terms of its predecessor F_{i-1} introduces some distortions. As a result, encoding frame F_{i+1} in terms of F_i increases the distortion. Even in lossless video compression, a frame may lose some bits. This may happen during transmission or after a long shelf stay. If a frame F_i has lost some bits, then all the frames following it, up to the next intra frame, are decoded improperly, perhaps even leading to accumulated errors. This is why intra frames should be used from time to time inside a sequence, not just at its beginning. An intra frame is labeled I, and an inter frame is labeled P (for *predictive*).

Once this idea is grasped, it is possible to generalize the concept of an inter frame. Such a frame can be coded based on one of its predecessors and also on one of its *successors*. We know that an encoder should not use any information that is not available to the decoder, but video compression is special because of the large quantities of data involved. We usually don't mind if the encoder is slow, but the decoder has to be fast. A typical case is video recorded on a hard disk or on a DVD, to be played back. The encoder can take minutes or hours to encode the data. The decoder, however, has to play it back at the correct frame rate (so many frames per second), so it has to be fast. This is why a typical video decoder works in parallel. It has several decoding circuits working simultaneously on several frames.

With this in mind we can now imagine a situation where the encoder encodes frame 2 based on both frames 1 and 3, and writes the frames on the compressed stream in the order 1, 3, 2. The decoder reads them in this order, decodes frames 1 and 3 in parallel, outputs frame 1, then decodes frame 2 based on frames 1 and 3. The frames should, of course, be clearly tagged (or time stamped). A frame that is encoded based on both past and future frames is labeled B (for *bidirectional*).

Predicting a frame based on its successor makes sense in cases where the movement of an object in the picture gradually uncovers a background area. Such an area may be only partly known in the current frame but may be better known in the next frame. Thus, the next frame is a natural candidate for predicting this area in the current frame.

The idea of a B frame is so useful that most frames in a compressed video presentation may be of this type. We therefore end up with a sequence of compressed frames of the three types I, P, and B. An I frame is decoded independently of any other frame. A P frame is decoded using the preceding I or P frame. A B frame is decoded using the preceding *and* following I or P frames. Figure 6.9a shows a sequence of such frames in the order in which they are generated by the encoder (and input by the decoder). Figure 6.9b shows the same sequence in the order in which the frames are output by the decoder and displayed. The frame labeled 2 should be displayed after frame 5, so each frame should have two time stamps, its coding time and its display time.

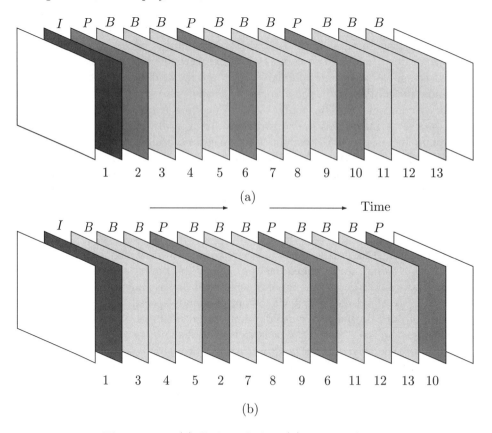

Figure 6.9: (a) Coding Order. (b) Display Order.

We start with a few intuitive video compression methods.

Subsampling: The encoder selects every other frame and writes it on the compressed stream. This yields a compression factor of 2. The decoder inputs a frame and duplicates it to create two frames.

Differencing: A frame is compared to its predecessor. If the difference between them is small (just a few pixels), the encoder encodes the pixels that are different by writing three numbers on the compressed stream for each pixel: its image coordinates, and the difference between the values of the pixel in the two frames. If the difference between the frames is large, the current frame is written on the output in raw format. Compare this method with relative encoding, Section 1.3.1.

A lossy version of differencing looks at the amount of change in a pixel. If the difference between the intensities of a pixel in the preceding frame and in the current frame is smaller than a certain threshold, the pixel is not considered different.

Block Differencing: This is a further improvement of differencing. The image is divided into blocks of pixels, and each block B in the current frame is compared to the corresponding block P in the preceding frame. If the blocks differ by more than a certain amount, then B is compressed by writing its image coordinates, followed by the values of all its pixels (expressed as differences) on the compressed stream. The advantage is that the block coordinates are small numbers (smaller than a pixel's coordinates), and these coordinates have to be written just once for the entire block. On the downside, the values of all the pixels in the block, even those that haven't changed, have to be written on the output. However, since these values are expressed as differences, they are small numbers. Consequently, this method is sensitive to the block size.

Motion Compensation: Anyone who has watched movies knows that the difference between consecutive frames is small because it is the result of moving the scene, the camera, or both between frames. This feature can therefore be exploited to get better compression. If the encoder discovers that a part P of the preceding frame has been rigidly moved to a different location in the current frame, then P can be compressed by writing the following three items on the compressed stream: its previous location, its current location, and information identifying the boundaries of P. The following discussion of motion compensation is based on [Manning 98].

In principle, such a part can have any shape. In practice, we are limited to equal-size blocks (normally square but can also be rectangular). The encoder scans the current frame block by block. For each block B it searches the preceding frame for an identical block C (if compression is to be lossless) or for a similar one (if it can be lossy). Finding such a block, the encoder writes the difference between its past and present locations on the output. This difference is of the form

$$(C_x - B_x, C_y - B_y) = (\Delta x, \Delta y),$$

so it is called a *motion vector*. Figure 6.10a,b shows a simple example where the sun and trees are moved rigidly to the right (because of camera movement) while the child moves a different distance to the left (this is scene movement).

Motion compensation is effective if objects are just translated, not scaled or rotated. Drastic changes in illumination from frame to frame also reduce the effectiveness of this method. In general, motion compensation is lossy. The following paragraphs discuss the main aspects of motion compensation in detail.

Frame Segmentation: The current frame is divided into equal-size nonoverlapping blocks. The blocks may be square or rectangles. The latter choice assumes

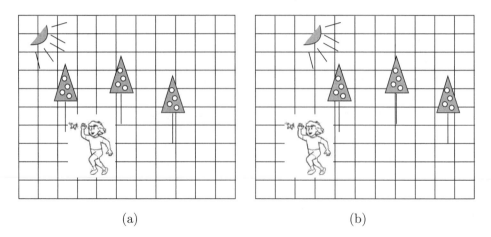

(a)   (b)

Figure 6.10: Motion Compensation.

that motion in video is mostly horizontal, so horizontal blocks reduce the number of motion vectors without degrading the compression ratio. The block size is important, since large blocks reduce the chance of finding a match, and small blocks result in many motion vectors. In practice, block sizes that are integer powers of 2, such as 8 or 16, are used, since this simplifies the software.

Search Threshold: Each block B in the current frame is first compared to its counterpart C in the preceding frame. If they are identical, or if the difference between them is less than a preset threshold, the encoder assumes that the block hasn't been moved.

Block Search: This is a time-consuming process, and so has to be carefully designed. If B is the current block in the current frame, then the previous frame has to be searched for a block identical to or very close to B. The search is normally restricted to a small area (called the *search area*) around B, defined by the *maximum displacement* parameters dx and dy. These parameters specify the maximum horizontal and vertical distances, in pixels, between B and any matching block in the previous frame. If B is a square with side b, the search area will contain $(b+2dx)(b+2dy)$ pixels (Figure 6.11) and will consist of $(2dx+1)(2dy+1)$ distinct, overlapping $b \times b$ squares. The number of candidate blocks in this area is therefore proportional to $dx \cdot dy$.

Distortion Measure: This is the most sensitive part of the encoder. The distortion measure selects the best match for block B. It has to be simple and fast, but also reliable. A few choices—similar to the ones of Section 4.12—are discussed below.

The *mean absolute difference* (or *mean absolute error*) calculates the average of the absolute differences between a pixel B_{ij} in B and its counterpart C_{ij} in a candidate block C:

$$\frac{1}{b^2} \sum_{i=1}^{b} \sum_{j=1}^{b} |B_{ij} - C_{ij}|.$$

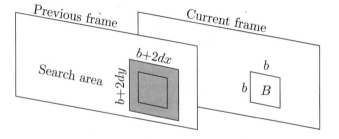

Figure 6.11: Search Area.

This involves b^2 subtractions and absolute value operations, b^2 additions, and one division. This measure is calculated for each of the $(2dx + 1)(2dy + 1)$ distinct, overlapping $b \times b$ candidate blocks, and the smallest distortion (say, for block C_k) is examined. If it is smaller than the search threshold, than C_k is selected as the match for B. Otherwise, there is no match for B, and B has to be encoded without motion compensation.

◇ **Exercise 6.5:** How can such a thing happen? How can a block in the current frame match nothing in the preceding frame?

The *mean square difference]* is a similar measure, where the square, rather than the absolute value, of a pixel difference is calculated:

$$\frac{1}{b^2} \sum_{i=1}^{b} \sum_{j=1}^{b} (B_{ij} - C_{ij})^2.$$

The *Pel difference Classification* (PDC) measure counts how many differences $|B_{ij} - C_{ij}|$ are smaller than the PDC parameter p.

The *integral projection* measure computes the sum of a row of B and subtracts it from the sum of the corresponding row of C. The absolute value of the difference is added to the absolute value of the difference of the columns sum:

$$\sum_{i=1}^{b} \left| \sum_{j=1}^{b} B_{ij} - \sum_{j=1}^{b} C_{ij} \right| + \sum_{j=1}^{b} \left| \sum_{i=1}^{b} B_{ij} - \sum_{i=1}^{b} C_{ij} \right|.$$

Suboptimal Search Methods: These methods search some, instead of all, the candidate blocks in the $(b + 2dx)(b + 2dy)$ area. They speed up the search for a matching block, at the expense of compression efficiency. Several such methods are discussed in detail in Section 6.4.1.

Motion Vector Correction: Once a block C has been selected as the best match for B, a motion vector is calculated as the difference between the upper-left corner of C and that of B. Regardless of how the matching was determined, the motion vector may be wrong because of noise, local minima in the frame, or because the matching algorithm is not ideal. It is possible to apply smoothing techniques to the motion vectors after they have been calculated, in an attempt to improve the matching. Spatial correlations in the image suggest that the motion vectors should also be correlated. If certain vectors are found to violate this, they can be corrected.

This step is costly and may even backfire. A video presentation may involve slow, smooth motion of most objects, but also swift, jerky motion of some small objects. Correcting motion vectors may interfere with the motion vectors of such objects and cause distortions in the compressed frames.

Coding Motion Vectors: A large part of the current frame (perhaps close to half of it) may be converted to motion vectors, so the way these vectors are encoded is crucial; it must also be lossless. Two properties of motion vectors help in encoding them: (1) They are correlated and (2) their distribution is nonuniform. As we scan the frame block by block, adjacent blocks normally have motion vectors that don't differ by much; they are correlated. The vectors also don't point in all directions. There are usually one or two preferred directions in which all or most motion vectors point; the vectors are thus nonuniformly distributed.

No single method has proved ideal for encoding the motion vectors. Arithmetic coding, adaptive Huffman coding, and various prefix codes have been tried, and all seem to perform well. Here are two different methods that may perform better:

1. Predict a motion vector based on its predecessors in the same row and its predecessors in the same column of the current frame. Calculate the difference between the prediction and the actual vector, and Huffman encode it. This method is important. It is used in MPEG and other compression methods.

2. Group the motion vectors in blocks. If all the vectors in a block are identical, the block is encoded by encoding this vector. Other blocks are encoded as in 1 above. Each encoded block starts with a code identifying its type.

Coding the Prediction Error: Motion compensation is lossy, since a block B is normally matched to a somewhat different block C. Compression can be improved by coding the difference between the current uncompressed and compressed frames on a block by block basis and only for blocks that differ much. This is usually done by transform coding. The difference is written on the output, following each frame, and is used by the decoder to improve the frame after it has been decoded.

6.4.1 Suboptimal Search Methods

Video compression includes many steps and computations, so researchers have been looking for optimizations and faster algorithms, especially for steps that involve many calculations. One such step is the search for a block C in the previous frame to match a given block B in the current frame. An exhaustive search is time-consuming, so it pays to look for suboptimal search methods that search just some of the many overlapping candidate blocks. These methods do not always find the best match, but can generally speed up the entire compression process while incurring only a small loss of compression efficiency.

Signature-Based Methods: Such a method performs a number of steps, restricting the number of candidate blocks in each step. In the first step, all the candidate blocks are searched using a simple, fast distortion measure such as pel difference classification. Only the best matched blocks are included in the next step, where they are evaluated by a more restrictive distortion measure, or by the same measure but with a smaller parameter. A signature method may involve several steps, using different distortion measures in each.

Distance-Diluted Search: We know from experience that fast-moving objects look blurred in an animation, even if they are sharp in all the frames. This suggests a way to lose data. We may require a good block match for slow-moving objects, but allow for a worse match for fast-moving ones. The result is a block matching algorithm that searches all the blocks close to B, but fewer and fewer blocks as the search gets farther away from B. Figure 6.12a shows how such a method may work for maximum displacement parameters $dx = dy = 6$. The total number of blocks C being searched goes from $(2dx + 1) \cdot (2dy + 1) = 13 \times 13 = 169$ to just 65, less than 39%!

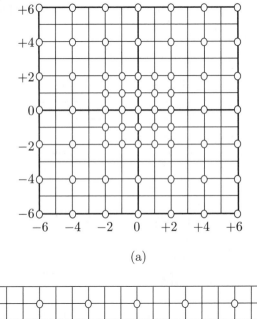

(a)

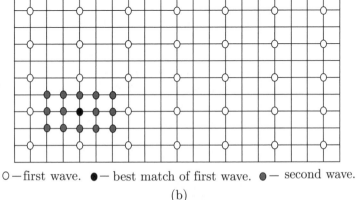

$\bigcirc$ —first wave. $\bullet$ — best match of first wave. $\bullet$ — second wave.

(b)

Figure 6.12: (a) Distance-Diluted Search For $dx = dy = 6$.
(b) A Locality Search.

Locality-Based Search: This method is based on the assumption that once a good match has been found, even better matches are likely to be located near it (remember that the blocks C searched for matches highly overlap). An obvious algorithm is to start searching for a match in a sparse set of blocks, then use the best-matched block C as the center of a second wave of searches, this time in a denser set of blocks. Figure 6.12b shows two waves of search, the first considers widely spaced blocks, selecting one as the best match. The second wave searches every block in the vicinity of the best match.

Quadrant Monotonic Search: This is a variant of locality-based search. It starts with a sparse set of blocks C that are searched for a match. The distortion measure is computed for each of those blocks, and the result is a set of distortion values. The idea is that the distortion values decrease as we move away from the best match. By examining the set of distortion values obtained in the first step, the second step may predict where the best match is likely to be found. Figure 6.13 shows how a search of a region of 4×3 blocks suggests a well-defined direction in which to continue searching.

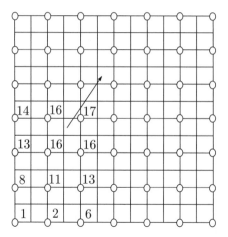

Figure 6.13: Quadrant Monotonic Search.

This method is less reliable than the previous ones since the direction proposed by the set of distortion values may lead to a local best block, whereas *the* best block may be located elsewhere.

Dependent Algorithms: As has been mentioned before, motion in a frame is the result of either camera movement or object movement. If we assume that objects in the frame are bigger than a block, we conclude that it is reasonable to expect the motion vectors of adjacent blocks to be correlated. The search algorithm can therefore start by estimating the motion vector of a block B from the motion vectors that have already been found for its neighbors, then improve this estimate by comparing B to some candidate blocks C. This is the basis of several *dependent algorithms*, which can be spatial or temporal.

Spatial dependency: In a spatial dependent algorithm, the neighbors of a block B in the current frame are used to estimate the motion vector of B. These, of course, must be neighbors whose motion vectors have already been computed. Most blocks have eight neighbors each, but using all eight may not be the best strategy (also, when a block B is considered, only some of its neighbors may have their motion vectors already computed). If blocks are matched in raster order, then it makes sense to use one, two, or three previously matched neighbors, as shown in Figure 6.14a,b,c. Because of symmetry, however, it is better to use four symmetric neighbors, as in Figure 6.14d,e. This can be done by a three-pass method that scans blocks as in Figure 6.14f. The first pass scans all the blocks shown in black (one-quarter of the blocks in the frame). Motion vectors for those blocks are calculated by some other method. Pass two scans the blocks shown in gray (25% of the blocks) and estimates a motion vector for each using the motion vectors of its four corner neighbors. The white blocks (the remaining 50%) are scanned in the third pass, and the motion vector of each is estimated using the motion vectors of its neighbors on all four sides. If the motion vectors of the neighbors are very different, they should not be used, and a motion vector for block B is calculated using a different method.

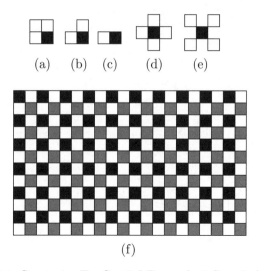

(a)　(b)　(c)　(d)　(e)

(f)

Figure 6.14: Strategies For Spatial Dependent Search Algorithms.

Temporal dependency: The motion vector of block B in the current frame can be estimated as the motion vector of the same block in the previous frame. This makes sense if we can assume uniform motion. After the motion vector of B is estimated this way, it should be improved and corrected using other methods.

More Quadrant Monotonic Search Methods: The following suboptimal block matching methods use the main assumption of the quadrant monotonic search method.

Two-Dimensional Logarithmic Search: This multistep method reduces the search area in each step until it shrinks to one block. We assume that the current block B is located at position (a, b) in the current frame. This position becomes the initial center of the search. The algorithm uses a distance parameter d that defines the search area. This parameter is user-controlled with a default value. The search area consists of the $(2d + 1) \times (2d + 1)$ blocks centered on the current block B.

Step 1: A step size s is calculated by

$$s = 2^{\lfloor \log_2 d \rfloor - 1},$$

and the algorithm compares B to the five blocks at positions (a, b), $(a, b + s)$, $(a, b - s)$, $(a + s, b)$, and $(a - s, b)$ in the previous frame. These five blocks form the pattern of a plus sign "+".

Step 2: The best match among the five blocks is selected. We denote the position of this block by (x, y). If $(x, y) = (a, b)$, then s is halved (this is the reason for the name *logarithmic*). Otherwise, s stays the same, and the center (a, b) of the search is moved to (x, y).

Step 3: If $s = 1$, then the nine blocks around the center (a, b) of the search are searched, and the best match among them becomes the result of the algorithm. Otherwise the algorithm goes to Step 2.

Any blocks that need be searched but are outside the search area are ignored and are not used in the search. Figure 6.15 illustrates the case where $d = 8$. For simplicity we assume that the current block B has frame coordinates $(0, 0)$. The search is limited to the 17×17-block area centered on block B. Step 1 calculates

$$s = 2^{\lfloor \log_2 8 \rfloor - 1} = 2^{3-1} = 4,$$

and searches the five blocks (labeled 1) at locations $(0, 0)$, $(4, 0)$, $(-4, 0)$, $(0, 4)$, and $(0, -4)$. We assume that the best match of these five is at $(0, 4)$, so this becomes the new center of the search, and the three blocks (labeled 2) at locations $(4, -4)$, $(4, 4)$, and $(8, 0)$ are searched in the second step.

Assuming that the best match among these three is at location $(4, 4)$, the next step searches the two blocks labeled 3 at locations $(8, 4)$ and $(4, 8)$, the block (labeled 2) at $(4, 4)$ and the "1" blocks at $(0, 4)$ and $(4, 0)$.

⋄ **Exercise 6.6:** Assuming that $(4, 4)$ is again the best match, use the figure to describe the rest of the search.

Three-Step Search: This is somewhat similar to the two-dimensional logarithmic search. In each step it tests eight blocks, instead of four, around the center of search, then halves the step size. If $s = 3$ initially, the algorithm terminates after three steps, hence its name.

Orthogonal Search: This is a variation of both the two-dimensional logarithmic search and the three step search. Each step of the orthogonal search involves a horizontal and a vertical search. The step size s is initialized to $\lfloor (d + 1)/2 \rfloor$, and the block at the center of the search and two candidate blocks located on either side of it at a distance of s are searched. The location of smallest distortion becomes the center of the vertical search, where two candidate blocks above and below the center, at distances of s, are searched. The best of these locations becomes the center of the next search. If the step size s is 1, the algorithm terminates and returns

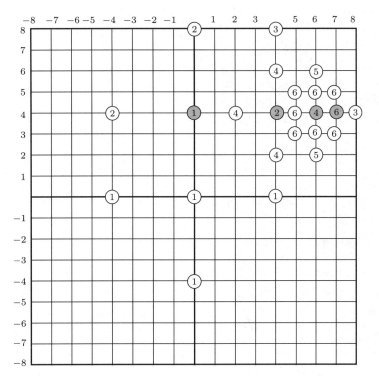

Figure 6.15: The Two-Dimensional Logarithmic Search Method.

the best block found in the current step. Otherwise, s is halved, and another set of horizontal and vertical searches is performed.

One-at-a-Time Search: In this type os search there are again two steps, a horizontal and a vertical. The horizontal step searches all the blocks in the search area whose y coordinates equal that of block B (i.e., that are located on the same horizontal axis as B). Assuming that block H has the minimum distortion among those, the vertical step searches all the blocks on the same vertical axis as H and returns the best of them. A variation repeats this on smaller and smaller search areas.

Cross Search: All the steps of this algorithm, except the last one, search the five blocks at the edges of a multiplication sign "$\times$". The step size is halved in each step until it gets down to 1. At the last step, the plus sign "$+$" is used to search the areas located around the top-left and bottom-right corners of the preceding step.

This has been a survey of quadrant monotonic search methods. We follow with an outline of two advanced search methods.

Hierarchical Search Methods: Hierarchical methods take advantage of the fact that block matching is sensitive to the block size. A hierarchical search method starts with large blocks and uses their motion vectors as starting points for more searches with smaller blocks. Large blocks are less likely to stumble on a local maximum, while a small block generally produces a better motion vector. A hierarchical search method is thus computationally intensive, and the main point is to speed it up by reducing the number of operations. This can be done in several ways as follows:

1. In the initial steps, when the blocks are still large, search just a sample of blocks. The resulting motion vectors are not the best, but they are only going to be used as starting points for better ones.

2. When searching large blocks, skip some of the pixels of a block. The algorithm may, for example, use just one-quarter of the pixels of the large blocks, one half of the pixels of smaller blocks, and so on.

3. Select the block sizes such that the block used in step i is divided into several (typically four or nine) blocks used in the following step. This way a single motion vector calculated in step i can be used as an estimate for several better motion vectors in step $i + 1$.

Multidimensional Search Space Methods: These methods are more complex. When searching for a match for block B, such a method looks for matches that are rotations or zooms of B, not just translations.

A multidimensional search space method may also find a block C that matches B but has different lighting conditions. This is useful when an object moves among areas that are illuminated differently. All the methods discussed so far compare two blocks by comparing the luminance values of corresponding pixels. Two blocks B and C that contain the same objects but differ in luminance would be declared different by such methods.

When a multidimensional search space method finds a block C that matches B but has different luminance, it may declare C the match of B and append a luminance value to the compressed frame B. This value (which may be negative) is added by the decoder to the pixels of the decompressed frame, to bring them back to their original values.

A multidimensional search space method may also compare a block B to rotated versions of the candidate blocks C. This is useful if objects in the video presentation may be rotated in addition to being moved. The algorithm may also try to match a block B to a block C containing a scaled version of the objects in B. If, for example, B is of size 8×8 pixels, the algorithm may consider blocks C of size 12×12, shrink each to 8×8, and compare it to B.

This kind of block search involves many extra operations and comparisons. We say that it increases the size of the *search space* significantly, hence the name *multidimensional search space*. It seems that at present there is no multidimensional search space method that can account for scaling, rotation, and changes in illumination and also be fast enough for practical use.

Bibliography

Manning (1998), URL `http://lemontree.web2010.com/dvideo/`.

6.5 MPEG

Started in 1988, the MPEG project was developed by a group of hundreds of experts under the auspices of the ISO (International Standardization Organization) and the IEC (International Electrotechnical Committee). The name MPEG is an acronym for Moving Pictures Experts Group. MPEG is a method for video compression, which involves the compression of digital images and sound, as well as synchronization of the two. There currently are several MPEG standards. MPEG-1 is intended for intermediate data rates, on the order of 1.5 Mbit/s. MPEG-2 is intended for high data rates of at least 10 Mbit/s. MPEG-3 was intended for HDTV compression but was found to be redundant and was merged with MPEG-2. MPEG-4 is intended for very low data rates of less than 64 Kbit/s. A third international body, the ITU-T, has been involved in the design of both MPEG-2 and MPEG-4. This section concentrates on MPEG-1 and discusses only its image compression features.

The formal name of MPEG-1 is the international standard for moving picture video compression, IS11172-2. Like other standards developed by the ITU and ISO, the document describing MPEG-1 has *normative* and *informative* sections. A normative section is part of the standard specification. It is intended for implementers, is written in a precise language, and should be strictly followed in implementing the standard on actual computer platforms. An informative section, on the other hand, illustrates concepts discussed elsewhere, explains the reasons that led to certain choices and decisions, and contains background material. An example of a normative section is the various tables of variable codes used in MPEG. An example of an informative section is the algorithm used by MPEG to estimate motion and match blocks. MPEG does not require any particular algorithm, and an MPEG encoder can use any method to match blocks. The section itself simply describes various alternatives.

The discussion of MPEG in this section is informal. The first subsection (main components) describes all the important terms, principles, and codes used in MPEG-1. The subsections that follow go into more details, especially in the description and listing of the various parameters and variable-size codes.

The importance of a widely accepted standard for video compression is apparent from the fact that many manufacturers (of computer games, CD-ROM movies, digital television, and digital recorders, among others) implemented and started using MPEG-1 even before it was finally approved by the MPEG committee. This also was one reason why MPEG-1 had to be frozen at an early stage and MPEG-2 had to be developed to accommodate video applications with high data rates.

There are many sources of information on MPEG. [Mitchell et al. 97] is one detailed source for MPEG-1, and the MPEG consortium [MPEG 98] contains lists of other resources. In addition, there are many web pages with descriptions, explanations, and answers to frequently asked questions about MPEG.

> Television? No good will come of this device. The word is half Greek and half Latin.
>
> —C. P. Scott

To understand the meaning of the words "intermediate data rate" we consider a typical example of video with a resolution of 360×288, a depth of 24 bits per pixel, and a refresh rate of 24 frames per second. The image part of this video requires $360 \times 288 \times 24 \times 24 = 59{,}719{,}680$ bits/s. For the sound part, we assume two sound tracks (stereo sound), each sampled at 44 KHz with 16 bit samples. The data rate is $2 \times 44{,}000 \times 16 = 1{,}408{,}000$ bits/s. The total is about 61.1 Mbit/s and this is supposed to be compressed by MPEG-1 to an intermediate data rate of about 1.5 Mbit/s (the size of the sound track alone), a compression factor of more than 40! Another aspect is the decoding speed. An MPEG-compressed movie may end up being stored on a CD-ROM or DVD and has to be decoded and played in real time.

MPEG uses its own vocabulary. An entire movie is considered a *video sequence*. It consists of *pictures*, each having three *components*, one luminance (Y) and two chrominance (Cb and Cr). The luminance component (Section 4.1) contains the black-and-white picture, and the chrominance components provide the color hue and saturation (see [Salomon 99] for a detailed discussion). Each component is a rectangular array of *samples*, and each row of the array is called a *raster line*. A *pel* is the set of three samples. The eye is sensitive to small spatial variations of luminance, but is less sensitive to similar changes in chrominance. As a result, MPEG-1 samples the chrominance components at half the resolution of the luminance component. The term *intra* is used, but *inter* and *nonintra* are used interchangeably.

The input to an MPEG encoder is called the *source data*, and the output of an MPEG decoder is the *reconstructed data*. The source data is organized in packs (Figure 6.16b), where each pack starts with a start code (32 bits) followed by a header, ends with a 32-bit end code, and contains a number of packets in between. A packet contains compressed data, either audio or video. The size of a packet is determined by the MPEG encoder according to the requirements of the storage or transmission medium, which is why a packet is not necessarily a complete video picture. It can be any part of a video picture or any part of the audio.

The MPEG decoder has three main parts, called *layers*, to decode the audio, the video, and the system data. The system layer reads and interprets the various codes and headers in the source data, and routes the packets to either the audio or the video layers (Figure 6.16a) to be buffered and later decoded. Each of these two layers consists of several decoders that work simultaneously.

6.5.1 MPEG-1 Main Components

MPEG uses I, P, and B pictures, as discussed in Section 6.4. They are arranged in groups, where a group can be open or closed. The pictures are arranged in a certain order, called the *coding order*, but are output, after decoding, and sent to the display in a different order, called the *display order*. In a closed group, P and B pictures are decoded only from other pictures in the group. In an open group, they can be decoded from pictures outside the group. Different regions of a B picture may use different pictures for their decoding. A region may be decoded from some preceding pictures, from some following pictures, from both types, or from none. Similarly, a region in a P picture may use several preceding pictures for its decoding, or use none at all, in which case it is decoded using MPEG's intra methods.

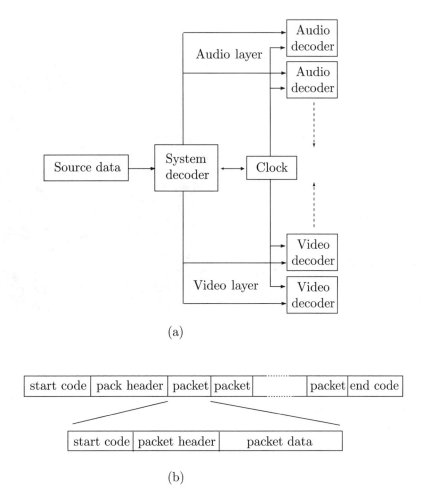

(a)

(b)

Figure 6.16: (a) MPEG Decoder Organization. (b) Source Format.

The basic building block of an MPEG picture is the *macroblock* (Figure 6.17a). It consists of a 16×16 block of luminance (grayscale) samples (divided into four 8×8 blocks) and two 8×8 blocks of the matching chrominance samples. The MPEG compression of a macroblock consists mainly in passing each of the six blocks through a discrete cosine transform, which creates decorrelated values, then quantizing and encoding the results. It is very similar to JPEG compression (Section 4.6), the main differences being that different quantization tables and different code tables are used in MPEG for intra and nonintra, and the rounding is done differently.

A picture in MPEG is organized in slices, where each slice is a contiguous set of macroblocks (in raster order) that have the same grayscale (i.e., luminance component). The concept of slices makes sense because a picture may often contain large uniform areas, causing many contiguous macroblocks to have the same grayscale. Figure 6.17b shows a hypothetical MPEG picture and how it is divided into slices.

Each square in the picture is a macroblock. Notice that a slice can continue from scan line to scan line.

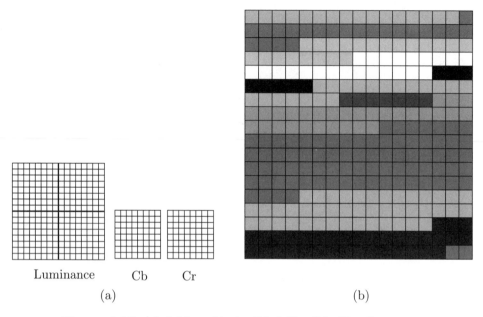

Luminance   Cb   Cr

(a)   (b)

Figure 6.17: (a) A Macroblock. (b) A Possible Slice Structure.

⋄ **Exercise 6.7:** How many samples are there in the hypothetical MPEG picture of Figure 6.17b?

When a picture is encoded in nonintra mode (i.e., it is encoded by means of another picture, normally its predecessor), the MPEG encoder generates the differences between the pictures, then applies the DCT to the differences. In such a case, the DCT does not contribute much to the compression, because the differences are already decorrelated. Nevertheless, the DCT is useful even in this case, since it is followed by quantization, and the quantization in nonintra coding can be quite deep.

The precision of the numbers processed by the DCT in MPEG also depends on whether intra or nonintra coding is used. MPEG samples in intra coding are 8-bit unsigned integers, whereas in nonintra they are 9-bit signed integers. This is because a sample in nonintra is the difference of two unsigned integers, and may therefore be negative. The two summations of the two-dimensional DCT, Equation (4.9), can at most multiply a sample by $64 = 2^6$ and may therefore result in an $8 + 6 = 14$-bit integer (see Exercise 4.22 for a similar case). In those summations, a sample is multiplied by cosine functions, which may result in a negative number. The result of the double sum is therefore a 15-bit signed integer. This integer is then multiplied by the factor $C_i C_j / 4$ which is at least $1/8$, thereby reducing the result to a 12-bit signed integer.

This 12-bit integer is then quantized by dividing it by a quantization coefficient (QC) taken from a quantization table. The result is, in general, a noninteger and has to be rounded. It is in quantization and rounding that information is irretrievably lost. MPEG specifies default quantization tables, but custom tables can also be used. In intra coding rounding is done in the normal way, to the nearest integer, whereas in nonintra rounding is done by truncating a noninteger to the nearest smaller integer. Figure 6.18a,b shows the results graphically. Notice the wide interval around zero in nonintra coding. This is the so-called *dead zone*.

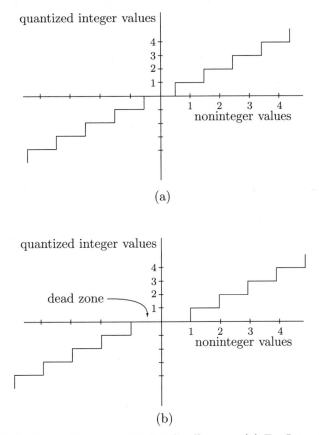

Figure 6.18: Rounding of Quantized DCT Coefficients. (a) For Intra Coding. (b) For Nonintra Coding.

The quantization and rounding steps are complex and involve more operations than just dividing a DCT coefficient by a quantization coefficient. They depend on a scale factor called `quantizer_scale`, an MPEG parameter that is an integer in the interval $[1, 31]$. The results of the quantization, and hence the compression performance, are sensitive to the value of `quantizer_scale`. The encoder can change this value from time to time and has to insert a special code in the compressed stream to indicate this.

We denote by DCT the DCT coefficient being quantized, by Q the QC from the quantization table, and by $QDCT$ the quantized value of DCT. The quantization tule for intra coding is

$$QDCT = \frac{(16 \times DCT) + \text{Sign}(DCT) \times \texttt{quantizer\_scale} \times Q}{2 \times \texttt{quantizer\_scale} \times Q}, \qquad (6.2)$$

where the function $\text{Sign}(DCT)$ is the sign of DCT, defined by

$$\text{Sign}(DCT) = \begin{cases} +1, & \text{when } DCT > 0, \\ 0, & \text{when } DCT = 0, \\ -1, & \text{when } DCT < 0. \end{cases}$$

The second term of Equation (6.2) is called the *rounding term* and is responsible for the special form of rounding illustrated by Figure 6.18a. This is easy to see when we consider the case of a positive DCT. In this case, Equation (6.2) is reduced to the simpler expression

$$QDCT = \frac{(16 \times DCT)}{2 \times \texttt{quantizer\_scale} \times Q} + \frac{1}{2}.$$

The rounding term is eliminated for nonintra coding, where quantization is done by

$$QDCT = \frac{(16 \times DCT)}{2 \times \texttt{quantizer\_scale} \times Q}. \qquad (6.3)$$

Dequantization, which is done by the decoder in preparation for the IDCT, is the inverse of quantization. For intra coding it is done by

$$DCT = \frac{(2 \times QDCT) \times \texttt{quantizer\_scale} \times Q}{16}$$

(notice that there is no rounding term), and for nonintra it is the inverse of Equation (6.2)

$$DCT = \frac{\big((2 \times QDCT) + Sign(QDCT)\big) \times \texttt{quantizer\_scale} \times Q}{16}.$$

The precise way to calculate the IDCT is not defined in MPEG. This can lead to distortions in cases where a picture is encoded by one implementation and decoded by another, where the IDCT is done differently. In a chain of inter pictures, where each picture is decoded by means of its neighbors, this can lead to accumulation of errors, a phenomenon known as *IDCT mismatch*. This is why MPEG requires periodic intra coding of every part of the picture. This *forced updating* has to be done at least once for every 132 P pictures in the sequence. In practice, forced updating is rare, since I pictures are fairly common, occurring every 10 to 15 pictures.

The quantized numbers $QDCT$ are Huffman coded, using the nonadaptive Huffman method and Huffman code tables that were calculated by gathering statistics from many training image sequences. The particular code table being used depends on the type of the picture being encoded. To avoid the zero probability problem (Section 2.18), all the entries in the code tables were initialized to 1 before any statistics were collected.

Decorrelating the original pels by computing the DCT (or, in the case of inter coding, by calculating pel differences) is part of the statistical model of MPEG. The other part is the creation of a symbol set that takes advantage of the properties of Huffman coding. Section 2.8 explains that the Huffman method becomes inefficient when the data contain symbols with large probabilities. If the probability of a symbol is 0.5, it should ideally be assigned a 1-bit code. If the probability is higher, the symbol should be assigned a shorter code, but the Huffman codes are integers and hence cannot be shorter than one bit. To avoid symbols with high probability, MPEG uses an alphabet where several old symbols (i.e., several pel differences or quantized DCT coefficients) are combined to form one new symbol. An example is run lengths of zeros. After quantizing the 64 DCT coefficients of a block, many of the resulting numbers are zeros. The probability of a zero is therefore high and can easily exceed 0.5. The solution is to deal with runs of consecutive zeros. Each run becomes a new symbol and is assigned a Huffman code. This method creates a large number of new symbols, and many Huffman codes are needed as a result. Compression efficiency, however, is improved.

Table 6.19 is the default quantization coefficients table for the luminance samples in intra coding. The MPEG documentation "explains" this table by saying, "This table has a distribution of quantizing values that is roughly in accord with the frequency response of the human eye, given a viewing distance of approximately six times the screen width and a 360×240 pel picture." Quantizing in nonintra coding is completely different, since the quantities being quantized are pel differences, and they do not have any spatial frequencies. This type of quantization is done by dividing the DCT coefficients of the differences by 16 (the default quantization table is thus flat), although custom quantization tables can also be specified.

8	16	19	22	26	27	29	34
16	16	22	24	27	29	34	37
19	22	26	27	29	34	34	38
22	22	26	27	29	34	37	40
22	26	27	29	32	35	40	48
26	27	29	32	35	40	48	58
26	27	29	34	38	46	56	69
27	29	35	38	46	56	69	83

Table 6.19: Default Luminance Quantization Table for Intra Coding.

In an I picture, the DC coefficients of the macroblocks are coded separately from the AC coefficients, similar to what is done in JPEG (Section 4.6.6). Figure 6.20 shows how three types of DC coefficients, for the Y, Cb, and Cr components of the I picture, are encoded separately in one stream. Each macroblock consists of four Y blocks, one Cb, and one Cr block, so it contributes four DC coefficients of the first type, and one coefficient of each of the other two types. A coefficient DC_i

is first used to calculate a difference $\Delta DC = DC_i - P$ (where P is the previous DC coefficient *of the same type*), and then the difference is encoded by coding a size category followed by bits for the magnitude and sign of the difference. The size category is the number of bits required to encode the sign and magnitude of the difference ΔDC. Each size category is assigned a code. Three steps are needed to encode a DC difference ΔDC: (1) The size category is first determined and its code is emitted; (2) if ΔDC is negative, a 1 is subtracted from its 2's complement representation; and (3) the *size* least-significant bits of the difference are emitted. Table 6.21 summarizes the size categories, their codes, and the range of differences ΔDC for each size. Notice that the size category of zero is defined as 0. This table should be compared with Table 4.55, which lists the corresponding codes used by JPEG.

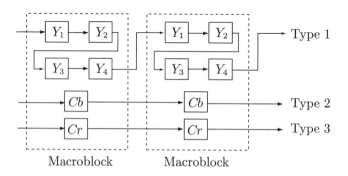

Figure 6.20: The Three Types of DC Coefficients.

Y codes	C codes	size	magnitude range
100	00	0	0
00	01	1	$-1,1$
01	10	2	$-3\cdots-2,2\cdots3$
101	110	3	$-7\cdots-4,4\cdots7$
110	1110	4	$-15\cdots-8,8\cdots15$
1110	11110	5	$-31\cdots-16,16\cdots31$
11110	111110	6	$-63\cdots-32,32\cdots63$
111110	1111110	7	$-127\cdots-64,64\cdots127$
1111110	11111110	8	$-255\cdots-128,128\cdots255$

Table 6.21: Codes for DC Coefficients (Luminance and Chrominance).

Examples: (1) A luminance ΔDC of 5. The number 5 can be expressed in three bits, so the size category is 3, and code 101 is emitted first. It is followed by the three least-significant bits of 5, which are 101. (2) A chrominance ΔDC of -3. The number 3 can be expressed in 2 bits, so the size category is 2, and code 10 is first emitted. The difference -3 is represented in twos complement as $\ldots 11101$.

When 1 is subtracted from this number, the 2 least-significant bits are 00, and this code is emitted next.

⋄ **Exercise 6.8:** Compute the code of luminance $\Delta DC = 0$ and the code of chrominance $\Delta DC = 4$.

The AC coefficients of an I picture (intra coding) are encoded by scanning them in the zigzag order shown in Figure 1.8b. The resulting sequence of AC coefficients consists of nonzero coefficients and run lengths of zero coefficients. A *run-level* code is output for each nonzero coefficient C, where *run* refers to the number of zero coefficients preceding C, and *level* refers to the absolute size of C. Each run-level code for a nonzero coefficient C is followed by the 1-bit sign of C (1 for negative and 0 for positive). The run-level code for last nonzero coefficient is followed by a special 2-bit end-of-block (EOB) code. Table 6.23 lists the EOB code and the run-level codes for common values of runs and levels. Combinations of runs and levels that are not in the table are encoded by the escape code, followed by a 6-bit code for the run length and an 8 or 16-bit code for the level.

Figure 6.22a shows an example of an 8×8 block of quantized coefficients. The zigzag sequence of these coefficients is

$$127, \ 0, \ 0, \ -1, \ 0, \ 2, \ 0, \ 0, \ 0, \ 1,$$

where 127 is the DC coefficient. Thus, the AC coefficients are encoded by the three run-level codes $(2, -1)$, $(1, 2)$, $(3, 1)$, followed by the EOB code. Table 6.23 shows that the codes are (notice the sign bits following the run-level codes)

$$0101\ 1|000110\ 0|00111\ 0|10$$

(without the vertical bars).

```
127 0 2 0 0 0 0 0     118 2 0  0 0 0 0 0
  0 0 0 0 0 0 0 0       0 0 0  0 0 0 0 0
 -1 0 0 0 0 0 0 0      -2 0 0 -1 0 0 0 0
  1 0 0 0 0 0 0 0       0 0 0  0 0 0 0 0
  0 0 0 0 0 0 0 0       0 0 0  0 0 0 0 0
  0 0 0 0 0 0 0 0       0 0 0  0 0 0 0 0
  0 0 0 0 0 0 0 0       0 0 0  0 0 0 0 0
  0 0 0 0 0 0 0 0       0 0 0  0 0 0 0 0
         (a)                   (b)
```

Figure 6.22: Two 8×8 Blocks of DCT Quantized Coefficients.

⋄ **Exercise 6.9:** Calculate the zigzag sequence and run-level codes for the AC coefficients of Figure 6.22b.

0/1	1s (first)	2	1/1	011s	4
0/1	11s (next)	3	1/2	0001 10s	7
0/2	0100 s	5	1/3	0010 0101 s	9
0/3	0010 1s	6	1/4	0000 0011 00s	11
0/4	0000 110s	8	1/5	0000 0001 1011 s	13
0/5	0010 0110 s	9	1/6	0000 0000 1011 0s	14
0/6	0010 0001 s	9	1/7	0000 0000 1010 1s	14
0/7	0000 0010 10s	11	1/8	0000 0000 0011 111s	16
0/8	0000 0001 1101 s	13	1/9	0000 0000 0011 110s	16
0/9	0000 0001 1000 s	13	1/10	0000 0000 0011 101s	16
0/10	0000 0001 0011 s	13	1/11	0000 0000 0011 100s	16
0/11	0000 0001 0000 s	13	1/12	0000 0000 0011 011s	16
0/12	0000 0000 1101 0s	14	1/13	0000 0000 0011 010s	16
0/13	0000 0000 1100 1s	14	1/14	0000 0000 0011 001s	16
0/14	0000 0000 1100 0s	14	1/15	0000 0000 0001 0011 s	17
0/15	0000 0000 1011 1s	14	1/16	0000 0000 0001 0010 s	17
0/16	0000 0000 0111 11s	15	1/17	0000 0000 0001 0001 s	17
0/17	0000 0000 0111 10s	15	1/18	0000 0000 0001 0000 s	17
0/18	0000 0000 0111 01s	15	2/1	0101 s	5
0/19	0000 0000 0111 00s	15	2/2	0000 100s	8
0/20	0000 0000 0110 11s	15	2/3	0000 0010 11s	11
0/21	0000 0000 0110 10s	15	2/4	0000 0001 0100 s	13
0/22	0000 0000 0110 01s	15	2/5	0000 0000 1010 0s	14
0/23	0000 0000 0110 00s	15	3/1	0011 1s	6
0/24	0000 0000 0101 11s	15	3/2	0010 0100 s	9
0/25	0000 0000 0101 10s	15	3/3	0000 0001 1100 s	13
0/26	0000 0000 0101 01s	15	3/4	0000 0000 1001 1s	14
0/27	0000 0000 0101 00s	15	4/1	0011 0s	6
0/28	0000 0000 0100 11s	15	4/2	0000 0011 11s	11
0/29	0000 0000 0100 10s	15	4/3	0000 0001 0010 s	13
0/30	0000 0000 0100 01s	15	5/1	0001 11s	7
0/31	0000 0000 0100 00s	15	5/2	0000 0010 01s	11
0/32	0000 0000 0011 000s	16	5/3	0000 0000 1001 0s	14
0/33	0000 0000 0010 111s	16	6/1	0001 01s	7
0/34	0000 0000 0010 110s	16	6/2	0000 0001 1110 s	13
0/35	0000 0000 0010 101s	16	6/3	0000 0000 0001 0100 s	17
0/36	0000 0000 0010 100s	16	7/1	0001 00s	7
0/37	0000 0000 0010 011s	16	7/2	0000 0001 0101 s	13
0/38	0000 0000 0010 010s	16	8/1	0000 111s	8
0/39	0000 0000 0010 001s	16	8/2	0000 0001 0001 s	13
0/40	0000 0000 0010 000s	16			

Table 6.23: Variable-Length Run-Level Codes (Part 1 of 2).

9/1	0000 101s	8	18/1	0000 0001 1010 s	13
9/2	0000 0000 1000 1s	14	19/1	0000 0001 1001 s	13
10/1	0010 0111 s	9	20/1	0000 0001 0111 s	13
10/2	0000 0000 1000 0s	14	21/1	0000 0001 0110 s	13
11/1	0010 0011 s	9	22/1	0000 0000 1111 1s	14
11/2	0000 0000 0001 1010 s	17	23/1	0000 0000 1111 0s	14
12/1	0010 0010 s	9	24/1	0000 0000 1110 1s	14
12/2	0000 0000 0001 1001 s	17	25/1	0000 0000 1110 0s	14
13/1	0010 0000 s	9	26/1	0000 0000 1101 1s	14
13/2	0000 0000 0001 1000 s	17	27/1	0000 0000 0001 1111 s	17
14/1	0000 0011 10s	11	28/1	0000 0000 0001 1110 s	17
14/2	0000 0000 0001 0111 s	17	29/1	0000 0000 0001 1101 s	17
15/1	0000 0011 01s	11	30/1	0000 0000 0001 1100 s	17
15/2	0000 0000 0001 0110 s	17	31/1	0000 0000 0001 1011 s	17
16/1	0000 0010 00s	11	EOB	10	2
16/2	0000 0000 0001 0101 s	17	ESC	0000 01	6
17/1	0000 0001 1111 s	13			

Table 6.23: Variable-Length Run-Level Codes (Part 2 of 2).

⬦ **Exercise 6.10:** How is a block with 63 zero AC coefficients coded?

A peculiar feature of Table 6.23 is that it lists two codes for run-level $(0, 1)$. Also, the first of those codes (labeled "first") is 1s, which may conflict with the EOB code. Th explanation is that the second of those codes (labeled "next"), 11s, is normally used, and this causes no conflict. The first code, 1s, is used only in nonintra coding, where an all-zero DCT coefficients block is coded in a special way.

The discussion so far has concentrated on encoding the quantized DCT coefficients for intra coding (I pictures). For nonintra coding (i.e., P and B pictures) the situation is different. The process of predicting a picture from another picture already decorrelates the samples, and the main advantage of the DCT in nonintra coding is quantization. Deep quantization of the DCT coefficients increases compression, and even a flat default quantization table (that does not take advantage of the properties of human vision) is effective in this case. Another feature of the DCT in nonintra coding is that the DC and AC coefficients are not substantially different, since they are the DCT transforms of differences. There is, therefore, no need to separate the encoding of the DC and AC coefficients.

The encoding process starts by looking for runs of macroblocks that are completely zero. Such runs are encoded by a macroblock address increment. If a macroblock is not all zeros, some of its six component blocks may still be completely zero. For such macroblocks the encoder prepares a *coded block pattern* (cbp). This is a 6-bit variable where each bit specifies whether one of the six blocks is completely zero or not. A zero block is identified as such by the corresponding cbp bit. A nonzero block is encoded using the codes of Table 6.23. When such a nonzero block is encoded, the encoder knows that it cannot be all zeros. There must be at least one nonzero coefficient among the 64 quantized coefficients in the block. If the first nonzero coefficient has a run-level code of $(0,1)$, it is coded as "1s" and there is no conflict with the EOB code since the EOB code cannot be the first code in such a block. Any other nonzero coefficients with a run-level code of $(0,1)$ are encoded using the "next" code, which is "11s".

6.5.2 MPEG-1 Video Syntax

Some of the many parameters used by MPEG to specify and control the compression of a video sequence are described in this section in detail. Readers who are interested only in the general description of MPEG may skip this section. The concepts of video sequence, picture, slice, macroblock, and block have already been discussed. Figure 6.24 shows the format of the compressed MPEG stream and how it is organized in six layers. Optional parts are enclosed in dashed boxes. Notice that only the video sequence of the compressed stream is shown; the system parts are omitted.

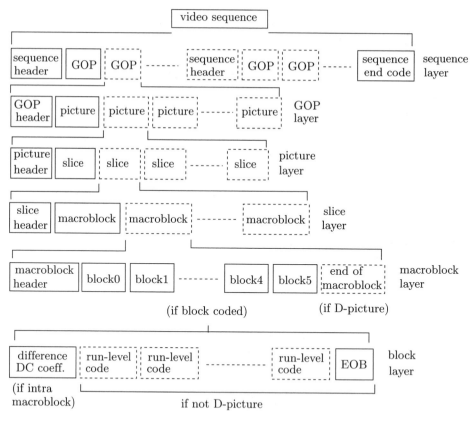

Figure 6.24: The Layers of a Video Stream.

The video sequence starts with a sequence header, followed by a group of pictures (GOP) and optionally by more GOPs. There may be other sequence headers followed by more GOPs, and the sequence ends with a sequence-end-code. The extra sequence headers may be included to help in random access playback or video editing, but most of the parameters in the extra sequence headers must remain unchanged from the first header.

A group of pictures (GOP) starts with a GOP header, followed by one or more pictures. Each picture in a GOP starts with a picture header, followed by one or more slices. Each slice, in turn, consists of a slice header followed by one or more macroblocks of encoded, quantized DCT coefficients. A macroblock is a set of six 8×8 blocks, four blocks of luminance samples and two blocks of chrominance samples. Some blocks may be completely zero and may not be encoded. Each block is coded in intra or nonintra. An intra block starts with a difference between its DC coefficient and the previous DC coefficient (of the same type), followed by run-level codes for the nonzero AC coefficients and zero runs. The EOB code terminates the block. In a nonintra block, both DC and AC coefficients are run-level coded.

It should be mentioned that in addition to the I, P, and B picture types, there exists in MPEG a fourth type, a D picture (for *DC coded*). Such pictures contain only DC coefficient information; no run-level codes or EOB is included. However, D pictures are not allowed to be mixed with the other types of pictures, so they are rare and will not be discussed further.

The headers of a sequence, GOP, picture, and slice all start with a byte-aligned 32-bit start code. In addition to these video start codes there are other start codes for the system layer, user data, and error tagging. A start code starts with 23 zero bits, followed by a single bit of 1, followed by a unique byte. Table 6.25 lists all the video start codes. The "sequence.error" code is for cases where the encoder discovers unrecoverable errors in a video sequence and cannot encode it as a result. The run-level codes have variable lengths, so some zero bits normally have to be appended to the video stream before a start code, to make sure the code starts on a byte boundary.

Start code	Hex	Binary
extension.start	000001B5	00000000 00000000 00000001 10110101
GOP.start	000001B8	00000000 00000000 00000001 10111000
picture.start	00000100	00000000 00000000 00000001 00000000
reserved	000001B0	00000000 00000000 00000001 10110000
reserved	000001B1	00000000 00000000 00000001 10110001
reserved	000001B6	00000000 00000000 00000001 10110110
sequence.end	000001B7	00000000 00000000 00000001 10110111
sequence.error	000001B4	00000000 00000000 00000001 10110100
sequence.header	000001B3	00000000 00000000 00000001 10110011
slice.start.1	00000101	00000000 00000000 00000001 00000001
...	...	
slice.start.175	000001AF	00000000 00000000 00000001 10101111
user.data.start	000001B2	00000000 00000000 00000001 10110010

Table 6.25: MPEG Video Start Codes.

Code	height/width	Video source
0000	forbidden	
0001	1.0000	computers (VGA)
0010	0.6735	
0011	0.7031	16:9, 625 lines
0100	0.7615	
0101	0.8055	
0110	0.8437	16:9 525 lines
0111	0.8935	
1000	0.9157	CCIR Rec, 601, 625 lines
1001	0.9815	
1010	1.0255	
1011	1.0695	
1100	1.0950	CCIR Rec. 601, 525 lines
1101	1.1575	
1110	1.2015	
1111	reserved	

Table 6.26: MPEG Pel Aspect Ratio Codes.

Code	nominal picture rate	Typical applications
0000		forbidden
0001	23.976	Movies on NTSC broadcast monitors
0010	24	Movies, commercial clips, animation
0011	25	PAL, SECAM, generic 625/50Hz component video
0100	29.97	Broadcast rate NTSC
0101	30	NTSC profession studio, 525/60Hz component video
0110	50	noninterlaced PAL/SECAM/625 video
0111	59.94	Noninterlaced broadcast NTSC
1000	60	Noninterlaced studio 525 NTSC rate
1001		
...		
1111	reserved	

Table 6.27: MPEG Picture Rates and Typical Applications.

horizontal_size $\leq$ 768 pels.
vertical_size $\leq$ 576 lines.
number of macroblocks $\leq$ 396.
(number of macroblocks)$\times$picture_rate $\leq 396 \times 25$.
picture_rate ≤ 30 pictures per second.
vbv_buffer_size ≤ 160.
bit_rate ≤ 4640.
forward_f_code ≤ 4.
backward_f_code ≤ 4.

Table 6.28: Constrained Parameters Bounds.

Video Sequence Layer: This starts with start code 000001B3, followed by nine fixed-length data elements. The parameters `horizontal_size` and `vertical_size` are 12-bit parameters that define the width and height of the picture. Neither is allowed to be zero, and `vertical_size` must be even. Parameter `pel_aspect_ratio` is a 4-bit parameter that specifies the aspect ratio of a pel. Its 16 values are listed in Table 6.26. Parameter `picture_rate` is a 4-bit parameter that specifies one of 16 picture refresh rates. Its eight nonreserved values are listed in Table 6.27. The 18-bit `bit_rate` data element specifies the compressed data rate to the decoder (in units of 400 bits/s). This parameter has to be positive and is related to the true bit rate R by

$$\texttt{bit\_rate} = \lceil R/400 \rceil.$$

Next comes a `marker_bit`. This single bit of 1 prevents the accidental generation of a start code in cases where some bits get corrupted. Marker bits are common in MPEG. The 10-bit `vbv_buffer_size` follows the marker bit. It specifies to the decoder the lower bound for the size of the compressed data buffer. The buffer size, in bits, is given by

$$B = 8 \times 2048 \times \texttt{vbv\_buffer\_size},$$

and is a multiple of 2K bytes. The `constrained_parameter_flag` is a 1-bit parameter that is normally 0. When set to 1, it signifies that some of the other parameters have the values listed in Table 6.28.

The last two data elements are 1-bit each and control the loading of the intra and nonintra quantization tables. When `load_intra_quantizer_matrix` is set to 1, it means that it is followed by the 64 8-bit QCs of the `intra_quantizer_matrix`. Similarly, `load_non_intra_quantizer_matrix` signals whether the quantization table `non_intra_quantizer_matrix` follows it or whether the default should be used.

GOP Layer: This layer starts with nine mandatory elements, optionally followed by extensions and user data, and by the (compressed) pictures themselves.

The 32-bit group start code 000001B8 is followed by the 25-bit `time_code`, which consists of the following six data elements: `drop_frame_flag` (1 bit) is zero unless the picture rate is 29.97 Hz; `time_code_hours` (5 bits, in the range $[0, 23]$), `time_code_minutes` (6 bits, in the range $[0, 59]$), and `time_code_seconds` (6 bits, in the same range) indicate the hours, minutes, and seconds in the time interval from the start of the sequence to the display of the first picture in the GOP. The 6-bit `time_code_pictures` parameter indicates the number of pictures in a second. There is a `marker_bit` between `time_code_minutes` and `time_code_seconds`.

Following the `time_code` there are two 1-bit parameters. The flag `closed_gop` is set if the GOP is closed (i.e., its pictures can be decoded without reference to pictures from outside the group). The `broken_link` flag is set to 1 if editing has disrupted the original sequence of groups of pictures.

Picture Layer: Parameters in this layer specify the type of the picture (I, P, B, or D) and the motion vectors for the picture. The layer starts with the 32-bit `picture_start_code`, whose hexadecimal value is 00000100. It is followed by a 10-bit `temporal_reference` parameter, which is the picture number (modulo 1024) in the sequence. The next parameter is the 3-bit `picture_coding_type` (Table 6.29), and this is followed by the 16-bit `vbv_delay` that tells the decoder how many bits must be in the compressed data buffer before the picture can be decoded. This parameter helps prevent buffer overflow and underflow.

Code	picture type
000	forbidden
001	I
010	P
011	B
100	D
101	reserved
...	...
111	reserved

Table 6.29: Picture Type Codes.

If the picture type is P or B, then this is followed by the forward motion vectors scale information, a 3-bit parameter called `forward_f_code` (see Table 6.34). For B pictures, there follows the backward motion vectors scale information, a 3-bit parameter called `backward_f_code`.

Slice Layer: There can be many slices in a picture, so the start code of a slice ends with a value in the range $[1, 175]$. This value defines the macroblock row where the slice starts (a picture can therefore have up to 175 rows of macroblocks). The horizontal position where the slice starts in that macroblock row is determined by other parameters.

The `quantizer_scale` (5 bits) initializes the quantizer scale factor, discussed earlier in connection with the rounding of the quantized DCT coefficients. The `extra_bit_slice` flag following it is always 0 (the value of 1 is reserved for future ISO standards). Following this, the encoded macroblocks are written.

Macroblock Layer: This layer identifies the position of the macroblock relative to the position of the current macroblock. It codes the motion vectors for the macroblock, and identifies the zero and nonzero blocks in the macroblock.

Each macroblock has an address, or index, in the picture. Index values start at 0 in the upper-left corner of the picture and continue in raster order. When the encoder starts encoding a new picture, it sets the macroblock address to -1. The `macroblock_address_increment` parameter contains the amount needed to increment the macroblock address in order to reach the macroblock being coded. This parameter is normally 1. If `macroblock_address_increment` is greater than 33, it is encoded as a sequence of `macroblock_escape` codes, each incrementing the macroblock address by 33, followed by the appropriate code from Table 6.30.

The `macroblock_type` is a variable-size parameter, between 1 and 6 bits long, whose values are listed in Table 6.31. Each value of this variable-size code is decoded into 5 bits that become the values of the following five flags:

1. `macroblock_quant`. If set, a new 5-bit quantization scale is sent.
2. `macroblock_motion_forward`. If set, a forward motion vector is sent.

Increment value	macroblock address increment	Increment value	macroblock address increment
1	1	19	0000 00
2	011	20	0000 0100 11
3	010	21	0000 0100 10
4	0011	22	0000 0100 011
5	0010	23	0000 0100 010
6	0001 1	24	0000 0100 001
7	0001 0	25	0000 0100 000
8	0000 111	26	0000 0011 111
9	0000 011	27	0000 0011 110
10	0000 1011	28	0000 0011 101
11	0000 1010	29	0000 0011 100
12	0000 1001	30	0000 0011 011
13	0000 1000	31	0000 0011 010
14	0000 0111	32	0000 0011 001
15	0000 0110	33	0000 0011 000
16	0000 0101 11	stuffing	0000 0001 111
17	0000 0101 10	escape	0000 0001 000
18	0000 0101 01		

Table 6.30: Codes for Macroblock Address Increment.

	Code	quant	forward	backward	pattern	intra
I	1	0	0	0	0	1
	01	1	0	0	0	1
	001	0	1	0	0	0
	01	0	0	0	1	0
	00001	1	0	0	1	0
P	1	0	1	0	1	0
	00010	1	1	0	1	0
	00011	0	0	0	0	1
	000001	1	0	0	0	1
	0010	0	1	0	0	0
	010	0	0	1	0	0
	10	0	1	1	0	0
	0011	0	1	0	1	0
	000011	1	1	0	1	0
B	011	0	0	1	1	0
	000010	1	0	1	1	0
	11	0	1	1	1	0
	00010	1	1	1	1	0
	00011	0	0	0	0	1
	000001	1	0	0	0	1
D	1	0	0	0	0	1

Table 6.31: Variable Length Codes for Macroblock Types.

cbp dec.	cbp binary	block # 012345	cbp code	cbp dec.	cbp binary	block # 012345	cbp code
0	000000	......	forbidden	32	100000	c.....	1010
1	000001	c	01011	33	100001	c....c	0010100
2	000010	....c.	01001	34	100010	c...c.	0010000
3	000011	cc	001101	35	100011	c...cc	00011100
4	000100	...c..	1101	36	100100	c..c..	001110
5	000101	...c.c	0010111	37	100101	c..c.c	00001110
6	000110	...cc.	0010011	38	100110	c..cc.	00001100
7	000111	...ccc	00011111	39	100111	c..ccc	000000010
8	001000	..c...	1100	40	101000	c.c...	10000
9	001001	..c..c	0010110	41	101001	c.c..c	00011000
10	001010	..c.c.	0010010	42	101010	c.c.c.	00010100
11	001011	..c.cc	00011110	43	101011	c.c.cc	00010000
12	001100	..cc..	10011	44	101100	c.cc..	01110
13	001101	..cc.c	00011011	45	101101	c.cc.c	00001010
14	001110	..ccc.	00010111	46	101110	c.ccc.	00000110
15	001111	..cccc	00010011	47	101111	c.cccc	000000110
16	010000	.c....	1011	48	110000	cc....	10010
17	010001	.c...c	0010101	49	110001	cc...c	00011010
18	010010	.c..c.	0010001	50	110010	cc..c.	00010110
19	010011	.c..cc	00011101	51	110011	cc..cc	00010010
20	010100	.c.c..	10001	52	110100	cc.c..	01101
21	010101	.c.c.c	00011001	53	110101	cc.c.c	00001001
22	010110	.c.cc.	00010101	54	110110	cc.cc.	00000101
23	010111	.c.ccc	00010001	55	110111	cc.ccc	000000101
24	011000	.cc...	001111	56	111000	ccc...	01100
25	011001	.cc..c	00001111	57	111001	ccc..c	00001000
26	011010	.cc.c.	00001101	58	111010	ccc.c.	00000100
27	011011	.cc.cc	000000011	59	111011	ccc.cc	000000100
28	011100	.ccc..	01111	60	111100	cccc..	111
29	011101	.ccc.c	00001011	61	111101	cccc.c	01010
30	011110	.cccc.	00000111	62	111110	ccccc.	01000
31	011111	.ccccc	000000111	63	111111	cccccc	001100

Table 6.32: Codes for Macroblock Address Increment.

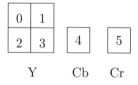

       Y   Cb   Cr

Figure 6.33: Indexes of Six Blocks in a Macroblock.

3. `macroblock_motion_backward`. If set, a backward motion vector is sent.

4. `macroblock_pattern`. If set, the `coded_block_pattern` code (variable length) listed in Table 6.32 follows to code the six `pattern_code` bits of variable `cbp` discussed earlier (blocks labeled "." in the table are skipped, and blocks labeled "c" are coded). These six bits identify the six blocks of the macroblock as completely zero or not. The correspondence between the six bits and blocks is shown in Figure 6.33, where block 0 corresponds to the most-significant bit of the `pattern_code`.

5. `macroblock_intra`. If set, the six blocks of this macroblock are coded as intra.

These five flags determine the rest of the processing steps for the macroblock.

Once the `pattern_code` bits are known, blocks that correspond to 1 bits are encoded.

Block Layer: This layer is the lowest in the video sequence. It contains the encoded 8×8 blocks of quantized DCT coefficients. The coding depends on whether the block contains luminance or chrominance samples and on whether the macroblock is intra or nonintra. In nonintra coding, blocks that are completely zero are skipped; they don't have to be encoded.

The `macroblock_intra` flag gets its value from `macroblock_type`. If it is set, the DC coefficient of the block is coded separately from the AC coefficients.

6.5.3 Motion Compensation

An important element of MPEG is *motion compensation*, which is used in inter coding only. In this mode, the pels of the current picture are predicted by those of a previous reference picture (and, perhaps, by those of a future reference picture). Pels are subtracted, and the differences (which should be small numbers) are DCT transformed, quantized, and encoded. The differences between the current picture and the reference one are normally caused by motion (either camera motion or scene motion), so best prediction is obtained by matching a region in the current picture with a different region in the reference picture. MPEG does not require the use of any particular matching algorithm, and any implementation can use its own method for matching macroblocks (see Section 6.4 for examples of matching algorithms). The discussion here concentrates on the operations of the decoder.

Differences between consecutive pictures may also be caused by random noise in the video camera, or by variations of illumination, which may change brightness in a nonuniform way. In such cases, motion compensation is not used, and each region ends up being matched with the same spatial region in the reference picture.

If the difference between consecutive pictures is caused by camera motion, one motion vector is enough for the entire picture. Normally, however, there is also scene motion and movement of shadows, so a number of motion vectors are needed, to describe the motion of different regions in the picture. The size of those regions is critical. A large number of small regions improves prediction accuracy, whereas the opposite situation simplifies the algorithms used to find matching regions and also leads to fewer motion vectors and sometimes to better compression. Since a macroblock is such an important unit in MPEG, it was also selected as the elementary region for motion compensation.

Another important consideration is the precision of the motion vectors. A motion vector such as $(15, -4)$ for a macroblock M typically means that M has been moved from the reference picture to the current picture by displacing it 15 pels to the right and 4 pels up (a positive vertical displacement is down). The components of the vector are in units of pels. They may, however, be in units of half a pel, or even smaller. In MPEG-1, the precision of motion vectors may be either full-pel or half-pel, and the encoder signals this decision to the decoder by a parameter in the picture header (this parameter may be different from picture to picture).

It often happens that large areas of a picture move at identical or at similar speeds, and this implies that the motion vectors of adjacent macroblocks are correlated. This is the reason why the MPEG encoder encodes a motion vector by subtracting it from the motion vector of the preceding macroblock and encoding the difference.

A P picture uses an earlier I picture or P picture as a reference picture. We say that P pictures use forward motion-compensated prediction. When a motion vector MD for a macroblock is determined (MD stands for *motion displacement*, since the vector consists of two components, the horizontal and the vertical displacements), MPEG denotes the motion vector of the preceding macroblock in the slice by PMD and calculates the difference dMD=MD–PMD. PMD is reset to zero at the start of a slice, after a macroblock is intra coded, when the macroblock is skipped, and when parameter `block_motion_forward` is zero.

The 1-bit parameter `full_pel_forward_vector` in the picture header defines the precision of the motion vectors (1=full-pel, 0=half-pel). The 3-bit parameter `forward_f_code` defines the range.

A B picture may use forward or backward motion compensation. If both are used, then two motion vectors are calculated by the encoder for the current macroblock, and each vector is encoded by first calculating a difference, as in P pictures. Also, if both are used, then the prediction is the average of both. Here is how the prediction is done in the case of both forward and backward prediction. Suppose that the encoder has determined that macroblock M in the current picture matches macroblock MB in the following picture and macroblock MF in the preceding picture. Each pel $M[i, j]$ in macroblock M in the current picture is predicted by calculating the difference

$$M[i, j] - \frac{MF[i, j] + MB[i, j]}{2},$$

where the quotient of the division by 2 is rounded to the nearest integer.

Parameters `full_pel_forward_vector` and `forward_f_code` have the same meaning as for a P picture. In addition, there are the two corresponding parameters `full_pel_backward_vector` and `backward_f_code`.

The following rules apply in coding motion vectors in B pictures:

1. The quantity PMD is reset to zero at the start of a slice and after a macroblock is skipped.

2. In a skipped macroblock, MD is predicted from the preceding macroblock in the slice.

3. When `motion_vector_forward` is zero, the forward MDs are predicted from the preceding macroblock in the slice.

4. When `motion_vector_backward` is zero, the backward MDs are predicted from the preceding macroblock in the slice.

5. A B picture is predicted by means of I and P pictures but not by another B picture.

6. The two components of a motion vector (the motion displacements) are to a precision of either full-pel or half-pel, as specified in the picture header.

Displacement Principal and Residual: The two components of a motion vector are motion displacements. Each motion displacement has two parts, a principal and a residual. The principal part is denoted by dMD_p. It is a signed integer that is given by the product

$$dMD_p = \texttt{motion\_code} \times f,$$

where `motion_code` is an integer parameter in the range $[-16, +16]$, included in the compressed stream by means of a variable-length code, and f, the scaling factor, is a power of 2 given by

$$f = 2^{rsize}.$$

The integer $rsize$ is simply `f_code` $- 1$, where `f_code` is a 3-bit parameter with values in the range $[1, 7]$. This implies that $rsize$ has values $[0, 6]$ and f is a power of 2 in the range $[1, 2, 4, 8, \ldots, 64]$.

The residual part is denoted by r and is a positive integer, defined by

$$\mathbf{r} = |dMD_p| - |dMD|.$$

After computing r, the encoder encodes it by concatenating the ones-complement of r and `motion_r` to the variable length code for parameter `motion_code`. The parameter `motion_r` is related to r by

$$\texttt{motion\_r} = (f - 1) - \mathbf{r},$$

and f should be chosen as the smallest value that satisfies the following inequalities for the largest (positive or negative) differential displacement in the entire picture

$$-(16 \times f) \leq \texttt{dMD} < (16 \times f).$$

Once f has been selected, the value of parameter `motion_code` for the differential displacement of a macroblock is given by

$$\texttt{motion\_code} = \frac{\texttt{dMD} + \text{Sign}(\texttt{dMD}) \times (f - 1)}{f},$$

where the quotient is rounded such that `motion_code` $\times f \geq$ `dMD`.

Table 6.34 lists the header parameters for motion vector computation ("p" stands for picture header and "mb" stands for macroblock header). Table 6.35 lists the generic and full names of the parameters mentioned here, and Table 6.36 lists the range of values of `motion_r` as a function of `f_code`.

Header parameter	set in header	number of bits	displacement parameter
full_pel_forward_vector	p	1	precision
forward_f_code	p	3	range
full_pel_backward_vector	p	1	precision
backward_f_code	p	3	range
motion_horizontal_forward_code	mb	vlc	principal
motion_horizontal_forward_r	mb	forward_r_size	residual
motion_vertical_forward_code	mb	vlc	principal
motion_vertical_forward_r	mb	forward_r_size	residual

Table 6.34: Header Parameters for Motion Vector Computation.

Generic name	Full name	Range
full_pel_vector	full_pel_forward_vector full_pel_backward_vector	0,1
f_code	forward_f_code backward_f_code	1–7
r_size	forward_r_size backward_r_size	0–6
f	forward_f backward_f	1,2,4,8,16,32,64
motion_code	motion_horizontal_forward_code motion_vertical_forward_code motion_horizontal_backward_code motion_vertical_backward_code	$-16 \rightarrow +16$
motion_r	motion_horizontal_forward_r motion_vertical_forward_r motion_horizontal_backward_r motion_vertical_backward_r	$0 \rightarrow (f-1)$
r	compliment_horizontal_forward_r compliment_vertical_forward_r compliment_horizontal_backward_r compliment_vertical_backward_r	$0 \rightarrow (f-1)$

Table 6.35: Generic Names for Motion Displacement Parameters.

f_code	r_size	f	$f-1$	r	motion_r
1	0	1	0		0
2	1	2	1	0,1	1,0
3	2	4	3	0–3	3,...,0
4	3	8	7	0–7	7,...,0
5	4	16	15	0–15	15,...,0
6	5	32	31	0–31	31,...,0
7	6	64	63	0–63	63,...,0

Table 6.36: Range of Values of motion_r as a Function of f_code.

6.5.4 Pel Reconstruction

The main task of the MPEG decoder is to reconstruct the pel of the entire video sequence. This is done by reading the codes of a block from the compressed stream, decoding them, dequantizing them, and calculating the IDCT. For nonintra blocks in P and B pictures, the decoder has to add the motion-compensated prediction to the results of the IDCT. This is repeated six times (or fewer, if some blocks are completely zero) for the six blocks of a macroblock. The entire sequence is decoded picture by picture, and within each picture, macroblock by macroblock.

It has already been mentioned that the IDCT is not rigidly defined in MPEG, which may lead to accumulation of errors, called *IDCT mismatch*, during decoding.

For intra-coded blocks, the decoder reads the differential code of the DC coefficient and uses the decoded value of the previous DC coefficient (of the same type) to decode the DC coefficient of the current block. It then reads the run-level codes until an EOB code is encountered, and decodes them, generating a sequence of 63 AC coefficients, normally with few nonzero coefficients and runs of zeros between them. The DC and 63 AC coefficients are then collected in zigzag order to create an 8×8 block. After dequantization and inverse DCT calculation, the resulting block becomes one of the six blocks that make up a macroblock (in intra coding all six blocks are always coded, even those that are completely zero).

For nonintra blocks, there is no distinction between DC and AC coefficients and between luminance and chrominance blocks. They are all decoded in the same way.

Bibliography

Mitchell, Joan L., W. B. Pennebaker, C. E. Fogg, and D. J. LeGall, eds., (1997) *MPEG Video Compression Standard*, New York, Chapman and Hall and International Thomson Publishing.

MPEG (1998), see URL `http://www.mpeg.org/`.

6.6 H.261

In late 1984, the CCITT (currently the ITU-T) organized an expert group to develop a standard for visual telephony for ISDN services. The idea was to send images and sound between special terminals, so that users could talk and see each other. This type of application requires sending large amounts of data, so compression became an important consideration. The group eventually came up with a number of standards, known as the H series (for video) and the G series (for audio) recommendations, all operating at speeds of $p \times 64$ Kbit/s for $p = 1, 2, \ldots, 30$. These standards are known today under the umbrella name of $p \times 64$ and are summarized in Table 6.37. This section provides a short summary of the H.261 standard.

Members of the $p \times 64$ also participated in the development of MPEG, so the two methods have many common elements. There is, however, one important difference between them. In MPEG, the decoder must be fast, since it may have to operate in real time, but the encoder can be slow. This leads to very asymmetric compression, and the encoder can be hundreds of times more complex than the decoder. In H.261, both encoder and decoder operate in real time, so both have to be fast. Still, the H.261 standard defines only the data stream and the decoder. The encoder can use

Standard	Purpose
H.261	Video
H.221	Communications
H.230	Initial handshake
H.320	Terminal systems
H.242	Control protocol
G.711	Companded audio (64 Kbits/s)
G.722	High quality audio (64 Kbits/s)
G.728	Speech (LD-CELP @16kbits/s)

Table 6.37: The $p \times 64$ Standards.

any method as long as it creates a valid compressed stream. The compressed stream is organized in layers, and macroblocks are used as in MPEG. Also, the same 8×8 DCT and the same zigzag order as in MPEG are used. The intra DC coefficient is quantized by always dividing it by 8, and it has no dead zone. The inter DC and all AC coefficients are quantized with a dead zone.

Motion compensation is used when pictures are predicted from other pictures, and motion vectors are coded as differences. Blocks that are completely zero can be skipped within a macroblock, and variable-size codes that are very similar to those of MPEG (such as run-level codes), or are even identical (such as motion vector codes) are used. In all these aspects, H.261 and MPEG are very similar.

There are, however, important differences between them. H.261 uses a single quantization coefficient instead of an 8×8 table of QCs, and this coefficient can be changed only after 11 macroblocks. AC coefficients that are intra coded have a dead zone. The compressed stream has just four layers, instead of MPEG's six. The motion vectors are always full-pel and are limited to a range of just ± 15 pels. There are no B pictures, and only the immediately preceding picture can be used to predict a P picture.

6.6.1 H.261 Compressed Stream

H.261 limits the image to just two sizes, the common intermediate format (CIF), which is optional, and the quarter CIF (QCIF). These are shown in Figure 6.38a,b. The CIF format has dimensions of 288×360 for luminance, but only 352 of the 360 columns of pels are actually coded, creating an active area of 288×352 pels. For chrominance, the dimensions are 144×180, but only 176 columns are coded, for an active area of 144×176 pels. The QCIF format is one-fourth of CIF, so the luminance component is 144×180 with an active area of 144×176, and the chrominance components are 72×90, with an active area of 72×88.

The macroblocks are organized in groups (known as GOB) of 33 macroblocks each. Each GOB is a 3×11 array (48×176 pels), as shown in Figure 6.38c. A CIF picture consists of 12 GPBs, and a QCIF picture is 3 GOBs, numbered as in Figure 6.38d.

Figure 6.39 shows the four H.261 video sequence layers. The main layer is the picture layer. It start with a picture header, followed by the GOBs (12 or 3, depending on the image size). The compressed stream may contain as many pictures

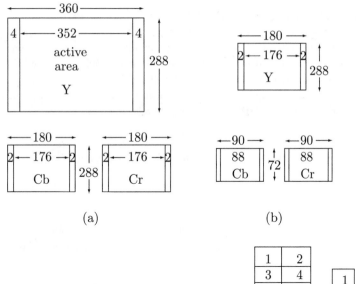

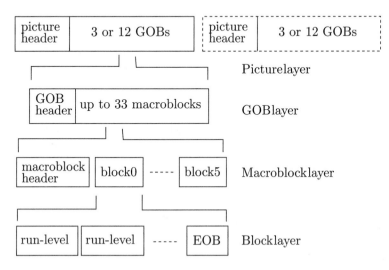

Figure 6.38: (a) CIF. (b) QCIF. (c) GOB.

Figure 6.39: H.261 Video Sequence Layers.

as necessary. The next layer is the GOB, which consists of a header, followed by the macroblocks. If the motion compensation is good, some macroblocks may be completely zero and may be skipped. The macroblock layer is next, with a header that may contain a motion vector, followed by the blocks. There are six blocks per macroblock, but blocks that are zero are skipped. The block layer contains the blocks that are coded. If a block is coded, its nonzero coefficients are encoded with a run-level code. A 2-bit EOB code terminates each block.

Bibliography

Liou, Ming (1991) "Overview of the p×64 kbits/s Video Coding Standard," *Communications of the ACM*, **34**(4):59–63, April.

I must say I find television very educational. The minute somebody
turns it on I go into the library and read a good book
—Groucho Marx [1890–1977]

7
Audio Compression

Text does not occupy much space in the computer. An average book, consisting of a million characters, can be stored uncompressed in about 1 Mbyte, since each character of text occupies one byte (the Colophon at the end of the book illustrates this with precise data from the book itself).

◇ **Exercise 7.1:** It is a handy rule of thumb that an average book occupies about a million bytes. Show why this makes sense.

In contrast, images take much more space, lending another meaning to the phrase "a picture is worth a thousand words." Depending on the number of colors used in an image, a single pixel occupies between one bit and three bytes. Thus, a 512×512-pixel image requires between 32 Kbytes and 768 Kbytes. With the advent of powerful, inexpensive personal computers came multimedia applications, where text, images, movies, and *sound* are stored in the computer, and can be displayed, edited, and played back. The storage requirements of sound are smaller than those of images or movies, but bigger than those of text. This is why audio compression has become important and has been the subject of much research and experimentation throughout the 1990s.

This chapter starts with a short introduction to sound and digitized sound. It then discusses those properties of the human auditory system (ear and brain) that make it possible to lose much audio information without losing sound quality. The chapter continues with a survey of simple audio compression methods, such as μ-law, A-law (Section 7.4), and ADPCM (Section 7.5). The chapter concludes with a description of the three methods (layers) of audio compression used by the MPEG-1 standard.

7.1 Sound

To most of us, sound is a very familiar phenomenon, since we hear it all the time. Nevertheless, when we try to define sound, we find that we can approach this concept from two different points of view, and we end up with two definitions, as follows:

An intuitive definition: Sound is the sensation detected by our ears and interpreted by our brain in a certain way.

A scientific definition: Sound is a physical disturbance in a medium. It propagates in the medium as a pressure wave by the movement of atoms or molecules.

We normally hear sound as it propagates through the air and hits the diaphragm in our ears. However, sound can propagate in many different media. Marine animals produce sounds underwater and respond to similar sounds. Hitting the end of a metal bar with a hammer produces sound waves that propagate through the bar and can be detected at the other end. Good sound insulators are rare, and the best insulator is vacuum, where there are no particles to vibrate and propagate the disturbance.

Sound can also be considered a wave, even though its frequency may change all the time. It is a longitudinal wave, one where the disturbance is in the direction of the wave itself. In contrast, electromagnetic waves and ocean waves are transverse waves. Their undulations are perpendicular to the direction of the wave.

As any other wave, sound has three important attributes, its speed, amplitude, and period. The frequency of a wave is not an independent attribute; it is the number of periods that occur in one time unit (one second). The unit of frequency is the hertz (Hz). The speed of sound depends mostly on the medium it passes through, and on the temperature. In air, at sea level (one atmospheric pressure), and at 20° Celsius (68° Fahrenheit), the speed of sound is 343.8 meters per second (about 1128 feet per second).

The human ear is sensitive to a wide range of sound frequencies, normally from about 20 Hz to about 22,000 Hz, depending on the person's age and health. This is the range of *audible frequencies*. Some animals, most notably dogs and bats, can hear higher frequencies (ultrasound). A quick calculation reveals the periods associated with audible frequencies. At 22,000 Hz, each period is about 1.56 cm long, whereas at 20 Hz, a period is about 17.19 meters long.

⋄ **Exercise 7.2:** Verify these calculations.

The amplitude of sound is also an important property. We perceive it as loudness. We sense sound when air molecules strike the diaphragm of the ear and apply pressure on it. The molecules move back and forth tiny distances that are related to the *amplitude*, not to the period of the sound. The period of a sound wave may be several meters, yet an individual molecule in the air may move just a millionth of a centimeter in its oscillations. With very loud noise, an individual molecule may move about one thousandth of a centimeter. A device to measure noise levels should therefore have a sensitive diaphragm where the pressure of the sound wave is sensed and is converted to electrical voltage, which in turn is displayed as a numeric value.

The problem with measuring noise intensity is that the ear is sensitive to a very wide range of sound levels (amplitudes). The ratio between the sound level of a cannon at the muzzle and the lowest level we can hear (the threshold of hearing) is about 11–12 orders of magnitude. If we denote the lowest audible sound level by 1, then the cannon noise would have a magnitude of 10^{11}! It is inconvenient to deal with measurements in such a wide range, which is why the units of sound loudness use a *logarithmic scale*. The (base-10) logarithm of 1 is zero, and the logarithm of 10^{11} is 11. Using logarithms, we only have to deal with numbers in the range 0 through 11. In fact, this range is too small, and we typically multiply it by 10 or by 20, to get numbers between zero and 110 or 220. This is the well-known (and sometimes confusing) decibel system of measurement.

⋄ **Exercise 7.3:** (For the mathematically weak.) What exactly is a logarithm?

The decibel (dB) unit is defined as the base-10 logarithm of the ratio of two physical quantities whose units are powers (energy per time). The logarithm is then multiplied by the convenient scale factor 10. (If the scale factor is not used, the result is measured in units called "Bel." The Bel, however, was dropped long ago in favor of the decibel.) Thus, we have

$$
\text{Level} = 10 \log_{10} \frac{P_1}{P_2} \text{ dB},
$$

where P_1 and P_2 are measured in units of power such as watt, joule/sec, gram·cm/sec, or horsepower. This can be mechanical power, electrical power, or anything else. In measuring the loudness of sound, we have to use units of acoustical power. Since even loud sound can be produced with very little energy, we use the microwatt (10^{-6} watt) as a convenient unit.

From the Dictionary

Acoustics: (1) The science of sound, including the generation, transmission, and effects of sound waves, both audible and inaudible. (2) The physical qualities of a room or other enclosure (such as size, shape, amount of noise) that determine the audibility and perception of speech and music within the room.

The decibel is the logarithm of a ratio. The numerator, P_1, is the power (in microwatts) of the sound whose intensity level is being measured. It is convenient to select as the denominator the number of microwatts that produce the faintest audible sound (the threshold of hearing). This number is shown by experiment to be 10^{-6} microwatt $= 10^{-12}$ watt. Thus a stereo unit that produces 1 watt of acoustical power has an intensity level of

$$
10 \log \frac{10^6}{10^{-6}} = 10 \log \left(10^{12}\right) = 10 \times 12 = 120 \text{ dB}
$$

(this happens to be about the threshold of feeling; see Figure 7.1), whereas an earphone producing 3×10^{-4} microwatt has a level of

$$10 \log \frac{3 \times 10^{-4}}{10^{-6}} = 10 \log \left(3 \times 10^2 \right) = 10 \times (\log 3 + \log 100) = 10 \times (0.477 + 2) \approx 24.77 \text{ dB}.$$

In the field of electricity, there is a simple relation between (electrical) power P and pressure (voltage) V. Electrical power is the product of the current and voltage $P = I \cdot V$. The current, however, is proportional to the voltage by means of Ohm's law $I = V/R$ (where R is the resistance). We can therefore write $P = V^2/R$, and use pressure (voltage) in our electric decibel measurements.

In practical acoustics work, we don't always have access to the source of the sound, so we cannot measure its electrical power output. In practice, we may find ourselves in a busy location, holding a sound decibel meter in our hands, trying to measure the noise level around us. The decibel meter measures the pressure Pr applied by the sound waves on its diaphragm. Fortunately, the acoustical power per area (denoted by P) is proportional to the square of the sound pressure Pr. This is because sound power P is the product of the pressure Pr and the speed v of the sound, and because the speed can be expressed as the pressure divided by the specific impedance of the medium through which the sound propagates. This is why sound loudness is commonly measured in units of dB SPL (sound pressure level) instead of sound power. The definition is

$$\text{Level} = 10 \log_{10} \frac{P_1}{P2} = 10 \log_{10} \frac{Pr_1^2}{Pr_2^2} = 20 \log_{10} \frac{Pr_1}{Pr_2} \text{ dB SPL}.$$

The zero reference level for dB SPL becomes 0.0002 dyne/cm^2, where the dyne, a small unit of force, is about 0.0010197 grams. Since a dyne equals 10^{-5} newtons, and since one centimeter is 0.01 meter, that zero reference level (the threshold of hearing) equals 0.00002 newton/meter^2. Table 7.2 shows typical dB values in both units of power and SPL.

The sensitivity of the human ear to sound level depends on the frequency. Experiments indicate that people are more sensitive to (and therefore more annoyed by) high-frequency sounds (which is why sirens have a high pitch). It is possible to modify the dB SPL system to make it more sensitive to high frequencies and less sensitive to low frequencies. This is called the dBA standard (ANSI standard S1.4-1983). There are also dBB and dBC standards of noise measurement. (Electrical engineers use also decibel standards called dBm, dBm0, and dBrn; see, for example, [Shenoi 95].)

Because of the use of logarithms, dB measures don't simply add up. If the first trumpeter starts playing his trumpet just before the concert, generating, say, a 70 dB noise level, and the second trombonist follows on his trombone, generating the same sound level, then the (poor) listeners hear twice the noise intensity, but this corresponds to just 73 dB, not 140 dB. To see this we notice that if

$$10 \log \left(\frac{P_1}{P_2} \right) = 70,$$

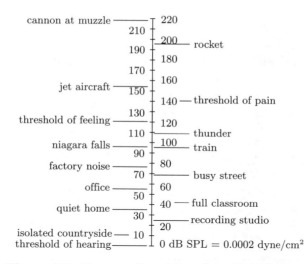

Figure 7.1: Common Sound Levels In dB PSL Units.

watts	dB	pressure n/m^2	dB SPL	source
30000.0	165	2000.0	160	jet
300.0	145	200.0	140	threshold of pain
3.0	125	20.0	120	factory noise
0.03	105	2.0	100	highway traffic
0.0003	85	0.2	80	appliance
0.000003	65	0.02	60	conversation
0.00000003	45	0.002	40	quiet room
0.0000000003	25	0.0002	20	whisper
0.000000000001	0	0.00002	0	threshold of hearing

Table 7.2: Sound Levels In Power and Pressure Units.

then

$$10 \log \left(\frac{2P_1}{P_2} \right) = 10 \left[\log_{10} 2 + \log \left(\frac{P_1}{P_2} \right) \right] = 10(0.3 + 70/10) = 73.$$

Doubling the noise level increases the dB level by 3 (if SPL units are used, the 3 should be doubled to 6).

⬦ **Exercise 7.4:** Two sound sources A and B produce dB levels of 70 and 79 dB, respectively. How much louder is source B compared to A?

Bibliography

Shenoi, Kishan (1995) *Digital Signal Processing in Telecommunications*, Upper Saddle River, NJ, Prentice Hall.

7.2 Digital Audio

Much as an image can be digitized and broken up into pixels, where each pixel is a number, sound can also be digitized and broken up into numbers. When sound is played into a microphone, it is converted into a voltage that varies continuously with time. Figure 7.3 shows a typical example of sound that starts at zero and oscillates several times. Such voltage is the *analog* representation of the sound. Digitizing sound is done by measuring the voltage at many points in time, translating each measurement into a number, and writing the numbers on a file. This process is called *sampling*. The sound wave is sampled, and the samples become the digitized sound. The device used for sampling is called an analog-to-digital converter (ADC).

The difference between a sound wave and its samples can be compared to the difference between an analog clock, where the hands seem to move continuously, and a digital clock, where the display changes abruptly every second.

Since the sound samples are numbers, they are easy to edit. However, the main use of a sound file is to play it back. This is done by converting the numeric samples back into voltages that are continuously fed into a speaker. The device that does that is called a digital-to-analog converter (DAC). Intuitively, it is clear that a high sampling rate would result in better sound reproduction, but also in many more samples and therefore bigger files. Thus, the main problem in sound sampling is how often to sample a given sound.

Figure 7.3a shows what may happen if the sampling rate is too low. The sound wave in the figure is sampled four times, and all four samples happen to be identical. When these samples are used to play back the sound, the result is a uniform sound, resembling a buzz. Figure 7.3b shows seven samples, and they seem to "follow" the original wave fairly closely. Unfortunately, when they are used to reproduce the sound, they produce the curve shown in dashed. There simply are not enough samples to reconstruct the original sound wave.

The solution to the sampling problem is to sample sound at a little over the *Nyquist rate* (page 466), which is twice the maximum frequency contained in the sound. Such a sampling rate guarantees true reproduction of the sound. This is illustrated in Figure 7.3c, which shows 10 equally spaced samples taken over four periods. Notice that the samples do not have to be taken from the maxima or minima of the wave; they can come from any point.

The range of human hearing is typically from 16–20 Hz to 20,000–22,000 Hz, depending on the person and on age. When sound is digitized at high fidelity, it should therefore be sampled at a little over the Nyquist rate of $2 \times 22000 = 44000$ Hz. This is why high-quality digital sound is based on a 44,100 Hz sampling rate. Anything lower than this rate results in distortions, while higher sampling rates do not produce any improvement in the reconstruction (playback) of the sound. We can consider the sampling rate of 44,100 Hz a lowpass filter, since it effectively removes all the frequencies above 22,000 Hz.

Many low-fidelity applications sample sound at 11,000 Hz, and the telephone system, originally designed for conversations, not for digital communications, samples sound at only 8 KHz. Thus, any frequency higher than 4000 Hz gets distorted when sent over the phone, which is why it is hard to distinguish, on the phone,

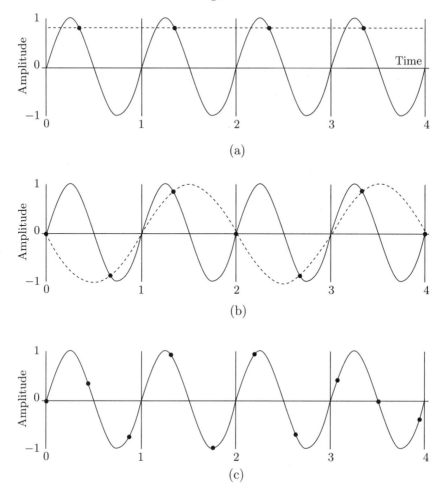

Figure 7.3: Sampling a Sound Wave.

between the sounds of "f" and "s." This is also why, when someone gives you an address over the phone you should ask, "Is it H street, as in EFGH?" Often, the answer is, "No, this is Eighth street, as in sixth, seventh, eighth."

> The meeting was in Mr. Rogers' law office, at 1415 *H* Street. My slip of paper said 1415 *8th* Street. (The address had been given over the telephone.)
> —Richard P. Feynman, *What Do YOU Care What Other People Think?*

The second problem in sound sampling is the sample size. Each sample becomes a number, but how large should this number be? In practice, samples are normally either 8 or 16 bits, although some high-quality sound cards may optionally use 32-bit samples. Assuming that the highest voltage in a sound wave is 1 volt, an 8-bit sample can distinguish voltages as low as $1/256 \approx 0.004$ volt, or 4 millivolts (mv). A quiet sound, generating a wave lower than 2 mv, would be sampled as zero and played back as silence. In contrast, a 16-bit sample can distinguish sounds as low as $1/65,536 \approx 15$ microvolt (μv). We can think of the sample size as a quantization of the original audio data. Eight-bit samples are more coarsely quantized than 16-bit ones. As a result, they produce better compression but poorer reconstruction (the reconstructed sound has only 256 levels).

⋄ **Exercise 7.5:** Suppose that the sample size is one bit. Each sample has a value of either 0 or 1. What would we hear when these samples are played back?

Audio sampling is also called *pulse code modulation* (PCM). We have all heard of AM and FM radio. These terms stand for *amplitude modulation* and *frequency modulation*, respectively. They indicate methods to modulate (i.e., to include binary information in) continuous waves. The term *pulse modulation* refers to techniques for converting a continuous wave to a stream of binary numbers. Possible pulse modulation methods include pulse amplitude modulation (PAM), pulse position modulation (PPM), pulse width modulation (PWM), and pulse number modulation (PNM). [Pohlmann 85] is a good source of information on these methods. In practice, however, PCM has proved the most effective form of converting sound waves to numbers. When stereo sound is digitized, the PCM encoder multiplexes the left and right sound samples. Thus, stereo sound sampled at 22,000 Hz with 16-bit samples generates 44,000 16-bit samples per second, for a total of 704,000 bits/s, or 88,000 bytes/s.

Bibliography

Pohlmann, Ken (1985) *Principles of Digital Audio*, Indianapolis, IN, Howard Sams & Co.

7.3 The Human Auditory System

The frequency range of the human ear is from about 20 Hz to about 20,000 Hz, but the ear's sensitivity to sound is not uniform. It depends on the frequency, and experiments indicate that in a quiet environment the ear's sensitivity is maximal for frequencies in the range 2 KHz to 4 KHz. Figure 7.4a shows the *hearing threshold* for a quiet environment.

⋄ **Exercise 7.6:** Suggest a way to conduct such an experiment.

It should also be noted that the range of the human voice is much more limited. It is only from about 500 Hz to about 2 KHz.

The existence of the hearing threshold suggests an approach to lossy audio compression. Just delete any audio samples that are below the threshold. Since the threshold depends on the frequency, the encoder needs to know the frequency spectrum of the sound being compressed at any time. The encoder therefore has to save several of the previously input audio samples at any time ($n-1$ samples, where n is either a constant or a user-controlled parameter). When the current sample is input, the first step is to transform the n samples to the frequency domain (Section 5.2). The result is a number m of values (called *signals*) that indicate the strength of the sound at m different frequencies. If a signal for frequency f is smaller than the hearing threshold at f, it (the signal) should be deleted.

In addition to this, two more properties of the human hearing system are used in audio compression. They are *frequency masking* and *temporal masking*.

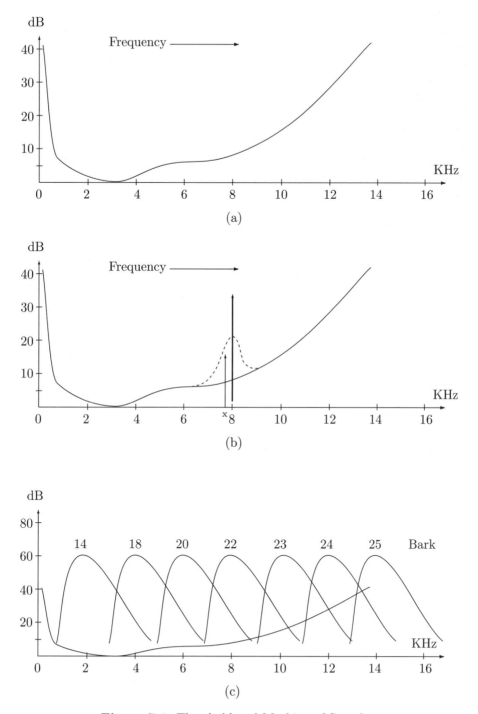

Figure 7.4: Threshold and Masking of Sound.

Frequency masking (also known as *auditory masking*) occurs when a sound that we can normally hear (because it is loud enough) is masked by another sound with a nearby frequency. The thick arrow in Figure 7.4b represents a strong sound source at 800 KHz. This source raises the normal threshold in its vicinity (the dashed curve), with the result that the nearby sound represented by the arrow at "x", a sound that would normally be audible because it is above the threshold, is now masked and is inaudible. A good lossy audio compression method should identify this case and delete the signals corresponding to sound "x", since it cannot be heard anyway. This is one way to lossily compress sound.

The frequency masking (the width of the dashed curve of Figure 7.4b) depends on the frequency. It varies from about 100 Hz for the lowest audible frequencies to more than 4 KHz for the highest. The range of audible frequencies can therefore be partitioned into a number of *critical bands* that indicate the declining sensitivity of the ear (rather, its declining resolving power) for higher frequencies. We can think of the critical bands as a measure similar to frequency. However, in contrast to frequency, which is absolute and has nothing to do with human hearing, the critical bands are determined according to the sound perception of the ear. Thus, they constitute a perceptually uniform measure of frequency. Table 7.5 lists 27 approximate critical bands.

Another way to describe critical bands is to say that because of the ear's limited perception of frequencies, the threshold at a frequency f is raised by a nearby sound only if the sound is within the critical band of f. This also points the way to designing a practical lossy compression algorithm. The audio signal should first be transformed into its frequency domain, and the resulting values (the frequency spectrum) should be divided into subbands that resemble the critical bands as much as possible. Once this is done, the signals in each subband should be quantized such that the quantization noise (the difference between the original sound sample and its quantized value) should be inaudible.

band	range	band	range	band	range
0	0–50	9	800–940	18	3280–3840
1	50–95	10	940–1125	19	3840–4690
2	95–140	11	1125–1265	20	4690–5440
3	140–235	12	1265–1500	21	5440–6375
4	235–330	13	1500–1735	22	6375–7690
5	330–420	14	1735–1970	23	7690–9375
6	420–560	15	1970–2340	24	9375–11625
7	560–660	16	2340–2720	25	11625–15375
8	660–800	17	2720–3280	26	15375–20250

Table 7.5: Twenty-Seven Approximate Critical Bands.

Yet another way to look at the concept of critical band is to consider the human auditory system a filter that lets through only frequencies in the range (bandpass) of 20 Hz to 20000 Hz. We visualize the ear–brain system as a collection of filters, each with a different bandpass. The bandpasses are called critical bands. They overlap and they have different widths. They are narrow (about 100 Hz) at low frequencies and become wider (to about 4–5 KHz) at high frequencies.

The width of a critical band is called its size. The widths of the critical bands introduce a new unit, the *Bark* (after H. G. Barkhausen) such that one Bark is the width (in Hz) of one critical band. The Bark is defined as

$$1 \text{ Bark} = \begin{cases} \frac{f}{100}, & \text{for frequencies } f < 500 \text{ Hz,} \\ 9 + 4 \log\left(\frac{f}{1000}\right), & \text{for frequencies } f \geq 500 \text{ Hz.} \end{cases}$$

Figure 7.4c shows some critical bands, with Barks between 14 and 25, positioned above the threshold.

Heinrich Georg Barkhausen

Heinrich Barkhausen was born on December 2, 1881, in Bremen, Germany. He spent his entire career as a professor of electrical engineering at the Technische Hochschule in Dresden, where he concentrated on developing electron tubes. He also discovered the so-called "Barkhausen effect," where acoustical waves are generated in a solid by the movement of domain walls when the material is magnetized. He also coined the term "phon" as a unit of sound loudness. The institute in Dresden was destroyed, as was most of the city, in the famous fire bombing in February 1945. After the war, Barkhausen helped rebuild the institute. He died on February 20, 1956.

Temporal masking may occur when a strong sound A of frequency f is preceded or followed in time by a weaker sound B at a nearby (or the same) frequency. If the time interval between the sounds is short, sound B may not be audible. Figure 7.6 illustrates an example of temporal masking. The threshold of temporal masking due to a loud sound at time 0 goes down, first sharply, then slowly. A weaker sound of 30 dB will not be audible if it occurs 10 ms before or after the loud sound, but will be audible if the time interval between the sounds is 20 ms.

7.3.1 Conventional Methods

Conventional compression methods, such as RLE, statistical, and dictionary-based, can be used to losslessly compress sound files, but the results depend heavily on the specific sound. Some sounds may compress well under RLE but not under a statistical method. Other sounds may lend themselves to statistical compression but may expand when processed by a dictionary method. Here is how sounds respond to each of the three classes of compression methods.

RLE may work well when the sound contains long runs of identical samples. With 8-bit samples this may be common. Recall that the difference between the two 8-bit samples n and $n+1$ is about 4 mv. A few seconds of uniform music, where the wave does not oscillate more than 4 mv, may produce a run of thousands of identical

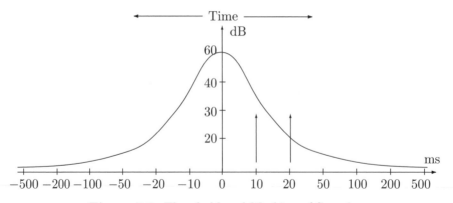

Figure 7.6: Threshold and Masking of Sound.

samples. With 16-bit samples, long runs may be rare and RLE, consequently, ineffective.

Statistical methods assign variable-size codes to the samples according to their frequency of occurrence. With 8-bit samples, there are only 256 different samples, so in a large sound file, the samples may sometimes have a flat distribution. Such a file will therefore not respond well to Huffman coding (See Exercise 2.21). With 16-bit samples there are more than 65,000 possible samples, so they may sometimes feature skewed probabilities (i.e., some samples may occur very often, while others may be rare). Such a file may therefore compress better with arithmetic coding, which works well even for skewed probabilities.

Dictionary-based methods expect to find the same phrases again and again in the data. This happens with text, where certain strings may repeat often. Sound, however, is an analog signal and the particular samples generated depend on the precise way the ADC works. With 8-bit samples, for example, a wave of 8 mv becomes a sample of size 2, but waves very close to that, say, 7.6 mv or 8.5 mv, may become samples of different sizes. This is why parts of speech that sound the same to us, and should therefore have become identical phrases, end up being digitized slightly differently, and go into the dictionary as different phrases, thereby reducing the compression performance. Dictionary-based methods are thus not very well suited for sound compression.

> I don't like the sound of that sound.
> —Heather Graham as Judy Robinson in *Lost in Space* (1998)

7.3.2 Lossy Sound Compression

It is possible to get better sound compression by developing lossy methods that take advantage of our perception of sound, and discard data to which the human ear is not sensitive. This is similar to lossy image compression, where data to which the human eye is not sensitive is discarded. In both cases we use the fact that the original information (image or sound) is analog and has already lost some quality when digitized. Losing some more data, if done carefully, may not significantly affect the played-back sound, and may therefore be indistinguishable from the original. We briefly describe two approaches, *silence compression* and *companding*.

The principle of silence compression is to treat small samples as if they were silence (i.e., as samples of zero). This generates run lengths of zero, so silence compression is actually a variant of RLE, suitable for sound compression. This method uses the fact that some people have less sensitive hearing than others, and will tolerate the loss of sound that is so quiet they may not hear it anyway. Audio files containing long periods of low-volume sound will respond to silence compression better than other files with high-volume sound. This method requires a user-controlled parameter that specifies the largest sample that should be suppressed. Two other parameters are also necessary, although they may not have to be user-controlled. One specifies the shortest run-length of small samples, typically 2 or 3. The other specifies the minimum number of consecutive large samples that should terminate a run of silence. For example, a run of 15 small samples, followed by 2 large samples, followed by 13 small samples may be considered one silence run of 30 samples, whereas a situation of 15, 3, 13 may become two distinct silence runs of 15 and 13 samples, with nonsilence in between.

Companding (short for "compressing/expanding") uses the fact that the ear requires more precise samples at low amplitudes (soft sounds), but is more forgiving at higher amplitudes. A typical ADC used in sound cards for personal computers converts voltages to numbers linearly. If an amplitude a is converted to the number n, then amplitude $2a$ will be converted to the number $2n$. A compression method using companding examines every sample in the sound file, and uses a nonlinear formula to reduce the number of bits devoted to it. For 16-bit samples, for example, a companding encoder may use a formula as simple as

$$\text{mapped} = 32767 \left(2^{\frac{\text{sample}}{65536}} - 1 \right) \tag{7.1}$$

to reduce each sample. This formula maps the 16-bit samples nonlinearly to 15-bit numbers (i.e., numbers in the range [0, 32767]) such that small samples are less affected than large ones. Table 7.7 illustrates the nonlinearity of this mapping. It shows eight pairs of samples, where the two samples in each pair differ by 100. The two samples of the first pair get mapped to numbers that differ by 34, whereas the two samples of the last pair are mapped to numbers that differ by 65. The mapped 15-bit numbers can be decoded back into the original 16-bit samples by the inverse formula

$$\text{Sample} = 65536 \log_2 \left(1 + \frac{\text{mapped}}{32767} \right). \tag{7.2}$$

Reducing 16-bit numbers to 15-bits doesn't produce much compression. Better compression can be achieved by substituting a smaller number for 32,767 in equations (7.1) and (7.2). A value of 127, for example, would map each 16-bit sample into an 8-bit one, producing a compression ratio of 0.5. However, decoding would be less accurate. A 16-bit sample of 60,100, for example, would be mapped into the 8-bit number 113, but this number would produce 60,172 when decoded by

Sample	Mapped	Diff	Sample	Mapped	Diff
100 →	35	34	30000 →	12236	47
200 →	69		30100 →	12283	
1000 →	348	35	40000 →	17256	53
1100 →	383		40100 →	17309	
10000 →	3656	38	50000 →	22837	59
10100 →	3694		50100 →	22896	
20000 →	7719	43	60000 →	29040	65
20100 →	7762		60100 →	29105	

Table 7.7: 16-Bit Samples Mapped to 15-Bit Numbers.

Equation (7.2). Even worse, the small 16-bit sample 1000 would be mapped into 1.35, which has to be rounded to 1. When Equation (7.2) is used to decode a 1, it produces 742, significantly different from the original sample. The amount of compression should thus be a user-controlled parameter, and this is an interesting example of a compression method where the compression ratio is *known in advance*!

In practice, there is no need to go through Equations (7.1) and (7.2), since the mapping of all the samples can be prepared in advance in a table. Both encoding and decoding are thus fast.

Companding is not limited to Equations (7.1) and (7.2). More sophisticated methods, such as μ-law and A-law, are commonly used and have been made international standards.

7.4 μ-Law and A-Law Companding

A simple logarithm-based function is used by these two international standards [ITU-T 89] to encode digitized audio samples for ISDN (integrated services digital network) digital telephony services, by means of nonlinear quantization. The ISDN hardware samples the voice signal from the telephone 8000 times per second, and generates 14-bit samples (13 for A-law). The method of μ-law companding is used in North America and Japan, and the A-law is used elsewhere. The two methods are similar; they differ mostly in their quantizations (midtread vs. midriser).

Experiments indicate that the low amplitudes of speech signals contain more information than the high amplitudes. This is why nonlinear quantization makes sense. Imagine an audio signal sent on a telephone line and digitized to 14-bit samples. The louder the conversation, the higher the amplitude, and the bigger the value of the sample. Since high amplitudes are less important, they can be coarsely quantized. If the largest sample, which is $2^{14} - 1 = 16,384$, is quantized to 255 (the largest 8-bit number), then the compression factor is $14/8 = 1.75$. When decoded, a code of 255 will become very different from the original 16,384. We say that because of the coarse quantization, large samples end up with high quantization noise. Smaller samples should be finely quantized, so they end up with low noise.

The μ-law encoder inputs 14-bit samples and outputs 8-bit codewords. The A-law inputs 13-bit samples and also outputs 8-bit codewords. The telephone signals are sampled at 8 KHz (8000 times per second), so the μ-law encoder receives 8000× 14 = 112,000 bits/s. At a compression factor of 1.75, the encoder outputs 64,000 bits/s. The G.711 standard also specifies output rates of 48 Kbps and 56 Kbps.

The μ-law encoder receives a 14-bit *signed* input sample x. The input is thus in the range $[-8192, +8191]$. The sample is normalized to the interval $[-1, +1]$, and the encoder uses the logarithmic expression

$$\text{sgn}(x)\frac{\ln(1 + \mu|x|)}{\ln(1 + \mu)}, \quad \text{where } \text{sgn}(x) = \begin{cases} +1, & x > 0, \\ 0, & x = 0, \\ -1, & x < 0, \end{cases}$$

(and μ is a positive integer), to compute and output an 8-bit code in the same interval $[-1, +1]$. The output is then scaled to the range $[-256, +255]$. Figure 7.8 shows this output as a function of the input for the three μ values 25, 255, and 2555. It is clear that large values of μ cause coarser quantization for larger amplitudes. Such values allocate more bits to the smaller, more important, amplitudes. The G.711 standard recommends the use of $\mu = 255$. The diagram shows only the nonnegative values of the input (i.e., from 0 to 8191). The negative side of the diagram has the same shape but with negative inputs and outputs.

The A-law encoder uses the similar expression

$$\begin{cases} \text{sgn}(x)\dfrac{A|x|}{1 + \ln(A)}, & \text{for } 0 \leq |x| < \frac{1}{A}, \\[2mm] \text{sgn}(x)\dfrac{1 + \ln(A|x|)}{1 + \ln(A)}, & \text{for } \frac{1}{A} \leq |x| < 1. \end{cases}$$

The G.711 standard recommends the use of $A = 255$.

The following simple calculations illustrate the nonlinear nature of the μ-law. The two (normalized) input samples 0.15 and 0.16 are transformed to outputs 0.6618 and 0.6732. The difference between the outputs is 0.0114. On the other hand, the two input samples 0.95 and 0.96 (bigger inputs but with the same difference) are transformed to 0.9908 and 0.9927. The difference between these two outputs is 0.0019; much smaller.

Bigger samples are decoded with more noise, and smaller samples are decoded with less noise. However, the signal-to-noise ratio (SNR, Section 4.2.2) is constant because both the μ-law and the SNR use logarithmic expressions.

Logarithms are slow to calculate, so the μ-law encoder performs much simpler calculations that produce an approximation. The output specified by the G.711 standard is an 8-bit codeword whose format is shown in Figure 7.9.

Bit P in Figure 7.9 is the sign bit of the output (same as the sign bit of the 14-bit signed input sample). Bits S2, S1, and S0 are the segment code, and bits Q3 through Q0 are the quantization code. The encoder determines the segment code by (1) adding a bias of 33 to the absolute value of the input sample, (2) determining the bit position of the most significant 1-bit among bits 5 through 12 of the input, and (3) subtracting 5 from that position. The 4-bit quantization code is set to the four bits following the bit position determined in step 2. The encoder ignores the remaining bits of the input sample, and it inverts (1's complements) the codeword before it is output.

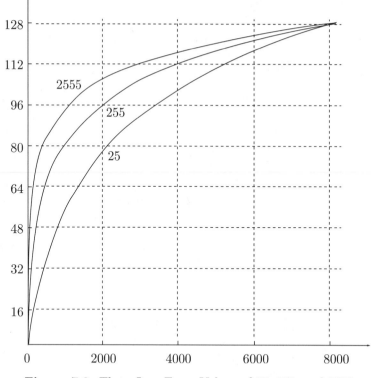

Figure 7.8: The μ-Law For μ Values of 25, 255, and 2555.

```
dat=linspace(0,1,1000);
mu=255;
plot(dat*8159,128*log(1+mu*dat)/log(1+mu));
```

Matlab code for Figure 7.8. Notice how the input is normalized to the range $[0,1]$ before the calculations, and how the output is scaled from the interval $[0,1]$ to $[0,128]$.

P	S2	S1	S0	Q3	Q2	Q1	Q0

Figure 7.9: G.711 μ-Law Codeword.

				Q3	Q2	Q1	Q0					
0	0	0	1	0	1	0	1	1	0	0	0	1
12	11	10	9	8	7	6	5	4	3	2	1	0

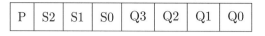

Figure 7.10: Encoding Input Sample −656.

We use the input sample -656 as an example. The sample is negative, so bit P becomes 1. Adding 33 to the absolute value of the input yields $689 = 0001010110001_2$ (Figure 7.10). The most significant 1-bit in positions 5 through 12 is found at position 9. The segment code is thus $9 - 5 = 4$. The quantization code is the four bits 0101 at positions 8–5, and the remaining five bits 10001 are ignored. The 8-bit codeword (which is later inverted) becomes

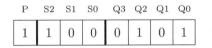

The μ-law decoder inputs an 8-bit codeword and inverts it. It then decodes it as follows:

1. Multiply the quantization code by 2 and add 33 (the bias) to the result.
2. Multiply the result by 2 raised to the power of the segment code.
3. Decrement the result by the bias.
4. Use bit P to determine the sign of the result.

Applying these steps to our example produces

1. The quantization code is $101_2 = 5$, so $5 \times 2 + 33 = 43$.
2. The segment code is $100_2 = 4$, so $43 \times 2^4 = 688$.
3. Decrement by the bias $688 - 33 = 655$.
4. Bit P is 1, so the final result is -655. Thus, the quantization error (the noise) is 1; very small.

Figure 7.11a illustrates the nature of the μ-law midtread quantization. Zero is one of the valid output values, and the quantization steps are centered at the input value of zero. The steps are organized in eight segments of 16 steps each. The steps within each segment have the same width, but they double in width from one segment to the next. If we denote the segment number by i (where $i = 0, 1, \ldots, 7$) and the width of a segment by k (where $k = 1, 2, \ldots, 16$), then the middle of the tread of each step in Figure 7.11a (i.e., the points labeled x_j) is given by

$$x(16i + k) = T(i) + k \times D(i), \tag{7.3}$$

where the constants $T(i)$ and $D(i)$ are the initial value and the step size for segment i, respectively. They are given by

i	0	1	2	3	4	5	6	7
$T(i)$	1	35	103	239	511	1055	2143	4319
$D(i)$	2	4	8	16	32	64	128	256

Table 7.12 lists some values of the breakpoints (points x_j) and outputs (points y_j) shown in Figure 7.11a.

The operation of the A-law encoder is similar, except that the quantization (Figure 7.11b) is of the midriser variety.. The breakpoints x_j are given by Equation (7.3), but the initial value $T(i)$ and the step size $D(i)$ for segment i are different

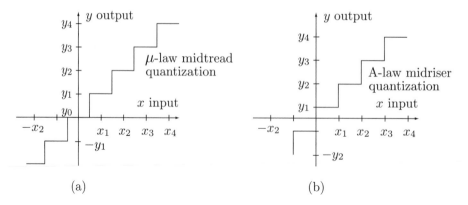

Figure 7.11: (a) μ-Law Midtread Quantization. (b) A-law Midriser Quantization.

segment 0		segment 1		$\cdots$	segment 7	
break points	output values	break points	output values		break points	output values
	$y_0 = 0$		$y_{16} = 33$	$\cdots$		$y_{112} = 4191$
$x_1 = 1$		$x_{17} = 35$			$x_{113} = 4319$	
	$y_1 = 2$		$y_{17} = 37$	$\cdots$		$y_{113} = 4447$
$x_2 = 3$		$x_{18} = 39$			$x_{114} = 4575$	
	$y_2 = 4$		$y_{18} = 41$	$\cdots$		$y_{114} = 4703$
$x_3 = 5$		$x_{19} = 43$			$x_{115} = 4831$	
	$y_3 = 6$		$y_{19} = 45$	$\cdots$		$y_{115} = 4959$
$x_4 = 7$		$x_{20} = 47$			$x_{116} = 5087$	
$\cdots$				$\cdots$		
$\cdots$				$\cdots$		
$x_{15} = 29$		$x_{31} = 91$			$x_{127} = 7903$	
	$y_{15} = 28$		$y_{31} = 93$	$\cdots$		$y_{127} = 8031$
$x_{16} = 31$		$x_{32} = 95$			$x_{128} = 8159$	

Table 7.12: Specification of the μ-Law Quantizer.

from those used by the μ-law encoder and are given by

i	0	1	2	3	4	5	6	7
$T(i)$	0	32	64	128	256	512	1024	2048
$D(i)$	2	2	4	8	16	32	64	128

Table 7.13 lists some values of the breakpoints (points x_j) and outputs (points y_j) shown in Figure 7.11b.

The A-law encoder generates an 8-bit codeword with the same format as the μ-law encoder. It sets the P bit to the sign of the input sample. It then determines the segment code by

segment 0		segment 1		$\cdots$	segment 7	
break points	output values	break points	output values		break points	output values
$x_0 = 0$		$x_{16} = 32$			$x_{112} = 2048$	
	$y_1 = 1$		$y_{17} = 33$	$\cdots$		$y_{113} = 2112$
$x_1 = 2$		$x_{17} = 34$			$x_{113} = 2176$	
	$y_2 = 3$		$y_{18} = 35$	$\cdots$		$y_{114} = 2240$
$x_2 = 4$		$x_{18} = 36$			$x_{114} = 2304$	
	$y_3 = 5$		$y_{19} = 37$	$\cdots$		$y_{115} = 2368$
$x_3 = 6$		$x_{19} = 38$			$x_{115} = 2432$	
	$y_4 = 7$		$y_{20} = 39$	$\cdots$		$y_{116} = 2496$
$\cdots$					$\cdots$	
$\cdots$					$\cdots$	
$x_{15} = 30$		$x_{31} = 62$			$x_{128} = 4096$	
	$y_{16} = 31$		$y_{32} = 63$	$\cdots$		$y_{127} = 4032$

Table 7.13: Specification of the A-Law Quantizer.

1. Determining the bit position of the most significant 1-bit among the seven most significant bits of the input.
2. If such a 1-bit is found, the segment code becomes that position minus 4. Otherwise, the segment code becomes zero.

The 4-bit quantization code is set to the four bits following the bit position determined in step 1, or to half the input value if the segment code is zero. The encoder ignores the remaining bits of the input sample, and it inverts bit P and the even-numbered bits of the codeword before it is output.

The A-law decoder decodes an 8-bit codeword into a 13-bit audio sample as follows:

1. It inverts bit P and the even-numbered bits of the codeword.
2. If the segment code is nonzero, the decoder multiplies the quantization code by 2 and increments this by the bias (33). The result is then multiplied by 2 and raised to the power of the (segment code minus 1). If the segment code is zero, the decoder outputs twice the quantization code, plus 1.
3. Bit P is then used to determine the sign of the output.

Normally, the output codewords are generated by the encoder at the rate of 64 Kbps. The G.711 standard also provides for two other rates, as follows:

1. To achieve an output rate of 48 Kbps, the encoder masks out the two least-significant bits of each codeword. This works, since $6/8 = 48/64$.
2. To achieve an output rate of 56 Kpbs, the encoder masks out the least-significant bit of each codeword. This works, since $7/8 = 56/64 = 0.875$.

This applies to both the μ-law and the A-law. The decoder typically fills up the masked bit positions with zeros before decoding a codeword.

Bibliography

ITU-T (1989) *CCITT Recommendation G.711: Pulse Code Modulation (PCM) of Voice Frequencies.*

Shenoi, Kishan (1995) *Digital Signal Processing in Telecommunications*, Upper Saddle River, NJ, Prentice Hall.

7.5 ADPCM Audio Compression

As always, compression is possible only because sound, and thus audio samples, tend to have redundancies. Adjacent audio samples tend to be similar in much the same way that neighboring pixels in an image tend to have similar colors. The simplest way to exploit this redundancy is to subtract adjacent samples and code the differences, which tend to be small numbers. Any audio compression method based on this principle is called DPCM (differential pulse code modulation). Such methods, however, are inefficient, since they do not adapt themselves to the varying magnitudes of the audio stream. Better results are achieved by an adaptive version, and any such version is called ADPCM.

Similar to predictive image compression, ADPCM uses the previous sample (or several previous samples) to predict the current sample. It then computes the difference between the current sample and its prediction, and quantizes the difference. For each input sample $X[n]$, the output $C[n]$ of the encoder is simply a certain number of quantization levels. The decoder multiplies this number by the quantization step (and may add half the quantization step, for better precision) to obtain the reconstructed audio sample. The method is efficient because the quantization step is modified all the time, by both encoder and decoder, in response to the varying magnitudes of the input samples. It is also possible to modify adaptively the prediction algorithm.

Various ADPCM methods differ in the way they predict the current sound sample and in the way they adapt to the input (by changing the quantization step size and/or the prediction method).

In addition to the quantized values, an ADPCM encoder can provide the decoder with *side information*. This information increases the size of the compressed stream, but this degradation is acceptable to the users, since it makes the compressed audio data more useful. Typical applications of side information are (1) help the decoder recover from errors and (2) signal an entry point into the compressed stream. An original audio stream may be recorded in compressed form on a medium such as a CD-ROM. If the user (listener) wants to listen to song 5, the decoder can use the side information to quickly find the start of that song.

Figure 7.14a,b shows the general organization of the ADPCM encoder and decoder. Notice that they share two functional units, a feature that helps in both software and hardware implementations. The adaptive quantizer receives the difference $D[n]$ between the current input sample $X[n]$ and the prediction $Xp[n-1]$. The quantizer computes and outputs the quantized code $C[n]$ of $X[n]$. The same code is sent to the adaptive dequantizer (the same dequantizer used by the decoder), which produces the next dequantized difference value $Dq[n]$. This value is added to the previous predictor output $Xp[n-1]$, and the sum $Xp[n]$ is sent to the predictor to be used in the next step.

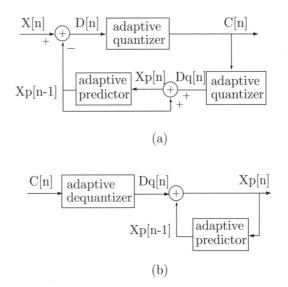

(a)

(b)

Figure 7.14: ADPCM Encoder (a) and Decoder (b).

Better prediction would be obtained by feeding the actual input X[n] to the predictor. However, the decoder wouldn't be able to mimic that, since it does not have X[n]. We see that the basic ADPCM encoder is simple, but the decoder is even simpler. It inputs a code C[n], dequantizes it to a difference Dq[n], which is added to the preceding predictor output Xp[n − 1] to form the next output Xp[n]. The next output is also fed into the predictor, to be used in the next step.

The following describes the particular ADPCM algorithm adopted by the Interactive Multimedia Association (IMA). The IMA is a consortium of computer hardware and software manufacturers, established to develop standards for multimedia applications. The goal of the IMA in developing its audio compression standard was to have a public domain method that is simple and fast enough such that a 20-MHz 386-class personal computer would be able to decode, in real time, sound recorded in stereo at 44,100 16-bit samples per second (this is 88,200 16-bit samples per second).

The encoder quantizes each 16-bit audio sample into a 4-bit code. The compression factor is thus a constant 4.

The "secret" of the IMA algorithm is the simplicity of its predictor. The predicted value Xp[n − 1] that is output by the predictor is simply the decoded value Xp[n] of the preceding input X[n]. The predictor just stores Xp[n] for one cycle (one audio sample interval), then outputs it as Xp[n − 1]. It does not use any of the preceding values Xp[i] to obtain better prediction. Thus, the predictor is not adaptive (but the quantizer is). Also, no side information is generated by the encoder.

Figure 7.17a is a block diagram of the IMA quantizer. It is both simple and adaptive, varying the quantization step size based on both the current step size and the previous quantizer output. The adaptation is done by means of two table lookups, so it is fast. The quantizer outputs 4-bit codes where the leftmost bit is a sign and the remaining three bits are the number of quantization levels computed for the current audio sample. These three bits are used as an index to the first table. The item found in this table serves as an index adjustment to the second table. The index adjustment is added to a previously stored index, and the sum, after being checked for proper range, is used as the index for the second table lookup. The sum is then stored, and it becomes the stored index used in the next adaptation step. The item found in the second table becomes the new quantization step size. Figure 7.17b illustrates this process, and Tables 7.15 and 7.16 list the two tables. Table 7.18 shows the 4-bit output produced by the quantizer as a function of the sample size. For example, if the sample is in the range $[1.5ss, 1.75ss)$, where ss is the step size, then the output is 0|110.

Table 7.15 adjusts the index by bigger steps when the quantized magnitude is bigger. Table 7.16 is constructed such that the ratio between successive entries is about 1.1.

Bibliography

ITU-T (1990), Recommendation G.726 (12/90), *40, 32, 24, 16 kbit/s Adaptive Differential Pulse Code Modulation (ADPCM)*. Available from `http://www.itu.int//itudoc/itu-t/rec/g/g700-799/index.html`.

7.6 MPEG-1 Audio Layers

The video compression aspects of the MPEG-1 standard are described in Section 6.5. Its audio compression principles are discussed here. Readers are advised to read the preceding sections of this chapter before trying to tackle this material.

The formal name of MPEG-1 is *the international standard for moving picture video compression, IS 11172*. It consists of five parts, of which part 3 [ISO/IEC 93] is the definition of the audio compression algorithm. Like other standards developed by the ITU and ISO, the document describing MPEG-1 has *normative* and *informative* sections. A normative section is part of the standard specification. It is intended for implementers, it is written in a precise language, and it should be strictly followed in implementing the standard on actual computer platforms. An informative section, on the other hand, illustrates concepts discussed elsewhere, explains the reasons that led to certain choices and decisions, and contains background material. An example of a normative section is the tables of various parameters and of the Huffman codes used in MPEG audio. An example of an informative section is the algorithm used by MPEG audio to implement a psychoacoustic model. MPEG does not require any particular algorithm, and an MPEG encoder can use any method to implement the model. The section itself simply describes various alternatives.

The MPEG-1 audio standard specifies three compression methods called *layers* and designated I, II, and III. All three layers are part of the MPEG-1 standard. A movie compressed by MPEG-1 uses only one layer, and the layer number is specified in the compressed stream. Any of the layers can be used to compress an audio file without any video. The functional modules of the lower layers are also used by the higher layers, but the higher layers have additional features that result in better compression. An interesting aspect of the design of the standard is that the layers

three bits quantized magnitude	index adjust
000	−1
001	−1
010	−1
011	−1
100	2
101	4
110	6
111	8

Table 7.15: First Table For IMA ADPCM.

Index	Step Size	Index	Step Size	Index	Step Size	Index	Step Size
0	7	22	60	44	494	66	4,026
1	8	23	66	45	544	67	4,428
2	9	24	73	46	598	68	4,871
3	10	25	80	47	658	69	5,358
4	11	26	88	48	724	70	5,894
5	12	27	97	49	796	71	6,484
6	13	28	107	50	876	72	7,132
7	14	29	118	51	963	73	7,845
8	16	30	130	52	1,060	74	8,630
9	17	31	143	53	1,166	75	9,493
10	19	32	157	54	1,282	76	10,442
11	21	33	173	55	1,411	77	11,487
12	23	34	190	56	1,552	78	12,635
13	25	35	209	57	1,707	79	13,899
14	28	36	230	58	1,878	80	15,289
15	31	37	253	59	2,066	81	16,818
16	34	38	279	60	2,272	82	18,500
17	37	39	307	61	2,499	83	20,350
18	41	40	337	62	2,749	84	22,358
19	45	41	371	63	3,024	85	24,633
20	50	42	408	64	3,327	86	27,086
21	55	43	449	65	3,660	87	29,794
						88	32,767

Table 7.16: Second Table For IMA ADPCM.

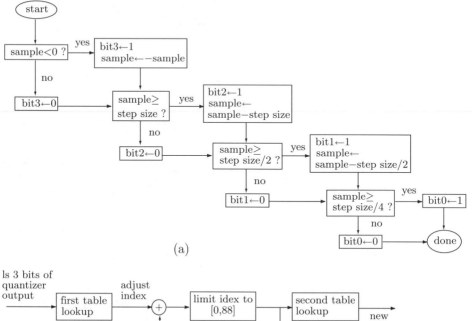

(a)

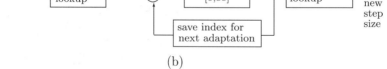

(b)

Figure 7.17: (a) IMA ADPCM Quantization. (b) Step Size Adaptation.

if sample is in range	4-bit quant	if sample is in range	4-bit quant
$[1.75ss, \infty)$	0|111	$[-\infty, -1.75ss)$	1|111
$[1.5ss, 1.75ss)$	0|110	$[-1.75ss, -1.5ss)$	1|110
$[1.25ss, 1.5ss)$	0|101	$[-1.5ss, -1.25ss)$	1|101
$[1ss, 1.25ss)$	0|100	$[-1.25ss, -1ss)$	1|100
$[.75ss, 1ss)$	0|011	$[-1ss, -.75ss)$	1|011
$[.5ss, .75ss)$	0|010	$[-.75ss, -.5ss)$	1|010
$[.25ss, .5ss)$	0|001	$[-.5ss, -.25ss)$	1|001
$[0, .25ss)$	0|000	$[-.25ss, 0)$	1|000

Table 7.18: Step Size and 4-bit Quantizer Outputs.

form a hierarchy in the sense that a layer-III decoder can also decode audio files compressed by layers I or II.

The result of having three layers was an increasing popularity of layer III. The encoder is extremely complex, but it produces excellent compression, and this, combined with the fact that the decoder is much simpler, has produced in the late 1990s an explosion of what is popularly known as .mp3 sound files. It is easy to legally and freely obtain a layer-III decoder and much music which is already encoded in layer III. So far, this has been a big success of the audio part of the MPEG project.

The MPEG audio standard [ISO/IEC 93] starts with the normative description of the format of the compressed stream for each of the three layers. It follows with a normative description of the decoder. The description of the encoder (it is different for the three layers), and of two psychoacoustic models follows and is informative; any encoder that generates a correct compressed stream is a valid MPEG encoder. There are appendices (annexes) discussing related topics such as error protection.

In contrast with MPEG video, where many information sources are available, there is relatively little in the technical literature about MPEG audio. In addition to the references at the end of this section, the reader is referred to the MPEG consortium [MPEG 00]. This site contains lists of other resources, and is updated from time to time. Another resource is the Association of Audio Engineers (AES). Most of the ideas and techniques used in the MPEG audio standard (and also in other audio compression methods) were originally published in the many conference proceedings of this organization. Unfortunately, these are not freely available and have to be obtained from the AES.

The history of MPEG-1 audio starts in December 1988, when a group of experts met for the first time in Hanover, Germany, to discuss the topic. During 1989, no fewer than 14 algorithms were proposed by these experts. They were eventually merged into four groups, known today as ASPEC, ATAC, MUSICAM, and SB-ADPCM. These were tested and compared in 1990, with results that led to the idea of adopting the three layers. Each of the three layers is a different compression method, and they increase in complexity (and in performance) from layer I to layer III. The first draft of the ISO MPEG-1 audio standard (standard 11172 part 3) was ready in December 1990. The three layers were implemented and tested during the first half of 1991, and the specifications of the first two layers were frozen in June 1991. Layer III went through further modifications and tests during 1991, and the complete MPEG audio standard was ready and was sent by the expert group to the ISO in December 1991, for its approval. It took the ISO/IEC almost a year to examine the standard, and it was finally approved in November 1992.

When a movie is digitized, the audio part may many times consist of two sound tracks (stereo sound), each sampled at 44.1 KHz with 16-bit samples. The audio data rate is therefore $2 \times 44,100 \times 16 = 1,411,200$ bits/s; close to 1.5 Mbits/s. In addition to the 44.1 KHz sampling rate, the MPEG standard allows sampling rates of 32 KHz and 48 KHz. An important feature of MPEG audio is its compression ratio, which the standard specifies in advance! The standard calls for a compressed stream with one of several bitrates (Table 7.19) ranging from 32 to 224 Kbits/s per audio channel (there normally are two channels, for stereo sound). Depending on the original sampling rate, these bitrates translate to compression factors of from 2.7 (low) to 24 (impressive)! The reason for specifying the bitrates of the compressed stream is that the stream also includes compressed data for the video and system parts. (These parts are mentioned in Section 6.5 and are not the same as the three audio layers.)

		Bitrate (Kbps)	
Index	Layer I	Layer II	Layer III
0000	free format	free format	free format
0001	32	32	32
0010	64	48	40
0011	96	56	48
0100	128	64	56
0101	160	80	64
0110	192	96	80
0111	224	112	96
1000	256	128	112
1001	288	160	128
1010	320	192	160
1011	352	224	192
1100	384	256	224
1101	416	320	256
1110	448	384	320
1111	forbidden	forbidden	forbidden

Table 7.19: Bitrates in the Three Layers.

The principle of MPEG audio compression is quantization. The values being quantized, however, are not the audio samples but numbers (called signals) taken from the frequency domain of the sound (this is discussed in the next paragraph). The fact that the compression ratio (or equivalently, the bitrate) is known to the encoder means that the encoder knows at any time how many bits it can allocate to the quantized signals. Thus, the (adaptive) *bit allocation algorithm* is an important part of the encoder. This algorithm uses the known bitrate and the frequency spectrum of the most recent audio samples to determine the size of the quantized signals such that the quantization noise (the difference between an original signal and a quantized one) will be inaudible (i.e., will be below the *masked threshold*, a concept discussed in Section 7.3).

The psychoacoustic models use the frequency of the sound that is being compressed, but the input stream contains audio samples, not sound frequencies. The frequencies have to be computed from the samples. This is why the first step in MPEG audio encoding is a discrete Fourier transform, where a set of 512 consecutive audio samples is transformed to the frequency domain. Since the number of frequencies can be huge, they are grouped into 32 equal-width frequency subbands (layer III uses different numbers but the same principle). For each subband, a number is obtained that indicates the intensity of the sound at that subband's frequency range. These numbers (called *signals*) are then quantized. The coarseness of the quantization in each subband is determined by the masking threshold in the subband and by the number of bits still available to the encoder. The masking threshold is computed for each subband using a psychoacoustic model.

MPEG uses two psychoacoustic models to implement frequency masking and temporal masking. Each model describes how loud sound masks other sounds that happen to be close to it in frequency or in time. The model partitions the frequency range into 24 critical bands and specifies how masking effects apply within each band. The masking effects depend, of course, on the frequencies and amplitudes of the tones. When the sound is decompressed and played, the user (listener) may select any playback amplitude, which is why the psychoacoustic model has to be designed for the worst case. The masking effects also depend on the nature of the source of the sound being compressed. The source may be tone-like or noise-like. The two psychoacoustic models used by MPEG are based on experimental work done by researchers over many years.

The decoder must be fast, since it may have to decode the entire movie (video and audio) at real time, so it must be simple. As a result it does not use any psychoacoustic model or bit allocation algorithm. The compressed stream must therefore contain all the information that the decoder needs for dequantizing the signals. This information (the size of the quantized signals) must be written by the encoder on the compressed stream, and it constitutes overhead that should be subtracted from the number of remaining available bits.

Figure 7.20 is a block diagram of the main components of the MPEG audio encoder and decoder. The ancillary data is user-definable and would normally consist of information related to specific applications. This data is optional.

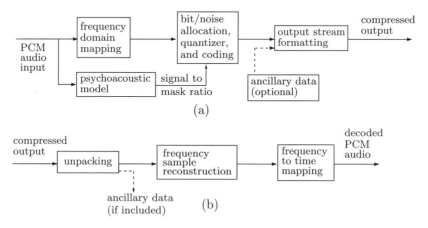

Figure 7.20: MPEG Audio Encoder (a) and Decoder (b).

7.6.1 Frequency Domain Coding

The first step in encoding the audio samples is to transform them from the time domain to the frequency domain. This is done by a bank of *polyphase filters* that transform the samples into 32 equal-width frequency subbands. The filters were designed to provide fast operation combined with good time and frequency resolutions. As a result, their design involved three compromises.

The first compromise is the equal widths of the 32 frequency bands. This simplifies the filters but is in contrast to the behavior of the human auditory system, whose sensitivity is frequency-dependent. Ideally, the filters should divide the input into the critical bands discussed in Section 7.3. These bands are formed such that the perceived loudness of a given sound and its audibility in the presence of another, masking, sound are consistent within a critical band, but different across these bands. Unfortunately, each of the low-frequency subbands overlaps several critical bands, with the result that the bit allocation algorithm cannot optimize the number of bits allocated to the quantized signal in those subbands. When several critical bands are covered by a subband X, the bit allocation algorithm selects the critical band with the least noise masking and uses that critical band to compute the number of bits allocated to the quantized signals in subband X.

The second compromise involves the inverse filter bank, the one used by the decoder. The original time-to-frequency transformation involves loss of information (even before any quantization). The inverse filter bank therefore receives data that is slightly bad, and uses it to perform the inverse frequency-to-time transformation, resulting in more distortions. Therefore, the design of the two filter banks (for direct and inverse transformations) had to use compromises to minimize this loss of information.

The third compromise has to do with the individual filters. Adjacent filters should ideally pass different frequency ranges. In practice, they have considerable frequency overlap. Sound of a single, pure, frequency can therefore penetrate through two filters and produce signals (that are later quantized) in two of the 32 subbands instead of in just one subband.

The polyphase filter bank uses (in addition to other intermediate data structures) a buffer X with room for 512 input samples. The buffer is a FIFO queue and always contains the most recent 512 samples input. Figure 7.21 shows the five main steps of the polyphase filtering algorithm.

1. Shift in 32 new input samples into FIFO buffer X

2. Window samples: $Z_i = C_i \times X_i$, for $i = 0, 1, \ldots, 511$

3. Partial computation: $Y_i = \sum_{j=0}^{7} Z_{i+64j}$, for $i = 0, 1, \ldots, 63$

4. Compute 32 signals: $S_i = \sum_{k=0}^{63} M_{i,k} \times Y_k$, for $i = 0, 1, \ldots, 31$

5. Output the 32 subband signals S_i

Figure 7.21: Polyphase Filter Bank.

The next 32 audio samples read from the input are shifted into the buffer. Thus, the buffer always holds the 512 most recent audio samples. The signals $S_t[i]$ for the 32 subbands are computed by

$$S_t[i] = \sum_{k=0}^{63} \sum_{j=0}^{7} M_{i,k} \big(C[k + 64j] \times X[k + 64j] \big), \; i = 0, \ldots, 31. \qquad (7.4)$$

The notation $S_t[i]$ stands for the signal of subband i at time t. Vector C contains 512 coefficients of the analysis window and is fully specified by the standard. Some of the subband filter coefficients C_i are listed in Table 7.22a. M is the analysis matrix defined by

$$M_{i,k} = \cos \left(\frac{(2i + 1)(k - 16)\pi}{64} \right), \; i = 0, \ldots, 31, \; k = 0, \ldots, 63. \qquad (7.5)$$

Notice that the expression in parentheses in Equation (7.4) does not depend on i, while $M_{i,k}$ in Equation (7.5) does not depend on j. (This matrix is a modified version of the well-known DCT, so it is called the MDCT matrix.) This feature is a compromise that results in fewer arithmetic operations. In fact, the 32 signals $S_t[i]$ are computed by only $512 + 32 \times 64 = 2560$ multiplications and $64 \times 7 + 32 \times 63 = 2464$ additions, which come to about 80 multiplications and 80 additions per signal. Another point worth mentioning is the decimation of samples (Section 5.7). The entire filter bank produces 32 output signals for 32 input samples. Since each of the 32 filters produces 32 signals, its output has to be decimated, retaining only one signal per filter.

Figure 7.24a,b illustrates graphically the operations performed by the encoder and decoder during the polyphase filtering step. Part (a) of the figure shows how the X buffer holds 64 segments of 32 audio samples each. The buffer is shifted one segment to the right before the next segment of 32 new samples is read from the input stream and is entered on the left. After multiplying the X buffer by the coefficients of the C window, the products are moved to the Z vector. The contents of this vector are partitioned into segments of 64 numbers each, and the segments are added. The result is vector Y, which is multiplied by the MDCT matrix, to produce the final vector of 32 subband signals.

Part (b) of the figure illustrates the operations performed by the decoder. A group of 32 subband signals is multiplied by the IMDCT matrix $N_{i,k}$ to produce the V vector, consisting of two segments of 32 values each. The two segments are shifted into the V FIFO buffer from the left. The V buffer has room for the last 16 V vectors (i.e., 16×64, or 1024, values). A new 512-entry U vector is created from 32 alternate segments in the V buffer, as shown. The U vector is multiplied by the 512 coefficients D_i of the synthesis window (similar to the C_i coefficients of the analysis window used by the encoder), to create the W vector. Some of the D_i coefficients are listed in Table 7.22b. This vector is divided into 16 segments of 32 values each and the segments added. The result is 32 reconstructed audio samples. Figure 7.23 is a flowchart illustrating this process. The IMDCT synthesis matrix

i	C_i	i	C_i	i	C_i
0	0.000000000	252	−0.035435200	506	−0.000000477
1	−0.000000477	253	−0.035586357	507	−0.000000477
2	−0.000000477	254	−0.035694122	508	−0.000000477
3	−0.000000477	255	−0.035758972	509	−0.000000477
4	−0.000000477	256	−0.035780907	510	−0.000000477
5	−0.000000477	257	−0.035758972	511	−0.000000477
⋮		⋮			

(a)

i	D_i	i	D_i	i	D_i
0	0.000000000	252	−1.133926392	506	0.000015259
1	−0.000015259	253	−1.138763428	507	0.000015259
2	−0.000015259	254	−1.142211914	508	0.000015259
3	−0.000015259	255	−1.144287109	509	0.000015259
4	−0.000015259	256	−1.144989014	510	0.000015259
5	−0.000015259	257	−1.144287109	511	0.000015259
⋮		⋮			

(b)

Table 7.22: Coefficients of (a) The Analysis and (b) The Synthesis Window.

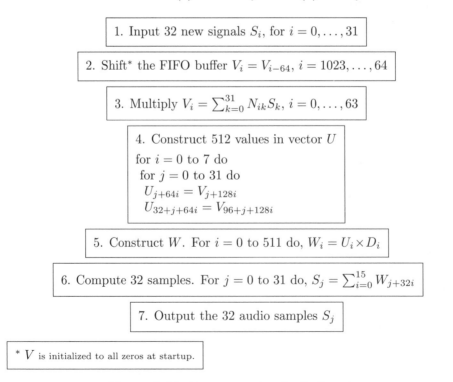

1. Input 32 new signals S_i, for $i = 0, \ldots, 31$

2. Shift* the FIFO buffer $V_i = V_{i-64}$, $i = 1023, \ldots, 64$

3. Multiply $V_i = \sum_{k=0}^{31} N_{ik} S_k$, $i = 0, \ldots, 63$

4. Construct 512 values in vector U
   for $i = 0$ to 7 do
   for $j = 0$ to 31 do
   $U_{j+64i} = V_{j+128i}$
   $U_{32+j+64i} = V_{96+j+128i}$

5. Construct W. For $i = 0$ to 511 do, $W_i = U_i \times D_i$

6. Compute 32 samples. For $j = 0$ to 31 do, $S_j = \sum_{i=0}^{15} W_{j+32i}$

7. Output the 32 audio samples S_j

* V is initialized to all zeros at startup.

Figure 7.23: Reconstructing Audio Samples.

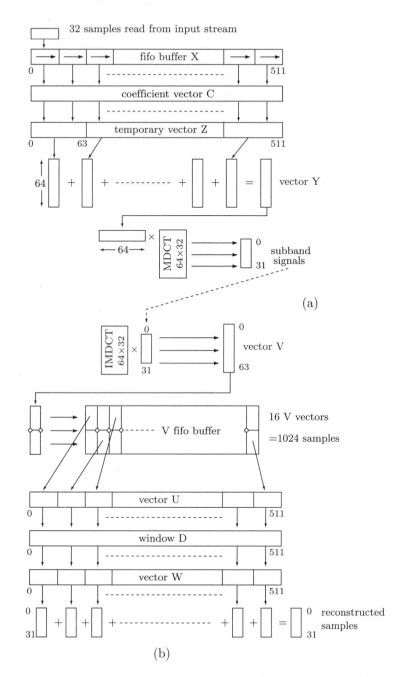

Figure 7.24: MPEG Audio Encoder (a) and Decoder (b).

$N_{i,k}$ is given by

$$N_{i,k} = \cos\left(\frac{(2k+1)(i+16)\pi}{64}\right), \ i = 0,\ldots,63, \ k = 0,\ldots,31.$$

The subband signals computed by the filtering stage of the encoder are collected and packaged into *frames* containing 384 signals (in layer I) or 1152 signals (in layers II and III) each. The signals in a frame are then scaled and quantized according to the psychoacoustic model used by the encoder and the bit allocation algorithm. The quantized values, together with the scale factors and quantization information (the number of quantization levels in each subband) are written on the compressed stream (layer III also uses Huffman codes to encode the quantized values even further).

7.6.2 Format of Compressed Data

In layer I, each frame consists of 12 signals per subband, for a total of $12\times32 = 384$ signals. In layers II and III, a frame contains 36 signals per subband, for a total of 1152 signals. The signals in the frame are quantized (this is how compression is achieved) and written on the compressed stream together with other information.

Each frame written on the output starts with a 32-bit header whose format is identical for the three layers. The header contains a synchronization code (12 1-bits) and 20 bits of coding parameters listed below. If error protection is used, the header is immediately followed by a 16-bit CRC check word (Section 3.23) that uses the generating polynomial $CRC_{16}(x) = x^{16} + x^{15} + x^2 + 1$. Next comes a frame of the quantized signals, followed by an (optional) ancillary data block. The formats of the last two items depend on the layer.

In layer I, the CRC 16-bit code is computed from the last 16 bits (bits 16–31) of the header and from the bit allocation information. In layer II, the CRC code is computed from these bits plus the scalefactor selection information. In layer III, the CRC code is computed from the last 16 bits of the header and also from either bits 0–135 of the audio data (in single-channel mode) or bits 0–255 of the audio data (in the other three modes, see field 8 below).

The synchronization code is used by the decoder to verify that what it is reading is, in fact, the header. This code is a string of 12 bits of 1, so the entire format of the compressed stream had to be designed to avoid an accidental occurrence of a string of 12 ones elsewhere.

The remaining 20 bits of the header are divided into 12 fields as follows:

Field 1. An ID bit whose value is 1 (this indicates that MPEG is used). A value of zero is reserved and is currently unused.

Field 2. Two bits to indicate the layer number. Valid values are 11—layer I, 10—layer II, and 01—layer III. The value 00 is reserved.

Field 3. An error protection indicator bit. A value of zero indicates that redundancy has been added to the compressed stream to help in error detection.

Field 4. Four bits to indicate the bitrate (Table 7.19). A zero index indicates a "fixed" bitrate, where a frame may contain an extra slot, depending on the padding bit (field 6).

Field 5. Two bits to indicate one of three sampling frequencies. The three values are 00—44.1 KHz, 01—48 KHz, and 10—32 KHz. The value 11 is reserved.

Field 6. One bit to indicate whether padding is used. Padding may add a slot (slots are discussed in Section 7.6.3) to the compressed stream after a certain number of frames, to make sure that the total size of the frames either equals or is slightly less than the sum

$$\sum_{\text{first frame}}^{\text{current frame}} \frac{\text{frame-size} \times \text{bitrate}}{\text{sampling frequency}},$$

where frame-size is 384 signals for layer I and 1152 signals for layers II and III. The following algorithm may be used by the encoder to determine whether or not padding is necessary.

```
for first audio frame:
  rest:=0;
  padding:=no;
for each subsequent audio frame:
  if layer=I
    then dif:=(12 × bitrate) modulo (sampling-frequency)
    else dif:=(144 × bitrate) modulo (sampling-frequency);
  rest:=rest−dif;
  if rest<0 then
    padding:=yes;
    rest:=rest+(sampling-frequency)
  else padding:=no;
```

This algorithm has a simple interpretation. A frame is divided into N or $N+1$ slots, where N depends on the layer. For layer I, N is given by

$$N = 12 \times \frac{\text{bitrate}}{\text{sampling frequency}}.$$

For layers II and II, it is given by

$$N = 144 \times \frac{\text{bitrate}}{\text{sampling frequency}}.$$

If this does not produce an integer, the result is truncated and padding is used.

Padding is also mentioned in Section 7.6.3

Field 7. One bit for private use of the encoder. This bit will not be used by ISO/IEC in the future.

Field 8. A two-bit stereo mode field. Values are 00—stereo, 01—joint-stereo (intensity-stereo and/or ms-stereo), 10—dual-channel, and 11—single-channel.

Stereo information is encoded in one of four modes: stereo, dual channel, joint stereo, and ms-stereo. In the first two modes, samples from the two stereo channels are compressed and written on the output. The encoder does not check for any correlations between the two. The stereo mode is used to compress the left and right stereo channels, while the dual channel mode is used to compress different sets of audio samples, such as a bilingual broadcast. The joint stereo mode exploits redundancies between the left and right channels, since many times they are identical, similar, or differ by a small time lag. The ms-stereo mode ("ms" stands for "middle-side") is a special case of joint stereo, where two signals, a middle value M_i and a side value S_i, are encoded instead of the left and right audio channels L_i and R_i. The middle-side values are computed by the following sum and difference

$$L_i = \frac{M_i + S_i}{\sqrt{2}}, \text{ and } R_i = \frac{M_i - S_i}{\sqrt{2}}.$$

Field 9. A two-bit mode extension field. This is used in the joint-stereo mode. In layers I and II the bits indicate which subbands are in intensity-stereo. All other subbands are coded in "stereo" mode. The four values are:

  00—subbands 4–31 in intensity-stereo, bound=4.
  01—subbands 8–31 in intensity-stereo, bound=8.
  10—subbands 12–31 in intensity-stereo, bound=12.
  11—subbands 16–31 in intensity-stereo, bound=16.

In layer III these bits indicate which type of joint stereo coding method is applied. The values are

  00—intensity-stereo off, ms-stereo off.
  01—intensity-stereo on, ms-stereo off.
  10—intensity-stereo off, ms-stereo on.
  11—intensity-stereo on, ms-stereo on.

Field 10. Copyright bit. If the compressed stream is copyright protected, this bit should be 1.

Field 11. One bit indicating original/copy. A value of 1 indicates an original compressed stream.

Field 12. A 2-bit emphasis field. This indicates the type of de-emphasis that is used. The values are 00—none, 01—50/15 microseconds, 10—reserved, and 11 indicates CCITT J.17 de-emphasis.

Layer I: The 12 signals of each subband are scaled such that the largest one becomes one (or very close to one, but not greater than one). The psychoacoustic model and the bit allocation algorithm are invoked to determine the number of bits allocated to the quantization of each scaled signal in each subband (or, equivalently, the number of quantization levels). The scaled signals are then quantized. The number of quantization levels, the scale factors, and the 384 quantized signals are then placed in their areas in the frame, which is written on the output. Each bit allocation item is four bits, each scale factor is six bits, and each quantized sample occupies between two and 15 bits in the frame.

The number l of quantization levels and the number q of bits per quantized value are related by $2^q = l$. The bit allocation algorithm uses tables to determine q for each of the 32 subbands. The 32 values $q-1$ are then written, as 4-bit numbers, on the frame, for the use of the decoder. Thus, the 4-bit value 0000 read by the decoder from the frame for subband s indicates to the decoder that the 12 signals of s have been quantized coarsely to one bit each, while the value 1110 implies that the 16-bit signals have been finely quantized to 15 bits each. The value 1111 is not used, to avoid conflict with the synchronization code. The encoder decides many times to quantize all the 12 signals of a subband s to zero, and this is indicated in the frame by a different code. In such a case, the 4-bit value input from the frame for s is ignored by the decoder.

◇ **Exercise 7.7:** Explain why the encoder may decide to quantize 12 consecutive signals of subband s to zero.

The decoder multiplies the dequantized signal values by the scale factors found in the frame. There is one scale factor for the 12 signals of a subband. This scale factor is selected by the encoder from a table of 63 scale factors specified by the standard (Table 7.25). The scale factors in the table increase by a factor of $\sqrt[3]{2}$.

Index	scalefactor	Index	scalefactor	Index	scalefactor
0	2.00000000000000	21	0.01562500000000	42	0.00012207031250
1	1.58740105196820	22	0.01240157071850	43	0.00009688727124
2	1.25992104989487	23	0.00984313320230	44	0.00007689947814
3	1.00000000000000	24	0.00781250000000	45	0.00006103515625
4	0.79370052598410	25	0.00620078535925	46	0.00004844363562
5	0.62996052494744	26	0.00492156660115	47	0.00003844973907
6	0.50000000000000	27	0.00390625000000	48	0.00003051757813
7	0.39685026299205	28	0.00310039267963	49	0.00002422181781
8	0.31498026247372	29	0.00246078330058	50	0.00001922486954
9	0.25000000000000	30	0.00195312500000	51	0.00001525878906
10	0.19842513149602	31	0.00155019633981	52	0.00001211090890
11	0.15749013123686	32	0.00123039165029	53	0.00000961243477
12	0.12500000000000	33	0.00097656250000	54	0.00000762939453
13	0.09921256574801	34	0.00077509816991	55	0.00000605545445
14	0.07874506561843	35	0.00061519582514	56	0.00000480621738
15	0.06250000000000	36	0.00048828125000	57	0.00000381469727
16	0.04960628287401	37	0.00038754908495	58	0.00000302772723
17	0.03937253280921	38	0.00030759791257	59	0.00000240310869
18	0.03125000000000	39	0.00024414062500	60	0.00000190734863
19	0.02480314143700	40	0.00019377454248	61	0.00000151386361
20	0.01968626640461	41	0.00015379895629	62	0.00000120155435

Table 7.25: Layers I and II Scale Factors.

◇ **Exercise 7.8:** How does this increase translate to an increase in the decibel level?

Quantization is performed by the following simple rule: If the bit allocation algorithm allocates b bits to each quantized value, then the number n of quantization levels is determined by $b = \log_2(n + 1)$, or $2^b = n + 1$. The value $b = 3$, for example, results in $n = 7$ quantization values. Figure 7.26a,b shows examples of such quantization. The input signals being quantized have already been scaled to the interval $[-1, +1]$, and the quantization is midtread. For example, all input

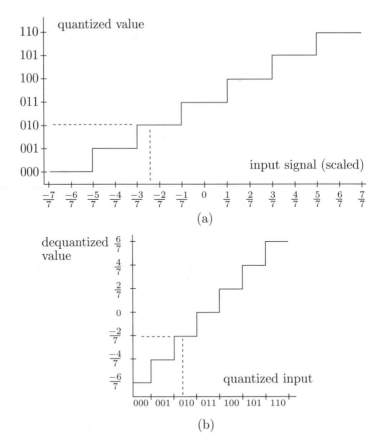

Figure 7.26: Examples of (a) Quantizer and (b) Dequantizer.

values in the range $[-1/7, -3/7]$ are quantized to 010 (dashed lines in the figure). Dequantization is also simple. The quantized value 010 is always dequantized to $-2/7$. Notice that quantized values range from 0 to $n-1$. The value $n = 11\ldots 1$ is never used, in order to avoid a conflict with the synchronization code.

Table 7.27 shows that the bit allocation algorithm for layer I can select the size of the quantized signals to be between 0 and 15 bits. For each of these sizes, the table lists the 4-bit allocation code that the encoder writes on the frame for the decoder's use, the number q of quantization levels (between 0 and $2^{15} - 1 = 32,767$, and the signal-to-noise ratio in decibels.

In practice, the encoder scales a signal S_i by a scale factor scf that is determined from Table 7.25, and quantizes the result by computing

$$S_{qi} = \left(A \left[\frac{S_i}{scf} \right] + B \right) \Big|_N,$$

where A and B are the constants listed in Table 7.28 (the three entries flagged by asterisks are used by layer II but not by layer I) and N is the number of bits needed

bit alloc	4-bit code	number of levels	SNR (dB)
0	0000	0	0.00
2	0001	3	7.00
3	0010	7	16.00
4	0011	15	25.28
5	0100	31	31.59
6	0101	63	37.75
7	0110	127	43.84
8	0111	255	49.89
9	1000	511	55.93
10	1001	1023	61.96
11	1010	2047	67.98
12	1011	4095	74.01
13	1100	8191	80.03
14	1101	16383	86.05
15	1110	32767	92.01
invalid	1111		

Table 7.27: Bit Allocation and Quantization in Layer I.

to encode the number of quantization levels. (The vertical bar with subscript N means: Take the N most significant bits.) In order to avoid conflicts with the synchronization code, the most significant bit of the quantized value S_{qi} is inverted before that quantity is written on the output.

Layer II Format: This is an extension of the basic method outlined for layer I. Each frame now consists of 36 signals per subband, and both the bit allocation data and the scale factor information are coded more efficiently. Also, quantization can be much finer and can have up to $2^{16} - 1 = 65,535$ levels. A frame is divided into three parts, numbered 0, 1, and 2. Each part resembles a layer-I frame and contains 12 signals per subband. The bit allocation data is common to the three parts, but the information for the scale factors is organized differently. It can be common to all three parts, it can apply to just two of the three parts, or it can be specified for each part separately. This information consists of a 2-bit scale factor selection information (sfsi). This number indicates whether one, two, or three scale factors per subband are written in the frame, and how they are applied.

The bit allocation section of the frame is encoded more efficiently by limiting the choice of quantization levels for the higher subbands and the lower bitrates. Instead of the four bits per subband used by layer I to specify the bit allocation choice, the number of bits used by layer II varies from 0 to 4 depending on the subband number. The MPEG standard contains a table that the encoder searches by subband number and bitrate to find the number of bits.

Quantization is similar to layer I, except that layer II can sometimes pack three consecutive quantized values in a single codeword. This can be done when the number of quantization levels is a power of 2, and it reduces the number of wasted bits.

number of levels	A	B
3	0.750000000	−0.250000000
5*	0.625000000	−0.375000000
7	0.875000000	−0.125000000
9*	0.562500000	−0.437500000
15	0.937500000	−0.062500000
31	0.968750000	−0.031250000
63	0.984375000	−0.015625000
127	0.992187500	−0.007812500
255	0.996093750	−0.003906250
511	0.998046875	−0.001953125
1023	0.999023438	−0.000976563
2047	0.999511719	−0.000488281
4095	0.999755859	−0.000244141
8191	0.999877930	−0.000122070
16383	0.999938965	−0.000061035
32767	0.999969482	−0.000030518
65535*	0.999984741	−0.000015259

Table 7.28: Quantization Coefficients in Layers I and II.

7.6.3 Encoding: Layers I and II

The MPEG standard specifies a table of scale factors. For each subband, the encoder compares the largest of the 12 signals to the values in the table, finds the next largest value, and uses the table index of that value to determine the scale factor for the 12 signals. In layer II, the encoder determines three scale factors for each subband, one for each of the three parts. It calculates the difference between the first two and the last two and uses the two differences to decide whether to encode one, two, or all three scale factors. This process is described in Section 7.6.4.

The bit allocation information in layer II uses 2–4 bits. The *scale factor select information* (sfsi) is two bits. The scale factor itself uses six bits. Each quantized signal uses 2–16 bits, and there may be ancillary data.

The standard describes two psychoacoustic models. Each produces a quantity called the *signal to mask ratio* (SMR) for each subband. The bit allocation algorithm uses this SMR and the SNR from Table 7.27 to compute the *mask to noise* ratio (MNR) as the difference

$$\text{MNR} = \text{SMR} - \text{SNR dB.}$$

The MNR indicates the discrepancy between waveform error and perceptual measurement, and the idea is that the subband signals can be compressed as much as the MNR. As a result, each iteration of the bit allocation loop determines the minimum MNR of all the subbands. The basic principle of bit allocation is to minimize the MNR over a frame while using not more than the number of bits B_f available for the frame.

In each iteration, the algorithm computes the number of bits B_f available to encode a frame. This is computed from the sample rate (number of samples input per second, normally $2 \times 44{,}100$) and the bitrate (number of bits written on the compressed output per second). The calculation is

$$\text{frames/sec} = \frac{\text{samples/second}}{\text{samples/frame}}, \quad B_f = \frac{\text{bits/second}}{\text{frames/second}} = \frac{\text{bitrate}}{\text{sampling rate}}.$$

Thus, B_f is measured in bits/frame. The frame header occupies 32 bits, and the CRC, if used, requires 16 bits. The bit allocation data is four bits per subband. If ancillary data are used, its size is also determined. These amounts are subtracted from the value of B_f computed earlier.

The main step of the bit allocation algorithm is to maximize the minimum MNR for all subbands by assigning the remaining bits to the scale factors and the quantized signals. In layer I, the scale factors take six bits per subband, but in layer II there are several ways to encode them (Section 7.6.4).

The main bit allocation step is a loop. It starts with allocating zero bits to each of the subbands. If the algorithm assigns zero bits to a particular subband, then no bits will be needed for the scale factors and the quantized signals. Otherwise, the number of bits assigned depends on the layer number and on the number of scale factors (1, 2, or 3) encoded for the subband. The algorithm computes the SNR and MNR for each subband and searches for the subband with the lowest MNR whose bit allocation has not yet reached its maximum limit. The bit allocation for that subband is incremented by one level, and the number of extra bits needed is subtracted from the balance of available bits. This is repeated until the balance of available bits reaches zero or until all the subbands have reached their maximum limit.

The format of the compressed output is shown in Figure 7.29. Each frame consists of between two and four parts. The frame is organized in slots, where a slot size is 32 bits in layer I, and 8 bits in layers II and III. Thus, the number of slots is $B_f/32$ or $B_f/8$. If the last slot is not full, it is padded with zeros.

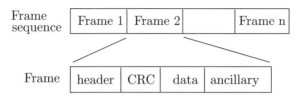

Figure 7.29: Format of Compressed Output.

The relation between sampling rate, frame size, and number of slots is easy to visualize. Typical layer I parameters are (1) a sampling rate of 48,000 samples/s, (2) a bitrate of 64,000 bits/s, and (3) 384 quantized signals per frame. The decoder has to decode $48{,}000/384 = 125$ frames per second. Thus, each frame has to be decoded in 80 ms. In order to output 125 frames in 64,000 bits, each frame must have $B_f = 512$ bits available to encode it. The number of slots per frame is thus $512/32 = 16$.

A similar example assumes (1) a sampling rate of 32,000 samples/s, (2) a bitrate of 64,000 bits/s, and (3) 384 quantized signals per frame. The decoder has to decode $32,000/384 = 83.33$ frames per second. Thus, each frame has to be decoded in 12 ms. In order to output 83.33 frames in 64000 bits, each frame must have $B_f = 768$ bits available to encode it. The number of slots per frame is thus $768/32 = 24$.

⋄ **Exercise 7.9:** Do the same calculation for a sampling rate of 44,100 samples/s.

7.6.4 Encoding: Layer II

A frame in layer II consists of 36 subband signals, organized in 12 granules as shown in Figure 7.30. Three scale factors $scf1$, $scf2$, and $scf3$ are computed for each subband, one scale factor for each group of 12 signals. This is done in six steps as follows:

Step 1: The maximum of the absolute values of these 12 signals is determined.
Step 2: This maximum is compared to the values in column "scalefactors" of Table 7.25, and the smallest entry that is greater than the maximum is noted.
Step 3: The value in column "Index" of that entry is denoted by scf_i.
Step 4: After repeating steps 1–3 for $i = 1, 2, 3$, two differences, $D_1 = scf1 - scf2$ and $D_2 = scf2 - scf3$, are computed.
Step 5: Two "class" values, for D_1 and D_2, are determined by

$$\text{Class}_i = \begin{cases} 1, & \text{if } Di \leq -3, \\ 2, & \text{if } -3 < Di < 0, \\ 3, & \text{if } Di = 0, \\ 4, & \text{if } 0 < Di < 3, \\ 5, & \text{if } Di \geq 3. \end{cases}$$

Step 6: Depending on the two classes, three scale factors are determined from Table 7.31, column "s. fact. used." The values 1, 2, and 3 in this column mean the first, second, and third scale factors, respectively, within a frame. The value 4 means the maximum of the three scale factors. The column labeled "trans. patt." indicates those scale factors that are actually written on the compressed stream.

Table 7.32 lists the four values of the 2-bit *scale factor select information* (scfsi).

As an example, suppose that the two differences D_1 and D_2 between the three scale factors A, B, and C of the three parts of a certain subband are classified as $(1, 1)$. Table 7.31 shows that the transmission factor is 123 and the select information is 0. The top rule in Table 7.32 shows that scfsi of 0 means that each of the three scale factors is encoded separately in the output stream as a 6-bit number. (This rule is used by both encoder and decoder.) The three scale factors occupy, in this case, 18 bits, so there is no savings compared to layer I encoding.

We next assume that the two differences are classified as $(1, 3)$. Table 7.31 shows that the scale factor is 122 and the select information is 3. The bottom rule in Table 7.32 shows that a scfsi of 3 means that only scale factors A and B need be encoded (since $B = C$), occupying just 12 bits. The decoder assigns the first six

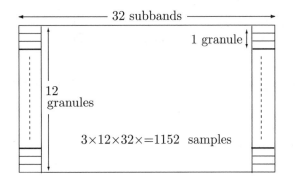

Figure 7.30: Organization of Layer II Subband Signals.

class 1	class 2	s. fact used	trans. patt.	s. fact. select	class 1	class 2	s. fact used	trans. patt.	s. fact. select
1	1	123	123	0	3	4	333	3	2
1	2	122	12	3	3	5	113	13	1
1	3	122	12	3	4	1	222	2	2
1	4	133	13	3	4	2	222	2	2
1	5	123	123	0	4	3	222	2	2
2	1	113	13	1	4	4	333	3	2
2	2	111	1	2	4	5	123	123	0
2	3	111	1	2	5	1	123	123	0
2	4	444	4	2	5	2	122	12	3
2	5	113	13	1	5	3	122	12	3
3	1	111	1	2	5	4	133	13	3
3	2	111	1	2	5	5	123	123	0
3	3	111	1	2					

Table 7.31: Layer II Scale Factor Transmission Patterns.

scsfi	# of coded scale factors	decoding scale factor
0 (00)	3	scf1, scf2, scf3
1 (01)	2	1st is scf1 and scf2
		2nd is scf3
2 (10)	1	one scale factor
3 (11)	2	1st is scf1
		2nd is scf2 and scf3

Table 7.32: Layer II Scale Factor Select Information.

bits as the value of A, and the following six bits as the values of both B and C. Thus, the redundancy in the scale factors has been translated to a small savings.

⋄ **Exercise 7.10:** How are the three scale factors encoded when the two differences are classifieds as $(3, 2)$?

Quantization in layer II is similar to that of layer I with the difference that the two constants C and D of Table 7.33 are used instead of the constants A and B. Another difference is the use of grouping. Table 7.33 shows that grouping is required when the number of quantization levels is 3, 5, or 9. In any of these cases, three signals are combined into one codeword, which is then quantized. The decoder reconstructs the three signals $s(1)$, $s(2)$, and $s(3)$ from the codeword w by

$$w = 0,$$
$$\text{for } i = 0 \text{ to } 2,$$
$$s(i) = w \bmod \text{nos},$$
$$w = w \div \text{nos},$$

where "mod" is the modulo function, "÷" denotes integer division, and "nos" denotes the number of quantization steps.

Figure 7.34a,b shows the format of a frame in both layers I and II. In layer I (part (a) of the figure), there are 384 signals per frame. Assuming a sampling rate of 48,000 samples/s and a bitrate of 64,000 bits/s, such a frame must be fully decoded in 80 ms, for a decoding rate of 125 frames/s.

⋄ **Exercise 7.11:** What is a typical frame rate for layer II?

7.6.5 Psychoacoustic Models

The task of a psychoacoustic model is to make it possible for the encoder to easily decide how much quantization noise to allow in each subband. This information is then used by the bit allocation algorithm, together with the number of available bits, to determine the number of quantization levels for each subband. The MPEG audio standard specifies two psychoacoustic models. Either model can be used with any layer, but only model II generates the specific information needed by layer III. In practice, model I is the only one used in layers I and II. Layer III can use either model, but it achieves better results when using model II.

The MPEG standard allows considerable freedom in the way the models are implemented. The sophistication of the model that is actually implemented in a given MPEG audio encoder depends on the desired compression factor. For consumer applications, where large compression factors are not critical, the psychoacoustic model can be completely eliminated. In such a case, the bit allocation algorithm does not use an SMR (signal to mask ratio). It simply assigns bits to the subband with the minimum SNR (signal to noise ratio).

A complete description of the models is outside the scope of this book and can be found in the text of the MPEG audio standard [ISO/IEC 93], pp. 109–139. The main steps of the two models are as follows:

number of steps	C	D	grouping	samples/code	bits/code
3	1.3333333333	0.5000000000	yes	3	5
5	1.6000000000	0.5000000000	yes	3	7
7	1.1428571428	0.2500000000	no	1	3
9	1.7777777777	0.5000000000	yes	3	10
15	1.0666666666	0.1250000000	no	1	4
31	1.0322580645	0.0625000000	no	1	5
63	1.0158730158	0.0312500000	no	1	6
127	1.0078740157	0.0156250000	no	1	7
255	1.0039215686	0.0078125000	no	1	8
511	1.0019569471	0.0039062500	no	1	9
1023	1.0009775171	0.0019531250	no	1	10
2047	1.0004885197	0.0009765625	no	1	11
4095	1.0002442002	0.0004882812	no	1	12
8191	1.0001220852	0.0002441406	no	1	13
16383	1.0000610388	0.0001220703	no	1	14
32767	1.0000305185	0.0000610351	no	1	15
65535	1.0000152590	0.0000305175	no	1	16

Table 7.33: Quantization Classes for Layer II.

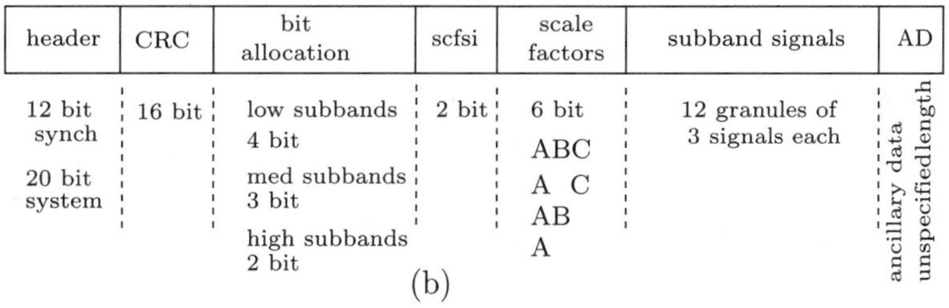

Figure 7.34: Organization of Layers I and II Output Frames.

1. A Fourier transform is used to convert the original audio samples to their frequency domain. This transform is separate and different from the polyphase filters because the models need finer frequency resolution in order to accurately determine the masking threshold.

2. The resulting frequencies are grouped into critical bands, not into the same 32 subbands used by the main part of the encoder.

3. The spectral values of the critical bands are separated into tonal (sinusoid-like) and nontonal (noise-like) components.

4. Before the noise masking thresholds for the different critical bands can be determined, the model applies a masking function to the signals in the different critical bands. This function has been determined empirically, by experimentation.

5. The model computes a masking threshold for each subband.

6. The SMR (signal to mask ratio) is calculated for each subband. It is the signal energy in the subband divided by the minimum masking threshold for the subband. The set of 32 SMRs, one per subband, constitutes the output of the model.

7.6.6 Encoding: Layer III

Layer III uses a much more refined and complex algorithm than the first two layers. This is reflected in the compression factors, which are much higher. The difference between layer III and layers I and II starts at the very first step, filtering. The same polyphase filter bank (Table 7.22a) is used, but it is followed by a modified version of the discrete cosine transform. The MDCT corrects some of the errors introduced by the polyphase filters and also subdivides the subbands to bring them closer to the critical bands. The layer III decoder has to use the inverse MDCT, so it has to work harder. The MDCT can be performed on either a short block of 12 samples (resulting in six transform coefficients) or a long block of 36 samples (resulting in 18 transform coefficients). Regardless of the block size chosen, consecutive blocks transformed by the MDCT have considerable overlap, as shown in Figure 7.35. In this figure, the blocks are shown above the thick line, and the resulting groups of 18 or 6 coefficients are below the line. The long blocks produce better frequency spectrum for stationary sound (sound where adjacent samples don't differ much), while the short blocks are preferable when the sound varies often.

The MDCT uses n input samples x_k (where n is either 36 or 12) to obtain $n/2$ (i.e., 18 or 6) transform coefficients S_i. The transform and its inverse are given by

$$S_i = \sum_{k=0}^{n-1} x_k \cos\left(\frac{\pi}{2n}\left[2k+1+\frac{n}{2}\right](2i+1)\right), \ i = 0, 1, \ldots, \frac{n}{2} - 1,$$

$$x_k = \sum_{i=0}^{n/2-1} S_i \cos\left(\frac{\pi}{2n}\left[2k+1+\frac{n}{2}\right](2i+1)\right), \ k = 0, 1, \ldots, n-1.$$

The size of a short block is one-third that of a long block, so they can be mixed. When a frame is constructed, the MDCT can use all long blocks, all short blocks (three times as many), or long blocks for the two lowest-frequency subbands and short blocks for the remaining 30 subbands. This is a compromise where the long

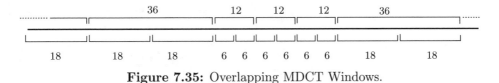

Figure 7.35: Overlapping MDCT Windows.

blocks provide finer frequency resolution for the lower frequencies, where it is most useful, and the short blocks maintain better time resolution for the high frequencies.

Since the MDCT provides better frequency resolution, it has to result in poorer time resolution because of the uncertainty principle (Section 5.3). What happens in practice is that the quantization of the MDCT coefficients causes errors that are spread over time and cause audible distortions that manifest themselves as preechoes (read: "pre-echoes").

The psychoacoustic model used by layer III has extra features that detect conditions for preechoes. In such cases, layer III uses a complex bit allocation algorithm that borrows bits from the pool of available bits in order to temporarily increase the number of quantization levels and thus reduce preechoes. Layer III can also switch to short MDCT blocks, thereby reducing the size of the time window, if it "suspects" that conditions are favorable for preechoes.

(The layer-III psychoacoustic model calculates a quantity called "psychoacoustic entropy" (PE) and the layer-III encoder "suspects" that conditions are favorable for preechoes if PE > 1800.)

The MDCT coefficients go through some processing to remove artifacts caused by the frequency overlap of the 32 subbands. This is called *aliasing reduction*. Only the long blocks are sent to the aliasing reduction procedure. The MDCT uses 36 input samples to compute 18 coefficients, and the aliasing reduction procedure uses a butterfly operation between two sets of 18 coefficients. This operation is illustrated graphically in Figure 7.36a with a C-language code shown in Figure 7.36b. Index i in the figure is the distance from the last line of the previous block to the first line of the current block. Eight butterflies are computed, with different values of the weights cs_i and ca_i that are given by

$$cs_i = \frac{1}{\sqrt{1 + c_i^2}}, \quad ca_i = \frac{c_i}{\sqrt{1 + c_i^2}}, \quad i = 0, 1, \ldots, 7.$$

The eight c_i values specified by the standard are -0.6, -0.535, -0.33, -0.185, -0.095, -0.041, -0.0142, and -0.0037. Figures 7.36c,d show the details of a single butterfly for the encoder and decoder, respectively.

Quantization in layer III is nonuniform. The quantizer raises the values to be quantized to 3/4 power before quantization. This provides a more consistent SNR. The decoder reverses this operation by dequantizing a value and raising it to 4/3 power. The quantization is done by

$$is(i) = \text{nint}\left[\left(\frac{xr(i)}{\text{quant}}\right)^{3/4} - 0.0946\right],$$

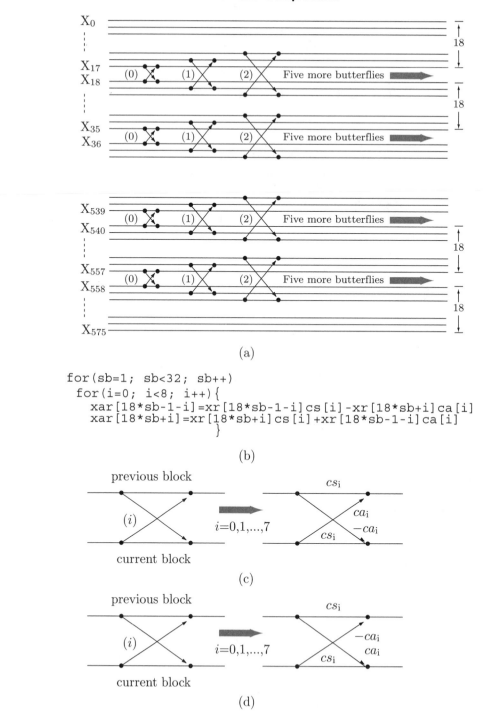

(a)

```
for(sb=1; sb<32; sb++)
  for(i=0; i<8; i++){
    xar[18*sb-1-i]=xr[18*sb-1-i]cs[i]-xr[18*sb+i]ca[i]
    xar[18*sb+i]=xr[18*sb+i]cs[i]+xr[18*sb-1-i]ca[i]
                }
```

(b)

(c)

(d)

Figure 7.36: Layer III Aliasing Reduction Butterfly.

where $xr(i)$ is the absolute value of the signal of subband i, "quant" is the quantization step size, "nint" is the nearest-integer function, and $is(i)$ is the quantized value. As in layers I and II, the quantization is midtread, i.e., values around zero are quantized to zero and the quantizer is symmetric about zero.

In layers I and II, each subband can have its own scale factor. Layer III uses *bands* of scale factors. These bands cover several MDCT coefficients each, and their widths are close to the widths of the critical bands. There is a noise allocation algorithm that selects values for the scale factors.

Layer III uses Huffman codes to compress the quantized values even further. The encoder produces 18 MDCT coefficients per subband. It sorts the resulting 576 coefficients ($= 18 \times 32$) by increasing order of frequency (for short blocks, there are three sets of coefficients within each frequency). Notice that the 576 MDCT coefficients correspond to 1152 transformed audio samples. The set of sorted coefficients is divided into three regions, and each region is encoded with a different set of Huffman codes. This is because the values in each region have a different statistical distribution. The values for the higher frequencies tend to be small and have runs of zeros, whereas the values for the lower frequencies tend to be large. The code tables are provided by the standard (32 tables on pages 54–61 of [ISO/IEC 93]). Dividing the quantized values into three regions also helps to control error propagation.

Starting at the values for the highest frequencies, where there are many zeros, the encoder selects the first region as the continuous run of zeros from the highest frequency. It is rare, but possible, not to have any run of zeros. The run is limited to an even number of zeros. This run does not have to be encoded, since its value can be deduced from the sizes of the other two regions. Its size, however, should be even, since the other two regions code their values in even-numbered groupings.

The second region consists of a continuous run of the three values -1, 0, and 1. This is called the "count1" region. Each Huffman code for this region encodes four consecutive values, so the number of codes must be $3^4 = 81$. The length of this region must, of course, be a multiple of 4.

The third region, known as the "big values" region, consists of the remaining values. It is (optionally) further divided into three subregions, each with its own Huffman code table. Each Huffman code encodes two values.

The largest Huffman code table specified by the standard has 16×16 codes. Larger values are encoded using an escape mechanism.

A frame F in layer III is organized as follows: It starts with the usual 32-bit header, which is followed by the optional 16-bit CRC. This is followed by 59 bits of side information. The last part of the frame is the main data. The side information is followed by a segment of main data (the side information contains, among other data, the length of the segment) but the data in this segment does not have to be that of frame F! The segment may contain main data from several frames because of the encoder's use of a *bit reservoir*.

The concept of the bit reservoir has already been mentioned. The encoder can borrow bits from this reservoir when it decides to increase the number of quantization levels because it suspects preechoes. The encoder can also donate bits to the reservoir when it needs fewer than the average number of bits to encode a frame. Borrowing, however, can be done only from past donations; the reservoir cannot have a negative number of bits.

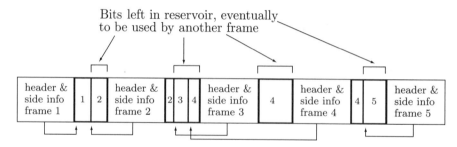

Figure 7.37: Layer III Compressed Stream.

The side information of a frame includes a 9-bit pointer that points to the start of the main data for the frame, and the entire concept of main data, fixed-size segments, pointers, and bit reservoirs is illustrated in Figure 7.37. In this diagram, frame 1 needed only about half of its bit allocation, so it left the other half in the reservoir, where it was eventually used by frame 2. Frame 2 needed a little additional space in its "own" segment, leaving the rest of the segment in the reservoir. This was eventually used by frames 3 and 4. Frame 3 did not need any of its own segment, so the entire segment was left in the reservoir, and was eventually used by frame 4. That frame also needed some of its own segment, and the rest was used by frame 5.

Bit allocation in layer III is similar to that in the other layers, but includes the added complexity of noise allocation. The encoder (Figure 7.38) computes the bit allocation, performs the actual quantization of the subband signals, encodes them with the Huffman codes, and counts the total number of bits generated in this process. This is the bit allocation inner loop. The noise allocation algorithm (also called analysis-by-synthesis procedure) becomes an outer loop where the encoder calculates the quantization noise (i.e., it dequantizes and reconstructs the subband signals and computes the differences between each signal and its reconstructed counterpart). If it finds that certain scale-factor bands have more noise than what the psychoacoustic model allows, the encoder increases the number of quantization levels for these bands, and repeats the process. This process terminates when any of the following three conditions becomes true:

1. All the scale-factor bands have the allowed noise or less.
2. The next iteration would require a requantization of ALL the scale-factor bands.
3. The next iteration would need more bits than are available in the bit reservoir.

⋄ **Exercise 7.12:** Layer III is extremely complex and hard to implement. In view of this, how is it that there are so many free and low-cost programs available to play .mp3 audio files on all computer platforms?

Bibliography

Brandenburg, KarlHeinz and Gerhard Stoll (1994) "ISO-MPEG-1 Audio: A Generic Standard for Coding of High-Quality Digital Audio," *Journal of the Audio Engineering Society*, **42**(10):780–792, October.

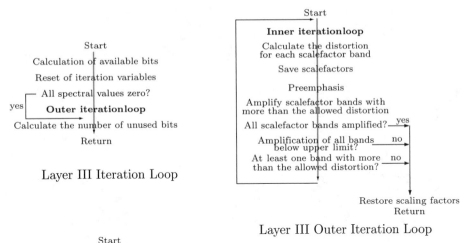

Layer III Iteration Loop

Layer III Outer Iteration Loop

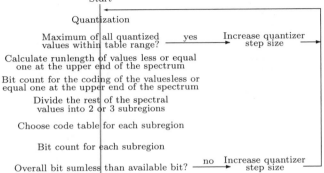

Layer III Inner Iteration Loop

Figure 7.38: Layer III Iteration Loop.

ISO/IEC (1993) International Standard IS 11172-3 "Information Technology—Coding of Moving Pictures and Associated Audio for Digital Storage Media at up to about 1.5 Mbits/s—Part 3: Audio."

MPEG (2000), see URL http://www.mpeg.org/.

Pan, Davis Yen (1995) "A Tutorial on MPEG/Audio Compression," *IEEE Multimedia*, **2**:60–74, Summer.

Rao, K. R., and J. J. Hwang (1996) *Techniques and Standards for Image, Video, and Audio Coding*, Upper Saddle River, NJ, Prentice Hall.

Shlien, Seymour (1994) "Guide to MPEG-1 Audio Standard," *IEEE Transactions on Broadcasting* **40**(4):206–218, December.

Sounds good to me.

—Jason James Richter (as Jesse), *Free Willy (1993)*

8
Other Methods

Previous chapters discuss the main classes of compression methods: RLE, statistical methods, and dictionary-based methods. There are data compression methods that are not easy to classify and do not clearly belong in any of the classes discussed so far. A few such methods are described here.

■ The Burrows-Wheeler method (Section 8.1) starts with a string S of n symbols and scrambles (i.e., permutes) them into another string L that satisfies two conditions: (1) Any area of L will tend to have a concentration of just a few symbols. (2) It is possible to reconstruct the original string S from L.

■ The technique of *symbol ranking* (Section 8.2) uses context to rank symbols rather than assign them probabilities.

■ ACB is a new method, based on an associative dictionary (Section 8.3). It has features that relate it to the traditional dictionary-based methods as well as to the symbol ranking method.

■ Section 8.4 is a description of the sort-based context similarity method. This method uses the context of a symbol in a way reminiscent of ACB. It also assigns ranks to symbols, and this feature relates it to the Burrows-Wheeler method and also to symbol ranking.

■ The special case of *sparse binary strings* is discussed in Section 8.5. Such strings can be compressed very efficiently due to the large number of consecutive zeros they contain.

■ Compression methods that are based on words rather than individual symbols are the subject of Section 8.6.

■ Textual image compression is the topic of Section 8.7. When a printed document has to be saved in the computer, it has to be scanned first, a process that converts it into an image typically containing millions of pixels. The complex method described here has been developed for this kind of data, which forms a special type of image, a *textual image*. Such an image is made of pixels, but most of the pixels are grouped to form characters, and the number of different groups is not large.

■   The FHM method (for Fibonacci, Huffman, and Markov) is an unusual, special-purpose method for the compression of curves.

■   Dynamic Markov coding uses finite-state machines to estimate the probability of symbols, and arithmetic coding to actually encode them. This is a compression method for two-symbol (binary) alphabets.

■   Sequitur, Section 8.10, is a method especially suited for the compression of semi-structured text. It is based on context-free grammars.

■   Section 8.11 is a detailed description of edgebreaker, a highly original method for compressing the connectivity information of a triangle mesh. This method and its various extensions may become the standard for compressing polygonal surfaces, one of the most common surface types used in computer graphics. Edgebreaker is an example of a *geometric compression* method.

8.1 The Burrows-Wheeler Method

Most compression methods operate in the *streaming mode*, where the codec inputs a byte or several bytes, processes them, and continues until an end-of-file is sensed. The Burrows-Wheeler (BW) method, described in this section, works in a *block mode*, where the input stream is read block by block and each block is encoded separately as one string. The method is thus also referred to as *block sorting*. The BW method is general purpose, it works well on images, sound, and text, and can achieve very high compression ratios (1 bit per byte or even better).

The main idea of the BW method is to start with a string S of n symbols and to scramble them into another string L that satisfies two conditions:

1. Any region of L will tend to have a concentration of just a few symbols. Another way of saying this is, if a symbol s is found at a certain position in L, then other occurrences of s are likely to be found nearby. This property means that L can easily and efficiently be compressed using the move-to-front method (Section 1.5), perhaps in combination with RLE. This also means that the BW method will work well only if n is large (at least several thousand symbols per string).

2. It is possible to reconstruct the original string S from L (a little more data may be needed for the reconstruction, in addition to L, but not much).

The mathematical term for scrambling symbols is *permutation*, and it is easy to show that a string of n symbols has $n!$ (pronounced "n factorial") permutations. This is a large number even for relatively small values of n, so the particular permutation used by BW has to be carefully selected. The BW codec proceeds in the following steps:

1. String L is created, by the encoder, as a permutation of S. Some more information, denoted by I, is also created, to be used later by the decoder in step 3.

2. The encoder compresses L and I and writes the results on the output stream. This step typically starts with RLE, continues with move-to-front coding, and finally applies Huffman coding.

3. The decoder reads the output stream and decodes it by applying the same methods as in 2 above but in reverse order. The result is string L and variable I.

4. Both L and I are used by the decoder to reconstruct the original string S.

> I do hate sums. There is no greater mistake than to call arithmetic an exact science. There are permutations and aberrations discernible to minds entirely noble like mine; subtle variations which ordinary accountants fail to discover; hidden laws of number which it requires a mind like mine to perceive. For instance, if you add a sum from the bottom up, and then from the top down, the result is always different.
>
> —Mrs. La Touche, *Mathematical Gazette*, v. 12

The first step is to understand how string L is created from S, and what information needs to be stored in I for later reconstruction. We use the familiar string "swiss⎵miss" to illustrate this process.

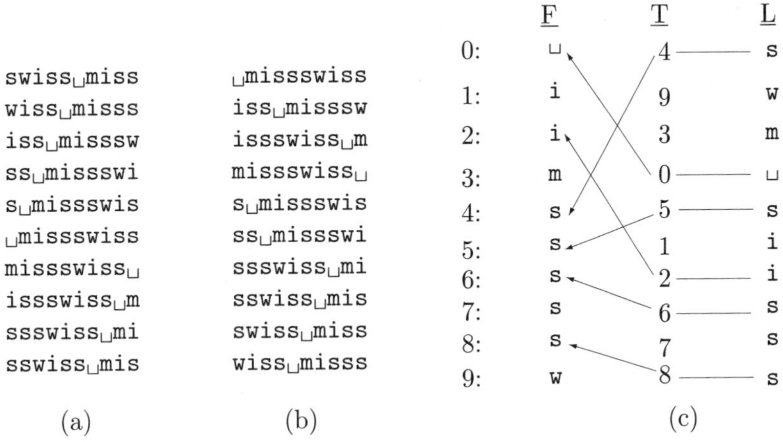

			F	T	L
swiss⎵miss	⎵missswiss	0:	⎵	4	s
wiss⎵misss	iss⎵misssw	1:	i	9	w
iss⎵misssw	issswiss⎵m	2:	i	3	m
ss⎵missswi	missswiss⎵	3:	m	0	⎵
s⎵missswis	s⎵missswis	4:	s	5	s
⎵missswiss	ss⎵missswi	5:	s	1	i
missswiss⎵	ssswiss⎵mi	6:	s	2	i
issswiss⎵m	sswiss⎵mis	7:	s	6	s
ssswiss⎵mi	swiss⎵miss	8:	s	7	s
sswiss⎵mis	wiss⎵misss	9:	w	8	s
(a)	(b)			(c)	

Figure 8.1: Principles of BW Compression.

The encoder constructs an $n \times n$ matrix where it stores string S in the top row, followed by $n-1$ copies of S, each cyclically shifted (rotated) one symbol to the left (Figure 8.1a). The matrix is then sorted lexicographically by rows (see Section 3.3 for lexicographic order), producing the sorted matrix of Figure 8.1b. Notice that every row and every column of each of the two matrices is a permutation of S and thus contains all n symbols of S. The permutation L selected by the encoder is the **last column** of the sorted matrix. In our example this is the string "swm⎵siisss". The only other information needed to eventually reconstruct S from L is the row number of the original string in the sorted matrix, which in our example is 8 (row and column numbering starts from 0). This number is stored in I.

It is easy to see why L contains concentrations of identical symbols. Assume that the words `bail`, `fail`, `hail`, `jail`, `mail`, `nail`, `pail`, `rail`, `sail`, `tail`, and `wail` appear somewhere in S. After sorting, all the permutations that start with `il` will appear together. All of them contribute an `a` to L, so L will have a concentration of `a`'s. Also, all the permutations starting with `ail` will end up together, contributing to a concentration of the letters `bfhjmnprstw` in one region of L.

We can now characterize the BW method by saying that it uses sorting to group together symbols based on their contexts. However, the method considers context on only one side of each symbol.

⬦ **Exercise 8.1:** (Easy.) The last column, L, of the sorted matrix contains concentrations of identical characters, which is why L is easy to compress. However, the first column, F, of the same matrix is even easier to compress, since it contains runs, not just concentrations, of identical characters. Why select column L and not column F?

Notice also that the encoder does not really have to construct the two $n \times n$ matrices (or even one of them) in memory. The practical details are discussed in Section 8.1.2, as well as the compression of L and I, but let's first see how the decoder works.

The decoder reads a compressed stream, decompresses it using Huffman and move-to-front (and perhaps also RLE), and then reconstructs string S from the decompressed L in three steps:

1. The first column of the sorted matrix (column F in Figure 8.1c) is constructed from L. This is a straightforward process, since F and L contain the same symbols (both are permutations of S) and F is sorted. The decoder simply sorts string L to obtain F.

2. While sorting L, the decoder prepares an auxiliary array T that shows the relations between elements of L and F (Figure 8.1c). The first element of T is 4, implying that the first symbol of L (the letter "s") is located in position 4 of F. The second element of T is 9, implying that the second symbol of L (the letter "w") is located in position 9 of F, and so on. The contents of T in our example is $(4, 9, 3, 0, 5, 1, 2, 6, 7, 8)$.

3. String F is no longer needed. The decoder uses L, I, and T to reconstruct S according to,

$$S[n - 1 - i] \leftarrow L[T^i[I]], \quad \text{for } i = 0, 1, \ldots, n - 1,$$
$$\text{where } T^0[j] = j, \text{ and } T^{i+1}[j] = T[T^i[j]]. \tag{8.1}$$

Here are the first two steps in this reconstruction:

$$S[10-1-0] = L[T^0[I]] = L[T^0[8]] = L[8] = s,$$
$$S[10-1-1] = L[T^1[I]] = L[T[T^0[I]]] = L[T[8]] = L[7] = s.$$

⋄ **Exercise 8.2:** Complete this reconstruction.

Before getting to the details of the compression, it may be interesting to understand why Equation (8.1) reconstructs S from L. The following arguments explain why this process works:

1. T is constructed such that $F[T[i]] = L[i]$ for $i = 0, \ldots, n$.
2. A look at the sorted matrix of Figure 8.1b shows that in each row i, symbol L[i] precedes symbol F[i] in the original string S (the word *precedes* has to be understood as *precedes cyclically*). Specifically, in row I (8 in our example), L[I] cyclically precedes F[I], but F[I] is the first symbol of S, so L[I] is the *last* symbol of S. The reconstruction starts with L[I] and reconstructs S from right to left.
3. $L[i]$ precedes $F[i]$ in S for $i = 0, \ldots, n-1$. Therefore $L[T[i]]$ precedes $F[T[i]]$, but $F[T[i]] = L[i]$. The conclusion is that $L[T[i]]$ precedes $L[i]$ in S.
4. The reconstruction thus starts with $L[I] = L[8] = \mathtt{s}$ (the last symbol of S) and proceeds with $L[T[I]] = L[T[8]] = L[7] = \mathtt{s}$ (the next-to-last symbol of S). This is why equation (8.1) correctly describes the reconstruction.

8.1.1 Compressing L

Compressing L is based on its main attribute, namely, it contains concentrations (although not necessarily runs) of identical symbols. Using RLE makes sense, but only as a first step in a multistep compression process. The main step in compressing L should use the move-to-front method (Section 1.5). This method is applied to our example L="swm␣siisss" as follows:

1. Initialize A to a list containing our alphabet A=("␣", "i", "m", "s", "w").
2. For $i := 0, \ldots, n-1$, encode symbol L_i as the number of symbols preceding it in A, and then move symbol L_i to the beginning of A.
3. Combine the codes of step 2 in a list C, which will be further compressed using Huffman or arithmetic coding.

The results are summarized in Figure 8.2a. The final list of codes is C = $(3, 4, 4, 3, 3, 4, 0, 1, 0, 0)$, illustrating how any concentration of identical symbols produces small codes. The first occurrence of i is assigned code 4 but the second one, code 0. The first two occurrences of s get code 3, but the next one gets code 1.

It is interesting to compare the codes in C, which are integers in the range $[0, n-1]$, to the codes obtained without the extra step of "moving to front." It is easy to encode L using the three steps above but without moving symbol L_i to the beginning of A. The result is $C' = (3, 4, 2, 0, 3, 1, 1, 3, 3, 3)$, a list of integers *in the same range* $[0, n-1]$. This is why applying move-to-front is not enough. Lists C and C' contain elements in the same range, but the elements of C are smaller on average. They should therefore be further encoded using Huffman coding or some other statistical method. Huffman codes for C can be assigned assuming that code 0 has the highest probability and code $n-1$, the smallest.

In our example, a possible set of Huffman codes is 0—0, 1—10, 2—110, 3—1110, 4—1111. Applying this set to C yields "1110|1111|1111|1110|1110|1111|0|10|0|0"; 29 bits. (Applying it to C' yields "1110|1111|110|0|1110|10|10|1110|1110|1110"; 32 bits.) Our original 10-character string "swiss␣miss" has thus been coded using 2.9 bits/character, a very good result. It should be noted that the Burrows-Wheeler

L	A	Code	C	A	L
s	⊔imsw	3	3	⊔imsw	s
w	s⊔imw	4	4	s⊔imw	w
m	ws⊔im	4	4	ws⊔im	m
⊔	mws⊔i	3	3	mws⊔i	⊔
s	⊔mwsi	3	3	⊔mwsi	s
i	s⊔mwi	4	4	s⊔mwi	i
i	is⊔mw	0	0	is⊔mw	i
s	is⊔mw	1	1	is⊔mw	s
s	si⊔mw	0	0	si⊔mw	s
s	si⊔mw	0	0	si⊔mw	s
	(a)			(b)	

Figure 8.2: Encoding/Decoding L by Move-to-Front.

method can easily achieve better compression than that when applied to longer strings (thousands of symbols).

⋄ **Exercise 8.3:** Given the string S="sssssssssh" calculate string L and its move-to-front compression.

Decoding C is done with the inverse of move-to-front. We assume that the alphabet list A is available to the decoder (it is either the list of all possible bytes or it is written by the encoder on the output stream). Figure 8.2b shows the details of decoding C = $(3, 4, 4, 3, 3, 4, 0, 1, 0, 0)$. The first code is 3, so the first symbol in the newly constructed L is the *fourth* one in A, or "s". This symbol is then moved to the front of A, and the process continues.

8.1.2 Implementation Hints

Since the Burrows-Wheeler method is efficient only for long strings (at least thousands of symbols), any practical implementation should allow for large values of n. The maximum value of n should be so large that two $n \times n$ matrices would not fit in the available memory (at least not comfortably), and all the encoder operations (preparing the permutations and sorting them) should be done with one-dimensional arrays of size n. In principle, it is enough to have just the original string S and the auxiliary array T in memory.

String S contains the original data, but surprisingly, it also contains all the necessary permutations. Since the only permutations we need to generate are rotations, we can generate permutation i of matrix 8.1a by scanning S from position i to the end, then continuing cyclically from the start of S to position $i - 1$. Permutation 5, for example, can be generated by scanning substring $(5, 9)$ of S ("⊔miss"), followed by substring $(0, 4)$ of S ("swiss"). The result is "⊔missswiss". The first step in a practical implementation would thus be to write a procedure that takes a parameter i and scans the corresponding permutation.

Any method used to sort the permutations has to compare them. Comparing two permutations can be done by scanning them in S, without having to move symbols or create new arrays.

Once the sorting algorithm determines that permutation i should be in position j in the sorted matrix (Figure 8.1b), it sets T[i] to j. In our example, the sort ends up with T = $(5, 2, 7, 6, 4, 3, 8, 9, 0, 1)$.

◊ **Exercise 8.4:** Show how T is used to create the encoder's main output, L and I.

Implementing the decoder is straightforward, since it does not need to create $n \times n$ matrices. The decoder inputs bits that are Huffman codes. It uses them to create the codes of C, decompressing each as it is created, using inverse move-to-front, into the next symbol of L. When L is ready, the decoder sorts it into F, generating array T in the process. Following that, it reconstructs S from L, T, and I. The decoder thus needs at most three structures at one time, the two strings L and F (having typically one byte per symbol), and the array T (with at least 2 bytes per pointer, to allow for large values of n).

Bibliography

Burrows, Michael, and D. J. Wheeler (1994) *A Block-Sorting Lossless Data Compression Algorithm*, Digital Systems Research Center report 124, Palo Alto, Calif, May 10.

Manber, U., and E. W. Myers (1993) "Suffix Arrays: A New Method for On-Line String Searches," *SIAM Journal on Computing* **22**(5):935–948, October.

McCreight, E. M. (1976) "A Space Economical Suffix Tree Construction Algorithm," *Journal of the ACM* **32**(2):262–272, April.

8.2 Symbol Ranking

Like so many other ideas, the idea of text compression by symbol ranking is due to Claude Shannon, the creator of information theory. In his classic paper on the information content of English text [Shannon 51] he describes a method for experimentally determining the entropy of such texts. In a typical experiment a passage of text has to be predicted, character by character, by a person (the examinee). In one version of the method the examinee predicts the next character and is then told by the examiner whether the prediction was correct or, if it was not, what the next character is. In another version, the examinee has to continue predicting until he obtains the right answer. The examiner then uses the number of wrong answers to estimate the entropy of the text.

As it turned out, in the latter version of the test, the human examinees were able to predict the next character in one guess about 79% of the time and rarely needed more than 3–4 guesses. Table 8.3 shows the distribution of guesses as published by Shannon.

# of guesses:	1	2	3	4	5	> 5
Probability:	79%	8%	3%	2%	2%	5%

Table 8.3: Probabilities of Guesses of English Text.

The fact that this probability is so skewed implies low entropy (Shannon's conclusion was an entropy of English text in the range of 0.6–1.3 bits per letter), which in turn implies the possibility of very good compression.

The symbol ranking method of this section [Fenwick 96] is based on the latter version of the Shannon test. The method uses the context C of the current symbol S (the N symbols preceding S) to prepare a list of symbols that are likely to follow C. The list is arranged from most likely to least likely. The position of S in this list (position numbering starts from 0) is then written by the encoder, after being suitably encoded, on the output stream. If the program performs as well as a human examinee, we can expect 79% of the symbols being encoded to result in 0 (first position in the ranking list), creating runs of zeros, which can easily be compressed by RLE.

The various context-based methods described elsewhere in this book, most notably PPM, use context to estimate symbol probabilities. They have to generate and output escape symbols when switching contexts. In contrast, symbol ranking does not estimate probabilities and does not use escape symbols. The absence of escapes seems to be the main feature contributing to the excellent performance of the method. Following is an outline of the main steps of the encoding algorithm.

Step 0: The *ranking index* (an integer counting the position of S in the ranked list) is set to zero.

Step 1: An LZ77-type dictionary is used, with a search buffer containing text that has already been input and encoded, and with a look-ahead buffer containing new, unprocessed, text. The most recent text in the search buffer becomes the *current context* C. The leftmost symbol, R, in the look-ahead buffer (immediately to the right of C) is the *current symbol.* The search buffer is scanned from right to left (from recent to older text) for strings matching C. This process is very similar to the one described in Section 3.14 (LZP compression). The longest match is selected (if there are several longest matches, the most recent one is selected). The match length, N, becomes the *current order.* The symbol P following the matched string (i.e., immediately to the right of it) is examined. This is the symbol ranked first by the algorithm. If P is identical to R, the search is over and the algorithm outputs the ranking index (which is currently zero).

Step 2: If P is different from R, the ranking index is incremented by 1, P is declared *excluded,* and the other order-N matches, if any, are examined in the same way. Assume that Q is the symbol following such a match. If Q is in the list of excluded symbols, then it is pointless to examine it, and the search continues with the next match. If Q has not been excluded, it is compared with R. If they are identical, the search is over, and the encoding algorithm outputs the ranking index. Otherwise the ranking index is incremented by 1, and Q is excluded.

Step 3: If none of the order-N matches is followed by a symbol identical to R, the order of the match is decremented by 1, and the search buffer is again scanned from right to left (from more recent text to older text) for strings of size $N-1$ that match C. For each failure in this scan, the ranking index is incremented by 1, and Q is excluded.

Step 4: When the match order gets all the way down to zero, symbol R is compared to symbols in a list containing the entire alphabet, again using exclusions and incrementing the ranking index. If the algorithm gets to this step it will find R in this list, and will output the current value of the ranking index (which will then normally be a large number).

Some implementation details are discussed here.

1. Implementing exclusion. When a string S that matches C is found, the symbol P immediately to the right of S is compared with R. If P and R are different, P should be declared excluded. This means that any future occurrences of P should be ignored. The first implementation of exclusion that comes to mind is a list to which excluded symbols are appended. Searching such a list, however, is time-consuming, and it is possible to do much better.

The method described here uses an array `excl` indexed by the alphabet symbols. If the alphabet consists, for example, of just the 26 letters, the array will have 26 locations indexed `a` through `z`. Figure 8.4 shows a simple implementation that requires just one step to determine whether a given symbol is excluded. Assume that the current context C is the string "...abc". We know that the `c` will remain in the context even if the algorithm has to go down all the way to order-1. The algorithm therefore prepares a pointer to `c` (to be called the *context index*). Assume that the scan finds another string `abc`, followed by a `y`, and compares it to the current context. They match, but they are followed by different symbols. The decision is to exclude `y`, and this is done by setting array element `excl[y]` to the context index (i.e., to point to `c`). As long as the algorithm scans for matches to the same context C, the context index will stay the same. If another matching string `abc` is later found, also followed by `y`, the algorithm compares `excl[y]` to the context index, finds that they are equal, so it knows that `y` has already been excluded. When switching to the next current context there is no need to initialize or modify the pointers in array `excl`.

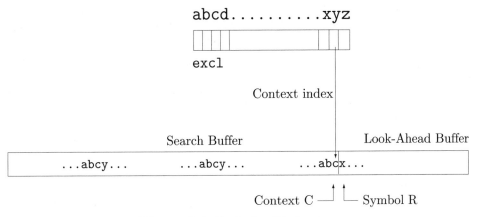

Figure 8.4: Exclusion Mechanism.

2. It has been mentioned earlier that scanning and finding matches to the current context C is done by a method similar to the one used by LZP. The reader should review Section 3.14 before reading ahead. Recall that N (the order) is initially unknown. The algorithm has to scan the search buffer and find the longest match to the current context. Once this is done, the length, N, of the match becomes the

current order. The process therefore starts by hashing the two rightmost symbols
of the current context C and using them to locate a possible match.

Figure 8.5 shows the current context "...amcde". We assume that it has already been matched to some string of length 3 (i.e., a string "...cde") and we try
to match it to a longer string. The two symbols "de" are hashed and produce a
pointer to string "lmcde". The problem is to compare the current context to "lmcde" and find whether and by how much they match. This is done by the following
three rules.

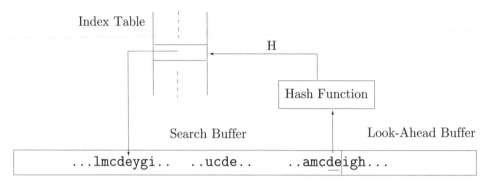

Figure 8.5: String Search and Comparison Method.

Rule 1: Compare the symbols preceding (i.e., to the left of) "cde" in the two
strings. In our example they are both "m", so the match is now of size 4. Repeat this
rule until it fails. It determines the order N of the match. Once the order is known
the algorithm may have to decrement it later and compare shorter strings. In such
a case this rule has to be modified. Instead of comparing the symbols *preceding* the
strings, it should compare the leftmost symbols of the two strings.

Rule 2: (We are still not sure whether the two strings are identical.) Compare
the middle symbols of the two strings. In our case, since the strings have a length
of 4, this would be either the c or the d. If the comparison fails, the strings are
different. Otherwise, Rule 3 is used.

Rule 3: Compare the strings symbol by symbol to finally determine whether
they are identical.

It seems unnecessarily cumbersome to go through three rules when only the
third one is really necessary. However, the first two rules are simple, and they
identify 90% of the cases where the two strings are different. Rule 3, which is slow,
has to be applied only if the first two rules have not identified the strings as different.
3. If the encoding algorithm has to decrement the order all the way down to 1, it
faces a special problem. It can no longer hash two symbols. Searching for order-1
matching strings (i.e., single symbols) therefore requires a different method which
is illustrated by Figure 8.6. Two linked lists are shown, one linking occurrences of
s and the other, of i. Notice how only certain occurrences of s are linked, while
others are skipped. The rule is to skip an occurrence of s which is followed by a
symbol that has already been seen. Thus the first occurrences of si, ss, s⊔, and sw
are linked, whereas other occurrences of s are skipped.

The list linking these occurrences of **s** starts empty and is built gradually, as more text is input and is moved into the search buffer. When a new context is created with **s** as its rightmost symbol, the list is updated. This is done by finding the symbol to the right of the new **s**, say **a**, scanning the list for a link **sa**, deleting it if found (not more than one may exist), and linking the current **s** to the list.

Figure 8.6: Context Searching for Order-1.

This list makes it easy to search and find all occurrences of the order-1 context "**s**" that are followed by different symbols (i.e., with exclusions).

Such a list should be built and updated for each symbol in the alphabet. If the algorithm is implemented to handle 8-bit symbols, then 256 such lists are needed and have to be updated.

The implementation details above show how complex this method is. It is slow, but it produces excellent compression.

Bibliography

Fenwick, P. (1996) *Symbol Ranking Text Compression*, Tech. Rep. 132, Dept. of Computer Science, University of Auckland, New Zealand, June.

Shannon, C. (1951) "Prediction and Entropy of Printed English," *Bell System Technical Journal* **30**(1):50–64, January.

8.3 ACB

Not many details are available of the actual implementation of ACB, a new, highly efficient text compression method by George Buyanovsky. The only documentation currently available is in Russian [Buyanovsky 94] and is already outdated. (An informal interpretation in English, by Leonid Broukhis, is available on the web at URL `http://www.cbloom.com/news/leoacb.html`.) The name ACB stands for "associative coder (of) Buyanovsky." We start with an example and follow with some features and a variant. The precise details of the ACB algorithm, however, are still unknown.

Assume that the text "`...swiss⎵miss⎵is⎵missing...`" is part of the input stream. The method uses an LZ77-type sliding buffer where we assume that the first seven symbols have already been input and are now in the search buffer. The look-ahead buffer starts with the string "`iss⎵is...`".

$$\boxed{\text{...swiss⎵m}\;\big|\;\text{iss⎵is⎵missing...}}\text{...}\leftarrow \text{text to be read}$$

While text is input and encoded, all contexts are placed in a dictionary, each with the text following it. This text is called the *content* string of the context. The six entries (context|content) that correspond to the seven rightmost symbols in the search buffer are shown in Table 8.7a. The dictionary is then sorted by contexts, *from right to left*, as shown in Table 8.7b. Both the contexts and contents are unbounded. They are assumed to be as long as possible but may include only symbols from the search buffer since the look-ahead buffer is unknown to the decoder. This way both encoder and decoder can create and update their dictionaries in lockstep.

...s|wiss␣m	1	...swiss␣|m
...sw|iss␣m	2	...swi|ss␣m
...swi|ss␣m	3	...s|wiss␣m
...swis|s␣m	4	...swis|s␣m
...swiss|␣m˙	5	...swiss|␣m
...swiss␣|m	6	...sw|iss␣m

(a)	(b)

Table 8.7: Six Contexts and Contents.

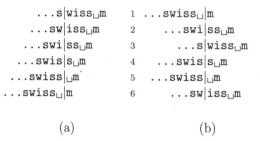

Figure 8.8: Dictionary Organization.

...s|wiss␣miss␣i	1	...swiss␣miss␣|i
...sw|iss␣miss␣i	2	...swiss␣|miss␣i
...swi|ss␣miss␣i	3	...swiss␣mi|ss␣i
...swis|s␣miss␣i	4	...swi|ss␣miss␣i
...swiss|␣miss␣i	5	...swiss␣m|iss␣i
...swiss␣|miss␣i	6	...s|wiss␣miss␣i
...swiss␣m|iss␣i	7	...swiss␣mis|s␣i
...swiss␣mi|ss␣i	8	...swis|s␣miss␣i
...swiss␣mis|s␣i	9	...swiss␣miss|␣i
...swiss␣miss|␣i	10	...swiss|␣miss␣i
...swiss␣miss␣|i	11	...sw|iss␣miss␣i

(a)	(b)

Table 8.9: Eleven Contexts and Their Contents.

8.3.1 The Encoder

The current context "...swiss␣m" is matched by the encoder to the dictionary entries. The best match is between entries 2 and 3 (matching is from right to left). We arbitrarily assume that the match algorithm selects entry 2 (the algorithm does not, of course, make arbitrary decisions and is the same for encoder and decoder). The current content "iss..." is also matched to the dictionary. The best content match is to entry 6. The four symbols "iss␣" match, so the output is $(6-2,4,$"i"$)$, a triplet that compresses the *five* symbols "iss␣i". The first element of the triplet is the distance d between the best content and best context matches (it can be negative). The second element is the number 1 of symbols matched (hopefully large, but could also be zero). The third element is the first unmatched symbol in the look-ahead buffer (in the spirit of LZ77). The five compressed symbols are appended to the "content" fields of *all* the dictionary entries (Table 8.9a) and are also shifted into the search buffer. These symbols also cause five entries to be added to the dictionary, which is shown, re-sorted, in Table 8.9b.

The new sliding buffer is

$$\boxed{\qquad\texttt{...swiss␣miss␣i}\,|\,\texttt{s␣missing...}}\texttt{...}\leftarrow \text{text to be read.}$$

The best context match is between entries 2 and 3 (we arbitrarily assume that the match algorithm selects entry 3). The best content match is entry 8. The six symbols "s␣miss" match, so the output is $(8-3,6,$"i"$)$, a triplet that compresses seven symbols. The seven symbols are appended to the "content" field of every dictionary entry and are also shifted into the search buffer. Seven new entries are added to the dictionary, which is shown in Table 8.10a (unsorted) and 8.10b (sorted).

(a)		(b)
...s|wiss␣miss␣is␣missi	1	...swiss␣miss␣is␣|missi
...sw|iss␣miss␣is␣missi	2	...swiss␣miss␣|is␣missi
...swi|ss␣miss␣is␣missi	3	...swiss␣|miss␣is␣missi
...swis|s␣miss␣is␣missi	4	...swiss␣miss␣i|s␣missi
...swiss|␣miss␣is␣missi	5	...swiss␣miss␣is␣mi|ssi
...swiss␣|miss␣is␣missi	6	...swiss␣mi|ss␣is␣missi
...swiss␣m|iss␣is␣missi	7	...swi|ss␣miss␣is␣missi
...swiss␣mi|ss␣is␣missi	8	...swiss␣miss␣is␣m|issi
...swiss␣mis|s␣is␣missi	9	...swiss␣m|iss␣is␣missi
...swiss␣miss|␣is␣missi	10	...s|wiss␣miss␣is␣missi
...swiss␣miss␣|is␣missi	11	...swiss␣miss␣is|␣missi
...swiss␣miss␣i|s␣missi	12	...swiss␣miss␣is␣mis|si
...swiss␣miss␣is|␣missi	13	...swiss␣mis|s␣is␣missi
...swiss␣miss␣is␣|missi	14	...swis|s␣miss␣is␣missi
...swiss␣miss␣is␣m|issi	15	..swiss␣miss␣is␣miss|i
...swiss␣miss␣is␣mi|ssi	16	...swiss␣miss|␣is␣missi
...swiss␣miss␣is␣mis|si	17	...swiss|␣miss␣is␣missi
..swiss␣miss␣is␣miss|i	18	...sw|iss␣miss␣is␣missi

Table 8.10: Eighteen Contexts and Their Contents.

The new sliding buffer is

$$\boxed{\texttt{...swiss}_\sqcup\texttt{miss}_\sqcup\texttt{is}_\sqcup\texttt{missi}\,|\,\texttt{ng...}}\ \texttt{...} \leftarrow \text{text to be read.}$$

(Notice that each sorted dictionary is a permutation of the text symbols in the search buffer. This feature of ACB resembles the Burrows-Wheeler method, Section 8.1.)

The best context match is now entries 6 or 7 (we assume that 6 is selected), but there is no content match, since no content starts with an "n". No symbols match, so the output is (0,0,"n"), a triplet that compresses the single symbol "n" (it actually generates expansion). This symbol should now be added to the dictionary and also shifted into the search buffer. (End of example.)

⋄ **Exercise 8.5:** Why does this triplet have a first element of zero?

8.3.2 The Decoder

The ACB decoder builds and updates the dictionary in lockstep with the encoder. At each step the encoder and decoder have the same dictionary (same contexts and contents). The difference between them is that the decoder does not have the data in the look-ahead buffer. The decoder does have the data in the search buffer, though, and uses it to find the best context match at, say, dictionary entry t. This is done before the decoder inputs anything. It then inputs a triplet (d,l,x) and adds the distance d to t to find the best content match c. The decoder then simply copies l symbols from the content part of entry c, appends symbol x, and outputs the resulting string to the decompressed stream. This string is also used to update the dictionary.

Notice that the content part of entry c may have fewer than l symbols. In this case, the decoding becomes somewhat more complicated and resembles the LZ77 example (from Section 3.2)

$$\texttt{...}\boxed{\texttt{alf}_\sqcup\texttt{eastman}_\sqcup\texttt{easily}_\sqcup\texttt{yells}_\sqcup\texttt{A}}\boxed{\texttt{AAAAAAAAAA}}\texttt{AAAAAH...}\ .$$

(The author is indebted to Donna Klaasen for pointing this out.)

A modified version of ACB writes pairs (distance, match length) on the compressed stream instead of triplets. When the match length l is zero, the raw symbol code (typically ASCII or 8 bits) is written, instead of a pair. Each output, a pair or raw code, must now be preceded by a flag indicating its type.

The dictionary may be organized as a list of pointers to the search buffer. Figure 8.8 shows how dictionary entry 4 points to the second "s" of "swiss". Following this pointer, it is easy to locate both the context of entry 4 (the search buffer to the left of the pointer, the past text) and its content (that part of the search buffer to the right of the pointer, the future text).

Part of the excellent performance of ACB is attributed to the way it encodes the distances d and match lengths l, which are its main output. Unfortunately, the details of this are still unknown.

It is clear that ACB is somewhat related to both LZ77 and LZ78. What is not immediately obvious is that ACB is also related to the symbol-ranking method (Section 8.2). The distance d between the best-content and best-context entries can be regarded a measure of ranking. In this sense ACB is a *phrase-ranking* compression method.

8.3.3 A Variation

Here is a variation of the basic ACB method that is slower, requiring an extra sort for each match, but is more efficient. We assume the string

$$\boxed{\quad\ldots\text{your}_\sqcup\text{swiss}_\sqcup\text{mis}\big|\text{s}_\sqcup\text{is}_\sqcup\text{mistress}\ldots}\ldots\leftarrow \text{ text to be read.}$$

in the search and look-ahead buffers. We denote this string by S. Part of the current dictionary (sorted by context, as usual) is shown in Table 8.11a, where the first eight and the last five entries are from the current search buffer "your$_\sqcup$swiss$_\sqcup$mis", and the middle ten entries are assumed to be from older data.

All dictionary entries whose context fields agree with the search buffer by at least k symbols—where k is a parameter, set to 9 in our example—are selected and become the *associative list*, shown in Table 8.11b. Notice that these entries agree with the search buffer by ten symbols, but we assume that k has been set to 9. All the entries in the associative list have identical, k-symbol contexts and represent dictionary entries with contexts similar to the search buffer (hence the name "associative").

The associative list is now sorted in ascending order by the **contents**, producing Table 8.12a. It is now obvious that S can be placed between entries 4 and 5 of the sorted list (Table 8.12b).

Since each of these three lines is sorted, we can temporarily forget that they consist of characters, and simply consider them three sorted bit-strings that can be written as in Table 8.13a. The "xx...x" bits are the part were all three lines agree (the string "swiss$_\sqcup$mis$|$s$_\sqcup$is$_\sqcup$"), and the "zz...z" bits are a further match between entry 4 and the look-ahead buffer (the string "mist"). All that the encoder has to output is the index 4, the underlined bit (which we denote by b and which may, of course, be a zero), and the length 1 of the "zz...z" string. The encoder's output is thus the triplet (4,b,1).

In our example S agrees best with the entry preceding it. In some cases it may best agree with the entry following it, as in Table 8.13b (where bit b is shown as zero).

◇ **Exercise 8.6:** Why is the configuration of Table 8.13c impossible?

The decoder maintains the dictionary in lockstep with the encoder, so it can create the same associative list, sort it, and use the identical parts (the intersection) of entries 4 and 5 to identify the "xx...x" string. It then uses 1 to identify the "zz...z" part in entry 4 and generates the bit-string "xx...x$\tilde{\text{b}}$zz...zb" (where $\tilde{\text{b}}$ is the complement of b) as the decompressed output of the triplet (4,b,1).

This variant can be further improved (producing better but slower compression) if instead of 1, the encoder generates the number q of $\tilde{\text{b}}$ bits in the "zz...z" part. This improves compression since q $\le$ 1. The decoder then starts copying bits from the "zz...z" part of entry 4 until it finds the (q + 1)st occurrence of $\tilde{\text{b}}$, which it ignores. Example: if b = 1 and the "zz...z" part is "01011110001011" (preceded by $\tilde{\text{b}}$ = 0 and followed by b = 1) then q = 6. The three lines are shown in

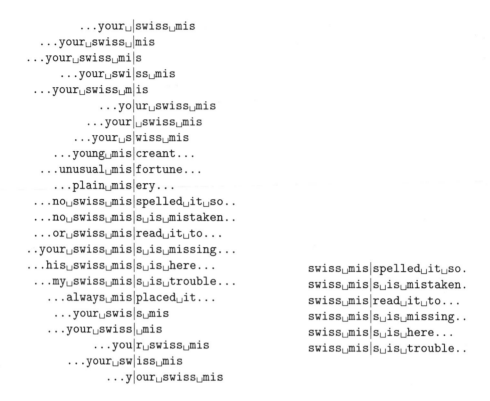

$$...\text{your}_\sqcup|\text{swiss}_\sqcup\text{mis}$$
$$...\text{your}_\sqcup\text{swiss}_\sqcup|\text{mis}$$
$$...\text{your}_\sqcup\text{swiss}_\sqcup\text{mi}|\text{s}$$
$$...\text{your}_\sqcup\text{swi}|\text{ss}_\sqcup\text{mis}$$
$$...\text{your}_\sqcup\text{swiss}_\sqcup\text{m}|\text{is}$$
$$...\text{yo}|\text{ur}_\sqcup\text{swiss}_\sqcup\text{mis}$$
$$...\text{your}|_\sqcup\text{swiss}_\sqcup\text{mis}$$
$$...\text{your}_\sqcup\text{s}|\text{wiss}_\sqcup\text{mis}$$
$$...\text{young}_\sqcup\text{mis}|\text{creant}...$$
$$...\text{unusual}_\sqcup\text{mis}|\text{fortune}...$$
$$...\text{plain}_\sqcup\text{mis}|\text{ery}...$$
$$...\text{no}_\sqcup\text{swiss}_\sqcup\text{mis}|\text{spelled}_\sqcup\text{it}_\sqcup\text{so}..$$
$$...\text{no}_\sqcup\text{swiss}_\sqcup\text{mis}|\text{s}_\sqcup\text{is}_\sqcup\text{mistaken}..$$
$$...\text{or}_\sqcup\text{swiss}_\sqcup\text{mis}|\text{read}_\sqcup\text{it}_\sqcup\text{to}...$$
$$..\text{your}_\sqcup\text{swiss}_\sqcup\text{mis}|\text{s}_\sqcup\text{is}_\sqcup\text{missing}...$$
$$...\text{his}_\sqcup\text{swiss}_\sqcup\text{mis}|\text{s}_\sqcup\text{is}_\sqcup\text{here}...$$
$$...\text{my}_\sqcup\text{swiss}_\sqcup\text{mis}|\text{s}_\sqcup\text{is}_\sqcup\text{trouble}...$$
$$...\text{always}_\sqcup\text{mis}|\text{placed}_\sqcup\text{it}...$$
$$...\text{your}_\sqcup\text{swis}|\text{s}_\sqcup\text{mis}$$
$$...\text{your}_\sqcup\text{swiss}|_\sqcup\text{mis}$$
$$...\text{you}|\text{r}_\sqcup\text{swiss}_\sqcup\text{mis}$$
$$...\text{your}_\sqcup\text{sw}|\text{iss}_\sqcup\text{mis}$$
$$...\text{y}|\text{our}_\sqcup\text{swiss}_\sqcup\text{mis}$$

swiss_mis|spelled_it_so.
swiss_mis|s_is_mistaken.
swiss_mis|read_it_to...
swiss_mis|s_is_missing..
swiss_mis|s_is_here...
swiss_mis|s_is_trouble..

(a)   (b)

Table 8.11: (a) Sorted Dictionary. (b) Associative List.

1 swiss_mis|read_it_to...
2 swiss_mis|s_is_here...
3 swiss_mis|s_is_missing...
4 swiss_mis|s_is_mistaken..
5 swiss_mis|s_is_trouble...
6 swiss_mis|spelled_it_so..

4. swiss mis|s is mistaken..
S. swiss mis|s is mistress..
5. swiss mis|s is trouble...

(a)   (b)

Table 8.12: (a) Sorted Associative List. (b) Three Lines.

4. xx...x0zz...z0A   4. xx...x0CC...   4. xx...x0CC...
S. xx...x0zz...z1B   S. xx...x1zz...z0B   S. xx...x1zz...z1B
5. xx...x1CC...   5. xx...x1zz...z1A   5. xx...x1zz...z0A

(a)   (b)   (c)

Table 8.13: (a, b) Two Possibilities, and (c) One Impossibility, of Three Lines.

Table 8.14. It is easy to see how the decoder can create the 14-bit "zz...z" part by copying bits from entry 4 until it finds the seventh 0, which it ignores. The encoder's output is thus the (encoded) triplet $(4, 1, 6)$ instead of $(4, 1, 14)$. Writing the value 6 (encoded) instead of 14 on the compressed stream improves the overall compression performance somewhat.

```
                zz..........z
     4. xx...x0|01011110001011|0A
     S. xx...x0|01011110001011|1B
     5. xx...x1 CC...
```

Table 8.14: An Example.

Another possible improvement is to delete any identical entries in the sorted associative list. This technique may be called *phrase exclusion*, in analogy with the exclusion techniques of PPM and the symbol-ranking method. In our example, Table 8.12a, there are no identical entries, but had there been any, exclusion would have reduced the number of entries to fewer than 6.

⋄ **Exercise 8.7:** How would this improve compression?

The main strength of ACB stems from the way it operates. It selects dictionary entries with contexts that are similar to the current context (the search buffer), then sorts the selected entries by content and selects the best content match. This is slow and also requires a huge dictionary (a small dictionary would not provide good matches) but results in excellent context-based compression without the need for escape symbols or any other "artificial" device.

8.3.4 Context Files

An interesting feature of ACB is its ability to create and use *context files*. When a file abc.ext is compressed, the user may specify the creation of a context file called, for example, abc.ctx. This file contains the final dictionary generated during the compression of abc.ext. The user may later compress another file lmn.xyz asking ACB to use abc.ctx as a context file. File lmn.xyz will thus be compressed by using the dictionary of abc.ext. Following this, ACB will replace the contents of abc.ctx. Instead of the original dictionary, it will now contain the dictionary of lmn.xyz (which was not used for the actual compression of lmn.xyz). If the user wants to keep the original contents of abc.ctx, its attributes can be set to "read only." Context files can be very useful, as the following examples illustrate.

1. A writer emails a large manuscript to an editor. Because of its size, the manuscript file should be sent compressed. The first time this is done, the writer asks ACB to create a context file, then emails both the compressed manuscript and the context file to the editor. Two files need be emailed, so compression doesn't do much good this first time.

The editor decompresses the manuscript using the context file, reads it, and responds with proposed modifications to the manuscript. The writer modifies the manuscript, compresses it again with the same context file, and emails it, this time without the context file. The writer's context file has now been updated, so the writer cannot use it to decompress what he has just emailed (but then he doesn't need to). The editor still has the original context file, so he can decompress the second manuscript version, during which process ACB creates a new context file for the editor's use next time.

2. The complete collection of detective stories by a famous author should be compressed and saved as an archive. Since all the files are detective stories and are all by the same author, it makes sense to assume that they feature similar writing styles and therefore similar contexts. One story is selected to serve as a "training" file. It is compressed and a context file created. This context file is permanently saved and is used to compress and decompress all the other files in the archive.

3. A shareware author writes an application `abc.exe` that is used (and paid for) by many people. The author decides to make version 2 available. He starts by compressing the old version while creating a context file `abc.ctx`. The resulting compressed file is not needed and is immediately deleted. The author then uses `abc.ctx` as a context file to compress his version 2, then deletes `abc.ctx`. The result is a compressed (i.e., small) file, containing version 2, which is placed on the internet, to be downloaded by users of version 1. Anyone who has version 1 can download the result and decompress it. All they need is to compress their version 1 in order to obtain a context file, then use that context file to decompress what has been downloaded.

Bibliography

Buyanovsky, G. (1994), "Associative Coding," (in Russian), *Monitor*, Moscow, #8, 10–19, August. (Hard copies of the Russian source and English translation are available from the author of this book. Send requests to the author's email address found in the Preface.)

Fenwick, P. (1996), "Symbol Ranking Text Compression," *Tech. Rep. 132*, Dept. of Computer Science, University of Auckland, New Zealand, June.

Lambert, Sean M. (1999) "Implementing Associative Coder of Buyanovsky (ACB) Data Compression," M.S. thesis, Montana State University (available from Sean Lambert at `sum1els@mindless.com`).

> This algorithm ... is simple for software and hardware implementations.
>
> —George Buyanovsky

8.4 Sort-Based Context Similarity

The idea of context similarity is a "relative" of the symbol ranking method of Section 8.2 and of the Burrows-Wheeler method (Section 8.1). In contrast to the Burrows-Wheeler method, the context similarity method of this section is adaptive.

The method uses context similarity to sort previously seen contexts by reverse lexicographic order. Based on the sorted sequence of contexts, a *rank* is assigned to the next symbol. The ranks are written on the compressed stream and are later used by the decoder to reconstruct the original data. The compressed stream also includes each of the distinct input symbols in raw format, and this data is also used by the decoder.

The Encoder: The encoder reads the input symbol by symbol and maintains a sorted list of (context, symbol) pairs. When the next symbol is input, the encoder inserts a new pair into the proper place in the list, and uses the list to assign a rank to the symbol. The rank is written by the encoder on the compressed stream and is sometimes followed by the symbol itself in raw format. The operation of the encoder is best illustrated by an example. Suppose that the string bacacaba has been input so far, and the next symbol (still unread by the encoder) is denoted by x. The current list is shown in Table 8.15 where λ stands for the empty string.

#	context	symbol
0	λ	b
1	ba	c
2	bacacaba	x
3	baca	c
4	bacaca	b
5	b	a
6	bacacab	a
7	bac	a
8	bacac	a

Table 8.15: The Sorted List For bacacaba.

Each of the nine entries in the list consists of a context and the symbol that followed the context in the input stream (except entry 2, where the input is still unknown). The list is sorted by contexts, but in reverse order. The empty string is assumed, by definition, to be less than any other string. It is followed by all the contexts that end with an "a" (there are four of them), and they are sorted according to the second symbol from the right, then the third symbol, and so on. These are followed by all the contexts that end with "b", then the ones that end with "c", and so on. The current context bacacaba happens to be number 2 in this list. Once the decoder has decoded the first eight symbols, it will have the same nine-entry list available.

The encoder now ranks the contexts in the list according to how similar they are to context 2. It is clear that context 1 is the most similar to 2, since they share two symbols. Thus, the ranking starts with context 1. Context 1 is then compared to the remaining seven contexts 0 and 3–8. This context ends with an "a", so is similar to contexts 3 and 4. We select context 3 as the most similar to 1, since it is shorter than 4. This rule of selecting the shortest context is arbitrary. It simply guarantees that the decoder will be able to construct the same ranking. The ranking so far is $1 \rightarrow 3$. Context 3 is now compared to the remaining six contexts. It is clear that it is most similar to context 4, since they share the last symbol. The ranking so far is therefore $1 \rightarrow 3 \rightarrow 4$. Context 4 is now compared to the remaining five contexts. These contexts do not share any suffixes with 4, so the shortest one, context 0, is selected as the most similar. The ranking so far is $1 \rightarrow 3 \rightarrow 4 \rightarrow 0$. Context 0 is now compared to the remaining four contexts. It does not share any suffix with them, so the shortest of the four, context 5, is selected. The ranking so far is $1 \rightarrow 3 \rightarrow 4 \rightarrow 0 \rightarrow 5$.

⋄ **Exercise 8.8:** Continue this process.

As the answer to the exercise shows, the final ranking of the contexts is

$$1 \to 3 \to 4 \to 0 \to 5 \to 6 \to 7 \to 8 \;.$$
$$\text{c} \quad \text{c} \quad \text{b} \quad \text{b} \quad \text{a} \quad \text{a} \quad \text{a} \quad \text{a} \tag{8.2}$$

This ranking of contexts is now used by the encoder to assign a rank to the next symbol x. The encoder inputs x and compares it, from left to right, to the symbols shown in Equation (8.2). The rank of x is one more than the number of distinct symbols that are encountered in the comparison. Thus, if x is the symbol "c", it is found immediately in Equation (8.2), there are no distinct symbols, and "c" is assigned a rank of 1. If x is "b", the encoder encounters only one distinct symbol, namely "c", before it gets to "b", so the rank of "b" becomes 2. If x is "a", its rank becomes 3, and if x is a different symbol, its rank is 4 [one more than the number of distinct symbols in Equation (8.2)]. The encoder writes the rank on the compressed stream, and if the rank is 4, the encoder also writes the actual symbol in raw format, following the rank.

We now show the first few steps in encoding the input string `bacacaba`. The first symbol "b" is written on the output in raw format. It is not assigned any rank. The encoder (and also the decoder, in lockstep) constructs the one-entry table (λ b). The second symbol, "a", is input. Its context is "b", and the encoder inserts entry (b a) into the list. The new list is shown in Table 8.16a with x denoting the new input symbol, since this symbol is not yet known to the decoder. The next five steps are summarized in Table 8.16b–f.

(a)	(b)	(c)	(d)	(e)	(f)
0 λ b	0 λ b	0 λ b	0 λ b	0 λ b	0 λ b
1 b x	1 ba x	1 ba c	1 ba c	1 ba c	1 ba c
	2 b a	2 b a	2 baca x	2 baca c	2 baca c
		3 bac x	3 b a	3 b a	3 bacaca x
			4 bac a	4 bac a	4 b a
				5 bacac x	5 bac a
					6 bacac a

Table 8.16: Constructing the Sorted Lists For `bacacaba`.

Equation (8.3) lists the different context rankings.

$$0\,, \qquad 0 \to 2\,, \qquad 0 \to 2 \to 1\,,$$
$$\text{b} \qquad \text{b} \quad \text{a} \qquad \text{b} \quad \text{a} \quad \text{c}$$
$$1 \to 0 \to 3 \to 4\,, \qquad 4 \to 0 \to 3 \to 1 \to 2\,,$$
$$\text{c} \quad \text{a} \quad \text{a} \quad \text{a} \qquad \text{a} \quad \text{b} \quad \text{a} \quad \text{c} \quad \text{c}$$
$$2 \to 1 \to 0 \to 4 \to 5 \to 6 \;.$$
$$\text{c} \quad \text{c} \quad \text{b} \quad \text{a} \quad \text{a} \quad \text{a} \tag{8.3}$$

With this information, it is easy to manually construct the compressed stream. The first symbol, "b", is output in raw format. The second symbol, "a", is assigned rank 1 and is also output following its rank. The first "c" is assigned rank 2 and is also output (each distinct input symbol is output raw, following its rank, the first time it is read and processed). The second "a" is assigned rank 2, because there is one distinct symbol ("b") preceding it in the list of context ranking. The second "c" is assigned rank 1.

⋄ **Exercise 8.9:** Complete the output stream.

⋄ **Exercise 8.10:** Practice your knowledge of the encoder on the short input string ubladiu. Show the sorted contexts and the context ranking after each symbol is input. Also show the output produced by the encoder.

The Decoder: Once the operation of the encoder is understood, it is clear that the decoder can mimic the encoder. It can construct and maintain the table of sorted contexts as it reads the compressed stream, and use the table to regenerate the original data. The decoding algorithm is shown in Figure 8.17.

```
Input the first item. This is a raw symbol. Output it.
while not end-of-file
  Input the next item. This is the rank of a symbol.
  If this rank is > the total number of distinct symbols seen so far
    then Input the next item. This is a raw symbol. Output it.
    else Translate the rank into a symbol using the current
         context ranking. Output this symbol.
  endif
  The string that has been output so far is the current context.
   Insert it into the table of sorted contexts.
endwhile
```

Figure 8.17: The Decoding Algorithm.

The Data Structure: Early versions of the context sorting method used a binary decision tree to store the various contexts. This was slow, so the length of the contexts had to be limited to eight symbols. The new version, described in [Yokoo 99a], uses a *prefix list* as the data structure, and is fast enough to allow contexts of unlimited length. We denote the input symbols by s_i. Let $S[1\ldots n]$ be the string $s_1 s_2 \ldots s_n$ of n symbols. We use the notation $S[i\ldots j]$ to denote the substring $s_i \ldots s_j$. If $i > j$, then $S[i\ldots j]$ is the empty string λ.

As an example, consider the 9-symbol string $S[1\ldots 9] = $ yabrecabr. Table 8.18a lists the ten prefixes of this string (including the empty prefix) sorted in reverse lexicographic order. Table 8.18b considers the prefixes, contexts and lists the ten (context, symbol) pairs. This table illustrates how to insert the next prefix, which consists of the next input symbol s_{10} appended to the current context yabrecabr. If s_{10} is not any of the rightmost symbols of the prefixes (i.e., if it is not any of abcery), then s_{10} determines the position of the next prefix. For example, if s_{10} is "x", then prefix yabrecabrx should be inserted between yabr and y. If, on the other hand, s_{10} is one of abcery, we compare yabrecabrs_{10} to the prefixes that precede it and follow it in the table, until we find the first match.

$$
\begin{array}{rc}
S[1\ldots 0] = & \lambda \\
S[1\ldots 7] = & \text{yabreca} \\
S[1\ldots 2] = & \text{ya} \\
S[1\ldots 8] = & \text{yabrecab} \\
S[1\ldots 3] = & \text{yab} \\
S[1\ldots 6] = & \text{yabrec} \\
S[1\ldots 5] = & \text{yabre} \\
S[1\ldots 9] = & \text{yabrecabr} \\
S[1\ldots 4] = & \text{yabr} \\
S[1\ldots 1] = & \text{y}
\end{array}
$$

λ	y
yabreca	b
ya	b
yabrecab	r
yab	r
yabrec	a
yabre	c
yabrecabr	s_{10} ↑↓
yabr	e
y	a

(a)   (b)

Table 8.18: (a) Sorted List For yabrecabr. (b) Inserting the Next Prefix

For example, if s_{10} is "e", then comparing yabrecabre with the prefixes that follow it (yabr and y) will not find a match, but comparing it with the preceding prefixes will match it with yabre in one step. In such a case (a match found while searching up), the rule is that yabrecabre should become the predecessor of yabre. Similarly, if s_{10} is "a", then comparing yabrecabra with the preceding prefixes will find a match at ya, so yabrecabra should become the predecessor of ya. If s_{10} is "r", then comparing yabrecabrr with the prefixes following it will match it with yabr, and the rule in this case (a match found while searching down) is that yabrecabrr should become the successor of yabr.

Once this is grasped, the prefix list data structure is easy to understand. It is a doubly linked list where each node is associated with an input prefix $S[1\ldots i]$ and contains the integer i and three pointers. Two pointers (*pred* and *succ*) point to the predecessor and successor nodes, and the third one (*next*) points to the node associated with prefix $S[1\ldots i+1]$. Figure 8.19 shows the pointers of a general node representing substring $S[1\ldots P.index]$. If a node corresponds to the entire input string $S[1\ldots n]$, then its *next* field is set to the null pointer *nil*. The prefix list is initialized to a special node H that represents the empty string. Some list operations are simplified if the list ends with another special node T. Figure 8.20 shows the prefix list for yabrecabr.

Here is how the next prefix is inserted into the prefix list. We assume that the list already contains all the prefixes of string $S[1\ldots i]$ and that the next prefix $S[1\ldots i+1]$ should now be inserted. If the newly input symbol s_{i+1} precedes or succeeds all the symbols seen so far, then the node representing $S[1\ldots i+1]$ should be inserted at the start of the list (i.e., to the right of special node H) or at the end

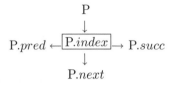

Figure 8.19: Node Representing $S[1 \ldots \text{P}.index]$.

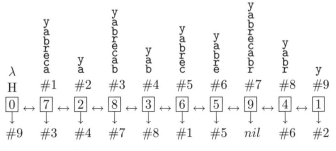

Figure 8.20: Prefix List For yabrecabr.

of the list (i.e., to the left of special node T), respectively. Otherwise, if s_{i+1} is not included in $S[1 \ldots i]$, then there is a unique position Q that satisfies

$$S[Q.index] < s_{i+1} < S[Q.succ.index]. \tag{8.4}$$

The new node for $S[1 \ldots i+1]$ should be inserted between the two nodes pointed to by Q and $Q.succ$.

If symbol s_{i+1} has already appeared in $S[1 \ldots i]$, then the inequalities in Equation (8.4) may become equalities. In this case, the immediate predecessor or successor of $S[1 \ldots i+1]$ has the same last symbol as s_{i+1}. If this is true for the immediate successor (i.e., if the immediate successor $S[1 \ldots j+1]$ of $S[1 \ldots i+1]$ satisfies $s_{j+1} = s_{i+1}$), then $S[1 \ldots j]$ precedes $S[1 \ldots i]$. The node corresponding to $S[1 \ldots j]$ should be the first node that satisfies $s_{j+1} = s_{i+1}$ in traversing the list from the current node to the start. We can test whether the following symbol matches s_{i+1} by following the pointer *next*.

Conversely, if the last symbol s_{j+1} of the immediate successor $S[1 \ldots j+1]$ of $S[1 \ldots i+1]$ equals s_{i+1}, then the node for $S[1 \ldots j]$ should be the first one satisfying $s_{j+1} = s_{i+1}$ when the list is traversed from the current node to the last node. In either case we start from the current node and search forward and backward, looking for the node for $S[1 \ldots j]$ by comparing the last symbols s_{j+1} with s_{i+1}. Once the node for $S[1 \ldots j]$ has been located, the node for $S[1 \ldots j+1]$ can be reached in one step by following the *next* pointer. The new node for $S[1 \ldots i+1]$ should be inserted adjacent to the node for $S[1 \ldots j+1]$.

[Yokoo 99a] has time complexity analysis and details about this structure.

The context sorting method was first published in [Yokoo 96] with analysis and evaluation added in [Yokoo 97]. It was further developed and improved by its developer, Hidetoshi Yokoo. It has been communicated to the author in [Yokoo 99b].

Bibliography

Yokoo, Hidetoshi (1996) "An Adaptive Data Compression Method Based on Context Sorting," in *Proceedings of the 1996 Data Compression Conference*, J. Storer Ed., Los Alamitos, CA, IEEE Computer Society Press, pp. 160–169.

Yokoo, Hidetoshi (1997) "Data Compression Using Sort-Based Context Similarity Measure," *The Computer Journal*, **40**(2/3):94–102.

Yokoo, Hidetoshi (1999a) "A Dynamic Data Structure For Reverse Lexicographically Sorted Prefixes," in *Combinatorial Pattern Matching, Lecture Notes in Computer Science 1645*, M. Crochemore and M. Paterson, eds., Berlin, Springer-Verlag, pp. 150–162.

Yokoo, Hidetoshi (1999b) Private Communication.

8.5 Sparse Strings

Regardless of what the input data represents—text, binary, images, or anything else—we can think of the input stream as a string of bits. If most of the bits are zeros, the string is *sparse*. Sparse strings can be compressed very efficiently, and this section describes methods developed specifically for this task. Before getting to the individual methods it may be useful to convince the reader that sparse strings are not a theoretical concept but do occur commonly in practice. Here are some examples.

1. A drawing. Imagine a drawing, technical or artistic, done with a black pen on white paper. If the drawing is not very complex, most of it remains white. When such a drawing is scanned and digitized, most of the resulting pixels are white, and the percentage of black ones is small. The resulting bitmap is an example of a sparse string.

2. A *bitmap* index for a large data base. Imagine a large data base of text documents. A bitmap for such a data base is a set of bit-strings (or bitvectors) that makes it easy to identify all the documents where a given word w appears. To implement a bitmap, we first have to prepare a list of all the distinct words w_j in all the documents. Suppose that there are W such words. The next step is to go over each document d_i and prepare a bit-string D_i that is W bits long, containing a 1 in position j if word w_j appears in document d_i. The bitmap is the set of all those bit-strings. Depending on the database, such bit-strings may be sparse.

(Indexing large databases is an important operation, since a computerized database should be easy to search. The traditional method of indexing is to prepare a *concordance*. Originally, the word concordance referred to any comprehensive index of the Bible, but today there are concordances for the collected works of Shakespeare, Wordsworth, and many others. A computerized concordance is called an *inverted file*. Such a file includes one entry for each term in the documents constituting the database. An entry is a list of pointers to all the occurrences of the term, similar to an index of a book. A pointer may be the number of a chapter, of a section, a page, a page-line pair, of a sentence, or even of a word. An inverted file where pointers point to individual words is considered *fine grained*. One where they point to, say, a chapter is considered *coarse grained*. A fine-grained inverted file may seem preferable, but it must use large pointers, and as a result, it may turn out to be so large that it may have to be stored in compressed form.)

3. Sparse strings have also been mentioned in Section 4.6.5, in connection with JPEG.

The methods described here (except prefix compression, Section 8.5.5) are due to [Fraenkel 85].

8.5.1 OR-ing Bits

This method starts with a sparse string L_1 of size n_1 bits. In the first step, L_1 is divided into k substrings of equal size. In each substring all bits are logically OR-ed, and the results (one bit per substring) become string L_2, which will be compressed in step 2. All zero substrings of L_1 are now deleted. Here is an example of a sparse, 64-bit string L_1, which we divide into 16 substrings of size 4 each:

$$L_1 = 0000|0000|0000|0100|0000|0000|0000|1000|0000$$
$$|0000|0000|0000|0010|0000|0000|0000.$$

After ORing each 4-bit substring we get the 16-bit string $L_2 = 0001|0001|0000|1000$.

In step 2, the same process is applied to L_2, and the result is the 4-bit string $L_3 = 1101$, which is short enough so no more compression steps are needed. After deleting all zero substrings in L_1 and L_2, we end up with the three short strings

$$L_1 = 0100|1000|0010, \qquad L_2 = 0001|0001|1000, \qquad L_3 = 1101.$$

The output stream consists of seven 4-bit substrings instead of the original 16! (A few more numbers are needed, to indicate how long each substring is.)

The decoder works differently (this is an asymmetric compression method). It starts with L_3 and considers each of its 1-bits a pointer to a substring of L_2 and each of its 0-bits a pointer to a substring of all zeros that is not stored in L_2. This way string L_2 can be reconstructed from L_3, and string L_1, in turn, from L_2. Figure 8.21 illustrates this process. The substrings shown in square brackets are the ones not contained in the compressed stream.

◇ **Exercise 8.11:** This method becomes highly inefficient for strings that are not sparse, and may easily result in expansion. Analyze the worst case, where every group of L_1 is nonzero.

8.5.2 Variable-Size Codes

We start with an input stream that is a sparse string L of n bits. We divide it into groups of l bits each, and assign each group a variable-size code. Since a group of l bits can have one of 2^l values, we need 2^l codes. Since L is sparse, most groups will consist of l zeros, implying that the variable-size code assigned to the group of l zeros (the zero group) should be the shortest (perhaps just one bit). The other $2^l - 1$ variable-size codes can be assigned arbitrarily, or according to the frequencies of occurrence of the groups. The latter choice requires an extra pass over the input stream to compute the frequencies. In the ideal case, where all the groups are zeros, and each is coded as one bit, the output stream will consist of n/l bits, yielding a compression ratio of $1/l$. This shows that in principle, the compression ratio can

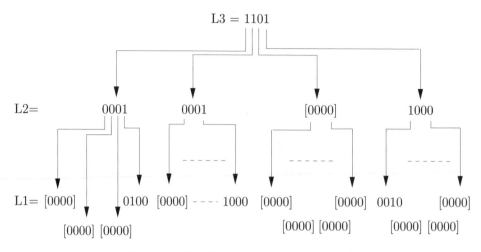

Figure 8.21: Reconstructing L_1 from L_3.

be improved by increasing l, but in practice, large l means many codes, which, in turn, increases the code size and decreases the compression ratio for an "average" string L.

A better approach can be developed once we realize that a sparse input stream must contain **runs** of zero groups. A run of zero groups may consist of 1, 2, or up to n/l such groups. It is possible to assign variable-size codes to the runs of zero groups, as well as to the nonzero groups, and Table 8.22 illustrates this approach for the case of 16 groups. The trouble is that there are $2^l - 1$ nonzero groups and n/l possible run lengths of zero groups. Normally, n is large and l is small, so n/l is large. If we increase l, then n/l gets smaller but $2^l - 1$ gets bigger. We thus always end up with many codes, which implies long codes.

Size of run length	Run of zeros	Nonzero group	
1	0000	1	0001
2	0000 0000	2	0010
3	0000 0000 0000	3	0011
⋮	⋮ ⋮	⋮	
16	0000 0000 ... 0000	15	1111
(a)		(b)	

Table 8.22: (a) n/l Run-lengths. (b) $2^l - 1$ Nonzero Groups.

A more promising approach is to divide the run lengths (which are integers between 1 and n/l) into classes, assign one variable-size code C_i to each class i, and assign a two-part code to each run length. Imagine a run of r zero groups, where r happens to be in class i, and happens to be the third one in this class. When a run of r zero groups is found in the input stream, the code of r is written to the output stream. Such a code consists of two parts: The first is the class code C_i, and the second is 2, the position of r in its class (positions are numbered from zero). Experience with algorithm design and binary numbers suggests the following definition of classes: A run length of r zero groups is in class i if $2^{i-1} \le r < 2^i$, where $i = 1, 2, \ldots, \lfloor \log_2(n/l) \rfloor$. This definition implies that the position of r in its class is $m = r - 2^{i-1}$, a number that can be written in $(i-1)$ bits. Table 8.23 shows the four classes for the case $n/l = 16$ (16 groups). Notice how the numbers m are written as $i - 1$-bit numbers, so for $i = 1$ (the first class), no m is necessary. The variable-size Huffman codes C_i shown in the table are for illustration purposes only and are based on the (arbitrary) assumption that the most common run lengths are 5, 6, and 7.

Run length	Code	$r - 2^{i-1}$	$i-1$	Huffman code|m
1	C_1	$1 - 2^{1-1} = 0$	0	00010
2	C_2	$2 - 2^{2-1} = 0$	1	00011|0
3	C_2	$3 - 2^{2-1} = 1$	1	0010|1
4	C_3	$4 - 2^{3-1} = 0$	2	0011|00
5	C_3	$5 - 2^{3-1} = 1$	2	010|01
6	C_3	$6 - 2^{3-1} = 2$	2	011|10
7	C_3	$7 - 2^{3-1} = 3$	2	1|11
8	C_4	$8 - 2^{4-1} = 0$	3	00001|000
9	C_4	$9 - 2^{4-1} = 1$	3	000001|001
$\vdots$				$\vdots$
15	C_4	$15 - 2^{4-1} = 7$	3	000000000001|111

Table 8.23: $\log_2(n/l)$ Classes of Run-Lengths.

It is easy to see from the table that a run of 16 zero groups (which corresponds to an input stream of all zeros) does not belong in any of the classes. It should thus be assigned a special variable-size code. The total number of variable-size codes required in this approach is therefore $2^l - 1$ (for the nonzero groups) plus $\lfloor \log_2(n/l) \rfloor$ (for the run lengths of zero groups) plus 1 for the special case where all the groups are zero. A typical example is a 1-megabit input stream (i.e., $n = 2^{20}$). Assuming $l = 8$, the number of codes is $2^8 - 1 + \log_2(2^{20}/8) + 1 = 256 - 1 + 17 + 1 = 273$. With $l = 4$ the number of codes is $2^4 - 1 + \log_2(2^{20}/4) + 1 = 16 - 1 + 18 + 1 = 34$; much smaller, but more codes are required to encode the same input stream.

The operation of the decoder is straightforward. It reads the next variable-size code, which represents either a nonzero group of l bits, or a run of r zero groups, or an input stream of all zeros. In the first case, the decoder creates the nonzero group. In the second case, the code tells the decoder the class number i. The decoder then reads the next $i - 1$ bits to get the value of m, and computes $r = m + 2^{i-1}$ as the size of the run length of zero groups. The decoder then creates a run of r zero groups. In the third case the decoder creates a stream of n zero bits.

Example: An input stream of size $n = 64$ divided into 16 groups of $l = 4$ bits each. The number of codes needed is $2^4 - 1 + \log_2(64/4) + 1 = 16 - 1 + 4 + 1 = 20$. We arbitrarily assume that each of the 15 nonzero groups occurs with probability $1/40$, and that the probability of occurrence of runs in the four classes are $6/40$, $8/40$, $6/40$, and $4/40$, respectively. The probability of occurrence of a run of 16 groups is assumed to be $1/40$. Table 8.24 shows possible codes for each nonzero group and for each class of runs of zero groups. The code for 16 zero groups is 00000 (corresponds to the 16 in italics).

Nonzero groups								Classes	
1	111111	5	01111	9	00111	13	00011	C_1	110
2	111110	6	01110	10	00110	14	00010	C_2	10
3	111101	7	01101	11	00101	15	00001	C_3	010
4	111100	8	01100	12	00100	*16*	00000	C_4	1110

Table 8.24: Twenty Codes.

⬦ **Exercise 8.12:** Encode the input stream

0000|0000|0000|0100|0000|0000|0000|1000|0000|0000|0000|0000|0010|0000|0000|0000

using the codes of Table 8.24.

8.5.3 Variable-Size Codes for Base 2

Classes defined as in the preceding section require a set of $(2^l - 1) + \lfloor \log_2(n/l) \rfloor + 1$ codes. The method is efficient but slow, since the code for a run of zero groups involves both a class code C_i and the quantity m. In this section we look at a way to handle runs of zero groups by defining codes R_1, R_2, R_4, $R_8, \ldots$ for run lengths of $1, 2, 4, 8, \ldots, 2^i$ zero groups. The binary representation of the number 17, e.g., is 10001, so a run of 17 zero groups would be coded as R_{16} followed by R_1. Since run lengths can be from 1 to n/l, the number of codes R_i required is $1 + (n/l)$, more than before. Experience shows, however, that long runs are rare, so the Huffman codes assigned to R_i should be short for small values of i, and long for large i's. In addition to the R_i codes, we still need $2^l - 1$ codes for the nonzero groups. In the case $n = 64$, $l = 4$ we need 15 codes for the nonzero groups and 7 codes for R_1 through R_{64}. An example is illustrated in Table 8.25 where all the codes for nonzero groups are 5 bits long and start with 0, while the seven R_i codes start with 1 and are variable-size.

The R_i codes don't have to correspond to powers of 2. They may be based on 3, 4, or even larger integers. Let's take a quick look at octal R_i codes (8-based). They are denoted by R_1, R_8, $R_{64}, \ldots$. To encode a run length of 17 zero groups ($= 21_8$) we need **two** copies of the code for R_8, followed by the code for R_1. The number of R_i codes is smaller, but some may have to appear several (up to 7) times.

The general rule is; Suppose that the R_i codes are based on the number B. If we identify a run of R zero groups, we first have to express R in base B, then

Nonzero groups		Run lengths	
1 0 0001	9 0 1001	R_1	1 1
2 0 0010	10 0 1010	R_2	1 01
3 0 0011	11 0 1011	R_4	1 001
4 0 0100	12 0 1100	R_8	1 00011
5 0 0101	13 0 1101	R_{16}	1 00010
6 0 0110	14 0 1110	R_{32}	1 00001
7 0 0111	15 0 1111	R_{64}	1 00000
8 0 1000			

Table 8.25: Codes for Base-2 R_i.

create copies of the R_i codes according to the digits of that number. If $R = d_3 d_2 d_1$ in base B, then the coded output for run length R should consist of d_1 copies of R_1, followed by d_2 copies of R_2 and by d_3 copies of R_3.

◇ **Exercise 8.13:** Encode the 64-bit input stream of Exercise 8.12 by using the codes of Table 8.25.

8.5.4 Fibonacci-Based Variable-Size Codes

The codes R_i used in the previous section are based on powers of 2, since any positive integer can be expressed in this base using just the digits 0 and 1. It turns out that the well-known Fibonacci numbers also have this property. Any positive integer R can be expressed as $R = b_1 F_1 + b_2 F_2 + b_3 F_3 + b_4 F_5 + \cdots$ (that is $b_4 F_5$, not $b_4 F_4$), where the F_i are the Fibonacci numbers $1, 2, 3, 5, 8, 13, \ldots$ and the b_i are binary digits. The Fibonacci numbers grow more slowly than the powers of 2, meaning that more of them are needed to express a given run length R of zero groups. However, this representation has the interesting property that the string $b_1 b_2 \ldots$ does not contain any adjacent 1's ([Knuth 73], ex. 34, p. 85). If the representation of R in this base consists of d digits, at most $\lceil d/2 \rceil$ codes F_i would actually be needed to code a run length of R zero groups. As an example, the integer 33 equals the sum $1 + 3 + 8 + 21$, so it is expressed in the Fibonacci base as the 7-bit number 1010101. A run length of 33 zero groups is therefore coded, in this method, as the four codes F_1, F_3, F_8, and F_{21}.

Table 8.26 is an example of Fibonacci codes for the run length of zero groups. Notice that with seven Fibonacci codes we can express only runs of up to $1 + 2 + 3 + 5 + 8 + 13 + 21 = 53$ groups. Since we want up to 64 groups, we need one more code. Table 8.26 thus has eight codes, compared to seven in Table 8.25.

◇ **Exercise 8.14:** Encode the 64-bit input stream of Exercise 8.12 using the codes of Table 8.26.

This section and the previous one suggest that any number system can be used to construct codes for the run lengths of zero groups. However, number systems based on binary digits are preferable, since certain codes can be omitted in such a case, and no code has to be duplicated. Another possibility is to use number systems where certain combinations of digits are impossible. Here is an example, also based on Fibonacci numbers.

Nonzero groups		Run lengths	
1 0 0001	9 0 1001	F_1	1 1
2 0 0010	10 0 1010	F_2	1 01
3 0 0011	11 0 1011	F_3	1 001
4 0 0100	12 0 1100	F_5	1 00011
5 0 0101	13 0 1101	F_8	1 00010
6 0 0110	14 0 1110	F_{13}	1 00001
7 0 0111	15 0 1111	F_{21}	1 00000
8 0 1000		F_{34}	1 000000

Table 8.26: Codes for Fibonacci-Based F_i.

The well-known recurrence relation these numbers satisfy is $F_i = F_{i-1} + F_{i-2}$. It can be written

$$F_{i+2} = F_{i+1} + F_i = (F_i + F_{i-1}) + F_i = 2F_i + F_{i-1}.$$

The numbers produced by this relation can also serve as the basis for a number system that has two interesting properties: (1) Any positive integer can be expressed using just the digits 0, 1, and 2. (2) Any digit of 2 is followed by a 0.

The first few numbers produced by this relation are 1, 3, 7, 17, 41, 99, 239, 577, 1393 and 3363. It is easy to verify the following examples:

1. $7000_{10} = 2001002001$ (since $7000_{10} = 2 \times 3363 + 239 + 2 \times 17 + 1$.
2. $168_{10} = 111111$.
3. $230_{10} = 201201$.
4. $271_{10} = 1001201$.

Thus a run of 230 zero groups can be compressed by generating two copies of the Huffman code of 99, followed by the Huffman code of 17, by two copies of the code of 7, and by the code of 1. Another possibility is to assign each of the base numbers 1, 3, 7, etc., two Huffman codes, one for two copies and the other one, for a single copy.

Bibliography

Fraenkel, A. S., and S. T. Klein (1985), "Novel Compression of Sparse Bit-Strings—Preliminary Report," in A. Apostolico and Z. Galil, eds., *Combinatorial Algorithms on Words*, Vol. 12, NATO ASI Series F:169–183, New York, Springer-Verlag.

Knuth, D. E. (1973), *The Art of Computer Programming*, Vol. 1, 2nd Ed., Reading, MA, Addison-Wesley.

8.5.5 Prefix Compression

The principle of the prefix compression method is to assign an address to each bit of 1 in the sparse string, divide each address into a prefix and a suffix, then select all the one-bits whose addresses have the same prefix and write them on the compressed file by writing the common prefix, followed by all the different suffixes. Compression will be achieved if we end up with many one-bits having the same prefix. In order for several one-bits to have the same prefix their addresses should be close. However, in a long, sparse string, the one-bits may be located far apart. Prefix compression tries to bring together one-bits that are separated in the string, by breaking up the string into equal-size segments that are then placed one below the other, effectively creating a sparse *matrix* of bits. It is easy to see that one-bits that are widely separated in the original string may get closer in this matrix. As an example consider a binary string of 2^{20} bits (a megabit). The maximum distance between bits in the original string is about a million, but when the string is rearranged as a matrix of dimensions $2^{10} \times 2^{10} = 1024 \times 1024$, the maximum distance between bits is only about a thousand.

Our problem is to assign addresses to matrix elements such that (1) the address of a matrix element is a single number and (2) elements that are close will be assigned addresses that do not differ by much. The usual way of referring to matrix elements is by row and column. We can create a one-number address by concatenating the row and column numbers of an element, but this is unsatisfactory. Consider, for example, the two matrix elements at positions $(1, 400)$ and $(2, 400)$. They are certainly close neighbors, but their numbers are 1400 and 2400, not very close!

We therefore use a different method. We think of the matrix as a digital image where each bit becomes a pixel (white for a zero-bit and black for a one-bit) and we require that this image be of size $2^n \times 2^n$ for some integer n. This normally necessitates extending the original string with zero bits until its size becomes an even power of two (2^{2n}). The original size of the string should therefore be written, in raw form, on the compressed file for the use of the decompressor. If the string is sparse, the corresponding image has few black pixels. Those pixels are assigned addresses using the concept of a *quadtree*.

To understand how this is done, let's assume that an image of size $2^n \times 2^n$ is given. We divide it into four quadrants and label them $\left(\begin{smallmatrix} 0 & 1 \\ 2 & 3 \end{smallmatrix}\right)$. Notice that these are 2-bit numbers. Each quadrant is subsequently divided into four subquadrants labeled in the same way. Each subquadrant thus gets a four-bit (two-digit) number. This process continues recursively, and as the subsubquadrants get smaller, their numbers get longer. When this numbering scheme is carried down to individual pixels, the number of a pixel turns out to be $2n$ bits long. Figure 8.27 shows the pixel numbering in a $2^3 \times 2^3 = 8 \times 8$ image and also a simple image consisting of 18 black pixels. Each pixel number is six bits (three digits) long, and they range from 000 to 333. The original string being used to create this image is

$$10000100010001000010010000011110001001000100010011000000110000000$$

(where the six trailing zeros, or some of them, have been added to make the string size an even power of two).

The first step is to use quadtree methods to figure out the three-digit id numbers of the 18 black pixels. They are 000, 101, 003, 103, 030, 121, 033, 122, 123, 132, 210, 301, 203, 303, 220, 221, 222, and 223.

The next step is to select a *prefix* value. For our example we select $P = 2$, a choice that is justified below. The code of a pixel is now divided into P prefix digits followed by $3 - P$ suffix digits. The last step goes over the sequence of black pixels

000 001 010 011	100 101 110 111
002 003 012 013	102 103 112 113
020 021 030 031	120 121 130 131
022 023 032 033	122 123 132 133
200 201 210 211	300 301 310 311
202 203 212 213	302 303 312 313
220 221 230 231	320 321 330 331
222 223 232 233	322 323 332 333

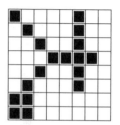

Figure 8.27: Example of Prefix Compression.

and selects all the pixels with the same prefix. The first prefix is 00, so all the pixels that start with 00 are selected. They are 000 and 003. They are removed from the original sequence and are compressed by writing the token 00|1|0|3 on the output stream. The first part of this token is a prefix (00), the second part is a count (1), and the rest are the suffixes of the two pixels having prefix 00. Notice that a count of one implies two pixels. The count is always one less than the number of pixels being counted. Sixteen pixels now remain in the original sequence, and the first of them has prefix 10. The two pixels with this prefix, namely 101 and 103, are removed and compressed by writing the token 10|1|1|3 on the output stream. This continues until the original sequence becomes empty. The final result is the nine-token string

$$00|1|0|3\ 10|1|1|3\ 03|1|0|3\ 12|2|1|2|3\ 13|0|2\ 21|0|0\ 30|1|1|3\ 20|0|3\ 22|3|0|1|2|3,$$

or in binary,

$$0000010011\ 0100010111\ 0011010011\ 011010011011\ 01110010$$
$$10010000\ 1100010111\ 10000011\ 10101100011011$$

(without the spaces). Such a string can be decoded uniquely, since each token starts with a two-digit prefix, followed by a one-digit count c, followed by $c+1$ one-digit suffixes. Preceding the tokens, the compressed file should contain, in raw form, the value of n, the original size of the sparse string, and the value of P that was used in the compression. Once this is understood, it becomes obvious that decompression is trivial. The decompressor reads the values of n and P, and these two numbers are all it needs to read and decode all the tokens unambiguously.

⋄ **Exercise 8.15:** Can adjacent pixels have different prefixes?

Notice that our example results in expansion because our binary string is short and therefore not sparse. A sparse string has to be at least tens of thousands of bits long.

In general, the prefix is P digits (or $2P$ bits) long, and the count and each suffix are $n-P$ digits each. The maximum number of suffixes in a token is therefore 4^{n-P}. The maximum size of a token is thus $P+(n-P)+4^{n-P}(n-P)$ digits. Each token corresponds to a different prefix. A prefix has P digits, each between 0 and 3, so the maximum number of tokens is 4^P. The entire compressed string thus occupies at most

$$4^P \left[P + (n - P) + 4^{n-P}(n - P) \right] = n \cdot 4^P + 4^n(n - P)$$

digits. To find the optimum value of P we differentiate the expression above with respect to P,

$$\frac{d}{dP} \left[n \cdot 4^P + 4^n(n - P) \right] = n \cdot 4^P \ln 4 - 4^n,$$

and set the derivative to zero. The solution is

$$4^P = \frac{4^n}{n \cdot \ln 4}, \quad \text{or} \quad P = \log_4 \left[\frac{4^n}{n \cdot \ln 4} \right] = \frac{1}{2} \log_2 \left[\frac{4^n}{n \cdot \ln 4} \right].$$

For $n = 3$ this yields

$$P \approx \frac{1}{2} \log_2 \left[\frac{4^3}{3 \times 1.386} \right] = \frac{\log_2 15.388}{2} = 3.944/2 = 1.97.$$

This is why $P = 2$ was selected in our example. A practical compression program should contain a table with P values precalculated for all expected values of n. Table 8.28 shows such values for $n = 1, 2, \ldots, 12$.

n:	1	2	3	4	5	6	7	8	9	10	11	12
P:	0.76	1.26	1.97	2.76	3.60	4.47	5.36	6.26	7.18	8.10	9.03	9.97

Table 8.28: Dependence of P on n.

```
Clear[t]; t=Log[4]; (* natural log *)
Table[{n,N[0.5 Log[2,4^n/(n t)],3]}, {n,1,12}]//TableForm
```

Mathematica Code for Table 8.28.

This method for calculating the optimum value of P is based on the worst case. It uses the maximum number of suffixes in a token, but many tokens have just a few suffixes. It also uses the maximum number of prefixes, but in a sparse string many prefixes may not occur. Experiments indicate that for large sparse strings (corresponding to n values of 9–12), better compression is obtained if the P value selected is one less than the value suggested by Table 8.28. However, for short sparse strings, the values of Table 8.28 are optimum. Selecting, for example, $P = 1$ instead of $P = 2$ for our short example (with $n = 3$) results in the four tokens

0|3|00|03|30|33   1|5|01|03|21|22|23|32   2|5|10|03|20|21|22|23   3|1|01|03,

which require a total of 96 bits, more than the 90 bits required for the choice $P = 2$.

In our example the count field can go up to three, which means that an output token, whose format is prefix|count|suffixes, can compress at most four pixels. A better choice may be to encode the count field so its length can vary. Even the simple unary code might produce good results, but a better choice may be a Huffman code where small counts are assigned short codes. Such a code may be calculated based on distribution of values for the `count` field determined by several "training" sparse strings. If the `count` field is encoded, then a token may have any size. The compressor thus has to generate the current token in a short array of bytes and write the "full" bytes on the compressed file, moving the last byte, which is normally only partly filled, to the start of the array before generating the next token. The very last byte is written to the compressed file with trailing zeros.

⋄ **Exercise 8.16:** Does it also make sense to encode the `prefix` and `suffix` fields?

One of the principles of this method is to bring the individual bits of the sparse string closer together by rearranging the one-dimensional string into a two-dimensional array. Thus, it seems reasonable to try to improve the method by rearranging the string into a three-dimensional array, a cube, or a rectangular box, bringing the bits even closer. If the size of the string is 2^{3n}, each dimension of the array will be of size 2^n. For $n = 7$, the maximum distance between bits in the string is $2^{37} = 2^{21} \approx 2$ million, while the distance between them in the three-dimensional cube is just $2^7 = 128$, a considerable reduction!

The cube can be partitioned by means of an *octree*, where each of the eight octants is identified by a number in the range 0–7 (a 3-bit number). When this partitioning is carried out recursively all the way to individual pixels, each pixel is identified by an n-digit number, where each digit is in the range 0–7.

⋄ **Exercise 8.17:** Is it possible to improve the method even more by rearranging the original string into a four-dimensional hypercube?

Decoding: The decoder starts by reading the value of n and constructing a matrix M of $2^n \times 2^n$ zeros. We assume that the rows and columns of M are numbered from 0 to $2^n - 1$. It then reads the next token from the compressed file and reconstructs the addresses (we'll call them *id numbers*) of the pixels (1-bits) included in the token. This task is straightforward and does not require any special algorithms. Next, the decoder has to convert each id into a row and column numbers. A recursive algorithm for that is shown here. Once the row and column of a pixel are known, the decoder sets that location in matrix M to 1. The last task is to "unfold" M into a single bit string, and delete any artificially appended zeros, if any, from the end.

Our recursive algorithm assumes that the individual digits of the id number are stored in an array `id`, with the most significant digit stored at location 0. The algorithm starts by setting the two variables `R1` and `R2` to 0 and $2^n - 1$, respectively. They denote the range of row numbers in M. Each step of the algorithm examines the next less-significant digit of the id number in array `id` and updates `R1` or `R2` such that the distance between them is halved. After n recursive steps, they meet at a common value which is the row number of the current pixel. Two more variables, `C1` and `C2`, are initialized and updated similarly, to become the column number of the current pixel in M. Figure 8.29 is a pseudo-code algorithm of a recursive procedure `RowCol` that executes this algorithm. A main program that performs the initialization and invokes `RowCol` is also listed. Notice that the symbol ÷ stands for integer division, and that the algorithm can easily be modified to the case where the row and column numbers start from 1.

```
procedure RowCol(ind,R1,R2,C1,C2: integer);
case ind of
0: R2:=(R1+R2)÷2; C2:=(C1+C2)÷2;
1: R2:=(R1+R2)÷2; C1:=((C1+C2)÷2)+1;
2: R1:=((R1+R2)÷2)+1; C2:=(C1+C2)÷2;
3: R1:=((R1+R2)÷2)+1; C1:=((C1+C2)÷2)+1;
endcase;
if ind≤n then RowCol(ind+1,R1,R2,C1,C2);
end RowCol;


main program
integer ind, R1, R2, C1, C2;
integer array id[10];
bit array M[2ⁿ,2ⁿ];
ind:=0; R1:=0; R2:=2ⁿ−1; C1:=0; C2:=2ⁿ−1;
RowCol(ind, R1, R2, C1, C2);
M[R1,C1]:=1;
end;
```

Figure 8.29: Recursive Procedure `RowCol`.

Bibliography

Salomon, D. (2000) "Prefix Compression of Sparse Binary Strings," *ACM Crossroads Magazine*, **6**(3), February.

8.6 Word-Based Text Compression

All the data compression methods mentioned in this book operate on small alphabets. A typical alphabet may consist of the two binary digits, the sixteen 4-bit pixels, the 7-bit ASCII codes, or the 8-bit bytes. In this section we consider the application of known methods to large alphabets that consist of *words*.

It is not clear how to define a word in cases where the input stream consists of the pixels of an image, so we limit our discussion to text streams. In such a stream a word is defined as a maximal string of either alphanumeric characters (letters and digits) or other characters (punctuations and spaces). We denote by A the alphabet of all the alphanumeric words and by P, that of all the other words. One consequence of this definition is that in any text stream—whether the source code of a computer program, a work of fiction, or a restaurant menu—words from A and P strictly *alternate*. A simple example is the C-language source line

"␣␣for␣(␣short␣i=0;␣i␣<␣npoints;␣i++␣)•",

where • indicates the end-of-line character (CR, LF, or both). This line can easily be broken up into the 15-word alternating sequence

"␣␣" "for" "␣(␣" "short" "␣" "i" "=" "0" ";␣" "i" "␣<␣" "npoints" ";␣" "i" "++␣)•".

Clearly, the size of a word alphabet can be very large and may for all practical purposes be considered infinite. This implies that a method that requires storing the entire alphabet in memory cannot be modified to deal with words as the basic units (symbols) of compression.

⋄ **Exercise 8.18:** What is an example of such a method?

A minor point to keep in mind is that short input streams tend to have a small number of distinct words, so when an existing compression method is modified to operate on words, care should be taken to make sure it still operates efficiently on small quantities of data.

Any compression method based on symbol frequencies can be modified to compress words if an extra pass is added, where the frequency of occurrence of all the words in the input is counted. This is impractical for the following reasons:

1. A two-pass method is inherently slow.
2. The information gathered by the first pass has to be included in the compressed stream, since the decoder needs it. This decreases the compression efficiency even if that information is included in compressed form.

It therefore makes more sense to come up with *adaptive* versions of existing methods. Such a version should start with an empty database (dictionary or frequency counts) and should add words to it as they are found in the input stream. When a new word is input, the raw, uncompressed ASCII codes of the individual characters in the word should be output, preceded by an escape code. In fact, it is even better to use some simple compression scheme to compress the ASCII codes. Such a version should also take advantage of the alternating nature of the words in the input stream.

8.6.1 Word-Based Adaptive Huffman Coding

This is a modification of the character-based adaptive Huffman coding (Section 2.9). Two Huffman trees are maintained, for the two alphabets A and P, and the algorithm alternates between them. Table 8.30 lists the main steps of the algorithm.

The main problems with this method are the following:

1. In what format to output new words. A new word can be written on the output stream, following the escape code, using the ASCII codes of its characters. However, since a word normally consists of several characters, a better idea is to code it by using the original, character-based, adaptive Huffman method. The word-based adaptive Huffman algorithm thus "contains" a character-based adaptive Huffman algorithm that is used from time to time. This point is critical, since a short input stream normally contains a high percentage of new words. Writing their raw codes on the output stream may degrade the overall compression performance considerably.
2. What to do when the encoder runs out of memory because of large Huffman trees. A good solution is to delete nodes from the tree (and to rearrange the tree after such deletions, so that it remains a Huffman tree) instead of deleting the entire tree. The best nodes to delete are those whose counts are so low that their Huffman codes are longer than the codes they would be assigned if they were seen for the

```
repeat
 input an alphanumeric word W;
 if W is in the A-tree then
  output code of W;
  increment count of W;
 else
  output an A-escape;
  output W (perhaps coded);
  add W to the A-tree with a count of 1;
  Increment the escape count
 endif;
 rearrange the A-tree if necessary;
 input an ''other'' word P;
 if P is in the P-tree then
  ...
  ... code similar to the above
  ...
until end-of-file.
```

Table 8.30: Word-Based Adaptive Huffman Algorithm.

first time. If there are just a few such nodes (or none at all), then nodes with low frequency counts should be deleted.

Experience shows that word-based adaptive Huffman coding produces better compression than the character-based version but is slower, since the Huffman trees tend to get big, slowing down the search and update operations.

3. The first word in the input stream may be either alphanumeric or other. The compressed stream should therefore start with a flag indicating the type of the first word.

8.6.2 Word-Based LZW

Word-based LZW is a modification of the character-based LZW method (Section 3.10). The number of words in the input stream is not known beforehand and may also be very large. As a result, the LZW dictionary cannot be initialized to all the possible words, as is done in the character-based original LZW method. The main idea is to start with an empty dictionary (actually two dictionaries, an A-dictionary and a P-dictionary) and use escape codes.

> You watch your phraseology!
> —Paul Ford as Mayor Shinn in *The Music Man* (1962)

Each phrase added to a dictionary consists of two strings, one from A and the other from P. All phrases where the first string is from A are added to the A-dictionary. All those where the first string is from P are added to the P-dictionary. The advantage of having 2 dictionaries is that phrases can be numbered starting from 1 in each dictionary, which keeps the phrase numbers small. Notice that two different phrases in the two dictionaries can have the same number, since the decoder knows whether the next phrase to be decoded comes from the `A`- or the `P`-dictionary. Table 8.31 is a general algorithm, where the notation "`S,W`" stands for string "`W`" appended to string "`S`".

```
 S:=empty string;
repeat
 if currentIsAlph then input alphanumeric word W
                  else input non-alphanumeric word W;
 endif;
 if W is a new word then
  if S is not the empty string then output string # of S; endif;
  output an escape followed by the text of W;
  S:=empty string;
 else
  if startIsAlph then search A-dictionary for string S,W
                 else search P-dictionary for string S,W;
  endif;
  if S,W was found then S:=S,W
  else
    output string numer of S;
    add S to either the A- or the P-dictionary;
    startIsAlph:=currentIsAlph;
    S:=W;
  endif;
 endif;
 currentIsAlph:=not currentIsAlph;
until end-of-file.
```

Table 8.31: Word-Based LZW.

Notice the line "`output an escape followed by the text of W;`". Instead of writing the raw code of `W` on the output stream it is again possible to use (character-based) LZW to code it.

8.6.3 Word-Based Order-1 Prediction

English grammar imposes obvious correlations between consecutive words. It is common, for example, to find the pairs of words "`the boy`" or "`the beauty`" in English text, but rarely a pair such as "`the went`". This reflects the basic syntax rules governing the structure of a sentence, and similar rules should exist in other languages as well. A compression algorithm using order-1 prediction can thus be very successful when applied to an input stream that obeys strict syntax rules. Such an algorithm should maintain an appropriate data structure for the frequencies of all the pairs of alphanumeric words seen so far. Assume that the text "$\ldots P_i\, A_i\, P_j$"

has recently been input, and the next word is A_j. The algorithm should get the frequency of the pair (A_i, A_j) from the data structure, compute its probability, send it to an arithmetic encoder together with A_j, and update the count of (A_i, A_j). Notice that there are no obvious correlations between consecutive punctuation words, but there may be some correlations between a pair (P_i, A_i) or (A_i, P_j). An example is a punctuation word that contains a period, which usually indicates the end of a sentence, suggesting that the next alphanumeric word is likely to start with an uppercase letter, and to be an article. Table 8.32 is a basic algorithm in pseudo-code, implementing these ideas. It tries to discover correlations only between alphanumeric words.

Since this method uses an arithmetic encoder to encode words, it is natural to extend it to use the same arithmetic encoder, applied to individual characters, to encode the raw text of new words.

Bibliography

Horspool, N. R. and G. V. Cormack (1992) "Constructing Word-Based Text Compression Algorithms," in *Proceedings of the 1992 Data Compression Conference*, J. Storer, ed., Los Alamitos, CA, IEEE Computer Society Press, pp. 62–71, April.

```
prevW:=escape;
repeat
  input next punctuation word WP and output its text;
  input next alphanumeric word WA;
  if WA is new then
    output an escape;
    output WA arithmetically encoded by characters;
    add AW to list of words;
    set frequency of pair (prevW,WA) to 1;
    increment frequency of the pair (prevW,escape) by 1;
  else
    output WA arithmetically encoded;
    increment frequency of the pair (prevW,WA);
  endif;
  prevW:=WA;
until end-of-file.
```

Table 8.32: Word-Based Order-1 Predictor.

When I use a word it means just what I choose it to mean—neither more nor less.

—Humpty Dumpty

8.7 Textual Image Compression

All of the methods described so far assume that the input stream is either a computer file or resides in memory. Life, however, isn't always so simple, and sometimes the data to be compressed consists of a printed document that includes text, perhaps in several columns, and rules (horizontal and vertical). The method described here cannot deal with images very well, so we assume that the input documents do not include any images. The document may be in several languages and fonts, and may contain musical notes or other notation instead of plain text. It may also be handwritten, but the method described here works best with printed material, since handwriting normally has too much variation. Examples are (1) rare books and important original historical documents that are deteriorating because of old age or mishandling, (2) old library catalog cards about to be discarded because of automation, and (3) typed manuscripts that are of interest to scholars. In many of these cases it is important to preserve *all* the information on the document, not just the text. This includes the original fonts, margin notes, and various smudges, fingerprints, and other stains.

Before any processing by computer, the document has, of course, to be scanned and converted into black and white pixels. Such a scanned document is called a *textual image*, since it is text described by pixels. In the discussion below, this collection of pixels is called *the input* or the *original image*. The scanning resolution should be as high as possible, and this raises the question of compression. Even at the low resolution of 300 dpi, an 8.5×11" page with 1-inch margins on all sides has a printed area of $6.5 \times 9 = 58.5$ square inches, which translates to $58.5 \times 300^2 = 5.265$ million pixels. At 600 dpi (medium resolution) such a page is converted to about 21 billion pixels. Compression makes even more sense if the document contains lots of blank space, since in such a case most of the pixels will be white.

One approach to this problem is OCR (optical character recognition). Existing OCR software uses sophisticated algorithms to recognize the shape of printed characters and output their ASCII codes. If OCR is used, the compressed file should include the ASCII codes, each with a pair of (x, y) coordinates specifying its position on the page.

◇ **Exercise 8.19:** The (x, y) coordinates may specify the position of a character with respect to an origin, perhaps at the top-left or the bottom-left corner of the page. What may be a better choice for the coordinates?

OCR may be a good solution in cases where the entire text is in one font, and there is no need to preserve stains, smudges, and the precise shape of badly printed characters. This makes sense for documents such as old technical manuals that are not quite obsolete and might be needed in the future. However, if the document contains several fonts, OCR software normally does a poor job. It also cannot handle accents, images, stains, musical notes, hieroglyphs, or anything other than text.

(It should be mentioned that recent releases of some OCR packages, such as Xerox Techbridge, *do* handle accents. The Adobe Acrobat Capture application goes even further. It inputs a scanned page and converts it to PDF format. Internally it represents the page as a collection of recognized glyphs and unrecognized bitmaps.

As a result it is capable of producing a PDF file that, when printed or viewed may be almost indistinguishable from the original.)

Facsimile compression (Section 2.13) can be used but does not produce the best results, since it is based on RLE and does not pay any attention to the text itself. A document where letters repeat all the time and another one where no character appears twice may end up being compressed by the same amount.

The method described here [Witten 92] is complex and requires several steps, but is general, it preserves the entire document, and results in excellent compression. Compression factors of 25 are not uncommon. The method can also be easily modified to include lossy compression as an option, in which case it may produce compression factors of 100 [Witten 94].

The principle of the method is to separate the pixels representing text from the rest of the document. The text is then compressed with a method that counts symbol frequencies and assigns them probabilities, while the rest of the document— which typically consists of random pixels and may be considered "noise"—is compressed by another, more appropriate, method. Here is a summary of the method (the reader is referred to [Witten 94] for the full details).

The encoder starts by identifying the lines of text. It then scans each line, identifying the boundaries of individual characters. The encoder does not attempt to actually recognize the characters. It treats each connected set of pixels as a character, called a *mark*. Often, a mark is a character of text, but it may also be part of a character. The letter "i", for example, is made up of two unconnected parts, the stem and the dot, so each becomes a mark. Something like "ö" becomes three marks. This way the algorithm does not need to know anything about the languages, fonts, or accents used in the text. The method works even if the "text" is made up of "exotic" characters, musical notes, or hieroglyphs. Figure 8.33 shows examples of three marks and some specks. A human can easily recognize the marks as the letters "PQR", but software would have a hard time at this, especially since some pixels are missing.

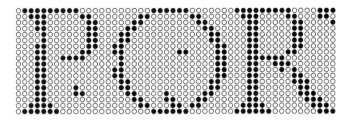

Figure 8.33: Marks and Specks.

Very small marks (less than the size of a period) are left in the input and are not further processed. Each mark above a certain size is compared to a library of previously found marks (called symbols). If the mark is identical to one of the symbols, its pixels are removed from the original textual image (the input). If the mark is "close enough" to one of the library symbols, then the difference between the mark and the symbol is left in the input (it becomes part of what is called the *residue*) and the rest is removed. If the mark is sufficiently different from all the library symbols, it is added to the library as a new symbol and all its pixels are removed from the input. In each of these cases the encoder generates the triplet

$$(\# \text{ of symbol in the library, } x, y),$$

which is later compressed. The quantities x and y are the horizontal and vertical distances (measured in pixels) between the bottom-left corner of the mark and the bottom-right corner of its predecessor; they are thus *offsets*. The first mark on a print line normally has a large negative x offset, since it is located way to the left of its predecessor.

The case where a mark is "sufficiently close" to a library symbol is important. In practice, this usually means that the mark and the symbol describe the same character but there are small differences between them due to poor printing or bad alignment of the document during scanning. The pixels that constitute the difference are therefore normally in the form of a *halo* around the mark. The residue is thus made up of halos (which are recognizable or almost recognizable as "ghost" characters) and specks and stains that are too small to be included in the library. Considered as an image, the residue is thus fairly random (and therefore poorly compressible), since it does not satisfy the condition "the near neighbors of a pixel should have the same value as the pixel itself."

When the entire input (the scanned document) has been scanned in this way, the encoder selects all the library symbols that matched just one mark and returns their pixels to the input. They become part of the residue. (This step is omitted when the lossy compression option is used.) The encoder is then left with the symbol library, the string of symbol triplets, and the residue. Each of these is compressed separately.

The decoder first decompresses the library and the list of triplets. This is fast and normally results in text that can immediately be displayed and interpreted by the user. The residue is then decompressed, adding pixels to the display and bringing it to its original form. This process suggests a way to implement lossy compression. Just ignore the residue (and omit the step above of returning once-used symbols to the residue). This speeds up both compression and decompression, and significantly improves the compression performance. Experiments show that the residue, even though made up of relatively few pixels, may occupy up to 75% of the compressed stream, since it is random in nature and thus compresses poorly.

The actual algorithm is very complex, since it has to identify the marks and decide whether a mark is close enough to any library symbol. Here, however, we will discuss just the way the library, triplets, and residue are compressed.

The number of symbols in the library is encoded first, by using one of the prefix codes of Section 2.3.1. Each symbol is then encoded in two parts. The first encodes the height and depth of the symbol (using the same code as for the number of symbols); the second encodes the pixels of the symbol using the two-level context-based image compression method of Section 4.16.

The triplets are encoded in three parts. The first part is the list of symbol numbers, which is encoded in a modified version of PPM (Section 2.18). The original PPM method was designed for an alphabet whose size is known in advance, but the number of marks in a document is unknown in advance and can be very large (especially if the document consists of more than one page). The second part is the list of x offsets, and the third part, the list of y offsets. They are encoded with adaptive arithmetic coding.

The x and y offsets are the horizontal and vertical distances (measured in pixels) between the bottom-right corner of one mark and the bottom-left corner of the next. In a neatly printed page, such as this one, all characters on a line, except those with descenders, are vertically aligned at their bottoms, which means that most y offsets will be either zero or small numbers. If a proportional font is used, then the horizontal gaps between characters in a word are also identical, resulting in x offsets that are also small numbers. The first character in a word has an x offset whose size is the interword space. In a neatly printed page all interword spaces on a line should be the same, although those on other lines may be different.

All this means that many values of x will appear several times in the list of x values, and the same for y values. What is more, if an x value of, say, 3 is found to be associated with symbol s, there is a good chance that other occurrences of the same s will have an x offset of 3. This argument suggests the use of an adaptive compression method for compressing the lists of x and y offsets.

The actual method used inputs the next triplet (s, x, y) and checks to see whether symbol s was seen in the past followed by the same offset x. If yes, then offset x is encoded with a probability

$$\frac{\text{the number of times this } x \text{ was seen associated with this } s}{\text{the number of times this } s \text{ was seen}},$$

and the count (s, x) incremented by 1. If x hasn't been seen associated with this s, then the algorithm outputs an escape code, and assigns x the probability

$$\frac{\text{the number of times this } x \text{ was seen}}{\text{the total number of } x \text{ offsets seen so far}},$$

(disregarding any associated symbols). If this particular value of x has never been seen in the past, the algorithm outputs a second escape code and encodes x using the same prefix code used for the number of library symbols (and for the height and width of a symbol). The y value of the triplet is then encoded in the same way.

Compressing the residue presents a special problem, since viewed as an image, the residue is random and thus incompressible. However, viewed as text, the residue consists mostly of halos around characters (in fact, most of it may be legible, or close to legible), which suggests the following approach:

The encoder compresses the library and triplets, and writes them on the compressed stream, followed by the compressed residue. The decoder reads the library and triplets, and uses them to decode the *reconstructed text*. Only then does it read and decompress the residue. Both encoder and decoder thus have access to the reconstructed text when they encode and decode the residue, and this fact is used to compress the residue! The two-level context-based image compression method of Section 4.16 is used, but with a twist.

A table of size 2^{17} is used to accumulate frequency counts of 17-bit contexts (in practice it is organized as a binary search tree or a hash table). The residue pixels

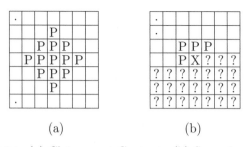

Figure 8.34: (a) Clairvoyant Context. (b) Secondary Context.

are scanned row by row. The first step in encoding a pixel at residue position (r, c) is to go to the same position (r, c) *in the reconstructed text* (which is, of course, an image made of pixels) and use the 13-pixel context shown in Figure 8.34a to generate a 13-bit index. The second step is to use the four-pixel context of Figure 8.34b *on the pixels of the residue* to add 4 more bits to this index. The final 17-bit index is then used to compute a probability for the current pixel based on the pixel's value (0 or 1) and on the counts found in the table for this 17-bit index. The point is that the 13-bit part of the index is based on pixels that *follow* the current pixel in the reconstructed text. Such a context is normally impossible (it is called *clairvoyant*) but can be used in this case, since the reconstructed text is known to the decoder. This is an interesting variation on the theme of compressing random data.

Even with this clever method, the residue still takes up a large part (up to 75%) of the compressed stream. After some experimentation the developers realized that it is not necessary to compress the residue at all! Instead, the original image (the input) can be compressed and decompressed using the method above, and this gives better results, even though the original image is less sparse than the residue, because it (the original image) is not as random as the residue.

This approach, of compressing the original image instead of the residue also means that the residue isn't necessary at all. The encoder does not need to reserve memory space for it and to actually create the pixels, which speeds up encoding.

The compressed stream thus contains two parts, the symbol library and triplets (which are decoded to form the reconstructed text), followed by the entire input in compressed form. The decoder decompresses the first part, displays it so the user can read it immediately, then uses it to decompress the second part. Another advantage of this method is that as pixels of the original image are decompressed and become known, they can be displayed, replacing the pixels of the reconstructed text and thus improving the decompressed image viewed by the user in *real time*. The decoder is therefore able to display an approximate image very quickly, and then clean it up row by row, while the user is watching, until the final image is displayed.

As has been mentioned, the details of this method are complex, since they involve a pattern recognition process in addition to the encoding and decoding algorithms. Here are some of the complexities involved.

Identifying and extracting a mark from the document is done by scanning the input from left to right and top to bottom. The first nonwhite pixel found is thus the top-left pixel of a mark. This pixel is used to trace the entire boundary of the mark, a complex process involving an algorithm similar to those used in computer graphics to fill an area. The main point is that the mark may have an inside boundary as well as an outside one (think of the letters "O," "P," "Q," and "Φ"), and there may be other marks nested inside it.

◇ **Exercise 8.20:** It seems that no letter of the alphabet is made of two nested parts. What are examples of marks that contain other, smaller marks nested within them?

Tracing the boundary of a mark also involves the question of connectivity. When are pixels considered connected? Figure 8.35 illustrates the concepts of 4- and 8-connectivity and makes it clear that the latter method should be used because the former may miss letter segments that we normally consider connected.

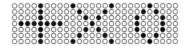

Figure 8.35: 4- and 8-Connectivity.

Comparing a mark to library symbols is the next complex problem. When is a mark considered "sufficiently close" to a library symbol? It is not enough to simply ignore small areas of pixels where the two differ, as this may lead to identifying, for example, an "e" with a "c". A more complex method is needed, based on pattern recognition techniques. It is also important to speed up the process of comparing a mark to a symbol, since a mark has to be compared to all the library symbols before it is considered a new one. An algorithm is needed that will find out quickly whether the mark and the symbol are too different. This algorithm may use clues such as large differences in the height and width of the two, or in their total areas or perimeters, or in the number of black pixels of each.

When a mark is determined to be sufficiently different from all the existing library symbols, it is added to the library and becomes a symbol. Other marks may be found in the future that are close enough to this symbol and end up being associated with it. They should be "remembered" by the encoder. The encoder therefore maintains a list attached to each library symbol, containing the marks associated with the symbol. When the entire input has been scanned, the library contains the first version of each symbol, along with a list of marks that are similar. To achieve better compression, each symbol is now replaced with an average of all the marks in its list. A pixel in this average is set to black if it is black in more than half the marks in the list. The averaged symbols not only result in better compression but also look better in the reconstructed text, making it possible to use lossy compression more often. In principle, any change in a symbol should result in modifications to the residue, but we already know that in practice the residue does not have to be maintained at all.

All these complexities make textual images a complex, interesting example of a special-purpose data compression method and show how much can be gained from a systematic approach in which every idea is implemented and experimented with before it is rejected, accepted, or improved upon.

Bibliography

Constantinescu, C., and R. Arps (1997) "Fast Residue Coding for Lossless Textual Image Compression," in *Proceedings of the 1997 Data Compression Conference*, J. Storer, ed., Los Alamitos, CA, IEEE Computer Society Press, pp. 397–406.

Witten, I. H., T. C. Bell, M. E. Harrison, M. L. James, and A. Moffat (1992) "Textual Image Compression," in *Proceedings of the 1992 Data Compression Conference*, J. Storer, ed., Los Alamitos, CA, IEEE Computer Society Press, pp. 42–51.

Witten, I. H., et al. (1994) *Managing Gigabytes: Compressing and Indexing Documents and Images*, New York, Van Nostrand Reinhold.

8.8 Dynamic Markov Coding

This is an adaptive, two-stage statistical compression method due to G. V. Cormack and R. N. Horspool [Cormack 87] (see also [Yu 96] for an implementation). Stage 1 uses a finite-state machine to estimate the probability of the next symbol. Stage 2 is an arithmetic encoder that performs the actual compression. Recall that the PPM method (Section 2.18) works similarly. Finite automata (also called finite-state machines) are introduced in an appendix in the book's web site.

> Three centuries after Hobbes, automata are multiplying with an agility that no vision formed in the seventeenth century could have foretold.
>
> —George Dyson, *Darwin Among the Machines* (1997)

A finite-state machine can be used in data compression as a model, to compute probabilities of input symbols. Figure 8.36a shows the simplest model, a one-state machine. The alphabet consists of the three symbols "a", "b", and "c". Assume that the input stream is the 600-symbol string "aaabbcaaabbc...". Each time a symbol is input, the machine outputs its estimated probability, updates its count, and stays in its only state. Each of the three probabilities is initially set to 1/3 and gets very quickly updated to its correct value (300/600 for "a", 200/600 for "b", and 100/600 for "c") because of the regularity of this particular input. Assuming that the machine always uses the correct probabilities, the entropy (number of bits per input symbol) of this first example is

$$-\frac{300}{600}\log_2\left(\frac{300}{600}\right) - \frac{200}{600}\log_2\left(\frac{200}{600}\right) - \frac{100}{600}\log_2\left(\frac{100}{600}\right) \approx 1.46.$$

Figure 8.36b illustrates a two-state model. When an "a" is input by state 1, it gets counted, and the machine switches to state 2. When state 2 inputs an "a" or a "b" it counts them and switches back to state 1 (this model will stop prematurely if state 2 inputs a "c"). Each sextet of symbols read from the input stream switches between the two states four times as follows:

$$a \xrightarrow{2} a \xrightarrow{1} a \xrightarrow{2} b \xrightarrow{1} b \xrightarrow{1} c \xrightarrow{1}.$$

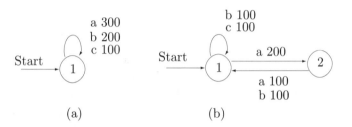

Figure 8.36: Finite-State Models for Data Compression.

State 1 accumulates 200 counts for "a", 100 counts for "b", and 100 counts for "c". State 2 accumulates 100 counts for "a" and 100 counts for "b". State 1 thus handles 400 of the 600 symbols, and state 2, the remaining 200. The probability of the machine being in state 1 is therefore $400/600 = 4/6$, and that of its being in state 2 is $2/6$.

The entropy of this model is calculated separately for each state, and the total entropy is the sum of the individual entropies of the two states, weighted by the probabilities of the states. State 1 has "a", "b", and "c" coming out of it with probabilities $2/6$, $1/6$, and $1/6$, respectively. State 2 has "a" and "b" coming out of it, each with probability $1/6$. The entropies of the two states are thus

$$-\frac{100}{600}\log_2\left(\frac{100}{600}\right) - \frac{200}{600}\log_2\left(\frac{200}{600}\right) - \frac{100}{600}\log_2\left(\frac{100}{600}\right) \approx 1.3899 \quad \text{(state 1)},$$

$$-\frac{100}{600}\log_2\left(\frac{100}{600}\right) - \frac{100}{600}\log_2\left(\frac{100}{600}\right) \approx 0.8616 \quad \text{(state 1)}.$$

The total entropy is thus $1.3899 \times 4/6 + 0.8616 \times 2/6 = 1.21$.

Assuming that the arithmetic encoder works at or close to the entropy, this two-state model encodes a symbol in 1.21 bits, compared to 1.46 bits/symbol for the previous, one-state model. This is how a finite-state machine with the right states can be used to produce good probability estimates (good predictions) for compressing data.

The natural question at this point is, given a particular input stream, how do we find the particular finite-state machine that will feature the smallest entropy for that stream. A simple, brute force approach is to try all the possible finite-state machines, pass the input stream through each of them, and measure the results. This approach is impractical, since there are n^{na} n-state machines for an alphabet of size a. Even for the smallest alphabet, with two symbols, this number grows exponentially: one 1-state machine, 16 2-state machines, 729 3-state machines, and so on.

Clearly, a clever approach is needed, where the algorithm can start with a simple one-state machine, and adapt it to the particular input data by adding states as it goes along, based on the counts accumulated at any step. This is the approach adopted by the DMC algorithm.

8.8.1 The DMC Algorithm

This algorithm was originally developed for binary data (i.e., a two-symbol alphabet). Common examples of binary data are machine code (executable) files, images (both monochromatic and color), and sound. Each state of the finite-state DMC machine (or DMC model; in this section the words "machine" and "model" are used interchangeably) reads a bit from the input stream, assigns it a probability based on what it has counted in the past, and switches to one of two other states depending on whether the input bit was 1 or 0. The algorithm starts with a small machine (perhaps as simple as just one state) and adds states to it based on the input. It is thus adaptive. As soon as a new state is added to the machine, it starts counting bits and using them to calculate probabilities for 0 and 1. Even in this simple form, the machine can grow very large and quickly fill up the entire available memory. One advantage of dealing with binary data is that the arithmetic encoder can be made very efficient if it has to deal with just two symbols.

In its original form, the DMC algorithm does not compress text very well. Recall that compression is done by reducing redundancy, and that the redundancy of a text file is featured in the text characters, not in the individual bits. It is possible to extend DMC to handle the 128 ASCII characters by implementing a finite-state machine with more complex states. A state in such a machine should input an ASCII character, assign it a probability based on what characters were counted in the past, and switch to one of 128 other states depending on what the input character was. Such a machine would grow to consume even more memory space than the binary version.

The DMC algorithm has two parts; the first is concerned with calculating probabilities, and the second is concerned with adding new states to the existing machine. The first part calculates probabilities by counting, for each state S, how many zeros and ones were input in that state. Assume that in the past the machine was in state S several times, and it input a zero s_0 times and a one s_1 times while in this state (i.e., it switched out of state S s_0 times on the 0 output, and s_1 times on the 1 output; Figure 8.37a). The simplest way to assign probabilities to the 2 bits is by defining the following:

The probability that a zero will be input while in state S is $\dfrac{s_0}{s_0 + s_1}$,

The probability that a one will be input while in state S is $\dfrac{s_1}{s_0 + s_1}$.

But this, of course, raises the *zero-probability problem*, since either s_0 or s_1 may be zero. The solution adopted by DMC is to assign probabilities that are always nonzero and that depend on a positive integer parameter c. The definitions are the following:

The probability that a zero will be input while in state S is $\dfrac{s_0 + c}{s_0 + s_1 + 2c}$,

The probability that a one will be input while in state S is $\dfrac{s_1 + c}{s_0 + s_1 + 2c}$.

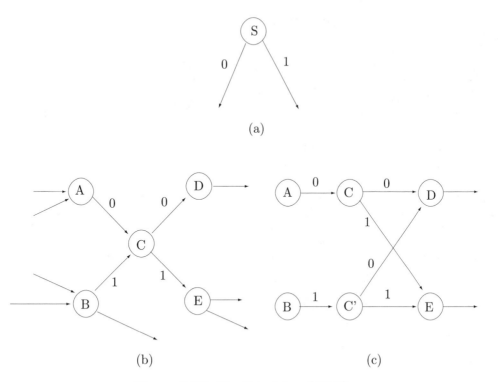

Figure 8.37: The Principles of DMC.

Assigning small values to c implies that small values of s_0 and s_1 will affect the probabilities significantly. This is done when the user feels that the distributions of the 2 bits in the data can be "learned" fast by the model. If the data is such that it takes longer to adapt to the correct bit distributions, larger values of c can lead to better compression. Experience shows that for very large input streams, the precise value of c does not make much difference.

$\diamond$ **Exercise 8.21:** Why is there c in the numerator but $2c$ in the denominator of the two probabilities?

The second part of the DMC algorithm is concerned with how to add a new state to the machine. Consider the five states shown in Figure 8.37b, which may be part of a large finite-state DMC model. When a 0 is input while in state A, or when a 1 is input while in state B, the machine switches to state C. The next input bit switches it to either D or E. When switching to D, e.g., some information is lost, since the machine does not "remember" whether it got there from A or from B. This information may be important if the input bits are correlated (i.e., if the probabilities of certain bit patterns are much different from those of other patterns). If the machine is currently in state A, it will get to D if it inputs 00. If it is in state B, it will get to D if it inputs 10. If the probabilities of the input patterns 00 and 10 are very different, the model may compute better probabilities (may produce better predictions) if it knew whether it came to D from A or from B.

The central idea of DMC is to compare the counts of the transitions $A \rightarrow C$ and $B \rightarrow C$, and if they are significantly different, to create a copy of state C, call it C', and place the copy such that $A \rightarrow C \rightarrow (D, E)$ but $B \rightarrow C' \rightarrow (D, E)$ (Figure 8.37c). This copying process is called *cloning*. The machine becomes more complex but can now keep better counts (counts that depend on the specific correlations between A and D, A and E, B and D, and B and E) and, as a result, compute better probabilities. Even adding one state may improve the probability estimates significantly since it may "bring to light" correlations between a state preceding A and one following D. In general, the more states that are added by cloning, the easier it is for the model to "learn" about correlations (even long ones) between the input bits.

Once the new state C' is created, the original counts of state C should be divided between C and C'. Ideally, they should be divided in proportion to the counts of the transitions $A \rightarrow C \rightarrow (D, E)$ and $B \rightarrow C \rightarrow (D, E)$, but these counts are not available (in fact, the cloning is done precisely in order to have these counts in the future). The next-best thing is to divide the new counts in proportion to the counts of the transitions $A \rightarrow C$ and $B \rightarrow C$.

An interesting point is that unnecessary cloning does not do much harm. It increases the size of the finite-state machine by one state, but the computed probabilities will not get worse. (Since the machine now has one more state, each state will be visited less often, which will lead to smaller counts and will therefore amplify small fluctuations in the distribution of the input bits, but this is a minor disadvantage.)

All this suggests that cloning be performed as early as possible, so we need to decide on the exact rule(s) for cloning. A look at Figure 8.37b shows that cloning should be done only when both transitions $A \rightarrow C$ and $B \rightarrow C$ have high counts. If both have low counts, there is "not enough statistics" to justify cloning. If A has a high count, and B a low count, not much will be gained by cloning C since B is not very active. This suggests that cloning should be done when both A and B have high counts and one of them has a much higher count than the other. The DMC algorithm thus uses two parameters $C1$ and $C2$, and the following rule:

> If the current state is A and the next one is C, then C is a candidate for cloning, and should be cloned if the count for the transition $A \rightarrow C$ is greater than $C1$ **and** the total counts for all the other transitions $X \rightarrow C$ are greater than $C2$ (X stands for all the states feeding C, except the current state A).

The choice of values for $C1$ and $C2$ is critical. Small values mean fast cloning of states. This implies better compression, since the model "learns" the correlations in the data faster, but also more memory usage, increasing the chance of running out of memory while there is still a lot of data to be compressed. Large values have the opposite effect. Any practical implementation should thus let the user specify the values of the two parameters. It also makes sense to start with small values and increase them gradually as compression goes along. This enables the model to "learn" fast initially, and also delays the moment when the algorithm runs out of memory.

⬦ **Exercise 8.22:** Figure 8.38 shows part of a finite-state DMC model. State A switches to D when it inputs a 1, so D is a candidate for cloning when A is the current state. Assuming that the algorithm has decided to clone D, show the states after the cloning.

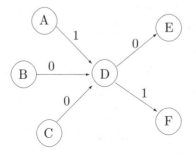

Figure 8.38: State D is a Candidate.

Figure 8.39 is a simple example that shows six steps of adding states to a hypothetical DMC model. The model starts with the single state 0 whose two outputs loop back and become its inputs (they are *reflexive*). In 8.39b a new state, state 1, is added to the 1-output of state 0. We use the notation $0, 1 \rightarrow 1$ (read: state 0 output 1 goes to new state 1) to indicate this operation. In 8.39c the operation $0, 0 \rightarrow 2$ adds a new state 2. In 8.39d,e,f states 3, 4, and 5 are added by the operations $1, 1 \rightarrow 3$; $2, 1 \rightarrow 4$; and $0, 0 \rightarrow 5$. Figure 8.39f, for example, was constructed by adding state 5 to output 0 of state 0. The two outputs of state 5 are determined by examining the 0-output of state 0. Since this output used to go to state 2, the new 0-output of state 5 goes to state 2. Also, since this output used to go to state 2, the new 1-output of state 5 becomes a copy of the 1-output of state 2, which is why it goes to state 4.

⬦ **Exercise 8.23:** Draw the DMC model after the operation $1, 1 \rightarrow 6$.

8.8.2 DMC Start and Stop

When the DMC algorithm starts, it needs to have only one state that switches to itself when either 0 or 1 are input, as shown in Figure 8.40a. This state is cloned many times and may grow very fast to become a complex finite-state machine with many thousands of states. This way to start the DMC algorithm works well for binary input. However, if the input consists of nonbinary symbols, an appropriate initial machine, one that takes advantage of possible correlations between the individual bits of a symbol, may lead to much better compression. The tree of Figure 8.40b is a good choice for 4-bit symbols, since each level corresponds to one of the 4 bits. If there is, for example, a large probability that a symbol $01xx$ will have the form $011x$ (i.e., a 01 at the start of a symbol will be followed by another 1), the model will discover it very quickly and will clone the state marked in the figure. A similar complete binary tree, but with 255 states instead of 15, may be appropriate as an initial model in cases where the data consists of 8-bit symbols.

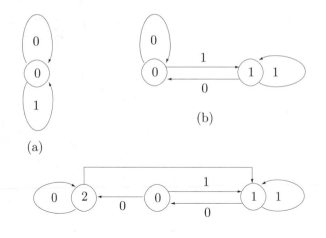

(a)

(b)

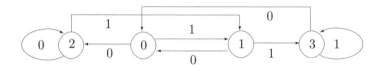

(c)

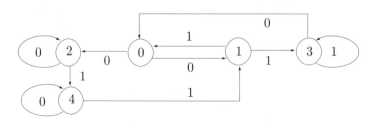

(d)

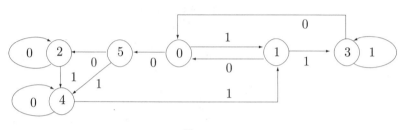

(e)

(f)

Figure 8.39: First Six States.

More complex initial machines may even take advantage of correlations between the last bit of an input symbol and the first bit of the next symbol. One such model, a *braid* designed for 3-bit input symbols, is shown in Figure 8.40c.

Any practical implementation of DMC should address the question of memory use. The number of states can grow very rapidly and fill up any amount of available memory. The simplest solution is to continue, once memory is full, without cloning. A better solution is to discard the existing model and start afresh. This has the advantage that new states being cloned will be based on new correlations discovered in the data, and old correlations will be forgotten. An even better solution is to always keep the k most recent input symbols in a circular queue and use them to build a small initial model when the old one is discarded. When the algorithm resumes, this small initial model will let it take advantage of the recently discovered correlations, so the algorithm will not have to "relearn" the data from scratch. This method minimizes the loss of compression associated with discarding the old model.

⋄ **Exercise 8.24:** How does the loss of compression depend on the value of k?

The main principle of DMC, the rule of cloning, is based on intuition and not on any theoretical principles. Consequently, the main justification of DMC is that it works! It produces very good compression, comparable to that achieved by PPM, while also being faster.

Bibliography

Cormack G. V. and R. N. S. Horspool (1987) "Data Compression Using Dynamic Markov Modelling," *The Computer Journal* **30**(6):541–550.

Yu, Tong Lai (1996) "Dynamic Markov Compression," *Dr Dobb's Journal* pp. 30–31, January.

8.9 FHM Curve Compression

The name FHM is an acronym that stands for Fibonacci, Huffman, and Markov. This method is a modification of the *multiring chain coding* method (see [Freeman 61] and [Wong 92]), and it uses Fibonacci numbers to construct squares of specific sizes around the current point, such that the total number of choices at any point in the compression is exactly 256.

The method is designed to compress curves, and it is especially suited for the compression of digital signatures. Such a signature is executed, at a point-of-sale or during parcel delivery, with a stylus on a special graphics tablet that breaks the signature curve into a large sequence of points. For each point $\mathbf{P}_i$ such a tablet records its coordinates, the time it took the user to move the stylus to $\mathbf{P}_i$ from $\mathbf{P}_{i-1}$, and the angle and pressure of the stylus at $\mathbf{P}_i$. This information is then kept in an archive and can be used later by a sophisticated algorithm to compare to future signatures. Since the sequence can be large (five items per point and hundreds of points), it should be archived in compressed form.

In the discussion below we consider only the compression of the coordinates. The resulting compressed curve is very close to the original one but any time, angle, and pressure information is lost. The method is based on the following two ideas:

1. A straight line is fully defined by its two endpoints, so any interior point can be ignored. In regions where the curve that is being compressed has small curvature

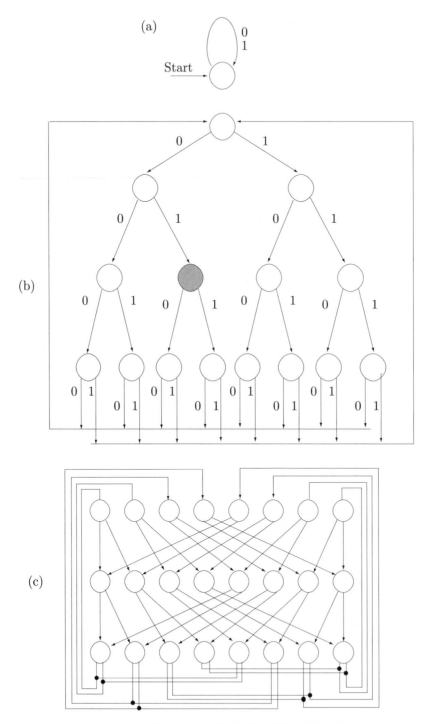

Figure 8.40: Initial DMC Models.

(i.e., it is close to a straight line) certain points that have been digitized by the tablet can be ignored without changing the shape of the curve.

2. At any point in the compression process the curve is placed inside a grid centered on the current *anchor point* A (the grid has the same coordinate size used by the tablet). The next anchor point B is selected such that (1) the straight segment AB is as long as possible, (2) the curve in the region AB is close to a straight line, and (3) B can be chosen from among 256 grid points. Any points that have been originally digitized by the tablet between A and B are deleted, and B becomes the current anchor point. Notice that in general B is not any of the points originally digitized. Thus, the method replaces the original set of points with the set of anchor points, and replaces the curve with the set of straight segments connecting the anchor points. In regions of large curvature the anchor points are close together. The first anchor point is the first point digitized by the tablet.

Figure 8.41a shows a 5×5 grid S_1 centered on the current anchor point X. There are 16 points on the circumference of S_1, and eight of them are marked with circles. We select the first point Y that's on the curve but is outside the grid, and connect points X and Y with a straight segment (the arrow in the figure). We select the two marked points nearest the arrow and construct the triangle shown in dashed. There are no points inside this triangle, which means that the part of the curve inside S_1 is close to a straight line. Before selecting the next anchor point, we try the next larger grid, S_2 (Figure 8.41b). This grid has 32 points on its circumference, and 16 of them are marked. As before, we select the first point Z located on the curve but outside S_2, and connect points X and Z with a straight segment (the arrow in the figure). We select the two marked points nearest the arrow and construct the triangle (in dashed). This time there is one point (Y) on the curve which is outside the triangle. This means that the part of the curve inside S_2 is not sufficiently close to a straight line. We therefore go back to S_1 and select point P (the marked point nearest the arrow) as the next anchor point. The distance between the next anchor and the true curve is therefore less than one grid unit. Point P is encoded, the grids are centered on P, and the process continues.

Figure 8.41c shows all six grids used by this method. They are denoted by S_1, S_2, S_3, S_5, S_8, and S_{13}, with 8, 16, 24, 40, 64, and 104 marked points, respectively. The total number of marked points is thus 256.

◇ **Exercise 8.25:** Where do the Fibonacci numbers come into play?

Since the next anchor point P can be one of 256 points, it can be written on the compressed stream in 8 bits. Both encoder and decoder should have a table or a rule telling them where each of the 256 points are located relative to the current anchor point. Experience shows that some of the 256 points are selected more often than others, which suggests a Huffman code to encode them. The 104 points on the border of S_{13}, for example, are selected only when the curve has a long region (26 coordinate units or more) where the curve is close to a straight line. These points should thus be assigned long Huffman codes. A practical way to determine the frequency of occurrence of each of the 256 points is to *train* the algorithm on many actual signatures. Once the table of 256 Huffman codes has been determined, it is built into both encoder and decoder.

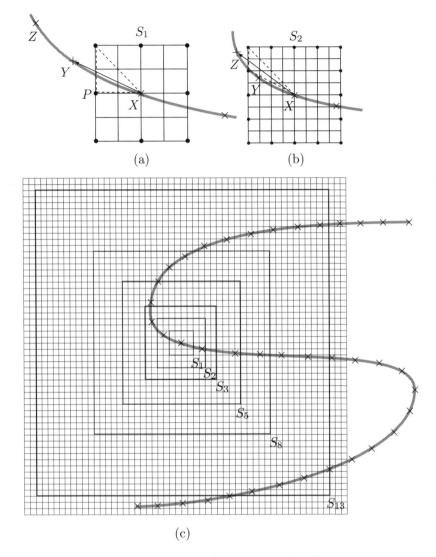

Figure 8.41: FHM Compression of a Curve.

Now for Markov. A Markov chain (or a Markov model) is a sequence of values where each value depends on one of its predecessors, not necessarily the immediate one, but not on any other value (in a k-order Markov model, a value depends on k of its past neighbors). Working with real signatures shows that the number of direction reversals (or near reversals) is small compared to the size of the signature. This implies that if a segment L_i between two anchor points goes in a certain direction, there is a good chance that the following segment L_{i+1} will point in a slightly different, but not very different, direction. Segment L_{i+1} thus depends on segment L_i but not on L_{i-1} or preceding segments. The sequence of segments L_i is thus a Markov chain, a fact that suggests using a different Huffman code table for each segment. A segment goes from one anchor point to the next. Since there are 256 different anchor points, a segment can point in one of 256 directions. We denote the directions by D_0, D_1,...,D_{255}. We now need to calculate 256 tables with 256 Huffman codes each; a total of $2^{16} = 65,536$ codes!

To calculate the Huffman code table for a particular direction D_i we need to analyze many signatures and count how many times a segment pointing in direction D_i is preceded by a segment pointing in direction D_0, how many times it is preceded by a segment pointing in direction D_1, and so on. In general, code j in the Huffman code table for direction D_i depends on the *conditional probability* $P(D_j|D_i)$ that a segment pointing in direction D_i is preceded by a segment pointing in direction D_j. Allocating 2^{16} locations for tables is not unusual in modern applications, and the main point is that the decoder can mimic all the encoder's operations.

⋄ **Exercise 8.26:** Estimate the conditional probability $P(D_i|D_i)$.

⋄ **Exercise 8.27:** Estimate the compression ratio of this method.

Bibliography

Fibonacci (1999), is file `Fibonacci.html` in URL
`http://www-groups.dcs.st-and.ac.uk/~history/References/`.

Freeman, H. (1961) "On The Encoding of Arbitrary Geometric Configurations," *IRE Transactions on Electronic Computers*, EC-10(2):260–268, June.

Vorobev, Nikolai N. (1983) Ian N. Sneddon (ed.), and Halina Moss (translator), *Fibonacci Numbers*, New Classics Library.

Wong, P. W. and J. Koplowitz (1992) "Chain Codes and Their Linear Reconstruction Filters," *IEEE Transactions on Information Theory*, IT-38(2):268–280, May.

8.10 Sequitur

Sequitur is based on the concept of context-free grammars, so we start with a short review of this field. A (natural) language starts with a small number of building blocks (letters and punctuation marks) and uses them to construct words and sentences. A sentence is a finite sequence (a string) of symbols that obeys certain grammar rules, and the number of valid sentences is, for all practical purposes, unlimited. Similarly, a formal language uses a small number of symbols (called *terminal symbols*) from which valid sequences can be constructed. Any valid sequence is finite, the number of valid sequences is normally unlimited, and the sequences are constructed according to certain rules (sometimes called *production rules*).

The rules can be used to construct valid sequences and also to determine whether a given sequence is valid. A production rule consists of a nonterminal symbol on the left and a string of terminal and nonterminal symbols on the right. The nonterminal symbol on the left becomes the name of the string on the right. In general, the right-hand side may contain several alternative strings, but the rules generated by sequitur have just a single string.

The entire field of formal languages and grammars is based on the pioneering work of Noam Chomsky in the 1950s [Chomsky 56]. The BNF notation, used to describe the syntax of programming languages, is based on the concept of production rules, as are also L Systems [Salomon 99].

We use lowercase letters to denote terminal symbols and uppercase letters for the nonterminals. Suppose that the following production rules are given: $A \rightarrow ab$, $B \rightarrow Ac$, $C \rightarrow BdA$. Using these rules we can generate the valid strings ab (an application of the nonterminal A), abc (an application of B), abcdab (an application of C), as well as many others. Alternatively, we can verify that the string abcdab is valid since we can write it as AcdA, rewrite this as BdA, and replace this with C. It is clear that the production rules reduce the redundancy of the original sequence, so they can serve as the basis of a compression method.

In a context-free grammar, the production rules do not depend on the context of a symbol. There are also context-sensitive grammars.

Sequitur (from the Latin for "it follows") is based on the concept of context-free grammars. It considers the input stream a valid sequence in some formal language. It reads the input symbol by symbol and uses repeated phrases in the input data to build a set of context-free production rules. Each repetition results in a rule, and is replaced by the name of the rule (a nonterminal symbol), thereby resulting in a shorter representation. Generally, a set of production rules can be used to generate many valid sequences, but the production rules produced by sequitur are not general. They can be used only to reconstruct the original data. The production rules themselves are not much smaller than the original data, so sequitur has to go through one more step, where it compresses the production rules. The compressed production rules become the compressed stream, and the sequitur decoder uses the rules (after decompressing them) to reconstruct the original data.

If the input is a typical text in a natural language, the top-level rule becomes very long, typically 10–20% of the size of the input, and the other rules are short, with typically 2–3 symbols each.

Figure 8.42 shows three examples of short input sequences and grammars. The input sequence S on the left of Figure 8.42a is already a (one-rule) grammar. However, it contains the repeated phrase bc, so this phrase becomes a production rule whose name is the nonterminal symbol A. The result is a two-rule grammar, where the first rule is the input sequence with its redundancy removed, and the second rule is short, replacing the *digram* bc with the single nonterminal symbol A. (The reader should review the discussion of digram encoding in Section 1.3.)

Figure 8.42b is an example of a grammar where rule A uses rule B. The input S is considered a one-rule grammar. It has redundancy, so each occurrence of abcdbc is replaced with A. Rule A still has redundancy because of a repetition of the phrase bc, which justifies the introduction of a second rule B.

Sequitur constructs its grammars by observing two principles (or enforcing two *constraints*) that we denote by $p1$ and $p2$. Constraint $p1$ is; No pair of adjacent symbols will appear more than once in the grammar (this can be rephrased as; Every digram in the grammar is unique). Constraint $p2$ says; Every rule should be used more than once. This ensures that rules are useful. A rule that occurs just once is useless and should be deleted.

The sequence of Figure 8.42a contains the digram bc twice, so $p1$ requires the creation of a new rule (rule A). Once this is done, digram bc occurs just once,

Input	Grammar
S → abcdbc	S → aAdA
	A → bc
(a)	
S → abcdbcabcdbc	S → AA
	A → aBdB
	B → bc
(b)	
S → abcdbcabcdbc	S → AA
	A → abcdbc
	S → CC
	A → bc
	B → aA
	C → BdA
(c)	

Figure 8.42: Three Input Sequences and Grammars.

inside rule A. Figure 8.42c shows how the two constraints can be violated. The first grammar of Figure 8.42c contains two occurrences of bc, thereby violating $p1$. The second grammar contains rule B, which is used just once. It is easy to see how removing B reduces the size of the grammar.

◇ **Exercise 8.28:** Show this!

The sequitur encoder constructs the grammar rules while enforcing the two constraints at all times. If constraint $p1$ is violated, the encoder generates a new production rule. When $p2$ is violated, the useless rule is deleted. The encoder starts by setting rule S to the first input symbol. It then goes into a loop where new symbols are input and appended to S. Each time a new symbol is appended to S, the symbol and its predecessor become the current digram. If the current digram already occurs in the grammar, then $p1$ has been violated, and the encoder generates a new rule with the current digram on the right-hand side and with a new nonterminal symbol on the left. The two occurrences of the digram are replaced by this nonterminal.

Figure 8.43 illustrates the operation of the encoder on the input sequence abcd-bcabcd. The leftmost column shows the new symbol being input, or an action being taken to enforce one of the two constraints. The next two columns from the left list the input so far and the grammar created so far. The last two columns list duplicate digrams and any underused rules. The last line of Figure 8.43a shows how the input symbol c creates a repeat digram bc, thereby triggering the generation of a new rule A. Notice that the appearance of a new, duplicate digram does not always generate a new rule. If, for example, the new, duplicate digram xy is created, but is found to be the right-hand side of an existing rule A → xy, then xy is replaced by A and there is no need to generate a new rule. This is illustrated in Figure 8.43b,

New symbol or action	the string so far	resulting grammar	duplicate digrams	unused rules
a	a	S → a		
b	ab	S → ab		
c	abc	S → abc		
d	abcd	S → abcd		
b	abcdb	S → abcdb		
c	abcdbc	S → abcdbc	bc	
enforce		S → aAdA		
p1		A → bc		
(a)				
a	abcdbca	S → aAdAa		
		A → bc		
b	abcdbcab	S → aAdAab		
		A → bc		
c	abcdbcabc	S → aAdAabc	bc	
		A → bc		
enforce		S → aAdAaA	aA	
p1		A → bc		
(b)				
enforce	abcdbcabc	S → BdAB		
p1		A → bc		
		B → aA		
(c)				
d	abcdbcabcd	S → BdABd	Bd	
		A → bc		
		B → aA		
enforce		S → CAC		B
p1		A → bc		
		B → aA		
		C → Bd		
enforce		S → CAC		
p2		A → bc		
		C → aAd		
(d)				

Figure 8.43: A Detailed Example of the Sequitur Encoder (After [Nevill-Manning and Witten 97]).

where a third occurrence of bc is found. No new rule is generated, and existing rule A is appended to S. This creates a new, duplicate digram aA in S, so a new rule B → aA is generated in Figure 8.43c. Finally, Figure 8.43d illustrates how enforcing $p2$ results in a new rule (rule C) whose right-hand side consists of three symbols. This is how rules longer than a digram can be generated.

⋄ **Exercise 8.29:** Why is rule B removed in Figure 8.43d?

One more detail, namely rule utilization, still needs to be discussed. When a new rule X is generated, the encoder also generates a counter associated with X, and initializes the counter to the number of times X is used (a new rule is normally used twice when it is first generated). Each time X is used in another rule Y, the encoder increments X's counter by 1. When Y is deleted, the counter for X is decremented by 1. If X's counter reaches 1, rule X is deleted.

As mentioned earlier, the grammar (the set of production rules) is not much smaller than the original data, so it has to be compressed. An example is file book1 of the Calgary Corpus (Table 3), which is 768,771 bytes long. The sequitur encoder generates for this file a grammar where the first rule (rule S) has 131,416 symbols, and each of the other 27,364 rules has 1.967 symbols on average. Thus, the size of the grammar is 185,253 symbols, or about 24% the size of the original data; not very impressive. There is also the question of the names of the nonterminal symbols. In the case of book1 there are 27,365 rules (including rule S), so 27,365 names are needed for the nonterminal symbols.

The method described here for compressing the grammar has two parts. The first part uses arithmetic coding to compress the individual grammar symbols. The second part provides an elegant way of handling the names of the many nonterminal symbols.

Part 1 uses adaptive arithmetic coding (Section 2.15) with an order-0 model. Constraint $p1$ ensures that no digram appears twice in the grammar, so there is no advantage to using higher-order models to estimate symbol probabilities while compressing a grammar. This is also the reason why compression methods that use high-order models, such as PPM (Section 2.18), would not do a better job in this case. Applying this method to the grammar of book1 yields compression of 3.49 bpc; not very good.

Part 2 eliminates the need to compress the names of the nonterminal symbols. The number of terminal symbols (normally letters and punctuation) is relatively small. This is typically the set of 128 ASCII characters. The number of nonterminals, on the other hand, can be huge (27,365 for book1). The solution is to not assign explicit names to the nonterminals. The encoder sends (i.e., writes on the compressed stream) the sequence of input symbols, and whenever it generates a rule, it sends enough information so the decoder can reconstruct the rule. Rule S represents the entire input, so this method is equivalent to sending rule S and sending other rules as they are generated.

When a nonterminal is found by the encoder while sending rule S, it is handled in one of three ways, depending on how many times it has been encountered in the past. The first time a nonterminal is found in S, its contents (i.e., the right-hand side of the rule) are sent. The decoder does not even know that it is receiving symbols that constitute a rule. The second time the nonterminal is found, a pair (pointer, count) is sent. The pointer is the offset of the nonterminal from the start of rule S, and the counter is the length of the rule. (This is similar to the tokens generated by LZ77, Section 3.2.) The decoder uses the pair to form a new rule that it can use later. The name of the rule is simply its serial number, and rules are numbered by both encoder and decoder in the same way. On the third and subsequent occurrences of the nonterminal, its serial number is sent by the encoder and is identified by the decoder.

This way, the first two times a rule is encountered, its name (i.e., its serial number) is not sent, a feature that greatly improves compression. Also, instead of sending the grammar to the decoder rule by rule, a rule is sent only when it is needed for the first time. Using arithmetic coding together with part 2 to compress book1 yields compression of 2.82 bpc.

◇ **Exercise 8.30:** Show the information sent to the decoder for the input string abcdbcabcdbc (Figure 8.42b).

Detailed information about the actual implementation of sequitur can be found in [Nevill-Manning 96].

One advantage of sequitur is that every rule is used more than once. This is in contrast to some dictionary-based methods that add (to the dictionary) strings that may never occur in the future and thus may never be used.

Once the principles of sequitur are understood, it is easy to see that it performs best when the data to be compressed consists of identical strings that are adjacent. In general, identical strings are not adjacent in the input stream, but there is one type of data, namely *semi-structured text*, where identical strings are many times also adjacent. Semi-structured text is defined as data that is human readable and also suitable for machine processing. A common example is HTML. An HTML file consists of text with markup tags embedded. There is a small number of different tags, and they have to conform to certain rules. Thus, the tags can be considered highly structured, in contrast to the text, which is unstructured and free. The entire HTML file is therefore semi-structured. Other examples of semi-structured text are forms, email messages, and data bases. When a form is stored in the computer, some fields are fixed (these are the highly structured parts) and other parts have to be filled out by the user (with unstructured, free text). An email message includes several fixed parts in addition to the text of the message. The same is true for a database. Sequitur was used by its developers to compress two large genealogical data bases [Nevill-Manning and Witten 97], resulting in compression ratios of 11–13%.

Sequitur can be used interactively at www.cs.waikato.ac.nz/sequitur.

Bibliography

Nevill-Manning, C. G. (1996) "Inferring Sequential Structure," Ph.D. thesis, Department of Computer Science, University of Waikato, New Zealand.

Nevill-Manning, C. G., and Ian H. Witten (1997) "Compression and Explanation Using Hierarchical Grammars," *The Computer Journal*, **40**(2/3):104–116.

8.11 Triangle Mesh Compression: Edgebreaker

Polygonal surfaces are commonly used in computer graphics. Such a surface is made up of flat polygons, and is therefore very simple to construct, save in memory, and render. A surface is normally rendered by simulating the light reflected from it (although some surfaces are rendered by simulating light that they emit or transmit). Since a polygonal surface is made of flat polygons, it looks angular and unnatural when rendered. There are, however, simple methods (such as Gouraud shading and Phong shading, see, e.g., [Salomon 99]) that smooth the reflection over the polygons, resulting in a realistic-looking smooth, curved surface. This fact, combined with the simplicity of the polygonal surface, has made this type of surface very common.

Any flat polygon can be used in a polygonal surface, but triangles are common, since a triangle is always flat (other polygons have to be tested for flatness before they can be used in such a surface). This is why a polygonal surface is normally a triangle mesh. Such a mesh is fully represented by the coordinates of its vertices (the triangle corners) and by its connectivity information (the edges connecting the vertices). Since polygonal surfaces are so common, compressing a triangle mesh is a practical problem. The edgebreaker algorithm described here [Rossignac 98] is an efficient method that can compress the connectivity information of a triangle mesh to about two bits per triangle; an impressive result (the list of vertex coordinates is compressed separately).

Mathematically, the connectivity information is a graph called the *incidence graph*. Edgebreaker is therefore an example of a *geometric compressor*. It can compress certain types of geometries. For most triangle meshes, the number of triangles is roughly twice the number of vertices. As a result, the incidence graph is typically twice as big as the list of vertex coordinates. The list of vertex coordinates is also easy to compress, since it consists of triplets of numbers (integer or real), but it is not immediately clear how to efficiently compress the geometric information included in the incidence graph. This is why edgebreaker concentrates on compressing the connectivity information.

The edgebreaker encoder encodes the connectivity information of a triangle mesh by traversing it triangle by triangle, and assigning one of five codes to each triangle. The code expresses the topological relation between the current triangle and the boundary of the remaining mesh. The code is appended to a history list of triangle codes, and the current triangle is then removed. Removing a triangle may change the topology of the remaining mesh. In particular, if the remaining mesh is separated into two regions with just one common vertex, then each region is compressed separately. Thus, the method is recursive, and it uses a stack to save one edge of each of the regions waiting to be encoded. When the last triangle of a region is removed, the encoder pops the stack and starts encoding another region. If the stack is empty (there are no more regions to compress), the algorithm terminates. The decoder uses the list of triangle codes to reconstruct the connectivity, following which, it uses the list of vertex coordinates to assign the original coordinates to each vertex.

The Encoding Algorithm: We assume that the original triangle mesh is homeomorphic to half a sphere, that is, it is a single region, and it has a boundary

B that is a closed polygonal curve without self intersections. The boundary is called a *loop*. One edge on the boundary is selected and is denoted by g (this is the current *gate*). Since the gate is on the boundary, it is an edge of just one triangle. Depending on the local topology of g and its triangle, the triangle is assigned one of the five codes C, L, E, R, or S. The triangle is then removed (which changes the boundary B) and the next gate is selected among one of the edges on the boundary. The next gate is an edge of the new current triangle, adjacent to the previous one.

> The term *homeomorphism* is a topological concept that refers to intrinsic topological equivalence. Two objects are homeomorphic if they can be deformed into each other by a continuous, invertible mapping. Homeomorphism ignores the geometric details of the objects and also the space in which they are embedded, so the deformation can be performed in a higher-dimensional space. Examples of homeomorphic objects are (1) mirror images, (2) a Möbius strip with an even number of half-twists and another Möbius strip with an odd number of half-twists, (3) a donut and a ring.

Figure 8.44e demonstrates how removing a triangle (the one marked X) may convert a simple mesh into two regions sharing a common vertex but not a common edge. The boundary of the new mesh now intersects itself, so the encoder divides it into two regions, each with a simple, non-self-intersecting boundary. An edge on the boundary of one region is pushed into the stack, to be used later, and the encoder continues with the triangles of the remaining region. If the original mesh is large, many regions may be formed during encoding. After the last triangle in a mesh has been assigned a code and has been removed (the code of the last triangle in a mesh is always E), the encoder pops the stack, and starts on another region. Once a code is determined for a triangle, it is appended to a compression history H. This history is a string whose elements are the five symbols C, L, E, R, and S, where each symbol is encoded by a prefix code. Surprisingly, this history is all that the decoder needs to reconstruct the connectivity of the original mesh.

Next, we show how the five codes are assigned to the triangles. Let **v** be the third vertex of the current triangle (the triangle whose outer edge is the current gate g, marked with an arrow). If **v** hasn't been visited yet, the triangle is assigned code C. Vertex **v** of Figure 8.44a hasn't been visited yet, since none of the triangles around it has been removed. The current triangle (marked X) is therefore assigned code C. A triangle is assigned code L (left) if its third vertex (the one that does not bound the gate) is exterior (located on the boundary) and immediately precedes g (Figure 8.44b). Similarly, a triangle is assigned code R (right) if its third vertex is exterior and immediately follows g (Figure 8.44d). If the third vertex **v** is exterior but does not immediately precede or follow the current gate, the triangle is assigned code S (Figure 8.44e). Finally, if the triangle is the last one in its region (i.e., if vertex **v** immediately precedes and immediately follows g), the triangle is assigned code E (Figure 8.44c).

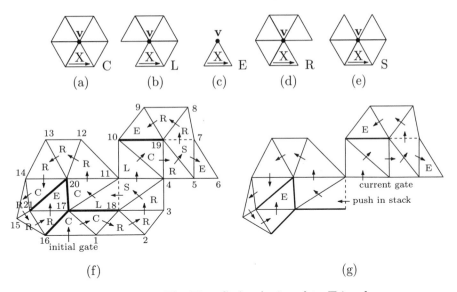

Figure 8.44: The Five Codes Assigned to Triangles.

Figure 8.44f shows an example of a mesh with 24 triangles. The initial gate (selected arbitrarily) is indicated. The arrows show the order in which the triangles are visited. The vertices are numbered in the order in which they are added to the list **P** of vertex coordinates. The decoder reconstructs the mesh in the same order as the encoder, so it knows how to assign the vertices the same serial numbers. The decoder then uses the list **P** of vertex coordinates to assign the actual coordinates to all the vertices. The third set of coordinates in **P**, for example, is assigned to the vertex labeled 3.

Initially, the entire mesh is one region. Its boundary is a 16-segment polygonal curve that does not intersect itself. During encoding, as the encoder removes more and more triangles, the mesh degenerates into three regions, so two edges (the ones shown in dashed lines) are pushed into the stack and are popped out later. Figure 8.44g shows the first two regions and the last triangles of the three regions. As the encoder moves from triangle to triangle, all the interior edges (except the five edges shown in thick lines) become gates. The encoder produces a list **P** of the coordinates of all 21 vertices, as well as the compression history

$$H = \text{CCRRRSLCRSERRELCRRRCRRRE.}$$

Notice that there are three triangles with a code of E. They are the last triangles visited in the three regions. Also, each C triangle corresponds to an interior vertex (of which there are five in our example).

The list **P** of vertex coordinates is initialized to the coordinates of the vertices on the boundary of the mesh (if the mesh has a boundary; a mesh that is homeomorphic to a sphere does not have a boundary curve). In our example, these are vertices 1–16. During the main loop, while the encoder examines and removes triangles, it appends (an interior) vertex to **P** for each triangle with a code of C. In our example, these are the five interior vertices 17–21.

A few more terms, as well as some notation, have to be specified before the detailed steps of the encoding algorithm can be listed. The term *half-edge* is a useful topological concept. This is a directed edge together with one of the two triangles incident on it. Figure 8.45a shows two triangles X and Y with a common edge. The common edge together with triangle X is one half-edge, and the same common edge together with triangle Y is another half-edge pointing in the opposite direction. An exterior edge is associated with a single half-edge. The following terms are associated with a half-edge h (Figure 8.45b,c):

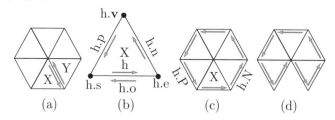

Figure 8.45: Manipulating Half-Edges.

1. The start vertex of h is denoted by h.s.
2. The end vertex of h is denoted by h.e.
3. The third vertex of X (the one that does not bound h) is denoted by h.v.
4. The half-edge that follows h in the triangle X is denoted by h.n.
5. The half-edge that precedes h in the triangle X is denoted by h.p.
6. The half-edge that is the opposite of h is denoted by h.o.
7. The half-edge that follows h in the boundary of the mesh is denoted by h.N.
8. The half-edge that precedes h in the boundary is denoted by h.P.

Figure 8.45c shows a simple mesh composed of six triangles. Six half-edges are shown along the boundary of the mesh. While the encoder visits triangles and removes them, the boundary of the mesh changes. When a triangle is removed, a half-edge that used to be on the boundary disappears, and two half-edges that used to be interior are now positioned on the boundary. This is illustrated in Figure 8.45d. To help the encoder manipulate the half-edges, they are linked in a list. This is a doubly linked, cyclic list where each half-edge points both to its successor and to its predecessor.

The algorithm presented here uses simple notation to indicate operations on the list of half-edges. The notation h.x = y indicates that field h.x of half-edge h should be set to point to y. The algorithm also uses two types of binary flags. Flags **v**.m mark each previously visited vertex **v**. They are used to distinguish between C and S triangles without having to traverse the boundary. Flags h.m mark each half-edge h located on the boundary of the remaining portion of the mesh. These flags are used during S operations to simplify the process of finding the half-edge b such that g.**v** is b.**e**. The last notational element is the vertical bar, used to denote concatenation. Thus, H=H|C indicates the concatenation of code C to the history so far, and **P**=**P**|**v** indicates the operation of appending vertex **v** to the list of vertex coordinates **P**.

The edgebreaker encoding algorithm can now be shown in detail. It starts with an initialization step where (1) the first gate is selected and a pointer to it is pushed into the stack, (2) all the half-edges along the boundary are identified, marked, and linked in a doubly-linked, cyclic list, and (3) the list of coordinate vertices **P** is initialized. **P** is initialized to the coordinates of all the vertices on the boundary of the mesh (if the mesh has a boundary) starting from the end-vertex of the gate.

The main loop iterates on the triangles, starting from the triangle associated with the first gate. Each triangle is assigned a code and is removed. Depending on the code, the encoder executes one of five cases (recall that B stands for the boundary of the current region). The loop can stop only when a triangle is assigned code E (i.e., it is the last in its region). The routine that handles case E tries to pop the stack for a pointer to the gate of the next region. If the stack is empty, all the regions that constitute the mesh have been encoded, so the routine stops the encoding loop. Here is the main loop:

```
if not g.v.m then case C   % v not marked
  else if g.p==g.P          % left edge of X is in B
     then if g.n==g.N then case E else case L endif;
     else if g.n==g.N then case R else case S endif;
        endif;
endif;
```

The details of the five cases are shown here, together with diagrams illustrating each case.

Case C: Figure 8.46 shows a simple region with six half-edges on its boundary, linked in a list. The bottom triangle gets code C, it is removed, and the list loses one half-edge and gains two new ones.

Case L: Figure 8.47 is a simple example of this case. The left edge of the bottom triangle is part of the boundary of the region. The triangle is removed, and the boundary is updated.

Case R: Figure 8.48 shows an example of this case. The right edge of the current triangle is part of the boundary of the region. The triangle is removed, and the boundary is updated.

Case S: Figure 8.49 shows a simple example. The upper triangle is missing, so removing the bottom triangle converts the original mesh to two regions. The one on the left is pushed into the stack, and the encoder continues with the region on the right.

Case E: Figure 8.50 shows the last triangle of a region. It is only necessary to unmark its three edges. The stack is then popped for the gate to the next region. If the stack is empty (no more regions), the encoder stops.

Compressing the History: The history string H consists of just five types of symbols, so it can easily and efficiently be compressed with prefix codes. An efficient method is a two-pass compression job where the first pass counts the frequency of each symbol and the second pass does the actual compression. In between the

```
H=H|C;                    % append C to history
P=P|g.v;                  % append v to P
g.m=0; g.p.o.m=1;         % update flags
g.n.o.m=1; g.v.m=1;
g.p.o.P=g.P; g.P.N=g.p.o; % fix link 1
g.p.o.N=g.n.o; g.n.o.P=g.p.o; % fix link 2
g.n.o.N=g.N; g.N.P=g.n.o; % fix link 3
g=g.n.o; StackTop=g;      % advance gate
```

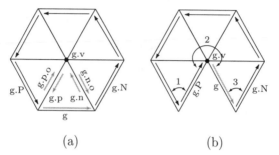

(a)   (b)

Figure 8.46: Handling Case C.

```
H=H|L;                    % append L to history
g.m=0; g.P.m=0; g.n.o.m=1; % update flags
g.P.P.n=g.n.o; g.n.o.P=g.P.P; % fix link 1
g.n.o.N=g.N; g.N.P=g.n.o; % fix link 2
g=g.n.o; StackTop=g;      % advance gate
```

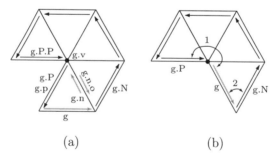

(a)   (b)

Figure 8.47: Handling Case L.

```
H=H|R;                    % append R to history
g.m=0; g.N.m=0; g.p.o.m=1;   % update flags
g.N.N.P=g.p.o; g.p.o.N=g.N.N.   % fix link 1
g.p.o.P=g.P; g.P.N=g.p.o;       % fix link 2
g=g.p.o; StackTop=g;            % advance gate
```

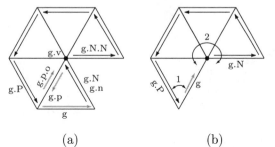

(a)   (b)

Figure 8.48: Handling Case R.

```
H=H|S;                    % append S to history
g.m=0; g.n.o.m=1; g.p.o.m=1; % update flags
b=g.n;                    % initial candidate for b
while not b.m do b=b.o.p;
                          % turn around v to marked b
g.P.N=g.p.o; g.p.o.P=g.P.       % fix link 1
g.p.o.N=b.N; b.N.P=g.p.o;       % fix link 2
b.N=g.n.o; g.n.o.P=b;           % fix link 3
g.n.o.N=g.N; g.N.P=g.n.o;       % fix link 4
StackTop=g.p.o; PushStack;  % save new region
g=g.n.o; StackTop=g;            % advance gate
```

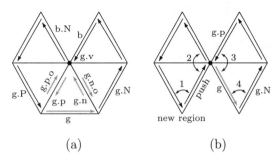

(a)   (b)

Figure 8.49: Handling Case S.

```
H=H|E;                          % append E to history
g.m=0; g.n.m=0; g.p.m=0;   % unmark edges
if StackEmpty then stop
 else PopStack; g=StackTop;% start on next region
endif
```

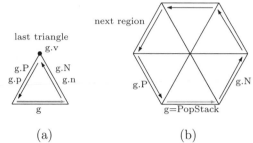

(a)　　　　　　　　　　　　　　　(b)

Figure 8.50: Handling Case E.

passes, a set of five Huffman codes is computed and is written at the start of the compressed stream. Such a method, however, is slow. Faster (and only slightly less efficient) results can be obtained by selecting the following fixed set of five prefix codes: Assign a 1-bit code to C and 3-bit codes to each of the other four symbols. A possible choice is the set 0, 100, 101, 110, and 111 to code C, S, R, L, and E, respectively.

The average code size is not hard to estimate. The total number of bits used to encode the history H is $c = |T| - |C| = |C| + 3(|S| + |L| + |R| + |E|)$. We denote by T the set of triangles in the mesh, by V_i the set of interior vertices of the mesh, and by V_e the set of exterior vertices. The size of V_i is the size of C $|C| = |V_i|$. We also use Euler's equation for simple meshes, $t - e + v = 1$, where t is the number of triangles, e is the number of edges, and v is the number of vertices. All this is combined to yield

$$|S| + |L| + |R| + |E| = |T| - |C| = |T| - |V_i|,$$

and $c = |V_i| + 3(|T| - |V_i|)$ or $c = 2|T| + (|T| - 2|V_i|)$. Since $|T| - 2|V_i| = |V_e| - 2$ we get $c = 2|T| + |V_e| - 2$.

The result is that for simple meshes, with a simple, short initial boundary, we have $|V_e| \ll |V_i|$ (the mesh is interior heavy), so $c \approx 2|T|$. The length of the history is two bits per triangle.

A small mesh may have a relatively large number of exterior edges and may thus be exterior heavy. Most triangles in such a mesh get a code of R, so the five codes above should be changed. The code of R should be 1 bit long, and the other four codes should be three bits each. This set of codes yields $c = 3|T| - 2|R|$. If most triangles have a code of R, then $|T| \approx |R|$ and $c \approx 1$; even more impressive.

We conclude that the set of five prefix codes should be selected according to the ratio $|V_e|/|V_i|$.

The Decoder: Edgebreaker is an asymmetric compression method. The operation of the decoder is very different from that of the encoder and requires two passes, preprocessing and generation. The preprocessing pass determines the numbers of triangles, edges, and vertices, as well as the offsets for the S codes. The generation pass creates the triangles in the order in which they were removed by the encoder. This pass determines the labels of the three vertices of each triangle and stores them in a table.

The preprocessing pass reads the codes from the history H and performs certain actions for each of the five types of codes. It uses the following variables and data structures:

1. The triangle count t. This is incremented for each code, so it tracks the total number of triangles.

2. The value of $|S| - |E|$ is tracked in d. Once the operation of the encoder is fully understood, it should be clear that codes S and E act as pairs of balanced brackets and that the last code in H is always E. After reading this last E, the value of d becomes negative.

3. The vertex counter c is incremented each time a C code is found in the history H. The current value of c becomes the label of the next vertex g.**v**.

4. Variable e tracks the value of $3|E| + |L| + |R| - |C| - |S|$. Its final value is $|V_e|$. When an S code is read, the current value of e is pushed by the decoder into a stack.

5. The number of S codes is tracked by variable s. When e is pushed into the stack, s is used to relate e to the corresponding S.

6. A stack into which pairs (e, s) are pushed when an S code is found. The last pair is popped when an E code is read from H. It is used to compute the offset.

7. A table O of offsets.

All variables are initialized to zero. The stack and table O start empty.

The operations performed by the preprocessing pass for each type of code are as follows:

> S code: $e- = 1$; $s+ = 1$; $\text{push}(e, s)$; $d+ = 1$;
> E code: $e+ = 3$; $(e', s') = \text{popstack}$; $O[s'] = e = e' - 2$; $d- = 1$; if $d < 0$, stop.
> C code: $e- = 1$; $c+ = 1$;
> L code: $e+ = 1$;
> R code: $e+ = 1$;

In addition, t is incremented for each code read. At the end of this pass, t contains the total number $|T|$ of triangles, c is the number $|V_i|$ of interior vertices, e is set to the number $|V_e|$ of exterior vertices, and table O contains the offsets, sorted in the order in which codes S occur in H.

Two points should be explained in connection with these operations. The first is why the final value of e is $|V_e|$. The calculation of e uses H to find out how many edges were added to the boundary B or deleted from it by the encoder. This number is then used to determine the initial size of B. Recall that the encoder deletes two edges from B and adds one edge to it while processing an R or an L code. Processing an E code by the encoder involves removing three edges.

⋄ **Exercise 8.31:** How does the number of edges change when the encoder processes a C code or an S code?

These edge-count changes imply that the initial number of edges (and thus also the initial number of vertices) in the boundary is $3|E| + |L| + |R| - |C| - |S|$. This is why e tracks this number.

The second point is the offsets. We know that S and E codes act as paired brackets in H. Any substring in H that starts with an S and ends with the corresponding E contains the connectivity information for a region of the original mesh. We also know that e tracks the value of $3|E| + |L| + |R| - |C| - |S|$ for the substring of H that has already been read and processed. Therefore, the difference between the values of e at the E operation and at the corresponding S operation is the number of vertices in the boundary of that region. We subtract 2 from this value in order not to count the two vertices of the gate g as part of the offset.

For each S code, the value of e is pushed into the stack. When the corresponding E code is read from H, the stack is popped and is subtracted from the current value of e.

The preprocessing pass is illustrated by applying it to the history

$$H = CCRRRSLCRSERRELCRRRCRRRE$$

that was generated by the encoder from the mesh of Figure 8.44f. Table 8.51 lists the values of all the variables involved after each code is read from H. The pair (e', s') is the contents of the top of the decoder's stack. The two offsets 1 and 6 are stored in table O. The final value of e is 16 (the number of exterior vertices or, equivalently, the number of vertices in B). The final value of c is 5. This is the number of interior vertices. The final value of t is, of course, 24, the number of triangles.

	C	C	R	R	R	S	L	C	R	S	E	R	R	E	L	C	R	R	R	C	R	R	R	E
t	1	2	3	4	5	6	7	8	9	10	11	12	13	14	15	16	17	18	19	20	21	22	23	24
d	0	0	0	0	0	1	1	1	1	2	1	1	1	0	0	0	0	0	0	0	0	0	0	-1
c	1	2	2	2	2	2	2	3	3	3	3	3	3	3	3	4	4	4	4	5	5	5	5	5
e	-1	-2	-1	0	1	0	1	0	1	0	3	4	5	8	9	8	9	10	11	10	11	12	13	16
s	0	0	0	0	0	1	1	1	1	2	2	2	2	2	2	2	2	2	2	2	2	2	2	2
e',s'						0,1	0,1	0,1	0,1	0,2	0,1	0,1	0,1											
$O[s']$											1			6										

Table 8.51: An Example of the Preprocessing Pass.

The generation pass starts with an initialization phase where it does the following:

1. Starts an empty table TV of triangle vertices, where each entry will contain the labels of the three vertices of a triangle.

2. Initializes a vertex counter c to $|V_e|$, so that references to exterior vertices precede references to interior ones.

3. Constructs a circular, doubly linked list of $|V_e|$ edges, where each node corresponds to an edge G and contains a pointer G.P to the preceding node, a pointer G.N to the successor node, and an integer label G.e that identifies the end vertex of edge G. The labels are integers increasing from 1 to $|V_e|$.

4. Creates a stack of references to edges and initializes it to a single entry that refers to the first edge G (the gate) in the boundary B. Notice that uppercase letters are used for the edges to distinguish them from the half-edges used by the encoder.

5. Sets a triangle counter $t = 0$ and a counter $s = 0$ of S operations.

The pass then reads the history H symbol by symbol. For each symbol it determines the labels of the three vertices of the current triangle X and stores them in TV[t]. It also updates B, G, and the stack, if necessary. Once the current gate, G, is known, it determines two of the three vertices of the current triangle. They are G.P.**e** and G.**e**. Determining the third vertex depends on the current code read from H. The actions for each of the five codes are shown here (the notation x++ means return the current value of x, then increment it, while ++x means increment x, then return its new value):

C code: TV[$+ + t$]=(G.P.**e**, G.**e**, $+ + c$);
    New Edge A; A. **e**=c;
    G.P.N=A; A.P=G.P;
    A.N=G; G.P=A;

R Code: TV[$+ + t$]=(G.P.**e**, G.**e**, G.N.**e**);
    G.P.N=G.N; G.N.P=G.P;
    G=G.N;

L Code: TV[$+ + t$]=(G.P.**e**, G.**e**, G.P.P.**e**);
    G.P=G.P.P; G.P.P.N=G;

E Code: TV[$+ + t$]=(G.P.**e**, G.**e**, G.N.**e**);
    G=PopStack;

S Code: D=G.N; repeat D=D.N; O[$+ + s$] times;
    TV[$+ + t$]=(G.P.**e**, G.**e**, D.**e**);
    New Edge A; A.**e**=D.**e**;
    G.P.N=A; A.P=G.P;
    PopStack; Push A;
    A.N=D.N; D.N.P=A;
    G.P=D; D.N=G;
    Push G;

These actions are illustrated here for the history

$$H = CCRRRSLCRSERRELCRRRCRRRE,$$

originally generated by the encoder from the mesh of Figure 8.44f. The preprocessing pass computes $|V_e| = 16$, so we start with an initial boundary of 16 edges and of 16 vertices that we label 1 through 16. The first edge (the one that is associated with vertex 1) is our initial gate G. Variable c is set to 16. The first C code encountered in H sets entry TV[1] to the three labels 16 (G.P.**e**), 1 (G.**e**), and 17 (the result of $++c$). The reader should use Figure 8.44f to verify that these are, in fact, the vertices of the first triangle processed and removed by the encoder. A new edge, A, is also created, and 17 is stored as its label. The new edge A is inserted before G by updating the pointers as follows: G.P.N=A, A.P=G.P, A.N=G, and G.P=A. The second C code creates triangle $(17, 1, 18)$ and inserts another new edge, with label 18, before G. (The reader should again verify that $(17, 1, 18)$ are the vertices of the second triangle processed and removed by the encoder.) The first R code creates triangle $(18, 1, 2)$, deletes gate G from the boundary, and declares the edge labeled 2 the current gate.

⋄ **Exercise 8.32:** Show the result of processing the second and third R codes.

The first S code skips the six vertices (six, because O[1] = 6) 5, 6, 7, 8, 9, and 10. It then determines that triangle 6 has vertices $(18, 4, 11)$, and splits the boundary into the two regions $(11, 12, 13, 14, 15, 16, 17, 18)$ and $(4, 5, 6, 7, 8, 9, 10)$. The bottom of the stack points to edge $(8, 11)$, the first edge in the first region. The top of the stack points to edge $(11, 4)$, the first edge in the second region. The L code creates triangle $(11, 4, 10)$ and deletes the last edge of the second region. At this point the current edge G is edge $(10, 4)$.

[Rossignac 98] has more details of this interesting and original method, including extensions of edgebreaker for meshes with holes in them, and for meshes without a boundary (meshes that are homeomorphic to a sphere).

Bibliography

Rossignac, Jarek (1998) "Edgebreaker: Connectivity Compression for Triangle Meshes," GVU Technical Report GIT-GVU-98-35, Georgia Institute of Technology.

Salomon, David (1999) *Computer Graphics and Geometric Modeling*, New York, Springer-Verlag.

> In comedy, as a matter of fact, a greater variety of
> methods were discovered and employed than in tragedy.
> —T. S. Eliot, [1888–1965], *The Sacred Wood*

Bibliography

Abelson, H., and A. A. diSessa (1982) *Turtle Geometry*, Cambridge, MA, MIT Press.

Adelson, E. H., E. Simoncelli, and R. Hingorani (1987) "Orthogonal Pyramid Transforms for Image Coding," *Proceedings SPIE*, vol. 845, Cambridge, MA, pp. 50–58, October.

Ahmed, N., T. Natarajan, and R. K. Rao (1974) "Discrete Cosine Transform," *IEEE Transactions on Computers* C-23:90–93.

Akansu, Ali, and R. Haddad (1992) *Multiresolution Signal Decomposition*, San Diego, CA, Academic Press.

Anderson, K. L., et al., (1987) "Binary-Image-Manipulation Algorithm in the Image View Facility," *IBM Journal of Research and Development* 31(1):16–31, January.

Anedda, C. and L. Felician (1988) "P-Compressed Quadtrees for Image Storing," *The Computer Journal*, 31(4):353–357.

ATT (1996) is URL http://www.djvu.att.com/.

Backus, J. W. (1959) "The Syntax and Semantics of the Proposed International Algebraic Language," in *Proceedings of the International Conference on Information processing*, pp. 125–132, UNESCO.

Banister, Brian, and Thomas R. Fischer (1999) "Quadtree Classification and TCQ Image Coding," in Storer, James A., and Martin Cohn (eds.) (1999) *DCC '99: Data Compression Conference*, Los Alamitos, CA, IEEE Computer Society Press, pp. 149–157.

Barnsley, M. F., and Sloan, A. D. (1988) "A Better Way to Compress Images," *Byte Magazine* pp. 215–222 January.

Barnsley, M. F. (1988) *Fractals Everywhere*, New York, Academic Press.

Bell, T. C., I. H. Witten, and J. G. Cleary (1990) *Text Compression*, Englewood Cliffs, NJ, Prentice-Hall.

Bell, T. C. (1986) "Better OPM/L Text Compression," *IEEE Transactions on Communications* COM-34(12):1176–1182, December.

Bentley, J. L. et al. (1986) "A Locally Adaptive Data Compression Algorithm," *Communications of the ACM* **29**(4):320–330, April.

Blackstock, Steve (1987) "LZW and GIF Explained," available from URL "`http://www.ece.uiuc.edu/~ece291/class-resources/gpe/gif.txt.html`".

Blinn, J. F. (1993) "What's the Deal with the DCT," *IEEE Computer Graphics and Applications* pp. 78–83, July.

Bloom, C. R., (1996) "LZP: A New Data Compression Algorithm," in *Proceedings of Data Compression Conference*, J. Storer, editor, Los Alamitos, CA, IEEE Computer Society Press, p. 425.

Bradley, Jonathan N., Christopher M. Brislawn, and Tom Hopper (1993) "The FBI Wavelet/Scalar Quantization Standard for Grayscale Fingerprint Image Compression," *Proceedings of Visual Information Processing II*, Orlando, FL, SPIE volume 1961, pp. 293–304, April.

Brandenburg, KarlHeinz, and Gerhard Stoll (1994) "ISO-MPEG-1 Audio: A Generic Standard for Coding of High-Quality Digital Audio," *Journal of the Audio Engineering Society*, **42**(10):780–792, October.

Brislawn, Christopher, Jonathan Bradley, R. Onyshczak, and Tom Hopper (1996) "The FBI Compression Standard for Digitized Fingerprint Images," in *Proceedings SPIE*, v. 2847, Denver, CO, pp. 344–355, August.

Burrows, Michael, et al. (1992) *On-line Data Compression in a Log-Structured File System*, Digital, Systems Research Center, Palo Alto, CA.

Burrows, Michael, and D. J. Wheeler (1994) *A Block-Sorting Lossless Data Compression Algorithm*, Digital Systems Research Center report 124, Palo Alto, Calif, May 10.

Burt, Peter J., and Edward H. Adelson (1983) "The Laplacian Pyramid as a Compact Image Code," *IEEE Transactions on Communications*, COM-31(4):532–540, April.

Buyanovsky, G. (1994), "Associative Coding" (in Russian), *Monitor*, Moscow, #8, 10–19, August. (Hard copies of the Russian source and English translation are available from the author of this book. Send requests to the author's email address found in the Preface.)

Cachin, Christian (1998) "An Information-Theoretic Model for Steganography," in *Proceedings of the Second International Workshop on Information Hiding*, D. Aucsmith, ed. vol. 1525 of *Lecture Notes in Computer Science*, Springer-Verlag, pp. 306–318.

Cappellini, V. (ed.) (1985) *Data Compression and Error Control Techniques with Applications*, New York, Academic Press.

Chaitin, Gregory J. (1977) "Algorithmic Information Theory," *IBM Journal of Research and Development*, **21**:350–359, July.

Chaitin, Gregory J. (1997) *The Limits of Mathematics*, Singapore, Springer-Verlag.

Chomsky, N. (1956) "Three Models for the Description of Language," *IRE Transactions on Information Theory* **2**(3):113–124.

Cleary, J. G., and I. H. Witten (1984) "Data Compression Using Adaptive Coding and Partial String Matching," *IEEE Transactions on Communications* COM-32(4):396–402, April.

Cole, A. J. (1985) "A Note on Peano Polygons and Gray Codes," *International Journal of Computer Mathematics* **18**:3–13.

Cole, A. J. (1986) "Direct Transformations Between Sets of Integers and Hilbert Polygons," *International Journal of Computer Mathematics* **20**:115–122.

Constantinescu, C., and J. A. Storer (1994a) "Online Adaptive Vector Quantization with Variable Size Codebook Entries," *Information Processing and Management*, **30**(6)745–758.

Constantinescu, C., and J. A. Storer (1994b) "Improved Techniques for Single-Pass Adaptive Vector Quantization," *Proceedings of the IEEE*, **82**(6)933–939, June.

Constantinescu, C., and R. Arps (1997) "Fast Residue Coding for Lossless Textual Image Compression," in *Proceedings of the 1997 Data Compression Conference*, J. Storer, ed., Los Alamitos, CA, IEEE Computer Society Press, pp. 397–406.

Cormack G. V., and R. N. S. Horspool (1987) "Data Compression Using Dynamic Markov Modelling," *The Computer Journal* **30**(6):541–550.

CREW 2000 is URL `http://www.crc.ricoh.com/CREW/`

Crocker, Lee Daniel (1995) "PNG: The Portable Network Graphic Format," *Dr. Dobb's Journal of Software Tools* **20**(7):36–44.

Culik, Karel II, and J. Kari (1993) "Image Compression Using Weighted Finite Automata," *Computer and Graphics*, **17**(3):305–313.

Culik, Karel II, and J. Kari (1994) "Image-Data Compression Using Edge-Optimizing Algorithm for WFA Inference," *Journal of Information Processing and Management*, **30**,6:829–838.

Culik, Karel II and Jarkko Kari (1994) "Inference Algorithm for Weighted Finite Automata and Image Compression," in *Fractal Image Encoding and Compression*, Y. Fisher, editor, New York, NY, Springer-Verlag.

Culik, Karel II, and Jarkko Kari (1995) "Finite State Methods for Compression and Manipulation of Images," in *DCC '96, Data Compression Conference*, J. Storer, editor, Los Alamitos, CA, IEEE Computer Society Press, pp. 142–151.

Culik, Karel II, and V. Valenta (1996), "Finite Automata Based Compression of Bi-Level Images," in Storer, James A. (ed.), *DCC '96, Data Compression Conference,* Los Alamitos, CA, IEEE Computer Society Press, pp. 280–289.

Culik, Karel II, and V. Valenta (1997), "Finite Automata Based Compression of Bi-Level and Simple Color Images," *Computer and Graphics,* **21**:61–68.

Culik, Karel II, and V. Valenta (1997), "Compression of Silhouette-like Images Based on WFA," *Journal of Universal Computer Science,* **3**:1100–1113.

Cushing, John Aikin, and Yukio Rikiso (1990) *Data Compression Algorithms for English Text Based on Word Frequency,* Institute of Economic Research, Kobe University of Commerce, Kobe, Japan.

Czech, Z. J., et al. (1992) "An Optimal Algorithm for Generating Minimal Perfect Hash Functions," *Information Processing Letters* **43**:257–264.

Dasarathy, Belur V. (ed.) (1995) *Image Data Compression: Block Truncation Coding (BTC) Techniques,* Los Alamitos, CA, IEEE Computer Society Press.

Daubechies, Ingrid (1988) "Orthonormal Bases of Compactly Supported Wavelets," *Communications on Pure and Applied Mathematics,* **41**:909–996.

Demko, S., L. Hodges, and B. Naylor (1985) "Construction of Fractal Objects with Iterated Function Systems," *Computer Graphics* **19**(3):271–278, July.

DeVore, R., et al. (1992) "Image Compression Through Wavelet Transform Coding," *IEEE Transactions on Information Theory* **38**(2):719–746, March.

Dewitte, J., and J. Ronson (1983) "Original Block Coding Scheme for Low Bit Rate Image Transmission," in *Signal Processing II: Theories and Applications—Proceedings of EUSIPCO 83,* H. W. Schussler, ed., Amsterdam, Elsevier Science Publishers B. V. (North-Holland), pp. 143–146.

Ekstrand, Nicklas (1996) "Lossless Compression of Gray Images via Context Tree Weighting," in Storer, James A. (ed.), *DCC '96: Data Compression Conference,* Los Alamitos, CA, IEEE Computer Society Press, pp. 132–139, April.

Elias, P. (1975) "Universal Codeword Sets and Representations of the Integers," *IEEE Transactions on Information Theory* IT-21(2):194–203, March.

Fang I. (1966) "It Isn't ETAOIN SHRDLU; It's ETAONI RSHDLC," *Journalism Quarterly* **43**:761–762.

Feder, Jens (1988) *Fractals,* New York, Plenum Press.

Federal Bureau of Investigation (1993) *WSQ Grayscale Fingerprint Image Compression Specification, ver. 2.0,* Document #IAFIS-IC-0110v2, Criminal Justice Information Services, February.

Feig, E., and E. Linzer (1990) "Discrete Cosine Transform Algorithms for Image Data Compression," in *Proceedings Electronic Imaging '90 East,* pages 84–87, Boston, MA.

Fenwick, P. (1996) *Symbol Ranking Text Compression*, Tech. Rep. 132, Dept. of Computer Science, University of Auckland, New Zealand, June.

Fiala, E. R., and D. H. Greene (1989), "Data Compression with Finite Windows," *Communications of the ACM* **32**(4):490–505.

Fibonacci (1999), is file `Fibonacci.html` in URL `http://www-groups.dcs.st-and.ac.uk/~history/References/`.

Fisher, Yuval (ed.), (1995) *Fractal Image Compression: Theory and Application*, New York, Springer-Verlag.

Floyd, R., and L. Steinberg (1975) "An Adaptive Algorithm for Spatial Gray Scale," in *Society for Information Display 1975 Symposium Digest of Technical Papers*, p. 36.

Floyd, Sally, and Manfred Warmuth (1993) *Sample Compression, Learnability, and the Vapnik-Chervonenskis Dimension*, Tech. report UCSC-CRL-93-13. Univ. of California, Santa Cruz.

Fox, E. A., et al. (1991) "Order Preserving Minimal Perfect Hash Functions and Information Retrieval," *ACM Transactions on Information Systems* **9**(2):281–308.

Fraenkel, A. S., and S. T. Klein (1985) "Novel Compression of Sparse Bit-Strings— Preliminary Report," in A. Apostolico and Z. Galil, eds. *Combinatorial Algorithms on Words*, Vol. 12, NATO ASI Series F:169–183, New York, Springer-Verlag.

Frank, Amalie J., J. D. Daniels, and Diane R. Unangst (1980) "Progressive Image Transmission Using a Growth-Geometry Coding," *Proceedings of the IEEE*, **68**(7):897–909, July.

Freeman, H. (1961) "On The Encoding of Arbitrary Geometric Configurations," *IRE Transactions on Electronic Computers*, EC-10(2):260–268, June.

Gabor, G., and Z. Gyorfi (1986) *Recursive Source Coding: A Theory for the Practice of Waveform Coding*, New York, Springer-Verlag.

Gardner, Martin (1972) "Mathematical Games," *Scientific American*, **227**(2):106, August.

Gersho, Allen, and Robert M. Gray (1992) *Vector Quantization and Signal Compression*, Boston, MA, Kluwer Academic Publishers.

Gharavi, H. (1987) "Conditional Run-Length and Variable-Length Coding of Digital Pictures," *IEEE Transactions on Communications*, COM-35(6):671–677, June.

Gilbert, Jeffrey M., and Robert W. Brodersen (1998) "A Lossless 2-D Image Compression Technique for Synthetic Discrete-Tone Images," in *Proceedings of the 1998 Data Compression Conference*, J. Storer, ed., Los Alamitos, CA, IEEE Computer Society Press, pp. 359–368, March. This is also available from `http://infopad.eecs.berkeley.edu/~gilbertj`.

Golomb, S. W. (1966) "Run-Length Encodings," *IEEE Transactions on Information Theory* IT-12(3):399–401.

Gonzalez, Rafael C., and Richard E. Woods (1992) *Digital Image Processing*, Reading, MA, Addison-Wesley.

Gottlieb, D., et al. (1975) *A Classification of Compression Methods and their Usefulness for a Large Data Processing Center*, Proceedings of National Computer Conference **44**:453–458.

Gray, Frank (1953) "Pulse Code Communication," United States Patent 2,632,058, March 17.

Haffner, Patrick, et al. (1998) "High-Quality Document Image Compression with DjVu," *Journal of Electronic Imaging*, **7**(3):410–425, SPIE. This is also available from URL `http://www.research.att.com/~leonb/biblio.html`.

Hafner, Ullrich (1995) "Asymmetric Coding in (m)-WFA Image Compression," Report 132, Department of Computer Science, University of Würzburg, December. (Available at `http://www-info2.informatik.uni-wuerzburg.de/staff/ulli/home/publications/` file `tr132.ps.gz`.)

Hamming, Richard (1950) "Error Detecting and Error Correcting Codes," *Bell Systems Technical Journal* **29**:147–160, April.

Hamming, Richard (1986) *Coding and Information Theory*, 2nd Ed., Englewood Cliffs, NJ, Prentice-Hall.

Harris, Matthew (1993) *The Disk Compression Book*, Indianapolis, IN, Que.

Havas, G., et al. (1993) *Graphs, Hypergraphs and Hashing* in Proceedings of the International Workshop on Graph-Theoretic Concepts in Computer Science (WG'93), Berlin, Springer-Verlag.

Heath, F. G. (1972) "Origins of the Binary Code," *Scientific American*, **227**(2):76, August.

Held, Gilbert, and Thomas R. Marshall (1991) *Data Compression: Techniques and Applications: Hardware and Software Considerations*, 3rd ed., New York, John Wiley.

Held, Gilbert, and Thomas R. Marshall (1996) *Data and Image Compression: Tools and Techniques*, 4th Ed., New York, John Wiley.

Held, Gilbert (1994) *Personal Computer File Compression: A Guide to Shareware, DOS, and Commercial Compression Programs*, New York, Van Nostrand.

Hilbert, D. (1891) "Ueber stetige Abbildung einer Linie auf ein Flächenstück," *Math. Annalen* **38**:459–460.

Hirschberg, D., and D. Lelewer (1990) "Efficient Decoding of Prefix Codes," *Communications of the ACM* **33**(4):449–459.

Hopcroft, John E., and Jeffrey D. Ullman (1979) *Introduction to Automata Theory, Languages, and Computation*, Reading, MA, Addison-Wesley.

Horspool, N. R. (1991) "Improving LZW," in *Proceedings of the 1991 Data Compression Conference*, J. Storer, ed., Los Alamitos, CA, IEEE Computer Society Press, pp .332–341.

Horspool, N. R. and G. V. Cormack (1992) "Constructing Word-Based Text Compression Algorithms," in *Proceedings of the 1992 Data Compression Conference*, J. Storer, ed., Los Alamitos, CA, IEEE Computer Society Press, pp. 62–71, April.

Howard, Paul G., and J. S. Vitter (1992a), "New Methods for Lossless Image Compression Using Arithmetic Coding," *Information Processing and Management*, **28**(6):765–779.

Howard, Paul G., and J. S. Vitter (1992b), "Error Modeling for Hierarchical Lossless Image Compression," in *Proceedings of the 1992 Data Compression Conference*, J. Storer, ed., Los Alamitos, CA, IEEE Computer Society Press, pp. 269–278.

Howard, P. G., and J. S. Vitter, (1993) "Fast and Efficient Lossless Image Compression," In *Proceedings of the 1993 Data Compression Conference*, J. Storer, ed., Los Alamitos, CA, IEEE Computer Society Press, pp. 351–360.

Howard, P. G., and J. S. Vitter (1994) "Fast Progressive Lossless Image Compression," Proceedings of the Image and Video Compression Conference, *IS&T/SPIE 1994 Symposium on Electronic Imaging: Science & Technology*, 2186, San Jose, CA, pp. 98–109. February.

Huffman, David (1952) "A Method for the Construction of Minimum Redundancy Codes," *Proceedings of the IRE* **40**(9):1098–1101.

Hunter, R., and A. H. Robinson (1980) "International Digital Facsimile Coding Standards," *Proceedings of the IEEE* **68**(7):854–867, July.

Huntley, H. E. (1970) *The Divine Proportion: A Study in Mathematical Beauty*, New York, Dover Publications.

ISO/IEC (1993) International Standard IS 11172-3 "Information Technology, Coding of Moving Pictures and Associated Audio for Digital Storage Media at up to about 1.5 Mbits/s—Part 3: Audio."

ISO/IEC (2000), International Standard IS 15444-1 "Information Technology— JPEG 2000 Image Coding System." This is the FDC (final committee draft) version 1.0, 16 March 2000.

ITU-T (1989) *CCITT Recommendation G.711: Pulse Code Modulation (PCM) of Voice Frequencies.*

ITU-T (1990), Recommendation G.726 (12/90), *40, 32, 24, 16 kbit/s Adaptive Differential Pulse Code Modulation (ADPCM).* Available from `http://www.itu.int//itudoc/itu-t/rec/g/g700-799/index.html`.

Jarvis, J. F., C. N. Judice, and W. H. Ninke (1976) "A Survey of Techniques for the Image Display of Continuous Tone Pictures on Bilevel Displays" *Computer Graphics and Image Processing* **5**(1):13–40.

Jarvis, J. F., and C. S. Roberts (1976) "A New Technique for Displaying Continuous Tone Images on a Bilevel Display" *IEEE Transactions on Communications* **24**(8):891–898, August.

Jordan, B. W., and R. C. Barrett (1974) "A Cell Organized Raster Display for Line Drawings," *Communications of the ACM*, **17**(2):70–77.

Joshi, R. L., V. J. Crump, and T. R. Fischer (1993) "Image Subband Coding Using Arithmetic and Trellis Coded Quantization," *IEEE Transactions on Circuits and Systems Video Technology*, **5**(6):515–523, Dec.

JPEG 2000 Organization (2000) is at URL `http://www.jpeg.org/JPEG2000.htm`.

Kespret, Istok (1994) *PKZIP, LHARC and Co.: The Ultimate Data Compression Book*, Grand Rapids, MI, Abacus.

Kespret, Istok (1996) *ZIP Bible*, Grand Rapids, MI, Abacus.

Kieffer, J., G. Nelson, and E-H. Yang (1996a) "Tutorial on the quadrisection method and related methods for lossless data compression." Available for downloading at URL
`http://www.ece.umn.edu/users/kieffer/index.html`.

Kieffer, J., E-H. Yang, G. Nelson, and P. Cosman (1996b) "Lossless compression via bisection trees," at `http://www.ece.umn.edu/users/kieffer/index.html`.

Knowlton, Ken (1980) "Progressive Transmission of Grey-Scale and Binary Pictures by Simple, Efficient, and Lossless Encoding Schemes," *Proceedings of the IEEE*,**68**(7):885–896, July.

Knuth, D. E. (1973) *The Art of Computer Programming*, Vol. 1, 2nd Ed., Reading, MA, Addison-Wesley.

Knuth, D. E. (1985) "Dynamic Huffman Coding," *Journal of Algorithms* **6**:163–180.

Knuth, Donald E., (1987) "Digital Halftones by Dot Diffusion," *ACM Transactions on Graphics* **6**(4):245–273.

Krichevsky, R. E., and V. K. Trofimov (1981) "The Performance of Universal Coding," *IEEE Transactions on Information Theory*, IT-27:199–207, March.

Krichevsky, R. E. (1994) *Universal Compression and Retrieval*, Boston, Kluwer Academic.

Lambert, Sean M. (1999) "Implementing Associative Coder of Buyanovsky (ACB) Data Compression," M.S. thesis, Montana State University (available from Sean Lambert at `sum1els@mindless.com`).

Langdon, G., and J. Rissanen (1981) "Compression of Black White Images with Arithmetic Coding," *IEEE Transactions on Communications* COM-29(6):858–867, June.

Langdon, Glen G. (1983) "A Note on the Ziv-Lempel Model for Compressing Individual Sequences," *IEEE Transactions on Information Theory* IT-29(2):284–287, March.

Langdon, Glen G. (1984) *On Parsing vs. Mixed-Order Model Structures for Data Compression*, IBM research report RJ-4163 (46091), January 18, 1984, San Jose.

Lewalle, Jacques (1995) "Tutorial on Continuous Wavelet Analysis of Experimental Data," available from `ftp.mame.syr.edu/pub/jlewalle/tutor.ps.Z`.

Lin, Shu (1970) *An Introduction to Error Correcting Codes*, Englewood Cliffs, NJ, Prentice-Hall.

Linde, Y., A. Buzo, and R. M. Gray (1980) "An Algorithm for Vector Quantization Design," *IEEE Transactions on Communications*, COM-28:84–95, January.

Lindenmayer, A. (1968) "Mathematical Models for Cellular Interaction in Development," *Journal of Theoretical Biology* **18**:280–315.

Liou, Ming (1991) "Overview of the p×64 kbits/s Video Coding Standard," *Communications of the ACM*, **34**(4):59–63, April.

Litow, Bruce, and Olivier de Val (1995) "The Weighted Finite Automaton Inference Problem," Technical report 95-1, James Cook University, Queensland.

Loeffler, C., A. Ligtenberg, and G. Moschytz (1989) "Practical Fast 1-D DCT Algorithms with 11 Multiplications," *Proceedings of the International Conference on Acoustics, Speech, and Signal Processing (ICASSP '89)*, pp. 988–991.

Lowe, Doug (1994) *Microsoft Press Guide to DOUBLESPACE: Understanding Data Compression with MS-DOS 6.0 and 6.2*, Redmond, WA, Microsoft Press.

Lynch, Thomas J. (1985) *Data Compression Techniques and Applications*, Belmont, CA, Lifetime Learning Publications.

Mallat, Stephane (1989) "A Theory for Multiresolution Signal Decomposition: The Wavelet Representation," *IEEE Trans. on Pattern Analysis and Machine Intelligence*, **11**(7):674–693, July.

Manber, U., and E. W. Myers (1993) "Suffix Arrays: A New Method for On-Line String Searches," *SIAM Journal on Computing* **22**(5):935–948, October.

Mandelbrot, Benoit (1982) *The Fractal Geometry of Nature*, San Francisco, CA, W. H. Freeman.

Manning (1998), URL `http://lemontree.web2010.com/dvideo/`.

Marking, Michael P. (1990) "Decoding Group 3 Images," *The C Users Journal* pp. 45–54, June.

Matlab (1999) is URL `http://www.mathworks.com/`.

McConnell, Kenneth R. (1992) *FAX: Digital Facsimile Technology and Applications*, Norwood, MA, Artech House.

McCreight, E. M (1976) "A Space Economical Suffix Tree Construction Algorithm," *Journal of the ACM* **32**(2):262–272, April.

Meyer, F. G., A. Averbuch, and J.O. Strömberg (1998) "Fast Adaptive Wavelet Packet Image Compression," submitted to the *IEEE Transactions on Image Processing*, revised June 1999.

Miller, V. S., and M. N. Wegman (1985) "Variations On a Theme by Ziv and Lempel," in A. Apostolico and Z. Galil, eds., NATO ASI series Vol. F12, *Combinatorial Algorithms on Words*, Springer, Berlin, pp. 131–140.

Mitchell, Joan L., W. B. Pennebaker, C. E. Fogg, and D. J. LeGall, eds. (1997) *MPEG Video Compression Standard*, New York, Chapman and Hall and International Thomson Publishing.

Moffat, Alistair, Radford Neal, and Ian H. Witten (1998) "Arithmetic Coding Revisited," *ACM Transactions on Information Systems*, **16**(3):256–294, July.

Moffat, Alistair (1990) "Implementing the PPM Data Compression Scheme," *IEEE Transactions on Communications* COM-38(11):1917–1921, November.

Moffat, Alistair (1991) "Two-Level Context Based Compression of Binary Images," in *Proceedings of the 1991 Data Compression Conference*, J. Storer, ed., Los Alamitos, CA, IEEE Computer Society Press, pp. 382–391.

MPEG (1998), see URL `http://www.mpeg.org/`.

Mulcahy, Colm (1996) "Plotting and Scheming with Wavelets," *Mathematics Magazine*, **69**(5):323–343, Dec. See also `http://www.spelman.edu/~colm/csam.ps`.

Mulcahy, Colm (1997) "Image Compression Using the Haar Wavelet Transform," *Spelman College Science and Mathematics Journal*, **1**(1):22–31, April. Also available as `http://www.spelman.edu/~colm/wav.ps`. (It has been claimed that any smart 15 year old could follow this introduction to wavelets.)

Murray, James D. (1994) and William vanRyper, *Encyclopedia of Graphics File Formats*, Sebastopol, CA, O'Reilly and Assoc.

Nahin, Paul J., (1998) *An Imaginary Tale: The Story of* $\sqrt{-1}$, Princeton, NJ, Princeton University Press.

Naur, P., et al. (1960) "Report on the Algorithmic Language ALGOL 60," *Communications of the ACM* **3**(5):299–314, revised in *Communications of the ACM* **6**(1):1–17.

Nelson, Mark, and Jean-Loup Gailly (1996) *The Data Compression Book*, 2nd Ed., New York, M&T Books.

Nesenbergs, M., *Image Data Compression Overview: Issues and Partial Solutions*, NTIA report; 89–252.

Netravali, A. and J. O. Limb (1980) "Picture Coding: A Preview," *Proceedings of the IEEE*, **68**:366–406.

Nevill-Manning, C. G. (1996) "Inferring Sequential Structure," Ph.D. thesis, Department of Computer Science, University of Waikato, New Zealand.

Nevill-Manning, C. G., and Ian H. Witten (1997) "Compression and Explanation Using Hierarchical Grammars," *The Computer Journal,* **40**(2/3):104–116.

Nix, R. (1981) "Experience With a Space Efficient Way to Store a Dictionary," *Communications of the ACM* **24**(5):297–298.

Okumura, Haruhiko (1998) see URL `http://www.matsusaka-u.ac.jp/~okumura/` directory `compression/history.html`.

Pan, Davis Yen (1995) "A Tutorial on MPEG/Audio Compression," *IEEE Multimedia,* **2**:60–74, Summer.

Peano, G. (1890) "Sur Une Courbe Qui Remplit Toute Une Aire Plaine," *Math. Annalen* **36**:157–160.

Peitgen, H. -O., et al. (eds.) (1982) *The Beauty of Fractals,* Berlin, Springer-Verlag.

Peitgen, H. -O., and Dietmar Saupe (1985) *The Science of Fractal Images,* Berlin, Springer-Verlag.

Pennebaker, W. B., and J. L. Mitchell (1988) "Probability Estimation for the Q-coder," *IBM Journal of Research and Development* **32**(6):717–726.

Pennebaker, W. B., J. L. Mitchell, et al. (1988) "An Overview of the Basic Principles of the Q-coder Adaptive Binary Arithmetic Coder," *IBM Journal of Research and Development* **32**(6):737–752.

Pennebaker, William B., and Joan L. Mitchell (1992) *JPEG Still Image Data Compression Standard,* New York, Van Nostrand Reinhold.

Phillips, Dwayne (1992) "LZW Data Compression," *The Computer Application Journal* Circuit Cellar Inc., **27**:36–48, June/July.

Pohlmann, Ken (1985) *Principles of Digital Audio,* Indianapolis, IN, Howard Sams & Co.

Press, W. H., B. P. Flannery, et al. (1988) *Numerical Recipes in C: The Art of Scientific Computing,* Cambridge University Press. (Also available on-line from `http://www.nr.com/`.)

Prusinkiewicz, Przemysław (1986) *Graphical Applications of L-systems,* in Proc. of Graphics Interface '86—Vision Interface '86, pp. 247–253.

Prusinkiewicz, P., and A. Lindenmayer (1990) *The Algorithmic Beauty of Plants,* New York, Springer-Verlag.

Prusinkiewicz, P., A. Lindenmayer, and F. D. Fracchia (1991) "Synthesis of Space-Filling Curves on the Square Grid," in *Fractals in the Fundamental and Applied Sciences,* edited by Peitgen, H.-O., et al., Amsterdam, Elsevier Science Publishers, pp. 341–366.

Rabbani, Majid, and Paul W. Jones (1991) *Digital Image Compression Techniques,* Bellingham, WA, Spie Optical Engineering Press.

Ramabadran, Tenkasi V., and Sunil S. Gaitonde (1988) "A Tutorial on CRC Computations," *IEEE Micro* pp. 62–75, August.

Ramstad, T. A., et al (1995) *Subband Compression of Images: Principles and Examples*, Amsterdam, Elsevier Science Publishers.

Rao, K. R., and J. J. Hwang (1996) *Techniques and Standards for Image, Video, and Audio Coding*, Upper Saddle River, NJ, Prentice Hall.

Rao, K. R., and P. Yip (1990) *Discrete Cosine Transform—Algorithms, Advantages, Applications*, London, Academic Press.

Rao, Raghuveer M., and Ajit S. Bopardikar (1998) *Wavelet Transforms: Introduction to Theory and Applications*, Reading, MA, Addison-Wesley.

Reghbati, H. K. (1981) "An Overview of Data Compression Techniques," *IEEE Computer* 14(4):71–76.

Robinson, John A. (1997) "Efficient General-Purpose Image Compression with Binary Tree Predictive Coding," *IEEE Transactions on Image Processing*, 6(4):601–607 April.

Robinson, P., and D. Singer (1981) "Another Spelling Correction Program," *Communications of the ACM* 24(5):296–297.

Rodriguez, Karen (1995) "Graphics File Format Patent Unisys Seeks Royalties from GIF Developers," *InfoWorld*, January 9, 17(2):3.

Roetling, P. G. (1976) "Halftone Method with Edge Enhancement and Moiré Suppression," *Journal of the Optical Society of America*, 66:985–989.

Roetling, P. G. (1977) "Binary Approximation of Continuous Tone Images," *Photography Science and Engineering*, 21:60–65.

Ronson, J., and J. Dewitte (1982) "Adaptive Block Truncation Coding Scheme Using an Edge Following Algorithm," *Proceedings of the IEEE International Conference on Acoustics, Speech, and Signal Processing*, Piscataway, NJ, IEEE Press, pp. 1235–1238.

Rossignac, J. (1998) "Edgebreaker: Connectivity Compression for Triangle Meshes," GVU Technical Report GIT-GVU-98-35, Georgia Institute of Technology.

Sacco, William, et al. (1988) *Information Theory, Saving Bits*, Providence, R.I., Janson Publications.

Sagan, Hans (1994) *Space-Filling Curves*, New York, Springer-Verlag.

Said, A., and W. A. Pearlman (1996), "A New Fast and Efficient Image Codec Based on Set Partitioning in Hierarchical Trees," *IEEE Transactions on Circuits and Systems for Video Technology*, 6(6):243–250, June.

Salomon, David (1999) *Computer Graphics and Geometric Modeling*, New York, Springer.

Salomon, D. (2000) "Prefix Compression of Sparse Binary Strings," *ACM Crossroads Magazine*, **6**(3), February.

Sampath, Ashwin, and Ahmad C. Ansari (1993) "Combined Peano Scan and VQ Approach to Image Compression," *Image and Video Processing*, Bellingham, WA, SPIE vol. 1903, pp. 175–186.

Sayood, K., and K. Robinson (1992) "A Differential Lossless Image Compression Scheme," *IEEE Transactions on Signal Processing* **40**(1):236–241, January.

Sayood, Khalid (2000) *Introduction to Data Compression*, 2nd Ed., San Francisco, CA, Morgan Kaufmann.

Shannon, C. (1951) "Prediction and Entropy of Printed English," *Bell System Technical Journal* **30**(1):50–64, January.

Shapiro, J. (1993) "Embedded Image Coding Using Zerotrees of Wavelet Coefficients," *IEEE Transactions on Signal Processing*, **41**(12):3445–3462, October.

Shenoi, Kishan (1995) *Digital Signal Processing in Telecommunications*, Upper Saddle River, NJ, Prentice Hall.

Shlien, Seymour (1994) "Guide to MPEG-1 Audio Standard," *IEEE Transactions on Broadcasting* **40**(4):206–218, December.

Sieminski, A. (1988) "Fast Decoding of the Huffman Codes," *Information Processing Letters* **26**(5):237–241.

Sierpiński, W. (1912) "Sur Une Nouvelle Courbe Qui Remplit Toute Une Aire Plaine," *Bull. Acad. Sci. Cracovie* Serie A:462–478.

Simoncelli, Eero P., and Edward. H. Adelson (1990) "Subband Transforms," in John Woods, editor, *Subband Coding*, Boston, Kluwer Academic Press, 143–192.

Smith, Alvy Ray (1984) "Plants, Fractals and Formal Languages," *Computer Graphics* **18**(3):1–10.

Starck, J. L., F. Murtagh, and A. Bijaoui (1998) *Image Processing and Data Analysis: The Multiscale Approach*, Cambridge University Press.

Stollnitz, E. J., T. D. DeRose, and D. H. Salesin (1996) *Wavelets for Computer Graphics*, San Francisco, CA, Morgan Kaufmann.

Storer, J. A. and T. G. Szymanski (1982) "Data Compression via Textual Substitution," *Journal of the ACM* **29**:928–951.

Storer, James A. (1988) *Data Compression: Methods and Theory*, Rockville, MD, Computer Science Press.

Storer, James A. (ed.) (1992) *Image and Text Compression*, Boston, MA, Kluwer Academic Publishers.

Storer, James A., and John H. Reif (eds.) (1991) *DCC '91: Data Compression Conference*, Los Alamitos, CA, IEEE Computer Society Press.

Storer, James A., and Martin Cohn (eds.) (1992) *DCC '92: Data Compression Conference*, Los Alamitos, CA, IEEE Computer Society Press.

Storer, James A., and Martin Cohn (eds.) (1993) *DCC '93: Data Compression Conference*, Los Alamitos, CA, IEEE Computer Society Press.

Storer, James A., and Martin Cohn (eds.) (1994) *DCC '94: Data Compression Conference*, Los Alamitos, CA, IEEE Computer Society Press.

Storer, James A., and Martin Cohn (eds.) (1995) *DCC '95: Data Compression Conference*, Los Alamitos, CA, IEEE Computer Society Press.

Storer, James A., (ed.) (1996) *DCC '96: Data Compression Conference*, Los Alamitos, CA, IEEE Computer Society Press.

Storer, James A., (ed.) (1997) *DCC '97: Data Compression Conference*, Los Alamitos, CA, IEEE Computer Society Press.

Storer, James A., and Harald Helfgott (1997) "Lossless Image Compression by Block Matching," *The Computer Journal* **40**(2/3):137–145.

Strang, Gilbert, and Truong Nguyen (1996) *Wavelets and Filter Banks*, Wellesley, MA, Wellesley-Cambridge Press.

Strømme, Øyvind, and Douglas R. McGregor (1997) "Comparison of Fidelity of Reproduction of Images After Lossy Compression Using Standard and Nonstandard Wavelet Decompositions," in *Proceedings of The First European Conference on Signal Analysis and Prediction (ECSAP 97)*, Prague, June. Also downloadable from `http://homepages.strath.ac.uk/~cadu02/research/publications.html`.

Strømme, Øyvind (1999) *On The Applicability of Wavelet Transforms to Image and Video Compression*, Ph.D. thesis, University of Strathclyde, February.

Sweldens, Wim and Peter Schröder (1996), *Building Your Own Wavelets At Home*, SIGGRAPH 96 Course Notes, available on the WWW.

Szilard, A. L. and R. E. Quinton (1979) "An Interpretation for D0L Systems by Computer Graphics," *The Science Terrapin* **4**:8–13.

Taubman, D. (1999) "High Performance Scalable Image Compression with EBCOT," to appear in *IEEE Transactions on Image Processing*. This is currently available from `http://maestro.ee.unsw.edu.au/~taubman/activities/preprints/ebcot.pdf`.

Thomborson, Clark, (1992) "The V.42bis Standard for Data-Compressing Modems," *IEEE Micro* pp. 41–53, October.

Udupa, Raghavendra U., Vinayaka D. Pandit, and Ashok Rao (1999), Private Communication (available from the authors or from the author of this book).

Ulichney, Robert (1987) *Digital Halftoning*, Cambridge, MA, MIT Press.

Vasudev, Bhaskaran, and Konstantinos Konstantinides (1995) *Image and Video Compression Standards: Algorithms and Architectures*, Boston, MA, Kluwer Academic Publishers.

Vetterli, M., and J. Kovacevic (1995) *Wavelets and Subband Coding*, Englewood Cliffs, NJ, Prentice-Hall.

Vitter, Jeffrey S. (1987) "Design and Analysis of Dynamic Huffman Codes," *Journal of the ACM* **34**(4):825–845, October.

Volf, Paul A. J. (1997) "A Context-Tree Weighting Algorithm for Text Generating Sources," in Storer, James A. (ed.), *DCC '97: Data Compression Conference*, Los Alamitos, CA, IEEE Computer Society Press, pp. 132–139, (Poster).

Vorobev, Nikolai N. (1983) Ian N. Sneddon (ed.), and Halina Moss (translator), *Fibonacci Numbers*, New Classics Library.

Wallace, Gregory K. (1991) "The JPEG Still Image Compression Standard," *Communications of the ACM* **34**(4):30–44, April.

Watson, Andrew (1994) "Image Compression Using the Discrete Cosine Transform," *Mathematica Journal*, **4**(1):81–88.

Weinberger, M. J., G. Seroussi, and G. Sapiro (1996) "LOCO-I: A Low Complexity, Context-Based, Lossless Image Compression Algorithm," in *Proceedings of Data Compression Conference*, J. Storer, editor, Los Alamitos, CA, IEEE Computer Society Press, pp. 140–149.

Welch, T. A. (1984) "A Technique for High-Performance Data Compression," *IEEE Computer* **17**(6):8–19, June.

Willems, F. M. J. (1989) "Universal Data Compression and Repetition Times," *IEEE Transactions on Information Theory*, IT-35(1):54–58, January.

Willems, F. M. J., Y. M. Shtarkov and Tj. J. Tjalkens (1995) "The Context-Tree Weighting Method: Basic Properties," *IEEE Transactions on Information Theory*, IT-41:653–664, May.

Williams, Ross N. (1991) *Adaptive Data Compression*, Boston, MA, Kluwer Academic Publishers.

Williams, Ross N. (1991), "An Extremely Fast Ziv-Lempel Data Compression Algorithm," in *Proceedings of the 1991 Data Compression Conference*, J. Storer, ed., Los Alamitos, CA, IEEE Computer Society Press, pp. 362–371.

Wirth, N. (1976) *Algorithms + Data Structures = Programs*, Englewood Cliffs, NJ, Prentice-Hall, 2nd ed.

Witten, Ian H., Radford M. Neal, and John G. Cleary (1987) "Arithmetic Coding for Data Compression," *Communications of the ACM*, **30**(6):520–540.

Witten, I. H., T. C. Bell, M. E. Harrison, M. L. James, and A. Moffat (1992) "Textual Image Compression," in *Proceedings of the 1992 Data Compression Conference*, J. Storer, ed., Los Alamitos, CA, IEEE Computer Society Press, pp. 42–51.

Witten, I. H., et al. (1999) *Managing Gigabytes: Compressing and Indexing Documents and Images*, 2nd edition, New York, Van Nostrand Reinhold.

Wolff, Gerry (1999) URL `http://www.sees.bangor.ac.uk/~gerry/` file `sp_summary.html`.

Wong, Kwo-Jyr, and C. C. Jay Kuo (1993) "A Full Wavelet Transform (FWT) Approach to Image Compression," *Image and Video Processing*, Bellingham, WA, SPIE volume 1903:153–164.

Wong, P. W., and J. Koplowitz (1992) "Chain Codes and Their Linear Reconstruction Filters," *IEEE Transactions on Information Theory*, IT-38(2):268–280, May.

Woods, John, editor, (1990) *Subband Coding*, Boston, Kluwer Academic Press.

Wright, E. V. (1939) *Gadsby*, Los Angeles, Wetzel. Reprinted by University Microfilms, Ann Arbor, 1991.

Wu, Xiaolin (1995), "Context Selection and Quantization for Lossless Image Coding," in Storer, James A., and Martin Cohn (eds.), *DCC '95, Data Compression Conference*, Los Alamitos, CA, IEEE Computer Society Press, p. 453.

Wu, Xiaolin (1996), "An Algorithmic Study on Lossless Image Compression," in Storer, James A., ed., *DCC '96, Data Compression Conference*, Los Alamitos, CA, IEEE Computer Society Press.

Yokoo, Hidetoshi (1991) "An Improvement of Dynamic Huffman Coding with a Simple Repetition Finder," *IEEE Transactions on Communications* **39**(1):8–10, January.

Yokoo, Hidetoshi (1996) "An Adaptive Data Compression Method Based on Context Sorting," in *Proceedings of the 1996 Data Compression Conference*, J. Storer, ed., Los Alamitos, CA, IEEE Computer Society Press, pp. 160–169.

Yokoo, Hidetoshi (1997) "Data Compression Using Sort-Based Context Similarity Measure," *The Computer Journal*, **40**(2/3):94–102.

Yokoo, Hidetoshi (1999a) "A Dynamic Data Structure for Reverse Lexicographically Sorted Prefixes," in *Combinatorial Pattern Matching, Lecture Notes in Computer Science 1645*, M. Crochemore and M. Paterson, eds., Berlin, Springer Verlag, pp. 150–162.

Yokoo, Hidetoshi (1999b) Private Communication.

Yoo, Youngjun, Younggap Kwon, and Antonio Ortega (1998) "Embedded Image-Domain Adaptive Compression of Simple Images," *Proceedings of the 32nd Asilomar Conference on Signals, Systems, and Computers*, Pacific Grove, CA, Nov. 1998.

Young, D. M. (1985) "MacWrite File Format," *Wheels for the Mind* **1**:34, Fall.

Yu, Tong Lai (1996) "Dynamic Markov Compression," *Dr Dobb's Journal* pp. 30–31, January.

Zalta, Edward N. (1988) "Are Algorithms Patentable?" *Notices of the American Mathematical Society*, **35**(6):796–799.

Zandi A., J. Allen, E. Schwartz, and M. Boliek, 1995, "CREW: Compression with Reversible Embedded Wavelets," in Storer, James A., and Martin Cohn (eds.) *DCC*

'95: Data Compression Conference, Los Alamitos, CA, IEEE Computer Society Press, pp. 212–221, March.

Zhang, Manyun (1990) *The JPEG and Image Data Compression Algorithms* (dissertation).

Zhao, Zhiyuan (1998) is an applet at
"`http://ra.cfm.ohio-state.edu/~zhao/algorithms/algorithms.html`".

Ziv, Jacob, and A. Lempel (1977) "A Universal Algorithm for Sequential Data Compression," *IEEE Transactions on Information Theory* IT-23(3):337–343.

Ziv, Jacob and A. Lempel (1978) "Compression of Individual Sequences via Variable-Rate Coding," *IEEE Transactions on Information Theory* IT-24(5):530–536.

Zurek, Wojciech (1989) "Thermodynamic Cost of Computation, Algorithmic Complexity, and the Information Metric," *Nature*, **341**(6238):119–124, September 14.

> Bibliography still helps us with a further glimpse of our characters. I have here before me a small volume (printed for private circulation: no printer's name; n.d.), "Poesies par Frederic et Amelie." Mine is a presentation copy, obtained for me by Mr. Bain in the Haymarket; and the name of the first owner is written on the fly leaf in the hand of Prince Otto himself.
>
> —Robert Louis Stevenson, *Prince Otto*

Glossary

ACB

A very efficient text compression method by G. Buyanovsky (Section 8.3). It uses a dictionary with unbounded contexts and contents to select the context that best matches the search buffer and the content that best matches the look-ahead buffer.

Adaptive Compression

A compression method that modifies its operations and/or its parameters according to new data read from the input stream. Examples are the adaptive Huffman method of Section 2.9 and the dictionary-based methods of Chapter 3. (See also Semiadaptive Compression, Locally Adaptive Compression.)

Affine Transformations

Two-dimensional or three-dimensional geometric transformations, such as scaling, reflection, rotation, and translation, that preserve parallel lines (Section 4.32.1).

Alphabet

The set of all possible symbols in the input stream. In text compression the alphabet is normally the set of 128 ASCII codes. In image compression it is the set of values a pixel can take (2, 16, 256, or anything else). (See also Symbol.)

Archive

A set of one or more files combined into one file (Section 3.20). The individual members of an archive may be compressed. An archive provides a convenient way of transferring or storing groups of related files. (See also ARC, ARJ.)

ARC

A compression/archival/cataloging program written by Robert A. Freed in the mid 1980s (Section 3.20). It offers good compression and the ability to combine several files into an archive. (See also Archive, ARJ.)

Arithmetic Coding

A statistical compression method (Section 2.14) that assigns one (normally long) code to the entire input stream, instead of assigning codes to the individual symbols. The method reads the input stream symbol by symbol and appends more bits to the code each time a symbol is input and processed. Arithmetic coding is slow, but it compresses at or close to the entropy, even when the symbol probabilities are skewed. (See also Model of Compression, Statistical Methods, QM Coder.)

ARJ

A free compression/archiving utility for MS/DOS (Section 3.21), written by Robert K. Jung to compete with ARC and the various PK utilities. (See also Archive, ARC.)

ASCII Code

The standard character code on all modern computers (although Unicode is becoming a competitor). ASCII stands for American Standard Code for Information Interchange. It is a $(1+7)$-bit code, meaning 1 parity bit and 7 data bits per symbol. As a result, 128 symbols can be coded (see appendix in book's web page). They include the upper- and lowercase letters, the ten digits, some punctuation marks, and control characters. (See also Unicode.)

Bark

Unit of critical band rate. Named after Heinrich Georg Barkhausen and used in audio applications. The Bark scale is a nonlinear mapping of the frequency scale over the audio range, a mapping that matches the frequency selectivity of the human ear.

Bayesian Statistics

(See Conditional Probability.)

Bi-level Image

An image whose pixels have two different colors. The colors are normally referred to as black and white, "foreground" and "background," or 1 and 0. (See also Bitplane.)

BinHex

A file format for reliable file transfers, designed by Yves Lempereur for use on the Macintosh computer (Section 1.4.3).

Bintrees

A method, somewhat similar to quadtrees, for partitioning an image into nonoverlapping parts. The image is (horizontally) divided into two halves, each half is divided (vertically) into smaller halves, and the process continues recursively, alternating between horizontal and vertical splits. The result is a binary tree where any uniform part of the image becomes a leaf. (See also Prefix Compression, Quadtrees.)

Bitplane

Each pixel in a digital image is represented by several bits. The set of all the kth bits of all the pixels in the image is the kth bitplane of the image. A bi-level image, for example, consists of two bitplanes. (See also Bi-level Image.)

Bitrate

In general, the term "bitrate" refers to both bpb and bpc. In MPEG audio, however, this term is used to indicate the rate at which the compressed stream is read by the decoder. This rate depends on where the stream comes from (such as disk, communications channel, memory). If the bitrate of an MPEG audio file is, e.g., 128Kbps. then the encoder will convert each second of audio into 128K bits of compressed data, and the decoder will convert each group of 128K bits of compressed data into one second of sound. Lower bitrates mean smaller file sizes. However, as the bitrate decreases, the encoder must compress more audio data into fewer bits, eventually resulting in a noticeable loss of audio quality. For CD-quality audio, experience indicates that the best bitrates are in the range of 112Kbps to 160Kbps. (See also Bits/Char.)

Bits/Char

Bits per character (bpc). A measure of the performance in text compression. Also a measure of entropy. (See also Bitrate, Entropy.)

Bits/Symbol

Bits per symbol. A general measure of compression performance.

Block Coding

A general term for image compression methods that work by breaking the image into small blocks of pixels, and encoding each block separately. JPEG (Section 4.6) is a good example, since it processes blocks of 8×8 pixels.

Block Decomposition

A method for lossless compression of discrete-tone images. The method works by searching for, and locating, identical blocks of pixels. A copy B of a block A is compressed by preparing the height, width, and location (image coordinates) of A, and compressing those four numbers by means of Huffman codes. (See also Discrete-Tone Image.)

Block Matching

A lossless image compression method based on the LZ77 sliding window method originally developed for text compression. (See also LZ Methods.)

Block Truncation Coding

BTC is a lossy image compression method that quantizes pixels in an image while preserving the first two or three *statistical moments*. (See also Vector Quantization.)

Burrows-Wheeler Method

This method (Section 8.1) prepares a string of data for later compression. The compression itself is done using the move-to-front method (Section 1.5), perhaps in combination with RLE. The BW method converts a string S to another string L that satisfies two conditions:

1. Any region of L will tend to have a concentration of just a few symbols.
2. It is possible to reconstruct the original string S from L (a little more data may be needed for the reconstruction, in addition to L, but not much).

CALIC

A context-based, lossless image compression method (Section 4.21) whose two main features are (1) the use of three passes in order to achieve symmetric contexts and (2) context quantization, to significantly reduce the number of possible contexts without degrading compression performance.

CCITT

The International Telegraph and Telephone Consultative Committee (Comité Consultatif International Télégraphique et Téléphonique), the old name of the ITU, the International Telecommunications Union, a United Nations organization responsible for developing and recommending standards for data communications (not just compression). (See also ITU.)

Cell Encoding

An image compression method where the entire bitmap is divided into cells of, say, 8×8 pixels each and is scanned cell by cell. The first cell is stored in entry 0 of a table and is encoded (i.e., written on the compressed file) as the pointer 0. Each subsequent cell is searched in the table. If found, its index in the table becomes its code and is written on the compressed file. Otherwise, it is added to the table. In the case of an image made of just straight segments, it can be shown that the table size is just 108 entries.

CIE

CIE is an abbreviation for Commission Internationale de l'Éclairage (International Committee on Illumination). This is the main international organization devoted to light and color. It is responsible for developing standards and definitions in this area. (See Luminance.)

Circular Queue

A basic data structure (Section 3.2.1) that moves data along an array in circular fashion, updating two pointers to point to the start and end of the data in the array.

Codec

A term used to refer to both encoder and decoder.

Codes

A code is a symbol that stands for another symbol. In computer and telecommunications applications, codes are virtually always binary numbers. The ASCII code is the defacto standard, although the new Unicode is used on several new computers and the older EBCDIC is still used on some old IBM computers. (See also ASCII, Unicode.)

Composite and Difference Values

A progressive image method that separates the image into layers using the method of *bintrees*. Early layers consist of a few large, low-resolution blocks, followed by later layers with smaller, higher-resolution blocks. The main principle is to transform a pair of pixels into two values, a composite and a differentiator. (See also Bintrees, Progressive Image Compression.)

Compress

In the large UNIX world, `compress` is commonly used to compress data. This utility uses LZW with a growing dictionary. It starts with a small dictionary of just 512 entries and doubles its size each time it fills up, until it reaches 64K bytes (Section 3.16).

Compression Factor

The inverse of compression ratio. It is defined as

$$\text{compression factor} = \frac{\text{size of the input stream}}{\text{size of the output stream}}.$$

Values greater than 1 mean compression, and values less than 1 imply expansion. (See also Compression Ratio.)

Compression Gain

This measure is defined as

$$100 \log_e \frac{\text{reference size}}{\text{compressed size}},$$

where the reference size is either the size of the input stream or the size of the compressed stream produced by some standard lossless compression method.

Compression Ratio

One of several measures that are commonly used to express the efficiency of a compression method. It is the ratio

$$\text{compression ratio} = \frac{\text{size of the output stream}}{\text{size of the input stream}}.$$

A value of 0.6 means that the data occupies 60% of its original size after compression. Values greater than 1 mean an output stream bigger than the input stream (negative compression).

Sometimes the quantity $100 \times (1 - \text{compression ratio})$ is used to express the quality of compression. A value of 60 means that the output stream occupies 40% of its original size (or that the compression has resulted in a savings of 60%). (See also Compression Factor.)

Conditional Image RLE

A compression method for grayscale images with n shades of gray. The method starts by assigning an n-bit code to each pixel depending on its near neighbors. It then concatenates the n-bit codes into a long string, and calculates run lengths. The run lengths are encoded by prefix codes. (See also RLE, Relative Encoding.)

Conditional Probability

We tend to think of probability as something that is built into an experiment. A true die, for example, has probability of 1/6 of falling on any side, and we tend to consider this an intrinsic feature of the die. Conditional probability is a different way of looking at probability. It says that knowledge affects probability. The main task of this field is to calculate the probability of an event A given that another event, B, is known to have occurred. This is the conditional probability of A (more precisely, the probability of A conditioned on B), and it is denoted by $P(A|B)$. The field of conditional probability is sometimes called *Bayesian statistics*, since it was first developed by the Reverend Thomas Bayes [1702–1761], who came up with the basic formula of conditional probability.

Context

The N symbols preceding the next symbol. A context-based model uses context to assign probabilities to symbols.

Context-Free Grammars

A formal language uses a small number of symbols (called *terminal symbols*) from which valid sequences can be constructed. Any valid sequence is finite, the number of valid sequences is normally unlimited, and the sequences are constructed according to certain rules (sometimes called *production rules*). The rules can be used to construct valid sequences and also to determine whether a given sequence is valid. A production rule consists of a nonterminal symbol on the left and a string of terminal and nonterminal symbols on the right. The nonterminal symbol on the left becomes the name of the string on the right. The set of production rules constitutes the grammar of the formal language. If the production rules do not depend on the context of a symbol, the grammar is context-free. There are also context-sensitive grammars. The sequitur method of Section 8.10 uses context-free grammars.

Context-Tree Weighting

A method for the compression of bit strings. It can be applied to text and images, but they have to be carefully converted to bit strings. The method constructs a context tree where bits input in the immediate past (context) are used to estimate the probability of the current bit. The current bit and its estimated probability are then sent to an arithmetic encoder, and the tree is updated to include the current bit in the context. (See also KT Probability Estimator.)

Continuous-Tone Image

A digital image with a large number of colors, such that adjacent image areas with colors that differ by just one unit appear to the eye as having continuously varying colors. An example is an image with 256 grayscale values. When adjacent pixels in such an image have consecutive gray levels, they appear to the eye as a continuous variation of the gray level. (See also Bi-level image, Discrete-Tone Image, Grayscale Image.)

Continuous Wavelet Transform

An important modern method for analyzing the time and frequency contents of a function $f(t)$ by means of a wavelet. The wavelet is itself a function (which has to satisfy certain conditions), and the transform is done by multiplying the wavelet and $f(t)$ and calculating the integral of the product. The wavelet is then translated and the process is repeated. When done, the wavelet is scaled, and the entire process is carried out again in order to analyze $f(t)$ at a different scale. (See also Discrete Wavelet Transform, Lifting Scheme, Multiresolution Decomposition, Taps.)

Convolution

A way to describe the output of a linear, shift-invariant system by means of its input.

Correlation

A statistical measure of the linear relation between two paired variables. The values of R range from -1 (perfect negative relation), to 0 (no relation), to $+1$ (perfect positive relation).

CRC

CRC stands for *Cyclical Redundancy Check* (or *Cyclical Redundancy Code*). It is a rule that shows how to obtain vertical check bits from all the bits of a data stream (Section 3.23). The idea is to generate a code that depends on all the bits of the data stream, and use it to detect errors (bad bits) when the data is transmitted (or when it is stored and retrieved).

CRT

A CRT (cathode ray tube) is a glass tube with a familiar shape. In the back it has an electron gun (the cathode) that emits a stream of electrons. Its front surface is positively charged, so it attracts the electrons (which have a negative electric charge). The front is coated with a phosphor compound that converts the kinetic energy of the electrons hitting it to light. The flash of light lasts only a fraction of a second, so in order to get a constant display, the picture has to be refreshed several times a second.

Data Compression Conference

A meeting of researchers and developers in the area of data compression. The DCC takes place every year in Snowbird, Utah, USA. It lasts three days and the next few meetings are scheduled for late March.

Data Structure

A set of data items used by a program and stored in memory such that certain operations (for example, finding, adding, modifying, and deleting items) can be performed on the data items fast and easily. The most common data structures are the array, stack, queue, linked list, tree, graph, and hash table. (See also Circular Queue.)

Decibel

A logarithmic measure that can be used to measure any quantity that takes values over a very wide range. A common example is sound intensity. The intensity (amplitude) of sound can vary over a range of 11–12 orders of magnitude. Instead of using a linear measure, where numbers as small as 1 and as large as 10^{11} would be needed, a logarithmic scale is used, where the range of values is $[0, 11]$.

Decoder

A decompression program (or algorithm).

Dictionary-Based Compression

Compression methods (Chapter 3) that save pieces of the data in a "dictionary" data structure (normally a tree). If a string of new data is identical to a piece already saved in the dictionary, a pointer to that piece is output to the compressed stream. (See also LZ Methods.)

Differential Image Compression

A lossless image compression method where each pixel p is compared to a *reference pixel*, which is one of its immediate neighbors, and is then encoded in two parts: a prefix, which is the number of most significant bits of p that are identical to those of the reference pixel, and a suffix, which is (almost all) the remaining least significant bits of p. (See also DPCM.)

Digital Video

Digital video is a form of video in which the original image is generated, in the camera, in the form of pixels. (See also High-Definition Television.)

Digram

A pair of consecutive symbols.

Discrete Cosine Transform

A variant of the discrete Fourier transform (DFT) that produces just real numbers. The DCT (Sections 4.4.3 and 4.6.2) transforms a set of numbers by combining n numbers to become an n-dimensional point and rotating it in n-dimensions such that the first coordinate becomes dominant. The DCT and its inverse, the IDCT, are used in JPEG (Section 4.6) to compress an image with acceptable loss, by isolating the high-frequency components of an image, so that they can later be quantized. (See also Fourier Transform, Transform.)

Discrete-Tone Image

A discrete-tone image may be bi-level, grayscale, or color. Such images are (with few exceptions) artificial, having been obtained by scanning a document, or grabbing a computer screen. The pixel colors of such an image do not vary continuously or smoothly, but have a small set of values, such that adjacent pixels may differ much in intensity or color. Figure 4.41 is an example of such an image. (See also Block Decomposition, Continuous-Tone Image.)

Discrete Wavelet Transform

The discrete version of the continuous wavelet transform. A wavelet is represented by means of several filter coefficients, and the transform is carried out by matrix multiplication (or a simpler version thereof) instead of by calculating an integral. (See also Continuous Wavelet Transform, Multiresolution Decomposition.)

Dithering

A technique for printing or displaying a grayscale image on a bi-level output device, such as a monochromatic screen or a black and white printer. The tradeoff is loss of image detail. (See also Halftoning.)

DjVu

Certain images combine the properties of all three image types (bi-level, discrete-tone, and continuous-tone). An important example of such an image is a scanned document containing text, line drawings, and regions with continuous-tone pictures, such as paintings or photographs. DjVu (pronounced "déjà vu"), is designed for high compression and fast decompression of such documents.

It starts by decomposing the document into three components: mask, foreground, and background. The background component contains the pixels that constitute the pictures and the paper background. The mask contains the text and the lines in bi-level form (i.e., one bit per pixel). The foreground contains the color of the mask pixels. The background is a continuous-tone image and can be compressed at the low resolution of 100 dpi. The foreground normally contains large uniform areas and is also compressed as a continuous-tone image at the same low resolution. The mask is left at 300 dpi but can be efficiently compressed, since it is bi-level. The background and foreground are compressed with a wavelet-based method called IW44, while the mask is compressed with JB2, a version of JBIG2 (Section 4.10) developed at AT&T.

DPCM

DPCM compression is a member of the family of differential encoding compression methods, which itself is a generalization of the simple concept of relative encoding (Section 1.3.1). It is based on the fact that neighboring pixels in an image (and also adjacent samples in digitized sound) are correlated. (See also Differential Image Compression, Relative Encoding.)

Embedded Coding

This feature is defined as follows: Imagine that an image encoder is applied twice to the same image, with different amounts of loss. It produces two files, a large one of size M and a small one of size m. If the encoder uses embedded coding, the smaller file is identical to the first m bits of the larger file.

The following example aptly illustrates the meaning of this definition. Suppose that three users wait for you to send them a certain compressed image, but they need different image qualities. The first one needs the quality contained in a 10 Kb file. The image qualities required by the second and third users are contained in files of sizes 20 Kb and 50 Kb, respectively. Most lossy image compression methods would have to compress the same image three times, at different qualities, to generate three files with the right sizes. An embedded encoder, on the other hand, produces one file, and then three chunks—of lengths 10 Kb, 20 Kb, and 50 Kb, all starting at the beginning of the file—can be sent to the three users, satisfying their needs. (See also SPIHT, EZW.)

Encoder

A compression program (or algorithm).

Entropy

The entropy of a single symbol a_i is defined (in Section 2.1) as $-P_i \log_2 P_i$, where P_i is the probability of occurrence of a_i in the data. The entropy of a_i is the smallest number of bits needed, on average, to represent symbol a_i. Claude Shannon, the creator of information theory, coined the term *entropy* in 1948, since this term is used in thermodynamics to indicate the amount of disorder in a physical system. (See also Entropy Encoding, Information Theory.)

Entropy Encoding

A lossless compression method where data can be compressed such that the average number of bits/symbol approaches the entropy of the input symbols. (See also Entropy.)

Error-Correcting Codes

The opposite of data compression, these codes (appendix in the book's web page) detect and correct errors in digital data by increasing the redundancy of the data. They use check bits or parity bits, and are sometimes designed with the help of generating polynomials.

EXE Compressor

A compression program for compressing EXE files on the PC. Such a compressed file can be decompressed and executed with one command. The original EXE compressor is LZEXE, by Fabrice Bellard (Section 3.22).

EZW

A progressive, embedded image coding method based on the zerotree data structure. It has largely been superseded by the more efficient SPIHT method. (See also SPIHT, Progressive Image Compression, Embedded Coding.)

Facsimile Compression

Transferring a typical page between two fax machines can take up to 10–11 minutes without compression, This is why the ITU has developed several standards for compression of facsimile data. The current standards (Section 2.13) are T4 and T6, also called Group 3 and Group 4, respectively. (See also ITU.)

FELICS

A Fast, Efficient, Lossless Image Compression method designed for grayscale images that competes with the lossless mode of JPEG. The principle is to code each pixel with a variable-size code based on the values of two of its previously seen neighbor pixels. Both the unary code and the Golomb code are used. There is also a progressive version of FELICS (Section 4.18). (See also Progressive FELICS.)

FHM Curve Compression

A method for compressing curves. The acronym FHM stands for Fibonacci, Huffman, and Markov. (See also Fibonacci Numbers.)

Fibonacci Numbers

A sequence of numbers defined by

$$F_1 = 1, \quad F_2 = 1, \quad F_i = F_{i-1} + F_{i-2}, \quad i = 3, 4, \ldots.$$

The first few numbers in the sequence are 1, 1, 2, 3, 5, 8, 13, and 21. These numbers have many applications in mathematics and in various sciences. They are also found in nature, and are related to the golden ratio. (See also FHM Curve Compression.)

Fourier Transform

A mathematical transformation that produces the frequency components of a function (Section 5.1). The Fourier transform shows how a periodic function can be written as the sum of sines and cosines, thereby showing explicitly the frequencies "hidden" in the original representation of the function. (See also Discrete Cosine Transform, Transform.)

Gaussian Distribution

(See Normal Distribution.)

GFA

A compression method originally developed for bi-level images that can also be used for color images. GFA uses the fact that most images of interest have a certain amount of self similarity (i.e., parts of the image are similar, up to size, orientation, or brightness, to the entire image or to other parts). GFA partitions the image into subsquares using a quadtree, and expresses relations between parts of the image in a graph. The graph is similar to graphs used to describe finite-state automata. The method is lossy, since parts of a real image may be very similar to other parts. (See also Quadtrees, Resolution Independent Compression, WFA.)

GIF

An acronym that stands for Graphics Interchange Format. This format (Section 3.17) was developed by Compuserve Information Services in 1987 as an efficient, compressed graphics file format that allows for images to be sent between computers. The original version of GIF is known as GIF 87a. The current standard is GIF 89a. (See also Patents.)

Golomb Code

A way to generate a variable-size code for integers n (Section 2.4). It depends on the choice of a parameter b and it is created in two steps:

1. Compute the two quantities

$$q = \left\lfloor \frac{n-1}{b} \right\rfloor, \qquad r = n - qb - 1.$$

2. Construct the Golomb code of n in two parts; the first is the value of $q + 1$, coded in unary (exercise 2.5), and the second, the binary value of r coded in either $\lfloor \log_2 b \rfloor$ bits (for the small remainders) or in $\lceil \log_2 b \rceil$ bits (for the large ones). (See also Unary Code.)

Gray Codes

These are binary codes for the integers, where the codes of consecutive integers differ by one bit only. Such codes are used when a grayscale image is separated into bitplanes, each a bi-level image. (See also Grayscale Image,)

Grayscale Image

A continuous-tone image with shades of a single color. (See also Continuous-Tone Image.)

Growth Geometry Coding

A method for progressive lossless compression of bi-level images. The method selects some *seed* pixels and applies geometric rules to grow each seed pixel into a pattern of pixels. (See also Progressive Image Compression.)

GZip

Popular software that implements the so-called "deflation" algorithm (Section 3.19) that uses a variation of LZ77 combined with static Huffman coding. It uses a 32 Kb-long sliding dictionary, and a look-ahead buffer of 258 bytes. When a string is not found in the dictionary, it is emitted as a sequence of literal bytes. (See also Zip.)

H.261

In late 1984, the CCITT (currently the ITU-T) organized an expert group to develop a standard for visual telephony for ISDN services. The idea was to send images and sound between special terminals, so that users could talk and see each other. This type of application requires sending large amounts of data, so compression became an important consideration. The group eventually came up with a number of standards, known as the H series (for video) and the G series (for audio) recommendations, all operating at speeds of $p{\times}64$ Kbit/s for $p = 1, 2, \ldots, 30$. These standards are known today under the umbrella name of $p{\times}64$.

Halftoning

A method for the display of gray scales in a bi-level image. By placing groups of black and white pixels in carefully designed patterns, it is possible to create the effect of a gray area. The tradeoff of halftoning is loss of resolution. (See also Bi-level Image, Dithering.)

Hamming Codes

A type of error-correcting code for 1-bit errors, where it is easy to generate the required parity bits.

Hierarchical Progressive Image Compression

An image compression method (or an optional part of such a method) where the encoder writes the compressed image in layers of increasing resolution. The decoder decompresses the lowest-resolution layer first, displays this crude image, and continues with higher-resolution layers. Each layer in the compressed stream uses data from the preceding layer. (See also Progressive Image Compression.)

High-Definition Television

A general name for several standards that are currently replacing traditional television. HDTV uses digital video, high-resolution images, and aspect ratios different from the traditional 3:4. (See also Digital Video.)

Huffman Coding

A popular method for data compression (Section 2.8). It assigns a set of "best" variable-size codes to a set of symbols based on their probabilities. It serves as the basis for several popular programs used on personal computers. Some of them use just the Huffman method, while others use it as one step in a multistep compression process. The Huffman method is somewhat similar to the Shannon-Fano method. It generally produces better codes, and like the Shannon-Fano method, it produces best code when the probabilities of the symbols are negative powers of 2. The main difference between the two methods is that Shannon-Fano constructs its codes top to bottom (from the leftmost to the rightmost bits), while Huffman constructs a code tree from the bottom up (builds the codes from right to left). (See also Shannon-Fano Coding, Statistical Methods.)

Information Theory

A mathematical theory that quantifies information. It shows how to measure information, so that one can answer the question; How much information is included in this piece of data? with a precise number! Information theory is the creation, in 1948, of Claude Shannon, of Bell labs. (See also Entropy.)

Interpolating Polynomials

Given two numbers a and b we know that $m = 0.5a + 0.5b$ is their average, since it is located midway between a and b. We say that the average is an *interpolation* of the two numbers. Similarly, the weighted sum $0.1a + 0.9b$ represents an interpolated value located 10% away from b and 90% away from a. Extending this concept to points (in two or three dimensions) is done by means of *interpolating polynomials* (see the book's web page). Given a set of points we start by fitting a parametric polynomial $\mathbf{P}(t)$ or $\mathbf{P}(u, w)$ through them. Once the polynomial is known, it can be used to calculate interpolated points by computing $\mathbf{P}(0.5)$, $\mathbf{P}(0.1)$, or other values.

ISO

The International Standards Organization. This is one of the organizations responsible for developing standards. Among other things it is responsible (together with the ITU) for the JPEG and MPEG compression standards. (See also ITU, CCITT, MPEG.)

Iterated Function Systems (IFS)

An image compressed by IFS is uniquely defined by a few affine transformations (Section 4.32.1). The only rule is that the scale factors of these transformations must be less than 1 (shrinking). The image is saved in the output stream by writing the sets of six numbers that define each transformation. (See also Affine Transformations, Resolution Independent Compression.)

ITU

The International Telecommunications Union, the new name of the CCITT, is a United Nations organization responsible for developing and recommending standards for data communications (not just compression). (See also CCITT.)

JBIG

A special-purpose compression method (Section 4.9) developed specifically for progressive compression of bi-level images. The name JBIG stands for Joint Bi-Level Image Processing Group. This is a group of experts from several international organizations, formed in 1988 to recommend such a standard. JBIG uses multiple arithmetic coding and a resolution-reduction technique to achieve its goals. (See also Bi-level Image, JBIG2.)

JBIG2

A recent international standard for the compression of bi-level images. It is intended to replace the original JBIG. Its main features are

1. Large increases in compression performance (typically 3–5 times better than Group 4/MMR, and 2–4 times better than JBIG).
2. Special compression methods for text, halftones, and other bi-level image parts.
3. Lossy and lossless compression.
4. Two modes of progressive compression. Mode 1 is quality-progressive compression, where the decoded image progresses from low to high quality. Mode 2

is content-progressive coding, where important image parts (such as text) are decoded first, followed by less important parts (such as halftone patterns).

5. Multipage document compression.

6. Flexible format, designed for easy embedding in other image file formats, such as TIFF.

7. Fast decompression. Using some coding modes, images can be decompressed at over 250 million pixels/second in software.

(See also Bi-level Image, JBIG.)

JFIF

The full name of this method (Section 4.6.9) is JPEG File Interchange Format. It is a graphics file format that makes it possible to exchange JPEG-compressed images between different computers. The main features of JFIF are the use of the YCbCr triple-component color space for color images (only one component for grayscale images) and the use of a *marker* to specify features missing from JPEG, such as image resolution, aspect ratio, and features that are application-specific.

JPEG

A sophisticated lossy compression method (Section 4.6) for color or grayscale still images (not movies). It also works best on continuous-tone images, where adjacent pixels have similar colors. One advantage of JPEG is the use of many parameters, allowing the user to adjust the amount of data loss (and thus also the compression ratio) over a very wide range. There are two main modes: lossy (also called baseline) and lossless (which typically gives a 2:1 compression ratio). Most implementations support just the lossy mode. This mode includes progressive and hierarchical coding.

The main idea behind JPEG is that an image exists for people to look at, so when the image is compressed, it is acceptable to lose image features to which the human eye is not sensitive.

The name JPEG is an acronym that stands for Joint Photographic Experts Group. This was a joint effort by the CCITT and the ISO that started in June 1987. The JPEG standard has proved successful and has become widely used for image presentation, especially in Web pages. (See also JPEG-LS, MPEG.)

JPEG-LS

The lossless mode of JPEG is inefficient and often is not even implemented. As a result, the ISO decided to develop a new standard for the lossless (or near-lossless) compression of continuous-tone images. The result became popularly known as JPEG-LS. This method is not simply an extension or a modification of JPEG. It is a new method, designed to be simple and fast. It does not use the DCT, does not use arithmetic coding, and uses quantization in a limited way, and only in its near-lossless option. JPEG-LS examines several of the previously seen neighbors of the current pixel, uses them as the *context* of the pixel, uses the context to predict the pixel and to select a probability distribution out of several such distributions, and uses that distribution to encode the prediction error with a special Golomb code. There is also a run mode, where the length of a run of identical pixels is encoded. (See also Golomb Code, JPEG.)

Kraft-MacMillan Inequality

A relation (Section 2.5) that says something about unambiguous variable-size codes. Its first part states; given an unambiguous variable-size code, with n codes of sizes L_i, then

$$\sum_{i=1}^{n} 2^{-L_i} \leq 1.$$

(This is Equation(2.1).) The second part states the opposite, namely, given a set of n positive integers $(L_1, L_2, \ldots, L_n)$ that satisfy Equation (2.1), there exists an unambiguous variable-size code such that L_i are the sizes of its individual codes. Together, both parts say that a code is unambiguous if and only if it satisfies relation (2.1).

KT Probability Estimator

A method to estimate the probability of a bit string containing a zeros and b ones. It is due to Krichevsky and Trofimov. (See also Context-Tree Weighting.)

L Systems

Lindenmayer systems (or L-systems for short) were developed by the biologist Aristid Lindenmayer in 1968 as a tool [Lindenmayer 68] to describe the morphology of plants. They were initially used in computer science, in the 1970s, as a tool to define formal languages, but have become really popular only after 1984, when it became apparent that they can be used to draw many types of fractals, in addition to their use in botany (see the book's web page).

Laplace Distribution

A probability distribution similar to the normal (Gaussian) distribution, but narrower and sharply peaked. The general Laplace distribution with variance V and mean m is given by

$$L(V, x) = \frac{1}{\sqrt{2V}} \exp\left(-\sqrt{\frac{2}{V}}|x - m|\right).$$

Experience seems to suggest that the values of pixels in many images are Laplace distributed, which is why this distribution is used in some image compression methods, such as MLP. (See also Normal Distribution.)

Laplacian Pyramid

A progressive image compression technique where the original image is transformed to a set of difference images that can later be decompressed and displayed as a small, blurred image that becomes increasingly sharper. (See also Progressive Image Compression.)

LHArc

This method (Section 3.21) is by Haruyasu Yoshizaki. Its predecessor is LHA, designed jointly by Haruyasu Yoshizaki and Haruhiko Okumura. These methods use adaptive Huffman coding with features drawn from LZSS.

Lifting Scheme

A method for calculating the discrete wavelet transform in place, so no extra memory is required. (See also Discrete Wavelet Transform.)

Locally Adaptive Compression

A compression method that adapts itself to local conditions in the input stream, and changes this adaptation as it moves from area to area in the input. An example is the move-to-front method of Section 1.5. (See also Adaptive Compression, Semiadaptive Compression.)

Luminance

This quantity is defined by the CIE (Section 4.6.1) as radiant power weighted by a spectral sensitivity function that is characteristic of vision. (See also CIE.)

Lossless Compression

A compression method where the output of the decoder is identical to the original data compressed by the encoder. (See also Lossy Compression.)

Lossy Compression

A compression method where the output of the decoder is different from the original data compressed by the encoder, but is nevertheless acceptable to a user. Such methods are common in image and audio compression, but not in text compression, where the loss of even one character may result in ambiguous or incomprehensible text. (See also Lossless Compression, Subsampling.)

LZ Methods

All dictionary-based compression methods are based on the work of J. Ziv and A. Lempel, published in 1977 and 1978. Today, these are called LZ77 and LZ78 methods, respectively. Their ideas have been a source of inspiration to many researchers, who generalized, improved, and combined them with RLE and statistical methods to form many commonly used adaptive compression methods, for text, images, and audio. (See also Block Matching, Dictionary-Based Compression, Sliding-Window Compression.)

LZAP

The LZAP method (Section 3.12) is an LZW variant based on the following idea: Instead of just concatenating the last two phrases and placing the result in the dictionary, place all prefixes of the concatenation in the dictionary. The suffix AP stands for All Prefixes.

LZFG

This is the name of several related methods (Section 3.7) that are hybrids of LZ77 and LZ78. They were developed by Edward Fiala and Daniel Greene. All these methods are based on the following scheme. The encoder produces a compressed file with tokens and literals (raw ASCII codes) intermixed. There are two types of tokens, a *literal* and a *copy*. A literal token indicates that a string of literals follow, a copy token points to a string previously seen in the data. (See also LZ Methods, Patents.)

LZMW

A variant of LZW, the LZMW method (Section 3.11) works as follows: Instead of adding I plus one character of the next phrase to the dictionary, add I plus the entire next phrase to the dictionary. (See also LZW.)

LZP

An LZ77 variant developed by C. Bloom (Section 3.14). It is based on the principle of context prediction that says "if a certain string 'abcde' has appeared in the input stream in the past and was followed by 'fg...', then when 'abcde' appears again in the input stream, there is a good chance that it will be followed by the same 'fg...'." (See also Context.)

LZSS

This version of LZ77 (Section 3.3) was developed by Storer and Szymanski in 1982 [Storer 82]. It improves on the basic LZ77 in three ways: (1) it holds the look-ahead buffer in a circular queue, (2) It holds the search buffer (the dictionary) in a binary search tree, and (3) it creates tokens with two fields instead of three. (See also LZ Methods.)

LZW

This is a popular variant (Section 3.10) of LZ78, developed by Terry Welch in 1984. Its main feature is eliminating the second field of a token. An LZW token consists of just a pointer to the dictionary. As a result, such a token always encodes a string of more than one symbol. (See also Patents.)

LZY

LZY (Section 3.13) is an LZW variant that adds one dictionary string per input character and increments strings by one character at a time.

MLP

A progressive compression method for grayscale images. An image is compressed in levels. A pixel is predicted by a symmetric pattern of its neighbors from preceding levels, and the prediction error is arithmetically encoded. The Laplace distribution is used to estimate the probability of the error. (See also Laplace Distribution, Progressive FELICS.)

MNP5, MNP7

These have been developed by Microcom, Inc., a maker of modems, for use in its modems. MNP5 (Section 2.10) is a two-stage process that starts with run length encoding, followed by adaptive frequency encoding. MNP7 (Section 2.11) combines run length encoding with a two-dimensional variant of adaptive Huffman coding.

Model of Compression

A model is a method to "predict" (to assign probabilities to) the data to be compressed. This concept is important in statistical data compression. When a statistical method is used, a model for the data has to be constructed before compression can begin. A simple model can be built by reading the entire input stream, counting the number of times each symbol appears (its frequency of occurrence), and computing the probability of occurrence of each symbol. The data stream is then input again, symbol by symbol, and is compressed using the information in the probability model. (See also Statistical Methods, Statistical Model.)

One feature of arithmetic coding is that it is easy to separate the statistical model (the table with frequencies and probabilities) from the encoding and decoding operations. It is easy to encode, for example, the first half of a data stream using one model, and the second half using another model.

Move-to-Front Coding

The basic idea behind this method (Section 1.5) is to maintain the alphabet A of symbols as a list where frequently occurring symbols are located near the front. A symbol s is encoded as the number of symbols that precede it in this list. After symbol s is encoded, it is moved to the front of list A.

MPEG

This acronym stands for Moving Pictures Experts Group. The MPEG standard consists of several methods for the compression of movies, including the compression of digital images and digital sound, as well as synchronization of the two. There currently are several MPEG standards. MPEG-1 is intended for intermediate data rates, on the order of 1.5 Mbit/s. MPEG-2 is intended for high data rates of at least 10 Mbit/s. MPEG-3 was intended for HDTV compression but was found to be redundant and was merged with MPEG-2. MPEG-4 is intended for very low data rates of less than 64 Kbit/s. A third international body, the ITU-T, has been involved in the design of both MPEG-2 and MPEG-4. A working group of the ISO is still at work on MPEG. (See also ISO, JPEG.)

Multiresolution Decomposition

This method groups all the discrete wavelet transform coefficients for a given scale, displays their superposition, and repeats for all scales. (See also Continuous Wavelet Transform, Discrete Wavelet Transform.)

Multiresolution Image

A compressed image that may be decompressed at any resolution. (See also Resolution Independent Compression, Iterated Function Systems, WFA.)

Normal Distribution

A probability distribution with the typical bell shape. It is found in many places in both theoretical and real-life models. The normal distribution with mean m and standard deviation s is defined by

$$f(x) = \frac{1}{s\sqrt{2\pi}} \exp\left\{ -\frac{1}{2}\left(\frac{x-m}{s}\right)^2 \right\}.$$

Patents

A mathematical algorithm can be patented if it is intimately associated with software or firmware implementing it. Several compression methods, most notably LZW, have been patented (Section 3.25), creating difficulties for software developers who work with GIF, UNIX `compress`, or any other system that uses LZW. (See also GIF, LZW, Compress.)

Pel

The smallest unit of a facsimile image; a dot. (See also Pixel.)

Phrase

A piece of data placed in a dictionary to be used in compressing future data. The concept of phrase is central in dictionary-based data compression methods since the success of such a method depends a lot on how it selects phrases to be saved in its dictionary. (See also Dictionary-Based Compression, LZ Methods.)

Pixel

The smallest unit of a digital image; a dot. (See also Pel.)

PKZip

A compression program for MS/DOS (Section 3.20) written by Phil Katz who has founded the PKWare company (`http://www.pkware.com`), which also markets the PKunzip, PKlite, and PKArc software.

Prediction

Assigning probabilities to symbols. (See also PPM.)

Prefix Compression

In an image of size $2^n \times 2^n$ each pixel can be assigned a $2n$-bit number using quadtree methods. The prefix compression method shows how to select a *prefix* value P. Once P has been selected, the method finds all the pixels whose numbers have the same P leftmost bits (same prefix). Those pixels are compressed by writing the prefix once on the compressed stream, followed by all the suffixes.

Prefix Property

One of the principles of variable-size codes. It states; Once a certain bit pattern has been assigned as the code of a symbol, no other codes should start with that pattern (the pattern cannot be the *prefix* of any other code). Once the string 1, for example, is assigned as the code of a_1, no other codes should start with 1 (i.e., they all have to start with 0). Once 01, for example, is assigned as the code of a_2, no other codes can start with 01 (they all should start with 00). (See also Variable-Size Codes, Statistical Methods.)

Progressive FELICS

A progressive version of FELICS where pixels are encoded in levels. Each level doubles the number of pixels encoded. To decide what pixels are included in a certain level, the preceding level can conceptually be rotated $45°$ and scaled by $\sqrt{2}$ in both dimensions. (See also FELICS, MLP, Progressive Image Compression.)

Progressive Image Compression

An image compression method where the compressed stream consists of "layers," where each layer contains more detail of the image. The decoder can very quickly display the entire image in a low-quality format, then improve the display quality as more and more layers are being read and decompressed. A user watching the decompressed image develop on the screen can normally recognize most of the image features after only 5–10% of it has been decompressed. Improving image quality over time can be done by (1) sharpening it, (2) adding colors, or (3) adding resolution. (See also Progressive FELICS, Hierarchical Progressive Image Compression, MLP, JBIG.)

PPM

A compression method that assigns probabilities to symbols based on the context (long or short) in which they appear. (See also Prediction, PPPM.)

PPPM

A lossless compression method for grayscale (and color) images that assigns probabilities to symbols based on the Laplace distribution, like MLP. Different contexts of a pixel are examined and their statistics used to select the mean and variance for a particular Laplace distribution. (See also Laplace Distribution, Prediction, PPM, MLP.)

Prefix Compression

A variant of quadtrees, designed for bi-level images with text or diagrams, where the number of black pixels is relatively small. Each pixel in a $2^n \times 2^n$ image is assigned an n-digit, or $2n$-bit, number based on the concept of quadtrees. Numbers of adjacent pixels tend to have the same prefix (most-significant bits), so the common prefix and different suffixes of a group of pixels are compressed separately. (See also Quadtrees.)

Psychoacoustic Model

A mathematical model of the sound masking properties of the human auditory (ear brain) system.

QIC-122 Compression

An LZ77 variant that has been developed by the QIC organization for text compression on 1/4-inch data cartridge tape drives.

QM Coder

This is the arithmetic coder of JPEG and JBIG. It is designed for simplicity and speed, so it is limited to input symbols that are single bits and it uses an approximation instead of a multiplication. It also uses fixed-precision integer arithmetic, so it has to resort to *renormalization* of the probability interval from time to time, in order for the approximation to remain close to the true multiplication. (See also Arithmetic Coding.)

Quadrisection

This is a relative of the quadtree method. It assumes that the original image is a $2^k \times 2^k$ square matrix M_0, and it constructs matrices M_1, M_2,...,M_{k+1} with fewer and fewer columns. These matrices naturally have more and more rows, and quadrisection achieves compression by searching for and removing duplicate rows. Two closely related variants of quadrisection are bisection and octasection (See also Quadtrees.)

Quadtrees

This is a data compression method for bitmap images. A quadtree (Section 4.27) is a tree where each leaf corresponds to a uniform part of the image (a quadrant, subquadrant, or a single pixel) and each interior node has exactly four children. (See also Bintrees, Prefix Compression, Quadrisection.)

Quaternary

A base-4 digit. It can be 0, 1, 2, or 3.

Relative Encoding

A variant of RLE, sometimes called *differencing* (Section 1.3.1). It is used in cases where the data to be compressed consists of a string of numbers that don't differ by much, or in cases where it consists of strings that are similar to each other. The principle of relative encoding is to send the first data item a_1 followed by the differences $a_{i+1} - a_i$. (See also DPCM, RLE.)

Reliability

Variable-size codes and other codes are vulnerable to errors. In cases where reliable transmission of codes is important, the codes can be made more reliable by adding check bits, parity bits, or CRC (Section 2.12 and Appendix in the book's web page). Notice that reliability is, in a sense, the opposite of data compression, since it is done by increasing redundancy. (See also CRC.)

Resolution Independent Compression

An image compression method that does not depend on the resolution of the specific image being compressed. The image can be decompressed at any resolution. (See also Multiresolution Images, Iterated Function Systems, WFA.)

RLE

A general name for methods that compress data by replacing a run length of identical symbols with one code, or token, containing the symbol and the length of the run. RLE sometimes serves as one step in a multistep statistical or dictionary-based method. (See also Relative Encoding, Conditional Image RLE.)

Scalar Quantization

The dictionary definition of the term "quantization" is "to restrict a variable quantity to discrete values rather than to a continuous set of values." If the data to be compressed is in the form of large numbers, quantization is used to convert them to small numbers. This results in (lossy) compression. If the data to be compressed is analog (e.g., a voltage that changes with time), quantization is used to digitize it into small numbers. This aspect of quantization is used by several audio compression methods. (See also Vector Quantization.)

SemiAdaptive Compression

A compression method that uses a two-pass algorithm, where the first pass reads the input stream to collect statistics on the data to be compressed, and the second pass performs the actual compression. The statistics (model) are included in the compressed stream. (See also Adaptive Compression, Locally Adaptive Compression.)

Semi-Structured Text

Such text is defined as data that is human readable and also suitable for machine processing. A common example is HTML. The sequitur method of Section 8.10 performs especially well on such text.

Shannon-Fano Coding

An early algorithm for finding a minimum-length variable-size code given the probabilities of all the symbols in the data (Section 2.6). This method was later superseded by the Huffman method. (See also Statistical Methods, Huffman Coding.)

Simple Image

A simple image is one that uses a small fraction of the possible grayscale values or colors available to it. A common example is a bi-level image where each pixel is represented by eight bits. Such an image uses just two colors out of a palette of 256 possible colors. Another example is a grayscale image scanned from a bi-level image. Most pixels will be black or white, but some pixels may have other shades of gray. A cartoon is also an example of a simple image (especially a cheap cartoon, where just a few colors are used). A typical cartoon consists of uniform areas, so it may use a small number of colors out of a potentially large palette. The EIDAC method of Section 4.11 is especially designed for simple images.

Sliding Window Compression

The LZ77 method (Section 3.2) uses part of the previously seen input stream as the dictionary. The encoder maintains a window to the input stream, and shifts the input in that window from right to left as strings of symbols are being encoded. The method is thus based on a *sliding window*. (See also LZ Methods.)

Space-Filling Curves

A space-filling curve (Section 4.29) is a function $\mathbf{P}(t)$ that goes through every point in a given two-dimensional area, normally the unit square. Such curves are defined recursively and are used in image compression.

Sparse Strings

Regardless of what the input data represents—text, binary, images, or anything else—we can think of the input stream as a string of bits. If most of the bits are zeros, the string is called *sparse*. Sparse strings can be compressed very efficiently by specially designed methods (Section 8.5).

SPIHT

A progressive image encoding method that efficiently encodes the image after it has been transformed by any wavelet filter. SPIHT is embedded, progressive, and has a natural lossy option. It is also simple to implement, fast, and produces excellent results for all types of images. (See also EZW, Progressive Image Compression, Embedded Coding, Discrete Wavelet Transform.)

Statistical Methods

These methods (Chapter 2) work by assigning variable-size codes to symbols in the data, with the shorter codes assigned to symbols or groups of symbols that appear more often in the data (have a higher probability of occurrence). (See also Variable-Size Codes, Prefix Property, Shannon-Fano Coding, Huffman Coding, and Arithmetic Coding.)

Statistical Model

(See Model of Compression.)

String Compression

In general, compression methods based on strings of symbols can be more efficient than methods that compress individual symbols (Section 3.1).

Subsampling

Subsampling is, possibly, the simplest way to compress an image. One approach to subsampling is simply to ignore some of the pixels. The encoder may, for example, ignore every other row and every other column of the image, and write the remaining pixels (which constitute 25% of the image) on the compressed stream. The decoder inputs the compressed data and uses each pixel to generate four identical pixels of the reconstructed image. This, of course, involves the loss of much image detail and is rarely acceptable. (See also Lossy Compression.)

Symbol

The smallest unit of the data to be compressed. A symbol is normally a byte but may also be a bit, a trit $\{0, 1, 2\}$, or anything else. (See also Alphabet.)

Symbol Ranking

A context-based method (Section 8.2) where the context C of the current symbol S (the N symbols preceding S) is used to prepare a list of symbols that are likely to follow C. The list is arranged from most likely to least likely. The position of S in this list (position numbering starts from 0) is then written by the encoder, after being suitably encoded, on the output stream.

Taps

Wavelet filter coefficients. (See also Continuous Wavelet Transform, Discrete Wavelet Transform.)

TAR

The standard UNIX archiver. The name TAR stands for Tape ARchive. It groups a number of files into one file without compression. After being compressed by the UNIX `compress` program, a TAR file gets an extension name of `tar.z`.

Textual Image Compression

A compression method for hard copy documents containing printed or typed (but not handwritten) text. The text can be in many fonts and may consist of musical notes, hieroglyphs, or any symbols. Pattern recognition techniques are used to recognize text characters that are identical or at least similar. One copy of each group of identical characters is kept in a library. Any leftover material is considered residue. The method uses different compression techniques for the symbols and the residue. It includes a lossy option where the residue is ignored.

Token

A unit of data written on the compressed stream by some compression algorithms. A token consists of several fields that may have either fixed or variable sizes.

Transform

An image can be compressed by transforming its pixels (which are correlated) to a representation where they are *decorrelated*. Compression is achieved if the new values are smaller, on average, than the original ones. Lossy compression can be achieved by quantizing the transformed values. The decoder inputs the transformed values from the compressed stream and reconstructs the (precise or approximate) original data by applying the opposite transform. (See also Discrete Cosine Transform, Fourier Transform, Continuous Wavelet Transform, Discrete Wavelet Transform.)

Triangle Mesh

Polygonal surfaces are very popular in computer graphics. Such a surface consists of flat polygons, mostly triangles, so there is a need for special methods to compress a triangle mesh. Such a method is edgebreaker (Section 8.11).

Trit

A ternary (base 3) digit. It can be 0, 1, or 2.

Unary Code

A way to generate variable-size codes in one step. The unary code of the nonnegative integer n is defined (Section 2.3.1) as $n - 1$ ones followed by one zero (Table 2.3). There is also a general unary code. (See also Golomb Code.)

Unicode

A new international standard code, the Unicode, has been proposed, and is being developed by the international Unicode organization (`www.unicode.org`). Unicode uses 16-bit codes for its characters, so it provides for $2^{16} = 64K = 65,536$ codes. (Notice that doubling the size of a code much more than doubles the number of possible codes. In fact, it *squares* the number of codes.) Unicode includes all the ASCII codes in addition to codes for characters in foreign languages (including complete sets of Korean, Japanese, and Chinese characters) and many mathematical and other symbols. Currently, about 39,000 out of the 65,536 possible codes have been assigned, so there is room for adding more symbols in the future.

The Microsoft Windows NT operating system has adopted Unicode, as have also AT&T Plan 9 and Lucent Inferno. (See also ASCII, Codes.)

V.42bis Protocol

This is a standard, published by the ITU-T (page 91) for use in fast modems. It is based on the older V.32bis protocol and is supposed to be used for fast transmission rates, up to 57.6K baud. The standard contains specifications for data compression and error correction, but only the former is discussed, in Section 3.18.

V.42bis specifies two modes: a *transparent* mode, where no compression is used, and a *compressed* mode using an LZW variant. The former is used for data streams that don't compress well, and may even cause expansion. A good example is an already compressed file. Such a file looks like random data, it does not have any repetitive patterns, and trying to compress it with LZW will fill up the dictionary with short, two-symbol, phrases.

Variable-Size Codes

These are used by statistical methods. Such codes should satisfy the prefix property (Section 2.2) and should be assigned to symbols based on their probabilities. (See also Prefix Property, Statistical Methods.)

Vector Quantization

This is a generalization of the scalar quantization method. It is used for both image and sound compression. In practice, vector quantization is commonly used to compress data that has been digitized from an analog source, such as sampled sound and scanned images (drawings or photographs). Such data is called *digitally sampled analog data* (DSAD). (See also Scalar Quantization.)

Video Compression

Video compression is based on two principles. The first is the spatial redundancy that exists in each video frame. The second is the fact that very often, a video frame is very similar to its immediate neighbors. This is called *temporal redundancy*. A typical technique for video compression should thus start by encoding the first frame using an image compression method. It should then encode each successive frame by identifying the differences between the frame and its predecessor, and encoding these differences.

Voronoi Diagrams

Imagine a petri dish ready for growing bacteria. Four bacteria of different types are simultaneously placed in it at different points and immediately start multiplying. We assume that their colonies grow at the same rate. Initially, each colony consists of a growing circle around one of the starting points. After a while some of them meet and stop growing in the meeting area due to lack of food. The final result is that the entire dish gets divided into four areas, one around each of the four starting points, such that all the points within area i are closer to starting point i than to any other start point. Such areas are called *Voronoi regions* or *Dirichlet Tessellations*.

WFA

This method uses the fact that most images of interest have a certain amount of self similarity (i.e., parts of the image are similar, up to size or brightness, to the entire image or to other parts). It partitions the image into subsquares using a quadtree, and uses a recursive inference algorithm to express relations between parts of the image in a graph. The graph is similar to graphs used to describe finite-state automata. The method is lossy, since parts of a real image may be very similar to other parts. WFA is a very efficient method for compression of grayscale and color images. (See also GFA, Quadtrees, Resolution-Independent Compression.)

WSQ

An efficient lossy compression method specifically developed for compressing fingerprint images. The method involves a wavelet transform of the image, followed by scalar quantization of the wavelet coefficients, and by RLE and Huffman coding of the results. (See also Discrete Wavelet Transform.)

Zero-Probability Problem

When samples of data are read and analyzed in order to generate a statistical model of the data, certain contexts may not appear, leaving entries with zero counts and thus zero probability in the frequency table. Any compression method requires that such entries be somehow assigned nonzero probabilities.

Zip

Popular software that implements the so-called "deflation" algorithm (Section 3.19) that uses a variant of LZ77 combined with static Huffman coding. It uses a 32 Kb-long sliding dictionary, and a look-ahead buffer of 258 bytes. When a string is not found in the dictionary, it is emitted as a sequence of literal bytes. (See also Gzip.)

> Necessity is the mother of compression.
> —Aesop (paraphrased)

Joining the Data Compression Community

People who are interested in a personal touch can join the "DC community" and communicate with researchers and developers in this area in person by attending the Data Compression Conference (DCC). It has taken place every year since 1991, in Snowbird, Utah, USA. The conference lasts three days and the next few meetings are scheduled for late March. Detailed information on the conference can be found at `http://www.cs.brandeis.edu/~dcc/index.html`. This web page includes information about the conference itself, the organizers, and the geographical location.

In addition to invited presentations and technical sessions, there is a poster session and "Midday Talks" on issues of current interest.

The poster session is the central event of the DCC. Each presenter places a description of recent work (including text, diagrams, photographs, and charts) on a 4-foot-wide by 3-foot-high poster. They then discuss the work with anyone interested, in a relaxed atmosphere, with refreshments served.

The Capocelli prize is awarded annually for the best student-authored DCC paper. This is in memory of Renato M. Capocelli [1940–1992].

The program committee reads like a who's who of data compression, but the two main figures are James Andrew Storer and Martin Cohn, both of Brandeis University, who chair the conference and the conference program, respectively.

The conference proceedings have traditionally been edited by Storer and Cohn. They are published by the IEEE Computer Society (`http://www.computer.org/`) and are distributed prior to the conference; an attractive feature.

A complete bibliography (in bibTEX format) of papers published in past DCCs can be found at `http://www.cs.mu.oz.au/~alistair/dccrefs.bib`.

> At first they approached each other with hesitation; then, joining right hands, they promised before the altars of their gods to punish the treachery of their enemies and to yield one to the other.
>
> —Tacitus, *Annals*

Index

How did he bank it up, swank it up,
the whaler in the punt, a guinea by a groat,
his index on the balance and such
wealth into the bargain, with the boguey
which he snatched in the baggage coach
ahead?

—James Joyce, *Finnegans Wake* (1920)

Colophon

The first edition of this book was written in a burst of activity during the short period June 1996 through February 1997. The second edition is the result of intensive work during the second half of 1998 and the first half of 1999. The book was designed by the author and was typeset by him with the TeX typesetting system developed by D. Knuth. The text and tables were done with Textures, a commercial TeX implementation for the Macintosh. The diagrams were done with Adobe Illustrator, also on the Macintosh. Diagrams that require calculations were done either with *Mathematica* or Matlab, but even those were "polished" by Adobe Illustrator. The following points illustrate the amount of work that went into the book:

- The book (including the auxiliary material located in the author's web site) contains about 215,600 words, consisting of about 1,226,800 characters. However, the size of the auxiliary material collected in the author's computer and on his desk while working on the book is about 10 times bigger than the entire book. This material includes articles and source codes available on the internet, as well as many pages of information collected from various sources.

- The text is typeset mainly in font cmr10, but about 30 other fonts were used.

- The raw index file contained about 3900 items.

- There are about 840 cross references in the book.

That which shrinks must first expand
—Lao-Tzu, verse 36 of *Tao Te Ching*